Routledge Handbook of Diplomacy and Statecraft

Edited by B. J. C. McKercher

Routledge
Taylor & Francis Group

LONDON AND NEW YORK

First published 2011
by Routledge
2 Park Square, Milton Park, Abingdon, Oxon, OX14 4RN

And by Routledge
711 Third Avenue, New York, NY 10017

First published in paperback 2015

Routledge is an imprint of the Taylor & Francis Group, an informa business

British Library Cataloguing in Publication Data
A catalogue record for this book is available from the British Library

Library of Congress Cataloging in Publication Data
A catalog record has been requested for this book

ISBN 13: 978-0-415-78110-7 (hbk)
ISBN 13: 978-1-138-90857-4 (pbk)
ISBN 13: 978-0-203-80780-4 (ebk)

Typeset in Bembo
by Integra Software Services Pvt. Ltd, Pondicherry, India

Printed and bound in Great Britain by
TJ International Ltd, Padstow, Cornwall

Routledge Handbook of Diplomacy and Statecraft

Despite post-Cold War arguments about their demise, 'Great Powers' not only continue to thrive, with lesser Powers they form the basis of the constellation of global politics. This topical new Handbook illustrates how and why the new international order has evolved – and is still evolving – since the end of the Cold War, through the application of diplomacy and statecraft.

Including cutting-edge contributions from over 40 scholars, the Handbook is structured around seven sections:

- Context of Diplomacy
- Great Powers
- Middle Powers
- Developing Powers
- International Organisations and Military Alliances
- International Economy
- Issues of Conflict and Co-operation.

Through analysis of a wide range of case studies, the Handbook assesses the diplomacy and statecraft of individual powers, offering insights into how they function, their individual perception of national interests, and the roles they play in modern statecraft. The contributors also seek to evaluate the organisations and contemporary issues that continue to influence the shaping of the new international order.

A comprehensive survey of diplomacy across the world, this work will be essential reading for scholars and professionals alike.

B.J.C. McKercher, FRHistS, is Professor of International History at the University of Victoria. He previously taught at the Royal Military College of Canada where he was a past Chair of War Studies. An expert on interwar international relations, his work centres on Britain as the only global Great Power. Since 2007, he has been editor of *Diplomacy & Statecraft*.

Contents

List of illustrations   *ix*
Contributors   *x*
Prologue: the international order and the new century
B.J.C. McKercher   *xv*

PART I
The Context of Diplomacy   **1**

1   Diplomatic history: a new appraisal   3
    Jeremy Black

2   Theorising diplomacy   15
    Christer Jönsson

PART II
The Great Powers   **29**

3   The United States: the contemporary world's indispensable nation?   31
    James M. Scott

4   The foreign policy of Great Britain   43
    Christoph Bluth

5   Unravelling the enigma: Russian foreign policy in the
    twenty-first century   53
    Jeffrey Mankoff

6   China: Great Power rising   64
    Robert D'A. Henderson

7   France: exercising power and influence across the ages   76
    Paul P. Vallet

Contents

8   German foreign policy mirrored in the achievements and
shortcomings of its chancellors   87
Christian Hacke

9   Japan's diplomacy and culture   96
Alexander Bukh

PART III
The Middle Powers   107

10   Brazil: making room at the main table   109
Sean W. Burges

11   Indian statecraft struggles to come to terms with
India's rise   120
Harsh V. Pant

12   Contemporary Canadian foreign policy: a middle Power
in a Great Power world   131
Stéphane Roussel

13   The Czech Republic: the domestic limits to foreign-policy
effectiveness   143
Dan Marek and Michael Baun

14   The foreign policy of Turkey   155
Dimitris Keridis

PART IV
The Developing Powers   167

15   Cuban revolutionary diplomacy 1959–2009   169
Carlos Alzugaray

16   Peru: a model for Latin American diplomacy and
statecraft   181
Ronald Bruce St John

17   Nigeria: the foreign policy of a putative African Power   192
Cyril I. Obi

18   Thailand: the enigma of bamboo diplomacy   204
Pavin Chachavalpongpun

19 Indonesia's foreign policy after the Cold War: political legitimacy,
    international pressure, and foreign-policy choices   215
    Kai He

PART V
International Organisations and Military Alliances   **227**

20 A global Great Power in the making?: the European Union in
    the emerging global order   229
    Rikard Bengtsson

21 The Great Powers and the United Nations   240
    Stephen Ryan

22 Reconciling different logics of security provision: the case
    of NATO   252
    Alexandra Gheciu

23 New regionalisms and the African Union:
    reflections on the rise of Africrats, regional economic
    integration, and inter-regional relations   264
    J. Andrew Grant and Thomas Kwasi Tieku

24 The non-aligned movement: collective diplomacy of the
    global South   274
    Jacqueline Anne Braveboy-Wagner

PART VI
The International Economy   **291**

25 The International Monetary Fund and the World Bank:
    the power of money?   293
    Morten Bøås

26 The European Union and the economic and financial crisis:
    reforming internal governance and external representation
    in turbulent times   303
    Daniela Schwarzer

27 The Organization of the Petroleum Exporting Countries
    and contemporary international politics and economy   314
    Houchang Hassan-Yari

Contents

28 From colonies to collective: ALBA, Latin American integration, and the
    construction of regional political power   325
    Larry Catá Backer

29 The G8 and the move to a globalised international economy   338
    Andreas Freytag and Leo Wangler

30 The opposition to the globalised international economy   349
    Bruno R. Wüest

PART VII
Issues of Conflict and Cooperation   **363**

31 International arms control   365
    David Mutimer

32 The strategy gap: contemporary civil–military relations
    and the use of military power   376
    Michael L. Roi

33 The Middle East: strategic and military balance of power   388
    Eyal Zisser

34 The balance of power in South Asia   398
    Sumit Ganguly

35 North Korea: the foreign policy of a 'rogue' state   405
    Balbina Y. Hwang

36 Failed states: Zimbabwe   417
    Jeremy R. Youde

37 Public versus private power: non-governmental organisations
    and international security   428
    Jonathan Goodhand and Oliver Walton

38 Soft power: overcoming the limits of a concept   441
    Kostas Ifantis

Bibliography   *453*
Index   *475*

List of illustrations

Figures

26.A1	GDP, constant prices, percent change (2005–11 (estimate))	312
26.A2	GDP based on purchasing-power-parity (PPP) share of world total	313
27.1	OPEC share of world crude oil reserves (2004)	320
27.2	OPEC shares of world crude oil reserves (2009)	320
27.3	World crude oil reserves (2000–2009), cumulative production versus net additions	321

Tables

20.A1	Ongoing Common Security and Defence Policy missions and operations	238
24.A1	The Founding Principles of the Non-Aligned Movement	285
24.A2	The Principles enshrined in the Declaration on the Purposes and Principles and the Role of the Non-Aligned Movement in the Present International Juncture adopted in the 14th NAM Summit in Havana	285
24.A3	Members of the Non-Aligned Movement (2010)	286

Contributors

Carlos Alzugaray Treto, Professor at the University of Havana, served in the Cuban Foreign Service from 1961 to 1996. He has received several awards for his writings and teachings on international relations and has been a Visiting Professor at universities in Spain, Canada, the United States, Italy, and Mexico.

Larry Catá Backer, the Founding Director, the Coalition for Peace and Ethics, Washington, DC, is the W. Richard and Mary Eshelman Faculty Scholar and Professor of Law and Professor of International Affairs, Pennsylvania State University.

Michael Baun is Marguerite Langdale Pizer Professor of International Relations at Valdosta State University, Valdosta, Georgia. One of his recent publications, with Dan Marek, is 'Czech Foreign Policy and EU Integration: European and Domestic Sources', *Perspectives on European Politics and Society* (2010).

Rikard Bengtsson is Associate Professor of Political Science and Deputy Director of the Centre for European Studies at Lund University, Sweden. His main research interests include global political order, regionalism and regional security, and European Union external relations.

Jeremy Black, MBE, is a British historian and Professor of History at the University of Exeter. He is a Senior Fellow at the Centre for the Study of America and the West at the Foreign Policy Research Institute and is a Fellow of the Royal Society of Arts.

Christoph Bluth, Professor of International Studies at the University of Leeds, has written widely on international security, in particular Soviet/Russian, United States, and NATO nuclear weapons policies, nuclear non-proliferation, Cold War History, and security on the Korean peninsula. His books include *Korea* (2008) (also translated into Korean and Bulgarian).

Morten Bøås, Head of Research at Fafo's Institute for Applied International Studies, has published extensively on global governance, multilateral development policies, and African politics. His works have appeared in journals like *Global Governance, Journal of Intervention and Statebuilding, Politique Africaine*, and *Journal of Modern African Studies*. His latest books published in English include *Global Development and Institutions. Framing the World?* (2004) and *International Development*, 4 Volumes (2010).

Jacqueline Anne Braveboy-Wagner, Professor of Political Science at The City College and The Graduate School and University Center of the City University of New York, is the author/editor of nine books and a large number of articles and reports. She specialises in foreign policy with an area focus on the Caribbean and the global South.

Alexander Bukh is Associate Professor of International Relations, University of Tsukuba, Ibaraki, Japan. He holds an LLM in International Law, University of Tokyo, and a PhD in International Relations, London School of Economics. He is the author of *Japan's Identity and Foreign Policy: Russia as Japan's 'Other'* (2009).

Sean W. Burges is Lecturer in International Relations, School of Politics and International Relations, and Senior Associate with the Australian National Centre for Latin American Studies, Australian National University. He has written *Brazilian Foreign Policy After the Cold War*, plus numerous articles and chapters on Brazilian foreign policy and inter-American affairs.

Pavin Chachavalpongpun, a former diplomat, is a Fellow and Lead Researcher for Political and Strategic Affairs at the ASEAN Studies Centre, Institute of Southeast Asian Studies, Singapore. He has written *Reinventing Thailand: Thaksin and His Foreign Policy* (2010) and *A Plastic Nation: The Curse of Thainess in Thai-Burmese Relations* (2005).

Andreas Freytag, a specialist in international relations and development and monetary policy, is Professor of Economics at the Friedrich-Schiller-University, Jena and Honorary Professor at the University of Stellenbosch. He is Senior Research Fellow at the European Centre for International Political Economy, Brussels, Senior Research Associate at the South African Institute of International Affairs, Johannesburg, and associated with the G8 Research Group, Toronto.

Sumit Ganguly is Professor of Political Science and holds the Rabindranath Tagore Chair in Indian Cultures and Civilization at Indiana University, Bloomington. He is the author, co-author, editor, or co-editor of twenty books on the international and domestic politics of South Asia.

Alexandra Gheciu is Associate Professor at the Graduate School of Public and International Affairs and Associate Director of the Centre for International Policy Studies, University of Ottawa. Her recent publications include *NATO in the New Europe* (2005) and *Securing Civilization?* (2008).

Jonathan Goodhand is Reader in Conflict and Development Studies in the Department of Development Studies, School of Oriental and African Studies, University of London. His primary research interests are the political economy of armed conflict, non-governmental organisations, and peace-building, and 'post-conflict' reconstruction. His books include *Aiding Peace? The Role of NGOs in Armed Conflict* (2006).

J. Andrew Grant is Assistant Professor of Political Studies at Queen's University, Kingston. His publications, based on field research conducted throughout Africa, focus on regional security, post-conflict reconstruction, natural resource governance, and conflict diamonds and the Kimberley Process. His three co-edited books examine regional political economy and security.

Christian Hacke was Professor of Political Science, University of the Army Forces, Hamburg, from 1980 to 2000 and then held the Chair of Political Science and Contemporary History at Bonn University. His research focuses on American and German foreign policy, and the history and theory of international relations. The author of several books, mostly on American and German foreign policy, he contributes frequently to German newspapers and magazines such as *Die Zeit* and *Frankfurter Allgemeine Zeitung*.

Houchang Hassan-Yari, Professor of Political Science at the Royal Military College of Canada, earned his degrees from universities in Iran and Canada. A member of the *Académie de Géopolitique de Paris*, he has taught in Teheran, Lyon, and Montreal. The author and editor of a number of books and articles, his research areas include Middle Eastern issues, geopolitics of resources, and comparative politics.

Kai He is Assistant Professor of Political Science at Utah State University. He is the author of *Institutional Balancing in the Asia Pacific: Economic Interdependence and China's Rise* (2009) and has published articles in *European Journal of International Relations*, *Review of International Studies*, *Security Studies*, and *The Pacific Review*.

Robert D'A. Henderson is an International Assessments Expert based in Ottawa and editor of *Brassey's International Intelligence Yearbook*. Previously, he was a senior international strategic analyst with the Canadian Government after almost twenty years of teaching international relations and security studies at universities in Canada and overseas.

Balbina Y. Hwang is Visiting Professor at Georgetown University and the National Defense University. She served as Senior Special Advisor to Ambassador Christopher Hill, Assistant Secretary for East Asian Affairs at the United States Department of State from 2007 to 2009.

Kostas Ifantis is Associate Professor of International Relations at the University of Athens. He has held visiting posts at Harvard and the London School of Economics. His papers have appeared in edited books and in periodicals such as *Democratization*, *Review of International Affairs*, *International Journal*, *Turkish Studies*, and *Southern Europe and the Balkans*.

Christer Jönsson is Professor Emeritus of Political Science at Lund University and a member of the Royal Swedish Academy of Sciences. His publications include *Communication in International Bargaining* (1990), *Essence of Diplomacy* (co-author 2005), and *Transnational Actors in Global Governance* (co-editor 2010), along with several articles in leading academic journals.

Dimitris Keridis is an Associate Professor of International Politics at the University of Macedonia and Director of the Navarino Network, a public policy think-tank, in Thessaloniki, Greece. He is co-editor of *The Future of Foreign Policy* (2004).

Jeffrey Mankoff is a Council on Foreign Relations (CFR) International Affairs Fellow. He was previously Associate Director of International Security Studies at Yale University and adjunct fellow for Russia Studies at the CFR.

Dan Marek is Jean Monnet Lecturer in European Politics at the Department of Politics and European Studies, Palacký University, Olomouc, Czech Republic. One of his recent publications, with Michael Baun, is *The Czech Republic and the European Union* (2011).

B.J.C. McKercher, FRHistS, is Professor of International History at the University of Victoria. He previously taught at the Royal Military College of Canada where he was a past Chair of War Studies. An expert on interwar international relations, his work centers on Britain as the only global Great Power. Since 2007, he has been editor of *Diplomacy & Statecraft*.

David Mutimer, Deputy Director of the York Centre for International and Security Studies and Associate Professor of Political Science at York University (Toronto), researches issues of contemporary international security, particularly arms control, through lenses provided by critical social theory and popular culture. He recently co-edited a special issue of *Contemporary Security Policy* on 'Arms Control for the 21st Century'.

Cyril I. Obi received his PhD from the University of Lagos and has published widely on African politics, political economy, and international relations. He is a Senior Researcher and Leader, Research Cluster on Conflict, Displacement and Transformation at the Nordic Africa Institute,

Uppsala, Sweden. Since 2005, he has been on leave from the Nigerian Institute of International Affairs, where he is an Associate Research Professor.

Harsh V. Pant, Department of Defence Studies, King's College, London, is also an Associate with the King's Centre for Science and Security Studies and an Affiliate with the King's India Institute. His current research focuses on Asian security issues. His most recent books include *Contemporary Debates in Indian Foreign and Security Policy* (2008).

Michael L. Roi is the Director of Strategic Operations Analysis at the Department of National Defence, Ottawa, and an Adjunct Professor of War Studies at the Royal Military College of Canada. From 1998 to 2002, he was the Executive Director of the Atlantic Council of Canada.

Stéphane Roussel is Professor in the Department of Political Science at the *Université du Québec à Montréal* and Canada Research Chair in Canadian Foreign and Defence Policy. His research interests concern Canada's relations with the United States and Europe, Arctic security, public opinion, and Canadian strategic culture.

Stephen Ryan is Senior Lecturer in the School of English, History and Politics at the University of Ulster. He is the author of *Ethnic Conflict and International Relations* (1995), *The United Nations and International Politics* (2000), and *The Transformation of Violent Intercommunal Conflict* (2007).

Ronald Bruce St John has lectured at the Diplomatic Academy of Peru and served as a consultant for Fortune 500 companies, government agencies, and media outlets. In addition to *The Foreign Policy of Peru* (1992) and *La Política Exterior del Perú* (1999), his publications include *Toledo's Peru: Vision and Reality* (2010) and *Libya: Continuity and Change* (2011).

Daniela Schwarzer is Head of the Research Division, European Integration at the German Institute for International and Security Affairs, Berlin. From 1999 until 2004, she served as editorialist and France correspondent for the *Financial Times Deutschland*. She has lectured at various universities and has held advisory positions in European Union member-states.

James M. Scott is Herman Brown Chair and Professor, Department of Political Science, Texas Christian University. The author, co-author, or editor of 30 publications, he is currently an Associate Editor of *Foreign Policy Analysis* and has been President of both the International Studies Association-Midwest (2000) and the Foreign Policy Analysis Section (2001) of the International Studies Association.

Thomas Kwasi Tieku teaches international relations and directs the African Studies Program at the University of Toronto. He specialises in international mediation and diplomacy, peace-building, and multilateral democracy promotion, which appears in *Democratization*, *Africa Today*, *African Affairs*, *Africa Today*, *African Security Review*, *Canadian Foreign Policy Journal*, and the *International Journal*.

Paul P. Vallet teaches history and international relations at *Sciences Po*—the *Institut d'Études Politiques de Paris*. He has degrees from *Sciences Po*, the Fletcher School of Law and Diplomacy at Tufts University, and received his PhD from Cambridge University. He was Visiting Professor at the Fletcher School in Spring 2011.

Oliver Walton is a Research Fellow at the Governance and Social Development Resource Centre, University of Birmingham. He has published and taught on issues relating to non-governmental organisations (NGOs), civil society, peace-building, and conflict resolution. He has worked for a number of NGOs in Britain and Sri Lanka.

Leo Wangler is currently teaching and research assistant for the Chair for Economic Policy at the Friedrich-Schiller-University in Jena. His main field of interest is climate change policy, which is also the topic for his PhD dissertation. He received his Diploma degree in 2007 from Albert-Ludwigs-University in Freiburg.

Bruno R. Wüest is a researcher at the University of Zurich and guest researcher at the New York University. He received his Master in Political Science and Economic history at the University of Zurich.

Jeremy R. Youde is Assistant Professor of Political Science at the University of Minnesota, Duluth. His research focuses on global health politics and southern African politics. His most recent book is *Biopolitical Surveillance and Public Health in International Politics* (2009).

Eyal Zisser is Dean of the Faculty of Humanities and the Director of the Moshe Dayan Center for Middle Eastern and African Studies at Tel Aviv University. He has written extensively on the history and the modern politics of Syria and Lebanon and the Arab–Israeli conflict.

Prologue

The international order and the new century

B. J. C. McKercher

I say that it is a narrow policy to suppose that this country or that is to be marked out as the eternal ally or the perpetual enemy of England. We have no eternal allies, and we have no perpetual enemies. Our interests are eternal and perpetual, and those interests it is our duty to follow.

Palmerston, March 1848[1]

Despite post–Cold War arguments about their demise, 'Great Powers' not only continue to thrive, with lesser Powers they form the basis of the constellation of global politics. The statement of Lord Palmerston, the British Foreign Secretary, to the House of Commons in early 1848 about Britain having no permanent allies and enemies, only permanent interests, came in response to domestic critics who disparaged the cordial tone of his Russian policy. Yet, despite their temporal distance from the second decade of the twentieth-first century, Palmerston's observations comprise a set of axioms about a world populated by Great and smaller Powers, about assessing their competing interests, and about finding the political and military means to preserve and enhance those interests. Significantly, these axioms are still relevant in understanding the nature of contemporary international politics. Of course, modern 'Great' Powers arose from the morass of Europe's religious wars more than two centuries before Palmerston first held public office; and in Asia, empires like those of China and the Mongols were earlier Great Powers.[2] Thus, he did not invent them. Rather, he was just one of an unbroken line of statesmen and stateswomen who, since the late sixteenth century, have had the responsibility for making and implementing foreign and military policies.

Unencumbered by 'theories' of international politics, these diplomatists (ranging from Cardinal Richelieu to Clemens von Metternich to Otto von Bismarck to Henry Kissinger and beyond[3]) have grasped the simple fact that Great Powers exist, they seek always to defend their strategic advantages and secure their wealth, and they have the ability to shape the contours of the international landscape in war and peace. Of course, not all the statesmen guiding the Great Powers have been successful.[4] And, just as important, Great Powers have never existed by themselves. So what has been true for their diplomatists over the past four centuries has been doubly so for those of middle and lesser Powers competing amongst themselves and the Great Powers for advantage and survival in an unforgiving world.[5]

As the Cold War ended in 1989–91, a new international order arose with the disintegration of Soviet Russia, the collapse of its Eastern European Empire, and the crumbling of its alliances. The international order that emerged after the Second World War, bipolar and dominated by two mutually antagonistic superpowers and their alliance coalitions, disappeared. In its place arose an order with a supposed single 'Hyper Power', the United States of America.[6] Under two Republican presidents, Ronald Reagan (1981–89) and George Bush, Sr (1989–93), American victory in the Cold War was a watershed in global politics. American diplomatists understood this transition and willingly pursued foreign and defense policies designed to ensure American international hegemony. The 1990–91 Gulf War can be considered the first overt action to ensure the emerging new international order. Although American missteps precipitated the crisis (Saddam Hussein, Iraq's dictator, thought the Bush Administration supported his annexationist ambitions[7]) the United States successfully forced the Iraqis from Kuwait by leading a coalition of Powers with an interest in secure Middle Eastern oil supplies. As one of the principal architects of Republican foreign and defense policy, Paul Wolfowitz, argued about American post-Cold War strategy:

> Our first objective is to prevent the re-emergence of a new rival, either on the territory of the former Soviet Union or elsewhere, that poses a threat on the order of that posed formerly by the Soviet Union. … we endeavor to prevent any hostile power from dominating a region whose resources would, under consolidated control, be sufficient to generate global power.[8]

Flowing from this argument, Wolfowitz outlined a second objective: 'to address sources of regional conflict and instability in such a way as to promote increasing respect for international law, limit international violence, and encourage the spread of democratic forms of government and open economic systems.' In different forms and, sometimes, with different emphasis, Wolfowitz's ideas about supposed American hegemony were shared by a range of American politicians, diplomatists, intellectuals, and journalists.[9] Thus, as the new international order emerged, influential elements of America's foreign policy-making elite had a strategic vision for ensuring their newly won primacy, and the United States had given the world a lesson in its readiness to enforce its image of international stability.

Beyond this practical expression of American *realpolitik*, there arose a philosophical explanation for the rise of American triumph over Soviet Russia. Just as the Berlin Wall crumbled, in a seminal, contentious, and widely circulated article, 'The End of History', the American neoconservative thinker Francis Fukuyama asserted that liberal democracy, tied to free enterprise capitalism and social democracy, had defeated the Soviet system's command economies.[10] Indeed, the abject failure of the Marxist socioeconomic experiment both domestically and in its ability to support effective foreign and defense policies lay at the base of what had been a titanic struggle between the first world of the United States and its allies and the second one of Soviet Russia and its Empire. And not only had free enterprise capitalism, social democratic mixed economies, and their corollary of liberal democracy girded successful external policies of the first world (concurrently providing its people with increasing living standards, employment, and personal liberty), they constituted the socioeconomic future for all states. History had ended; the great fight over competing socioeconomic systems, in various guises since at least the French Revolution, had been decided; Fukuyama did not say that problems, crises, and wars would disappear, but the long struggle over how men and women should govern themselves socioeconomically was over.

Fukuyama was not the only thinker reflecting on the United States' emergence as the Hyper Power.[11] But these arguments (as diverse in form and emphasis as those about the practical politics of safeguarding and extending American international hegemony) provoked a reaction from critics in the United States and the wider world. Animated by philosophical distaste for free enterprise capitalism, by support for other socioeconomic systems, by opposition to American foreign-policy goals, or, simply, by base anti-Americanism, these critics took the United States and its foreign policies to task.[12] In France, Jacques Derrida, a leading post-modernist, disparaged the gross inadequacies of American capitalism, arguing that its brand of liberal democracy could not be transplanted to other places in the world.[13]

The varied criticism of supposed American omnipotence after 1989–91 reached its apogee with the rise of anti-globalisation organisations in most parts of the world. Globalisation (what the World Bank defines as 'the growing integration of economies and societies around the world'[14]) did not suddenly begin after 1989; in many respects the fifteenth-century northern European Hanseatic League and nineteenth-century German *zollverein* were earlier successful efforts of at least economic consolidation;[15] in the latter half of the twentieth century, regional blocs like the European Economic Community and the Council for Mutual Economic Assistance were avowedly integrationist;[16] and, perhaps, best of all, the British Empire for almost ninety years after the 1848 repeal of the Corn Laws constituted a real global marketplace.[17] Indeed, as a result of the international economic dislocation caused by the Great Depression of the 1930s and the Second World War, the establishment of the International Monetary Fund, the General Agreement on Tariffs and Trade (GATT), and the World Bank provided a framework for greater international economic and financial cooperation and planning.[18] But it was the extension of American economic power through trade and investment after 1989–91 by United States-based international corporations that provoked widespread activist opposition to 'globalisation'. Although the equally aggressive expansion of other First World international corporations was as pronounced (from Britain, Canada, France, Germany, and other countries[19]), the size and strength of American corporate institutions, tied to the potency of the world's largest economy and its modern military, provoked activist dissent and criticism.[20] That Washington played a major role in replacing GATT with the World Trade Organization (WTO) in 1995, and that the United States occupied a paramount place in that body, only added to criticisms of globalisation.[21]

Therefore, three intertwined elements shaped the contours of international politics for two decades after the Berlin Wall collapsed: United States power; strengthened capitalist and social democratic socioeconomic systems; and American-led globalisation, which critics argue undercut the particularism and political and economic sovereignty that defined nation-states. Here was a new international order and, given the potency of the capitalist United States, the argument emerged that the era of Great Power rivalry had ended.[22] Indeed, in international relations theory, there has been a trend to redefine international politics as being post-modern: change is constant; absolute values are illusory, thus, relative values are the norm; on this basis there are no absolute or universal truths; and, suffusing everything, all human endeavors (art, politics, economics, and more) are moulded by the cultural context of a distinct time and space.[23] Following this argument, the distinction between domestic affairs and foreign policy blurs; the use of armed force to resolve crises repudiated; reliance placed on codified and self-enforced rules of conduct under organisations as diverse as the United Nations (UN), the WTO, and the North Atlantic Treaty Organization (NATO); a supposed emerging irrelevance of borders caused by globalisation, legal and illegal immigration, the lethality of modern weapon systems, and the encroaching of space-based surveillance systems; and, finally, enhanced national security by open diplomacy, economic and political interdependence, and shared vulnerability to attack.

Suffused by notions of American international hegemony, this theoretical construct suggests that Great Power rivalry disappeared (or at the least became anachronistic) in the new order.[24] This theory has penetrated the public mind to the extent that it informs the public pronouncements of Western leaders. In October 1992, the American presidential candidate, Bill Clinton, remarked that 'in a world where freedom, not tyranny, is on the march, the cynical calculus of pure power politics simply does not compute'.[25] By the same token, Tony Blair, early in his tenure as British Prime Minister in 1999, took a similar tack before a Chicago audience: 'The defining characteristic of our modern world is interdependence. We live in the age of the interconnected.'[26]

Yet, these declarations, and others (disparaging realism, old diplomatic and military nostrums in international politics, and supposed antiquated methods of conducting foreign and defense policies[27]) are in reality subsets of theories. And as helpful as theories are, the wonderful thing about them is that they cannot be proved. As theoreticians like to pronounce, theories can only be tested.[28] Accordingly, in contradistinction to theories about the emerging post-modern world and hyper power, 'Great' Powers simply have not disappeared. Nor have the Palmerstonian (or Richelieuien, Metternichian, Bismarckian, or Kissingerian) axioms that govern how they compete with one another to pursue their interests and find the political and military means to preserve and enhance those interests.

New international orders are not unique. The 1648 Peace of Westphalia ending the Thirty Years War established a 'new' Europe by formalising the existence of Great Powers.[29] For almost a century and a half, wars of religion tied to dynastic interest had been fought by the European Powers. By the mid-seventeenth century, Habsburg Spain fell to second-class status, its Austrian cousin, the Holy Roman Empire, emerged as the bulwark against the expansive Ottomans in the East, Poland dominated north-eastern Europe, Sweden the north, and France and England, the undisputed victors, emerged as the leading Great Powers and were beginning significant overseas expansion. Over the next three hundred years, new international orders came and went: after 1714 in the War of the Spanish Succession, after the War of the Austrian Succession in the 1740s, after the Seven Years War in 1763, the Napoleonic Wars in 1814–15, the German wars of unification in 1871, the First World War in 1918, and the Second World War in 1945. Hence, the transition that emerged in 1991 was no more or less significant than any other.

As international politics evolved, Great Powers rose and fell for various reasons, for example, Prussia–Germany after 1648. When the Thirty Years War ended, Lutheran Prussia was just one of more than three hundred German states existing under the aegis of the Roman Catholic Holy Roman Emperor. It slowly built and consolidated over a century; then, under the brilliant leadership of a militaristic, Enlightenment king, Frederick the Great, emerged as a recognised Great Power after the War of the Austrian Succession and the Seven Years War. It suffered setbacks during the Napoleonic Wars but, through skilful diplomacy and by taking a prominent part in defeating France in 1814–15, it thereafter rivalled the Austrian Empire for leadership amongst now thirty-nine German states. Military reforms after 1815 gave a weapon to Bismarck and aristocratic and conservative German nationalists in Prussia to use between 1864 and 1871 to unify Germany politically under the Prussian crown. But the united *Kaiserreich* lasted less than half a century, defeated in the First World War by falling prey to the strategic nightmare of fighting a two-front land war against three first-class Great Powers (its chief ally, Austria-Hungary, was ineffective) and a maritime war in which its expensive High Seas Fleet did virtually nothing. But Germany revived by the late 1930s, under the expansionist Nazi regime of Adolf Hitler. As occurred to the *Kaiserreich* in1914–18, Hitler's *Reich* overreached itself after 1939; again, fighting a two-front war against first-class Great Powers and being tied to a weak ally, this time fascist Italy. Defeated Germany was then divided into four zones of occupation by the victorious Powers in 1945; by 1949, Cold War divisiveness produced two Germanys: a liberal democratic, capitalist West Germany tied to the United States and NATO; and a Marxist-Leninist, socialist East Germany tied to Soviet Russia and the Warsaw Pact. Only after East Germany collapsed in 1989–90 did Germany reunite and move into the post-Cold War new international order.

Prussia–Germany in one guise or another entered each and every new international order since the Peace of Westphalia. It did so as a weak Power, a divided Power, a defeated Great Power, a victorious Great Power, and, at least twice, the dominant European Great Power. And what is true for Prussia–Germany is true for all the other existing Great Powers of the modern period: tsarist, Bolshevik, Soviet, and post-Cold War Russia; monarchical, revolutionary, Imperial, and republican France; Imperial and liberal democratic Japan; Manchu, nationalist, and communist China; and so on. Similarly, some Great Powers have ceased to exist; the Holy Roman Empire and its Habsburg Austrian and Austro-Hungarian successors are exemplary.

There are telling observations to make about Great Powers and new international orders. These orders arise from the chaos of war, when one Great Power or a group of Great Powers see losses on the battlefield translated directly into losses of territory, transfers of population, payment of reparations, and, in some cases, like that of Poland in 1795, complete obliteration.[30] Victor Powers determine the geographical, economic, political, and strategic contours of the new order through usually difficult and disputatious bargaining; during the Congress of Vienna in 1814–15, the possibility of Russia's former allies going to war against it over the Polish question seemed a real possibility.[31] In any post-war period, victorious Great Powers tend to view each other suspiciously and, sometimes, as emergent threats to their perceived national interests. Thus, in the War of the Austrian Succession, Britain supported Austria against Prussia, the reason being that France, Britain's main rival, backed Prussia.[32] Less than five years after this struggle, Austria won French support for renewed war against Prussia; with an effective Army and an assertive Frederick the Great, Prussia now threatened both France and Austria and their new ally, Russia. Britain shifted its support to Prussia; again, to weaken France, take its Empire in North America, and stabilise the continental balance of power so necessary for British security.[33] The same kind of situation emerged after the First World War in terms of Anglo-French relations, and after the Second World War, for Soviet Russian relations with Britain and the United States.

Often in creating new international orders, one victorious Power emerges as the greatest of the Great Powers and retains this position for extended periods. After 1648, Bourbon France occupied the center of political, economic, and military gravity in Europe. Louis XIV squandered this advantage in two ways: extended wars against the Dutch, English, and their allies provided no strategic victory; and the huge drain on the French exchequer over more than two decades to build Versailles Palace created endemic fiscal domestic weakness until after the French Revolution.[34] Still, France remained a Great Power because it supported its foreign policy with armed force and effective diplomacy; and it was not until Napoleon I's defeat, a century after Louis XIV died, that French expansionism was finally checked.[35] The record of British arms in the one hundred and fifty years before 1815 was generally one of success, a notable exception being its defeat by usurpers in the 'Thirteen Colonies' in North America in 1782.[36] However, by 1815, girded by the Royal Navy's preeminence after victory over its French enemy at Trafalgar in 1804 and the expansion of trade routes and colonial holdings during the Napoleonic Wars when it was denied access to the European market, Great Britain emerged as the only truly World Power.[37] Supported by an expanding franchise, successive British leaders were able to defend the 'eternal and perpetual interests' of the nation and Empire until the Second World War.[38]

As suggested above, grand theories of political intercourse have rarely animated Great Power statesmen, their advisors, diplomatists, and soldiers, sailors, and airmen.[39] The world inhabited by the Great Powers has always been one where competing concrete interests, as well as interests touching religion and ideology, and the defense or extension of territory has at times been brutal. Frederick the Great's ambition to exploit Habsburg weakness in 1740 to annex Silesia, Palmerston's willingness to use armed force to open the Chinese market to British trade in 1839, and Joseph Stalin's employment of the Red Army to extend the Soviet Russian Empire into Eastern Europe between 1944 and 1948 are examples of what one critic of Great Power diplomacy in 1914 called 'the international anarchy'.[40]

Of course, efforts have been made to eliminate (or, at least, ameliorate) this anarchy. Although Christian beliefs supposedly provided a moral base for the foreign policies of temporal European monarchs, restraint had rarely if ever been effective. In the wars of religion after the Protestant Reformation, Christian precepts were used to justify war by Protestant and Roman Catholic sovereigns one against each other.[41] In this context, the lengthy struggle between Spain and its rebellious Dutch provinces was especially blood-soaked.[42] In reaction to these seemingly interminable hostilities, a body of writings emerged that looked to natural rather than religious law as to control war. The three-tome book, *On the Laws of War and Peace*, by the Dutch philosopher Hugo Grotius published in 1625 had three main arguments: war was sometimes justified; wars can be fought for self-defense, the reparation of injury, and retribution; and should war occur, rules exist concerning its conduct whether the combatant Powers have a just cause or not.[43] Grotius's ideas laid the basis for modern international law, and the development of legal constraints to direct how Powers great and small governed their affairs.[44]

However, the Great Powers rarely allowed morality to limit their foreign and military policy objectives. In Palmerston's view, sometimes they would cooperate with one another; sometimes they would not. Time and circumstance dictated how each Great Power's leaders moved to protect their 'eternal and perpetual' interests. Accordingly, the Roman Catholic France dominated by Richelieu had little compunction in seeking to limit the influence of the Roman Catholic Holy Roman Emperor in Germany by supporting Protestant Sweden in the first phase of the Thirty Years War.[45] In this circumstance, it is not surprising that Richelieu apparently coined the term, *raison d'état*.[46] Thus, Great Powers would cooperate only when it was in their interest to do so. Perhaps the most effective effort at such cooperation came after the Allied defeat of Napoleonic France in 1814–15. Exhausted by twenty-five years of war and revolution and desirous of reestablishing stability to the continent based on conservative aristocratic control of governments, the victorious Great Powers created the Congress of Europe. Under Metternich's deft diplomatic hand, the Great Powers met in five congresses between 1814 and 1822 to settle crises amongst themselves without recourse to war; that Austrian forces could enter Italy under the Congress' writ to restore order or that France, a member of the Congress system after 1818, could receive permission to send troops into Spain to quell a rebellion was quite a different thing.[47]

Still, the Congress was short-lived. It met last in 1822, when Britain withdrew; British leaders saw no threat to the continental balance and, consequently, no need to involve themselves in the daily machinations of European politics. Moreover, the death in 1825 of the Western-oriented Russian Tsar, Alexander I, saw Russia begin to pursue a more independent foreign policy.[48] But in place of the Congress system, there evolved a less formal diplomatic mechanism to resolve European crises with the potential for war: the Concert of Europe.[49] The Great Powers, including Britain, would convene *ad hoc* to find a collective agreement to resolve disputes. For the most part, the Concert worked, for instance when the Powers met at Berlin in June–July 1878 to find a workable settlement of a Russo-Turkish crisis in the Balkans. But occasionally, the Concert did not work, for instance, in the endless Balkan crises after 1902 that threatened to pit tsarist Russia (backed by France) against Austria–Hungary (backed by Germany).[50] Two Balkan wars, in 1912 and 1913, had actually been resolved by the intervention of the Concert Powers, called together by the British Foreign Secretary, Sir Edward Grey.[51] But when a third war threatened in summer 1914 after the assassination of the heir-apparent to the Habsburg throne by Serbian-sponsored terrorists, the Great Powers did not meet. The Germans argued that this crisis involved only Austria–Hungary and Russia and not the Concert Powers; Great Power tensions increased, the 1914 'July Crisis' was spawned, and, by early August, the Great War (the First World War) had broken out amongst the European Great Powers.[52]

Only with the devastation caused by this war was a serious international effort made to find diplomatic means to regulate the Powers' behavior. 1914–18 saw the first 'total' war in Great Power history. Citizens at home had been drafted into the war effort to maximise industrial and agricultural production.[53] Soldiers and citizens paid a huge price in blood and treasure to fight the war so that, as the fighting progressed, public opinion within all the belligerent Powers looked for means to make peace permanent once the struggle ended.[54] The result in 1919 was the creation of the League of Nations, the first permanent international organisation dedicated to maintaining international peace and security. Yet, the League had limitations because all the Great Powers were never members at the same time.[55] The United States refused to join. Germany became a member only in 1926, but left in 1934 after Hitler's revolution. Looking for collective security against Nazi Germany, Soviet Russia then joined for the first time. But the League failed. Although it could check the transgressions of smaller Powers (like Greece during the 1923 Corfu crisis[56]) it could not restrain the naked ambitions of Great Powers: Japan's conquest of Manchuria in 1931–32 and the Italian descent on Abyssinia thee years later.[57] Both of these Great Powers left the League; in 1939, the organisation could do nothing to stop the outbreak of Great Power war for the second time in twenty-five years. The post-1945 international system saw a new organisation, the UN, replace the League.[58] Although the UN made some seminal con- tributions in maintaining peace and security (the advent of peace-keeping in 1956, for instance[59]), it suffered the same weakness as the League: it could not force Great and Super Powers to disgorge conquests or limit warfare. Soviet Russia's suppression of the Hungarian Uprising in 1956, French policies in Algeria after 1954, and American violations of Cambodian neutrality during the Vietnam War are spectacular instances in which UN inadequacy manifested itself.[60] As happened since Grotius put pen to paper, Great Powers were independent in pursuit of perpetual national interests.

The persistence of the Great Powers can best be appreciated by looking at the architecture of the international system they inhabit and the strategic bases of foreign and defense policy. A distinguishing feature of Great Powers is a willingness (and, sometimes, dire need) to find and hold allies to help protect their existence and their interests. Before the Second World War, the best example of a Great Power that used alliances effectively was Great Britain. From the struggle against Louis XIV through the Napoleonic wars to the Crimean War and the two World Wars of the twentieth century, Britain never fought alone.[61] The strategic predicament that it faced in 1940 was that its principal ally, France, and its huge land-based army were unexpectedly defeated.[62] Thus, Britain suddenly had to fight two Great Powers in Europe and face the menace of a third in the Far East without a Great Power ally. In 1941, Soviet Russia and the United States joined Britain in confronting the Axis Powers and Japan; Britain had major allies but, now, given American and Russian economic, industrial, and manpower resources, Britain became a junior ally.[63] Of course, reliance on alliances has not always been successful, as Britain's Second World War experience showed; and this British experience was not unique.[64] Nonetheless, because they augment the diplomatic and military resources of states, alliances have always been integral to the persistence of the Great Powers.

And successful alliances can disintegrate. With the disappearance of the common threats of Italian fascism, German Nazism, and Japanese militarism by 1945, the Super Power victors of the Second World War fell out as peace dawned.[65] In the resulting bipolar Cold War world, the United States-led NATO alliance confronting the Soviet Russian-led Warsaw Pact defined Great and Super Power rivalry in Europe for two generations.[66] Outside Europe with varying degrees of success, Western alliances like the Australia, New Zealand, United States Security (ANZUS) Treaty, the Southeast Asia Treaty Organization (SEATO), and even the Canadian-American North American Air Defence agreement were integral elements of the international system.[67]

Soviet Russian treaties of mutual assistance with various non-European minor Powers during the Cold War (with at various times Cuba, Egypt, Syria, Angola, and Mozambique[68]) added to the international edifice.

Between the UN and the regional alliances lay a host of international organisations that looked to better the conditions of Powers and populations. GATT, the World Bank, and the International Monetary Fund were post-Second World War efforts to prevent the kind of international economic dislocation caused by the Great Depression of the 1930s that led supposedly to the disaster of the Second World War.[69] But these organisations were just part of a plethora of others composed of member-states that clustered around the UN. The UN Economic, Social, and Cultural Organisation, the World Health Organization, the Food and Agricultural Organization, the International Atomic Energy Agency, and more were part and parcel of the Cold War order and beyond.[70] The creation of the European Economic Community in 1958, its transformation in the 1980s into the European Union, and its expansion thereafter demonstrated new approaches to preserving and enhancing Powers' interests by multilateral agreement.[71] And governmental organisations were joined after 1945 by non-governmental organisations (NGOs) that sometimes worked with governments, but more often worked independently, to minister to peoples whose homelands had been ravaged by war, pestilence, and poverty.[72] As the Cold War ended, unchecked by the rigidity brought by East–West struggle, NGOs proliferated and became an accepted component of the architecture of international politics, but one still dominated by Great Powers. Indeed, international organisations became a medium in which the Great Powers and their alliances continued to compete: in the Congo in the late 1950s, over the Arab Powers' lengthy efforts to isolate Israel, or in the Balkans in the 1990s; yet, NGOs ply their trade only because of Great Power tolerance, Great Power protection, or Great Power willingness to use NGO resources rather than their own to alleviate social and economic distress.

Finally, the strategic bases of foreign policy have defined the long era of Great Powers in international politics. What emerged at Westphalia was the strategic prescription of the balance of power.[73] If a single Great Power or group of Great Powers moved to upset the balance in their favor (imperilling the security and interests of other Great Powers), the other Great Powers would align and meet the threat diplomatically or militarily. Such action explains British opposition to France for more than one hundred and fifty years after Westphalia. It explains Prussian policy towards Austria in the Seven Years War; and in the Cold War, it explains NATO and the Warsaw Pact balancing one against the other in case of a potential war that might upset the post-1945 Europe equilibrium.

Some scholars and others argue that the balance of power never really existed, or even exists today.[74] They are wrong. The 'Eastern Question', the nineteenth-century contest to benefit from the disintegration of the Ottoman Empire in the Balkans, is a case in point.[75] But whether in the Balkans, in other regions of Europe, or in the wider world, belligerent Powers' hegemonic designs were always constrained by other Great Powers either diplomatically or, in extreme situations, resorting to military strength. Importantly, the concept of the balance was often used by policy-makers as a historical explanation for diplomatic strategy that informed policy rather than a theoretical model for diplomatic practice or an analytical tool.[76] And although some Great Powers might follow policies founded on hegemonic goals rather than see themselves limited by the prescripts of the balance and the quest for stability, the balance served always to check their ambitions. In this context, in their different ways, the expansionist aspirations of Louis XIV's France in the late seventeenth and early eighteenth centuries, those of Tsar Nicholas I's Russia in the mid-1850s, and Adolph Hitler's Germany in 1939–45 were each doused by the concerted action of their Great Power rivals.

But whereas relying on the balance has been the lynch-pin of Great Power rivalry since the 1640s if not before (Elizabethan England certainly worked to build counterveiling weight to Philip II's Spain[77]), other strategic prescriptions exist and have been tried. These approaches have arisen either because of unique circumstances or the conscious desire of particular statesmen critical of the balance, who have sought different means to protect their state's national interests. It might be surprising, but appeasement (granting concessions to avoid costly confrontation) has a long and spotted history amongst the Great Powers. In the late eighteenth century, in one instance, the Habsburgs sought to appease Catherine the Great's Russia as it looked to bolster its position in Central Europe and expand its territories at Ottoman expense.[78] In 1939, Bolshevik Russia concluded the so-called Ribbentrop–Molotov pact to improve its relations with Nazi Germany at a moment when it was weak and when Stalin believed war between Germany and the Western Powers was inevitable.[79] Even the United States has endorsed appeasement, pursuing Cold War *détente* in the late 1960s and early 1970s.[80] But, of course, the most spectacular instance of a Great Power relying on appeasement was Britain in the late 1930s.[81] The British premier after May 1937, Neville Chamberlain, scorned the balance because he believed it had produced the Great War of 1914–18. Reckoning that Britain needed time to rearm to contain excessive German ambitions, he looked to buy time by making concessions to Hitler that would allow peaceful territorial changes in Central Europe to bring all German-speaking peoples within the Reich.[82] But he misjudged Hitler, who broke his word about not seeking non-German-speaking territories when Nazi Germany annexed the rump of Czechoslovakia in March 1939.[83] Chamberlain's brand of appeasement was a rational policy (*realpolitik* of a high order) based on the demands of British voters, the economic strength of the state, and armed forces needing strengthening. But when it failed (spectacularly) Britain found itself at war in September 1939 and its leaders looking to the reestablishment of the European balance as a war aim.

Another strategy with a long pedigree has been a reliance on conference diplomacy. The series of diplomatic meetings that produced the Peace of Westphalia, the Congress of Vienna and its subsequent meetings, and the Concert of Europe were tangible manifestations of the Powers' willingness to settle important international questions face to face. After the First World War, despite the League, the Powers used conference diplomacy to resolve a number of pressing problems; the Paris Peace Conference began the process and, because that Conference left unresolved a series of issues and because of new difficulties, other multilateral meetings followed: the Washington conference, 1921–22, to settle Pacific, Chinese, and naval questions; the Geneva Naval Conference, 1927; The Hague Conferences on reparations, 1929–30; the World Disarmament Conference, 1932–35; the Ottawa tariffs conference, 1932; the World Economic Conference, 1933; and two London naval conferences, 1930 and 1935–36. But long-term resolution of international problems proved impossible because all Powers did not attend, domestic political considerations compelled leaders to pursue independent policies, or fascist Italy, militaristic Japan, and Nazi Germany were prepared to use force to restructure the constellation of power in their interests.

And what was true of the interwar period was equally so for the Cold War and after. Admittedly, efforts dealing with social concerns mounted by UN appendages have been some-what successful,[84] but those dealing with security and disarmament less so. For instance, the nuclear arms race from the late 1950s to the late 1980s (the Soviet Russian decision to build intercontinental ballistic missiles or the American pursuit of so-called 'Star Wars' technology, let alone the decisions of other Powers as diverse as France, India, and Israel to develop nuclear weapons) was only mildly tempered by negotiations that produced the Nuclear Non-Proliferation Treaty of 1968, the Anti-Ballistic Missile Treaty of 1972, and the Strategic Arms Limitation Treaty of 1974.[85] A new idea about conferring amongst the Great Powers did emerge in the Cold War, although its antecedents lay with the Chamberlain–Hitler discussions that produced the 1938 Munich agreement.[86] It entailed 'summit meetings' of leaders to address a series of arms limitation and political questions. But whether American presidents met with Soviet leaders (John F. Kennedy and Nikita Khrushchev, Richard Nixon and Leonid Brezhnev, and Ronald Reagan and Mikhail Gorbachev) the results were minimal. Despite a willingness of leaders to converse privately, Great Powers' machinations in pursuit of 'eternal and perpetual' interests drove and drive international politics. Thus, in one instance, although Reagan and Gorbachev discussed limiting nuclear weapons in the 1980s, the Reagan Administration pushed ahead with its Star Wars program to force Soviet Russian concessions.[87] The annual meetings of the present G8 nations is an expression of post-Cold War summitry but their record, too, is less than successful, as the wars in Iraq and Afghanistan, Russia's invasion of Georgia, and China's brutal suppression of Tibetan nationalism demonstrate.[88]

A third strategy to replace the balance is collective security. This concept emerged in 1924 from work by the League to define better its mandate to ensure international peace and security.[89] But as noted earlier, although the League could collectively resolve crises that involved smaller Powers, it could not do so when Great Powers expanded their interests by the use or threat of armed force. When the Allied Great Powers created the UN in 1945 to replace the League, they sought to improve the new organisation's ability to maintain international peace and security via the collective strength of its Great Power members. Hence, whereas both permanent and non-permanent members of the League Council had veto power, the UN Charter gave this right only to the five permanent members of the Security Council: the United States, China, France, Britain, and Soviet Russia. But in Cold War crises with Great Powers at odds (the interminable Middle Eastern disequilibrium beginning in 1948, Korea in 1950, United States involvement in Vietnam in the 1960s–70s, and Soviet Russian invasions of Hungary in 1956, Czechoslovakia in 1968, and Afghanistan in 1979) effective UN collective security proved hollow.[90] Even after the Cold War, in the Balkans and Rwanda in the 1990s and in Darfur, Tibet, North Korea, and Zimbabwe after the turn of the twentieth-first century,[91] Great Power deadlock in the Security Council translated into the pursuit of narrow national interests. Moreover, because the UN was to provide universal collective security after the Second World War, regional peacetime military alliances were thought unnecessary. Yet, the dynamics of the Cold War produced NATO, the North American Aerospace Defense Command, and the Warsaw Pact, plus a plethora of smaller defensive alliances like ANZUS, SEATO, and Soviet Russian agreements with Cuba, its Middle Eastern clients like Egypt and Syria, and so on. Collective security has proved more an ideal than a reality, at best limited and suffused by continuing Great Power rivalry.

Ultimately, the balance of power was and is the most efficacious means for Great Powers to regulate their affairs. It was used with success by a range of Great Power leaders, from Marlborough to Metternich, Bismarck, Grey, and Kissinger. Hence, the failure of the balance did not lead to the 1914 'July Crisis'. Germany's determination to break the Entente Powers (to overturn the balance) precipitated the First World War. That that war was longer and more ruinous than pre-war politicians, military planners, diplomats, and the citizens of the eventual belligerents ever believed is unimportant in why the Great Powers went to war. And the same can be said about Hitler's foreign-policy ambitions in the 1930s, as well as those of fascist Italy and militaristic Japan in the same period. During the Cold War, the bipolar world dominated by Washington and Moscow provided a strategic equilibrium that allowed for the Powers on each side of the divide (including neutral Powers) to pursue their interests short of all-out nuclear war. Of course, crises did emerge that threatened the international edifice (the 1962 Cuban missile crisis foremost[92]) but the Great Powers always receded from the brink of war. International stability remained the essence of foreign policy, although it is crucial to understand that stability and peace were two different things. American involvement in Vietnam, Soviet Russia's thrust into Afghanistan, and the Anglo-Argentinean Falklands War attest to this fact. And as the Cold War bipolar world ended and the Soviet Russian Empire disintegrated, the Great Powers still functioned in a balanced world.[93] In many senses, Europe after 1991 returned to that of the interwar period; and in the wider world, the advent of new *loci* of emerging regional Great Powers like China, Iran, and India saw the emergence of global multipolarity within the context of a wider balance.

In a general sense, the strategic alternatives to the balance had limited effectiveness because they were always short term. Habsburg appeasement in the latter half of the eighteenth century, American prescriptions for *détente*, and the British variant under Chamberlain were all designed to give breathing space to Great Powers that, whilst not ending international rivalry, were designed to buy time to strengthen economies and armed forces. Reliance on conference diplomacy tended to arise after long and exhaustive wars. Accordingly, when France sought later to steal a march on the other Great Powers after 1667 by annexing the Spanish Netherlands, conference diplomacy would not guarantee British, Spanish, Dutch, or Habsburg security.[94] Europe did experience a century of relative stability after the Congress of Vienna (despite the dangerous revolutions of 1848[95]) but the Great Powers were in an almost constant military and diplomatic equilibrium.[96] Even the German wars of unification between 1864 and 1871 did not upset that equipoise: lesser Powers like Denmark, Saxony, and Bavaria learnt the bitter lesson of confronting a Great Power, defeated Habsburg Austria restructured itself as Austria–Hungary; and united Germany under Prussian leadership was perceived to be a new element balancing an aggressive France.[97] But in the nineteenth century, European rivalry continued, outside the subcontinent, both in peripheral places and violently like the Crimea in the mid-1850s and in colonial rivalry in South and East Asia and Africa.[98] Although ushering in a new international order, the Paris Peace Conference soon saw its work undermined by German revanchism and Italian and Japanese aggressiveness. The newest strategic alternative before and after 1945, collective security, worked only as long as the Great Powers joined to contain crises with the potential to upset international stability or, ironically, were balanced one against the other by military alliances like NATO and the Warsaw Pact after the mid-1950s. Moreover, strategic alternatives to the balance like defense in depth, nuclear deterrence, collective defense, and others were and are tactical approaches to ensure strategies like the balance and the lesser approaches work.[99]

Thus, what does this say about the future of international politics in an era still marked by Great Power rivalry (the Hyper Power United States being a myth), the strengthening of capitalist and social democratic socioeconomic systems, and economic globalisation that critics argue undercuts the particularism and political and economic sovereignty that define nation-states? The answer is simple: *plus ça change, plus c'est la même chose.* The Great Powers not only exist, they dominate international politics; just as in Palmerston's day and before, they have only permanent interests; the architecture and strategic bases of international politics might be modified (there have been new additions to the small group of Great Powers in the past fifteen years) but the edifice that existed for at least three and a half centuries remains largely untouched. Accordingly, just as Louis XIV's France learnt in the late seventeenth century or as Victorian British statesmen understood in the nineteenth, the United States today, its supporters, and its critics must understand that preeminence is not omnipotence. The United States is just one of a number of Great Powers.

To enforce these points, several recent case studies propel themselves forward. After the Cold War, Great Powers new and old have not been remiss in seeking to entrench and expand their foreign-policy interests *vis-à-vis* other Powers, including against those of the United States. In the 1990s, post-Soviet Russia supported Serbia diplomatically during the 1990s Balkans' crisis; it continued doing so after the turn of the twenty-first century in the face of NATO opposition. In 2007–08, Russia staked out territorial claims in the Arctic (crucial to future exploitation of natural resources in that region) by planting a flag on the Arctic Ocean floor; more traditionally, by using armed force, it took advantage of an ill-conceived offensive by Georgia and extended Russian influence in the eastern Black Sea region and, thereby, informing expanded NATO that a limit existed to Moscow's forbearance about the security of Russia's western flank. It also sought to cow its former Polish satellite to acquiesce in Russian interests in Eastern Europe that conformed to long-standing Russian ambitions stretching back to the late eighteenth century.[100] Apart from a dalliance in Africa by backing Robert Mugabe against Western Power interference in Zimbabwe's 2008 elections, Communist China's consistent support of North Korea and Iran in their development of nuclear weapons shows Beijing's intention to keep and hold allies to limit the influence of the United States, Britain, Japan, and other rival Great Powers in East and Central Asia. And Beijing's determination to protect what its leaders perceive as China's national security, shown in its truculent reaction to Western suggestions that Tibet is an occupied country, cannot be doubted.[101]

Although international relations theories might trumpet new ideas about how and why international politics function in a changing world, centers of international power are emerging along established Great Power lines. As just mentioned, Beijing is not averse to using foreign policy, backed by its growing economic and conventional and nuclear military muscle, to protect and extend perceived Chinese national interests. So, too, are India, Iran, Israel, and Pakistan, each with or with the potential to back their diplomatic initiatives with significant conventional and nuclear force. And each does so within well-defined borders, fashioned by war, that define them as national entities. Because unilateral efforts are often weak, the new Great Powers like the established ones seek allies to defend interests and project will; and just as often, these alliances formal and informal shift because interests are eternal and perpetual whereas allies are not. Thirty years ago, Iran under Shah Reza Pahlevi stood as a firm American ally in the Middle East. Today, under Islamic fundamentalist and nationalist leaders, Iran is carving a dominant regional position with decidedly strong anti-American policies to exploit the strategic vacuum created by Iraq's collapse and the reshaping of the Middle Eastern balance of power.[102] Even supposedly staunch American allies are not averse to asserting their national interests against Washington, as Israeli intelligence penetration of the American Government attests.[103]

Historians tend to adhere to the sage words of the Canadian philosopher, Hector (Toe) Blake, who once observed: 'Predictions are for gypsies'.[104] However, the persistence of the Great Powers has not been undermined in the post-Cold War international order. The Great Powers still exist and, as international politics evolve, the basic architecture of foreign-policy-making ('no eternal allies', 'no perpetual enemies', only interests 'eternal and perpetual') has not changed since before Westphalia and beyond. Change can probably come only with the decline of the nation-state. But as the course of Great Power politics has shown for almost four hundred years, the primacy of the nation-state whether in transitory alliances, in the Concert of Europe, or, despite 'open diplomacy' in more recent international organisations like the League, the UN, and the WTO has only strengthened. History has not ended. Theories to explain international relations rise and fall out of fashion. Critics of what Great Powers do, how they protect and extend their national interests, and the often hard edge of their policies do not necessarily lack truth. But what Louis XIV, Metternich, Palmerston, the present Russian leadership, and the leaders of Great and small Powers have always understood is that they are in positions to shape events for good, or ill. Their tendency for rivalry is and will be for the foreseeable future constant and absolute.

This *Handbook* is built around the premise that seven Great Powers constitute the core of modern international politics. After this 'Prologue' about the persistence of the Great Powers in the new world order, specialists provide insight into how the foreign-policy-making elite of each of these Powers perceives national interests, how their policy-making processes determine grand strategy, and how effective their foreign policy is in meeting their strategic objectives when it is implemented. Clustering around the Great Powers is a range of Middle and Developing Powers. The next two sections of the book deal with these states; and because they are too numerous to have separate chapters, representative Middle and Developing Powers from the Americas, Europe, Africa, and South and East Asia are analysed. This analysis follows the same lines as that for the Great Powers: probing perception of national interests; assaying the determination of grand strategy; and determining how effective their individual foreign policies are in meeting their strategic objectives. Along the same lines, the domestic and international limitations on their diplomacy and statecraft are examined.

Flowing from the analyses of individual Powers, the next two sections of the book look at important international organisations and military alliances and the international economy. Specialists on the UN, NATO, the World Bank, and more have a wider analytical brush to paint the political, military, and economic context of the new international order. And they do so showing the effectiveness of these organisations (and, if necessary, their inadequacies) in a complex world where both cooperation and conflict amongst all Powers great and small are the norm. The last section deals with a series of contemporary problems in conflict and cooperation that are having and will have influence in shaping the evolution of the new international order: international arms control; civil–military relationships and policy-making; the interminable Middle Eastern crisis; the South Asian balance of power; rogue and failed states; and NGOs. In this context, 'soft power' has increasing relevance.

Whilst international relations theories seek to explain how and why international politics function in a changing world, centers of international power have emerged since 1989–91 along established Great Powers lines. They are not averse to using their foreign policies (backed by their economic and conventional and, in some cases, nuclear, military muscle) to protect and extend perceived national interests. So, too, are Middle and Developing Powers, each with or with the potential to back their diplomacy and statecraft with the economic and military resources available to them. And each does so within well-defined borders, fashioned by war and diplomacy that define them as national entities. But contemporary international politics are also shaped by international organisations, military alliances, the functioning of the international economy, private NGOs, and a series of issues marked by the possibility of conflict or cooperation. The scholars contributing to this book collectively show how and why the new international order has evolved (and is still evolving) since the end of the Cold War.

Acknowledgements

I would like to thank the staffs of the libraries of the Royal Military College of Canada, Queens' University (Kingston), and the Université de Rouen, as well as the Österreichische Nationalbibilothek (Vienna), for their assistance.

Notes

1 Palmerston, Speech to the House of Commons, 1 March 1848, *Hansard*, 123.
2 See J. Black, *Quest for Power: The World Order Since 1500* (London, 2007); H.M. Scott, *The Birth of a Great Power System, 1740–1815* (Essex, UK, 2006).
3 Cf. G.D. Cleva, *Henry Kissinger and the American Approach to Foreign Policy* (London, 1989); M. Haehl, *Les affaires étrangères au temps de Richelieu: le secrétariat d'État, les agents diplomatiques, 1624–1642* (Bruxelles,

New York, 2006); K. Müller, *1866: Bismarcks deutscher Bruderkrieg: Königgrätz und die Schlachten auf deutschem Boden* (Graz, 2007); P.W. Schroeder, *Metternich's Diplomacy at Its Zenith, 1820–1823* (Austin, TX, 1962).

4   For example, M.S. Anderson, *The War of the Austrian Succession, 1740–1748* (New York, London, 1995); I. Kershaw, *Hitler, 1936–1945: Nemesis* (New York, 2000).

5   See A.F. Cooper, *Niche Diplomacy: Middle Powers After the Cold War* (Basingstoke, New York, 1997); G. Hermet, 'Les Nouveaux centres de pouvoir dans le systéme international: Entre l'Utopie et la Stratégie. La hiérarchie des nations dans le systéme mondial', *Revue Française de Science Politique*, 30(1980), 205–21; T. Schieder, 'Die Mittleren Staaten im System der Grossen Mächte', *Historische Zeitschrift*, 232(1981), 583–604.

6   'Hyper Power' is a disputatious term. Cf. A. Chua, *Day of Empire. How Hyperpowers Rise to Global Dominance—And Why They Fail* (New York, 2007); E.Cohen. 'History and the Hyperpower', *Foreign Affairs*, Vol.83, No. 4(2004), 49–63.

7   H.W. Brand, 'George and the Gulf War of 1991', *Presidential Studies Quarterly*, 34(2004), 113–14; L. Geld, 'Foreign Affairs; Mr Bush's Fateful Blunder', *New York Times* (17 July 1991).

8   This and the next quotation from an excerpt of a Department of Defense planning document, 'Prevent the Re-Emergence of a New Rival', February 1992, enclosed in P.E. Taylor, 'U.S. Strategy Plan Calls for Insuring No Rivals Develop. A One-Superpower World', *New York Times* (8 March 1992).

9   For example, M. Byers and G. Nolte, eds, *United States Hegemony and the Foundations of International Law* (Cambridge, 2003); R. Foot, S.N. MacFarlane, and M. Mastanduno, *US Hegemony and International Organizations* (Oxford, 2003); J.L. Gaddis, *We Now Know: Rethinking Cold War History* (New York, 1997); C. Krauthammer, ' "The Unipolar Moment", in Council on Foreign Relations', *America and the World 1990/91*, 70(1991), 23–33.

10 F. Fukuyama, 'The End of History?', *National Interest* (Summer 1989).

11 R. Vitalis, 'Theory Wars of Choice. Hidden Casaulties in the "Debate" Between Hegemony and Empire', in C.-P. David and P. Grondin, eds., *Hegemony or Empire? The Redefinition of US Power under George W. Bush* (Aldershot, 2006), 21–31.

12 For examples of the first three critiques, see F. Cameron, *US Foreign Policy after the Cold War: Global Hegemon or Reluctant Sheriff* (London, 2002); N. Chomsky, *World Orders, Old and New* (New York, 1994); R.W. Merry, *Sands of Empire: Missionary Zeal, American Foreign Policy, and the Hazards of Global Ambition* (New York, 2005); J.-F. Revel. *L'obsession anti-americaine: Son fonctionnement, ses causes, ses inconsequences* (Paris, 2002). For examples of base anti-Americanism, see M. Barlow, *Too Close for Comfort: Canada's Future Within Fortress North America* (Toronto, 2005); A.S. Markovits, *Amerika, Dich hasst's sich besser: Antiamerikanismus und Antisemitismus in Europa* (Hamburg, 2004). Then cf. the articles in *American Historical Review Forum*, 111(2006), 1092–1119.

13 J. Derrida (P. Knauf, translator), *Specters of Marx, the State of the Debt, the Work of Mourning, and the New International* (London, 1994).

14 'Globalization': www1.worldbank.org/economicpolicy/globalization/.

15 See H. Wernicke, *Städtehanse, 1280–1418: Genesis, Strukturen, Funktionen* (Weimar, 1983); D. Stage, *Frankfurt am Main im Zollverein; die Handelspolitik und die öffentliche Meinung der Freien Stadt Frankfurt in den Jahren 1836 bis 1866* (Frankfurt, 1971).

16 See J. Gillingham, *European Integration, 1950–2003: Superstate or New Market Economy?* (Cambridge, New York, 2003); A. Zwass, *Rat für Gegenseitige Wirtschaftshilfe 1949 bis 1987: der dornige Weg von einer politischen zu einer wirtschaftlichen Integration* (Wien, New York, 1988).

17 See P.J. Cain and A.G. Hopkins, *British Imperialism: Innovation and Expansion, 1688–1914* (London, New York, 1993). Cf. I.M. Drummond, *Imperial Economic Policy, 1917–1939; Studies in Expansion and Protection* (London, 1974).

18 M.G. De Vries, *IMF in a Changing World, 1945–85* (Washington, DC, 1986); D. Kapur, J.P. Lewis, R. Webb, *World Bank: Its First Half Century* (Washington, DC, 1997); T.W. Zeiler, *Free Trade, Free World: The Advent of GATT* (Chapel Hill, NC, 1999). And there were others like the North American Free Trade Agreement. See S. Weintraub, *NAFTA's Impact on North America The First Decade* (Washington, DC, 2004).

19 For examples of non-American multinationals benefiting from and fostering globalisation: Germany's Volkswagen corporation, see F. Piëch, *Auto.Biographie* (Hamburg, 2002); the Royal Bank of Canada, D. McDowall, *Quick to the Frontier: Canada's Royal Bank* (Toronto,1993).

20 On globalisation generally, see G. Jones, 'The End of Nationality? Global Firms and "Borderless Worlds," ' *Zeitschrift für Unternehmensgeschichte*, 51(2006), 49–165; N. Klein, *No Logo* (London, 2001); A. Starr, *Naming the Enemy. Anti-Corporate Movements Confront Globalization* (London, 2000). Cf.

S.G. Bunker and P.S. Ciccantell, *Globalization and the Race for Resources* (Baltimore, MD, 2005); A. Mathers, *Struggling for a Social Europe: Neoliberal Globalization and the Birth of a European Social Movement* (Aldershot, Burlington, VT, 2007); G. Rénique, 'Strategic challenges for Latin America's anti-neoliberal insurgency', in T. Ballvé and V. Prasha, eds., *Dispatches from Latin America: On the Frontlines Against Neoliberalism* (Cambridge, MA, 2006), 35–46.

21 D.Z. Cass, *Constitutionalization of the World Trade Organization: Legitimacy, Democracy, and Community in the International Trading System* (New York, 2005); P.-T. Stoll and F. Schorkopf, *WTO – Welthandelsordnung und Welthandelsrecht* (Köln, 2002). Then see A. Cockburn and J. St Clair, *Five Days That Shook the World: Seattle and Beyond* (London, New York, 2000).

22 D. Deudney and G.J. Ikenberry, 'Realism, Structural Liberalism, and the Western Order', in E. B. Kapstein and M. Mastanduno, eds., *Unipolar Politics. Realism and State Strategies After the Cold War* (New York, 1999), 103–81; W.C. Wohlfarth, 'The Stability of a Unipolar World', *International Security*, 24(1999), 10–22.

23 M. Albert, '"Postmoderne" und Theorie der Internationalen Beziehungen,' *Zeitschrift für Internationale Beziehungen*, 1(1994), 45–63; S. Smith, 'Epistemology, Postmodernism and International Relations Theory: A Reply to Østerud', *Journal of Peace Research*, 34(1997), 330–36; R.D. Spegele, 'Political Realism and the Remembrance of Relativism,' *Review of International Studies*, 21(1995), 211–36. Cf. D.S.L. Jarvis, *International Relations and the Challenge of Postmodernism: Defending the Discipline* (Charleston, SC, 2000).

24 H. Cleveland, *The Birth of a New World: An Open Moment in International Leadership* (San Francisco, CA, 1993); G. Dussouy, *Quelle géopolitique au XXIe siècle?* (Brussels, 2001); S.P. Huntington, *The Clash of Civilizations and the Remaking of World Order* (New York, 1996).

25 'The 1992 Campaign; Excerpts From Speech By Clinton on U.S. Role', *New York Times* (2 October 1992).

26 T. Blair, *A Global Alliance for Global Values* (London, 2006), 7.

27 For an example of the post-Cold War debate over 'realism', see J.W. Legro and A. Moravcsik, 'Is Anybody Still a Realist?', *International Security*, 24(1999), 5–55; P.D. Feaver. G. Hellman *et al.*, 'Correspondence. Brother Can You Spare a Paradigm (Or Was Anybody Ever a Realist?)', *International Security*, 25(2000), 165–93. Cf. P.W. Schroeder, 'Historical Reality vs. Neorealist Theory,' in Michael E. Brown, Sean M. Lynn-Jones, and Steven E. Miller, eds., *The Perils of Anarchy: Contemporary Realism and International Security* (Cambridge, MA, 1995), 421–61.

28 J. Mayall, 'Globalisation and International Relations', *Review of International Studies*, 24(1998), 239–50; R. Szostak, *Classifying Science. Phenomena, Data, Theory, Method, Practice* (Dordrecht, Norwell, MA, 2004), 204–12.

29 L. Braun, *Zwischen Katholizismus und Protestantismus: Franken nach dem Westfälischen Frieden von 1648: das Reichskirchenrecht des Westfälischen Friedens und seine Auswirkungen auf Franken* (Bamberg, 2001); H. Langer, *1648, der Westfälische Frieden: Pax Europaea und Neuordnung des Reiches* (Berlin, 1994).

30 See J. Lukowski, *Partitions of Poland, 1772, 1793, 1795* (New York, 1999).

31 Paul Schroeder, *Transformation of European politics, 1763–1848* (Oxford, London, 1994), 524–36. Cf. H. Haussherr, 'Russland und Europa in der epoche des Wiener Kongresses', *Jahrbucher fur Geschichte Osteuropas*, 88(1960), 10–31.

32 M.S. Anderson, *War of the Austrian Succession, 1740–1748* (London, New York, 1995); R. Browning, *The War of the Austrian Succession* (Stroud, 1994).

33 J. Black, 'Pitt the Elder and the foundation of an imperial foreign policy', in T.G. Otte, ed., *The Makers of British Foreign Policy: From Pitt to Thatcher* (Basingstoke, 2001), 35–52; K.W. Schweizer, *Frederick the Great, William Pitt and Lord Bute: The Anglo-Prussian Alliance, 1756–1763* (Oxford, 1991).

34 H. Hasquin, *Louis XIV face à l'Europe du Nord: l'absolutisme vaincu par les libertés* (Bruxelles, 2005); B. Jeanmougin, *Louis XIV à la conquête des Pays-Bas espagnols: la uerre oubliée, 1678–1684* (Paris, 2005). Then see A. Maurois, *Louis XIV à Versailles* (Paris, 1955); G. Sabatier, *Versailles, ou, La Figure du Roi* (Paris, 1999); G. Walton, *Louis, XIV's Versailles* (London, 1986).

35 D.G. Chandler, *Waterloo, the hundred days* (New York, 1981); J.P. Lawford, *Napoleon: the last campaigns, 1813–15* (New York, 1977).

36 J. Black, *British Foreign Policy in the Age of Walpole* (Edinburgh, Atlantic Highlands, NJ, 1985); A. D'Arjuzon, *Castlereagh (1761–1822), ou, Le défi à l'Europe de Napoléon* (Paris, 1995); S.P. Oakley, *William III and the Northern Crowns during the Nine Years War, 1689–1697* (New York, 1987).

37 C.A. Bayly, *Imperial Meridian: The British Empire and the World, 1780–1830* (London, New York, 1989); M.E. Chamberlain, *British Foreign Policy in the Age of Palmerston* (London, 1980); C.I. Hamilton, *Anglo-French Naval Rivalry, 1840–1870* (Oxford, New York, 1993).

38 G.H. Bennett, *British Foreign Policy during the Curzon Period, 1919–24* (London, New York, 1995); A. Clayton, *British Empire as a Superpower, 1919–39* (Basingstoke, 1986); C.C. Eldridge, *Disraeli and the Rise of a New Imperialism* (Cardiff, 1996); J.R. Ferris, *Men, Money, and Diplomacy: c, 1919–26* (Ithaca, NY, 1989); G. Hicks, *Peace, War and Party Politics: the Conservatives and Europe, 1846–59* (Manchester, 2007); I. H. Nish, *Anglo-Japanese Alliance; The Diplomacy of Two Island Empires, 1894–1907* (London, 1966); M. L. Roi, *Alternative to Appeasement: Sir Robert Vansittart and Alliance Diplomacy, 1934–1937* (Westport, CT, London, 1997).

39 The issue of ideology, which includes religious precepts and is not the same as theory, is different. Cf. B. Coward, *Cromwellian Protectorate* (Manchester, New York, 2002); M. Heseman, *Hitlers Religion: die fatale Heilslehre des Nationalsozialismus* (München, 2004); K. Boeckh, *Stalinismus in der Ukraine: die Rekonstruktion des soujetischen Systems nach dem Zweiten Weltkrieg* (Wiesbaden, 2007).

40 G. Lowes Dickinson, *The International Anarchy, 1904–1914* (New York, 1926). Cf. Anderson, *War of the Austrian Succession, 1740–1748*; B. Inglis, *The Opium War* (London, 1976); V. Mastny, *Russia's Road to the Cold War: Diplomacy, Warfare, and the Politics of Communism, 1941–1945* (New York, 1979).

41 A. Bitzel, *Anfechtung und Trost bei Sigismund Scherertz: ein lutherischer Theologe im Dreissigjährigen Krieg* (Göttingen, 2002); G. Rystad, *Kriegsnachrichten und propaganda während des Dreissigjährigen Krieges: die Schlacht bei Nördlingen in den gleichzeitigen, gedruckten Kriegsberichten* (Lund, 1960).

42 A. Kohler, 'Vom Habsburgischen gesamtsystem Karls V. zu den teilsystemen Philipps II. und Maximilians II', *Wiener Beitraege zur Geschichte der Neuzeit*, 19(1992), 13–37; M.C. Waxman, 'Strategic Terror: Philip II and Sixteenth-Century Warfare', *War in History*, 4(1997), 339–47.

43 H. Grotius, *Law of War and Peace (De jure belli ac pacis)* (New York, 1949).

44 Cf. M.H. Keen, *Laws of War in the Late Middle Ages* (London, 1965); S.C. Neff, *War and the Law of Nations: A General History* (Cambridge, UK, New York, 2005).

45 This and the next sentence are based on C.J. Burckhardt, *Richelieus Aussenpolitik.* (Basel, Stuttgart, 1968); W. Mommsen, *Richelieu, Elsass und Lothringen; ein Beitrag zur elsass-lothringischen Frage* (Berlin, 1922); J. Wollenberg, *Richelieu: Staatsräson u. Kircheninteresse: zur Legitimation d. Politik d. Kardinalpremier* (Bielefeld, 1977).

46 F. Hildesheimer, *Richelieu, une certaine idée de l'Etat* (Paris, 1985).

47 G. de Bertier de Sauvigny, 'Metternich et l'intervention française en Espagne en 1822', *Bulletin de la Société d'Histoire Moderne*, Vol. 57, No.5(1958), 19–21; A. Nicolle, 'Ouvrard and the French Expedition in Spain in 1823', *Journal of Modern History*, Vol. 17, No. 3(1945), 193–201; A.J. Reinerman, *Austria and the Papacy in the Age of Metternich*, Volume I: *Between Conflict and Cooperation, 1809–1830* (Washington, DC, 1979).

48 T. Chapman, 'Russia under Tsar Nicholas I: 1825–56', *Modern History Review*, Volume 12, No. 2(2000): 14–17; W.B. Lincoln, *Nicholas I: Emperor and Autocrat of all the Russias* (Bloomington, IN, 1978).

49 J.-B. Duroselle, 'Le "Concert Européen"', *Relations Internationales*, 39(1984), 271–85; W. Baumgart, *Europäisches konzert und nationale bewegung: internationale beziehungen, 1830–1878* (Paderborn, 1999).

50 See W.N. Medlicott, *Congress of Berlin and After; A Diplomatic History of the Near Eastern Settlement 1878–1880* (Hamden, CT, 1963); B. Waller, *Bismarck at the Crossroad: The Reorientation of German Foreign Policy after the Congress of Berlin, 1878–1880* (London, 1974). Then cf. M. Bourquin, 'La Desintegration de l'Europe et la politique des alliances à la fin du XIX Siècle', *Cahiers de Bruges*, Vol.5, No. 2(1955), 128–32.

51 R.C. Hall, *The Balkan Wars, 1912–1913: Prelude to the First World War* (London, 2000), 101–2, 123–29; K. Robbins, *Sir Edward Grey. A Biography of Lord Grey of Fallodon* (London, 1971), 264–67.

52 The classic study is L. Albertini, *Origins of the War of 1914*, 2 volumes (New York, 1952–57). For more recent and insightful analyses, see J. Joll, *Origins of the First World War* (London, New York, 1984); D. Stevenson, *Armaments and the Coming of War: Europe, 1904–1914* (Oxford, New York, 1996); H. Strachan, *The First World War*, Vol. I: *To Arms* (Oxford, 2001), 1–207.

53 For an early assessment, see L. Daudet, *Guerre totale* (Paris, 1918). Then see B.P. Beckwith, *Total War; The Economic Theory of a War Economy* (Boston, 1943); G.D. Feldman, *Army, Industry, and Labor in Germany, 1914–1918* (Princeton, NJ, 1966).

54 For example, F.E. Buisson, *Principes de la Société des Nations* (Paris, 1917); Deutsche Liga für Völkerbund, *Deutschland und der Völkerbund* (Berlin, 1926). Then see G.W. Egerton, *Great Britain and the Creation of the League of Nations: Strategy, Politics, and International Organization, 1914–1919* (Chapel Hill, NC, 1978).

55 P. David, *Histoire de la Société des Nations: l'esprit de Genève: vingt ans d'efforts pour la paix* (Geneva, 2000); F.P. Walters, *History of the League of Nations* (London, New York, 1960).

56 J. Barros, *Corfu Incident of 1923: Mussolini and the League of Nations* (Princeton, NJ, 1965).

57 On Manchuria, see I.H. Nish, *Japan's Struggle with Internationalism: Japan, China, and the League of Nations, 1931–3* (London, New York, 1993); C. Thorne, *The Limits of Foreign Policy; The West, the League, and the Far Eastern Crisis of 1931–1933* (New York, 1972). On Abyssinia, see F. Hardie, *Abyssinian Crisis* (London, 1974); P. Terhoeven, *Liebespfand fürs Vaterland: Krieg, Geschlecht und faschistische Nation in der italienischen Gold-und Eheringsammlung 1935/36* (Tübingen, 2003).

58 P. Gerbet, *Réve d'un Ordre Mondial: de la SDN à l'ONU* (Paris, 1996); T. Hoopes and D. Brinkley, *FDR and the Creation of the U.N.* (New Haven, CT, 1997).

59 N. Briscoe, *Britain and UN Peacekeeping, 1948–67* (New York, 2003); A.M. James, *Peacekeeping in International Politics* (Basingstoke, New York, 1990); G. Pearson, *Seize the Day: Lester B. Pearson and Crisis Diplomacy* (Ottawa, 1993).

60 On Hungary, see P. Lendvai, *Ungarnaufstand 1956: Eine Revolution und ihre Folgen* (München, 2006). On Algeria, L. Aggoun and J.-B. Rivoire, *Françalgérie, crimes et mensonges d'Etats: histoire secrète, de la guerre d'indépendance à la "troisième guerre" d'Algérie* (Paris, 2004). On Cambodia, W. Shawcross, *Sideshow: Kissinger, Nixon, and the destruction of Cambodia* (New York, 1979).

61 See J. Charmley, 'Castlereagh and France', *Diplomacy & Statecraft*, 17(2006): 665–73; C.I. Hamilton, 'Anglo-French Seapower and the Declaration of Paris', *International History Review*, 4(1982), 166–90; J.B. Hattendorf, *England in the War of the Spanish Succession: A Study of the English View and Conduct of Grand Strategy, 1702–1712* (New York, 1987); M. Kitchen, *British Policy towards the Soviet Union during the Second World War* (Basingstoke, 1986); A.D. Lambert, *The Crimean War: British Grand Strategy, 1853–56* (Manchester, 1990); P.J. Philpott, *Anglo-French Relations and Strategy on the Western Front, 1914–18* (New York, 1996); H. Wentker, 'Der "Pitt-Plan" von 1805 in krieg und frieden: Zun kontinuitätsproblem der Britischen Europapolitik in der ära der Napoleonischen kriege', *Francia 2: Frühe Neuzeit*, 29(2002), 129–45; D. Reynolds, *Creation of the Anglo-American Alliance, 1937–41: Study in Competitive Co-operation* (London, 1981).

62 P.M.H. Bell, *Certain Eventuality: Britain and the Fall of France* (Farnborough, 1974).

63 W.R. Louis, *Imperialism at Bay, 1941–1945: The United States and the Decolonization of the British Empire* (Oxford, 1977); D. Reynolds, W.F. Kimball, and A.O Chubarian, eds., *Allies at War: The Soviet, American, and British Experience, 1939–1945* (New York, 1994).

64 Fascist Italy's alliance with Nazi Germany is an excellent case in point. See F.W. Deakin, *Brutal Friendship: Mussolini, Hitler, and the Fall of Italian Fascism* (London, 1962); M. König, *Kooperation als Machtkampf: das faschistische Achsenbündnis Berlin-Rom im Krieg 1940/41* (Köln, 2007).

65 Still the best study is J.L. Gaddis, *The United States and the Origins of the Cold War, 1941–1947* (New York, 1972). Cf. Gaddis, *We Now Know*, 1–25. Then see V. Mastny and G. Schmidt, *Konfrontationsmuster des Kalten Krieges 1946 bis 1956* (München, 2003); P. Wright, *Iron Curtain: From Stage to Cold War* (Oxford, New York, 2007).

66 On NATO, see L.S. Kaplan, *United States and NATO: The Formative Years* (Lexington, KY, 1984); C. Zorgbibe, *Histoire de l'OTAN* (Bruxelles, 2002). On the Warsaw Pact, V. Mastny and M. Byrne, eds., *Cardboard Castle? An Inside History of the Warsaw Pact, 1955–1991* (New York, 2005); F. Umbach, *Rote Bündnis: Entwicklung und Zerfall des Warschauer Paktes 1955 bis 1991* (Berlin, 2005).

67 On ANZUS, see W.D. McIntyre, *Background to the ANZUS Pact: Policy-Making, Strategy and Diplomacy, 1945–55* (London, New York, Christchurch, 1995). On SEATO, see L. Buszynski, *SEATO, the Failure of an Alliance Strategy* (Singapore, 1983). On NORAD, J.J. Jockel, *No Boundaries Upstairs: Canada, the United States and the Origins of North American Air Defence, 1945–1958* (Vancouver, 1987).

68 On Cuba, see Y. Pavlov, *Soviet-Cuban Alliance, 1959–1991* (New Brunswick, NJ, 1994). On Egypt, I. Ginor, '"Under the Yellow Arab Helmet Gleamed Blue Russian Eyes": Operation "Kavkaz" and the War of Attrition, 1969–70', *Cold War History*, 3(2002), 127–56. On Angola, O.A. Westad, 'Moscow and the Angolan Crisis, 1974–76: A New Pattern of Intervention', *Cold War International History Project Bulletin*, 8–9(1996–97), 21–32. On Mozambique, L. Abegunrin, 'Angola and the Soviet Union', *Current Bibliography on African Affairs*, 18(1985–86), 231–43.

69 On GATT, see T.W. Zeiler, *Free Trade, Free World: The Advent of GATT* (Chapel Hill, NC, 1999). On the World Bank, A. Chhibber, R.K. Peters, and B.J. Yale, eds., *Reform and Growth: Evaluating the World Bank Experience* (New Brunswick, NJ, 2006). On the IMF, see J.M. Boughton, *Silent Revolution: The International Monetary Fund 1979–1989* (Washington, DC, 2001).

70 C. Bekri, *UNESCO, une 'entreprise erronée'?* (Paris, 1991); S. Dutt, *UNESCO and a Just World Order* (New York, 2002). On WHO, Y. Beigbeder, *Organisation mondiale de la santé* (Paris, 1995). On FAO, J.C. Abbott, *Politics and Poverty: A Critique of the Food and Agriculture Organization of the United Nations*

(London, New York, 1992). On the IAEC, E. Häckel and G. Stein, eds., *Tightening the Reins: Towards a Strengthened International Nuclear Safeguards System* (Berlin, New York, 2000).

71 J. Gillingham, *European Integration, 1950–2003: Superstate or New Market Economy?* (Cambridge, New York, 2003); G. Thiemeyer, *Vom 'Pool Vert' zur Europäischen Wirtschaftsgemeinschaft: europäische Integration, kalter Krieg und die Anfänge der gemeinsamen europäischen Agrarpolitik 1950–1957* (München, 1999).

72 S. Ahmed and D. Potter, *NGOs in International Politics* (Bloomfield, CT, 2006); S. Krüger, *Nachhaltigkeit als Kooperationsimpuls: Sozialökologische Bündnisse zwischen NGOs und Gewerkschaften* (Münster, 2002).

73 The literature on the 'balance of power' is immense. But see E.V. Gulick, *Europe's Classical Balance of Power; A Case History of the Theory and Practice of One of the Great Concepts of European Statecraft* (New York, 1967); E. Luard, *The Balance of Power: The System of International Relations, 1648–1815* (New York, 1992); M. Sheehan, *Balance of Power: History and Theory* (London, New York, 1996).

74 Cf. J. Charmley, *Splendid isolation? Britain, the Balance of Power and the Origins of the First World War* (London, 1999); P. Krüger, 'Mythen des europäischen Staatensystems: Gleichgewicht, europäisches Konzert, Integration', *Zeitschrift fuer Religions und Geistesgeschichte*, 51(1999), 100–114; K. Walz, *Man, the State, and War. A Theoretical Analysis* (New York, 2001), 217.

75 The classic study is M.S. Anderson, *Eastern Question, 1774–1923: A Study in International Relations* (London, Melbourne, New York, 1966). Cf. G. Schöllgen, *Imperialismus und Gleichgewicht Deutschland, England und die Orientalische Frage, 1871–1914* (München, 1984).

76 For the example of British diplomatists between 1919 and 1939, see B.J.C. McKercher and M.R. Roi, 'Ideal and "Punch-Bag": Conflicting Views of the Balance of Power and Their Influence on Interwar British Foreign Policy', *Diplomacy & Statecraft*, 12(2001), 47–78.

77 W. McCaffrey, *Elizabeth I: War and Politics, 1588–1603* (Princeton, 1992); R.B. Wernham, *The Making of Elizabethan Foreign Policy, 1558–1603* (Berkeley, CA, 1981).

78 H.L. Dyck, 'Pondering the Russian Fact: Kaunitz and the Catherinian Empire in the 1770s', *Canadian Slavonic Papers*, 22(1980), 451–69; M.Z. Mayer, 'The Price for Austria's Security: Part I – Joseph II, the Russian Alliance, and the Ottoman War, 1787–89', *International History Review*, 26(2004), 257–99.

79 G. Gorodetsky, 'The Impact of the Ribbentrop-Molotov Pact on the Course of Soviet Foreign Policy', *Cahiers du Monde Russe et Sovietique*, 31(1990) 27–41; G. Roberts, *The Unholy Alliance: Stalin's Pact with Hitler* (Bloomington, IN, 1989).

80 For the 1930s, see R.F. DeBedts, *Ambassador Joseph Kennedy, 1938–1940: An Anatomy of Appeasement* (New York, 1985); F.W. Marks, 'Six Between Roosevelt and Hitler: America's Role in the Appeasement of Nazi Germany', *Historical Journal*, 28(1985), 969–82. For the period of detente, T. Draper, 'Appeasement and Detente', *Commentary*, Vol.61, No.2(1976), 27–38; K.L. Nelson, *The Making of Détente: Soviet-American Relations in the Shadow of Vietnam* (Baltimore, MD, 1995).

81 This subject is disputatious. Cf. R.J. Caputi, *Neville Chamberlain and Appeasement* (Cranbury, NJ, 2000); B.J.C. McKercher, 'Deterrence and the European Balance of Power: The Field Force and British Grand Strategy, 1934–38', *English Historical Review*, 123(2008), 98–131; R.A.C. Parker, *Chamberlain and Appeasement: British Policy and the Coming of the Second World War* (New York, 1993).

82 As he said just after becoming Prime Minister: 'I believe the double policy of rearmament and better relations with Germany and Italy will carry us safely through the danger period'. In I. Colvin, *The Chamberlain Cabinet* (New York, 1971), 46.

83 P. Le Goyet, *15 mars 1939: Le premier 'coup de Prague'* (Paris, 1989); T. Prochazka, *The Second Republic: The Disintegration of Post-Munich Czechoslovakia, October 1938-March 1939* (New York, 1981). Then see the diary entries for 15 March–2 April 1939 of Sir Alexander Cadogan, the Foreign Office Permanent Under-Secretary, in D. Dilks, ed., *The Diaries of Sir Alexander Cadogan, O.M., 1938–1945* (London, 1971), 62–67.

84 See A. Staples, *The Birth of Development: How the World Bank, Food and Agriculture Organization, and World Health Organization Changed the World, 1945–1965* (Kent, OH, 2006). Then cf. R. Hankins, 'The World Health Organization and Immunology Research and Training, 1961–74', *Medical History*, 45(2001), 243–66; M.C. Maio, 'UNESCO and the Study of Race Relations in Brazil: Regional or National Issue?', *Latin American Research Review*, 36(2001), 118–36; L. Phillips and S. Ilcan, 'Numerical Governance and Expertise: The FAO Before WID', *Atlantis*, Vol.26, No.2(2002), 33–38. But criticism of these social conferences exists; see A. De Grieff, 'The Politics of Noncooperation: The Boycott of the International Centre for Theoretical Physics', *Osiris*, 21(2006), 86–109; C.F. Scheutz, 'UN Food Office in Cairo Closed by Arab Pressure', *International Perspectives*, (September–October 1980), 22–24.

85 On the nuclear arms race, see O. Bukharin, 'US Atomic Energy Intelligence Against the Soviet Target, 1945–70', *Intelligence and National Security*, 19(2004), 655–79; R. Dietl, 'In Defence of the West: General Lauris Norstad, NATO Nuclear Forces and Transatlantic Relations 1956–63', *Diplomacy & Statecraft*, 17

(2006), 347–92; J.G. Mathers, *The Russian Nuclear Shield from Stalin to Yeltsin* (New York, 2000); H. V. Pant, 'India's Nuclear Doctrine and Command Structure: Implications for Civil-Military Relations in India', *Armed Forces and Society*, 33(2007), 238–64; Z. Shalom, *Israel's Nuclear Option: Behind the Scenes Diplomacy between Dimona and Washington* (Brighton, UK, Tel Aviv, 2005). On the Non-Proliferation treaty, the ABM Treaty, and SALT, see H. Brands, 'Non-Proliferation and the Dynamics of the Middle Cold War: The Super Powers, the MLF, and the NPT', *Cold War History*, 7(2007), 389–423; R. L. Garthoff, *Policy versus the Law: The Reinterpretation of the ABM Treaty* (Washington, DC, 1987); G. Korniyenko, 'A "Missed Opportunity": Carter, Brezhnev, SALT II, and the Vance Mission to Moscow, November 1976-March 1977', *Cold War International History Project Bulletin*, 5(1995), 140–54.

86 D. Reynolds, *Summits. Six Meetings that Shaped the Twentieth Century* (New York, 2007). Cf. D.H. Dunn, ed., *Diplomacy at the Highest Level: The Evolution of International Summitry* (London, 1996).

87 S. Bjork, *The Strategic Defence Initiative. Symbolic Containment of the Nuclear Threat* (Albany, NY, 1992); D. Mikheev, *Soviet Perspective on the Strategic Defense Initiative* (Washington, DC, 1987).

88 For instance, on Iraq, see 'President Bush, Prime Minister Blair Discuss Iraq at G8 Summit. Remarks by the President and Prime Minister Blair of the United Kingdom in a Photo Opportunity. Dunbar House, Sea Island, Georgia' (9 June 2004): www.whitehouse.gov /news/releases/2004/06/20040609-1.html; É. Toussaint, 'Iraq, War, Debt and the G8', 26 April 2003: www.cadtm.org/spip.php?article263.

89 B.J.C. McKercher, 'The League of Nations and the Problem of Collective Security 1919–39', in U.-M. Ruser, ed., *The League of Nations 1920–1946* (New York, Geneva, 1996), 70–71.

90 In order following the text, M. Rossi, 'L'O.N.U. et la crise du Proche-Orient de 1967', *Politique Étrangère*, 40(1975), 525–5; B. Catchpole, *The Korean War* (New York, 2000); M.S. Rajan and T. Israel, 'The United Nations and the Conflict in Vietnam', *International Studies*, 12(1973), 511–40; C. Békés, 'The Hungarian Question on the UN Agenda: Secret Negotiations by the Western Great Powers, October 26th–November 4th 1956. British Foreign Office Documents', *Hungarian Quarterly*, 41 (2000), 103–22; V. Mastny, 'Was 1968 a Strategic Watershed of the Cold War?', *Diplomatic History*, 29 (2005), 149–77; A. Saikal, 'The UN and Afghanistan: A Case of Failed Peacemaking Intervention?', *International Peacekeeping*, 3(1996), 19–34.

91 In order following the text, W. Maley, 'The United Nations and Ethnic Conflict Management: Lessons From the Disintegration of Yugoslavia', *Nationalities Papers*, 25(1997), 559–73; T. Piiparinen, 'Reconsidering the Silence from the Ultimate Crime: A Functional Shift in Crisis Management from the Rwandan Genocide to Darfur', *Journal of Genocide Research*, 9(2007), 71–91; Tibet Justice Center, 'The United Nations and Tibet': tibetjustice.org/reports/un.html; N. Onishi, 'Questions grow over UN curbs on North Korea', *International Herald Tribune* (17 October 2006): www.iht.com/articles/2006/10/ 16/asia/web.1016nations.php; Associated Press, 'China, Russia nix U.N. sanctions for Zimbabwe; new focus on S. Africa efforts', *Daily News* (12 July 2008): www.nydailynews.com/news/us_world/2008/07/ 12/2008-07-12_china_russia_nix_un_sanctions_for_zimbab.html.

92 Cf. T. Diez Acosta, *In the Threshold of Nuclear War: The 1962 Missile Crisis* (Havana, 2002); M. Dobbs, *One Minute to Midnight: Kennedy, Khrushchev, and Castro on the Brink of Nuclear War* (New York, 2008); B. Greiner, *Kuba Krise: 13 Tage im Oktober: Analyse, Dokumente, Zeitzeugen* (Nördlingen, 1988).

93 S. Wall, *Stranger in Europe: Britain and the EU from Thatcher to Blair* (Oxford, New York, 2008); D. Webber, ed., *New Europe, New Germany, Old Foreign Policy? German Foreign Policy Since Unification* (London, 2001). Cf. W. Hilz, *Europas verhindertes Führungstrio: die Sicherheitspolitik Deutschlands, Frankreichs und Grossbritanniens in den Neunzigern* (Paderborn, 2005).

94 O. Reshef, 'La Guerre de Devolution', *Information Historique*, 1988 50(3–4), 89–103.

95 S. Aprile et al., *La révolution de 1848 en France et en Europe* (Paris, 1998); R. Fleck, *Gleichheit auf den Barrikaden: die Revolutionen von 1848 in Europa: Versuch über die Demokratie* (Wien, 1991).

96 The still-to-be-surpassed study of this issue is A.J.P. Taylor, *The Struggle for Mastery in Europe, 1848–1918* (Oxford, 1954). Cf. G. Fesser, *Europa 1815–1914: vom Wiener Kongress bis zum Ersten Weltkrieg* (Erfurt, 2002).

97 M. Embree, *Bismarck's First War: The Campaign of Schleswig and Jutland 1864* (Sollihull, UK, 2007); K. Hildebrand, *No Intervention: die Pax Britannica und Preussen 1865/66–1869/70: eine Untersuchung zur englischen Weltpolitik im 19. Jahrhundert* (München, 1997); K. Müller, *1866: Bismarcks deutscher Bruderkrieg: Königgrätz und die Schlachten auf deutschem Boden* (Graz, 2007).

98 On the Crimean war, W. Baumgart, *Crimean War: 1853–1856* (London, New York, 1999); T. Royle, *Crimea: The Great Crimean War, 1854–1856* (London, 1999). On Great Power rivalry in Africa, the classic study is R. Robinson and J. Gallagher, with A. Denny, *Africa and the Victorians. The Official Mind of Imperialism*, 2nd edition (London, 1988). Cf. M.E. Chamberlain, *The Scramble for Africa* (Harlow, UK, 1981); A.J.P. Taylor, *Germany's First Bid for Colonies 1884–1885* (London, 1938).

99 T. Enders, *Franz Josef Strauss, Helmut Schmidt und die Doktrin der Abschreckung* (Koblenz, 1984); D.N. Schwartz, *NATO's Nuclear Dilemmas* (Washington, DC, 1983).

100 N. Kulish, 'Georgian Crisis Brings Attitude Change to a Flush Poland', *New York Times* (20 August 2008); 'Russia-Georgia Conflict. Polish support for missile deal soars', *Welt* Online (18 August 2008): welt.de/english-news/article2322942/Polish-support-for-missile-deal-soars.html.

101 Reported in 'Commentary. Dalai Lama is Spewing Lies', *China View* (30 April 2008): www.news.xinhuanet.com/english/2008-04/30/content_8082923.htm.

102 Cf. J.L. Esposito, ed., *The Iranian Revolution: Its Global Impact* (New York, 2001); D. Harris, *The Crisis: the President, the Prophet, and the Shah – 1979 and the Coming of Militant Islam* (New York, 2004).

103 For example, R.J. Olive, *Capturing Jonathan Pollard: How One of the Most Notorious Spies in American History was Brought to Justice* (Annapolis, MD, 2006).

104 J. Reed, 'Canadiens-Leafs', December 2005: www.jeffreyreedreporting.com/ hockeydynasties.doc. Cf. W.W Rostow, 'Beware of Historians Bearing False Analogies', *Foreign Affairs*, 66 (1988), 863–68.

Part I

The Context of Diplomacy

1

Diplomatic history

A new appraisal

Jeremy Black

Diplomatic history has long been an area of scholarly endeavour where Whiggish ideas of improvability and of improvement have a central role—with little qualification. The standard theme is of progress in terms of bureaucratic processes, notably systematisation. This *leitmotif* has an especial chronological configuration. In particular, there is a commonly held negative interpretation of medieval diplomacy and the improved practices of the early modern period. This typical explanation remains deeply teleological, tying the advance of modern diplomacy with the emergence of strong Powers, centralised government, and what is frequently called the European states system.

The best recent advocate of this typology was an eighteenth-century specialist, Matthew Anderson; he investigated longer-term development and used the customary chronological outline, one genuflecting to the persuasive efforts of Garrett Mattingly. Accordingly, when discussing the 'origins of modern diplomacy', Anderson observed: 'The sixteenth century saw the emergence for the first time of a network of organised diplomatic contacts which linked together more or less continuously the states of western Europe. ... It was in Italy that [the] situation first changed decisively and permanently'.[1] His slant aligned with a common view of medieval and modern Europe that reaches towards the Renaissance suffused with new beginnings and looking to before the medieval period for suitable Classical roots, references, and models. However, this view needs qualification through a deeper appreciation of medieval diplomacy and reflecting on the early-modern condition (in so far as the two can be separately defined in satisfactory fashion).

In contrast to the established view and emerging in the medieval period, permanent embassies signify modern diplomacy's advent. But this development requires qualification. Permanence is relative. During the Middle Ages, long-term embassies by accredited 'diplomats' were not unique;[2] in one instance, in the 1390s, France enjoyed consistent diplomatic relations with Milan, Florence, and Naples.[3] Moreover, some individuals were diplomatic specialists: well-informed about certain kingdoms, dynasties, or intercourt negotiations in general. Moreover, medieval diplomatic reportage could be knowledgeable and perceptive. Interests, power balances, and coalitions were also abundantly assessed. Although these analyses inclined towards the episodic and centred on immediate issues (and were held within a context stressing dynasticism and the politics of eminence), this condition was also mirrored in the early-modern period.

Nonetheless, modifications occurred in the early-modern period such as the notion about diplomats' efforts not endangering their personal honour, or that diplomats need not feel humiliated should their monarchical master ask them to mouth falsehoods or if they had to lie because of their ruler's actions. The concept of state or royal service not despoiling personal honour emerged in England about 1500.[4] This notion of state service also related to the increase in ideological conflict, substantial during Europe's Wars of Religion fostered by the Protestant Reformation of the sixteenth century. Underscoring the argument that Renaissance changes have been too heavily emphasised by scholars, medieval popes asserted that typically disreputable acts in papal-approved policies (say, undermining a heretic) did not dishonour those following orders. In addition, the sustained practice of employing aristocrats as diplomats fortified, and mirrored, an ancient assurance of personal honour that continued well into the modern period.

Juxtaposed with the expansionism of most of the Powers and the resolve of seigniorial families to entrench their position, medieval Italy's balkanised politics encouraged conflict. Conflict, in turn, produced pressure for diplomacy. The Gonzaga and Visconti families employed resident envoys, with Gian Galeazzo Visconti, Duke of Milan (reigned 1378–1402) being especially adept. His emissaries found support from an effective chancery that functioned as a nascent ministry of foreign affairs. The model of Italy's 'despots' was followed by the republics, notably Venice. In 1435, by sending Zacharias Bembo to Rome as 'Orator' to strengthen the republic against Filippo Maria Visconti, Venice became the first Italian republic to appoint a resident agent. The republics then began employing permanent or resident envoys in a fixed system of official diplomatic practice.

The prolonged conflict following the collapse of the Visconti in 1402 concluded with the 1454 Peace of Lodi, mediated by Pope Nicholas V. Lodi afforded an opportunity to amalgamate major territorial expansion by Florence and Venice. Like Westphalia in 1648, it also stimulated a broadening of the diplomatic system in which resident diplomacy extended from a method of protecting alliances to working with former adversaries. With a system of permanent embassies, Italy's leading states were now interconnected diplomatically.[5] With Italians at the centre, the system expanded. Western European coalition politics in war and peace concentrated on Italy but went further afield, principally because of relationships with interests outside the peninsula. Perhaps the first resident envoy was used by Luigi Gonzaga of Mantua and sent to the court of the Holy Roman Emperor, Ludwig IV, 'the Bavarian' (reigned 1314–47). The Emperor claimed suzerainty in northern Italy, which allowed successive emperors a key and enduring role there, something traced back to Charlemagne's revival of the Holy Roman Empire in 800. By the latter half of the fifteenth century, permanent Italian embassies had proliferated. For instance, the Duchy of Milan had missions amongst others in the major capitals of Paris, Venice, and, by the 1490s, London. Venice sent diplomats to the Turkish Empire, Spain, and England.[6] Florence established diplomatic links with Milan, Naples, the Vatican, and the courts in France and Burgundy. With permanent embassies came the growth of diplomatic archives, as well as expositions on the new system, specifically on the character and duties of the ambassador.[7] In turn, this literature helped create a normative pattern.

Crucial to modern concepts of diplomacy and the international system, this supposition is only one of several concerning diplomatic means that needs to be considered in terms of fitness-for-purpose and without any sense of hierarchy in quality. Thus, Korea's tribute relationship with, first, Ming and, then, Manchu China produced stability until the 1870s. Vassalage guaranteed non-interference, a practice mediated by despatching treaty envoys. This relationship ended with Japan's intervention in Korea; it created not a 'modern' diplomatic system but a variant form of imperial relations. A colonial Power, Japan, annexed Korea in 1910.[8] This evolution accentuates the hazards of assuming European patterns and chronology as normative international diplomacy. Even in Europe, the international system and diplomatic condition, including diplomatic means, would have beheld differently had the perspective been from 1810 or 1941, when Napoleon and Hitler, respectively, dominated.

There were also important conceptual limitations to diplomacy. Beginning in the medieval period, the character of communication with non-European Powers remained obscure to most contemporaries. Distance apart, discussing and hypothesising occurred over what was poorly, if at all, comprehended. Suffusing all was the tendency to see the distant world as an extension of the proximate, especially its problems, outline, and patterns of causation. As a means of contact and a medium for recording contact, diplomacy remained part of this process. Spanish paintings of the 1690s portraying the conquest of Aztec Mexico in 1519–21, for instance, showed Cortés, the Spanish leader, dining with Montezuma's ambassadors as part of a process of grounding the conquest as a process of legitimate expansion. Europeans generalised their forms of statehood, social hierarchy, and notions of cause and effect on other Powers; concurrently, they repeatedly inclined to simplify, if not primitivise, the latter.[9] Thus, European history was used to explain non-Western societies and Powers: Turkish sultans viewed as contemporary forms of pre-Christian tyrants of Imperial Rome, notably Nero, and African polities as if they were European states. Not surprisingly, diplomacy aided the advance of Western interests, rather than understanding Turkish or African society and culture.

This form of interaction intensified as the European Powers expanded overseas in commerce and colonisation. Consequently, foreign Powers or the aboriginal confederations and communities in North America and other places were perceived principally by their associations with rival European Powers and by the pattern of European politics. Exaggerating the significance and potential of links with the European Powers, this approach undervalued the independence of non-European states. And the pattern extended to the present, especially with the tendency during the Cold War to measure Third World Powers by referring to their politics. The same was true of the 'War on Terror' in the 2000s.

Because diplomacy was designed to use force to ensure profit (just as force was the medium to achieve foreign policy goals) it is not unexpected that both standing armies and diplomatic networks emerged at the same period. The Italian Wars weakened the Italian principalities and their ruling families; in fact, several Italian territories and principalities were annexed by neighbouring and foreign Powers: the Habsburgs acquired Milan and Naples; Florence, the republics of Pisa (for the second time) and Siena. These results saw diplomacy become essential in the search for security, let alone aggrandisement, and as a facet of institutional innovation in an extremely competitive political milieu. Whilst needing the support of military force, Venice demonstrated the value of skilful diplomacy to adapt to changing circumstances.[10] Likewise, despatching and accepting embassies demonstrated legitimacy and counterbalanced the assertions of opponents, notably exiles. Legitimacy and aggrandisement were allied, as when the Medici negotiated themselves into the rank of Grand Dukes of Tuscany.

The Italian Wars encouraged the Italian idea of permanent embassies elsewhere in Europe. With domains in southern Italy, Ferdinand of Aragon stood as a vital link between Italy and the rest of Europe; he appointed the first non-Italian resident envoys outside Italy in the 1480s; France and England each dispatched their first permanent embassies in 1509; the French court had ten by 1547. Yet, at this juncture, expansion on this scale did not include Scandinavia, Poland, or Russia.

Limitations arose not only within Europe. Globally, states' weakness not their strength remained crucial in European international relations. At the beginning of the sixteenth century, no European Power brandished the power of Ming China or Ottoman Turkey. These robust Powers required diplomacy rather less than Tudor England, Valois France, or Sforza Milan. European Powers needed diplomacy to win allies should they rely on war or, equally, seek to avoid it. Diplomacy's prominence ensured that weakness and failure in international politics led to tangible or latent instability.

Linked to this weakness was another defining aspect of European international relations: its multipolar character, which provided cause and opportunity for frequent diplomacy. Thus, the development of European diplomacy can be located in terms not so much of a theory of modernisation through government development as of the contingent nature of a state system that was distinctive, rather than modern. This distinctiveness was readily apparent in contrast with East Asia or the 'pre-contact' (that is, pre-Spanish) Americas, but was scarcely unique. The development of diplomacy in Antiquity had similar political contexts. More than multipolarity provided by competing Powers lay in European developments. It is useful to compare Europe's condition with that in the Middle East, where, between 1480 and 1530, a series of Islamic states, notably Ottoman Turkey, Mamluk Egypt, and Safavid Persia, looked to delineate their relations. A degree of similarity exists with Western Europe. The Ottomans acquired a vital advantage by Mamluk and Safavid inability to collaborate,[11] a failure paralleled by the Christian Powers' unwillingness to cooperate against Ottoman expansion. Yet, major differences existed because unlike Christian Europe, the Middle East lacked second- and third-rank Powers; the Christian Powers needed diplomacy to secure alliances.

The position of monarchs constitutes an element of the attempted modernisation of pre-1800 diplomacy: seeking modern elements and modernising trends and weighing a period by how it conformed to modernisation. Such an approach is archaic. Other assumptions exist, like over-estimating training (as opposed to social skills) in *ancien régime* diplomacy and the propensity to modulate religious motivation and ecclesiastical topics in relations. Whether or not archaism is at issue, it is practical to ask how far the modern assumption that diplomacy establishes and replicates mutuality and equality in representation and negotiation can be applied in the past without qualification.

There were also important ideological factors at play in the Middle East that limited the development of a comparable international system to that seen in Habsburg–Valois rivalry. In particular, rivalry over claims to be the true Islamic polity introduced a potent element of hostility, and this rivalry was exacerbated by confessional differences between the Safavids and the Ottomans, and by the willingness of the former to encourage heterodox religious tendencies in Anatolia.[12] Such issues remain significant to diplomacy in the modern Middle East, with the organisation of the haj, the annual pilgrimage of the faithful to Mecca, and the safety of the pilgrims, providing a particular irritation.[13] But Europe, too, confronted a religious schism after the advent of the Protestant Reformation in 1517. For almost a century and a quarter, the European Wars of Religion produced a heavy reliance on war and diplomacy.

The Thirty Years' War (1618–48) constituted the zenith of unrelenting religious animosity within Europe, especially before full-scale French entry into the struggle in 1635 against the Catholic Habsburg Powers, Austria and Spain. The ferocity of the struggle encouraged diplomacy: peace negotiations occurred sporadically, often concurrent with military operations and being affected by them or by reports and rumours about them, a situation that put a premium on intelligence.[14] Searching for allies also stimulated diplomacy. Hence, in the example of Denmark: rather than impromptu diplomatic missions, beginning in the 1620s, there emerged diplomats residing permanently at foreign courts. Stockholm received the first. Then, around 1630, other permanent residents were in Paris and The Hague and, by the 1640s, at Vienna, Madrid, and Brussels.

Alliances negotiations and the operations of armed forces sometimes conducted over decided distances put pressure on diplomacy. Communication difficulties heightened the complex problem of accredited diplomats not committing their political masters to bargains without clear direction. Such a question affected the Treaty of Regensburg in 1630. Cardinal Richelieu repudiated the treaty, claiming duplicitously that his envoys had exceeded their orders by both agreeing that France would not aid the Holy Roman Emperor's enemies and signing the treaty with the Emperor. Known as the Peace of Westphalia, with treaties signed at Münster and Osnabrück in 1848, a peace settlement finally ended this war. Westphalia is held as a milestone in the progress of international relations and, hence, diplomacy. In fact, the peace treaties are commonly held up as the genesis of the modern state system. Sovereign independence became an accepted concept: Spain accepted Dutch independence, ending the Dutch Revolt that began in 1566; with the important exception of Hungary, Austrian Habsburg control over their domains, chiefly Bohemia, was acknowledged and ended these domains' quest for autonomy.[15]

That Westphalia is a fundamental departure in the growth of the modern state system also derives from the treaty avowing that German princes could pursue their own foreign policies. Such recognition ended the myth of Christian unity that the Holy Roman Empire had provided since the ninth century. The weakening of the Imperial ideal has been trumpeted as the shift from medievalism to modernity: the Westphalian concept of sovereignty and its state system are expressions since used extensively. Hinging on the belief that individual states are sovereign bodies accountable only to themselves, it contrasts with supranational institutions and theories like those advanced by advocates of Imperial Holy Roman Empire ideals before 1648 and liberal universalists in the 1990s.[16] However, such an analysis places too much emphasis on the changes wrought by Westphalia, making it the dawn of a new diplomacy. But medieval and Renaissance diplomacy had already long set the pace, notably the development of resident embassies.

In practice, Westphalia's impact on Germany was narrow and its wider consequences blurred. Although princes within the Empire had long enjoyed effective autonomy (they negotiated accordingly), imperial discord and the effective sovereignty of each prince had been markedly advanced by the Protestant Reformation. Thus, rather than a milestone, Westphalia's changes represented the reworking of a frail federal system in which interstate diplomacy was already well established. They bear little reference to the more circumspect shift in the relationships between the emperor, his Empire, and the princes before and after 1648.[17] Several German states were too minor to pursue earnest independent foreign policies; this fact, in part, explains the Emperor's and the Empire's sustained role and importance. And if a limited parallel existed between earlier conceptions of the Holy Roman Empire and Chinese assumptions about themselves (that China was the centre of the world) rudiments of these previous conceptions remained, particularly the Emperor's lofty esteem.[18]

Moreover, curbs on the German states through clauses in Westphalia permitted princes to ally with each other and with foreign Powers to defend their security, which was not for offensive purposes. These alliances were satisfactory on condition that they were not directed against the Emperor, the Empire, or the treaty. During the War of the Spanish Succession, two French allies, the Electors of Bavaria and Cologne, suffered an Imperial injunction in 1706, removing their rights and privileges, which they regained only in 1714, when the Treaty of Rastatt ended the war. More generally, international relations in the century after Westphalia were not too different from those in the preceding century.[19]

Rather than a milestone for European diplomacy, Westphalia addressed current and new issues in the latter half of the seventeenth century that saw the value of diplomats for reporting and negotiation. The advent in 1649 of an English Republic and its external ambitions under, first, the Rump Parliament and, later, from 1653 to 1658, Oliver Cromwell, stood as an early challenge to the continental Powers. Its challenge was heightened by perceptions of England as both unstable and a forceful Power. A Swedish ambassador in the mid-1650s, Christer Bonde, recounted: 'this regime is riddled with intrigues and with such jealousies that I have some reason to doubt whether there may not be those who deliberately confuse sensible policies so that matters may go ill'.[20] Cromwell exploited Franco-Spanish differences to secure an alliance of France, which, hitherto, supported the English Royalists.[21]

New issues were also distinguished by the policies and affectations of Louis XIV, who controlled French policy after 1661, and their implications within Europe. For example, Austro-Turkish and Austro-French relations were interconnected in that Turkish policies were perceived as being consequential for Western European power relationships. And, instead of emphasising Westphalia's innovative character, it is more appropriate to be less teleological. The Thirty Years' War had disturbed the development of the resident diplomat system, only to see it resume afterwards.[22] In turn, the reciprocal character of representation saw a greater spread of resident diplomacy, although it remained still far from comprehensive; for instance, Italian state representation in London in 1665–72 was inconsistent.[23] Likewise, bureaucratic developments in directing foreign policy, chiefly in France, have been questioned by scholarly enquiry indicating the pliability of organisational practices and the degree to which fixed methods were constrained by personal connections and factional politics.[24]

However, Westphalia initiated a sequence of protracted peace congresses ending major wars, congresses that validated diplomatic skills. These congresses and the negotiating talents that produced them invigorated an appreciation of the multiple interactions of Powers within an international system that was multilateral and in which distant issues might be consequential even for those not directly involved. In addition, the congresses emulated French diplomatic style and method, an approach viewed as effective and increasingly successful.[25] Moreover, they reflected complex changes in the political values of international relations, with a greater faith in arbitration within what should be a naturally benign international system, plus a requirement to respond to changing legal concepts about war.[26] Ideas advanced in 1672 by Samuel, Freiherr von Pufendorf's *De Jure Naturae et Gentium Libri Ôcto* underwrote these developments. Indeed, emerging international law proved significant in shaping political thought and the norms of international relations.[27] The implications for diplomacy strengthened its practice as a means for conducting relations amongst all other states, instead of just between allies and, thus, generally at the expense of others. Equality as a basis for negotiations proved important at congresses and to the procedures there adopted.[28]

Just as Westphalia was not necessarily a novel departure, the same was true for the violent replacement of the Ming dynasty in China in the mid-seventeenth century. The Manchu, the new dynasty, brought together Chinese and non-Han traditions and influences, and its rulers upheld the essentials of the Ming world-view: the Son of Heaven, the Emperor, presided over an orderly civilisation to which respectful barbarians were to be admitted. Korea had already recognised the Manchu ruler as the tributary overlord in 1636. Alongside the bureaucratic administrative hierarchy, a key to China's power lay with the feudal-type suzerainty enjoyed by the Emperor over vassals within his dominions. The latter practice was extended to the outside world, where all Powers were comprehended as tribute-offering vassals. These suppositions in 1593 made the entreaties of Hideyoshi, Japan's new ruler, for equality with the Wan Li Emperor a major trial. Hideyoshi sought investiture as the King of the Ming (to legitimate his seizure of power in Japan) and to acquire the privileges of tribute trade. The Chinese required Hideyoshi to take a more subordinate status, for example, corresponding to Altan Khan, the Mongol ruler, but their efforts were vetoed in 1596, when Hideyoshi determined China's intent, which Chinese envoys endeavoured to obscure to obviate a failure in negotiations. Equally, Menelik II of Abyssinia disallowed Italian employment of an Italian version of the treaty signed in 1889, a different text to permit Italy to assert a protectorate.

Rather than the seventeenth-century crisis ushering in a new Chinese system, as happened in Europe to an extent, virtue in China was sustained not in the norms and actions of an international system of sovereign states (the European model) but in the laudable example of the Son of Heaven. Barbarians revered his merit through tribute and performing due genuflection, especially kowtowing; thus was maintained an order expressed in, and upheld via, a universal kingship. Alongside theory, the reality of Chinese diplomacy included fundamentals familiar to Western rulers, like playing off barbarians against each other. Another contrast involved the degree to which negotiations appeared to safeguard peace by what could be perceived as the fraudulent bridging of contradictory pretensions and claims, but what was also an endeavour to save face and status by this deceit.[29]

Saving face was not just a vital aim of Chinese diplomacy. Chinese rejection of any equality of status saw Japan use diplomacy (sending and receiving envoys) to assert the Tokugawa Shogunate's legitimacy in 1689 and save face in part by restricting its diplomatic links in the seventeenth and eighteenth centuries largely to Korea and to the conquered kingdom of Ryukyu.[30] This policy was also emphasised by restricting links with European Powers. The Portuguese were expelled from Japan in 1639, and contact with the Dutch curtailed in 1641. In contrast, the Europeans desired trading rights in China, such as a Dutch East India Company embassy received in 1656.

By the late seventeenth century, most major Western and Central European Powers reciprocally maintained permanent peacetime embassies that, together, constituted the diplomatic corps. This corps stood as an increasingly defined and self-conscious world, with precise privileges and methods of procedure. It attracts attention in analyses of the development of a diplomatic system; but instead of focusing exclusively on form, it also conveys an understanding of the degree by which the system developed and adapted in response to particular needs and anxieties. Three key European exceptions to the expansion of the system of peacetime embassies were Russia, which established its first permanent embassy in Poland in 1688; the Turkish Empire; and the Papacy, whose representation was restricted to Catholic courts. Initiating diplomatic relations with England in the 1550s, Russia despatched an envoy to Paris in 1615 and an agent to Stockholm in 1635–36; but these links remained *ad hoc*, on the former pattern for specific purposes and a limited period.

Whereas the major Christian Powers set up embassies at Constantinople, the Turkish Empire did not establish permanent embassies until 1793, previously sending individual missions for particular negotiations. In 1689, one reached Vienna but failed to negotiate a peace settlement for a war in which the Turks were increasingly losing. Led by Zulfikar Efendi, the head of the Chancery, and Alexander Mavrocordato, the chief interpreter to the Imperial Divan, the special embassy reflected the gravity of the diplomacy—conveying more than a resident envoy.[31] Matters of status complicated relations with the Turks. Russia concluded peace with Turkey in late 1739, but unresolved issues remained: the titles by which Sultan and Tsar would be addressed; the exchange of slaves; border demarcation; and demolishing the Azov fortifications.[32] Resolution took two years (until May 1741); treaty ratification did not occur until that September.

In a system of growing conformity, other Powers frequently used individual missions, even when they had permanent embassies. Their purpose involved handling crucial negotiations and fulfilling ceremonial functions like congratulations on accessions, marriages, and births or installations with chivalric orders. Diplomatic choice was twofold: where to send envoys and whom to send. The fundamental concern for the former involved the nature of relations. If the recipient Powers were poor, diplomatic links were severed or reduced, which ensured that the range and nature of representation were greatly affected by periods of conflict. There were also disputes that severed diplomatic links. However, most rulers did not maintain permanent embassies in more than a few capitals, if that. Cost, the finding of suitable diplomats, and a lack of matters requiring negotiations were determining factors. Thus, an integrated diplomatic network ignores the rulers who had no, or very few, permanent embassies.

Consequently, diplomacy assumes different forms and has diverse consequences. The standard account focussing on the Western model of permanent embassies is constricted; thus it is crucial to understand what is on offer. Diplomacy has always been a privileged aspect of general systems of information-gathering, representation, and negotiation. In this sense, it is not the approach enshrined in the classic analysis by the British diplomat, Sir Ernest Satow, who retired in 1906. He defined diplomacy as 'the application of intelligence and tact to the conduct of official relations between the governments of independent states, extending sometimes also to their reactions with vassal states; or, more briefly still, the conduct of business between states by peaceful means'.[33] Harold Nicolson, a British diplomat of a younger generation, saw diplomacy as 'the process and machinery by which ... negotiation is carried out'[34]; surprisingly, his definition excluded much of what diplomats do. More laconically, a historian, Peter Barber, reckoned diplomacy constitutes 'the peaceful management of international relations'; but as others have done, he discussed the actions of diplomats rather than others involved in foreign policy-making and execution.[35] In reality, monarchs and presidents, prime ministers and Cabinets, foreign ministries and other bureaucratic advisors in other departments of state and the armed services, accredited ambassadors and diplomats, trade officials, military attachés, and more are diplomats.

Putting aside diplomacy's essence (preparing for war, assembling coalitions and misleading rival and neutral Powers) it hardly equals peaceful management—an approach differing significantly from that which, much more loosely, extends diplomats and diplomacy to other forms of representation, power projection and negotiation. Consequently, for James Der Derian, an international relations theorist, diplomacy becomes 'mediation between estranged individuals, groups or entities'.[36] Indeed, today, juxtaposed with the growing international schema of foreign services and diplomacy, plus the complex interaction with domestic issues and actors, diplomats and diplomacy embrace cultural or sporting activities,[37] so that anyone abroad is a diplomat for his or her country.

Thus, 'diplomats' can also describe those without formal diplomatic accreditation such as editors or important correspondents of authoritative newspapers or other media, like Valentine Chirol, the anti-German Foreign Editor of the *Times* from 1899 to 1911. He was received by the Japanese Emperor and described by President Theodore Roosevelt as the 'godfather' of the Anglo-Japanese treaty of 1902.[38] Along the same lines, prominent politicians and others can fulfil the same role. In October 2009, John Bencow, the Speaker in the British House of Commons, saw his role as being 'Ambassador for Parliament'.[39]

An example of the complexity of diplomacy that touches government policy, but reaches more widely than the narrow purview of foreign ministries, is 'dollar diplomacy'. Initially used by *Harper's Weekly* in April 1910 to describe the efforts by Secretary of State Philander Knox to augment American foreign investment, after 1945 'dollar diplomacy' was applied to the delivery of United States economic aid, principally to Latin American states, and often in return for supervision by American economic advisers. The key agency was generally not the State Department. Yet, the core of this support often mirrored more formal diplomacy, namely economic and political stabilisation and/or promoting democracy.[40] In this approach, diplomacy is loosely defined as international political activity. However, such a flexible definition minimises the distinct character of diplomacy as the execution of policy through accredited persuasion. Still, no unblemished distinction exists between making and realising policy, and persuasion is not the only means, nor accredited agents the only ones, to play a role.

And given the attention on diplomats, the discourse on diplomacy is usually overly narrow. Its role in cultural exchange is unambiguously significant and has been so in the past, and not only in

Europe but also in East Asia and elsewhere.[41] For another habitually undervalued aspect of diplomacy, information-gathering has a key role given government dependency on information; and acquiring accurate material is fundamental to the success of any diplomatic system. As such, diplomats constitute just part of the mechanism to obtain information, and often not the most important part.[42] Consequently, where diplomacy is integral to information-gathering, and also representation, it does not serve as the sole means. Certainly, part of diplomatic history must be to explain how far these processes have been conducted through, or under the control of, the formal foreign policy mechanisms. In practice, this has always been the case only to a limited extent.

Whilst information-gathering is least likely to be controlled by the formal diplomatic process, diplomats were habitually best placed to corroborate and trade information; an essential professional skill is distinguishing the certain from the uncertain.[43] However, to validate and exchange information, diplomats remained reliant on their governments providing information. If unable to obtain, and thus offer, such information, their credibility suffered. In this situation, it would be problematic to acquire intelligence and provide the informed counterfactuals indispensable to their function in the policy-making process. This theme underscores the mutuality between states that is basic to diplomatic processes.

Other sources of knowledge about foreign countries have traditionally included commercial and military individuals and institutions, and today, new extraofficial sources like non-governmental organisations are involved. This point serves as an important reminder of the degree to which the diplomatic system, understood as that centred on diplomats and their political masters, does not control the diplomatic process (the management peaceful or otherwise of international relations). A similar conclusion can be made about the extent to which the use of force is not simply a matter of the formal military mechanisms of the state. Financial, political, and special interest entities have sometimes brought pressures to bear short of war.

Hence, the formal diplomatic system did not govern diplomatic practice as normally assumed: the absence of inclusiveness was also so for representation and negotiation. The latter has been managed primarily by diplomats, although mitigated somewhat by the part played by sovereigns, heads of state, ministers, and favourites of sovereigns not given diplomatic rank. The travels of heads of government are closely linked to diplomacy, as with David Lloyd George, British prime minister from 1916 to 1922. He headed the British delegation at the Paris Peace Conference in 1919, when the Treaty of Versailles with defeated Germany was negotiated amongst the victorious Allied Powers. And he then travelled to a series of post-Versailles conferences at Genoa, Cannes, and other places that refined the Peace Settlement.

Distrustful of the British Foreign Office and Diplomatic Service, which he saw as a bastion of aristocratic privilege (and critical of the tradition of pursuing the balance of power that he reckoned helped lead to the First World War) he pursued high-level diplomacy that lacked a strategic basis. Whilst professional British diplomats fought back successfully to reassert their primacy in the foreign policy-making process (assured when Lloyd George fell from power in October 1922), the possibility of prime ministerial control of foreign policy remained. Indeed, the direct involvement of heads of state and ministers has been amplified since with the decided advances in air travel and the progress made in communications technology.

Yet, the perception and practice of diplomacy warrants that mistreating diplomats and embassies are particularly serious. Cuban and Venezuelan envoys in Honduras were detained during a military coup in June 2009, leading Venezuela's president, Hugo Chavez, to threaten retaliation should his representative be maltreated. Members of the deposed government sought sanctuary in foreign embassies (not unusual in such circumstances), which significantly complicated normal diplomatic relations: the new Honduran government pushed for severing relations with Venezuela.

As a concept, and adding complexity, diplomacy can be detached from notions of formal accreditation. For instance, intelligence agencies can advance government strategy; thus, Syrian agents in Beirut who assassinated Rafiq al-Hariri, a prominent Lebanese politician and former premier, on 14 February 2005 cannot gainfully be viewed as diplomats. But they can be characterised as crucial entities of a Power in which intelligence organs have a central governmental role, and in which legal concepts have limited applicability. Moreover, at that time, al-Hariri's slaying can be portrayed as Syria's method of managing its relations with Lebanon through guiding, or at least influencing, Lebanese politics: al-Hariri opposed Damascus' influence and Lebanon's Syrian-backed president, Émile Lahoud. Little usefulness exists in treating such actions as detached from diplomacy because doing so risks pushing aside from analysis similar conduct by many Powers across history.

The essential fact (Syrian agents pursuing state policy abroad although not official diplomats) conforms to a functional definition of diplomacy; and, notwithstanding, relations between diplomatic services and intelligence agencies can be difficult, as in France in the 1930s.[44] In addition, the increased level of Cold War intelligence operations endured after 1990–91, something seen with Russian and Chinese operations against Britain and the United States. However, these actions have a lesser part in the public dimension of international politics than had been the case during the Cold War, when Powers exploited their revelation for political advantage. In 1984, for instance, Britain expelled the KGB resident in London after arresting a British citizen recruited as a spy; the next year, the defection of Oleg Gordievsky, the KGB Resident-Delegate, saw twenty-five Soviet intelligence officers expelled.

The orthodox European-based concept of diplomatic developments until, during the twentieth century, they encompassed the globe is an insufficient guiding principle for writing diplomatic history. It is therefore essential to rethink it so that the 'non-West' receives its deserved share of attention: in the way diplomacy was conceived by its practitioners and in the analysis of diplomatic events. This 'global' challenge includes not only the need to discuss non-Western notions of diplomacy, but also to consider its encounters with Western concepts. In this context, there exist major themes: the development of professional diplomacy, tensions between ideology and realism, and the impact of the proliferation of Powers in the last century. Moreover, there are issues of empires and diplomacy, hegemonic diplomacy, diplomacy and totalitarianisms, and the role of both supranational institutions and non-governmental organisations. There also needs to be emphasis on the complexity of developments, which transforms into a warning against relying too much on synoptic models. In doing so, there is the formidable challenge of writing history to cover a long time span and a worldwide canvas.

Notes

1 M. S. Anderson, *The Origins of the Modern European State System, 1494–1618* (Harlow, 1998), 52–53. Cf. G. Mattingly, *Renaissance Diplomacy* (London, 1955); O. Krauske, *Die Entwickelung der ständigen Diplomatie* (Leipzig, 1885).

2 P. Zutshi, 'Proctors acting for English Petitioners in the Chancery of the Avignon Popes (1305–78)', *Journal of Ecclesiastical History*, 35(1984), 27.

3 J. Sumption, *The Hundred Years War*, Volume III: *Divided Houses* (London, 2009), 785.

4 M. E. James, *English Politics and the Concept of Honour, 1485–1642* (Oxford, 1978).

5 G. Mattingly, 'The first resident embassies: medieval Italian origins of modern diplomacy', *Speculum*, 12 (1937), 423–39.

6 For example, R. A. Griffiths and J. Law, eds., *Rawdon Brown and the Anglo-Venetian Relationship* (Stroud, 2005). Cf. R. Fubini, 'Diplomacy and Government in the Italian City-States of the Fifteenth Century (Florence and Venice)', in D. Frigo, ed., *Politics and Diplomacy in Early Modern Italy. The Structure of Diplomatic Practice, 1450–1800* (Cambridge, 2000), 48.

7 B. Behrens, 'Treatises on the ambassador written in the fifteenth and early sixteenth centuries', *English Historical Review*, 51(1936), 616–27.

8 M.C. Wright, 'The adaptability of Ch'ing diplomacy: The Case of Korea', *Journal of Asian Studies*, 17 (1958), 363–81.

9 D. Goffman, *Britons in the Ottoman Empire, 1642–1660* (London, 1998).

10 R. Finlay, *Venice Besieged. Politics and Diplomacy in the Italian Wars, 1494–1534* (Farnham, 2008).

11 P. Brummett, *Ottoman Seapower and Levantine Diplomacy in the Age of Discovery* (Albany, NY, 1994).

12 N.R.K. Keddie and R. Matthee, eds., *Iran and the Surrounding World: interactions in culture and cultural politics* (Seattle, WA, 2002); M. Mazzaoui, ed., *Safavid Iran and her neighbors* (Salt Lake City, UT, 2003).

13 H. Fürtig, *Iran's Rivalry with Saudi Arabia between the Gulf Wars* (Reading, 2002).

14 D. Croxton, '"The Prosperity of Arms Is Never Continual": Military Intelligence, Surprise, and Diplomacy in 1640s Germany', *Journal of Military History*, 64 (2000), 981–1004, especially 991, 1001.

15 For an English abridgement of the terms, G. Symcox, ed., *War, Diplomacy and Imperialism, 1618–1763* (London, 1974), 39–62. Recent work can be approached through K. Bussmann and H. Schilling, eds., *1648: War and Peace in Europe*, 3 Volumes (Münster, 1998); H.J. Duchhardt, ed., *Der Westfälische Friede* (Munich, 1998), 369–91.

16 K.J. Holsti, *Peace and War: Armed Conflicts and International Order, 1648–1989* (Cambridge, 1991), 39; L. Bély, ed., *L'Europe des Traités de Westphalie: Esprit de la Diplomatie et Diplomatie de l'Esprit* (Paris, 2000); R. Lesaffer, ed., *Peace Treaties and International Law in European History* (Cambridge, 2004). For a recent example of the widespread application of the term, F.H. Lawson, 'Westphalian Sovereignty and the Emergence of the Arab States System: The Case of Syria', *International History Review*, 22(2000), 529–56; idem., *Constructing International Relations in the Arab World* (Stanford, California, 2006).

17 D. Croxton, 'The Peace of Westphalia and the origins of sovereignty', *International History Review*, 21 (1999), 569–91.

18 P.H. Wilson, *German Armies. War and German Politics, 1648–1806* (London, 1998).

19 Jeremy Black, *Eighteenth Century Europe 1700–1789* (New York, 1990); Heinz Duchhardt, *Altes Reich und europäische Staatenwelt, 1648–1806* (München, 1990).

20 M. Roberts, ed., *Swedish Diplomats at Cromwell's Court, 1655–1656* (London, 1988), 301.

21 T. Venning, *Cromwellian Foreign Policy* (Basingstoke, 1995).

22 D. Croxton, *Peacemaking in Early-Modern Europe: Cardinal Mazarin and the Congress of Westphalia, 1643–1648* (Selinsgrove, PA, 1999); A. Tischer, *Französische Diplomatie und Diplomaten auf dem Westfälischen Friedenskongress. Aussenpolitik und Richelieu und Mazarin* (Münster, 1999).

23 Clayton, *Diplomats and Diplomacy*, 16.

24 M. Haehl, *Les Affaires étrangères au temps de Richelieu: Le Secrétariat d'État, les Agents Diplomatiques, 1624–1642* (Brussels, 2006).

25 L. Bély, 'Méthodes et perspectives dans l'étude des négociations internationales à l'époque moderne', in R. Babel, ed., *Frankreich im europäischen Staatensystem der Frühen Neuzeit* (Paris, 1995), 219–34.

26 S.C. Neff, *War and the Law of Nations: A General History* (Cambridge, 2005).

27 O. Asbach, ed., *War, the State and International Law in Seventeenth-Century Europe* (Farnham, 2010).

28 Congress of Cambrai, Stowe Mss fol. 73 (British Library, London).

29 K.R. Robinson, 'Centering the King of Chosŏn: Aspects of Korean Maritime Diplomacy, 1392–1592', *Journal of Asian Studies*, 59(2000), 109–25; K.M. Swope, 'Deceit, Disguise, and Dependence: China, Japan, and the Future of the Tributary System, 1592–96', *International History Review*, 24(2002), 763; H.G. Marcus, *A History of Ethiopia* (Berkeley, CA, 1994), 89–90.

30 R.P. Toby, *State and Diplomacy in Early Modern Japan: Asia in the Development of Tokugawa Bakufu* (Stanford, CA, 1991); E.H. Kang, *Diplomacy and Ideology in Japanese-Korean Relations from the Fifteenth to the Eighteenth Century* (New York, 1997).

31 C.J. Heywood, 'English Diplomatic Relations with Turkey, 1689–98', in W. Hale and A.I. Bağiş, eds., *Four Centuries of Turco-British Relations* (Walkington, 1984), 29; I. Parev, *Habsburgs and Ottomans between Vienna and Belgrade, 1683–1739* (Boulder, CO, 1995). For a later special embassy, N. Itzkowitz and M. Mote, eds., *Mubadele—an Ottoman/Russian exchange of ambassadors* (Chicago, IL, 1970).

32 Russia was allowed to retain control of this position, contested since the 1690s, as long as it was unfortified.

33 E. Satow, *A Guide to Diplomatic Practice* (London, 1917), 1.

34 H. Nicolson, *Diplomacy* (Oxford, 1963), 3–4.

35 P. Barber, *Diplomacy* (London, 1979), 6.

36 J. Der Deriam, 'Mediating estrangement: a theory for diplomacy', *Review of International Studies*, 13 (1987), 9.

37 J.C.E. Gienow-Hecht, *Transmission Impossible: American Journalism as Cultural Diplomacy in Postwar Germany, 1945–1955* (Baton Rouge, LA, 1999); R.T. Arndt, *The First Resort of Kings: American Cultural Diplomacy in the Twentieth Century* (Dulles, VA, 2005).

38 L.B. Fritzinger, *Diplomat without Portfolio: Valentine Chirol, His Life, and 'The Times'* (London, 2006).

39 Ten o'Clock News, BBC 1 (15 October 2009).

40 F. Adams, *Dollar Diplomacy: United States Economic Assistance to Latin America* (Aldershot, 2000).

41 P.Y. Beaurepaire, *Le mythe de l'Europe française au XVIIIe siècle: Diplomatie, culture et sociabilités au temps des Lumières* (Paris, 2007).

42 For diplomats as negotiators, intelligence sources, and cultural contacts, see M.J. Levin, *Agents of Empire: Spanish Ambassadors in Sixteenth-Century Italy* (Ithaca, NY, 2005); P.M. Drover, 'Letters, Notes and Whispers: Diplomacy, Ambassadors and Information in the Italian Renaissance Princely State' (PhD Dissertation, Yale, 2002).

43 John Burnaby (private secretary to James, Earl Waldegrave, British envoy, Paris) to Horatio Walpole (envoy, The Hague), 1 February 1735, State Papers (National Archives, Kew, London) 84/341 fols 56–57.

44 P. Jackson, *France and the Nazi Menace: Intelligence and Policy Making, 1933–1939* (Oxford, 2000).

2

Theorising diplomacy

Christer Jönsson

Whilst there is a rich and growing literature on diplomacy, theories of diplomacy are less abundant. In view of its pivotal role in international relations (IR), diplomacy has received surprisingly little attention amongst theoretically oriented IR scholars. Indeed, diplomacy has been described as 'particularly resistant to theory',[1] and the well-known Israeli diplomat and foreign minister, Abba Eban, has argued that the 'intrinsic antagonism' between theory and practice is more acute in diplomacy than in most other fields.[2] Why, then, has diplomacy not been the object of more theorising? There may be several reasons for the relative dearth of diplomatic theory. Two major factors have to do with the conceptualisation of diplomacy and the character of the authors writing about diplomacy.

There is no consensual conceptualisation of diplomacy that can serve as a foundation for theorising. The words 'diplomacy' and 'diplomatic' are used with several different meanings. In fact, the words have been characterised as 'monstrously imprecise', simultaneously signifying 'content, character, method, manner and art'.[3] According to Sir Peter Marshall, at least six related meanings may be distinguished.

First, 'diplomacy' sometimes refers to the *content* of foreign affairs as a whole. Diplomacy then becomes more or less synonymous with foreign policy. This means that theories of foreign policy are applicable. Second, 'diplomacy' may connote the *conduct of foreign policy*. The word is then used as a synonym of statecraft. Henry Kissinger's book, *Diplomacy*, which draws on his experiences as United States Secretary of State, is a case in point.[4] A third connotation of diplomacy focuses on the management of IR by *negotiation*. Thus, the *Oxford English Dictionary* defines diplomacy as 'the conduct of international relations by negotiation'. Adam Watson offers a similar definition as 'negotiations between political entities which acknowledge each other's independence'.[5] Theories of negotiation, which are well developed, are then what is needed to understand diplomacy. Fourth, diplomacy may be understood as the use of diplomats, organised in a *diplomatic service*. This usage is more time-bound, as the organisation and professionalisation of diplomacy are rather recent. Fifth, diplomacy, and especially the adjective 'diplomatic', often refers to the *manner* in which relations are conducted. To be diplomatic means to use 'intelligence and tact', to quote Ernest Satow's classic formulation.[6] A sixth, related conceptualisation is to understand diplomacy more specifically as the art or *skills* of professional diplomats.

One definitional controversy concerns the peaceful character of diplomacy. Some authors conceptualise diplomacy in terms of 'the peaceful conduct of relations'[7] or 'the establishment and development of peaceful contacts',[8] regarding diplomacy as the opposite to war or any use of force. On the other hand, other scholars are reluctant to draw such a clear-cut line, arguing either that the opposition of war and diplomacy is a Western notion,[9] or that the blurring of the line between diplomacy and violence is one of the characteristics of modern diplomacy.[10] During the

Cold War, the phrase 'coercive diplomacy' was coined to denote the use of threats or limited force in diplomatic persuasion.[11]

In short, the lack of an agreed definition has been a stumbling block to rigid theorising. As developed below, different conceptualisations of diplomacy entail different theoretical approaches.

A second major factor impeding the development of theory concerns the authorship of most works on diplomacy. The bulk of the vast literature on diplomacy has been written either by practitioners or diplomatic historians. Neither category of authors has been particularly interested in theory-building. Practitioners have tended to be anecdotal rather than systematic, and diplomatic historians idiographic rather than nomothetic.[12] Just as historians are interested in a particular past, practitioners draw on their own particular experiences. Neither practitioners nor diplomatic historians have been prone to generalise from different historical experiences and insights.

Diplomats have been prolific writers. Many have had scholarly ambitions and credentials. Diplomats have reflected on their own practice to an extent that few other professions can match. Much of this literature is in the form of memoirs. In these works there is a clear prescriptive bent. What characterises the good diplomat? How should diplomacy best be conducted? These are questions occupying authors from antiquity to today. In addition to this prescriptive tendency, modern-day ambassadorial memoirs tend to emphasise and exaggerate the profound changes that their authors claim to have experienced in their time of service, whilst overlooking elements of continuity.

Diplomatic historians, for their part, have amassed a wealth of information about specific eras or incidents from antiquity onwards, but have failed to forge any strong links with IR theorists. Although diplomatic history and IR have been characterised as 'brothers under the skin',[13] academic parochialism as well as stereotypical and caricatured readings of one another's subfield have hampered interdisciplinary cross-fertilisation.

These and other aggravating factors notwithstanding, a number of theoretical approaches to diplomacy have been developed. The remainder of this chapter reviews the most important of these, beginning with the long tradition of prescriptive tracts, offering observations and advice concerning the conduct of diplomacy. Realism, which became the predominant school of thought in IR scholarship after the Second World War, encompasses a conceptualisation of diplomacy tied to state power in an anarchic world. The so-called English School offers a rivalling approach and different understanding of diplomacy, anchored in an international society with rules and institutions guiding state behaviour. After juxtaposing these two chief alternative approaches, the chapter proceeds to discuss other, more recent attempts at theorising diplomacy, drawing on post-modern approaches, diplomatic understandings of IR, suggestive metaphors, and social anthropology.

Reflections on diplomacy can be found throughout history. For instance, the Ancient Indian treatise on statesmanship, *Arthasastra*, written by Kautilya in the fourth century BC, offers observations and advice concerning the conduct of diplomacy. But it was only in seventeenth-century Europe that diplomatic practice had become sufficiently standardised to make practitioners able to theorise about it. As early as 1436 Bernard du Rosier, provost of Toulouse, who frequently served as an ambassador, wrote the first European textbook of diplomatic practice entitled *Short Treatise About Ambassadors*. The development of a diplomatic system based on resident ambassadors in Renaissance Italy saw the production of hundreds of similar works over the next few centuries. The proper behaviour and necessary skills of an ambassador were common themes of these early works. To mention a few prominent examples, in 1620 the Spanish scholar, courtier, and diplomat Don Juan Antonio De Vera published *El Embajador*. It was translated into French (its title became *Le parfait ambassadeur*) and Italian and was read thoroughly by most aspiring diplomats throughout the next century.

In *L'Ambassadeur et ses fonctions*, the Dutch diplomat and purveyor of political intelligence, Abraham de Wicquefort, criticised De Vera. First published in 1681, it was translated into English in 1716 as *The Embassador and His Functions*.[14] Wicquefort identified the resident ambassador as the principal institutional device, tracing its development over two centuries. De Vera and several other authors focused on resident ambassadors as well, but they tended to describe an ideal of conduct. Dismissing this type of moral speculation, Wicquefort was equally critical of the literature produced by jurists, which was preoccupied with an envoy's legal status rather than his functions. He aimed at delineating what, in practice, makes for a successful ambassador, paying tribute to the diplomats he most admired. Focusing on the representational significance of diplomacy, Wicquefort saw ambassadors as primarily representatives of sovereigns and regarded 'the right of embassy' as a crucial mark of sovereignty. Representing one sovereign whilst being dependent upon the whims of another, the ambassador's insecure predicament was described by Wicquefort as that of 'an honourable spy', an expression enjoying wide currency at the time. In short, *The Embassador and His Functions* has been described as 'the first guide to the diplomatic practice of the European States-system as it emerged from the Congress of Westphalia'.[15]

The most renowned work on the European diplomatic system, based on the activities of resident envoys, is François de Callières' *De la manière de négocier avec les souverains*, published in 1716. Along with Wicquefort's book, it became one of the standard references on diplomatic practice throughout the eighteenth century.[16] Callières was active as a diplomat in the service of Louis XIV. Whilst he built on Wicquefort in describing actual diplomatic practice, what mattered, in his view, was not so much the attributes of individual ambassadors as the character of the European system of interdependent sovereigns. He viewed diplomacy as an essentially moderating influence, making the pursuit of state interests compatible with civilised behaviour. The self-assertive European states could therefore be '*membres d'une même république*'. Callières thus contributed to an understanding of diplomacy as an international institution. Like Richelieu before him, Callières emphasised the need for continuous diplomacy, arguing that negotiation should not be a one-time affair, but a constant and necessary ingredient in collecting the information needed for policy-making. Callières was the first to regard diplomacy as a profession in its own right. In fact, he was active in launching the first school devoted to the training of future diplomats, and he probably wrote his book with the school in mind. His short book, reprinted several times, has been hailed as 'a mine of political wisdom' by Ernest Satow[17] and as 'the best manual of diplomatic method ever written' by Harold Nicolson.[18]

Satow and Nicolson can be seen as modern followers of the early tradition. Both had a background as professional diplomats in the British Diplomatic Service. An exceptional linguist and noted Orientalist, Satow maintained his scholarly interest throughout his distinguished diplomatic career. He shared a taste for history with such writers as Wicquefort and Callières and was also a trained lawyer. In his view, diplomatic manners may change over time, but the essence of sound diplomacy will not. His most famous work, *A Guide to Diplomatic Practice*, was first published in 1917 and has since appeared in several revised editions. Satow's famous definition of diplomacy, 'the application of intelligence and tact to the conduct of official relations between the governments of independent states,' is frequently quoted.

Nicolson entered the diplomatic service in 1909 and distinguished himself as a member of the British Delegation at the Paris Peace Conference in 1918–19. After the conference, he was appointed private secretary to Sir Eric Drummond, the first secretary-general of the newly established League of Nations. An erstwhile Wilsonian idealist, Nicolson grew increasingly disillusioned in the immediate post-war years. In 1929 he gave up his diplomatic career to become a journalist and eventually a Member of Parliament. His reputation as a writer on diplomacy rests largely on his *Diplomacy* (1939) and the smaller treatise, *The Evolution of Diplomatic Method* (1954). They both join Satow´s encyclopedic work as modern-day classics. To Nicolson, diplomacy was a lubricant that guaranteed the smooth conduct of international affairs. His examination of diplomacy has been described as 'an attempt to render an *a posteriori* justification of his own conversion in the 1920s from a Wilsonian idealist to a more pragmatic realist'.[19]

Authors from du Rosier to Nicolson were practitioners, who not only aimed to describe and explain diplomacy but also had a clear prescriptive bent, offering recommendations as to how diplomacy should best be conducted. In this long tradition of prescriptive tracts, one can find similar but rather vacuous advice; 'the striking thing is how little over the centuries the recommendations have changed'.[20] Garrett Mattingly comments on the continuity from Bernard du Rosier to his own time, arguing that the clichés of the fifteenth century were similar to those of the twentieth and that students in foreign service schools around the world were still learning much of the same generalities.[21] In short, although the term diplomatic theory is often used when referring to these early works, they cannot be said to offer anything amounting to a positive theory of diplomacy. Containing a wealth of useful information in need of systematisation, these prescriptive and value-laden treatises can rather be seen as embryos of a normative theory of diplomacy.

With Nicolson, as mentioned, the study of diplomacy took a step away from idealism in the direction of realism, the school of thought that came to dominate the study of IR after the Second World War. Classic realism provides a state-centric perspective on IR. Proceeding from a core assumption that world politics unfolds in an international anarchy, that is, a system with no overarching authority, realists conceive of international politics as a struggle for power amongst states, ensuing in inevitable conflicts ultimately resolved by war. States are seen as protectors of their territory, population, and way of life and are assumed not to see beyond their national interests in the conduct of their foreign policy.

War and military strategy are treated in greater detail than diplomacy in realist works. To the extent that realists pay attention to diplomacy at all, they tend to regard it as an asset of states. Diplomacy then becomes a component, or reflection, of state power. Hans Morgenthau, the pioneering realist thinker, is emblematic of this perspective. In his *Politics Among Nations*, he includes 'the quality of diplomacy' amongst elements of national power.[22] Considering all the other factors that determine national power as the raw material of power, Morgenthau argues that the quality of a nation's diplomacy combines these different factors into an integrated whole, turning potentialities into actual power. To Morgenthau, the conduct of a nation's foreign affairs by its diplomats is for national power in peace what military strategy and tactics by its military leaders are for national power in war.

Diplomacy, in this view, is included amongst, and is dependent on, other more material capabilities; hence, it reflects state power. On the other hand, the quality of diplomacy may modify the value of other elements of state power. Thus, skilful diplomacy can increase a nation's power beyond what one would expect in view of other material factors. Conversely, poor diplomacy may prevent otherwise powerful states from making full use of their power potentials. As an example of an outclassed state in material terms wielding power chiefly by virtue of its brilliant diplomacy, Morgenthau cites France in the period from 1890 to 1914. Furthermore, he argues that British power covaried with the quality of British diplomacy, and that the first decades of skilful US diplomacy were followed by a long period of mediocrity or even ineptitude.

> Thus, diplomacy is seen as a second-order lever or instrument used to communicate promises or threats to deploy other instruments.

To put it another way, the advantages diplomacy confers are more likely to come from being good at it, rather than possessing a lot of it. Diplomacy, in short, is to be regarded as what economists and strategists call a multiplier, not an element of power in itself.[23]

Whilst recognising the role of individual diplomats (asking rhetorically what the power of France would have been without Richelieu, Mazarin and Talleyrand) Morgenthau concludes that 'it is of the utmost importance that the good quality of the diplomatic service be constant', and that 'constant quality is best assured by dependence upon tradition and institutions rather than upon the sporadic appearance of outstanding individuals'.[24]

Raymond Aron, another classic realist, views diplomacy and war as 'complementary modalities, one or the other dominating in turn, without one ever entirely giving way to the other except in the extreme case either of absolute hostility, or of absolute friendship or total federation'.[25] Citing Clausewitz, Aron espouses the subordination of war to policy.[26] Drawing on the experience of the First World War, he warns of diplomacy becoming a prisoner of military mechanisms prepared in advance.[27] According to Aron, 'diplomacy might be called the art of convincing without using force—*convaincre*—and strategy the art of vanquishing at the least cost — *vaincre*'.[28] Like Morgenthau, Aron understands diplomacy as an element of state power. On one hand, diplomacy implies the use of economic, psycho-political, and violent means and the choice of appropriate ones amongst them; on the other, 'pure' diplomacy relies on persuasion alone, without economic and political pressure or violence. Yet Aron doubts that pure diplomacy exists. To be sure, states may make every effort to convince both adversaries and onlookers that they want to persuade or convince, not to constrain; and adversaries may have the illusion of freedom, even when they are in fact yielding to force. Yet according to Aron, persuasion that is not backed by power has little chance of success.[29]

In 1979 Kenneth Waltz published his influential book, *Theory of International Politics*, which became the main source of inspiration for so-called neo-realism. Whilst proceeding from similar assumptions about an anarchic system of independent states, Waltz departs from classic realism by ignoring its normative concerns and by trying to provide a scientific IR theory inspired by economics. Whereas state leaders are at the centre of attention in classic realism, the structure of the system is the central analytical focus in neo-realism. Aron had argued that 'the principal actors have determined the system more than they have been determined by it'.[30] Waltz, by contrast, posits that structures, rather than individual actors, determine action. His is a theory of international politics, not of foreign policy.[31]

In the neo-realist system-level approach, diplomacy loses its relevance as an analytical category. Diplomacy may matter only occasionally 'as one of those contingent factors about which it is neither possible nor necessary to theorize'.[32] Diplomatic skills are epiphenomenal; the decentralised structure of anarchy between functionally similar states provides the continuity and shifting balances of power in the dynamics of international politics. It is symptomatic that 'diplomacy' does not appear at all in the index of Waltz's book. Nor have other neo-realist authors taken any interest in diplomacy. If neo-realism implies a move from unit-level to system-level analysis, it posits an anarchic system without any institutional constraints. In the words of one leading neo-realist, 'institutions have minimal influence on state behavior'.[33] However, if institutions are allowed into the picture, diplomacy assumes renewed importance in system-level analysis.

An institutionalist perspective on diplomacy is primarily associated with the so-called English School (ES). Adherents of this school argue, in opposition to realists, that beyond an international system, however anarchic, there exists an international society reflected in certain international institutions with concomitant norms, rules, and practices. Diplomacy is seen as one of these institutions. Martin Wight, in fact, characterises diplomacy as 'the master-institution' of IR,[34] and other authors in the ES tradition count diplomacy amongst the central international institutions along with sovereignty, war, and international law.

As one of the major institutions of the society of states, diplomacy is seen to have a moderating influence on state power, 'taming the sovereigns', in Kalevi Holsti's words.[35] Diplomacy is one crucial component in the set of institutional arrangements that for the most part allows states to coexist peacefully, and to interact in rule-bound environments that enhance the opportunities for mutual communication, trade, and flows of people and ideas. By providing links of communication and representation between states and regulating their day-to-day intercourse, diplomacy sets limits to the unrestricted use of state power.

There is today a revived interest in the ES.[36] In his useful overview of ES studies of diplomacy, Iver Neumann argues that the first generation of ES scholars (Martin Wight and Herbert Butterfield, in particular) did place diplomacy at the centre of IR, producing taxonomic and historical studies of diplomacy. However, these studies did not focus on diplomacy as a practice or diplomacy as an integrated part of social life but aimed at formulating a philosophy of history.[37]

The next generation of ES scholars, represented by Hedley Bull and Adam Watson, by and large discarded Wight and Butterfield's writings on diplomacy as speculation and rumination. Both had experience of serving as diplomats. Bull listed diplomacy as one of five central institutions of IR, along with the balance of power, international law, war, and Great Power concert. To Wight's list of diplomacy's functions (information, negotiation and information gathering) Bull added 'minimisation of the effects of friction' and 'symbolising the existence of the society of states'.[38] In addition to emphasising diplomacy's symbolic functions, he postulated the existence of a diplomatic culture, defined as 'the common stock of ideas and values possessed by the official representatives of states',[39] but never fully developed the idea. Bull, in short, conceived of diplomacy as reflecting, rather than constituting, international society. His treatment of diplomacy was primarily taxonomical.[40]

Watson focused much more on diplomacy as a practice. Following Wight, he saw diplomacy as dialogue, emphasising that this dialogue has a recorded history stretching back to the Amarna Letters from the fourteenth century BC. Rather than making sovereignty a pre-condition, he defines diplomacy as 'negotiation between political entities which acknowledge each other's independence'.[41] Watson was interested in the institution of diplomacy rather than its different manifestations: 'To Watson, then, diplomacy is a practice which by preceding, succeeding and also accompanying war emerges as a constant institution of international society'.[42]

In sum, the contributions by the second generation of ES scholars consisted of further developing the historical perspective and improving upon the taxonomical work of the first generation. Bull and Watson provided several fruitful and stimulating observations rather than full-fledged theories of diplomacy.[43]

In recent decades, Barry Buzan has made significant efforts to revive and reappraise the ES approach. In his ambition to build on previous ES research to develop a rigorous theoretical framework on the foundation that can be applied to contemporary globalisation, Buzan highlights conceptualisations of world society and international institutions.[44] He makes a distinction between 'primary' and 'secondary' institutions. Primary international institutions are durable and recognised practices that are constitutive of both polities and international society, whereas secondary institutions regulate practices amongst political units once legitimate actors are established, the basic rules are in place, and the game of IR is under way. The distinction between primary and secondary institutions is not always easy to uphold, and different authors suggest varying lists of primary international institutions.[45] However, most ES writers, including Buzan, include diplomacy amongst the primary institutions. Buzan suggests that the various issue-based regulative arrangements analyzed by regime theorists can be said to represent secondary institutions.

The ES has followers beyond the British Isles. For example, the Canadian Kalevi Holsti investigates change over time in eight major international institutions: statehood, territoriality, sovereignty, international law, diplomacy, international trade, colonialism, and war.[46] Reminiscent of Buzan, he makes a distinction between 'foundational' and 'procedural' institutions, in which foundational ones define and give privileged status to certain actors and procedural ones regulate interactions and transactions between actors. He places diplomacy amongst the procedural institutions, along with trade, colonialism, and war. Foundational institutions, according to Holsti, include statehood, sovereignty, territoriality, and international law.[47]

Holsti dates the institutionalisation of diplomacy to the end of the seventeenth century.[48] By then, diplomatic practices had become increasingly standardised; there was growing consensus on how to understand diplomacy; norms of sovereign representation, immunity, and extraterritoriality of the permanent embassy had been established; the administration of foreign relations had become bureaucratised; and the diplomatic career had taken its first steps towards professionalisation. Before then, 'diplomatic practices were so diverse, unpatterned, and unregulated by custom, etiquette, or formal rules that the degree of institutionalization was low'.[49]

Focusing on institutional change, Holsti distinguishes different notions of change: novelty or replacement, addition or subtraction, increased/decreased complexity, transformation, reversion, obsolescence.[50] He characterises changes in diplomacy since the end of the seventeenth century as increased complexity and addition, refuting arguments about its obsolescence, or transformation.[51] States have multiplied, and their interconnectedness has grown; means of rapid communication have been developed that have facilitated summits and multilateral conferences; and the scope of diplomacy has expanded to encompass the whole range of issues generated by modern societies. All this has added complexity, according to Holsti, but the traditional functions of diplomacy have stayed intact and the diplomatic institution remains robust.

With the exception of Adam Watson, writers in the ES tradition have been interested primarily in the significance of institutions generally in international society and have identified sets of institutions of varying importance, rather than singling out diplomacy for in-depth treatment. The effort by Christer Jönsson and Martin Hall to formulate a pre-theory of diplomacy, drawing on the ES and historical sociology, is an exception.[52] They aim to make IR theory relevant to diplomacy and diplomacy relevant to IR theory. Jönsson and Hall view diplomacy as a transhistorical phenomenon, as a perennial international institution structuring relations not only amongst states, but amongst different kinds of political authorities through the ages, so-called polities. Proceeding from an approach focusing on processes and relationships contributing to the differentiation of political space, they focus on processes of institutionalisation and ritualisation. Their theorising aims at uncovering those timeless parameters, within which change occurs in a long-term historical perspective. At a high level of abstraction, Jönsson and Hall argue, diplomacy can be analyzed as the mediation of universalism and particularism. Thus, diplomacy

> in a sense *constitutes* and *produces* international society. Each combination of universalism and particularism—whether settled in a treaty or, more commonly, continuously negotiated—represents a differentiation of political space. Each resolution specifies, often implicitly, who 'we' are and which competence we have (universalism), and who 'I' am and which competence I have (particularism).[53]

They then identify three essential dimensions of diplomacy that capture the mechanisms involved in mediating universalism and particularism: communication, representation, and reproduction of international society. Their conception of communication emphasises its constructive elements and poses diplomats as 'intuitive semioticians'. They point to the perennial quest for a common diplomatic language, both in the literal, linguistic sense and in the sociological sense of common codes and conventions of expression. Drawing on the literature on representative democracy, Jönsson and Hall distinguish between representation as behaviour (acting for others) and status (standing for others), arguing that representation is best understood as a process of mutual interaction between principals and agents. And they refer to diplomatic recognition and socialisation as key mechanisms by which diplomacy contributes to the reproduction of a given international society, contrasting contemporary exclusive recognition practices (only states are recognised as legitimate entities) with more inclusive practices in the past. In short, Jönsson and Hall emphasise the continuity of basic parameters whilst pointing to constant change within these parameters, painting an overall picture of an institution characterised by great resilience and adaptability.

In 1987 James Der Derian published *On Diplomacy*, a 'post-classical' theoretical treatise building on a doctoral thesis supervised by Hedley Bull and dedicated to his memory. It has been characterised as 'the most mature work on diplomacy to emerge out of the English School',[54] but takes it in a new direction. Whilst acknowledging his debt to Wight and Bull, Der Derian draws on the work of Nietzsche and Foucault in developing a genealogy of diplomacy, a history of the present told in terms of the past. And he deploys the theories of Hegel, Feuerbach Marx, Sartre, and others to explain how diplomacy arises as a mediation of mutual estrangement between individuals, groups, or entities, suggesting that

> Hegel's philosophical account of alienation can be used to explain two critical moments in diplomatic history: when the *mutual* estrangement *of* states *from* Western Christendom gives rise to an international diplomatic system; and when the Third World's revolt against Western 'Lordship' precipitates the transformation of diplomacy into a truly global system.[55]

Der Derian views diplomacy as embedded in a larger social order. In other words, the practice of diplomacy is integrated with other social practices and must be studied in its historical context. Diplomacy, in his view, is defined not only by Great Powers and great events, but as much by 'the "petty" *rituals* and *ceremonies* of power'.[56] He analyzes the origins and transformations of diplomacy in terms of 'six interpenetrating paradigms': mytho-diplomacy, proto-diplomacy, diplomacy, anti-diplomacy, neo-diplomacy, and techno-diplomacy.

Mytho-diplomacy emerged from mediation of man's alienation from God, as chronicled in the Bible and systematised by Augustine. The cleric, the warrior, and the trader are seen as prototypes of diplomacy,[57] and Carolingian *missi* as links 'in a chain of mediatory relations between rulers of various ranks, stretching from the late stages of mytho-diplomacy to the early stages of proto-diplomacy'.[58] Diplomacy 'develops as a mediation of *mutual* estrangements *between* states'.[59] Anti-diplomacy refers to the intra-national estrangement in the newly formed states, giving rise to utopianism aiming at ending diplomacy. The French and the Russian revolutions transformed anti-diplomacy into neo-diplomacy; and recent global communication processes have given rise to techno-diplomacy.

A different post-modern approach, without any anchoring in the ES, is taken by Costas Constantinou, who builds on the work of Derrida and others in using textual analysis to capture social phenomena.[60] Proceeding from the assumption that diplomacy is a primary example of a practice in which the textual plays a key role, Constantinou focuses on the language that underwrites and directs diplomacy. He notes that, etymologically, the word 'diplomacy' is derived from the Greek verb *diploun*, 'to double', and from the Greek noun *diploma*, which refers to an official document written on double leaves joined together and folded.[61] *Diploma* has the double connotations of a secret message and an official paper conferring certain rights to the bearer.

Constantinou examines the career of the word *theoria* and its etymological-philosophical association with both theory and diplomacy. In particular, he focuses on linguistic reflections of common associations of diplomacy with deception, ambiguity, and the manipulation of ambiguous identities. He notes that in ancient Greece, Hermes was the god not only of diplomacy but also of language and travellers as well as deceit and double-talk, and he points to the etymological links with hermeneutics.[62] In his multifaceted deconstruction of diplomacy, Constantinou comments on such different aspects as the representation of diplomacy in art and gastronomic diplomacy. A pervading theme is that the duplicity associated with diplomacy is present in all social life.

This theme recurs in a more recent essay by Constantinou on the human dimension and the spiritual, transformative potential of diplomacy.[63] He coins the term 'homo-diplomacy' to bring together these neglected aspects of diplomatic practice. Specifically, he distinguishes three interrelated features of homo-diplomacy: the stoic idea of introspective negotiation (a form of 'creative idleness', in which stoics were forced to confront themselves); the Paulian notion of reverse accreditation (viewing Paul's ecumenical embassy functions as a precursor of universalism); and gnostic discourse (bridging the chasm between the Self, the Other, and the divine, seeing all three as identical). Diplomacy, in this view, points the way out of the conceptual and practical gaols of conventional understandings.

Whilst most other theorising efforts involve applying IR approaches to diplomacy, Paul Sharp identifies a specifically diplomatic tradition of international thought that can say interesting and useful things about IR as well as human relations in general.[64] He is interested in what diplomats themselves, rather than IR scholars, have had to say about IR, contending that diplomatic theory (a coherent and distinctive set of propositions) 'can be derived if not from the utterances of diplomats always, then from the place which is distinctly theirs in international relations'.[65] Sharp draws on the ES in different ways. First, he uses Martin Wight's schema of three traditions of Western thought about IR (the Machiavellian or realist, the Grotian or rationalist, and the Kantian or revolutionary tradition) to develop his argument that diplomacy and diplomats remain peripheral and mysterious in IR theories. Second, he uses Hedley Bull's attempts to identify international theory as his point of departure for developing diplomatic theory. Third, the international society idea is central in his theorising.

Conditions of separateness are at the core of the diplomatic theory that Sharp outlines. Diplomacy is a response to a plural world in which groups of people want to live separately whilst seeing the need to conduct relations with others. These conditions provide the space in which diplomacy and diplomats work. Diplomats occupy positions between human communities. They are, as it were, professional strangers, experiencing distance from both home and abroad. This makes for a specifically diplomatic understanding of the world, 'with a sense of distance from the issues and interests which their senders and receivers think that their international relations are about'.[66] This understanding, in turn, makes them think diplomatically about specific issues in IR.

The diplomatic tradition, Sharp argues, suggests three relations of separateness.[67] Encounter relations occur when peoples, actually or figuratively, run into each other for the first time. In discovery relations, peoples attempt to render their respective cultures mutually intelligible. Re-encounter relations involve keeping known others at arm's length by reproducing and emphasising differences. Sharp explores the diplomatic understanding of these relations in three different dimensions: when an international society is integrating or disintegrating, expanding or contracting, and concentrating or diffusing power. He concludes that these dimensions acquire a second-order character in the diplomatic understanding. 'What matters is how relations are to be maintained in the midst of these and other processes, and in the midst of the arguments to which they give rise'.[68]

Similarly, thinking diplomatically about specific issues (Sharp discusses specifically problems of rogue states, economic globalisation, religion and public diplomacy) emphasises sustaining dialogue and seeking modes of coexistence, rather than taking an unequivocal stand. Prescriptively, diplomatic thinking implies, first, that one should accord the content of existing worldviews, including one's own, a provisional and relative character; second, that one should regard the existence of peoples holding different worldviews as a primary fact of IR.[69] In conclusion, Sharp identifies three injunctions that anyone engaged in diplomatic theorising or diplomatic practice has to follow: be slow to judge; be ready to appease; and doubt most universals.[70]

Metaphors are essential parts of our conceptual systems and often constitute building blocks in scientific theories. Two metaphors, in particular, have inspired theorising about diplomacy: Raymond Cohen's use of 'theatre' as a metaphor for the repertoire of visual and symbolic tools used by diplomats and statesmen, and Robert Putnam's coinage of 'two-level games' to direct our attention to the nexus between internal and external negotiations.

Cohen proposes a dramaturgical approach to diplomatic signalling. 'The international system is like a great stage on which the states are, at one and the same time, both actors and audience'.[71] He identifies three ways in which diplomatic communication differs from interpersonal communication. First, it is bound to seek cross-cultural comprehensibility; hence the development of a specific language of diplomacy. Second, it is always the product of careful deliberation. Third, it cannot escape from an insatiably inquisitive audience.[72] Cohen emphasises the dramaturgical tasks of leadership and the importance of stage-managing. In diplomacy, as in the theatre, there is a script, a basically prearranged text. The setting is meticulously prepared, and every gesture is premeditated, whether the length of a handshake or the warmth of an embrace. In the dramaturgical analogy, the conventional distinction between words and actions, or appearance and substance, loses a lot of its usefulness. Cohen emphasises non-verbal signalling in particular. One of its advantages lies in its being ambiguous and disclaimable. Moreover, non-verbal communication is able to capture the attention and interest of mixed audiences, and possibly to induce them to act.[73] Whilst culturally specialised gestures pose difficulties, protocol and diplomatic convention permit dialogue even in the absence of shared cultural assumptions.[74]

Putnam's two-level game metaphor resonates with the experience of diplomatic negotiators, who often emphasise the problems of internal bargaining, arguing they spend as much or even more time achieving consensus within their own side.[75] The metaphor draws attention to the fact that diplomacy has internal as well as external aspects. An edited volume uses this metaphor as a 'conceptual springboard'[76] to analyze the interaction of domestic and international processes in various episodes of diplomatic negotiations. Diplomacy, in this perspective, involves influencing domestic and international actors simultaneously.

> Diplomatic strategies and tactics are constrained both by what other states accept and by what domestic constituencies will ratify. Diplomacy is a process of strategic interaction in which actors simultaneously try to take account of and, if possible, influence the expected reactions of other actors, both at home and abroad.[77]

Analyses of such 'double-edged' diplomacy tend to focus on statesmen, rather than diplomatic agents, as the central strategic actors. The 'win-set' in any international negotiation is determined not only by strategies at the interstate level, but by preferences and coalitions as well as institutions at the national level. The empirical studies suggest that the relative autonomy of statesmen decreases over the course of diplomatic negotiations. They may be in the driver's seat as international agendas are being formulated, but become increasingly constrained by mobilised interest groups as international options become more clearly defined.[78]

Whereas the theoretical efforts discussed thus far have taken their point of departure in, or have been formulated in counterpoint to, IR theory, diplomacy has attracted attention in other disciplines as well. Notably, social anthropological approaches have addressed two aspects: the origin and ubiquity of diplomats, on the one hand, and the daily experience of being a diplomat, on the other. Ragnar Numelin's inquiry into 'the general human and social groundwork of diplomatic relations'[79] is an early study of diplomacy amongst less differentiated (in his terminology 'primitive') societies. He notes that the inviolability of messengers seems to be an accepted principle amongst aboriginal peoples[80] and points to the exchange of gifts as a primordial method to create goodwill and peaceful relations.[81] Numelin traces the oriental roots of the ritualised courtesy we associate with diplomats. 'The East had ... long been accustomed to a studied courtesy, and it was from its more polished manners that Western Europe was later to acquire those polite forms of intercourse which marked the age of chivalry'.[82] Similar, more recent works in this genre have dealt with such specific topics as diplomacy amongst American Indians and in pre-colonial Africa. However, they tend to be more descriptive than analytical or theoretical.

A prime example of theoretically informed anthropology, using the method of participant observation, is Iver Neumann's study of how diplomats experience the world.[83] He proceeds from the anthropological assumption that 'no analysis of social interaction is complete if it does not incorporate the meanings that permeate people's actions'.[84] Drawing on Charles Taylor's general scripts for the Western self, he proposes that being a diplomat implies balancing three scripts of self: the bureaucratic, the hero, and the mediator scripts. The heroic script (making a difference in the world) is usually seen as dominant and has numerous overachievers, whereas the bureaucratic script (following previously established routines) is more seldom overfulfilled. The mediator script posits the diplomat in a self-effacing role. Arguing that these scripts cannot be reconciled, only juggled, Neumann points to contextual clashes of scripts. The tensions between home life and job life as well as between life at home and life abroad are examples of such clashes.

As this overview has demonstrated, there are several different attempts at theorising diplomacy but no single widely accepted theory. The absence of a consensual definition of diplomacy has contributed to this situation, in combination with the lack of theoretical aspirations in much of the literature on diplomacy. A number of contested issues can be identified in the existing theoretical attempts.

First, there is a dividing line between those who associate diplomacy with individual actors and those who regard it as an international institution. The former view diplomacy either as an asset of states, speaking for example of British, French, and Chinese diplomacy; or they relate it to individual agents, such as Talleyrand, Metternich, or Kissinger. The latter see diplomacy as a universal institution that constitutes, and is constituted by, international society rather than individual states.

Another disagreement concerns the relative emphasis on continuity or change. Those observers, who highlight continuity, point to the timeless features of diplomacy, such as diplomatic immunity, ceremonial, and protocol. Several fundamental ingredients of diplomacy, they argue, have existed throughout recorded history. Those who emphasise change usually point to the role of technological developments. For instance, the revolution in information and communication technology is often seen as transforming diplomacy, depriving diplomats of their former monopoly of cross-border communication. A middle position in this controversy may be to try to 'uncover those timeless parameters, within which change occurs in a long-term historical perspective'.[85]

Whether diplomacy should be linked exclusively to the powers that be, or exists beyond formal political authority, is another issue. Whereas diplomacy has traditionally been regarded as state-to-state activity, monopolised by professional diplomats representing sovereigns or governments, many argue that examples exist of diplomatic agents and practices beyond that narrow circle throughout history. The role of non-state actors in contemporary diplomacy has attracted considerable attention. For example, one overview of current scholarship on diplomacy distinguishes between traditional, nascent, and innovative schools of diplomatic thought, based on the relative importance they ascribe to new, unorthodox variants of diplomacy and diplomatic agents.[86]

A final observation concerns the existing dearth but potential usefulness of multidisciplinary approaches. Most diplomatic studies have been carried out within the disciplinary borders of history and IR. Yet a broader spectrum of social sciences and humanities seem relevant to the study of such a multifaceted phenomenon as diplomacy. Anthropology has demonstrated its value, but psychology may be equally useful.[87] And linguistic approaches appear pertinent to studying diplomacy as a practice in which the production of texts is a key component.[88] In short, just as diplomacy entails crossing physical borders, there is a need to cross disciplinary borders in approaching diplomacy theoretically.

Notes

1 J. Der Derian, 'Mediating estrangement: a theory for diplomacy', *Review of International Studies*, 13 (1987), 91.

2 A. Eban, *The New Diplomacy* (London, 1983), 384–85.

3 P. Marshall, *The Dynamics of Diplomacy* (London, 1990), 7.

4 H.A. Kissinger, *Diplomacy* (New York, 1994).

5 A. Watson, *Diplomacy: The Dialogue Between States* (London, 1982), 33.

6 E. Satow (Lord Gore-Booth, ed.), *Satow's Guide to Diplomatic Practice*, 5th edition (London, New York, 1979), 3.

7 K. Hamilton and R. Langhorne, *The Practice of Diplomacy: Its Evolution, Theory and Administration* (London and New York, 1995), 1.

8 J.C. De Magalhães, *The Pure Concept of Diplomacy* (New York, 1988), 59.

9 R. Cohen, 'Reflections on the New Global Diplomacy: Statecraft 2500 BC to 2000 AD', in J. Melissen, ed., *Innovation in Diplomatic Practice* (London, New York, 1999), 4.

10 R.P. Barston, *Modern Diplomacy* (London, New York, 1988), 1.

11 A.L. George, *Forceful Persuasion: Coercive Diplomacy as an Alternative to War* (Washington, DC, 1991); A. L. George and W.E. Simons, eds, *The Limits of Coercive Diplomacy* (Boulder, CO, 1994).

12 Cf. J.S. Levy, 'Explaining events and developing theories: history, political science, and the analysis of international relations', in C. Elman and M.F. Elman, eds, *Bridges and Boundaries: Historians, Political Scientists, and the Study of International Relations* (Cambridge, MA, 2001); J.S. Levy, 'Too important to leave to the other: history and political science in the study of international relations', *International Security*, 22(1997), 22–33.

13 S. Haber, D.M. Kennedy, and S.D. Krasner, 'Brothers under the skin: diplomatic history and international relations', *International Security*, 22(1997), 34–43.

14 See M. Keens-Soper, 'Wicquefort', in G.R. Berridge, M. Keens-Soper, and T.G. Otte, *Diplomatic Theory from Machiavelli to Kissinger* (Basingstoke, 2001).

15 Ibid., 92.

16 Cf. M. Keens-Soper, 'François De Callières and diplomatic theory', in C. Jönsson and R. Langhorne, eds, *Diplomacy*, Volume I (London, 2004); K.J. Holsti, *Taming the Sovereigns: Institutional Change in International Politics*, (Cambridge, UK, 2004), 184.

17 As quoted in M. Keens-Soper, 'Callières', in Berridge et al., *Diplomatic Theory*, 107.

18 H. Nicolson, *The Evolution of Diplomatic Method* (London, 1954); reprinted (1998) by the Diplomatic Studies Programme, Centre for the Study of Diplomacy, University of Leicester.

19 T.G. Otte, 'Nicolson', in Berridge et al., *Diplomatic Theory*, 154.

20 H. Bull, *The Anarchic Society: A Study of Order in World Politics* (London, 1977), 182.

21 G. Mattingly, *Renaissance Diplomacy* (London, 1955), 39.

22 H.J. Morgenthau, *Politics Among Nations: The Struggle for Power and Peace*, 3rd edition (New York, 1966), 139–43.

23 P. Sharp, *Diplomatic Theory of International Relations* (Cambridge, UK, 2009), 56.
24 Morgenthau, *Politics Among Nations*, 141.
25 R. Aron, *Peace and War: A Theory of International Relations* (New York, 1966), 40.
26 Ibid., 45.
27 Ibid., 43.
28 Ibid., 24.
29 Ibid., 61.
30 Ibid., 95.
31 K.N. Waltz, *Theory of International Politics* (Reading, MA, 1979).
32 Sharp, *Diplomatic Theory*, 55.
33 J.J. Mearsheimer, 'The false promise of international institutions', *International Security*, Volume 19, Number 3(1995), 7.
34 M. Wight, *Power Politics* (Leicester, 1978), 113.
35 Holsti, *Taming the Sovereigns*.
36 Cf. T. Dunne, *Inventing International Society: A History of the English School* (London, 1998); B. Buzan, *From International to World Society? English School Theory and the Social Structure of Globalisation* (Cambridge, UK, 2004).
37 I.B. Neumann, 'The English School on Diplomacy', *Discussion Papers in Diplomacy*, No. 79 (The Hague, 2002), 7.
38 Bull, *Anarchic Society*, 171–72.
39 Ibid., 316.
40 Neumann, 'English School', 9.
41 A. Watson, *Diplomacy: The Dialogue Between States* (London, 1982), 33.
42 Neumann, 'English School', 11.
43 Cf. Ibid., 14.
44 Buzan, *From International to World Society?*
45 See Ibid., 167–76.
46 Holsti, *Taming the Sovereigns*.
47 Ibid., 24–27.
48 Ibid., 179–89.
49 Ibid., 180–81.
50 Ibid., 12–17.
51 Ibid., 190–210.
52 C. Jönsson and M. Hall, *Essence of Diplomacy* (Basingstoke, 2005).
53 Ibid., 37.
54 Neumann, 'English School', 17.
55 J. Der Derian, *On Diplomacy: A Genealogy of Western Estrangement* (Oxford, 1987), 23.
56 Ibid., 114.
57 Ibid., 80–95.
58 Ibid., 73.
59 Ibid., 110.
60 C.M. Constantinou, *On the Way to Diplomacy* (Minneapolis, MN, 1996).
61 Ibid., 77.
62 Ibid., 35, 150–51.
63 C.M. Constantinou, 'Human Diplomacy and Spirituality', *Discussion Papers in Diplomacy*, No. 103 (The Hague, 2006).
64 Sharp, *Diplomatic Theory*.
65 Ibid., 7.
66 Ibid., 102.
67 Ibid., 89–92.
68 Ibid., 192.
69 Ibid., 294.
70 Ibid., 296–311.
71 R. Cohen, *Theatre of Power: The Art of Diplomatic Signalling* (London and New York, 1987), 21.
72 Ibid., 2–3.
73 Ibid., 19–42.
74 Ibid., 103.

75 R.D. Putnam, 'Diplomacy and domestic politics: the logic of two-level games', *International Organzation*, 42(1988), 428–60.
76 The volume is P.R. Evans, H.K. Jacobson, and R.D. Putnam, eds., *Double-Edged Diplomacy* (Berkeley and Los Angeles, CA, 1993). The quotation is from P.B. Evans, 'Building an integrative approach to international and domestic politics', in Ibid., 398.
77 A. Moravcsik, 'Introduction: integrating international and domestic theories of international bargaining', in Ibid., 17.
78 Evans, 'Building an integrative approach', in ibid., 399.
79 R. Numelin, *The Beginnings of Diplomacy: A Sociological Study of Inter-tribal and International Relations* (Oxford, 1950), 14.
80 Ibid., 147–52.
81 Ibid., 254.
82 Ibid., 305.
83 I.B. Neumann, 'To be a diplomat', *International Studies Perspectives*, 6(2005), 72–93.
84 Ibid., 72.
85 Jönsson and Hall, *Essence of Diplomacy*, 3.
86 S. Murray, 'Consolidating the gains made in diplomacy studies: a taxonomy', *International Studies Perspectives*, 9(2008), 22–39.
87 Cf. T. Gärling, G. Backenroth-Ohsako and B. Ekhammar, eds, *Diplomacy and Psychology: Prevention of Armed Conflicts after the Cold War* (Singapore, 2006).
88 Cf. Neumann, 'English School', 25.

Part II
The Great Powers

3

The United States

The contemporary world's indispensable nation?

James M. Scott

On 20 January 1997, America's forty-second President, William Jefferson Clinton, used his second inaugural address to proclaim that 'America stands alone as the world's indispensable nation'.[1] Calling attention to United States centrality to the post-Cold War order, Clinton's assertion also hinted at the recognition of the evolving nature of power and influence in the emerging international environment. With the bipolarity of the Cold War giving way to a more complex distribution of power in which traditional forms and levers of power are complicated by the complexities of an increasingly globalised and interconnected world, the United States (and all major Powers) face new challenges and constraints. For the United States, the shift to greater multipolarity and the relative rise of major Powers like China, Japan, Britain, France, Germany, Russia, India, Brazil, and perhaps others, complicate the status of the United States as the sole global Power able to extend its reach around the world. Moreover, the increasingly important role of non-state and transnational actors in international politics muddies traditional conceptions of national power and national interests. All of these combine to establish a complex international environment in which major Powers, middle Powers, developing Powers, and non-state and transnational actors interact. As Clinton's assertion suggests, the United States may occupy a central and privileged place in this order, but 'indispensability' is a far cry from 'dominance'.

Many Americans have the perception that American foreign policy was isolationist until the Second World War and internationalist thereafter. However, if one defines isolationism to mean non-involvement, clearly the United States has never been isolationist:

> Only by the loosest conceivable definition of the term, however, could 'isolation' be said to represent the reality of United States policy during the first century-and-a-half of American independence. A nation that by 1900 had quadrupled its land mass at the expense of other claimants, engaged in multiple wars of conquest, vigorously pursued access to markets in every quarter of the globe, and acquired by force an overseas empire could hardly be said to have been 'isolated' in any meaningful sense.[2]

If 'isolationism' and 'internationalism' are poor guides to American engagement with the world, how can the historical context be better understood?

In fact, since achieving its independence, American engagement with the rest of the world has passed through three major periods.[3] The first was the Continental Era (1776–1860s), in which the United States focused on building an independent country safe from its neighbors, expanding territorial control over North America, constructing a strong national economy, and establishing a stable democratic polity. After the American Civil War, a Regional Era (1860s–1940s) ensued, in which American foreign policy was increasingly motivated by a growing sense of a 'manifest destiny' that emphasised 'the special virtues of the American people and their institutions; their mission to redeem and remake the world in the image of America; and the American destiny under God to accomplish this sublime task'.[4] During this period, American foreign policy was geared toward promoting and maintaining political stability, whilst seeking economic expansion abroad, often engaging in military intervention and occupation, especially in Latin America and Asia. Toward the end of this period, the United States became increasingly involved in Europe as well, first entering the First World War and, then, after isolationist sentiment amongst the American public and a strong peace movement contributed to Washington's rejection of American participation in the League of Nations, through other forms of active involvement. Nevertheless, whilst becoming increasingly important to the international political economy, the United States continued promotion of trade protectionism and was unwilling to take a strong leadership position with a declining Britain, which contributed to the world falling into the Great Depression.

The Second World War catapulted the United States into a Global Era (1940s–present). In the aftermath of the war, American leaders built on the foundation of international engagement established by Franklin Roosevelt in the war to assume a position of global leadership. From the Truman Administration to the Vietnam War, American leaders generally agreed on a global strategy that involved two related strands: a 'containment order' and a 'liberal economic order'. In essence, American strategy included the pursuit of global security and stability during the Cold War and in the face of the perceived Soviet expansionism, and the promotion of a liberal international market economy based upon the principles of free, open trade, fixed exchange rates, and multilateral management. With strong bipartisan support, Presidents Harry Truman and Dwight Eisenhower created a global American military presence, an unmatched nuclear arsenal, and an intelligence service that frequently engaged in covert operations overseas, some of which included forceful regime change in such countries as Guatemala and Iran. In the early 1960s, President John F. Kennedy expanded American foreign assistance whilst maintaining an aggressive anti-communist security policy.

However, the Vietnam War shattered this Cold War consensus and severely damaged both the Johnson and Nixon administrations.[5] The backlash against Vietnam prompted persistent struggles over the ends and means of American foreign policy for two decades. In contrast to the Cold War years, it became difficult after Vietnam for any President or administration to devise a foreign policy that responded successfully to changes in the global environment and obtain substantial domestic support. Neither Jimmy Carter's attempt to make human rights the 'soul of American foreign policy' nor Ronald Reagan's efforts to re-establish more confrontational Cold War policies reconstructed consensus. As these struggles persisted, the Cold War came to an end and the new international order emerged.

The preceding overview indicates the trajectory of power, influence, and engagement of the United States in world politics since its conception as in independent state. Its general outline suggests some of the underlying tensions that have characterised the American approach to the world. Understanding the trajectory, and the variation and debates underlying it, requires attention to the societal and institutional contexts that have shaped the American response to the constraints, imperatives, and opportunities of world politics over time.

The societal context of American foreign policy influences 'the manner in which members of society, including the state elite, define themselves and their place in the larger global setting'.[6] Whilst the societal context does not determine foreign policy, its nature gives shape to possible actions and helps shape the perceptual maps of policy-makers. As one authority suggests, the notion of 'interests' is deeply embedded in the societal context and political culture.[7] The heart of the societal context consists of a set of core values, a 'creed', through which Americans define themselves and their engagement with the world.

First amongst these values is 'democratic liberalism'. The United States is liberal in that it emphasises the individual and the rights and freedoms to which he or she is entitled, with a particular commitment 'to individual liberty and the protection of private property; to limited government, the rule of law, natural rights, the perfectibility of human institutions, and the possibility of human progress'.[8] The United States is democratic in the sense of a commitment to three things: the principle that there are specific procedures to follow for filling government positions (ie, elections) and making government decisions; popular sovereignty, or the view that the citizens are the source of government authority and, thus, the government must be accountable to them; and majority rule with respect and protection for the rights of minorities. Democratic liberalism therefore calls for limited and accountable government that should be responsive to and formed with the participation of the citizenry.

Other elements of the societal context concern relations amongst individuals and groups in society, and between them and the government. For example, the United States tends toward 'egalitarianism', in that there is broad agreement that citizens ought to have equal political standing and generally equal opportunities in society. Whilst much of American history has involved a struggle to define and apply these principles of equality (especially as regards racial, ethnic, and gender differences) in the main, the commitment is real and has militated against various forms of social and class distinctions, preferences, and discrimination that have been more common elsewhere. In addition, the United States is 'pluralist', accepting decisions that result in the victory of one group over another as long as individuals are free to associate with groups of their choice and there are no systematic barriers blocking the right of any group or individual to advocate for their preferences. Moreover, the United States tends to be 'legalist', a 'law-oriented society' with a preference for law-making to resolve conflict and a broad belief that 'ideas embodied in legal precepts are entitled to respect and obedience'.[9] Finally, a general 'universalism/exceptionalism' underlies these preceding features, a sense that 'the American way' is a model for others. Americans widely believe that values discussed above are and should be embraced by others. Hence, universalism essentially leads Americans to believe that commitments to democratic liberalism, constitutional government, and the like are superior preferences suitable and desirable for all people and countries.

One way to simplify the complex connection between these aspects of culture and foreign affairs is to identify the 'societal impulses' and 'foreign policy orientations' the culture generates. These may be considered in terms of two continua. The societal impulse continuum ranges between moralism/idealism at one end to pragmatism/realism at the other. Involving the 'forceful assertion of society's ideological principles',[10] moralism/idealism describes the impulse to promote certain values in foreign policy, rather than to defend various interests. Moralists/idealists argue that the United States should involve itself internationally for ethical reasons and in defense of moral principles. Furthermore, moralism/idealism rests on the presumption of the benevolence and moral superiority of American purposes and values and, thus, involves a sense of duty and destiny best defined as the 'United States' mission'.[11]

On the other hand, pragmatism/realism involves *ad hoc* problem-solving that eschews broad moral, ideological, or doctrinal purposes in favour of a concern with concrete interests and a results-based standard of evaluation.[12] Values such as democracy and pluralism lend themselves to the development of mutually acceptable compromises as solutions to problems. Within the broad parameters of American values, the impulse toward pragmatism means 'case-by-case-ism', reactive rather than proactive approaches, and the focus on the short term rather than the long term.

A foreign policy orientation continuum (based on broad attitudes toward US policy) ranges between isolationism and internationalism. Isolationism may be simply defined as the desire to keep the United States out of substantial political and military involvement with the world. It is, in short, a preference for a passive response to the world whereby the United States serves chiefly as an example, without assuming responsibilities, acting as an agent to reform the world, or intervening in the affairs of others. It is in this sense that John Winthrop's frequently repeated 'city upon a hill' metaphor is apt. In contrast, internationalism suggests that the United States should be actively involved in the world's political affairs to protect American interests and provide the necessary leadership. In this view, the United States has interests and responsibilities that must be served through participation and leadership. In practice, internationalism includes the willingness to exercise power, to intervene politically, militarily, and economically in global politics, to exercise leadership in world affairs, and even to transplant American values and institutions.

These apparently opposite orientations spring from the same political culture. Not only do both orientations exist simultaneously, helping to generate a fundamental ambivalence amongst Americans toward world affairs, but the orientations themselves are bound together by a common element: the sense of an American mission to lead the world into better forms of political, social, and economic relationships. In effect, the orientations divide over the means to achieve the mission. Both depend on a unique sense of American duty and destiny.

If the societal context shapes the mode of international interactions and the definition of interests, the institutional context constitutes the players, structures, and processes that shape the particular policy strategies and decisions guiding American involvement in the world. This context begins in the United States Constitution. Without delving too deeply into the constitutional distribution of powers and responsibilities over various aspects of foreign affairs, several points should be noted. The Constitution provides for accountability and access on the part of the public, making American foreign policy the legitimate target of public pressure, and causing its makers to be rightfully concerned with public acceptance. Institutionally, the Constitution establishes the principles of separation of powers and checks and balances by which policy-making power is divided, distributed, and balanced amongst three branches of government. Furthermore, the Constitution does not assign to any branch 'the foreign policy power'. Instead, it breaks this power into pieces and assigns various portions to the Congress and the Executive, generally forcing a sharing of responsibility. Yet, the Constitution does not specify which branch is to lead in foreign policy, providing an 'invitation to struggle' to the political branches.[13]

In spite of the Constitution's ambiguity, it is common practice to refer to 'the pre-eminence of Presidents' over American foreign policy. In fact, the predominant model of American foreign policy-making is a series of concentric circles beginning with the President and expanding outward to include advisors, bureaucracies, Congress, and the public. According to this model, the influence and relevance of actors decreases with the distance from the centre of the circles. To the extent that this model suggests that the White House is central to the foreign policy process, it is generally useful. However, it is often taken to mean the White House is always the center of policy-making, which is less accurate. As a former member of the National Security Council staff notes, policy-making begins 'before the decision memorandum reached the President's desk and continues after it has gone into the out-box'.[14] In addition to the White House, it is possible for the bureaucracy or Congress to be at the center of policy-making or, at least, to exercise significant influence. Moreover, actors from the public sector, including public opinion, interest groups, and the media may also play an important role. Thus, a more accurate image of the institutional context of American foreign policy is a series of shifting constellations formed by the White House (the President and key advisers), the foreign policy bureaucracy, and Congress, which are embedded in and affected by a societal circle of non-governmental actors. Foreign policy may emerge from shifting and uncertain interactions between the White House, Congress, bureaucratic agencies, and private sector groups and individuals. To be sure, the White House may dominate, but it does not necessarily always dominate.[15]

Understanding this complex institutional context is central to explaining how American foreign policy-makers formulate policy and address and adapt to the challenges of the international environment. It indicates that American strategies and responses to the world are structured by its foreign policy culture, and by the structures and processes of its institutional setting. Foreign policy emerges from a political process involving the interaction of the White House, the foreign policy bureaucracy, and Congress. The role of the President and top aides and advisers stems from the President's position as the chief executive. This circle commands the executive branch and, hence, has access to its expertise, information, and capabilities for implementing policy. Moreover, the ability of this group to set the agenda and seize the initiative, mobilise opinion, set the bureaucracy in motion, exert pressure on Congress, and force it to react, in addition to such powers as are bestowed on the commander-in-chief, chief executive, chief diplomat, and chief legislator of the United States government, provide persistent opportunities to lead policy-making.

The bureaucracy (or that part with foreign policy responsibility) is also significant in making American foreign policy. This circle consists of the State Department, Defence Department, Central Intelligence Agency, and economic agencies created to provide advice and implement policy decisions. The bureaucracy's expertise and control of information give it a position in policy formulation by performing much of the generation and consideration of policy alternatives. Moreover, the various agencies of the foreign policy bureaucracy shape policy by their primary role in its implementation. In both of these roles, disagreements amongst different officials and agencies affect both the nature of the policy and the process by which it is formulated and implemented. Its policy behaviour is affected by its fragmentation, disagreement, 'turf wars', and organisational characteristics such as parochialism, risk avoidance, and routinisation.

The congressional circle influencing foreign policy includes the leadership, committees, caucuses, and individual members and staffs of both houses of Congress. Whilst limited by many structural characteristics and electoral constraints, including its size, decentralised nature, limited access to information, and procedures, the institution and its individual members have access to potentially potent avenues of influence: the ability to pass laws; the constitutional and statutory authority to hold oversight hearings; requiring reports and requesting individual briefings; the advise and consent authority over treaties and appointments; and the 'power of the purse'. In addition, less direct and less formal instruments such as threatening to legislate, expressing a 'mood', issuing requests and warnings directly to executive branch personnel, or passing non-binding resolutions also provide a means for congressional influence.

The role and influence of each of these potentially important players varies within a policy, across different policies, and over different policy or historical settings. Thus, the 'constellations' change: leadership and influence amongst the three groups can shift and societal actors may affect a given policy. Amongst the factors that may account for these shifts are policy types (for example, crisis, strategic, or structural) timing, policy stage, or policy cycle; issue area; situation (crisis or non-crisis); and policy instrument (for instance, aid, troop deployment, diplomacy). Hence, the particular approach to the world embraced by the United States at any given time is in part a function of political variables at the societal and institutional levels.

The preceding overview provides the historical, societal, and institutional circumstances for understanding American foreign-policy strategies for engaging with the world. These forces are shaped by and influence the global context in which foreign policy takes place. The global context affects the underlying conditions or parameters of United States foreign policy, and particular world events and relationships often have an immediate impact. For example, the general patterns that prevail throughout the globe affect American power and the United States role, whilst international crises such as the 9/11 attacks on New York and Washington can catapult an issue onto the political agenda and have an impact on both politics and policies.

The global context in which the United States found itself shaped its strategies and engagement with the world from its inception. After 1945, bipolarity, American power, and the rise of the Cold War led to assertive engagement in the world. United States diplomacy and statecraft were dominated by a view of the Soviet Union as an evil enemy attempting to achieve world domination. Consequently, Washington intervened throughout the world to contain Soviet communist aggression and counter threats to the *status quo* arising from political instability and insurgency. The United States also became the bulwark of the Bretton Woods international political economy, promoting what has been called 'nation building' in Third World countries in accord with the American liberal model of political and economic development.

Combined with the relative decline of American power, the growth of interdependence, the rise of new economic challengers in Europe and Asia, and the powerful forces of nationalism in the developing world made it increasingly difficult for the United States to pursue its Cold War policies abroad, something best illustrated by the American failure in the Vietnam War and the ending of the Bretton Woods economic system. As the world became noticeably more pluralistic and interdependent, the United States ability to influence the world declined relative to its post-Second World War apex.

The end of the Cold War produced a complicated world, with contradictory implications for American power and foreign policy. The collapse of communism in the Soviet Union and Eastern Europe resulted in a single, integrated international political economy of growing interdependence and complexity, re-enforced by the tremendous rise of international economic transactions and trade with countries such as China as well as the development of the North American Free Trade Agreement (NAFTA) and the creation of the World Trade Organisation (WTO). Accordingly, all states and parts of the world, including the United States, are increasingly interdependent economically as the world has become a single international political economic system or globalised world.

The United States, the West, and liberal capitalism appeared to have prevailed as many optimistically proclaimed.[16] Yet, the international economic crises of the late 1990s and early twenty-first century, such as the collapse of the Mexican peso, the 'Asian tiger' economies, the Argentinean and other South American economies, and, most recently, the 2008 global economic meltdown, highlight the extent to which the United States is heavily interwoven in the fabric of the larger global economic system. Such a world of global complexity, interdependence, economic growth, and instability increasingly affected American foreign-policy priorities and actions.

The end of the Cold War did not signify the end of conflict in the world. In some ways, the greater complexity in which global issues proliferated and power diffused produced more, albeit different, crises and challenges for American statecraft. In the present context, especially for Americans, the most obvious conflict revolves around terrorism. Although the issues and problems surrounding international terrorism have existed for some time, they became salient for most Americans in the wake of the 9/11 attacks on important national symbols on American soil: the World Trade Center towers in New York City, which were completely destroyed, and the Pentagon in Washington, DC. As the recent experiences in Iraq and Afghanistan testify (and unlike the Persian Gulf [1991] or Kosovo [1999] wars) the war on terrorism has not been, nor will be, an easy one against easily identifiable enemies that can be accomplished quickly and convincingly.

In addition to terrorism, other types of international conflict persist: disputes arising from traditional rivalries and over national frontiers such as in the Middle East and between India and Pakistan; changes in the authority and influence of Powers like China, Russia, and the European Union; ethnic strife over and within state boundaries; the demand and need for scarce resources like water; the movement and migration of peoples, demographic change, and growth of refugee populations; economic competition and the growing inequality between rich and poor within regions and states; the environment and pollution, such as deforestation and global warming; and more. These and other problems create difficult challenges for American foreign policy and the conversion of United States power into preferred outcomes.

Clearly, whilst the post-Cold War era saw both greater opportunities and constraints for the evolution and exercise of American power, there has been little consensus over how best to address these issues. Not surprisingly, given the collapse of the Soviet Union and communism, no dominant and consistent foreign-policy pattern prevailed during George H.W. Bush's Administration (1988–92). Instead, it displayed a 'mixture of competence and drift, of tactical mastery set in a larger pattern of strategic indirection'.[17] In other words, the first Bush Administration's foreign policy appeared to be caught between the legacy of the Cold War past and the great uncertainty of a post-Cold War future. After entering office in 1993, the Clinton Administration initiated several significant foreign policy actions in Haiti, Mexico, Bosnia, and the Middle East, as well as engineered the expansion of the North Atlantic Treaty Organization alliance to include Powers from the former Soviet alliance. For the most part, major national security failures were avoided whilst the Administration highlighted domestic policy and international economics. Most prominent in this regard were passage of NAFTA and the Uruguay round of the General Agreement on Tariffs and Trade agreement that produced the WTO. However, neither administration succeeded in developing a coherent foreign policy approach to the changed environment.

The American response to the challenges of the twenty-first century has varied significantly across the two administrations in power since 2001. The strategies of engagement embraced by the George W. Bush and Barack Obama Administrations both reflected core elements of the American foreign-policy culture and attempted to address the central features of international context. However, each approach was driven by decidedly different conceptions of power and roles for the United States as a Great Power (perhaps *the* only global Power of the era).

In George W. Bush's 2000 presidential election campaign, foreign-policy emphasis was on the need to reduce American commitments, emphasise vital national interests, and exercise greater humility abroad in response to what was commonly described as a more benign international environment.[18] However, not long into the Bush Administration's first year, a distinct approach to American power and influence began to take shape: a 'hegemonist' view of American foreign policy, committed to United States power and the willingness to use it. Numerous members of the Administration tended to view power, especially military power, as the essential ingredient for American security, whilst also rejecting traditional emphases on deterrence, containment, multilateralism, and international rules and agreements. It was, in short, a view fundamentally committed to maintaining what they characterised as a unipolar world and acting unilaterally.[19] Even before the terrorist attacks of September 2001, Bush's Administration rejected multilateral agreements such as the Kyoto Protocol and the International Criminal Court as well as other international commitments. This approach was fuelled by 11 September 2001. In reaction to the terrorist strikes, the Administration openly embraced a more aggressive foreign policy, revolving around a global war on terrorism, preemption, and the pursuit of international primacy. In the words of Bush's National Security Advisor, Condoleezza Rice: 'I really think that this period is analogous to 1945 to 1947 in that the events so clearly demonstrated that there is a big global threat, and that it's a big global threat to a lot of countries that you would not have normally thought of as being in the coalition. That has started shifting the tectonic plates in international politics'.[20]

New enemies (Osama bin Laden and al-Qaeda, Saddam Hussein and Iraq, and terrorism) replaced the old enemy of communism. After 9/11, in the minds of members of the Bush Administration, the 'United States was [now] faced with an irreconcilable enemy; the sort of black-and-white challenge that had supposedly been transcended in the post-Cold War period, when the great clash of ideologies [had] ended, [and] had now reappeared with shocking suddenness'.[21] Bush's global war on terrorism resulted in a major defence build-up, an emphasis on 'homeland security', an effort to distinguish between friends and foes, and a heavy reliance on the use of force abroad. The Administration's strategy became much more unilateral in orientation, saw little relevance of international organisations like the United Nations (UN), and officially emphasised the threat and use of 'overt' preemptive (or preventive) strikes. Together, such a policy orientation has become known as the Bush Doctrine as reflected in Bush's 2002 foreign policy address at West Point.[22]

Bush immediately set about refocusing his Administration to engage in a global war on terrorism, beginning with Afghanistan to overthrow the Taliban and turning to Iraq to depose Saddam Hussein. No issue seemed more central than Iraq. Despite international resistance and some internal disagreement, once Bush decided to use force to remove Hussein's regime, Administration officials and the President himself forcefully advanced the case that Iraq's possession of weapons of mass destruction and ties to al-Qaeda required assertive military action.[23] After securing congressional support and despite resistance from much of the international community, especially France, Russia, and China on the UN Security Council, the Administration, in concert with a 'coalition of the willing' composed chiefly of Great Britain and a few other countries, invaded Iraq in March 2003. By May, American forces had captured Baghdad, the Hussein regime collapsed, and Bush officially declared 'mission accomplished' on 2 May 2003.

At first, the public and Congress rallied around this action. However, with the initial military campaign over, the more difficult task of rebuilding the Iraqi government and nation-building ensued. Whilst resistance to the American occupation soon grew and violence seemed to increase daily, the weapons of mass destruction that Iraq was alleged possess were never found; American-led search units soon concluded officially that they had never existed. Nor were any ties to al-Qaeda discovered, although al-Qaeda soon became active in the insurgency against American forces and the Iraqi regime that Washington sought to empower. Moreover, Bush's rejection of the international community left the United States isolated and widely distrusted overseas. By late 2006, citizens in thirty-three of thirty-five countries surveyed believed that the war in Iraq had increased the likelihood of terrorist attacks around the world.[24] Ninety-eight percent of European Commission members and 68 percent of members in the European Parliament disapproved of Bush's foreign policies.[25] At home, a July 2008 survey found 'improving America's standing in the world' to be the general public's top United States foreign policy priority.[26]

With the costs of the war spiralling upward, Bush began to face increased unrest and challenges, and his public approval began to decline steadily. Distance from the 9/11 attacks, coupled with increasing costs in Iraq, persistent questions about the success of his global war on terrorism, and the decline of American prestige and reputation around the world (combined with domestic economic problems and other challenges) eroded Bush's support. It exacerbated his lame-duck status to the point that his presidency was effectively crippled in November 2006, when the Democrats seized control of both houses of Congress in a stunning political backlash against Bush.

Riding public discontent with the Bush Administration, the Democrat, Barack Obama. emerged as the victor in the 2008 presidential elections; he promised to restore American prestige and reputation and re-engage with the world so as to repair relations with friends and allies and assert American power and influence in a softer and more conciliatory fashion. Whilst contending with the so-called 'Great Recession' of 2007–9, Obama effectively sought 'indispensability' instead of primacy or dominance. Although the problems Obama faced as he began his efforts were not so dramatic as those of the economic depression and global war of the 1930s and 1940s, few Presidents since the Second World War have faced such a daunting array of challenges. In addition to contending with the legacy of the Iraq invasion, he faced challenges stemming from the deteriorating situation in Afghanistan and Pakistan (where the Taliban and al-Qaeda had re-emerged as viable opponents), a severe global economic crisis, urgent environmental and energy policy issues, and regional security and non-proliferation challenges in North Korea and Iran. Obama also confronted a political environment in Washington DC more divided along partisan lines than ever before in recent memory.

A considerable portion of Obama's foreign policy involved trying to engineer a multilateral response through the G20 countries and international financial institutions to the global economic crisis. In addition to urgently needed attention on foreign economic policy, the Obama Administration also had to deal with a variety of national security issues that it inherited from previous administrations. The most pressing efforts concerned withdrawing American troops from Iraq and turning the war there over to the Iraqis whilst increasing American troop levels and involvement in Afghanistan and Pakistan, given the deteriorating and increasingly unstable situations in those countries. In addition, other issues needed to be addressed including the Arab-Israeli conflict, the future of Russia, oil dependency, immigration, global warming, and North Korea, Iran, and nuclear proliferation. Furthermore, substantive debates and divisions deepened on questions about the proper nature, uses, and balance amongst foreign instruments including diplomacy, force, aid, and others. The President and other Administration officials also actively sought to restore confidence in American leadership and promote the likelihood of multilateral responses in attempting to react and address such global problems.

According to the Obama team, the Bush White House was principally responsible for the decline of American standing in the international community. Questionable policy choices, unilateralism, unabashed claims of predominance and disregard for international institutions, agreements, and cooperation were especially blamed. In contrast to Bush, Obama argued that American power was most effectively applied in the velvet glove of cooperation.[27] He thus aggressively pursued diplomatic engagement and multilateral cooperation, and he exhibited greater reliance on soft power and greater concern for global problems. The new Administration stressed a conception of American national interest that incorporated transnational concerns; a conception of power that included 'soft' as well as 'hard' forms; an emphasis on diplomacy and economic statecraft to a greater degree relative to military power; and greater involvement in multilateral institutions and support for international law.[28]

Obama elaborated on his approach at an April 2009 press conference in Trinidad:

> … the United States remains the most powerful, wealthiest nation on Earth, but we're only one nation, and that the problems that we confront, whether it's drug cartels, climate change, terrorism, you name it, can't be solved just by one country. And I think if you start with that approach, then you are inclined to listen and not just talk. And so in all these meetings what I've said is, we have some very clear ideas in terms of where the international community should be moving; we have some very specific national interests … but we recognize that other countries have good ideas, too, and we want to hear them. … Countries are going to have interests, and changes in foreign policy approaches by my administration aren't suddenly going to make all those interests that may diverge from ours disappear. What it does mean,

though, is, at the margins, they are more likely to want to cooperate than not cooperate. It means that where there is resistance to a particular set of policies that we're pursuing, that resistance may turn out just to be based on old preconceptions or ideological dogmas that, when they're cleared away, it turns out that we can actually solve a problem.[29]

In the administration's first national security strategy, released in May 2010, Obama laid out the rationale for his course change in American foreign policy:

> Our national security strategy is, therefore, focused on renewing American leadership so that we can more effectively advance our interests in the 21st century. We will do so by building upon the sources of our strength at home, while shaping an international order that can meet the challenges of our time. This strategy recognizes the fundamental connection between our national security, our national competitiveness, resilience, and moral example. And it reaffirms America's commitment to pursue our interests through an international system in which all nations have certain rights and responsibilities.[30]

Time will tell whether the new Administration is successful in these efforts to grapple with the constraints and imperatives of the current international context.

The ultimate global challenge for the current Administration (indeed, for all Presidents since the end of the Cold war) might be called the 'challenge of hegemony' and the 'challenge of legitimacy'. Clearly, in the current global environment:

> The preeminence of American power today is unprecedented in modern history. No other great power has enjoyed such formidable advantages in military, economic, technological, cultural, or political capabilities. We live in a one-superpower world, and there is no serious competitor in sight. Other states rival the United States in one area or another, but it is the multi-faceted character of American power that makes it so commanding, far reaching, and provocative.[31]

Such global predominance obviously brings advantages, but it poses challenges as well. Amongst the most significant are the fear and uneasiness that it provokes in other countries, even those that are commonly allied with the United States.

Three types of global reactions are often generated in response to the rise of hegemonic Powers. First, the predominance of American strength can prompt other Powers to align with the United States for self-interested reasons. To accommodate and cooperate with the United States, Powers may 'bandwagon' (join in), 'bond' (build close ties and hope to influence United States decision-making as a trusted ally), or attempt to 'penetrate' American politics (take advantage of the open society and multiple access points to American officials in the executive branch and Congress to persuade decision-makers to adopt favourable policies). Second, United States hegemony is likely to trigger efforts by other states to rein in American power and resist American domination. Their efforts would include 'balancing' American power, 'balking' (ignoring United States requests) or foot-dragging in carrying them out to hinder American efforts. They also include 'binding', or attempting to use norms and institutions such as the UN and others to constrain American freedom of action, as well as 'blackmail', which involves threatening to take action that Washington opposes unless the United States offers compensation. Finally, to encourage resistance to American efforts, others may attempt 'delegitimisation', portraying the United States as irresponsible, arrogant, and selfish (actions readily seen in a variety of places in recent years).[32]

American decision-makers will increasingly struggle to grapple with these responses to the global power of the United States. In one estimation,

September 11 reminded those Americans with a rosy view that not all the world sees U.S. primacy as benign. ... American global primacy is one of the causes of this war. It animates both the terrorists' purposes and their choice of tactics. To groups like al-Qaeda, the United States is the enemy because American military power dominates their world, supports corrupt governments in their countries, and backs Israelis against Muslims; American cultural power insults their religion and pollutes their societies; and American economic power makes all these intrusions and desecrations possible. Japan, in contrast, is not high on al-Qaeda's list of targets, because Japan's economic power does not make it a political, military, and cultural behemoth that penetrates their societies.[33]

In other words, the vastness and pervasiveness of American power have complex and contradictory implications. In addition, 'if a new world order is to be established under American aegis, then the United States must appear as a just and trustworthy leader'.[34] Given the world's complexity and diversity and the United States' tendency to act unilaterally (usually in the name of liberalism, democracy, and human rights) it is likely that the United States will not only remain the most powerful country in the world. It may slowly, but inevitably, experience greater challenges to its power and foreign policy in the future, more balancing and delegitimation than bandwagoning. Such may be the paradoxical nature of American power in contemporary and future international politics.

In the end, confronting these problems may capture the priorities for American foreign policy under the Obama Administration and its successors, focusing on building multilateral responses to international issues, setting values-based examples in word and deed, and adapting to cultural and ideological differences. For United States diplomacy and statecraft, being 'indispensable' in this way may address foreign apprehensions about America's predominant power and leadership in international affairs. However, to be successful, such an approach must be rooted in the fabric of American foreign-policy culture and, as well, navigate the increasingly contentious political environment in Washington DC. Consensus is necessary for coherent, sustained, White House-led foreign policy. Consensus, however, rests on clarity of threat, purpose, and interest, making it a rare commodity in the post-Cold War world.

Notes

1 United States Congress, Joint Congressional Committee on Inaugural Ceremonies, *Inaugural addresses of the presidents of the United States: from George Washington to George W. Bush.* (Washington, DC, 2001): www.bartleby.com/124/pres65.html.
2 A.J. Bacevich, 'Charles Beard, Properly Understood', *National Interest*, 35(1994), 75.
3 Jerel A. Rosati and James M. Scott, *The Politics of United States Foreign Policy*, 5th edn (New York: Cengage, 2011), chapter 11.
4 William Earl Weeks, *Building the Continental Empire: American Expansion from the Revolution to the Civil War* (Chicago, IL, 1961), 61.
5 Richard A. Melanson, *American Foreign Policy since the Vietnam War* (Armonk, NY, 2005).
6 Daniel Deudney and G. John Ikenberry, 'The International Sources of Soviet Change', *International Security*, Volume 16, Number 3 (1991), 111.
7 Aaron Wildavsky, 'Choosing Preferences by Constructing Institutions: A Cultural Theory of Preference Formation', in Arthur Asa Berger, ed., *Political Culture and Public Opinion* (New Brunswick, NJ, 1989), 21–46.
8 John Dumbrell, *The Making of US Foreign Policy* (Manchester, 1990), 6.
9 Cecil V. Crabb, *The Doctrines of American Foreign Policy: Their Meaning, Role and Future* (Baton Rouge, LA, 1982), 375.
10 Crabb, *American Foreign Policy*, 377.
11 Edward M. Burns, *The American Idea of Mission: Concepts of National Purpose and Destiny* (New Brunswick, NJ, 1957).
12 Crabb, *American Foreign Policy*, 1–2.
13 Edward S. Corwin, *The President: Office and Powers, 1787–1957*, revised edition (New York, 1957), 171.

14 Philip Zelikow, 'Foreign Policy Engineering: From Theory to Practice and Back Again', *International Security*, Volume 18, Number 4 (1994), 156.

15 See James M. Scott, *Deciding to Intervene: American Foreign Policy and the Reagan Doctrine* (Durham, NC, 1996); James M. Scott, ed., *After the End: Making American Foreign Policy in the Post-Cold War World* (Durham, NC, 1998).

16 See F. Fukuyama, 'The End of History?', *National Interest*, (Summer 1989), 3–18.

17 Terry L. Deibel, 'Bush's Foreign Policy: Mastery and Inaction', *Foreign Policy*, 84(1991), 3.

18 Condoleezza Rice, 'Campaign 2000: Promoting the National Interest', *Foreign Affairs*, 79(2000).

19 Ivo H. Daalder, and James M. Lindsay, *America Unbound: The Bush Revolution in Foreign Policy* (Washington, DC, 2003); G. John Ikenberry, 'America's Imperial Ambition', *Foreign Affairs*, 81(2002), 2–15.

20 Quoted in Nicholas Lemann, 'The Next World Order: The Bush Administration May Have a Brand-New Doctrine of Power', *New Yorker* (1 April 2002), 42–44.

21 Michael Hirsh, 'Bush and the World', *Foreign Affairs*, 81(2002), 18.

22 A more elaborate and detailed account of the Bush Administration's post-9/11 strategy can be found in White House, *The National Security Strategy of the United States of America* (Washington, DC, 2002).

23 See Bob Woodward, *Plan of Attack* (New York, 2004).

24 'World public says Iraq War has increased global terrorist threat', World Public Opinion, Global Public Opinion on International Affairs: www.worldpublicopinion.org/pipa/articles/international_security_bt/172.php.

25 'European elites survey: Survey of members of the European Parliament and top European Commission officials; Key findings 2006', Centre for the Study of Political Change at the University of Siena: www.circap.unisi.it/ees/ees_overview.

26 'Anxious Americans seek a new direction in United States foreign policy: Results of a 2008 survey of public opinion', Chicago Council on Global Affairs: www.thechicagocouncil.org/UserFiles/File/POS_Topline%20Reports/POS%202008/2008%20Public%20Opinion%202008_US%20Survey%20Results.pdf.

27 See Stephen M. Walt, 'Keeping the world off-balance: Self-restraint and U.S. foreign policy', in G. John Ikenberry, ed., *America Unrivaled: The future of the balance of power* (Ithaca, NY, 2002); Stephen M. Walt, *Taming American Power: The global response to U.S. primacy* (New York, 2005).

28 Steven W. Hook and James M. Scott, *US Foreign Policy Today: American Renewal?* (Washington, DC, 2011).

29 Barack Obama, 'Press Conference', (19 April 2009), Hilton Hotel. Port of Spain, Trinidad and Tobago.

30 White House, *National Security Strategy* (Washington, DC, 2010), 1. Also see Barack Obama, *Remarks by the President in Address to the Nation on the End of Combat Operations in Iraq* (Washington, DC, 31 August, 2010).

31 Ikenberry, *Imperial Ambitions*, 1.

32 Walt, *Taming American Power.*

33 Richard K. Betts, 'The Soft Underbelly of American Primacy: Tactical Advantages of Terror', *Political Science Quarterly*, 117(2002), 33.

34 Trobjorn L. Knutsen, *The Rise and Fall of World Orders* (Manchester, 1999), 67.

4

The foreign policy of Great Britain

Christoph Bluth

It has been said of the period after the Second World War that Great Britain had lost an Empire and was in search of a new role in the international system.[1] During the Cold War, Britain managed to maintain a role as one the world's major Powers through its special relationship with the United States that provided access to a formidable nuclear deterrent and as one of the two leading European North Atlantic Treaty Organisation (NATO) Powers with troops deployed in Germany and one of the four Powers that controlled the city of Berlin.[2]

The end of the Cold War reduced Britain's special status as the defence of Western Europe diminished as a global security concern and the focus of threats to international security moved outside the traditional NATO area. The extent to which the British Government actually articulated a 'grand strategy' for the post-Cold War world is debatable.[3] But there was some degree of continuity with the past, as the central elements of British foreign and security policy were the 'special relationship' with the United States and a leading role in NATO and the European Union (EU).[4] In this respect the Labour Government that came to office in 1997 under the leadership of Tony Blair shifted direction somewhat. Whereas the Conservatives had become increasingly Eurosceptic, Blair was determined that Britain should play a leadership role in the EU. This resolve manifested itself in the transformation of the Western EU, a rather amorphous security organization whose membership did not fully coincide with that of the EU, into European Security and Defence Policy (ESDP).

The meaning of the 'new international order' is contested,[5] and the British Government has not produced a clear conceptualisation of either what this order is or Britain's role in international security. Nevertheless, one can discern some general principles. The West European Powers no longer fear major armed conflict with any other state and therefore enjoy an unprecedented level of national security. Not just in Europe, but on a global scale, armed conflict between and amongst Powers has become rare. Not only has the armed confrontation between Great Powers ended with the Cold War but, in most parts of the globe, countries no longer fear attacks by other states. There is practically no potential for interstate armed conflict in the Western hemisphere.[6] West and Central European states have no plausible enemies; Russia does not have to fear a military attack from anyone; China is predicating its international reputation on the 'peaceful rise of China'; South-East Asian states are not intending to invade each other; Australia and New Zealand do not fear military attack; and interstate conflict in Africa is also practically non-existent. A risk of armed conflict remains confined to South Asia (the arc from Afghanistan to India), the Korean peninsula, and certain parts of the Middle East. As a consequence, military establishments throughout the world have been emasculated.[7] The Soviet Army collapsed as a result of the Treaty on Conventional Armed Forces in Europe, its withdrawal from Central Europe, and the dissolution of the Soviet Union. The Russian Army is not able to engage in large-scale high-intensity warfare because of the low number of combat-capable units.[8] The number of strategic nuclear warheads deployed by the United States and Russia has been dramatically cut and is targeted to reach a level of 15 percent of that in 1991. The Western European Powers have reduced their defence budgets to such a level that they can no longer meet significant military challenges out of area. Almost all modern states have abandoned conscription, drastically reduced their military manpower, and have comparatively low defence expenditures, with some notable exceptions such as the United States, whose defence expenditure now equals that of all other states combined.

Clearly the major risk to international security in the time following the post-Cold war period resides in the so-called new wars, sub-state conflicts that arise from ethnic disputes, failed states in regions of low development, or international terrorism.[9]

When the Labour Party came to power in 1997, it conducted a strategic review to define Britain's strategic priorities. It concluded that Russia no longer presented a threat to European security. However, it was likely that Britain would continue to be involved in peace-keeping operations. Furthermore, British forces would be involved in joint operations with those of other allies in other parts of the world. Whilst it remained unclear how this new global vision of international security was to be resourced, it signalled a fundamental shift in the conceptual approach. It could best be described as a cautious departure from the *realpolitik* of the past towards an acceptance of the need for collective security. Essentially, the Government led by Prime Minister Blair adopted a cautiously institutionalist approach that it justified in public as the best way of defending the national interest. It was successful in restoring Britain's role in Europe to a significant extent by playing an important leadership role in developing the EU's Common Foreign and Security Policy through the Amsterdam Treaty.

The problem was that the military conflicts that broke out in Europe and other parts of the world were not susceptible simply to peace-keeping. John Mearsheimer predicted in a seminal article that the collapse of the Soviet Union would result in a multipolar world that would be especially conflict prone and that the Powers and their populations would 'soon miss the Cold War'.[10] He also predicted that Germany and Japan would acquire nuclear weapons to confront the newly arising security threats. However, none of this came to pass. The new conflicts in Europe were not a consequence of multipolarity, but rather had to do with the break-up of artificially constructed states. In the Soviet case, a war of dissolution was avoided, but not in the former Yugoslavia. As for the other East European Powers, their main ambition was to join NATO and the EU, which required meeting various political and economic criteria and precluded the outbreak of armed conflict between or amongst them. The European response to the Balkans conflict after 1995 was half-hearted, but Blair became convinced that Britain and the other Western Powers had a duty to confront Serbian aggression. At the request of Blair's Chief of Staff, Jonathan Powell, Professor Lawrence Freedman, a strategic studies specialist at King's College, London, prepared a document on humanitarian intervention that listed various criteria that should be applied to any decision on becoming involved in a military intervention. These criteria were included in an April 1999 speech that Tony Blair gave in Chicago:

1. Are we sure of our case? 2. Have we exhausted all diplomatic options? 3. Are there military operations that we can sensibly and prudently undertake? 4. Are we prepared for the long term? 5. Do we have national interests at stake?'[11]

The fundamental problem for humanitarian interventions was that it was difficult to find a justification in international law unless they were supported by a mandate from the United Nations (UN) Security Council, but the Prime Minister had concluded that it would be difficult to obtain such a mandate due to the Council's make-up. In particular, he believed that in the cases of Kosovo and Iraq, there would be at least one veto against military intervention. In his Chicago speech he argued that the UN needed to be reformed to enable intervention in cases in which dictatorial regimes were carrying out atrocities against their own people. Efforts by the UN Secretary General Kofi Annan to have principles for humanitarian intervention adopted were rejected by the Security Council.[12] British involvement in Kosovo was largely supported by the general public and resulted in outcomes considered to be a success, despite the extreme reluctance on the part of the Americans to use ground forces. The Freedman doctrine met a severe test in the 2003 interventions in Iraq and, later, Afghanistan.

The post-Cold War era has posed novel strategic problems for Britain in this respect, which were put into sharp relief by the Iraq conflict. If the world is inhabited by only one superpower (the United States) and even although the United States is a democratic country that shares fundamental values with Britain and the rest of the EU, how can this country be contained? In other words, for example, how can American allies ensure that the United States acts within the strictures of international law? How can Britain and the EU prevent unilateral actions by a Power with military preponderance? This issue played heavily in the Iraq war. Britain was extremely concerned about ensuring that there remained some kind of unity between Europe and the United States, and that the United States would not really go out on its own and develop a unilateral policy. In this context, the disdain shown by the administration of President George W. Bush, especially in its first term, for multilateral organizations and its tendency toward unilateralism was considered to be alarming and dangerous by other Powers.

American unilateralism also posed the important question as to who is the global security manager. Or, more prosaically, who holds responsibility for dealing with international security crises around the globe? Technically the UN Security Council does so, but it does not have any military resources of its own, and it is really a political body in which there is no fundamental consensus on global security, so much so that the British Government came to view the G20 as the international forum in which international security issues could be effectively addressed.[13]

Answering this question imparted momentum to the EU's ESDP: a programme to develop EU civilian and military capabilities for international crisis management and conflict prevention, thus helping facilitate the maintenance of international peace and international security in accord with the UN Charter. The Union had to stop sitting on the sidelines and assume a proactive role because, if the United States existed as the only global security manager, it would be impossible to complain about the actions it decided to take. In Blair's view, it was not desirable that the United States should be left not only to carry the burdens of global security but also be allowed, by default, to make those decisions unilaterally. Since the Iraq War, a debate has started in Britain about to what extent the special relationship with the United States exists and can be maintained, and to what extent the relationship is in Britain's interests. There is a widespread belief that one of the major reasons why Blair agreed to participate in the war against Iraq was to maintain the special relationship. The evidence shows that such a way of looking at it is rather simplistic. And there were other factors to consider. In the case of Iraq, because the United States was going to bypass the UN completely, Britain was extremely concerned lest any American action be taken without the consent of the UN and be seen as a violation of international law. The British strategy was to cooperate with the United States to keep the Americans within UN boundaries. The French, on the other hand, believed that they could actually stop the United States and, therefore, embarked on a course of obstruction. Those two strategies negated each other, with the result that the United States went to war without the full backing of the Security Council, even though it is not clear that the war had no legal foundation.[14]

According to public statements by Blair, Jack Straw, the Foreign Secretary, and other spokespersons, the British Government perceived threat posed by the regime of Saddam Hussein as follows. After 9/11, all states with clandestine weapons of mass destruction (WMD) programmes had to be considered a threat and had to be confronted about their activities in this field. Although there was no proven link between Saddam's regime and Al-Qaeda, in the age when terrorists sought to cause mass casualties, it had to be considered as a realistic prospect that the possibility that a Power with substantial stocks of biological and chemical weapons would make them available to terrorists. Saddam Hussein was contained, but had shown such an inclination towards aggression in the past that Iraq remained a threat to the region, especially given the effort to maintain WMD capabilities. Iraq was believed to seek to develop ballistic missiles with greater ranges and therefore would emerge as a strategic threat in the future. Even although Iraq did not have nuclear weapons, it had sufficient expertise that at some point in the future a nuclear capability could emerge. Finally, the Iraqi regime was an imminent threat to its own people.

The obvious question is how such a threat assessment justifies the use of force. Blair's answer was that it was a serious threat that needed to be addressed; that it needed to be addressed urgently because it could not be predicted when it would materialize (for example, terrorists could obtain WMD from Iraq at any time); that the only alternative way of meeting this threat, namely containment and peaceful disarmament, was not viable; and that the Iraqi people should not be asked to endure this inhumane regime any longer.[15] Although initially the British Government had the support of Parliament and even of a majority in the general population for the action against Iraq, public opinion turned against the war, and also against Blair. This turn arose with the later revelation that there were no stockpiles of chemical or biological weapons in Iraq and because the multiple insurgencies that arose in post-Saddam Iraq generated an enormous level of violence. In aggregate, these issues convinced many Britons that the intervention had been a huge and costly mistake.

One international security issue that has risen to the fore dramatically since the end of the Cold War is that of nuclear proliferation. The British Government considers nuclear proliferation and its prevention a strategic issue. How serious is this threat? The non-proliferation regime has turned out to be robust and has become more so over the last 20 years because many more Powers have acceded to the Nuclear Non-proliferation Treaty (NPT). Whilst there has been one defection from the NPT (North Korea), in fact, only four countries in the world are not within the treaty. In many respects, the NPT is one of the most successful international regimes of any kind.

Powers that were clearly considering going nuclear (in Latin America, for example) have turned away from the acquisition of such weapons. Libya gave up its nuclear programme, and South Africa eliminated an existing nuclear weapons capability. The countries of the former Soviet Union, namely, Ukraine, Kazakhstan, and Belarus, gave up the nuclear weapons based in their territory, thereby foregoing the option of becoming nuclear-weapons states in their own right. In that sense, there is no doubt that the NPT has been successful.

For Britain there is the issue as to whether Britain should remain a nuclear-weapons state, and whether it should give up its nuclear capacity as the issue of replacing the Trident system is now coming to the fore. The Trident issue played a minor role in the 2010 General Election campaign, with the Liberal Democrat (LibDem)–Conservative coalition reaffirming the previous government's commitment to replace the Trident system, but not before the next election. It is unlikely that Britain will part with its nuclear weapons for the foreseeable future for the simple reason that a legitimate nuclear status is considered to be a unique privilege; moreover, for any Prime Minister giving it up once and for all is almost an impossible decision to take. Although Britain does not face any direct nuclear threats at this time, the national security strategy published by the coalition

Government in October 2010 (the *Strategic Defence and Security Review*) refers to the uncertainty of emerging future threats, and the rationale for maintaining a deterrent:

> No state currently has both the intent and capability to threaten the independence or integrity of the UK. But we cannot dismiss the possibility that a major direct nuclear threat to the UK might reemerge—a state's intent in relation to the use of threat of use of its capabilities could change relatively quickly … we cannot rule out a major shift in the international security situation which would put us under grave threat.[16]

For example, it may be the case that in the future, Iran will have nuclear capability and will have missiles that can reach Britain, even although this is not the case at present. The maintenance of a minimum credible and effective nuclear deterrent thus remained at the core of British defence policy. This in turn committed the Government to the replacement of the submarines on which a renewed Trident system would be based. To minimize the impact of Trident renewal on the plan to reduce Britain's budget deficit, the decisions on replacing the nuclear warhead for Trident were deferred, the life of the Vanguard submarines was extended, and the finalization of detailed procurement plans deferred until 2016. The maximum number of nuclear warheads to deploy on each submarine is to be reduced from 48 to 40, decreasing the number of operationally available warheads to a total of at most 120 from the current 160. The *Strategic Defence and Security Review* affirms that Britain's long-term goal is a nuclear-free world to be achieved through multilateral disarmament.

So even although there is no specific threat upon which the nuclear deterrent is focused, however, the counterargument is that, first, the future is uncertain and, second, the privilege of being one of the five permanent members of the UN Security Council means that Britain is accepted as a legitimate nuclear Power. This latter argument is not made explicit in the *Strategic Defence and Security Review*, but it underlies its central logic and is hinted at in the section (§ 3.6) that emphasizes the role of Britain as a responsible nuclear weapons state party to the NPT. This recognition is probably the main reason why the UK will continue to maintain a nuclear arsenal, although there is now an agreement with France on technical cooperation in nuclear matters. And there is another point to be taken into consideration: as long as China and Russia remain nuclear Powers, it is not desirable for Europe that there be only one other Western Power possessing nuclear weapons. In other words, if France and Britain were to give up their nuclear arsenals, the United States would again bear the Western security burden by being its sole nuclear Power; Europe's political and strategic position would be weakened.

It is often said that the nuclear non-proliferation regime is threatened by the fact that the nuclear Powers have not done enough to reduce their own arsenals. But this assertion is wide of the mark. First, these Powers have reduced substantially; Russia and the United States, in particular, have limited their arsenals dramatically. Second, it is not desirable at this time (as long as there are nuclear Powers outside the NPT) that the five permanent Powers on the UN Security Council should abandon their nuclear weapons. Paradoxically, the stability of the NPT depends to some extent on these five Powers. If the United States were not giving nuclear guarantees to Japan, South Korea, or the Arab states in the Middle East, then the nuclear programmes in Iran and North Korea would precipitate both the pursuit of nuclear programmes and a chain reaction against the NPT in these regions. The viewpoint of Prime Minister David Cameron's Government is that unilateral British disarmament will not result in reciprocal actions by other nuclear Powers, it will not make a positive contribution to prevent proliferation, and it will not have an impact on the nuclear decision-making of either Iran or North Korea. Instead, Britain is prepared to put its nuclear weapons on the table of any multilateral arms control negotiations.

The third element of the international security landscape to consider is regional crises. In the past decade and a half, such crises have occurred in confined areas in which there is the prospect of interstate conflict in the foreseeable future: in Europe, there was the Balkan imbroglio; there is the continuing problem of South Asia centring on Afghanistan; the Middle East can be classified as a crisis region; and there is the security dilemma on the Korean Peninsula. Britain participated in the complete shift of security strategy in Europe. Collective defence is now obsolete. Consequently the use of the word 'defence', even in the ESDP, is oxymoronic because none of the European Powers faces military threats from outside. The only external threat, if that phrase may be used, might be international terrorism. Consequently, NATO and the EU have transformed their strategy to focus on intervention in crises outside their own region that do not involve direct threats to their security but nevertheless are important for international security. This was a long and painful process, obviously one the legitimacy of which has to be questioned at times. It was also difficult because of the decline in European military capabilities since the end of the Cold War and the lack of crisis intervention capacities. Finally, the experience of the Iraq war after 2003 has raised doubts about interventionism and the extent to which Europe should be involved in crises and conflicts outside its own territory. The conflict in Afghanistan is currently a major test for NATO. If its intervention should fail, serious doubts will be raised about the future role of the Alliance. The lacklustre commitment of many NATO members has already sidelined the organization, the International Security Assistance Force in Afghanistan, which is in charge of NATO operations. In reality, NATO does not really own the strategy in Afghanistan, which is led and controlled by the United States.[17]

All Western leaders have struggled to articulate the reasons for the engagement in Afghanistan. The same is true for the British Government. Prime Minister Gordon Brown, who led the Labour Government from 2007 to 2010, defined it purely in terms of national security interests. Clearly, there is a national security interest: a terrorist threat that would increase if Afghanistan once again came under the power of the Taliban. But one could also make the case that the destabilization of that region is not in Britain's interests and that in some ways the West owes something to the people of Afghanistan after Western intervention in 2001. Brown's case also suffered from the fact that the British engagement was clearly underresourced. Not only was the number of troops inadequate for the tasks that the Government set for them, but many of the daily needs of the troops for radios and protective armour were not sufficiently met. After United States President Barack Obama announced a troop surge in Afghanistan in 2009, Britain's role in Helmand province was taken over by the United States Army. While the British Army performed extraordinarily well, the same cannot be said for the strategic judgment of those in charge in Whitehall. The situation is not likely to improve under the coalition Government. Prime Minister Cameron has signalled strongly that he would like to withdraw British troops soon, although this has been qualified by the commitment to achieve the objectives of the campaign, without specifying what these might be.[18]

One theme that dominates international security at the moment is, of course, the 'war on terrorism'. The national security strategy published by the Conservative-led coalition Government identified international terrorism as one of the main security threats faced by Britain. However, for London the threat of terrorism also resides in terms of domestic internal Islamic radicalization (something seen starkly in the 2005 bombings of London Transport), so that the country faces this threat from within as well as from without. Nevertheless, since 9/11, when Prime Minister Blair declared Britain's unequivocal support for the United States and the 'war on terror', there has been a shift of emphasis. In the first place, the term 'war on terrorism' is problematic in the sense that when there is talk about such a war, it is a phenomenon that is boundless and infinite. Any kind of war should have more precisely defined and limited objectives.

The use of the language of 'war' also gives legitimacy to the opponent that is not warranted; another view might be that what Britain and the other Powers are dealing is a form of organized criminality that has no legitimacy of any kind. Moreover, military force has only a limited role in combating terrorism. Counterterrorism involves mostly defensive measures and intelligence operations. The use of military force in Afghanistan is obviously part of a strategy to defeat terrorism, with the aim of depriving terrorists of the use of the resources of a failed state to organize their campaigns.

Britain did not agree with the United States that the Iraq intervention was part of the 'war on terror'. Here lies an important conceptual distinction. The British Government agreed that the war against Iraq was necessary because of the regional security threat posed by the Saddam Hussein regime, but it did not conflate those issues because it did not believe that Iraq had any links with al-Qaeda, was in any sense responsible for 9/11, or engaged in that type of international terrorism. The Obama Administration in concert with the Labour Government reconceptualized the campaign in the Afpak area as an effort to promote regional stability and abandoned the concept of the 'war on terror'. This transition was based on the belief that the Bush Administration's conceptualization of the 'war on terror' is not really appropriate in terms of dealing with the phenomenon with which Britain, the United States, and their allies are dealing.[19] The Iraq War obviously created an enormous problem in transatlantic relations because of the serious opposition, especially in Germany and France, to Western involvement. Moreover, the manner in which the EU afterwards refused to take any kind of responsibility for its aftermath was also a bitter experience.

The domestic political backlash in Britain against the Iraq war generated a certain spill-over into the 'war on terror'. Although it had its own 9/11 in 7/7 (the London Transport attacks on 7 July 2005, in which 52 people were killed and 700 injured) the British Government had difficulty garnering support for its counterterrorism measures and its involvement in the counterinsurgency in Afghanistan. The events of 7 July showed the risk of home-grown terrorism in Britain and the radicalization of British-born Muslims who received training and support in Pakistan or Somalia. British involvement in the intervention in Iraq seems to have been the tipping point for many young British Muslims that caused them to become involved in the *jihad*. In response, the British Government proposed a new counterterrorism strategy in 2006 known as CONTEST (Countering International Terrorism), which focused on preventing or countering the radicalization of Muslims in the United Kingdom. In the same year, a sophisticated plot to detonate ten airliners over the Atlantic by assembling liquid explosives taken aboard clandestinely was uncovered, resulting in dramatic changes to airport security measures. On 9 November 2006 the Head of MI5, Eliza Manningham-Buller, revealed that the agency was monitoring 30 active terrorist plots and 200 groups involving over 1,600 persons.[20]

In terms of economic foreign policy, Britain initially stayed aloof from the EU. This distance obviously had to do with the fact that in the aftermath of the Second World War, Britain still saw itself as a global Power. In the late 1940s, Britain's international role was defined by three overlapping areas of commitment enunciated in 1948 by the former wartime prime minister, Winston Churchill, in his *Three Circles Doctrine*.[21] The first circle consisted of the British Commonwealth and Empire; the second, the English-speaking world, including the United States and Canada; and the third, Europe. But the international system had changed, with the United States having emerged as the dominant western Allied Power. Nevertheless, it was not really until the mid-1960s that the British political elite understood that the time of the British Empire was over. In 1966, the very deliberate turn towards Europe took place, leading to the decision to join the European Economic Community (EEC), the precursor of the EU. It was under the Conservative Government of Margaret Thatcher that Britain acceded to the Maastricht

Treaty, although it stayed out of the European Monetary Union, especially after the debacle with the European exchange rate.

It was the policy of Blair's Labour Government that Britain should eventually adopt the euro as its currency. This issue became a matter of serious contention between the Prime Minister and his Chancellor of the Exchequer, Gordon Brown. Brown defined six tests that the British economy had to pass before it could use the euro; but Britain never joined the euro, and it has become clear from the memoirs of Blair and his Chief of Staff, Jonathan Powell, that Brown obstructed all efforts to put the issue to the British people in a referendum. Whether such a referendum would have favoured using the euro remains unknown. But apart from Brown's attitude, it seems the decision to join has never been able to garner enough political support. British policy was very much oriented towards widening the EU as a way of preventing its deepening. In the 1960s and 1970s, Labour was increasingly anti-European, and it was the Conservatives who led Britain into the EEC. Since then the positions have reversed and, under Thatcher, the Conservatives became increasingly Eurosceptic. The Conservatives, who have led the coalition Government since May 2010, have declared their opposition to further European integration and pledged to oppose any additional transfer of sovereignty to the EU.

'New Labour' on the other hand (and Blair in particular) were keen that Britain should play a full and leading role in the EU. Thus the British Government supported the controversial Lisbon Treaty, signed in December 2007, the genesis of which was a proposal for a European constitution. Initially the Labour Government, now led by Brown after Blair's retirement, had committed itself to bring any European constitution before British voters in a referendum; but with the Lisbon Treaty no longer being officially deemed a EU constitution, the Labour Government did not bring it to referendum. The new LibDem–Conservative coalition will also not be able to do so since the Lisbon Treaty came into effect in December 2009. The Labour Government also took the decision to incorporate the European Convention on Human Rights into Britain's domestic law. This action was designed to show the Government's commitment to human rights and end a series of cases in the European Court of Human Rights by which decisions by British domestic courts had been frequently and embarrassingly overturned.

In terms of military cooperation, the British Government had been unwilling for a long time to participate in a meaningful way with the EU; it saw NATO as the primary security organization in Europe; this attitude was linked to the British approach towards European integration. Attitudes changed under Blair. They changed because of the extraordinarily painful experiences associated with Bosnia and Kosovo. First, the EU was revealed to the world as an impotent actor in international security affairs; and, second, although wanting to stay out of the Balkans conflict and let Europe take a leading role, the United States had to intervene through the instrument of NATO after being frustrated by the EU's inability to act effectively.

EU weakness led to a dramatic change: the creation of the ESDP, which has developed military and civilian instruments of intervention. These instruments are modest simply because the EU Powers had important gaps in their military capabilities: heavy lift capabilities, intervention capabilities, and reliance on the United States for satellite-based capabilities. But nevertheless, through the development of the European Rapid Reaction Force, available EU military resources are now capable; and the ESDP has been involved in a number of missions, two of which are military missions and one involving substantial military deployments. Thus, the ESDP has become a more credible asset in the military field and, with the Berlin Plus agreement (permitting the EU to rely on some of NATO's military resources in its own peace-keeping operations) it also has forged a link to NATO so that it can make use of the alliance's capabilities.[22]

For British foreign policy, more important and less discussed, perhaps, are the civilian instruments, the crisis management mechanisms involved in ESDP that are extremely important and that NATO lacks. Consequently an interesting situation has arisen in which NATO can still provide military capabilities, but the EU and ESDP provide civilian ones for conflict resolution. The spat between the United States and Europe over ESDP has to some extent ended with an agreement that ESDP is not going to take away from NATO, but in a sense add to the alliance. NATO is very much on trial because its current testing ground is Afghanistan, where, again, from the American point of view, the Europeans are not really meeting their responsibilities. The interesting thing about NATO is that since its inception, its purpose was to keep the Americans in Europe and make sure that they would be committed to its defence; now, its purpose seems to be to keep the Europeans committed and make certain that they participate actively in international security given that there is much questioning as to whether Europe should be involved in conflicts outside its own territory. How successful this has been so far is questionable. The Europeans have so far not shown the capability of taking a leadership role. In the Balkan conflicts (Bosnia and Kosovo) NATO became involved after the Americans, having tired of European prevarication, took the initiative.

It was in this context that the British Government conducted the 2010 national security and defence review.[23] Its outcome was in some respects paradoxical. It affirmed the intention to maintain a full spectrum of military capabilities, including intervention with global reach and the capacity to engage in large-scale high-intensity warfare. At the same time, capabilities are to be scaled down. Two aircraft carriers procured by the previous Labour Government were obvious candidates for cuts, but they were retained because the cost of cancellation was greater than the cost of completion. However, the fleet of Harrier fighter bombers is to be scrapped, resulting in the ironic situation that Britain will not have any planes to deploy on the new carriers until Joint Strike Fighters currently in development are available. The strategic defence review announced that the Government had decided to operate only one of the carriers with just 12 Joint Strike Fighters (instead of 36) and possibly 12 Chinook or Merlin Helicopters and/or up to eight Apache helicopters. Again, this projection is based on the analysis that Britain is not likely to engage in high-intensity operations but, rather, precision operations in which the key task is air defence suppression and a military strike capability in a regional theatre for counterinsurgency operations. Overall, British armed forces will shrink, with the retention of a modest high-readiness force, armed assets capable of intervention, stabilization forces, and military and police capacities to combat terrorism.

The transformation of the global international security environment since 1990 created some degree of uncertainty about the nature of the emerging international system and Britain's role in it. With the *National Security Review and Defence Review*, the Government has articulated a grand strategy that is commensurate with a realistic assessment of the security threats that it faces in the foreseeable future. This strategy means a shift from the development of technologically advanced weapons platforms designed for large-scale, high-intensity warfare to the procurement of equipment required for counterinsurgencies, although Britain remains committed to deploying and modernizing a strategic nuclear deterrent. International terrorism and cyber-warfare have moved to the top of the hierarchy of potential threats to British security. It reaffirms the commitment to European defence collaboration, NATO, and the special relationship with the United States (albeit with some rather vague qualifications related to the British national interest). However, it remains unclear what degree of responsibility either Britain or its European allies together will be willing to assume for global security. Prime Minister Cameron has made it clear that in his view Britain must accept that it cannot play the role of world policeman and that there are limits to what it can do. This vision signalled that the coalition Government would not only like to end the commitment in Afghanistan as soon as it can without losing face but also that it would be unlikely to enter similar commitments again and that spending on Britain's armed forces would have to be reduced in the short and medium term. Future military operations would only take place if Britain's own national interest was at stake. While based on a realistic appraisal of national security interests of the United Kingdom, it leaves it with a diminishing and uncertain role in the future.

Notes

1 David Sanders, *Losing an Empire, Finding a Role* (London, 1990).
2 Christoph Bluth, *Britain, Germany and Western Nuclear Strategy* (Oxford, 1995).
3 Michael Clarke, *British External Policy-making in the 1990s* (London, 1992).
4 John Dumbrell, *A Special Relationship: Anglo-American Relations from the Cold War to Iraq* (Aldershot, 2006).
5 T.V. Paul and John A. Hall, eds., *The International Order and the Future of World Politics* (Cambridge, UK, 1999).
6 Michael Mandelbaum, *The Dawn of Peace in Europe* (New York, 1996).
7 International Institute for Strategic Studies, *Military Balance 2010–11* (Abingdon, 2010).
8 Christoph Bluth, 'Russian Military Policy: Constraints and Capabilities', in Roy Allison and Christoph Bluth, eds, *Security Dilemmas in Russia and Eurasia* (London, 1998), 67–93.
9 Mary Kaldor, *New and Old Wars: Organised Violence in a Global Era* (Stanford, CA, 2007).
10 John J. Mearsheimer, 'Back to the Future', *International Security*, 15(1999), 5–56.
11 Jonathan Powell, *The New Machiavelli* (London, 2010), Chapter 11.
12 John Sloboda and Chris Abbott, 'The "Blair doctrine" and after: five years of humanitarian intervention', *Open Democracy*, 21(April 2004).
13 Powell, *New Machiavelli*, Chapter 11.
14 Christoph Bluth, 'The British Road to War: Blair, Bush and the decision to invade Iraq', *International Affairs*, 80(2004), 851–72.
15 Tony Blair, *A Journey* (London, 2010), Chapter 13.
16 Great Britain Prime Minister, Cm 7948: *Securing Britain in an Age of Uncertainty: The Strategic Defence and Security Review*, (London, 2010), §3.2.
17 Sean M. Maloney, *Enduring The Freedom: A Rogue Historian In Afghanistan* (Dulles, VA, 2005).
18 James Fergusson, *A Million Bullets: The Real Story of the British Army in Afghanistan* (London, 2009); Patrick Wintour, 'Afghanistan Withdrawal Before 2015, says Cameron', *Guardian* (26 June 2010).
19 Bob Woodward, *Obama's Wars* (New York, 2010); Julian Borger, 'War on Terror Was a Mistake Says Miliband', *Guardian* (15 January 2009).
20 Steve Hewitt, *The British War on Terror* (London, 2008), xxi.
21 Christoph Bluth, *Western Nuclear Strategy*, 10 f.
22 Jolyon Howorth, *Security and Defence Policy in the European Union* (Basingstoke, 2007).
23 Great Britain Prime Minister, Cm 7953: *A Strong Britain in an Age of Uncertainty: the National Security Strategy* (London, 2010); *Securing Britain in an Age of Uncertainty*.

5

Unravelling the enigma

Russian foreign policy in the twenty-first century

Jeffrey Mankoff

Ever since the collapse of the Soviet Union, Russian officials have struggled to articulate a new intellectual framework for their country's foreign policy. The process has been uneven, in part because the Russian Federation was fundamentally new as a state, its identity and interests still loosely defined for several years after independence in 1991. What is Russia? Not a nation-state, given its vast territorial expanse and wide range of ethnic groups inhabiting its territory, but no longer an empire either; and clearly not a superpower (although it continues to maintain the world's second largest nuclear arsenal and a permanent seat on the United Nations [UN] Security Council). But whilst the Soviet Union may have lost the Cold War, it was not bombed out, crushed, and occupied the way Germany and Japan were in 1945. Post-1991 Russia remained a major, if diminished Power, especially in its own neighbourhood, where other new states were still weaker, more chaotic, and continued to look to Moscow as the principal arbiter of regional conflicts.

Russia was also (as it had always been) a European state and a member of the European state system. In historical and cultural terms, Russia has always been a major player inside Europe; one only has to think of the giant contributions to European culture made by Tolstoy, Chekhov, and Tchaikovsky, not to mention those ambassadors of Russian culture inside Europe such as Kandinsky and Nabokov. But with more than two-thirds of its territory and most of its natural resources behind the Urals, Russia is also in Asia, if not precisely of it. The Soviet collapse actually drove Russia's frontiers farther from the centre of Europe. After 1991 Russia no longer bordered Germany and Czechoslovakia in the West; it bordered Ukraine and Belarus instead. Moreover, the post-Cold War years saw the European and 'Euro-Atlantic' communities rapidly expanding, taking in Russia's one-time Warsaw Pact satellites, but not Russia itself. If being European meant being a member (or aspiring member) of the European Union and the North Atlantic Treaty Organization (NATO), where did that leave Russia, which was neither?

This uncertainty about what precisely the Russian Federation is spilled over into debates about the country's foreign policy as well. Debates about foreign policy are a staple of political life in practically all states, at least those not subject to rigid autocratic control. What distinguished, and continues to distinguish, the debate in Russia is the extent to which it centres on basic principles as much as on specific policy choices. In the United States, for instance, there is general bipartisan agreement that the United States should support a liberal international order and cultivate friendships with other liberal democracies, even as analysts and political figures fiercely argue over how to implement those principles in practice: for instance, should the United States go to war to spread democracy or seek to work with authoritarian states that reject Washington's democratic principles? In Russia, on the other hand, the debates focus more on first principles, in large part because of the lingering uncertainty about Russia's identity as a state and an actor in the international system. Should the focus of Russia's diplomatic activity be on the West or its post-Soviet neighbours, or perhaps on East Asia? Can Russia ultimately merge its identity with that of the West, in the same way that Germany joined its one-time enemies in the post-Second World War European Economic Community and post-Communist states such as Poland became part of NATO and the European Union (EU) more recently? Or is Russia just too big and too foreign, condemned always to play a separate role on the world stage? Can Russia become a modern, technologically driven economy, or is its perpetual role to be a supplier of oil and gas to its more developed neighbours?

Answering these and similar questions has provided the substance to much of the debate about foreign policy within the Russian academic and analytic community since the end of the Cold War, even before the actual collapse of the Soviet Union. Force of circumstance has helped answer some of them. Even after several years of solid economic growth, the Russian Federation is too poor to inherit the superpower role of the Soviet Union, especially given that it lacks the ideological underpinnings that made Soviet Russia attractive as a patron and model in much of the world. The political and socioeconomic decay that the country has endured over the past two decades make it difficult for Russia to pursue an overly audacious foreign policy. Internal restoration has to take priority over external adventurism, particularly since the war and economic crisis of 2008.

Nonetheless, Russia's leadership and elite remain largely in agreement that large, powerful states will continue to be the drivers of international affairs in the twenty-first century, and that Russia itself must remain one of these leading Powers. This outlook is in many ways at odds with the focus on shared sovereignty animating the EU, not to mention the emphasis on multilateral responses to global challenges that many Western Powers inside and outside Europe have articulated since the end of the Cold War. Russian foreign policy continues to focus on other states (and those multilateral institutions, such as the G20 and the UN) that remain major Power clubs and do not impose Western-derived behavioural norms on their members. Hard security issues remain fundamental as well, with the Russian Government continuing to spend large sums to modernise and upgrade the military even as austerity has increasingly affected military budgets throughout the West; meanwhile Russia is for the time being a fairly marginal player in addressing global challenges such as climate change and pandemic disease. Russia's foreign assistance capacity pales in comparison with that of the United States, the EU, or Japan.

Central to Russian thinking about the world and Russia's place in it is the concept of multi-polarity (*mnogopolyarnost*). Russian thinkers from across the spectrum reject the right of the United States or the West more broadly to define the parameters for acceptable behaviour, internationally as well as domestically. They see unilateral American actions in the security sphere, such as the bombing of Yugoslavia in 1999 or the invasion of Iraq in 2003, as profoundly destabilising to a world order based on a roughly balanced concert of major Powers. Instead, they subscribe to a worldview in which international law, as embodied in the consensual decisions of the UN Security Council (of which Russia is a veto-wielding permanent member) is the principal source of legitimacy. In this view, Russia is neither an actual nor an aspiring member of the West as a geopolitical construct, but one major Power amongst several that bear ultimate responsibility amongst themselves for upholding world order.[1] This worldview does not of necessity condemn Russia to a confrontational relationship with the West. Indeed, Russian diplomats have repeatedly emphasised their desire for good relations with the United States and the other major Powers, insofar as those Powers are willing to respect Russia's interests and not seek to undermine Russian security through military expansion or the promotion of political change (like democracy promotion in countries Russia considers vital to its own security).

Relations with the West have in fact gone through cycles of *rapprochement* and confrontation over the course of the two decades since the collapse of the Soviet Union, even as Russian views on the nature and goals of foreign policy have remained reasonably consistent. In the early 1990s, a coterie of liberal Westernisers around President Boris Yeltsin sought to bring Russia rapidly into Western institutions. Their failure prompted a backlash in the mid- to late 1990s, punctuated by serious clashes over the Balkans and Russia's invasion of Chechnya. With the arrival to power of Vladimir Putin at the beginning of 2000, relations began warming again, particularly in the aftermath of the 9/11 attacks in the United States and the despatch of American forces to Afghanistan, which Moscow viewed as a hotbed of radicalism and instability threatening its Central Asian allies as well as Russia itself. The Iraq invasion in 2003 and Putin's increasingly authoritarian rule at home bred renewed confrontation, which reached its climax during Russia's five-day war with Georgia in August 2008. Barely six months later, however, the new United States president, Barack Obama. was proclaiming his intention to 'reset' relations with Moscow, and a new era of partnership appeared on the horizon.

The year 2008 was in many ways pivotal for Russia and its place in the world. The year saw a war that, whilst providing a quick triumph against a small foe, had far-reaching political and diplomatic consequences for Russia. The war helped spark an economic crisis that increasingly called into question the belief that Russia had overcome its internal challenges and should be included on the list of rapidly rising Powers alongside China, India, Brazil, and others. Although Russia recovered from the economic crisis relatively quickly, the severity of the downturn forced a reassessment of the assertive foreign policy pursued by Putin, as well as the commodity-dependent economic model Russia inherited from the Soviet Union. In the shadow of the war and economic crisis, Russia also went through its second post-Communist political transition, with Putin stepping down (into the role of Prime Minister) in favour of the younger, more liberal-seeming Dmitry Medvedev.

The Deep Purple-loving, technologically savvy Medvedev brought a new style to Russian foreign policy, but his accession, coupled with the exogenous crises buffeting Russia at the beginning of his term, also heralded something of a reconfiguration and refocusing of priorities. No longer could Russia's ascent to the ranks of the major Powers be taken for granted. Rather, fixing Russia's ills, setting the stage for durable economic growth, and restoring its international standing were increasingly portrayed as long-term tasks. Diversifying the economy away from dependence on resource extraction increasingly became a national security priority. The corollary of diversification was a foreign policy that looked increasingly to the West and to the rapidly modernising states of East Asia as partners and the source of solutions to Russia's domestic problems. The turn toward the West and toward globalisation, symbolised by the reset of relations between Russia and the United States and Russia's active campaign to, at last, join the World Trade Organization (WTO) was less a repudiation of Russia's Great Power ambitions than a recognition that being a Great Power in the twenty-first century required more than tanks. It required a modern economy, a population enjoying higher living standards, and the economic and cultural soft power to win over allies without resorting to coercion.

With the end of the Soviet Union and of the bipolar world in which it existed, Russia's elite has had to construct a new framework for participation in world affairs. How a country defines its interests in the world has much to do with its understanding of itself.[2] As Russia emerged from its Soviet past in the early 1990s, its identity as a state remained very much contested territory. This struggle to define Russia's identity spilled over in to foreign policy. Some argued that shorn of the distorting veneer of Marxism–Leninism, Russia was rejoining the European/Western family from which it had been cut off 70 years earlier, and it should embrace the norms and institutions of the West just as its one-time satellites in Eastern Europe were doing. Others saw the Russian Federation more as the lineal descendant of the Soviet Union, arguing that the new country should continue to resist the spread of American hegemony that the end of the Cold War appeared ready to unleash. Other, more idiosyncratic visions found space as well, such as the one, promoted by a range of populist movements, that portrayed Russia as a state for its ethnic Russian majority at risk of being overrun by hordes of migrants from its largely Muslim, largely poor post-Soviet neighbours to the south.

However, the principal axis around which the identity/foreign policy debate has circled is the question of Russia's position vis-à-vis the West. Of course, this debate is hardly new. Peter the Great's opening to Europe in the early eighteenth century provoked a furious reaction from a clerical and aristocratic establishment that viewed Russia as a unique civilisation defined by its autocratic and Orthodox heritage. For much of the nineteenth century, too, Russian intellectual life was defined by the debate between Westernisers such as Aleksandr Herzen and Slavophiles, amongst the most prominent of whom was Fyodor Dostoevsky. The Cold War largely subsumed this debate, since what defined the Soviet Union as a global Power was less its Russian heritage than its promotion of Marxist–Leninist ideology.[3] Unlike the Soviet Union, the Russian Federation lacks an official ideology and global appeal. What it retains is its historical position on the eastern edge of Europe, with borders stretching deep into Asia and a traditional aspiration to play a central role in world affairs.

The group of officials who came to power with Russia's independence in 1991 largely saw the country as an aspiring outpost of the West. During their heyday in the early 1990s, the young reformers around Yeltsin pursued integration with Western institutions and the reshaping of Russia along Western lines. Yeltsin's first foreign minister, Andrey Kozyrev, argued that Russia should move as rapidly as possible to bind itself to the West in large part to cement Russia's own post-Communist political transition. Indeed, one of the central tenets of the liberal camp throughout the post-Soviet period had been that domestic reform and a pro-Western foreign policy are intimately linked: integration with international institutions operating on Western norms (such as the WTO) will not only enhance Russia's voice on the international stage, it will provide a foundation for difficult reforms at home. For the liberal camp, the basic tenets of Russian foreign policy should therefore be close cooperation with the West, integration into global institutions, and the institution of liberalism and democracy domestically.

This pursuit of liberalism and integration foundered in the mid-1990s, in part because the economy plunged into a steep crisis that called into question the reforms that Yeltsin's Government was undertaking. Equally important was the perception that the West itself was unwilling to accept Russia as a full-fledged member of the club. Rather than the Marshall Plan with which the United States greeted Europe at the end of the Second World War, Russia after the Cold War received limited financial assistance from a West eager to enjoy a post-Cold War peace dividend; along with a significant amount of advice from Western financial advisers and consultants about how to institute a market economy. When that experiment brought about a steeper economic decline in percentage terms than the Great Depression, many Russians turned against the Westernisers in Yeltsin's Government, and against the West itself, for leading Russia down the road to ruin.

At the same time that the West was peddling what many Russians saw as disastrous and self-serving economic advice, it was busy consolidating its strategic position in Russia's backyard. Most galling was the decision to expand NATO, bringing an alliance whose *raison d'être* was containment of Soviet power, closer to the frontiers of the new Russia. If the Warsaw Pact no longer existed and Russia was no longer an enemy, why should the West expand NATO, unless it was still committed to surrounding and weakening the new Russia? As Kozyrev had presciently warned, NATO expansion would only vindicate those inside Russia arguing that the West remained a foe and calling for a less accommodating approach to foreign policy.[4]

Indeed, the beneficiaries of this backlash were those who stood for both a curbing of the market economy and a foreign policy that focused less on joining the West than on restoring Russian influence within the borders of the former Soviet Union. The main apostle of this approach inside the Government was Kozyrev's successor as foreign minister, the ex-spymaster Yevgeny Primakov, who took over the reins of Russian foreign policy in 1996. Primakov argued that Russia could not accept a subordinate role to the major Western Powers, and it should instead focus on reestablishing itself as a major independent pole in the world, not necessarily opposed to the West, but apart from it, whilst focusing its attention on dominating the post-Soviet space. Primakov and his successors found intellectual backing from a philosophical movement known as Eurasianism (sometimes neo-Eurasianism to distinguish it from its White Russian and Soviet antecedents), whose adherents emphasise Russia's special role as a civilisation straddling the boundaries between East and West.[5] Whilst the Eurasianists cover a spectrum from relative moderates, who see Russia as a bridge between East and West, to more extreme figures for whom Russia is destined to serve as the nucleus for a group of states that will stand up to the creeping hegemony of the United States, they share a conviction that Russia is something other than Western, and that its foreign policy should aim above all at restoring Russian influence over the states of the former Soviet Union whilst keeping the West at arm's length.

The Eurasianists' influence has waxed and waned throughout the post-Soviet period, enjoying a particular vogue in the late 1990s and early 2000s. It remains prominent amongst members of the military and the security services (the so-called *siloviki*) many of whom were appointed to prominent positions by former President Putin. Whilst Kozyrev saw the former Soviet Union (especially culturally distinct Central Asia) as an impediment to Russia's progress toward the West, Eurasianists saw former Soviet territories as Russia's natural zone of 'privileged interests', thanks to the common Soviet heritage and a linked infrastructure of roads, railways, and pipelines that can facilitate deeper economic, and possibly political, integration. Through institutions such as the Collective Security Treaty Organization, the Euro-Asian Economic Cooperation forum, and the Russia-Belarus-Kazakhstan Customs Union, as well as through cross-border infrastructure investment, the push for post-Soviet integration has been a Eurasianist priority.

Eurasianist sentiments also underpin the sensitivity that Russia has shown toward the expansion of Western influence, and the extension of Western military power, into the post-Soviet space. One of the principal reasons for the anti-Western backlash that characterised Russian foreign policy under Primakov and a decade later Putin was a belief that the West (above all the United States) was taking advantage of Russian weakness to pursue what amounted to a neo-containment policy. NATO expansion was a particular *bête noir* for Moscow, but other Western initiatives in the post-Soviet space (and Eastern Europe) also contributed to this narrative. American support was instrumental in bringing about the construction of the Baku-Tbilisi-Ceyhan oil pipeline, which allowed Azerbaijan and Kazakhstan to export oil directly to Europe, bypassing Russia's pipeline network and weakening Russian diplomatic leverage in the Caspian. After unilaterally withdrawing from the Anti-Ballistic Missile Treaty, which Moscow considered a cornerstone of strategic stability, the Bush Administration's decision to build a missile defence system in Poland and the Czech Republic was interpreted in Moscow as an attempt to undermine Russia's deterrent capability, breaking with the logic of mutually assured destruction that had enforced restraint on both sides during the Cold War.

Washington's hand was also detected behind the so-called 'coloured revolutions' that broke out in several post-Soviet countries starting with Georgia in 2003. In each case, disaffection with corruption and misrule, coupled with prodemocracy movements that had received some degree of assistance from the United States, replaced governments in Georgia, Ukraine, and Kyrgyzstan considered acceptable in Moscow with new leaders who, in the cases of Georgia and Ukraine, were overtly pro-Western in their sympathies and became more so as Moscow sought to undermine them. Some Russians even believed that the United States saw these revolutions as trial runs for bringing about similar change inside Russia itself.

The anti-Western wave crested in 2008 with the war between Russia and Georgia. Georgian President Mikheil Saakashvili, who had come to power in early 2004 at the head of Georgia's Rose Revolution (the first of the 'coloured revolutions') sought to position his country as a Western outpost in the Caucasus. Whilst he undermined several oligarchs with ties to Russia and made a show of unmasking Russian spies allegedly laying the foundation for his ouster, his two biggest sins in Russian eyes were his ambition for Georgia to join NATO and his attempts to reassert control over the breakaway provinces of South Ossetia and Abkhazia, which had enjoyed *de facto* autonomy under Russian protection since the early 1990s. Although Moscow took a variety of steps to weaken Saakashvili, from imposing a trade embargo on Georgia's most important exports of wine and mineral water to expelling Georgian citizens living in Russia who sent remittances to their families in Georgia, it failed to dissuade the mercurial Georgian leader.

After a string of Russian provocations, Saakashvili ordered his forces to retake South Ossetia in early August 2008, confident that his close relationship with the Bush Administration would deter Russia from direct intervention. Saakashvili badly miscalculated, and barely a day later, Russian troops launched a counteroffensive. After five days, although the Russians suffered significant casualties, Georgian forces were routed and both South Ossetia and Abkhazia were under Russian control. The two statelets then proclaimed their independence, which Russia quickly recognised. In a television interview following the conflict, Russia's new president, Medvedev, laid out a five-point programme for Russian foreign policy in which he emphasised that the post-Soviet space constituted a zone of 'privileged interests' for Russia.[6] Medvedev argued that whilst Russia was not seeking conflict with the West, it could not accept undue interference in a region it still considered fundamental to its security. In this interview Medvedev reemphasised the importance of a multipolar world order, essentially telling the West that what Russia did in the Caucasus was none of its business; and Russia justified its recognition of the breakaway regions by pointing to American and European support for Kosovo's campaign to break away from the Russian ally, Serbia. Many informed Russian observers argued that Medvedev's five-point scheme was drawn up by Russia's leading Eurasianist thinker, the Moscow State University professor, Aleksandr Dugin.[7]

Of course, the importance of the ideological split between Westernisers and Eurasianists should not be overstated. Most Russian officials have tended to fall somewhere in between, favouring cooperation with the West when possible but willing to push back when they see Russian national interests being threatened. Equally, a significant factor in many Russian foreign-policy decisions appears to be little more than the naked search for profit. Particularly under Putin, Russia saw a close fusion between big business and the state, with state-owned companies playing an increasingly prominent role not only in the vital energy sector, but across the economy. Alongside the gas monopoly, Gazprom, state companies such as Rosneft (oil), Rostekhnologii (defence), Rosnano (nanotechnology), and United Shipbuilding were established with top political figures in important executive positions. Many, although not all, of these political figures were Putin's *silovik* allies. Amongst others, Medvedev, who served as one of Putin's Deputy Prime Ministers before becoming President in 2008, was also chairman of the board of Gazprom.

The consolidation of state control over key sectors of the economy facilitated an increasingly mercantilist approach to foreign policy during the Putin years. The most notable example was the long-running dispute with Ukraine over gas.[8] After the Orange Revolution, which brought the pro-Western Viktor Yushchenko to power in 2004, Gazprom pushed to wean Ukraine from the subsidies it enjoyed as a reliable Russian ally. These subsidies, which cost Gazprom (and hence, the Russian state) billions of dollars a year, gave Moscow an important lever with which to influence Ukrainian politics. When Yushchenko sought to move Ukraine out of Russia's sphere of influence (signing a strategic partnership agreement with the United States and campaigning for NATO membership) Moscow decided it no longer had any reason to continue throwing money at Kyiv.[9] Twice the resulting standoffs led Russia to cut its shipments, which affected not only Ukraine but also countries further downstream that relied on Russian gas piped through Ukraine to power their factories and heat their homes. The diplomatic damage to Russia's reputation was severe, especially during the first crisis in 2006, but the resulting accords were highly profitable to Gazprom and its well-connected shareholders, above all the Russian state itself. Nor was this battle over gas prices confined to Ukraine. During Putin's second term, Russia moved to raise energy prices to all of its post-Soviet neighbours, although reliably pro-Russian countries such as Armenia and, for a time, Belarus continued to receive preferential treatment, highlighting the ingrained tension between mercantilist and geopolitical goals that has often characterised Russian foreign policy.

Paradoxically, the war with Georgia helped push Russian foreign policy back in a more pro-Western direction. Notwithstanding its battlefield success, the war left Russia isolated on the international stage. Even its closest allies such as Belarus and Kazakhstan refused to endorse the independence of South Ossetia and Abkhazia, despite extensive Russian lobbying. China, which confronted its own separatist challenges in Tibet and Xinjiang, was adamantly opposed as well, despite its vocal support for the idea of a multipolar world. Yet the war also affected the West, which was forced largely to shelve the idea of further NATO expansion into the former Soviet Union. Major European Powers like France and Germany, which had never been keen on NATO membership for Georgia or Ukraine, now became less deferential to Washington's desire to continue pressing the issue. The December 2008 NATO Ministerial Meeting rejected the Bush Administration's initiative to extend formal membership action plans to Kyiv and Tbilisi, choosing instead to establish an open-ended programme to help Georgia and Ukraine meet membership criteria.[10] The August 2008 war had left both Russia and the West chastened and more inclined to seek compromise as they sought to get their relationship back on track.

Russia had another reason for wanting to end the standoff with the West. The war coincided with the beginning of a serious economic crisis that saw Russia's rapid growth of the previous five years go into reverse. Foreign investors were spooked by the war and by hints that Putin was considering a renewed crackdown on private investment, similar to the 2003 assault on Mikhail Khodorkovsky's Yukos oil company. Meanwhile, sparked by the housing meltdown in the United States, the unfolding global recession pushed energy demand sharply lower, reducing prices for Russia's most important exports. Russia's stock market lost more than 90 percent of its value before recovering. Overall gross domestic product decreased by 7.9 percent in 2009, amongst the worst performance by any major economy. Foreign direct investment also decreased precipitously.[11] Even though the economy began to recover by the end of 2009, the elite increasingly realised that the dependence of the Russian economy on commodity exports left it vulnerable to similar future downturns given the violent price swings to which commodities are often subject. The crisis strengthened the faction within the elite arguing for a more modernised, technologically advanced economy, which could be constructed only in close cooperation with the advanced economies of the West and East Asia.

Medvedev became the public face of this campaign for modernisation. In an article penned for the liberal-leaning website, *Gazeta.ru*, he argued that not only had Russia's commodity dependence left it vulnerable to the recent downturn, but it prevented Russia's voice from being taken seriously in international forums. To overcome these weaknesses, Medvedev argued that Russia needed to modernise its economy, taking advantage of its intellectual potential, and create a democratised, accountable political system capable of supporting such an economy. These transformations required that 'petulance, conceit, insecurity, mistrust, and above all enmity must be mutually removed from relations between Russia and the leading democratic states'.[12]

The emphasis on reconciliation with the West as the *sine qua non* for the transformation of the Russian economy is a theme Medvedev has sounded on a number of occasions. In his 2009 State-of-the-Nation address to Parliament, he argued that the success or failure of Russia's foreign policy rested solely on its ability to improve the standard of living inside the country, and that Russia should not 'puff out its cheeks' ('not be full of hot air' in the official English translation) to threaten other countries if it wanted them to invest their money in Russia.[13] A strategy paper leaked by the Ministry of Foreign Affairs in May 2010 provided more detail. It called for 'modernisation alliances' with the developed countries of the West as well as East Asia, whereby the expansion of close political relations would pave the way for an influx of foreign investment and technology transfers that would allow Russia to overcome its dependence on oil and gas extraction.[14]

Some of Medvedev's allies outside government have gone further. The Institute for Contemporary Development (INSOR), which Medvedev nominally chairs, produced a report in January 2010 arguing that Russia needed economic modernisation not only as a means of improving the lives of its own citizens, but because economic growth and development would enhance Russia's international standing. According to the INSOR report, attempts to promote integration in the post-Soviet space, for instance, would remain doomed to failure unless Russia itself provided an attractive model for its neighbours to emulate with both a robust economy and a political system responsive to public needs. In its most daring suggestion, the report argued that Russia should put an end to its continued standoff with the West on security issues by simply joining NATO.[15]

In part, renewed cooperation with the West in the aftermath of the Russia–Georgia war is also the result of changes in Western behaviour. In addition to backing away from the American commitment to further NATO expansion, Obama's desire to 'reset' relations with Russia remains one of his top foreign policy priorities. During its first two years in office, the Obama Administration signed a major new arms control treaty with Moscow (New START), reconfigured the proposed missile defence system in Europe to meet Russian concerns, signed an agreement to ship soldiers and supplies to Afghanistan across Russia, created a bilateral commission to expand cooperation into a variety of new spheres, and pushed for greater security cooperation both bilaterally and in the context of NATO and the Organization for Security and Cooperation in Europe.

Russia proved receptive. Yet the resulting *rapprochement* has not changed the underlying bases of Russian foreign policy, above all the desire to be accorded the respect of a major Power with a right to strategic independence. This emphasis on pursuing an independent foreign policy, in the context of a world that is becoming increasingly multipolar, is what sets the Medvedev-era approach to foreign policy apart from that of Kozyrev and his fellow Westernisers in the early 1990s.

Moreover, the current round of *rapprochement* is not confined to the West. When Russian diplomats speak of modernisation alliances, for instance, they focus on the developed states of East Asia such as South Korea and Singapore in addition to the United States and its European allies (Japan is less of a priority because of the lingering territorial dispute between Tokyo and Moscow over a chain of four islands in the Sea of Okhotsk). The leaked Foreign Ministry strategy document emphasises the importance of these Powers to Russia's modernisation quest, especially in the context of the underdeveloped Russian Far East; it also emphasises that Russia will not abandon its demand to play a leading role in the post-Soviet space.[16] Indeed, Russian diplomacy has become more active across Asia during Medvedev's presidency. Apart from good relations with China, which Russia has pursued since the mid-1990s, Moscow has more recently sought a more active role in Asian regional forums (including the Asia Pacific Economic Cooperation forum, whose summit will be held in Vladivostok in 2012) and has deepened its bilateral cooperation with select partners such as Vietnam, Malaysia, and India.

Nor, in contrast to the early 1990s, has Russia turned its back on the former Soviet Union, which Moscow continues to regard as a region where it has 'privileged interests'. Rather, the war in Georgia has produced a largely favourable dynamic from the Russian perspective in which the West has become more cautious about the type of engagement it pursues with Russia's neighbours and these countries themselves have awoken to the importance of good relations with Moscow. The end of Ukraine's Orange Revolution and the election of the more Russophile Viktor Yanukovych as Ukrainian President in early 2010 produced a government in Kyiv with which Moscow thought it could do business, even as Russia continues to boycott contacts with Georgia as long as Mikheil Saakashvili remains in power. In Central Asia, the worsening security situation in and around Afghanistan led Moscow to conclude that cooperation with the United States was preferable to Afghanistan's complete collapse and a return to power by the Taliban. Rather than castigating Washington for its decision to maintain an air base in Kyrgyzstan, Russia coordinated closely with the United States when Kyrgyzstan's internal politics spiralled into chaos during spring–summer 2010.

Of course, it is too soon to know whether the post-2008 *rapprochement* between Russia and the West will prove more durable than its predecessors. To be sure, there are reasons for optimism. The war with Georgia highlighted the limits of Russian power even inside the post-Soviet space, whilst bringing home to the Russian elite the dangers of renewed international isolation. Abkhazia and especially South Ossetia have become diplomatic and financial burdens that Russia would like to rid itself of if it could find a face-saving way to do so. The appetite for a renewed post-colonial conflict in the former Soviet Union is close to nil; when Kyrgyzstan's weak provisional government all but begged Moscow to send troops to contain pogroms that rocked the southern part of the country in mid-2010, Russia refused to be drawn in.

In the aftermath of the conflict in Georgia, Russia began undertaking a wholesale reform of its military. Belatedly, Moscow realised that the mass army of conscripts it inherited from the Soviet Union was wholly incapable of dealing with the twenty-first century security challenges Russia faces: not a conventional land war with NATO forces on the plains of central Europe, but a rising tide of insurgencies and small wars around its borders. Despite the overwhelming strategic necessity of military reform, the Kremlin's effort remains deeply unpopular with the tens of thousands of officers slated to be cashiered as Russia moves to a smaller, more technologically advanced, and better-trained volunteer force.[17] As it pushes through with these painful, unpopular reforms, the Kremlin has little capacity to embark on any new foreign adventures; when and if the reforms are completed, the Russian military will look vastly different, its capacity to pose a serious threat to the West (apart from its possession of nuclear weapons) vastly diminished.

More broadly, Russia's strategic environment is changing. Whilst Russia like the West suffered significant losses in the global economic crisis that began in late 2008, China did not. Chinese economic growth slowed only slightly, and Beijing was able to deploy its massive stock of foreign reserves into a depressed market to purchase resources, infrastructure, and other assets to strengthen its strategic position over the longer term. Many of these investments were in Central Asia, a region Russia has long regarded as an integral piece of its zone of 'privileged interests'. Chinese investment brought to fruition a major new gas pipeline from Turkmenistan, which had previously been almost entirely dependent on Russia for its access to global markets. China also invested large sums to finance a separate oil pipeline from Russia itself (the East Siberia-Pacific Ocean pipeline), in the process throwing a life raft to Russia's indebted state energy firms in exchange for significant price concessions. The growing disparity between Russia and China has forced many Russian analysts to conclude that the only way for Moscow to avoid becoming a raw materials appendage of China is to seek deeper economic integration and political cooperation with the West. What forms such cooperation will take remains to be decided, but China's rise will constitute one of the most profound challenges to Russian influence in the near to medium-term future.

Nonetheless, one of the most important factors for the future of Russia's relationship with the West is the West's own openness to Russia. The framework adopted by the United States and its allies in the 1990s, in which Russia would essentially follow the path laid out by Japan and Germany after the Second World War failed: that is trading geopolitical autonomy to become part of a collective security community dominated by the United States. It failed primarily because Russia's leaders were not prepared to surrender their strategic autonomy. Notwithstanding the economic crisis, the rise of China, and the United States–Russia reset, that aspect of Russian foreign policy has not changed.

The United States and its allies will need to be more creative in finding ways to engage Russia, ways that respect Russia's desire for an autonomous role but that advance mutual interests. Areas such as missile defence and European security will have to be at the forefront of that effort, and they will likely require the United States and its allies to go much further in making Russia a full partner, with a real say in the design of institutions, than they have been willing to do so far. Precisely because Russia is so tied to Europe by its history and culture, the Europeans and the Americans who continue to underwrite their security have little choice in the long run but to seek Russia's integration in one form or another into the full range of European institutions. With its vast size and murky politics, Russia will not be an easy fit; many institutions may have to be redesigned or created from scratch, particularly insofar as Russia does not share many of the underlying normative principles that lie at the heart of the collective entity known as 'the West'. Russia's politics may evolve over time to become more open and democratic but, in the meantime, the security imperatives for Russia as well as the West dictate the necessity for enhanced foreign policy cooperation and integration, regardless of Russia's progress (or lack thereof) toward democracy. For the West, designing a path for Russia's deeper integration whilst acknowledging the West's inability to fashion a Russia in its own image will be the greatest challenge of all. As the memory of the Cold War fades on both sides of the old Iron Curtain, the West as well as Russia will have an opportunity to move forward without the political and psychological baggage of the past. It is an opportunity they will need courage, patience, and determination to embrace.

Notes

1 See Jeffrey Mankoff, *Russian Foreign Policy: The Return of Great Power Politics* (Lanham, MD, 2009), Chapter 2.

2 Alexander Wendt, *Social Theory of International Politics* (New York, 1999) 1–7; Ted Hopf, *Social Construction of International Politics: Identities & Foreign Policies, Moscow 1955 and 1999* (Ithaca, NY, 2002), 156.

3 Other countries related to the Soviet Union primarily as the leader of the global Communist Bloc, even if the actual imperatives driving Soviet foreign policy were, as George Kennan argued in his famous 'X article', drawn from Russian history. See George Kennan ('X'), 'The Sources of Soviet Conduct', *Foreign Affairs*, 25(July 1947), 566–82.

4 Andrei Kozyrev, 'The Lagging Partnership', *Foreign Affairs*, 73(May/June 1994).
5 For a more thorough analysis of the Eurasianist movement, see especially Marlène Laruelle, *Russian Eurasianism: An Ideology of Empire* (Washington, DC, 2008).
6 'Interv'yu Dmitriya Medvedeva telekanalam <Rossiya>, Pervomu, NTV' (31 August 2008): www.kremlin.ru/text/appears/2008/08/205991.shtml.
7 Fred Weir, 'Moscow's moves in Georgia track a script by right-wing prophet', *Christian Science Monitor* (20 September 2008).
8 Simon Pirani, Jonathan Stern, and Katja Yafimava, 'The Russo-Ukrainian gas dispute of January 2009: A Comprehensive Assessment', Oxford Institute for Energy Studies (February 2009): www.oxfordenergy.org/pdfs/NG27.pdf.
9 'Dvoinoi standarty "gazovoi voiny"', *Izvestiya* (3 January 2006).
10 'NATO Ministerial Chairman's Statement', 3 December 2008: www.nato.int/cps/en/natolive/official_texts_46248.htm?selectedLocale=en.
11 Ministry of Economic Development and Trade, 'Ob itogakh sotsial'no-ekonomicheskogo razvitiya Rossiiskoi Federatsii v 2009 godu', (3 February 2009): www.economy.gov.ru/minec/activity/sections/macro/monitoring/doc20100203_01.
12 Dmitry Medvedev, 'Rossiya, Vpered!', *Gazeta.ru* (10 September 2009): www.gazeta.ru/comments/2009/09/10_a_3258568.shtml.
13 Dmitry Medvedev, 'Presidential Address to the Federal Assembly of the Russian Federation' (12 November 2009): http://eng.kremlin.ru/transcripts/297.
14 Russian Ministry of Foreign Affairs, 'Programma effektivnogo ispol'zovaniya na sistemnoi osnove vneshnopoliticheskikh faktorov v tselyakh dolgosrochnogo razvitiya Rossiiskoi Federatsii" (11 May 2010).
15 'Rossiya XXI veka: Obraz zhelaemogo zavtra', INSOR (January 2010): http://insor-russia.ru/files/Obraz_gel_zavtra_0.pdf.
16 Ministry of Foreign Affairs, 'Programma effektivnogo ispol'zovaniya'.
17 The military has been slow to embrace the new threat environment as well. The official 'Military Doctrine' released in 2009 continues to regard NATO expansion and out-of-area operations as direct threats to Russian security. Voennaya doktrina Rossiiskoi Federatsii (5 February 2010): http://news.kremlin.ru/ref_notes/461.

6

China

Great Power rising

Robert D'A. Henderson

In late 2006, China's state-run television channel Chinese Central TV2 carried a multi-episode documentary on 'The Rise of the Great Powers' twice in prime time. Each episode centred on the basic question of how did 'so many tiny, population-constrained, resource-poor, often warring, mostly European states make it so big on the world stage?' Whilst left unstated, this series raised the complementary question for Chinese viewers: why with its huge population, iron and coal resources, inventive efforts, and unified country, China had not risen to such Great Power status in modern times?[1]

Is the rising of a Great Power the result of a set of factors sometimes referred to as 'politics of geography' (geopolitics) or even international power politics? In his seminal book *The Rise and Fall of the Great Powers*, Paul Kennedy argued that a critical relationship exists between economic power and military power, namely that nations project their military power based on their economic resources and in defense of broad national economic interests. Kennedy went on to argue that the cost of projecting such military power is more than even the largest economics can afford indefinitely (a point with direct relevance to the United States as the current 'sole superpower' and to China in the late twenty-first century).[2]

Since the early 1990s as China increasingly built on its domestic economic reforms under Deng Xiaoping and a rapid growth of almost ten per cent annually to extend its global economic reach, the expression 'China Rising' has come to be used to describe this rapid development. Over the same period, the Chinese communist Government made double-digit annual increases in its defense budget. Nevertheless Chinese leaders preferred to call China's Great Power emergence a 'peaceful rising' or a 'path to peaceful development'. By 2010, the People's Republic of China (PRC) (*Zhonghua Renmin Gonlkgheguo*) had become an economic superpower with the second largest economy in the world (behind the United States and ahead of Japan) with global reach. But it was still a regional military power, despite its nuclear weapons state status since October 1964, a small intercontinental ballistic missile force, and a growing arsenal of sophisticated conventional weapons systems including missile frigates, nuclear submarines, fourth-generation jet fighters, short- and medium-range ballistic missiles, and surveillance satellites. By 2003, China had become the third Power after Russia and the United States to send a person into space, with current plans to place a Chinese national on the moon before 2020.

Many China observers consider that China is already a Superpower. At the turn of the twenty-first century, there were many warnings of an emerging 'China Threat'. Some writers have noted that China's ascent to power is no different than the rise of other Great Powers since 'power is necessarily expansionist',[3] and, because it is 'usually rising powers that provoke wars', that it is important not to confront China but rather to encourage it to act like a major Power and follow international rules amongst sovereign states.[4] China's assertiveness on the world stage, its military build-up, and its sovereignty claims on regional issues (such as over disputed islands in the East China Sea and South China Sea) are seen as evidence of this striving for regional power or hegemony.[5] But Chinese writers counter that the Western view of world politics is deeply rooted in the belief that 'every rising power will eventually pursue regional and world hegemony', a view drawn from their own historical experience overseas that is 'irrelevant in China's case'.[6]

But China's rise to Great Power status has been subject to various constraints. Domestically, its sustained and rapid economic growth has produced increased economic inequities, huge social problems, and new problems of governance. It has also brought populist reactions and nationalist impulses. And externally, there have been difficulties in managing its immediate rivalry with Japan and the long-term relationship with the United States.[7] China has over 22,000 kilometres of land borders with 14 countries and 14,500 kilometres of coastlines on the Yellow Sea, the East China Sea, and the South China Sea, with international passages through each of them. Based on its favorable location on the Euro-Asian map, China's influence is expanding on land and at sea, from Central Asia to the South China Sea and from the Russian Far East to the Indian Ocean. Yet it has not fought a war or border conflict since 1979. China's mounting demand for energy and natural resources is driving its international strategic policy, and, with it, China's growing political and economic influence and military force projection in Asia and further overseas.[8] Rather than pursuing a reputed strategic plan for world domination, like all rising Great Powers, it is following the needs of its economic growth to play a greater and more influential international role.

Even as China has been experiencing 'growing pains' during its emergence as a Great Power, so it has had to determine in concrete terms what are its core national interests and what it wants its Great Power image to be in the international community. Twenty years ago, China was a struggling, self-described Third World nation, and in many ways it is still a developing country with a $6600 per capita GDP (in 2009, 128 in the world).[9] For its large 1.3 billion population, it lacks sufficient clean water and electricity and confronts extensive industrial pollution and other development problems. But now the Chinese leadership 'has to have a foreign policy for everything' as China emerges as a Great Power in the international community,[10] at the same time that its communist leadership was to have greater influence over world affairs that affect the country.

The PRC is an authoritarian one-party state established in October 1949 by the Chinese Communist Party (CCP), following its victory on the mainland over Kuomintang—Nationalist Party (KMT) forces in the Chinese civil war. In its preamble, the 1982 State Constitution of the PRC (as amended to 2004) declares that, along the road of Chinese-style socialism, the country is under the leadership of the CCP. But economically the CCP led by Deng changed China in the 1980s and 1990s from a socialist to a state-led capitalist economy. Politically, the CCP maintains a highly centralised party structure under the principle of 'democratic centralism', whereby each level of the Party can theoretically have policy input into the level above but, once a decision has been made at a higher level, that decision must be followed and implemented.[11] In practice, the CCP is the supreme source of political power in the country. Senior party leaders hold all top government, military, and police positions at the national and regional levels. Ultimate authority for policy-making rests with the 25 members of the CCP Politburo, and within it, those who hold the nine seats in the Politburo's Standing Committee, the party's main decision-making body. The Politburo and Standing Committee members hold senior positions in the party's almost 370-member Central Committee, as well as in the 12-member Party Secretariat and the 9-member party Central Military Commission (CMC).

Under the state constitution (Article 93), the CCP leadership has direct command through the CMC over the People's Liberation Army (PLA), as the military is constitutionally under the CMC (the party) and not the state. PLA forces are composed of the Chinese army, navy (PLAN), air force (PLAAF), and strategic rocket forces. In addition, the CMC has the authority to make all senior military promotions, appointments, and dismissals. Its chairman is responsible to the National People's Congress (NPC) and its Standing Committee under Article 94 of the State Constitution. At present, President Hu Jintao and Vice-President Xi Jinping are the only civilians sitting on the CMC. Although Hu chairs this body (with Xi appointed CMC Vice-Chair in September 2010) many China observers suggest that he and senior party officials continue to feel the necessity of building up the loyalty of the military commanders with annual defense budget increases for modernisation and weapons purchases. During the revolutionary period, CCP leaders were also military commanders, 'dual elites being both political and military'. But, since the passing of Deng and the first- and second-generation leaders, current CCP leaders have not had any military experience.[12] As such, the PLA and its commanders can be seen as an 'interest group living on the party' with strong influence on the setting of the country's foreign affairs and security objectives, in exchange for not challenging the political leadership and the CCP's political agenda.[13]

In theory, the NPC, which meets every five years, with the 18th NPC meeting scheduled for Autumn 2012, is the highest party organ. But in operation, the members of the party's Standing Committee, Politburo, and CMC exercise all decision-making authority, with some senior communist leaders holding positions in each of these leadership bodies as well as senior government posts. Parallel to the CCP is the state structure, with the head of state being the State President, whilst the head of government is the State Premier, who is chairman of the State Council (the cabinet of ministers and state councillors). The top government, party, and military posts are respectively the State President, the CCP Secretary-General, and CMC Chairman, currently held by Hu, whilst Wen Jinbao is State Premier and party Standing Committee member.

China has a unicameral legislature, the NPC, which meets annually for two weeks to review and confirm legislation prepared by the NPC Standing Committee. The NPC is composed of almost 3,000 members elected by municipal, regional, and provincial people's congresses to serve five-year terms. But its Standing Committee acts for the NPC when it is not in session, including approving legislation. In addition, a range of state and semi-state structures have arisen to deal with economic, technical, science, defense production, commercial, social, and other issues. There are a range of official and quasi-official policy research groups and think tanks, plus the national academic and university community. In the area of science, technology, and commercial and defense production, there are many state-owned enterprises (SOEs), multinational commercial groups, and even growing private business interests. Over the past two decades, many of these bodies have increasingly sought to ensure that their institutional interests are expressed to senior party and government leaders. In addition, a strong interlink exists between party and state positions in China, which has led to extensive personal affiliations developed from past party and governmental postings. More recently, there have been popular domestic protests in urban centres (as well as rural areas), some of which have been nationalistic, with their focus on foreign issues that have an impact on China's declared core interests, such as the sovereignty over small islets in the East China Sea and the South China Sea, access claims to potential oil and gas deposits, secure passage for seaborne oil imports, and more.

The Chinese communist leadership's historical view has constantly pointed to China's 'Century of Humiliation' that began in the mid-nineteenth century when foreign Powers gained 'extraterritorial control' over treaty ports and commercial concessions in its prosperous coastal areas whilst oppressing the Chinese people. These concessionary leases and surrendered border territories and offshore islands had been exhorted through so-called 'Unequal Treaties' with foreign Powers resulting from wars lost or ultimatums imposed. In the 1911 Chinese revolution, the Qing

Dynasty was overthrown and replaced by the Republic of China (ROC) under Sun Yat-sen and the KMT. After his death in 1925, General Chiang Kai-shek assumed leadership of the KMT and, throughout the 1930s, conducted an internal conflict with the CCP under Mao Zedong. During this same period, the Imperial Japanese Army seized Manchuria in 1931, followed by the invasion of northern China six years later, beginning the Sino-Japanese War, which would become part of the Second World War in Asia. After Japan's surrender to the United States and its allies in 1945, the CCP and KMT resumed their pre-war civil war, leading to CCP victory on the mainland by 1949 and KMT forces retreating to Taiwan.

Only months after proclaiming the PRC, Chinese 'volunteer' armed forces entered the Korean War and fought alongside the North Koreans for two years, until the 1953 armistice. Throughout the remainder of the 1950s and into the early 1960s, under Mao's 'Leaning to One Side', China's foreign policy placed itself within the international communist movement under the Soviet Union and signed a bilateral friendship and security treaty with it. During this period, the CCP leadership perceived China as part of the Third World of underdeveloped countries. But increasingly ideological and political differences with the post-Stalinist Soviet leadership led to a Sino-Soviet split in the early-1960s, with Beijing positioning China as a leader of the Third World and as the centre of its declared communist world revolution.

In October 1971, the PRC gained enough votes in the United Nations (UN) to displace the ROC and take the 'China' seat in the UN, including its permanent seat on the Security Council. Increasingly, countries switched diplomatic relations from the ROC to the PRC, further augmenting the international influence of the mainland regime. By the late 1970s, the PRC was able to establish diplomatic relations with all the other Great Powers, including the United States in 1979, although these countries still retained semidiplomatic ties with the ROC through economic and cultural offices in Taipei. After Mao's death in 1976 and the ouster of radical Cultural Revolution factions including the 'Gang of Four', Deng was reconfirmed in the concurrent posts of Party Vice-Chairman, Politburo Standing Committee member, PLA Chief of Staff, and Vice-State Premier. From these positions of political power, he began economic reforms known as the 'Four Modernisations' strategy (development of China's agriculture, industry, science and technology, and defense sectors) to turn China into an advanced industrialised country by the year 2000.

In June 1989, in the twilight of the Cold War, thousands of peaceful Chinese demonstrators in Beijing began calling for democracy in China. In response, a hard-line portion of the CCP leadership ordered PLA forces to remove the prodemocracy demonstrators from Tiananmen Square; PLA troops and tanks killed 2,500 demonstrators. As a result of this massacre as well as subsequent crackdowns on human rights throughout the country, the United States, the European Union (EU), and other countries implemented sanctions on technology transfers and high-tech arms sales to China intended to pressure the CCP leadership into permitting democratic reforms and an end to human rights abuses. These prohibitions have remained in place to various degrees to the present.[14]

At the beginning of the twenty-first century, Beijing began promoting a 'new concept of security' for the international community in which China (based upon its rapid economic growth) would play an increasingly important role in promoting international strategic stability and global economic integration. This new security concept was intended to reestablish international strategic stability that had ended with the collapse of the bipolar Cold War confrontation between the United States and the Soviet Union.[15] In this new international era of 'unipolarity', the United States was seen as the 'sole superpower' with global military and economic reach as well as the leading nation in the remaining major military alliance, the North Atlantic Treaty Organization. From this international perspective, China's leadership saw the United States enforcing its military and economic hegemony over many of the regions of the world, especially in East Asia. As a result, PRC foreign policy increasingly supported the principles of state sovereignty, non-interference in internal affairs of other states, and 'multilateralism' (*duo jihua*), with China as one of the poles in the new order. Moreover, there was the need to build up state-to-state cooperation in international economic affairs to obtain the raw materials, especially oil, necessary for China's continued rapid economic development.

The PRC has its decision-making centralised in the CCP Standing Committee and Politburo, which maintains a 'consensus leadership' style to decide on policies in the domestic and international spheres. But information is compartmentalised within both the bureaucratic party and state structures, and the hierarchical 'stove-pipe' nature of these structures restricts the flow of timely information and intelligence to senior party leaders. From the 1950s to the early 1970s, China's decision-making process (particularly during crisis periods) was highly centralised and concentrated in the person of the CCP chairman, Mao, and a small group of close senior civilian and military advisors from the revolutionary period. Chinese foreign policy was largely determined by domestic factors, mainly 'the primary of politics, the right of the past and the importance of ideology.'[16]

During his period of reforms from the mid-1970s to the early-1990s, Deng Xiao-ping pursued a wider degree of party and military consultation (and arguably compromise) with senior party, government, and PLA officials, including retired party cadres from the revolutionary and early state formation periods, respectively, the First- and Second-Generation party leaders. Under his pragmatic policies, the PRC undertook considerable economic reforms with the 'Four Modernisations'; and China's foreign policy followed that which supported the country's economic growth, namely the primacy of state-led economics that permitted capitalist enterprise. To this end, in the early 1980s, Deng called for China to pursue an 'independent foreign policy of peace'. But the violent suppression in Tiananmen Square set back China's emergence as a Great Power, as the United States, the EU, Japan, and other Powers imposed stiff sanctions to encourage China to act as a 'normal country' following international norms in the post-Cold War world.

Under Jiang Zemin and Third-Generation party leaders (mid-1900s to early 2000s) and Hu and the Fourth Generation (early 2000s to 2010s) Chinese foreign-policy decision-making has maintained its focus through leadership consensus on national economic growth being placed ahead of military power. Foreign activities that favoured economic growth, like energy security through long-term oil contracts and minority shareholdings in foreign oil companies, took priority over military expenditure. But there have been questions about the continuing restrictions in the flow of information to senior leadership due to the 'stove-pipe' nature of both the party and state bureaucracies. In addition, there are questions as to the nature and timeliness of information from senior PLA commanders and Chinese military intelligence, including collection and processing. Although it does not appear that PLA commanders can override senior party leadership decisions, the PLA may be in some crises the sole source of information to senior leaders, such as the 1995–96 Taiwan Strait missile crises and the 2001 EP-3 mid-air collision in the South China Sea.[17]

According to State Councillor for Foreign Affairs Dai Bingguo in July 2009, the national core interests of China are to defend its fundamental systems and national security, preserve national sovereignty and unification, and maintain the steady and sustainable development of the country's economy and society. In addition to territorial claims to Taiwan and Tibet, the oceanic areas of the East China Sea, the South China Sea, and, recently, the Yellow Sea have been added as core interests. Some Chinese military commanders and strategists have also sought to include outer space and such areas as the vast oceans traversed by Chinese oil freighters on this list.

In September 2010, a new chapter was added to the Ministry of Foreign Affairs' (MFA'S) annual report on China's foreign policy. It noted that border and maritime issues concern the country's 'sovereignty, security and development interests' and constitute an 'important component' of Chinese diplomacy. With its development of a 'Blue Water' navy, including its small PLAN squadron tour around the world in 2006 and its PLAN squadron participation in UN international anti-piracy patrols in the Gulf of Aden since January 2009, PLAN has signalled its intent to expand its seaward defenses (including enforcing sea denial) past the 'first island chain' in the East China Sea and into the Western Pacific Ocean.[18]

With the end of the Cold War and the start of the twenty-first century, China began advocating a 'New Concept of Security' for the international community. It felt that it was 'imperative for mankind to establish a new security concept (as) the old security concept based on military alliances and build-up of armaments will not help ensure global security, still less will it lead to a lasting world peace'.[19] This new concept had to meet the 'needs of the times and to explore new ways to safeguard world peace'. Under this new concept, China has participated with its Eurasian neighbouring states, including Russia, in 'Peace Mission' joint military exercises, particularly under the auspices of the recently established Shanghai Cooperation Organization. Despite the continuing publicity around this 'New Concept', recent discussions with Chinese researchers and observers suggest that the Chinese Government is still lacking a stated national security concept; rather, it has only guiding principles when crises arise. There had been reports that China might establish a government 'National Security Council' on the American model in which senior party leaders, government officials, and military commanders meet to discuss national security policies and emerging crises. But the PLA is thought to strongly oppose this proposal because it would reduce its influence on national security issues.

China's rapid rise to Great Power status in the past two decades has been subject to various constraints. With the start of the twenty-first century, the foreign-policy formulation process in China has become increasingly complex. There is an expanding pluralism from the growing market economy ('Socialism with Chinese Characteristics') within Chinese society and the country's growing economic and political interdependence with the international community. The result has been the need for greater involvement by party and state structures as well as the emergence of a new range of foreign-policy actors. But foreign and security decision-making remains the sole prerogative of the senior CCP leadership. This widening arena of party, state, military, and semi- and non-government institutes and groupings provides information and assessments on China's foreign affairs, whilst often attempting to influence or pressure senior decision-makers for favourable policy outcomes, as well as to influence other interest groups and Chinese public opinion.

China's primary decision-making bodies on foreign policy and security issues are *ad hoc* committees placed under the State Council. Currently, these are understood to include the Foreign Affairs Leading Small Group, the National Security Leading Small Group, and the Taiwan Leading Small Group, created in 2000 and only meeting as determined by their chair. Such Leading Small Groups (LSGs) enable the State Council to coordinate the work of several departments and agencies on designated issues as well as to maintain a CCP party overview into the activities of government bodies. These LSGs are chaired by the State President and party leader, Hu, who designates senior party leaders to participate in the groups' deliberations. There is some question whether these LSGs take firm decisions on foreign and security policies and crises, or only seek consensus on guiding principles for government and military implementation. Under the PRC constitution, the security of China includes defending its sovereignty and territorial integrity, as well as continuing its economic and social development and maintaining its international stature. At present, there is no declared 'National Security' set of principles such as the 1947 National Security Act in the United States that established its National Security Council.

State Councillor Dai Bingguo heads the State Council Secretariat that coordinates the work of these bodies. In addition, its attached International Studies and Research Centre (also attached to the Ministry of State Security [MSS] [*Guoanbu*]) compiles the necessary classified intelligence assessments for their consideration. The secretariat then disseminates their policy decisions or guidelines to the relevant government ministers and their departments and agencies. It also facilitates the growing practice of senior leaders consulting with the country's prominent experts and think-tank institutes on specialised international and security affairs issues. In addition, the CMC, also chaired by Hu, can discuss issues brought to the Chairman's attention and determined by him for deliberation, although at this time, the nine-member CMC has only two civilian members, Hu and Xi. The CCP International Liaison Department has responsibility for main-taining party-to-party relations with foreign communist parties, foreign ruling parties, and foreign political parties with complementary views and objectives.

The State Council, the Cabinet, is chaired by head of government, the State Premier. In addition to the MFA, many Cabinet-level departments are increasing their linkages to foreign countries and international organisations, such as the Ministry of Health to the World Health Organization. But these non-party bodies exercise less power in decision-making than CCP party organs and mostly act to implement policy determined by senior party leaders.

The MFA is the government body responsible for bilateral relations with foreign states and PRC membership in international organisations, including the UN Security Council. But rather than being a major part of the foreign-policy process, it is commonly seen as implementing foreign-policy decisions taken by senior party leaders. This result is partly seen in the appointment of career diplomats to the post of foreign minister with a careful view to CCP policy-lines. But the MFA's Policy Planning Department appears to be upgraded to provide international reporting to CCP structures, as well as to the Minister of Foreign Affairs and the MFA geographical depart-ments. The Institute for International Studies in Beijing and the Shanghai Institute for International Studies are attached to the MFA, providing it with international assessments and background studies.

The Ministry of Commerce (formerly known as the Ministry of Foreign Trade and Economic Cooperation) has responsibility for regulating China's international trade and foreign investment, negotiating bilateral and multilateral trade agreements, and regulating direct foreign investments within China. In 2001, China joined the World Trade Organization as a full member. Because commercial SOEs are increasingly pursuing foreign sales and/or raw resources purchases, these activities have increasingly led to their involvement in China's foreign affairs and, with it, the need for the Commerce Ministry to oversee their activities.

The MSS was established under the State Council in 1983 with responsibility for state security against espionage and counterrevolutionary activities. It is also responsible for civilian foreign intelligence collection abroad and counterintelligence activities within China. The Institute of Contemporary International Relations in Beijing acts as the intelligence collation and strategic intelligence assessment centre for the MSS and provides classified assessments to the State Council.[20]

The Ministry of National Defense (MND) is responsible for managing the country's defense, its PLA armed forces, and its defense budget. In addition, the Ministry acts as the connection for the PLA's relations with the outside world and foreign countries' militaries. The Minister of National Defense is usually a serving PLA general, to whom the PLA Chief of Staff and regional military commanders as well as the PLA General Staff Department report; and who, in turn, reports to the State Premier and the party CMC. Chinese defense officials have repeatedly stated in foreign forums that the country's defense development is not aimed at challenging or threatening anyone; instead, it is to ensure China's 'own security and promote international and regional peace and stability', and that China 'pursues a defense policy that is defensive in nature.' More recently, MND officials have been highlighting the point that non-traditional (that is, non-state) security issues such as tsunamis, earthquakes, typhoons, and floods pose grave challenges to Asian regional security. The Institute for International Strategic Studies (IISS) in Beijing is attached to the MND as a strategic assessment body.[21]

Whilst most observers agree that PLA General Staff and military regional commanders remain under the control of the senior CCP leadership through CMC, there is increasing evidence that the influence of a newly assertive Chinese military is growing over foreign policy. At the beginning of China's 'peaceful rise' as a Great Power, the Chinese leadership placed emphasis and resources on economic growth. But, as the country's growth has increased, greater resources have been made available for modernising the armed forces through increased high-tech training and acquisition of newest-generation weapons systems, particularly for PLAN and PLAAF. There has been more than a decade of double-digit annual increases in the defense budget. As the country's security requirements have increased during the past decade, the PLA's range of operational activities beyond China's borders has also seen enormous growth, from UN peacekeeping operations to joint exercises with foreign militaries as well as humanitarian assistance and disaster relief. After the success of its 2007 anti-satellite missile test, some observers have suggested that the PLA's influence both domestically and on international issues will grow in the run-up to the 2012 CCP leadership transition.

Operating both domestically and overseas, China's SOEs are not seen as having an active role in foreign policy, but they can complicate the country's diplomacy. According to a recent report on 108 central government-led enterprises in 2009, the telecom giant, China Mobile, was the country's most profitable SOE, followed by the China National Petroleum Corporation and the China Petrochemical Development Corporation, each of which has made major investments in foreign oil production and oil supply contracts to provide for China's increasing energy needs. But in their pursuit of raw materials, particularly oil and commercial deals, such large SOEs have disrupted China's foreign-policy activities as a result of global concerns about a variety of issues including human rights in Sudan, Myanmar, and Zimbabwe, energy security in Central Asia, and political interference in South and Southeast Asia.[22] Foreign companies have complained that Chinese SOEs have won major contracts in third-party countries by means of 'price-dumping, aggressive financing, and generous risk-guarantees' from the Chinese Government, thereby creating bilateral political fiction with the national governments of those competing companies.[23] There have also been cases in which Chinese SOEs have been accused of violating international arms control accords, resulting in direct confrontations with other Great Powers, particularly the United States. In 2003, Washington imposed sanctions (because of China's weak implementation of its export control regulations and control lists) on the North China Industries Corporation for allegedly supplying missile technology to Iran.

As a result of the expanding government, commercial, and public interest in international affairs in China, as well as the country's growing political and economic interdependence with the international community, the PRC's foreign-policy formulation process is increasingly complex. New actors and interest groups have emerged as China has developed broad political, economic, and commercial needs, leading to involvement in formulating China's foreign policy or drawing China into foreign issues. Most ministries and agencies have attached think tanks like the IISS that provide specialised assessment reports and expert consultation to their government units as well as to central party officials when requested.[24]

The Xinhua (New China) News Agency is the state-run news agency with a network of more than 90 bureaus around the world. In addition, it maintains a foreign news monitoring centre in

Beijing on news broadcasts to compile, translate, and assess worldwide reporting on international events. In addition to providing a Chinese perspective on world events, the Xinhua News Agency provides a daily analytical input to both senior party and government officials.

The PRC does not have a historical pattern of public input into Chinese policy-making outside CCP activities; rather it has a history of rural suppression operations in the 1950s, the chaotic activities of the Revolutionary Red Guards in the Cultural Revolution of the 1960s, and the violent crushing of the prodemocracy movement in Tiananmen Square. But, in the most recent decade, there have been an increasing number of public protests, against local cases of corruption, party nepotism, and others but also regarding international events that reflect on China's sovereignty and public image. Concerning the latter, an example is the 2010 Japanese seizure of a Chinese fishing boat and arrest of its captain for ramming a Japanese Coast Guard vessel within Japanese-administrated islets in the East China Sea that China also claims. Such public protests on international issues appear to arise from growing Chinese nationalist emotions; there are questions about whether these protests are instigated by party authorities or outside their control.[25] Similarly, there are rising numbers of cyber-protests against the websites of foreign governments and their agencies and against the websites of foreign critics of the PRC Government, although there is no evidence to establish if the cyber-protesters are Chinese Government-instigators or individual 'netizens'.

In November 2010, Zheng Bijian, former Vice-President of the Party School of the CPC Central Committee, said publicly that the 'peaceful development' concept that emphasised pragmatic foreign policy and mutual benefit would 'continue to define China's international strategy, despite challenges and others' doubts', whereas Wang Chen, Information Office director at the China State Council, at the same venue stated that 'China's own development requires a peaceful international environment', and that (its) growth 'contributes to world peace'. This view of China's peaceful development (or peaceful rising) in a stable international environment is the repeatedly declared image that China's leadership wishes to project abroad in the twenty-first century.[26]

Chinese foreign policy under Deng and Jiang was essentially to hold back in international initiatives and never to take the lead. But under Hu, China has used its full array of hard and soft power instruments, including foreign aid assistance, trade concessions, foreign direct investment, weapons sales, PLA naval ship visits, voting power in international organisations, participation in international peace-keeping operations, widening cultural exchanges including leasing out their famous national treasure pandas, extending its international communications networks, and others.

There have been suggestions by long-time China observers that hard-line elements amongst party officials and military commanders will attempt strongly to sway PRC foreign and security policies toward their factional interests during the current generation change in the CCP party leadership, leading up to the National Party Congress in 2012.[27] One argument is that whilst Hu appears 'willing to consider dovish as well as hawkish approaches to key issues such as the definition of China's core interests (*hexin liyi*)', a number of nationalist party and military hard-liners have been 'pushing for the broadest possible—and ever-expanding—definition of *hexin liyi*.' Whilst some of the party leadership may only be pursuing a strong Chinese nationalist approach, PLA generals may also have seized upon the current downward spiral in Sino-American linkages as well as overall tension in the Asia-Pacific Region 'to lobby for more economic and political resources' to upgrade their weapons arsenal. And as 'China becomes stronger—and requires more resources to sustain its march toward superpower status—its list of core interests will grow accordingly'.[28]

At the 2012 National Party Congress, Fourth-Generation leader Hu will step down as Party Secretary, and as State President the following year. Although Hu can remain

Commander-in-Chief of the PLA until 2017, via his position as CMC chairman, it is expected that Xi will be his Fifth-Generation replacement as Party Secretary and Head of State. Xi was named CMC Vice-Chairman in September 2010, cementing his status as China's next national leader.[29] But the incoming Fifth-Generation party leadership has little foreign experience or schooling outside China. Similarly, there is little international experience amongst senior PLA commanders.[30] Even with on-and-off contacts, some senior PLA officers have interacted with the United States and other countries' militaries, although generally limited to occasional bilateral visits, regional conferences, and exchanges of speeches and statements. PLAN has taken tentative steps towards extending its operational reach beyond the First Island chain into the Western Pacific Ocean. But the latest Pentagon report on China's military power surmised that the PRC remains a regional military force with a focus on its near-abroad (especially Taiwan) and was not yet an extraregional Power.[31] Nevertheless, with China's growing influence both in economic and military capabilities, many Asian countries are looking to the United States as a regional balancing force to China whilst not provoking a preventable conflict.

There has been a return of authoritarian Great Powers to the world stage, with the former communist countries, Russia and China, now using a state-led model of market development. Whilst noting that China could become a 'true authoritarian superpower', Azar Gat wrote that the rise of authoritarian Great Powers 'would not necessarily lead to a non-democratic hegemony or a war.'[32] In addition to being a regional military Power, China is a global economic Power with the second-largest economy in the world. It enjoys a trade surplus with most of the G9 economies including the United States and Japan, although Taiwan has a large trade surplus with mainland China as a result of its exports to Taiwanese companies on the mainland that then export their final products to global markets. In addition, China's foreign exchange reserves are the largest in the world, estimated at US$2.5 trillion.

On the world stage, China is likely to increase its international activities under the UN, as well as use its growing influence in such world bodies as the UN Security Council, the G20 group of major economies, the World Bank, the World Trade Organization, the Asia-Pacific Economic Cooperation group, as well as regional organisations such as the Shanghai Cooperation Organisation. It has even been suggested that over the next 50 years, the BRIC economies (Brazil, Russia, India, China and South Africa) could come to dominate the agenda of G20 and with it that of the world economy.

Nevertheless, Chinese leaders still need the economy to grow by eight or nine percent annually for the next 20 years, for maintaining social stability and preserving CCP political control. To do so, China will need to continue to have access to growing sources of foreign natural resources, especially energy supplies, which in turn will continue to drive its foreign policy. China's foreign and defense policies (like those of other Great Powers) are largely determined by its domestic policy requirements and the necessity for the CCP leadership to maintain its exclusive hold on political power and the party's legitimacy. The past three decades of sweeping economic reforms have transformed China with a widening range of groupings, factions, and interest groups expressing their views on China's foreign policies. Domestically, there have been rising voices for political reforms[33] at the same time as an escalating suppression of political activists and human rights groups.

In this century unlike the historical pattern of the past two, China wants to translate its economic power into greater political and military influence.[34] But its widening range of foreign-policy actors are displaying increasingly nationalist perspectives, including the view that China is being 'contained' by the United States and its allies. Still, questions remain as to whether the current foreign disputes are due to Chinese leadership's overconfidence and policy miscalculations or Western lack of acceptance of China's ascent as a Great Power. There is also the growing uncertainty as to American 'outsider' intentions in Asian regional affairs, which can partly account for China's 'hawks' overreacting to various territorial disputes and foreign military forces in neighbouring waters. Even Chinese national policy-makers appear to fear that claiming ever-wider national 'core issues' will only enflame the 'China Threat' amongst Powers in the Asian region and further abroad, rather than the image of 'Peaceful Rising'. Linked with the CCP leaders' own sense of insecurity, there is a growing Chinese nationalism and assertiveness in the country as it feels stronger and more powerful.[35] In the decades beyond 2012, a major question will remain whether China as a Great Power will become a 'normal country' acting responsibly in international affairs or acting increasingly as a belligerent 'regional hegemon'.

Notes

I am very grateful for the knowledgeable and always cheerful assistance of the late Robert W. Chen on this writing, as well as on many previous East Asian writings.

1 Stephen Green, 'The World according to CCTV', *Far Eastern Economic Review*, Volume 170, Issue 2 (2007), 41–45. The Chinese documentary series surveyed the rise in order of appearance: Portugal, Spain, Holland, Britain, France, Germany, Russia, Japan, and the United States.
2 Paul M. Kennedy, *The Rise and Fall of the Great Powers: Economic Change and Military Conflict from 1500 to 2000* (New York, 1987), xv–xxv.
3 Harsh V. Pant, 'China—A Great Power like Any Other', *ISN Security Watch* (15 February 2010). Also see John J. Mearsheimer, 'China's Unpeaceful Rise', *Current History*, Volume 105, Issue 690(2006), 160–69.
4 Susan Shirk, *China: Fragile Superpower* (New York, 2007).
5 See Hugo Restall, 'China's Bid for Asian Hegemony', *Far Eastern Economic Review*, 4(May 2007), 42–45; David Shambaugh, 'The Year [of the Tiger 2010] China Showed Its Claws', *Financial Times* (16 February 2010).
6 For a recent example, see Xinhua writer Yang Qingchuan, 'Western hegemony theory not apply to China-Asia relations', *Xinhua News Agency*, Beijing, (14 November 2010).
7 Michael B. Yahuda, *The International Politics of the Asia Pacific*, second revised edition (London, 2004), 268–69.
8 Robert D. Kaplan, 'The Geography of Chinese Power: How far can Beijing reach on land and at sea?', *Foreign Affairs*, 89(May–June 2010).
9 'China', *CIA World Factbook 2010*: www.cia.gov/library/publications/the-world-factbook/geos/ch.html.
10 For a discussion of his interview with Chinese Premier Wen Jiabao, see Fareed Zakaria, 'U.S.-China split would be a catastrophe', *CNN International*, October 1, 2010: http://edition.cnn.com/2010/OPINION/10/01/zakaria.china.trade/?hpt=Sbin.
11 *The Constitution of the People's Republic of China* (Beijing, 1982—as amended March 14, 2004): http://english.peopledaily.com.cn/constitution/constitution.html). According to the preamble, the PRC is 'under the leadership of the Communist Party of China and under the guidance of Marxism-Leninism, Mao Zedong Thought, Deng Xiaoping Theory and the important thought of 'Three Represents'.'
12 The First Generation was Mao Zedong and the revolutionary-era party-military leaders; the Second Generation was Deng and party leaders with military experience; the Third Generation was Jiang at the core of a collective party leadership, the Fourth Generation was Hu and Wen Jiabao leading a collective party leadership with a government of technocrats; and the Fifth Generation is expected to be led by Xi and Li Keqiang. For a forward view, see Willy Lam, *Changing of the Guard: Beijing Grooms Sixth-Generation Cadres for 2020s* (Washington DC, 2010).
13 Ko Shu-ling, 'Politics and the Military Blur in China', *Taipei Times* (5 October 2010).
14 Robert Henderson, 'China's military build-up must be checked', *Taiwan Journal*, (27 October 2006).
15 Government of China. Ministry of Foreign Affairs, *New Concept of Security Advocated by China* (Beijing, 2004). The MFA statement: http://no.china-embassy.org/eng/wjzc/cjjk/dw/t110949.htm. Also see Zhong Jing and Pan Zhenqiang, 'Redefining Strategic Stability in a Changing World: A Chinese View', *Contemporary Security Policy*, 25(2004), 123–35.
16 For a useful 50-year survey, see Thomas W. Robinson, 'Chinese Foreign Policy from the 1940s to the 1990s', in Thomas W. Robinson and David Shambaugh, eds., *Chinese Foreign Policy: Theory and Practice* (Oxford, 1994), 555–602.

17 See Michael D. Swaine, 'Chinese Crisis Management', in Andrew Scobell and Larry M. Wortzel, eds., *Chinese National Security Decisionmaking under Stress* (Carlisle PA), 5–55.

18 Quoted in Da Wei, 'A clear signal of 'core interests' to the world', *China Daily*, (2 August 2010). See also 'China foreign policy white paper gets new chapter on maritime rights', *Kyodo News* (27 September 2010).

19 Chinese Permanent Mission to the United Nations in Geneva, *New Concept of Security Advocated by China* (16 April 2004); Embassy of the PRC in the United States of America, *Joint Military Exercises Testify New Concept of Security* (26 August 2005).

20 See Robert D'A. Henderson, 'China–National Intelligence Community', *Brassey's International Intelligence Yearbook* (Washington DC, 2003), 33–52.

21 See 'China to Enhance Army's Capabilities for National Interest: Defense Minister Liang Guanglie', *Xinhua News Agency*, (1 August 2010);'Defense Minister Liang Guanglie Makes Use of ASEAN Meeting to Boost Regional Peace and Stability', *Xinhua News Agency* (12 October 2010). Cf. Jeremy Page, 'China's [PLA] Army Extends Sway', *Wall Street Journal* (4 October 2010).

22 For example, see Su Peike, 'The Truth behind [China's] SOEs Excessive Profits', *WatchChinaTimes* (27 September 2010).

23 For example, see 'German warning on 'aggressive' Chinese [corporate] rivals', *Financial Times* (15 October 2010).

24 See Thomas Bondiguel and Thierry Kellner, 'The Impact of China's Foreign Policy Think Tanks', *Asia Papers*, Volume 5, Issue 5(April 2010).

25 On growing public protests in China, see Willy Lam, 'Is China afraid of its own people?', *Foreign Policy* (28 September 2010).

26 "Peaceful development' concept continues to define China's international strategy', *Xinhua News Agency*, (7 November 2010).

27 David Lai, 'The Coming of Chinese Hawks', *Strategic Studies Institute Newsletter* (October 2010), 1–3.

28 Willy Lam, 'Hawks vs. Doves: Beijing Debates 'Core Interests' and Sino-U.S. Relations', *China Brief*, 10 (19 August 2010). Also see Kerry Brown, 'The Power Struggle among China's Elite', *Foreign Policy* (14 October 2010).

29 Willy Lam, 'China's New President Xi Jinping', *Asia Sentinel*, Hong Kong (19 October 2010).

30 David Zweig, 'Spooked by China's Hawks? So Are the Chinese', *Asia Wall Street Journal* (11 November 2010).

31 United States Government. Office of the Secretary of Defense, *Annual Report to Congress: Military and Security Developments Involving the People's Republic of China 2010* (Washington DC, August 2010).

32 Azar Gat, 'The Return of Authoritarian Great Powers', *Foreign Affairs*, 86(July/August 2007).

33 See 'China has to pursue gradual political reform – Editorial', *Global Times*, (15 October 2010).

34 For example, see Shen Dingli, 'Modern Makeover [for China]', *American Review*, 2(May 2010). Professor Shen Dingli is Executive Dean of the Institute of International Affairs, Fudan University, Shanghai.

35 Quoted in Geoff Dyer, 'China: View from the inside', *Financial Times* (5 October 2010).

7

France

Exercising power and influence across the ages

Paul P. Vallet

Power, as well as its exercise on the international stage, poses a recurrent problem to France and its leaders. The French Republic is one of the five permanent members of the United Nations (UN) Security Council since 1945, one of eight officially declared nuclear-armed Powers since 1960, a founding member of the European Union (EU), a founding member of both the G8 and G20. It belongs to many other international organizations, like the *Organisation Internationale de la Francophonie*; it is estimated there are some 175 million French speakers around the world. France therefore appears to possess considerable means of power despite its population being only 62.3 million, which ranks it twentieth in the world, but its economy is the sixth largest in GDP. Throughout a long history, French leaders, whether kings, emperors, or presidents, have expressed the ambition to lead their people into playing a preeminent, if not front-rank, role in international relations. In early 2010, the *Revue Défense Nationale*, an official publication of the French Defense Ministry, reflected on French strategic interests.[1] One section of the essay, 'Interests, values and responsibilities, the engine of France's external action', stated:

> The performances aimed at by this engine are well-known: first, in the security interest of France, European defense must be reinforced and the area must be stabilized; [for French] values [to prevail], peace and security must be promoted as well as development while respecting diversity; and finally, *regarding its responsibilities*, [the international community] *must be made to appreciate the pertinence of the French principles in world organization which are based on a strong cultural, institutional and multilateral heritage.*[2]

The reference to heritage is an expression of the particular character of French ambitions towards the exercise of international Power.

In medieval times, the area in which this ambition played out was Europe, or 'Christendom', in which the 'Eldest Daughter of the Church' struggled to affirm its independence.[3] With the Age of Discoveries, France's international vision and stage increased gradually to become truly global in scope. From the sixteenth century, France carried out a relentless drive to expand its borders (which it did under Richelieu and his successors), characterized as a quest for its 'Natural Borders'. Whilst increasing the centralization and consolidation of the state, France also engaged in a match for power, dominance, and hegemony with successive competitors on European fields and across new reaches of the globe. The Habsburgs of Austria and Spain were France's first indomitable enemy in this power struggle from the Italian Wars in 1503 to the Treaty of the Pyrenees in 1659.

France exited the Thirty Years' War in a position to claim Western European hegemony, but then a new rival, England, emerged. The increase of French power in Europe during the reign of Louis XIV (1639–1715) engendered opposition from rival Powers (the Habsburgs, the Netherlands, and England); but French ambitions had also turned to the Americas and West Indies and, there, England emerged as France's nemesis in what some see as a new Hundred Years' War during the long eighteenth century, culminating with the wars of the French Revolution and of Napoleon.

Despite France's front-rank status among continental European Powers, it suffered heavy defeats outside Europe;[4] yet it had the capacity to rebound and regain its strategic edge. Intervention in the American War of Independence to settle scores with England bankrupted the French monarchy, ushering in the Revolution. This new stage in France's political experiments introduced an era of even greater French ambition. The ideals of the French Revolution, considered to be universal, incited the *Grande Nation* to live up to this qualification, both literally and metaphorically. French revolutionary leaders, including Napoleon, dreamt to touch the destinies of the most far-flung human communities. Even after the end of the Napoleonic era, France remained a Great European Power, later acquiring the second-largest colonial empire in the world after Britain's. It met an even greater defeat than that of 1815 in 1870–71, before its newest rival, Germany. In the next war (1914–18) France could not achieve victory in a struggle that drained its forces. In 1940, Germany again so completely defeated France that this raised the question at the end of the Second World War of France's suitability to occupy the ranks of the victorious Powers, let alone those of the Great Powers. Yet France strove to retain that rank. Modern France has become a Republic, which has traded its earlier Christian-based messianic endeavors for a similarly ambitious vision of universal grandeur and leverage founded on the ideals of the Revolution of 1789.[5] These ambitions were all the more powerful in that they relied on memories, imprinted on the national consciousness and on the minds of successive French leaders up to the present and transmitted to later generations with the advent of a universal education system during the latter part of the Nineteenth Century. Georges Clemenceau, France's Premier during the First World War, aptly summed up this ambition in his victorious proclamation to the French Chamber of Deputies on 11 November 1918: 'France, yesterday the soldier of God, today the soldier of Humanity, will always be the soldier of the Ideal'.[6]

This notion illustrates France's ambitious aim, past and present, in managing to exert power on the international stage, to stand visibly in the front ranks of the Powers, as an actor and as an object of reference for other nations. This ambition remains true although France no longer has a colonial empire and is no longer one of the most populous or prosperous states. The primary political objective of France remains to make its views known and heard and, at best, adopted by others. The exercise of power matters, but influence is also seen as power. In the French understanding, 'influence' is what 'soft power' is to the United States. Power and influence are therefore the notions that the French historian, Maurice Vaïsse, used as the title for his recent study of France in the world since 1958.[7] That the French consider influence as a desirable objective, equal with the leverage provided by effective power, is not surprising: it is the result of the historical experience of making do in adverse conditions, such as overcoming the disasters suffered in 1871, 1914, and 1945 through a capacity to rebuild and renew the foundations of its power and influence. France's capacity to continue to do so today is perhaps an even more remarkable trait than the varying degrees of success which it has met. It pursues power and influence on the global stage, but it is increasingly doing so within the framework of an integrating Europe in which France has engaged herself since the early post-World War II years. The evolution of French political institutions since those years has played no small role in allowing France to exert its power to shape the international context rather than as a subordinate to more powerful forces and entities.

French political institutions matter in successfully meeting ambitious goals for international influence, leverage, and relevance. After 1870, the Republican regime's challenge was to provide inspiring international leadership to a democratic community more concerned with its own domestic security and prosperity. The two Bonapartist imperial experiments (in 1804–15 and 1852–70) fell through military defeat rather than from internal disaffection. The Third Republic (1870–1940) also met its end through a devastating collapse of its arms, invasion, and the occupation of the French territory. The Fourth Republic (1946–58) foundered on the shocks delivered by the protracted Algerian War of Independence. It was therefore the Fifth Republic's task, since the adoption of its constitution in 1958, to build on past lessons, provide the country with solid institutions and practices, reinforce the authority of its government, and improve its capacity to deliver in both the domestic and international fields. The first Fifth Republic President, General Charles de Gaulle, governed from 1958 to 1969, giving him ample time to set policy lines and practices that went some way towards achieving these goals.[8]

Nevertheless, some legacies of the Third and Fourth Republics are important to understand institutional traits of the Fifth and its international political practices. Most evident appears to be the fundamental role devolved to the Executive.

The Third Republic institutions were founded on three Constitutional Laws passed in 1875. Of these, the *Law On the Organization of Public Powers* and the *Law On Relations Between the Public Powers* had the most significant role.[9] The conservative majority of lawmakers in 1875 desired to balance parliamentary institutions with a head of state having the strong attributes of a monarch: a President holding a renewable seven-year term of office.[10] This President's long mandate allowed the overseeing of substantial policies, and the seven-year term became a tradition that persisted to the Fifth Republic until a five-year term was introduced in 2000.[11] The President's task as head of the administration and Commander-in-Chief of the armed forces was to oversee and execute the policy of the government, whose head, the *Président du Conseil*,[12] formed a Cabinet at presidential bidding. The President represented France abroad, appointed all civilian and military officers, as well as ambassadors, and received the accreditations of foreign envoys.[13] However, not being responsible before either of the two Chambers of the French Parliament (the Deputies and the Senators) the President's foreign policy actions were valid only when countersigned by the relevant Minister of Foreign Affairs,[14] who also accompanied the President on state visits abroad.[15] This did not prevent the President from negotiating and ratifying international treaties, which might be communicated to the Chambers 'as soon as the interest and safety of the State may allow'.[16] Declaring war, on the other hand, required a vote by both Chambers.[17] Reviewing these powers, John Keiger has characterized the presidential role as 'potentially powerful ... the President could effectively make foreign affairs his domain';[18] and, indeed, the political tradition of France has been to the present day to refer to foreign policy as belonging to a *domaine réservé* of the Head Of State. Yet the political practice of the Third and Fourth Republics did not see the president exercising such monarchial powers. These parliamentary regimes checked presidential power in practice by giving the essential initiative and implementation of foreign policy to the Cabinet through the Premier and Foreign Minister.[19] Despite the impediment of frequent ministerial crises, some able foreign ministers gave France considerable stature and importance in international politics: for instance, Théophile Delcassé and Aristide Briand under the Third Republic, and Robert Schuman under the Fourth. The unstable nature of French political life left considerable latitude to French ambassadors, as well as high-ranking military officers, to weigh on policy decisions affecting the country's international standing. Such a system, however, proved inefficient to prevent France falling into wars that wreaked havoc with its European and global ranking. To avoid their repetition, the constitution of 1958 consolidated executive presidential powers.[20]

As first President, de Gaulle displayed this reinforced role, setting an example in statecraft which has been unavoidable for all of his successors, even his one-time arch-rival François Mitterrand. As Vaïsse wrote: 'The successors of General de Gaulle have not only re-taken the style but also the contents of the foreign policy of the founder of the Fifth Republic ...'.[21] Three of the General's five presidential successors have had 'Gaullism' as their essential political reference and affiliation. Presidential powers defined in Title II of the Constitution (Articles 5 to 19) make the President the guarantor of national independence and of the application of France's international treaties (Article 5);[22] he appoints the Prime Minister and his Cabinet colleagues (Article 8), all civilian and military officers of State (Article 13), accredits French diplomats (Article 14) and, as head of the Armed Forces, presides over defense councils and committees (Article 15).[23] Article 16, granting the President the occasional assumption of emergency powers, specifies among the required conditions that France be 'prevented from executing its international obligations'.[24] The exercise of all other powers not specified by these articles requires the Prime Minister and the relevant minister to countersign presidential acts. One can see that the *domaine réservé* still belongs to political tradition rather than constitutional requirements. Indeed, the Government 'determines and conducts the policy of the Nation. It disposes of the administration and armed forces' (Article 21).[25] The prime minister 'directs the action of the Government. He is responsible for National Defense'; he may also appoint some civilian and military officers and delegate these tasks to ministers (Article 22).[26] This ensures strong executive primacy over France's external policy and the exercise of power abroad. The practice has been a tandem of President and Foreign Minister, the Prime Minister intervening only occasionally. Vaïsse observes: 'Under the Fifth Republic, foreign policy is defined at the Élysée'.[27] For Keiger, 'The Cabinet generally ratifies decisions taken in the Élysée';[28] and he further notes that in the first case of cohabitation between a President and a government of different parties in 1986–88, 'Jacques Chirac attempted to challenge presidential dominance ... under Mitterrand but was unsuccessful'.[29] Only instances of presidential weakness coming through illness have given Prime Ministers some possibility of leeway.[30] The much longer cohabitation of Jacques Chirac, now President, and Lionel Jospin in 1997–2002 also represented a different case, in which the Prime Minister had more time to shape policy; however, policy was still essentially conducted between Chirac and Foreign Minister Hubert Védrine, who had previous experience as Chief of Staff to President Mitterrand and mastered the workings of the President's office.[31]

De Gaulle's model has therefore persisted: a President who conceptualizes the main lines of France's international strategy towards the maximization of its power and influence. This direct role has been emphasized by the frequency of presidential trips abroad and attendance at multi-lateral summits, either at the G8, the European Council,[32] or the North Atlantic Treaty Organization (NATO) and the United Nations (UN). When de Gaulle assumed power, he benefitted from both past experience and prestige as leader of the Free French (1940–44) and then President of the Provisional Government (1944–46), and his capacity to formulate policy and make use of statecraft was unquestioned.

> The Man of 18 June had already entered history. ... His conception of the world was marked by pragmatism ... De Gaulle did not seek to overturn the constraints of geography and therefore always reasoned in a historical perspective. For him, the struggle of national interests constituted the foundation of international life. ... With an ambition for the greatness of France, General de Gaulle's foreign policy had two objectives: for France, [to achieve] national independence founded on a strong State with an adapted military instrument; abroad, to change the international status quo.[33]

De Gaulle retained the same Foreign Minister, Maurice Couve de Murville, a career diplomat, for a decade, unlike his successors (with the exception of President Nicolas Sarkozy), who have had three to five different Ministers on average during their terms. The General also set the pattern for taking foreign-policy decisions in close cooperation with his own staff, rather than the Foreign Ministry. Bernard Tricot, as Secretary-General of the Presidency, was a trusted adviser of the General during several international crises, whereas Jacques Foccart played a particular role as direct intermediary between the Head Of State and the governments of the newly independent African countries.[34] In particular, France's African policy has been determined mostly at the Élysée. From the origins of the G7 meetings, French presidents have also appointed their diplomatic advisers as 'sherpas' to prepare the summits with them. Mitterrand entrusted this to Jacques Attali,[35] and also appointed his son, Jean-Christophe, to head the 'African affairs cell' of the Presidency.[36] Like Mitterrand before him, Chirac also selected a career diplomat, Dominique de Villepin, as his Secretary-General as well as diplomatic adviser and, afterwards, appointed him Foreign Minister.[37] Sarkozy has both innovated and followed tradition in his appointments. His Secretary-General, Claude Guéant, a long-standing friend, has undertaken several diplomatic missions on the President's behalf, especially on the African continent, where he has considerable contacts. Sarkozy also selected as his diplomatic adviser an experienced diplomat, Jean-David Lévitte, who has been France's permanent UN representative and Ambassador to the United States. Lévitte has at times been styled the French equivalent of the American National Security Advisor, not least because of his direct Washington contacts.[38]

The possibility for French Foreign Ministers to formulate policy during the Fifth Republic has thus been limited; and the President and his advisors have planned policy and then put the Minister in charge of executing it when the President did not take a particular role, in particular in direct bilateral contact with his peers. Of the Fifth Republic's 19 Foreign Ministers, eight have been career diplomats and two former Secretary-Generals of the Élysée. Michel Barnier, a former member of the European Union (EU) Commission,[39] represented an interesting exception considering that French foreign policy is now fundamentally linked to the EU. Recent years have seen an important role played by the Secretary of State for European Affairs, the Foreign Minister's subordinate, in preparing the ever-frequent Councils of Ministers in Brussels. This post was especially strategic during France's latest presidency of the European Council in July– December 2008. Sarkozy had selected a civil servant from the Treasury for the position, Jean-Pierre Jouyet, who had close contacts in Germany. The tandem was seen to function well in a period of high visibility for France, which was credited with prompt reactions to the crisis ignited by the Russo-Georgian War of August 2008 and the outbreak of the financial crisis in September 2008.[40] However, one must recognize that the prominent role Sarkozy has taken, alongside his closest advisers, Guéant and Lévitte, as well as Jouyet, has meant that the foreign minister, Bernard Kouchner, an atypical choice for such a post,[41] has not had the influence over French decision-making that had been expected on his appointment.

The president's role as main formulator of policy and practitioner of international statecraft has therefore met little challenge from de Gaulle to Sarkozy. Parliamentary oversight of the executive's policy has tended to diminish in both the domestic and foreign fields. Sarkozy's recent constitutional reforms have aimed to rehabilitate these capacities. The current prime minister, François Fillon, declared following the adoption of the revision that 'the Parliament must be considered as an actor of our diplomacy';[42] but the political opposition remains skeptical that this has actually occurred, and foreign policy has continued to remain a somewhat marginal pre-occupation for parliamentarians. Some issues, such as French participation in NATO operations in Afghanistan or France's full reintegration into NATO, have been occasions for passionate debate. However, significantly, presidential decisions have not been altered or overturned by these discussions. De Gaulle's principal guidelines in foreign policy have had remarkable longevity given that they were formulated nearly fifty years ago. Vaïsse has identified eight principal areas in which the policy rules set by de Gaulle have been generally followed by his successors: European integration, an independent-minded interpretation of the transatlantic alliance, overture to Eastern Europe, policy towards Africa, policy towards the Arab world, outreach towards the rest of the developing countries, multilateralism, and cultural diplomacy.

Europe is not only a policy choice made by France, but also a venue through which French power can be exercised.[43] The move towards European integration was made by Schuman and the governments of the Fourth Republic, in line with the recommendation formulated by Winston Churchill in his Zurich Speech of 1946, and following the integrationist logic of the Marshall Plan after 1947. Despite de Gaulle's reservations towards the supranational ambitions of the European Economic Community (EEC) (the first expression of integration) the Fifth Republic further deepened its commitment on condition that intergovernmental institutions allowed France to play a visible, leading role. De Gaulle forcefully imposed this role on the other five partner states of the EEC during the 'Empty Chair Crisis' of 1965, in which he effectively boycotted the Brussels institutions. He also imposed, through two rejections of British membership applications, a generally grudging and conditional French acceptance of EEC and later EU enlargement.[44] French influence was also decisive and sufficiently strong in keeping EEC policy overly focused on the Common Agricultural Policy, which remains to this day the most important segment of the EU budget despite the considerable diversification of EU policies since the 1980s.

This particular guideline did not prevent the General's successors from playing their own original part in the setting of new courses for Europe. With the German Chancellor Helmut Schmidt, President Valéry Giscard d'Estaing gave pioneering impulse to European monetary cooperation with the European Monetary System of 1979, which later made the European Monetary Union possible. Mitterrand carried on this cooperative track with Schmidt's successor, Helmut Kohl. However, Mitterrand and the man he brought to the presidency of the European Commission, Jacques Delors, also played a decisive role in the formulation of further political integration through the Single European Act and the Treaty of Maastricht. If a sufficient number of France's European partners were convinced to adopt this step forward into integration, the French population, when consulted, showed considerable reluctance to ratify the Treaty on European Union: only 50.9% voted in favor. This vote split French political parties and pre-figured French voter rejection of the Constitutional Treaty in 2005, despite the prominent role played by French leaders in its drafting.[45] Enlargement had also somewhat diluted French influence in EU policy-making and has been the occasion for renewed complaints, often expressed by the French President himself, towards admission of new member-states. The French presidency of the Council in 2008 may have been successful,[46] but it was the last projected for several decades. The Treaty of Lisbon has since brought in a new President of the European Council, elected for a two-and-a-half year term, a post that, tellingly, France did not seek. Paris has considered it of greater strategic importance to maintain one of its own at the direction of the European Central Bank and as Single Market Commissioner. Concerning the position of EU High Representative in charge of the Common Foreign and Security Policy, France did not seek the post but helped win it for its preferred candidate, from Britain.[47] It has also placed a French diplomat as Secretary-General for the new European External Action Service.[48] The president of the EU Military Committee is the former French Armed Forces Chief of Staff, General Henri Bentégeat.

An autonomous European defense policy is also an area in which France sought to exert greater influence in Europe and beyond. Although the concept was anathema to de Gaulle, who opposed the European Defense Community planned in the 1950s, building a purely European defense establishment has been consistently and vocally backed by French Presidents since Mitterrand. He took initiatives alongside Germany for creating integrated military units as well as setting up a political – military chain of command within EU institutions. However, French ambitions ran afoul of more Atlanticist EU members, revealing a difficult truth of the post-Cold War period: France's long estrangement from NATO, decided by de Gaulle in 1966 as he sought to impose the existence of an independent French nuclear deterrent, also contributed to creating (despite French professions of loyalty to the Atlantic alliance) an atmosphere of mistrust of French intentions when defense policy was discussed among Europeans. Yet the first Gulf War in 1991 revealed the inadequacy of French military capabilities, according to the model posed by de Gaulle after the Algerian War and relying on nuclear deterrence as well as aloofness from NATO structures. This defect was further verified in Bosnia. Determined to carry out a restructuring of French defense, Chirac decided to end conscription in 1996 and attempted to negotiate a tailored reintegration of France into NATO; but this policy failed when the French negotiators insisted on obtaining NATO's Mediterranean command, which the United States would not consider.[49] France then had to overcome British objections towards reinforcing Europe's Common Defense Identity, but it succeeded in doing so only when dealing with a Europhile British Prime Minister, Tony Blair, at the bilateral summit of Saint-Malo in 1998.

At least France does possess a consequent military to speak authoritatively in favor of integrated European defense capabilities. The end of conscription has shrunk the forces to 240,995, which still possess both air- and sea-launched nuclear capabilities and a proven record in overseas interventions, valuable lessons learnt in UN peace-keeping operations as well as a growing number of EU operations in which France has played a leading role.[50] Although defense of national territory remains an important commitment, French armed forces are openly seen as an instrument for external force or influence projection. The five stated missions of the forces are to know and anticipate, to prevent, to deter, to protect, to intervene.[51] In prevention and intervention, the external character of this mission is explicit:

> Placing forces in proximity to seats of tension allows confidence to emerge with local populations … prevention strategy relies on multiple means: diplomatic, economic, military, legal and cultural, associated in coordinated fashion and undertaken on national, European and international scale. …
>
> Intervention remains an essential means of action of the armed forces, especially outside the national territory. The capacity to intervene guarantees our strategic interests and our international responsibilities. Most often, intervention will take place in a multinational cadre. …[52]

This role also includes rescue missions and the capacity of the French military to assist in disaster relief (most recently in Haiti) albeit at the cost of some verbal sparring by some French officials and journalists dismayed by the size of the American military deployment to the ravaged island.[53] If France therefore has some significant military capabilities, it has had to recognize that it can hardly use them on its own; hence the importance given to cooperation with NATO allies and EU partners. Little popular enthusiasm exists for foreign expeditions, despite the apparent public sympathy with the concepts of humanitarian intervention developed by Kouchner and others over the past twenty years. French public opinion was so startled by the loss of ten paratroopers in Afghanistan in August 2008, shortly after Sarkozy decided to reinforce the French contingent with the International Security Assistance Force, that over two-thirds of people polled favored an immediate withdrawal. The president then pointedly referred, in his public eulogy for the fallen, to the responsibility he felt as Commander-in-Chief, as well as to that of the country as a Permanent Member of the UN Security Council. The public have seen more reinforcements head for Afghanistan with resignation, but Sarkozy has successfully resisted calls by the Barack Obama Administration for a larger commitment beyond the 3,700 troops France has sent. One might note there are still over 10,000 troops stationed on the African continent, for the most part under the terms of mutual defense agreements signed soon after independence. Although a review of these deployments had been part of Sarkozy's electoral platform in 2007, this reassessment has not fully occurred, and France's African policy is believed to have continued in the mode practiced by previous presidents.[54] Mitterrand took responsibility for intervening in Rwanda from 1990 on the side of the Hutu majority government against rebel forces of the Rwanda Patriotic Front, an alignment that later gave rise to accusations of French complicity in the genocide of 1994.[55] As a result, on Villepin's advice, Chirac quickly intervened in the Ivory Coast in 2003 and, if large-scale civil war was averted and France managed to coordinate its initially unilateral operation with the UN and African Union, the Ivorian conflict has not in itself been solved. French influence over this once very close African ally has receded, and large numbers of French expatriates have had to flee.[56]

The use of the military has therefore prompted an intense debate. The defense expert, Louis Gautier, observed that since de Gaulle, defense policy had been as constant as the foreign-policy doctrine.[57] A first White Paper on defense was published in 1974, confirming the guidelines set by the General. The next one came only in 1994, a result of the disillusions of the first Gulf War. But while conceding some necessary post-Cold War adaptations, it did not advocate a radical overhaul and, more importantly, did not generate greater funding; defense expenditure shrank along with that of all France's European partners. However, in 2008, a most comprehensive review took place to produce a White Paper on Defense[58] almost simultaneously with a White Paper on foreign policy.[59] The former document reaffirmed that French efforts to be a major global player would continue, because 'its perceptions, capabilities and mediations are much in demand'.[60] The latter formulated twelve recommendations to upgrade the efficiency of French external action through better coordination of concerned ministries and agencies.

Requested by Sarkozy, these two White Papers mark an effort to replace the French exercise of power in a world undergoing deep change, for which the rhetoric inspired by de Gaulle as well as guidelines set in the 1960s are no longer sufficient. In foreign policy, the pace of European integration, defense, trans-Atlantic relations, and policy towards the developing world that now includes real emerging Powers, France has appeared out of step several times since the 1990s. It has evoked the notion of multipolarity in opposition to the United States' contention that it might exercise a lone, if benevolent hegemony.[61] Yet France is hard pressed to retain the means of being one of these alternate poles or to inspire the EU to become one. In the 1970s, Giscard d'Estaing ruefully admitted: 'France is a medium-sized power'. Since then, it has not lost the will to act beyond this constraining status, but the White Paper debates, as much as the original 'rupture' agenda on which Sarkozy ran for President, have revealed doubts that France's traditional means remain up to the task.[62] France maintains the second-largest diplomatic network in the world, with some originality: development aid is now solely within the Foreign Ministry's remit, whilst it also supports considerable infrastructure to promote cultural and educational activities to boost French influence.[63] Efforts to promote the use of the French language in international organizations also fall under this defensive strategy.[64] Placing French officials at key posts in major multilateral organizations, like the International Monetary Fund, the World Trade Organization, the European Central Bank, and the European Bank for Reconstruction and Development may not be an option in the future as emerging Powers demand and obtain their share of postings. Most of all, France's diminished demographic and economic standing that is projected within the next decades will put greater strain on its strategy of being seen and heard.[65] This older Power stands at a crossroads where it cannot yet be certain that its European ambitions will succeed in allowing it to continue to wield its influence indirectly, or whether it will find other ways and other leaders who may carry French voices across the international stage with powerful effect.

Notes

1 All translations from the French are by the author.
2 J. Dufourcq, 'Intérêts stratégiques français', *Revue Défense Nationale*, n° 726(2010), 9.
3 Against authorities claiming higher rank, such as the Holy Roman Emperor or the Papacy. See J.-C. Allain, F. Autrand, L. Bély, P. Contamine, P. Guillen, T. Lentz, G.-H. Soutou, L. Theis, M. Vaïsse, *Histoire de la Diplomatie française* (Paris, 2005). Quotations for this chapter come from the pocket edition in two volumes, namely from volume II, *De 1815 à nos jours*, Perrin, Paris: 2007. See also P. Renouvin, ed., *Histoire des relations internationales*, 3 volumes (Paris, 1953–55 [new edition 1994]).
4 The 1763 Treaty of Paris marking the loss of nearly all the American and Indian colonies was a particular low point. Allain *et al.*, *Histoire de la diplomatie française*, 377.
5 This has domestic implications as well. Jean Dufourcq noted that the basis for French internal security in today's globalised world, 'rests fundamentally on the vigor of a national identity slowly fashioned over a millennium, on a Christian basis first, then a republican and secular one, and multiple [factors] today'. Dufourcq, *'Intérêts stratégiques*, 9.
6 Jean-Baptiste Duroselle, *Clemenceau* (Paris, 1988), 719.
7 Maurice Vaïsse, *La Puissance ou l'Influence? La France dans le monde depuis 1958* (Paris, 2009). This is also the title of Professor Vaïsse's contribution to Allain *et al.*, *Histoire de la diplomatie française*.
8 de Gaulle was followed in office by Georges Pompidou (1969–74), Valéry Giscard d'Estaing (1974–81), François Mitterrand (1981–95), Jacques Chirac (1995–2007), and Nicolas Sarkozy (since 2007).
9 "Loi du 25 février 1875" and "Loi constitutionnelle du 16 juillet 1875", both in *Les constitutions de la France de la Révolution à la IVème République* (Paris, 2009), 292–93, 296–99.
10 'Loi du 25 février 1875', Article 2.
11 The Presidential term is currently five years, renewable once. *Constitution de la République française, texte intégral de la Constitution de la Vème République à jour des dernières révisions constitutionnelles* (Paris, 2010).
12 The 'President of the Council of Ministers' was in effect an *ad hoc* prime minister. The lengthy title of the Third and Fourth Republic official is often abridged to 'Premier' by anglophone writers on French history and politics.
13 'Loi du 25 février 1875', Article 3.
14 Ibid.
15 This became more frequent at the beginning of the 1900s. Serge Berstein, *Chef de l'État. L'histoire vivante de 22 présidents à l'épreuve du pouvoir* (Paris, 2002), 79–94.
16 'Loi constitutionnelle du 16 juillet 1875', article 8. 'Treaties of peace, of commerce, engaging the State's finances, affecting the person and property of French people abroad' required a confirmation vote by both Chambers.
17 Article 9, Ibid.
18 J.F.V. Keiger, *France and the World since 1870* (London, 2001), 41–42.
19 In the absence of an official Prime Minister's Office and Services until 1934, most Premiers had to combine their position with an ordinary portfolio, often that of the Interior, which gave them control over the central administration of the French State. Some exceptionally chose to govern with the portfolio of Foreign Affairs, especially at critical times of international tension. Ibid., 44–46.
20 Ibid., 43.
21 Vaïsse, *La Puissance*, 20.
22 Vaïsse quotes another scholar, Marie-Christine Kessler, who asserts that Article 5 of the Constitution 'was authored by General de Gaulle himself'. M.-C. Kessler, *La politique étrangère de la France* (Paris, 1999), 25, in Vaïsse, *La Puissance*, 17n1.
23 *Constitution de la République française.*
24 Ibid.
25 Ibid.
26 Ibid.
27 Vaïsse, *La Puissance*, 16.
28 Keiger, *France*, 45.
29 Ibid.
30 In 1973–74 when President Pompidou was dying of an undisclosed condition, he had a loyal Prime Minister belonging to the same party, but in 1994 at the time of the Rwandan genocide, President Mitterrand's cancer had considerably weakened him. However, the cohabitation Prime Minister, Édouard Balladur, had been Pompidou's Chief of Staff during his agony and elected not

to take advantage of the situation. However, it did give the then Foreign Minister, Alain Juppé, occasion for more initiatives in the Rwandan and Bosnian crises. See M. Vaïsse, 'Alain Juppé', in L. Bély, G.-H. Soutou, L. Theis, M. Vaïsse, eds., *Dictionnaire des Ministres des Affaires étrangères 1589–2004* (Paris, 2005), 612–15.

31 Robert Frank, 'Hubert Védrine' in Bély *et al., Dictionnaire*, 618–24. As Foreign Minister, Védrine coined the term 'hyperpower' to qualify the United States' unchallenged geopolitical position of the 1990s, but he failed to anticipate that the adjective 'hyper' might be construed pejoratively rather than the intended comparative.

32 The original G5 Forum was created by President Giscard d'Estaing, and the European Council; although not mentioned in original European Treaties, it has also been strongly supported by successive French Presidents.

33 Vaïsse, *La Puissance*, 17–18.

34 Ibid., 18.

35 And, later, to Anne Lauvergeon. Vaïsse, *La Puissance*, 26.

36 Ibid., 27.

37 Samy Cohen, 'Dominique de Villepin' in Bély *et al., Dictionnaire*, 624–61. Also Vaïsse, *La Puissance*, 29–32. Villepin's most famous moment was his forceful speech in the UN Security Council rebutting the American case for the invasion of Iraq in 2003, rhetoric so inspiring that contrary to procedure, it was met by a most unusual round of applause by the other delegations.

38 Among whom, most of all, were the National Security Advisors to Presidents Bush and Obama: Stephen Hadley and James Jones. However, his main task appears confined to foreign policy more than national security.

39 To which he was reappointed in 2010. The French government battled for him to be awarded the strategic portfolio of the Single Market, in charge of defending the future regulation of financial markets. See Vaïsse, *La Puissance*, 40–41.

40 See Jouyet's memoir, J.-P. Jouyet and S. Coignard, *Une présidence de crise: les six mois qui ont bousculé l'Europe* (Paris, 2009). Also on this topic, Florence Autret, *Sarkozy à Bruxelles* (Paris, 2008).

41 Like Jouyet, Kouchner had been a member of the opposition Socialist Party and served as a minister under Mitterrand: Under-Secretary for Humanitarian Aid, with prominent roles during the Somalia relief operations and the Bosnian civil war in 1992. He has also been head of the UN Provisional administration for Kosovo. However, he is best known as the founder of *Médicins sans Frontières* (Doctors without Borders) and a frequent advocate for the *droit d'ingérence*, international intervention on humanitarian grounds regardless of a state's sovereignty rights.

42 Speech of 28 August 2008; 30 August 2008, *Le Monde*: quoted in Vaïsse, *La Puissance*, 17.

43 Vaïsse, *La Puissance*, 94–95. See also C. Lequesne, *La France dans la nouvelle Europe* (Paris, 2008).

44 L. Binet, 'Supporting Europe and Voting No?', and D.J. Howard 'Using Europe to Keep the World at Bay: French Policy on EU Economic Governance', in M. Maclean and J. Szarka, eds., *France on the World Stage. Nation State Strategies in the Global Era* (Basingstoke, 2008).

45 L. Binet, 'Supporting Europe', N. Startin, 'The French Rejection of the 2005 EU Constitution in a Global Context: A Public Opinion Perspective', in Maclean and Szarka, *France*, 91–110.

46 An important role was played by the French Permanent Representative to the EU, Pierre Sellal, who served an unusually long term in Brussels (2002–9). Sellal is now Secretary-General of the French Foreign Ministry.

47 France's preferred candidate was the then British Foreign Secretary, David Miliband, but the post went to outgoing EU Commissioner for External Trade, Catherine Ashton.

48 Pierre Vimont, previously Ambassador to the United States, appointed in October 2010.

49 On this subject, see Charles Cogan, *French Negotiating Behavior. Dealing with la Grande Nation* (Washington DC, 2003). This is a rare book on French foreign policy-making by a foreigner, which has been translated into French. Charles Cogan (with Nicolas Roussellier and Hubert Védrine), *Diplomatie à la française* (Paris, 2008).

50 The first two operations in 2003 were 'CONCORDIA' in the former Yugoslav Republic of Macedonia in 2003, and 'ARTEMIS', a limited policing operation in the Democratic Republic of Congo. France acted as 'core nation' for this operation alongside Germany and smaller observer teams from the rest of the EU states.

51 French Ministry of Defense website: www.defense.gouv.fr

52 Ibid.

53 The disgruntled comments equating the American relief mission to an occupation were made by the French Under-Secretary for Development Aid, Alain Joyandet. This led to a prompt statement by the Élysée that such views did not reflect those of the French Government. For French press coverage of this incident, see for instance coverage by France 24: www.france24.com/en/20100120-france-seeks-dispel-tensions-with-us.

54 Y. Gounin, *La France en Afrique. Le combat des Anciens contre les Modernes* (Brussels, 2009), 69–85.

55 Ibid., 45–47.

56 Ibid., 61–68.

57 Gautier was defense adviser to Prime Minister Lionel Jospin. Louis Gautier, *La défense de la France après la Guerre froide* (Paris, 2009).

58 Gouvernement de France, *Livre Blanc sur la Défense et la Sécurité nationale* (Paris, 2008); and idem., *Défense et Sécurité nationale. Livre Blanc. Les Débats* (Paris, 2008). With some originality on the part of the French Government, a translation in English has been published as *The French White Paper on Defence and National Security* (New York, 2008).

59 Alain Juppé and Louis Schweitzer, eds., *La France et l'Europe dans le monde. Livre blanc sur la politique étrangère et européenne de la France 2008–2020* (Paris, 2008).

60 *French White Paper on Defense*, 299.

61 The rhetoric promoting multipolarity was used frequently during the Franco-American rift over Iraq. Attempts at *rapprochement* began with the obvious weakening of the United States after it failed to reach its objectives in its Middle Eastern campaigns.

62 The question is highlighted by some recent essays by scholars, including F. Charillon, *La France peut-elle encore agir sur le monde? Éléments de réponse* (Paris, 2010). See Maclean and Szarka, *France*, especially M. Maclean and J. Szarka, 'Globalization and the Nation State: Conceptual Lenses on French Ambitions in a Changing World Order', 1–19, and Albrecht Sonntag, 'The Burdensome Heritage of Prestige Politics', 77–90, which are illuminating.

63 France has 162 Embassies and 235 Consular posts, staffed by 16,000 personnel. Its Foreign Ministry also supports a network of 147 cultural centres in 89 countries, 228 *Alliance Française* institutes, and 461 schools. Yet the Foreign Ministry's budget represents only 1 per cent of France's state expenses.

64 In 2006, French was still the second language in the UN and EU, used by 14 per cent and 30 per cent of delegates, respectively.

65 Since the crisis of the Eurozone in spring 2010, the French Government has become acutely aware of the possibility that its sovereign credit may be degraded by ratings agencies, after years of accumulated deficits. Economies have already led Alain Juppé and Hubert Védrine to express in a joint open letter the fear that France's external action may no longer be possible under such circumstances. Yet the 2011 budget presented on 29 September 2010 is one of further expected cutbacks, because the Foreign Ministry has not been explicitly sheltered from them according to previous statements from the French Government.

8

German foreign policy mirrored in the achievements and shortcomings of its chancellors

Christian Hacke

When looking back on more than sixty years of German foreign policy, it seems to be a remarkable success both in the context of German history and in international comparison: from the collapse of the Third Reich to the powerless occupied Germany to a partner integrated in the Western community of democracies and, finally, to the reunited European Power. These significant steps since 1945 did not occur solely as a result of deliberate political decisions but came into being gradually as the result of a specific constellation in world politics, as the product of the Second World War and the Cold War. Germany's evolution progressed in an uneasy mix of the old territorial-geostrategic mode of international relations, a new military-strategic mode shaped by nuclear weapons, and a modern economic-interdependent mode that seemed impervious to considerations either of territory or the nuclear balance[1].

No German politician would have been able to pursue an autonomous policy in defeated, divided, and occupied Germany after 1945. This limited political responsibility was assumed by the older generation who had supported the Weimar Republic and had lived in silent opposition or been members of the resistance movements after the rise of the National Socialist regime in 1933. Yet moral credibility (a term that today is well worn beyond recognition) still had a significance in 1945 that caused emotions for German leaders like Kurt Schumacher, chairman of the Social Democratic Party (SDP), Konrad Adenauer, the leading Christian Democratic Union (CDU) politician, and Jakob Kaiser, the founder of the Berlin CDU.

How did they perceive and react to the new constellation of power at the beginning of the Cold War? Schumacher was too socialist, too nationalistic, and too uncompromising to be successful. Kaiser was overly committed to a neutral, reunited Germany, which put him at odds with the new realities and with his party leader, Adenauer.[2] Consequently the former mayor of Cologne was the only one who recognised early on the new dynamics of the Cold War and drew realistic conclusions. Adenauer saw no alternative to the rising partition of Germany and Europe. Therefore Germans had neither the power nor the legitimacy to conduct their own foreign policy. Thus when Adenauer became Chancellor of the newly formed Federal Republic of Germany in 1949 (a post he held till 1963), he was not a sovereign politician but the representative of a less economically well-off and politically inferior state. He was forced to build up Germany's sovereignty and amplify its foreign-policy effectiveness step by step. Adenauer's primary foreign policy aim was to entrench that sovereignty and, with it, a legal and political base for German diplomacy. Between 1949 and 1955, when the United States and the Soviet Union struggled over a new European order, the competing alliances of the North Atlantic Treaty Organization (NATO) and the Warsaw Pact hardened the division of both Germany and Europe and drew the boundaries of the American and Soviet spheres of influence.

Adenauer became a key player for American interests in Europe. He used this new position shrewdly to enhance the interests of West Germany: looking for chances to assert its sovereignty. And he seized such chances by joining integrative organisations such as NATO and European Economic Community via, respectively, the Paris treaty of 1955 and the treaty of Rome of 1957. In this perspective, integration and equality became and remain the central precepts of the Federal Republic's Western policies. The creation of integrative Western European and Atlantic institutions accelerated the political and economic recovery of West Germany, provided institutions for controlling it, and, therefore, made the restoration of German sovereignty less risky for the western Powers. In this context the quest for security and the aim of political stability and economic recovery became mutually reinforcing.

By 1960 West Germany had achieved an astonishing economic revival and its political leverage had increased enormously. Whilst this success made West Germany the European centrepiece of the American global containment policy, Adenauer's policy of strength also accelerated Germany's partition. Consequently, the division of Germany and Europe became a major stabilising element in the Cold War outside Germany, but until the 1960s, it called for a revision of the political and legal inhibitions of Bonn's *Ostpolitik* (its approach to the Soviet Union and its Eastern European empire that centred on improving the possibility of German reunification). Increasing stability stood in the way of a dynamic approach to German unity. Even today, Adenauer's policy towards the western Powers remains a central feature of the Federal Republic's *raison d'état*, as does his ability to pursue a balancing policy: for instance, putting the European Union (EU) Powers under the obligation to act collectively in Europe's interests. As a result of Adenauer's prestige, Germany seemed to replace Britain in its traditional role as the arbiter of the European equilibrium, a role that both Superpowers watched in the following decades not without envy and slight mistrust. Adenauer's long-term dream of extending the European Economic Community (EEC) to all of Europe finally became a reality after the fall of the Soviet empire in 1989. From then on, his genuine aspiration, Europe balancing not only in the East–West context but on a global scale, came slowly but steadily into being.

In this perspective, Adenauer was a political revolutionary and visionary. He made the Federal Republic a part of the Atlantic civilisation and, at the same time, created the prerequisites for the unification of a free and democratic Germany within the framework of a reunited Europe on the basis of democracy, a market economy, and human rights. But Adenauer's inventive and revolutionary approach towards the West stood in stark contrast to his harsh and *status quo*-oriented policy towards Eastern Europe. Without any East–West *rapprochement*, West Germany could not hope to improve the chances for reunification.

From a foreign-policy perspective, Adenauer's successors, Ludwig Erhard (1965–66) and Kurt Georg Kiesinger (1966–69), were interim chancellors. Both were looking for new ways in foreign policy, primarily in *Ostpolitik*, but the time was not yet ripe for change. Only when the Soviet Union signalled a new readiness for negotiations, could Chancellor Willi Brandt (1969–74) initiate his brand of *Ostpolitik*, which was more accommodating to the Soviet Union, East Germany (the German Democratic Republic [GDR]) and Poland. With his new *Ostpolitik*, Brandt made a distinctive and essential contribution to the development of a policy for the management of *détente*.[3] This policy combined continuity and change, pushing German foreign policy successfully in a new direction. A package of bilateral treaties with the Soviet Union, Poland, and the GDR were essential for the Berlin four-Power agreement of 1971, which ended East–West tensions over the city, and the Helsinki Accords of 1975, which stabilised Europe's borders. Brandt's *Ostpolitik* encased a dual strategy: a readiness for dialogue and cooperation with the Soviet Union and Eastern Europe whilst keeping a military balance between NATO and the Warsaw Pact. *Ostpolitik* was closely connected with security issues; and by recognising territorial realities, Brandt developed a constructive attitude towards arms control and adjusted Bonn's policy to the dynamics of *détente*.

At the same time, *détente* sharpened and reflected a central paradox: whilst the Germans perceived *détente* as a prerequisite to overcome the division of Germany and Europe, for the Soviets it became a central element to solidify their imperial status in Europe. These treaties can be interpreted as expressions of conflict control. They did not solve fundamental problems, like the German question; they merely isolated them in discreet diplomatic capsules. In the course of the revolutionary developments of 1989–90, these capsules finally burst open and made the treaties obsolete.[4] But the growing prestige and strength that evolved worldwide out of the new Ostpolitik energised all aspects of German foreign policy. It enlarged Bonn's role in the Third World, in international organisations, and, most of all, in the United Nations. Also the translation of West Germany's economic power into political and moral leverage was significantly assisted by the new *Ostpolitik*.

Brandt led a coalition government composed of the SPD and the liberal Free Democrats (FDP). In 1974, when Brandt resigned over the discovery that his personal assistant was an East German spy, *Ostpolitik*'s dynamics had become irreversible and would not be altered fundamentally by his successors, Helmut Schmidt (1974–82) and Helmut Kohl (1982–98). Led by Schmidt as Chancellor and Hans Dietrich Genscher as Foreign Minister, the continuing SPD–FDP coalition faced new challenges in the West. Problems were aggravated by Washington's failure to keep the dollar strong in international markets and its pressing Germany into assuming a new role as economic locomotive. But Schmidt as well as Kohl was unwilling to finance American overconsumption at Germany's cost. Schmidt took a tough stand against President Jimmy Carter in almost all issues, which ranged from defence strategy to human rights and *détente*. Schmidt consequently opposed all Carter's efforts to presume leadership by declaring: 'the leadership role can be assumed only by the United States; however, they are not prepared to lead. Instead, isolationist, American-centred, hegemonic and internationalist tendencies struggle for supremacy.'[5]

Personal animosities between Carter and Schmidt deepened political problems that significantly eroded the German–American partnership. Consequently, Schmidt intensified European ties and sought a closer Franco-German partnership in which President Valéry Giscard d'Estaing became his favoured partner and personal friend. Both invented the G5 summit to limit American influence not only in economic terms; and they moved towards a major new initiative, a European Monetary Union, to coordinate more closely the currencies and economics of the EEC. Their purpose was a regional effort at creating a new monetary order as a practical step toward a more self-assertive Europe.

For Schmidt, who had become increasingly sceptical about the United States, in general, and Carter, in particular, the Euro-strategic balance became a test of alliance management. In this sense, NATO's Double Track decision of 1979 became essential: mutually limiting medium-range and intermediate-range ballistic missiles with the Warsaw Pact in combination with the threat that in the event of disagreement, NATO would deploy more middle-range nuclear weapons in Western Europe. Schmidt had outlined the basic problems in a famous speech in 1977 in London.[6] He represented a new self-confident Germany. He warded off economic dangers and protected the Republic's *Ostpolitik* flank against any confrontation of the Superpowers. Schmidt mastered world politics but, in the matter of the NATO dual-track decision, his own party did not follow him.

The change of government in October 1982 (a CDU/Christian Social Union [CSU]–FDP coalition) and the confirmation of Helmut Kohl as the new Chancellor by elections in March

1983 was the price the SPD paid for its lack of realism in security policy. Kohl and Genscher, still the Foreign Minister, reiterated their support for the double-track decision. The continuity of Ostpolitik had been a precondition for the FDP decision to join the new coalition with the CDU/ CSU. With regard to the Americans, Kohl was determined to create a more harmonious diplomatic climate. But Ronald Reagan's Strategic Defence Initiative, his harsh Cold War rhetoric, and American disarray on strategic matters and lack of interest in arms control profoundly disquieted the German Government, especially Genscher, who kept a low profile. Nonetheless the Kohl Government was successful in consolidating the West German–American relationship.

From 1986 to 1989, Mikhail Gorbachev, the new Soviet leader's, *glasnost* and *perestroika* favoured conditions for Germany's *Ostpolitik*. Gorbachev indirectly and unintentionally expanded the scope of action of the Federal Republic whilst putting the GDR leadership under pressure to reform. Even before the revolutionary changes of 1989, the Kohl–Genscher Government had set new standards for *détente* and arms control and hastened Western European integration. And before November 1980, the Federal Republic had grown into *the* European Central Power,[7] but against its will. German reunification in 1990 did not initiate this process; it seemed only to accelerate it. From 1949 to 1989, West Germany's foreign policy was built on cooperation instead of war, on the pursuit of wealth rather than military power, on a quest for integration through transfer of sovereignty instead of a vain search for autonomy. And Germany projected the rules of this system onto relations with other states in Europe and the world whilst openly rejecting the past anti-West German *Sonderweg*.[8] Thus, pacifism, democracy, and respect for human rights emerged as powerful core values expressed in the attitudes of an idealistic civilian power towards world politics.

The unification diplomacy of the Kohl–Genscher Government was a masterstroke achieved with the strong assistance of the United States. London and Paris followed hesitantly as the collapsing Soviet Empire had to give away its western outpost of the GDR: 'the irony is that the Cold War could not have ended and Germany could not have been unified without the Soviet Union's renunciation of conflict and class struggle in Europe.'[9]

German unification, the end of the Cold War, and the demise of the Soviet Empire represented monumental shifts. Germany became once again Europe's largest country. In theory, Germany was free to return to its old role of one of Europe's Great Powers. But this development might have reignited fears of a resurgent German problem as a geopolitical challenge because of the new and growing imbalance within the European system and the assumed assertiveness of a new post-war generation less constrained by the Nazi legacy. However, the reunited country showed no desire to depart from its post-war foreign-policy traditions and, wedded to the primacy of civilian political power, insisted strongly on continuity in its integration. To dispel anxiety about a potentially more powerful Germany, Kohl reaffirmed Germany's commitment to multi-lateralism, to the EU, and his aversion to military force. Enlargement of NATO was promoted by his government in this sense, but also because it was critical for German security that stability was created in Central and Eastern Europe for the new democracies.

Enlargement seemed to diminish tendencies for further destabilisation or renationalisation in Central Europe, as the historic German fear of isolation was replaced by a revolutionary new situation. For the first time, Germany was surrounded by allies and friends. And by moving NATO farther east, Germany has become the geopolitical centre of the alliance whilst, at the same time, Berlin views itself as the door for the membership aspirations of new European democracies with regard to the EU. Promoting unified Germany as the advocate for Eastern European integration put the Kohl Government side by side with Washington, but with some 'soft-Power' advantages: Germany's economic presence in Eastern Europe exceeds that of any other Western Power; Germany is now the leading Western economic Power in the region, a fact that adds to regional stability. Kohl also believed that EU eastward enlargement would serve German and European interests by fostering democracy and social improvement. And despite its post-war hesitancy to employ military power outside the narrow compass of NATO Europe, Germany began to enhance its military role in a multilateral context and within a pronounced civilian power paradigm.[10]

Perhaps the most profound change since the end of the Cold War is Germany's deployment of troops outside Europe for the first time since the Second World War. Germans never believed that they would be called to intervene militarily in extra-European conflicts. Living safely under the American security umbrella for decades had not made them more aware of threats or more willing to increase their readiness to meet them. Consequently, in the early 1990s, public opposition and constitutional constraints prevented Germany from offering more than financial support to combat and peacekeeping efforts in the Persian Gulf and the Balkans. But after 1994, a Constitutional Court ruling enabled the Kohl Government to deploy troops abroad. The country has since then participated in a number of UN- and NATO-sanctioned combat, peace-keeping, reconstruction, and stabilising missions. Today, over 7000 *Bundeswehr* soldiers are deployed in missions ranging from Afghanistan (International Security Assistance Force [ISAF]) to the UN mission in Lebanon. As a consequence of Europe's failure to respond quickly and forcefully to the Balkans conflicts during the mid-1990s, Kohl's Government was also a strong supporter of a European Security and Defense Policy as a means to pool defense resources. However, since then there exists a widening gap between Germany's institutional commitments and its defense posture. Budget allocations in defense have decreased by 30 to 40 percent since the late 1980s.

An SPD government under Chancellor Gerhard Schröder, with Joschka Fischer as Foreign Minister, took office in October 1998. In coming to power, it faced the challenge of the first German combat mission since 1945: NATO's air campaign to prevent ethnic cleansing in Kosovo. Against strong domestic opposition, Schröder and Fischer argued that German history did not hinder, it obligated Germany to intervene militarily in Kosovo to stop atrocities similar to those perpetrated by Germany during World War II. 'Auschwitz' became the unwarranted synonym for exaggerations of German power, this time in a moral sense. Without a UN mandate, Schröder's Government implicitly accepted the principle of limited sovereignty in this war.

As a response to 9/11, the Schröder Government again aided the United States and sent German forces to Afghanistan in support of Operation 'Enduring Freedom' because the Taliban regime had allowed al-Qaeda to attack a NATO ally. But Schröder's Government then strongly opposed the war in Iraq because the Bush Administration transformed the United States (not only in the eyes of Germans) from the world's favourite protector into its leading disturber of peace.[11] Both Bush and Schröder bear responsibility for the misunderstanding that emerged over Iraq. Schröder's categorical and preemptive 'No' to UN Security Council resolutions not only encouraged Saddam Hussein but were hardly an option for a country aspiring for a permanent seat there. His supposed 'German Way' in foreign policy (opposing the Iraq was indicative) and seeking a Paris–Berlin–Moscow axis in Europe represented a chain of missteps that weakened Germany's international role; in domestic elections, he gained by turning openly anti-American. All the shared values and interests that bound the United States and Germany could not prevent the astonishingly rapid deterioration of relations between nations that had been close allies for fifty years.

Schröder disarranged German foreign-policy coordinates; in fact he torpedoed three pillars of influence: Germany's image as a dependable American partner, its weight in the EU, and its role as honest-broker in the trans-Atlantic world. Most of all, the Iraq war showed that the German concept of civilian power crumbles when confronted with the determination of actors who do not shy away from the use of hard power. Today, the German political culture no longer gives any US government the benefit of doubt. At the beginning of the twenty-first century, it is less than clear whether the common strategic interests that remain can be shaped to give the German–American relationship a realistic basis.[12]

As a consequence, Schröder pursued close relations with Russia to counterbalance American influence in Europe. Since the end of the Cold War, Germany has consistently sought to ensure that Russia feels unthreatened by the EU and NATO enlargement. Germany is also Russia's largest trading partner, relying on Russia for close to 40 percent of its natural gas and 30 percent of its crude oil needs. German dependence on Russian energy resources and the pursuit of bilateral agreements by Schröder's Government to secure further energy supplies might threaten broader European energy security and undermine the West's ability to reach consensus on energy matters. Central and Eastern European countries also have been critical about the German–Russian gas pipeline agreement negotiated by Schröder. Russia's subsequent manipulation of oil and gas supplies is evidence of Moscow's ability to use its energy wealth to divide Europe and weaken the trans-Atlantic fabric.

No wonder that when Angela Merkel, the CDU leader, succeeded Schröder in November 2005 (becoming the first woman chancellor and heading a grand coalition including the SPD) she made a concerted effort to improve ties with Germany's eastern neighbours to reassure them that good relations with Russia are no threat to European unity or security. Negotiating a new EU–Russia Partnership and Cooperation Agreement was one of Merkel's primary goals during her EU presidency in 2007. However, she allowed negotiations to collapse when faced with strong Polish opposition and Russian intransigence.

Germany is likely to continue an increasingly tenuous middle path between Russia and the new European democracies. As Russia's most important political partner and largest gas customer, Germany is in many ways Russia's major Western interlocutor.[13] Since Brandt's *Ostpolitik*, the German–Russian relationship has become the defining feature of European politics. Since the 1970s, there has been a remarkable continuity in German *Ostpolitik* regardless of which party coalition holds power. This course is a product of geography, history, and, increasingly, mutual economic interests.

Whilst Schröder described Vladimir Putin, the Russian President, as a 'flawless democrat', Merkel's rhetoric is more restrained but her policies are similar. On the whole, Germany takes Russia's sensitivities and interests in account more than most of its neighbours (especially in the East), who remain for historical reasons highly suspicious and sceptical about Russia's behaviour. Germany's opposition to further NATO enlargement and her exclusively close ties in energy policy and low-key human-rights position regarding Russia are in contrast to the more critical attitude of many Europeans. Merkel also seeks to bolster German–American relations, but a new German–United States tandem mirroring that of the Cold War is unlikely to reemerge. Nevertheless, shared values, common interests, and economic interdependence still make the United States the most important ally of Germany and Europe. The financial and economic crisis after 2008, as well as reactions to terrorism, organised crime, climate change, and other crises show the need for close trans-Atlantic cooperation, a vital German–American relationship, and United States–European cooperation on the world stage.

But despite President Barack Obama's politics of reform, not only the United States but also Europe seem to be on the decline. Whilst the financial crises take a painful toll on the United States and many EU members, Germany seems to handle them more successfully. Compared with other Powers in the trans-Atlantic world, Germany's economy holds a relatively comfortable position. But Germany's most important foreign policy consideration, the EU, is in trouble. German unification opened the door to European unification through the eastward enlargement. Yet rapid enlargement to the east and south, new demands of globalisation, renationalisation, a paradox of overburdened but mostly ineffective military engagement, and a split into pro-Atlanticist and anti-American parts weakens the continent politically. European politics becomes less European and more national, whilst too many checks and balances in Brussels inhibit effective decisions. Therefore the EU might become a union in name only. Germany alone cannot keep the engine of integration running.

European participation in the wars in Iraq and Afghanistan has added to this weariness. German forces deployed in Asia would have been unthinkable in the pacifist Germany of twenty years ago. But in 1992 German soldiers were sent to Somalia for logistic support, in 1995 to Bosnia-Herzegovina, in 1999 in the first 'fighting humanitarian intervention' in Kosovo and, after the 9/11 attacks in Afghanistan, Germany's armed forces are participating more and more in military action. Whilst the United States and other NATO members engaging in heavy combat operations have put enormous pressure on the Merkel Government to provide more troops to join the fight and step up its overall engagement, the vast majority of Germans oppose *Bundeswehr* deployment vigorously.

German engagement in Afghanistan, a decade long in 2011, is longer than in either the First or Second World Wars, but the outlook for successful stabilisation darkens from day to day: what is at stake? What are the costs? How long will it take? What is the likelihood of success or failure? How many lives a year is Afghanistan worth? Is it really the mission of ISAF to see that Afghanistan will be free and democratic? And how is the assessment of the German engagement to be judged? Despite having the third-largest troop contingent in Afghanistan, the Merkel Government faces pointed criticism, particularly from Washington, for too many national caveats that prevent German soldiers from being deployed to Afghanistan's more dangerous regions.

But Iraq parallels Afghanistan. The United States seems to replace a rogue state that was successfully contained with a failed state that threatens to require indefinite occupation. No Western Power seems willing to agree to this perspective, especially Germany. Since 2009, the Merkel Government remains reluctant and hard pressed to justify increased German military engagement abroad to a persistently sceptical German public, even within a NATO or EU framework. It emphasises instead the importance of civilian components to multilateral peace-keeping. Negative trends in defense spending and the slow pace of defense reform highlight a regrettable discrepancy between articulated high goals and too little action to realise these aims.

It was Germany's fate till 1945 that without a democratic fabric at home, balanced national interests, and a liberal vision abroad, its foreign policy degenerated into racism, suppression, and war. And before 1933, Germany lacked a stable democratic tradition. But the Germans of the Federal Republic learnt their historic lessons and turned the country into a model of reconciliation, liberalism, and social welfare. In this context, what about the impact of the old GDR society today? Since unification, has there been a specific eastern German element on German foreign policy?

East Germans suffered more and longer from the consequences of the Second World War. The Soviets did not liberate but occupied and installed a brutal dictatorship. Soviet tanks against East German workers in summer 1953, violent squashing of the rebellion in Hungary 1956, the Wall in 1961, and the Soviet invasion of Prague in 1968 offer a totally opposite experience of ideas and reality than that of their West German neighbours. Torn between anticapitalist propaganda and West German television and radio, denied the freedom to travel, East Germans sought to validate world politics whilst being unable to see the world.

Antifascism created not only an ideological basis for the GDR Government's claims to power but served also as an argument for affiliation with the Soviet Union. In this context, East Germans accepted Soviet power as a historical consequence of Hitler and anti-Western arguments in the framework of socialist world view. Gorbachev fuelled these hopes for socialist reforms in domestic and foreign policy. For the first time since 1945, East Germans felt that they were on the right side of world politics, on the side with a better superpower because of a better leader; Reagan's anticommunist rhetoric was unpopular and his 'Tear down this wall' bombast seemed totally unrealistic.

Consequently in the collective consciousness of East Germans until today, the heroes of unification are still Kohl and Gorbachev. In a way, Gorbachev's downfall therefore was regretted by East Germans, as was America's rise to superficial imperial omnipotence. Therefore with East Germans as a whole having a 'leftist', more critical attitude towards NATO enlargement, the war on the Balkans, and Kosovo with German participation, they show more scepticism towards the EU. And they have more sympathy for Russian objections with regard to these questions. Consequently they look at the wars in Iraq and Afghanistan more doubtfully and refuse totally German military engagement and participation.

There exists a fundamental scepticism in East Germany toward NATO and anything military related, including the *Bundeswehr* and defense expenditures. A political party like the former Party of Democratic Socialism (today the Left Party, which is a *Volkspartei* in the East with 20 per cent of the vote) finds and creates much agreement when it calls for withdrawal of the *Bundeswehr* in Afghanistan, Germany's exit from NATO, the rejection of the Lisbon Treaty, or anti-American slogans. Especially in the east of Germany, President George W. Bush lost political capital during the 'war on terror'; Obama can hardly reset the clocks alone.

All the more important, eastern German politicians disagree with these views and take pro-Western positions like Merkel and others. So a specific eastern German interest in foreign policy at the federal level is difficult to recognise. But pronounced eastern German accents on German foreign and security policy are indirectly present. There is a specific eastern German sentiment in German foreign policy since unification. Not in day-to-day politics, but because eastern Germans can influence the party system and its foreign-policy agenda by vote in the federal elections. And in education, mass media, and elsewhere, there are a lot of chances to influence indirectly the fabric of society with ideas and interests that radiate a different voice than heard in the traditional foreign policy establishment of the old Bonn Republic. Whether this will lead to a new *Mitte* (a centre) in the Federal Republic and its foreign policy awaits to be seen.

Therefore, today, Germany as a member of NATO, EU, and the Organization for Security and Cooperation in Europe seeks as a primary objective cooperative relations with Moscow and, then, with Washington and Paris. But can it hold this delicate balance? These goals do not necessarily add up to a coherent whole: the French connection seldom fits with the Atlantic one, and the Central European option clashes with the Russian relationship as well as with the necessity of keeping a homogeneous EU for the purpose of deepening and widening. Germany's grand strategy of maximising options and minimising hard commitments is in reality not so grand as it sounds. 'Europeanist' initiatives have caused much unease in Washington, London, and other pro-Atlanticist capitals.

What is still missing at the beginning of the twenty-first century is a new global outlook in which a new balance is found between power and ethics, responsibility and interest, and amongst the nation's interests, regional integration, and global commitments. Germany's model as a civilian-controlled Power, a trading Power, the European locomotive of integration, and a pacemaker for *détente* have served the cause of an Atlantic civilisation for more than fifty years. For the first time in its history, unified Germany has become a part of the West, part of a great civilisation in which the heritage of the nineteenth century and cosmopolitan humanism is integrated. But now as global challenges have grown and authoritarian Powers are gaining more influence in world politics, more self-assertion is needed, not only for Germany, but for all the Powers that comprise Western civilisation. Such an approach is necessary to maintain their values, interests, and welfare (a more courageous geostrategic vision for the free world) of the Atlantic civilisation that is in high danger.

Notes

1 Wolfram Hanrieder, *Germany, America, Europe—Forty Years of German Foreign Policy* (New Haven, CT, 1989), xii.

2 Christian Hacke, *Die Außenpolitik der Bundesrepublik Deutschland—von Konrad Adenauer bis Gerhard Schröder* (Berlin 2003), 27ff.

3 Philip Windsor, *Germany and the Management of Detente* (London 1971), 202f.

4 Hacke, *Von Adenauer bis Schröder*, 188ff.

5 Helmut Schmidt, A Grand Strategy for the West (New Haven, CT, 1985), 50ff.

6 Helmut Schmidt, 'The 1977 Alastair Buchan Memorial Lecture', *Survival*, 20(1978), 2–10.

7 Hans Peter Schwarz, *Die Zentralmacht Europas. Deutschlands Rückkehr auf die Weltbühne* (Berlin, 1994).

8 '*Sonderweg*' ('special path') was a concept used by German conservatives in the late nineteenth century Wilhelmine period to explain Germany's 'superior' form of government: eschewing both tsarist autocracy and the ineffectual and decadent liberal democratic governance of Britain and France. A robust military and authoritarian state ensured enlightened rule, bringing rational reform from above instead of pandering to outlandish demands from below. After 1945, historiographical debate over the 'German catastrophe' saw scholarly examination of Germany's cultural, economic, intellectual, political, and social history to learn why democracy failed during the Weimar period (1919–33) and what produced National Socialism. Some historians concluded that Germany's failure to nurture stable democratic institutions before 1914 ensured the breakdown of the Weimar Republic. After 1945, *Sonderweg*'s affirmative connotations were replaced by negative ones. See Gérard Raulet, *Historismus*, Sonderweg *und dritte Wege* (Frankfurt am Main, 2001).

9 Philip Zelikow and Condoleezza Rice, *Germany Unified And Europe Transformed. A Study In Statecraft* (Cambridge, MA, 1995), 369.

10 Hanns Maull, ed., *Germany's Uncertain Power: Foreign Policy of the Berlin Republic* (New York, 2006).

11 David Calleo, *Follies of Power, America's Unipolar Fantasy* (Cambridge, UK, New York 2009), 13.

12 Stephen F. Szabo, *Parting Ways. The Crisis in German-American Relations* (Washington, DC, 2004), 140.

13 Angela Stent, 'Berlin's Russia Challenge,' *National Interest*, Number 46(2007): http://nationalinterest.org/tag/energy-in-russia.

9

Japan's diplomacy and culture

Alexander Bukh

Modern Japan's diplomacy started in 1853 with the arrival of Commodore Matthew Perry, who demanded opening of Japan to trade with the United States. This event triggered Japan's semi-forceful incorporation in 'European International Society'.[1] During the next nine decades, Japan transformed from a semi-colonial entity tied by the so-called 'unequal treaties' into a mighty empire capable of forcing other nations to signing unfavourable treaties (for example, the Treaty of Annexation with Korea signed in 1910; Korea became a colony within the Japanese Empire). At its peak, this empire ruled over territory stretching from Manchuria in the north to Papua New Guinea in the south. This period of Japan's status as one of the Great Powers ended with its defeat in the Second World War and its acceptance of unconditional surrender on 2 September 1945, on the USS *Missouri* anchored victoriously in Tokyo Bay. Defeat in the war against the United States and its allies resulted in the loss of all of the territories acquired after the enactment of the Meiji Constitution of 1890, and it left Japan in possession of only three of its initial colonies: Hokkaido in the north and, in the south, Okinawa and the Bonin Islands (*Ogasawara* in Japanese).[2] Seven years of total national mobilisation (Japan's war began in July 1937 with its invasion of China south of the Great Wall) combined with the Allied aerial attacks culminating in the atomic bombings of Hiroshima and Nagasaki exhausted the population. The acceptance of surrender on 15 August 1945 officially transformed Japan into an occupied nation governed by United States General Douglas MacArthur, the Supreme Commander of the Allied Powers.

However, the occupation ended in April 1952 after the Treaty of Peace with Japan signed in San Francisco on 8 September 1951 entered into force. The rapid economic growth of the next two decades propelled by United States military procurements during the Korean War (1950–53) transformed Japan from a defeated nation into the second largest economy of the 'free world'. This second makeover of Japan, similar to that of the second half of the nineteenth century, thus saw its revival as a Great Power; but this time Japan's strength came from trade and economic diplomacy (based on the economic 'miracle') rather than by territorial expansion. However, like in the previous century, Japan was viewed in the West with a mixture of admiration and fear.[3]

Despite its indisputable status as an economic superpower, Japan in terms of its foreign policy has been considered as an odd child among other Great Powers. The oddity of Japan's Cold War foreign policy seems to be self-evident: despite its economic prowess and unlike other Great Powers, Japan did not seek to secure or expand its interests through military means but remained largely withdrawn from international politics.[4] The main principle guiding Japan's post-war foreign policy has been the so-called 'Yoshida Doctrine', named after Yoshida Shigeru, Japan's prime-minister in 1946–47 and 1948–54, and a key participant in the process of shaping post-war Japan. Succinctly, Yoshida envisioned post-war Japan as a 'merchant nation', which meant a focus on the economy and reliance on the United States for defense against outside threats.[5] As such during the Cold War, Japan refrained from direct involvement in military conflicts in Asia (like the Korean War and the Indochina wars, in regions that traditionally were considered vitally important for its prosperity) and generally kept a low profile in international politics.

While closely following American foreign-policy objectives, Tokyo did engage at times in diplomacy that diverged from that of Washington. Examples of this 'autonomous policy' are Japan's trade relations with the People's Republic of China (PRC) in the 1950s and 1960s, normalisation talks with the Soviet Union in 1955–56, Japan's participation in the Arab boycott of Israel that followed the 1973 Israeli–Arab war, and the Fukuda doctrine of 1977 that argued for Japan's distinct role in Southeast Asia to help stabilise the region through provision of aid to all the countries in the region regardless of their political system.[6] However, amongst these examples, only Japan's participation in the boycott against Israel can be considered as genuinely autonomous. The negotiations with the Soviet Union fell short of concluding a peace treaty partially because of American intervention.[7] Despite trade relations that existed under the slogan of separation of politics and economy, diplomatic relations with Beijing were established after the Richard Nixon Administration fundamentally changed United States China policy in 1971 by giving the PRC diplomatic recognition. This sudden change in American policy was a 'shock' to Japanese policy-makers, because it came completely unexpectedly and did not involve any consultations with Japan, the United States' major partner in East Asia.[8] The Fukuda Doctrine was revised two years after its pronouncement. Then, with the evaporation of Soviet–American *détente* in the late 1970s and after Vietnam's invasion of Cambodia in 1979, Japan backed away from an earlier promise to assist the Communist Vietnam economically.[9] As such, Japan's participation in the Arab boycott, which remained intact despite United States pressure, can be regarded as an exception that underlined the validity of the rule.

This deviation in Japan's foreign policy from traditional Great Power practices (economic prowess usually goes hand in hand with military might and active participation in international politics) gave rise to numerous explanations of the Japan puzzle.[10] Many of these focused on explaining Japan's reluctance to despatch its forces overseas. Followers of the 'rational choice' approach argued that Japan was a free rider, enjoying economic prosperity while relying on the United States for its security. An alternative view construed Japan as a potential challenger to the American hegemony, arguing that its economic prowess is bound to result in clashes between the two Powers. The constructivist argument that emerged in the 1990s challenged the pre-dominant 'rational actor' approach by providing an alternative explanation for Japan's passive military posture. Emphasising the importance of norms, identities, and culture in shaping states' behaviour in international politics, it argued that Japan's reluctance to participate in external military operations resulted from a unique anti-militarist identity that developed in Japan in the post-Second World War years.

The two decades that have passed since the end of the Cold War have seen a number of important changes in Japan's defense policy. The shift towards more active participation in international affairs began in 1992 with the enactment of the *Law Concerning Cooperation for United Nations*, which, while imposing strict conditions, legally enabled the despatch of Japan's Self-Defense Forces for UN peacekeeping and humanitarian operations. Importantly, it must be noted that it was not the end of the Cold War that brought about this change but, rather, the first Gulf War, in which Japan's 'cheque book diplomacy' was not met with understanding by other major Powers and resulted in a 'national humiliation'.[11] However, the most important changes occurred during the Junichiro Koizumi administration (2001–6). Despite fierce protests from the opposition, Koizumi swiftly enacted a number of laws that enabled Japan's participation in the 'war on terror' in Afghanistan and in the United States-led invasion and occupation of Iraq.[12] Furthermore, in December 2006, Japan's Defense Agency was upgraded to a Ministry.

This process was not a symbolic gesture. After the upgrade and for the first time since the establishment of the Agency in 1954, the executive head of Japan's military acquired the legal authority to introduce legislative bills at Cabinet meetings. Furthermore, the question of the revision of Japan's 'Peace Constitution' (drafted mainly by United States occupation authorities in 1947) ,which in the past was voiced solely by right-wing or right-leaning politicians and activists, became an integral part of the political and public debates. Public opinion on this issue has fluctuated over the years and, as of 2010, the drive towards revision had lost its political momentum. However, opinion polls conducted by major newspapers have shown that the need for the whole or partial revision of the so-called 'pacifist' Article 9 is supported by a large part of the population.[13] As the Article is considered to be one of the main impediments in Japan's contribution of troops to international missions, this kind of public mood can be considered as another indicator of the changes in Japan's recent security posture.

Scholars of Japan have responded in different ways to these foreign-policy changes and the intensification of related domestic debates. Some perceive these shifts as indicators of a, however reluctant, gradual normalisation of Japan.[14] Some of the constructivists admitted the inability of constructivist theory to explain these changes and, instead, proposed analytical eclecticism, according to which different aspects of Japan's foreign policy can be explained by different international relations theories.[15]

Overall, however, Japan's diplomacy in the post-Cold War era has remained without a comprehensive vision of Japan's place and role in the new international order. Unlike many who had hoped (or feared) during the twilight of the Cold War the vision of *Pax Nipponica*,[16] the idea of Japan achieving a hegemonic status in international society has disappeared. Despite recent frictions over relocation of the United States airbase in Futenma, Okinawa, the American alliance has remained the central pillar of Japan's foreign policy.[17] Japan's relations with other regional Powers are complex. Issues related to Japan's historical memory of its expansionist past continue to weigh heavily over its relations with South Korea and the PRC.[18] Territorial disputes with both of these Powers add further complexity to their bilateral relationships with Japan. Tokyo's diplomacy *vis-à-vis* Russia, another important regional player, has focused on fostering the return of four islands, known in Japan as the 'Northern Territories'. These islands were captured by the Soviet forces in August–September 1945 and, later, were incorporated into Russia's Maritime Province. In the two decades since the collapse of the Soviet Union, the negotiation process has been marked by ups and downs. But Tokyo's reluctance to compromise on the scope of the territory it wants returned has led to an impasse that has prevailed since 2001.[19] The relationship between the two Powers did improve when compared to the Cold War, but it can hardly be viewed as warm. As a result of the impasse in the territorial dispute negotiations, Japan and Russia are still to conclude a peace treaty that will officially end the hostilities of the Second World War. Furthermore, as can be seen in the recent designation of 2 September as a 'Victory over Japan Day', Russia is growing increasingly impatient with the Japanese preoccupation with the territories.

Issues tied to historical memory as well as the territorial disputes can be seen as a complex legacy of the Cold War and are often used by each side for domestic purposes.[20] At the same time, however, in other geographical areas free from the burden of historical and territorial issues, Japan's diplomacy can hardly be regarded as impressive. One of the best examples is Central Asia, an area that has no historical disputes with Japan. Japan's interest in the region emerged almost simultaneously with the collapse of the Soviet Union.[21] Its strategy towards the region, however, was formulated much later, in a 24 July 1997 foreign-policy speech given by Prime Minister Ryutaro Hashimoto before the Japan Association of Corporate Executives. Hashimoto introduced the notion of 'Eurasian Diplomacy', which emphasised Japan's identity as an Asian country and stipulated three principles for Japanese diplomacy towards the Central

Asian region: building mutual trust and understanding; cooperation in the development of economies and natural resources; and cooperation for building and preserving peace.[22] Obviously, despite apparent altruism, access to natural resources plays an important role in shaping Japan's interests in the region.[23] At the same time, however, a romantic vision of Central Asia as resembling Japan's own past and Japan's self-conception as Asia's leader (rather similar to Japan's pre-1945 'Orientalism') also plays a certain role in Japan's interest in the region.[24] Despite numerous exchanges of visits and declarations, as well as a formidable allocation of development assistance, Japan's achievements in the region are modest. In terms of public opinion, Japan not only failed to wrestle Central Asia away from Russia, but it is also losing to (or, at the best) is on a par with other newcomers to the region, such as China and South Korea.[25] The involvement of these two Powers in the region is more pragmatic and involves less humanitarian projects. For example, in fiscal year 2005, Japanese grants to Uzbekistan amounted to US$25.24 million, while that of South Korea was only US$2.83 million, that is, just over one-tenth of Japan's aid.[26] At the same time, when Uzbekistanis were asked about other Powers' influence on their country, Japan was selected by 52 per cent as having good or rather good influence; South Korea received 68.7 per cent; Russia received 90.9 per cent.[27] In terms of the struggle over energy resources, which are considered vital for import-dependent Japan, the Japanese are losing to the Chinese and South Koreans.[28]

Other attempts to engage in autonomous diplomacy, like attempting to strengthen Japan's position on the Korean peninsula thorough engagement with North Korea and recent involvement in the Azadegan oilfield in Iran, have resulted in failure. In the case of North Korea, Japan's preoccupation with the abductees issue resulted in the failure to normalise relations with Pyongyang and, later, to the sidelining of Japan in the Six-Party Talks devoted to finding a peaceful solution of the security concerns concerning North Korea's development of nuclear weapons.[29] In case of Iran, Japan succumbed to United States pressure and pulled out of the oil development project.[30]

Whilst Japan's participation in the wider world has experienced a number of changes, like participating in the reconstruction of Iraq and the 'war on terror' in Afghanistan, its overall diplomacy can hardly be seen as successful. There are obviously multiple reasons behind Japan's inability to develop a clear and consistent vision that will guide its diplomacy. Among these reasons are its political system, in which prime ministers and cabinets change almost on a yearly basis, its economic stagnation (which has resulted in a sharp decrease in Japan's developmental model appeal), the emergence of China as one of the world's leading economic and political Great Powers, and the continuous dependence on the United States in terms of conventional security. At the same time, if we share the constructivist premise that culture serves as the fundamental basis for the conception of national interest and related strategy, the state of Japan's culture should also be scrutinised.

The creation of modern Japan's identity in the second half of the nineteenth century was dominated by the quest for 'casting off Asia' formulated by the leading intellectual of that time, Fukuzawa Yukichi (1835–1901). A simple adoption of the Western Enlightenment model would have meant a denial of Japan's past and would have doomed Japan to a 'perpetual state of inferiority' as a barbarian nation, standing at the periphery of civilisation.[31] Therefore, an integral part of Japan's internalisation of Western paradigms constituted a struggle to maintain or recreate political and cultural independence; Japanese intellectuals sought to rescue Japan from the category of the backward Orient and create a unique place for it in the universal history of humankind. The academic discipline of Oriental history emerged as an integral part of this struggle to find an alternative conception of the universal. In Japanese historiography, the Orient became the Origin, the cultural past of Japan from which it developed and grew.[32] Japan was constructed as a nation that emerged from the Orient, inheriting all the positive aspects of Asian culture, but went on to develop and gain a degree of cultural and historical autonomy comparable with that of the West. This creation of Japan's own 'Orient' in turn enabled the creation of Japan's own history of development into a modern nation; as such it has provided a world vision, a new totality, a variant of the Western model of universal history, through which Japan could favorably position itself relative to both Asia and the West. As a result of the new universality created by Oriental historiography, Japan became spatially unified with Asia but, at the same time, temporally unified with the West in that both have achieved modernity. The other regions of Asia were relegated to the status of 'incomplete variations of Japan' whose options were either to follow 'historical development' as defined and demonstrated by Japan or resist the flow of universal history.

This construction of the Orient and attempt to transcend the East–West dichotomy provided legitimacy for Japan's claims for equality with the West. However, the need for the consolidation of Japan as a nation, resulting from the sense of societal disintegration attributed to Western cultural influence during the Taisho Period (1911–25), and the continuing preponderance within the international hierarchy of the West over Japan, gave birth to the discourse on Japan's cultural uniqueness. This distinctiveness was achieved through the creation of Japan's unique history of assimilation and transformation of many pasts (Asian and Western alike). Japan came to epitomise all that the West was not. As opposed to the individualism, self-interest, greed, conflict, competition, and imperialism of the West, Japan's essence was characterised by cohesion, co-operation, and loyalty: positive values found in the antiquity of the Orient.[33] Gradually, this notion of Japanese uniqueness blended with pan-Asian ideology. The latter was initially based on such ideas as a racial union of Asian nations based on common culture, race, and a shared struggle against Western imperialism.[34] Gradually, however, there evolved the idea of a 'New Order' in East Asia that envisaged Japan as the leader of the Greater East Asia Co-Prosperity Sphere. Obviously, it would be an oversimplification to argue that the ideology of pan-Asianism caused Japan's expansionism, as the ideology itself developed together with Japan's expansionist policies.[35] Furthermore, the conceptions of Japanese culture, its history, and racial belonging were far from having a clear and stable set of arguments; indeed, they contained many contradictory elements.[36] However, policy and the discourse on culture existed in a discursive symbiosis, feeding and shaping each other. For example, in colonial Korea, the policy of encouraging intermarriage between Japanese and Koreans was promoted by the Japanese Government-General from 1930s onwards. It found basis on the idea of the racial unity between the two nations that constituted an integral part of the Imperial ideology.[37]

When Japan regained its independence in April 1952 with the Peace Treaty, another agreement, a Security Treaty with the United States, came into force simultaneously. By laying out the basic structure of the Japan–American alliance and incorporating Japan into the United States Cold War policy, these two treaties created the fundamental framework for postwar Japan's foreign policy.[38] The conservative Japanese Government then in office, while correcting some of the perceived mistakes of the Occupation, continued the project of constructing a 'free and democratic Japan'.[39] However, the process of creating a new Japan occurred within the context of a fierce struggle with the political Left, which in the 1950s and 1960s enjoyed formidable support among the people of Japan.

As Dower notes, 'culture', 'peace', and 'democracy' became the dominant signifiers that defined the Japanese political struggle. However, the meaning of 'culture' underwent a number of significant changes. After defeat in the Pacific War, cognitive structures that traced Japan's militarism to peculiar cultural traits were adopted by many domestic intellectuals, following the broader pattern of domestic incorporation or modification of Western images of Japan.[40] The negative conception of Japanese traditional culture as feudalistic and as being a direct cause of the pre-1945 militarism and ultranationalism dominated academic and public discourses alike.[41] Arguably, it is this understanding of Japanese traditional culture that guided the argument about the need to build a 'culture state' that was contained in Prime Minister Tetsu Katayama's speech to the Diet (the parliament) in 1947.[42] That 'culture' was associated not with Japanese traditional modes of behaviour but with Western-style democracy and a construction of a 'culture state' meant a thorough pursuit of Western-style democracy.[43]

In the 1950s and 1960s, the biggest challenge faced by the conservative Japanese establishment in its struggle over public support was not related to 'culture', but over the definition of 'peace,' 'democracy', and 'liberty.' This struggle was particularly fierce in the context of Japan's military alliance with the United States, denounced by the Left but considered one of the main pillars of Japan's foreign policy by the conservative mainstream. Importantly, during the first two post-war decades, there was a broad-based popular opposition in Japan to the military alliance. Although marginal in today's politics, the non-communist Left (mainly the Socialist Party and a significant number of Left leaning but unaffiliated public intellectuals) played a crucial role in shaping domestic public discourse during the Cold War years, particularly in the 1950s and 1960s, when Japan's politics were basically defined by a two-party system centred on the conservative and the socialist blocs. After political realignment in 1955, Japan's Socialist Party (JSP) became the largest opposition party and its critique of the military alliance with the United States resonated well with broader anti-war sentiment. The changes sought by the Japanese Left were to be achieved through peaceful and democratic revolution, as opposed to the violent, anti-democratic Russian revolution that led to the creation of the Soviet Union. From the early post-war days, 'peace,' 'independence', and 'democracy' were the main slogans of the Left.[44] Within this Leftist discourse, these goals could be achieved only through the advent of domestic socialism, on the one hand, and, on the other, in terms of foreign policy, through abolition of the American–Japanese military alliance and the institution of permanent unarmed neutrality. Needless to say, the principal 'other' in this discourse was 'American imperialism' and most of the rhetoric, narrating Japan as still occupied and subordinated, was directed at the United States.[45]

The Socialist Party platform that emerged from a compromise that produced the merger of the Left and Right socialist parties in 1954–55 reflected the strong suspicion of communism among some of the dominant members of the newly formed JSP, as well as the rivalry with the pro-Soviet Japanese Communist Party over the progressive vote. Thus, the JSP argued for Japan's neutrality, emphasising independence from both the capitalist and communist camps.[46] In general the socialists, while criticising American military policies in Japan and Asia, did not necessarily oppose Western-style liberal democracy and argued the liberation and development of the individual to be their main goal.[47] In terms of Japan's place in the Cold War, the progressives warned that the alliance with the United States would bring eventual destruction to Japan and, hence, argued for the urgent need to adopt a neutral stance and to abolish the security treaty with the United States. In this vision, Japanese security would be guaranteed through a 'Locarno style' collective security pact that will include United States, Japan, Soviet Russian, and the PRC, or by a 'UN army' to be stationed in Japan.[48]

In contrast to the leftist paradigm of 'neutrality,' the conservative discourse consistently emphasised the necessity of the American alliance, arguing that 'neutrality' was not a realistic option in the context of the global Cold War. The alliance was presented as the only realistic way not just to preserve regional stability, but also to pursue Japan's post-war values of peace and freedom.[49] While the left argued that Japan's interests and sovereignty were being subordinated to the United States, the alliance was portrayed in conservative discourse as integral to Japan's post-war identity as free and democratic. The preservation of domestic peace and democracy with its 'respect for personal freedom and human rights' became an integral and inseparable part of Japan's path of 'peace and prosperity' within the camp of 'free nations.' The security treaty was presented as the guarantee for this membership and, by default, as the basis for domestic peace and democracy. As such, the leftist vision of a neutral Japan, which, according to conservatives, was a pretext for joining the 'anti-democratic' communist camp, was argued to lead inevitably to the collapse of democracy in Japan and Japan's 'isolation' in Asia.[50]

As such, the battle over Japan's identity between the conservative and the progressive camps evolved around the definitions of such political paradigms as 'peace' and 'democracy' but did not touch on the notion of culture. As Harry Harootunian has perceptively noted in the context of Japanese discourse on the emperor, the domestic Left in general has not been able 'to take seriously the discourse on culture'.[51] 'Culture' reemerged as a distinct concept in the conservative political discourse in the 1970s, along with Japan's accession to the status of an economic superpower. The 1970s saw the emergence of a body of academic, quasi-academic, and popular literature known as *nihonjinron* (the theory of Japaneseness) that explored the various sociocultural and historical aspects of the Japanese nation. While being rather diverse in terms of methodology and the focus of inquiry, the unifying thread of this discourse has been a consistent commitment to the idea of Japanese uniqueness, whether the sources of this distinctiveness are located in history, biology, climate, diet, or orthography (for detailed analysis of *nihonjinron* see Dale 1986, Befu 1987 and 2001, Minami 1994, Clammer 2001 and Kowner 2002).[52] In general, *nihonjinron* replicated the pre-1945 debates on Japanese uniqueness. It construed Japan as radically different from other nations, perceived it as racially and socially homogeneous and historically continuous, and presented an array of arguments in favour of the positive distinctiveness of the Japanese socio-cultural characteristics. In general, this body of literature, through the juxtaposition of Japan with the West, argued the former to be a consistently harmonious, communal, and peaceful society. Japan was argued to be a racially homogenous island nation, rich in nature, which prevails over the man. Unlike the West, Japanese society is depicted as vertical and hierarchical, emotional, tolerant, and peaceful.[53]

In late 1970s, *nihonjinron* became an integral part of the political discourse with the birth of Ōhira Cabinet (1978–80). Masayoshi Ōhira established a number of policy study groups whose overall aim was to develop a new national agenda for Japan.[54] In the context of Japan's relations with Asia, particularly important was the report of the 'Pacific Basin Cooperation Group', which argued for 'open regionalism' and interdependence based on cooperation and respect for the diversity of cultures in the region.[55] Ōhira also declared the coming of the age of culture in the policy speech to the Diet made on 25 January 1979.[56] In this speech, for the first time in Japan's post-war politics, 'culture' was construed as an autonomous concept, independent from 'democracy', 'peace', and 'trade'.[57] This declaration was followed by the establishment of a 'Study Group on the Age of Culture', headed by one of the main *nihonjinron* authors, Yamamoto Shichihei (best known for his *Japanese and the Jews* written under the penname of Isaiah Bendasan). One would expect the report to follow the *nihonjinron* argument affirming the unique cultural traits of Japan, paralleling the above-mentioned vision of the Pacific Basin as a region of diverse cultures by establishing Japan's position and role within this diversity. However, the report noted the current 'demand for culture', discussed various forms of cultural exchange, but failed to outline what exactly was meant by Japanese culture. Ironically, the root of the failure was the implicit attempt to follow the idea of equality of cultures voiced by both the Pacific Basin report and Ōhira.[58] As such, the writers of the report noted and criticised the existing definitions of Japanese culture through a 'superior/inferior' dichotomy in relation to the West and Asia.[59] The attempt of the authors to transcend this trend results in inability to define the essence of Japanese culture and the only reference to Japan's cultural uniqueness is made in the context of its unique secularism.[60]

As such, in the 1980s, following the reemergence of the notion of 'culture' in the domestic public discourse, there were two conceptions of Japanese culture. One was provided by *nihonjin-ron*, narrating Japanese culture through juxtaposition with the West and ignoring Asia. Its dichotomous depiction of the Japan–West relations completely ignored Japan's political alliance with the West and, through this course, excluded culture from the political. Furthermore, its assumption of Japanese inherent and transhistorical uniqueness, and the inability of others to internalise its spirit, eliminated its possibility to serve as the basis for Japan's foreign policy. The other conception of Japan's culture, provided by the Study Group on the Age of Culture, argued for cultural relativism; but in its attempt to transcend the 'superior/inferior' dichotomy, it failed to define the essence of Japanese culture. For obvious reasons, however, most of the attempts to appeal to Japanese culture in the political discourse used the *nihonjinron* conception. Among the adherents to the *nihonjinron* argument, one can count Prime Minister Yasuhiro Nakasone (1982–87) with his statements about Japan's superiority over the United States in that it lacked problematical ethnic minorities, and Tokyo's current governor Shintaro Ishihara, the coauthor of the infamous *Japan That Can Say 'No'*. Yet, paradoxically, Nakasone's strongly pro-American policy epitomised in his relationship with President Ronald Reagan (1981–89) (the 'Ron-Yasu' relationship) underscored the impossibility of operationalising *nihonjinron* in international affairs. Ishihara's argument focused mainly on criticising the United States and constituted a mirror-image of Japan-bashing in the United States. While arguing about the need for a more independent security policy for Japan, it did not provide any broad ideas that could serve as a basis for Japan's policy.

Most of the recent attempts to define Japan's culture have occurred within the debate on Japan's soft power. The concept of 'soft power' became overwhelmingly popular in Japan in the early 2000s. This popularity stemmed from a number of factors. During this time, two American publications argued for Japan's exceptional 'soft power' potential. One was *Soft Power: The Means to Success in World Politics*, the widely acclaimed book by Joseph Nye, in which he argued that Japan has more potential soft power resources than any other Asian country.[61] The other was an article by Douglas McGray entitled 'Japan's Gross National Cool'.[62] Initially appearing in *Foreign Policy*, it was later reprinted in Japan's influential *Chūō Kōron*. In this article, McGray argued that despite its economic recession, Japan has reinvented itself as a cultural superpower, whose popular culture exercises global influence. The idea of Japan as a 'cultural superpower' was received as a pleasant surprise in Japan, because of its favorable view of Japanese culture and its global influence and because, before these publications, the domestic elites did not pay much attention to Japan's popular culture and its political potential. Another important factor in the sudden popularity of 'soft power' in Japan was the premiership of the charismatic Koizumi, who was seeking to boost Japan's role in international affairs. In 2004, he established an *ad hoc* think tank called 'A Discussion Group on the Promotion of Cultural Diplomacy'. The purpose of the group, whose members included representatives of academia, artists, and writers, centred on the importance of cultural diplomacy and bringing width and depth to Japan's diplomacy by providing it with a firm cultural basis.[63] The report published by the Group in the following year argued that Japan managed to protect its own identity in the process of modernisation and, therefore, has the unique ability to understand the problems faced by other non-Western states. Following an already-established pattern, the report argued that Japan has the potential to become the bridge between various cultures. In terms of Japanese culture, the report emphasised the importance of popular culture such as *manga*, pop music, and motion pictures, in many ways repeating the argument made by McGray in 'National Cool'. However, the most interesting part of the report is the plan for action to be taken by Japan in its exercise of culture diplomacy; it focuses not on the resources of Japan's soft power but on the behavior that should use these resources.[64] Here, the Group argues, the most important cultural value Japan can contribute to the world in the pursuit of its role as the bridge between different cultures and values is the 'spirit of *wa* and coexistence'. According to the report, the latter refers to Japan's unique pursuit of coexistence with the natural environment. *Wa* is explained as a distinct Japanese concept, meaning harmony, peace, fusion, and consideration towards others. Japanese culture, it is argued, emerged as a unique fusion of both Western and Eastern cultures, and *wa* is its most essential element.[65]

Besides the obvious bending of historical facts in this idyllic definition of Japan's culture and behavior, the report perceives Japan simply as an intermediary, a bridge between different cultures. Furthermore, the fascination with the 'cool Japan' concept completely ignored the fact that McGray also dubbed Japan as 'postmodern'.[66] Unlike the case of American popular culture, he argued, the political values behind Japanese cultural products are unclear if not non-existent. Cultural attraction that lacks normative underpinning can hardly be seen as a successful exercise of 'soft power' because it does not necessarily mean political acceptance of the source of the cultural products. The best example of this lack of correlation is the anti-Japanese protests in China that took place in 2005, the same year that the aforementioned report was published. The fascination with Japanese pop music and *anime* did not prevent Chinese youth from participating *en masse* in violent anti-Japanese protests.[67] As such, recent attempts to define Japan's culture, while showing certain sophistication, have failed to define premises that could serve as a basis for Japan's proactive foreign policy.

Lacking a clearly defined cultural basis, Japan's engagement with other countries is explicitly apolitical. That with Russia is rather illustrative. Unlike other major capitalist democracies that, after the collapse of the Soviet Union, rushed to democratise and liberalise Russia, neither the Japanese Government nor Japan's non-governmental organisations have felt the need to engage in the sociopolitical or politicised realms of Russian society. The activities of the 'Japan Centres,' whose status and *raison d'être* are otherwise comparable with that of the British Council, for example, are symbolic of Japan's engagement with Russia. Established in 1994 and currently operating in seven major Russian cities, the centres engage solely in the provision of Japanese language classes and technical training for Russian specialists expected to become the 'pillars of the future Russian economy', as well as business consulting to both Russian and Japanese entrepreneurs.[68]

Nye argued in his *Soft Power* that Japan stands out among Asian countries in its potential 'soft power' resources because of its being the first non-Western country that achieved full modernisation and reached equality with the West in terms of income and technology.[69] Arguably, however, if Japan's modernisation is construed as being accomplished in the post-war years, along with its democratisation and adoption of the capitalist model, the same traits can also be seen as the greatest impediment to its 'soft power'. Namely, as the result of internalisation of Enlightenment thinking in the mid-nineteenth century, most importantly the 'West–East' dichotomy and related binary oppositions, Japan's cultural identity could be defined only through its juxtaposition with the West. At the same time, Japan's political agenda in the post-war years came to be defined by such keywords as 'democracy' and 'market economy', concepts of Western cultural origin. Consequently, both culture and political agenda have been defined by Western paradigms. The former aimed at creating particularism; the latter has been conceived as universal. Arguably, this contradiction underlies Japan's inability to define the cultural basis of its diplomacy.

Notes

1 S. Suzuki, 'Japan's Socialization into Janus-Faced European International Society', *European Journal of International Relations*, 11(2005), 137–64.
2 Japan's sovereign control over the Bonin Islands was restored in 1968 and over Okinawa in 1972.

3 For example, G. Friedman and M. Lebard, *The Coming War with Japan* (New York, 1991); E. Vogel, *Japan as Number One: Lessons for America* (Cambridge, MA, 1979).

4 K.B. Pyle, *Japan Rising* (New York, 2007), 1.

5 For a concise analysis of the "Yoshida Doctrine", see T. Kawasaki, 'The Yoshida Doctrine: A Conceptual Analysis'. Paper presented at the International Studies Association Annual Conference (Honolulu, 2005).

6 M. Yahuda, *The International Politics of the Asia-Pacific, 1945–1995* (London, 1996), 229–47.

7 H. Wada, *Hoppōryōdo mondai* (Tokyo, 1999), 229–60.

8 M. Yokibe, *Sengo nihon gaikōshi* (Tokyo, 1999), 147–48.

9 J. Inada, 'ODA seisaku ni miru sengo nihon gaikō no "kihan" ', in Y. Hasegawa, ed., *Nihon gaikō no aidentiti* (Tokyo: 2004), 82–83.

10 The rest of this paragraph is based on Thomas U. Berger, *Cultures of Antimilitarism: National Security in Germany and Japan* (Baltimore, MD, 1998); P.J. Katzenstein, 'Coping with Terrorism: Norms and Internal Security in Germany and Japan', in Judith Goldstein and Robert O. Keohane, eds., *Ideas and Foreign Policy: Beliefs, Institutions and Political Change* (Ithaca, NY, London, 1993).

11 M. Green, *Japan's Reluctant Realism* (New York, 2001), 269.

12 For details see T. Shinoda, *Koizumi Diplomacy* (Seattle, WA, 2007).

13 *Basic Documents on the Constitution* (*Kenpō ni kan suru kihon shiryō*): www.k3.dion.ne.jp/~keporin/siryou.htm.

14 For example, Green, *Reluctant Realism*.

15 J.J. Suh, P.J. Katzenstein, and A. Carlson, eds., *Rethinking Security in East Asia* (Stanford, 2004).

16 Vogel, *Number One*.

17 For example, N. Kan, 'Policy Speech 11.6.2010' (2010): http://dtcn-wisdom.jp/00001-2010-6-11kannsouri.p.

18 Green, *Reluctant Realism*, 187.

19 See A. Bukh, *Japan's Identity and Foreign Policy: Russia as Japan's "Other"* (London, 2009) for details.

20 K. Hara, *Cold War Frontiers in the Asia-Pacific* (London, 2007).

21 C. Len, 'Japan's Central Asian Diplomacy: Motivations, Implications and Prospects for the Region', *China and Eurasia Forum Quarterly*, 3(2005), 127–49.

22 Tanaka Akihiko Data Base, *Sekai to nihon*: www.ioc.u-tokyo.ac.jp/~worldjpn/.

23 Len, 'Central Asian Diplomacy', 130.

24 Ibid., 132; T. Uyama, 'Japan's Diplomacy Towards Central Asia in the Context of Japan's Asian Diplomacy and Japan-US Relations', in C. Len, T. Uyama, and T. Hirose, eds., *Japan's Silk Road Diplomacy* (Singapore, 2008), 108.

25 See T. Inoguchi, *et al.*, *Asia Barometer* (2005): www.asiabarometer.org/en/findings/General%20findings/2005/Q26.

26 Ministry of Foreign Affairs, Japan, *Roshia ni okeru nihon senta no jigyō* (Tokyo, 2006); Ministry of Foreign Affairs and Trade, Republic of Korea, ODA Korea (2010): www.odakorea.go.kr/eng/operations/Europe/Uzbekistan.php.

27 Inoguchi et al, *Asia Barometer*.

28 J. Townsend and A. King, 'Sino-Japanese Competition for Central Asian Energy: China's Game to Win', *China and Eurasia Forum Quarterly*, 5(2007), 23–45.

29 S. Snyder, 'The Korean Peninsula and Northeast Asian Stability', in D. Shambaugh and M. Yahuda, eds., *International Relations of Asia*. (New York, 2008), 266. The six parties were North Korea, South Korea, the PRC, the United States, Russia, and Japan.

30 Y. Yamao and M. Kitagawa, 'Hinomaru yuden gaiatsu ni kusu', 1 October 2010, *Asahi Shimbun*.

31 S. Tanaka, S., *Japan's Orient* (Berkeley, CA, 1993), 266–67.

32 Ibid., 103–4.

33 Ibid.

34 S. Saaler, 'Pan-Asianism in Modern Japanese History', in S. Saaler and V.J. Koschmann, eds., *Pan-Asianism in Modern Japanese History: Colonialism, Regionalism and Borders* (London, 2007), 10.

35 Ibid., 12–13.

36 E. Oguma, *A Geneology of 'Japanese' Self-Images* (Melbourne, 2002).

37 Ibid., 209–16.

38 J.W. Dower, 'Peace and Democracy in Two Systems', in A. Gordon, ed., *Postwar Japan as History* (Berkeley, CA, 1993), 4.

39 E. Takemae, *Inside GHQ: The Allied Occupation of Japan and Its Legacy* (London, 2002), 516–60. Cf. for example, Prime Minister Yoshida's speech in the Diet, 12 October 1951: Tanaka Akihiko Data Base.

40 H.D. Harootunian, 'America's Japan/Japan's Japan', in H.D. Harootunian and M. Miyoshi, eds., *Japan in the World* (London, 1993), 7.
41 T. Aoki, *Nihonbunkaron no henyō* (Tokyo, 1999), 56–67.
42 Quoted in K. Hirano, Sengo nihon gaikō ni okeru 'bunka', in A. Watanabe, ed., *Sengo nihon no taigai seisaku* (Tokyo, 1985), 344.
43 Ibid., 345.
44 J.A. Stockwin, *The Japanese Socialist Party and Neutralism; A Study of Political Party and Its Foreign Policy* (Carlton, 1968).
45 Ibid., 1–20; Oguma, *"Japanese" Self-Images*, 447–98.
46 Stockwin, *Japanese Socialist Party*, 71–97.
47 Y. Seki, 'Minshushugi no kisō rinen', in Minshushakaishugi renmei, ed., *Tōitsu shakaitō kōryō sōan to sono kaiseutsu* (Tokyo, 1955).
48 Y. Sakamoto, 'Chūritsu nihon no boei kōsō', *Sekai*, 164(1959), 31–47. The Locarno treaty of December 1925 brought stability to post-First World War Europe by an Anglo-Italian guarantee of the Franco-German border. See G. Johnson, *Locarno Revisited: European Diplomacy, 1920–1929* (London, 2004).
49 M. Kosaka, 'Genjitsu shugisha no heiwaron', *Chūō Kōron*, 78(1963), 38–49.
50 See, for example, Prime Minister Nobusuke Kishi's 'Speech at the National Press Club', 21 June 1957: Tanaka Akihiko Data Base.
51 D. Harootunian, *Overcome by Modernity* (Princeton, NJ, 2000), 625–26.
52 H. Befu, *Ideorogi to shite no nihonbunkaron* (Tokyo, 1987); idem. *Hegemony of Homogeneity*, Melbourne (2001); J. Clammer, *Japan and its Others* (Melbourne, 2001); P.N. Dale, *The Myth of Japanese Uniqueness* (New York, 1986); R. Kowner, R. 2002 "Deconstructing the Japanese National Discourse: Laymen's Beliefs and Ideology", in R. Donahue, ed., *Exploring Japaneseness*. (Westport, CT, 2002); H. Minami, *Nihonjin ron: meiji kara kon'nichi made* (Tokyo, 1994).
53 Dale, *Myth*, 44–46.
54 Yahuda, *International Politics*, 246.
55 Pacific Basin Cooperation Study Group, *Kan taiheiyō rentai kōsō* (Tokyo, 1980): www.ioc.u-tokyo.ac.jp/~worldjpn/documents/texts/APEC/19800519.O1J.html.
56 Tanaka Akihiko Data Base.
57 Hirano, 'Sengo nihon', 361.
58 For example, see Ōhira speech, Oakland, California, 18 January 1980: Tanaka Akihiko Data Base.
59 Study Group on the Age of Culture, *Bunka no jidai* (Tokyo, 1980), 23–25.
60 Ibid., 34–35.
61 Joseph S. Nye, *Soft Power: The Means to Success in World Politics* (New York, 1984), 85.
62 Douglas McGray, 'Japan's Gross National Cool', *Foreign Policy*, (May 2002), 44–54.
63 Cabinet Office, *Bunka gaikō no sokushin ni kan suru kondankai no kaisai ni tsuite* (2004): www.kantei.go.jp/jp/singi/bunka/konkyo.html.
64 Cabinet Office, 'Bunka kouryuu no heiwa kokka" nihon no souzou o' (2005): www.kantei.go.jp/jp/singi/bunka/kettei/050711houkoku_s.pdf.
65 Ibid., 14–15.
66 McGray, 'National Cool', 48–49.
67 Y. Nakano, 'Shared Memories: Japanese Pop Culture in China', in Y. Watanabe and D. McConnell, eds., *Soft Power Superpowers* (London, 2008), 111–12.
68 Ministry of Foreign Affairs, *Roshia ni okeru, 4.*
69 Nye, *Soft Power*, 85.

Part III
The Middle Powers

10

Brazil

Making room at the main table

Sean W. Burges

A quick perusal of Brazilian diplomatic history can bring a few surprises for readers grounded in the standard Western texts on twentieth-century events. Brazil was at the table when the Treaty of Versailles was negotiated after the First World War and held a place on the Council of the League of Nations. It was the only active South American participant in the Second World War, sending troops to fight in the Italian campaign. Brazil contributed to the formation of the United Nations (UN) system, winning the honour of giving the first speech at each year's UN General Assembly, although not acquiring the much-desired permanent seat on the Security Council. Brazil was one of the seventeen nations that negotiated the formation of the General Agreement on Trade and Tariffs. In short, Brazil has a long history of actively engaging in global governance institutions and the substance of international diplomacy. But much to the annoyance of its diplomats working in the Foreign Ministry's Itamaraty Palace, Brazil also has a long history of being largely ignored or marginalised by the Great Powers in global affairs and strong-armed or side-stepped in regional matters. The idea that Brazil matters and that the country's counsel is desired and actively sought at major international meetings is something that has generally not received much public attention, despite the sustained official consultations that have been conducted by influential individuals such as Henry Kissinger.[1] The change seen today is that major Powers are openly giving credence to Brazil's voice, resulting in Brazilian inclusion at globally important diplomatic tables.

Two such tables have preoccupied Brazilian diplomats, and their interwoven story has helped transform Brazil into a Power of global significance. First is the international negotiating table, where issues of global importance are discussed and direction given to international politics. From its inception in 1902, the modern Brazilian Foreign Ministry conforms to traditions established by the Baron of Rio Branco, José Maria da Silva Paranhos Junior, and has been dedicated to ensuring that Brazil has a seat at the main global table. Brazilian diplomatic history is a consistent story of attempts to use the national and regional context as a springboard for inclusion at international diplomatic tables to protect national sovereignty and preserve autonomy in governmental policy-making.[2] But it is only since 2000 that these attempts at international leadership have gained serious traction, suggesting that the future may finally be here for a country that cynics have often quipped is perpetually waiting for its destiny to arrive.

How Brazil managed to establish itself as a serious candidate for inclusion in post-Cold War global diplomatic forums can be divided into four broad periods. First was the 'fight for survival' (1990–95), which addressed efforts to set Brazil's internal political and economic house in order. The second stage, 'building credibility' (1995–2004), looked at the solidification of economic stability in Brazil and the transformation of South America from a region of fiscally moribund despotic regimes to one of serious and stable political economies. In 'searching for a seat' (2005–9), the third phase, attention turned to how the Luiz Ignacio Lula da Silva Government used the legacy of stability left by the Fernando Henrique Cardoso presidency to claim a greater international presence. Finally, the fourth stage (2009–10) has been one of 'trying the seat out for size', as Brazilian diplomacy adapts to the country's arrival as an accepted important Power in global councils.

The second diplomatic table is where the domestic decision-making elite determines Brazil's foreign policy. In its preliminary stages, the composition of this table was rather uncomplicated. Drawing on the domestic apolitical traditions that Rio Branco made a condition for taking control of the Foreign Ministry,[3] the Itamaraty Palace succeeded through much of the twentieth century in convincing the elite that foreign policy was largely a technocratic exercise best left to professional diplomats. Until about 2000, this ring-fencing of diplomatic thinking was facilitated by the relative unimportance of international affairs to most Brazilians, and to the national Congress in particular. But the rapid internationalisation of Brazilian business, as well as the integration of Brazil into regional energy and economic matrices, created a quickly shifting situation that saw business and political actors demand a greater voice in the policy-making process. Where Cardoso had pushed the boundaries of presidential diplomacy to compel the Itamaraty to broaden its internal thinking, Lula forced the Palace doors open and ushered in voices from both the reactionary left wing of his governing Worker's Party as well as the increasingly assertive agro-industrial sector. The result is a more complicated international position that combines hard-nosed trade policy with elements of an ideology of global solidarity. What has not changed is Brazil's commitment to ensuring respect for the principle of state sovereignty, as well as vouchsafing the autonomy to pursue national policy.[4]

At the beginning of the 1990s Brazil faced an additional set of challenges beyond discerning the shape of the post-Cold War international system. Democracy was still new in both Brazil and the wider region of South America. Concerns about competing economic blocs that dominated North American thinking paled compared with the domestic economic travails of Brazil, which experienced the confusion of four different currencies between 1990 and 1994 in addition to inflation rates that went as high as 2,700 percent in 1993. As if the problems of spiralling national debt and wildly inefficient state-owned companies were not enough to preoccupy presidential advisors, there were also lingering questions about confidence building with long-time security rival Argentina, as well as the question of how to prevent Paraguay descending into disorder and chaos as the health of its last caudillo, General Andres Rodriguez, failed. Tied to these regional and economic challenges was the political crisis caused by President Fernando Collor de Mello's 1992 resignation amidst a Congressional process to impeach him on charges of corruption. He was succeeded by Itamar Franco (1992–95). Foreign policy during the Collor–Franco period was one of transition and adaptation to new domestic and international challenges.[5]

Although tarred by his impeachment on influence-peddling charges, Collor's presidency stands out for launching many of the reforms that made possible the stabilisation policies of Cardoso and the poverty eradication measures of the Lula presidency. As part of his promise to 'finish the Maharajahs' in Brasília living large on the public purse, Collor broke with the inward-looking developmental traditions of Brazilian public policy, turning instead to a relatively orthodox approach to economic policy. In foreign policy, this necessitated a series of revisions about how diplomats should shape their country's international engagement. The proposal put forward by Celso Lafer was to return to some of the traditions of the *política externa independente*, taking a view that Brazil should determine the priority of its own interests before becoming aligned in a tight alliance with one or another of the rising industrial regional blocs that preoccupied analysts at the time.[6] This determination remained a shared common thread in the succeeding foreign ministries of Fernando Henrique Cardoso and Celso Amorim, with both building on the theme of Brazil constructing its own path forward in a changing global context despite considerable domestic economic restraints.

The challenge for Itamaraty was that the move towards an independently minded foreign policy was precipitated by the liberalising policies of the Collor presidency rather than a considered process of change within the Foreign Ministry. Moreover, it was a relatively quick change in direction for a bureaucracy known for its more measured approach to shifts in policy direction. As Celso Lafer reflected on his first period as foreign minister, 'the pace of foreign policy is, as a general rule, slower, and consequently is distinct from the pace of domestic politics.'[7] In searching for a new strategic framework, Itamaraty turned partially inwards to the lessons held in the ministerial archives; and at the prompting of ministers such as Lafer and Cardoso, it also invited selected outsiders to contribute to a series of seminars rethinking Brazil's role in the world. An extensive internal report on these meetings was generated for internal use and could be found online with the correct search terms.[8] A more carefully edited version for public consumption was published in two volumes in 1994 to explain where Brazilian foreign policy was going.[9]

Three options faced Itamaraty: seeking tighter allegiance with a dominant Power such as the United States or European Union, pursuing a pragmatically independent foreign policy, or seeking an inwardly oriented and almost isolationist approach. Policy-makers chose the middle option, articulating a clear identity for Brazil as an internationally engaged actor in favour of multilateralism with the persona of a 'global trader'.[10] The answer to the question of how Brazil might go about fulfilling this persona from a position of relative international weakness was regionalism, most immediately in the form of the Common Market of the South, *Mercosul* (*Mercosur* in Spanish). This decision cut away from a traditional strategy of using regional integration with Argentina, Paraguay, and Uruguay to defuse a host of regional security tensions, vouchsafe the still-uncertain democracies in the grouping, and create a large internal economic space that could be used to prepare member-country firms for global competition.[11] Over the course of the next five years, intrabloc trade flows boomed and, more significantly for Brazil's larger ambitions of restoring its international reputation and securing at least a tacit regional leadership role, brought stability and security to the Southern Cone.

Whilst *Mercosul* has subsequently settled into a more staid routine involving a sufficient number of petty trade squabbles so that its utility is being questioned,[12] the bloc and its regionalist principals remain the foundation for Brazil's foreign policy strategy. As Itamaraty Secretary-General Antonio Patriota noted in 2010:

> Mercosul is really the building block, the founding stone of what we are trying to accomplish more broadly in terms of South American integration. Without Argentina and Brazil having become so closely associated on the trade and economic front, as they did through Mercosul, the other developments wouldn't have been possible.[13]

Indeed, *Mercosul* and the regional presence it created was the cornerstone of Cardoso's efforts to restore Brazil's global economic credibility. To start, there was a surge in intrabloc exports (from US$10 billion in 1993 to US$20.3 billion in 1998) with value-added products dominating bilateral flows. The shelter of the *Mercosul* common external tariff provided Brazil's industrial sector with a space to consolidate and expand operations throughout the bloc, using competition from Argentina as an intermediate test for the viability of longer-term operations. The result was that after the forced devaluation of the *real* in 1999, Brazilian industry emerged stronger and more capable of exporting value-added products into global markets, which in turn provided a major contribution to the restoration of national economic stability that would make the poverty reduction achievements of the Lula presidency possible.

The *Mercosul*-induced surge in economic activity combined with the continuation of Brazilian–Argentine political dialogue begun in the 1980s to attract the attention of European leaders ever-vigilant to nurture proto-EU groupings. German Chancellor Helmut Kohl was direct in courting Cardoso, strongly suggesting that Brazil should seize the moment and use its larger size and increasingly dynamic economy to accelerate formation of a deep regionalist project in South America.[14] Whilst Kohl's attention combined with Cardoso's international scholarly reputation won the Brazilian president invitations to some of the more interesting international blue-sky thinking events like the 'Third Way' summits,[15] economic reality in Brazil and throughout South America dictated a more modest approach. Despite gains coming from intra-*Mercosur* trade, Brazil remained hostage to the vagaries of international capital markets and lacked the internal economic resources necessary to serve as the anchor Power of an EU-style bloc. Indeed, Brazil's fiscal situation was such that international investors more or less expected the Brazilian economy to implode. Much to the international community's surprise, this implosion did not happen. Instead, Brazilian-made economic policies of the *real* plan were constantly reshaped to fit the shifting sands of the global economy.[16] More impressive was the rapid stabilisation of the *real* in early 1999, when aftershocks of an Asian financial crisis forced its uncontrolled and rapid devaluation. Where the International Monetary Fund (IMF) predicted sudden economic decline, what emerged was a temporary blip in the economic numbers followed by a strong and lasting recovery as currency devaluation provided a three-fold boost in the price-competitiveness of Brazilian exports.

By 2000, these repeated economic successes began to give added credence to the economic commentary and thinking coming from Brazil. This in turn played into a steady stream of calls by the Brazilian President and his ministers for substantive reform of global governance institutions, particularly economic governance groups such as the World Bank. In what remains emblematic of Brazil's approach to global governance, Cardoso's call was not for the destruction or wholesale reengineering of organisations such as the World Bank or IMF; instead, he looked for a meaningful tweaking of procedures and a reevaluation of contributors to ensure that these institutions remained able to continue efficiently managing global economic disruptions.[17] At the heart of this entrance into global governance discussions was the strong technocratic capacity of graduates from the economics departments of Brazilian universities (for example, the *Universidade de São Paulo* and the *Universidade Nacional de Brasília*) as well as technocrats in the Central Bank, Finance Ministry, and quasi-autonomous research institutes like the *Instituto de Pesquisa Econômica Aplicada*. The quiet expansion of thinking from these different groups into the global policy milieu that began during the Cardoso years started to take visible form early in the Lula presidency: international financial agencies such as the IMF began to suggest that Brazilian ideas be adopted as new global norms.[18]

The creativity and adaptability of macro-economic policy was duplicated in foreign and foreign economic policy. Whilst Brazil certainly lacked the economic strength to serve as the regional anchor advocated by Kohl, there were other avenues for making use of economic linkages to strengthen Brazil's nascent regional leadership. Chief amongst them was a process of strategic trade diversion. The decision to purchase grain from Argentina was an early precursor of this tactic designed to ease the tensions in the bilateral trade imbalance. A later and wider-reaching example was the decision to shift energy sourcing away from the Middle East to neighbouring countries, most notably by constructing a gas pipeline from Bolivia to supply the São Paulo–Rio de Janeiro industrial corridor.[19] The nature of regional exports to Brazil conformed to this general model, with manufactured goods representing a significantly higher percentage of total bilateral trade than was the case with exports to the global market. This form of simultaneous economic penetration and absorption was sustained during the Lula years when it provided a model for deeper engagement with South America and the surge in bilateral linkages with a number of African countries.[20]

These attempts at regional and global economic engagement drew directly on the liberalising legacy of the Collor presidency and, significantly, were largely pushing Brazilian business and civil society forward rather than responding to demands from these groups. Indeed, much of the liberalisation agenda pursued by the Cardoso Government (and which later became the bedrock of the Lula presidency's international engagement strategy) was actively opposed by Lula's Workers Party in the Brazilian Congress. For the most part, Congressional interest in foreign policy was restricted to international junkets and attendance at receptions for visiting dignitaries. It took major crises like the World Trade Organization (WTO) enquiry into Brazilian aircraft financing practices or wounds to national pride such as the technicality-driven Canadian decision to ban imports of Brazilian beef to rouse Congress into any form of noticeable action.[21] Business interest in foreign opportunities was equally insipid in the early stages of the Cardoso presidency, with concern rising only after 1999 when Brazilian firms realised that there were opportunities in Argentina. Indeed, by 2002, the Brazilian agro-industrial sector had begun seriously to penetrate international markets and was losing patience with the slow speed of government policy changes on the international trade and phytosanitary files.[22]

The foreign policy-making autonomy that wider civil society and Congress were granting the Cardoso presidency by default appears all the more strange when considering some of the non-economic ventures that Brazil pursued in the name of demonstrating its ability to maintain stability and security in South America. Amongst the first crises that Cardoso faced as President was the eruption of a shooting war between Ecuador and Peru. Settling this long-standing border dispute is highlighted by both Cardoso and his Foreign Minister, Luiz Felipe Lampreia, as a critical achievement and a clear demonstration of Brazil's ability to manage regional security issues.[23] Similar emphasis was put on the Brazilian use of *Mercosul* membership conditions to ensure that democracy remained the institutional norm in Paraguay during a series of crises in the 1990s. Whilst less public discussion has been given to the use of the Rio Group to sideline the Organization of American States and the United States to protect sovereignty and democratic processes during other political disputes in Ecuador, Peru, and Venezuela, the pattern during the Cardoso years was one of Brazil quietly demonstrating an ability to maintain essential minimal levels of stability and due process throughout South America. Whilst not in itself anything particularly surprising, the twist added by Cardoso's approach to Brazil's regional husbandry was an embedded concern with using these disruptions to nurture the development of sustainable domestic political practices in regional countries experiencing crisis.[24]

In short, Cardoso's presidency would seem to be a period when Brazil emerged as an internationally credible actor worthy of at least standing at the edge of the grand decision-making tables of global governance. In reality, this situation was not quite the case. Cardoso's foreign policy was marked by the very strong use of presidential diplomacy, with Cardoso acting as the chief driver and fountainhead of his country's foreign relations.[25] Major innovations such as promoting South America as an active geopolitical space during the 2000 Brasília Summit of South American Presidents was an initiative that the presidential palace compelled Itamaraty to undertake. Even the tone in Brazilian diplomatic discourse was altered by Cardoso during his time as Foreign Minister and President, shifting towards acceptance of a less-formal discourse reflective of the proliferation of global civil society, not the staid formality of Westphalian diplomacy.

Whilst Brazil was ostensibly accepted on the international stage as a rising Power, it was the prestige and confidence in Cardoso and his presidential diplomacy that formed the bedrock of Brazil's growing credibility. Consequently, after the victory by the left-wing Lula in the 2002 presidential election, international concern emerged about the end of sensible policies in Brazil. To his credit, Cardoso made clear that this was not going to be the case and, even if there was a hint of ambiguity in Lula not continuing with sensible economic policies, it was dispelled by public pre-election announcements that he would maintain existing macro-economic policy and bring in Henrique Meirelles to run the Central Bank and Antonio Palocci the Finance Ministry. It took slightly more than one year and a strong primary fiscal surplus to gain international acceptance that the substance of Brazil's rising place in the world was vested as much in bureaucratic structures as presidential charisma. Whilst Lula's charm played a central role in earning him simultaneous invitations to address the World Economic Forum in Davos and the counter-World Social Forum, it was the liberal rationality of his economic policies and the continuation of an internationally oriented foreign policy and economic model that eased the frayed nerves of Western observers. Within a year, they realised that what Lula's Government was proposing through its foreign policy was not a dismantling of the global system, but a clarion call for the global South to exercise some self-belief and explore economic opportunities by engaging regional and global partners.[26]

By 2005 Lula's Brazil was being accepted as a potentially valuable participant in global affairs and, thus, worthy of a seat at the main international tables. At the heart of this global acceptance lay the strength of Brazil's domestic consensus on economic policy and the global credibility that Lula acquired in advocating for Southern development, as an explicit foreign policy goal and not simply electorate-appeasing genuflection.[27] Whilst this shift towards Southern solidarity as the lynch-pin for Brazilian foreign policy was grounded in the South American turn initiated by Cardoso, it reflected a much deeper shift in domestic dynamics at the diplomatic table.

Lula's Worker's Party took office with definite ideas on foreign policy grounded in the leftist activism of key figures such as presidential advisor Marco Aurelio Garcia and career diplomat Samuel Pinheiro Guimarães.[28] With the highly experienced Celso Amorim serving as Foreign Minister and overseer of North–South linkages and WTO questions, many diplomatic functions were effectively subdivided between Marco Aurelio, who shepherded South American affairs, and Samuel Pinheiro, who used his position as Itamaraty Secretary-General, to manage the broader approach to Southern solidarity. An informal checks-and-balances system emerged, with Amorim putting the brake on overambitious ideas emanating from Lula and his two chief foreign policy advisors. An example of this system can be seen after the WTO Cancun ministerial meetings in September 2003, when Lula mused that the success at the meeting of the G20 coalition of developing countries suggested space for a larger integrative project. Amorim quickly placed this proposition on the back-burner. But similar ideas did proceed, most notably the launching of an arrangement called the India–Brazil–South Africa Dialogue Forum (IBSA), which sought patiently to build pragmatic trilateral links amongst business, civil society, and bureaucrats.[29] Existing regional linkages were reinterpreted in a similar manner, with Lula's team repackaging Cardoso's South American vision as the Union of South American Nations (UNASUR) and working to bring Venezuela into *Mercosul* as a full partner.

The firm retention of foreign-policy strategy in the Planalto presidential palace was matched by a push to bring more voices into the discussion process. Towards the end of the Cardoso presidency, the São Paulo business community and the agro-industrial sector were beginning to express dissatisfaction with the shape of Brazil's global trade policy. Two of the leading figures in the call for change were Luiz Fernando Furlan, a leading agro-industrial executive, and Marcos Jank, an agricultural economist who had returned from the Interamerican Development Bank to establish ICONE, the Institute for International Trade Negotiations. Whilst Furlan lobbied behind the scenes, Jank engaged in a sustained assault upon Brazilian trade policy via the op-ed pages of leading Brazilian newspapers. Their respective voices were heard: Furlan became Minister of Development and International Trade in 2003, whereas Jank's think tank became the central research resource for Brazilian negotiations with the WTO.

This transformation represented a major change for Itamaraty, which suddenly received intricate technocratic input on foreign trade questions at a rate that exceeded its institutional analytical capacity. Its response was two-fold. First, recruitment was expanded and an emphasis put on acquiring the expertise needed to grapple with the sorts of technical issues that blurred the lines between economics and politics. Second, Itamaraty neatly repositioned itself as the Brazilian Government's diplomatic voice, taking on the role of coordinating interministerial and public discussions and brokering government-wide consensus positions that could then be projected externally.[30] In an even more innovative twist in at least the area of WTO negotiations, Itamaraty actively used the diversity of voices at the domestic policy table to formulate language and approaches that were more likely to receive acceptance at the heterogeneous G20 trade consultation table in Geneva.

This expansion of voices in the economic foreign policy-making process spread across other areas. A new defense policy was launched in 2008, which included a major international element by positing the pursuit of a South American-wide web of interoperable military systems. Congressional interest in Brazilian foreign policy grew significantly after the May 2006 surprise nationalisation of the natural gas industry in Bolivia. This single act, holding the prospect of cutting close to one-quarter of São Paulo's energy supplies, highlighted the extent to which the Lula presidency had succeeded in internationalising the daily reality of the Brazilian economy. It was soon followed by a string of trenchant attacks on the South–South tenor of Brazil's foreign policy. Most telling was the retirement of Roberto Abdenur, who left his post as ambassador to Washington, DC with an interview in the news magazine, *Veja*, that highlighted the anti-Americanism of Lula's coterie. Broader questions were raised by recently departed senior diplomats about the intelligence of a foreign policy predicated on South–South solidarity that appeared unable to protect critical national interests such as access to Bolivia's natural gas.

One of the central issues for these critics was the extent to which Lula appeared intent on constantly giving the benefit of the doubt to regional partners and engaging in an unprecedented expansion of activities in Africa, including the launch of a burgeoning foreign-aid program under the guise of bilateral technical cooperation.[31] Yet, this was precisely the point to the strategy devised by Lula's advisors, cogently summarised in a journal article subtitle: 'The search for autonomy through integration.'[32] Like Cardoso before him, Lula realised that Brazil lacked the power to stand alone in the global system and thus had to head a coalition that would magnify Brazil's importance. In a quirk of logic, Lula's approach to making this strategy work was actually more liberal and embracing of globalisation than the supposedly neoliberal policies of his predecessor. Running through the writing and thoughts of Lula's inner coterie of advisors was the belief that only through solidarity would Brazil be able to advance, that the country's future prosperity was predicated on bringing neighbouring countries and the global South to a higher level of socioeconomic development.[33] In short, globalisation was an opportunity to be collectively managed for mutual benefit, not simply rejected as an imperialist ruse.

Running underneath this idealistic approach to the internationalisation of national development is a more realist argument. As part of their long-range thinking, Brazilian diplomats are keenly aware that they face massive border- and immigration-related security problems if Brazil continues to grow in a rapid and sustainable manner and neighboring countries in South America do not. Whilst the war against poverty in Brazil is far from over, there is already a strong flow of illegal migrant workers from Bolivia and Paraguay into São Paulo and other places. A second aspect of the realist underpinnings to the logic of solidarity comes from Brazil's experience in the WTO Doha round negotiations (which began in 2001 and stalled in 2008), when it became clear that access to the markets of Europe and North America would, at best, be difficult. The untapped reserve markets are Latin America, which Brazil has already penetrated, and Africa, where demand exists for the sorts of low-end consumer goods produced in Brazil and in a regulatory ambience that displays the same sort of formal and informal institutional fluidity familiar to Brazilian entrepreneurs. Overlaying the pursuit of exports is the plethora of resource extraction and infrastructure construction opportunities in Africa. Brazilian firms have been quick to step into this market; and they have succeeded in winning contracts in competition with Western and Chinese firms. They have done so by drawing on the Lula Government's solidarity approach to foreign affairs to take a decennial time-line in profit-making rather than the dominant quarterly approach demanded by equity markets. The Brazilian Government has supported this process by creating the appropriate export credit lines at the National Bank for Economic and Social Development, which disbursed R$144 billion in 2009 (US$86 billion).

Whilst there are certainly mercantilist elements to Brazil's engagement with the global South, there is a sense that it lacks some of the harder-edged predatory aspects found in Western and Chinese engagement. This perception has contributed to Brazil being accepted by large swaths of the South as an acceptable interlocutor with the North, although it would be stretching the point considerably to suggest that the countries interacting most with Brazil completely trust it to protect and advance their interests. Rather, Brazil is seen as an international actor that at least faces the same challenges and limitations as other developing countries and, because it is willing to discuss these issues openly with potential partners, is likely to bring these perspectives to global decision-making tables. As the now-collapsed G8 Heiligendamm outreach process and the post-Global Financial Crisis G20 meetings demonstrate, other Great and Middle Powers are effectively turning to Brazil as a representative of the South that has the technocratic capability to contribute positively to the management of major issues. The corollary is that those Powers also expect Brazil to deliver the South and bring developing countries on board to support decisions made at the core global governance decision tables.

Brazil's welcome at these tables was publicly unveiled at the April 2009 G20 meeting in London. United States President Barack Obama broke off a conversation with another world leader during the obligatory photo opportunity to stop a passing Lula, grab his hand, and loudly announce: 'That's my man right here. Love this guy. He's the most popular politician on earth.' More formal gravitas was added to this benediction later in the year when Brazil was elected to one of the rotating UN Security Council seats. For the foreign policy advisors in the Planalto and Itamaraty palaces, this achievement was a sure sign that the future had arrived for Brazil. The problem that emerged was what to do with this future.

In Brazil's rise to global prominence, it has actively embraced some of the key characteristics of a Middle Power, chiefly coordinating consensus positions, framing alternate approaches to problems, and seeking inclusive policies to build the multilateral system to ensure the stability of global system. Within these bounds, there is considerable space for advancing new ideas and interpretations,[34] which is precisely how Brazil under Cardoso and Lula won its place at global diplomatic tables. However, this place is neither fixed nor guaranteed, and it is subject to a continuous process of reevaluation by the established Powers. To make matters more confusing for policy-makers, this place does not come with an instruction guide setting out clear limits on what sorts of activities are acceptable, which was problematic for a Lula team full of confidence that Brazil was now one of the central actors in international relations.

Brazil pushed the envelope in situations such as the 2010 Haitian earthquake recovery process by initially seeking to supplant countries such as Canada, France, and the United States as the leader in the island's reconstruction. In this case, the stakes were not particularly high for the other major Powers; and because there was a sufficiently strong international effort to coordinate programing, no country seriously tried to take over management and responsibility for the rebuilding of Haiti. Such assertiveness met with an altogether different reaction when it began to impinge on core international security questions. Lula's decision to work with Turkey in Spring 2010 to broker a nuclear enrichment deal with Iran was met with deep scepticism by senior

Itamaraty diplomats, who were effectively overruled by presidential advisors in the Planalto Palace. The result was nearly a withdrawal of Brazil's seat at the main global table. Although Lula's announcement of the May 2010 nuclear deal in Teheran prompted Brazilian television commentators literally to bounce in their seat with delight at their country's diplomatic victory, the more important reaction from United States Secretary of State Hillary Clinton was terse and blunt: 'Certainly we have very serious disagreements with Brazil's diplomacy vis-à-vis Iran.'[35] After further communications in the wake of a Brazilian UN Security Council vote against expanded sanctions against Iran, Itamaraty took the warnings on board and talked Lula down from his defence of the deal, which all but vanished from Brazilian diplomatic discourse within a few short weeks.

The short but stiff diplomatic fracas with the United States over Iran was quickly forgotten, but it remains illustrative of one of the key challenges that continue to face Brazilian diplomacy. The country's claims for global leadership are not based on traditional sources of power. Although Brazil loaned the IMF US$10 billion in the midst of the global financial crisis in 2008–9, in realistic terms this act was more a symbolic gesture to indicate the health of the Brazilian economy than a suggestion that the country might be a saviour for an embattled global economy. Traditional military power capabilities are if anything weaker than Brazil's economic power. Despite being the foremost military force in South America, the Brazilian military does not have force-projection capabilities, and certainly not the sort of offensive capability that would be needed to help control piracy off the coast of Somalia, let alone enforce a nuclear enrichment deal with Iran. Of course, Brazilian diplomats would respond that such actions would not be consistent with their country's pacific history and commitment to multilateralism and negotiation. This diplomatic tradition is also precisely why Brazil has been invited to take a seat at the main global diplomatic tables. The challenge that diplomats faced during the last two years of Lula's presidency was explaining this reality to domestic voices seeking to influence foreign policy-making. It is also a discussion that will continue during the presidency of Dilma Rouseff, Lula's Worker's Party successor, who took office on 1 January 2011 and retained some of the key advisors who helped guide Brazil to the center of the international system.

Notes

1 Matias Spektor, *Kissinger e o Brasil* (Rio de Janeiro, 2009).
2 E. Bradford Burns, *The Unwritten Alliance: Rio Branco and Brazilian-American Relations* (New York, 1966); Amado Luiz Cervo and Clodoaldo Bueno, *História da Política Exterior do Brasil* (Brasília, 2002); Joseph Smith, *Unequal Giants: Diplomatic Relations Between the United States and Brazil, 1889–1930* (Pittsburgh, PA, 1991); André Luiz Reis da Silva, *A Diplomacia Brasileira Entre a Segurança e o Desenvolvimento: A Política Externa do Governo Castelo Branco (1964–1967)* (Porto Alegre, 2004); Cíntia Vieira Souto, *A Diplomacia do Interesse Nacional: A Política Externa do Governo Medici* (Porto Alegre, 2003).
3 Rubens Ricupero, *Rio Branco: O Brasil no Mundo* (Rio de Janeiro, 2000).
4 Luiz Felipe Lampreia and Ademar Seabra da Cruz Junior, 'Brazil: Coping with Structural Constraints,' in Justin L Robertson and Maurice A East, eds., *Diplomacy and Developing Nations: Post-Cold War Foreign Policy-making Structures and Processes* (London, 2005).
5 Ney Canani, *Política Externa no Governo Itamar Franco, 1992–1994* (Porto Alegre, 2004).
6 Ministério das Relações Exteriores, *A Inserção Internacional do Brasil: A Gestão do Ministro Celso Lafer no Itamaraty* (Brasília, 1993).
7 Celso Lafer, 'Introduction', in Ministério das Relações Exteriores, *A Inserção Internacional do Brasil: A Gestão do Ministro Celso Lafer no Itamaraty* (Brasília, 1993), 25. [author translation].
8 Ministerio de Relações Exteriores, *Reflexões Sobre a Política Externa Brasileira* (Brasília, 1993).
9 Gelson Fonseca Júnior and Sérgio Henrique Nabuco de Castro, eds., *Temas de Política Externa Brasileira* (São Paulo, 1994).
10 Rubens Antônio Barbosa and Luís Panelli César, 'O Brasil como "Global Trade",' in Ibid.

11 Luigi Manzetti, 'Argentine-Brazilian Economic Integration: An Early Appraisal,' *Latin American Research Review*, Volume 25, Number 3 (1990), 109–40; Dominique Fournier, 'The Alfonsín Administration and the Promotion of Democratic Values in the Southern Cone and the Andes,' *Journal of Latin American Studies*, 31(1999), 39–74; Jeffrey Cason, 'On the Road to Southern Cone Economic Integration,' *Journal of Interamerican Studies and World Affairs*, 42(2002), 23–42; idem., 'Democracy Looks South: Mercosul and the Politics of Brazilian Trade Strategy,' in Peter R. Kingstone and Timothy J. Power, eds., *Democratic Brazil: Actors, Institutions, and Processes* (Pittsburgh, PA, 2000).

12 Juan Arias, 'Los socialdemócratas en Brasil apuestan por un tratado con la UE que no dependa de Mercosur: El candidato presidencial de la oposición cree que Brasil debe "avanzar solo",' *El País* (Spain) (17 July 2010); Jerônimo Teixeira, 'Mercado incomum', *veja.com* (19 May 2010).

13 Antonio de Aguiar Patriota, 'Keynote address by Ambassador Antonio de Aguiar Patriota Secretary-General of External Relations of Brazil,' to 'Canada and Brazil in the 21st Century' conference, Ottawa, Canada (10 May 2010).

14 Fernando Henrique Cardoso, *A Arte de Política: A História que Vivi* (Rio de Janeiro, 2006), 617–18.

15 Ted G. Goertzel, *Fernando Henrique Cardoso: Reinventing Democracy for Brazil* (Boulder, CO, 1999).

16 Maria Clara R.M. do Prado, *A Real História do Real: Uma Radiografia da Moeda que Mudou o Brasil* (Rio de Janeiro, 2005); Cardoso, *Arte de Política*, Chapter 3; Eliana Cardoso, 'Monetary and Fiscal Reforms,' in Mauricio A. Font and Anthony Peter Spanakos, eds., *Reforming Brazil* (New York, 2004).

17 Fernando Henrique Cardoso, *Discurso no Almoço com o Presidente do México na Fiesp* (São Paulo, 1999); idem., 'An Age of Citizenship,' *Foreign Policy*, 119(2000), 40–43; idem., 'Towards a Democratic Global Governance: A Brazilian Perspective,' The Cyrill Foster Lecture, University of Oxford (13 November 2002).

18 Paulo Sotero, 'Brasil vai testar novo modelo de investimento,' *O Estado de São Paulo*, 26 April 2004.

19 Mauro Brasil Francisco de Holanda, *O Gás no Mercosul: Uma Perspectiva Brasileira* (Brasília, 2001).

20 J. Peter Pham, 'Brazil Expanding Links in Africa: Lula's Positive Legacy' (12 October 2010): www.familysecuritymatters.org/publications/id.7624/pub_detail.asp.

21 Jean Daudelin, 'Trapped: Brazil, Canada and he Aircraft Dispute,' in Norman Hillmer and Maureen Appel Molot, eds., *Canada Among Nations 2001: A Fading Power* (Toronto, 2002), 256–79; Senado do Brasil, 'Notas Taquigráficas do Depoimento do Ministro Celso Lafer no Senado, 13 de Março de 2001,' *Inforel* No. 015/2001 (15 March 2001).

22 Pedro da Motta Veiga, 'Política Comercial no Brasil: Características, Condicionantes Domésticos e Policy-Making,' in Marcos Sawaya Jank and Simão Davi Silber, eds., Políticas Comerciais Comparadas: Desempenho e *Modelos Organizacionais* (São Paulo, 2007).

23 Monica Herz and João Pontes Nogueira, *Ecuador vs. Peru: Peacemaking Amid Rivalry* (Boulder, CO, 2002); Cardoso, *Arte da Política*, 634–40.

24 Jean Daudelin and Sean W. Burges, 'Brazil: How Realists Defend Democracy,' in Thomas Legler, Sharon F. Lean, and Dexter S. Boniface, eds., *Promoting Democracy in the Americas* (Baltimore, MD 2007).

25 Sérgio Danese, *Diplomacia Presidencial: História e Crítica* (Rio de Janeiro, 1999).

26 Sean W Burges, '*Auto-Estima* in Brazil: The Logic of Lula's South-South Foreign Policy,' *International Journal*, 60(2005), 1133–51.

27 Jean Daudelin, 'Joining the Club: Lula and the End of the Periphery for Brazil,' in Peter Birle, Sérgio Costa and Horst Nitschack, eds., *Brazil and the Americas: Convergences and Perspectives* (Madrid, 2008).

28 Paulo Roberto de Almeida, 'A Política Internacional do Partido dos Trabalhadores: Da Fundação à Diplomacia do Governo Lula,' *Revista Sociológica Política*, 20(June 2003), 87–102.

29 Chris Alden and Marco Antonio Vieira (2005), 'The New Diplomacy of the South: South Africa, Brazil, India and Trilateralism,' *Third World Quarterly*, 26(2005), 1077–95; João Genésio de Almeida Filho, *O Fórum de Diálogo Índia, Brasil e África do Sul (IBAS): Análise e Perspectivas* (Brasília, 2009).

30 Jeffrey W Cason and Timothy J Power, 'Presidentialization, Pluralization, and the Rollback of Itamaraty: Explaining Change in Brazilian Foreign Policy Making in the Cardoso-Lula Era,' *International Political Science Review*, Volume 30, Number 2(2009), 117–40.

31 Miriam Gomes Saraiva, 'As Estratégias de Cooperação Sul-Sul nos marcos da Política Externa Brasileira de 1993 a 2007,' *Revista Brasileira de Política Internacional*, Volume 50, Number 2(2007), 42–59; Luiz Alberto Moniz Bandeira, 'Política Exterior do Brasil—de FHC a Lula,' *Plenarium*, ano 2, n. 2 (Brasília, 2005), 64–82; Thiago Gehre Galvão, 'América do Sul: Construção Pela Reinvenção,' *Revista Brasileira de Política Internacional*, Volume 52, Number 2(2009), 63–80; Shiguenoli Miyamoto, 'O Brasil e a Comunidade dos Países de Língua Portuguesa,' Ibid., 22–42.

32 Tullo Vigevani and Marcello Fernandes de Oliveira (2007), 'Brazilian Foreign Policy in the Cardoso Era: The Search for Autonomy Through Integration,' *Latin American Perspecitves*, 34(2007), 58–80.

33 Author anonymous interview with senior presidential foreign-policy advisors, Brasília, May 2010.

34 Andrew Cooper, Richard Higgott, and Kim Richard Nossal, *Relocating Middle Powers: Australia and Canada in a Changing World Order* (Vancouver, 1993).

35 D. Gollust, 'Clinton Criticizes Brazil's Iran Diplomacy,' VOAnews.com (27 May 2010): www.voanews.com/english/news/Clinton-Criticizes-Brazils-Iran-Diplomacy-95064654.html.

11

Indian statecraft struggles to come to terms with India's rise

Harsh V. Pant

In November 2008, the financial capital of India, Mumbai, was struck by terrorists whom the Indian (as well as American and British) intelligence later confirmed had received extensive training from the Pakistan-based group, *Lashkar-e-Toiba* (Army of the Pure). Given the sophistication of planning and execution involved, it became apparent that this commando-style operation had the possible involvement of another state. As physical evidence mounted in terms of satellite phone calls, equipments, and boats used for the attack, Pakistan's hand was seen in the operation. Although India conceded that the newly installed civilian administration in Islamabad of Asif Ali Zardari was probably not behind the attacks, the army and Inter-Services Intelligence, Pakistan's principal intelligence agency, were seen as the main culprit.[1]

Public outcry after the Mumbai attacks was strong enough for the Indian Government to consider using the military option *vis-à-vis* Pakistan. But it soon emerged that India had neither the capability of imposing quick and effective retribution on Pakistan nor the kind of conventional superiority over its regional adversary that it had for the previous five decades.[2] This fact was surprising for a nation that the international community regarded as a major global economic and military Power, pursuing a defence modernisation programme estimated to be over US$50 billion over the next five years.

A year earlier, in another incident that confounded observers, India's Cabinet Secretary circulated a note to all Government ministers advising them against attending a function organised by the Gandhi Peace Foundation on behalf of the Dalai Lama.[3] A number of reasons were deduced for such an action. Perhaps the prime minister wished to assuage the concerns of the Indian Communist Parties, then part of the ruling coalition, that Indian foreign policy was tilting towards Washington; he wanted to send the message that India desired to preserve the upward trajectory in Sino-Indian ties. It is also possible that the Government wanted to thank China for the successful visit to that country by Congress Party President, Sonia Gandhi, during which some media reports suggested that China seemed to take a more favourable view of the United States–India nuclear deal then being negotiated.[4]

Yet outside observers remained perplexed about the goals of the Indian Government, since it contravened India's long-held position that the Dalai Lama is a not a mere political dissident but a widely revered Indian spiritual leader. Indeed some argued that India's genuflection to Chinese concerns about the Dalai Lama were probably not even in India's national interest. Delhi's position neither lived up to ideals for which India often claims it stands nor clearly enhanced India's strategic interests towards China. When Chinese authorities subsequently cracked down on Tibetan protests in Lhasa and elsewhere during the 2008 Olympic torch relay, India's

Government could not even condemn forcefully China's behaviour.[5] For the Government, it seemed a tough balancing act, but for the rest of the world it was a supine foreign-policy posture by a state that wants to be recognised as an emerging Great Power.

These episodes are symptomatic of the fundamental crisis facing Indian foreign policy at the beginning of the new millennium. As India's weight has grown in the international system in recent years, a perception exists that India is on the cusp of achieving 'Great Power' status. It is repeated *ad nauseum* in the Indian and global media, and India is already being asked to behave like one. There is just one problem: Indian policy-makers are unclear about what Great Power status entails. At a time when India's foreign-policy establishment should be vigorously debating the nature and scope of Indian engagement with the world, it is disappointingly silent. This intellectual vacuum has allowed Indian foreign policy to drift without any sense of direction, with the result that as the world is looking to India to help shape the emerging international order, it has little to offer except platitudinous rhetoric that does great disservice to its rising global stature.

As India makes its ascent in international politics, two issues will emerge as a major constraint. First, India will have to exploit the extant structure of international system to its advantage; structural constraints are the most formidable ones a state encounters in driving towards major Power status. Yet, Indian foreign policy continues to be reactive to the strategic environment and the constraints it imposes rather than trying to shape the strategic realities. Whilst such an *ad hoc* response to structural imperatives carried little cost when India was on the periphery of global politics, it can have grave consequences when Indian capabilities have risen to a point at which it seems poised to play a significant role in global politics. The second constraint is India's discomfort with the very notion of power and in particular, its wariness of the use of 'hard power.' All major Powers throughout history have demonstrated an ability to use skilfully their military as an effective instrument of national policy. India's reluctance to evolve a more sophisticated understanding of power, especially military power, will continue to underline the strategic diffidence that has come to be associated with Indian foreign and security policy.

If the global balance of power is indeed shifting from the Atlantic to the Pacific, then the rise of India (and China) is the indisputable reality that few can no longer dare to dismiss. Consequently, India is now being invited to G8 summits, is being called upon to shoulder global responsibilities from the challenges of nuclear proliferation to the instability in the Persian Gulf, and is increasingly being viewed as more than a mere 'South Asian' Power. From a nation that was mortgaging its gold reserves in 1990 to one whose foreign exchange reserves are overfull, from a nation that was marginal in the global distribution of economic might to one that is increasingly emerging as a centre of the modern global economy, India has come a long way. Its economy is one of the fastest growing in the world; it possesses nuclear weapons, a status being grudgingly accepted by the world; its armed forces are highly professional, moving toward rapid modernisation; and its vibrant democratic institutions, with the world's second-largest Muslim population, are attracting global attention at a time when the Islamic world is passing through turbulent times.

According to the United States National Intelligence Council Report, 'Mapping the Global Future,' the international community by 2020 will have to confront the military, political, and economic dimensions of the rise of China and India.[6] This report has likened the emergence of these Powers in the early twenty-first century to the rise of Germany in the nineteenth and America in the twentieth, with an impact potentially as dramatic. The Central Intelligence Agency has labelled India the key 'swing state' in international politics and predicts that by 2015, India will emerge as the fourth most important Power in the international system. According to Goldman Sachs, the four largest economies by 2040 will be China, the United States, India, and Japan.[7] India will overtake the G6 economies faster than expected; and its gross domestic product will probably surpass that of the United States before 2050, making it the second largest economy after China. After decades of marginalisation as a result of the vagaries of Cold War, its obsolescent model of economic management, and the seemingly never-ending tensions with Pakistan, India is starting to display flashes of self-confidence that accompany growing capabilities. Its global and regional ambitions are rising, showing aggressiveness in its foreign policy not heretofore seen. Yet it remains far from obvious that in line with these trends, India is crafting a foreign policy in tandem with its rising international stature. Whilst ignoring structural imperatives carried little cost when India occupied the periphery of global politics, it is being suggested that such disregard can have grave consequences when Indian capabilities have risen to a point at which it seems poised to play a significant international role.[8]

A nation's foreign policy flows from several sources: the international system, its domestic political imperatives, and cultural factors that underlie its society to the personal characteristics and perceptions of individual decision-makers. Like that of most nations, Indian foreign policy is a result of these varied factors at different levels of analysis interacting and transforming each other. But as a nation's weight in the global balance rises, it becomes imperative to pay greater attention to systemic constraints.[9] States do not emerge as Great Powers because they excel in one or another kind of capability. They rely on combined capabilities to serve their interests. Therefore, economic, military, territorial, demographic, and political capabilities cannot be weighed in isolation from each other.[10] Great Powers dominate and shape international politics, their behaviour largely a product of their external environment. The structure of the international system more than anything else shapes the foreign policies of Great Powers.

By any objective measure of material capability, India is a rising Power, and the consequences are visible in the international system. India is not yet a Great Power, although it is most certainly a leading contender for that status. India's increasing wealth and large population is latent power that India is and will be using to build up its military might.[11] As a result, it is not surprising that India is being asked to shoulder responsibilities consonant with its rising global stature. What is less clear is whether Indian foreign policy is up to the task and whether Indian policy-makers are willing to make hard choices.

Throughout the Cold War, India was concerned about getting entangled in the superpower rivalry. It made sense to choose a non-aligned foreign policy posture that at least in theory preserved India's decision-making autonomy. Behind the rhetoric of so-called Third World solidarity, there was cool-headed calculation aimed at protecting vital Indian interests. And these interests were fairly limited in scope given India's relatively restricted economic and military capabilities. Pakistan's security strategy was India's most immediate threat, thus India's obsession with Pakistan was not unexpected. But beyond Pakistan, there was little clarity, something brought home vividly in the stunning defeat at the hands of the Chinese in 1962. And even on Pakistan, there is little evidence to suggest that India had a coherent strategy.

Immediately at Independence, before any foreign-policy framework could be established, India's first Prime Minister, Jawaharlal Nehru, was required to address two interrelated problems: Kashmir and relations with Pakistan, which have remained important strands in Indian foreign policy ever since. But little evidence exists to suggest that India has ever evolved a coherent policy for countering Pakistan's security strategy, still less for resolving the Kashmir problem. Instead, India has reacted to events. The wars with Pakistan kept coming, and India kept fighting them without ever apparently making an assessment of whether a policy could be crafted to obviate war. It is instructive that for the last six decades, India has struggled to deal with the malevolence of a single hostile neighbour one-eighth its size.

More generally, Nehru wanted to construct a distinctive Indian approach to foreign policy, taking a certain distance from the views of its former colonial master. For almost two decades, his concerns about getting entangled in superpower rivalry found expression in support for the non-aligned movement (NAM) that, at least in theory, preserved India's foreign-policy decision-making autonomy. NAM was started when not wanting to join either of the two military blocs, the newly decolonised nations combined to assert their autonomy and pleas for disarmament and greater development aid. NAM possessed a certain weight in the era of decolonisation, yet mere reiteration of their non-aligned credentials did not prevent individual nations from having close relations with major Powers like the United States, the Soviet Union, and Britain. For all their pious declarations on global peace, non-aligned Powers have rarely shared significant convergent interests and have even fought among themselves. NAM was an impotent observer to the eight-year long Iran–Iraq conflict and several other direct and indirect conflicts among its member-states. And behind all the Indian rhetoric about Third World solidarity, there was cool calculation aimed at protecting vital Indian interests that were restricted in scope given India's relatively limited economic and military capabilities.

In 1962, the limitations of this policy were brought home by the Sino-Indian war, which virtually spelled the end of the Nehru era in Indian politics. But there was no real change in the direction of Indian foreign policy and, in 1971, India was again forced to reckon with global forces in the run-up to the war with Pakistan over Bangladesh. Since the very beginning, Pakistan had been a close American ally, thereby effectively balancing Indian preponderance in the subcontinent. When it became clear that the West, especially the United States, would not support India against Pakistan, Prime Minister Indira Gandhi was forced to court the Soviet Union to ensure that India would be able to prosecute its war without Great Power involvement. Thus, even though Washington dispatched the USS *Enterprise* to the Bay of Bengal to show support for Pakistan, India, with the Soviet Union on its side, successfully fought against Pakistan, and Bangladesh was born.

The one arena of foreign and security policy where India has had a long-term perspective is its approach to the nuclear question. Although at times the overall policy was contradictory (and its various strands at cross-purpose) India carved out a coherent policy that served its needs with great efficacy. The Chinese exploded their nuclear device in 1964. Coming on the heels of Indian defeat in 1962, this explosion shook the Indian foreign-policy elite and gave a sense of urgency to the Indian nuclear programme. The first option was support from the West, essentially seeking a nuclear umbrella. When the Indian efforts were rebutted, there was no option but to consolidate its own indigenous nuclear weapons programme. India's efforts in the nuclear realm culminated in what the then Indian Government rather disingenuously termed the 'Peaceful Nuclear Explosion' in 1974. Immediate sanctions were imposed by the international community and India was left out of the global high-technology regime, with long-term consequences for its economic and technological development.

These sanctions were also a result of India's opposition to the 1968 Nuclear Non-Proliferation Treaty (NPT), which India argued was discriminatory in nature by creating a two-tiered system of nuclear haves and have-nots. The five states allowed to keep their nuclear programmes had become nuclear Powers before 1968, whilst the remaining Powers were not to pursue nuclear weapons programmes. India argued that only global and comprehensive nuclear disarmament was acceptable and, in its absence, would be unwilling to surrender its right to pursue its nuclear weapons programme if its security interests so demanded. India viewed the NPT as an instrument of the nuclear Powers to legitimise their stockpiles by the comity of nations and, therefore, a tool to perpetuate their nuclear hegemony. It was a *realpolitik* approach to the global nuclear politics, and India successfully played this card until it developed an indigenous nuclear weapons capability that it demonstrated to the world in 1998. Today, when India has emerged as a *de facto* nuclear weapons state, it wants to be a part of the same 'hegemonistic' security architecture that it once so vociferously decried. The two mainstream political parties, the Congress and the Bharatiya Janata

Party (BJP), have had similar approaches on nuclear issues ever since the former Prime Minister, Rajiv Gandhi, initiated weaponisation in the late 1980s. Traditionally, only the Indian Communist parties have not supported the nuclear weapons programme, but they have generally been marginal in national security decision-making.

The Bangladesh War initiated twenty years of close relations between India and the Soviet Union, so close that India did not criticise the Soviet misadventure in Afghanistan in 1979. But India's balance of power approach, although skilful, was still reactive, not based on any strategic assessment of its long-term foreign-policy priorities. Although the era of decolonisation had largely ended, NAM's principles were still upheld, and India's self-identification with the colonised found expression in Rajiv Gandhi's criticisms of Margaret Thatcher's policy on Rhodesia/ Zimbabwe. In the mid-1980s, Indian policy-makers seem to have been attracted by a more assertive policy towards India's neighbours, although this 'Regional Gendarme' role had mixed results. The economic blockade of Nepal certainly helped bring down its absolute monarchy, but intervention in Sri Lanka caused more problems than it solved, and incidentally led to Rajiv's assassination. But the disintegration of the Soviet Union and the consequent collapse of the Indian economy soon occupied centre stage. In some ways, the end of the Cold War came as a blessing in disguise because Indian policy-makers were forced to adapt to new global political and economic realities. The economic crisis that India faced in the early 1990s forced it to move from the dominant Nehruvian socialist paradigm towards economic liberalisation and greater integration into the global economy. Concurrently, the demise of the former Soviet Union changed the nature of the international system.

Many of the central assumptions about Indian foreign policy had to be reviewed in light of changed circumstances. The shape of the world changed, signalling the possibility of a new Indian foreign and national security strategy. A rapidly shifting geostrategic landscape confronted India as it made its way up the interstate hierarchy. At the beginning of the new millennium, India is on the threshold of achieving the status of a major global Power, emerging as an indispensable, albeit reluctant, element of the new global order exemplified not only by its growing economic and military might but also the attraction of its political and cultural values. But even as India's rise in that hierarchy continues steadily, its policy-makers act as if India can afford the luxury of responding to foreign-policy challenges on a case-by-case basis without the requirement of a long-term strategic policy framework. The same *ad hocism* that characterised Indian foreign policy in the past continues. It is two decades since the Cold War ended, and India still debates the relevance of NAM. Whatever the merits or otherwise of NAM, India's foreign-policy establishment holds rigidly to the concepts and intellectual frameworks that may have been useful when they were developed but which have become outmoded in the present strategic context.

How states respond to their relative material rise or decline has long been central to understanding the forces that shape international politics:

> Similar security policies recur throughout history and across the international system in states that, whatever their differences, occupy similar positions in the international system ... The security policies of very strong states are different from those of very weak ones, and both differ from those of states that are neither very strong nor very weak.[12]

Structural constraints, in other words, force states towards particular foreign policies in line with their relative position in the international system. As that position undergoes change, so does foreign policy. As Robert Gilpin explains, 'a more wealthy and a more powerful state ... will select a larger bundle of security and welfare goals than a less wealthy and less powerful state,'[13] thereby using the tools at its disposal to gain control over its strategic environment. A state, hence, will become more ambitious in defining the scale and scope of its foreign policy as its relative material power capabilities increase and *vice versa*. Indian policy-makers will have to make some crucial and necessary foreign-policy choices as India reaches a turning point in its relations with the rest of the world, the most important of which will deal with how best to exploit the extant structure of the international system to national advantage.

But a fundamental foreign-policy quandary that has long dogged India and has become more acute with India's ascent in the international order is what Sunil Khilnani has referred to as India's lack of an 'instinct for power.' Power lies at the heart of international politics. It affects the influence that states exert over one another, thereby shaping political outcomes. Foreign-policy success and failure is largely a function of a nation's power and the manner in which that power is wielded. The exercise of power can be shocking, and at times corrupting, but power is absolutely necessary to fight the battles that must be fought. India's ambivalence about power and its use has resulted in a situation in which even as India's economic and military capabilities have gradually expanded, it has failed to evolve a commensurate strategic agenda and requisite institutions to mobilise and use its resources optimally.

India faces a unique conundrum: its political elites desperately want global recognition for India as a major Power and all the prestige and authority associated with it. Yet, their reticence about acquiring and using power in foreign affairs continues. Most recently, this ambivalence was expressed by the Indian Minister of Commerce when he suggested that 'this word power often makes me uncomfortable.'[14] Although talking about the economic rise of India and the challenges that it faces as it continues to strive for sustained economic growth, his discomfort with the notion of India as a rising Power indicated a larger reality in the Indian polity. This ambivalence about using power in international politics, where 'any prestige or authority eventually rely upon traditional measures of power, whether military or economic',[15] is curious, because the Indian political elites have rarely shied away from the maximisation of power in domestic politics, thereby corroding the institutional fabric of liberal democracy in the country.

In what has been diagnosed as a 'mini-state syndrome,' those states lacking the material capabilities to make a difference to outcomes at the international level often denounce the concept of power in foreign-policy making.[16] India had long been one of these states, viewing itself as an object of the foreign policies of a small majority of powerful nations. Thus, its political and strategic elite developed a suspicion of power politics, with the word 'power' acquiring a pejorative connotation concerning foreign policy. The relationship between power and foreign policy was never fully understood, leading to a progressive loss in India's ability to wield power effectively in the international realm.

Vital interests, in the ultimate analysis, can be preserved and enhanced only if the nation has sufficient power capabilities at its disposal. India's lack of an instinct for power is most palpable in military affairs, in which, unlike other major global Powers of the past and the present, India has failed to master the creation, deployment, and use of its military resources in support of its national objectives.[17] Nehru envisioned making India a global leader without any help from the nation's armed forces, arguing, 'the right approach to defense is to avoid having unfriendly relations with other countries—to put it differently, war today is, and ought to be, out of the question.'[18] War has, thus, been systematically factored out of India's foreign policy and national security matrix, with a resulting ambiguity about India's ability to withstand future major wars.

Few nations face the kind of security challenges confronting India. Yet, since independence, the military was never seen as central in achieving Indian national priorities; the tendency of Indian political elites is to downplay the importance of military power. India ignored the defence sector after independence and paid inadequate attention to its defence needs. Even though the policy-makers themselves had little knowledge of critical defence issues, the armed forces had almost no role in the formulation of defence policy till 1962.[19] Divorcing foreign policy from military power was a recipe for disaster, as India realised in 1962 when even Nehru was forced to concede that 'military weakness has been a temptation, and a little military strength may be a deterrent.'[20] A state's legitimacy is tied to its ability to monopolise the use of force and operate effectively in an international strategic environment; India has lacked clarity on the relationship between the use of force and its foreign-policy priorities.

After Independence, Indian politicians viewed the Indian Army with suspicion, seeing it as the last supporter of the British Raj, and did their best to isolate the military from policy-making. This attitude was further reinforced by the views of two giants of the Indian nationalist movement, Mahatma Gandhi and Nehru. Gandhi's ardent belief in non-violence left little room for accepting the use of force in an independent India. It also shaped the views of the first generation of post-independence political leaders on military and defence. But more important has been the legacy of Nehru, who laid the institutional foundations for Indian civil–military relations. His obsession with economic development was matched only by his disdain and distrust of the military, resulting in the sidelining of defence planning.[21] He also ensured that the experiences in neighbouring Pakistan, where the military had become the dominant political force soon after Independence, would not be repeated in India. He thus institutionalised civilian supremacy over the country's military apparatus. The civilian elite also did not want the emergence of a rival elite with direct access to political leadership.

Along with Nehru, another politician who left a lasting impact on the evolution of civil–military relations was V.K. Krishna Menon, the Minister of Defence from 1957 to 1962. During his tenure, described as the most controversial stewardship of the Indian Defense Ministry, he heralded a number of organisational changes unpopular with the armed forces.[22] Despite any military experience, Nehru and Menon were actively involved in operational level planning before the outbreak of the Sino-Indian war of 1962. They 'directly supervised the placement of individual brigades, companies, and even platoons, as the Chinese and Indian forces engaged in mutual encirclement of isolated outposts.'[23] Consequently, when China won a decisive victory, the blame was laid at the doors of Nehru and Menon. Menon resigned, whereas Nehru's reputation suffered a lasting damage. Defeat also made clear both to the civilians and the military that purely operational matters were best left to military experts. Some have argued that since then a convention has been established whereby operational directives are laid down by the political leadership and the actual planning of operations is left to the chiefs of staff.[24]

In his study of the impact of societal structures on the military effectiveness of a state, Stephen Rosen argues that the separation of the military from Indian society, whilst preserving the coherence of the Indian Army, has reduced the effective military power of the Indian state.[25] Whilst India has been successful in evolving a sustained tradition of strict civilian control over the military since its independence, unlike its immediate neighbours, it has been unable to evolve institutions and procedures that allow substantive military participation in the national security decision-making processes. This process has significantly reduced the effectiveness with which India can wield its military as an instrument of national power.

A state can promulgate law and pursue strategy once it has not only achieved a legitimate monopoly on violence, but also when it is free of the coercive violence of other states.[26] It is not a surprise therefore that India's ability to think strategically on issues of national security remains at best questionable. George Tanham, in his landmark study on Indian strategic thought, observed that Indian elites have shown little evidence of having thought coherently and systematically about national strategy. He argued that this lack of long-term planning and strategy owes largely to India's historical and cultural developmental patterns. These patterns include the Hindu view of life as largely unknowable, thereby being outside man's control, and the Hindu concept of time as eternal, thereby discouraging planning. In consequence, Tanham asserted that India has been on the strategic defensive throughout its history, reluctant to assert itself except within the subcontinent.[27]

India's former Minister for External Affairs, Jaswant Singh, has also examined the evolution of strategic culture in both Indian society and its political decision-making class with particular reference to post-1947. He also finds Indian political elites lacking the ability to think strategically about foreign-policy and defence issues, although he trains his guns on Nehru, pointing to his 'idealistic romanticism' and unwillingness to institutionalise strategic thinking, policy formulation, and implementation.[28] It is ironic, however, that even when Singh was the External Affairs minister, there is little evidence that anything of substance really changed in so far as the strategic dimension of India's foreign policy is concerned. For all the blame that Singh lays at Nehru's door, even he and his Government did not move towards the institutionalisation of strategic thinking, policy formulation, and implementation. Perhaps, the Indian strategic culture became too powerful a constraint for even him to overcome.

A major outcome of the lack of Indian strategic culture is a perceptible need for institutionalisation of foreign-policy making in India. At its very foundation, Indian democracy is sustained by a range of institutions from the more formal ones of the executive, legislative, and the judiciary to the less formal of the broader civil-society. It is these institutions that in large measure have allowed Indian democracy to thrive and flourish for more than fifty years despite a number of constraints that have led to the failure of democracy in many other societies. However, in foreign policy, the lack of institutionalisation has allowed a drift to set in without any long-term orientation. Some have laid the blame on Nehru for his unwillingness to construct strategic planning architecture because he single-handedly shaped Indian foreign policy during his tenure.[29] But even his successors have failed to pursue institutionalisation in a consistent manner. The BJP-led National Democratic Alliance came to power in 1999 promising to establish a National Security Council (NSC) to analyze the military, economic, and political threats to the nation and to advise the Government on meeting these challenges effectively.

Whilst setting up the NSC in the late 1990s and defining its role in policy formulation, this Government neglected to institutionalise the NSC and build up its capabilities to play the role assigned to it. It thereby failed to underpin national security by structural and systematic institutional arrangements. Important national security decisions were taken in an *ad hoc* manner without using the Cabinet Committee on Security, the Strategic Policy Group (comprising key secretaries, service chiefs, and heads of intelligence agencies) and officials of the National Security Advisory Board. Moreover, as has been rightly pointed out, the NSC structure makes long-term planning impossible, thereby negating the very purpose of its formation; and its effectiveness remains hostage to the weight of the National Security Advisor (NSA) in national politics.[30] The NSA has become the most powerful authority on national security, sidelining the NSC.

Whilst the Congress-led United Progressive Alliance came to power in 2004 promising to make the NSC a professional and effective institution and blaming the NDA for making only cosmetic changes to institutional arrangements, it has so far failed to make it work in an optimal manner whereby the NSC anticipates national security threats, coordinates the management of national security, and engenders long-term planning by generating new and bold ideas. An effective foreign-policy institutional framework would not only identify the challenges but it would also develop a coherent strategy to deal with it, organise and motivate the bureaucracy, and persuade and inform the public. The NSC, by itself, is not a panacea, particularly in light of the inability of the American NSC to mediate successfully in the bureaucratic wars and effectively coordinate policy. But the lack of an effective Indian NSC is reflective of Delhi's *ad hoc* foreign-policy decision-making process. If there is any continuity in India's approach to foreign policy and national security, it is the inability and unwillingness of policy-makers, across political ideologies, to give strategic vision to the nation's foreign-policy priorities.

There is clearly an appreciation in the Indian policy-making circles of India's rising capabilities. It is reflected in a gradual expansion of Indian foreign-policy activity in recent years, in the attempt to reshape Indian defence forces, and in the desire to seek greater global influence. But this process is happening in an intellectual vacuum with the result that micro issues dominate the foreign-policy discourse in the absence of an overarching framework. Because foreign policy does not tend to win votes, little incentive exists for political parties to devote serious attention to it; the result is *ad hoc* responses to crises as they emerge. The recent debates on the United States–India nuclear deal, on India's role in the Middle East, on engagements with Russia and China in the so-called 'Strategic Triangle,' and on India's policy towards its immediate neighbours are all important; but ultimately they are of little value because they fail to clarify the singular issue facing India today: what should be the trajectory of Indian foreign policy when India is emerging from the structural confines of the international system as a rising Power on way to a possible Great Power status?

There was a long-held myth propagated by the political elites that there has been a general consensus across political parties on major foreign-policy issues. Aside from the fact that such a consensus has more been a result of intellectual laziness and apathy than any real attempt to forge a coherent grand strategy that cuts across ideological barriers, it is most certainly an exaggeration. Until the early 1990s, the Congress Party's dominance over the Indian political landscape was almost complete and there was no political organisation of an equal capacity to bring to bear its influence on foreign and security policy issues in the same measure. It was the rise of the Hindu nationalist BJP that gave India a different foreign-policy voice. But more important, it is the changes in the international environment that have forced Indian policy-makers to challenge some of the assumptions underlying their approach to the outside world.

To the extent that it is taking place, the strategic debate is grounded in two abstractions. The left-liberal side sees economics as a substitute for strategy, steadfast in their belief that India only needs to keep focusing on its economic growth and the world will soon recognise India as a major power. The policy prescription that follows is that Indian foreign policy should be geared towards deepening its economic engagement with friends and foes alike. Influenced by this approach, the present Indian Prime Minister has articulated a vision of Indian foreign policy, according to which it exists to push pragmatic economic goals (especially as India integrates more and more with the global economy) and also to build a world of open inclusive nations. This understanding of foreign policy unambiguously identifies India with other liberal democracies of the world. The Prime Minister has also suggested that the global environment has never been more conducive for India's economic development than today and the world wants to help India achieve its full potential. He has argued that India should engage other Great Powers like the United States and China to the fullest, and neither should be treated as an adversary.[31] The right of the political spectrum already sees India as a Great Power and argues that India should start behaving as one without worrying about the constraints on its ability to pursue its ends. This view would like India to take on the United States as well as China at the same time and disregards any structural constraints that might impinge on the behaviour of India as a rising Power. Both of these mainstream foreign-policy approaches ignore the practical realities that a rising Power must encounter to be able to leverage its power effectively in an international system to achieve its national interests.

In debating the nature and scope of its engagement with the world, India will have to bring its commitments and power into balance or in a different context in which its means equal its purposes and its purposes are within its means. To this end, India will need an intellectual and political leadership, which seems in short supply at the moment. Its foreign-policy elite remains mired in the exigencies of day-to-day pressures emanating from the immediate challenges at hand rather than evolving a grand strategy that integrates the nation's multiple policy strands into a cohesive whole, to preserve and enhance Indian interests in a rapidly changing global environment. The assertions, therefore, that India does not have a China policy or an Iran policy or a Pakistan policy are irrelevant. India does not have a foreign policy, period. This lack of strategic orientation often results in a paradoxical situation in which, on one hand, India is accused by various domestic constituencies of angering this or that country by its actions whilst, on the other, India's relationship with almost all major Powers is termed as a 'strategic partnership' by Delhi.

More recently, the Indian Government has been accused of betraying its time-tested friends such as Iran and Russia, as if the only purpose of foreign policy is to make friends. A nation's foreign policy cannot be geared towards trying to keep every other country in the world in good humour. India has been extremely fortunate in encountering a benign international environment for the last several years, making it possible for it to expand its bilateral ties with all the major Powers simultaneously. This trend has given rise to some rather fantastic suggestions such as India being well-placed to be a 'bridging power,' enjoying harmonious relations with all major Powers (the United States, Russia, China, and the European Union). Such a suggestion not only implies that the major global Powers are willing to be 'bridged' but also that India has the capabilities and influence to be such a 'bridge.' It is mere wishful thinking that cannot be a substitute for serious policy, however desirable it may appear on the surface. Moreover, the period of stable major Power relations is rapidly coming to an end and, soon, difficult choices will have to be made. Indian policy-makers should have enough self-confidence to make those decisions even when they go against their long-held predilections. But a foreign policy lacking intellectual and strategic coherence will ensure that India will forever remain poised on the threshold of Great Power status but will not be quite able to cross it.

India is being told that it is on the verge of becoming a Great Power. But no one is clear what India intends to do with the accretion of economic and military capabilities and with its purported great power status. India today, more than at any other time in its history, needs a view of its role in the world quite removed from the shibboleths of the past, allowing India to shed its defensive attitude in framing its interests and grand strategy. Despite enormous challenges that it continues to face, India is widely recognised today as a rising Power with enormous potential. The portents are hopeful if only the Indian policy-makers have the imagination and courage to seize some of the opportunities.

Notes

1 Raj Chengappa, 'The Real Boss,' *India Today*, 11 December 2008.
2 Shekhar Gupta, 'No First Use Options,' *Indian Express*, 17 January 2009.
3 'Pleasing Beijing, Govt tells its Ministers Don't Attend Dalai Lama Honour Function,' *Indian Express*, 4 November 2007.
4 For a detailed examination of the United States–India negotiations on the civilian nuclear energy cooperation pact, see Harsh V. Pant, *Contemporary Debates in Indian Foreign and Security Policy: India Negotiates Its Rise in the International System* (New York, 2008), 19–37.
5 Somini Sengupta, 'India Tiptoes in China's Footsteps to Compete but Not Offend,' *New York Times*, 4 April 2008.
6 The report is available at: www.cia.gov/nic/NIC_globaltrend2020.html
7 The report is available at: www2.goldmansachs.com/insight/research/reports/99.pdf
8 C.R. Mohan, 'India's Grand Strategy in the Gulf', in Gulf Research Centre and the Nixon Centre, *India's Growing Role in the Gulf Implications for the Region and the United States* (Dubai, Washington, DC, 2009), 55–70.
9 Christopher Layne, 'The Unipolar Illusion: Why New Great Powers Will Rise?', *International Security*, Volume 17, Number 4(1993), 9–10.

Harsh V. Pant

10 On the identification of Great Powers by the measurement of capabilities, see Kenneth Waltz, *Theory of International Politics* (Reading, MA, 1979), 129–31.
11 On why it makes sense to define power in terms of material capabilities rather than outcomes, see John J. Mearsheimer, *The Tragedy of Great Power Politics* (New York, 2001), 55–82.
12 Michael Mandelbaum, *The Fates of Nations: The Search for National Security in the Nineteenth and Twentieth Centuries* (Cambridge, UK, 1988), 2, 4.
13 Robert Gilpin, *War and Change in World Politics* (Cambridge, UK, 1981), 22–23, 94–95.
14 The full transcript of this speech is available at: www.iiss.org.uk/conferences/iiss-citi-india-global-forum/igf-plenary-sessions-2008/opening-remarks-and-dinner-address/dinner-address-kamal-nath
15 Michael Sheehan, *The Balance of Power: History and Theory* (London, 1996), 7.
16 K. Subrahmanyam, *Indian Security Perspectives* (New Delhi, 1982), 127.
17 This point has been eloquently elaborated in Ashley J. Tellis, *Future Fire: Challenges Facing Indian Defense Policy in the New Century*, Delivered at the India Today Conclave, New Delhi, 13 March 2004: www.ceip.org/files/pdf/futurefire.pdf.
18 Quoted in P.V.R. Rao, *India's Defence Policy and Organisation Since Independence* (New Delhi, 1977), 5–6.
19 K. Subrahmanyam, *Perspectives in Defence Planning* (New Delhi, 1972), 126–33.
20 Lorne J. Kavic, *India's Quest for Security: Defence Policies, 1947–1965* (Berkeley, CA, 1967), 192.
21 Stephen P. Cohen, *India: Emerging Power* (New Delhi, 2001), 127–30.
22 P.R. Chari, 'Civil-Military Relations in India,' *Armed Forces and Society*, 4(1977), 13–15.
23 S. Cohen, *The Indian Army. Its Contribution to the Development of a Nation* (Berkeley, CA, 1971), 176.
24 P.R. Chari, 'Civil-Military Relations of India,' *Link* (15 August, 1977), 75.
25 Stephen P. Rosen, *Societies and Military Power: India and Its Armies* (Ithaca, NY, 1996), 250–53.
26 Philip Bobbitt, *The Shield of Achilles: War, Peace, and the Course of History* (New York, 2003), 336.
27 George Tanham, *Indian Strategic Thought: An Interpretive Essay* (Santa Monica, CA, 1992).
28 Jaswant Singh, *Defending India* (New York, 1999), 1–58.
29 Ibid., 34.
30 Ashley J. Tellis, *India's Emerging Nuclear Posture: Between Recessed Deterrent and Ready Arsenal* (New York, 2001), 658.
31 The Prime Minister's speech at the India Today Conclave delivered on 25 February 2005: http://pmindia.nic.in/speeches.htm.

12

Contemporary Canadian foreign policy

A middle Power in a Great Power world

Stéphane Roussel

Canada is the middle Power *'par excellence'*. At the first sight, Canada seems to match closely with the concept as it is usually understood: neither a Great Power nor a small Power; some significant international interests but not the resources to defend or to promote them unilaterally; and displaying some elements linked with the notion of Great Power, but not all. The Canadian Government can thus count on some resources (like a developed economy, a highly educated population, or the control over some strategic raw materials) to gain some international influence; but it clearly lacks others (for instance, significant military power or a large population). Canadian officials were amongst the first to use the concept of 'middle Power' during and after the Second World War to secure Canada's place in the post-war international order; reminding the Great Powers that they could not dominate the world in a restricted Concert without the support of the other smaller Powers whose contributions were significant, if not crucial, to the victory of 1945.

The concept of middle Power was useful for Canadian decision-makers and politicians to express their demands and expectations. But when academics attempted with mixed results to reframe the same concept for analytical purposes, they reached its limits quickly: if the concept of middle Power can show what Canada (or Australia, Brazil, Poland, India, or South Africa) is *not*, which is neither a Great Power nor a small one, it remains nonetheless difficult to say what *is* a middle Power. In fact, the foreign policies of the states usually labelled as 'middle Powers' bear little in common. Even the notion of 'regional Power' is unhelpful because whilst some of these states can dominate in their region (say Brazil or South Africa) many others (like Canada) lack a 'natural' region or share it with a Great Power that obliterates their potential leadership.

The concept of middle Power remains useful in a normative perspective (how it guides policy-makers and is used in political discourse) but cannot be used to describe an *objective* reality. Is it a reason to discard the concept of power as an analytical tool in considering Canada? Certainly not. The notion of power helps to understand the international behaviour of these states when used in a relative and subjective perspective. First, it is crucial to take into account the specific qualities of each 'middle Power' beyond the fact that they do not enjoy a certain level of strength sufficient to promote their international interests; second, to qualify the nature of their relationship with the Great Powers; and last, to understand the worldviews and perceptions of the political elites regarding power relationships and Canada's place in the international power hierarchy.

Contemporary Canadian foreign policy emerged during the second half of the Second World War. Whilst the First World War accelerated dramatically the emergence of the country as an independent international agent, it nevertheless took another twenty-five years to develop a real, consistent, and working foreign-policy doctrine. The Second World War clarified for the new generation of Canadian diplomats that the country had a strong and significant international interest and that a policy of isolationism (which dominated Canadian foreign policy between the two Wars) no longer had utility. To the contrary, to guarantee its security, prosperity, and newly acquired sovereignty, Canada had to engage the world. In 1945, all the central pieces of the new foreign policy were in place: strong commitments to multilateralism and international organisations, a clear anchor in the Western camp, promotion of liberal values, a growing concern for trade issues, and a defiance or reluctance toward purely military solutions to political problems.

Hence, Canada was one of the most enthusiastic founding members of the United Nations (UN), the North Atlantic Treaty Organization (NATO), and almost all other post-war institutions.[1] Institutions were perceived as the best way to balance relationships with the Great Powers by providing the opportunity for small and middle Powers to work together to create a counterweight. International institutions were also viewed as a forum where Canadian political and diplomatic viewpoints could influence the world's Great Powers. More generally, multilateralism and international institutions reflected the idea that they represented the best, if not the only way, for a middle Power to protect and promote its international interests.[2] But global multilateralism was always subordinated to a regional one when applied to transatlantic relations. Whilst the same principles were applied in the North Atlantic region, Canadians never hide that they are first and foremost linked to the Western world, above any other relationship. 'Atlanticism' in Canadian foreign policy finds its source in the historical roots of Canada's French and English colonies; in a set of shared values and culture; in the strong economic ties established over the nineteenth century with the British Isles; and that Canadian politicians and diplomats simply preferred to not stay alone with their powerful North American neighbour.[3] Canada's commitment to Atlanticism is just the modern version of an older concept, the 'North Atlantic Triangle'(or 'Triangle ABC', because it was applied to a relationship between Americans, British and Canadians), in which Canadians sought both stability and balance between its two main partners.[4] More than sixty years after its creation, NATO remains a central pillar of Canada's foreign and defense policies.

Both as a cause and consequence of Canada's close relations with the Western world, the defense and promotion of Western values and culture emerged as a core feature of Canadian foreign policy. Called 'The values of the Christian civilization' in 1947,[5] they could be associated today with a contemporary version of the classical liberal philosophy. Here, the promotion of democracy, human rights, and a free market economy are mixed with some 'centre leftist values', such as social justice and wealth redistribution, to create the prominent features of Canadian international action. This philosophy also explains Canadian faith in institutions as a solution to conflicting interests. Even if the same can be said about the foreign policy of numerous other Western (and even non-Western) states, since 1945, Canadians were probably amongst the most vocal in pursuing these values.

Evidence of this idealist dimension in Canadian foreign policy can be found regularly since 1945.[6] The Canadian Government earned a solid reputation by promoting international norms of human rights or human security. One of the most celebrated aspects of this idealism (by Canadians themselves) was the Canadian commitment to UN peace-keeping missions during and immediately after the Cold War. The concept of the 'blue helmet' was suggested by Canada's Minister of External Affairs, Lester B. Pearson, during the 1956 Suez Crisis; and Canada remained one of the most stalwart contributors to these missions over the next forty years.

Canadian foreign policy is heavily shaped by some of its specific national features that make it different from any other so-called 'middle Power'. These features can largely explain Canada's international behaviours, as well as its particularities. First, geography is a key variable to understanding the evolution of Canadian foreign policy. As the second largest country in the world (10 million square kilometres) it possesses the longest coastlines (202,000 kilometres), bordering three oceans. For such a huge territory, Canada has relatively few neighbours. If the borders with Denmark (Greenland) and France (St-Pierre-et-Miquelon) do not require constant attention except over minor issues or conflicts, the one with the United States does. It is the longest in the world and has a tremendous impact on Canadian politics in terms of security, trade, and culture. Canada has a fourth neighbour, Russia, even if there is no common border. But since it is possible that Russia's continental shelf is connected with North America's somewhere under the Arctic Ocean, the two countries could be considered as geographically closer than it would initially seem.

These geographical features mean that Canada is located away from historical axes of instability (Europe, the Middle East or South West Asia), it has been spared the fear of a foreign invasion since the end of the nineteenth century, and it has never seriously suffered from destruction or occupation by foreign military.[7] With the exception of the United States, no Power seriously posed a threat against Canadian security or sovereignty until the development of Soviet long-range bombers and nuclear weapons in the early Cold War. Considering Canada's obvious weaknesses (a huge territory and a limited workforce) this absence of threat was a great asset. In a few words, Canada is too huge to be defensible and too isolated to be vulnerable. A lack of a tragic history could explain the attitude of Canadian political leaders and public opinion that displays a reluctance to spend significant resources on defence in peacetime. War always remains something at a distance; even the emergence of weapons of mass destruction and international terrorism did not really change that attitude. Moreover, Canadian society never paid a discernible price for neglecting its armed force in peacetime.[8] In fact, the absence of collective trauma and its sense of immediacy partly explain why Canadian diplomacy can afford the luxury of bearing a good dose of idealism.

Of course, geography also placed Canada in the immediate vicinity of the international system's dominant power. Such proximity means that Canadian–American relations are different from any other relationship that Washington may develop with other middle or small Powers, with the possible exceptions of Mexico and some Caribbean states. Since the beginning of the twentieth century, Americans and Canadians have had to discuss a variety of issues, including fisheries, border management, the environment, technical standardisation, transport infrastructure, labour, and immigration. Surprisingly, Canadians did very well in their relations with their American counterpart, and the middle Power was rarely, if ever, 'dominated' by its powerful neighbours.

'Canada', according to Herman Kahn, 'is a regional power without a region';[9] this statement recognises the country's importance in the international system and the consequences of its isolation. Nevertheless, three oceans surrounding the country could be viewed as gateways for developing relationships with other regions. For a long while, Europe was the privileged region for Canadians thanks to colonial links and the transatlantic bridge. But Europe lost part of its importance as a privileged region in the last decades of the twentieth century. In the mid-1990s, the Pacific Rim emerged as a potential contender as Canada's new privileged region, but those hopes never materialised.[10] In the early 2000s, global warming and dramatic changes in the Arctic forced Canadians to take a fresh look at the circumpolar relations; but the unilateral and very defensive approach taken by Ottawa after 2004 prevented the development of a strong circumpolar diplomacy.

Another feature that explains a good deal of Canadian diplomacy is that Canada is a merchant country, a society whose prosperity is strongly tied to international trade. Roughly one-third of the Canadian national wealth derives from international trade. However, its trade structure is uneven: the American market absorbs between 70 and 80 percent of Canadian exports, sometimes peaking to 85 percent. The Canadian economy is deeply integrated with the American one on all levels: finance, production, distribution, and knowledge-based. The situation can be viewed from different perspectives: nationalists like to describe this relationship as one of 'Canadian dependence', whilst others prefer the word 'interdependence'. The importance of external trade to Canadian prosperity heavily shapes Canadian diplomacy. Ottawa can be described as a 'stability seeker', seeking a predictive, organised, and institutionalised environment that encourages and promotes international trade.

The 'stability seeker' is at work in Canada's relationship with the United States when protecting Canadian trade from radical changes in the American market. Three strategies have traditionally been promoted. The first was protectionism, used in the nineteenth century and on some occasions in the early twentieth century; it is no longer a viable option. Used regularly since the mid-nineteenth century, the second seeks deeper integration between the two economies by concluding free-trade agreements. The strategy is designed to prevent any attempt by the United States Congress to adopt measures that could impede access to the American market for Canadian goods and services. The first expression of this strategy occurred in 1854 with the conclusion of the Canadian–American Reciprocity Treaty. Other agreements were negotiated during the twentieth century, the most important being the Auto Pact of 1965 on automotive production, the Canadian–American Free Trade Agreement of 1988 and the 1992 North American Free Trade agreement amongst Canada, the United States, and Mexico. Institutions are viewed here as the best guarantee against unforeseeable circumstances. Finally, the third option is to diversify trade with other regions to reduce trade reliance with the United States in relative terms and, thus, to reduce Canadian dependence. The Pierre Trudeau Government of the 1970s explicitly used this strategy, but the results were anything but convincing because the trade with the United States also grew throughout that same period.

But Canada is also a 'stability seeker' at the global level. Since the middle of the Second World War, Canadian diplomats conceived international economic institution as a central pillar of Canada's post-war trade policy. This attitude can be traced first in the negotiations surrounding the creation of the UN and its specialised agencies, as well as those leading to the creation of the General Agreement on Tariffs and Trade.[11] Interestingly, stability was not only seen as a precondition for trade but also its consequence. Encouraging trade and denouncing protectionist policies was perceived as a key to strengthening peaceful relationships amongst states, especially liberal ones confronting the communist challenge. In Canadian post-war strategic thinking, trade was as important as the military component in approaching international problems. In 1948–49, whilst negotiating the terms of the North Atlantic treaty, Canadians were anxious to add an economic dimension (as well as a political and social one) to the military approach reinforcing alliance unity; although its content was seriously diluted during the negotiation process, Article 2 of the treaty resulted from this demand and the reform of the Organization for European Economic Development after the Marshall Plan ended.[12] For these same economic and strategic reasons, Canadians contributed to the Colombo Plan of 1951, the first international economic development assistance efforts. Whilst the practice since the 1950s was unable to match the enthusiasm of the discourse, rationales supporting trade and aid policies remains central to Canadian foreign policy.

Another feature worth mentioning is demography. First, the Canadian population is relatively small compared with the size of the country (34 million people living in 10 million square kilometres) and the vast majority of the citizens live within 200 kilometres of the American border in the south of the country. Consequently, vast stretches of territory, especially the Arctic, are almost empty. This demographic poses many problems, not only technical (such as communication between communities or control of the territory by the government agencies) but also in terms of national identity. Regional divisions exist: Atlantic Canada (Nova Scotia, New Brunswick, Prince Edward Island, and Newfoundland and Labrador), Central Canada (Ontario and Quebec), Western Canada (Manitoba, Saskatchewan, Alberta and, to a lesser degree, British Columbia), and the North (Nunavut, Northwest Territories, and Yukon). Each region has different priorities, interests, and, over some issues, its own values.[13]

But the demographic factor that has historically played the most important role is the linguistic division of the country. Whilst coexistence between the conquered French colony and their English occupiers and colonists after the Treaty of Paris of 1763 remained relatively easy and pacific, strongly divergent views between the anglophone majority and the francophone minority arose over some foreign-policy issues, such as military commitments overseas. Today, the linguistic division remains a factor in shaping Canadian diplomacy and defence policy, even if the difference in the attitude of French- and English-speaking Canadians is not so sharp as it was until the end of the Second World War.[14] Because of both regional and linguistic divisions, but also because of the proximity to the United States, with whom Canadians share many cultural elements, Canadian national and international identity is probably one of the weakest in the Western world. It is not enough that Canadians must find a common denominator, but they must also find what makes them distinct from their powerful neighbour. Consequently, Canadian foreign policy bears the important dimension of an 'identity quest'. Difficulty exists in finding foreign-policy issues that reinforce the Canadian sense of nationhood and national unity. Amongst the rare issues that could create a consensus nationwide are peace-keeping operations, the protection of Canadian sovereignty in the Arctic, and the promotion of human rights.[15]

More important is the demographic change fostered by new Canadians arriving from all regions of the world. Since the 1980s, the term 'multiculturalism' has supplemented the traditional 'biculturalism' to describe Canadian cultural identity. On the foreign-policy side, consequences of multiculturalism are both obvious and unclear. On one hand, the presence of diasporas keeps the attention of the Canadian Government on issues and countries that may otherwise be ignored. The presence of significant diasporas also means that Canadians can gain privileged access to foreign societies and develop stronger trade or social relations than would otherwise be possible. Of course, Canadians can be trapped in foreign conflicts or see the development of foreign criminal or terrorist activities on their territory.[16] In this way, Canada is no different than the vast majority of other Western countries. But what remains unclear is how the deep changes in the fabric of Canadian identity brought by the growing presence of non-European cultures in Canadian society will affect foreign policy. Contrary to that of many other Western societies, Canada's identity seems to be weak and subject to change more quickly because of demographic changes.[17]

A final point is that Canada possesses one of the most educated societies in the world. Its small population is productive and embracing of new transnational concepts, including trade, science, communication technology, energy exploitation, and transportation. And Canadian diplomats and its military are in general highly educated and display a high degree of professionalism, opposed to societies in which diplomatic nominations are largely a political process or in which military personnel are conscripted. All of these factors augment Canadian policy at the international level.[18]

Like many small or middle Powers, Canadian diplomacy is largely driven by relations with the Great Powers. Two interesting observations can be made here. Since the creation of the modern

Canada in 1867 (if not since the first settlements in New France in the early seventeenth century) the country relied heavily on a Great Power for its physical security and to guarantee a form of stability in the international system. Focusing on this dimension could lead an observer to believe that Canada is just a 'semi-independent' state, which simply follows the Great Powers and has limited manoeuvrability to promote its own interests. However, Canada is doing remarkably well in its relationships with the Great Powers, maximising benefits and limiting costs, and retaining the right to refuse the Great Powers' dictums if Ottawa considers them to run counter to Canadian interests. These two observations together draw a nuanced portrait of Canadian foreign policy.

Canada has always been under the benevolent leadership and protection of a Great Power: first, the British Empire and, then, since 1940, the United States. It is probably because Canada was a part of the British Empire that it did not join the United States in the second half of the nineteenth century, when the Americans were contemplating annexing Canada.[19] And, between 1940 and 1947, when Britain could no longer offer any security guarantee to Canada, Ottawa did not hesitate to seek American support—the organised the defense of North America: first against Axis Powers, than against the Soviet Union during the Cold War.[20] From this perspective, it is tempting to perceive Canadians as free-riders: relying on the protection of powerful allies whilst using their own limited resources in support of other non-military projects. But Canadians learned that these relationships involved an element of reciprocity. To ensure British or American protection, Canadians had a duty to contribute to their protector's security both at home and overseas. By the late nineteenth century, and maybe with an exception between the two World Wars, Canadian diplomatic and military strategy involved a significant overseas commitment.

In 1899, approximately 8,000 Canadians served in South Africa against the Boers; 242 lost their lives. In the First World War, hundreds of thousands of Canadians served in France and Belgium against the German Empire, which cost 66,000 lives and countless permanent injuries, the worst war in Canadian history. From 1940 to 1945, Canadian forces again crossed the Atlantic and fought Nazi Germany along with other British allies. Canadian soldiers served also in Korea (1950–53), the Persian Gulf (1990–91), Serbia (1999), Afghanistan (since 2001), and Libya (2011). And from 1951 to 1991, a substantial part of Canadian forces were deployed in West Germany as a contribution to the defence of NATO's central front. Hence, overseas commitments in coalition and under the direction of the protecting Great Power became a dominant feature of contemporary Canadian foreign policy.

These regular overseas commitments can be easily justified as the defense of Canadian interests. In the first place, encouraging a Great Power ally to remain engaged in the international system (in other words, to avoid isolationism) helps provide international stability. This strategy became prominent in Canadian diplomacy immediately after the Second World War concerning the United States and was a central objective in Canadian involvement in NATO in 1949 and afterwards. More generally, even if Canadian decision-makers and diplomats frequently suggest reforms of the international system or an improvement of international institutions, these demands are rarely radical. Canada remains first and foremost a *status quo* state. For this reason, Canadian and American international interests are easily reconciled because the United States is also committed to the preservation of the status quo.[21]

Flowing from conjoined international interests, contributing to a Great Power's involvement overseas is usually perceived as a means to obtain influence over that Power (in London or, later, in Washington). Canadian involvement on Britain's side in the First World War was conceived as a way to obtain the right to be consulted on the direction of the British Empire as well as to gain some autonomy. During the Cold War, contributing to NATO's common efforts was justified as the entry fee for Canadians to get a 'seat at the table'. After 2001, Canadian involvement in Afghanistan served as a means for Canada to gain credibility in other allies' eyes, especially American ones. Accordingly, it is rare that Canadians think of their international activities as an expression of 'national' interest. In international affairs, the reference point is usually not Canada by itself but a wider group or, to use one cogent assessment, 'a broader "realm," than [Canada's] national territory'.[22] Finally, it is also possible to understand the Canadian commitment to coalitions as an expression of shared identity. Until the Second World War, many Canadians identified themselves as 'British', and it was normal that as a component of a wider entity, Canada fought where the Empire required assistance. The same idea applies today: many Canadians perceive Canada's involvement in Western institutions or coalitions, led by the United States, as a normal duty for a member of the Western community.

Naturally, a 'follower' attitude touches just one side of the relationship that Canada maintains with the Great Powers. As a sovereign state, it is Ottawa's duty to keep a safe distance from them and to ensure that 'cooperation' is not a euphemism for 'domination'. And as the representatives of any society with a weak or unstable national identity, policy-makers have a duty to adopt policies that distinguish their country from those of the Great Power and to set a distinctive image for the international stage. The word 'sovereignty' is, therefore, central in the official discourse on Canadian foreign policy. International commitments at the side of the dominant Great Power are often conceived as means to obtain and maintain Canada's sovereignty. Hence, Canada's military performance in the First World War is commonly viewed as the beginning of a process that culminated with the formal diplomatic independence of the Dominion in December 1931. In the same vein, security and defence measures put in place during the Second World War, the Cold War, and after the attacks of September 2001 were largely viewed as 'sovereignty driven' in the sense that the objective was, partly, not to provide any reasons for the Americans to adopt unilateral measures that could harm Canadian sovereignty.

But a close relationship with the USA is not without danger. As Machiavelli warned 500 years ago, it is always risky for a weak state to enter in an alliance with a powerful one. The weaker risks being constrained, dominated, or absorbed by its ally. From a certain perspective, this is the case for Canada. Whilst Canadians remain officially in charge of the defence of their territory, the definition of threat, as well as the general orientation to meet it, is made in Washington. Therefore, even if Canadians are not really concerned by, say, the terrorist threat, they have no choice but to accept some defensive measures: not to meet their own fears, but those expressed by their American counterparts. On the trade side, Canadians have very little leverage over what happens in the United States market and have no other choice but to adapt to changing economic conditions.

Moreover, public opinion could constitute another source of concern for policy-makers. Getting too close to the Americans is sometimes not well received by the Canadian population. The first major wave of English-speaking migrants to Canada comprised Loyalists who fled the American Revolution and, as long as British Imperialism held a significant place in the Canadian political spectrum, any *rapprochement* with the United States was perceived as a betrayal to the 'Mother Country'. Since the Second World War, criticism of the United States is usually expressed by groups and individuals associated with the left of the political spectrum or those who hold a discourse tainted with Canadian 'nationalism' or 'patriotism'. Any step that brings Canada closer to the United States could create a backlash of public opinion, especially when the resident of the White House is viewed as too conservative for the majority of Canadians (the case with Ronald Reagan [1980–88] and George W. Bush [2000–8]). In recent years, many debates dealing with foreign policy in Canada were associated with the Canadian attitude toward the United States, like the conclusion of the Free Trade Agreement in 1988 or the seemingly endless debate about a possible Canadian contribution to the American missile defence system (1995–2005).

   This does not mean that Canadians are anti-American (in fact, Canadian 'anti-Americanism' is probably more contextual than structural since it can change quickly) but Canadians are both critical of certain values they do not share, such as individualism or the use of force to enforce order; and they are anxious to express their differences from Americans. At the same time, the vast majority of Canadians are culturally and politically close to their American neighbours. In this context, it is not surprising to note a distinct ambivalence amongst decision-makers concerning the best attitude to adopt toward the United States. Some prime ministers were elected by emphasising the need to keep a distance from the United States, like the Liberals Pierre Elliott Trudeau (1968–84) or Jean Chrétien (1993–2003). Others, usually staggered between those seeking distance, are elected with an alternative promise of being a 'super' American ally. This alternative was the case with the Conservatives Brian Mulroney (1984–93) and Stephen Harper (since 2006), or the Liberal Paul Martin (2004–6).[23]

   Despite occasional conflicts on specific issues (and usually conflicts between the United States and Canada are compartmentalised so as not to affect other issues) Canadian–American relations are generally functional and friendly. The most telling observation is probably that there has been no war between the two countries since the bulk of the British troops left Canada in 1871 and Canada was dependent on its own resources for protection. Moreover, relations between Washington and Ottawa do not reflect the huge difference in power between Canada and the United States; conflict and negotiations do not systematically reflect the position of the more powerful of the two states; bilateral institutions are usually built on the principle of equal representation with the same number of Americans and Canadians; almost all territorial and sovereignty conflicts, usually the most delicate in any bilateral relationship, have been settled to the satisfaction of the two parties;[24] and finally, Canada always has the possibility to refuse any agreement or any project that seems to run against Canadian interests without suffering any American retaliation. The classic example respecting the latter involved the Canadian Government's refusal to join the 'Coalition of the Willing' against Iraq in 2003.

   Many factors explain why Canada is successful in its relations with Great Powers, especially the United States. They include economic interdependence, convergence of interests, balance of power, convergence of political values (democratic peace) or cultural proximity.[25] But if these systemic or dyadic variables say anything about the context of these relations, they are less useful in understanding the strategies used by Canadian decision-makers and diplomats. Strategies to manage relations with the United States have changed over time, depending on the worldview of the decision-makers, and whether this vision is largely shared by Canadian society; this 'worldview' is a set of assumptions about Canada's power attributes, its place in the international hierarchy, the nature of its relations with the Great Powers, and its overall national and international interests.[26] Various worldviews can be linked to philosophical traditions about international relations, each reflecting a different ideological set of values. Naturally, because of these variations, each set of values supposes a difference in political agenda and doctrine.

   Put simply, there are in the contemporary debates concerning Canadian foreign policy three clashing worldviews: internationalism, critical nationalism, and continentalism. Internationalism is frequently labelled as the 'default setting' of Canadian foreign policy, because it is the most commonly held amongst decision-makers, if not always amongst the citizenry. Emerging during the Second World War amongst Canadian diplomats based on their wartime experience and immediate objectives, it remained dominant for the next 60 years in one form or another, even during the premiership of Pierre Trudeau, who tried to distance himself from this set of ideas. Key figures in the formulation of the internationalist approach have been civil servants, including

Lester Pearson (who rose from within the Department of External Affairs to become Minister of External Affairs and, later, Prime Minister) and other high-ranking diplomats like Escott Reid, Hume Wrong, and John Holmes.

The central internationalist assumption is that Canada is a middle Power, which means essentially two things. First, it has global interests but without the resources to promote them alone; the question then is *how* to advance these interests. Second, Canada can make a significant contribution towards maintaining international stability and cannot be ignored by the Great Powers. Canadian experience during the Second World War taught its diplomats to avoid a strictly bilateral relationship with the United States, because it could lead to temporary infringements of Canada's sovereignty.[27] Rooted in liberal political philosophy, internationalism shares liberal assumptions that inform many of its foreign-policy solutions. Another internationalist assumption is that Canada is a 'natural' member of larger groups of states, that being Canadian means being a 'citizen of the world' but first and foremost of the West. And an emerging assumption is implicit recognition of American international leadership, a clear break from the isolationist attitude of the 1920s and 1930s.

The principal concern of internationalists was to avoid another major global conflict like the Second World War and guarantee the advancement of Canadian interests. Both of these concerns were related to the Great Powers' behaviour, in general, and Canada's relationship with the United States, in particular. As with liberal philosophy, institutions provide a first element of solution. Having Great Powers constrained by institutions and international law will reduce the risk of major war and any disrespect for lesser Powers. Multilateralism and institutionalism consequently became a central element of Canada's international strategy. Canada's idealistic promotion of international law and institutions belied the cold calculation of national interests underneath; multilateral institutions were also considered forums where secondary Powers could gather and concert to constrain the Great Powers. Counterweights and balance were explicit components of the internationalist strategy.[28] Another crucial element of internationalist strategy involved accepting some responsibilities and roles to uphold international norms as peace-keepers and mediators. The purpose of these roles was to reinforce international stability and international institutions, obviate major clashes between the Great Powers, and conduct activities that could establish a clear distinction between Canada and the United States or the dominant European Powers. Internationalist strategies were predominant during the Cold War, but their legacy can also be traced in Chrétien's foreign policy during 1993–2003 and, to a lesser extent, in his successors' policies.[29]

In that it questions the foundations of Canadian foreign policy, the second significant worldview can be labelled as 'critical'; it appeared in the early 1960s at the crossroads of two emergent ideas. On one hand, this period witnessed the rehabilitation of Marxist ideas in the Western world, as the impact of 'American imperialism' and the complicity of the local élites in reproducing the capitalist system was actively questioned. On the other, Canadian nationalism was stimulated when the size and importance of American capital in the Canadian economy was suddenly revealed. For critical nationalists, Canada was no longer a 'middle Power' but, instead, a 'satellite of the United States': a simple off-shoot of the American economy whose government was deprived of any real autonomy. International institutions were no longer the perfect forum for a middle Power to establish coalitions or to implement new norms, but were instead tools wherein American imperialists controlled other states. The central values associated with this approach were clearly inspired by a leftist political agenda and included social justice, solidarity, redistribution of wealth, and, later, sustainable development.

On the normative side, this worldview advocates a foreign policy that keeps the largest possible distance from the Great Powers. Its radical version advocates leaving the alliances, adopting neutralism, and establishing closer relationships with developing countries. On the trade side, Canadian critical nationalists searched for measures to reduce Canada's dependence on American capital and its market economy. Only one modern Canadian government (the Trudeau Government [1968–84]) seems to have been inspired by this worldview. Trudeau tried to refocus Canadian foreign policy: reduce Canada's contribution to NATO and increase defence resources dedicated to the protection of Canadian territory and sovereignty; diversify Canadian exports by developing new markets; establish relationships with governments demonised by Washington (especially Cuba and the People's Republic of China); launch a national energy programme; and create procedures to limit foreign control of critical economic sectors. Very few of these adopted measures gave the expected results, and almost all of them were abandoned or lost their significance. Nevertheless, the spirit of critical nationalism is still alive in debates on Canadian foreign policy. In assessing the merit of the two free-trade agreements linking Canada, the United States, and Mexico, in discussing the creation of a North American security perimeter, or in evaluating the rationale behind Canada's participation in the war in Afghanistan, arguments borrowing the logic of 'critical nationalism' are still frequently used.[30]

In many ways, whilst still very different from internationalism, continentalism is the antithesis of the critical nationalism and emerged from trade priorities. Taking their cues from the Trudeau Government's inability to diversify Canadian trade and facing repeated attempts by the United States Congress to adopt protectionist measures, a growing number of businesspeople demanded a radical shift in trade policy: Canada must seek greater economic integration with the United States. In other words, 'if you can't beat 'em, join 'em'. This idea was accepted by Mulroney's Conservative Government in 1985; three years later, a first bilateral agreement was concluded, followed by a trilateral one that included Mexico in 1992.

The continentalist world view goes far beyond an economic rationale. It is based on three suppositions. First, Canada is not a small or middle Power; it is a 'foremost' or a 'prominent' Power. When considering certain crucial strategic resources, like energy or water, Canada is even becoming a 'superpower'. This idea emerged in the late 1970s, when the energy crisis gave Canada new leverage to exert influence on the international stage. With its highly educated population, strong commodity-based economy, and small but professional military force, Canada deserves to be amongst the most powerful nations in institutions such as the G7 and G8. Second, the United States represents Canada's most important ally and trade partner and, as such, there can be no higher priority than keeping a functional relationship with Washington. Any break in mutual confidence or slowdown in the trade between the two Powers would have terrible consequences for Canadian prosperity. Third, the assumption remains that if Ottawa wants any international influence, it must first gain influence in Washington. The United States represents the hegemonic Power, and it is only by maintaining credibility with the American leadership that Canada can hope to maintain a significant influence on the international stage.

The continentalist agenda has two broad objectives. The first is to remove any obstacle that could prevent Canadian products from reaching American consumers. This objective can be achieved by deepening North American economic integration through a customs union, a common currency, or a single market. The attacks of 11 September 2001 added a security dimension to this objective. Washington reacted to the attacks by dramatically slowing all border traffic, an effect far more damaging than any protectionist legislation. To avoid repeating the 'September 12' situation, continentalists suggest the creation of a 'security perimeter', which includes measures like harmonising security procedures and the closest cooperation amongst Canadian and American security agencies. Partly inspired by the Schengen Agreement in Europe, the idea is to improve the surveillance of travellers and goods originating outside North America to reduce border impediments between Canada and the United States. The second objective is to back American international initiatives, especially those aimed at maintaining global order. Canadian troops must be deployed to the same theatre as their American counterparts, whilst Canadian diplomats must support American initiatives in multilateral forums. This objective is aimed primarily at reinforcing Canada's credibility in Washington, but also at maintaining an environment favourable to trade.

In terms of political philosophy, continentalism is closer to conservative values such as the imposition of law and order or the belief in the benefits of economic competition, rather than wealth redistribution. But contrary to internationalism or critical nationalism, continentalism pays little attention to questions concerning national identity. On one hand, the issue is brushed aside by the argument that living in a 'foremost Power', Canadians should not fear American competition. On the other, continentalism frames foreign-policy issues in terms of national interest, leaving little room for values or identity concerns. From this perspective, continentalism is probably a Canadian incarnation of the classical *realpolitik*. This worldview is growing in popularity. Whilst Jean Chrétien's Liberal Government avoided that discourse, it clearly informed that of his Liberal successor, Paul Martin, and the present Conservative one under Stephen Harper (since 2006). But it remains to be seen if continentalism can really supplant internationalism as the dominant worldview in Canadian foreign policy.

Canadian foreign policy can be seen as driven by a quest for international stability, a need to express national identity, a relatively low concern for security and defence, and a good dose of idealism. It is tempting to consider these goals as the quintessence of a middle Power approach to international relations. But this 'model' can hardly be applied to any other secondary Power, because this particular foreign policy is not a consequence of Canada's position in the international hierarchy, but one of a unique history, geography, and demography. Contrary to many other so-called middle Powers like Australia or Poland, Canadians rarely using a diplomatic language that is associated with classical *realpolitik* discourse based on a rational assessment of national interest and usually ranking power and security first in the priority list. From this point of view, the Canadian experience is original and gives some credit to the argument that Canada might be 'arguably the first post-modern state par excellence'.[31]

Acknowledgements

I wish to thank Maryanne Lewell, Saint John High School, Saint John, New Brunswick, for her advice and suggestions.

Notes

1 With the notable exception of the Organization of the American States [OAS], perceived as too openly controlled by the United States. Canada joined the OAS only in 1990.
2 After the title of the book edited by the former diplomat John Holmes, *No Other Way. Canada and International Security Institutions* (Toronto, 1986).
3 Kim Richard Nossal, 'Un pays européen? L'histoire de l'atlantisme au Canada', in J. English and N. Hillmer, eds., *La politique étrangère canadienne dans un ordre international en mutation. Une volonté de se démarquer?* (Québec, 1992): 131–60. See also Justin Massie, "Making Sense of Canada's 'Irrational' International Security Policy. A Tale of Three Strategic Cultures", *International Journal*, 64(2009), 625–45.
4 On the North Atlantic Triangle, see B.J.C. McKercher and Lawrence Aronsen, eds., *The North Atlantic Triangle in a Changing World. Anglo-American-Canadian Relations, 1902–1956* (Toronto, 1996); David G. Haglund, *The North Atlantic Triangle Revisited. Canadian Grand Strategy at Century's End* (Toronto, 2000).
5 Louis St-Laurent, 'The Foundation of Canadian Policy in World Affairs', *Statements and Speeches*, Number 47/2 (Toronto, 1947).
6 Rosalind Irwin, ed., *Ethics and Security in Canadian Foreign Policy* (Vancouver, 2001); Costas Melakopides, *Pragmatic Idealism. Canadian Foreign Policy, 1945–1995* (Montréal, 1998); Prosper Bernard, Jr., 'Canada and

Human Security: From the Axworthy Doctrine to Middle Power Internationalism', *American Review of Canadian Studies*, 36(2006), 233–61; Greg Donaghy, 'All God's Children: Lloyd Axworthy, Human Security and Canadian Foreign Policy, 1996–2000', *Canadian Foreign Policy*, 10(Winter 2003), 39–59.

7 See John Keegan's map of the world's military–non-military zones. With the exception of southern Ontario and Quebec, Canada belongs almost entirely to the 'non-military' zone. John Keegan, *A History of Warfare* (London, 1993), 69.

8 Desmond Morton, 'The Military Problems of an Unmilitary Power', *Revue internationale d'histoire militaire*, 54(1982), 3. See also idem., 'Defending the Indefensible: Some Historical Perspectives on Canadian Defence 1867–1967', *International Journal*, 42(1987), 627–44.

9 Quoted in Peter C. Dobbell, *Canada's Search for New Roles. Foreign Policy in the Trudeau Era* (Toronto, 1972), 4.

10 Haglund, *North Atlantic Triangle*, 63–69.

11 Michael Hart, *A Trading Nation. Canadian Trade Policy from Colonialism to Globalization* (Vancouver, 2002), 131–41.

12 John C. Milloy, *The North Atlantic Treaty Organization, 1948–1957. Community or Alliance?* (Montréal, 2006), 35–66.

13 See, for example, Justin Massie, 'Regional Strategic Subculture? Canadians and the Use of Force in Afghanistan and Iraq', *Canadian Foreign Policy*, 14 (Spring 2008), 19–48.

14 Stéphane Roussel and Jean-Christophe Boucher, 'The Myth of the Pacific Society: Quebec's Contemporary Strategic Culture', *American Review of Canadian Studies*, 38 (Summer 2008), 165–87.

15 Justin Massie and Stéphane Roussel, 'Au service de l'unité: Le rôle des mythes en politique étrangère canadienne', *Canadian Foreign Policy*, 14(Spring 2008), 67–93.

16 Kim Richard Nossal, Stéphane Roussel, and Stéphane Paquin, *International Policy and Politics in Canada* (Toronto, 2011), 85–91.

17 For recent contributions about the consequences of demographic changes on Canadian foreign policy, see David Carment and David Bercuson, eds., *The World In Canada: Diasporas, Demography, and Domestic Policy* (Montreal, 2008); Rima Berns-McGown and Jack Jedwab, guest eds., 'Diasporas. What it Now Means to be Canadian', *International Journal*, 63(Winter 2007–8), 1–159.

18 Evan H. Potter, *Branding Canada: Projecting Canada's Soft Power through Public Diplomacy* (Montreal, Kingston, 2009); Pierre Pahlavi, 'La diplomatie publique du Canada: Virage ou figure de style ?', *Canadian Foreign Policy*, 14(2007), 3–29.

19 Stéphane Roussel, *The North American Democratic Peace: Absence of War and Security Institution-Building in Canada-US Relations, 1867–1958* (Montreal, Kingston, 2004), 111–17.

20 J.L. Granatstein, *How Britain's Weakness Forced Canada into the Arms of the United States* (Toronto, 1989).

21 This attitude was observable in recent military operations overseas, for instance the Kosovo war. See Kim Richard Nossal and Stéphane Roussel, 'Canada and the Kosovo War: the Happy Follower', in Pierre Martin and Mark Brawley, eds., *Alliance Politics, Kosovo, and NATO's War: Allied Force or Forced Allies?* (New York, 2000), 181–99.

22 Kim Nossal, 'Defending the 'Realm': Canadian Strategic Culture Revisited', *International Journal*, 59 (2004), 504.

23 Nossal, Roussel, and Paquin, *International Policy*, 192–204.

24 Roussel, *Democratic Peace*.

25 Ibid.

26 The concept of worldview as defined here approximates the one of 'dominant ideas' used in Nossal, Roussel, Paquin, *International Policy*, 117–53.

27 Especially in Canada's North, where American forces conducted numerous projects without asking permission from Ottawa. See Shelagh D. Grant, *Sovereignty or Security? Government Policy in the Canadian North, 1936–1950* (Vancouver, 1988).

28 David G. Haglund and Stéphane Roussel, 'Escott Reid, the North Atlantic Treaty, and Canadian Strategic Culture', in Greg Donaghy and Stéphane Roussel, eds, *Escott Reid, Diplomat & Scholar* (Montréal, 2004), 44–66.

29 Nossal, Roussel, and Paquin, *International Policy*, 135–43.

30 Stephen Clarkson, *Uncle Sam and US Globalization, Neoconservatism, and the Canadian State* (Toronto, Washington, DC, 2002); Stephen Clarkson, *Does North America Exist? Governing the Continent after NAFTA and 9/11* (Toronto, 2008).

31 Peter J. Katzenstein, 'Conclusion', in idem., ed., *The Culture of National Security: Norms and Identity in World Politics* (New York, 1996), 518n48, 535.

13

The Czech Republic

The domestic limits to foreign-policy effectiveness

Dan Marek and Michael Baun

As a relatively small country in the heart of Europe, the Czech Republic is not a major foreign-policy actor. Nevertheless, it does have its own national interests to protect and extend, and as a member of major Western political, economic, and security communities (chiefly the European Union [EU] and the North Atlantic Treaty Organization [NATO]) as well as other international organisations, it has expanded possibilities of doing so. However, aside from successfully attaining the fundamental objectives of EU and NATO membership, the Czech Republic has often been less than effective in pursuing and achieving its foreign-policy goals. The problem is not so much the definition of basic national interests, on which a broad consensus amongst political actors and within society exists, but rather the inability to achieve a consistent and coherent strategy for promoting those interests and disagreement over specific foreign-policy goals. For this failure, the high degree of polarisation between political elites and a fragmented institutional system for foreign-policy decision-making are largely to blame.

After gaining independence from communism and Soviet domination in the 1989 'Velvet Revolution' (so-called because of its relatively peaceful character) Czechoslovakia's main foreign-policy objective was to secure its newly acquired freedom, independence, and sovereignty. A key step in this direction involved the successful withdrawal of Soviet troops from Czechoslovak soil in June 1991, followed the next month by abolition of the Warsaw Pact. Simultaneously, Czechoslovakia pursued integration into Western economic, political, and security institutions in an effort to rejoin the international community that was generally understood as the 'return to Europe.' In 1993, federal Czechoslovakia split into two independent states (the Czech Republic and the Slovak Republic) in a process often referred to as the 'Velvet Divorce.' However, the basic concept of national interests for the Czech Republic remained almost unchanged.[1]

The new state's first official foreign-policy document, the 1993 *Conception of the Foreign Policy of the Czech Republic*, declared that the country's main strategic goal was membership of European and Euro-Atlantic organisations, especially the EU, NATO, and the Western European Union (WEU).[2] In a 1998 Policy Statement, the Czech Government defined the country's vital interests as 'the survival of the state, securing its sovereignty and territorial integrity, the maintenance of constitutional order and democracy, and the security of citizens.'[3] It further specified that the Czech Republic wanted to assist in creating and strengthening favourable international conditions, in which 'war is an unacceptable method of resolving disputes between states, where nations jointly identify and … where various forms of political and economic cooperation are promoted.'

Also stating that the Czech Republic desired 'a united, democratic, socially just, prosperous, peaceful and tension-free Europe,' it emphasised the creation of external conditions favourable for the country's economic growth and prosperity.

The Conception of Czech Foreign Policy for the 2003–2006 Period (the most recent foreign-policy document) declares that the primary interest of the Czech Republic is ensuring the continuation of the state, with all its typical attributes; in other words, maintenance of the country's physical survival, sovereignty, independence, and security, with the aim of remaining 'a democratic state based on rule of law, freedom, equality, justice, tolerance to differences and respect for the weaker, endangered and defenseless.'[4] It emphasises the Czech Republic's interest in a peaceful, uniting, stable, safe, and prospering Europe and the development of international political and economic cooperation. It also declares the Czech Republic's interest in the promotion of international conditions suitable for the country's increased prosperity and competitiveness. A completely new element that appears in this document is the fight against terrorism, which reflects the altered nature of the international arena and demands for better and more effective security after the terrorist attacks in New York in September 2001, Madrid in March 2004, and London in July 2005.

National interests are determined by numerous factors, including economic, ideological, military security, moral, legal, cultural, and ethnic issues.[5] They can also be derived from other determinants, such as a nation's historical experience or its geographical position. In this context, internal factors shape Czech national interests, specifically national identity, public opinion, and the views of political parties and elites.

In the Czech Republic, national identity is to a great extent shaped by the country's difficult history, during which the Czech lands have often been an object of other states' power ambitions: 'The Czech nation managed to survive four hundred years of Habsburg oppression, six years of Nazi German occupation, and forty-three years of communism and Soviet domination. It also experienced two failed attempts to establish an independent democratic state, the first falling victim to German aggression in 1939, and the second to communist machinations in 1948.'[6] Consequently, whilst the Czech people do not identify much with the state and national identity tends to be rather weak, Czechs also continue to be suspicious of larger European Powers. Apart from positive features of Czech national identity (such as democratic spirit and ability to learn) there is a typical aspect that can be characterised as Czech 'littleness' or 'smallness.' This concept refers to the country's assumed lack of power to change the course of events and make decisions in its own right, a trait that can have important consequences for Czech foreign policy.[7]

Public opinion is another domestic factor influencing the construction of national interests. In the 1990s, public opinion played only a marginal role in discussions about the direction of Czech foreign policy; a broad public consensus favoured the chief foreign-policy goals of EU and NATO membership. Public opinion started to exert stronger influence on Czech foreign policy only later, particularly in connection with the Iraq war, with many Czechs unhappy about their Government's support for the United States invasion, and more recently in relation to EU affairs. In a 2003 referendum, a large majority (77.3 percent) of Czechs voted in favour of EU accession. Since the Republic became a member-state in 2004, Czechs have usually reflected the EU average in public opinion polls on most issues, although they tend to be slightly more eurosceptical than the citizens of other new member-states.[8] However, in this context, it is important to realise that even though the country is sometimes labelled as 'eurosceptic,' Czech euroscepticism differs from what is commonly seen in most other EU member-states in that it tends to be more ideological and non-populist in nature.[9] Opinion polls also regularly show that the wider public is more Euro-optimistic than the Czech political leadership.[10] In April 2010, for example, 34 percent of Czechs considered EU membership to be a good thing, whilst 13 percent claimed the opposite and 45 percent expressed a neutral opinion.[11] Another foreign-policy issue that has recently mobilised public interest is the possible installation of United States missile defense facilities in the Czech Republic, with many Czechs opposing the Government's cooperation with American plans.

A crucial role in the Czech Republic's parliamentary system of government is exercised by political parties. Because of a proportional representation electoral system and the fact that Czech governments tend to be coalitions, political parties exert a strong influence on Czech foreign policy.[12] Nevertheless, in the early 1990s, Czech political parties were not consolidated enough and played almost no role in the formulation and conduct of the foreign policy. At that time, the international orientation of the Czech Republic was influenced mainly by prominent individuals of the post-communist era, such as President Václav Havel (1993–2003) and Prime Minister Václav Klaus (1993–98). Gradually, however, political parties consolidated and became more important in the foreign-policy decision-making process.

Overall, it can be argued that Czech national interests are varied but have retained considerable continuity. Since the early 1990s, the Republic's primary national interests have aimed at preservation and enhancement of the country's political autonomy, physical survival, independence, sovereignty, security, and culture, as well as the pursuit of wealth, economic growth, and power. Another consistent national interest has been a favourable international environment, meaning a united, democratic, just, prosperous, and peaceful international community with a respect for human rights. The only significant new development is the importance currently given to the fight against terrorism. Thus, it seems that EU and NATO membership has not significantly changed basic perceptions of Czech national interests, which 'for the most part continue to be determined by the [pre-1989] historical experience of external domination by larger European powers and perceptions of geopolitical vulnerability.'[13]

One of the main contours of Czech foreign policy is strong support for multilateral cooperation, since the country understands membership in international organisations as a suitable means to advance and protect its national interests.[14] In fact, some experts claim that the Czech Republic has been much more successful in multilateral cooperation than in establishing direct bilateral ties.[15] A major priority of Czech foreign policy after the Velvet Revolution was membership of the EU. Understood as the main vehicle of the country's return to Europe, EU membership was to provide a profitable economic and secure political space for the country's future development. Even though the Czech Republic was one of the last candidate countries to submit its official application in January 1996, it soon became a member of the so-called Luxembourg Group, comprising the most advanced candidates in terms of membership preparations. Together with seven other Central and Eastern European countries (Estonia, Latvia, Lithuania, Hungary, Poland, Slovenia, and Slovakia) as well as Cyprus and Malta, the Czech Republic finally joined the EU on 1 May 2004, thus ending an almost 15-year effort to return to Europe.[16]

As a fully fledged EU member, the Czech Republic actively participates in all EU policies, including its Common Foreign and Security Policy (CFSP) and Common Security and Defense Policy (CSDP). Because of EU membership, the Czech Republic's influence on international policy is potentially greater than its limited size, power, and geographical location would otherwise allow. The Czech Republic realises this fact and views CFSP as an important foreign-policy instrument and means to promote the Czech agenda and pursue its own national interests. Czech CFSP priorities, which strongly mirror the country's general foreign-policy goals, encompass close partnership with and a coherent policy towards Eastern Europe, integration of the western Balkans into the EU, and the worldwide promotion of democracy and human rights.[17] Moreover, it pushes for enhanced energy security, good transatlantic relations, greater cooperation between the EU and NATO, and the expansion of free trade.[18]

All of these issues were reflected in the policy priorities of the Czech EU presidency in the first half of 2009. The EU presidency, held on a rotating six-month basis by an individual member-state, gives that Power a chance to influence significantly the bloc's foreign-policy agenda. The Czech Republic was only the second new member-state to hold the EU presidency, after Slovenia in early 2008. Thus, according to the Czech Ministry of Foreign Affairs, it was a 'unique opportunity to participate in EU policymaking and show the maturity and reliability of a full-fledged EU member'.[19] Apart from external developments and the evolving EU agenda, the Czech presidency priorities reflected the ideological predispositions of the country's center-right government and its perceptions of basic national interests.[20] Under the motto 'Europe without barriers,' the presidency priorities featured three Es: economy, energy, and European Union in the world. As the circumstances later demonstrated, these priorities proved to be relevant and valid.[21]

Membership of NATO was another major foreign-policy priority of the Czech Republic and a major instrument for promoting national interests and safeguarding national security. In 1994, the Czech Republic joined the Partnership for Peace, and on 12 March 1999 it became a full member of NATO.[22] NATO membership was supported across the political spectrum by all major political parties, except the Communists. In fact, together with Hungary and Poland, the Czech Republic belonged to the most eager NATO supporters amongst the ten Central and Eastern European countries that were applying to join. After initial hesitation and some inconsistent steps (for instance, in policy towards Kosovo) the Czech Republic has gradually established its reputation as a reliable and active member, supporting further NATO enlargement and institutional reform.[23] Even after EU accession, NATO has remained the primary security reference for the Czech Republic.[24]

Indeed, a typical feature of Czech foreign policy is its 'internationalism,' embodied by its long-term efforts to balance its position between the EU (Continentalism) on one hand, and NATO (Atlanticism) on the other.[25] The Czech Republic's aspiration to balance its foreign policy between Brussels and Washington is clearly evident in its preference for the closest possible cooperation and functional complementarity of both organisations.[26]

Despite the Czech Republic's positive attitude towards European security cooperation and its high level of participation in CSDP actions, it does not view CSDP as a means of achieving independence from NATO, but rather as a supplement to the trans-Atlantic security alliance that will guarantee the EU's effective defense.[27] The Czech position on CSDP is influenced by the deep-rooted idea that whilst the EU should engage in the civil dimension of crisis management, military operations belong to NATO. Because the Czech Republic believes that the EU and NATO should not compete with each other, or unnecessarily duplicate the others' capacities and abilities, it supported the French EU presidency's initiative in 2008 to unblock the EU–NATO relationship, later making this policy one of its own EU presidency priorities.[28]

Czech efforts to sustain a halfway position between Washington and Brussels have led to certain disagreements with the EU, since the country still tends to make key foreign-policy decisions outside the EU framework, especially in matters relating to the United States. This tendency was obvious, for example, in Czech support of US policy in Iraq (although this happened before EU accession) or in the question of placing American missile defense facilities in the country. In the latter case, the Czech Government pursued unilateral negotiations with Washington without any consultations with other EU member-states, thus generating mutual political tensions.

In the realm of multilateral diplomacy, the Czech Republic also supports the United Nations (UN) and its agencies. In this respect, the Czech Republic has been very active in the UN Commission for Human Rights. In fact, the human rights agenda is considered one of the best formulated and most dynamic areas of Czech foreign policy.[29] For historical and political reasons, the country's special interest is the situations in Cuba and Belarus. Yet, it is interesting to note that despite the activities of numerous Czech non-governmental organisations (NGOs), Czech policy towards the infringement of human rights in China and Tibet is rather inactive and submissive.

The Czech Republic is also a member and supporter of other organisations that encourage international cooperation.[30] In 1993, it became a member of the Council of Europe and, in May 1994, an Associate Partner of the WEU. The next year, it entered another important organisation, the Organization for Economic Cooperation and Development, thus becoming the first post-communist country in Central and Eastern Europe to do so. It is a founding member of the Visegrad Group, an alliance of four Central European states (the Czech Republic, Hungary, Poland, and Slovakia) established in 1991 to increase mutual cooperation and pursue common interests. This initiative reflected the general preference of the early Czechoslovak leadership for cooperative and multilateral approaches to international relations. In the mid-1990s, Visegrad cooperation ceased to be a priority (when compared with the period before 1993) but was reinvigorated by the accession of the four countries to the EU.[31] Nowadays, it remains a useful forum for multilateral cooperation in a number of fields of common interest, with projects including student scholarships and shared embassies.[32] Another subregional organisation that the Czech Republic strongly supports is the Central European Initiative.[33]

The promotion of amicable bilateral relationships with neighbouring (Austria, Poland, Slovakia, and Germany) and other countries constitutes another principal instrument of Czech foreign policy. Germany is a crucial neighbour of the Czech Republic, mainly because of numerous commercial and investment-related contacts between the two countries. Although Germany's share of the Czech Republic's foreign trade has been gradually decreasing in favour of other European countries, with a 30 percent share it retains its position as the main importer of Czech goods and also as one of the country's main sources of foreign investment.[34] Germany's importance is also confirmed by public opinion polls, with 61 percent of Czechs considering it the country's most important neighbor.[35] An important tool for enhancing good relations with Germany was the Czech–German Declaration of 1997, which focused on overcoming sensitive historical issues in Czech–German relations. Still, even though the main animosities have been removed, some discord continues, appearing from time to time. One example is Germany's concern about the Czech Republic's ability to secure its borders, which prevented it and other new Central European member-states from joining the EU's passport-free zone (the Schengen Area) until 2007.[36] Although such misunderstandings are quickly solved, they suggest that the Czech–German relationship is still not completely natural and normal.[37] In this context, it is interesting to note that except for Germany, the Czech Republic has failed to establish close political ties with other major players on the European arena such as France, Great Britain, Italy, or the Benelux countries.[38]

Czech trade and economic relations with Austria have traditionally been intensive and qualitatively good. Yet, the volume of mutual exports and imports steadily decreases: whilst in 2004, Austria was the Republic's third-biggest trading partner with a share of 5 percent of total trade, in 2008 it was eighth, with a share of 4.2 percent.[39] Certain animosities in Czech–Austrian relations remain, although the Melk Agreement signed in 2000 resolved the main disputes.[40] Austrian opposition to the Temelín nuclear power plant has generated tensions, whilst the Czech Republic's negative response to the participation of Jörg Haider's ultraconservative Freedom Party in the Austrian coalition government formed in 2000, and the Austrian attempt to make repeal of the Beneš Decrees a precondition of Czech EU membership, have also cooled relations.[41] As a result, in 2003 only 48 percent of Czechs rated Czech–Austrian relations as good, with 49 percent viewing them negatively.[42]

The Czech Republic attaches great importance to good relations with the Slovak Republic, which for a long time has been its second-biggest trading partner, accounting for 7.5 percent of Czech foreign trade in 2008.[43] In its 2003 foreign-policy concept paper, the Czech Government declared further intensification of cooperation with the Slovak Republic, at both bilateral and regional levels, to be a key goal: 'The Czech Republic is particularly committed to extending this cooperation in the field of economic relations. It expects new opportunities to arise including new dimensions of cooperation at the European level after the entry of the two countries into the EU'.[44] And the Republic pursues amicable relations with Poland, the country's third-biggest trading partner, accounting for 6.2 percent of total foreign trade. Bilateral trade relations have developed dynamically, with Czech exports exceeding imports; in 2008, the Czech Republic invested more in Poland than any other country.[45] The 2003 concept paper specifies that bilateral cooperation should particularly intensify in the construction of transport infrastructure and the further development of trade and cultural relations.

As already indicated, good relations with the United States remain an unequivocal cornerstone of Czech foreign policy.[46] Prague places particular emphasis on strengthening cooperation between the United States (and thus NATO) and the EU. Yet, it is important to stress that the Czech Republic has 'never been decidedly uncritical of the US and staunchly Atlanticist'.[47] Common with Central and Eastern European countries, the Czech Republic has adopted a generally critical and cautious stance towards Russia.[48] In the mid-1990s, Czech–Russian relations were even deemed 'not good and unfriendly'.[49] Although not so hostile today as in the case of Poland or the Baltic states, they have lately cooled because of the natural-gas disputes between Russia and Ukraine in 2006 and 2009, and Russia's military action in Georgia in August 2008.[50]

One constant in Czech foreign policy is its strong regional interest in close cooperation with Eastern Europe and the Western Balkans, which partly derives from geographical proximity but also from historical, cultural, and political factors. Taking part in all CSDP operations in the Balkans, the Czech Republic also contributed troops to NATO operations in Bosnia beginning in 1996. However, although the Czech military, experts, and NGOs are active in this region, the potential of mutual relations has not yet been fully realised. Indeed, according to Drulák, Czech support for the region has been mainly rhetorical, the most notable exception being Czech visa policy towards the region.[51] The Czech Republic is a strong supporter of EU policies (the European Neighbourhood Policy and the Eastern Partnership Initiative) that seek to improve political and economic ties with the countries of Eastern Europe (Belarus, Ukraine, Moldova) and the South Caucasus (Armenia, Azerbaijan, Georgia); in fact, the Czech Republic made the further development of EU Eastern policy one of the main priorities of its 2009 EU presidency.[52]

As a member of both the EU and the international community of democratically and economically developed countries, the Czech Republic 'respects the principle of solidarity and accepts its share of responsibility in dealing with global problems'.[53] It thus regards foreign development assistance as integral to its foreign policy and provides it on both a bilateral and multilateral basis in line with international principles and its own interests. Nevertheless, although the country is now a more generous donor of foreign humanitarian and development aid than in the early1990s, it still does not fulfil international obligations committing the Czech Republic to allocate a minimum of 0.17 percent of its gross national income by 2010, and 0.33 percent by 2015, to development assistance. Czech bilateral foreign development aid is currently directed towards nine priority countries (Angola, Zambia, Vietnam, Mongolia, Yemen, Moldova, Bosnia and Herzegovina, Serbia, and Montenegro) as well as to project countries such as Iraq and Afghanistan, Kosovo, Cambodia, Ethiopia, and the Occupied Palestinian Territories.[54]

The main objective of Czech foreign policy has been to safeguard national security and prosperity through integration into Western institutions and structures, primarily the EU and NATO, with strong trans-Atlantic cooperation as an equalising aspect and security guarantee. Yet, as Wallat points out, Czech foreign policy in the first decade after independence was not linear and, sometimes, even displayed contradictory tendencies:

it oscillated between a very pro-European and a distinctly eurosceptic policy; it went from calling for the abolition of NATO in 1990 to joining it in 1999; it was one of the main initiators of the East Central European Visegrad cooperation as well as the main obstacle to such cooperation.[55]

Similarly, in the aftermath of the 1989 Velvet Revolution Czech political elites strongly supported European integration; then in the mid-1990s the country became notorious for its eurosceptic position, with the pendulum swinging back towards a pro-European stance in 1998.[56]

EU membership in 2004 has affected Czech foreign policy, as the country began actively participating in CFSP/CSDP activities and coordinating its foreign-policy decision-making with other EU members. However, it has not altered the basic contours of Czech foreign policy; and it can be argued that the level of Europeanisation of Czech foreign policy is low when compared with the influence of domestic political factors, such as changes of government and the beliefs and actions of national leaders. What has been modified by EU membership is mainly the methods and instruments that the Czech Republic uses to achieve its foreign-policy goals and safeguard its national priorities.[57]

Recording both successes and failures, Czech foreign policy has been the subject of much debate, praise, and criticism both domestically and abroad. Whilst the country has managed to secure membership in key international organisations and it participates actively in their activities, its foreign policy has not always been so effective, strong, and successful as it could be. There is the example of the 2009 EU presidency, which had a significant impact on the Republic's international position and reputation.[58] The Czech EU presidency recorded several successes, including *inter alia* progress in the area of energy security, on EU Eastern policy, and in relation to the Middle Eastern situation. Unfortunately, the entire presidency was negatively marked by the embarrassing mid-term collapse of the Czech Government, a result of political score-settling and partisan manoeuvring that overshadowed its achievements. There are other cases in which the Czech Republic has behaved neither effectively nor diplomatically, including its delay in ratifying the EU's Lisbon Treaty and its decision to negotiate unilaterally with Washington on both the visa waiver programme and Central European missile defense. As a result, the Czech Republic has not earned the reputation in the EU of either a reliable partner that can be counted on or an actor that frequently comes up with new initiatives and fresh ideas.[59]

There are several reasons for this rather poor and uncoordinated foreign-policy decision-making and implementation. A major factor is the high degree of polarisation amongst Czech political actors on most foreign-policy issues. As previously indicated, Czech political disunity is evident not only in EU affairs, but also on international security matters. Czech policy-makers and politicians have disagreed on several crucial issues, including the future course of European integration, NATO's bombing campaign against Serbia during the Kosovo war, modernisation of the Czech air force, the Iraq war, and United States missile defense plans.[60]

In fact, only a few examples exist of wide cross-party agreement on Czech foreign-policy goals. One is joining NATO, which was a priority that all major political parties (with the exception of the Communists) supported. A similar consensus existed regarding the EU, with all major parliamentary parties (except the Communists and extremist Republicans) showing consistent support for joining the EU as quickly as possible.[61] Indeed, most analysts assume that even if there had been a different government in the pre-accession period, the Czech Republic would have most probably joined the EU anyway. According to Drulák, it was the only national interest that the country managed to agree on and to accomplish, and there has been no such consensual theme ever since.[62] In fact, recent research by the Czech Institute of International Relations suggests that no consensus on major foreign-policy issues is possible in the Republic's current contentious political environment. Common accord is to be found only on marginal matters, because nobody cares too much about them and it is not costly.[63] Where does this low degree of consensus on Czech foreign-policy goals originate?

For Wallat, the major force behind significant swings in the concepts, styles, and focus of policy has been the 'exceptionally strong role of individuals and their ideational background'.[64] This was particularly so in the 1990s, with strong influence over foreign policy being exercised by Havel and Klaus, men with strong personalities and ideological beliefs, although of a very different sort. Since 2003, a strong role in foreign policy has been pursued by Klaus, now President.

There have also been many different governments ruling the Czech Republic (eleven in 18 years): four centre-right coalitions, four centre-left coalitions, a minority Social Democratic government, and two caretaker governments, with foreign policy thus being heavily influenced by the partisan composition and ideological orientation of individual cabinets. Although all of the main parties (except the Communists) basically support Western integration and internationalist principles, there are major differences in orientation between 'Atlanticists' (mainly the Civic Democratic Party [ODS]), who prefer closer cooperation with the United States, and 'Continentalists' (mainly the Social Democratic Party [ČSSD]), who favour more European integration.[65] These differences have grown since the 2001 Iraq war and EU accession, further strengthening their role and influence in foreign-policy formulation.

The ODS, the major Czech right-wing party, is often described in scholarly literature as being 'soft eurosceptic'.[66] On closer scrutiny, it began moving in a more eurosceptical direction after going into opposition after the June 1998 elections. Although it still supported EU accession, the ODS became increasingly critical of certain aspects of European integration: it preferred a more loosely organised intergovernmental model of cooperation for the EU. In particular, the party favoured a 'Europe of nations,' in which countries retain their basic sovereignty and national interests and identities are respected. The ODS also linked its disagreement with deeper European integration to nationalist themes and the defense of Czech national interests, exploiting historically based fears of Germany that are widespread amongst many Czechs; it argued 'that the EU's development in a federalist direction favored German interests and designs for dominating Europe'.[67]

The ČSSD, the country's major left-wing party, has been generally pro-European, supporting deeper integration and considering the EU a suitable arena in which to promote Czech national interests. In the party's view, the Czech Republic can only benefit from a more integrated Europe: 'this would also enhance the country's own weight and influence. For the ČSSD, therefore, a strong Europe means a strong Czech Republic'.[68] The party thus prefers strong European institutions that would allow the EU to strengthen its position on the international scene, as well as the continuation of the enlargement process.

Another factor undermining a more effective Czech foreign policy is the constitutional set-up of executive power. The Czech constitution identifies three power centres that share foreign-policy-making (the President, Prime Minister, and Minister of Foreign Affairs) but does not introduce any effective coordinating mechanism to ensure that all three speak with one voice externally,[69] or clearly state which organ should have the final and decisive voice in determining the Republic's foreign-policy orientation. This naturally creates space for overlaps and disagreements, especially in the case of ideological differences amongst the actors. Although Article 63 of the Constitution attributes the privileged role in conducting Czech foreign policy to the Government, it also confers certain foreign-policy powers on the President. Thus, foreign policy represents a policy area in which (compared with other policies) the President's prerogatives are amongst the most extensive.

During the last twenty years, there have been ebbs and flows of presidential dominance in Czech foreign-policy formulation. In general, both Czech Presidents (Havel and Klaus) have been active in the foreign-policy realm, but they have not always pursued a political line consistent with the Government's concept. The situation is even more complicated in the case of Klaus, who is well known for his eurosceptic views. Clashes between the Government and the President deepened in 2008, and especially in 2009, in relation to Kosovo's independence, the Georgia–Russia military crisis, and the Lisbon Treaty.[70] In fact, Klaus became one of the Lisbon Treaty's toughest opponents in Europe, claiming that it threatened Czech national interests. He also made his signature conditional with a number of requirements, such as the Czech Constitutional Court's statement that the treaty did not violate the Czech constitution, a positive second Irish referendum, and, finally, an opt-out for the Czech Republic from the treaty's Charter of Fundamental Rights.[71] In light of these latest developments, Klaus' foreign-policy role has unprecedentedly increased[72] and, once again, in the Czech political arena, the President can act autonomously, unaccountable to anything or anybody.[73] Nevertheless, disagreements do not arise only between the President and the Government, as illustrated by the example of dissonance between Prime Minister Miloš Zeman and his Minister of Foreign Affairs, Jan Kavan, on the Palestinian question in 2002.[74]

It is obvious that the Czech Republic's role, position, and influence in contemporary international politics have changed significantly since the 1989 Velvet Revolution. As a member of many international organisations, the country is firmly integrated in stable security and economic structures on regional, European, Euro-Atlantic and global levels. The Republic seeks to present itself as a politically, economically, and socially stable democratic state in Central Europe that promotes not only its own interests but also assumes its share of responsibility for the development of Europe and the international community as a whole.[75]

Yet, the Czech Republic's global reach and its capacities to influence the international situation autonomously and effectively are limited. Indeed, although the political leadership in the early years after the Velvet Revolution firmly believed that small Czechoslovakia could influence wider European and international developments, successive foreign-policy elites returned to the perception that the Czech Republic can exert only limited international influence.[76] As a relatively small and still inexperienced country, the Czech Republic has generally not sought to play an activist or leadership role on the global scene.[77] In addition, as a country with an open economy highly dependent on trade and lacking in natural resources, the Czech Republic is largely reliant on international cooperation.[78] According to Kořan, a small or middle-size country is successful to the extent that it manages to use its limited potential.[79] Unfortunately, however, in the Czech case, a significant portion of Prague's foreign-policy potential is being wasted.

The problem is not so much that the still-maturing Czech political system tends to produce narrow parliamentary majorities and weak coalition governments, because similar situations exist in other countries with proportional representation electoral systems without the same consequences for their foreign policy.[80] Instead, the political context of Czech foreign-policy formulation has been significantly worsened by such factors as the unclear division of foreign-policy competences and powers, the increasing domination of the executive branch, the irrational polarisation of the Czech political scene, political rivalry and maneuvering, internal ideological divisions within political parties, intraparty bargaining, and the short-sighted opportunism of some domestic politicians.[81] Despite the fact that when in government, the right-wing parties act more pro-European and the left-wing parties more pro-Atlanticist than their previous rhetoric would have suggested,[82] the mutual antagonism of the political parties has unfortunate consequences for the Czech Republic's position, performance, and influence in modern statecraft.

The strong polarisation of Czech political parties and elites on most foreign-policy issues and their general unwillingness to compromise seriously hampers the conduct of a cooperative, complex, and confident foreign policy. These antagonisms also make it extremely difficult to formulate a coherent national strategy with clear positions on foreign-policy priorities, and they have also resulted in delays when it comes to the preparation of strategic and conceptual documents. For instance, the last foreign-policy and security framework documents for the Czech Republic were adopted in 2003, for the period 2003–6.[83] As a result, Czech foreign policy has sometimes been contradictory, chaotic, controversial, and unreadable.[84] In some cases it has also lacked a strong mandate, and many of its priorities have failed to be realised. Currently, a widespread 'policy of disinterest' and the subordination of foreign policy to domestic political interests seriously weaken or even paralyze the Czech Republic's international position and prevent it from becoming a reliable, stable, and constructive foreign-policy actor.

Whilst there has been considerable consensus on core national interests in the Czech Republic, the consistency of foreign-policy strategy and instruments in advancing those interests has been significantly less. In other words, Czech national interests are more static than the instruments used to pursue them. Concrete foreign-policy goals and priorities are more likely to become subject to change than national interests themselves, as they are regularly reviewed and updated according to current developments and momentary turns in the political environment. In the final analysis, however, both must complement each other for a country's foreign policy to be effective. For the Czech Republic, this synchronisation of national interests with foreign-policy strategy and instruments remains to be accomplished.

Notes

1 Petr Drulák, 'Jediný národní zájem, na němž jsme se dokázali shodnout a naplnit ho, byl vstup do Evropské unie', *Mezinárodní politika*, Volume 34, Number 5(2010), 19–20.
2 Jiří Šedivý, 'Czech-NATO Relations: A Dynamic Process', in Tadayuki Hayashi, ed., *The Emerging New Regional Order in Central and Eastern Europe* (Hokkaido, 1996), 131.
3 Ministerstvo zahraničních věcí [MZV], *Czech Foreign Policy: Points of Departure, Principles, Interests and Objectives* (Praha, 12 August 1998): http://pdc.ceu.hu/archive/00002560/01/conc_basis.pdf.
4 MZV, *Koncepce zahraniční politiky České republiky na léta 2003–2006* (Praha, 3 March 2003): www.mzv.cz/servis/soubor.asp?id=4191.
5 Daniel Papp, *Contemporary International Relations. Frameworks for Understanding* (New York, 1991), 40.
6 Dan Marek and Michael Baun, *The Czech Republic and the European Union* (London, New York, 2011), 28.
7 Ibid.
8 Ibid., 30.
9 Mats Braun, 'Understanding Klaus. The Story of Czech Eurorealism,' *EPIN Working Paper*, Number 26 (November 2009), 1–2.
10 Vit Beneš and Mats Braun, 'Evropský rozměr české zahraniční politiky', in Michal Kořan, ed., *Česká zahraniční politika v roce 2009* (Praha, 2010), 80.
11 Sociologický ústav AV ČR, *Občané o členství České republiky v Evropské unii* Centrum pro výzkum veřejného mínění (Sociologický ústav Akademie věd České republiky, 2010), 2: www.cvvm.cas.cz/upl/zpravy/101034s_pm100429.pdf.
12 Petr Drulák, 'The Czech EU Presidency: Background and Priorities', *Studies & Research*, Number 67 (2008), 11.
13 Michael Baun and Dan Marek, 'Czech Foreign Policy and EU Integration: European and Domestic Sources,' *Perspectives on European Politics and Society*, Volume 11, Number 2(2010), 17.
14 Veronika Bílková, 'Multilaterální rozměr české zahraniční poliky,' in Kořan, *Česká zahraniční politika ... 2009*, 289; MZV, *MZV, Koncepce zahraniční ... 2003–2006*.
15 Kai-Olaf Lang, 'Má dáti – dal: česká zahraniční politika na prahu vstupu do Evropské unie,' *Mezinárodní politika*, Volume 28, Number 2(2004), 13.
16 Marek and Baun, *European Union*, 9.
17 MZV, *Koncepce zahraniční ... 2003–2006*.
18 Baun and Marek, 'EU Integration', 17.
19 MZV, *Zpráva o zahraniční politice České republiky za rok 2008* (Praha, 4 April 2009), 6: www.mzv.cz/jnp/cz/zahranicni_vztahy/vyrocni_zpravy_a_dokumenty/zprava2008.html.

20 Marek and Baun, *European Union, 133.*
21 MZV, *Zpráva o zahraniční politice České republiky za rok 2009* (Praha, 21 May 2010), 7, 26: www.mzv.cz/jnp/cz/zahranicni_vztahy/vyrocni_zpravy_a_dokumenty/zprava2009.htm.
22 Jiří Šedivý, *Dilema rozšiřování* NATO (Praha, 2001), 23.
23 Jiří Schneider, 'Budoucnost transatlantických vztahů z pohledu České republiky,' *Mezinárodní politika,* Volume 29, Number 4(2005), 8–9; MZV, *Bezpečnostní strategie ČR,* (Praha, 2003): www.mzv.cz/jnp/cz/zahranicni_vztahy/bezpecnostni_politika/bezpecnostni_strategie_cr_1/index.html.
24 Baun and Marek, 'EU Integration', 10.
25 Petr Drulák, 'Česká zahraniční politika v době počínajícího politického rozkladu', in Kořan, *Česká zahraniční politika v roce 2008* (Praha, 2009), 373; Radek Khol, *Česká republika a Společná zahraniční a bezpečnostní politika EU* (2003), 6: www.europeum.org/doc/arch_eur/EPF_SZBP.pdf; MZV, *Koncepce zahraniční ... 2003–2006.*
26 MZV, *Bezpečnostní strategie ČR* (Praha, 2003), 4: www.mzv.cz/jnp/cz/zahranicni_vztahy/bezpecnostni_politika/bezpecnostni_strategie_cr_1/index.html.
27 Khol, *Česká republika,* 6.
28 Vit Střítecký, 'Bezpečnostní rozměr české zahraniční politiky', in Kořan, *Česká zahraniční politika ... 2008,* 87.
29 Vladimír Handl and Otto Pick, 'Česká zahraniční politika 1993–2005 od návratu do Evropy k evropeizaci, 1. část,' *Mezinárodní politika,* Volume 29, Number 8(2005), 14.
30 MZV, *Koncepce zahraniční ... 2003–2006.*
31 Baun and Marek, 'EU Integration', 4, 12.
32 Petr Drulák, 'Závěrem: Český nezájem se prosazuje', in Kořan, *Česká zahraniční politika ... 2008,* 359.
33 MZV, *Koncepce zahraniční ... 2003–2006.*
34 MZV, *Zpráva o zahraniční politice ... 2009.*
35 Lukáš Novotný, 'Hodnocení současných vztahů mezi Českou republikou a SRN,' *Mezinárodní politika,* 30(2006), 20.
36 Vladimír Handl, 'Česká politika vůči Spolkové republice Německo: od normalizace k evropeizaci', in Kořan, *Česká zahraniční politika ... 2008,* 37.
37 Drulák, 'Jediný národní zájem', 20–21.
38 Drulák, 'Závěrem', 358.
39 MZV, *Zpráva o zahraniční, 163.*
40 Miroslav Šepták, 'Místo Rakouska v české (československé) zahraniční politice', in Michal Kořan, ed., *Česká zahraniční politika v zrcadle sociálně-vědního výzkumu* (Praha, 2009), 44–55.
41 Lang, 'Má dáti – dal'; Miroslav Šepták, 'Místo Rakouska v české (československé) zahraniční politice', in Kořan, *Česká ... sociálně-vědního výzkumu,* 45–48.
42 Sociologický ústav, *Vztah ČR k,* 1.
43 Otto Pick, 'Uskutečnění původních priorit české zahraniční politiky', *Mezinárodní politika,* Volume 28, Number 1(2004), 7; MZV, *Zpráva o zahraniční politice ... 2009,* 166.
44 MZV, *Koncepce zahraniční ... 2003–2006.*
45 MZV, *Zpráva o zahraniční politice ... 2008,* 161.
46 Ondřej Ditrych, 'Spojené státy americké v české zahraniční politice', in Kořan, *Česká zahraniční politika ... 2009,* 165; Schneider, 'Budoucnost transatlantických', 8.
47 Jiří Šedivý and Marcin Zaborowski, 'Old Europe, New Europe and Transatlantic Relations,' *European Security,* Volume 13, Number 3(2004), 189.
48 Marek and Baun, *European Union, 12.*
49 Lang, 'Má dáti – dal', 15.
50 Petra Kuchyňková, 'Rusko v české zahraniční politice', in Kořan, *Česká zahraniční politika ... 2009,* 189–203; Marek and Baun, *European Union,* 121.
51 Drulák, 'Jediný národní zájem', 21.
52 Baun and Marek, 'EU Integration', 12.
53 MZV, *Zpráva o zahraniční politice ... 2009,* 220.
54 Ibid., 220–21.
55 Josefine Wallat 'Czechoslovak/Czech Foreign and Security Policy 1989–99,' *Perspectives—The Central European Review of International Affairs,* Volume 9, Number 17(2001), 14.
56 Ibid., 25.
57 Baun and Marek, 'EU Integration', 3.
58 The rest of this paragraph is based on Marek and Baun, *European Union,* 127, 150; Baun and Marek, 'EU Integration', 15–16, 17; Drulák, 'Jediný národní zájem', 21–22; Drulák, 'Závěrem', 359.

Dan Marek and Michael Baun

59 Drulák, 'Jediný národní zájem', 21.
60 Ibid., 21; Handl and Pick, 'Česká zahraniční politika 1993–2005', 15.
61 Marek and Baun, *European Union*, 36.
62 Drulák, 'Jediný národní zájem', 21.
63 Ibid.
64 Wallat, 'Foreign and Security Policy', 26.
65 Drulák, European Presidency, 7–10.
66 Braun, 'Understanding Klaus', 1.
67 Marek and Baun, *European Union*, 38.
68 Ibid., 41.
69 Handl, 'Česká politika', 38.
70 Kořan, 'Politický kontext', 26.
71 Marek and Baun, *European Union*, 49–50.
72 Drulák, 'Závěrem', 357.
73 Kořan, 'Politický kontext', 26.
74 Handl and Pick, 'Česká zahraniční politika', 15.
75 MZV, *Koncepce zahraniční … 2003–2006*.
76 Wallat, 'Foreign and Security Policy', 26.
77 Marek and Baun, *European Union*, 150.
78 MZV, *Koncepce zahraniční … 2003–2006*.
79 Kořan, 'Politický kontext', 15.
80 Marek and Braun, *European Union*, 152.
81 Kořan, 'Politický kontext', 15.
82 Drulák, 'Jediný národní zájem', 21.
83 Tomáš Weiss (2009) 'Jaké vlastně jsou zahraničně-politické zájmy České republiky?' *NATOAktual* (2009): www.natoaktual.cz/jake-vlastne-jsou-zahranicne-politicke-zajmy-ceske-republiky-pur-/na_analyzy.asp?c=A090511_095911_na_analyzy_m02.
84 The rest of this paragraph is based on Drulák, 'Česká zahraniční politika', 375, 378; Drulák, 'Závěrem', 357.

14

The foreign policy of Turkey

Dimitris Keridis

There is increased international interest in the foreign policy of Turkey for a number of reasons. These include Turkey's economic success, coupled with a young and growing population, the politics of a democratically elected, mildly Islamist government, and a favourable geostrategic position. All these assets have turned Turkey into a regional leader and a 'middle Power', with rising aspirations for some global influence.[1]

Turkey is a country of 77 million people.[2] It is estimated that its population will reach 100 million people by the middle of the twenty-first century.[3] Thanks to a falling fertility rate, it will then stabilise around that mark. And with an average median age of 28 years, Turkey's population is at least ten years younger on average than that of Europe. For the next 20 to 30 years, Turkey will enjoy a demographic window of opportunity, with more people of working age supporting a decreasing number of dependents. Turkey is a member of the G20, the group of the world's leading economies. The size of its gross domestic product (GDP) will soon reach US$ one trillion.[4] In 2010 Turkey's economy grew by 8 percent, whilst the average annual rate of growth between 2002–8 was 6 percent.[5] Tayip Erdogan, the current Turkish Prime Minister, has set the goal of having Turkey join the top ten biggest economies in the world by 2023, the centennial of the founding of the Turkish Republic.

Turkey's public finances are in good shape.[6] With a public debt that stands at a manageable 50% of GDP, many European countries would be envious of the solvency of the Turkish treasury. For the first time in living memory, Turkish inflation has dropped to single digits and the Turkish lira is strong and credible.[7] As a result, Turkey's international credit ratings have continued to be upgraded.[8] Moreover, Turkey is the only sizeable exporter of manufactured goods in southeastern Europe and the Middle East. In recent years, it has emerged as a leading tourist destination and an important energy hub, whilst Turkish companies dominate the construction market in much of the Middle East and the former Soviet Union.

The story of Turkey's economic success began with liberal reforms in 1980 that transformed a closed, protectionist, imports-substitution economy into an export-oriented manufacturer.[9] However, budgetary discipline remained lax and prone to politicking, fueling persistent high, double-digit inflation.[10] Stop-and-go cycles of growth and recession ended dramatically in 2001, when Turkey lost one-quarter of its national income to save its banks. Since then, Turkey has consolidated its public finances, reformed its banking sector, and restructured several parts of its economy.[11] Today, the Turkish economy is stronger and more diverse than ever before.[12]

Beyond its economic prowess, Turkey is interesting for its politics as well. Turkey enjoys a long democratic tradition, unique in the Muslim world. The first constitution was introduced by Ottoman reformers in 1876 followed, one year later, by the first-ever parliamentary elections in the Muslim world.[13] Since 1950, governments have largely been chosen by the ballot box.

Although the military has intervened in Turkish politics several times in the past,[14] its political influence today is waning and the possibility of a military coup appears remote. In reality, Turkish society today is too complex and difficult to rule single-handedly, whilst the immediate economic costs of a coup seem to deter any potential adventurism on the part of the generals.

In addition, the Turkish media are, more or less, independent, the police is becoming more accountable, and the respect for human rights, although far from impeccable, is gradually improving.[15] Overall, the political and social atmosphere in Ankara is more relaxed than almost anywhere else in the Middle East and, definitely, compared with the atmosphere in Cairo or Teheran. The country is, currently, ruled by Tayip Erdogan's mildly Islamist government, first elected in 2002. Erdogan has dominated Turkish politics for two main reasons. The first had to do with the crisis of the old politics of weak coalition governments that badly misruled Turkey in the 1990s. But, whereas the crisis of Italy's *ancien régime* gave way to the ineffective rule of Silvio Berlusconi, that in Turkey brought to power a group of mildly Islamist, strong-willed reformers. Thus, the second reason relates to the modernisation of traditional Turkish Islamism under the leadership of Erdogan and Abdullah Gül, the Minister of Foreign Affairs from 2003 to 2007 and the President since.[16] They made the Justice and Development Party (AKP) more appealing and electable than any Islamist party of the past. Turkey has traditionally been politically conservative, and the AKP's emergence as the dominant force on the right established it as the natural party of government.

It is often said that today is the age of democracy.[17] However, historically, the opening of political systems to popular participation does not necessarily produce more rights for citizens; liberalisation does not always lead to liberalism. This situation is especially true in the Muslim world, where the contradictions and, occasional, bankruptcy of the West's secular ideologies have contributed to the rise of political Islam.[18] But political Islam does not have to be radical and violent and, in most of the Muslim world, it is neither.[19] In the struggle to accommodate democracy with modernisation and the reconciliation of cultural identities (first and foremost, Islam) with liberalism, Turkey has emerged as a primary battleground.[20] It is true that the gradual liberalisation of Turkish politics has put enormous pressure on the unyielding, officially sanctioned secularism dictated by modern Turkey's founder, Kemal Ataturk, and has reinvigorated the people's traditional, Islam-centred, cultural identity.[21] On the surface, there exists the following paradox: the more Turkey 'Europeanises', the more oriental it seems to become; the more it looks to the West, the more it turns to the East. The successful resolution of this paradox, without recourse to force and repression, entails many risks but has made Turkish politics particularly interesting for the world at large.[22]

Thanks to its experience with democracy and secularism, at least at the level of state institutions, the potential success of Erdogan's government, in establishing a prosperous, well-functioning democracy along European norms, would have important ramifications not only for Turkey but internationally, starting with the Turks' brethren in Central Asia and their Arab and Iranian neighbours in the Middle East. It is here, in its own neighbourhood, where Turkey enjoys its third comparative advantage, beyond the economy and politics. Turkey is uniquely endowed with a privileged geostrategic position. Few powers can claim such a central position.[23] Lying between Europe and Asia, Turkey controls large parts of the Black Sea and the Eastern Mediterranean, including the Bosporus and the Dardanelles Straits, which connect the two. It borders the Caucasus, the Middle East, and Southeastern Europe, three of the world's most unstable and conflict-ridden regions, which attract a great share of international news coverage.

In the past, this regional instability often made Turkey feel vulnerable. Today, it stands above the other two historically Great Middle Eastern powers, Egypt and Iran. Despite lacking oil income or an equivalent to the revenue-producing Suez Canal, Turkey has grown stronger and freer than most of its neighbours.[24] Seeking equality with its historical nemesis, Russia, it also has opinions about regional matters and defends them vigorously, even if it brings conflict with Israel and its powerful patron, the United States.[25]

In sum, Turkey's economic and political resources coupled with recent developments and the weakness of most of its neighbors have infused Turkish foreign policy with a new-found self-confidence. Turks believe in their power and influence abroad to a degree that would have been unthinkable only a few years ago.[26] However, caution is required. It is not the first time there has been this Turkish self-perception. In the early 1990s, following a period of growth under Turgut Özal and the collapse of the Soviet Union, Turkey put itself forward as a regional leader in the Caucasus, Central Asia, and the Balkans.[27] However, it soon became evident that Russia remained the dominant force in the Caucasus and Central Asia, whereas the Balkan imbroglio was resolved only after United States' intervention.

Furthermore, Turkey is in danger of overreaching itself. Its recent success remains somewhat fragile. Turkey is divided in several important ways: ethnically between a Turkish majority and a Kurdish, often marginalised, minority;[28] religiously between Sunni and Alevi;[29] culturally between the secular elites of Istanbul and the Aegean, the so-called White Turks, and the pious masses of Anatolia; economically between a developed west and an underdeveloped and still struggling east; and socially between an upper class and a vast underclass. Progress is real but, in some cases, growth has accentuated inequalities and tensions.[30]

The average Turk is still less than one-third as wealthy as the average European. The national savings rate is low, and the economy depends on foreign capital and knowledge to develop.[31] At the same time, corruption is endemic.[32] Whilst the Prime Minister and his Islamist colleagues appear suspicious and vengeful towards critics, the opposition has failed to offer a credible alternative.[33] Until it does, democratic politics will remain lopsided and unconsolidated. Thus, before Turkish elites embark on a forward-looking foreign policy, they should have a more realistic understanding of their country's potential, needs, and vulnerabilities. Such caution is not to mean that a confident Turkey, constructively engaged abroad, is not to be welcomed. But any thought for some kind of Ottoman revival is dangerous and grossly misplaced.[34]

Modern Turkey has traditionally looked to the West.[35] Since 1952, a loyal member of the North Atlantic Treaty Organization (NATO), it has been allied with the United States.[36] Turkey's drive westwards was initiated by Ottoman reformers in the nineteenth century as a response to the crisis of the Ottoman state.[37] Until the eve of the First World War, Ottoman Turkey was allied with Great Britain against a southward-looking, expansionist Russia. The Young Turks' repositioning towards Germany after 1908 led to the Ottoman Empire's destruction in 1918. After the war, Mustafa Kemal led a Turkish nationalist movement that succeeded in establishing a republic in the heartland of Asia Minor and Eastern Thrace.[38] The founding document establishing the new order was the 1923 Treaty of Lausanne delineating (with minor adjustments in later years) Turkey's present borders. Whilst the British kept Mosul and present-day northern Iraq out of Turkey, Kemal succeeded in reclaiming Turkey's full sovereignty over the Straits in 1936 and the province of Hatay-Alexandretta, along the border with Syria, in 1939.[39]

During the interwar period, Kemal concentrated Turkish energy on domestic reconstruction and modernisation. Unlike some Young Turks, he denounced pan-Turkism and any interest in the fate of Turks and Turkic-speakers outside the borders of the republic. Pursuing a neutralist policy, Turkey worried about Benito Mussolini's imperialist ambitions in the Mediterranean and supported an ineffective Balkan pact based on reconciliation with Greece.[40] The crowning achievement of Kemalist disengagement was Turkish neutrality during the Second World War under Kemal's loyal ally and successor, Ismet Inonü. However, the war's end found Stalin demanding a series of concessions from Turkey. Ankara quickly sought an alliance with the United States, Britain's successor as the preeminent maritime power in the Mediterranean and the new arbiter of the European and Middle Eastern order.[41]

With the proclamation of the Truman Doctrine and the Marshall Plan in 1947, Turkey began to receive American aid. In 1950 Turkey sent troops to Korea to support the American-led anti-communist forces; it joined into NATO in 1952; and, beginning in 1954, it signed renewable Defense Cooperation Agreements that provided basing rights for American forces.[42] Two opposing developments colored Turkey's position inside the Western alliance. The first devolved from the decolonisation of Cyprus that caused sometimes violent differences between Greek and Turkish nationalists regarding the future of the ethnically divided island.[43] American intervention to ensure stability on NATO's southeastern flank and deny the Soviets an opportunity to divide the United States' allies was, occasionally, perceived by Turkey as hostile to its national interests.[44] Thus, Cyprus clouded Turkey's relationship not only with Greece but with its principal Western allies, including the United States. The best example of this dilemma involved an American arms embargo briefly imposed on Turkey following the latter's invasion of Cyprus in 1974. And, today, Cyprus continues to be the biggest stumbling block to Turkey's full membership in the European Union (EU).[45] Turkey cannot hope to realise its ambition to join the EU without accepting a substantial loss of control over Cyprus. The second development has worked in the other direction: enhancing Turkey's importance for and position in the Western alliance. This has to do with the rise, first, of Arab nationalism and, then, political Islam in the Middle East. The 1979 anti-American Iranian Revolution and the Iraqi crisis after 1990 have strengthened Turkey's bargaining power.[46]

Turkish foreign policy can be thought of as comprising three concentric circles. The first is regional, because Turkey has had difficult relations with many of its neighboring powers. Problems with Syria stemmed from Damascus' support for the Kurdistan Workers' Party (PKK)-led Kurdish insurgency in Turkey's southeast,[47] a dispute over sharing the waters of the Euphrates river after the completion of Turkey's GAP project,[48] and the old border dispute over the partially Arab-speaking province of Hatay-Alexandretta.[49] In the past, there were many occasions when Turkey and Greece mobilised militarily against each other. Often, a regional war was averted only thanks to American diplomatic intervention. The deterioration of the Greco-Turkish relations in the 1950s was caused by conflict over Cyprus. In later years, a dispute over the delineation of the Aegean continental shelf and related matters further poisoned the situation.[50] Turkey also objected strongly to Bulgaria's attempts to bulgarise its large Turkish minority during communism's final years in the 1980s. In 1993, Ankara closed the border with Armenia in reaction to the latter's occupation of Nagorno-Karabakh. Finally, Turkey invaded northern Iraq several times in pursuit of PKK guerrillas using safe heavens on Iraqi territory.

The second circle contains Turkey's relations with the West, mainly the United States and Europe and, in juxtaposition, with Russia. Historically, Turkey looked to the West to counter-balance the threat that tsarist and then Soviet Russia posed from the north. During the Cold War, dependent on American diplomatic support and military aid, Ankara's relationship with Washington remained of paramount importance. The relationship solidified through Turkey's NATO membership and a series of bilateral, mostly military, agreements signed between Turkey and the United States. However, the Russian revival after 1999 has produced an explosion in the volume of trade and cross-border investments between Turkey and Russia. This economic *rapprochement* has spilled over into geoeconomics, with a Russo-Turkish partnership in energy and closer cooperation in places such as the Caucasus, Central Asia, and the Balkans.

In parallel, Turkey showed an early and keen interest in European integration. It applied for associate membership of the European Communities in 1959 and signed the corresponding agreement in 1963. However, full membership into the ever-closer EU has remained elusive. Prime Minister Turgut Özal did submit a formal application in 1987 but it was coolly received by the European Commission. Furthermore, for all the bonds of alliance forged during the 40-year Cold War, Turkey was quickly bypassed after 1990 by Eastern European countries such as Poland and even Bulgaria, which became EU members in 2004 and in 2007, respectively. Offered and entering a full customs union with the EU in 1996, Turkey was finally accepted as a candidate in 1999 and accession negotiations began in 2005.[51] Since then, the momentum for Turkey's accession has weakened for a number of factors.[52] They include Europe's economic troubles, the intractability of the Cyprus problem, and the strong opposition of Nicolas Sarkozy, the President of France, and Angela Merkel, the Chancellor of Germany.[53]

In recent years, Turkey's European policy has become a highly contested issue both within Turkey and in several EU countries.[54] It is often argued that Erdogan is a Europeanist out of convenience rather than conviction. He might be better than some of his predecessors, who did nothing to support Turkey's Europeanisation, but is he good enough? To answer this question, it is worth describing the ruling Islamists' complicated relationship with Europe. Erdogan increased the pace of EU-inspired reforms first started by his predecessors, including a plethora of constitutional amendments. It has been a remarkable development given the origins and social background of the AKP. Coming from the most conservative, traditionalist, and pious strata of Turkish society, most AKP supporters feel uncomfortable with many components of what might be called European modernity. Nevertheless, for Erdogan and his comrades, Europeanisation has proved a useful tool for weakening the army's and the entrenched bureaucracy's hold on power by increasing the decision-making role of the Turkish parliament. There, Erdogan maintains a decisive majority. According to one observer, 'the AKP benefited from the fact that EU membership represented the climax of the Kemalist aim of reaching the level of contemporary civilisations and enjoyed an above-politics common good status in Turkey.'[55]

However, there have been two sets of doubts casting a heavy cloud over Turkey's reform efforts. The first centers on Erdogan's slowness in adopting Europe-mandated reforms that run counter to his domestic agenda, as is the case with women and minority rights. The second has to do with Erdogan's persistent attempt to concentrate all power in his and his close associates' hands. This has brought him into conflict with the media and has led to the expansion of a non-transparent and corrupt network of relations between his AKP and various state-dependent business interests. The best-known example of this trend has been the charges for tax evasion that the Erdogan Government brought against Turkey's biggest publisher, Aydin Dogan.[56] Although there might be some truth in the charges, one cannot fail to notice the startling parallels with Vladimir Putin's similar tactics in Russia.[57] In conclusion, ambivalence on the part of the Turkish leadership, coupled with the rising tide in Europe against enlargement in general and Turkey's membership in particular, have slowed considerably the pace of the accession negotiations and have pushed the goal of full membership further into the future.[58]

The third circle of Turkish foreign policy concerns the wider world. Traditionally, lacking the resources and being fully preoccupied with its own security, Turkey was not much concerned with issues of wider international importance. But, today, it looks at itself as a rising power with some global influence, projecting the image of moderate Islam, reconciled with modernity and the West, in opposition to ultraconservative, radical, and anti-Western versions emanating from places such as Saudi Arabia and Iran.[59] Thus, Turkey has been spending more than ever before on building schools and cultural centers in places once ruled by the Ottomans, such as Bosnia, Kosovo, the former Yugoslav Republic of Macedonia and elsewhere in the Caucasus and

Central Asia. This new spending does not come solely from the state. A primary source has been the privately funded network of schools by Fethullah Gülen, a conservative, pro-market Muslim preacher.[60]

In general, Turkish Islam has been, comparatively speaking, more open, pragmatic, and tolerant of heterodox practices best exemplified by the strength of Sufism in its midst.[61] Furthermore, the Ottomans built an empire by ruling over sizeable communities of non-Muslims. They were, primarily, concerned with the practicalities of politics rather than the metaphysics of theology.[62] In addition, they initiated a program of reforms in 1839 that paved the way for the Young Turks revolution in 1908 and Kemal's proclamation of a Turkish Republic in 1923.[63] As a result, Turkey has modernised institutionally, economically, and socially, probably, more than any other Muslim society in the world. Since the 1980s, the rise of a dynamic but pious entrepreneurial class in the Anatolian heartland (which knows how to accumulate wealth in the modern world and engages in manufacturing and exports competitively in large numbers[64]) runs counter to all Western stereotypes about the backwardness of Islam and its irreconcilability with capitalism. This constitutes an achievement about which many nationalist Turks, secular and Islamist alike, feel proud and would like to share with the rest of the world. Some analysts have even drawn comparisons between recent socioeconomic developments in Turkish towns such as Kayseri and Konya with the early fusion of Protestantism and capitalism and have talked of a similar phenomenon that they call 'Islamic Calvinism.'

For all the exaggeration involved, Erdogan is keen about the image of a modern, entrepreneurial, dynamic, and yet pious Turkey that breaks from the chains of economic *étatism*, protectionism, and state authoritarianism. After all, it is these newly empowered Anatolian elites of Islamo-Calvinists that have been his firmest supporters. In that regard, together with the Spanish Prime Minister, Jose Luis R. Zapatero, Erdogan has underwritten the 'Alliance of Civilizations' initiative meant to foster respect and dialogue between Islamic and Western societies.[65]

Furthermore, it should not be forgotten that for centuries Istanbul ruled over a vast empire, stretching from Algeria to the Persian Gulf, the Danube, and Crimea. It forged a common, post-Ottoman cultural space where, for all the national differences, many affinities still survive. Turks are very familiar with the hotspots in their region that have attracted international attention. From Bosnia and Kosovo in the Balkans to Palestine and Iraq, Turkey is well versed in the local conditions and can prove useful in fostering regional peace and stability. Thus, Ankara has recently mediated a *rapprochement* between Belgrade and Sarajevo and has forged a close relationship with Serbia, despite its well-known sympathies for the Muslims of Bosnia and Kosovo.[66]

For Turkey to play this wider role, it must disentangle from some regional disputes that, over the years, have proved intractable. The current Foreign Minister, Ahmet Davotuglu, an imaginative and outspoken professor of international relations with a strong Islamist background, has described a policy of zero problems with neighbors.[67] He sounds ambitious given the often bloody past separating Turks and some of these neighbors. However, it is true that there have been some breakthroughs recently, and that the overall atmosphere is more relaxed today than was the case only a few years ago.

Three disputes (with the Armenians, Kurds, and Greeks) stand out as the most troublesome. The problems with Armenia are well known and have to do with both the painful memories of the Armenian genocide and Armenia's occupation of Nagorno-Karabach. Turkey has aggressively resisted the recognition of the Young Turks' genocide of Armenians in 1915, denied access to its state archives, and refused to cooperate in shedding light on one of the darkest chapters of the First World War. However, in recent years there has been a thaw, starting with civil society and, later, moving to the state level. President Gül visited Yerevan and Davutoğlu signed an agreement with his Armenian counterpart, Edward Nalbandian, in October 2009, establishing diplomatic relations and opening the border, between the two countries, which Turkey has kept closed since 1993. The agreement provided for a joint commission including foreign experts to examine the past. However, the agreement was not ratified by either country's parliament.

Turkey and Greece form a rare couple in that they have fought their wars of independence against each other. Historically, relations between the two powers have been antagonistic as an irredentist Greece sought to expand to the Greek-populated lands of Ottoman Turkey. However, a period of peace and cooperation emerged after the signing of the Treaty of Lausanne between 1930 and 1955. The catalyst for a new deterioration in the Greco-Turkish relationship was the decolonisation of Cyprus and, then, the discovery of oil in the Aegean. In the past, the United States provided some useful crisis management between its two allies. But repeated crises led to an arms race and, until 1999, a diplomatic war in every possible forum available. Since then, Greece has appeared supportive of Turkey's EU membership, provided a judicious resolution of the Aegean and Cypriot disputes is forthcoming.

The problems with Kurds are probably Turkey's gravest concern given the number of Kurds living within Turkey and the armed struggle against Kurdish separatist guerrillas that has been going on since 1984.[68] From the founding of the Turkish Republic, traditionalist and religious Kurds opposed the abolition of the caliphate and Kemal's modernising reforms.[69] Intolerant Turkish nationalism with which the new republic was infused from early on left no room for the cultural, let alone the political, expression of Kurds. Although many Kurds have assimilated into Turkey's dominant culture and moved up the social ladder, often by migrating to Istanbul and other urban centres in western Turkey, the majority remain stuck in poverty in the under-developed southeast. The violence of the guerrilla fighting and the state's counterinsurgency response after 1984 has aggravated the Kurds' situation. Whole areas have been cleansed and their populations moved to the cities by the Turkish army.

Turkey objected strongly to American designs against Saddam Hussein in 2003. Turks warned the Americans of the possibility of a bloody Iraqi break-up if Saddam was abruptly removed. For the Turks, who had fought many wars in Ottoman times to keep Shi'ite Iran out of Mesopotamia, America's ill-prepared invasion opened the pandora's box. Predictably, it led to the establishment of an autonomous Kurdistan in northern Iraq outside the control of Baghdad. Initially, Ankara viewed the emergence of this new entity along the Turkish border as an existential threat. Nevertheless, Turkey has profited economically from business opportunities produced by the recent changes. Soon thereafter, Ankara proved pragmatic in its relations with the Kurdistan Autonomous Region, although it continues to support the unity of Iraq and the Arab control of Kirkuk.

Generally speaking, all three problems are intimately linked with domestic developments within Turkey and the ongoing process of liberalisation, democratisation, and the overall modernisation of Turkish society and polity. In a sense, the central problem still resides with the successful resolution of the contradictions brought about by the disintegration of the old Ottoman imperial order and its replacement by inward-looking, ultranationalist, insecure, and xenophobic nation-states. The normalisation of relations between the Turkish state and its neighbours and citizens undoubtedly passes through a reconceptualisation of the Turkish identity and national idea. Kemalism's authoritarian and intolerant nationalism might have been well suited in the interwar period but it is not so in the twenty-first century of globalisation and increased cross-cultural interactions. Hence, in a sense, the main struggle for the success of a policy of zero problems abroad is not one for Turkish diplomats and their foreign counterparts but for the elites and the peoples of Turkey about their vision of the future.

There is an intensifying debate, mainly in the United States and Israel, with an echo in Europe, about the real destination of Turkey under the current government of Erdogan. Two schools of thought exist: a growing minority viewing Erdogan with suspicion and rising hostility and a shrinking majority seeing him as the best and most effective prime minister Turkey has had in a very long time. For the former, Erdogan is a die-hard Islamist who is turning Turkey away from its traditional partnership with the West and towards an alliance with rogue states and players in the Middle East and the Third World such as Iran and Hamas.[70] For this group, a special alarm sounded with Turkey opposing Western-sponsored sanctions against Iran in the UN Security Council, Erdogan's verbal attack against Israel's president, Shimon Peres, at the 2009 Davos Economic Forum after Israel's invasion of Gaza, and Turkey's fury at Israel when Israeli commandos killed nine Turkish citizens on board a flotilla heading for Gaza in summer 2010. For his critics, Erdogan's agenda is no longer hidden: he is an Islamist determined to undo Kemal's legacy. As a result, they would have little problem siding with the military in Erdogan's domestic struggle against the Kemalist establishment. It might not be an exaggeration to claim that these people would welcome a military coup to topple Erdogan, stop what they perceive as the increasing Islamisation of the Turkish state and society, and reconfirm Turkey's position within NATO as a staunch supporter of the West, the United States, and Israel.

However, best exemplified by the British weekly, *The Economist*,[71] the majority opinion accepts Erdogan as a reformer in practice. Whether his reformist drive is the product of conviction and true ideological commitment or of convenience is of little importance to his supporters. Even as a survival tactic against an all-too-powerful military and judiciary-led Kemalist establishment, which had no problem in jailing Erdogan in the past, he should be judged favorably by his deeds. Against the background of a succession of fragmented and ineffective coalition governments and a meddling military, Erdogan has kept a steady hand, deepened the political and economic reforms of his predecessors, and provided the most effective government Turkey has seen in decades. For this school of thought, Erdogan is an Islamic democrat, drawing parallels with Europe's Christian democrats. His Islamism is mild, democratic, and popular with the majority of Turks. Turkey's problem is not its elected Prime Minister but an authoritarian military and state bureaucracy that has exaggerated a number of threats to defend its power and privileges, primarily an Islamist takeover and supposed subsequent imposition of sharia.[72] Furthermore, Erdogan's antagonism towards Israel might be genuine, given Tel Aviv's policies against the Palestinians and the effect this has had on Turkish public opinion. Erdogan's government reckons that Turkey is powerful enough to speak its mind confidently and defend what it believes to be right, even when this approach raises opposition by the United States.

In conclusion, it is obvious that the foreign policy debate will only intensify as Turkey comes of age and finds its new place and role in the world.[73] Turkey is no longer an American client state in need of foreign aid against a powerful Soviet Union. Nor is it an economic basket case on Europe's periphery in need of EU aid. On the contrary, Turkey has emerged as the fourth power in Europe, behind Germany, Britain and France, ahead of Italy and Spain; the most successful and powerful nation in the Middle East, ahead of Iran, Egypt, and Saudi Arabia; and an assertive power, with global concerns in league and, occasionally, in coordination with other rising powers such as Brazil.[74] It is only natural that this new, stronger Turkey flexes its muscles, for better or worse. The issue is not about Islam but nationalism and power. But, of course, only Turkish leaders can make good use of Turkey's assets. Nothing could benefit Turkey more than resolving the Kurdish problem, which has consumed enormous resources and poisoned the country's development, politically and otherwise, to a regrettable extent. Whereas fear is often a bad councillor, confidence is a prerequisite for generosity and wisdom. It is time for Turkey to be more attentive to the needs of its disadvantaged Kurdish citizens for both its and their sake.

For Turkish foreign policy to be effective, it has to preserve some modesty and an understanding of regional sensitivities. Furthermore, in opposition to all those who look for alternatives, it should be acknowledged that the West remains Turkey's most important trading partner by far and the only inspiring political model for an increasingly complex and cosmopolitan society. At the same time, the West and Europe should recognise the progress that Turkey has made and welcome its power, dynamism, regional experience, and connections. It often seems that when Europeans talk of Turks, they are hostage to the image of the poor *gastarbeiter*, the Anatolian guest workers of the 1960s, and they fail to recognise how fast Turkey is changing today. Turkey is not lost simply because it does not do as it is told. On the contrary, in many respects, it has found its way after years of stagnation, false starts, reversals, and failures. Its new foreign-policy activism is a reflection of its success and the interdependence of today's world. After all, there are few Muslim powers with which the West shares as many common values and interests as Turkey.

Notes

1 For the current Turkish foreign minister, Ahmet Davutoğlu, Turkey is not simply a regional Power but an aspiring global one. 'A conversation with Ahmet Davutoğlu', Council on Foreign Relations (14 April 2010): www.cfr.org.
2 CIA, *World Factbook*: www.cia.gov/library/publications.
3 UN Department of Economic and Social Affairs' World Population Prospects (2008 revision): http://esa.un.org.
4 International Monetary Fund reported in *Invest in Turkey* website: www.invest.gov.tr.
5 'OECD foresees higher growth rate than Turkish government', *Hurriyet Daily News* (19 November 19 2010); 'Doing it by the book', *Economist* (21 October 2010).
6 For more information: www.turkisheconomy.org.uk.
7 Since the introduction of the new Turkish lira in January 2005, Turkey's currency has lost little value against the American dollar.
8 See www.worldbulletin.net/news_detail.php?id=64779.
9 In 2010, the export of manufactured goods, including automobiles, will reach US$100 billion. Economist Intelligence Unit, *2010 Country Report on Turkey*: http://country.eiu.com/.
10 S. Togan and V. N. Balasubramanyam, eds., *The Economy of Turkey since Liberalization* (New York, 1996).
11 The hero of this transformation was Kemal Dervis, Minister of the Economy in the Government of Bülent Ecevit and the main architect of the economic recovery program launched in 2001.
12 'Doing it by the book'.
13 This first Ottoman parliament was comprised of 69 Muslim millet representatives, including many Arabs, and 46 representatives of other millets, including Greeks, Jews, and Armenians.
14 Nicole Pope and Hugh Pope, *Turkey Unveiled, A History of Modern Turkey* (New York, 1996), 94–108.
15 For more, see the reports of Human Rights Watch, the European Commission, and other international bodies.
16 Gül is currently the President of the Turkish Republic, having served as Prime Minister and Foreign Minister before.
17 See Larry Diamond and Marc F. Plattner, eds., *The Global Resurgence of Democracy*, second edition (Baltimore, MD, 1996).
18 John Micklethwait and Adrian Wooldridge, *God is Back, How the Global Revival of Faith Is Changing the World* (New York, 2009).
19 John L. Esposito, *Political Islam: Revolution, Radicalism or Reform* (New York, 1997).
20 Richard Tapper, ed., *Islam in Modern Turkey, Religion, Politics and Literature in a Secular State* (London, 1993).
21 Hakan M. Yavuz, ed., *The Emergence of a New Turkey: Democracy and the AK Party* (Salt Lake City, UT, 2006).
22 Sylvia Kedourie, ed., *Turkey, Identity, Democracy, Politics* (London, 1998).
23 Graham E. Fuller and Ian O. Lesser, *Turkey's New Geopolitics, From the Balkans to Western China* (Boulder, CO, 1993).
24 The World Bank sets Turkey's per capita income in 2009 at US$8,730, Iran's US$4,530, and Egypt's US 2,070: http://siteresources.worldbank.org. In Freedom House's 2010 rankings, Turkey is considered to be 'partly free', whereas Egypt and Iran are classified as 'not free': www.freedomhouse.org.
25 Vojtech Mastny and R. Craig Nation, eds., *Turkey Between East and West, New Challenges for a Rising Regional Power* (New York, 1996).

26 'The Davutoğlu effect', *Economist* (21 October 2010).

27 In 1992, Özal went as far as to declare that 'the next century will be a Turkish century'. In 'Turgut Özal Period in Turkish Foreign Policy: Özalism', *U.S.AK Yearbook of International Politics and Law*, 2(2009), 153–205.

28 David McDowall, *The Kurds, A Nation Denied* (London, 1992).

29 David Shankland, *The Alevis in Turkey: The Emergence of a Secular Islamic Tradition* (London, 2007).

30 According to the United Nations Development Programme Human Development Index, Turkey is ranked eighty-third in a list of 169 countries and is placed at the bottom of the 'High Human Development' countries. The Gini coefficient, measuring income inequality, stood at 43.6 in 2007, ten points higher than the European average: http://hdr.undp.org.

31 According to Refik Erzan: 'Turkey has a long-term annual growth record of around 4 percent ... this places Turkey in the lower rank of successful emerging markets ... Turkey must address ... raising the overall savings rate, which has been 15–20 percent of GDP, compared to 30–35 percent in fast-growing emerging economies. ... The other long-term constraint on growth is education.' 'Turkey's Economic Prospects: As Good as It Gets?', *Carnegie Endowment for International Peace International Economic Bulletin* (29 June 2010).

32 In the 2010 Corruption Perception Index, compiled by the Transparency International, Turkey is ranked fifty-sixth amongst 178 countries, with a score of 4.4, with 10 being the top: www.transparency.org.

33 In the 2007 parliamentary elections, the main opposition party, the Republican People's Party (CHP), got 20.85 percent of the total vote. On the other hand, the incumbent AKP increased its share of the vote by 12.38 percent to 46.66 percent.

34 'The trouble with Ottomania', *Economist* (22 November 2010): www.economist.com.

35 Lewis Bernard, *The Emergence of Modern Turkey* (Oxford, 2001).

36 Ahmad Feroz, *The Making of Modern Turkey* (London, 1993).

37 Stanford J. Shaw and Ezel Kural Shaw, *History of the Ottoman Empire and Modern Turkey* (Cambridge, UK, 1977).

38 Eic Zurcher, *Turkey: A Modern History* (London, 2004).

39 Sylvia Kedourie, ed., *Turkey Before and After Ataturk, Internal and External Affairs* (London, 1999).

40 A Balkan Pact was signed by Greece, Turkey, Romania, and Yugoslavia in 1934.

41 Zurcher, *Turkey*.

42 See Alexander Cooley, *Base Politics: Democratic Change and the U.S. Military Overseas* (Ithaca, NY, 2008), 95–136; Douglas T. Stuart, 'Continuity and Change in the Southern Region of the Atlantic Alliance', in James R. Golden et al, eds., *NATO at Forty, Change, Continuity and Prospects* (Boulder, CO, 1989), 74–97.

43 See David Hannay, *Cyprus, The Search for a Solution* (London, 2004).

44 This was the case when President Lyndon Johnson warned against Turkey's planned intervention in Cyprus in 1964. See Stearns Monteagle, *Entangled Allies: U.S. Policy toward Greece, Turkey and Cyprus* (New York, 1992).

45 'Turkey still has not complied with its obligations. ... There is no progress towards normalization of bilateral relations with the Republic of Cyprus'. Commission to the Council and the European Parliament, *Enlargement Strategy and Main Challenges 2010–2011*: http://ec.europa.eu/enlargement/.

46 Henri J. Barkey, ed. *Reluctant Neighbor. Turkey's Role in the Middle East* (Washington, DC, 1996).

47 The PKK is a Marxist-leaning, separatist, Kurdish organisation founded in 1978 and often classified as a terrorist group that has been fighting an armed struggle against the Turkish state.

48 GAP stands for Southeastern Anatolian Project and is about the irrigation and development of Turkey's poor southeast.

49 Lenore L. Martin, 'Turkey's Middle East Foreign Policy', in Lenore G. Martin and Dimitris Keridis, *The Future of Turkish Foreign Policy* (Cambridge, MA, 2004), 157–89.

50 Panayotis J. Tsakonas and Thanos P. Dokos, 'Greek-Turkish Relations in the Early Twenty-first Century: A view from Athens', in Martin and Keridis, *Turkish Foreign Policy*, 101–26.

51 Kalypso Nicolaidis, 'Europe's Tainted Mirror: Reflections on Turkey's Candidacy Status after Helsinki', in Dimitris Keridis and Dimitrios Triantaphyllou, eds., *Greek-Turkish Relations in the Era of Globalization* (New York, 2001), 245–77; 'A very special relationship, Why Turkey's EU Accession Process Will Continue', *European Stability Initiative* (November 2010).

52 Sezer Ozcan, 'Historical evolution of the Europeanization process of Turkey', *Portuguese Journal of International Affairs*, 3(Spring/Summer 2010), 33–40.

53 'The Great Debate: Germany, Turkey and the Turks', *European Stability Initiative*, (October 2010); Nicolaidis Kalypso, 'Turkey is European ... for Europe's sake', The Netherlands: Ministry of Foreign

Affairs, *Turkey and the European Union: From association to accession*: www.sant.ox.ac.uk/ext/knicolaidis/sortedpubs.htm#EUenlargement.

54 'A very special relationship, Why Turkey's EU Accession Process Will Continue', *European Stability Initiative* (November 2010); Aktar Cengiz, 'The present and future of Turkey's membership negotiations with the EU', Global Political Trends Center, *A Policy Brief* (Istanbul, October 2010).

55 Cinar Menderes, 'Disassociation of Europeanization and Democratization in Turkey', 'Europe's and NATO's Unfinished Business: The Balkans', a workshop organised by the Navarino Network in Chalkidiki, Greece, 20–21 February 2010: www.navarinonetwork.org.

56 In 2009, Turkey's tax authorities fined Dogan Holding the equivalent of US$2.5 billion.

57 Another interesting case was the restriction of access to the YouTube website. Human Rights Watch Report 'The criminalization of opinion remains a key obstacle to the protection of human rights in Turkey …' (2010): www.hrw.org.

58 Ioannis N. Grigoriadis, *Trials of Europeanization: Turkish Political Culture and the European Union* (New York, 2009).

59 Graham E. Fuller, *New Turkish Republic: Turkey as a Pivotal State in the Muslim World* (Washington, DC, 2007).

60 See Fethullah Gülen's official website: http://en.fgulen.com/.

61 Cemal Kafadar, *Between Two Worlds, The Construction of the Ottoman State* (Berkeley, CA, 1995).

62 Halil Inalcik, *An Economic and Social History of the Ottoman Empire* (Cambridge, UK, 1994).

63 Shaw and Shaw, *Ottoman Empire*.

64 Togan and Balasubramanyam, *Economy of Turkey*.

65 The Alliance has come under the auspices of the United Nations: www.unaoc.org.

66 Since 2009, the Foreign Ministers of the three countries have been meeting regularly.

67 Ahmet Davotuglu, *Strategic Depth* (Ankara, 2001).

68 Kemal Kirisci and Gareth M. Winrow, *The Kurdish Question and Turkey, An Example of a Trans-State Ethnic Conflict* (London, 1997).

69 Stephen Kinzer, *Crescent and Star, Turkey Between Two Worlds* (New York, 2001), 109–35.

70 An excellent exposé of this kind of thinking is Soner Cagaptay, 'Is Turkey Leaving the West? An Islamist Foreign Policy Puts Ankara at Odds With Its Former Allies', *Foreign Affairs*, 57(September/October 2009). He asserts: 'The foundation of Turkey's 60-year-old military and political cooperation with the West may be eroding.'

71 See, for example, *The Economist*'s Special Report on Turkey on 21 October 2010. Cf. Zahedi Dariush and Gokhan Bacik, 'Kemalism is Dead, Long Live Kemalism, How the AKP Became Ataturk's Last Defender', *Foreign Affairs*, 88(March/April 2010). The authors assert that 'the AKP may be the best defender of Western values that Turkey has.'

72 This tactic reached the level of paranoia with the case brought against the AKP by the state prosecutor in 2007. In the prosecutor's indictment, Erdogan was essentially presented as the reincarnation of Iran's Ayatollah Khomeini.

73 Dario D'Urso, 'Shifting Turkey. Ankara's new dynamics under the AKP government.' *Portuguese Journal of International Affairs*, 3(Spring/Summer 2010), 15–23.

74 Morton Abramowitz and Henri J. Barkey, 'Turkey's Transformers, The AKP Sees Big', *Foreign Affairs*, 87 (November/December 2009).

Part IV
The Developing Powers

15

Cuban revolutionary diplomacy 1959–2009

Carlos Alzugaray

On 26 October 2010, by a vote of 187 for, two against, and three abstentions, the United Nations (UN) General Assembly endorsed a Cuban-sponsored resolution reproving the United States' unilateral illegal economic sanctions against the island and demanding its end.[1] The two votes opposing came from the American and Israeli delegations. Washington's most important allies, including the European Union (EU), Canada, Japan, and Australia, joined Cuba. It was the nineteenth consecutive time that the General Assembly had taken such an unbalanced pronouncement. How is it possible that a small state, lacking in the necessary attributes of 'hard power', is able to produce such a diplomatically successful outcome against the world's largest superpower? One answer is that even Great Powers make mistakes and that the sanctions against Cuba, adopted during the Cold War, are a case in point. But it does not reveal the whole truth. Even if Washington's Cuba policy is one of the most absolutely unilateral actions taken by its policy-making elite, it does not reasonably explain how Cuban diplomacy has garnered the support of practically the whole world, including countries that, in the last analysis, coincide with the United States in their 'regime change' policy towards Cuba.

The response can be found in the way that the Cuban Government has carried out its diplomacy since the Revolution in 1959. Cuban revolutionary diplomacy has been generally successful in achieving its main policy goals, and there has been a clear definition of the fundamentals on which Cuba's national interest has been defined. Successful diplomacy must be constructed on the basis of the material and cultural factors that determine a state's position in the world. Cuban revolutionary diplomacy was constructed on the basis of a redefinition of the national interest in 1959.[2] That interest is based upon a number of material and cultural premises that determine a specific vision of Cuba, its role in world politics, and its links with the immediate surrounding environment.

In the first place, Cuba's foreign policy is influenced by the physical characteristics of the island's geography and geopolitical location. Because of its size and position, Cuba and its adjacent keys and archipelagos were the object of hegemonic ambitions of a variety of Powers with expansionary designs in the Caribbean, but especially by the United States. Even before the 1895–98 War of Independence, Washington yearned to annex Cuba. In 1898 it occupied the island and imposed a *de facto* protectorate through various means. This control continued until 1959.[3] Bearing in mind this geopolitical reality, it is only logical that any definition of the Cuban national interest should be based on the protection of its independence and self-determination.[4] This obviously applies mostly to United States interference, but it also applies to any other Great Power. A determined opposition, and indeed a refusal to accept any foreign intervention of any kind, has become the first and most important element of the Cuban national interest.

A second element lies in the vulnerability of Cuba's economy, which requires a deep insertion in the world economy, creating more often than not situations of dependency that have been used to put pressure on the Cuban Government. Because of its insular character, its tropical climate, and its relatively small geographical mass and population, the country cannot develop a self-sufficient economy; it has to depend to a great extent on its external relations in terms of both trade and services. Domestic energy sources are particularly lacking. Under these conditions, a clear necessity exists for Cuba to establish a strong international economic network, avoiding an exclusive dependency on a single partner or small group of partners. Therefore, it is in Cuba's national interest to build and to develop a system of external relationships that are both sufficient for its economic and social development but that can be protected from external pressures, an apparently insurmountable contradiction.

Another decisive influence on Cuba's national interest is the multiethnic origin and development of Cuban society. The prevention of internal conflicts and the achievement of social stability require a just social, economic, and political system, with a high degree of inherent fairness and cohesion. Considering that its strategic position and the structure of its natural resources make Cuba extremely vulnerable to external pressures, it is therefore important to minimise all social differences. The result is that the creation and preservation of an economic and political regime that has as its primary foundation the promotion of social justice is a matter of high national priority.[5] For a majority of Cubans, the socialist system established after 1959, even recognising some of its failures and shortcomings, has been the most capable of attaining this objective. In the cultural sphere, several social and intellectual legacies have enriched Cuban nationality. It can be argued that there is a persistent tradition of defending the national identity, whilst engaging and seeking a fair global system. The Cuban people lived under Spanish colonial domination until 1898 and passed on, practically without any break, to become the object of United States neocolonialism from 1898 to 1959. That experience contributed to the reinforcement of a strong sense of the need for independence and sovereignty.

Notwithstanding, there exists in the Cuban national character a strong tendency of openness to foreign influences largely as the result of its multiethnic nature, its geopolitical location at a significant crossroads of global movements, and ideological trends. This factor blends with another important aspect of Cuban culture: concern with the value of human solidarity, reflected in José Martí's oft-cited observation: 'Fatherland is Humanity'. For the last fifty years, these cultural and ideological premises have been reinforced by the formation inside Cuban society of a radical, progressive, and emancipatory sociopolitical thought based upon the Marxist vision of society. It is not a dogmatic and paralyzed Marxism, like that which prevailed in some European socialist countries in the past; rather, it consists of a rich and diverse image that recognises the contributions of other philosophical and political inclinations. Moreover, it reaffirms that the development of human society requires emancipation combined with material progress.[6]

On the basis of these premises, the Cuban national interest can be defined in terms of the following preferences:

- Preserving and defending the independence, sovereignty, self-determination, and security of the Cuban nation as the primary mission
- Establishing external economic relations that will promote its development without being used as a means of external pressure
- Assuming and protecting a popular, democratic, and participatory form of government based on its own traditions

- Establishing and promoting a prosperous and fair socioeconomic system in which 'the full dignity of the human being should be the first law of the Republic'
- Safeguarding and protecting Cuba's cultural identity and sociopolitical values
- Projecting Cuba's cultural and ideological values internationally at a level of involvement proportional to its real possibilities as an effective member of international society.

For the revolutionary Government established on 1 January 1959, there were three crucial international priorities: redesigning Cuba's relationship with the United States on the basis of respect for its sovereignty and independence; strengthening the links with Latin American and Caribbean countries, especially with those that had overthrown right-wing pro-American military dictatorships similar to the Batista regime in Cuba; and searching for new economic and political allies and partners in Europe, Asia, and Africa. All these priorities would have to develop into a more active and autonomous foreign policy.

Redesigning the relationship with the United States was the most elusive and intricate problem for Cuban revolutionary diplomacy. The new Government had promised to implement a number of changes that had been demanded by different sectors of Cuban society for many years, the most important amongst them agrarian reform. The promised changes would obviously affect important American interests attained over the years. But, at the same time, the worse possible scenario had to be avoided: military conflict and United States intervention and occupation. In a visit to the United States in April 1959, Fidel Castro went out of his way to emphasise two points: there were problems in Cuba that required decisive government actions, which might affect some American interests, although their intention was not to affect the Americans but to solve Cuban problems; and Havana was interested in maintaining the best possible relations with Washington.[7]

A month after this visit, the Cuban revolutionary Government enacted the *Agrarian Reform Law*. It was an extremely popular measure and a logical step demanded not only by progressive groups but by many economists. The American reaction was swift: through diplomatic channels, it questioned the validity of the measure and demanded that American property owners be swiftly compensated, in cash and at the price demanded by the owners. The Cuban Government rejected the United States position. The exchange of verbal notes that ensued clearly demonstrated the nature of the conflict: Cuba asserting its sovereign right to implement agrarian reform, the United States questioning that right and pressuring the Cuban Government to reverse the decision or modify it in a way that would favor American interests.[8]

Immediately after this incident, in June 1959, the Eisenhower Administration changed its initial attitude of cautious critical scepticism towards the revolutionary Government. As Livingston Merchant, Deputy Under-Secretary of State, told a meeting of the National Security Council chaired by the President on 14 January 1960, American policy now decided to have as its main objective 'to adjust all our actions in such a way as to accelerate the development of an opposition in Cuba which would bring about a change in the Cuban Government, resulting in a new government favorable to US interests'.[9]

That decision led to a 'regime change' strategy that exists until today (with the possible exception of the Carter years [1977–81]). Such a policy has encompassed every possible instrument, excluding direct military intervention, but including at different times covert violent operations (terrorism, sabotage, and assassination attempts), subversion, black propaganda, diplomatic isolation, and illegal unilateral economic sanctions, the most permanent of its components. In terms of developments between 1959 and 1968, the policy led to the break in diplomatic relations in January 1961, the April 1961 Bay of Pigs American-sponsored invasion and defeat, and the Missile Crisis of October 1962. During this short period of two years and ten months, the danger of an outright invasion of Cuba by United States military forces was real. American policy towards Cuba aimed not only at regime change; it also included a containment component, most evident when John F. Kennedy's Administration implemented its Alliance for Progress in 1961 and when President Lyndon Johnson ordered the occupation of the Dominican Republic in 1965.

In political terms, Cuba responded in an anti-hegemonic manner, which materialised in three diplomatic lines: demonstrate that even if unwilling to accept Washington's imposition, it was ready to find a negotiated solution; attempt to neutralise the diplomatic isolation tactics of the State Department using direct and public diplomacy in Latin America and the Caribbean; and search for solidarity and support from the rest of the world, including important diplomatic actions in the United Nations and other international forums. Cuba went as far as to put forward a gentlemen's agreement through Ernesto Che Guevara during a conversation with Richard Goodwin, Kennedy's advisor for Latin America, at the Organization of American States (OAS) conference in Punta del Este, Uruguay in August 1961.[10] None of this worked. The Eisenhower, Kennedy, and Johnson administrations continued with 'regime change' and 'containment', although, at one point, Kennedy contemplated normalisation, something recalled by Carlos Lechuga, Cuban Ambassador to the UN in the early 1960s.[11] Cuba reacted positively to this initiative, which was aborted when the President was assassinated in November 1963.

During the 1962 Missile Crisis, Cuba put forward five demands: cessation of economic sanctions, cessation of spy flights over its territory, cessation of terrorist and other acts carried out from United States territory, cessation of all subversive and destabilising activities carried on by the Central Intelligence Agency (CIA), and the return of Guantánamo Naval Base.[12] Even though both superpowers tried to ignore Cuba in their bilateral negotiations to end the Crisis, the threat of an invasion receded after 1962, probably in part because of United States involvement in the Vietnam War in 1963–64, but also because a 'limited security regime' was accepted between Cuba and the United States.[13] The Missile Crisis had a collateral benefit for Havana's revolutionary diplomacy. At the height of the Cold War, when the world was on the verge of all-out nuclear war, this small state refused to be treated as a pawn in a power struggle between two major Powers and stood its ground. The example of Cuba defying both the United States and the Soviet Union, reinforced its political position *vis-à-vis* other Third World Countries, particularly within the Non-Aligned Movement that Cuba had joined in its founding summit in Yugoslavia in 1961.

The conflict between Cuba and the United States in the 1960s expanded to Latin America and the Caribbean. Washington tried to isolate Cuba from the rest of the world, particularly in the Western hemisphere. Using its hegemony over the OAS, the Eisenhower, Kennedy, and Johnson administrations obtained the suspension of the Cuban revolutionary Government in 1962 and the adoption of sanctions in 1964. Cuban diplomats tried to avoid isolation in the continent, but the region was strongly under American influence. Democratically elected governments in Argentina and Brazil were overthrown by right-wing military coups when they did not comply with Washington's wishes. Only Mexico and Canada in the Western hemisphere maintained their diplomatic relationship with Havana.

But the most dangerous actions were related to the support that several governments gave the CIA to conduct its covert regime change actions against Cuba, as was the case with Guatemala, Nicaragua, and Venezuela, amongst others. After losing the battle to avoid diplomatic isolation, Cuba responded by supporting revolutionary groups all over the region, Che Guevara's guerrilla operation in Bolivia being the most significant example. When Johnson succeeded Kennedy, Washington's containment policy included the support for repressive right-wing military dictatorships after 1964 and the invasion of the Dominican Republic in 1965. By 1967, when Guevara was captured and murdered, Washington had succeeded and Havana had failed. Guerrilla movements in Venezuela, Argentina, Bolivia, and Guatemala had been annihilated.

The third priority for the Cuban revolutionary Government was to expand its international relations, mainly for economic but also for security reasons. These actions focused basically on Third World countries and, to a lesser degree, Europe. In the early months of the Revolution, Cuba did not seek a new relationship with the Soviet Union and other members of the socialist community of nations, except in the framework broadening its external economic relations. The first Soviet representative arrived in Havana in October 1959. The next year a Soviet Trade Exhibition included Cuba in a tour of Latin American countries and both governments signed a trade agreement to exchange sugar for oil. By May 1960, Cuba reestablished diplomatic relations with the Soviet Union and opened embassies in Eastern Europe. Shortly after that, the revolutionary Government recognised the People's Republic of China and broke off relations with Taiwan. The logic behind these steps was originally economic, later security-related, as the conflict with the United States and the danger of a military aggression became more real. However, as Cuban internal politics became more radicalised, there were clear ideological motivations.

The relationship with the Soviet Union deserves a specific analysis. The initiative was Soviet, not Cuban. Evidence exists that there was a Cuban debate about the future of Cuban–American relations and the possibility of a security alliance with Moscow. But what is objectively true is that American hostile actions, which developed rapidly and strongly in the period 1959–60, left the revolutionary Government no other option but to seek allies wherever they could be found. Raúl Castro himself has recently recognised: 'Every new aggression strengthened and radicalised the Revolution across all sectors and levels'.[14]

Between May 1960, when full diplomatic relations with Moscow were reestablished after the signing of the trade agreement, and August 1968, when Fidel Castro supported critically the intervention of Warsaw Pact forces in Czechoslovakia, relations with the Soviet Union and its allies were difficult and controversial. Moscow, not without some hesitation, embraced the Cuban Revolution and gave its economic and military support. But at the same time, some of its representatives and diplomats started to behave in Cuba in ways that were unacceptable to Havana. Crises broke out in 1962 and 1968 over the issue. Furthermore, Fidel Castro was very critical of Nikita Khrushchev's decision to withdraw missiles from Cuba without consulting the revolutionary Government. In 1963–64, however, he visited the Soviet Union and returned home with beneficial economic agreements. But relations deteriorated after 1965. Between that date and 1968, several factors came to divide the allies: the United States escalated the Vietnam War and the Soviet bloc took what Havana thought was a complacent line; the Soviet and the Chinese parties clashed over leadership of the international communist movement, with the former stressing peaceful coexistence with the capitalist world to the detriment of countries like Cuba; the Cuban Communist Party emphasised armed revolutionary struggle as the only path to socialism in the Third World, especially in Latin America and the Caribbean; and it followed a radical brand of socialism at home, when market reforms were the name of the game in the European Soviet bloc. Signs of the deterioration in relations were evident at the end of 1967 and early 1968, when Moscow announced a reduction of its oil exports.

The Cuban decision to support the Soviet invasion of Czechoslovakia in August 1968 was difficult and came after a long process of discussion. In a speech on the subject, Fidel Castro revealed all the criticisms that Cuba had levelled at the Soviet Union; these included lack of sufficient support for North Vietnam; complacency towards United States and Western aggressive tactics in the Third World; and market reforms in the European socialist countries. But, for

Moscow, Cuban support was very important given Chinese criticism. Therefore, in a manner very similar to Trollope's ploy, the Soviet Union changed course and renewed all the economic agreements that had been put into question in early 1968, when it had announced that it would reduce the amount of oil sold to the island.

One final strand of Cuban revolutionary diplomacy in the period 1959–68 was the new relationships developed with the Afro-Asian world. The victory of the Cuban Revolution coincided with the upsurge of the Afro-Asian liberation movements and recently independent nations. The Bandung Conference had taken place in 1955; 1960 was proclaimed the Year of Africa by the UN both for the number of African countries that became independent in those years and the foundation of the Organization of African Unity, which had as one of its aims the elimination of colonialism in the continent; 1961 saw the founding Summit of the Non-Aligned Movement. In this favourable international climate, the Cuban revolutionary Government became an important player, establishing relations with all the newly independent nations, joining the Non-Aligned Movement, and supporting the national liberation struggles of the remaining colonies, especially in Africa. Havana was the venue of the Tricontinental Conference in 1966 at which the Organization for Solidarity amongst the Peoples of Asia, Africa and Latin America was founded.

In 1962, Cuba had carried out its first internationalist mission in Africa by sending both medical doctors and soldiers to Algeria. The doctors treated wounded combatants from the liberation struggle against France in Oran and the military supported Algerian forces in their frontier conflict with Morocco. Before his Bolivian mission, Che Guevara tried to organise a guerrilla movement in the Congo in 1965, where Patrice Lumumba had been assassinated and a pro-Western right-wing dictatorship had been established. This mission had the support of Tanzania and other progressive governments in Africa. From his headquarters in the Congolese jungle, Guevara proclaimed his intention to launch 'Two, three, many Vietnams' as part of the struggle against imperialism.[15] There is no doubt that Cuban support for Third World Afro-Asian countries and for national liberation struggles constituted a substantial contribution and helped enhance the role of Cuba's revolutionary diplomacy.

In this context, the revolutionary transformation of Cuban diplomacy occurred under the leadership of Raúl Roa, Foreign Minister between 1959 and 1976. If Fidel Castro gave Cuba a mission, Roa supplied the tactical abilities of a revolutionary conduct of foreign policy. By the end of this period, the Cuban Ministry of Foreign Affairs had transformed from a typical oligarchic institution subservient to Washington's designs into a radical representative of the Cuban state.[16] Cuban revolutionary diplomacy had obtained several important successes at some cost: it had successfully resisted American encroachment on its autonomous decision-making process at the cost of near war and losing the natural market for its products; it had found a new major ally, but relations had been rocky; it had been isolated from the rest of Latin America and the Caribbean, with the exception of Mexico; it had been able to maintain a decent level of relationships with United States allies from Canada to Japan, including most European Powers; and it had established itself as an important player in Third World politics.

From 1968 to 1989, Cuban revolutionary diplomacy had a very satisfactory performance. The main objectives during that period were:

- Maintaining its security and independence *vis-à-vis* the United States, which continued implementing its regime change policy toward Cuba with the exception of the four years of the Carter administration (1977–81)
- Strengthening its alliance with the Soviet Union and the European socialist community and benefiting economically and militarily from it

- Taking advantage of the opportunities that materialised to normalise its relations with Latin America and the Caribbean
- Maintaining a high degree of diplomatic influence in Third World countries
- Continuing its normal relations with the United States' main allies in order to block the possibility of an internationalisation of the unilateral economic sanctions and benefiting from possibilities to increase trade and investment
- Underlining the role of Cuba as a very active player in the international scene, as a small anti-hegemonic state.

Although during this period United States aggressiveness towards Cuba never attained the level that characterised its policy in the early 1960s, Washington in no way actually modified its 'regime change' strategy. The only exception was during the Carter Administration, which set as its policy goal normalisation of relations. Even during this latter period, the illegal unilateral economic sanctions were not lifted, only marginally modified in 1975–77. As a signal of its acceptance of this incipient *rapprochement*, Cuba abandoned its demand that the sanctions be lifted before engaging the United States and accepted the establishment of quasi-embassies, so-called Interest Sections, in each other's capitals.

But relations remained strained over three basic issues: Cuba's global activism, especially in Africa, where it deployed troops to aid Angola and Ethiopia defeat external military aggressions from South Africa and Somalia in 1975 and 1978; Havana's support for Nicaragua's Sandinista Government and Central American revolutionary movements in the late 1970s; and immigration. On many occasions, the American Government perceived wrongly Cuban actions as part of its Cold War conflict with the Soviet Union when, in reality, Havana's policies were nationally motivated.[17] This misperception was the case in Africa and Central America.

On immigration, the conflict had its origins in the previous period, when Washington adopted a policy of instigating illegal emigration by the *Cuban Adjustment Act* of 1967. Under this law, any Cuban national who enters the United States illegally or legally has the right to stay and, after one year, obtain resident status; the 1980 Mariel boatlift emigration crisis with the United States was a direct result of this policy. Cuba's position was that the emigration of its nationals to the United States should be subject to governmental regulation through a bilateral agreement. During this period, it tried unsuccessfully to bring the United States to the negotiating table on this issue.

Relations with the Soviet Union and its main allies in Europe developed in the framework of the Council for Mutual Economic Assistance (COMECON). What is important to underline is that the economic, financial, and trade agreements signed with these countries ensured Cuba of the necessary elements to carry on its economic development in terms highly favorable to the social justice vision projected by the revolutionary leadership. It also played an important role in enhancing Cuban security, especially significant after 1980 when the Ronald Reagan Administration renewed military threats.

Finally, Cuban revolutionary diplomacy exploited its growing role in Third World politics to become a power-broker in the links between these two blocs: the socialist community and the developing countries. This process was very real after the 1974 Non-Aligned Summit in Algeria, the first time that Fidel Castro attended such a gathering. Nevertheless, there were times when Moscow's actions created problems for Havana, as was the case with the invasion of Afghanistan in 1979, precisely the same year that Cuba hosted the Sixth Non-Aligned Summit and became Chairman of the Movement. No doubt, this factor cost Cuba dearly when it failed to be elected as a non-permanent member of the UN Security Council.

The years between 1968 and 1989 were significant for the normalisation of relations between Cuba and Latin America and the Caribbean. It began with the establishment of informal links with the left-wing military governments in Panama and Peru in 1969, the reestablishment of diplomatic relations with Chile under the short Government of Salvador Allende (1970–73), and the diplomatic recognition of Cuba by the Anglophone Caribbean countries that became independent in the early 1970s. By 1975, the movement towards normalisation had been so forceful that the OAS, at the request of several governments, lifted the sanctions imposed in 1964, allowing all member-states to reestablish diplomatic and economic relations with Cuba. The United States did not oppose this decision.

This normalisation process suffered some setbacks in the 1980s, motivated to a great degree by the Reagan Administration, which mounted a counteroffensive against revolutionary governments in Nicaragua and Grenada (the latter country, the object of a military intervention). But by the end of the 1980s, Cuban revolutionary diplomacy was able to overcome these setbacks. In its regional diplomacy during this period, Cuba played an important role in a series of initiatives: the search for a peaceful solution to the conflicts in Central America that led to the signature of the Esquipulas Agreements; the mid-1980s campaign to demand the elimination of the external debt; the garnering of Third World support for Argentina in the conflict with Great Britain over the Malvinas (Falkland) Islands.

Cuba also carried out those two military operations in the defense of Angola and Ethiopia against aggressions from South Africa and Somalia. Whilst its diplomatic representatives gained the support of the Non-Aligned Movement and the Organization of African Union, Cuba's policy in Asia and Africa was not limited to its security contribution. As it had done in Algeria, Cuba sent its doctors and teachers to underdeveloped countries in a demonstration of South – South cooperation, variously described as 'medical diplomacy' or 'medical internationalism'.[18] But probably the most successful diplomatic initiative involved the negotiation and signing of the Southwest African peace agreements at the UN in December 1988; it occurred after a year-long negotiation with Angola and South Africa; the United States participated as mediator. This agreement allowed for the disengagement of Cuban troops in Angola after the military victory of Cuito Cuanavale in 1987–88.

In this period Cuban revolutionary diplomacy was also successful in maintaining the most satisfactory relations possible with the United States' allies in North America, Europe, and Asia. The paradigmatic case is Canada. In 1975, Prime Minister Pierre Elliott Trudeau visited Cuba at the invitation of Fidel Castro, underlining the high level of the association between the two countries that included trade and cooperation. Although relations suffered in later years, they remained close enough and never led to a break. Irritants were overcome by a positive political will from both sides.[19]

Relations with Western Europe were limited for economic reasons. Cuban sugar exports were affected by the European Community's agricultural and preferential trade policies with African, Caribbean, and Pacific countries that were signatories of the 1975 Lomé Convention; at the end of the period, Cuba had accumulated an important external debt with most European economies. A final factor was Havana's membership of COMECON, which limited what Cuba could do in terms of giving diplomatic recognition to the European Community. Relations with these countries and with Japan did not go beyond correctness, in part because of economic limitations, in part because their alliances with the United States introduced an element of caution from their part.

1968–89 was very important in terms of Cuban revolutionary diplomacy using and benefiting from the international system's governance mechanisms. In the immediate post-Revolution period, although Havana had been active in promoting its image as an effective member of the UN and other international institutions (with the exception of the International Monetary Fund and the World Bank, which it abandoned), it had emphasised its revolutionary role by promoting alternative anti-hegemonic institutions, like the Tricontinental Organization. Without totally abandoning its anti-hegemonic and counterdependency efforts, the emphasis in 1968–89 was on organisations like the United Nations Educational, Scientific, and Cultural Organisation, the United Nations Children's Fund, and the United Nations Conference on Trade and Development. As a result, Cuba succeeded in being elected a member of the UN Security Council in October 1989.

The demise of the Soviet Union and the implosion of the socialist community in 1989–91 was a severe blow for Cuba. Its revolutionary diplomacy had to adapt in a very short period to a completely transformed international environment, in which its major adversary adopted an attitude of open triumphalism. The first order of business was to contribute to the survival of the socialist system in very negative circumstances. The political forces that had bet on the end of the Cuban revolutionary experiment activated themselves to what they considered to be an endgame. To guarantee the 'soft landing' of the Cuban economy was of paramount importance. The decision was to open up to international tourism and foreign investment. The newly formed EU was the first and most important candidate as Cuba's new main economic and trading partner. However, relations with Brussels have been the subject of many ups and downs for political reasons. Although Cuba has pursued a policy of establishing some sort of institutional framework, either through a bilateral trade and cooperation agreement or its access via the Lomé Accords to the Africa, Caribbean, and Pacific countries, political obstacles have remained. In 1996, at the behest of the right-wing Aznar Government in Spain, the EU adopted a so-called 'Common Position' (a clearly discriminatory and interventionist initiative, according to the Cuban Government) and in 2003 adopted limited sanctions reacting to domestic political developments in the island. The Common Position continues to be an important obstacle, but Cuba diplomacy has been effective in avoiding its becoming a major hindrance for the development of tourism, investment, and trade with major European countries.

The most successful Cuban diplomatic initiative in these years with American allies, again, has been with Canada. Although there have been changes of government in Ottawa, relations have remained stable and fruitful for both sides, with Canada transforming itself into Cuba's first tourist market, first Western investment associate, and fourth-largest trading partner. But in economic terms, the most important countries for Cuba have been China and Venezuela, also political allies in their own right. It would be impossible to describe in a short analysis like this one, all the initiatives that underline the importance of these two countries and the achievements of Cuban revolutionary diplomacy. Suffice it to say that agreements with China have guaranteed Cuba access to investments and technology, whilst Venezuela has become the major supplier of oil and investments. Respecting Venezuela, both Havana and Caracas have emphasised that they are working towards an economic union. On its side, Cuba has given Venezuela medical and technical support for its socialist transformation.

Since the early 1990s, Cuba had to neutralise Washington's renewed 'regime change' policy, which was evident not only in the administrations of George W.H. Bush (1989–93) and George W. Bush (2001–9) but also under that of Bill Clinton (1993–2001), which approved the Helms-Burton Act in 1996 re-enforcing US illegal unilateral economic sanctions. During this period, Cuba has displayed two parallel efforts towards the United States. On one side, it has maintained its intractable resistance position, not agreeing to any concession in the most difficult economic circumstances as was the case in 1989–94. On the other, it has been willing to work with the United States in negotiating an end of conflict and the beginning of normalisation. In the context of both initiatives, rejecting American pressures, Cuba reiterated again and again the defense of its national sovereignty and security.

Three examples present themselves. In 1990, the United States carried on important military maneuvers in the Caribbean combining Global Shield, Ocean Venture, and regular exercises in the Guantánamo Naval Base. Havana responded with its own Cuban Shield military exercises, at which its Mig29 advanced interceptor jets were shown for the first time. A second occasion was in 1996, when Cuban jets brought down two airplanes operating from Florida airports by the Brothers to the Rescue counterrevolutionary organisation. Cuba tried to solve the problem of the violation of its air space by these flights through diplomatic channels and applied force only as a last resort. The third occasion was between 2003 and 2004, when the George W. Bush administration reinforced its regime change policy.

Nevertheless, Cuba has continued to demonstrate its will to reach diplomatic and confidence-building agreements with the United States. Two instances can be pointed out: the negotiation and signing of the 1994–95 immigration accords and the creation of a confidence-building regime in the Guantánamo Naval Base area between the armed forces of both countries. Notwithstanding that the Barack Obama Administration gave some signals that it would be inclined to adopt a new policy towards Cuba, developments since April 2009 do not warrant any hope that both countries can reach a process of normalisation of their relations.

In the meantime, Cuban diplomacy has attained its objective of getting the UN General Assembly to condemn and demand the end of the economic sanctions. That issue was raised for the first time in 1992 and, as nor earlier (and, perhaps, surprisingly) a majority of Powers supported the Cuban position. Cuba has also condemned the terrorist acts of 11 September 2001 and produced a positive press release when the United States decided to use the Guantánamo Naval Base as a prison for terrorist detainees in 2002. As the revelations of gross violations of human rights in the Base became known, Cuba joined the condemnation by the international community. It has criticised the United States 'war on terror' but, at the same time, has proposed to Washington the signing of an anti-terrorist agreement. The American response has been to keep Cuba on the list of terrorism-sponsoring states, a charge that can hardly be justified.

In Latin America and the Caribbean since the end of the Cold War, Cuban revolutionary diplomacy has been able to take advantage of the triumph of left and centre-left leaders in almost a dozen countries, beginning with the victory of Hugo Chávez in the 1998 Venezuelan elections. Havana strengthened its relations not only with the more revolutionary leaderships in Caracas, La Paz, and Quito, but also with the moderate ones in Brasilia, Santiago, and Buenos Aires. A significant element of Cuban diplomacy has been to exploit its strengths to reinforce its relations even with conservative administrations in Mexico, Colombia, and Panama. The Cuban Government has expanded its 'medical diplomacy' in the region and demonstrated a capacity to cooperate in areas like education, sports, and energy. Obama himself recognised the value of 'medical diplomacy' at a press conference during the Summit of the Americas in Trinidad and Tobago in April 2009.[20]

Recently, Cuba was able to consolidate its position as an important player in the region. In 2008, the Rio Group admitted the Cuban Government; shortly thereafter Costa Rica and El Salvador normalised their diplomatic relations with Havana; and in 2009, the OAS General Assembly in Honduras lifted all sanctions. Although Havana refused to return to the OAS, it has become, together with Caracas, one of the main supporters of the Alianza Bolivariana para las Américas, the most recent and dynamic regional integration institution. Between 1989 and 2009, Cuban revolutionary diplomacy continued to exercise an important role in the Third World. Part of that result was due to the extension of its 'medical internationalism'. But Havana has used more traditional methods. The effort was rewarded in 2006 when Cuba became one of the few Powers that have hosted a Non-Aligned Movement Summit two times.

Cuban revolutionary diplomacy has been basically an instrument of the country's anti-hegemonic foreign policy (anti-hegemonic in two senses: defending itself against the United

States' and other Powers' attempts to impose changes from the outside; and contributing to Third World resistance to imperialism and neocolonialism). Starting from a Marxist Neo-Gramscian conception of world politics,[21] it has been nevertheless surprising how Cuba has used the instruments available in all theoretical perspectives prevalent in international political economy. From a Marxist globalist and Neo-Gramscian perspective, Cuban diplomacy has behaved as revolutionary, promoting attitudes that challenge the *status quo*. However, this principle has not been adopted by Havana in a dogmatic way; rather, it has adapted when it has been necessary. A successful foreign policy is one that combines principles and interests and, in that sense, Cuban revolutionary diplomacy has passed the test of time. But Cuba has also behaved according to a realist paradigm, searching for alliances with key players of the international system in each period since the Revolution. Concurrently, Havana has been very active in international institutions, thereby performing as a liberal state. Finally, some strands of its diplomacy have been constructivist in trying to establish new norms for the international system. The main weakness of Cuban revolutionary diplomacy can probably be found in the economic sphere. Its political decisions have at times created grave economic difficulties for the Cuban population. However, these difficulties have had more to do with its own domestic policies and with American economic sanctions.

Notes

1 There is a debate about how to designate the sanctions. Washington favours 'embargo'; Havana prefers the term 'blockade'. The resolution accepts the Cuban version.
2 The concept of national interest is controversial and historically and socially determined. For pre-revolutionary Cuba's ruling classes, the national interest was linked indissolubly to their subordination to American hegemony.
3 Louis A. Pérez Jr., *Cuba in the American Imagination: Metaphor and Imperial Ethos* (Chapel Hill, NC, 2008).
4 Carlos Alzugaray, 'Problems of National Security in the Cuban-U.S. Historic Breach', in Jorge I. Domínguez and Rafael Hernández, eds., *U.S.-Cuban Relations in the 1990s* (Boulder, CO, 1989), 85–116; ídem., 'La seguridad nacional de Cuba frente a los Estados Unidos: conflicto ¿cooperación?', *Temas* 62–63(2010), 45–53.
5 Alejandro de la Fuente, *A Nation for All: Race, Inequality and Politics in Twentieth Century Cuba* (Chapel Hill, NC, 2001); Antoni Kapcia, *Cuba: Island of Dreams* (Oxford, New York, 2000).
6 Aurelio Alonso, *El laberinto tras la caída del muro* (La Habana, 2006); Fernando Martínez, *El ejercicio de pensar* (La Habana, 2008).
7 Celia Sánchez Manduley, *Resumen de un Viaje (Textos Taquigráficos de los Discursos que Figuran Insertos)* (La Habana, 1960), 13, 54–55.
8 United States Department of State, *Foreign Relations of the United States, 1958–1960*, Volume VI: *Cuba* (Washington, DC, 1991), 530 ff.
9 Ibid., 742.
10 See Goodwin memorandum, 'Conversation with Comandante Ernesto Che Guevara of Cuba', 22 August 1961: www.gwu.edu/~nsarchiv/bayofpigs/19610822.pdf.
11 Carlos Lechuga, *En el Ojo de la Tormenta: F. Castro, N. Jruschov, J.F. Kennedy y la Crisis de los Misiles* (La Habana, North Melbourne, 1995).
12 James G. Blight, Bruce J. Allyn, and David A. Welch, eds., *Cuba on the Brink: Castro, the Missile Crisis, and the Soviet Collapse* (New York, 1993): Jorge I. Domínguez, *To Make the World Safe for Revolution: Cuba's Foreign Policy* (Cambridge, MA, 1989), 42; Lechuga, *En el Ojo de la Tormenta*.
13 Domínguez, *Cuba's Foreign Policy*, 47–49.
14 Raúl Castro, *El gobierno cubano insta al Presidente Obama a que sea consecuente con su compromiso en la lucha antiterrorista* (6 de octubre de 2010): www.cubadebate.cu/raul-castro-ruz/2010/10/06/el-gobierno-cubano-insta-al-presidente-obama-a-que-sea-consecuente-con-su-compromiso-en-la-lucha-antiterrorista/.
15 Piero Gleijeses, *Conflicting Missions: Havana, Washington, and Africa, 1959–1976* (Chapel Hill, NC, 2001).
16 Carlos Alzugaray, 'La creación de una Cancillería revolucionaria 1959–65', in Ana Cairo, ed., *Raúl Roa: Imaginarios* (La Habana, 2008).

17 Domínguez, *Cuba's Foreign Policy*; ídem., *La política exterior de Cuba* (Madrid, 2009); H. Michael Erisman, *Cuba's International Relations: The Anatomy of a Nationalistic Foreign Policy* (Boulder, CO, 1985); Gleijeses, *Conflicting Missions*.

18 See Julie M. Feinsilver, *Healing the Masses: Cuban Health Politics at Home and Abroad* (Berkeley, CA, 1993); John M. Kirk, and H. Michael Erisman, *Cuban Medical Internationalism: Origins, Evolution, and Goals* (London, 2009).

19 See John M. Kirk and Peter McKenna, *Canada-Cuba Relations: The Other Good Neighbor Policy* (Gainesville, FL, 1997).

20 Obama said: 'One thing that I thought was interesting—and I knew this in a more abstract way but it was interesting in very specific terms—hearing from these leaders who when they spoke about Cuba talked very specifically about the thousands of doctors from Cuba that are dispersed all throughout the region, and upon which many of these countries heavily depend'.: www.whitehouse.gov/the-press-office/press-conference-president-trinidad-and-tobago-4192009.

21 See Robert W. Cox, 'Gramsci, Hegemony and International Relations: An Essay in Method', in Louis Amoore, ed., *The Global Resistance Reader* (Cambridge, UK, 2005), 35–47; Mark Rupert, 'Globalizing Common Sense: A Marxian-Gramscian (Re)Vision of the Politics of Governance/Resistance', *Review of International Studies*, 29(2003), 181–98.

16

Peru

A model for Latin American diplomacy and statecraft

Ronald Bruce St John

After winning its independence from Spain, the Republic of Peru quickly distinguished itself in terms of the professionalism of its diplomacy and statecraft. It was the first Latin America state to pass a diplomatic law worthy of the name and also the first to conclude a treaty with Japan. In the interim, Peru created a consultative commission at the Ministry of Foreign Affairs, consisting of experts in the field, on foreign-policy issues, and decades later it established the Peruvian Diplomatic Academy, one of the first of its kind in Latin America. In early August 1821, General José de San Martín, soon after declaring Peru independent from Spain, established the Ministry of State and Foreign Relations and appointed Juan García del Río as the first Minister of Foreign Affairs of Peru. Less than five months later, García del Río was sent abroad in the attempt by the nascent republic to establish formal diplomatic relations with other states, and Bernardo Monteagudo replaced him as Foreign Minister.[1] Over the next two decades, the conduct of foreign affairs was largely the purview of a small coterie of often highly competent aristocrats, some of whom had previous experience in the Spanish administration.

With the decisive patriot victory at Ayacucho in 1824, Peruvian independence was secured, and the capabilities, options, and constraints of Peruvian foreign policy began to clarify. As with many of its neighbours, Peru's boundaries were in dispute and would remain so well into the next century. These territorial issues were often complicated by the commercial advantages at stake as the Pacific coast states of South America quarrelled over trade routes and seaports. Peru shared with its neighbors a profound awareness of interlocking interests; consequently, bilateral disputes often assumed multilateral dimensions as states shifted alliances in search of relative advantage. The conflicting demands of independence and interdependence, as determined by this potpourri of domestic and international forces, influenced the content and expression of Peruvian foreign policy long after 1824.[2]

The first two decades after independence were a time of considerable internal strife, bordering on civil war, in which Peruvian *caudillos* battled to determine the future of the state.[3] In this confused and shifting milieu, successive administrations struggled to define the frontiers of Peru, not in the narrow sense of planting boundary markers, but in the broader sense of determining whether Peru would be divided, federate with Bolivia, or stand alone. Like many new states, Peru achieved statehood long before it achieved nationhood, and in its early years, it struggled to maintain the former as it strove to develop the latter. It was not until the first half of the 1840s that Peru finally attained a more or less defined territory and government.

The election of Ramón Castilla to the presidency of Peru in April 1845 proved a milestone in the development of Peruvian foreign policy. Before his administration, Peru was a weak, divided nation with only vague, limited ambitions. Under Castilla, Peru acquired for the first time the degree of internal peace, centralised and efficient state organisation, adequate and reliable public funding, and emerging sense of national unity necessary for the formulation, articulation, and execution of an active foreign policy. The President also was able to draw on the nation's newly developed guano wealth to create the machinery and professionalism required to pursue its international aims and without which foreign policy itself would have been valueless.[4]

Peru's approach to foreign relations in 1821–45 mirrored that of its neighbors in that it lacked direction and structure; therefore, a high priority of the first Castilla administration (1845–51) was a thorough reorganisation of the consular and diplomatic services to improve their efficiency and effectiveness.[5] The President was motivated by the indignities suffered by Peru in the past either because it did not command respect abroad or because it lacked a vigorous foreign service capable of presenting its case competently to foreign governments. Castilla was ably assisted in his efforts to upgrade the Ministry of Foreign Affairs by José Gregorio Paz Soldán, widely considered the most efficient Peruvian Minister of Foreign Affairs in the nineteenth century.

On 31 July 1846, Castilla signed draft legislation, known as decree 90, reorganising the consular and diplomatic corps and outlining job classifications as well as remuneration and retirement practices.[6] Ratified by the congress in 1853, it was the first diplomatic law worthy of the name in Peru or elsewhere in Latin America, and it would become the longest-standing diplomatic legislation in Peru. Additional statutes later strengthened the structure outlined in the 1853 law, notably decree 553, which in 1856 detailed the duties of the Minister of Foreign Relations. Castilla took full advantage of the new legislation to upgrade the quality of Peruvian diplomats and to expand the number of missions abroad. By 1851, he had reorganised the diplomatic corps, improved the professionalism of Peruvian diplomats, and established or upgraded missions in a number of American and European locations. By 1857, Peru enjoyed widespread diplomatic representation abroad with missions throughout Latin America, the United States, and Europe. In 1862, the final year of the second Castilla administration, one-half of the 36 appointed consuls were salaried when only two had been so 15 years earlier.[7]

Serving non-consecutive terms, Castilla influenced the formation and execution of Peruvian foreign policy for a period longer than any other nineteenth-century chief executive. During his tenure, Peru experienced for the first time an administration that outlined a foreign policy at the outset of its term and then worked to achieve its stated objectives. The increased professionalism of the diplomatic corps, together with the improved structure of the Ministry of Foreign Relations, enabled Peru to support more effectively a wider range of foreign-policy goals. A broad diplomatic effort like that which supported the 1856 Continental Treaty, for example, would have been well beyond the scope of the state's capabilities only 20 years earlier. As a result of Castilla's efforts, Peruvian foreign policy became increasingly coherent and comprehensive, and Peru assumed a leadership role in continental affairs.[8]

When Castilla left office, the challenge for his successors was to build upon his achievements in a manner that advanced the national interests of Peru. Unfortunately, little new or lasting was accomplished in the 1860s, a decade lost largely in terms of advancing the goals of Peruvian foreign policy. The Spanish intervention of 1863–66 produced a temporary alliance of Andean republics, but the volatile nature of the coalition, coupled with the meager results of the Second Lima Conference (1864–65), highlighted the limited prospects for broader hemispheric unity. Moreover, rivalry with Chile, temporarily set aside during the Spanish intervention, resumed with a new intensity, eventually leading to armed conflict less than ten years later.[9]

During the 1870s, Peru enjoyed another opportunity to put its political and economic house in order and regain the sense of direction and regional leadership achieved under Castilla. The

Manuel Pardo (1872–76) and Mariano Ignacio Prado (1876–79) governments tried unsuccessfully to ensure Peru's security and compensate for reduced military strength by entering into treaties with neighbouring states.[10] These pacts took both bilateral and multilateral forms as Peru sought to strengthen the role of international law in regional affairs. To move away from excessive state reliance on foreign loans, Peru also restructured the marketing of guano and nationalised the nitrate industry.[11] Unfortunately, the economic policies of the Pardo and Prado administrations were not wholly successful and later contributed to Peru's defeat in the War of the Pacific (1879–83). In the interim, the ongoing need for labor led to new efforts at European immigration and groundbreaking treaties with China and Japan.[12] The 1873 treaty with Japan was Peru's first with an Asian state as well as Japan's first with a Latin American country.

In August 1872, in a natural extension of Castilla's efforts to enhance the foreign-policy machinery of the state, Pardo authorised the creation of a consultative commission at the Ministry of Foreign Affairs. This newly created commission consisted of past foreign ministers, congressional experts on foreign policy, former diplomats, and eminent scholars and international lawyers. The first Consultative Commission of Foreign Relations was named on 31 August 1872, and a second was named in June 1886 during the administration of Andrés Avelino Cáceres (1886–90).[13]

The relative positions of Bolivia, Chile, and Peru on the Pacific coast made naval power the crucial factor in the War of the Pacific. Once Chile gained control of the sea, the outcome of the war was inevitable. After four years of bloody fighting and protracted negotiations, the 1883 Treaty of Ancón reestablished peace between Peru and Chile. It was a punitive pact, with heavy indemnities, guaranteed to retard any improvement in regional relations. The treaty provisions related to the final disposition of the Peruvian provinces of Tacna and Arica were particularly unfortunate because they constituted an open sore that poisoned hemispheric relations for decades to come.[14] In the post-war period, Peruvian diplomacy concentrated on the recovery of the two provinces. After 10 years of Chilean occupation, the Treaty of Ancón called for a plebiscite to be held to determine whether Tacna and Arica would remain Chilean or revert to Peru. However, the ten-year period came and went without a plebiscite because the two sides could not agree on the terms of its execution. In the interim, Chile initiated a policy of Chileanisation in Tacna and Arica to ensure it would win any future plebiscite.[15]

Whilst Chile remained the central issue on the foreign-policy agenda, Peruvian diplomacy also made some progress in its complicated, often interrelated, boundary disputes with Bolivia, Brazil, Colombia, and Ecuador. In the Espinosa-Bonifaz Convention, Peru and Ecuador agreed in 1887 to submit their territorial dispute to arbitration by the King of Spain, a process that promised an outcome favorable to Peru. Later, Peru and Colombia agreed to a papal arbitration of their dispute, subject to the outcome of the Ecuador–Peru dispute. Bilateral relations with the United States, soured by Washington's amateurish diplomacy during the War of the Pacific, also improved. Given the economic and political ascendancy of the United States, Lima's ongoing need for development capital and diplomatic support clearly dictated better relations with Washington.[16]

Between 1908 and 1930, President Augusto B. Leguía served two non-consecutive terms, totalling 15 years. The first Leguía administration (1908–12) accomplished several major achievements, including the resolution of the boundary disputes with Bolivia and Brazil. The 1909 treaty with Brazil conceded to the latter only the territory over which it had *de facto* possession, whereas the treaty with Bolivia, an agreement based on an earlier arbitral decision, awarded 60 percent of the disputed territory to Peru.[17] During Leguía's second administration (1919–30), he negotiated the 1922 Salomón-Lozano Treaty with Colombia, granting the latter frontage on the Amazon River in return for ceding to Peru territory south of the Putumayo River that Colombia had received from Ecuador in 1916. Even though the agreement greatly enhanced Peru's regional position *vis-à-vis* Ecuador, its terms were poorly understood and widely condemned by Peruvian nationalists. In 1929, Leguía concluded an agreement with Chile that divided the two occupied provinces: Tacna going to Peru and Arica remaining with Chile. Weary of the dispute, the 1929 treaty and additional protocol were well received by a majority of citizens in both Peru and Chile; nevertheless, fulfilling their provisions remained a subject of debate for the remainder of the century.[18]

Leguía felt that offshore capital was the key to rapid economic growth and encouraged a dramatic increase in its role in Peru, aggressively recruiting foreign investment, technicians, and administrators, in particular from the United States. Leguía's close association with American interests, combined with his controversial territorial settlements, especially the division of Tacna and Arica, alienated influential segments of the population and nurtured the growth of a nascent Peruvian nationalism. The latent current of anti-American feeling that developed in Peru by the time Leguía was ousted in 1930 would influence Peruvian foreign policy for years to come.[19]

Over the next three decades, the challenges and opportunities of Peruvian foreign policy expanded in scope and direction, and Peru regained the leadership role in continental affairs that it earlier had abandoned. Having withdrawn from participation in the League of Nations after that body refused to consider the Tacna – Arica question, Peru was a founding member of the United Nations (UN) in 1945 and the Organization of American States (OAS) in 1948. It also joined the Latin American Free Trade Association when it was created in 1960. Dissatisfied with private investment as the primary means to generate economic development, Peru explored alternative sources for financial and technical assistance, including the UN and the OAS. Tentative steps in the direction of an increasingly multilateral approach to foreign affairs paralleled a decline in the power and prestige of the United States. In response, Peruvian foreign policy was marked by a heightened sense of nationalism, in which successive Peruvian governments displayed the capability and determination to resolve international issues on their own terms.[20]

Peru also demonstrated a growing interest in regional economic cooperation and development, participating in multilateral conferences on mineral resources and maritime fishing. In 1947, Peru stated its intent to exercise national sovereignty over the continental shelf and insular seas to a distance of 200 nautical miles; and in 1954, Peru, Chile, and Ecuador issued a joint declaration stating they would not unilaterally diminish without prior agreement their common claim to exercise national sovereignty over the continental shelf and insular seas out to 200 nautical miles. Over the next decade, Peru participated in a series of international conferences on this question, and the issue was also on the agenda of the Law of the Sea conferences held in Geneva in 1958 and 1960.[21]

To better manage the mounting level of international discourse, President Oscar R. Benavides (1933–39) earlier had reconstituted the Consultative Commission of Foreign Relations, which had ceased to function after 1903. Thereafter, this small group of foreign-policy specialists regularly contributed advice on key foreign-policy issues, like the Leticia dispute with Colombia in 1932–34 and the 1942 Rio Protocol and the 1998 Brasilia Accords with Ecuador. In 1999, the Commission also played a role in the negotiation of a package of agreements executing the 1929 Tacna and Arica Treaty and Additional Protocol, ending 70 years of controversy with Chile.[22]

Peru continued concurrently to improve the professionalism of the diplomatic corps through more stringent recruitment, better training, and higher advancement standards. During the Manuel Prado administration (1939–45), the Organic Foreign Relations Bill in 1941 and the Review of the Peruvian International Law Society in 1944 advanced a plan for training diplomats, leading to the creation in 1955 of the Peruvian Diplomatic Academy. It was one of the first such institutions in Latin America and, over time, it became a first-class educational body with a strong faculty and a demanding curriculum, eventually earning university status in 2005. In the process, it became the sole entry point into the diplomatic service, turning out generations of well-trained diplomats.[23] In conjunction with the growing strength and increased capability of the diplomatic corps, Peruvian foreign policy after 1962 moved in new directions as Peruvian diplomats addressed unfamiliar issues, adopted fresh approaches, and solidified new ties. Over the next three decades, successive administrations diversified arms transfers, expanded trade links, advocated a radical reorganisation of the inter-American economic and political system, and pressed for enhanced sub-regional economic cooperation.[24]

Peru was a founding member of the sub-regional trade bloc known as the Andean Group in 1969, and it joined other Powers in signing the multilateral Treaty for Amazonian Cooperation in 1978. Peru was also a founding member in 1980 of the Andean Reserve Fund, a lending facility associated with the Andean Group, as well as the 1988 Latin American Reserve Fund, an extension of the Andean Reserve Fund. At the same time, the second Belaúnde Terry administration (1980–85) pursed a more open economic system, a policy seen by some observers as softening Peru's commitment to Andean development. Thought to have been resolved in 1942, the boundary dispute with Ecuador led to renewed conflict in 1981 and, the next year, Peru refused to sign the UN Law of the Sea Convention on the grounds that it was unconstitutional.[25]

The second Belaúnde administration searched for a more positive relationship with the United States but, in the end, the conflicting demands of Peruvian nationalism and the need for American support to achieve key foreign-policy goals left little room for improvement. Economically, Peru clashed with the United States over the level of economic aid and American imposition of countervailing tariffs on Peruvian textiles. Politically, the harsh methods used by Peru to stem a growing wave of terrorism created a storm of protest from United States human rights groups. Diplomatically, Peru criticised American support for Britain in the 1982 Falklands War and the United States intervention in Grenada in 1983; and the United States criticised Peruvian backing for the Contadora Support group, which advocated a negotiated peace in war-torn Central America.[26]

The Alan García Pérez administration (1985–90) played an active role in the Non-Aligned Movement, opposed apartheid in Southern Africa, and promoted a close association with social democratic groups in Western Europe. Bilateral talks with Bolivia and Ecuador produced limited results, and an otherwise unproductive disarmament initiative led to the creation in Lima in 1986 of the UN Regional Centre for Peace, Disarmament, and Development in Latin America and the Caribbean. To avoid being labelled communist, García's administration attempted to maintain an independent posture toward the socialist states of the world; however, its activist foreign policy left little room for improvement in relations with the United States. In addition to García inheriting a number of unresolved and contentious issues from the Belaúnde administration, President García's opposition to US policy in Central America put him in direct conflict with the Reagan Administration. Peru's response to narcotrafficking and terrorist activities won limited praise from Washington, but the García administration's confrontational style left bilateral relations strained as the decade ended.[27]

With the end of the Cold War, Peruvian diplomacy continued to focus on many of the issues with which it had dealt since the conclusion of the Second World War. At the same time, the national interests of Peru evolved and matured; and successive administrations worked to expand and refine Peruvian statecraft in pursuit of new or redefined concerns. Peru strengthened ties to the international economy and increased its participation in regional and international organisations. It also nurtured key bilateral relationships, especially those with its Andean neighbours and the United States. In the 1990s, President Alberto Fujimori enjoyed more success in advancing the core goals of Peruvian foreign policy than any other administration in the second half of the century. In terms of regional cooperation and development, Fujimori attended the Andean Pact Summit in La Paz in late 1990, where dialogue centered on how best to reactivate the Andean process; and in February 1991, he presided at the opening meeting of the Andean Parliament when it convened in Lima. Three months later, Fujimori joined the chief executives of Bolivia, Colombia, Ecuador, and Venezuela in committing to the establishment of a free trade zone by January 1992 and a common market by 1995. In August 1992, after Fujimori suspended the 1979 constitution, padlocked the Congress, and dismantled the judiciary in a so-called *autogolpe*, Peru suspended temporarily its cooperation with the Andean Group; however, by 1998, it had returned to full participation.[28]

In August 1991, Peru joined Chile and Mexico in renewing calls for active membership of the Pacific Economic Cooperation Council, a goal that all three states later achieved; and with Japanese support, Peru became a full member of the Asia-Pacific Economic Cooperation (APEC) forum. Eager to cement bilateral relations with Japan, the land of his ancestors, Fujimori completed his tenth visit to Japan in 1999 whilst chief executive, marking the one-hundredth anniversary of the first wave of Japanese emigration to Peru. The Fujimori administration also advocated the integration of Peru and other Latin American states into the North American Free Trade Agreement as part of a strategy to create an economic grouping of developing countries.[29] The Fujimori administration also concluded important bilateral agreements with neighboring states: trade agreements with Colombia, Ecuador, and Venezuela. In support of Bolivia's perennial quest for a seaport, it gave La Paz an industrial park and duty-free port on the Pacific Ocean at Ilo in return for similar facilities at Puerto Suarez on the Paraguay River. In October 1998, Fujimori negotiated the Brasilia Accords with Ecuador, ending the longest-standing boundary dispute in the Americas. In December 1999, Peru also concluded an agreement with Chile, resolving the issues outstanding from the 1929 Tacna and Arica Treaty and Additional Protocol and ending another contentious and prolonged foreign-policy issue.[30]

Recognising the need for American support to restore the international standing of Peru after the disastrous policies of the García administration, Fujimori concentrated initially on the related issues of drug production and narcotrafficking, the policy concerns of greatest interest to Washington. Later, the bilateral relationship expanded to include other areas of mutual interest, including debt, democracy and human rights, development, and defense issues. By the end of the decade, under the Fujimori administration, Peru enjoyed the most positive relationship with the United States since the second Leguía administration.[31]

The Alejandro Toledo administration pursued nine interrelated foreign-policy goals. First, it promoted democracy and human rights, often tying the second policy goal, the struggle against poverty, to the promotion of democracy. Neither of these objectives was new to Peru; nevertheless, the enthusiasm and determination with which they were pursued after 2001 was notable. Third, the administration worked to broaden bilateral relations with neighboring states, emphasising economic development in the borderlands. Fourth, it encouraged a reduction in regional arms spending, arguing that money saved should be used to reduce poverty. Fifth, Toledo's administration promoted increased unity and stronger integration within the Andean Group; and sixth, it targeted stronger relations with the major industrialised Powers and the Asia–Pacific region. The seventh goal called for the Ministry of Foreign Affairs to become more effective in promoting the domestic economy abroad, and the eighth encouraged it to do a better job of serving Peruvians overseas. Initiatives in these two areas marked a renewed concern for the lives of Peruvians at home and abroad, and they also displayed recognition of the growing interdependence of domestic and foreign policies in the new millennium. Finally, the Toledo administration promised to reform personnel practices at the Ministry of Foreign Affairs, a goal driven by the scandalous treatment of diplomats in the Fujimori years.[32]

From the outset of his tenure in office (reflecting personal persuasion as much as a reaction to the authoritarian policies of the Fujimori regime) Toledo emphasised the central role of democratic values and the respect for human rights in any workable strategy to eliminate poverty. In so doing, he repeatedly stressed the need to reduce arms spending throughout Latin America, arguing the money would be better spent on education, health, and social welfare programs. Toledo's emphasis on arms control was reminiscent of the earlier García initiatives with the important difference that Toledo planned to use any money saved to reduce poverty whilst García had aimed to reduce Peru's external debt. In the end, the two arms reduction initiatives were also similar in their general absence of success, in large part because a Middle Power like Peru lacked the diplomatic and other resources to achieve them.[33]

The Toledo administration also continued the familiar Peruvian emphasis on expanded integration with sub-regional, regional, and extraregional bodies, from the Andean Community of Nations (CAN) to the OAS to the UN. In January 2004, an Extraordinary Summit of the Americas adopted a Peruvian proposal, the Declaration of Nuevo Leon, saying no American state should be a refuge for corruption or corrupt people. Later in the year, Peru hosted the Third Summit of South American Presidents, which witnessed the creation of the South American Community of Nations, later known as the Union of South American Nations. This new body targeted a gradual convergence of CAN with the Southern Common Market (MERCOSUR). In 2005, Peru was elected to a two-year term on the UN Security Council. Active in a plethora of international organisations, Peru suffered from what might be termed summit overload, an affliction common to Middle Powers. All of them belong to a growing number of economic and political groupings, most of which hold annual summits that heads of state are expected to attend, putting a severe strain on the limited capacity of Middle Powers to staff them.[34]

The Toledo administration also worked to promote regional cooperation and development through stronger bilateral ties with its Andean neighbours. In the wake of the 1998 Brasilia Accords, relations with Ecuador focused on executing the provisions of the accords, principally borderland development, whereas dialogue with Colombia mostly centered on the related issues of terrorism and narcotrafficking. In 2004, Peru concluded a tripartite accord with Brazil and Colombia aimed at combating criminal activity on the rivers that border the three countries. In 2003, Toledo met with Brazilian President Luiz Inácio Lula da Silva and signed a strategic alliance that proved to be a major foreign-policy success. The agreement provided for increased economic cooperation within the context of the Initiative for Integration of Regional Infrastructure in South America, a multiyear plan to crisscross Latin American with ten hubs of economic development, three of which passed through Peru. The two parties also agreed to promote bilateral trade and investment, and Brazil granted Peru access to two electronic surveillance systems that it had developed to track illicit activities in the Amazon Basin.[35]

Peruvian relations with Bolivia were generally positive in the early years of the Toledo administration but deteriorated after Bolivian President Evo Morales was inaugurated in January 2006. Morales moved Bolivian domestic and foreign policy in new directions that were often antithetical to the policies of Toledo. Bilateral relations with Venezuela were also strained as the personalities, philosophies, and policies of Toledo and Venezuelan President Hugo Chávez Frías could not differ more. In addition to the implementation of the 1999 agreement, Peru's main policy concerns with Chile were the Chile–Peru maritime boundary and the high level of Chilean arms purchases, which threatened to provoke a regional arms race. The Toledo administration failed to achieve a Chilean commitment to regional disarmament or to resolve the maritime dispute; however, that failure was as much due to Chilean intransigence as it was to any deficiency in Peruvian diplomacy.[36]

The policies of the Fujimori administration had enjoyed a high level of congruence with core elements of United States foreign policy in the post-Cold War era; consequently, Toledo inherited a highly favorable bilateral climate. In March 2002, President George W. Bush became the first sitting American President to visit Peru, and over the next four years, Peruvian–American relations moved from strength to strength. In December 2002, the Bush administration saluted Toledo's efforts to promote democracy and free markets, and Peru reaffirmed its role as a key United States ally in the struggle against international terrorism. In February 2003, the Peace Corps returned to Peru after a 28-year hiatus; and in 2006, the Toledo administration succeeded in concluding a free trade agreement with the United States.[37]

Even as it maintained a positive working relationship with Washington, the Toledo administration was able to challenge core elements of American policy, an indication of the professionalism of Peruvian statecraft. Peru opposed the United States invasion and occupation of Iraq, advocated UN Security Council reform, and pushed for a regional approach to combat drug trafficking. It also accepted the jurisdiction of the International Criminal Court, turning aside entreaties from Washington to conclude a bilateral immunity agreement shielding United States citizens from prosecution. Several factors contributed to the success of Peruvian diplomacy, including the strong personal relationship that developed between Presidents Bush and Toledo. In addition, the Bush Administration embraced the Peruvian approach in policy, touching the promotion of democracy, human rights, and free trade in a region in which populist, socialist regimes were offering alternatives unacceptable to Washington.[38]

The foreign policy of the second García administration blended the old with the new but, when taken as a whole, largely mirrored the policies of the Toledo administration. Support for market-friendly economic policies replaced the emphasis on socialism in the first García administration, and multiple visits to the White House contrasted with the earlier policy of confrontation with the United States. Having questioned the wisdom of the free trade agreement with the United States during the election campaign, García once in office embraced the agreement. García did not achieve the close personal relationship with Bush enjoyed by his predecessor, but his three invitations to the Bush White House were a decided accomplishment for a chief executive who was in effect *persona non grata* in Washington by the end of his first term. In mid-2010, García also visited the Obama White House.[39]

In the course of the 2006 election campaign, García pledged to give priority to bilateral relations with neighboring states, and in so doing, his administration largely followed the approach of his predecessor. With Ecuador, the focus remained on the implementation of the agreements constituting the 1998 Brasilia Accords, with major emphasis on development of the borderlands. In the case of Chile, García's administration finalised a commercial accord that had been largely negotiated during the Toledo administration; and it secured the extradition from Chile to Peru of former President Fujimori, a policy holdover from the previous government. García also supported Toledo's decision to take the maritime dispute with Chile to the International Court of Justice, a judicial process well under way in 2010 but expected to take years to complete. The second García administration also advocated reduced arms purchases in the region, in general, and in Chile, in particular, a policy it had championed in 1985–90, and one adopted by the Toledo administration.[40]

With Brazil, the García administration worked to strengthen the strategic relationship negotiated by Toledo. Early in García's tenure, new agreements were signed covering technical cooperation, health, education, biotechnology, energy-mining, and Amazon security. Later, commercial and other accords were concluded. In the case of Colombia, bilateral relations continued to center on border issues related to questions of national defense and security. As evidence mounted that Colombian guerrilla units engaged in the illicit drug trade were operating on both sides of the Colombia–Peru border, the García administration promoted economic development in the frontier zone, together with increased commerce and stronger collaboration against narcotrafficking.[41]

When it came to Bolivia and Venezuela, García faced many of the same problems encountered by his predecessor. Harshly critical of presidents Morales and Chávez during the presidential campaign, García reached out to them after his election in an attempt to calm the rhetoric. At the same time, he cast his administration, with its emphasis on democracy and free markets, as the antithesis to Bolivia and Venezuela, an approach that played well in Washington but not in La Paz or Caracas. With Bolivia, the more divisive issues included a Bolivian agreement with Venezuela for the latter Power to fund military bases along the Bolivia–Peru border and Bolivia's reluctance to accept the modifications to the CAN agreement required for Peru to implement its free trade agreement with the United States. With Venezuela, there was ongoing concern over the activities and goals of the Venezuelan-funded Bolivian Alternative for the Americas and periodic complaints that Venezuela continued to meddle in the domestic affairs of Peru.[42]

Elsewhere, García continued the participatory policies of the Fujimori and Toledo administrations in a wide variety of regional and international organisations like the OAS and UN. In May 2008, Peru hosted the Fifth Summit of the Heads of State and Government of Latin America, the Caribbean, and the European Union and, six months later, the Sixteenth APEC Summit. The García administration also continued Toledo's efforts to increase trade with China and to attract Chinese investment to Peru, as well as earlier efforts to broaden commercial relations with Japan and South Korea. The García administration negotiated free trade agreements with China and Singapore, in addition to others with Canada and the European Union. On the other hand, García was not so aggressive as his predecessor in championing initiatives to promote democracy in international forums, and although he articulated a policy of arms control and reduced arms spending, his administration agreed to a major rearmament of the Peruvian armed forces, compromising his position on the issue.[43]

Unlike the Great Powers, stable governments, secure societies, strong economies, and significant military strength have all, at one time or another, been a problem for Peru. At the end of the Toledo administration in mid-2006, a prominent Lima newspaper noted that Peru for the first time in decades would have a change of government without a serious economic or political crisis. As Peru addressed the shortcomings of its political economy, it was able to widen the scope of its foreign policy, expanding its ties to multilateral organisations and the international economy. In the process, the focus of Peruvian foreign policy gradually evolved from one centered largely on bilateral questions, notably the resolution of multiple boundary issues, to one impacting on a variety of regional and international issues.

In pursuit of the national interests of Peru, its politicians and diplomats have regularly used economic, military, and political means, the traditional attributes of power; however, it was the professionalism of its diplomatic service that often separated Peruvian diplomacy and statecraft from that of neighboring states. Concerted efforts to improve the effectiveness of the diplomatic corps began after independence, increased in the mid-nineteenth century, and continued to the present time. On more than one occasion, the executive branch attempted to politicise the Ministry of Foreign Affairs, with the Fujimori administration being the most recent example, but for the most part, the chief executives of Peru have looked to the professionals in the Ministry of Foreign Affairs to guide the external relations of the state. At the same time, the stature and decisiveness of certain chief executives, like Ramón Castilla, Augusto B. Leguía, Alberto Fujimori, and Alejandro Toledo, clearly played a major role in shaping political outcomes. In a more institutionalised state, the role of the chief executive in leading the foreign-policy process might not be so important, but in a Middle Power like Peru, it was critical. Working with the professionals in the Ministry of Foreign Affairs, strong chief executives implemented well-thought-out, coherent foreign policies that reflected domestic concerns and interests and were well suited to the international milieu.

Notes

1 Juan Miguel Bákula, *Perú: Entre la Realidad y la Utopía, 180 Años de Política Exterior*, Volume 1 (Lima, 2002), 51–59; Pedro Ugarteche, *Valija de un Diplomático Peruano* (Buenos Aires, 1965), 21–22.
2 Alberto Wagner de Reyna, *Historia diplomática del Perú, 1900–1945*, Volume 1 (Lima, 1964), 9–14; Ronald Bruce St John, *The Foreign Policy of Peru* (Boulder, CO, 1992), 10–11, 20.
3 Modesto Basadre y Chocano, *Diez Años de Historia Política del Perú (1834–1844)* (Lima, 1955), 1–166; Alvaro Pérez del Castillo, *Bolivia, Colombia, Chile y el Perú: Diplomacia y Política, 1825–1904* (La Paz, 1980), 13–128, 144–86, 196–202.
4 Rosa Garibaldi, *La Política exterior del Perú en la era de Ramón Castilla: Defensa hemisférica y defensa de la jurisdicción nacional* (Lima, 2003), 23; St John, *Foreign Policy of Peru*, 45.
5 Garibaldi, *La Política exterior*, 23–24; Bákula, *Perú*, 1, 172–96.
6 Jorge Basadre, *Historia de la república del Perú, 1822–1933*, 6th edition, Volume 3 (Lima, 1968), 113–14; Garibaldi, *La Política exterior*, 24–32.
7 Garibaldi, *La Política exterior*, 32–38.
8 St John, *Foreign Policy of Peru*, 62–63; Garibaldi, *La Política exterior*, 252–304.
9 Basadre, *Historia*, Volume 5, 201–363; St John, *Foreign Policy*, 80–81.
10 Evaristo San Cristoval, *Manuel Pardo y Lavalle: Su vida y su obra* (Lima, 1945), 49–262; Peter Flindell Klarén, *Peru: Society and Nationhood in the Andes* (Oxford, 2000), 172–82.
11 Heraclio Bonilla, *Guano y Burguesía en el Perú*, 3rd edition. (Quito, 1994), 127–90; Robert G. Greenhill and Rory M. Miller, 'The Peruvian Government and the Nitrate Trade, 1873–79', *Journal of Latin American Studies* 5(1973), 107–31.
12 Watt Stewart, *Chinese Bondage in Peru: A History of the Chinese Coolie in Peru, 1849–1874* (Durham, NC, 1951), 175–76, 189–90; Amelia Morimoto, *Los japoneses y sus descendientes en el Perú* (Lima, 1999), 32–33.
13 Pedro Ugarteche, *La Comisión Consultiva de Relaciones Exteriores del Perú* (Lima, 1948), 1–15.
14 For an introduction to the extensive literature on the War of the Pacific, see William F. Slater, *Chile and the War of the Pacific* (Lincoln, NE, 1986); Bruce W. Farcau, *The Ten Cents War: Chile, Peru, and Bolivia in the War of the Pacific, 1879–1884* (Westport, CT, 2000).
15 Raúl Palacios Rodríguez, *La Chilenización de Tacna y Arica, 1883–1929* (Lima, 1974).
16 Juan Miguel Bákula, *Perú y Ecuador: Tiempos y testimonios de una vecindad*, Volume 3 (Lima, 1992), 19–170; Heraclio Bonilla, *Un siglo a la deriva: Ensayos sobre el Perú, Bolivia y la Guerra* (Lima, 1980), 71–105.
17 Alberto Ulloa, *Posición Internacional del Perú* (Lima, 1941), 229–34; René Hooper López, *Leguía: ensayo biográfico* (Lima, 1964), 153–62; Bákula, *Perú*, Volume 1, 519–28, 712–14.
18 Pedro Ugarteche, *La Política Internacional Peruana durante la dictadura de Leguía* (Lima, 1930), 69–93; Manuel A. Capuñay, *Leguía: Vida y obra del constructor del gran Perú* (Lima, 1951): 206–52; López, *Leguía*, 163–76.
19 Lawrence A. Clayton, *Peru and the United States: The Condor and the Eagle* (Athens, GA, 1999), 104–41; St John, *Foreign Policy*, 164, 166, 168.
20 Fernando Belaúnde Terry, President of Peru (1963–68, 1980–85), interview with author, Denver, Colorado, 16 May 1969; Luis Velaochaga, *Políticas Exteriores del Perú: Sociología, Histórica y Periodismo* (Lima, 2001), 187–203; Cynthia McClintock and Fabian Vallas, *The United States and Peru: Cooperation at a Cost* (London, 2003), 18–25.
21 Félix C. Calderón U., *La Negociación del Protocolo de 1942: mitos y realidades* (Lima, 1998); Manuel Rodríguez Cuadros, *Delimitación Marítima con Equidad: El caso de Perú y Chile* (Lima, 2007), 59–74, 141–87.
22 St John, *Foreign Policy*, 176.
23 Ugarteche, *Valija de un Diplomático Peruano*, 9–20.
24 Pedro-Pablo Kuczynski, *Peruvian Democracy under Economic Stress: An Account of the Belaúnde Administration, 1963–1968* (Princeton, NJ, 1977), 106–25, 152–61, 260–76; C. Hélan Jaworski 'Peru: The Military Government's Foreign Policy in Its Two Phases (1968–80),' in Heraldo Muñoz and Joseph S. Tulchin, eds., *Latin American Nations in World Politics* (Boulder, CO, 1984), 200–215.
25 Fernando Belaúnde Terry, President of Peru (1963–68, 1980–85), interview with author, Lima, Peru, 11 July 1983; Eduardo Ferrero Costa, 'Peruvian Foreign Policy: Current Trends, Constraints and Opportunities', *Journal of Interamerican Studies and World Affairs* 29(1987), 55–78.

26 Velaochaga, *Políticas Exteriores del Perú*, 224–42; St John, *Foreign Policy*, 206–9.
27 John Crabtree, *Peru under García: An Opportunity Lost* (Pittsburgh, PA, 1992), 40–41, 78–82, 188–209; Velaochaga, *Políticas Exteriores del Perú*, 242–58; Clayton, *Peru and the United States*, 264–65, 288–89.
28 Ronald Bruce St John, *La Política Exterior del Perú* (Lima, 1999), 218–21.
29 Ronald Bruce St John, 'Peru: Atypical External Behavior,' in Gordon Mace and Jean-Philippe Thérien, eds., *Foreign Policy & Regionalism in the Americas*, (Boulder, CO, 1996), 133–34; Mark Huband, 'Fujimori looks for a place in Nafta, a place in the world,' *Financial Times*, 14 May 1998.
30 Fernando de Trazegnies Granda, Foreign Minister of Peru (1998–2000), interview with author, Lima, Peru, 2 September 1999; Ronald Bruce St John, *The Ecuador-Peru Boundary Dispute: The Road to Settlement* (Durham, 2000); idem., 'Chile and Peru: The Final Settlement', *Boundary and Security Bulletin* 8 (Spring 2000), 91–100; Bákula, *Perú*, 2: 1133–44.
31 David Scott Palmer, 'Relaciones entre Estados Unidos y el Perú durante el decenio de 1990: dinámicas, antecedentes y proyecciones,' *Política Internacional*, 53 (July-September 1998), 23–45; St John, *La Política Exterior*, 213–18.
32 Diego García-Sayán, Foreign Minister of Peru (July 2001–July 2002), interview with author, 11 March 2008; José Manuel Rodríguez Cuadros, Deputy Foreign Minister of Peru (July 2001–December 2003), Foreign Minister of Peru (December 200–August 2005), interview with author, Lima, Peru, 14 March 2008.
33 Alejandro Toledo Manrique, President of Peru (2001–6), interview with author, Lima, Peru, 19 April 2006.
34 Óscar Maúrtua de Romaña, Foreign Minister of Peru (August 2005–July 2006), interview with author, Lima, Peru, 18 April 2006; Perú, Ministerio de Relaciones Exteriores, *Un Líder sin Fronteras: Diplomacia Presidencial, 2001–2006* (Lima, 2006), 235–40.
35 José Manuel Rodríguez Cuadros, Deputy Foreign Minister of Peru (July 2001–December 2003), Foreign Minister of Peru (December 2003–August 2005), interview with author, Lima, Peru, 4 March 2008; Ronald Bruce St John, *Toledo's Peru: Vision and Reality* (Gainesville, FL, 2010), 137–42, 147–53.
36 Alejandro Toledo Manrique, President of Peru (2001–6), interview with author, Palo Alto, California, 12 September 2008; St John, *Toledo's Peru*, 142–47, 153–60.
37 Alejandro Toledo Manrique, President of Peru (2001–6), interviews with author, Lima, Peru, 9 May 2003 and 19 April 2006; St John, *Toledo's Peru*, 174–76.
38 Allan Wagner Tizón, Foreign Minister of Peru (1985–88, July 2002–December 2003), interview with author, Lima, Peru, 9 May 2003; Óscar Maúrtua de Romaña, Foreign Minister of Peru (August 2005–July 2006), interview with author, Lima, Peru, 18 April 2006; St John, *Toledo's Peru*, 176–80.
39 Cynthia McClintock, 'An Unlikely Comeback in Peru,' *Journal of Democracy*, Volume 17, Number 4 (2006), 107; 'Barack Obama felicitó a Alan García: 'El Perú ha tenido un éxito extraordinario,' *El Comercio*, 1 June 2010.
40 'Equipo peruano inició el análisis de la contramemoria chilena,' *El Comercio*, 12 March 2010; 'Rafael Correa: "La Paz entre Ecuador y el Perú es irreversible",' *El Comercio*, 9 June 2010.
41 'Alan García: "Estoy satisfecho de que el presidente Lula salido a empuñar la bandera de la integración," ' *El Comercio*, 16 June 2010; 'Jefe del Comando Conjunto de las FF.AA. descartó presencia de las FARC en territorio peruano,' *El Comercio*, 3 August 2010.
42 'El Perú y Venezuela tendrán relaciones plenas con llegada de embajador,' *El Comercio*, 12 August 2009; "Evo Morales no tiene autoridad para criticar al Perú",' *El Comercio*, 1 October 2009.
43 'AGP aboga por transparencia y homologación de gasto militar,' *La República*, 4 June 2010; 'Lo positivo y negativo de los cuatro años de gestión de Alan García,' *El Comercio*, 11 July 2010.

17

Nigeria

The foreign policy of a putative African Power

Cyril I. Obi

In a recent forum at the Council for Foreign Relations in Washington, DC, Nigeria's president, Goodluck Jonathan, was quoted as expressing the view that 'our main focus is to see that at least within the continent of Africa, we have true democracies'.[1] He was alluding to the two main strands of continuity in his country's foreign policy: Nigeria's connection of its national interest to an Afrocentric external policy thrust; and its African leadership claims within the global context. Thus, in spite of its domestic challenges, the country projects itself as a key player in Africa and in international politics.

Nigeria is potentially the richest country in Africa given its vast oil and gas reserves, natural wealth, large population, diverse cultures and multiethnicity, and vast reservoir of highly skilled professionals and educated people within the country and in the diaspora. Underscoring Nigeria's centrality to the energy security interests of the world's emerging and established Powers, these qualities make it the continent's leading oil producer and regional Power.[2] Nigeria exports an estimated 40 percent of its oil to the United States (it is its fifth largest supplier of crude) whilst also accounting for between 10 and 12 percent of American oil imports. Nigeria is similarly critical to the oil supplies to the European Union (EU) and the emerging Asian Powers of China and India. But despite abundant natural and human resources,[3] the majority of Nigerians are poor in the context of widening inequalities, which has some implications for the country's diplomacy.

Externally, Nigeria has discharged itself fairly well in international peace-keeping under the auspices of the United Nations (UN), the African Union (AU), and the Economic Community of West African States' (ECOWAS) peacekeeping mission, ECOMOG. Providing leadership in the establishment of ECOWAS and ECOMOG, Lagos (later Abuja) proved crucial in peace and security, regional integration, and development in its immediate sub-region and the rest of the continent.[4] If anything, Nigeria has in the past fifty years consistently played a leadership role based on the Afrocentric principles on which its foreign policy has been based. The Nigerian case presents two specific challenges that lay in the evolution of the country's foreign policy: notions of national security and power; and a 'manifest destiny' to act as a regional Power and African leader.

The end of the Cold War has created new challenges in Africa that have called for a greater commitment to the demands for regional development, democratic accountability, conflict resolution, security, and global peace. A transforming regional and global context has posed more challenges to Nigeria's leadership role in the continent, as Africa grapples for a place of increased reckoning in an emerging post-Cold War international order. However, changes at the domestic level (economic, political, and social) as well as those attendant by the end of the Cold War and increased globalisation with the emergence of some non-state transnational actors and the blurring of the lines between the domestic, regional, and global spheres, and the post-9/11 international security agenda, also define the current challenges confronting the country.[5] These underscore the view recently expressed that the country 'most urgently needs a new foreign policy architecture'.[6]

This view is important given the challenges that have faced Nigeria since the return to civilian rule in 1999, and the high domestic and international expectations that the country would rise to the occasion and see the promise of its immense potential translated into leadership for African development, integration, peace, and security. Also relevant is Nigeria's response, on one hand, to global economic multipolarity represented by the emergence of Brazil, Russia, China, and India as 'new' Powers in the context of traditional relations with 'old' Western Powers and, on the other, the hegemonic unipolarity of the United States as the world's surviving superpower. There is evidence that Nigeria is broadening its relations through new economic partnerships with the emerging Asian giants of China and India even although it remains strongly connected to its Western economic partners.

What the foregoing does imply is that there are constants and changes in the way Nigeria has responded to the transformation of the domestic and international contexts. The constants relate to the country's definition of its national interests, despite changes devolving from the emerging post-Cold War world order. Much has depended on the primacy of the domestic structure in shaping of Nigeria's foreign policy. However, it is equally important that in some respects, this foreign policy has 'defied' its domestic base; but this process has usually been largely *ad hoc*, reactive, and personality driven, relying on providential national endowments or international expectations of Nigeria as one of Africa's most influential states. The foreign policy of this putative Power is therefore shaped by its domestic, regional, and global contexts.

The historical context of Nigeria's foreign policy is intimately intertwined with the origins and evolution of the Nigerian state. It can be traced to the long-standing trade and diplomatic relations dating as far back as the fifteenth century or earlier: between kingdoms and city-states of what later became Nigeria and merchants from Britain, Holland, Portugal, Spain, and France, or the earlier trans-Saharan trade with North Africa. After the abolition of the trans-Atlantic slave trade and its replacement with legitimate trade in the nineteenth century, these city-states and kingdoms were to be later forcibly annexed into the Nigerian colony by Britain. The country was the product of what in global imperial history could be described as 'the scramble for Africa', when the major European Powers met in Berlin in 1884–85 to determine the principles for carving up both the continent and its wealth amongst themselves. Colonialism implied the destruction of indigenous institutions and the subordination of the 'foreign policies' of the precolonial 'Nigerian' entities such as the Benin and Oyo empires, the Sokoto Caliphate, and the Niger Delta city-states of Bonny and Brass to British Imperial power. Under colonial rule, 'Nigeria' lost the power to formulate its 'foreign policy' to the British. It was not until the mid-1950s when Nigeria's independence was imminent that the British began to organise a Nigerian foreign-policy apparatus.[7]

The first set of Nigerian diplomatic officers were trained in a British university and attached to various British embassies and high commissions.[8] The institutional arm of Nigeria's foreign policy was the Ministry of Foreign and Commonwealth Relations. Becoming the Ministry of External Affairs in 1963, it was headed formally by a minister advised by a permanent secretary, deputy-permanent secretary, and divisional heads.[9] However, the Prime Minister, Sir Abubakar Tafawa Balewa, largely acted as his own External Affairs minister. To assist him, he had a foreign policy elite mainly made up of ministry officials as well as members of his party, the Northern People's Congress (NPC). Other ministries that made inputs into the policy formulation process were those of Finance, Defence, Trade, Education, Industry, Economic Development, and Information.

In July 1961, Jaja Wachuku was appointed Minister of External Affairs, although the premier was 'still Super Foreign Affairs Minister'.[10] This course was partly because Wachuku came from a junior coalition partner, the National Council of Nigerian Citizens, and lacked the clout possessed by NPC members. It is hardly surprising therefore that Wachuku did not last long and subsequently lost his portfolio in 1964. Because of Belawa's influence over foreign policy, his values and attitudes rubbed off on the institutions and processes of Nigeria's foreign policy. And they did so against the background of the regionalised and divisive ethnocentric politics of the First Republic and the 'radical' posture of the opposition to foreign-policy matters. Balewa's foreign policy was conservative, pro-British, and pro-Western. Indeed, in one of his earliest speeches, he allegedly enthused that: 'We are grateful to the British … who we have known as masters, then as leaders, and finally as partners, but always as friends'.[11]

Apart from the prime minister's ideological disposition, the institutions and processes of foreign-policy formulation were poorly organised.[12] Divisions within the populace and the low level of knowledge about international affairs militated against any concerted or organised public input into the policy formulation process. Although Nigeria was a member of the Non-Aligned Movement and the Organization of African Unity (OAU), and contributed troops to United States peace-keeping operations in Congo, its foreign policy remained moderate and pro-Western until the outbreak of the Nigerian Civil War (1967–70). This war occurred because Biafra, the eastern region of the country, sought independence. During the war, some elements within government felt that the Western Powers were not doing enough to help crush Biafran secession and reached out to the Soviet Union and Eastern bloc countries. Although Nigeria bought arms from the Soviet Union and some East bloc countries during the war, trade levels remained relatively low and did not assume ideological dimensions.

In the evolution of Nigeria's foreign-policy formulation and implementation before the return to civilian rule in 1999, 'no other corporate group or national institution in Nigeria has influenced the country's foreign policy to the same extent and in the same manner that the Nigerian military has done'.[13] Under General Gowon (1966–75), Nigeria diffused its pro-Western foreign-policy orientation based largely on the lessons of the Nigerian civil war.[14] This development implied building a strong regional bulwark around Nigeria and reducing external economic dependence through policies of good neighbourliness and regional integration. Apart from the oil-buoyed 'radical pan-Africanist' episode in the Murtala-Obasanjo military era (1975–79), when a Nigerian foreign-policy elite largely based in the Cabinet Office and universities 'crossed swords' with the West over apartheid South Africa and Namibia and the decolonisation of Lusophone Africa (and when General Sanni Abacha in the 1990s retaliated against alleged Western lack of understanding and interference in Nigeria's internal affairs), Nigeria's foreign policy has more often than not been framed in broadly pro-Western terms.

This process meant having cordial relations with Western Powers and pragmatic ones with the Soviet Union and its East bloc allies during the Cold War. Since the end of the Cold War, cordial relations with the Western Powers have remained more or less at the same level, whilst those with the former East bloc Powers declined. In its place, the emergent Asian powers of China and India have made a strong showing in Nigeria's external relations. However, it is too early to determine fully what the impact of Nigeria's new engagement with the emerging Asian Powers will have on its traditional ties with the West.[15]

In this context, the principles of Nigeria's foreign policy are crucial. They refer to the philosophical underpinnings of policy, the international objectives of the state, and the basic approaches and areas of emphasis in Nigeria's interaction with the international environment.[16] It has been noted that the main objective of 'Nigeria's foreign policy is to promote and protect the country's national interests in its interactions with the outside world and its relations with specific countries'.[17] Inherent in determining the national interest is Nigeria's organic link to Africa's interests in what is referred to as the 'Africa centre-piece doctrine'. Overall, the principles thus derived have remained largely unchanged over time and have defined the broad framework for Nigeria's foreign policy. The design of policy has occurred around 'concentric circles' in which the core interest is embedded, but with some modifications and shifting priorities linked to the personalities of various heads of state and in response to changes in the domestic, regional, and international contexts.

Since 1999, Nigeria has been instrumental in transforming the OAU into the AU, the fast-tracking of the ECOWAS integration project, and the New Partnership for Africa's Development (NEPAD), which seeks a new relationship with the G8 countries on the basis of an African-owned development initiative. Nigeria's foreign policy under the Obasanjo presidency (1999–2007) reflected the personal style of the President, based on his prominent international profile as an African statesman, providing regional leadership as well as representing the African 'presence' at global forums. After Obasanjo, the Yar' Adua presidency pursued what was referred to as 'citizen-diplomacy'. It was based on prioritising the interest of the citizen in the country's interaction with the international community, a notion grounded in a definition of Nigeria's national interests. To drive this point home, Nigeria's former Foreign Affairs Minister, Ojo Maduekwe, framed the fundamental challenge of a 'citizen-centred' diplomacy in the question: 'how does it benefit Nigeria and Nigerians?'; and he noted that 'it is a way of strengthening our commitment to Africa'.[18] Nigeria's foreign policy under President Jonathan has largely kept to the traditional principles.

Since 1999, Nigeria's foreign policy has combined a measure of pragmatism and realism with continuity. It has also engaged the emerging post-Cold War international order that is dominated by processes of globalisation and transnationalisation, particularly as they relate to regional security, peace and development, and the projection of national interests on to the national stage. The new challenge appears to be how Nigeria can effectively reorganise itself internally to provide leadership for Africa's survival and development in a rapidly globalising world. Although largely resting on the foregoing theoretical basis, the ability of Nigeria's foreign policy to respond to these challenges is dependent on the domestic context, national endowments such as oil, the fortunes of which have been fluctuating with adverse implications for the economy, and the capacity and commitment of the foreign-policy elite. Here the mantle of the urgent task of generating new ideas and thinking to enable Nigeria to meet its external challenges has fallen upon the elite.

The conceptual issues hinge upon the nature of the Nigerian state (whose institutions define the principles that underpin its foreign policy) and the policies that promote the national interest. Largely resting on a realist approach to international relations, Nigeria's foreign policy seeks to protect and project the country's core values and maximise its national interests in a competitive regional and global environment. The Nigerian state is a sovereign political entity. Through its laws and policies, it works for the good governance, welfare, defence, and security of Nigerians. In terms of the Eastonian model, the Nigerian state should be a neutral umpire, mediating competing demands and claims made on it from within, and also from outside.[19] Foreign policy could be said to approximate the state's output and feedback loop, based on demands placed on it by the foreign-policy elite, the public, as well as the response to international constraints or the global environment.

In reality Nigeria's state role in decision-making is more complex depending on its capacity and its relationship with the domestic structure and dominant elite. Rather than being a neutral umpire, the Nigerian state has limited autonomy: '… the state is institutionally constituted in such a way that it enjoys little independence from the social classes, particularly the hegemonic class, and so is immersed in the struggle of the classes'.[20] The state has operated largely as an arena of power jostling amongst several factions of the dominant elite. Thus, the stakes in controlling power are high, and state institutions tend to be dominated by the faction in power, limiting state autonomy with regard to its relations with the larger society. The implication of the limited autonomy of the Nigerian state is that it tends to favour the dominant elite, which is divided along ethnic, religious, and regional lines, but united in the quest for power and control of public resources. Given that its politics is largely 'normless', it has fed into deep alienation and distrust amongst competitors and the wider populace. It has also fuelled a 'politics of anxiety' and an obsession with gaining power at any cost, thus leading to instability and crisis.[21]

The limited autonomy of the Nigerian state also reflects its relationship with external economic actors. The economy has remained monocultural, dependent largely on oil exports whilst also acting as a ready market for the manufactured goods of the world's Powers. Foreign dominance of the economy, particularly the strategic oil sector, exposes the dependency of the state, moreso as the ruling elite acts as a partner of foreign capital whose central role in the local economy has direct implications for Nigeria's autonomy and foreign policy.[22]

Since the 1970s, oil has accounted for over 80 percent of Nigerian federal revenues, and over 90 percent of foreign exchange earnings.[23] Although from the 1970s the Government took majority ownership in oil company investments in Nigeria's petroleum industry through joint ventures and other oil contracts, oil multinationals have largely operated an enclave oil industry with little or no linkages to other sectors of the economy. Given its strategic role in Nigeria's political economy, oil has become a volatile issue both with regard to national politics, and the relationship between the local people in the oil-producing communities and the oil companies. With an oil-dependent monocultural economy that is weighed down by massive developmental challenges, Nigeria can ill afford to confront any major Power that buys or imports the bulk of its petroleum and gas. Even though these Powers also depend on Nigerian oil, the fact that their multinationals control the country's oil industry tips the balance of power in their favour. Thus, Nigeria's foreign policy has to some extent been reliant on the oil factor.

This factor served Nigeria well during the 1970s oil boom, when the country assumed the status of a 'frontline state' and provided leadership for the international campaign against apartheid in South Africa and for the independence of African countries still under the yoke of colonialism. However by the late 1990s, diminished oil clout saw a tactical retreat from expensive regional peacekeeping campaigns as reduced oil revenues were directed towards addressing urgent domestic priorities. The internationalisation of oil also provided a channel for Niger Delta groups to vent their grievances, globalise local protests and struggles, and bypass the state to connect the international community.

Consequently, the Nigerian state is an unstable policy environment. More fundamental perhaps is that the ruling elite have not been able to hegemonise its rule or homogenise or fully resolve Nigeria's nation-state and citizenship challenges. Thus, it is difficult to refer to a Nigerian nation-state, as the Government presides over a multiplicity of ethnic 'nations', whilst, since the 1990s, the integrative nation-state project begun after the Nigerian civil war in 1970 has been buffeted by demands for federal restructuring, decentralisation, and resource control. The Nigerian state therefore cannot in real terms articulate and implement a foreign policy that is wholly independent, neutral, or autonomous. An example can be seen from the challenges to the state by initially peaceful protests in the Niger Delta. Such protests against the Government and oil companies in the early 1990s began with the Movement for the Survival of Ogoni People (MOSOP), which adopted a strategy of the internationalising its protests and demands, and bypassing the Nigerian state, to appeal directly to a global audience.

Although the non-violent MOSOP was dealt a hard blow when nine of its leaders were hanged on the orders of a military tribunal in November 1995, a decade later, other ethnic minority organisations like the insurgent Movement for the Emancipation of the Niger Delta followed the path of protest; this time a repertoire of violence in pursuit of its objectives led to full-scale insurgency by militias targeting oil installations and Government forces.[24] The turn to violence in the Niger Delta, which also targets the global media,[25] has made state response problematic. Whilst the insurgency has been largely brought under control by combined military operations and an amnesty to militias willing to lay down their arms, the situation is far from stable. The legitimacy of the Nigerian state has been continuously questioned in the Niger Delta by groups that perceive the state–oil multinational business partnership as one of the main sources of their suffering and poverty, and a target for demands, protests, and attack; Nigeria's oil-dependent foreign policy continues to be influenced by contradictions and trends in its monocultural economic base and its related politics. In such a troubled context in which state legitimacy is questioned and challenged, foreign policy is constrained by domestic realities.

The domestic context provides a basis for understanding the institutions and processes of foreign-policy formulation in Nigeria. In a seminal work, Aforka Nweke refers to the 'domestic structure' as a 'complex entity both human and non-human, organised in a system of roles, interests and actions interacting within the internal and external processes which link one state with other states.'[26] He identifies four forces: cultural and historical issues; socioeconomic structure; class formation and relations; and institutional framework and processes. The first three provide the context for the fourth. Since institutions and processes do not function in a vacuum, it is apposite to dwell on the social and cultural context to facilitate better an evaluation of the 'framework' of policy.[27]

Nigeria is a multireligious and multiethnic society, which has implications for its domestic structure. The politicisation of religious and ethnic differences creates divisions that undermine national unity and cohesion, which in turn limit foreign-policy effectiveness. At the same time, some policy decisions may alienate certain sections of the country, sometimes leading to controversy, friction, and unnecessary tension. An example involved the decision of Nigeria under the Babangida administration to join the Organization of Islamic Conference. This choice caused some tension in the multireligious, multiethnic domestic context, igniting a debate about the secularity of the Nigerian state and the need to avoid giving the impression that Nigeria had adopted a particular faith as a state religion. The debate recurred after Nigeria returned to democratic rule in 1999 and some states in the northern part of the country extended the application of Islamic law beyond civil to criminal law. Tensions and even religious conflict emerged in some states, suggesting that the country had to devote time and resources to resolving such domestic issues, rather than embark on rather costly foreign adventures.

It terms of socioeconomic structure, Nigeria is a class society dominated by a relatively small elite with strong connections to the state, the oil economy, and international capital. Because of Nigeria's origins as a colonial state, and the divisions sown amongst the elite by regionalism, ethnicity, and personal rivalries, it has been difficult for this group to reach a clear consensus about broadly acceptable national goals. This process is further compounded by distrust and zero-sum competition over power and resources at the national level. This elite has been variously criticised as corrupt, inept, and visionless. Indeed, in about four decades of Nigeria's existence, it has not been able to articulate properly a national ideology, beyond broad references to national development and, now, deregulation, democracy, and market-led growth. It has not engaged in any far-reaching grassroots mobilisation or consultation directed at popularising or legitimising its ideological orientation. The combination of the character of Nigeria's ruling elite and the weak and extraverted nature of the oil economy severely limits the amount of power the nation can project internationally.

Closely related is the issue of class formation and relations. Under colonialism, a Western-educated emergent elite began to see themselves as the natural successors to the British. When the

Second War World ended and Nigerian nationalism was at its peak, elite-led political parties engaged in constitutional talks with the British on the transfer of power. The political elite were divided along ethnoregional lines and lacked a strong economic base *vis-à-vis* British and European firms. Thus, they turned to the state to provide the much-needed economic base for the class formation project. The legacy of this relationship that has been further compounded by the oil-dependent and *rentier* nature of the Nigerian economy is two-fold: high levels of capital flight, corruption, and economic dependency; and a tendency to foster a policy environment that gives primacy to the preservation of the status quo.

On the political front, elite strategy to use ethnicity and religion to mobilise support amongst the people, creating and nurturing ethnoreligious cleavages, has weakened societal cohesion over a long period. Ethnicity featured as a central factor in the political instability of Nigeria's First Republic (1960–66), which was violently overthrown by the military and contributed to the outbreak of civil war. Despite several post-war government policies directed at promoting unity amongst the country's diverse ethnic groups, ethnicity remains a divisive issue, usually the result of manipulation by elites engaging in competition for power and public office. Accordingly, the 'national interest that the formal foreign policy machinery seeks to promote is often subverted internally, or supported by insufficient domestic consensus'.[28]

Another domestic factor relevant to Nigerian foreign policy is that of leadership. Given the socioeconomic and political context described earlier, the head of state has considerable leverage over the content and direction of diplomacy. Thus, the personality of the president reflects in the nature of foreign policy. General Murtala Mohammed is remembered for his forceful pan-African foreign policy in the 1970s, when Nigeria took a frontline position in the liberation of Southern African countries then under colonial rule. This logic underlined policy under General Abacha, whose actions, including the abrupt aborting of a democratic transition programme and the hanging of the 'Ogoni Nine', contributed to the international isolation of the country. However, from 1999 to 2007, drawing on his earlier status as a military head of state, an African statesman who helped end apartheid in South Africa, and a member of missions to other African trouble spots, President Obasanjo's active personal diplomacy featured prominently in Nigeria's foreign policy. In his second coming as a head of state, Obasanjo proved instrumental to ECOWAS' success in bringing peace to Sierra Leone and Liberia, as well as the international endorsement of the NEPAD. However his successors, Yar'Adua and Jonathan, have kept a much lower profile with a less-robust foreign policy.

Analysis of the domestic structure would be incomplete without focusing on three of the institutions that are largely responsible for the formulation of Nigeria's foreign policy: the Ministry of Foreign Affairs, the Presidential Advisory Council on International Relations (PACIR), and the Nigerian Institute of International Affairs (NIIA). The Ministry of Foreign Affairs is the main institution for foreign-policy formulation. It operates at essentially two levels: within the cabinet or federal executive council or at the presidential level. The Minister for Foreign Affairs acts as the main presidential adviser on foreign matters. Administrative issues are handled by the Permanent Secretary, who is often assisted by a deputy, and other officials. Under some administrations, apart from the main Minister for Foreign Affairs, there is also a Minister of State for Foreign Affairs.[29]

In its early phase the Ministry was headed by a bureaucrat, the Permanent Secretary, assisted by the Deputy-Permanent Secretary and heads of divisions. However between 1968 and 1969, there were two Permanent Secretaries; and it reached a point in the 1980s and 1990s when there was the main Minister, a Minister of State, a Permanent Secretary as Director-General, and five others of the same rank overseeing five regions. In the 1960s, the Ministry comprised eleven divisions based on the functional and geographical classification of their responsibilities and activities.[30] These divisions were headed by First Secretaries. Recruitment of personnel was done through the Federal Public Service Commission, with the presence and involvement of top Ministry officials. In terms of policy formulation, much depends on the relationship between the President and the Foreign Affairs Minister.[31] Policy could be initiated from within the Ministry and articulated by the Minister in the form of advice to the President on special foreign-policy issues. On the other hand, the President may seek the Ministry's opinion on some issues. But in the final analysis, after consulting with the Minister for Foreign Affairs and other related ministries, experts, and advisers, the President ultimately formulates policy.

The PACIR is a relatively recent creation. Established by Obasanjo in 2001, it comprises distinguished Nigerians widely respected for their experience and expertise in the fields of diplomacy and international affairs. Their assignment is purely non-stipendiary, implying that they work not for personal gain, but in the spirit of selfless service to the Nigerian nation. PACIR's main objective was to provide alternative policy options for the President.[32] The Council is chaired by Chief Emeka Anyaoku, a former Minister for Foreign Affairs and retired Secretary-General of the Commonwealth. Other members include Ambassador Hamzat Ahmadu, Ambassador Jibrin Chinade, Ambassador Akporode Clark, Professor U. Joy Ogwu, Nigeria's Permanent Representative to the United Nations, and Professor 'Jide Osuntokun, Dean of the College of Humanities, Redeemers University, Mowe, Nigeria.

The Council meets periodically to brainstorm on issues pertinent to Nigeria's foreign policy or in response to specific presidential requests. It meets with the President to review international developments, particularly in the Commonwealth and Africa,[33] and examine policy options. According to Professor Osuntokun, its advice and recommendations led to the restructuring and rationalisation of the Ministry of Foreign Affairs, streamlining foreign-policy institutions, and reducing the number of Nigeria's embassies in ways that promote professionalism, efficiency, and cost cutting.[34] In a related sense, the Council has advocated for professionalising the Ministry of Foreign Affairs and limiting the number of politicians appointed to diplomatic positions. However, two points stand clear. This is not the first time a Nigerian President has established an advisory body on international affairs, even if it is the first time it has assumed such a prominent profile. And, second, PCIR still remains advisory. In the final analysis, the President may decide to use or reject their inputs.

Established in 1961 by a group of Nigerians with support from the Prime Minister, NIIA straddles the fields of research and foreign policy. Very much in the tradition of the Royal Institute of International Affairs in Britain, it seeks to define Nigeria's international role.[35] The Institute recruited its staff from the mid-1960s onwards and, by 1971, the federal Government took over. This action reflected the mood of post-civil war nationalism when Nigerian military rulers had learnt to appreciate the relevance of informed opinion and research on the policy process. In fundamental terms, therefore, NIIA is a policy-research body. Its core activities revolve around the Research and Studies Department, which conducts research and produces policy papers for Government, organises policy dialogues and conferences, seminars, roundtables, and workshops. It also publishes books, monographs, and a journal. Policy papers are produced either upon request or in anticipation of international events and trends relevant to Nigeria's foreign policy.

The Institute's Directors-General and Research Fellows serve on Special Government Committees and official delegations to various multilateral forums. NIIA has been able to intellectualise the discourse of Nigerian foreign policy and play a role in the articulation of Nigeria's role in Africa, including West Africa; and at a point, it contributed to the debate on economic diplomacy, which in the late 1980s defined the new emphasis in Nigeria's external relations.[36] Although little doubt exists that NIIA makes inputs into the policy process, it must be emphasised that its role is complementary and supportive of that process. Much depends on the relationship between the Director-General and the President in ensuring that the Institute makes inputs into the foreign-policy process.[37]

During the Cold War, Nigeria maintained an official policy of non-alignment, straddling between a moderate foreign policy underpinned by the principle of 'concentric circles or rings'[38] Afrocentric principles focused first on the country's immediate neighborhood (West Africa), then Africa and the world. However, the end of the Cold War threw up specific challenges. These were related to an initial relative decline in Africa's strategic significance following the collapse of both the Soviet Union and, with advance of multiparty democracy, most of Africa's one-party military or authoritarian regimes. A rising tide of intrastate conflicts and state collapse in some countries in West Africa, the Horn, and the Great Lakes region, amongst others, contributed to responses by African regional organisations (originally designed to address market integration and regional development) to the challenge of conflict resolution, peace-keeping, and security within the rubric of 'African solutions to African problems'.

Nigeria's response to such emerging regional challenges is well documented.[39] It played a key role in establishing ECOMOG, the West African peace-keeping force that contributed to the ending of civil war in Liberia and Sierra Leone, and the launch of a sophisticated mechanism for West African regional peace and security.[40] The country also responded to emerging transnational security threats in the sub-region by contributing to ECOWAS initiatives and protocols against the proliferation of small arms, human trafficking, and financial crimes.[41] Indications so far are that Nigeria and ECOWAS 'will need to respond more proactively to transnational and cross-border crimes and risks alongside intrastate conflicts'.[42] As noted earlier, Nigeria's influence goes beyond West Africa to include other regions of the continent. Thus, Nigeria's contribution to the transformation of the OAU into the AU in 2002, the drawing up of the NEPAD document as a strategy of regional economic cooperation and international development, and numerous conflict resolution and peace missions on the continent. In the emerging post-Cold War order, Nigeria's policy towards its immediate sub-region and the rest of Africa remains unchanged, even if the ongoing transformations demand more innovation and clearer definition of the principles that shape the country's Afrocentric policy.

Although the national and pan-Africanist underpinnings of Nigeria's foreign policy sometimes conflict with the national interests of Western Powers in Africa, several developments since the end of the Cold War have ensured more continuity, rather than radical shifts in traditionally close ties. These developments include Nigeria's increased strategic importance as Africa's most populous country and largest democracy, and its status as a state central to regional stability, security, and development. As such, the United States views Nigeria both as a Power crucial to promoting electoral democracy on the African continent and a strategic ally.[43] As a source of growing oil and gas supplies to the Western Powers, especially the United States and the EU, Nigeria is vital to Western national energy security interests. Two American oil giants (Chevron-Texaco and Exxon-Mobil) hold substantial investments in Nigeria's oilfields. From Nigeria's perspective, the United States is also an important strategic and economic partner; but this relationship is based on an understanding that such a partnership should not be taken for granted or be at the expense of Nigeria's national interests and sovereignty. Also there is a large immigrant Nigerian population in the United States with some interest in American policies towards Nigeria.

Although marked by ups and downs, Nigeria's relations with the EU have been generally warm, underlined in the case of Anglo-Nigerian relations by close economic, sociocultural, and people-to-people ties. Royal Dutch Shell, the largest corporate producer of Nigeria's oil, is partly British-owned. Nigeria's relations with Germany, Italy, and France have also been largely economic, although elements of cultural ties are developing rapidly. Nigeria's location in the oil-rich Gulf of Guinea, coupled with its influence on regional security and development in Africa in a post-9/11 world, has meant that its relations with the West have been underlined by mutual security interests and cooperation. Nigeria is partnering in several American-led security programmes on the continent targeting transnational threats in the Sahel region and the Gulf of Guinea.[44] It could be argued that security and development form the pillars of relations in an emerging post-Cold war era in West Africa.

Although Nigeria has had long-standing diplomatic ties with China since 1972 and India since 1960, the recent upswing in relations is linked to openings resulting from the decade of structural adjustment (the mid-1980s to mid-1990s) and Nigeria's return to democratic rule in 1999. This period coincided with the growing economic strength of both China and India, whose accelerated economies saw a rise in demand for overseas energy sources, the development of markets for manufacturers, and a quest for global influence. Africa's place in this calculus was one of a 'natural ally' both for South–South solidarity and a history of struggle against external domination and underdevelopment. On the Nigerian side, the ruling elite was eager to reach out to both Powers to attract investment and because of the 'no-strings-attached' development cooperation offered by China, the latter was preferred to the stringent conditions imposed by Western donors and international financial institutions.

After visits by top-level officials on all sides, trade between Nigeria and both Asian Powers has increased tremendously. Whereas Nigeria–India trade figures for 2009 have been estimated at US $10.5 billion,[45] making Nigeria India's largest trading partner in Africa, Nigeria – China trade has been estimated at US$6.5 billion.[46] However, both are less than the figures for Nigeria's trade with the United States and EU. China has gained the upper hand over its Asian rival, particularly with regard to Nigerian oil. The Chinese National Overseas Oil Corporation acquired a 45 percent stake in an offshore oil bloc in 2005;[47] and in 2009 another Chinese oil company, Sinopec, acquired offshore oilfields previously owned by Swiss-controlled Addax Oil Nigeria, where oil was reportedly struck in 2010.[48]

China has also signed a US$23 billion deal with the Nigerian Government to build three new refineries and a petrochemical plant in the country.[49] Although Nigeria currently accounts for between 8 and 12 percent of India's oil imports, Indian state oil corporations have not been so successful as their Chinese counterparts in acquiring concessions in Nigeria. Rather, their efforts have been limited to guarantees for increased oil supplies, whilst biding their time to win concessions. Although the last decade witnessed a rapid expansion in Chinese and Indian trade and investment, neither matches the economic clout of Western interests in Nigeria. However, they present an alternative and some space for Nigeria to negotiate and obtain more advantageous trade and economic terms in line with its national interests. In terms of the broader security-strategic framework, Chinese and Indian bilateral engagements with Nigeria have largely remained economic and cultural.

Nigeria possesses the potential resources and power, as well as institutions, to formulate a vibrant foreign policy. The seeming constraints on foreign-policy institutions and processes lay more in domestic factors and challenges. As noted earlier, the notion of national interest is problematic because of domestic socioeconomic challenges, the politicisation of cultural and ethnic diversities, lack of coherence amongst political elites, and the impact of globalisation on the society, including transnational threats that transcend national borders. The rather elitist and centralised policy-making structure also gives the country's foreign policy a distant and personalised character, the fortunes of which are inextricably linked to the skills and actions of those at the helm of affairs.

In terms of its possibilities, Nigeria's foreign policy remains critical to regional and pan-continental unity and development.[50] This African giant, if unfettered by its domestic contradictions and with a committed and visionary leadership, could act as an anchor for a robust and responsive Africa in the context of a highly competitive post-Cold War world. As Nigeria continues to grapple with its own domestic challenges, whilst at the same time projecting itself within its immediate sub-region and Africa as a pivotal state and regional Power, the fundamental principles of its foreign policy have remained largely unchanged. However, its nature, priorities, and strategies are being adjusted and require radical reinvention to define better national interests and effectively engage domestic and external challenges in the context of a complex and rapidly transforming world.

Notes

1 Cited in Editorial, Next (17 April 2010): http://234next.com/csp/cms/sites/Next/Home/5556059-146/nigerias_foreign_policy-.csp.
2 Cyril Obi, 'Scrambling for Oil in West Africa', in Roger Southall and Henning Melber, eds., A New Scramble for Africa (Scottsville, 2009).
3 Eghosa Osaghae, Crippled Giant: Nigeria Since Independence (London, 1998).
4 Cyril Obi, 'Economic Community of West African States on the Ground: Comparing Peacekeeping in Liberia, Sierra Leone, Guinea Bissau and Cote D'Ivoire', in Fredrik Söderbaum and Rodrigo Tavares, eds., Regional Organizations in African Security (London, New York, 2010), 52–54.
5 Cyril Obi, 'Nigeria's foreign policy and transnational security challenges in West Africa', Journal of Contemporary African Studies, 26(2008), 183–90.
6 Olu Adeniji, 'Foreword', in Adekeye Adebajo and Raufu Mustapha, eds., Gulliver's Troubles: Nigeria's Foreign Policy after the Cold War (Scottsville, 2008), xix.
7 Gordon Idang, Nigeria's Internal Politics and Foreign Policy (1960–1966) (Ibadan, 1973), 109.
8 Ibid., 107; Olu Adediji, 'Implementation and Administration of Foreign Policy: A Note on the Relationship between the Ministry of External Affairs and the Nigerian Missions Abroad', in Gabriel Olusanya and Rafiu Akindele, eds., The Structure and Processes of Foreign Policy Making and Implementation 1960–1990 (Lagos, 1990), 143–58.
9 Idang, Foreign Policy, 107–8.
10 Ibid., 113.
11 Ibid., 49.
12 Ibid., 113.
13 W. Alade Fawole, Nigeria's External Relations and Foreign Policy Under Military Rule (1966–1999) (Ile-Ife, 2003), 1.
14 Olajide Aluko, Essays in Nigerian Foreign Policy (London, 1981), 117–28.
15 Cyril Obi, 'African oil in the energy and security calculations of China and India', in Fantu Cheru and Cyril Obi, eds., The Rise of China and India in Africa (London, 2010), 190–91.
16 B. Okolo, 'Assessing the Principles of Nigerian Foreign Policy', in Stephen Olugbemi, ed., Alternative Political Futures for Nigeria (Lagos, 1987), 483–505.
17 Gabriel Olusanya and Rafiu Akindele, 'The Fundamentals of Nigeria's Foreign Policy and External Economic Relations', in Gabriel Olusanya and Rafiu Akindele, eds., Nigeria's External Relations: The First Twenty Five Years (Ibadan, 1986), 2.
18 Quoted in Chuks Okocha and Onwuka Nzeshi, 'Nigeria: Country to Adopt Citizenship Diplomacy', This Day (12 September 2007).
19 The Eastonian model distinguishes between system inputs and system outputs and, in the political process, these differences are apparent between policy formulation and policy implementation. See David Easton, A Systems Analysis of Political Li/e (New York, 1965).
20 Claude Ake, 'The Nigerian state: antimonies of a periphery formation', in Claude Ake, ed., Political Economy of Nigeria (London, Lagos, Longmans, 1985), 9.
21 Ibid., 10.
22 Ibid.
23 Cyril Obi, 'The Politics of the Nigerian Oil Industry: Implications for Environmental Governance', in Akinjide Osuntokun, ed., Democracy and Sustainable Development in Nigeria (Lagos, 2002).
24 Cyril Obi, 'Oil extraction, dispossession, resistance and conflict in the Niger Delta', Canadian Journal of International Affairs, 30(2010), 219–36.
25 Ibid.

26 Aforka Nweke, 'The Domestic Structure and Processes of Nigeria's Foreign Policy', in Olusanya and Akindele, *External Relations*, 23.

27 Ibid.

28 Abdul Raufu Mustapha, 'The three faces of Nigeria's foreign policy: Nationhood, identity and external relations', in Adekeye Adebajo and Raufu Mustapha, eds., *Gulliver's Troubles: Nigeria's Foreign Policy after the Cold War* (Scottsville, 2008). 51. Also see Rotimi Suberu, *Federalism and Ethnic Conflict in Nigeria* (Washington, DC, 2001), 9–17.

29 Idang, *Foreign Policy*.

30 Ibid., 108–9.

31 Interview, Professor Jide Osuntokun, University of Lagos and former Nigerian Ambassador to the Federal Republic of Germany, Lagos (26 June 2003).

32 Ibid.

33 Ibid.

34 Ibid.

35 A.O. Banjo, 'Nigerian Institute of International Affairs 1961–86: The Journey So Far', *NIIA Monograph Series*, Number 12 (1986).

36 Joy Ogwu, and Adebayo Olukoshi, eds., *The Economic Diplomacy of the Nigerian State*, revised edition (Lagos, 2002).

37 Interview, Professor Gabriel Olusanya, former NIIA Director-General and former Nigerian Ambassador to France (3 December 2003).

38 Idumange John, 'Re-defining Nigeria's National in World Diplomacy' (1 October 2010): www.pointblanknews.com/artopn2188.html.

39 Obi, 'Nigeria's foreign policy', 183–96; Akekeye Adebajo, *Liberia's Civil War: Nigeria, ECOMOG and Regional Security in West Africa* (Boulder, CO, 2002).

40 Obi, 'Economic Community', 51.

41 Obi, 'Nigeria's foreign policy', 92.

42 Obi, 'Economic Community', 64.

43 Gwendolyn Mikell, 'Players, policies and prospects: Nigeria-US relations', in Adebajo and Mustapha, *Gulliver's Troubles*, 283.

44 Cyril Obi, 'Terrorism in Africa: Real, emerging or imagined threats?', *African Security Review*, 15(2006); Michael Klare and Daniel Volman, 'The African oil rush and US national security', *Third World Quarterly*, 27(2006), 609–28.

45 Nigeria Factsheet, Indian High Commission, Abuja: www.indianhcabuja.com/Nigeria-Fact-Sheet.htm.

46 China Economy Blog (21 February 2010): http://ceconomy.blogspot.com/2010/02/nigeria-china-trade-reaches-65-billon.html

47 Obi, 'African oil', 185.

48 Reuters Africa, 'Sinopec Addax strike oil at Nigerian Block' (12 July 2010): http://af.reuters.com/article/investingNews/idAFJOE66B00P20100712.

49 Trevor Johnson, 'China signs $23 Billion Oil Deal with Nigeria', Global Research, (28 May 2010): www.globalresearch.ca/index.php?context=va&aid=19390.

50 Obi, 'Nigeria's foreign policy', 193–94.

18

Thailand

The enigma of bamboo diplomacy

Pavin Chachavalpongpun

Despite being a medium-sized country with an unstable political system, Thailand has long been recognised for its practice of shrewd diplomacy, which successfully served to maintain its independence throughout difficult periods in the country's history.[1] Thai leaders demonstrated that the art of diplomacy was carefully crafted not only to defend their nation from all kinds of threat, but also to raise the global Thai profile as one of the predominant players in mainland Southeast Asia. In retrospect, there are at least two major international events that put the art of Thai diplomacy to the test: the colonial period and the Second World War. These historical episodes allowed Thai leaders to sharpen their diplomatic skills as they dealt with the outside world. Siam, the former name of Thailand, was the only country in Southeast Asia never to have been officially colonised by foreign Powers.[2] It was able to escape colonialism, according to the majority of Thai historians, because of the resilience and flexibility of Thai diplomacy, buttressed by two factors: its geographical position as a buffer state between Britain and France and the far-sightedness and ingenuity of King Chulalongkorn (1868–1910).[3] The King apparently attempted to create a balance of power between two European nations by blurring the line of allegiance to make the kingdom somewhat independent. Equally sharp-witted diplomacy was continually practiced during the Second World War, when Thailand succeeded in being on both sides, the Axis and the Allies. Whereas the Phibun Songkhram Government (1936–44) formed an alliance with Japan and declared war on the United States, the Thai ambassador in Washington, Seni Pramoj, lent his support to the pro-Allied 'Free Thai' movement. At the war's end, the Free Thai movement claimed to represent the real stance of wartime Thailand, an argument broadly accepted by the Americans. This reflected a rare feat of foreign-policy flexibility. Through centuries, Thai leaders have prided themselves on a mastery of 'bamboo diplomacy'.[4]

As Thailand entered another difficult period characterised by the ideological conflict of the Cold War, Thai leaders resurrected the 'bending with the prevailing wind' strategy to cope with changes in the country's foreign affairs. The fact that the United States came to Thailand's rescue at the end of the Second World War and that it rapidly emerged as a superpower leading the Western world compelled Thailand to endorse a pro-American foreign policy. Internal and external circumstances reinforced Thailand's pro-American stance, ranging from the persistent military regimes at home to the outbreak of the communist threat in the neighborhood. The United States was content to tolerate Thailand's despotic regimes so long as Bangkok continued to implement an anti-communist foreign policy.[5] Aligning with the United States, in return, legitimised the role of the military in politics, in which protecting national security represented the most quintessential goal in the conduct of Thai diplomacy.

Hence, as the regional balance of power shifted with the fallout between the Union of Soviet Socialist Republics and China and the departure of the United States at the end of the Vietnam War, the ruling elite needed to find a new guarantor of national security. They breathed new life into the famous bamboo diplomacy, with the establishment of diplomatic relations with communist China in 1975, despite the latter previously being perceived as a threat to national security. Together with China, Thailand, as a frontline state, fully engaged in the Cambodian conflict, providing arms and ammunition to the Khmer Rouge to battle against the advancing Vietnamese menace. At the same time, Thailand sought support from the Association of Southeast Asian Nations (ASEAN), established in 1967, of which it was a founding member, to regionalise its anti-communist policy. The Thai strategy reiterates a survival technique of a developing Power on a mission to define and redefine its own national interests whenever the regional order was reorganised, to overcome certain limitations in the conduct of diplomacy, and to strike a balance in its dealings with outside Powers to ensure a degree of autonomy and create room for policy maneuvering. The post-Cold War world has witnessed a similar pattern of traditional Thai diplomacy at work, albeit under rather different and more complex circumstances that have been shaped by both the current political crisis in Thailand and the region's new geopolitical landscape.

Most studies of Thailand's diplomacy and statecraft seem to agree on one finding: the flexibility of Thai foreign policy and the ability to adjust to the altering balance of power.[6] Arne Kislenko noted that an ancient Siamese proverb likens foreign policy to the 'bamboo in the wind': always solidly rooted but flexible enough to bend whichever way the wind blows in order to survive. More than mere pragmatism, this adage reflects a long-cherished, philosophical approach to international relations, the precepts of which are very much enshrined in Thai cultural and religion.[7] The Thai traditional perception of national interests is explicit: Thai leaders have sought to maintain as far as possible national sovereignty and territorial integrity and to minimise external interference with the domestic system.[8] Without failure, the sentiment of having to safeguard national sovereignty was fortified by successive regimes. However, as a mid-range Power constrained by certain vulnerabilities, Thailand possessed a few alternatives in the determination of foreign-policy strategy.

Adopting pragmatism was one option, and it had so far proved effective. The uncertainty of international politics obliged Thailand to bend with the wind so as to retain its influence whilst managing its foreign affairs *vis-à-vis* foreign Powers and neighboring countries. For example, Siam's relations with China in ancient times, through the despatch of envoys and royal gifts (a symbol of political submission) in exchange for economic benefits reflected a high degree of pragmatism in the kingdom's foreign-policy thinking.[9] Siam was traditionally sensitive to shifts in the distribution of power. The arrival of the first Portuguese trade envoy in the kingdom of Ayutthaya in 1511 and the subsequent appearance of European merchants were an indication of a change of regional order and political landscape to the Siamese kings. China was no longer the region's supreme Power in Siamese eyes. The European colonialists represented both a real and present danger as well as an opportunity for Siamese kings. Understanding the limits and constraints of foreign policy, Siam took the stance of accommodation to appease the hegemons of the day so that it could preserve its autonomy and gain other benefits, both in its relations with foreign Powers and in its own internal power arrangement.

The key understanding of Thai foreign-policy pragmatism is that Thai leaders came to terms with their country's capabilities and acted eagerly in response to the reality, rather than to idealist goals or uninhibited ambitions. They made foreign policy based on practicality, seeing the country in terms of its history, form of government, and relationship with foreign Powers.[10] Meanwhile, they pursued a conventional strategy of adjusting to whatever stance best maintained friendly relations with Great Powers. Opportunism, alliance, and bandwagoning were vital elements of this strategy. Thai leaders also learnt to be assertive if situations permitted and to be compliant when choices in foreign policy seemed to be inadequate. The principle of pragmatism and resilience has been passed to the subsequent generations of Thai leaders in designing Thailand as a bamboo that leans with the prevailing wind. But doing so also induced a policy dilemma for Thailand.

Because of the lack of colonial experience, and unlike its neighboring countries, Thailand tended to entertain the politics of alliance usually with extraregional Powers instead of strictly upholding neutralism and non-alignment. Thai foreign policy heavily depended on the interests and policies of other Powers, whilst also taking advantage from them in the fulfilment of the country's interests. Thailand kept its open-door policy, despite some brief periods of isolationism, and invited external Powers to compete amongst themselves to win over their alliance with the kingdom. This was a component of Thailand's balance-of-power strategy. Thailand comprehended that its survival rested on the ability to bend with the wind and its appeasement of external Powers, even at the expense of occasionally compromising its own moral stance and principles.

The end of the Cold War brought about a new urgency for Thailand to reformulate its foreign policy to react more appropriately to the region's new distribution of power. Thai leaders were challenged by the reality in which the United States, a long-term guardian of Thai national security, was reducing its presence in Southeast Asia and, therefore, its influence on the region. American policy created a power vacuum, but it also paved the way for China, a rising Asian Power, to assert its role as it readjusted the regional equilibrium to its own benefit. Thailand felt that it could no longer depend on the United States alone in times of trouble. The Asian financial crisis that hit Thailand in 1997 reaffirmed this belief. Thailand was disappointed that the United States did not rush to its aid, particularly since the financial crisis was regarded as a new form of threat to the country's economic security. Instead, the Chinese and the Japanese contributed substantial amounts to the International Monetary Fund (IMF) bailout fund for Thailand.[11]

A reduced United States presence was not the only major phenomenon in the post-Cold War period. There have been a number of rising international trends that required Thailand to rethink its traditional foreign policy, which, hitherto, was primarily concerned with the state and the quest to protect its national sovereignty. The new world order is the world of multipolarity, a world with several balancing centres of power driven by the force of globalisation.[12] In Southeast Asia, the mushrooming of new regional and multilateral platforms has gradually eroded the traditional concept of state sovereignty. A corollary to this development is the diversification of actors like non-governmental organisations and multinational conglomerates, as well as increasingly important non-traditional issues and challenges such as environmental protection, humanitarian disaster relief, terrorism, and epidemics.

Under these circumstances, the need to redefine what constituted national interests to survive the latest shift in international politics was imperative. Domestic conditions equally contributed to the remolding of perceptions of national interest. Traditionally, the foreign policy decision-making process was dominated by a tiny elite in the military and the bureaucracy. Together, they often depicted the international environment as a highly dangerous domain filled with uncertainties. With the compelling thrust to safeguard national security constantly in their minds, they had been searching for protection from outside Powers; and by doing so, it legitimised their role in foreign-policy formulation. It explains why they were reluctant to abandon the traditional concept even after the Cold War had ended: they feared that they could lose their legitimacy in the conduct of diplomacy.

When a new administration led by General Chatichai Choonhavan (1988–91), the first elected prime minister since 1976, was installed in Thailand with an ambition to detraditionalise the conduct of Thai diplomacy, it immediately initiated the process of reinventing the Thai national interest concept. The period saw a decline of the military's role in foreign affairs, coinciding with Thailand's rapid economic growth throughout the 1980s, which peaked with an annual growth rate of 13.2 percent in 1988. Local business communities in Thailand urgently requested the new Government to downplay its security-centric foreign policy and implement a business-oriented one. The intervention of the public sector highlighted the role of non-state actors in the foreign policy-making process. Across the border, signs of the Cambodian conflict reaching its final phase were increasingly evident, including the withdrawal of Vietnamese troops from Cambodia in 1989, paving the way for the signing of the Agreements on a Comprehensive Political Settlement of the Cambodia Conflict in Paris in 1991 and the general elections in 1993 sponsored by the United Nations (UN) Transitional Authority for Cambodia.

Chatichai was keen to exploit new developments both within and outside Thailand for his political advantage. He thus established a group of well-educated and iconoclastic advisors, the so-called *Ban Phitsanulok* team, to remake a foreign policy aimed at turning 'the battlefield in Indochina into a marketplace' for Thai businesses.[13] The end of the Cold War, for Chatichai, was an opportune moment for Thailand to pursue an independent foreign policy. Thus, in December 1988, he daringly declared: 'The age of bending with the wind, a metaphor used to describe traditional foreign policy, had come to an end.'[14] Chatichai's declaration suggested that Thailand was embracing a revised definition of national interests. 'Economic prosperity' was now a priority for the Chatichai Government, taking center stage in Thai diplomacy and statecraft. It was juxtaposed with the old concept of 'national security' as equally significant aspects of the national interest.

In reality, Chatichai did not abandon the traditional bending-with-the-wind strategy, even when a new definition of national interests was introduced. Thailand under his premiership apparently blended itself with the new international order in which economic diplomacy super-seded guns and bullets. Chatichai concentrated mostly on taking full advantage from globalisation to revitalise the Thai economy, opening the country for foreign investment and tourists and finding new niche markets for Thai exports, a direction that had been closely followed by his successors, including billionaire Prime Minister Thaksin Shinawatra (2001–6). But his shift of foreign-policy focus was perceived as too radical and a threat to the power of the military and bureaucracy. In 1991, the army staged a coup against the Chatichai administration. Yet, the military won only a pyrrhic victory. Chatichai's marketplace policy, anticipating many new business opportunities in post-civil war Cambodia, proved that Thailand was on the right track and that the military was behind the times and out of touch of the reality of regional politics. When Thaksin later followed in the footsteps of Chatichai, he, too, was ousted in the military coup of 2006. The elusiveness of unlocking the traditional mode of thinking about foreign policy amongst the Thai elite, to a certain extent, represents a major hindrance to the work of Thai diplomacy.

In the context of Thailand's Great Powers politics, it is only relevant to focus the attention on the role of China, the only Great Power in the region supposedly capable of contesting United States influence on Thailand's foreign affairs. China epitomises the most commensurate contender to face United States supremacy since both Powers have been competing to win Thailand's alliance, willing to invest resources, and perfecting strategies to accomplish their goals. So far, European Great Powers have exercised little leverage in the way Thai diplomacy has been conducted. In fact, their role in Thailand's foreign affairs has plunged into obscurity since the end of the colonial period. Likewise, certain obstacles delay the improvement of bilateral relations between Thailand and Russia, including the lack of a real interest, and perhaps capability, on the part of Moscow to venture beyond its immediate Asian frontier. In other words, Russia has given more emphasis on its Northeast Asian neighbors compared with those in Southeast Asia, including Thailand.

As for Japan, it has been trying hard to grasp an opportunity in a multipolar world, whilst consolidating its power position economically to compensate for its lack of a military role in Southeast Asia. In the wake of the Asian financial crisis, Japan contributed generously to the IMF rescue program amounting to US$4 billion, and it even went further by providing the Miyazawa Fund to help stimulate a recovery of the Thai economy. Moreover, Japan has continued to give technical and financial assistance to Thailand. In general, Thai – Japanese ties are particularly cordial partly because of the close links between the two countries' royal families. However, Japan's domestic conditions, with the collapse of the Japanese 'bubble economy' and growing political uncertainty, have effectively lessened its influence on both Thailand and the Southeast Asian region.

The strategic shift at the regional level has opened the door for Thailand to reformulate a new foreign policy that conveniently accommodates China's rise, instead of having to rely on the United States as the sole provider of peace and security as in the past. Analysts have interpreted Thailand's accommodation with China in various ways, but all seem to have followed the similar theme of 'bamboo diplomacy'. For example, some consider it as the traditional strategy of 'bending with the wind', by which Thailand grasped the political and economic opportunities that came with China's rise to assert its own interests. Some construe Thailand's move to strengthen ties with China as a return of a balance-of-power policy in which counterweights are used against the US influence. Others also liken the Thai accommodation as a policy of bandwagoning, in which Thailand overtly sides with China at the same time that China is building its own exclusive spheres of influence to create a sphere of influence of its own.[15] Amid various analyses, the rise of China creates a space for Thailand to construct its foreign policy in a less restricted manner because of the decentralisation of the international order. As China gets politically stronger and economically more robust, it is also increasingly becoming Thailand's most attractive partner and ally.

In this period, Thailand has diversified its sources of political and economic benefits. Never having to put all its diplomatic eggs in one basket has effectively meant not being held foreign-policy hostage, as was evident during the Cold War. For Beijing, befriending a middle-sized Thailand could help cement its status as the rising Asian Great Power. Thailand has gone the extra distance to please China because of clear advantages that would ensue. First, China clarifies its position of not interfering in Thai domestic affairs. For instance, it refused to criticise the heavy-handed policy of Thaksin *vis-à-vis* the Muslim separatists in the south of Thailand. The question of Thaksin's legitimacy at home was purposefully downplayed by China. Non-interference also served the Chinese regime. Thaksin chose not to condemn China for alleged violations of human rights against its minorities on several occasions. Thai Prime Minister Samak Sundaravej (January–September 2008) insisted on adhering to the non-interference principle as he remained absolutely silent over China's brutal crackdown on Tibetan pro-democracy protesters before the Olympic Games in August 2008.[16]

These mutual benefits have boosted Thailand's confidence as it played the game of Great Powers politics. At a deeper level, as the regional order has moved away from the use of hard power as seen in the Cold War, the rise of China symbolises another softer aspect of diplomacy under the modernised term of 'soft power'. China's growing economic clout simply means business opportunities for Thailand. The thrust for closer economic relations with China has met with an encouraging response from Thailand's commerce-driven policies and capitalist agenda. The economic rise of China, in particular, has set the tone of Asia's international affairs in which business interests have priority at the expense of political issues, such as the promotion of democracy and respect for human rights. As a result, the Sino-Thai free trade agreement (FTA), the first between China and a Southeast Asian country, was signed and took effect on 1 October 2003. The FTA, part of the 'Early Harvest Programme' under the 2010 ASEAN-China FTA, was initiated to slash tariffs for the fruit and vegetable flows in each other's markets. The Thaksin Government, the driving force behind the Sino-Thai FTA, claimed that bilateral trade reached US$31 billion, a 23 percent increase in 2007 when compared with that of the previous year.[17]

Thailand has been quietly sliding into China's warm, embracing arms. Most Thai cabinet ministers, including many former Prime Ministers and powerful businesses in Thailand,[18] have significant investments in China. Thailand's Charoen Pokphand, one of Southeast Asia's largest companies, has been doing business in China since 1949. Bangkok Bank still has the largest foreign branch on Shanghai's Bund waterfront, and only recently have a few other foreign banks gained token footholds on China's preeminent business address.[19] Activities between Thai and Chinese business conglomerates were regularly conducted, with the exchange of visits and the sharing of business information. The Thai–Chinese Chamber of Commerce highlights on its website that 'all business activities must remain apolitical.'[20] In the cultural realm, Patrick Jory argued that since the Chinese language has been reintroduced into Thailand's schools and universities after a long period of official sanction, Chinese popular culture is much celebrated, and imported Chinese soap operas have been highly popular.[21] New Chinese language schools have been mushrooming in Bangkok and in major cities throughout the kingdom. 'Thailand has been taking the Chinese language seriously', Michael Vatikiotis wrote, 'so seriously that Thaksin asked China to send teachers'.[22]

In January 2006, China's Deputy Education Minister Zhang Xin-sheng was in Bangkok to sign an agreement to help train 1,000 Mandarin language teachers every year for Thailand. China also offered 100 scholarships for Thai students to study in China, and it dispatched 500 young volunteers to teach Chinese in Thailand.[23] According to the Chinese Ministry of Education, Thai students studying in China reached 1,554, making them the sixth largest group of foreign students in the country, after South Korea, Japan, the United States, Vietnam, and Indonesia.[24] 'The number of Thai students studying in Chinese universities has grown six- or seven-fold within the past few years,' said Tekhua Pung, director of a local Chinese-language teaching school.[25] Ultimately, bending with the Chinese wind seems to correspond with a new surge in the Thai public awareness about China's rise. A recent poll showed that more than 70 percent of Thais considered China as Thailand's most important external influence and wanted the Government to continue to craft a China-favored policy for a closer relationship with Beijing.[26]

Overall, Thailand's national interests have appeared to be in league with those of China. But at other moments, friction has occurred, although to date none has become severe or damaged Thailand's core national interests and the foundation of its relationship with China. Thailand's policy of exerting influence over its immediate neighbours was sometimes viewed as a deliberate attempt to overcome tense competition from China, which has also been in a similar process of expanding its control over them. For example, Thailand's contract farming program in Laos was said to be initiated to offset similar projects between Laos and China. Currently, Laos produces corn, soybeans, and cardamom under contract farming for export to China.[27] Laos itself has been seeking to reduce its dependence on Thailand and reaching out to China, as well as Vietnam, to help rejuvenate its moribund economy.

After diplomatic normalisation in 1988, China has overwhelmed Laos with financial and technical assistance in an attempt to pull Vientiane into its orbit and out of Thailand's sphere of influence. In another instance, Thailand cooperated with ASEAN in neutralising a perceived Chinese threat, as China and four other ASEAN members (the Philippines, Brunei, Vietnam and Malaysia) have fiercely engaged in territorial claims over various features and ocean space in the

South China Sea.[28] Although Thailand is not one of the claimants, it supported the signing of the Declaration on the Conduct of Parties in the South China Sea in 2002. This Declaration stresses the need to resolve the territorial and jurisdictional disputes by peaceful means, without resorting to the threat or use of force, through friendly consultations, and negotiations by sovereign states directly concerned.

Noticing the growing intimacy between Thailand and China, the United States, although criticised for neglecting Southeast Asia, has not really been a passive Great Power in this part of the world. It has participated in a number of regional frameworks that involve both Thailand and China, such as the Asia-Pacific Economic Cooperation (APEC), the ASEAN Regional Forum (ARF), and the East Asia Summit (EAS).[29] The United States and China have been locked in a new form of 'Cold War' involving other Great and Middle Powers in Northeast Asia, a situation reflected by their disagreement on numerous issues. The problems include nuclear proliferation on the Korean Peninsula, cross-straits relations (China–Taiwan), the American military base in Japan, and human rights violations inside China. Ian Bremmer asked: 'As the world's two Great Powers are growing dangerously hostile to one another, could this be worse than the Cold War?'[30] Not only have bittersweet Sino-US relations governed the balance of power in Asia's northern hemisphere; they have also reconfigured the political landscape of Southeast Asia. In the Thai case, Washington has been competing against China to regain its influence on the kingdom, albeit using a different approach than Beijing.

In 2003, as a reward for supporting the American 'war on terror' Thailand was awarded major non-North Atlantic Treaty Organization ally status, which made the kingdom eligible for priority delivery of defence materials and military cooperation. Bilateral relations have been further strengthened through the annual 'Cobra Gold' military exercise, the largest in Asia. 'Cobra Gold' later lent its form to the Chinese leaders, who proposed a similar annual military exercise with Thailand. The George W. Bush Administration also went ahead with FTA negotiations with Thailand, but these are now in a stage of inertia because of the onset of a political crisis in Thailand. Unlike the Chinese, the Americans have been directly involved in the Thai political turmoil, rekindling its Cold War policy strategy of maintaining its command over Thailand's domestic and international political life. More importantly, for Washington, this strategy serves to maintain the level of American dominance in Thailand and Southeast Asia at a time when the rise of China and its expanding influence in the region are increasingly threatening United States regional interests.

What does this mean to Thailand? Thailand has gleefully opened itself up to both as the United States and China vie for a Thai alliance. In particular, if one of them ever turns hostile to Thailand, Bangkok could play one off against the other, thus revisiting bamboo diplomacy. Thaksin was a master of manipulating Thailand's bending-with-the-wind strategy. When the United States failed to defend the Thaksin Government against the UN's criticism of his brutal war on drugs in 2003, which led to more than 2,500 Thais being killed, Thaksin labelled Washington as a 'useless friend'. He then flirted with China, attaching great importance to solidifying bilateral economic linkages to the point at which Bangkok often bent over backwards to avoid offending Beijing on a range of political issues.[31] It can be argued that Thaksin's embrace of Chinese power was a strategic response to the United States' ambivalent position toward his Government. The dynamism imbued within the complex relations between Thailand and two Great Powers has been seen more clearly and sensationally as the country has fallen deeper into its political crisis: the crisis in which China and the United States have been contesting with each other to entrench further their positions inside Thailand.

Since the 2006 military coup, Thailand has continued to sink deeply into political stalemate. The protracted conflict and the political polarisation in Thai society deserve a separate in-depth analysis. To provide context for the following discussion, the current crisis can be explained in terms of conflict between two profoundly divided and opposing camps for ultimate political control: the red-shirted supporters of Thaksin and those who back the country's 'network monarchy', a term coined by Duncan McCargo referring to a loose alliance of the palace, the military, and the Democrat Party led by former Prime Minister Abhisit Vejjajiva.[32]

Throughout the crisis, the United States and China have undertaken what is seen as a fierce competition for influence in Thailand. Thai Government spokesman Panitan Wattanayagorn stated in 2010:

> Our interests and international relations are becoming more complex. We see advantages in the competition between superpowers. The United States has high stakes in Thailand and actively pursues it interests. China is less active and uses an indirect approach and its handling of this situation was no different. China-Thailand ties are becoming more and more dynamic and China is very pragmatic, but very keen in getting information and reacting.[33]

Shawn Crispin suggested that the United States and China have been pursuing two different approaches: whereas China practiced a more pragmatic diplomacy, the United States chose an interventionist approach that has occasionally irked the traditional elite in Bangkok.[34] To protect the country's autonomy as much as their own interests from the potential intervention of the United States in domestic politics, Thai leaders have moved closer to China. The idea is to counterbalance America's dominant role. Nonetheless, Thai leaders have been careful not to damage the country's traditional status as a 'permanent friend' of the United States. Thus, they have been cautious not to be viewed as adopting an overtly hostile attitude toward the United States even when they disapproved of the American diplomatic style. This course highlighted a conventional Thai strategy of engineering a foreign policy that is less reliant on one single Power, which would restrain their diplomatic freedom.

Beijing's soft power illustrates its resilience in the Thai crisis in which China has gained a great deal of trust and respect from Bangkok. This trust is translated into even more cordial economic and military relations between Thailand and China. As a result of their FTA, total exports from Thailand to China have risen from US$11.8 billion in 2006 to US$16.2 billion in 2008; at the same time, imports from China grew from US$13.6 billion to US$20.1 billion. These figures reflect Thailand's trade deficit *vis-à-vis* China, registered at US$1.8 billion in 2006 and US$3.9 billion in 2008.[35]

In the military field, the first Sino-Thai joint naval exercises in the Gulf of Thailand took place in 2005 as an equivalent military exercise, albeit on a much smaller scale, to the American 'Cobra Gold'. Not only have these joint naval exercises been designed to cement military links between the two countries, they have served to erase the image of a Chinese threat in the eyes of the Thai leaders; and they have acted to undermine traditional United States–Thai strategic ties underpinned by a supposed common enemy. In an interview with the *Asia Times*, China's ambassador to Bangkok, Guan Mu, who speaks Thai fluently and has served in Thailand for 18 years in different capacities, underscored his country's strategy of befriending Thailand by avoiding interference in its domestic problems.[36] It is apparent that China has been ramping up economic and cultural diplomacy, all encapsulated within a discourse of Chinese soft power, which is more relevant and attuned to Thailand's future interests than the United States' still strong emphasis on security issues.[37]

The United States, on the contrary, has frequently intervened in Thailand's domestic politics, throughout both the Cold War era and in the present period. In an attempt to influence Thailand's domestic policy and dictate the behavior of certain political actors in the current crisis, Washington has managed to peeve both sides of Thailand's political divide. It was reported that United States intelligence officials eavesdropped on Thaksin and warned the Abhisit Government against possible sabotage during the red-shirts' rally, supposedly at the order of Thaksin.[38] This report infuriated red-shirt leaders, who felt that the United States did nothing to support their pro-democracy movement. At other times, the United States displeased the traditional elite in the anti-Thaksin camp by demanding a meeting between core red-shirted leaders and United States Assistant Secretary of State Kurt Campbell, who was keen to mediate between the two opposing factions. The meeting was arranged by American Ambassador to Bangkok, Eric John, who was later criticised by the Thai Government for inappropriately interfering in Thailand's domestic politics and for lacking cultural sensitivity and diplomatic skills.

Viewing such intervention as a violation to the country's national interests, Bangkok used statecraft to reprove the United States' indiscreet and ill-advised diplomacy; it sent a special envoy, Kiat Sitheeamorn, to Washington to protest against American intervention. Kiat said: 'The position of the United States has always been if we call for help and support, they will extend a helping hand, but it is up to us to request and we have not asked.'[39] In the meantime, to show his country's favorable view of China, Kiat commented that the closeness between Thailand and China has been unique and special. 'Do we have the same ties with the United States? Not similar, not at the same level'.[40]

From the perspective of the two Great Powers, Thailand represents their primary interest as a country strategically located in the heart of mainland Southeast Asia. As a long-time ally of Thailand, the United States has continued to exert its influence and power over the kingdom and demand its allegiance, even when the regional balance of power has shifted. The American interventionist approach did nothing but drive Thailand into the arms of China. China has quietly bid to capitalise on Washington's indiscreet approach and is now locked in a subtle, and intensifying, competition with the United States for Thai influence. Ultimately, China's soft power can be seen as the front edge of a longer-view strategy to neutralise the United States' strategic presence in this part of the world.[41] Because of its neutral position in the Thai crisis, China will be able to work with whichever side triumphs in the Thai conflict and in a future government. In this power game, it is thus likely that China stands to gain what the United States may lose.

When faced with a threat, Thailand traditionally seeks help from another Power. The rise of China had widened foreign-policy choices for Thailand and, hence, given more room for diplomatic maneuvering. In many ways, Thai leaders have taken an opportunistic approach that allowed Thailand to gain from the mounting rivalry between China and the United States in Southeast Asia. In its search to counterbalance the United States, Thailand has invited China to take a stake in the region and the kingdom, for instance, through bilateral cooperation in wider regional platforms like ASEAN and the EAS. It is clear that, despite its persistent political crisis, Thailand will continue to play a major role in American and Chinese foreign-policy considerations. But for now, Thailand is seeing its interests aligned more with those of China and will therefore cement its intimate ties with Beijing. As Kislenko once observed: 'Whatever new winds blow in the region, Thailand will undoubtedly try to accommodate them. With an emphasis on flexibility, and a remarkable history of continuity, Thai foreign policy—like the bamboo—faces the 21st century with solid roots.'[42]

Notes

1 The description of Thailand experiencing an 'unstable political system' is based on the fact that Thailand, since the abolition of absolute monarchy in 1932, has endured 18 military coups, and that throughout much of the Cold War, the country had been dominated by a series of military regimes with short interventions of civilian rule.

2 During the first Phibul Songkhram administration (1936–44), in 1939 the name of the country was changed from Siam to Thailand, purportedly because it was suitable to call the nation by a name that represented the country's majority and was popular with the people, an argument that remains fiercely debatable to this date.

3 Likhit Dhiravegin, *Siam and Colonialism (1855–1909): An Analysis of Diplomatic Relations* (Bangkok, 1975), 78.

4 See Duncan McCargo in his foreword in Pavin Chachavalpongpun, *Reinventing Thailand: Thaksin and His Foreign Policy* (Singapore, 2010), vii.

5 Daniel Fineman, *A Special Relationship: The United States and Military Government in Thailand, 1947–1958* (Honolulu, HI, 1997), 3.

6 See Russell F. Fifield, *The Diplomacy of Southeast Asia: 1945–1958* (New York, 1958), 230; D. Insor, *Thailand* (New York, 1963), 125; Donald E. Neuchterlein, *Thailand and the Struggle for Southeast Asia* (Ithaca, NY, 1965), 23; Charles E. Morrison, *Strategies of Survival: The Foreign Policy Dilemma of Smaller Asian States* (New York, 1979), 109.

7 Arne Kislenko, 'Bending with the Wind: The Continuity and Flexibility of Thai Foreign Policy', *International Journal*, 57(2002), 537. Also see, William J. Klausner, *Reflections on Thai Culture* (Bangkok, 1981), 79–80.

8 Anuson Chinvanno, *Thailand's Policies towards China, 1949–1954* (Oxford, 1992), 20. Cf. Likhit, *Siam and Colonialism*, 78–79; Tej Bunnag, *The Provincial Administration of Siam, 1892–1915: The Ministry of the Interior under Prince Damrong Rajanubhab* (Kuala Lumpur, 1977).

9 Sarasin Viraphol, *Tribute and Profit: Sino-Siamese Trade, 1652–1853* (Cambridge, MA, 1977), 1.

10 For further discussions, see Chachavalpongpun, *Reinventing Thailand*, 67–70.

11 Kusuma Snitwongse argued that the United States became the main target of a resurgent Thai nationalism, which sometimes degenerated into xenophobia. See Kusuma Snitwongse, 'Thai Foreign Policy in the Global Age: Principle of Profit?', *Contemporary Southeast Asia*, 23(2001), 206.

12 Cailean Bochanan, 'Globalisation: Multipolar World or New World Order?', in *These New Times*, 11 March 2010: http://inthesenewtimes.com/2010/03/11/globalisation-multipolar-world-or-new-world-order/.

13 Sunai Phasuk, *Nayobai Tang Prathet Khong Thai: Suksa Krabuankarnkamnod Nayobai Khong Ratthaban Pon-ek Chatichai Choonhavan Tor Panha Kumphucha, Si Singhakom 1988 – 23 Kumphaphan 1991* (Bangkok, 1997), 69–73.

14 Leszek Buszynski, 'Thailand's Foreign Policy: Management of a Regional Vision', *Asian Survey*, 34 (1994), 724. Buszynski also noted that the pursuit of an independent foreign policy was made possible because Thailand's reliance on external security support was slowly being removed after the end of the Cold War.

15 Various scholars and analysts have interpreted the Thai position *vis-à-vis* China differently. For example, Chulacheeb Chinwanno argued that Thailand has pursued a balanced engagement policy with external powers in order to achieve national interests. See his 'Thai-Chinese Relations: Security and Strategic Partnerships', RSIS Working Paper, Number 155 (Singapore, 2008), 25. To the contrary, Kavi Chongkittavorn explicitly asserted that Thailand, under Thaksin, sometimes spoke on behalf of China and this may lead other ASEAN members to think of Thailand as a conduit for China's foreign policy. Quoted in Chantasasawat, 'Burgeoning Sino-Thai Relations', 11.

16 In August 2008, Prime Minister Samak Sundaravej, largely known as Thaksin's political nominee, declared his pro-China position in the aftermath of the brutal crackdown on the Tibetan demonstrators. See 'Thai PM Proud to Host Olympic Torch', *USA Today* (18 April 2008).

17 Department of East Asian Affairs, Ministry of Foreign Affairs of Thailand.

18 Many former Thai Prime Ministers are in some way of Chinese descent, including Chuan Leekpai, Banharn Silpa-Archa, Chavalit Yongchaiyuth, Thaksin Shinawatra, and Premier Abhisit Vejjajiva.

19 David Fullbrook, 'So Long U.S., Hello China, India', *Asia Times* (4 November 2004).

20 www.thaiccc.or.th/eng-main.html.

21 Patrick Jory, 'Multiculturalism in Thailand: Cultural and Regional Resurgence in a Diverse Kingdom' *Harvard Asia-Pacific Review*, 4(2000), 18–22.

22 'The Soft Power of Happy Chinese', *International Herald Tribune* (18 January 2006).

23 Ibid.

24 Ministry of Education of China: www.moe.edu.cn/english/international_3.htm.

25 'Soft Power of Happy Chinese'.

26 Joshua Kurlantzick, 'China's Charm: Implications of Chinese Soft Power', *Policy Brief*, 47(2006), 1.

27 See Anthony M. Zola, 'Contract Farming for Exports in ACMECS: Lessons and Policy Implications', a paper presented at the meeting on 'Investment, Trade and Transport Facilitation in ACMECS', Bangkok, Thailand, 13 March 2007. Author's copy.

28 Mark J. Valencia, *The South China Sea Brouhaha: Separating Substance from Atmospherics*, in Nautilus Institute for Security and Sustainability (10 August 2010): www.nautilus.org/publications/essays/napsnet/policy-forums-online/security2009–10/the-south-china-sea-brouhaha-separating-substance-from-atmospherics.

29 APEC, a forum for 21 Pacific Rim Economies that seeks to promote free trade and economic cooperation throughout the Asia-Pacific region was established in 1989. Founded in 1994, ARF has two major goals: to foster constructive dialogue and consultation on political and security issues of common interest and concern; and to make significant contributions to efforts towards confidence-building and preventive diplomacy in the Asia–Pacific region. The EAS is an annual forum of leaders of 16 countries in the East Asian region. EAS meetings are held after annual ASEAN leaders' meetings. The first summit was held in Kuala Lumpur on 14 December 2005.

30 Ian Bremmer, 'China VS America: Fight of the Century', *Prospect*, Issue 169(March 2010): www.prospectmagazine.co.uk/2010/03/china-vs-america-fight-of-the-century/.

31 See Busakorn Chantasasawat, 'The Burgeoning Sino-Thai Relations: Seeking Sustained Economic Security', *China: An International Journal*, 4(March 2006), 86–112.

32 Duncan McCargo, 'Thailand', *Regional Outlook: Southeast Asia 2010–2011* (Singapore, 2010), 54.

33 Quoted in Shawn W. Crispin, 'US Slips, China Glides in Thai Crisis', *Asia Times Online* (20 July 2010): www.atimes.com/atimes/Southeast_Asia/LG20Ae01.html.

34 Ibid.

35 Sompop Manarungsan, 'Thailand-China Cooperation in Trade, Investment and Official Development Assistance', in Kagami Mitsuhiro, ed., *A China-Japan Comparison of Economic Relations with the Mekong River Basin Countries* (Tokyo, 2009), 295–96.

36 Crispin, 'US Slips, China Glides'.

37 Guan Mu estimated that there are 12 million Sino-Thais amongst Thailand's 65 million population. Ibid.

38 'UDD Submits Letter to US Embassy', *Bangkok Post*, 17 March 2010.

39 Crispin, 'US Slips, China Glides'.

40 Ibid.

41 Ibid.

42 Kislenko, 'Bending with the Wind', 561.

19

Indonesia's foreign policy after the Cold War

Political legitimacy, international pressure, and foreign-policy choices

Kai He

This chapter examines Indonesia's foreign policy after the Cold War. Although Indonesia officially has claimed a 'free and independent' foreign policy since its independence, as a middle Power it faces a political dilemma in designing its foreign policy. On one hand, Indonesia intends to play an important role in international affairs if opportunity permits. On the other, its middle Power status constrains its international ambitions since it lives amongst Great Powers like the United States, China, and Japan. After the Cold War, a dramatic change took place in the international environment because of the demise of the Soviet Union, the sustained 'unipolar moment', and the rise of China.[1] Although Indonesia lost the economic and security privileges it enjoyed in the Western camp during the Cold War, the changing international environment offered new opportunities to play a more important role on the world stage.

Domestically, in 1998, Indonesia experienced a turbulent political transition from an authoritarian regime to a democratic system. After 32 years in power, in May 1998, the Indonesian dictator, President Soeharto, stepped down. Indonesian politics began a new phase of democratisation. Four Presidents, B.J. Habibie (May 1998–October 1999), Abdurrahman Wahid (October 1999–July 2001), Megawati Sukarnoputri (July 2001–October 2004), and Susilo Bambang Yudhoyono (October 2004–present) successively came to power. During democratisation, Indonesian leaders faced tremendous domestic pressures and constraints from the electorate on their foreign-policy decision-making. Because of the fierce political struggle during democratisation, Indonesian leaders had to concentrate on domestic instead of international affairs. However, diplomacy can be used sometimes as a political tool for political leaders to boost domestic support and consolidate power.

Indonesia's foreign policy after the Cold War was shaped by two major factors: international pressure and leadership legitimacy. In the anarchic international system, Indonesia like other states is constrained by the power configuration of that system. In the bipolar world during the Cold War, Indonesia could choose either side of the two camps in which to seek its security. With unipolarity after the Cold War, Indonesia faced international pressures mainly from the United States, the remaining Superpower. How to balance and accommodate pressures and demands from the United States became the major task for Indonesian foreign-policy makers.

Leadership legitimacy is measured by the domestic support given Indonesia's President, the major designer of Indonesia's foreign policy. Under strong leadership legitimacy, Indonesia's foreign policy is more likely to be confident and decisive. Under weak leadership legitimacy, its foreign policy is more likely to be reluctant and responsive. Leadership legitimacy is built on different foundations in different regimes. Whereas leadership legitimacy is mainly based on ideology, economic performance, and political control in an authoritarian regime, democratic leaders' legitimacy is determined by the political support of constituencies through elections.[2]

After the Cold War, the interplay of international pressure and leadership legitimacy shaped Indonesia's foreign policy. Through exploring continuities and changes in Indonesia's foreign policy from Soeharto to Yudhoyono, this chapter suggests that the further consolidation of democratisation increased the confidence of Indonesia's foreign policy. The new power configuration in the international system accompanying China's rise provided a new opportunity for Indonesia to play a more important role in world politics.

Soeharto came to power after the 1965 coup and stayed in office until 1998. During his 'new order,'[3] Indonesia's economy sustained relatively high rates of growth and its social and political development was relatively stable. From 1970 to 1996, Indonesia's annual economic growth averaged more than 6%.[4] Because of rapid economic growth, Indonesia's absolute poverty rate dropped from 40% of the population in 1976 to 11% in 1996.[5] Indonesia also transformed itself from a low-income to a middle-income country, with an estimated income per capita of approximately $1,030 in 1995.[6] In the early 1990s, one World Bank report praised the East Asian economic miracle and categorised Indonesia as a 'newly industrializing economy' along with Malaysia and Thailand.[7]

Politically, Soeharto relied on the military to maintain his power. The military enjoyed the constitutional right to be involved in domestic politics because of the dual-function (*dwifungsi*) role of the military in the 'New Order.' Under the dual function, the military became both a 'security force' and a 'social political force' in Indonesia.[8] Consequently, Indonesia's foreign policy under Soeharto was heavily influenced by the military.

Indonesia's economic success and political stability provided Soeharto with strong political legitimacy in the 'New Order'. However, the bipolar international system left limited diplomatic room for Indonesia to maneuver during the Cold War. With the military's support, Soeharto adopted a pro-Western and anti-communist foreign policy, although Indonesia officially insisted on non-alignment. Western economic support and investment became one of the major reasons for Indonesia's economic takeoff in the 1980s. Regionally, Soeharto terminated the military confrontation with Malaysia in 1966 and supported the formation of the Association of Southeast Asian Nations (ASEAN) in 1967 to concentrate on economic development.

In the mid-1980s, Soeharto started to become more active in foreign policy as a result of his increasing political confidence in domestic politics. During the 1983 presidential election, Soeharto was the only candidate nominated by all three political parties in Indonesia. Moreover, there were no violence or student demonstrations during the parliamentary and presidential elections.[9] This unprecedented political stability signified Soeharto's strong political legitimacy after 20 years in power, and this legitimacy, in turn, encouraged him to play a more active foreign-policy role.

First, Indonesia tried to regain its Third World leader status, which it enjoyed during Sukarno's regime. In 1985, Indonesia hosted the thirtieth anniversary celebration of the Afro-Asian conference in Bandung. In 1987, Soeharto sent his Vice-President to attend the Non-Aligned Movement (NAM) conference in Zimbabwe and also indicated his desire to be the chairman of the next conference. Because of Indonesia's pro-Western stand during the Cold War, NAM did not agree to Indonesia's leadership in 1987.[10] However, Soeharto continued to pursue a leadership role in NAM; in 1991, Indonesia eventually became the chair of NAM. Besides boosting his international prestige, Soeharto also intended to strengthen his domestic support from the Muslim population through active diplomacy in the NAM.[11]

Second, Soeharto actively pursued a leadership role in Southeast Asia. In 1986, he personally mediated in a dispute between Singapore and Malaysia to show his regional leadership and, in 1987, insisted on attending the third ASEAN summit despite the widespread security concerns in Manila. The success of the ASEAN summit once again confirmed Soeharto's leadership amongst ASEAN countries.[12] Indonesia also played an important role in ASEAN's efforts in mediating the Kampuchean problem. In 1990, it actively initiated the unofficial Workshop on Managing Potential Conflicts in the South China Sea, which included China and other involved countries. After the Cold War, Indonesia actively supported the establishment of ASEAN Regional Forum (ARF) as a security dialogue mechanism to cope with the strategic uncertainty in the Asia Pacific. ARF's practices of consultation and consensus are actually rooted in Indonesia's traditional political culture (*musyawarah* and *mufakat*). In other words, Indonesia intended to play a leadership role in the newly established security institution through forming ARF's rules.

Third, Soeharto used diplomacy to promote economic development and strengthen his political legitimacy. One notable diplomatic maneuver was to normalise relations with China in 1990. Indonesia had frozen its diplomatic relations with China for 23 years because of China's alleged involvement in the 1965 coup in Indonesia. Soeharto's decision to normalise relations with Beijing was a surprise to many Indonesia watchers for two reasons: some Indonesian military high-ranking officials opposed publicly the normalisation with China; and Western countries, led by the United States, imposed economic and diplomatic sanctions on China after the 1989 Tiananmen incident.[13]

There are two possible explanations for Soeharto's bold decision. Normalisation could enhance Indonesia's regional influence, particularly efforts to resolve the Kampuchean problem.[14] Then, as Rizal Sukma suggests, the foundation of Soehart's political legitimacy in the late 1980s had changed from anti-communism to improved economic performance.[15] China's huge domestic market and economic potential attracted his attention logically and rationally. Besides the normalisation of relations with China, Soeharto also actively promoted regional economic cooperation through hosting the Asia-Pacific Economic Cooperation (APEC)) meeting in 1994, which declared the Bogor goals that set the timetable for both industrialised and developing countries to achieve free and open trade and investment in the APEC region.

Last, the East Timor issue became the diplomatic flashpoint between Indonesia and the West after the Cold War. East Timor, a former Portuguese colony, declared independence on 28 November 1975 under the left-wing party, the Revolutionary Front for an Independent East Timor (*Frente Revolucionária de Timor-Leste Independente*). Soeharto worried that the independence of East Timor would cause a chain reaction for other secessionist movements in Indonesia. Therefore, he sent troops to East Timor in December 1975 after the United States gave him the green light. Washington also feared the falling of another communist domino in Southeast Asia.[16] The United Nations (UN) passed two resolutions to confirm the inalienable East Timorese right to self-determination and demanded that Indonesia withdraw from the territory in 1976. However, Soeharto insisted on Indonesia's sovereignty over East Timor and tried hard to legitimise its annexation through negotiating with Portugal under UN mediation.

In November 1991 the Indonesian military used force to suppress a demonstration in Dili. It was reported that more than 200 East Timorese were killed and many wounded. Indonesia's military action in Dili was harshly criticised by the Western countries, which after the Cold War were more concerned about human rights issues than communism.[17] The Netherlands, Australia, Denmark, and Canada suspended economic aid to Indonesia. To ease international pressure,

Soeharto was forced to investigate the Dili tragedy and later remove two territorial commanders in East Timor. In 1993, the United States Congress terminated the International Military Education and Training Program (IMET) with Indonesia because of its military's notorious human rights record in East Timor.

Since then, the East Timor issue and the related human rights violations have become the black spot of Indonesia's diplomacy with the West. Although Soeharto made technical concessions, such as firing or prosecuting some military officers involved in human rights violations, East Timor's sovereignty was a non-negotiable issue. To a certain extent, Indonesia's diplomatic international enthusiasm after the Cold War was also rooted in Soeharto's belief that a more active foreign policy could help Indonesia balance the pressures from the West and eventually solve the East Timor issue in Indonesia's favor.

As a result of the deepening economic crisis and political turmoil, Soeharto was forced to resign and transfer power to the Vice-President, Habibie, in May 1998. However, Habibie, a long-term supporter of Soeharto, was unable to resolve the complex economic and political crisis in Indonesia. Under his rule, Indonesia's economy deteriorated and domestic political chaos continued. Internationally, Habibie's succession was unwelcome. The International Monetary Fund (IMF) threatened to suspend a next loan disbursement of $1 billion until the political situation in Indonesia stabilised: 'the fund was skeptical about the depth of the commitment by Habibie to root out the cronyism and corruption.'[18] With a similar wait-and-see tone, James Rubin, an American State Department spokesman, said 'the United States would wait for changes in Indonesia's political and economic policy before supporting any further loans by the international institutions.'[19]

Habibie faced severe domestic challenges to his political legitimacy. His Government was inherently weak in terms of political legitimacy as a result of the transformation of power during democratisation. Pro-reform forces, especially students, did not want him in power. As one activist from the University of Indonesia mentioned, 'Habibie is part of the Soeharto regime, [and] although he promised to make changes in the electoral laws, we are skeptical that he will make any real changes in the system.' Political elites and the military also showed reluctant and limited support to the new President.[20]

Aware of the low legitimacy of his presidency, Habibie tried to increase his political legitimacy by distancing himself from his patron Soeharto. Domestically, he restored press freedom, released political prisoners, and introduced legislation allowing for regional devolution of political and fiscal authority. Internationally, Habibie broke Indonesia's East Timor taboo to please the international community and in hopes of financial support. However, these approaches won little support either because the implementation of new policies was hindered by domestic political struggles or because policy changes themselves were too little and too late. East Timor is a good example of Habibie's failed attempts.

After taking office, he made a policy breakthrough over the East Timor issue. In January 1999 Habibie decided to allow a referendum (Indonesia's Government used the phrase, 'popular consultation', instead of 'referendum') in East Timor. If the East Timorese rejected Habibie's autonomy proposal, East Timor would be separated from Indonesia. The referendum of August 1999 saw 78.5% of the Timorese vote for independence. Mass violence and killing occurred after the referendum. To end the humanitarian disaster, the Australia-led International Force for East Timor under UN auspices entered East Timor in late September 1999. In October 1999 Indonesia's *Majelis Permusyawaratan Rakyat* (MPR) (the People's Consultative Assembly) endorsed the referendum. East Timor was then under UN administration until it obtained full independence and self-governance in May 2002 with a general election.

Why did Habibie agree to hold a referendum in East Timor in early 1999? And why did he allow international intervention forces to enter East Timor after the referendum? Regarding the first question, the weak political legitimacy of Habibie's Government offers a satisfactory answer. As mentioned before, Habibie intended to do 'what Soeharto did not do' to gain internal and external legitimacy after coming to power. The East Timor referendum proposal is a perfect 'what-Soeharto-did-not-do' issue. As Dewi Fortuna Anwar, Assistant Minister/State Secretary for Foreign Affairs during the Habibie Government, pointed out, Habibie wished to 'make his mark by resolving the East Timor issue once and for all as part of his plan both to strengthen his democratic credentials at home and his credentials abroad.'[21]

Besides weak political legitimacy, intense international pressure played an important role in driving Habibie's policy changes. Critical pressure on Habibie came mainly from the United States and Australia. In the annual Consultative Group on Indonesia meeting in Paris in late June 1998, the Americans raised concerns about human rights abuses in East Timor. In October, the United States Congress voted to continue the suspension of the IMET program in Indonesia because of ongoing abuses in East Timor. It should be noted that American pressure focused mainly on human rights, not the political status of East Timor. However, this kind of pressure in the context of economic crisis pushed the Indonesian Government to consider an 'alternative' approach to fix the problem, that is, compromising over the political status of East Timor to obtain economic support.

The well-known trigger for Habibie's decision on the referendum proposal stemmed from a private letter that Habibie received from the Australian Prime Minister John Howard in December 1998. Howard's letter outlined a proposal for an eventual vote on self-determination in East Timor and formally expressed a readiness to accept an independent East Timor. Since Australia had been one of the few Western countries to recognise Indonesian sovereignty over the territory of East Timor, a stance it adopted in 1978, the Howard letter dealt a hard blow to Habibie's Government.

The United States also played a key role in forcing Habibie's Government to accept international intervention after the violence and mass killing erupted in East Timor. On 9 September 1999, President Bill Clinton suspended American military sales, commercial transfers, and training programs to Indonesia. At the APEC forum in New Zealand in mid-September, he lobbied to pressure Habibie to invite a multilateral force into East Timor. The United States House of Representatives passed a harshly worded resolution on 28 September urging the MPR to ratify the 30 August vote. In the meantime, high-level Pentagon officers contacted General Wiranto and other senior officers to send political messages regarding East Timor. American Defense Secretary William Cohen met with Habibie and Wiranto in late September in Jakarta and also reportedly sent private letters urging the military to rein in the East Timor militia. Consequently, Wiranto replaced the East Timor provincial commander and other military officers accused of fomenting trouble in East Timor.[22]

In sum, Habibie's policy changes on East Timor were a joint result of high levels of international pressures and low political legitimacy. The low political legitimacy drove Habibie to initiate the 'autonomy' proposal to distance him from the old Soeharto regime and please Western donors for economic support. Under high pressure, especially from the United States and Australia, Habibie began to lose control over East Timor policy. His final reluctant acceptance of international intervention was an unintended consequence for his Government, resulting from combined American and Western government pressure.

Compared with Habibie, Wahid enjoyed a higher level of political legitimacy because of his election-based power transition. Under Indonesia's unique quasi-parliamentary system,[23] Wahid was elected by the MPR to balance between the nationalist pro-Megawati forces and conservative anti-Megawati Muslim parties. Although Wahid's party, the National Awakening, only held 11% of DPR seats, his charisma and traditional Muslim background helped him achieve a thin victory over Megawati by a vote of 373 to 313 in the MPR. He then nominated Megawati as Vice-President and shared power with other main parties in the DPR through a national unity cabinet consisting of representatives of all the major parties.

Although this multiparty coalition was inherently problematic and weak in terms of cabinet unity and power, Wahid nevertheless initially enjoyed high political legitimacy because he was the opposition leader during the Soeharto era, symbolising a new hope for Indonesia's democracy. In February 2000, Wahid removed Wiranto from his position as Coordinating Minister because of his alleged responsibility for the East Timor violence in 1999. A pro-Wiranto armed forces backlash did not occur, and the military reiterated their support for Wahid. This event was widely hailed as a successful test of Wahid's political legitimacy and power.

Internationally, Wahid was also widely praised and supported after he won the presidential election. United States Assistant Secretary of State for East Asian and Pacific Affairs Stanley Roth said the new Indonesian President had been 'quite impressive in terms of his breadth of knowledge on the issues and intentions towards the United States.' Australian Prime Minister John Howard said that as a leading religious and public figure, Wahid had been a strong supporter of political reform in Indonesia.[24] However, positive comments did not lower Western demands on the Indonesian Government, which focussed on economic reforms and human rights investigations over the East Timor violence. International intervention in East Timor and its separation were largely viewed by Indonesians as a deliberate humiliation by the West during the crisis. In September 1999 Wahid, as a religious reformist leader, supported the Habibie Government's decision to cancel the security cooperation agreement of 1995 with Australia because of its 'unfriendly' action in East Timor.

In June 2000, the United States pressured Wahid to remove his brother, Hasyim Wahid, from a key position in the Indonesian Bank Restructuring Agency (IBRA), one of the financial institutions under the IMF financial aid programs. As the *Far Eastern Economic Review* reported, at a meeting in mid-May with Foreign Minister Alwi Shihab, the American Secretary of State, Madeleine Albright, 'took the unusual step of calling for Hasyim to quit IBRA.'[25] Responding to tough IMF conditions for financial aid, Amien Rais, the Speaker of MPR, even suggested the Government stop receiving IMF aid from the IMF because of its encroachment on 'economic sovereignty'.

Soon after becoming President, Wahid announced a 'looking towards Asia' policy to balance the West. The main idea of this initiative was to enhance relationships amongst Indonesia, India, China, Japan, and Singapore to counter Western influence and reduce dependency on the West. Although it is an exaggeration to equate Wahid's policy to Sukarno's 'coalition of newly emerging forces' in the 1960s, this policy was designed to allow Indonesia to offset pressure from the West by forging formal or informal alignments with China, India, and other Asian states, especially after the East Timor intervention and the economic crisis. To implement this policy, Wahid chose China for his first state visit in December 1999 to boost bilateral Sino-Indonesian relations. In the first four months after taking office, Wahid visited 26 countries in the Asia–Pacific, the Indonesian Foreign Ministry explaining that Wahid's goal was to 'rebuild the good image of Indonesia in the eyes of the international community.'[26]

Wahid's 'looking towards Asia' policy had multiple purposes. First, the mild, anti-West orientation of this policy differentiated him from the Habibie regime, which favored relations with the West. Although the real policy change was labeled as ambiguous by skeptics,[27] it helped Wahid win domestic support in the short run. Second, Wahid worried about further national disintegration after the separation of East Timor, such as in Aceh, Irian Jaya, and Maluku. NATO's humanitarian intervention in Kosovo pushed Indonesia to look for international support for territorial integrity and sovereignty. China and other developing countries then became natural friends to Indonesia because of shared concerns. Last, Wahid hoped that his visits would generate more financial aid and investment for Indonesia, seen as key to Indonesian economic recovery.

Megawati came to power unexpectedly after the Parliament impeached Wahid in July 2001 for corruption and cronyism, failures in making economic reforms, and inept handling of deteriorating internal security. However, as many observers argue, the real trigger for Wahid's downfall stemmed from his mismanagement and abandonment of the fragile political coalition, which had helped him in October 1999.[28] Although facing similar domestic difficulties, such as uneasy relationships with other parties, a tough economic situation, and an unstable social environment, Megawati enjoyed some advantages in terms of political legitimacy and power when she was elected. First, her party was the largest party in the Parliament, holding 31% of seats, whereas Wahid's party had only 11%. Although Megawati still needed to forge coalitions and seek support from other parties, she enjoyed more leverage and faced fewer constraints than Wahid. Second, with her father's past glory, Megawati, Sukarno's eldest daughter, had won critical support from the military, which Wahid lacked. Finally, although Megawati's leadership skills were widely doubted and criticised, she was the best amongst the worst. Rather than challenging Megawati immediately, most parties prepared for the electoral race in 2004. In other words, no one wanted to get trapped in the mess left by Wahid. Megawati's political legitimacy, therefore, was at least as high as Wahid's, but her foreign policy was less assertive compared with Wahid's balancing strategy.

Megawati changed the high-profile external balancing policy under Wahid to a low-profile neighbor-first policy. Learning from Wahid's failure, Hassan Wirayuda, the new Foreign Minister, recognised that 'it will be very difficult to launch many initiatives with the current fragile (domestic) stability.'[29] Therefore, Megawati's priority was domestic, and the importance of foreign policy was downgraded. In her first state-of-the-nation address on 16 August 2001, there was only one paragraph on foreign policy, in which she mentioned the importance of ASEAN and the ASEAN Free Trade Area.[30] Further, rather than seeking support and alignment with major Powers in Asia and the wider world as Wahid did, the Foreign Ministry stated that ASEAN countries were the first 'concentric circle' of Indonesia's foreign-policy priorities.[31] Since ASEAN was Indonesia's traditional vehicle to extend its policy influence on the larger international stage, this 'neighbor-first policy' was a strategy to strengthen internal consolidation and revive ASEAN to counter external pressures. It may be the underlying reason why Indonesia became proactive in constructing 'economic, social and cultural and security communities' in ASEAN at the 2003 ASEAN Summit.

Besides the neighbor-first orientation, Megawati also used foreign policy to solve domestic problems. A good example is her cautious anti-terrorism policy and the hard-line Aceh policy. Although Megawati strongly condemned the 11 September attacks during her United States visit in September 2001, she publicly criticised the American counterattack on Afghanistan and opposed United States intervention in Iraq. Indonesia's official position emphasised the role of the UN and multilateral cooperation for resolving problems and rejected all *unilateral* decisions taken outside the framework of the UN. Being the leader of the world's most populous Muslim nation, Megawati had to act cautiously in her anti-terrorism policy, considering the constraints of public opinion and potential attacks from other competitive parties that might erode her legitimacy.

Megawati's less cooperative anti-terrorism policy changed significantly after Jemaah Islamiyah (JI) terrorist bombings in Bali in October 2002 and Jakarta in August 2003. The Indonesian Government cooperated with the American and Australian intelligence agencies to investigate and arrest terrorist suspects from JI, believed to be affiliated with al-Qaeda. In addition, the Indonesian Government passed tougher anti-terrorist laws that allowed terrorist suspects to be detained for six months and introduced classified materials into court hearings.[32] After the Bali nightclub bombing, the Indonesian Government arrested Abu Bakar Bashir, JI's spiritual leader, after requests from the United States and Australia. However, the four-year jail sentence given to Bashir and his exoneration from the Bali blast was disappointing to Washington and Canberra, both of which saw it as a setback for Indonesia's 'war on terror'.[33]

Soon after the September 11 tragedies, the United States changed its high-handed policy towards Indonesia, driven by human rights issues, to a low-pressure and cooperative policy. Indonesia had become an important American partner in the fight against global terrorism. During Megawati's 2001 visit, President George W. Bush offered a package of financial aid worth $657 million and promised to lift the embargo on commercial sales of non-lethal defense equipment. The Americans also replaced Robert Gelbard, the 'abrasive and controversial' Ambassador to Jakarta, with Ralph Boyce, an experienced career diplomat.[34] In mid-July 2002, the Senate Appropriations Committee lifted restrictions imposed three years earlier on military training programs with Indonesia, which was seen as the first Congressional step to lifting the ban against American training programs for the Indonesian military. In August 2002, Secretary of State Colin Powell stated that the United States was considering resuming military aid to Indonesia and fully normalising military-to-military relations.[35]

Although the United States declined Indonesia's request to place the *Gerakan Aceh Merdeka* (*GAM:* Free Aceh Movement) on the list of international terrorist organisations or to link the anti-separatist war with the global 'war on terrorism', Washington did not seriously criticise Indonesia's military actions in Aceh. It is true that the United States Congress blocked the renewal of military-to-military ties partly because of Indonesia's offensive in Aceh. However, as Anthony Smith argues: 'Aceh will not derail the broader Indonesia-U.S. relationship, especially as the United States needs good relations with Indonesia to proceed with the war against terrorism in Southeast Asia.'[36] Bush still called Indonesia a vital partner and a friend to America during his short visit to Indonesia in October 2003 and stated that the United States 'appreciates Indonesia's strong cooperation in the war on terror'.[37]

To a certain extent, Indonesia's Government under Megawati played to American interests in the 'war on terror' and seized the opportunity of weak United States pressure to try to solve its own separatist headache in Aceh. Although the United States did not accede to Indonesia's demand to link the Aceh rebels to terrorism, American acquiescence was the second-best result for Indonesia compared with Washington's strong position over East Timor two years before. The intention of Megawati's Aceh policy is clear: to crack down on Aceh separatist rebels to prevent further disintegration of Indonesia and restore domestic order to facilitate economic recovery.

Compared to Wahid, elected by the MPR under the old constitutional framework, Yudhoyono was the first directly elected President in Indonesia. Although Yudhoyono's own party, the Democratic Party, won only 7.5% of the popular vote in the legislative election, Yudhoyono and his presidential running mate, Jusuf Kalla, won a landslide victory, gaining 60.6% of the vote against the incumbent Megawati in the presidential election in September 2004. Both Yodhoyono and Kalla served in the Megawati Government. Whilst Yodhoyono was the Coordinating Minister for Political and Security Affairs, Kalla was the Coordinating Minister for People's Welfare. A major reason for Yodhoyono's victory was the pervasive dissatisfaction with Megawati's leadership, criticised as 'aloof and ineffectual.'[38]. However, Yodhoyono was seen as 'decisive, charismatic, inspiring, and honest,' according to a public survey after the presidential election.[39]

Although Yodhoyono enjoyed a very high political legitimacy as a result of his victory through direct election, he faced serious pressures and challenges from the Parliament controlled by his opponents, including Megawati's party. Using cabinet appointments to forge political coalitions in the Parliament, Yodhoyono was not initially effective. The major breakthrough was achieved in December 2004 when Kalla won the chairmanship of Golkar, the largest party in the Parliament.

Since then, Golkar, which had been the major opposition of the President, has started to support Yodhoyono. Yodhoyono's major challenge was to hasten the recovery of Indonesia's economy. Although Indonesia's economy was slowly revived under the three presidencies following Soeharto, Indonesia's speed of recovery lagged far behind other Southeast Asian countries. One major reason was Indonesian political instability and social unrest after the downfall of Soeharto. Using diplomacy as a political tool to stabilise domestic politics and gain international support became the major goal of Yodhoyono's foreign policy.

Differing from Megawati's hard-line policy toward the Aceh separatist movement, Yodhoyono seized the opportunity given by the 2004 tsunami to start peace negotiations with GAM. The tsunami struck the northern and western coasts of Aceh and killed 169,000 people. Because of the horrendous disaster, GAM agreed to peace negotiations with the Indonesian Government. In early 2005, under the auspices of the Crisis Management Initiative, headed by former Finnish President Martti Ahtisaari, GAM and the Indonesian Government signed a memorandum of understanding for a cease-fire agreement. Although GAM recognised Indonesian sovereignty over Aceh, Indonesia's Government allowed GAM to organise a political party to contest local elections in Aceh. The peace agreement has become one of the greatest political achievements for Yodhoyono.[40] It not only prevented further disintegration of Indonesia after East Timor's independence, it boosted Yodhoyono's political credibility in both the domestic and international arenas.

Indonesian–United States relations improved dramatically under Yodhoyono. Compared with Megawati's cautious attitude toward the American anti-terrorism campaign, Yodhoyono was decisive and practical in cracking down on the terrorist networks in Indonesia. When serving as the Coordinating Minister in Megawati's Government, he was in charge of cooperating with the United States in investigating the Bali and Marriot bombings. In September 2004 and October 2005 two JI-related terrorist attacks hit Indonesia again. Yodhoyono actively cooperated with the United States and Australia to crack down on the JI network in Indonesia; and in a November 2005 shoot-out, Indonesian police killed Azahari Husin, one of the most wanted terrorists in Southeast Asia, who was believed responsible for all terrorist suicide bombings in Indonesia.

The United States started to augment its military ties with Indonesia. In February 2005, the United States resumed the IMET program, which was suspended after the 1992 Dili killing. In addition, it lifted a series of restrictions on military assistance, such as non-lethal foreign military sales and foreign military financing. The United States and Indonesia also conducted several joint military counterterrorism exercises.[41] In 2004 and 2009, Washington actively provided humanitarian assistance to the Indonesian Government after the natural disasters in Aceh and Sumatra. In 2008, Yudhoyono proposed a strategic partnership between Jakarta and Washington. In February 2009, during her visit to Indonesia, Secretary of State Hillary Clinton committed the United States to 'working with Indonesia to pursue such a partnership with a concrete agenda.'[42] It is reported that the United States will sign a comprehensive partnership document with Indonesia during President Barack Obama's official visit to Indonesia (a visit twice postponed).

Why did the United States renew its interests in Indonesia? There are two principal reasons. First Indonesia, the largest Muslim country in the world, is a model of successful democratic transition. Close ties with Indonesia will help the United States improve its relations with the Muslim world. Second, as the largest country in Southeast Asia, Indonesia is a perfect candidate for the United States to countervail China's strategic rise.

Indonesia apparently understood the strategic intention of the United States. However, besides embracing American support, Yodhoyono chose a more balanced diplomatic strategy to boost Indonesia's international profile. On one hand, Indonesia stood firmly with the Muslim world to criticise Israel's conflict with Hezbollah in Lebanon and with Hamas in the West Bank. Although this policy caused some tension with the United States, it pleased Indonesia's domestic constituencies.

On the other, Indonesia improved its economic and political relations with China. In 2005, Yodhoyono visited Beijing to sign a strategic partnership agreement. The agreement included promoting trade, investment, and commercial links plus strengthening defense ties.[43] During his Beijing visit, Yodhoyono warned the United States not to intervene in Indonesia's domestic affairs in responding to the United States Congress passing a bill on Papua.[44] Although some critics suggest that the Indonesia–China military security relations lost momentum after Yodhoyono's visit, a close tie with China will still be an important diplomatic card for Indonesia in coping with pressures from the United States.[45]

Yodhoyono also conducted an active foreign policy to improve Indonesia's international profile. In 2007–8, Indonesia served as a non-permanent member of the UN Security Council. From late 2007 to early 2008, it hosted a series of international events, from the UN Climate Change summit to a large UN conference on anti-corruption measures.[46] In 2009, the upgrade of the G20 into the world's main council for economic cooperation increased Indonesia's diplomatic regional weight. As the only ASEAN state with G20 membership, Indonesia regained its leadership confidence and ambition in ASEAN. In October 2009, Indonesia suggested that other ASEAN states co ordinate with Jakarta before future G20 summits so that Indonesia could deliver a stronger ASEAN voice in the summit.[47] Despite domestic pressure in the legislative elections, Yodhoyono attended the G20 London summit in April 2009. In the later Pittsburgh meeting, he was invited to be the keynote speaker on climate change. Although there are many criticisms of Yodhoyono's speeches, in particular, and his G20 diplomacy, in general, Indonesia has gradually regained its lost international prestige under his leadership.[48]

Since the end of the Cold War, Indonesia has faced a dramatic change in both the international environment and domestic politics. The Soviet Union's collapse made the communist threat obsolete. As a middle Power, Indonesia faced new challenges and opportunities in the emerging unipolar world. In domestic politics, Soeharto's downfall in 1998 started Indonesia's new journey towards democracy. From Habibie to Yodhoyono, Indonesia transformed from an authoritarian regime to a successful democracy.[49]

Indonesia's foreign policy experienced dramatic shifts under the five presidents after the Cold War. As a longtime dictator, Soeharto conducted a 'strong man' foreign policy. The robust political legitimacy based on economic performance and political stability provided Soeharto with the political confidence to play a leadership role in regional security and economic cooperation after the Cold War. In turn, his international ambitions served to promote Indonesia's economic development and strengthen his political rule in Indonesia.

As a transitional political figure, Habibie's political legitimacy was inherently weak because of the 'transformation' of power transition. Facing a high level of international pressure from the West over East Timor, Habibie had no alternative but to compromise and finally give up Indonesia's sovereign claim over the island region. Enjoying relatively high political legitimacy, given their (indirectly) election-based victories, Wahid and Megawati experienced unstable domestic control because of shaky, multiparty coalitions formed in the Parliament. Whilst Wahid chose a strong external balancing policy to counter high pressure from the West on East Timor and economic reforms, Megawati employed a neighbor-first diplomacy in the presence of low American pressure to strengthen Indonesia's regional and domestic control, especially on the Aceh issue.

Yudhoyono is the first directly elected president in Indonesia. His political legitimacy is built on a landside electoral victory and therefore is the strongest amongst these four presidents after Soeharto. Although Yodhoyono also faced challenges and pressures from the Parliament, his political coalition skills and high popularity helped him manage shaky relations with the Parliament and the opposition parties. Although there were many criticisms of his dealings with domestic corruption and military reform, his successful reelection in 2009 vindicated his unchallenged political status in Indonesia.

The inherently strong political legitimacy encouraged Yodhoyono to conduct a more active foreign policy to boost Indonesia's international profile. Indonesia's unique identity as both a successful democracy and the largest Muslim country also attracted American attention. Consequently, the United States has tightened its security and economic ties with Indonesia since 2005. However, Yodhoyono conducted a multidimensional diplomacy to maximise Indonesia's international weight. Indonesia's firm stand on Middle Eastern issues and active participation in international institutions, especially the G20, made Indonesia an important Power on the world stage. The future challenge for Indonesia's foreign policy lies in the shifting power structure in the international system. How to deal with the seemingly inevitable competition between the United States and China will be the major task for Yodhoyono and his successors.

Notes

1 Charles Krauthammer, 'The Unipolar Moment.' *Foreign Affairs*, 70(1990), 23–33.
2 For political legitimacy in democracy and authoritarian regime, see Seymour Martin Lipset, *Political Man: The Social Bases of Politics*, expanded edition (Baltimore, MD, 1981).
3 The 'new order' is the term coined by President Suharto to contrast his rule with that of his predecessor, President Sukarno, the 'old order.'
4 See Econimost Intelligence Unit Country Profile, *Indonesia 1998* (London, 1999).
5 Thee Kian Wie, 'Indonesia's Economic Performance under President Soeharto's New Order,' *Seoul Journal of Economics*, 20(2007), 263–81.
6 EIU Country Profile 'Indonesia 1998,' London: Economist Intelligence Unit, 1999.
7 World Bank, *The East Asian Miracle: Economic Growth and Public Policy* (Oxford, 1993), 1.
8 See Michael Vatikiotis, *Indonesian Politics under Suharto*, 3rd edition (London, New York, 1993).
9 See Leo Suryadinata, *Indonesia's Foreign Policy Under Soeharto: Aspiring to International Leadership* (Singapore, 1996), 50–51.
10 See Dewi Fortuna Anwar, *Indonesia in ASEAN: Foreign Policy and Regionalism* (Singapore, 1994); Leo Suryadinata, *Indonesia's Foreign Policy*.
11 See Rizal Sukma, 'Recent Developments in Sino-Indonesian Relations: An Indonesian View.' *Contemporary Southeast Asia*, 16(1994), 35–45; Suryadinata, *Indonesia's Foreign Policy*.
12 See Suryadinata, *Indonesia's Foreign Policy*, 52.
13 Rizal Sukma, *Indonesia and China: The Politics of a Troubled Relationship* (London, New York, 1999); Kai He, 'Interpreting China-Indonesia Relations: "Good-Neighborliness," "Mutual Trust", and "All-Round Cooperation"', *SDSC Working Paper*, No. 349 (Canberra, 2000).
14 Ji Guoxing and Hadi Soesastro, eds., *Sino-Indonesian Relations in the Post-Cold War Era* (Jakarta, 1992), 134.
15 Sukma, *Indonesia and China*, 208.
16 Regarding American acquiescence in Soeharto's invasion to East Timor, see recently declassified United States Government documents on President Gerald Ford and Secretary of State Henry Kissinger' visits to Indonesia in 1975, available at the National Security Archive in George Washington University, www.gwu.edu/~nsarchiv/NSAEBB/NSAEBB62/.
17 See Suryadinata, *Indonesia's Foreign Policy*.
18 Richard Stevenson, 'U.S., IMF Await Evidence of Economic Change from Habibie.' *New York Times* (22 May 1998).
19 Ibid.
20 John McBeth, Michael Vatikiotis, and Margot Cohen, 'Into the Void,' *Far Eastern Economic Review* (4 June 1998), 16–18.
21 Dewi Fortuna Anwar, 'The East Timor Crisis: An Indonesian View', in Bruce Brown, ed., *East Timor-the Consequences* (Wellington, 2000), 20.
22 Margot Cohen, 'Captives of the Cause.' *Far Eastern Economic Review* (2 September 1999), 16–18.
23 Indonesia's President was elected by the People's Consultative Assembly [MPR: *Majelis Permusyawaratan Rakyat*], which consisted of members of the DPR [the Parliament] and regional and social group representatives. In the Soeharto era, the Assembly had 1,000 members, one-half from the 500-member

DPR and one-half appointed by Soeharto to represent the 27 provinces and a wide variety of governmental, social, and political groups. In the DPR, the military retained 100 seats until 1995, when Soeharto reduced their number to 75. However, DPR military seats were appointed by Soeharto. These regional and group representatives were also appointed by the President rather than elected. Therefore, Soeharto's ruling party ensured a majority of seats in the Assembly. In the 1999 election, the number of non-Parliament members was reduced from 500 to 200, with 135 representing the regions and 65 representing non-partisan social groups. Whereas regional delegates were to be selected by the newly elected provincial legislators, the social groups would be chosen by the National Election Commission rather than the President. For details, see William Liddle, 'Indonesia in 1999: Democracy Restored,' *Asian Survey*, 40(2000), 32–42.

24 BBC News, 'Asia-Pacific International Praise for Wahid', *BBC News Online*, 20 October 1999.
25 John McBeth and Dan Murphy. 'Ring of Scandal', *Far Eastern Economic Review*, (15 June 2000), 24–25.
26 Alwi Shihab, 'The Indonesian Foreign Policy Outlook.' Keynote Address at the Conference of the Indonesian National Press Day, 17 February 2000.
27 Some scholars argue that Wahid's 'looking towards Asia' policy was more rhetoric rather than practice because Indonesia needed Western economic aid to revive the economy. See Anthony Smith, 'Indonesia's Foreign Policy under Abdurrahman Wahid: Radical or Status Quo State', *Contemporary Southeast Asia*, 22(2000), 498–527. I basically agree with this assessment, but prefer to differentiate the policy from the consequence or outcome of the policy. Rather than asserting that Wahid's 'looking towards Asia' policy is rhetoric at the beginning, the policy outcome was a failure in terms of forging an anti-West alliance because other states, including China, did not actively respond to Wahid's proposal.
28 Irman Lanti, 'Indonesia: The Year of Continuing Turbulence', *Southeast Asian Affairs 2002* (Singapore, 2003), 111–29; Tim Huxley, *Disintegrating Indonesia? Implications for Regional Security*, Adelphi Paper 349 (London, 2002), 20–21.
29 Fabiola Unidjaja 'Emphasis on Bilateral Ties Back on Foreign Agenda', *Jakarta Post* (22 August 2001).
30 Kornelius Purba, 'Foreign Policy, Neighbors First', *Jakarta Post* (22 August 2001).
31 The other two concentric circles are the ASEAN +3 and the United States and the European Union. For Indonesia's official foreign policy documentation, see Indonesia's Foreign Ministry website, www.deplu.go.id.
32 Anthony Smith, 'Indonesia's Aceh Problem: Measuring International and Domestic Costs', *Asia-Pacific Security Studies*, 2(2003), online version.
33 Jeremy Wagstaff, 'Cold Comfort', *Far Eastern Economic Review* (11 September 2003), 18.
34 Michael S. Malley, 'Indonesia in 2001: Restoring Stability in Jakarta', *Asian Survey*, 42(2002), 130–31.
35 Colin Powell, 'Remarks with Indonesian Foreign Minister Hassan Wirajuda', 2 August 2002, www.state.gov/secretary.rm/2002/12426.htm.
36 Smith, 'Indonesia's Aceh Problem'.
37 F. F. Unidjaja and W. Boediwardhana, 'Bush makes stopover in Bali, lends support to Megawati', *Jakarta Post* (23 October 2003).
38 EIU country profile 'Indonesia 2008.' London: Economist Intelligence Unit, 2008, 5.
39 R. William Liddle and Saiful Mujani. 'Indonesia in 2004: The Rise of Susilo Bambang Yudhoyono.' *Asian Survey* 45, no. 1 (2005), 123.
40 R. William Liddle and Saiful Mujani, 'Indonesia in 2005: A New Multiparty Presidential Democracy.' *Asian Survey* 46, no. 1 (2006), 132–39.
41 Liddle and Mujani, 'Indonesia in 2005,' 139.
42 VOA, 'U.S.-Indonesia Cooperation', *VOA News*, (21 May 2010), www1.voanews.com/policy/editorials/US-Indonesia-Cooperation-94605954.html.
43 Dewi Fortuna Anwar. 'A Journey of Change: Indonesia's Foreign Policy', *Global Asia*, Volume 4, Number 3(2009), 16–20.
44 Liddle and Mujani, 'Indonesia in 2005', 139.
45 See Ian Storey, 'China and Indonesia: Military security Ties Fail to Gain Momentum,' *China Brief*, IX, Number 4(2009), 6–9.
46 See Marcus Mietzner, 'Indonesia in 2008: Yodhoyono's Struggle for Reelection', *Asian Survey* 49, 1 (2009), 146–55.
47 'ASEAN Seeks Stronger G20 Voice', *Jakarta Post* (25 October 2009).
48 For criticisms on Yodhoyono's diplomacy, see Mietzner, 'Indonesia in 2008'; idem., 'Indonesia in 2009.'
49 See Marcus Mietzner, 'Indonesia in 2009: Electoral Contestation and Economic Resilience', *Asian Survey*, 50(2010), 193.

Part V

International Organisations and Military Alliances

20

A global Great Power in the making?

The European Union in the emerging global order

Rikard Bengtsson

The European Union is inevitably a global player ... it should be ready to share in the responsibility for global security and in building a better world.

European Council, 2003[1]

The passage above stems from the European Security Strategy (ESS) adopted by the member-states of the European Union (EU) in 2003 and revised in 2008. The aim of the ESS is to develop a strategic perspective towards the main challenges for and threats to the EU in a globalised world. One of the central messages of this key document is that the EU ought to play a primary role in international relations, not only out of narrow self-interest but also because it has an obligation to contribute to global development and the promotion of human rights and democracy. This reasoning also permeates the foreign-policy provisions of the Lisbon Treaty, which entered into force in 2009 and is the current legal basis for the EU. Nonetheless, disunity amongst European states in the foreign policy area is a recurrent phenomenon that renders such ambitions in doubt.

Is the EU a foreign-policy actor? If so, what are the main elements of its external policy and do the member-states and EU-level institutions collectively carry any weight internationally? These questions are both simple and dramatically different to answer. Judging by the ambitions of key EU institutions (the European Commission, the European Parliament, the Council of Ministers, and the European Council) to influence matters beyond the territory of the member-states, the answer is definitely in the affirmative. The same goes for certain policy areas, most notably trade policy, in which the EU rests on a single market internally and in which trade policy in relation to the outside world is a matter of so-called exclusive EU competence with clear supranational elements. In 'classic' foreign, security, and defense policy, the issue is fundamentally more complex. Organisationally, structures have developed in this area under the heading of the Common Foreign and Security Policy (CFSP) (set up in 1993), and the EU now has a number of policy instruments at its disposal. The Lisbon Treaty develops these aspects even further. At the same time, there are numerous examples of disunity, even competition, amongst the EU member-states in this field, which justifies the conclusion that, thus far, it has largely been a situation of parallel foreign policies on both the member-state and European level. Moreover, ambitions are not transformed automatically into impact. In terms of trade policy, the situation is one of clear EU leadership: the EU is the world's largest economic entity, trading bloc, and development assistance provider and occupies a key role for instance in the World

Trade Organization. In foreign policy, the picture is different. In the Middle East, for instance, the EU has long tried to change its posture from being a 'payer' to becoming a 'player', but with limited success. This example also indicates that outsiders' perceptions of the EU (not only its internal institutional capacity and agenda) play a key role for the actorness of the EU.

One of the special features of the EU is, thus, that its foreign policy is uneven in character. In some areas, the case for a Union policy is easy to make, in terms of both organisation and impact. In the realm of classic foreign, security, and defense policy, the situation is fundamentally more complex. The EU's emergence in global politics is a principally important issue, both because newcomers are relatively rare in the international arena and because the *sui generis* character of the EU (combining supranational qualities with the intergovernmental logic of traditional international organisation) brings conceptualisations of international actorness to the fore. The key to understanding the EU as an international actor is to focus on the relationship between member-states and the various institutions of the EU system. That relationship has evolved over time, both in terms of formal structures and regarding the mind-sets of European politicians. Ultimately, a major obstacle for developing an effective foreign policy at the EU level lies with the diverging views of the member-states on important issues, reducing the EU foreign policy to a least-common-denominator outcome.[2] Nonetheless, the common denominator on many issues may be advanced and proactive partly because of the socialisation effects of advanced collaboration outside the foreign-policy realm proper, for instance on the Europeanisation of foreign policy.[3]

A fruitful point of departure regarding actorness is to draw on Roy Ginsberg's distinction between presence and actorness, in which the former denotes a passive or latent form of agency and the latter independent activity based on strategy and concrete capabilities.[4] Using such a conceptualisation, one may begin unpacking observations of increasing EU involvement on the global stage. In all relevant aspects (frequency, scope and depth) the EU has been increasing its international presence over the last decade.[5] But does EU foreign policy contribute in any independent way to global processes or events? Do EU-level institutions add any autonomous value or are the EU dimensions of European foreign policy simply the sum of the foreign policies of EU member-states? To what extent do others recognise the EU as an actor in its own respect?

Although it certainly remains important to analyze EU-internal developments (such as institutional changes) to understand the development of EU foreign-policy actorness, the EU does not exist in a vacuum. In the end, what is fundamentally important is to take account of these developments from the perspective of different actors involved in the current order and how their actions are influenced by (and influence) EU action. Overall, this implies an analytical framework based on strategic interaction and the reciprocal constitution of actorness.

Recognition (the mutual constitution of a relationship through parallel actor-internal developments and external expectations) helps conceptualise the elusive notion of actorness. Although an actor may hypothetically have great ambitions in a given issue area, this matters little as long as others do not recognise the impact of the actor. Conversely, external expectations may be rather substantial in some cases whilst, at the same time, preconditions in terms of actual capacity to deliver may be limited. The argument rests on constructivist logic in focusing on how perceptions shape and are shaped by actual behavior in a constantly ongoing process.[6]

For instance, this behavior forms the basis of the analysis of Charlotte Bretherton and John Vogler regarding the EU as a global actor.[7] A central argument on their part is that both internal capacity ('capability') and external events ('opportunity') are of importance, and how the former relates to the latter influences the 'presence' of an actor on the international stage. Presence should not be regarded in terms of concrete (purposive) action but, rather, as a 'consequence of being'.[8] Their analysis highlights that there are essentially two elements to actorness. One concerns an actor's power resources in terms of ability or capacity to influence a desired outcome. The other concerns the image (or identity) of the actor in the eyes of others.

Taking note of the increasing ambitions of the EU on the world stage begs the questions of how the Union sees itself and what kind of goals and ends it wants to pursue. But before analyzing the emergence of EU structures for foreign policy cooperation and the means at its disposal, the issues of the identity and international agenda of the EU need consideration. The most authoritative expression of the EU self-image is in the Preamble of the Lisbon Treaty:

> The Union is founded on the values of respect for human dignity, freedom, democracy, equality, the rule of law and respect for human rights, including the rights of persons belonging to minorities. The Union's aim is to promote peace, its values and the well-being of its peoples.[9]

Regarding the international ambitions, the following passage of the Lisbon Treaty is to guide subsequent external policy development:

> The Union's action on the international scene shall be guided by the principles which have inspired its own creation, development and enlargement, and which it seeks to advance in the wider world: democracy, the rule of law, the universality and indivisibility of human rights and fundamental freedoms, respect for human dignity, the principles of equality and solidarity, and respect for the principles of the United Nations Charter and international law. The Union shall seek to develop relations and build partnerships with third countries, and international, regional or global organisations which share the principles referred to (above). It shall promote multilateral solutions to common problems, in particular in the framework of the United Nations.[10]

Three main conclusions derive from these official expressions, as well as from numerous statements by EU representatives. First, the EU constitutes a community of values, in essence a security community in the Deutschian sense, but not a military alliance (although there are expressions of political solidarity, and in the Lisbon Treaty provision is made for mutual assistance in times of severe crisis, however without specifying the form of such support). Second, the EU has an external agenda (a willingness; indeed, an obligation) to promote its values on the international scene. Third, the values referred to above are not unique for the EU, or for Europe, but are at least embraced by the Organisation for Economic Co-operation and Development countries and the Western zone of peace;[11] or they form part of what Karen Smith calls 'normative globalisation'.[12] In the end, what may be special about the EU (strength or weakness depending on the observer) is the combination of resources and strategies available to or used by the EU (a strong reminder never to forget the member-states' input for the capacity of the EU) and the peculiar posture of the organisation itself. The most important thing about the EU as an external actor is not what it says or what it does, but what it is.[13] This international identity of the EU (a 'difference engine', labelled by Manners and Whitman) has given rise to an industry of academic writing and labeling, most notable in terms of normative power, but also expressed as ethical power, civilian power, and normative Great Power to mention just a few.[14]

Smith's analysis of EU foreign policy identifies (much in parallel to official sources referred to above) five major foreign-policy objectives in the realm of the CFSP: fostering regional cooperation, promoting human rights, promoting democracy and good governance, preventing violent conflict, and fighting international crime. Smith makes a number of observations of relevance to this analysis. First, these objectives clash with one another and with other objectives from time to time, implying that as for other foreign-policy actors, a coherent profile may be difficult to sustain over time. Second, these objectives have been on the EU agenda for some time; whilst not novel in relation to the Lisbon Treaty, they have been part of the evolution of foreign-policy cooperation. Third, one may question how distinctly EU-oriented these objectives are; Smith argues that apart from regional cooperation, the objectives are readily embraced by member-state foreign policies, in turn both a prerequisite and a weakness for the CFSP.[15]

Foreign policy cooperation amongst EU states has a long history, although it took time before it became part of formal treaty regulation. Aimed at coordinating the foreign policies of individual member-states, the so-called European Political Cooperation already evolved in the 1970s, but outside the organisation's formal structures. The Maastricht Treaty formally establishing the EU (signed in 1991, entering into force in 1993) introduced the EU's so-called pillar structure. The first pillar contained already existing cooperation, in short the Single Market and adjacent areas, whereas the second and third pillars were new and based on strictly intergovernmental logic. The EU in effect became a very complex organisation, with different political logics (varying elements of supranationality and institutional competences) for different policy areas. The second pillar contained the CFSP, whereas the third involved Justice and Home Affairs (JHA), another sovereignty-sensitive area hitherto not formally subject to cooperation.[16]

The CFSP as well as subsequent developments may have been largely events driven. Fundamentally, the development of the CFSP cannot be explained without reference to the end of the Cold War and the new geopolitical landscape in Europe and globally. Specifically, the conflicts in the former Yugoslavia are often seen as catalysts for this development. The intergovernmental nature of CFSP cooperation, in effect granting all participants veto power, simultaneously made it acceptable to the member-states and contributed to its inherent weakness. To be sure, the label of common policy was misdirected and, from the outset, the CFSP was plagued by a lack of resources and an obvious 'capability–expectations gap',[17] which EU representatives have contributed to themselves by claiming that the EU was indeed going to make a difference, not least in the greater European context. The ongoing conflicts in the Balkans showed that despite the CFSP formally in place, the EU was not a coherent actor making such a difference.

Again, largely events driven, the CFSP in the late 1990s took two steps that with the benefit of hindsight were fundamentally important. The first was to construct the office of the High Representative for the CFSP, formally in place through the Amsterdam Treaty of 1999. Thought by many as a top civil-servant position, EU leaders chose to assign Javier Solana, the former North Atlantic Treaty Organization Secretary-General, to the task. Formally, the position of High Representative rested on diffuse ground (to assist the six-month, rotating Presidency of the Council of Ministers) but with entrepreneurial efforts, tireless global diplomacy, and skilful staff at the Council Secretariat, Solana came to play a distinctly important role in giving the EU a face in the rest of the world. However, this process occurred in parallel to the rotating Presidency and the Commission also being involved in external relations, resulting in bureaucratic turf wars and a certain amount of competition for visibility if not in substance amongst the top people involved.[18]

The other important development in the late 1990s was the decision to enter into security and defense collaboration under an EU heading. This initiative, taken originally by France and Great Britain at St Malo in 1998 but formally agreed to at the Cologne European Council in Spring 1999 under the heading of European Security and Defence Policy (ESDP), opened up the area of civilian and military crisis management (dealing with so-called Petersberg tasks). The first Headline Goal of the EU was established in 1999 (by 2003, deployment within sixty days of 50,000–60,000 persons, sustained for one year) and upgraded in 2004. The EU has subsequently set up some 25 ESDP missions of civilian, military, or joint civil–military nature. Most have been small, reflecting the nature of civilian undertakings, although the military missions in the Balkans and in Congo have been relatively large (see Appendix).[19] Creating the office of the High Representative and setting up the ESDP proved to be mutually reinforcing in that Solana took on a leadership role in an area in which member-state priorities were not yet fully fixed.[20]

Finally, there exists the issue of institutional developments. In the aftermath of the St Malo and Cologne decisions, a number of organisations have been created within the CFSP/ESDP, the most important being the Political and Security Committee, charged with developing crisis management policy as well as overseeing concrete operations and reporting directly to the Council. Over time, this body has become the central locus of CFSP/ESDP institutional development. In addition, more specific organs have been developed for different military and civilian purposes, such as the EU Military Staff, the EU Military Committee, and the Committee for Civilian Crisis Management.[21]

Despite the evolution of the CFSP across time, some generic problems have remained: internal regarding the institutional division of labour; external regarding visibility and impact. Some of the major provisions of the Lisbon Treaty speak directly to these problems. Five issues require emphasis in the foreign-policy order of the EU. The first concerns abolishing the pillar structure. From the perspective of the 1993 Treaty on the EU, a number of issues in the JHA pillar have been transferred to the first pillar, whilst the drawbacks of having some external policy issues in the first pillar and others in the second have been all too evident. The Lisbon Treaty does away with the pillar structure and instead introduces two policy domains: internal and external. The result is that all aspects of external relations (trade, development, security, and defense policy) fall under the same heading. However (and fundamentally important), the CFSP remains intergovernmental in nature, implying that differences in competences and decision-making procedures remain along with the inherent problems that these differences entail. Still, the preconditions for policy coherence and a holistic perspective on security and development as set forth in the ESS and elsewhere have improved.

The second element concerns the institutional structure of foreign-policy making. Before Lisbon, three institutional actors were active in the foreign policy area: the Commission, the Council headed by the Presidency, and the High Representative. Changes to the treaty have ended effectively formal presidency involvement in CFSP. The novelty was to merge the post of the High Representative and the Commissioner for External Relations into a combined one, which again improves the preconditions for effective policy-making and decreases the likelihood for bureaucratic competition. Created on 1 December 2009, the new position is the High Representative of the Union for Foreign Affairs and Security Policy; its first incumbent is Baroness Catherine Ashton, a British politician. The High Representative is thus accountable to the EU system in total, rather than only to the Council, and is potentially important because it encompasses simultaneously serving as Vice-President of the Commission and presiding over the Foreign Affairs Council, comprising the foreign ministers of the member-states. Still it is important to underline that decisions in the Council are made unanimously, implying that the impact of the High Representative will continue to be subject to the spectrum of national interests. On the other hand, the position opens certain elements of agenda-setting and framing.

The third novelty of the Lisbon Treaty concerns the assignment of a permanent President of the European Council, the highest political institution in the EU comprising the heads of governments (and in a few cases, the heads of state) of the member-states. Earlier, the country holding the Presidency occupied that position as part of the responsibilities of the rotating six-month term. Now, a permanent President (at present, the former Belgian premier, Herman Van Rompuy) holds the post for a two-and-a-half- year term, with a possible one-time reelection. In the realm of foreign policy, this means that the President represents the EU to the outside world in parallel with the High Representative. The division of labor between the two is not clear and may well give rise to confusion inside and outside the EU.

Fourthly, the Lisbon Treaty creates the European External Action Service (EEAS), a foreign ministry of sorts for the EU. The basis for this institution is the already existing 130-odd European Commission Delegations around the world. The mandate of the EEAS will not be consular but, rather, to coordinate and represent the Union, report to the High Representative, and promote the EU's trade, development, enlargement, and security policies. The EEAS is staffed by formerly Commission Council Secretariat officials, and by diplomats from national foreign ministries. It is imperative to note that the EEAS does not replace the national foreign ministries; indeed, severe tensions between EU-level institutions and the national bureaucracies have already been evident.

Finally, the new treaty opens up enhanced cooperation, that is, the possibility for groups of member-states to cooperate more closely in issues in which not all member-states welcome further integration (so-called permanent structured cooperation). This possibility also includes the CFSP and the Common Security and Defence Policy (the former ESDP), in essence allowing for further military integration to undertake more advanced crisis-management operations.[22]

A tentative conclusion about the novelties of the Lisbon Treaty concerning foreign policy is that some of the weaknesses of the old system are being alleviated and the preconditions for effective external action are improved. However, fundamental challenges remain, both in inter-institutional terms and as far as the relationship between the member-state level and EU-level logics is concerned. What are the instruments at disposal for EU foreign policy? The discussion above reveals the predominance of civilian means, but the EU also includes military resources assigned specifically for EU purposes.

In concrete terms, a standard distinction amongst economic, diplomatic, and military means can fruitfully be employed. When discussing economic instruments in the context of the CFSP, the long line of preferential trade agreements is not of immediate interest; what is more important are economic instruments (cooperative agreements or imposing sanctions to change the behavior of third countries outside the EU in a direction desired by the EU), good governance, democracy, human rights, and so on. More precisely, it concerns if and how political conditionality may be attached to prospects of economic interaction, in effect inducing political and societal change in third countries via the market attraction of the EU: single market, preferential trade rules, and the like. Such a practice of conditionality has been widely employed; since 1995 all agreements entered into by the EU contain human rights conditionality of this kind, an issue of principal interest in the context of ongoing negotiations on so-called partnership and cooperation agreements (PCA) between the EU and China and the EU and Russia, respectively. The negative instruments of economic and financial sanctions are used primarily in relation to specific individuals (such as President Robert Mugabe of Zimbabwe) or goods (such as 'blood diamonds' as part of the Kimberley Process).[23]

Diplomatic instruments employed by the EU come in a various forms. They can involve sending démarches, making public statements, or conducting political dialogue and engaging in high-level visits with countries across the globe. It can also entail sending election observers where deemed needed; sending special representatives to conflict regions such as Africa and the Middle East, or civilian experts to state-building processes (for instance in Kosovo and Iraq); making cease-fire or peace proposals; employing diplomatic sanctions, visa, and travel bans; or imposing arms embargoes, for instance *vis-à-vis* the Belarussian Government.[24] As a foreign-policy actor, the EU thus holds a broad range of diplomatic instruments at its disposal. Some of these are primarily declaratory in nature, and often criticised for not being sharp enough, whereas others are part of informal or formal negotiation processes. A special political-diplomatic instrument (unique for the EU) is to offer membership. Such an offer is a strong but geographically limited instrument.

The military part of the arsenal of instruments is the newest instrument, a principally important one in that it changes the profile of EU external action.[25] The EU has developed a set of battle groups (formed by individual member-states or groups of states) to be employed in crises; however, such groups have not actually ever been used. As was mentioned above, the EU has deployed a number of military missions, including some joint civilian–military ones, under the EU flag (see Appendix). It needs to be stressed that military missions are voluntary for member-states in terms of participation and funding.

This inventory gives rise to two critical and related questions: one regarding consistency, the other effectiveness. The EU is facing consistency problems in terms of equal, or at least similar, application of instruments across cases. For instance, addressing human rights violations equally across countries; in the relationship between individual member-state foreign policy and EU-level policy (vertical consistency); and in the various institutions involved on the EU level (horizontal consistency), primarily between the Commission and the Council.[26] In the final analysis, the problem for the EU as a foreign-policy actor is to conduct a credible foreign policy by means that yield few, if any, immediate and tangible results. With the profile it has chosen (or been granted by member-states largely unwilling to cede sovereignty in this area) criticism for inefficiency and inability to deliver will likely be enduring.

EU foreign-policy instruments can be conceptualised in power terms. Four different forms of power exist: compulsory power (direct control by one actor over another); institutional power (indirect control over another through previously established formal and informal rules and procedures); structural power (the position of one actor is determined by the position of the other); and productive power (discursive processes and practices that give social meaning to subjects and shape conceptions of what is desirable and normal).[27] Joseph Nye's notions of soft power (the power of persuasion rather than coercion) thus fall into the latter category.[28] The instruments explicated above show that the EU possesses all these power resources, but to different degrees depending on context.

Interestingly enough, the *sui generis* character of the EU entity may provide the organisation with part of its resources. In short, the logic goes, the success of the EU (economically, but in this context primarily politically) may inspire others to follow, practically and intellectually. If so, it would mean that the EU possesses not only compulsory, institutional, and structural power in terms of existing relationships and its insistence on regulated, institution-based interaction, but also, importantly, productive power, through the ability to influence others about how to think about issues such as security, human rights, and welfare. It may be that these discursive means give the EU an edge in the CFSP domain, but this is hard to establish methodologically.

The previous sections have dealt with general institutional issues and the global profile of the EU. Although the EU remains contested as a global political actor, the picture is different in a regional, greater European perspective. Here, the EU exercises leadership in many contexts; and here, the actorness of the EU is undisputed. There are three major forms of EU interaction in greater Europe: the enlargement process, relations with what may be called Wider Europe primarily in the form of the European Neighbourhood Policy (ENP), and the strategic relationship with Russia.[29]

It has been argued that enlargement is the true success story of EU foreign policy; with a view to potential EU membership, many countries go far to reform their countries in a direction desired by the EU. The so-called Copenhagen criteria for membership (democratic system of government, market economy, and the administrative-judicial capacity to take on the obligations of EU membership) provide a strong form of conditionality *vis-à-vis* candidate countries. The

Eastern enlargement of 2004–7 is a good illustration of this logic: ten transition countries from the former Warzaw Pact, some even former republics in the Soviet Union, transformed their societies rapidly and often hurtfully to meet the demands of the EU. Cyprus and Malta were also part of this enlargement round. In the enlargement sphere, the EU exercises what is called normative leadership; drawing on various power resources discussed above, the EU determines the discourse (the meaning of being a European state), the process (structure of membership negotiations), and the outcome (evaluation of progress and possible offer of membership). There is good ground for expecting that the EU will remain a key actor in this part of the world. Negotiations are under way, albeit with very different pace, with three candidate countries (Croatia, Iceland, and Turkey), whereas Macedonia is recognised as a candidate country but has yet to start negotiations. The rest of the Western Balkan countries (Bosnia-Herzegovina, Serbia, Montenegro, Kosovo, and Albania) have all been officially recognised by the EU as prospective candidates for future membership.

Also in relation to the group of countries at its borders, the EU is a normative Great Power. In parallel to the 2004 enlargement, the EU developed the ENP with the ambition to create a 'ring of friends' with neighbors by an internationalist logic, acknowledging the interdependent nature of the relationships between these countries and the EU. Originally established in relation to the EU's Eastern neighbors, the ENP has also developed into covering all neighbors to the southeast and south, all in all 16 countries: Algeria, Armenia, Azerbaijan, Belarus, Egypt, Georgia, Israel, Jordan, Lebanon, Libya, Moldova, Morocco, the Palestinian Authority, Syria, Tunisia, and Ukraine. Russia was originally included in the plans, but it has subsequently left the format in favor of developing its bilateral relationship with the EU. Concrete ENP cooperation is bilateral in character, reflecting the very different interests, needs, and capacities of the ENP countries. As with enlargement, the EU is clearly a normative Great Power in the ENP context; the EU determines the institutional construction, and all countries, except Israel, are heavily dependent on EU aid. Most importantly, the program finds basis on the same kind of positive conditionality as the enlargement logic, although there are no formal links to future membership, which do not keep some ENP countries, such as Ukraine and Georgia, from repeatedly stating their long-term goal of EU membership. In essence, the ENP offers deeper economic and political integration (ultimately, a share in the internal market of the EU) if neighboring states adapt to core EU liberal norms. A critical examination of the ENP shows that in relation to many of the countries, domestic actors and/or processes slow and often challenge the Europeanisation processes. That means that in the wider Europe, the impact of the EU can be questioned. However, one interesting indication of EU leadership in the foreign-policy area is that a number of ENP countries, not least Ukraine, have aligned themselves publicly and repeatedly with CFSP statements issued by the EU.[30]

Finally, concerning Russia, the situation is fundamentally different. Both sides are seeking a regulated, negotiated relationship, but it proves difficult to go beyond formal diplomatic procedure. The relationship is highly institutionalised in that summits between the Russian President and EU leaders in troika format (the President of the European Council, the President of the Commission and the High Representative) are held twice a year. Agreements on advancing the PCA of 1997 have been made; at the summit in St Petersburg in May 2003, the parties agreed to intensify relations through four so-called Common Spaces for cooperation (economics, internal security, external security, and people-to-people contacts) and, two years later, four road maps for the implementation of cooperation were established. Still, the PCA agreement is not yet renegotiated (interrupted amongst other things by the serious rift over the 'Georgia war' in August 2008) and there is a lack of a clear and constant Russia policy on the side of the EU. The explanation for this situation may be found in at least two different corners: one concerning the dramatic but, amongst EU states, very uneven dependence on Russian energy, especially natural gas; the other from the geohistorical legacy of the Cold War and geopolitical considerations of future Russian aspirations. Both factors contribute to radically different interpretations and feelings about Russia and what kind of relationship to seek with it. In conclusion, the normative leadership so evident in other parts of greater Europe is largely absent from the Russian case because of divergent interests and perceptions amongst the EU members and Russia's own posture.[31]

The theoretical logic that informs this chapter pinpoints recognition as a key aspect of actorness. The chief importance of others' perceptions of the image and impact of a foreign-policy actor is of even greater significance for a new, non-state actor seeking to make a lasting impression on the global order. For the EU, numerous indications point in the direction that it is increasingly recognised as a Great Power in the security and political sphere; a recognition long held in the economic sphere concerning trade and aid. Simultaneously, inherent problems of member-state diversity and egoistic interests have a negative impact on such recognition.

The cases of the United States and Russia are exemplary. Based on official sources as well as interviews, grounds exist for stating that the United States increasingly recognises the EU as a global Great Power. The rift over Iraq is a good illustration that this recognition has not always been the case, but the perception has changed gradually during the George W. Bush Administration. The basis for such recognition is that the ideological compatibility and deep interdependence of the two sides make the EU a natural partner in American global policy.[32] There are indications of American appreciation for the changes brought about by the Lisbon Treaty, as argued by Secretary of State Hillary Clinton in September 2010: 'The post-Lisbon EU is expanding its role in world affairs, and the United States values our growing partnership with the EU and we see it as a cornerstone of global peace and security.'[33] However, the logic differs markedly in Russia's case. Russian recognition of the EU as a Great Power is based on deep interdependence and a set of common interests on international security issues, but also on competition for normative framing and ideological assertiveness, not least in the shared wider Europe.[34]

Other categories of states perceive the EU as a normative Great Power, projecting different forms of leadership based on a broad set of power resources.[35] This includes countries in Eastern Europe and North Africa and, not least, the African, Caribbean, and Pacific countries, with colonial links to individual EU members and recipients of great amounts of EU aid. However, it should be stressed that recognition varies within these groups, as does the impact of EU leadership. Not least in the North African context, it is evident that EU power projection yields very different outcomes, with limited impact on societal change in countries such as Syria, Egypt, and Algeria.[36]

Returning to the questions posed initially, there is good ground for concluding that the EU is developing into a Great Power in the foreign and security field, an area long reserved only for member-state policy-making. Institutional structures for action have been substantially developed over time, not least through the Lisbon Treaty, and a number of concrete instruments have been set up and put to use. Moreover, various other actors recognise the EU as a leading actor in key issues in the current international agenda.

However, there are also reasons to qualify such a positive picture. Although much activity is now taking place at the EU level, the substance of this policy development reflects positions only on which the member-states agree; on a whole array of issues, they have diverging interests, are deeply split, and do not think in all-European terms. Critics of EU foreign policy often claim that these differences are enduring and make potent action impossible. Others open up for transformation of national interests in a common direction (arguing that processes of Europeanisation in other areas have yielded such outcomes) in consequence allowing for greater scope and increasing effectiveness in foreign policy. The gap between expectations of the EU to take a leading role in global politics and its capabilities for doing so has been widely recognised. In part, the proactive rhetoric of European leaders and EU representatives exacerbates this problem. The post-Lisbon EU has a much-improved capacity for external action, potentially reducing the gap. However, the commitment of the member-states to use this capacity remains to be confirmed.

Appendix

Table 20.A1 Ongoing Common Security and Defence Policy missions and operations

Name	Nature	Initiated
EU police mission in Bosnia and Herzegovina (EUPM)	Civilian	2003
EU military operation in Bosnia and Herzegovina (EUFOR Althea)	Military	2004
EU advisory and assistance mission for security reform in DR Congo (EUSEC RD Congo)	Civilian	2005
EU integrated rule of law mission for Iraq (EUJUST LEX)	Civilian	2005
EU police mission in the Palestinian territories (EUPOL COPPS)	Civilian	2005
EU border assistance mission in Gaza (EUBAM Rafah)	Civilian	2005
EU border assistance mission in Moldova and Ukraine (EUBAM Moldova/Ukraine)	Civilian	2005
EU police mission in Afghanistan (EUPOL Afghanistan)	Civilian	2007
EU security sector reform in DR Congo (EUPOL RD Congo)	Civilian	2007
EU civilian monitoring mission in Georgia (EUMM Georgia)	Civilian	2008
EU rule of law mission in Kosovo (EULEX Kosovo)	Civilian	2008
EU anti-piracy mission off the Somali coast (EUNAVFOR Atalanta)	Military	2008
EU training mission in Somalia (EUTM Somalia)	Military	2010

Source: http://www.consilium.europa.eu/eeas/security-defence/eu-operations.aspx?lang=en; for analysis see Grevi et al 2009.

Notes

1 European Council, 'European Security Strategy. A Secure Europe in a Better World' (2003), 1: www.consilium.europa.eu/uedocs/cmsUpload/78367.pdf.
2 S. Keukeleire and J. MacNaughtan, *The Foreign Policy of the European Union* (Basingstoke, 2008), Chapter 5; K.E. Smith, *European Union Foreign Policy in a Changing World*, 2nd edition (Cambridge, UK, 2008), 9–12.
3 Reuben Wong, 'The Europeanisation of Foreign Policy', in Christopher Hill and Michael Smith eds., *International Relations and the European Union* (Oxford, 2005), 134–53.
4 R.H. Ginsberg, *The European Union in International Politics: Baptism by Fire* (Lanham, MD, 2001).
5 See Maria Strömvik, *To Act as a Union: Explaining the Development of the EU's Collective Foreign Policy* (Lund, 2005).
6 See R. Bengtsson, *The EU and the European Security order: Interfacing Security Actors* (London, 2009).
7 C. Bretherton and J. Vogler, *The European Union as a Global Actor*, 2nd edition (London, 2006).
8 Ibid., 12–36, quote on 27.
9 'Treaty of Lisbon amending the Treaty on the European Union and the Treaty establishing the European Community', signed at Lisbon, 13 December 2007: http://www.eur-lex.europa.eu/JOHtml.do?uri=OJ:C:2007:306:SOM:EN:HTML.
10 Article 10A, Ibid.
11 For elaboration, see R. Bengtsson, 'Constructing Interfaces: The neighbourhood discourse in EU external policy', *Journal of European Integration*, 30(2008), 597–617; Bengtsson, *European Security Order*.
12 Smith, *Union Foreign Policy*, 19–21. Also see Andrew Linklater, 'A European Civilising Process?', in C.J. Hill and M. Smith, eds., *International Relations and the European Union* (Oxford, 2005), 367–87.
13 I. Manners, 'Normative power Europe: a contradiction in terms?', *Journal of Common Market Studies*, 40 (2002), 240. Also see Smith, *Union Foreign Policy*, 17–19.
14 I. Manners and R. Whitman, 'The "difference engine": constructing and representing the international identity of the EU', *Journal of European Public Policy*, 10(2003), 380–404. Then following the text, see

Manners, 'Normative Power'; idem., 'Normative Power Europe reconsidered: beyond the crossroads', *Journal of European Public Policy*, 13(2006), 182–99; H. Sjursen, 'What kind of power?', *Journal of European Public Policy*, vol. 13(2006), 169–81; L. Aggestam, 'Introduction: Ethical Power Europe?', *International Affairs*, 84(2008), 1–11; M. Telò, *Europe: A Civilian Power? European Union, Global Governance, World Order* (Houndsmills, 2006); R. Bengtsson, and O. Elgström, 'Reconsidering the EU's Role in International Relations: Self-conceptions, expectations, and performance', in S. Harnisch, C. Frank, and H.W. Maull, eds, *Role Theory in International Relations* (London: Routledge, 2011).

15 Smith, *Union Foreign Policy*, 19–21.

16 For descriptions of historical developments, see David J. Howarth, 'Making and Breaking the Rules: French policy on EU "gouvernement économique" and the Stability and Growth Pact', European Integration online Papers, Number 15, 9(2005): http://eiop.or.at/eiop/texte/2005–15a.htm; Keukeleire and MacNaughtan, *Foreign Policy*; Chapter 5.

17 C. Hill, 'The capability-expectations gap, or conceptualising Europe's international role', *Journal of Common Market Studies*, 31(1993), 305–25.

18 D. Allen and R. Bengtsson, 'Exploring a Triangular Drama: The High Representative, the Council Presidency and the Commission', in G. Müller-Brandeck-Bocquet and Carolin Rüger, eds, *The High Representative for the EU Foreign and Security Policy – Review and Prospects* (Baden-Baden: Nomos Verlag, 2011).

19 G. Grevi, D. Helly, and D. Keohane, eds., *European Security and Defence Policy: The First Ten Years (1999–2009)* (Paris, 2009); Keukeleire and MacNaughtan, *Foreign Policy*; Smith, *Union Foreign Policy*.

20 G. Grevi, 'ESDP institutions', in Grevi, Helly, and Keohane, *European Security*, 21–67; Allen and Bengtsson, 'Exploring a triangular drama'.

21 Grevi, 'ESDP institutions', 31–46.

22 Ibid.

23 See Smith, *Union Foreign Policy*, 56–63.

24 Ibid., 63–72.

25 Manners, 'Normative power'.

26 S. Nuttall, 'Coherence and Consistency', in Hill and Smith, *International Relations*, 91–112; Smith, *Union Foreign Policy*, 73–74.

27 M. Barnett and R. Duvall, eds., *Power in Global Governance* (Cambridge, 2005), 8–22.

28 Joseph S. Nye, 'Security and Smart Power', *American Behavioral Scientist*, 51(2008), 1351–56.

29 For further analysis, see Keukeleire and MacNaughtan, *Foreign Policy*, Chapters 10–11.

30 For further analysis of the ENP, see Bengtsson, 'Constructing interfaces'; idem., *European Security Order*.

31 See Bengtsson, *European Security Order*; C. Wagnsson, *Security in a Greater Europe: The Possibility of a Pan-European Approach* (Manchester, 2008), Chapter 6.

32 Bengtsson, *European Security Order*, Chapter 7.

33 United States Mission to the European Union. *Clinton, EU High Representative Ashton After Their Meeting* (29 September 2010): www.uspolicy.be/Article.asp?ID=A62A6157–6441A–40D3–8DD8–F9AFA3257661; see also Bengtsson, *European Security Order*, Chapter 7.

34 Bengtsson, *European Security Order*, Chapter 6.

35 Ibid., Chapter 5; Bengtsson and Elgström, 'Reconsidering the EU's Role'; O. Elgström, 'Outsiders' Perceptions of the European Union in International Trade Negotiations', *Journal of Common Market Studies*, 45(2007), 949–67.

36 Bengtsson, *European Security Order*, Chapter 5.

21

The Great Powers and the United Nations

Stephen Ryan

> No international organization can be stronger than the structure of relationships among the Great Powers that underlies it.
>
> George Kennan[1]

There are those who see an inevitable tension between the needs of Great Powers and a strong role for global institutions such as the United Nations (UN). Whereas the former are assumed to be guided by narrow concerns of *realpolitik*, the latter draw inspiration from ideals that include a prohibition on aggressive action, respect for human rights, a commitment to the rule of law, and the replacement of the balance of power with collective security. Realists often view such ideas as naive. So Mearsheimer in a critique of 'institutionalist' theories, examines the 'false promise' of organisations like the UN and claims that they 'are based on the self-interested calculations of the Great Powers, and they have no independent effect on state behaviour'.[2] Supporters of the UN, on the other hand, claim that positive change is both achievable and desirable through these institutions.

What makes the study of the UN so fascinating is that it is a site where these two world views (along with others) come into contact and conflict on a daily basis. The UN represents both the ideal of a better type of international politics but remains deeply rooted in traditional nation-state thinking, striving for a balance between 'the desirable and the possible'.[3] Given this duality it is not surprising that commentators are attracted to the idea of mutual incompatibility, and there are at least two popular, but opposed, perspectives that share this assumption.

The first emphasises how a noble experiment to improve international relations has been undermined by cynical powers, who for reasons of self-interest have paralysed the organisation. The consequence for the UN, according to Hazzard, was 'arrested moral development' and unfulfilled potential.[4] This, in turn, has resulted in 'a human occasion that has not been risen to'.[5] Malvern condemns the hypocrisy and immaturity of the Council, where governments maintain secret agendas and 'corrupt the UN system'.[6] Sometimes this viewpoint condemns the Great Powers as a bloc; sometimes specific Powers are singled out for condemnation. In Somalia, for example, Polman claims that the United States 'first holed the ship and then abandoned it'.[7]

In response to these cogent criticisms it is important to note several things. The first is that the UN is not an alternative to the sovereign state system. As a former American Ambassador to the UN has pointed out, the 'authority of the UN flows entirely from its members; it is servant, not master'.[8] Hence, one has the famous saying that the UN Secretary-General is more secretary than general. It is important to keep an accurate view of what is possible at the UN because overoptimism can quickly lead to disillusionment.[9]

Second, it is undeniable that UN action has been thwarted on occasions by the use of the veto, or the threat of the veto. However, this was the price for Great Power membership of the organisation. Nor is it clear that the existence of the veto was always a bad thing. Claude argues that it could be a safety valve that warned proponents of a particular course of action to back off if it was opposed by one or more Great Powers.[10] Stoessinger agrees, pointing out that blaming the veto for the failures of the UN is to confuse the symptom with the real causes for inaction.[11]

Third, the claim that the UN has failed because of the Great Powers can be overstated. Focusing on a few high-profile catastrophes cannot produce a fair assessment of the organisation. On the plus side, the UN has played a major role on the development of international peace-keeping and peace-building. Its mediators have helped to settle key international and intercommunal conflicts. It has helped develop international law and new norms for the protection of human rights (including the rights of women, children, and refugees) and the environment. Through its specialised agencies, it has helped to protect vulnerable groups, coordinate global responses to diseases such as smallpox and human immunodeficiency virus/acquired immune deficiency syndrome (HIV/AIDS), and helped to promote development in poorer states. Fourth, there is a fear that focusing too much on the P5 to explain the UN's shortcomings might remove the incentive to focus on internal action. Blaming the Great Powers for its failures might distract attention from problems that exist within the organisation itself, thus inhibiting reform.[12]

The second perspective, found especially in the centers of decision-making in the capitals of the Great Powers is that strong support for the UN can be incompatible with the pursuit of their own national interests. In the early 1980s, Jean Kirkpatrick led the Reagan Administration's attack on the organisation as the US Ambassador to the UN and seemed to view the UN as a 'troublesome sideshow'.[13] The Secretary-General at the time claimed that critics in Washington believed the 'entanglement of the United States in the multilateralism represented by the UN would limit U.S. freedom of action and compromise its capacity to defend democracy'.[14] More recently such an attitude was clear in the remarks of United States Vice-President Dick Cheney in the debates leading to the coalition invasion of Iraq. 'Go tell them [the UN] it's not about us. It's about you. You are not important', he is reported to have said.[15]

Of course, any attempt to make use of the UN by any state involves giving other members a say in what is done. Parsons has pointed out that Western governments are 'wary of resorting to this cumbrous and unreliable mechanism as a place in which to conduct serious business'[16] Yet, as Hoffmann noted, if states use the UN as an instrument of policy, they have to submit to the influence of other states that are able to exploit skilfully the structures and procedures of the Organisation.[17] Also the UN has played an important role in creating international norms and this creates the corresponding disapproval of norm violation. So '[e]ven great powers can hardly escape this pressure, strengthened as it is by international public opinion'.[18]

So why would the Great Powers want to turn to the UN if it could restrict their freedom of action? In fact there are many reasons. The UN, especially during the Cold War, was able to play an important role in managing crises that the superpowers did not wish to see escalate to the point where they might be dragged towards a nuclear confrontation. Since the end of the Cold War this has been less important but the UN has been more useful in providing authority for armed interventions in conflicts that threaten international peace and security. It is uniquely placed to give a moral and legal authority to Great Power foreign policies: what Luck called 'coupling legitimacy with power'.[19] The organisation is also useful for providing a face-saving device for members when they get into trouble during a problematic intervention and want to get rid of an issue or to find a scapegoat for its own failings. Polman has called this 'blue rinsing'.[20]

In an age in which the dangers of globalisation are becoming more apparent it seems that many threats to human security (environmental destruction, the spread of weapons of mass destruction, global terrorist networks and infectious diseases such as swine flu and HIV/AIDS) require global responses, and the UN and its specialised agencies offer sites where these can be refined and coordinated.

So it is not surprising that Barack Obama, before becoming United States President, could state that 'no country has a bigger stake than we do in strengthening international institutions—which is why we pushed for their creation in the first place, and why we need to take the lead in improving them'.[21] Nor was this just campaign rhetoric, because after taking his office, in his first address to the UN General Assembly as President, he argued that the UN could play an important role in strengthening action in areas that that 'are fundamental to the future'.[22] The US also took up its seat on the Human Rights Council.

In reality, therefore, the UN has a complex relationship with the Great Powers, and attitudes to the UN rise and fall against the background of changes in world politics and domestic circumstances. This will be the theme of the rest of this chapter, as the interaction between UN and the Great Powers is explored through three distinct periods: the Cold War, the post-Cold War era of United States unipolarity, and the present era of relative American decline that heralds a return to either bipolarity or multipolarity. Any discussion of the last of these periods is going to have to acknowledge a much stronger role for China in international politics and the importance of Security Council reform.

The UN, The Great Powers, And The Cold War

The defining feature of this period was the impact that superpower rivalry had on the UN and the consequent failure of the organisation to work as its planners had intended. Eban notes that 'Great Power cooperation was built so deeply into the international idea that the structure could not bear the collapse of the central assumption'.[23] Between 1945 and the end of the Cold War, Chapter VII collective security measures were employed just three times: to authorise military action in Korea and to impose sanctions on South Africa and Rhodesia. Instead of an effective system of global security based on the Charter, the Cold War was characterised by spheres of influence and the balance of terror. The UN was side-lined in nearly all of the major conflicts involving the superpowers during this time.

Another theme was the growing disillusionment with the UN in the United States, its most ardent Great Power supporter in 1945. There had always been a section of American opinion that was hostile to the UN, especially on the right, but this increased in the 1960s as the United States lost its natural majority in the General Assembly. Decolonisation expanded the number states in the General Assembly that were more interested in north–south rather than the east–west issues.[24] These issues included justice, self-determination, development, and anti-racism. In the Security Council, the United States did not cast its first veto until 1970, but is now the P5 state most likely to use this device. By the 1960s American criticisms of the UN could be summed up as follows:

> it had not brought peace; it cost too much; its voting procedures were unreasonable and inimical to the United States; Afro-Asian nations were irresponsible on colonial issues; our desire to please them had divided NATO; the UN controlled U.S. foreign policy ... the UN's peacekeeping role was dangerous because it might someday be used against the US.[25]

This is not to imply that the UN did nothing of significance during this era. Violent conflicts associated with decolonisation offered opportunities for positive involvement. Secretary-General Dag Hammarskjold, in particular, was able to enhance the role of his office through 'executive action'.[26] Most famously, Hammarskjold, working with Lester Pearson of Canada and some of the Middle Powers, was able to develop UN peace-keeping, a term not found in the Charter. Peace-keeping was a poorly defined idea that was employed on an *ad hoc* basis to establish missions in a number of conflict zones.[27]

However, in the polarised Cold War atmosphere, any strong action by the Secretary-General was likely to raise problems. Trygve Lie, the first Secretary-General, was effectively driven out of office by Moscow, who objected to the UN's role in Korea. Hammarskjold, at the time of his death in a plane crash on 18 September 1961, was under fire from the USSR and France, which objected to paying their assessed contributions for the mission in the Congo. This triggered a financial crisis for the UN and led the USSR to propose replacing the post of Secretary-General with a 'troika'.

The USSR had always viewed the UN with suspicion, regarding it as 'an extension and instrument of American policy'.[28] In the 1950s the 'experience as a minority power seeking to frustrate the efforts of the hostile majority' did nothing to encourage warm feelings from the Kremlin.[29] Yet, as Nicholas points out, whatever their doubts the Soviets 'arrived at a settled conclusion that it was better to be in rather than out',[30] even if the policy was to keep it 'alive but weak' as a forum for diplomatic contacts, propaganda, and intelligence gathering.[31]

Britain has had a more critical attitude to the UN than the United States, and so never experienced the decline in support that happened across the Atlantic. At the same time, it never displayed some of the open hostility directed at the UN from Moscow. Just over ten years after it was created, Goodwin could sum up the British attitude as a viewpoint that saw the UN as 'little more than a dispassionately acknowledged fact, generally conceded to be a "good thing", but little more'.[32] Generally, the attitude was 'rather tepid'.[33] However, it is also true to say that British distrust of the UN never reached the heights of Gaullist governments in Paris in the 1960s. France's policy towards the UN was influenced by the fear of American hegemony and the memory of poor relations during the war between the Roosevelt administration and de Gaulle's government-in-exile.[34] France became one of the P5 states in 1945, but it had not participated in many of the key discussions that led to the San Francisco Conference. However, a permanent seat on the Council was an important affirmation of France's Great Power status and, like the other P5 states, it was happy to use this status to pursue its own interests.

The outlook for the UN often looked especially 'bleak' during the 1980s.[35] It was battered by complaints from Washington, experienced a serious funding crisis (arising in large part because of opposition in Congress) and was unable to play a significant role in major conflicts. One indication of the torpor into which the UN had fallen is that between 1978 and 1988, no new peace-keeping missions were created. The Reagan Administration rejected the Law of the Sea Treaty and took the United States out of UNESCO (the United Nations Educational, Scientific and Cultural Organization), a 'situation that would have amazed Franklin Roosevelt'.[36] It also revealed contempt for the International Court of Justice over a case involving its actions against Nicaragua.

Yet even as Washington was becoming more confrontational, the USSR, under its dynamic new leader, Mikhail Gorbachev, moved closer to the organisation. His first address to the General Assembly on 7 December 1988 made this shift apparent when he referred to the de-ideologisation of interstate relations and emphasised the common goals of ending wars, aggression, and poverty, where the UN could be a 'unique international center in the service of peace and security'.[37]

Gorbachev's positive assessment seemed to hint at a more positive role for the UN and indeed the end of the Cold War did act as a catalyst for reassessments of the organisation. During the superpower confrontation Eban claimed that:

> collective security failed to take root as the central principle of international life, not because its adherents were unworthy of its vision or because its opponents were of small mind and ignoble disposition, but more simply, because it is not a very rational idea.[38]

However, although this might have been an accurate assessment during the Cold War, as some basic features of Great Power politics began to shift, opportunities for collective security began to emerge in ways that Eban could not have envisaged just a few years earlier. As the Soviet Union imploded and superpower rivalry abated, there occurred a 'return to the UN',[39] although in reality it was not just an attempt to resurrect previous successes but to adjust to a new type of global politics.

The UN, The Great Powers, and the New World Order

The 1991 Gulf War, authorised by the UN under Chapter VII of the Charter, was important in improving relations between the United States and the UN and in reviving interest in collective security. On 21 January 1992, the first-ever Security Council meeting involving heads of state was held in New York and, later that year, the Secretariat published *An Agenda for Peace* proposing that trends in world politics were supportive of a stronger global role for the UN.[40] Even before the start of the 1990s, the organisation played a significant mediation role in ending the Iran–Iraq war and in facilitating Soviet withdrawal from Afghanistan. It also launched 'second-generation peace-keeping' in Namibia in 1988, followed by a burst of activity in other conflicts including Cambodia, El Salvador, and Haiti. The demand for peace operations began to swell just when the UN was more able and willing to supply missions to conflict zones.[41] All of this was made possible by the 'rejuvenation of the UN Security Council'.[42]

During the period 1988–95, the UN revealed itself to be more dynamic and flexible than some of its detractors believed possible.[43] In addition to conventional UN responses like mediation and peace-keeping, the more activist Security Council authorised other types of action. These included: the prosecution of war crimes through *ad hoc* tribunals in the former Yugoslavia and Rwanda; the revival of Chapter VII actions through military interventions and economic sanctions; expanded jurisdiction (for instance, responding to the threat of international terrorism) and the use of technical commissions for compensation and boundary disputes and arms control (in the case of Iraq after the first Gulf War).[44] Even conventional instruments were developed in interesting directions. Richmond has tracked the development of UN missions from 'first-generation' deployments to 'multidimensional' peace operations with wider mandates.[45] The organisation developed an interest in 'post-conflict peacebuilding'.[46] Indeed in 2005, the UN created a Peacebuilding Commission to support peace efforts in societies emerging from destructive conflict. Whilst in Macedonia the UN Preventive Deployment Force (UNPREDEP) took the organisation into 'preventive peacekeeping' for the first and only time.[47]

Yet, by its fiftieth anniversary in 1995, the organisation's prestige had been severely dented.[48] There were a number of factors that contributed to this, and their relative importance varied from case to case. The most important were declining American support for UN action and a lack of unity amongst the P5 and between the Security Council and the Secretary-General about what needed to be done. In addition, the UN was poorly equipped for complex and dangerous peace enforcement operations in places like Bosnia and Somalia, and the 'international community' might have underestimated the difficulties attached to the growing practice of 'humanitarian operations' under UN authorisation.[49] Kennan once warned about attempts to strengthen the UN that would 'encumber it with responsibilities that must obviously break its back'.[50] By the mid-1990s, the world seemed to be dangerously close to this state of affairs as the UN failed to stop genocide in both Rwanda and Srebrenica despite a peace-keeping presence in both situations.

The new Clinton presidency had encouraged the expectation that the White House would be more willing to work constructively with the international organisation. However, hopes were quickly dashed on the streets of Mogadishu, where the deaths of American troops demonstrated the limits of US toleration of international action through the UN. The Somali case also showed how useful the organisation was as a scapegoat for US failures.[51] It was a 'tragedy' for US–UN relations.[52] One aspect of this was a review of UN peace-keeping known as PDD-25, which placed tight restrictions on American participation in such operations and, although not made public until after the April 1994 genocide in Rwanda, 'the new psychology of saying no was already well in place'.[53] So, even before the presidency of George W. Bush, the UN had fallen out of favour in Washington.

Nonetheless, after 9/11, Washington adopted an even more confrontational style. As far as the US was concerned, the belief was that 'multilateral institutions are neither essential nor necessarily conducive to American interests'.[54] This was despite the fact that it had been supportive of the American position after the attacks on New York and Washington by enhancing its role in combating international terrorism through Security Council Resolution 1373 and creating a new Counter-Terrorism Committee.[55] However, Washington's policy to the UN was symptomatic of a more general feeling that it should be more assertive in exploiting its position as the dominant Power. The best known statement of this notion was the September 2002 National Security Strategy and its explicit adoption of the idea of preventive war. Many commentators at the time saw this as a direct challenge to the UN Charter.[56]

As the United States became more assertive, other Great Powers began to see the UN as a way of trying to constrain the American 'hyperpower'. France, Germany, Russia, and China all began emphasising the importance of multipolarity during the Bush presidency.[57] Weiss and Daws argue that 'contemporary UN debate could be compared with the Roman Senate's effort to control the emperor'.[58] If so this was always going to be a losing battle for the brutal fact is that those key decision-makers in the United States who wanted to act unilaterally were also those who were most likely to be dismissive of the UN if it tried to restrict Washington. The run-up to the Gulf War led

> the French, among others, to overestimate the price that the Bush administration was prepared to pay in order to get Security Council authorisation for an invasion. They did not ask themselves what polling would show if Americans were asked whether France, Russia or China should jointly or severally possess a right of veto over actions defined by an American president as necessary for his country's self-defense.[59]

There were always alternatives such as 'coalitions of the willing' to which the US could turn if it felt the UN was too limiting, and from the mid-1990s we see *ad hoc* American-led multilateral interventions in Bosnia (IFOR/SFOR), Kosovo (KFOR), Iraq, and Afghanistan.

During the Cold War, the UN's role as an instrument of international peace and security was severely restricted by superpower competition. In the post-Cold War world, despite initial optimism, American dominance resulted in an aggressive foreign policy that relegated the organisation to a secondary place and directly challenged some of its basic norms. The failure of the UN to stop military action against Iraq in 2003, despite the fact that the majority of the

Security Council was opposed to action at that time, represented a low point in US–UN relations. In one rather bleak assessment of the period, '1989 added to the great disappointments of 1919 and 1945'.[60]

The Future: Beyond The P5?

The UN did try to learn lessons from the Iraq case. The ineffectualness of the organisation in early 2003 led to the decision to set up a High Level Panel in November of that year. This made recommendations in 2004 that formed the basis of a report by Kofi Annan titled *In Larger Freedom*.[61] The Panel noted lost vitality in the General Assembly, a lack of legitimacy and credibility in the Security Council and the Human Rights Commission (renamed the Human Rights Council in 2005), a gap in addressing countries under stress, the need for new institutional arrangements to address economic and social threats, and the need for a more professional and better-organised Secretariat. *In Larger Freedom* advocated reform based on these concerns, and these were considered at a summit of world leaders in September 2005, the sixtieth anniversary of the organisation. The most controversial issue was Security Council reform, an old problem.[62] *In Larger Freedom* argued that the Security Council should be 'broadly representative of the realities of power' and proposed two different reform plans, neither of which envisaged new permanent members with the right of veto. These were 'effectively killed' when recently appointed United States Ambassador John Bolton tabled over 750 amendments a month before the summit.[63] One problem with Council reform is that the P5 states can veto any proposed changes to their special status. Another is that once the principle of new permanent members is accepted, who will be entitled to this special status? The P5 do not agree on this. There are also a number of competing plans for reform and no consensus about which is the best to follow.[64]

Yet, by the end of the 1990s, it was hard to defend the *status quo* and there 'was wide agreement that the Security Council did not represent power realities and needed to be reformed and enlarged'.[65] The states with the strongest case to become new permanent members are Japan and Germany, the defeated Axis Powers in 1945. For this reason, both were late joiners of the organisation, and there are still sensitive issues related to military action by both states. Japan is the second-largest contributor to the UN's regular budget; Germany is ranked third. Both have a preference for 'soft power' and neither aspire to be nuclear-weapon states.

Japan joined the UN in 1956, but it adopted a low-key role in international politics. Inoguchi referred to Japan as a 'combination of economic giant and political pygmy'.[66] The guiding light was the 'Yoshida doctrine', which put a strong reliance on the United States for Japanese security.[67] Japan would subordinate a lot of its foreign and security policy to Washington's lead, reflected recently in defense agreements in 1997 and 2005.[68] The 'no war' clause of the 1947 'Peace' Constitution also restricted the ability of Japan's Self Defence Forces (SDF) to participate in military operations. There were significant developments after the end of the Cold War. In 1992 the *Peace Cooperation Act* allowed SDF participation in UN operations, but only in a very limited manner. The first overseas deployment was to the UN Transitional Authority in Cambodia (UNTAC) in 1992.

The Federal Republic of Germany and the German Democratic Republic joined the UN as separate states in September 1973: a single German seat was established in October 1990. Germany has joined with Japan, India, and Brazil to create the G4 to coordinate their efforts to become permanent members. Britain and France have expressed some support for expansion, but there is also significant opposition. German membership has not attracted strong American support; it has given only unequivocal approval to Japanese elevation. One way to incorporate Germany would be for Britain and France to give up their separate seats so that the EU could become a permanent member. Germany has stated its long-term goal of an EU seat but does not believe this is achievable in the immediate future. Apart from opposition to this from the UK and France, there is no provision under the Charter for such an arrangement because the EU is not a member-state. Yet can the UK and France reasonably expect to retain their own special status given the changes that have occurred in world politics since 1945? One view is that the Security Council 'is too much of a retirement home for former world powers while major powers like India ... and Japan ... are excluded'.[69] In the German case it is interesting how in the talks with Iran over nuclear proliferation, Berlin has been included with the permanent members under the P5+1 formula, whereas in the discussions with North Korea, the six-party talks have included the two parts of Korea, the United States, China, Russia, and Japan, but not Britain and France. Here one may be witnessing what Castaneda referred to as 'de facto participation in lieu of formal membership'.[70]

Whoever becomes a permanent member of the Security Council in the coming years, the dominant fault line in global politics is likely to be between the United States and China: a Sino-American Cold War.[71] If true, how will the UN fare in such a world? There are some reasons to avoid pessimism because at present both Washington and Beijing are engaging with the UN in a relatively constructive manner. On the American side, the 2010 National Security strategy certainly has a different tone to the one endorsed by the Bush administration. Whereas the 2002 document makes no direct reference to the UN, the one published in May 2010 contains several positive references and pledges a greater willingness to work constructively with it:

> In recent years America's frustration with international institutions has led us at times to engage the UN system on an ad hoc basis. But in a world of transnational challenges, the United States will need to invest in strengthening the international system, working from inside international Institutions.[72]

However, in softening American attitudes to the UN, the Obama administration has also thrown down a challenge set out in the President's address to the General Assembly on 23 September 2009:

> We have also re-engaged the United Nations. We have paid our bills. We have joined the Human Rights Council. We have signed the Convention on the Rights of Persons with Disabilities. We have fully embraced the Millennium Development Goals. And we address our priorities here, in this institution – for instance, through the Security Council meeting that I will chair tomorrow on nuclear non-proliferation and disarmament, and through the issues that I will discuss today.[73]

He then went on to say that the UN had to be more effective in supporting four fundamental 'pillars' of world order: stopping the spread of nuclear weapons and seeking the goal of a world without them; the pursuit of peace; the preservation of the planet; and the creation of a global economy that advances opportunity for all people.

What about the emerging superpower? The People's Republic of China became a UN member only in 1971, when General Assembly resolution 2758 was passed on 25 October by 76–35–17. This allowed Beijing to replace the Republic of China (Taiwan) as the legitimate representative of China. By this time, Washington regarded the attempt to deny Beijing the Chinese seat as a 'doomed rearguard action', whilst supporting a dual representation formula that would stop Taiwan being ejected from the organisation.[74] This failed, an indication of America's declining influence over the General Assembly. China, of course, is the only P5 state that has been on the receiving end of UN Collective Security action, when it intervened in the Korean War in 1950. This may, in part, explain its suspicion of UN authorised military action.

After 1971, Beijing tended to adopt a low-key approach on the Security Council, preferring to withdraw or abstain rather than use the veto except in exceptional circumstances.[75] In the Assembly, it regarded itself as one of the leaders of the Third World bloc. Although there is a perception that Beijing obstructs UN action, since 1971 the United States has been twenty times more likely to use the veto than China.[76] One reason China uses the veto is to punish governments viewed as pro-Taiwan; hence the vetoing of a UN deployment to Guatemala and the extension of the peace-keeping mission in Macedonia. Both of these states still had diplomatic relations with the Republic of China. The veto has also been used to try to limit Western criticisms of the human rights record of states such as Zimbabwe (2008) and Burma (2007).

In the past decade, China has begun to take a more active role at the UN; this does not necessarily equate with supporting a more active role for the UN. As cases such as Sudan and Zimbabwe show, a more active role might also be a more obstructionist one. Yet the surge in Chinese activity in New York has also seen a growth in support for UN peace operations, including the deployment of small contingents to a number of missions. At the start of 2010, for example, China contributed a total of 2,131 troops, police, and military experts to missions in Western Sahara, Haiti, the Democratic Republic of Congo, Darfur, Liberia, Timor-Leste, and the Ivory Coast.[77] This made China only the fourteenth-largest contributor overall, but it was more than any other P5 state and either Japan or Germany.[78]

Whilst agreeing in principle that Security Council reform is required, China has opposed what it regards as artificial timeframes and wants a broad-based discussion to ensure geographical balance, with Africa and Latin America the top priorities.[79] The issue of permanent status for Japan causes Beijing particular problems. The last time this issue received serious attention, in the run-up to the 2005 Summit, there were anti-Japanese protests in Chinese cities, boycotts of Japanese goods, and over 22 million Chinese citizens signed an on-line petition.[80] Apart from the memory of the Japanese invasion of China in the 1930s and the refusal of many in Japan to acknowledge the extent of atrocities that accompanied this act of aggression, there are more contemporary reasons for strains in Beijing–Tokyo relations, including Taiwan (Japan is tied to American policy to defend the island) and a territorial dispute over the Senkaku/Diaoyutai Islands, which are the key to the exploitation of energy resources in the surrounding waters.

Russia states that it supports the idea of enlargement but, given that no one proposal can obtain general support, prefers to move forward with an 'intermediate' proposal that would see an increase in non-permanent members with the option of subsequent reelection, giving some states a sort of semi-permanent membership. However, it is clear that 'the present exclusive rights of its permanent members, including the right to veto, should remain unchanged'.[81] Indeed, Russia used its veto in 2009 to stop an extension of the UN mission in Georgia and had earlier joined with China in vetoing resolutions condemning Zimbabwe and Burma.

The controversies aroused by Security Council reform illustrate how difficult it can be to introduce fundamental change at the UN. Indeed, such change seems unlikely.[82] Yet, with the move to a more multipolar world, there may be opportunities in the years ahead to play a more vital role. As Claude noted, the 'mission assigned to the UN by its founders and endorsed by its members is … to make the world safe for pluralism—and pluralism safe for the world'.[83] If the global system returns to greater multipolarity the UN could be better suited to playing a stronger role than was the case in the Cold War or the brief era of US dominance. As we have seen, the UN was weakened by superpower rivalry. It had to operate in a system Hoffmann called 'revolutionary' and Aron termed 'heterogeneous'.[84] In such a world there was a high degree of conflict and an absence of consensus about basic norms. In the post-Cold War era, the UN was weakened by American dominance, which encouraged an aggressive unilateralism.[85] So the 'old power structure gave the Soviet Union an incentive to deadlock the council; the current power structure encourages the United States to bypass it'.[86] The next stage of global politics is likely to be multipolar, with no 'revolutionary' Great Power. For even China has so moderated its attitudes since becoming a member that many informed commentators believe that for a number of years, it has been 'playing the role of a status quo Power in the international system'.[87]

Of course conflicts will still exist. Any organisation with over 190 members that recognise no superior authority over their actions and who possess considerable capacity for destructive behavior is going to generate its fair share of dangerous disagreements. This probability is especially likely given the UN's weak authority and its inability to offer a credible deterrent to states that want to violate key norms of international behavior. As someone quipped many years ago, the UN is really a mixture of United Notions and Untied Nations, thus collective action is never easy to implement. One source of tension at the UN at present that is likely to continue into the future is between the United States and Western Europe, which favor a more activist and interventionist organisation, and China and Russia, stronger supporters of respect for state sovereignty. Both China and Russia share many key assumptions about how to structure the post-Cold War order, including 'the primacy of the UN in global decision making' and a rejection of Western conceptions of 'humanitarian intervention and limited sovereignty'.[88] It is, Lo admits, an 'elitist vision' based on a world where 'a few great powers … make the big decisions'.[89] Although given the primacy of economic concerns in Sino-American relations (the trade deficit, American debt, low levels of Chinese consumption, cheap Chinese imports, green tariffs, manipulation of the *renminbi*) Garrett could be right to point to the G20 rather than the UN as the key international arena for managing relations between the '*de facto* G2'.[90]

When the UN does act, it cannot depend on the strong leadership of the Great Powers. None are likely to be reliable supporters in all circumstances. Yet there will be times when certain constellations of overlapping interests will allow the UN to play a significant role. Maybe the best that can be hoped for in the area of international peace and security is a strengthening of peace-keeping and peace-building capacity along with 'limited collective security', which can be applied to smaller Powers, but not to the Great Powers or their clients.[91] For there is still some truth in the old witticism that when the UN engages in a conflict between two small states, the conflict disappears; when it gets involved in a conflict between a small state and a Great Power, the small state disappears; but when there is a conflict between the Great Powers, the UN disappears.

Notes

1 A. Dallin, *The Soviet Union at the United Nations* (New York, 1962), 231.
2 John J. Mearsheimer, 'The False Promise of International Institutions', *International Security*, 19 (1995), 7.
3 R. Thakur and A. Schnabel, 'Cascading generations of peacekeeping: Across the Mogadishu line to Kosovo and Timor' in R. Thakur and A. Schnabel, eds., *United Nations Peacekeeping Operations* (Tokyo, 2001), 23.
4 S. Hazzard, *Countenance of Truth: The United Nations and the Waldheim Case* (London, 1991), 33.
5 S. Hazzard, *Defeat of an Ideal: the Self-destruction of the United Nations* (London, 1973), 249.
6 L. Malvern, *The Ultimate Crime: Who Betrayed the UN and Why?* (London, 1995), 354.
7 L. Polman, *We Did Nothing* (Harmondsworth, 2004), 16.
8 M. Albright, *The Mighty and the Almighty* (Basingstoke, 2006), 82.
9 For example, A. Boyd, *United Nations: Piety, Myth and Truth* (Harmondsworth, 1962).
10 I.L. Claude, Jr. *Swords into Plowshares*, 4th edition (New York, 1984).
11 J.G. Stoessinger, *The United Nations and the Superpowers*, 4th edition (New York, 1977), 20.
12 A. Lebor, "*Complicity with Evil*": *The United Nations in the Age of Modern Genocide* (New Haven, CT, 2006).

13 B. Urquhart, *A Life in Peace and War* (London, 1987), 327.

14 J.P. de Cuellar, 'Reflecting on the Past and Contemplating the Future', *Global Governance*, 1(1969), 155.

15 B. Woodward, *Plan of Attack* (New York, 2004), 157.

16 A. Parsons, *From Cold War to Hot Peace: UN Interventions 1947–1995* (Harmondsworth, 1995), 247.

17 S. Hoffmann, *Gulliver's Troubles, Or the Setting of American Foreign Policy* (New York, 1968), 37.

18 S.B. Gareis and J. Varwick. *The United Nations: An Introduction* (Basingstoke, 2005), 253.

19 E.C. Luck, *UN Security Council: Practice and Promise* (London, 2006), 129.

20 Polman, *We Did Nothing*, viii.

21 B. Obama, *The Audacity of Hope* (Edinburgh, 2007), 327.

22 B. Obama, 'UN General Assembly Speech', (2009): www.guardian.co.uk/world/2009/sep/23/barack-obama-un-speech.

23 A. Eban, *The New Diplomacy* (New York, 1983), 276.

24 For example, E. Luard, *History of the United Nations*, Volume 2: *The Age of Decolonization 1955–1965* (Basingstoke, 1989).

25 Richard Gardner quoted in J.B. Martin, *Adlai Stevenson and the World* (Garden City, NY, 1978), 585.

26 L. Gordenker, *The UN Secretary-General and Secretariat* (London, 2005); B. Urquhart, *Hammarskjold* (New York, 1972).

27 S. Ryan, 'United Nations Peacekeeping: A Matter of Principles?', *International Peacekeeping*, 7(2006), 27–47.

28 D. Yergin, *Shattered Peace* (Harmondsworth, 1977), 146.

29 Dallin, *Soviet Union*, 182.

30 H.G. Nicholas, *The United Nations as a Political Institution*, 3rd edition (Oxford, 1967), 195.

31 Dallin, *Soviet Union*, 185.

32 G.L. Goodwin, *Britain and the United Nations* (London, 1957), 419.

33 Ibid.

34 N. Atkin, *The Fifth French Republic* (Basingstoke, 2005); R. Gildea, *France Since 1945* (Oxford, 2002).

35 D. Armstrong, L. Lloyd, and J. Redmond, *International Organizations in World Politics* (Basingstoke, 2004), 79.

36 P. Kennedy, *The Rise and Fall of the Great Powers* (London, 1988), 530.

37 S. White, *Gorbachev in Power* (Cambridge, 1990), 160.

38 Eban, *New Diplomacy*, 264.

39 G.R. Berridge, *Return to the UN* (Basingstoke, 1991).

40 Boutros, Boutros-Ghali, *An Agenda for Peace* (New York, 1992).

41 R. Paris, *At War's End: Building Peace After Civil Conflict* (Cambridge, 2004).

42 Armstrong et al., *International Organizations*, 116.

43 See, for example, P.F.Diehl, *Peace Operations*, Cambridge, 2008); W.A. Knight, ed., *Adapting the United Nations to a Postmodern Era* (Basingstoke, 2001); J. Matheson, *Council Unbound* (Washington, DC, 2006); R. Thakur, *The United Nations, Peace and Security* (Cambridge, 2006); T.G. Weiss, D.R. Forsythe, and P.A. Coate, eds., *The United Nations and Changing World Politics* (Boulder, CO, 1994).

44 Matheson, *Council Unbound*.

45 O.P. Richmond, *Maintaining Order, Making Peace* (Basingstoke, 2002).

46 See, for example, V. Chetail, ed., *Post-Conflict Peacebuilding: A Lexicon* (Oxford, 2009); R. Paris and T. Sisk, eds., *The Dilemmas of Statebuilding: Confronting the Contradictions of Postwar Peace Operations* (Oxford, 2009).

47 H.J. Sokalski, *An Ounce of Prevention: Macedonia and the UN Experience in Preventive Diplomacy* (Washington DC, 2003).

48 S. Ryan, *The United Nations and International Politics* (Basingstoke, 2000), Chapter 5.

49 S. Hoffmann, *The Ethics and Politics of Humanitarian Intervention* (Notre Dame, IN, 1997); D. Rieff, *At the Point of a Gun: Democratic Dreams and Armed Intervention* (New York, 2005); T.G. Weiss, *Military-Civilian Interactions: Intervening in Humanitarian Crises* (Lanham NJ, 1999).

50 G.F. Kennan, *Realities of American Foreign Policy* (Princeton NJ, 1954), 46.

51 L. Murray, *Clinton, Peacekeeping and Humanitarian Intervention* (London: 2008).

52 D. Halberstam, *War in a Time of Peace: Bush, Clinton and the Generals* (London, 2001), 264.

53 J.F. Harris, *The Survivor: Bill Clinton in the White House* (New York, 2005), 126.

54 I.H. Daalder and J.M. Lindsay. 'Bush's foreign policy revolution', in F. Greenstein, ed., *The George W. Bush Presidency* (Baltimore, 2003), 108.

55 J. Boulden and T.G. Weiss, eds. *Terrorism and the UN* (Bloomington, IN, 2004); J. Dhanapala, 'The United Nations' Response to 9/11', *Terrorism and Political Violence*, 17(2005), 17–23.

56 S. Ryan, 'The United Nations', in M. Buckley and R. Singh, eds., *The Bush Doctrine and the War on Terrorism* (London: 2006), 173–88.

57 M.J. Glennon, 'The UN Security Council in a Unipolar World', *Virginia Journal of International Law*, 44 (2003–4), 91–112.

58 T.G. Weiss and S. Daws, 'World Politics: Continuity and Change since 1945', in T.G. Weiss and S. Daws, eds., *The Oxford Handbook on the United Nations* (Oxford, 2007), 9.

59 W.R. Mead, *Power, Terror, Peace, and War* (New York, 2004), 93.

60 B.K. Booth and N.J. Wheeler, *The Security Dilemma* (Basingstoke, 2008), 27.

61 K. Annan, *In Larger Freedom* (New York: UN Document A/59/2005).

62 D. Bourantonis, *The History and Politics of UN Security Council Reform* (London, 2005).

63 R.W. Mansbach and K.L Rafferty, *Introduction to Global Politics* (London, (2008), 430–31.

64 See J.S. Lund, *The Pros and Cons of Security Council Reform* (2010): www.globalpolicy.org/security-council/security-council-as-an-institution/security-council-reform/general-articles/48674.html.

65 P.R. Baehr and L. Gordenker, *The United Nations at the end of the 1990s*, 3rd edition (Basingstoke, 1999), 156.

66 T. Inoguchi, *Japan's International Relations* (London, 1991), 1.

67 See M.A. Barnhart, *Japan and the World Since 1868* (London, 1995).

68 B.W. Jentleson, 'America's Global Role After Bush', *Survival* 49(2007), 179–200.

69 W.R. Mead, *Power, Terror, Peace, and War* (New York, 2004), 133.

70 J.G. Castaneda, 'Not ready for Prime Time', *Foreign Affairs*, 89(2010), 59.

71 Booth and Wheeler, *Security Dilemma*.

72 Cf. United States Government. *The National Security Strategy of the United States of America* (2002): www.globalsecurity.org/military/library/policy/national/nss-020920.pdf; United States Government. *National Security Strategy* (2010): www.whitehouse.gov/sites/default/files/rss_viewer/national_security_strategy.pdf.

73 Obama, 'General Assembly Speech'.

74 H. Kissinger, *White House Years* (Boston, MA, 1979), 770.

75 M. Yahuda. *China's Foreign Policy after Mao* (Basingstoke, 1978).

76 Michael Fullilove. 'Angel or dragon: China and the United Nations', *National Interest*, (September–October 2006).

77 United Nations, *UN Mission's Contribution by Country* (New York, 2010): www.un.org/en/peacekeeping/contributors/2010/june10_1.pdf.

78 United Nations, *Ranking of Military and Police Contributions to UN Operations* (2010): www.un.org/en/peacekeeping/contributors/2010/june10_2.pdf.

79 For example, see J.M. Malik, 'Security Council reform: China signals its veto', *World Policy Journal*, XXII (2005), 19–29.

80 A. Bezlova, 'China's Quandary over Japan's UN bid', *Asia Times*, 7 April 2005.

81 Permanent Mission of the Russian Federation to the United Nations, 'Position of the Russian Federation at the 64th Session of the United Nations General Assembly', (2010): www.un.int/Russia/new/MainRoot/index_plain.htm.

82 For example, see Gareis and Varwick. *United Nations*.

83 I.L. Claude Jr, 'Peace and Security: Prospective Roles for the Two United Nations', *Global Governance*, 2(1996), 297.

84 S. Hoffmann, 'The future of the international political system', in S. Hoffmann, *Janus and Minerva* (Boulder, CO, 1987); Aron, *Peace and War*.

85 M.J. Glennon, 'The UN Security Council in a Unipolar World', *Virginia Journal of International Law*, 44 (2003–4), 91–112.

86 M.J. Glennon, 'Why the UN Security Council Failed', *Foreign Affairs*, 82:3(2003), 16–34.

87 Yahuda, *China's Foreign Policy*, 101.

88 B. Lo, 'The long sunset of strategic partnership: Russia's evolving China policy', *International Affairs*, 80 (2004), 296.

89 Ibid.

90 G. Garrett, 'G2 in G20: China, the United States and the World after the Global Financial Crisis', *Global Policy*, 1(2010), 29.

91 E.M. Smith, 'Collective Security: Changing Conceptions and Institutional Adaptation', in W.A Knight, ed., *Adapting the United Nations to a Postmodern Era* (Basingstoke, 2001), 41–51.

22

Reconciling different logics of security provision

The case of NATO

Alexandra Gheciu

As the title suggests, this chapter examines the challenges faced by the North Atlantic Treaty Organization (NATO) in its efforts to combine multiple logics of security provision in a rapidly changing security environment. Contemporary analyses of NATO tend to start from the observation that the Atlantic Alliance has become a victim of its own success. Having emerged from the Cold War as (what was widely regarded as) the most successful alliance in history, NATO soon found itself facing difficult questions regarding its future. However, contrary to numerous gloomy predictions, NATO managed to embark on a comprehensive process of reform and enlargement to adapt to the rapidly changing security environment. Yet, that ambitious (and, in some ways at least, highly effective) process of adaptation did not entirely address major questions regarding the future role of NATO.

It would be impossible to engage here in an exhaustive analysis of NATO's post-Cold War adaptation. Instead, my focus is on the evolution of the relationship between the logic of inclusion and the logic of exclusion embedded in practices enacted by NATO. Contrary to the conventional wisdom that portrays it as no more than a geostrategic arrangement, NATO has always tried to combine the inclusive and exclusionary logics of security. Thus, NATO has been, at once, an alliance aimed at excluding inimical armies from the territory of member-states, as well as an institution aimed at integrating its members into the structures of a liberal-democratic security community. In efforts to redefine its mission following the collapse of communism, and then again in the aftermath of the 9/11 attacks, allied officials have built their arguments concerning NATO's continued relevance around the alliance's (allegedly) unique ability to combine inclusive practices of security community building (via the socialisation of new partners into the norms of the community) and practices of exclusion: keeping enemies outside the territory and away from the populations of allied states. But, as the final section of the chapter shows, that combination of practices of inclusion and exclusion has become particularly problematic in recent years.

Conventional realist wisdom about NATO portrays it as no more than an expression of the eternal dynamic of balancing behavior dictated by the perpetual competition for power in the international arena. In this case, the story goes, the American-led Western world created NATO in the context of growing geopolitical rivalry with the Soviet Union in the post-war era.[1] Yet, this picture cannot capture the complexity of NATO's story.[2] The Atlantic Alliance was never reducible to the concern with the practices associated with the logic of *exclusion* (in that case, the exclusion of the Soviet Union and its allies from NATO territory). Rather, a significant emphasis was also placed on the Kantian-inspired politics of *inclusion*: protecting liberal-democratic polities from internal weakness as well as from external aggression by including them in strong institutional structures. From the start, NATO defined itself as the security arm of a community of liberal-democratic norms and values, regarded as the core values of the Western world.[3] For the first forty years of NATO's existence, its political dimension, built around Article 2, was often subordinated to (although never completely annihilated by) the military dimension.[4]

However, the end of the Cold War led the allies to focus on Article 2 to an unprecedented degree, in a situation in which NATO embarked on a process of adaptation to the new environment. For the most part, NATO's efforts at reinventing itself involved a strengthening of its political dimension, as the allies sought to maintain support for NATO by reminding both their publics and their international partners that their security organisation had never been just a military alliance against the Soviet Union.[5] In the 1990s, against the background of instability in some of the countries of the former Warsaw Pact and the former Soviet Union, the allies came to share the idea that, to fulfil its traditional role of protecting its members, NATO had to become an exporter of democratic security to help stabilise Europe and prevent the spread of violent nationalist politics.[6] This occurred in a situation in which, as noted earlier, following the end of the Cold War, a Kantian-inspired democratic peace discourse came to prevail in Western decision-making circles: the best way to ensure long-lasting international stability involves the establishment and maintenance of liberal democratic polities, rather than the creation of particular geostrategic arrangements (say balances of power) as propounded by conventional international relations theory.[7]

As the then-NATO Secretary General Manfred Wörner noted: 'NATO must play its part alongside other Western institutions in extending the security and stability we enjoy to all European nations'.[8] In the new context, the alliance's principal mission came to be defined in terms of projecting stability to the former communist bloc.[9] Thus, in the 1990s, NATO became deeply involved in reshaping ex-communist polities. In particular, NATO representatives enacted a complex set of practices aimed at socialising Central and East European political and military elites into the norms, principles, and rules of Western liberal democracy, particularly in the field of security, and helping them build new institutions around those norms.[10] As a corollary to that view of security, the relationship between the members of the Western security community and former enemies (members of the ex-communist bloc) was not defined in terms of a dichotomy between self/dangerous others. Rather, those *others* were seen as potential friends: societies who, with the right guidance, had the capability to evolve into Western-like polities.[11] In that context, the most important dimension of the relationship between self/other was not spatial (for example, reinforced boundaries between them) but rather temporal, focusing on the potential future evolution of *others* into *selves*.

In short, after the end of the Cold War, NATO seemed to be moving towards a clear logic of conditional inclusion of others into the structures of the Western security community. In the 1990s, at least, the logic of exclusion of enemies from the territory of member states seemed to have been firmly put on the back burner, not least because it was not clear that an unambiguous, dangerous enemy could be identified.

And yet, the story of NATO's post-Cold War evolution did not end there because on 9/11, the terrorist attacks in the United States forced NATO to revisit the question of its role and relevance in the post-Cold War era. In response to 11 September, NATO acted quickly to invoke for the first time in its history the mutual defense clause (Article 5). The alliance then proceeded to redefine its role in the new world of elusive threats to international security. NATO's senior officials pointed out that the organisation would have to adapt to a new environment, an environment in which many threats come from non-conventional sources, such as non-state terrorist actors, possibly in possession of weapons of mass destruction (WMDs), operating across national boundaries.[12] In the new security situation, addressing terrorism came to be identified as 'a core mission for NATO'.[13]

NATO's post-11 September agenda revolves around a new definition of the enemy as highly elusive, often 'hidden among us', and taking advantage of the transnational flows of a globalising world to operate both within and outside the Euro-Atlantic area. According to the NATO defense ministers, the alliance must adapt to meet new challenges in an 'uncertain world', in which many of its enemies are hard to identify.[14] The notion involved here is that, in the new context, NATO must be prepared to deal with an enemy that is 'like cancer', operating anywhere and, potentially, everywhere, simultaneously attacking the West in different ways and on multiple fronts.[15]

In light of the growing prominence of non-conventional enemies and threats, allied officials argued, NATO must be increasingly able and willing to adopt a preventive approach to security, 'preventing instability from growing into crises and managing crises before they get too out of hand . . . if we wish to prevent the organised crime spawned by these conflicts from darkening our doorsteps'.[16] What is more, there is no end in sight to this new preventive approach, for it is not clear when or how there might be a definite end to the struggle against the new enemies.[17]

In a broader analytical perspective, it could be argued that NATO's post-9/11 emphasis on preventive action wherever necessary in response to fluid, non-conventional enemies, and the insistence on security as a process with no end in sight indicates the alliance's acceptance of the view that security provision needs to conform to the principles of risk management. In contrast to the promise of a peaceful 'new world order', which was so popular in the early years of the post-Cold War period, post-9/11 NATO statements and documents reflect a more cautious view of security. In the twenty-first century NATO discourse, there is little talk about definitive solutions to security challenges and a stable, peaceful new world order.[18] Instead, the emphasis is on security as a process of risk management in the face of a plurality of fluid security challenges.

The concept of risk management occupies a prominent position in the analyses put forward by scholars concerned with a general sense of insecurity that, they argue, prevails in our ('late modern') era.[19] In their view, the current international concern with risk is largely a product of globalisation, and a related sense of vulnerability in being part of a world system in which old protections (usually provided by nation-states) are increasingly becoming obsolete.[20] As Ulrich Beck, amongst others, famously argued, an unprecedented anxiety about risks is common to 'second modernity' or 'late modernity,' that is, a period when humanity is more sober about progress and about the future.[21] Thus, whilst many accept that things may still progress, they also recognise that there is a price to be paid, for instance, in terms of global, often unanticipated consequences of our actions.

Particular attention is paid to global risks, which cannot be delimited spatially (say, the threat of a nuclear attack, or even an attack by terrorist groups using WMD) just as they cannot be delimited in time, for actions taken today can have unforeseen consequences affecting future generations.[22] Beck has persuasively argued that that risk society 'is not an option which could be chosen or rejected in the course of political debate'.[23] Instead, it represents an inescapable structural condition of advanced industrialisation in which the produced hazards of that system 'undermine and/ or cancel the established safety systems of the provident state's existing risk calculation'.[24] Risk theorists argue that terrorism represents yet another manifestation of the 'world risk society'.[25] For Beck, 11 September demonstrated that we now live in a world risk society, a society that has to face unpredictable dangers that defy the traditional approach to the management of risk: insurance.

The sense of uncertainty and the emphasis on risk management as a characteristic of the new security environment was evident at NATO's Riga Summit in November 2006. Thus, the

Comprehensive Political Guidance (the key strategic document produced by the allies at the summit) states that NATO must be prepared to face 'unpredictable challenges' that 'arise at very short notice.' Under these circumstances, the priority for the alliance is to develop procedures and capabilities that enable it to 'respond quickly to unforeseen circumstances,' for instance by launching and sustaining 'concurrent major joint operations and smaller operations for collective defense and crisis response on and beyond Alliance territory, on its periphery and at strategic distance'.[26]

NATO's current focus on risk management has translated into a dual approach to the pursuit of security.[27] This involves an attempt to broaden and deepen the Western security community by *inclusive* practices aimed at cultivating or enhancing support for liberal norms outside the allied territory, especially by diffusing liberal norms and seeking to construct polities worthy of inclusion into that community. On the other hand, there has been a renewed emphasis on *exclusionary* practices aimed at identifying, excluding from allied space (or at least from the normal political and socioeconomic life of allied states) and defeating that new category of dangerous others. Particularly dangerous, according to the NATO discourse, are those actors accused of involvement in or support for Islamist terrorism, who allegedly pose a threat not only to the allied publics but more broadly to the values of civilisation.

Building on practices carried out in the 1990s, NATO has sought to intensify its effort to shape transitional, potentially unstable polities in an attempt to turn them into 'like-minded' liberal-democratic countries. The logic behind this approach to security is the same Kantian-inspired logic of building international security via an 'inside' approach, which became prevalent in the 1990s. Now, however, there is an additional rationale for engaging in building 'good,' self-disciplined liberal-democracies: these polities are seen as more reliable partners to address the risks posed by international terrorist groups and other non-conventional enemies.[28]

In the name of helping build self-disciplined, democratic societies, NATO has continued to carry out a plethora of socialisation practices. Its efforts at international norm promotion have involved, in particular, a series of initiatives designed to strengthen and expand the Partnership for Peace (PfP) Programme and to continue the process of NATO enlargement.[29] The PfP's explicit aim of spreading the alliance's ways of thinking and acting, and its emphasis on programs that teach people from transitional or non-democratic states Western-defined norms and rules, can be seen as significant indicators of the importance attached by the alliance to the construction of self-disciplined liberal (or at least pro-liberal) subjects who can presumably act as 'like-minded' partners and potential future members of the Euro-Atlantic security community.

The summit held by NATO in Istanbul in June 2004 was especially important for partnerships, not least because the alliance decided to establish some partnership programs built on the PfP model in the Mediterranean region and even in the so-called 'Broader Middle East', including the Caucasus and Central Asia. The Istanbul Cooperation Initiative (ICI) was extended to interested countries of the broader Middle East region, especially the members of the Gulf Cooperation Council,[30] to foster mutually beneficial bilateral relationships and thus enhance regional and international security and stability. The ICI supplements NATO's activities in Afghanistan and is thus part of NATO's post-9/11 strategy to use partnership and region-building practices to stabilise and (according to the allies) spread democratic norms to and thus help reform the Broader Middle East.

NATO has also reaffirmed its commitment to the 'open-door' policy and has sought to (re) shape the countries seeking inclusion into the alliance.[31] At present, NATO has completed three waves of post-Cold War enlargement, thereby incorporating most of the former communist states in Central/Eastern Europe, as well as several ex-Soviet republics (the Baltic states). The accession of most of those states followed a long period of accession dialogues and reforms monitored, and partly guided, within the framework of NATO's Membership Action Plan (the program designed to provide guidance and monitor the performance of countries wishing to join the Alliance). And, despite the strong opposition expressed by Moscow and even the concerns voiced by some of the European allies, at the Bucharest Summit in 2008 NATO went so far as to promise eventual membership to Georgia and Ukraine, although the allies did not put forward a timeline for their accession.

If NATO has sought to expand the security community that it claims to embody, it has also focused on efforts to exclude from the territory of that community a new type of dangerous *others*. In other words, whilst one can point to a certain continuity in terms of NATO's adoption of a mix of practices of inclusion/exclusion, it is important to note a certain post-9/11 transformation in the nature of practices of exclusion: based on the prevailing assumption within NATO that the predominant enemies of the alliance were no longer states but rather unconventional, non-state actors. The new enemies (the others to be subject to practices and exclusion and punishment) have been identified as being primarily terrorist groups who 'pose a threat to civilization itself' because of their alleged refusal to transcend their irrational behavior as reflected in the 'mindless slaughter of so many innocent civilians'; and their 'willingness to commit acts of violence without precedent in the modern era'[32] *Vis-à-vis* such actors (most notably, al-Qaeda and their supporters, both non-state and state actors) NATO's self-defined role is not that of a guide in the process of transition from an unlawful state of nature (borrowing a Kantian term) to a 'lawful state', a state governed by liberal norms. Indeed, those actors' wilful acts of violence 'against civilization' have made such a course of action impossible: according to the NATO discourse, terrorists and their supporters not only insist on living in an 'unlawful state,' but they explicitly seek to destroy the lawful world. Therefore, it is argued, it is necessary to find the right coercive measures to 'combat this scourge' and thus to prevent terrorists and their sponsors from harming the 'civilized nations'.[33] In the words of Lord Robertson, then NATO Secretary General, in the twenty-first century it is particularly important for the Alliance to find effective ways to protect its citizens 'from criminal terrorists and criminal states, especially when they are armed with weapons designed for massive and indiscriminate destruction'.[34]

The most obvious (although certainly not the only) expression of the contemporary version of the inclusion/exclusion combination of practices enacted by NATO can be found in Afghanistan. Afghanistan, of course, represents NATO's first out-of-area operation, justified via the argument that in the face of non-conventional enemies and challenges that cannot be confined to a particular space, the alliance must be (and is) able to act anywhere in the world. The Afghanistan mission has repeatedly been invoked by allied officials as clear evidence that NATO remains as relevant as ever because it has uniquely valuable material capabilities (particularly military might and flexibility) as well as cultural-symbolic capital: the knowledge and experience not only in fighting wars but also reconstructing war-torn societies around good norms of governance.[35]

The idea underpinning NATO's involvement in Afghanistan is that only a comprehensive operation, combining military and non-military dimensions, can promote stability and keep the country from (re)emerging as a safe haven for terrorism. Provincial Reconstruction Teams [PRTs], small teams of military and civilian personnel, are meant to be the leading edge of the NATO-led International Security Assistance Force (ISAF) presence in Afghanistan. The PRT concept marries the presence of a military force to provide security (primarily by helping government forces to fight insurgents and extend its authority and control over territory) with direct involvement in post-conflict reconstruction tasks, such as the construction of schools and hospitals and the digging of wells. They are meant to be a key component of a three-part strategy for Afghanistan (security, governance, development), seeking to help spread stability across the country.

As a perceived precondition for the establishment of stable institutions of good governance, ISAF has become involved in a series of practices of mentoring Afghans, aimed at helping to construct the kind of self-disciplined actors that can be governed by (and can be trusted to reproduce) such institutions. In seeking to socialise Afghans into new norms, NATO sought to perform functions conventionally attributed to domestic agencies rather than military alliances: teaching Afghans not only how to fight but also how to build security institutions, and how to structure the relationship between the armed forces and political leaders ostensibly around norms of democratic control of the military. Simultaneously, ISAF commanders have stressed the importance of developing adequate methods for identifying, containing, and defeating those individuals and groups that refuse to be governed by norms and rules of good (democratic) governance. Revealingly, senior NATO officers have repeatedly pointed out that the alliance put great emphasis on improving cooperation with Afghan actors, and that cooperation could be achieved only by winning the hearts and minds of the local population.[36] Concurrently, they noted that NATO did 'not hesitate to use appropriate measures against those disruptive elements opposed to democracy and the rule of law in Afghanistan, including military force.'[37]

In essence, NATO-led ISAF has sought the same, two-pronged approach to the pursuit of security discussed above. This involves a set of practices of inclusion (conventionally associated with domestic agencies rather than military alliances) aimed at educating and working with local actors who support NATO's agenda of establishing stable institutions and norms of 'good' governance. The idea behind this agenda is that international actors need to train and include pro-reform Afghans in practices of security governance as part of a broader process of helping the locals turn their country into the kind of modern, peaceful, well-governed state that deserves the respect and trust of the community of established democracies. At the same time, however, ISAF has also stressed the importance of practices of exclusion, involving the identification, exclusion from Afghan political and socioeconomic activities, and defeat of those groups that radically oppose the agenda for change prescribed by the international community.[38]

On this logic, the portrayal of Taliban insurgents as particularly dangerous enemies both *vis-à-vis* the Afghan Government/Afghan society and the international community was for a long time perceived as sufficient justification for the application of massive military force against their suspected bases, even at the risk of killing civilians caught in the crossfire. In other words, the modern rules of self-restraint designed to govern the application of coercion, particularly in the context of relations between a government and its citizens, seemed to be suspended in relations with Taliban insurgents. Afghan Government forces have cooperated with ISAF in the application of military power, even as President Karzai has reminded the international community that 'most Taliban fighters are Afghan citizens.'[39] In recent months, there has been a growing shift within the alliance towards the view that any long-term solution in Afghanistan requires the participation of some Taliban actors. But even in this context the inclusion/exclusion duality persists in a situation in which there is a clear effort to differentiate between moderate Taliban (the potential subjects of inclusion in governance arrangement) and the more extremist insurgents, seen as the enemies of modern values and civilisation itself and, hence, as actors who must be excluded from political negotiations and defeated as soon as possible.

The irony is that these new types of practices, meant to renew NATO and save it from difficult questions regarding its post-Cold War relevance, generated an immediate, very different kind of problem. For newer NATO members, this particular interpretation of practices of exclusion entailed the unacceptable marginalisation of the more conventional realist emphasis on collective defence against potential aggression carried out by inimical states. This problem became particularly acute in a situation in which (in the eyes of some former communist states) Russia was (re) launching a set of power policies and practices in its neighborhood.

As a recent policy brief published by the Centre for European Reform correctly noted, many of the countries that have joined NATO since the late 1990s worry that the alliance has been erroneously neglecting the possibility of 'old-fashioned' conflicts, possibly involving Russia, in favour of global risk management efforts.[40] The crisis generated by the war in Iraq in 2003, when the allies failed to maintain a common front, and the debates surrounding (and weak response to) the 2008 war in Georgia exacerbated the new members' concerns about their security situation. As a senior official from one of the Baltic States asked:

> what if the next time it will be a Baltic country rather than Georgia that is attacked by Russia? We need to be sure that the alliance will really be there for us, and at the moment many people in my country are not at all convinced that this would be the case.[41]

Under these circumstances, several former communist countries that are now members of NATO have insisted that NATO's new strategic concept, due to be adopted in November 2010, should include clear provisions to 'reassure' the Central/East Europeans that the alliance would, indeed, come to their defence in a security crisis, whether military or non-military, such as a cyber-attack.[42]

In this climate of concern regarding the credibility of NATO's defense commitments, the allies need to perform a fine balancing act when they formulate the new strategic concept. An interesting prelude to the themes that are likely to arise in official discussions regarding the new strategic concept can be found in a report issued in May 2010 by the Group of Experts chaired by Madeleine Albright.[43] Because the Report has already been made public and is the result of widespread consultations, it will probably be difficult for the alliance to distance itself from the ideas and vision of the future outlined by the Albright Group. Therefore, it is interesting to examine the report to get a better sense of the kinds of steps that NATO is likely to seek to take in the coming years.

The Albright Report can be read as an exercise in constructive ambiguity, because it outlines a vision of NATO as an institution that effectively combines inclusive and exclusionary security practices, but (not surprisingly) gives little indication as to how these are to be combined. The ideas put forward are inspiring and, if implemented, could help to turn NATO into an effective twenty-first century security institution. But the implementation of those ideas is likely to be more difficult than the Report seems to suggest. In describing the international security environment in which NATO is likely to operate in the next decade, the report paints a complex picture: 'provided NATO stays vigilant', the prospect of a direct military attack across the borders of the alliance remains 'slight'. The more immediate threats seem to be non-conventional ones: terrorism, the danger of 'efforts to harm society through cyber assaults or the unlawful disruption of critical supply lines', as well as the danger of proliferation of attacks with WMDs.

In this complex security environment, the report outlines a vision of the alliance with the ability to be a highly effective security institution if it combines inclusive security practices (continuing to build and expand the liberal security community) with two types of practices of exclusion. Thus, emphasis is placed both on the more conventional practices of deterrence and on practices aimed at containing and defeating non-conventional actors, such as the insurgents in Afghanistan. Thus, the Albright team insists:

> NATO's core commitment—embodied in Article 5 of the North Atlantic Treaty—is unchanged, but the requirements for fulfilling that commitment have shifted in shape. To remain credible, this pledge to shield members states from armed aggression must be backed up not only by basic military capabilities but also by the contingency planning, focused exercises, force readiness, and sound logistics required to preserve the confidence of Allies whilst minimizing the likelihood of miscalculation on the part of potential adversaries.

In addition to maintaining and enhancing its ability to deter potential enemies and defend the territory of its allies, NATO must enhance 'its ability to prevail in military operations and broader security missions beyond its borders'. Far from being directed against entire populations, those missions will require NATO to become more effective in developing a 'comprehensive' civil–military approach that combines military and non-military skills and assets and is aimed not simply at containing/defeating inimical individuals and groups (like al-Qaeda and the extremist Taliban in Afghanistan) but also at the creation of stable polities in areas emerging from conflict. Whilst performing these functions, NATO must continue to engage in inclusive security practices by maintaining an 'open-door' policy *vis-à-vis* countries that fulfill conditions of membership and must launch 'a new era of partnerships', including a stronger partnership with Russia.

The Albright Report invokes NATO's considerable material resources and experience in acting both as a collective defense organisation (having successfully protected the allies from the Soviet threat) and a security community based on liberal-democratic values to insist that the alliance can and should become an effective twenty-first century organisation that combines a multitude of inclusive and exclusionary practices of security. This combination is seen as necessary in the era of risk management, an era dominated not by clearly defined threats but by uncertainty and by the prominence of non-conventional dangers.

In essence, the report outlines the multiple functions and security practices that NATO needs to enact to remain relevant, without dwelling on the tensions that are likely to arise in attempts to reconcile these functions. Such constructive ambiguity was probably necessary to produce a report that would be acceptable to all the allies. But such constructive ambiguity also risks generating significant disagreement and tensions in the future implementation of the ideas contained in the report, and likely in the new strategic concept.

The situation that NATO will face in the foreseeable future is that, in an era of multiple, often fluid global and regional risks and few clearly identified enemies and threats, the allies are likely to have to reconcile multiple interpretations of the relative importance of those risks. The world of risk management is often characterised by debates and disagreements regarding the best way to juggle the multitude of risks that are present at any given moment, and these kinds of debates and possible disagreements are certainly likely to be present within NATO. As the 2002–3 debates surrounding the war in Iraq and the mission in Afghanistan demonstrate, what appears to one ally (in the American case) to be an unacceptable risk (the danger that a totalitarian regime might seek to develop WMDs, to take the case of Iraq) can appear to other member-states as being insufficiently urgent to warrant immediate military action by the alliance. In a similar vein, what appears to some Central/East European members of NATO to be a growing danger (Russia's increased assertiveness) can appear to the more established members of the alliance, particularly some of the West Europeans, as a far less significant source of threat to allied as security, and, as such, an issue that should be subordinated to the need for greater cooperation with Russia.[44]

In this atmosphere, significant interallied disagreements regarding the best way to combine inclusive and exclusionary security policies can be expected in the coming years. For instance, substantial disagreements are likely to make it difficult to achieve the dual goal inscribed in the Albright report: include Russia in Euro-Atlantic partnership structures and practices, whilst at the same time reassure those allies that are increasingly worried about Moscow's assertiveness in the region. It will be at best a very difficult balancing act.

The report states that 'NATO should pursue a policy of engagement with Russia whilst reassuring the allies that their security and interests will be defended'. But that emphasis on reassuring the allies (including the former Soviet republics of Estonia, Latvia, and Lithuania) is likely to be seen by Moscow as further evidence to support its claim that Europe and the eastern enlargement of NATO constitutes a military threat to Russia.[45] This is particularly so in a situation in which for some of the new NATO members, any credible measures of 'reassurance' need to include a military dimension. Indeed, several allies have demanded that NATO prepare contingency plans for any member-state that asks for one and, in early 2010, the rest of the allies agreed to do so.[46] But given Moscow's sensitivities and suspicion, it is hard to see how NATO can make visible military preparations against a possible attack (particularly in the Baltic countries) in ways that are at once reassuring to states concerned about a possible repetition of the Georgian war and seen as benign by Moscow.

In a similar vein, tensions are likely to arise in relationship to a NATO policy of inclusion that is particularly problematic for Russia: the open-door policy. At the 2008 Bucharest summit, under pressure from the Americans, the allies promised that NATO would eventually include Georgia and Ukraine. This promise occurred despite the fact that Moscow has always expressed particularly strong opposition to the accession to NATO of those two countries, which it regards as part of its region of influence. Ironically, domestic developments in those states (unresolved conflicts in Georgia and broad public opposition to NATO membership in the Ukraine) have temporarily relieved the allies of the pressure of having to make a decision in this area. But should those circumstances change, any discussion concerning the prospect of NATO membership for Georgia and Ukraine will likely fuel tensions between Moscow and the allied governments, making it even more difficult to build a strong, lasting Russia – NATO partnership.

To place this discussion in a broader perspective: even leaving aside the difficulties that the allies are likely to encounter in articulating a policy *vis-à-vis* Russia, NATO can expect to face substantial difficulties in finding the resources needed to carry out the combination of inclusive/exclusionary security practices outlined in the Albright Report. In recognition of the constraints associated with limited NATO resources, the Albright team argued that NATO has to place unprecedented emphasis on partnerships, especially with the European Union (EU). Thus, the Albright team clearly states that, 'as NATO moves toward 2020, it will generally not operate alone.' In its 'comprehensive approach', it will work with 'national governments and non-governmental entities', as well as the UN, the EU, the Organization for Security and Cooperation in Europe, and an array of other institutions. The emphasis on the need to cooperate with the EU marks a clear shift away from what used to be a significant concern on the part of some NATO members, especially the United States: any move towards a stronger dimension for the Union threatens to undermine NATO. Instead, the report unreservedly welcomes European defense efforts to regional and global security.

As two organisations that claim to embody the values of liberal-democracy (and share more than twenty members) the vision of closer EU – NATO partnership seems perfectly logical. In fact, this could be a perfect recipe for ensuring that the allies do more with less, particularly in a situation in which the allies have to cope with the serious effects of the economic crisis. Yet, an effective EU – NATO partnership in the area of security cannot be taken for granted. The Iraq war was a reminder that there is no guarantee that the EU can speak with one voice in matters of international security. Meanwhile, the different 'national caveats' upon which various European members of NATO insist in Afghanistan indicate two things: not only the difficulty of reaching agreement about the acceptable limits of allied involvement in peace-building operations, but also that within the EU, there are very different types of national legal and cultural constraints regarding the deployment of military forces.

These persisting differences can significantly undermine the ability of European states to turn the EU into an effective actor in various security missions that include a military dimension. Furthermore, it is well known that there is a growing gap in terms of defense capabilities between the Americans and the Europeans. Already, the United States expends about 70 percent of total NATO defense spending, three times more per soldier than the European Allies, and six times more on research and development.[47] This gap raises difficult questions about burden-sharing within NATO; some prominent American voices have repeatedly complained that should this trend continue, the value of European allies will diminish rapidly. Simultaneously, European reluctance to spend on defense (understandable though it may be, particularly in the current economic climate) also raises questions regarding the EU's ability to contribute to regional/global security. The problem is that in the absence of an effective partnership with the EU, it is more difficult to see how NATO can secure the resources needed to perform the multitude of inclusive/ exclusionary security practices envisaged in the Albright Report and indicated in recent statements by senior allied officials.[48]

In conclusion, this chapter has examined the ways in which NATO has sought to adapt to a rapidly changing security environment by invoking and building upon its historical repertoire of inclusive and exclusionary security practices. At present, the alliance has embarked upon another stage of its process of adaptation by starting to prepare a new strategic concept (the first since 1999). The preliminary set of recommendations for the new concept presented in the Albright report are a useful indicator of ways in which the alliance is likely to combine inclusive and exclusionary security practices in an effort to evolve into (and secure international recognition as) an effective security institution in the twenty-first century. However, the combination of inclusive and exclusionary security practices is likely to be more problematic than the Albright report seems to suggest. This is not to argue that NATO is doomed; indeed, despite recent economic difficulties and the problems encountered in Afghanistan, the alliance continues to have significant material and symbolic resources at its disposal and to be regarded by many policy-makers within allied states as an indispensable international security institution.[49] Nonetheless, the next stage in the alliance's process of post-Cold War adaptation may be particularly challenging.

Notes

1 John J. Mearsheimer, 'Back to the Future: Instability in Europe after the Cold War,' *International Security*, 14(1990), 5–56; Kenneth Waltz, 'The Emerging Structure of International Politics.' *International Security*, Volume 18, Number 2 (1990), 75–76.

2 Alexandra Gheciu, *NATO in the 'New Europe': The Politics of International Socialization after the Cold War* (Stanford, CA, 2005).

3 Escott Reid, *Time of Fear and Hope: The Making of the North Atlantic Treaty, 1947 1949* (Toronto, 1977); Thomas Risse-Kappen, 'Collective Identity in a Democratic Community,' in Peter Katzenstein, ed., *The Culture of National Security* (New York: 1996).

4 Gheciu, *'New Europe'*.

5 Alexandra Gheciu, *Securing Civilization?* (Oxford, 2008).

6 Ronald Asmus, *Opening NATO's Door; How the Alliance Remade Itself for a New Era* (New York, 2002).

7 This can be traced back to Immanuel Kant's *Perpetual Peace*. For analyses of the ways in which NATO embodies Kantian-inspired ideas see Risse, 'Collective Identity'; Michael C. Williams and Iver Neumann, 'From Alliance to Security Community: NATO, Russia and the Power of Identity,' *Millennium: Journal of International Studies*, 29(2000), 357–87.

8 Manfred Wörner, 'Opening Statement to the NATO Summit Meeting,' London, 5 July 1990, www. nato.int/docu/speech/1990/s900705a_e.htm.

9 Gheciu, *'New Europe'*.

10 Trine Flockhart, '"Masters and Novices": Socialisation and Social Learning through the NATO Parliamentary Assembly', *International Relations*, 18(2004), 361–80; Gheciu, *'New Europe'*; Frank Schimmelfennig, *The EU, NATO and the Integration of Europe. Rules and Rhetoric* (Cambridge, 2003).

11 Gheciu, *Securing Civilization?*

12 Chris Donnelly, 'Security in the 21st Century: New Challenges and New Responses.' Paper in NATO's online library (June 2003): www.nato.int.proxy.bib.uottawa.ca/docu/speech/2003/ s030605a.htm.

13 George Robertson, 'Defence and Security in an Uncertain World,' Keynote Speech, Forum Europe, Brussels, 17 May 2002, www.nato.int/docu/speech/2002/s020517a.htm.

14 NATO, 'Informal NATO Defence Ministers Meeting, Warsaw,' 24–25 September 2002, www.nato.int/docu/comm/2002/0209-wrsw.htm.
15 Donnelly, 'Security in the 21st Century'.
16 Robertson, 'Uncertain World'.
17 NATO, 'Prague Summit Declaration.' Press Release (2002)127, 21 November 2002, www.nato.int/docu/pr/2002/p02-127e.htm.
18 Gheciu, *Securing Civilization?*
19 For particularly interesting analyses see Ulrich Beck, *World Risk Society* (Cambridge, 1999); Mary Douglas and Aaron Wildavsky, *Risk and Culture: An Essay on the Selection of Technical and Environmental Dangers,* (Berkeley, 1982); Christopher Coker, *Globalization and Insecurity in the Twenty-First Century: NATO and the Management of Risk.* Adelphi Paper Number 345 (London, 2002); Mikkel Vedby Rasmussen, 'A Parallel Globalization of Terror: 9–11, Security and Globalization,' *Cooperation and Conflict,* 37(2002), 323–49; Michael J. Williams, *NATO, Security and Risk-Management: From Kosovo to Kandahar* (London, 2009). In criminology, especially influential has been Richard Ericson and Kevin Haggerty, *Policing the Risk Society* (Toronto, 1997).
20 Coker, *Globalization and Insecurity;* Rasmussen, 'Parallel Globalization'.
21 Beck, *World Risk;* idem., 'The Terrorist Threat: World Risk Society Revisited,' *Theory, Culture and Society* Volume 19, Number 4(2002), 39–55.
22 Coker, *Globalization and Insecurity.*
23 Ulrich Beck, 'World Risk Society as Cosmopolitan Society? Ecological Questions in a Framework of Manufactured Uncertainties,' *Theory, Culture and Society,* Volume 13, Number 4(1996), 28.
24 Ibid., 31.
25 Beck, 'Terrorist Threat,' 39–55.
26 'Comprehensive Political Guidance.' Endorsed by NATO Heads of State and Government, 29 November 2006: www.nato.int/issues/com_political_guidance/index.html.
27 Gheciu, *Securing Civilization?*
28 Interview with senior NATO official, Brussels, May 2005.
29 Isabelle François, 'Partnership: One of NATO's Fundamental Security Tasks,' *NATO Review,* 48(2000), www.nato.int/docu/review.htm.
30 More specifically Bahrain, Kuwait, Oman, Qatar, Saudi Arabia, and the United Arab Emirates.
31 Gheciu, *'New Europe';* idem., *Securing Civilization?*
32 North Atlantic Council, 'Statement by the North Atlantic Council,' NATO Press Release PR/CP(2001) 122, 11 September 2001, www.nato.int/docu/pr/2001/p01-122e.htm.
33 Ibid.
34 This and the next quotation are from Robertson, 'Uncertain World'.
35 Gheciu, *'New Europe'; idem., Securing Civilization?*
36 Communication with senior NATO officers, March 2006–March 2010, Brussels, Oxford, London, Ottawa.
37 Ibid.
38 For a more detailed analysis see Gheciu, *Securing Civilization?*
39 Communication with a senior British official, 30 May 2007, Oxford.
40 Ronald Asmus, Stefan Czmur, Chris Donnelly, Aivis Ronis, Tomas Valasek, and Klaus Wittman, *NATO, New Allies and Reassurance* (London 2010).
41 Author's interview with senior Baltic official, 20 March 2010.
42 Ibid. See also Asmus et al., *NATO.*
43 At their April 2009 Summit, allied leaders directed NATO Secretary General Anders Fogh Rasmussen to convene a group of independent experts to prepare the ground for a new NATO Strategic Concept. This group published its full report, entitled *NATO 2020: Assured Security, Dynamic Engagement,* in May 2010.
44 A revealing illustration of those disagreements can be found in different reactions by the allies in response to the Russian call for a new security architecture, which would significantly weaken NATO. Whereas the United States, Britain, and most of the former communist states were opposed, some West European states (for example, France) appeared more supportive of at least discussing the principles inscribed in the Russian proposal. See NATO Parliamentary Assembly, *Russia, the West and the Future of Euro-Atlantic Security* (Brussels, 2009); Dmitri Trenin, Andrew Kuchins and Thomas Gomart, *Toward a New Euro-Atlantic 'Hard' Security Agenda* (Paris, Washington, 2008).
45 In 2010, Russian President Medvedev approved a new Russian military doctrine that describes NATO expansion as a military threat that undermines efforts to improve Moscow's ties with the West.

46 See Asmus et al., *New Allies*. Contingency plans are drafted by the alliance in peacetime to hone defenses against the most probable threats.

47 Jamie Shea, 'NATO's New Strategic Concept', *Turkish Policy Quarterly*, 9(2010), 48–59.

48 Because of space constraints, I do not examine challenges of collaboration with other international actors.

49 Gheciu, *Securing Civilization?*

23

New regionalisms and the African Union

Reflections on the rise of Africrats, regional economic integration, and inter-regional relations

J. Andrew Grant and Thomas Kwasi Tieku

The African Union [AU] is representative of the post-Cold War international order that is witnessing increasing regional integration and co-operation across the globe. In the absence of intense ideological competition between the United States and Soviet-led blocs that marked the Cold War era, regional organisations have become increasingly prominent in international politics. The importance and relevance of regions and regional dynamics have also come to the fore within the practice of diplomacy and statecraft, fomenting change within the current international order. A 'new regionalisms approach' [NRA] allows a better understanding of such trends within the present international order.[1] This approach is applied as an analytical lens to address contemporary issues of relevance to the AU. Whether it is the influence of bureaucrats behind the scenes, understanding episodes of sustained violent conflict, or locating the role of civil society in governance schemes, the NRA places the implications of such issues in regional context. In the *Constitutive Act of the African Union*, the importance of civil society can be read into Article 3(g), which states that the AU will 'promote democratic principles and institutions, popular participation and good governance'.[2] Civil society can influence the AU through participation on special committees, expert panels, and sectorial meetings of the AU Commission. Ideas of civil society groups may be transmitted through these channels to 'Africrats'—bureaucrats within the AU. If accepted by Africrats, these ideas may result in a policy proposal being put forward for consideration by the AU Assembly, which is the most important body or organ of the organisation.[3] The result is an opening up of a small yet important space for civil society within the institutional framework of the AU.[4] Although the importance of civil society and its participation in contributing to good governance is often referenced in AU documents and declarations, members of non-governmental organisations [NGOs] are often persecuted in member states such as Zimbabwe and Eritrea or face severe restrictions in countries such as Angola and Sudan.

The NRA is a useful lens for understanding the new international order, for regions are increasingly salient in global affairs. Regions range from the micro-level to the meso-level to the macro-level. In the African context, examples of regional levels of formal regionalism include West Africa's Mano River Union, the Community of Sahel-Saharan States (Communauté des états sahélo-sahariens), and the continent-wide AU, respectively. The three levels of region each contain both formal and informal processes. The former is associated with institutions and inter-state agreements, whilst the latter witnesses a wide range of networks such as small-scale female traders to seasonal migration flows to smuggling conduits for illicit goods. These regional entities can also be purely informal, such as the Parrot's Beak in West Africa.[5] The NRA emphasises the importance of relations between and amongst states and non-state actors. The political economy of armed militias or individual entrepreneurs or NGOs has a reach that extends in both directions: from the regional to the local, and from the regional to the global.

The Organisation of African Unity [OAU] was founded on 25 May 1963, thereby making its debut during the height of the Cold War. On one hand, the Pan-African symbolism of the OAU and its aims of de-colonisation served as an important counter-weight to the push and pull of the Cold War era.[6] On the other, the OAU's lack of robust action was symptomatic of an era that considered state sovereignty as sacrosanct. Wide-scale human rights abuses and violent conflict occurred within member states—the cases of Nigeria-Biafra, Rwanda, Somalia, and the Democratic Republic of Congo—just to name a few. The OAU was largely impotent in its reaction to such humanitarian crises.

Despite committing to de-colonisation, the OAU did not provide much support for African secessionist movements. The plight of Cabinda is illustrative of the OAU stance on secessionist movements—even if these groups could substantiate their claims based on separate treaties signed with former colonial Powers. Following the 1885 Berlin Conference Cabinda, allocated to Portugal, was known as the 'Portuguese Congo'. The Portuguese also signed a series of treaties with local kingdoms in the Congo region, culminating in the 1885 Treaty of Simulambuco. In the early 1960s, the OAU drew up a list of European colonies across the continent that deserved independence. The regional grouping deemed Cabinda to be the thirty-ninth African 'state' to be de-colonised—only four places behind Angola. Yet, when Portugal's colonial possessions were finally granted independence in the mid-1970s, Angola claimed oil-rich Cabinda as part of its territory. Despite protests by Cabinda, which argued that it had been a separate and distinct Portuguese colonial possession, and hence deserving of independent statehood, the OAU remained silent on the matter.[7]

The AU replaced the OAU on 26 May 2001 (when the *Constitutive Act of the African Union* entered into force). On 9 July 2002, the AU officially debuted with much fanfare and optimism to counter the previous decade of so-called 'Afro-pessimism'. Expectations of good governance and transparency were touted by AU advocates, but securing good governance and greater transparency would incur greater financial costs for the 53-member[8] organisation. The AU inherited a legacy of 'membership payment defaults and a highly inept staff' from its predecessor.[9] Whereas the OAU's operating budget was approximately US$30 million per annum, the AU's annual budget is in the range of US$90 million.[10]

A more optimistic view of the OAU's legacy exists, contending that the AU represents the latest evolution of Pan-Africanism.[11] Admittedly, its exponents are cautiously optimistic that Pan-Africanism's goals of unity and freedom from exploitation and violent conflict may be achieved through the AU's institutional framework under the *Protocol Relating to the Establishment of the Peace and Security Council of the African Union*.[12] However, the regional body has been slow to intervene in member states. The absence of robust intervention by the AU in member states is due to lack of capacity—for example, funding, logistics, trained personnel, equipment—and lack of political will. The latter is a holdover from the OAU's reluctance to intervene in member states based on the norm of non-interference:

> The OAU was largely a club of heads of state and, given that heads of state were often the prime perpetrators of human rights abuse during the Cold War era, humanitarian

intervention remained an unlikely course of action. The principle of non-interference continued to be favoured at the expense of human rights.[13]

Pan-Africanism reinforced this norm of non-interference, which was misplaced given its initial aim of non-interference by former colonial Powers. This situation helps explain why despite having the right to intervene in its member states, the AU rarely exercises this right. It is particularly vexing considering that the *Constitutive Act of the African Union*, Article 3 (f) is frank in its commitment that one of the AU's primary objectives is to 'promote peace, security, and stability on the continent'.[14]

Over the past several years, some incremental change has occurred in contradiction to the norm of non-interference amongst African states. The *Constitutive Act of the African Union*, Article 4 (h) was amended during the Maputo summit in 2003 and reads:

> the right of the Union to intervene in a Member State pursuant to a decision of the Assembly in respect of grave circumstances, namely: war crimes, genocide and crimes against humanity *as well as a serious threat to legitimate order to restore peace and stability to the Member State of the Union upon the recommendation of the Peace and Security Council.*[15]

The amended version of Article 4 (h) has yet to come into force, as only 25 of the requisite 35 AU members have ratified the document. This lack of full ratification notwithstanding, the case may be made that the norm of non-interference amongst African states is weakening. Sudanese President Omar Hassan al-Bashir was forced to cancel his attendance at the third Africa-European Union [EU] summit held in Tripoli in November 2010, despite being invited by Libya in July.[16] However, AU members did not precipitate this decision. Nor was it an instance of grandstanding by Muammar Gaddafi, the Libyan leader. Since the AU's inception, Gaddafi has been viewed as trying to sway the organisation's objectives and goals, under the auspices of his 'new found'—or at least attempt at—Pan-Africanist credentials.[17] Rather, Libya bowed to behind-the-scene pressure by the EU, which threatened to have its 27 members walk out of the summit if al-Bashir was in attendance. In March 2009, the International Criminal Court [ICC] issued an arrest warrant for al-Bashir on charges of war crimes and crimes against humanity in Darfur. This action was followed by a second arrest warrant on charges of genocide in July 2010. The AU's Peace and Security Council has since lobbied the ICC to defer these arrest warrants against al-Bashir.

International bureaucracies have become ubiquitous characteristics and the public face of contemporary regional institutions. It is no different for the AU, wherein its bureaucrats, known as 'Africrats', set the agenda for meetings, initiate new policy for member states, implement decisions made by political leaders, and manage institutional resources. Within the OAU and AU, Africrats have never been mere servants of politicians, nor has the role they have played been a merely peripheral one in African regionalisms.[18] Rather, they have shaped, and continue to shape, African politics and diplomacy. Even well developed states such as South Africa rely on the African Union Commission [AUC] for policy directions at the regional level. The AUC has become a key source of policy ideas and long term strategic policy formulation.

The emergence of the Commission as an independent agent is interesting because the original intention of African leaders when they established the OAU Secretariat in 1963 was to prevent the establishment of a supranational entity. Their main objective for agreeing to the OAU regime was to consolidate the Westphalian state system. As a result, only institutions, rules, norms, and administrative mechanisms that strengthened sovereign prerogatives and the territorial integrity of African states were developed or allowed to operate properly. Institutions such as the

Commission for Mediation, Arbitration, and Conciliation, which could have chipped away some of the sovereign prerogatives of African states, remained on paper, and many institutional restrictions were put in the OAU Charter to make the organisation's Secretariat dependent on member states.

In the early days of the OAU, an interim work force dominated by Ethiopians and, in particular, former employees of the Ethiopian Ministry of Foreign Affairs, was recruited to keep the Provisional General Secretariat running until African leaders agreed on a permanent OAU structure. Many institutional restrictions were put in place to prevent the Administrative Secretary-General from becoming a supranational entity. A major change in the structure of the Secretariat occurred in 1979. The assertive Edem Kodjo, then OAU's Administrative Secretary-General, felt that the Secretariat required a 'fresh orientation' and new structures.[19] Kodjo persuaded the political leaders to make two significant decisions. First, the Assembly agreed to establish a committee to review the OAU Charter at its Sixteenth Ordinary Session held in Monrovia in 1979 to strengthen the OAU Secretariat so as to promote regional integration. Second, he got the approval of the leaders to restructure the OAU Secretariat. He increased its institutional departments and, perhaps more crucially, renamed the 'Administrative Secretary-General' the 'Secretary-General'. That shift meant that the Secretariat could do more than provide administrative support to OAU organs and organise annual summits. It now had the added responsibility of proposing new agenda items for summit meetings and OAU organs, commissioning studies, implementing decisions, and monitoring compliance with OAU decisions by member states.

These changes should have enhanced Africrat powers, but the kinds of people employed at the Secretariat prevented it from playing a more assertive role in the regionalism process. Many of them either were political appointees or recruited from member states' ministries of foreign affairs. Whilst the majority of the political appointees lacked the requisite skills, the qualified people recruited from the ministries saw the Secretariat as a retirement home, a place where they could get a decent severance package, something not available from most civil services in Africa. The competent ones stayed away from key issues that governments deemed sensitive, as they did not want to risk their retirement packages, and those who did not have to be extremely cautious lacked the expertise to tackle the big issues. As a consequence, the Secretariat continued to perform purely administrative functions, instead of becoming a supranational entity, as Kodjo hoped when he introduced the changes. The Secretariat became cumbersome and ineffective.[20]

By 1989 it had become clear that the Secretariat required radical reforms, and needed to redirect its 'attention and limited resources [to] priority activities and [to] tackling those issues and problems which are of the utmost priority' to the continent.[21] The then Secretary-General Salim Ahmed Salim set out to restructure the OAU 'to improve its capacity to deliver and to change the OAU's managerial setup, staff work ethics, and the process of recruiting, promoting and assessing staff at the Secretariat and regional offices'.[22] In brief, Salim wanted to build the capacity of the OAU administrative apparatus to ensure efficiency and to 'bring the levels of remuneration and staff performance to the highest standards possible'.[23] As part of the process of ensuring that 'quality and not quantity' is 'the guiding principle in retention and recruitment of people',[24] Salim set out to eliminate political appointments. Thus, he hired an independent consultant, Mohamed Halfani, to recruit OAU bureaucrats on the basis of merit. While at the University of Toronto, Halfani had written a doctoral thesis on administrative reforms and was eager to put some of his ideas into practice. Salim, armed with Halfani's proposed reforms, introduced new rules for the staff, changed the work ethics, replaced many of the notably unqualified staff at the Secretariat, ran the OAU Secretariat as if it were the office of a prime minister of a state, and produced voluminous reports about the best ways to make the Secretariat effective. Administrative reform ideas produced during Halfani's tenure (1989–2003), together with reports of consultants hired to audit the OAU Secretariat, led to the creation and adoption of a new administrative structure at the Maputo summit in July 2004. The Secretariat was transformed into a 10-member AU Commission led by a chairperson and a deputy chairperson, elected by the Assembly.

Reform of the OAU Secretariat under Salim, whilst not curing all of its many ills, transformed it from a typically inefficient administrative bureaucracy into a relatively efficient and knowledge-driven one. Beginning to take on work that went beyond its administrative responsibility, it teamed with the United Nations Economic Commission for Africa [UNECA] and independent consultants to assign studies on a range of issues, including regional integration, the state of Africa's economies, and conflict prevention. For instance, the Commission and UNECA jointly-published the *Economic Report on Africa*. The increase in the technical competence of senior management enabled the Secretariat and the Commission to play assertive roles in shaping policies of the OAU and the AU.

Almost all key policy directives that have guided the OAU and the AU since 1990 have come from Africrats, and three documents especially have shaped the work of the Pan-African organisation during this period: Africa's response to the end of the Cold War; the *Vision of the African Union and the Mission of the African Union Commission*; and the 2004–7 *Strategic Framework of the African Union Commission*. Developed during Salim's tenure as Secretary-General, the first document has had an enduring impact on the Pan-African organisation. Alpha Oumar Konaré, Chairperson of the AU Commission between 2003 and 2008, led the development of the rest of the documents. All three were composed with little, if any, input from the political organs of the OAU and the AU. The process of development left little policy space for African states to contribute to or comment on them, though civil society groups got the chance to contribute to the AU's vision and mission— and the strategic mechanisms. Konaré's regime brought civil society into the policy process of the AU.

The exclusion of member states from the process was in one part a result of legal requirements and, in the second, because of the technocrat-driven nature of OAU and AU policy-making. Africrats are barred by Article 4(1) of the *Constitutive Act of the African Union* from seeking or receiving instructions or directives from any member state of the Pan-African organisation unless the political organs and, in particular, the Assembly authorised it. Hence, Africrats could not consult any government officials on the documents without prior approval by the Assembly or the Council. The political organs adopted the documents not only without debate, but also without even asking Africrats to consult member states.

Africrats are providing policy direction and developing specific policies for the AU in spite of the fact that the political organs are formally supposed to perform that role. The Assembly, assisted by the Executive Council and the Permanent Representatives Committee [PRC], is hypothetically bound to set broad policy guidelines and mandate a strategic vision for the organisation. In the phraseology of the AU Constitutive Act and rules of procedure, the Assembly is the 'supreme organ of the Union' and determines 'its priorities'.[25] The specific policy proposals are supposed to come from the Executive Council. The Assembly and the Council have, however, been unable to perform these roles because of at least three factors. Strangely, the two bodies are neither designed nor equipped for developing policy directives. Apart from the obvious fact that the one-year rotational chairmanship of the Assembly and Council leadership does not encourage long term thinking, chairpersons of both institutions have no powers to initiate policy, set agendas, or provide policy direction for the organisation. African leaders intentionally disabled the positions of the chairs of the Assembly and of the Council primarily because of the fear that an ambitious chairperson might take advantage of the position to become pseudo-president of Africa. The decision to prevent the chairs of the Council and the Assembly from setting priorities for the Pan-African organisation reflects the general reluctance of African governments in 1963 to cede sovereign prerogatives to the OAU. And, unlike other institutions of the AU, those two bodies remained unreformed since that year.

Second, meetings of both the Assembly and the Council are not conducive to strategic thinking and policy formulation. Meetings are infrequent and too large, and many of the attendees have a weak policy background in most of the issues under consideration. Both institutions require at least 35 members to form a quorum. On average, 40 attend each meeting of the Assembly and the Council. The sheer size of these meetings discourages in-depth policy debate and discussions, and therefore the discussions are not well-informed enough to generate innovative ideas and policy prescriptions. The agendas of meetings are usually overloaded and, often, it is impossible for members to examine thoroughly the numerous reports that usually accompany the agendas of Assembly and Council meetings. The majority of issues under consideration are adopted without debate; at best, they are discussed in a superficial way. Members have no time to read carefully or discuss reports and agenda items, and thus, most of the proposals that reach them through the PRC are approved. The result is that the PRC has become a key institution in the development of AU policies and rules. It turns the 'AU agenda into the day to day reality of government business in capital cities around the [African] continent'.[26] It is also where most ideas are killed; particularly the most innovative ones related to monetary implications for member states. The PRC is famous for its gatekeeping role and for turning clearly-developed proposals into vague and largely unreadable texts.

A major problem with the PRC is that it is composed of diplomats who are usually capable of looking at only the political dimensions of issues. Most do not have technical knowledge of the specific issues that are put before them. The situation is not helped by the fact that they get no meaningful technical support from either their states or their missions. The unwritten rule that they have developed is to reject proposals they do not understand and to vote down new proposals that will require additional resources to be implemented. They also sometimes reword expensive proposals so that they cannot be implemented. The PRC's obstructionist attitude is a major source of frustration for Africrats. It was a very significant problem, particularly during Konaré's administration. Konaré felt he had to explain things like a primary school teacher whenever he submitted a proposal to the PRC, whilst PRC members felt that Konaré behaved like a president giving instructions to subordinates whenever he appeared before them. The often acrimonious relationship between Konaré and the PRC largely accounted for his departure after only one term. In addition, the PRC suffers from almost all the limitations associated with the Assembly and Council, except that members of the PRC are allowed to meet more often than the Assembly and the Council. But they are actually unable to do so because AU work is one of many responsibilities with which PRC members deal as ambassadors to Ethiopia and the AU. These factors have prevented the PRC from initiating policies on their own. It has made the PRC and the entire AU system dependent on Africrats for new ideas and policies.

Regional integration also focuses on economic matters ranging from trade to fiscal and monetary policy. As a response to the proliferation of regional trade blocs—such as the EU, the North American Free Trade Agreement, and the *Mercado Común del Sur*—the framers of the AU announced that cross-border trade within Africa would be made easier by reducing barriers to trade for member states. A central bank and monetary union were envisioned, which were initially expected to begin operations by 2004. A common African currency, known as the 'afro', was expected to follow in subsequent years. The logistics of founding a central bank and setting up a common currency have proved daunting.[27] Revised estimates now place a common currency supported by a full-functioning African Central Bank [ACB] to appear by the mid-2020s at the earliest. Aside from some modest gains to reduce trade barriers for member states of sub-regional groupings such as the Southern African Development Community, the East African

Community, and the Economic Community of West African States, goods are often held up by sluggish customs agencies imposing Byzantine sets of trade regulations.

Yet, these same sub-regional groupings are expected to be absorbed into the African Economic Community [AEC] despite not being signatories to the AEC treaty. Rather than establish a common free trade zone or customs union amongst all AU members, the AEC foresees economic integration to occur by absorbing the continent's different sub-regional economic communities in a series of complex stages.[28] The legality of moving towards a full-fledged AEC may face additional logistical challenges. As regards the African Court of Justice, individuals and firms cannot bring forward legal action against AEC laws because they have not—and cannot as non-state actors—ratify the Protocol of the Court. In other words, the current legal structure:

> makes the dispute settlement process unavailable to some of the most important players in the integration process, including consumers, traders, corporate bodies and investors. It fails to utilise a principal medium through which the community-state relationship is strengthened in economic integration.[29]

Given the above logistical challenges—not to mention the AU's large number of member states, 53—veritable economic integration for the AU will take some time.[30]

In recent years, an inter-regional relationship of sorts has evolved between the EU and the AU on issues ranging from the transfer of technical knowledge to a variety of capacity-building initiatives to trade agreements. This relationship is supported by EU-Africa trade, as roughly €200 billion worth of goods per year are now exchanged between the two regions. Yet, sensitivities to the possible perception of European paternalism in economic and political relations between the two regional bodies remain. Although the AU and its member states are content to receive technical and capacity-building assistance, they have largely resisted EU pressure to open up their economies to European goods and services through various economic partnership agreements [EPAs]. Many of the proposed EPAs would entail that government procurement contracts become open to bidding from European firms, hence reducing the ability of African governments to provide political 'rewards' to locals and stimulate domestic economies. In addition to opening up African markets to manufactured and agricultural goods from Europe, the EPAs also require the removal of export taxes with particular emphasis on natural resources. The economic impact of removing such taxes is monumental, for a sizable portion of African government revenues rely on commodity exports. Furthermore, the revenue collection capacity of most African countries is constrained by the fact that it is often difficult for the state to collect personal income taxes as well as corporate taxes from domestic firms.

The issue of EPAs with Europe was a leading topic of discussion during the 2010 AU Conference of Ministers of Trade in Kigali. At the conclusion of the conference, the Kigali Declaration was passed, with much of the wording centred on EPAs. The following paragraph is representative of the overall tone of the document:

> We, Ministers of Trade of the Member States of the African Union … hereby … express our deep concern about the pressure exerted by the European Commission on some countries and Regions to sign the interim EPAs, thus prejudicing the progress made in the negotiation process.[31]

One of the African trade ministers was quoted as depicting the EPA networks as being similar to 'placing African countries into the mouth of a lion in a repeat of the colonial experience'.[32] Creative analogies aside, this concern is reasonable given that the relatively small population and market size of the majority of AU member states hampers competitiveness in both the context of EPAs and the broader global economy. Given the resistance by AU member states towards EPAs, economic linkages will remain tentative and thus quite modest in scope in comparison to the EU's inter-regional relationship with the Association of Southeast Asian Nations [ASEAN].[33]

Two decades after the end of the Cold War, the international order remains in flux. Humanitarian crises continue to occur and countries such as China, Venezuela, Iran, North Korea, and Zimbabwe continue to pursue foreign policies that preclude a tranquil or static international order. Although the rise of regional organisations has provided a measure of stability within the evolving international order, such groupings face pressure to reform. The OAU's transformation to the AU represented one of the more ambitious changes. The G8 has expanded to become the G20 to incorporate emerging Powers such as Brazil, India, and China. Long regarded as the leading example of regional economic integration, the EU is straining under the burden of balance-of-payment assistance schemes for weakened European economies, those of Greece and Ireland, for instance, which has led to internal calls for reform.

The NRA seeks to shed light on such trends within the broader international order. This approach offers cogent analysis here by unpacking the state and examining the role of bureaucrats within the AU, as well as the prospects for regional economic integration in Africa. It also sheds light on some of the legacies bequeathed by the OAU to the AU. In spite of the institutional challenges they face, Africrats are able to shape African regionalisms in a fundamental way—their role going beyond being servants of politicians. Africrats perform more than mere functional duties for states. They provide ideas, broad policy directives, and specific proposals for political organs such as the PRC, the Council, and the Assembly to examine. And they also take advantage of their role as sources of ideas and policy options for states by controlling the set of choices about ideas and proposals that form the building blocks of African regionalism. In many instances, Africrat ideas and proposals are adopted without debate or change.

Inter-regional relationships also fall under the purview of NRA literature. The case of the EU-AU relationship on EPAs is particularly compelling because it has implications for economic integration in Africa. Over and above fears that EPAs with Europe would result in a flood of European goods and services and the reduction of government revenues owing to the removal export taxes on natural resources, African trade ministers have been concerned that such trade deals would hinder regional integration efforts. The basis for trepidation amongst African ministers is that EPAs would redirect a sizable portion of intra-Africa trade towards European goods and services. Since African economic integration is predicated in part on facilitating intra-regional trade of African goods and services, any diversion of such trade flows would retard the overall enterprise. The AU would prefer to establish a continent-wide common market of its own. This goal is reflected in a statement made during the 2010 AU Conference of Ministers of Trade in Kigali:

> Time has therefore come for us to speed up the establishment of the African Economic Community, which has been on the drawing board for almost two decades. A Pan-African Common Market of 1 billion people without internal borders will unleash the enormous economic growth and development potentials of Africa and strengthen economic independence of the continent.[34]

This statement contains many merits given the growth of regional trade blocs within the global economy. The envisioned AEC and common market would, in theory, provide greater power in negotiating a singular EPA with the EU. However, these important components of economic integration have yet to emerge within the AU and still face several logistical barriers. Nonetheless, the AU offers a chance for increasing regional integration and co-operation in Africa.

Acknowledgements

J. Andrew Grant would like to acknowledge the funding provided by an Advisory Research Committee award from Queen's University. Thomas Kwasi Tieku wishes to thank the University of Toronto for financial support. The authors would like to thank B.J.C. McKercher and Dickson Eyoh for their guidance and assistance during the writing of this chapter.

Notes

1 See for example: J.A. Grant and F. Söderbaum, 'Introduction: The New Regionalism in Africa', in J.A. Grant and F. Söderbaum, eds., *The New Regionalism in Africa* (Aldershot, 2003), 1–17; D.C. Bach, 'Revisiting a Paradigm', in D.C. Bach, ed., *Regionalization in Africa: Integration and Disintegration* (Oxford, 1999), 1–14; F. Söderbaum and I. Taylor, eds., *Afro-Regions: The Dynamics of Cross-Border Micro-Regionalism in Africa* (Uppsala, 2008); T.M. Shaw, J.A. Grant, and S. Cornelissen, eds., *The Research Companion to Regionalisms* (Aldershot, 2011); F. Söderbaum and T.M. Shaw, eds., *Theories of New Regionalism: A Palgrave Reader* (Basingstoke, 2003); M. Bøås, M.H. Marchand, and T.M. Shaw, eds., 'Special Issue: New Regionalisms in the New Millennium', *Third World Quarterly*, 20(1999) 897–1070; B. Hettne and F. Söderbaum, 'The New Regionalism Approach', *Politeia*, 17(1998), 6–21.
2 *The Constitutive Act of the African Union*, [adopted in Lomé, 11 July 2000] (Addis Ababa, 2000).
3 For a detailed overview of the functions of the AU's various organs, see S.M. Makinda and F. Wafula Okumu, *The African Union: Challenges of Globalization, Security, and Governance* (New York, 2007), 40–52.
4 For a good description of civil society in the AU, see for example B. Moyo, 'Civil Society and the African Union Architecture: Institutional Provisions and Invented Interfaces', in S. Adejumobi and A. Olukoshi, eds., *The African Union and Strategies for Development in Africa* (Amherst, MA, 2008), 275–96.
5 J.A. Grant, 'Informal Cross-Border Micro-Regionalism in West Africa: The Case of the Parrot's Beak', in Söderbaum and Taylor, eds., *Afro-Regions*, 105–20.
6 For more information on Pan-Africanism, see K. Nkrumah, *Africa Must Unite* (London, 1963); C. Legum, *Pan-Africanism* (London, 1962); L. Adele Jinadu, 'Nkrumah, Pan-Africanism, and the Future of Africa', in Adejumobi and Olukoshi, *African Union*, 23–38.
7 For further analyses regarding Cabinda's secessionist claims, see for example F.R. Bembelly, 'L'évolution juridique et politique de la question Cabindaise', *Revue Juridique et Politique, Indépendance et Coopération*, 50 (1996), 77–90; J.A. Grant, 'New Regionalism and Micro-Regionalism in South-Western Africa: The Oil-Rich Enclave of Cabinda', in Grant and Söderbaum, *New Regionalism*, 125–43.
8 Morocco is the only African country that has not joined the AU. In 1984, Morocco left the OAU to protest the February 1982 admission of Western Sahara—which Morocco claims as part of its territory after annexing the region in 1975—to the regional organisational as a separate country known as the Sahrawi Arab Democratic Republic. If post-referendum negotiations on South Sudan's secession proceed in a peaceful manner, the country will likely become the fifty-fourth member of the AU.
9 Makinda and Okumu, *African Union*, 57.
10 Ibid.
11 See for example, T. Murithi, *The African Union: Pan-Africanism, Peacebuilding and Development* (Aldershot, 2005); and idem., *The African Union: Pan-Africanism, Peacebuilding and Development*, second edition (Aldershot, 2010).
12 *Protocol Relating to the Establishment of the Peace and Security Council of the African Union* [adopted in Durban, 9 July 2002] (Addis Ababa, 2002).
13 J. Sarkin, 'Intervention and the Responsibility to Protect in Africa', in J. Akokpari and D.S. Zimbler, eds., *Africa's Human Rights Architecture* (Auckland Park, Cape Town, 2008), 46.
14 *Constitutive Act of the African Union*.
15 *Protocol on Amendments to the Constitutive Act of the African Union* [adopted in Addis Ababa, 3 February 2003 and Maputo, 11 July 2003] (Addis Ababa, 2003). The expanded wording in Article 4(h) has been italicised by the authors.
16 The Tripoli meeting follows earlier summits in Cairo in 2000 and Lisbon in 2007. The next summit is expected to be held in Brussels in 2013.
17 Although Gaddafi's ambition to establish and become 'president of a united AU' ebbs and flows, he has competed for attention with Nigeria and South Africa during past AU meetings, particularly when

Olusegun Obasanjo and Thabo Mbeki were in office. After much lobbying, Gaddafi was finally selected as AU Chairperson, serving a one-year term from 2 February 2009 to 31 January 2010.

18 Parts of this chapter draw upon T.K. Tieku, 'The Evolution of the African Union Commission and Africrats: Drivers of African Regionalisms', in Shaw, Grant, and Cornelissen, eds., *Companion to Regionalisms*.

19 E. Kodjo, *Report of the Administrative Secretary-General covering the period September 1970 to February 1971* (Addis Ababa, 1971), 351.

20 A. Salim, *Ushering the OAU into the Next Century: A Programme for Reform and Renewal* (Addis Ababa, 1997).

21 A. Salim, *The Political and Socio-Economic Situation in Africa and the Fundamental Changes Taking Place in the World* (Addis Ababa, 1989), 4.

22 Ibid.

23 Ibid., 5.

24 Ibid.

25 Article 4(a) of the 'Rules of Procedures of the Assembly of the African Union'.

26 I. Kane and N. Mbelle, *Towards a People-Driven African Union: Current Obstacles and New Opportunities* (London, 2007), 14.

27 Most Francophone African countries employ a common currency in the form of the *Communauté Financiére Africaine* [CFA] franc. However, the CFA franc predates the AU and, more importantly, the currency is guaranteed by the French government through its Treasury and pegged to the euro.

28 R. Frimpong Oppong, 'The African Union, the African Economic Community and Africa's Regional Economic Communities: Untangling a Complex Web', *African Journal International and Comparative Law*, 18(2010) 93–94.

29 Ibid., 101.

30 An interesting initiative that may inform the economic integration process is the AU's establishment of a peer-reviewed publication entitled the *African Integration Review*. The journal, which focuses on issues relating to the continent's economic integration, was founded in 2007 and publishes articles on a bi-annual basis that are available electronically (at no charge) on its website: www.africa-union.org/root/ UA/Newsletter/EA/Contenueng.htm.

31 African Union Commission, Sixth Ordinary Session of AU Ministers of Trade, *Kigali Declaration on the Economic Partnership Agreement Negotiations*, (Kigali, 2 November 2010), preamble and paragraph 9.

32 M. Khor, 'Africa is Resisting the Threat of Europe's Free Trade Agreements', *The China Post* (24 November 2010).

33 For a review that contrasts some of the positive developments with problematic issues relating to EU efforts to establish EPA networks in Africa, see U. Engel and H. Asche, eds., *Negotiating Regions: Economic Partnership Agreements between the European Union and the African Regional Economic Communities* (Leipzig, 2008). For additional insights into EU-ASEAN ties and other inter-regional relationships, see A.C. Robles, *The Political Economy of Interregional Relations* (Aldershot, 2004).

34 Statement by H.E. Mr. Erastus Mwencha, Deputy Chairperson, African Union Commission, Sixth Ordinary Session of AU Ministers of Trade, (Kigali, 1 November 2010), 3–4.

24

The non-aligned movement

Collective diplomacy of the global South

Jacqueline Anne Braveboy-Wagner

The Non-Aligned Movement (NAM) celebrated its fiftieth anniversary in 2011. Having come into existence during the ideologically polarised 1960s, this organisation, aimed at articulating the ambitions of newly decolonised countries, has faced major questions since the end of the Cold War: how relevant can it be when its *raison d'être* no longer exists? How can an organisation that promoted non-alignment continue to exist when only one superpower has survived? Yet NAM has persisted; in fact, it has been engaged in a revitalisation process for the last two decades. This ability to survive suggests that the organisation is still seen by its members as occupying a unique and beneficial diplomatic space.

Barring significant international turmoil, intergovernmental organisations (IGOs) have a low death-rate, whether based on rational state calculations or the deeply embedded values these organisations have helped to establish.[1] Although global South states have joined or created organisations for the same reasons as other states, two crucial factors set them apart when it comes to their expectations. First, without prejudice to the histories of 'greatness' of some of these countries, South states emerged to independence as small 'Powers' in a world dominated by superpowers and Great Powers. Security options for small Powers are usually described as either balancing against, or bandwagoning with, the Great Powers.[2] However, the option of neutrality has also been historically available, even if neutral territories were sometimes swallowed by their larger neighbors. In this sense, NAM was created as a neutralist option in a world divided between communists and Western liberal democrats. In the second place, global South states have long focused less on the effects of international anarchy than on the hierarchical nature of the international system because, even as they have legal equality with other states as sovereign states, the global hierarchy has reduced them to a position of inferiority. Thus Southern foreign policy, including organisational activity, is best seen as geared toward reducing global *hierarchy*. NAM diplomacy must be understood in the context of these two considerations.

As the Cold War hardened in 1945–46, Asian nations focused their energy on gaining independence from the colonial Powers weakened by the Second World War. In particular, in East, South, and Southeast Asia, decolonisation had begun in earnest.[3] By the late 1940s, Asian decolonisation was complicated in some places by the Cold War rivalry manifest in Europe. Thus Vietnam's provisional government ended up fighting, first, a nationalist battle against France, followed by a long war that pitted the North, allied with the Soviet Union and the People's Republic of China (PRC), against the South, allied with the United States. The Cold War also intruded on post-war Korea, divided between the communist north and the non-communist south. Malaya's independence had to be delayed until 1957 because of a communist rebellion. Post-independence Indonesia was embroiled in conflict between pro-China communists and the anti-communist military. And China was rent by civil war between the nationalist Kuomintang forces and communist rebels who eventually seized power in 1949. In sum, by the 1950s, the East–West conflict could no longer be isolated from the anti-colonial one in Asia.

In their anti-colonial struggle, Asians lagged behind Latin American nations that fought and earned their independence from Spain and Portugal in the nineteenth century. By 1948 habits of collaboration had already taken hold among Latin American governments through practices including holding inter-American conferences and establishing pan-American institutions.[4] It would be a long while before most Latin Americans began seeing commonalities with Asia and Africa. Instead, turning to Washington for protection from Europe and for other forms of assistance, Latin Americans were not involved in the early efforts to bring together the non-aligned. On the other hand, Asia was just ahead of sub-Saharan Africa in the pace of decolonisation, and the Africans could easily identify with Asian experiences. Not that pan-African sentiment was new: diasporic and continental Africans had been meeting since 1900. However, in the 1940s, nationalists were finally beginning to build the anti-colonial movement in sub-Saharan Africa.

In this context, India sponsored an Asian Relations Conference in 1947 to discuss issues arising from the anticipated end of the European presence in the region. The conference met under the auspices of the non-profit Indian Council of World Affairs, and invitations were issued to all Asian countries including Palestine (represented by a Jewish delegation), Egypt, and the Soviet Asian republics. Twenty-four countries attended, as well as observers from the Arab League, Australia, Turkey, Britain, and the United States. It was the first opportunity for Asians, until then divided by different colonial Powers, to get to know one another.

Because the conference was billed as a cultural one to deflect international criticism, political and economic issues could be discussed only insofar as they related in some way to culture. Thus discussion groups included migration, women, and social services as well as national movements for freedom.[5] Politically, participant-states agreed on the need for Asian unity against 'Western exploitation', and under the rubric of 'National Movements', underscored the basic principle of anti-colonialism.[6] The sense in which 'neutrality' was used was that of refraining from war and denying belligerents war material. Accordingly, a proposal for neutrality, although not adopted, 'seemed to command wide sympathy.'[7] This conference was important in bringing the newly emerging nations together and placing anti-colonialism and related issues on both the regional and international agendas. It also served as a leadership platform on which India and China competed for the attention of what became known as the 'Third World.'

Intra-Asian disagreements prevented the holding of a scheduled conference in China two years later.[8] Instead Asians met in New Delhi in January 1949 to discuss Dutch efforts to reintroduce colonial rule in Indonesia. New to this meeting were Ethiopia, Iraq, Lebanon, Pakistan, Saudi Arabia, Syria, and Yemen. Observers came from China, Nepal, New Zealand, and Siam.[9] The Soviet Republics were not invited, and neither was Israel. The conference adopted a resolution calling for Dutch withdrawal and the handover of power to Indonesia with the assistance of the United Nations (UN) Security Council and its appointed peace-making bodies.[10] After 1949, India's prominence was challenged by other Powers, including Indonesia and Ceylon.[11] In particular, once Indonesia achieved independence, its leader, Achmed Sukarno, staked a strong claim to Asian leadership. His lasting contribution to non-alignment came in the form of a meeting of Asian and African states held at Bandung in 1955.

The 'Spirit of Bandung' refers to the energy and hopefulness that characterised this conference of mostly newly emancipated Asian and African states brought together to share ideas and formulate common strategies to deal with colonialism, racialism, and development. Sponsored by the leaders of five nations (Burma, Ceylon, India, Indonesia, and Pakistan, the so-called Colombo Group that met in 1954), the Conference was the brainchild of Sukarno's Prime Minister, Ali Sastroamidjojo. One commentator remarked at the time, 'Asia's objective is to constitute with Africa an autonomous power alongside Europe and America as well as a bulwark of peace and conciliation between the major power blocs.'[12] Twenty-nine nations attended. Asian participants included Japan and China, the latter under communist rule. Five African nations (Egypt, Ethiopia, Libya, Sudan, and Gold Coast) participated.[13] The Cold War intruded on the invitations process because various countries were denied admission, 'almost always due to Cold War wars and alignments that predetermined political stances. Most obviously, these included the Koreas, but also Indochina.'[14]

In seeking a *modus operandi* over Tibet, which the PRC had conquered in 1950, India and China agreed on five principles of co-existence (the *Panchsheel*) to govern their relations: respect for each other's sovereignty and territorial integrity; mutual non-aggression; non-interference in each other's affairs; equality and mutual benefit; and peaceful coexistence. These principles became the basis of ten principles agreed to at Bandung in a declaration of solidarity and co-operation. They are regularly cited by NAM as foundational (see Table 24.A1 in the Appendix).

The Bandung participants agreed on many issues that carried over into NAM. On economic matters, *inter alia*, they agreed to cooperate with one another, initiating the long-standing call for South–South cooperation. They agreed to share information, support commodity stabilisation agreements to improve trade, and push for a special UN fund that later became the UN Development Programme. In contrast to the more nationalist approach adopted in the 1970s, they called for greater access to foreign investment and aid. They supported multilateralism (as NAM countries have since done), especially multilateral international financial institutions. In cultural areas, they called for assistance from the more advanced developing states, mutual cultural exchanges, and exchanges of information. Respect for human rights and self-determination were principles roundly endorsed whereas racial discrimination was condemned. Politically, anti-colonialism and support for dependent peoples were reemphasised. Bandung participants called for disarmament, that is, the total prohibition of nuclear weapons, along with increased regulation of armaments in general. Another 'foundational' theme was the call for UN reform: Asian–African countries should acquire non-permanent seats on the Security Council, which should admit more members.

Not surprisingly, clashes occurred at Bandung, in particular over membership of military alliances. Pro-West Lebanon and states such as the Philippines, Thailand, and Pakistan, which had all recently joined the South-East Asia Treaty Organization (SEATO), as well as Turkey, Iran, and Iraq, members of the Central Treaty Organization (CENTO), clashed with neutralist India, Indonesia, Ceylon, Burma, and Egypt, which wanted participants to eschew military alliances altogether. Egypt, Yemen, and Saudi Arabia were also neutralist, leading to clashes with their pro-West colleagues.[15]

Another dispute arose over the definition of colonialism. Turkey and Iraq asked unsuccessfully that 'subversion' and 'infiltration' be mentioned as expressions of a certain type of 'colonialism'; one observer noted, 'Colonialism, it must be said, was not precisely defined at Bandung; it is merely described as domination, exploitation and oppression without any reference to the specific forms that such domination, exploitation and oppression might take.'[16] Finally, Egypt's Colonel Gamal Abdel Nasser was apparently 'very disappointed at the Indian Prime Minister's [Nehru's] reluctance to get involved in quarrels between Arab countries, and particularly in the Palestinian question, on which he was in favor of adopting an extremely moderate motion, or in any event one that was much too moderate for their liking.'[17]

The conference is generally viewed as a Chinese triumph and somewhat of a disappointment for India. China's foreign minister, Zhou en Lai, adopted conciliatory stances that won favor amongst the various participants and assuaged fears about China's dominance as well as the role of overseas Chinese. On the difficult issue of Taiwan, China unexpectedly agreed to hold talks with the United States, although Washington hastily rejected the offer. In contrast to Zhou, the Philippine Foreign Minister recalled that Nehru was 'pedantic, dogmatic and unyielding' and, as a result, alienated many delegates, including the Indonesians and Ceylonese.[18] Despite the differences, Bandung is said to have succeeded because these diverse and geographically distant countries 'made friends with each other.'[19] Moreover, one of the overlooked outcomes amid the conference's more salient highlights was the endorsement of an Asian role in Africa. As Nehru noted in his closing speech: 'Whether it is racial, whether it is political, whatever it may be, it is there, and it is up to Asia to help Africa, to the best of her ability, because we are sister continents.'[20] That tone of unity and cooperation was carried forth into NAM.

Plans for a second conference to be held in Algiers in 1965 were scuttled because the Algerian leader, Ahmed Ben Bella, was deposed ten days before its scheduled opening. In addition, Indonesia had moved closer to China, and differences between Indonesia and India (whose relationship with China had begun to deteriorate, notwithstanding *Panchsheel*) had become increasingly sharp. Nasser was also in the neutralist camp, as was Marshal Tito of Yugoslavia but for different reasons. Coming to power on the strength of his popularity and nationalism, Tito looked to maintain Yugoslav independence *vis-à-vis* the Soviet Union. During the 1950s, he visited a number of Asian, African, and Latin American countries and, in July 1956, invited Nasser and Nehru to meet with him.[21] Thus began a regular round of meetings. Joined by Sukarno despite his differences with Nehru, and Kwame Nkrumah of Ghana, the three began promoting the concerns of uncommitted countries at the UN. In 1961, they issued invitations to a preparatory meeting of uncommitted countries to be held in Cairo. Representatives of twenty nations attended this June meeting, where they adopted the rubric 'non-aligned' instead of 'uncommitted.' This meeting was followed by the first Summit of Non-Aligned Countries in Belgrade in September.

NAM borrowed from, but completely overshadowed, the original Afro-Asian movement.[22] Of the twenty-five states that met in Belgrade, one Latin American country, Cuba, participated as a full member. Bolivia, Brazil, and Ecuador attended as observers. Thus NAM reached beyond Afro-Asia. To be a member meant to espouse peaceful coexistence, non-alignment, support for movements of national independence, and non-involvement in military alliances.[23] NAM would not adopt the traditional passive neutrality of older countries but, rather, seek an active international role to support stated principles.

1961 was a time of tension between moderate and radical Arab and African states. The Congo crisis had aggravated splits among African states between the moderate Brazzaville group (comprised of former French territories except for Guinea, as well as Libya) and the more militant Casablanca group comprising Morocco, Egypt, Ghana, Guinea, Mali, and the Algerian Provisional Government. Attendance at NAM's meeting reflected these splits, with only the more radical states participating.

The conference reiterated earlier Afro-Asian calls for ending colonialism, for independence and self-determination, and non-interference, as well as general and complete disarmament. Participants called for international economic reforms and greater intra-NAM cooperation, and supported the equitable representation of developing countries in such UN bodies as the Security Council and the Economic and Social Council. Given the Cuban–American conflict, they supported Cuba's right to determine its political system and called for members to avoid either political or economic blocs. In the China–Taiwan dispute, they noted, diplomatically, that *many* countries supported Taiwan's replacement by the PRC in the UN Security Council. This position was later adopted by the movement as a whole.

Since the 1961 conference did not institutionalise NAM, it was unclear what direction the movement would take. Even as plans were still being promoted by Sukarno for another Asia-Africa conference, a second NAM conference met in Cairo in 1964 on the initiative of Nasser, Nehru, Tito, and the Ceylonese Prime Minister, Solomon Bandanaraike. Attendance doubled to 47 countries, with ten observers plus the recently formed Organisation of African Unity (OAU) and various liberation movements.[24] The participants expanded NAM's focus on anti-colonialism to include support for various liberation movements, while calling again for policies and reforms proposed in 1961. In calling for strengthening intra-NAM educational, scientific, and cultural ties, the final declaration promoted cultural cooperation as well. Importantly, a few months earlier, the first UN Conference on Trade and Development had convened in Geneva, primarily through the persistent efforts of the developing and non-aligned nations. At that conference, the developing nations formed the Group of 77 (G77). The Cairo conference therefore endorsed the G77's proposals.

Another major theme was expanded in Cairo: military bloc non-membership. In 1961 NAM established as a criterion for membership a state's non-involvement in military alliances. The final declaration of the Cairo conference emphasised that Great Power coalitions had aggravated the Cold War and that non-aligned countries were therefore 'opposed to taking part in such pacts and alliances.'[25]

Between 1964 and 1970 NAM did not convene. It entered a period of decline after Nehru's death and the deposing of Nkrumah, Sukarno, and Ben Bella. African states were also ideologically split, and Arab ones were preoccupied with the war against Israel.[26] At Lusaka in 1970, however, the commitment to non-alignment was renewed and the institutionalisation of the movement begun. Triennial summit meetings (the Conference of Heads of State and Government) were established as the highest decision-making body. Summit meetings have since been held regularly, with only one gap occurring between 1998 and 2003, a period of tension between the nuclear Powers India and Pakistan, as well as global tensions arising from the advent of Islamic terrorism. Apart from the triennial summit, NAM conducts business through a Co-ordinating Bureau established in the 1970s and based at the UN headquarters. Bureau membership, initially limited to 25 regionally selected states, is now open to all member-states. NAM foreign ministers meet annually to coordinate policy before the General Assembly meets, and there are a number of working groups. Discussions also take place amongst the 'troikas', comprising the former, current, and future chairs at summit, ministerial, and ambassadorial levels.

NAM's collective diplomatic efforts can be assessed by looking at three areas: organisational adaptability, organisational cohesion, and credibility. Given that NAM has persisted whilst the global environment has changed, in particular with the end of the Cold War, the organisation has demonstrated an ability to adapt. Otherwise it would have stagnated and died (as did SEATO and CENTO), achieved its goals and died (for example, UN peace-keeping missions are time limited), or been replaced with an 'updated' version of itself (the OAU to African Union, for example). Instead, NAM has devoted energy to revitalising itself over the past twenty years. Further, if adaptability is reflected in the ability of an institution to refresh, although not necessarily change, its goals to suit a changed environment, NAM scores well.

NAM initially directed its attention to achieving decolonisation as well as disarmament. However, as most colonies received independence in the 1960s, and whilst remaining focused on persistent problem areas like Southern Africa, NAM turned its attention to 'neocolonialism': economic distortions caused by imbalances in the global economic and financial system as well as within member-state economies. Both were perceived to be the result of colonialism. Indeed, this turn to economics facilitated

NAM's expansion to Latin America, which now perceived common interests with Africa and Asia. In 1970 in Lusaka, NAM issued a 'Declaration on Non-Alignment and Economic Progress', which expressed concern about the poverty and economic dependence of developing countries deriving from colonialism. It pressed for reform of the global economic system and decided to foster mutual cooperation and exchange of information in trade, in industrial, mineral, agricultural, and marine production, in the development of infrastructure, and the application of science and technology. It urged the UN to employ international machinery to facilitate a rapid transformation of the world economy through assistance in production and marketing, preferential trade, preferential access for commodities, financial transfers of one percent of gross national product (GNP) from each developed country, and support for the cooperative initiatives of developing countries. This economic turn was expanded at Algiers in 1973 when developing countries began to exert some leverage on the basis of their natural resources. Participants issued an 'Economic Declaration and Action Programme' for a new international economic order that was intended to ensure greater equality between developed and developing countries. These proposals led to the UN General Assembly's adoption in May 1974 of the landmark 'Declaration and Action Program on the Establishment of a New International Economic Order' (NIEO) at its Sixth Special Session on raw materials and development.[27]

Until this time, NAM was gaining strength and bargaining power within the international community. However, the organisation had to adapt to a new environment in the late 1980s as a result of a global recession and because developed countries, led by the United States, now demanded global neoliberal reforms. In the 1950s and 1960s, developing countries had called for more foreign investment and aid, but they had become more economically nationalistic by the 1970s. They were now forced into structural adjustment programs and heavy borrowing from international financial institutions. Moreover, the Soviet Union's demise in 1990–91 posed new problems. No longer could they depend on Soviet sympathy and assistance; instead, the new international order was unipolar, one in which the United States expected conformity to its political and economic principles.

By the ninth summit held in Belgrade in September 1989, member-state enthusiasm for NAM was fading.[28] Faced with the prospect of irrelevance, NAM adapted in three ways: by expanding its agenda to reflect new global concerns; by reiterating the validity of its original principles and goals but applying them to the new context; and by adopting (with some scepticism) new liberal norms. With respect to expansion, at the 1992 summit in Jakarta, and in particular the 1995 Colombia summit, some new foci began to be elaborated. Thereafter, these grew to include social issues: global health concerns (human immunodeficiency virus/acquired immune deficiency syndrome prominent amongst them); progress in gender rights and empowerment; the status of children, especially in war zones; environmental issues; and the information gap. New governance concerns included democracy, corruption, and the violation of human rights, and new security issues such as ethnic conflict, small arms and drug trafficking, and terrorism were raised. These issues were accompanied by new economic challenges: indebtedness, poverty alleviation, unequal distribution of the benefits of globalisation, and obstacles to liberalisation. There were also cultural foci such as the promotion of a dialogue of civilisations rather than Western notions of a cultural clash. Of course, older issues remained on NAM's agenda. In fact, thematic consistency has been the hallmark of the NAM. At the 1995 meeting, for example, the governments committed to seeking continued progress in disarmament and eradicating the 'remnants of colonialism, foreign occupation and interventionism.'[29] Multilateralism in all respects retained strong support amongst the non-aligned.

On the other hand, NAM has adapted its original principles to the new context. The new order has engendered a rephrasing of concerns about non-interference and coercion into language targeting unipolarity and unilateralism. The 'Final Document' of the 2003 Malaysia Summit, issued against the backdrop of American intervention in Iraq, illustrates the repackaging of old wine in new bottles. It warns against new practices: 'policies of hegemony and domination'; unilateralism; emerging trends towards a unipolar world where 'unilateral and hegemonic policies could violate the basic principles of the Non-Aligned Movement and the United Nations Charter' (Article 15); the 'labelling of countries as good or evil and repressive based on unilateral and unjustified criteria' (Article 15); the 'so-called right' of humanitarian intervention and concerns about the similarities between that and the 'responsibility to protect' (Article 16); 'imposing sanctions without clearly defined objectives and specified time frames' (Article 33); the 'unsubstantiated allegations of non-compliance with relevant instruments of Weapons of Mass Destruction' (Article 85); and 'attempts to equate the legitimate struggle of peoples under colonial or alien domination and foreign occupation, for self-determination and national liberation with terrorism in order to prolong occupation and oppression of the innocent people with impunity' (Article 106). In fact, in a strong sign of adaptation, at Havana in 2006, Bandung's original principles were officially expanded to suit the 'present international juncture' without doing any notable injustice to the originals (Article 2).

Finally, with respect to adopting new liberal norms, NAM has done so albeit with some scepticism. For example, at the fourteenth summit in Havana in 2006, participants stressed that there can be no single model of democracy, that democracy must be linked to development, and that international aspects of democracy should be addressed along with the domestic.[30] Cuba's Foreign Minister, Felipe Roque, emphasised: '... although all democracies have common characteristics, there is no single model of democracy and ... this one is not the patrimony of any country or region'.[31] Although NAM members have called for (but not always adhered to) respect for human rights since the early days of the movement, they continue to request equal treatment for both economic and civil rights and are particularly focused on the 'right to development' and evolving rights to food and water. In economic areas, the non-aligned now call for increased foreign investment (as in the movement's earlier days) and most member-states have embraced free trade. However, they still express concerns about coercive measures and economic pressures, unfair trade practices and Northern subsidies, obstacles to liberalisation, inadequate levels of aid transfers, and their lack of adequate voice in global discussions on human security, poverty alleviation, and even the deliberations on the Millennium Development Goals. Rather surprisingly, considering that the NIEO dialogue of the 1970s proved so unproductive, the 2009 summit at Sharm el Sheikh, Egypt resurrected the idea by reaffirming the 'Declaration and Action Programme on the Establishment of a NIEO' and the 'validity of the major principles underlying that document.'[32]

Overall, NAM's reinvention has been helped by its ability to garner new members in the post-Cold War period. One key member has been South Africa, which emerged from apartheid in 1994 and hosted the twelfth summit in 1998. Central American and Caribbean countries previously dubious about the seemingly pro-Soviet NAM have joined in the 1990s and 2000s, as have the former Soviet states of Belarus, Turkmenistan, and Uzbekistan. Other former Soviet states have been granted observer status (see Table 24.A3 in the Appendix). NAM now boasts a membership of 118 countries compared with the 101 that attended the 1986 Harare meeting, held before the Cold War ended. More important, only Burma, Argentina, Cyprus, and Malta have voluntarily given up membership. The last two did not withdraw because of any dispute but simply ceased to be members in 2004 when they joined the European Union (EU). Burma (now Myanmar) withdrew in 1980 for ideological reasons but returned in 1992. Argentina withdrew in 1995 but returned as a guest in 2006 and an observer in 2009.

Apart from adaptation, NAM can be judged on its cohesion. NAM's record on this is mixed: although there have been several small and certainly one overarching internal dispute over the years (see below), the organisation has found ways to focus the attention of diverse countries from three continents on seemingly shared interests. To prevent countries from leaving the coalition, members must see some benefit in remaining, a benefit that outweighs the costs of membership. The costs have included Western/Northern hostility, in some cases the disapproval of some domestic constituencies, and the constraints on foreign-policy choices posed by any IGO membership. Fortunately, NAM's basic principles have proven broad enough to accommodate moderate as well as militant national foreign policies. A few conservative states, including Singapore and Saudi Arabia, have also held on to NAM membership.

Early contentious disagreements about military alliances and the nature of colonialism could have disrupted the organisation. NAM membership criteria regarding the non-involvement in military alliances and rejection of foreign bases meant that countries such as the Philippines and Pakistan could not become members. In the colonial and post-colonial context, however, it was recognised that countries did not always have a choice in the matter. As time went on, this prohibition became problematic as countries actively sought military alignments with East or West for their own ideological purposes. NAM resolved the issue by simply ignoring it.

That the participants at Bandung and early NAM summits could outline common principles and agree on certain strategies was an accomplishment in itself, achieved through the skilled diplomacy of the five founding leaders (Nehru, Nasser, Nkrumah, Sukarno, and Tito) as well as Bandaranaike, Ben Bella, and others. Continuing successes owe much to the efforts of the NAM Chairs. The Chair's role is not to 'direct or dictate to the Movement, but to co-ordinate and motivate in a manner that can best be characterised as that of a "consensus leader."'[33] Indeed, one key way in which NAM has maintained cohesion and avoided the traditional coalition politics of log-rolling has been through the early adoption of the principle that decision-making by equal member-states should be by consensus. Consensus (not to be confused with unanimity) was seen as the best way to preserve unity in diversity.[34] The method had its early critics among more conservative members who felt that their voice was not being heard and their proposals unlikely to be accepted. But their concern was met at the second summit in Cairo by allowing oral or written reservations to the Final Document. The procedure has been used liberally, with reservations focusing on a particular issue or broad concerns about any matter in the Final Document that might not be consistent with a country's basic foreign policy.[35]

Notwithstanding NAM's promotion of 'unity in diversity', one of the early differences among states concerned the meaning of 'peaceful coexistence.' Tito argued that it meant distancing oneself from both the East and the West, whereas the majority felt that it implied a broader and more proactive anti-colonialism and anti-imperialism.[36] This confusion returned in the form of a far bigger battle over the meaning of non-alignment. By the 1973 Algiers conference, some countries grumbled that the Movement was becoming too closely aligned with the communist bloc.[37] In fact there were three groups developing: states that accepted China's thesis that there were 'two imperialisms' and that the principal division in the world was between North and South; others espousing anti-Western imperialism and seeing the Soviet Union as a natural ally; and moderates that agreed with Tito that equidistance from both superpowers was desirable to maintain a country's independence.

Ideological tensions in NAM reached a peak when Cuba was chosen as chair in 1979. This choice was divisive, especially because Cuba had become militarily involved in Angola to counter South African intervention. Cuba articulated the view that only the United States was imperialist and that the Soviet Union was a natural ally. It was widely believed both within NAM and externally that Cuba would use the summit to guide NAM into the Soviet orbit. That this shift did not occur was credited to Tito, who made a strong plea for equidistance. Not that most NAM members favored a strict version of equidistance, but, rather, most countries wanted to remove ideological distractions and return to a more moderate path. The next summit, chaired by India, convened in a more cooperative atmosphere. In fact, the United States was so appreciative of NAM's turn to moderation that President Ronald Reagan sent a congratulatory letter to Prime Minister Indira Gandhi expressing American commitment to the basic non-aligned principles.[38] Although ideological differences did not end with the Indian conference, debates became more muted.

With the Cold War's end, NAM faced fresh disagreements between member-states virulently opposed to American 'hegemony' and to Washington-promoted ideas about liberalisation and those that embraced the new liberal norms. However, as of the early 2000s, militant countries (particularly Cuba, Bolivia, Venezuela, Iran, and North Korea) are the minority. In fact, one of NAM's most important members, India, has established close relations with the United States, leading some to wonder if it was going to abandon the grouping. However, India has continually reiterated its commitment to non-alignment, which Prime Minister Manmohan Singh described as a 'state of mind'.[39] The end of the Cold War also brought the rise of bilateralism and regionalism as rival strategies to multilateralism. Regionalism, in the form of regional cooperation, has actually been historically promoted by NAM. Yet, both bilateralism and regionalism have also created divisions among the Africans, Asians, and Latin Americans inasmuch as each country and region defines and prioritises its own agendas. This process has been seen as weakening NAM's tricontinental efforts.

On the last issue, credibility, although NAM may have been able to adapt and cohere (and it is still being revitalised), it has struggled to have its voice heard and achieve a measure of credibility in the eyes of developed nations. NAM seeks to bring collective pressure from developing countries to bear on the developed nations on selected issues. It can, in other words, be seen as a lobby for countries seeking greater voice and benefits within the international system. But lobbying is not by nature focused on compromise. Lobbies want their positions adopted and, as such, NAM tends not to compromise. NAM is not a forum for bargaining or negotiation. Rather, most of its diplomacy is waged at the UN and its agencies, where the *declaratory and normative positions* outlined in NAM documentation are applied to various issues. Therefore, it can be argued that NAM's diplomacy *vis-à-vis* developed countries has been too rigidly pursued to achieve its goals.

Before 1961, Asian and African states were bitterly anti-colonial but more moderate in their declarations toward the West and East. At the 1947 Asian conference, Western and Soviet concerns that a new hostile bloc was forming were assuaged by an overall-moderate conference tone and outcome.[40] At Bandung, the Soviets and the West each feared a loss of relative influence among this group of countries. The developed countries therefore maneuvered behind the scenes to ensure an acceptable outcome. Western Powers such as Britain and the United States made concerted efforts to counter the influence of neutrals like India and Indonesia and offered 'coaching' and 'guidance' to their allies (Pakistan, Turkey, and the Philippines, as well as Ceylon).[41] Washington was primarily concerned about the use of the conference by China as a propaganda platform, whereas the British simply wanted to maintain good relations with the participants.[42] France had concerns about anti-colonialism, its observers complaining strongly about the constant and even virulent criticism meted out to them; at that time, France was extricating itself in varying degrees from Indo-China and North Africa.[43] In the end, the Western Powers seemed pleased with the outcome, crediting this result to their pro-Western allies at the meeting.[44]

However, in the 1960s the newly independent countries, boosted by successes in decolonisation and development, adopted increasingly anti-Western postures. While Western governments, the United States in particular, still sought to influence NAM on some resolutions (for example, the

American embargo of Cuba), they found little success because moderate elements within NAM had weakened. Soon Washington and its allies began to deride the movement as pro-Soviet. Indeed, Moscow had gained inroads into NAM on the basis of its anti-colonial record as well as its energetic support for many of the grouping's economic proposals. China, too, had earned the respect of many NAM members since Bandung. Although PRC supporters constrained Soviet influence to an extent, it was only when the Soviets invaded Afghanistan in 1979 that NAM divisions on the Soviet role sharpened.

As the increasing dominance of pro-Soviet, pro-Chinese, and socialist-leaning member-states distanced NAM from key Western nations, it adopted a more radical stand on reform of the international economic system. The NIEO declaration contained much that was seen as anti-liberal by Western countries. The ensuing negotiations on this new order, the 'North–South dialogue,' were contentious because developing countries, including NAM members, engaged in strident rhetoric, took rigid stances, and set goals that had little chance of approval by the less-than-accommodating northern countries.[45] As the movement toward liberalisation began in the late 1980s, Northern Powers abandoned these negotiations and pressed for bilateral discussions instead.

In the post-Cold War era, NAM changed its tone to a more collaborative, if still highly conditional, one. Final documents issued in post-Cold War summits call for dialogue and engagement with developed countries in socioeconomic areas.[46] This relative moderation characterised even the 2006 Havana summit, which was preceded by media speculation about contention between radicals and conservatives. The presence of Iran, Sudan, Venezuela (now under socialist-leaning Hugo Chavez) as well as Bolivia (under the left-leaning Evo Morales), and North Korea raised media expectations that the document submitted by Cuba would be radical in tone.[47] Nonetheless, the final document hewed to the normal style and content of NAM documents. This does not mean that speeches by some members did not make explicit anti-American references, but such posturing would have occurred anywhere, not just in Havana. Instead the focus was on continuing to revitalise the movement.

A practical sign of the perception of NAM as more collaborative today is the fact that the organisation's summit guest list, usually comprised of smaller European countries, has expanded. At Durban in 1998, the United States, Britain, Russia, and France were guests for the first time. Canada and Germany had attended the previous summit. These Powers have continued to be guests, although the United States opted not to attend the 2006 Cuban summit. Still, the American approach to NAM remains cautious. In 2001 Richard Holbrooke, the United States UN Ambassador, pointedly remarked that he had 'not seen a single issue in which NAM positions actually benefited the African group.'[48] Despite subsequent governmental changes, little reason exists to think that the United States views NAM as a significant grouping. But another sign of a changing NAM is its UN interaction with the EU, as well as its stated interest in institutionalising meetings with the G8. On the other hand, creating a Non-Aligned News Network (launched by Malaysia in 2006) and reaffirming the NIEO have left some Northern analysts wondering how much has changed.

Overall, NAM's persistent promotion of its ideas has resulted in some major *normative* successes. Through the actions of the non-aligned and their supporters, decolonisation has been achieved in most of the world, under the normative umbrella of the 'Declaration on the Granting of Independence to Colonial Countries and Peoples.' Legitimising of the validity of national liberation movements has produced many positive outcomes. Non-aligned countries pressed assiduously for action against South Africa's apartheid regime. They have cultivated racial and cultural tolerance, today reflected in the call for intercultural dialogue. They have underscored the importance of multilateralism in all areas. In the important economic arena, they have been the main force behind what may be called the 'development regime', which includes a number of conventions, resolutions, agencies, and principles. At the core is the idea that the North must help the South, not only for moral reasons but because a healthy international economy benefits the industrialised nations. However, it should be noted that today's governance agenda, with its attention to democracy and good and inclusive governance, was largely devised 'from above', a result of pressure from the developed countries.

In recent years, although member-states have supported creating a NAM mechanism for conflict prevention and resolution and post-conflict peace-building,[49] it remains to be established. An incipient collective security mechanism has been proposed, asking members to provide 'moral, material and other forms of assistance' to any member suffering harm from embargoes, unilateral sanctions, and other economic, political, or military acts.[50] Moral support might be the most forthcoming. In the absence of these mechanisms, NAM's *ad hoc* mediation is complemented by its facilitation of bilateral discussions on the sidelines of its meetings. In 2009, for instance, India's President Manmohan Singh met with Pakistan's Prime Minister Asif Raza Gilani, only the second meeting between the two sides since some 170 persons were killed in the Mumbai terror attacks in 2008.

Despite championing disarmament, NAM has been peripheral to global efforts to reduce vertical proliferation; these negotiations remained at the Great Power level. Although most NAM members signed the Non-Proliferation Treaty as well as various regional denuclearisation arrangements, some key members, specifically India, Pakistan, North Korea, and Iran, have been engaged in controversial nuclear activities, with the first three openly classified as nuclear club members. In the area of general disarmament, NAM has little credibility given that many of its members have tended to devote large percentages of GNP to military expenditures, driven by interstate rivalries and intrastate conflicts.

Many NAM members, and certainly many Northern analysts, may actually be surprised that the organisation has persisted and grown in the post-Cold War period. After a period of uncertainty, fresh leadership has emerged from Colombia, South Africa, and Malaysia among other states. The changes in the global environment offer the organisation new opportunities to speak out on a varied and broad range of topics, particularly in social and economic spheres. Still, that revitalisation has been going on for two decades suggests that the process is more difficult than expected. First, bilateral and regional policies are being given priority over multilateralism. Countries tend to pay lip service to NAM while engaging in self-interested diplomacy. Second, since NAM's strength is in the normative arena, and also in coordination, it cannot easily show the same negotiating successes as other institutions (for example, the G20). However, it would be redundant for NAM, especially given the size and unwieldiness of the group, to be a negotiating assemblage itself. Instead, current plans to initiate and/or strengthen its outreach to important international groupings and work for a greater voice in the UN Security Council through non-permanent NAM members are preferred strategies.

Unnecessary radicalisation fractionalised the movement in the past and reduced its credibility. NAM's enduring image as a talk shop for radical states has yet to be expunged. Despite now being dominated by moderates, it remains somewhat uncompromising in its language and proposals. Finally, there have been calls for NAM to open its deliberations to civil society. It has endorsed the deepening of interaction with 'parliamentarians, civil society and non-governmental organisations, and the private sector of Non-Aligned Countries',[51] but it remains, like many NAM declarations, only a recommendation. In short, there seems room in the international community for an African–Asian–Latin American organisation, but it has to be one that conducts its diplomacy in a moderate, coherent, credible and proactive manner.

Appendix

Table 24.A1 The Founding Principles of the Non-Aligned Movement

1. Respect for fundamental human rights and for the purposes and principles of the Charter of the United Nations;
2. Respect for the sovereignty and territorial integrity of all nations;
3. Recognition of the equality of all races and of the equality of all nations, large and small;
4. Abstention from intervention or interference in the internal affairs of another country;
5. Respect for the right of each nation to defend itself singly or collectively, in conformity with the Charter of the United Nations;
6. (a) Abstention from the use of arrangements of collective defense to serve the particular interests of any of the big powers and;
   (b) Abstention by any country from exerting pressures on other countries;
7. Refraining from acts or threats of aggression or the use of force against the territorial integrity or political independence of any country;
8. Settlement of all international disputes by peaceful means such as negotiation, conciliation, arbitration, or judicial settlement or other peaceful means of the parties' own choice, in conformity with the Charter of the Untied Nations;
9. Promotion of mutual interests and co-operation;
10. Respect for justice and international obligations.

Table 24.A2 The Principles enshrined in the Declaration on the Purposes and Principles and the Role of the Non-Aligned Movement in the Present International Juncture adopted in the 14th NAM Summit in Havana

- Respect for the principles enshrined in the Charter of the United Nations and International Law.
- Respect for sovereignty, sovereign equality and territorial integrity of all States.
- Recognition of the equality of all races, religions, cultures and all nations, both big and small.
- Promotion of a dialogue among peoples, civilizations, cultures and religions based on the respect of religions, their symbols and values, the promotion and the consolidation of tolerance and freedom of belief.
- Respect for and promotion of all human rights and fundamental freedoms for all, including the effective implementation of the right of peoples to peace and development.
- Respect for the equality of rights of States, including the inalienable right of each State to determine freely its political, social, economic and cultural system, without any kind of interference whatsoever from any other State.
- Reaffirmation of the validity and relevance of the Movement's principled positions concerning the

- Condemnation of genocide, war crimes, crimes against humanity and systematic and gross violations of human rights, in accordance with the UN Charter and International Law.
- Rejection of and opposition to terrorism in all its forms and manifestations, committed by whomever, wherever and for whatever purposes, as it constitutes one of the most serious threats to international peace and security. In this context, terrorism should not be equated with the legitimate struggle of peoples under colonial or alien domination and foreign occupation for self-determination and national liberation.
- Promotion of pacific settlement of disputes and abjuring, under any circumstances, from taking part in coalitions, agreements or any other kind of unilateral coercive initiative in violation of the principles of International Law and the Charter of the United Nations.
- Defence and consolidation of democracy, reaffirming that democracy is a universal value based on the freely expressed will of people to determine their own political, economic, social, and cultural systems and their full participation in all aspects of their life.

(continued on the next page)

Table 24.A2 (continued)

right to self-determination of peoples under foreign occupation and colonial or alien domination.
- Non-interference in the internal affairs of States. No State or group of States has the right to intervene either directly or indirectly, whatever the motive, in the internal affairs of any other State.
- Rejection of unconstitutional change of Governments.
- Rejection of attempts at regime change.
- Condemnation of the use of mercenaries in all situations, especially in conflict situations.
- Refraining by all countries from exerting pressure or coercion on other countries, including resorting to aggression or other acts involving the use of direct or indirect force, and the application and/ or promotion of any coercive unilateral measure that goes against International Law or is in any way incompatible with it, for the purpose of coercing any other State to subordinate its sovereign rights, or to gain any benefit whatsoever.
- Total rejection of aggression as a dangerous and serious breach of International Law, which entails international responsibility for the aggressor.
- Respect for the inherent right of individual or collective self-defence, in accordance with the Charter of the United Nations.

- Promotion and defence of multilateralism and multilateral organisations as the appropriate frameworks to resolve, through dialogue and cooperation, the problems affecting humankind.
- Support to efforts by countries suffering internal conflicts to achieve peace, justice, equality and development.
- The duty of each State to fully and in good faith comply with the international treaties to which it is a party, as well as to honour the commitments made in the framework of international organisations, and to live in peace with other States.
- Peaceful settlement of all international conflicts in accordance with the Charter of the United Nations.
- Defence and promotion of shared interests, justice and cooperation, regardless of the differences existing in the political, economic and social systems of the States, on the basis of mutual respect and the equality of rights.
- Solidarity as a fundamental component of relations among nations in all circumstances.
- Respect for the political, economic, social and cultural diversity of countries and peoples.

Source: XV Summit of Heads of State and Government of the Non-Aligned Movement, Sharmel Sheikh, Egypt, 11th to 16th of July 2009 (NAM2009/FD/Doc.1), Annex III.

Table 24.A3 Members of the Non-Aligned Movement (2010)

Afghanistan	Burkina Faso	Democratic People's Republic of
Algeria	Burundi	Democratic Republic of the Congo
Angola	Côte d'Ivoire	Djibouti
Antigua and Barbuda	Cambodia	Dominica, Commonwealth of
Bahamas	Cameroon	Dominican Republic
Bahrain	Cape Verde	Ecuador
Bangladesh	Central African Republic	Egypt
Barbados	Chad	Equatorial Guinea
Benin	Chile	Eritrea
Bhutan	Colombia	Ethiopia
Bolivia	Comoros	Gabon
Botswana	Congo	Gambia
Brunei Darussalam	Cuba	Ghana

(continued on the next page)

Table 24.A3 (continued)

Grenada	Mauritius	Sierra Leone
Guatemala	Mongolia	Singapore
Guinea	Morocco	Somalia
Guinea-Bissau	Mozambique	South Africa
Guyana	Myanmar	Sri Lanka
Haiti	Namibia	Sudan
Honduras	Nepal	Suriname
Iran (Islamic Republic of)	Nicaragua	Swaziland
Iraq	Niger	Syrian Arab Republic
Jamaica	Nigeria	Thailand
Jordan	Oman	Timor Leste
Kenya	Pakistan	Togo
Korea	Palestine	Trinidad and Tobago
Kuwait	Panama	Tunisia
Lao People's Democratic	Papua New Guinea	Turkmenistan
Lebanon	Peru	Uganda
Lesotho	Philippines	United Arab Emirates
Liberia	Qatar	United Republic of Tanzania
Libyan Arab Jamahiriya	Republic	Uzbekistan
Madagascar	Rwanda	Vanuatu
Malawi	Saint Kitts and Nevis	Venezuela
Malaysia	Saint Lucia	Vietnam
Maldives	Saint Vincent and the Grenadines	Yemen
Mali	Senegal	Zambia
Mauritania	Seychelles	Zimbabwe

Notes

1 Richard Cupit, Rodney Whitlock, and Lynn Williams Whitlock, 'The [Im]mortality of International Governmental Organizations,' in Paul F. Diehl, ed., *The Politics of Global Governance: International Organizations in An Interdependent World*, (Boulder, CO, 2001), 58–59; Robert O. Keohane, *After Hegemony: Cooperation and Discord in the World Political Economy* (Princeton, NJ, 1984). Then see Kenneth W. Abbott and Duncan Snidal, 'Why States Act Through Formal International Organizations,' in Diehl, *Global Governance*, 51–32; Judith Goldstein and Robert O. Keohane, eds., *Ideas and Foreign Policy: Beliefs, Institutions, And Political Change* (Ithaca, NY, 1993); Oran Young, 'Political Leadership and Regime Formation: On the Development of Institutions in International Society,' *International Organization*, 45(1991), 281–309; Martha Finnemore, *National Interests in International Society* (Ithaca, NY, 1996); Alexander Wendt, 'Collective Identity Formation and the International State,' *American Political Science Review* 88(1994), 384–96.

2 Kenneth Waltz. *Theory of International Politics* (Reading, MA, 1979); Stephen M. Walt, *The Origins of Alliances* (Ithaca, NY, 1987).

3 In the region Thailand, the only country that had escaped formal European colonisation, also managed to escape Japanese occupation by collaborating with Japan. Afghanistan had never been colonised but had been the target of Anglo-Russo rivalry and had seen British control of its foreign affairs until 1919.

4 For an analysis of pan-Americanism, see Jacqueline Anne Braveboy-Wagner, *Institutions of the Global South* (London, 2009), 64–76.

5 Nicholas Mansergh, 'The Asian Conference,' *International Affairs*, 23(1947), 295, 299.

6 Ibid., 309.

7 Ibid.

8 Arab states also opposed holding such a conference. See Rahul Mukherji, 'Appraising the Legacy of Bandung: A View from India,' in Seng Tan and Amitav Acharya, eds., *Bandung Revisited: The Legacy of the 1955 Asian-African Conference for International Order* (Singapore, 2008), 160–79.

9   See *Resolution on the Indonesian Question, Adopted by the Security Council, January 28, 1949*, Document S/1234, January 28, 1949, *International Organization*, 3(1949), 387–89.

10 See *Resolution on the Indonesian Question*.

11 Peter Calvocoressi, *World Politics since 1945* (London, 1991), 144.

12 Maxim Fackler, 'The World after Bandung', *Suddeutsche Zeitung* (26 April 1955): www.ena.lu.

13 The attendees were the five organisers plus Afghanistan, Cambodia, Egypt, Ethiopia, Gold Coast [Ghana], Iran, Iraq, Japan, Jordan, Laos, Lebanon, Liberia, Libya, Nepal, the Philippines, the PRC, Saudi Arabia, Sudan, Syria, Thailand, Turkey, the democratic Republic of Vietnam, the state of Vietnam, and Yemen. This section draws heavily from Jacqueline Braveboy-Wagner, 'Tricontinental Diplomacy: The Non-Aligned Movement,' in idem., *Global South*, 13–29.

14 Itty Abraham, 'Bandung and State Formation in Post-colonial Asia,' in Tan and Acharya, *Bandung Revisited*, 59.

15 *Letter from Renaud Sivan to Antoine Piray* (Jakarta, 27 April 1955), www.cna.lu.

16 Fackler, 'World after Bandung.'

17 *Letter from Renaud Sivan.*

18 Anthony Reid, 'The Bandung Conference and Southeast Asian Regionalism,' in Tan and Acharya, *Bandung Revisited*, 24.

19 *Statement by the Indian Delegation at the Closing Session* (Bandung, 17 to 24 April 1955): www.ena.lu.

20 Ibid.

21 A.W. Singham and Shirley Hume, *Non-Alignment in an Age of Alignments* (London, 1986), 69.

22 The Second Asian–African Conference was eventually held in Bandung in 2005, on the fiftieth anniversary of the original conference. It was chaired by Indonesia and South Africa and attended by 89 heads of state or government and their special envoys, 20 other countries, and 21 organisational representatives. See Braveboy-Wagner, *Global South*, 22.

23 Peter Willetts, *The Non-Aligned Movement: The Origins of a Third World Alliance* (New York, 1978), 18–19.

24 New attendees were Angola, Burundi, Cameroon, Central African Republic, Chad, Congo-Brazzaville, Dahomey, Jordan, Kenya, Kuwait, Laos, Liberia, Libya, Malawi, Mauritania, Nepal, Nigeria, Senegal, Sierra Leone, Syria, Tanganyika, Togo, and Zambia.

25 *Conference of Heads of State or Government of Non-Aligned Countries, Programme for Peace and International Co-operation, Declaration as Adopted by the Conference*, Section VIII, Military Pacts, Foreign Troops & Bases, NAC-II/Heads/5, Cairo (10 October 1964).

26 Noted in Braveboy-Wagner, *Global South*, 16.

27 These documents can be accessed at: www.un-documents.net/s6r3201.htm.

28 S.K. Sahni, 'The Non-Aligned Movement: Bandung to Durban,' *Non-Aligned World* 26(October 1998), 24.

29 *The Call From Colombia*, 11th Summit of the Non-Aligned Movement, Cartagena, Colombia (18–20 October 1995), NAC11.Doc 6, point 5.

30 *Final Document, 14th Summit Conference of Heads of State or Government of the Non-Aligned Movement*, Havana, Cuba (11–16 September 2006): NAM 2006/Doc.1/Rev.3, Articles 120, 121, 124, 234.7.

31 Press Conference (16 September 2006) [Presentation of Felipe Perez Roque, Minister of Foreign Affairs of the Republic of Cuba]: www.cubanoal.cu/ingles/Conferencias/160906.htm.

32 *Final Document, XV Summit of Heads of State and Government of the Non-Aligned Movement*, Sharm el Sheikh, Egypt, 1(11–16 July 2009), Article 296.

33 Ibid., 309.

34 Ibid., 115. Citation is from the guidelines explained in the chair's statement, Preparatory Conference for Algiers Summit (1973), Kabul, Afghanistan.

35 'Appendix', *Reservations to the Final Document*, 11th Summit, Colombia, 1995.

36 Singham, *Non-Alignment*, 90–91.

37 Ibid., 1124.

38 Ibid., 308.

39 'India to US: NAM Still Relevant,' *Indian Express*, (29 June 2007): www.indianexpress.com/news/india-to-us-nam-still-relevant/203350/.

40 Mansergh, 'Asian Conference,' 305.

41 Amitav Acharya and See Seng Tan, 'Introduction,' in idem., *Bandung Revisited*, 13.

42 Ang Chen Guan, 'The Bandung Conference and the Cold War International History,' in ibid., 30.

43 *Letter from Renaud Sivan; Letter from General Ely to Antoine Pinay (Saigon, 28 April 1955)*: www.ena.lu.

44 Guan, 'Bandung', 36.

45 Braveboy-Wagner, *Global South*, 29; see also 44–45.
46 For example, in 2009, they agreed to: 'generate, expand and deepen a more dynamic relationship and co-operation with developed and industrialised countries, in particular with the Group of Eight, firmly rooted in mutual respect, mutuality of benefits, shared and differentiated responsibilities, constructive engagement and dialogue, broad partnership and genuine independence. ...' See *Final Document*, 2009, Article 176.
47 'Cuba Revives Non-Aligned Movement with a Successful Summit.' *NotiCen, Central American and Caribbean Affairs* (21 September 2006).
48 United States Mission to the UN (USUN) Press release #7(01), 17 January 2001.
49 See *Final Document*, 14th Summit, Havana (2006), Article 22.4; and *Final Document*, 15th Summit, Sharm el Sheikh (2009), Article 24.3.
50 *Final Document* (2009), Article 13.
51 Ibid., Article 14.2.

Part VI
The International Economy

The International Monetary Fund and the World Bank

The power of money?

Morten Bøås

In November 2010, the Executive Board of the International Monetary Fund (IMF) approved far-reaching reforms suggesting the end of the power structure that had prevailed ever since this multilateral institution was conceived at the Bretton Woods conference in 1944. Speaking to the press immediately after the Board's decision, the IMF's then managing director, Dominique Strauss-Kahn, hailed this process as 'a historical reform, increasing the voice and representation of emerging markets and developing countries in the IMF'.[1] In practice, this means that BRIC (Brazil, Russia, India, and China) will now be amongst the IMF's top shareholders as a result of a shift of six percent of the total quota shares. Because 80 percent of this shift comes from advanced economies (the United States and Europe mainly), when this reform takes full effect in October 2012, there will be two fewer seats for Europe on the IMF Executive Board and two more for emerging market countries. As the reforms will have significant consequences for the power structure of other important multilateral institutions, the World Bank included, this decision is one of systemic magnitude that reflects how much the world has changed since the IMF and the World Bank were created as the institutional anchors of the post-Second World War order established by the United States and its allies in 1944. The World Bank has yet to see equally significant changes, but here emerging economies also play a larger role today than only some years ago. Currently, eight member-states of the World Bank select the Executive Director directly: the United States, Japan, Germany, France, Britain, China, Russia, and Saudi Arabia.[2] The first five comprise the largest shareholders. The remaining executive directors are chosen amongst member country constituencies.

The IMF and the World Bank have undoubtedly occupied an important role in global economic affairs since they were established by providing both much-needed loans and technical assistance. Much has been written about them, and there is no shortage of technical information concerning their financing, lending, and impact; but what is more difficult to find is a concise introduction that treats them as what they really are, namely political institutions that form an integral part of modern-day economic statecraft and diplomacy. Because these institutions are not only political in their very nature, but also vast and complex international bureaucracies performing a wide range of different tasks, they cannot be approached as unitary actors totally under the control of majority shareholders. What is needed is an approach that highlights their internal processes and politics.

As already mentioned, in 1944 a conference was convened in Bretton Woods in the United States by the emerging victorious Powers in the Second World War. It was there that the IMF and the World Bank were born in the hope that they would provide the foundations for a peaceful and prosperous international future. The goal involved devising a stable global economic system that would avert calamities such as the Great Depression and its lingering effects, which had culminated in the Second World War. The 'Bretton Woods' system comprised the IMF and the World Bank (the International Bank for Reconstruction and Development). The IMF was charged with providing a stable international monetary system that could promote trade, whereas the World Bank was to aid in the reconstruction of Western Europe, essentially by channelling American money to European development. The IMF and the World Bank also represented a form of international cooperation that the world had not experienced before 1945, an evolution from the League of Nations and United Nations models in which all member countries had an equal voice and vote. The structure of the IMF and the World Bank, on the other hand, was inspired by the joint-stock model of private capitalist corporations, in which members are shareholders whose voting powers vary with their relative economic importance. In other words, each member country's share of the votes is weighted in accordance with the combined amount of capital that it contributes and guarantees. All member countries are organised in country constituencies, headed by an executive director who controls the combined votes of his or her constituency and sits on the institution's Board of Directors. The size and composition of the country constituencies may vary, but the principle of organisation is similar.[3]

The capital construction of all multilateral organisations was established with the formation of the World Bank. It was recognised as an institution whose capital would be provided by government, not by private sources. Its initial capitalisation of US$10 billion consisted of 20 percent in paid capital and 80 percent in guaranteed capital. This distinction is crucial. Each member-state subscription is divided into two parts. The larger one is so-called 'guaranteed capital'. This amount is not actually paid by the member-states, but each guarantees a certain sum of money. The credit rating of the World Bank and IMF is in effect based on the amount guaranteed by the richest member-states. It provides them with the best possible credit rating (for instance, triple A), making it possible either to lend money on international capital markets and relend it to poorer member countries or, in the case of IMF, to member-states in need of short-term loans to stabilise their finances and financial sectors. These financial arrangements would not have been possible without the membership of the strongest economies in the world and, therefore, it constitutes the backbone of their power in these institutions.[4] The IMF and the World Bank could not function without their wealthy member-states, and this knowledge, shared by all the actors involved, implies that votes are rarely used. Quite simply, votes are rarely needed because the power relations on the Board of Directors are transparent, and the consequences of constantly working against them obvious to everyone concerned.[5]

The reasoning for the IMF is the same as the World Bank, but its establishment differs because it resulted from lengthy discussions of four alternative proposals (American, British, Canadian, and French) during the Second World War. The British and American plans were more important. Britain's Keynes Plan proposed an international clearing union that would create an international means of payment called 'bancor'. The rival American plan, named after Harry Dexter White from the United States Treasury, suggested a currency pool to which members would make specified contributions only, and from which countries could borrow to help themselves over short-term balance-of-payments deficits. In essence, the major difference between these two plans was that the Keynes' emphasised national autonomy, whilst the White Plan considered exchange-rate stability to be of primary importance. In the end, it was the thinking behind the White Plan that came to constitute the IMF framework.

When the IMF began operations from its headquarters in Washington DC in 1946, its primary task was to monitor and manage a system of stable exchange rates in which the value of all currencies was based on gold and the American dollar. To ensure the stability of this system, Washington guaranteed the value of the dollar in gold at a set rate of US$35 per ounce. The IMF's second major function was to provide countries with short-term financing from its vast reserves of foreign currencies and gold to help them overcome temporary balance-of-payments deficits and support their exchange-rate values. These reserves came from the contributions by IMF member-states based on the size of their economy. Until the United States abandoned the gold standard in 1971 as a result of inflationary pressure and the costs of the war it was fighting in Vietnam, these remained the two main functions of the IMF. After President Richard Nixon unilaterally abandoned the gold standard, the IMF's main responsibility has been short-term loans for balance-of-payment deficits.

IMF membership is open to any country willing to adhere to the IMF charter of rights and obligations. Currently 187 countries are members and, on joining, each contributes a certain amount of money called a quota subscription. These quotas serve the following purposes:

- They form the pool of money that the IMF can draw from to lend to member-states in financial difficulties;
- They are the basis for determining how much money a member-state can borrow from the IMF or receive from the IMF in periodic allocations (known as special drawing rights); and
- They determine the voting power of each member-state.[6]

These quotas are reviewed every five years, and they can be raised or lowered according to both the needs of the IMF and the economic prosperity or decline of the member-state in question. The quotas also constitute the basis for IMF funds. However, the quotas themselves may not provide sufficient money to meet the borrowing needs of members in a period of great stress in the world economy. The Asian financial crisis in 1997 or the financial crisis that broke out globally in 2007 are examples. Such a situation is why the so-called 'general arrangements to borrow' were established in 1962. This arrangement is a line of credit with a number of governments and banks throughout the world to which the IMF pays interest on whatever it borrows and undertakes to repay the loan in five years. The IMF system for raising external funds is therefore different from that utilised by the World Bank but, in essence, the principle is the same. Both institutions borrow money on international capital markets based on the money paid in and guaranteed by its most affluent members.[7]

It should also be stressed that contrary to the World Bank, the IMF is not a development institution. Its mission is much narrower, lending to member-states with payment problems; that is, to countries that do not earn enough foreign currency to pay for what they buy from abroad. The economic logic is, thus, quite simple: a country with a payments problem is spending more than it is earning and this situation has to stop. Reform is needed; but if the country goes to the IMF, it cannot choose any kind of reform. It must adopt measures that can be approved by the IMF, and this procedure has had developmental consequences. In accordance with the neoliberal dogma of the IMF, reform plans should contain the following standard components: reduce government expenditure, tighten monetary policy, and deal with structural weaknesses by, for example, privatising inefficient public utilities and enterprises. More recently, some 'softer' items have also been added to this list: adequate social safety nets, 'good' government spending, and good governance. It is often unclear what these terms mean in practice, but all potential borrowers have learnt the importance of including such items in their applications.

Formally, the IMF is not granted much autonomy. The chain of command is supposed to run directly from the governments of member-states to the organisation. Thus, when working out lending arrangements, including conditionalities, the IMF formally acts not on its own, but as an intermediary between the will of the majority of its membership and the individual member-states. Yet, it is also clear that those who contribute the most to IMF possess the strongest voices in determining policies. The reality is that the IMF, if it is an intermediary, is one between the strongest economies in the world and individual member-states, and not necessarily between the majority and individual members. Just as in the case of the World Bank, the IMF has a Board of Directors that constitutes resident representatives in Washington DC. And just as in the World Bank, it is rare that the Board makes decisions based on formal voting. The usual procedure is the formation of a consensus; but this consensus is artificial given the distribution of voting power amongst the Board members.

Consequently, the IMF and the World Bank like other multilateral institutions still reflect the power relationship prevailing at their time of origin; and initially, at least, they tend to facilitate world views and beliefs (like the merits of neoliberal economics) in accord with these power relations.[8] This does not mean that initial power relations are cemented forever and that once a hegemon, always a hegemon. Multilateral institutions like the IMF and their original strongest member countries will sooner or later be forced to take global economic realities into consideration. Moreover, outcomes are also determined not simply by the distribution of power amongst member countries, but also by the institution itself, which can affect how choices are framed and outcomes reached. The IMF and the World Bank should therefore also be approached as social constructions,[9] which involve political, economic, and social actors, operating not only through the state's foreign-policy apparatus but also transnationally.

The IMF and the World Bank were originally established to solve one specific problem more than anything else: the reconstruction of Europe. However, because this took place at a faster pace than anticipated with little if any assistance from the IMF and the World Bank, it was done through the Marshall plan; the World Bank was geared toward the 'problem' of development, or the lack of it. The United States played an important role in this regard; President Harry Truman's inaugural speech on 20 January 1949 is commonly held to mark the beginning of the modern development enterprise.[10] In this speech, the transfer and transfusion of scientific and expert knowledge were presented as the solution to poverty and misery. Although transfers and transfusions were to be the means, increased prosperity and closer resemblance to Western societies were not only the original objective; they were clearly part of that age's geopolitical necessities.

What has changed, however, are the means not the ends. And the changes that have taken place have been incremental, most often without any attempt to place the objectives in a logical, prioritised order. The process of change that has taken place in the IMF and the World Bank therefore mainly resembles 'change by adaptation'.[11] The reason is that both organisations confront specific challenges when faced with demands to incorporate new issue areas. Their mission is never simple and straightforward because both member-states and other actors in their external environment may disagree on the interpretation of the mission (the ends) as well as on the tasks (the means) that need to be carried out if the mission is to be accomplished. In social units that function under such circumstances, organisational routines, and standard operating procedures are preferred to substantive change. They therefore favor one particular way of arranging and routinising their activities. Because the IMF and the World Bank have to satisfy not only their various member-states constituencies but also, increasingly, civil society organisations, they try to avoid articulating competing views. Consensus therefore becomes an objective in itself, but the kind of consensus established in the IMF and the World Bank is constructed on the basis of the power structure prevailing in the two institutions. This process means that consensus in the IMF and the World Bank is by and large artificial.

This way of reasoning is important because it helps to explain why the preferred approach of the IMF and the World Bank in promoting development has been that of the 'engineer'.

Development (or its lack) was defined as a technical and not a political issue concerning the distribution of wealth and resources. If the challenges of development and the new ideas supposed to resolve them could be defined in technical terms, the possibility increased getting a proposal for action approved internally as well as by member-states. Over time, a limited reexamination of the means used to reach the ends was made possible when new issue-areas were presented in the same language as the old and familiar knowledge. By applying such a strategy of depoliticisation, new and potentially challenging discussions were kept within the framework of already existing standard operating procedures. Hence, it was possible to treat potentially highly sensitive political issues, such as governance, as technical issues, and thereby the underlying political conflicts could be controlled at least in part. For example, it was the ability to define governance in strictly economic and technical terms that facilitated this issue-area's incorporation into the IMF and the World Bank.

Projects, policies, and approaches have been modified by the inclusion of new social and environmental components and regulatory safeguards to ensure that environmental and social damage is avoided as much as possible. However, the IMF and the World Bank approach is still of an engineering problem-solving type, with policies and project papers written in the technical language familiar to staff, management, and the boards of the institutions.

In the 1950s and 1960s, this strategy worked remarkably well. But in the 1970s and 1980s, it was gradually called into question; by the mid-1990s, it was fully apparent that new development challenges could no longer be tackled by narrow technical approaches, and the IMF and the World Bank in particular started to experience more severe difficulties. The question was no longer simply a matter of finding the right technical solution to a functional problem. In the twenty-first century, the challenge is to construct some sort of consensus around an increasingly politicised agenda, constituting a whole range of new cross-cutting themes: political, economic, and financial governance, involuntary resettlement, and indigenous peoples. The technocratic consensus has reached its limits. It is no longer possible, in any credible way, to define development solely in a technical and functional manner. As a consequence, the internal artificial consensus is disappearing, not only between donor and borrowing member-states of the World Bank and the IMF, but also internally in these institutions. This agenda makes the process of political manoeuvring between donor and recipient countries and other stakeholders (civil society and private sector actors) increasingly difficult.

The role of the United States is crucial in understanding both the establishment and early development of the World Bank and the IMF, as well as the policies pursued in the 1980s and 1990s. The multilateral institutions that emerged out of Bretton Woods was firstly an American creation, secondly Anglo-Saxon, and only thirdly international. The United States supplied most of the resources necessary for making loans and was also served as the predominant market for their securities. Over the years, there have been two conflicting opinions of American influence in the World Bank. One held by many members of the US Congress argues that the United States has too little influence on World Bank activities. The World Bank, it is claimed, is run by highly paid, aloof bureaucrats, unresponsive to American concerns and accountable only to themselves. The opposite view, held by a substantial number of World Bank staff and many outsiders (most notably non-governmental organisations [NGOs] and some borrowing member-states) maintains that the World Bank is run by the United States. A more sober analysis supports neither of these extreme positions: American influence in the World Bank is important, but not absolute.[12]

Nonetheless, throughout the history of the World Bank, the United States has been the largest shareholder and the most influential member country. American support for, pressure on, and criticism of the World Bank have been central to its growth and the evolution of its policies, programs, and practices. Underlying more than half a century of American-World Bank relations has been a fundamental ambivalence on the part of the United States toward both development assistance and multilateral cooperation in general.[13] However, United States support for the World Bank has been based on the view that promoting economic growth and development in other parts of the world is in the national interest, and that multilateral cooperation is a particularly effective way of both leveraging and allocating resources for development purposes that serve American national interests. The United States Treasury Department has consistently emphasised these points, and it has viewed both the IMF and the World Bank as instruments of foreign policy to be used in support of specific American aims and objectives. Thus, whilst various American administrations have supported the IMF and the World Bank for their capacity to leverage funds and influence borrowing countries' economic policies, the United States has also been uneasy with the autonomy on which the development role of the World Bank and the financial role of the IMF depend, and the power sharing that accompanies burden sharing.

This ambivalence, a preoccupation with first containing and, more recently, concern about the relative change in United States power in the world, explains much of the evolution of American relations with the IMF and the World Bank over the past decades. The United States Congress, unlike the legislatures in other member-states, has been a major influence on the policies of multilateral institutions, in general, and the IMF and the World Bank, in particular. For example, within the context of changing foreign-policy concerns, congressional involvement has significantly affected the style and approach of American participation in the World Bank. Having promoted the establishment, early financial growth, and expansion of the World Bank program, the United States in the 1970s often found itself at odds with the Bank. However, the debt crisis in the South, in particular in Latin America, and the collapse of the Soviet Union's sphere of influence in Eastern Europe led to renewed American interest in the World Bank; and it occurred at the same time as pressure from NGOs caused the United States to push it to be more environmentally aware. However, renewed United States attention to the World Bank was accompanied from the 1980s by a strange combination of a continuing decline in the American share of World Bank funding and a unilateral, dogmatic assertiveness on matters of World Bank policies. This combination antagonised several other member-states (borrowing and donor members alike). As long as the United States was regarded as the sole superpower and the economic powerhouse of the world, the American Congress's use of its power of the purse to direct as well as restrict American financial participation in the World Bank was tolerated; but as United States economic hegemony is decreasing, American power in the Bank is increasingly contested by BRIC and other emerging middle Powers.

However, it is important to recognise that the relationship between the United States and the World Bank–IMF is ambiguous. As a starting point, foreign aid has never been popular in the Congress. Although objections were muted just after the Second World War, Congress quickly became dissatisfied and distrustful of multilateral institutions. As a consequence, most members of Congress were uninterested and uninformed about World Bank operations. Even on key committees, there was much misunderstanding of what the World Bank did and how it operated.[14] Increased appropriation requests became attractive targets. Over time, there has also been a breakdown of discipline and effective leadership in Congress, making it increasingly difficult to maneuver unpopular aid requests through the labyrinthine authorisation and appropriation procedures. For example, no fewer than five committees have significant jurisdiction over American policy towards the World Bank. The most important ones are the House Banking Sub-committee on International Development Institutions and Finance, and the Appropriations Sub-committee of Foreign Relations. This kind of institutional arrangement provides multiple entry points for interest groups with specific policy agendas (for example, environmental NGOs) and it creates a situation in which strategically placed members of Congress, and specific issues, may gain disproportional weight in the policy process.[15] As long as Congress was passive in making policy towards toward the World Bank and IMF, its basic dislike of foreign aid and multilateral institutions and its cumbersome legislative procedures were of limited significance. However, as it became less deferential on matters of foreign policy, these factors became formative for American policy toward, and participation in, the World Bank and IMF.

The basis of US influence derives from the origins of the World Bank and the fact that its Charter and guiding principles have a distinctly American character. Traditionally it has been American thinking about the roles of government and markets that provided the conceptual centre of gravity for World Bank debates, rather than that of Europe, Japan and other Asian countries, and developing countries. Over the years, the United States has used its influence to ensure that those principles are not disregarded. Other sources of influence include its position as the largest shareholder in the World Bank, the importance of its financial market as a source of capital for the World Bank and other multilateral institutions, and its hold on the position of the presidency of the World Bank and other senior management positions. These factors are reinforced by the World Bank's location in Washington, DC. The great majority of the World Bank's economists and other staff members, whatever their nationality, also tend to have a postgraduate qualification from a North American university. And there are many subtle ways in which the Bank's location in the heart of Washington, DC, adjacent to the White House, Treasury, and Washington-based think tanks, helps contribute to the way in which American premises structure the very mind set of most World Bank staff. They read American newspapers, watch American television, and American English is their *lingua franca*.[16] Although the relative importance of the United States in many of these fields and dimensions has declined, it remains the dominant member-state in the World Bank, in large part because no other country or group of countries such as Japan, China, or the European Union (EU) has so far chosen deliberately to challenge the American leadership position in the Bank.[17]

Words spoken by the United States Treasury clearly carry a great deal of weight in the IMF, but the United States is not entirely dominant, and the multilateral institutional arrangement that the IMF represents does place some constraints on Treasury ability to act unilaterally in international financial politics. In theory, there are clear limits to American power. Washington controls only 16.74 percent of the votes. The managing director of IMF is by convention a European, and Japan (6.01 percent), Germany (5.87 percent), France (4.85 percent), and Britain (4.85 percent) could easily outvote the United States if they combined in a coordinated manner. It remains highly unlikely that a real challenge to American hegemony will come from EU Powers. If it ever emerged, it would be from BRIC and the Asian countries. But even if gaining importance in the IMF, these Powers are still far from exercising this type of authority. Accordingly, in practice, and despite the IMF becoming more and genuinely multi-polar, the United States is usually able to achieve the major decisions it desires, exercising influence behind the scenes, often in informal interactions between the First Deputy-Managing Director of the IMF (by convention an American) and the Deputy-Secretary of the United States Treasury.[18]

In normal times, the United States by and large does not get much involved. The IMF's main activity is surveillance, an activity that Washington feels comfortable leaving to the organisation. American power is exercised mainly under two circumstances: first, when the IMF is called upon to rescue a country in deep financial crisis, a situation in which the IMF and the United States Treasury have the leverage to extract commitments in return for financial rescue packages; and second, when American strategic interests are involved. The experience with the South Korean rescue package in December 1997 illustrates how this collaboration may work under such extraordinary circumstances.

As South Korea slipped within days of running out of hard currency to pay its debts in December 1997, it sent a secret envoy, Kim Kihwan, to work out a rescue package. 'I didn't bother going to the IMF', Mr. Kim recently recalled. 'I called Mr. Summers' office at the Treasury from my home in Seoul, flew to Washington and went directly there. I knew this was how this would be done'.[19]

The agreement was then reached and presented to the IMF and the other multilateral institutions involved as a done deal. IMF staff were not happy about this process, but they were not in a position to renegotiate the deal struck between the Treasury and the South Korean Government. They had no say over the deal, but were left with the task of putting the financial rescue package together.

The only member-state that has really tried to challenge some of the underlying premises that the United States seeks to protect and promote in the Bank is Japan. These encounters took place in the few years of Asia-euphoria, before the emergence of the Asian financial crisis in 1997. At the centre of the debate was the role of the state in development. This dispute was a consequence of the World Bank's neoliberal economic orthodoxy in the 1980s and 1990s, when the Bank under the influence of the Reagan Administration and Thatcher Government in, respectively, the United States and Britain almost endorsed the principle of the self-adjusting market: the necessity of 'getting the prices right' and providing a 'level playing field'. This Anglo-American ideology claimed that a single set of rules should apply to all Powers, and the basis of these rules was the idea that the proper role of the state was to provide the framework for private sector activity in a financial system based on private capital.

Before the advent of the Reagan Administration, Japan had few quarrels with the American emphasis on the merits of market forces, privatisation, and economic liberalisation. However, during the 1980s, Japan came increasingly to question the neoliberal economic model, particularly its appropriateness for Asia. The Japanese Government, especially the Ministry of Finance, resented what they interpreted as inflexible American attempts to apply neoliberal economic principles to Asian countries that lacked a strong private sector tradition and benefited from government intervention in the economy.[20] This critique clearly reflected Japan's own experience as a developmental Power with a state-controlled bank-based financial system. Hence, in the late 1980s and early 1990s, Tokyo began to use its financial muscle to take a more active role in the multilateral system: not simply adapting, but also debating. Its objective was to modify the approach of the World Bank and other multilateral economic institutions (including the IMF) so as to be more in line with the economic systems of Japan and East Asia. In response to intense Japanese pressure over an extended period of time, the World Bank agreed to conduct a study of the causes of economic growth in East Asia. The United States Treasury opposed the idea but, when Japan promised to pay for the whole study, agreement was finally reached.

The study cost the Japanese Government more than US$1.2 million and, for Japan and other East Asian countries that hoped that it would contribute to renewed reflections in the World Bank about the role of the state, the conclusion was a huge disappointment. According to the *East Asia Miracle Report*, the lessons to be learnt from East Asia had no implications for the World Bank's approach to development; rather, the Bank argued, a careful analysis of what had taken place in East Asia confirmed the validity of their position on the role of the state.[21] In one critical commentary on the World Bank's approach:

> Through the 1980s, the Bank had pressed the view that the central problem of developing countries is that they provided only a weak 'enabling environment' for private sector growth: they failed to provide adequate infrastructure, macroeconomic stability, a framework for law and property rights, transparency in policy-making and universal education. The *East Asian Miracle* finds that the presence of such an enabling environment in East Asia is the main

explanation of the region's superior performance. Conversely, selective industrial policies fortunately turn out to have been largely ineffective, despite the popular image of these countries as champions of industrial policies.[22]

One may argue that this was the only conclusion possible for the World Bank: if industrial policies had emerged from the study as the main explanation of East Asia's success, both the World Bank message and its image as the intellectual leader of the development debate would have been significantly damaged. To critical observers, it was obvious that the World Bank could not tolerate any other finding, because that would mean its preaching to client countries for the previous decade had been wrong. It was therefore argued that the conclusions of the report had been tailor-made to fit with the worldview of the United States Treasury. Debate continued in the World Bank, the IMF, and several other agencies across the multilateral system until the 1997 Asian financial crisis dealt a devastating blow to the Japanese and Asian economies. EU coordination in the World Bank and the IMF is slowly becoming more evident, but so far this group has neither been willing nor able to challenge the dominant position of the United States; and it remains to be seen if China is content with its current position in the IMF and the World Bank or whether it will be the leading force in a new Asian challenge to American hegemony.

The IMF and the World Bank are amongst the world's most powerful international organisations. As the institutional 'anchors' of the post-Second World War order, they reflected and still reflect the power relations prevailing at their time of origin. They have therefore also tended to facilitate world views in accordance with these power relations. This situation may be about to change because the IMF and the World Bank are primarily economic institutions and, thereby, bound to reflect global economic realities, and from an economic perspective, these realities are currently changing the world in a multipolar direction. However, it is also important to recognise that even if power relations are important for understanding the projects, policies, and approaches of the World Bank and the IMF, power is most often exercised carefully and through more subtle means than the direct power of money that capital subscriptions and quotas may allow. Votes are very rarely used; rather it has been American hegemony that for the better part of the post-1945 era that has made possible the United States exercise of its considerable influence.

Votes are important because they constitute the basis for the artificial consensus, but just as important for understanding the diplomacy and statecraft that revolves around the IMF and the World Bank are the more informal pathways of American power: their distinctively American Charters, the United States hold on the presidency of the World Bank and the First Deputy Managing Director of the IMF, and the United States as the centre of gravity for their conceptual debates amongst Washington, DC-based staff. In sum, it is probable that the United States will continue to be the most important member-state of the World Bank and the IMF; and even if global economic realities may be pointing towards China and Asia, the power relations prevailing in this type of international institutions will change only gradually and over a considerable time span. The argument is not that these power relations are cemented forever but, rather, they demonstrate that the exercise of influence in institutions such as the IMF and the World Bank is nested in sources of power of both a material and an ideational nature.

Notes

1 IMF, *IMF Board Approves Far-Reaching Governance Reforms* (Washington, DC, 2010).
2 As of 1 November 2010 the United States controls 16.36 percent of the total number of votes, and Japan 7.85 percent, Germany 4.48 percent, France 4.30 percent, and the United Kingdom 4.30 percent, whereas Russia, China, and Saudi Arabia each controls 2.78 percent of the votes.

3 Morten Bøås and Desmond McNeill, *Multilateral Institutions—a Critical Introduction* (London, 2003); Morten Bøås, 'Multilateral institutions and the developing world—changes and challenges', in Vandana Desai and Robert B. Potter, eds., *The Companion to Development Studies*, second edition (London, 2008), 547–50.

4 However, this is not the only source of power in the IMF and the World Bank.

5 Bøås, 'Multilateral institutions'.

6 As of November 2010, the United States is the largest country in the IMF with 16.74 percent of the total number of votes. Other large shareholding countries include Japan (6.01 percent), Germany (5.87 percent), France (4.85 percent), United Kingdom (4.85 percent), China (3.65 percent), Saudi Arabia (3.16 percent), and Russia (2.69 percent).

7 Bøås and McNeill, *Multilateral Institutions*.

8 Robert Cox, 'Multilateralism and world order', *Review of International Studies*, Volume 18, Number 2 (1992), 161–80; Robert Wade, 'U.S. hegemony and the World Bank: the fight over people and ideas', *Review of International Political Economy*, Volume 9, Number 2 (2002), 201–29.

9 Fredrich Kratochwil and John G. Ruggie, 'International organization: a state of the art or an art of the state', *International Organization*, 40(1986), 753–75.

10 Knut Nustad, 'The development discourse in the multilateral system', in Morten Bøås and Desmond McNeill, eds., *Global Institutions and Development: Framing the World?* (London, 2004), 13–23.

11 Ernst B. Haas, *When Knowledge Is Power: Three Models of Change in International Organizations* (Berkeley, CA, 1990).

12 See Bøås and McNeill, *Multilateral Institutions*.

13 Catherine Gwin, *U.S. Relations with the World Bank 1945–92* (Washington, DC, 1994); Morten Bøås and Desmond McNeill, 'Introduction: power and ideas in multilateral institutions: towards an interpretative framework', in Morten Bøås and Desmond McNeill, eds., *Global Institutions and Development: Framing the World?* (London, 2004), 1–12.

14 Lars Schoultz, 'Politics, economics and U.S. participation in multilateral development banks', *International Organization*, 36(1982), 537–74.

15 Morten Bøås, 'Multilateral development banks, environmental impact assessments and nongovernmental organizations in U.S. foreign policy', in Paul G. Harris, ed., *The Environment, International Relations and U.S. Foreign Policy* (Washington D.C., 2001), 178–96.

16 Robert Wade, 'Showdown at the World Bank', *New Left Review*, 7(January/February 2001), 124–37.

17 For example, the number of total votes that the United States controls has diminished from 34.1 percent of total votes to 16.36 in 2010.

18 See Bessma Momani, 'American politicization of the International Monetary Fund', *Review of International Political Economy*, Volume 15, Number 5 (2004), 880–904.

19 David E. Sanger, 'Runaway agency or U.S. pawn?', in L. John McQuillian and Paul C. Montgomery, eds., *The International Monetary Fund: Financial Medic to the World?* (Stanford, CA, 1999), 23.

20 Morten Bøås, *Governance, Leadership and Ownership: the Case of the African Development Bank and the Asian Development Bank 1979–1996* [Doctoral Dissertation, University of Oslo, 2001].

21 World Bank, *The East Asian Miracle: Economic Growth and Public Policy* (Washington DC, 1993).

22 Robert Wade, 'Is the East Asian Miracle right?', in Arthur Fishlow, Catherine Gwin, Stephen Haggard, Dani Rodrik, and Robert Wade, eds., *Miracle or Design: Lessons from the East Asian Experience* (Washington DC, 1994), 56.

26

The European Union and the economic and financial crisis

Reforming internal governance and external representation in turbulent times

Daniela Schwarzer

The global financial and economic crisis has severely hit the 27 member states of the European Union (EU). This situation is particularly true for the Eurozone, which forms the most integrated part of the EU. In 2009, for the first time since its creation ten years earlier, the Eurozone slipped into recession, resulting in a massive increase in unemployment and pressure on public finances. Later in the year, a sovereign debt crisis started to unfold, which accelerated to such a degree in 2011, that the end of the single currency is now openly debated.

One of the reasons for this debate is that the current crisis, like the previous economic downturn in the years of 2002–3, has not hit all members of the Eurozone with the same impact. Divergence in competitiveness and fiscal performance has tremendously increased between member-states, which provokes economic imbalances, severe market reactions, political power shifts, and strongly diverging national interests amongst member-states. Hence, the crisis management capacities of the governments and the European Central Bank (ECB) are put to a tough test. In parallel, conclusions have been drawn on how the Eurozone, which otherwise has been evaluated as a great success for the EU, could have slipped into such a situation. In the midst of crisis management, a broad reform process has been launched with the objective of fighting the root causes of today's crisis of the Eurozone. The historically unique structure of the European Monetary Union (EMU) with an integrated monetary policy and only rather loosely coordinated national budgetary and economic policies, weak European surveillance structures for member states, and financial markets and no permanent mechanism to solve sovereign debt crises is changing considerably. However, today it is not clear whether there will be more or less Europe (both internally and in its external representation) at the end of this process.

The current crisis affects the EU economically in the sense that the divergence between North and South in Europe has increased markedly and runs straight through the Eurozone; at the same time, the old East–West divide amongst member-states is losing importance. And fairly good recovery rates in 2010–11 cannot hide the fact that Europe has lost economic strength compared with other world regions. In addition, the crisis has had an impact on economic governance within both the EU and the Eurozone, affecting the broad reform process that was launched in 2010. But despite radical decisions in crisis management and a broad reform agenda, these efforts may still not be ambitious enough to ensure the sustainability of the single currency (the euro).

Europe's economic performance has lately been characterised by internal divergence and a loss of relative weight in global comparison. Since the euro was launched in 1999, the newly created ECB has been under close scrutiny. Initial fears that the EMU could add significantly to inflationary pressures within the EU has thus far proven to be unfounded. With an average of *circa* 2 percent in the decade 1999–2009, inflation in the Eurozone was low both in international and historical comparison; United States inflation was 2.7 percent in the same period. As the ECB quickly gained credibility in the markets and inflation expectations were revised downwards, interest rates in the money and capital markets sank. An exception occurred in 2008, with an estimated increase of 3.4 percent, mainly as a result of rising prices in the energy and food sectors, as well as rising wages. But in 2010, the ECB took an active part in managing the sovereign debt crisis. When markets began to react unfavorably, as part of the overall stabilisation strategy, the ECB started to buy sovereign bonds of the most-indebted countries to save them from bankruptcy. There are, hence, new concerns about inflationary pressure building up in the Eurozone.

The growth performance of the Eurozone had meanwhile caused concern well before the current crisis and the resulting recession. Even before the outbreak of the financial crisis, from 1999 to 2008, the gross domestic product (GDP) of the EMU countries grew by only 2.2 percent; in the same period, United States GDP grew by 2.8 percent, whereas the EU's overall GDP advanced by 2.5 %. The years 2002 (0.9 percent GDP growth in the Eurozone) and 2003 (0.8 percent GDP growth) had been particularly weak. The unemployment rate stabilised around 7 percent on EMU average during the first decade of the Euro's existence. As a consequence of the financial crisis, the Eurozone and EU slipped into a recession in 2009–10 in contrast to other world regions (see Table 26.A1 in the Appendix). Unemployment has since climbed to record levels, reaching over 10 percent in the Eurozone. Whilst this performance is giving rise to a severe debate on the EU's long-term growth prospects, it is widely acknowledged that the disappearance of exchange rates amongst the EMU countries has prevented an even worse performance in the crisis. The now 17 member-states (mirroring the sharp slump following the end of the New Economy boom after the turn of the twenty-first century) benefit from the fact that the serious downturn is not aggravated by additional costs caused by currency movements amongst the participating countries.

Since the beginning of 2010, the European economy on average has recovered modestly from the severe economic downturn. This improvement happened in spite of the severe turbulence in sovereign debt markets, which obliged (for the time being) two member-states to request rescue packages from the EU and International Monetary Fund (IMF). Economic activity in the EU has increased mostly to the predominantly export-driven demand in Germany (GDP growth of 3.3 percent in 2010). There are also some smaller member-states such as Finland, Slovakia, and Slovenia where growth rates have recovered. However, the recovery of average growth cannot hide the fact that there are pronounced differences in the developments across member-countries. Even before the outbreak of the economic and financial crisis in 2008, economic divergence emerged as a problem in the Eurozone.[1] In times of economic slump, they have become all the more visible. An important indicator for economic divergence is the development of current-account balances. Germany and the Netherlands, for instance, have net surpluses *vis-à-vis* their EU partners. After recording a deficit from 1999 to 2007, Germany jumped to a strong surplus of 6.7 percent of GDP in 2008. Meanwhile, countries like Spain, Portugal, or Italy recorded comparatively high current-account deficits that indicate a loss of competitiveness.

Because they go along with external debt, high current-account deficits can cause longer-term problems: for instance, paying back the debt can inhibit the development of domestic demand.

The evolution of unit labor costs as a result of repeated exaggerated wage increases is the major reason for the loss of competitiveness. Since the EMU began, unit labor costs increased by roughly 20 percent in Italy and Spain.[2] In Germany, these costs have remained stable as a result of moderate wage agreements and successes in restructuring and reforming the economy. Wage constraint has led to very low inflation rates and, hence, a real devaluation. Germany's economic activity strongly rebounded in 2010 because of robust manufacturing exports but also to an improvement in both private consumption and investment. But given its strong export orientation, Germany's growth prospects depend largely on demand developments in other world regions (mostly the United States and China). Given Germany's economic and financial pre-eminence (27 percent of Eurozone GDP), its substantial trade relationships, and links through production, the country has the potential to boost demand in the Eurozone. For the time being, for instance in France, the Eurozone's second-largest economy that competes less well internationally, growth is picking up much more slowly as private consumption is weakened by high unemployment and budgetary austerity. In Italy, both exports and investment picked up in the first half of 2010, but persistent competitiveness problems limit the scope for export growth and planned fiscal consolidation is likely to weaken private demand.

The situation is much worse in those European states that face serious sovereign debt problems. The economies of Portugal, Ireland, Greece, and Spain have either grown with very slow rates or shrunk. These countries find themselves in a negative spiral of tight austerity measures, increasing deficits, and low or negative growth rates and low competitiveness. It is not clear at present how sustainable the political reform process is, both in terms of structural reforms to improve competitiveness and with regard to budgetary consolidation. There is a risk that the countries will not be able to break the vicious circle and regain growth, unless there is a huge effort by the other member-states to support the adaptation process; this process will have to go beyond the EU and IMF packages that have been granted to Greece and Ireland in return for ambitious reform programs. The alternative would probably be a partial default on their sovereign debt.

Meanwhile, the Central and Eastern European member-states that joined the EU on 1 May 2005 are no longer the rather homogeneous group they used to be. Two clusters of countries can be distinguished. On the one hand, there are those that have major impediments to recovery, for instance Bulgaria or Latvia, which had previously experienced unsustainable booms. Hungary, Latvia, and Romania had or have severe problems with public debt levels and were compelled to request balance-of-payment loans from the EU and the IMF. On the other hand, with relatively strong private and public sector balances, some member-states like Poland and the Czech Republic were able to create a competitive export base during the pre-crisis period. Thanks to their recovery, and budgetary austerity in some Central and Eastern European member-states, they are converging economically and politically with the Eurozone's north (Germany, the Netherlands, Austria, Finland). Yet, even though the future prospects for these Central and Eastern European countries are good, their economies remain vulnerable to the growth performance of the EU, in general, and the Eurozone, in particular. Their domestic demand is not robust, and lower growth in the euro area will put further stress on the banking sector and reduce capital flows to Central and Eastern Europe. It could delay the revival of credit growth and domestic demand, or it might fuel a depreciation of some currencies.

Given these developments, a new economic map of the EU emerges. Until the economic crisis, there was a rather clear East–West divide, with most Western European countries belonging to the EMU, which promised them a comparable degree of stability in the first two years of the crisis. But, now, there are four Eurozone member-states that have severe public finance problems and struggle with low degrees of competitiveness. Greece, Ireland and Portugal have already received IMF- and EU-backed credits and guarantees as a result of which they do not need to issue more bonds until 2013. Other countries such as Spain may follow, and the €750 billion rescue fund now in place may have to be considerably increased. One of the most important risks to economic recovery (even in those member-states that are not hit by the sovereign debt crisis themselves) is that the financial sector suffers further stress. This eventuality could cause a credit crunch as banks are less and less willing to provide credit to the corporate sector. Demand could break down as a result, as could the impact of fiscal austerity that weighs heavily on domestic consumption in some member-states.[3] An overarching challenge is the reestablishment of trust by financial market actors who are increasingly prudent in their decisions to invest in public debt issued in the EU.

Despite the economic recovery, European growth rates are clearly below those in other economic areas. In particular, emerging markets grow with higher rates, like in pre-crisis times (see Table 26.A1 in the Appendix). Of course, emerging economies start from a much lower level of wealth, for example, measured in GDP per capita. But the fact that the recovery is quicker in emerging economies implies that the catch-up process is sped up compared with pre-crisis times. Hence, the loss of relative economic weight of the EU and the Eurozone will probably accelerate. Table 26.A2 in the Appendix shows the current trends in the distribution of regional shares in world GDP.

This relative loss of economic weight has strategic consequences for the EU and the Eurozone. First, Europe will further lose influence in global discussions on developments in international economics and finance. For instance with regard to financial market regulation or macroeconomic policy coordination, an economically weakened EU will be less and less likely to succeed in convincing its partners about European preferences. This trend is especially true in a G20-world that many observers see emerging, and in which the major policy choices influencing the international economic order are being made by China and the United States. It may put pressure on the European governments to pool their strength and to formally improve the external representation of the EU in matters of international economics and finance. Europe will be able to secure its place amongst the major players only if it combines a sound economic base (in terms of growth and internal convergence) with an effective representation of its interests on the global scale. If this combination is not assured and if internal divergences grow further and increase political tensions, the Eurozone (which, technically, from a macroeconomic perspective is one economy as long as the single currency and the single market exist) will continue not to be perceived and treated as such.

Under the exigencies of the sovereign debt crisis that has shaken the EU since the end of 2009, a broad reform process was launched in spring 2010. Reforms are supposed to ensure that a crisis similar to that which began in 2008 will never happen again. To tackle its root causes, reforms concern three areas: European surveillance and coordination of national budgetary policies; European surveillance and coordination of national economic policies; and the creation of a mechanism to solve and prevent sovereign debt crises. This agenda anticipates a revision of the EU Treaty, which Germany sees as necessary to create a permanent crisis resolution mechanism. Such a mechanism will include a rescue fund that will have to be compatible with the legal bases of the EU. The reform calendar foresees major decisions in 2011 and 2012.

In spring 2010, the EU's heads of state and government established the so-called Van Rompuy Task Force. It was a reaction to the creation of the €750 billion rescue fund mounted to provide credit to Eurozone member-states facing a liquidity crisis. Some member-states, in particular Germany, insisted that emergency aid should be accompanied by reforms that, in the future, would prevent similar crises in the Eurozone. The working group chaired by the new EU

Council president, Herman Van Rompuy, tabled its reform proposals in October 2010. In parallel, the European Commission published first drafts for related legislation, after having sketched its own proposals in several communications published since spring 2010. The details of the reforms are the subject of heated negotiations between the member-states and the European Parliament, which co-decides on four of six proposed regulations. But the major elements of the renewed economics governance rules in the Eurozone can still rather safely be forecast.

The EMU is unique in the world in that its single monetary policy is not matched by a unified fiscal or economic policy. These remain a national responsibility. But since the advent of the EMU, there have been rules and procedures that are supposed to prevent irresponsible budgetary policies and should ensure sound economic policies. The European rules for fiscal policy co-ordination are about to be modified for the third time since the negotiation of the 1992 Maastricht Treaty that created the EU.[4] In 1997, the 'Stability and Growth Pact' was adopted. Even before the EMU, this Pact added details and hardened the rules of the Maastricht Treaty, spelling out the terms for a more speedy procedure leading to sanctions. At the time, the Pact was widely seen as being one of the key guarantors of stability for the single currency. The architects of the Pact, notably the German Government, did not expect the sanction mechanism ever to be applied. That it existed was supposed to be enough of a deterrent to ensure sound fiscal policies under-pinning monetary stability.

Then, in 2005, the Pact was reformed to enable more political discretion in its application, in particular with the objective to allow governments to take into account cyclical conditions in single member-states because the stabilising role of fiscal policy had become a concern. Before this second reform, Powers like Germany, France, Portugal, and Italy had breached the deficit rules in the years of low economic growth (2002–4) and were about to face sanctions. The German and French Governments, in particular, pressured the Economic and Financial Affairs Council (Ecofin) (composed of the EU's finance ministers) to postpone temporarily the application of the sanctioning procedures. Pointing to the need to grant national fiscal policies a sufficient stabilising role, they won Ecofin support. However, a subsequent ruling of the European Court of Justice declared part of the Ecofin decision illegal, which reinforced the political dynamic towards further restructuring of the Pact.

In 2010, therefore, confronting the sovereign debt crisis, a new reform of the Stability Pact was initiated. This time it is part of a broader reform package to reinforce surveillance and coordination of national policies. A new surveillance cycle has been introduced, the so-called 'European Semester', the object of which is to connect better both the coordination of budgetary and economic policies and European and the national policy cycles. In the future, scrutiny on the European level should come timely enough actually to influence national debates and decisions, for instance on the annual budget. To ensure the effectiveness of European surveillance on national policy choices, a high degree of political ownership on the national level and political legitimacy needs to be ensured. A means to achieve this objective might involve national parliaments in the debates. In addition to these procedural innovations, a likely outcome of reforming the Stability Pact is that the variables subject to supervision will be expanded, paying particular attention to excessive debt; previously, the focus was primarily on deficits. The enforcement of the rules will be strengthened, meaning more efficient procedures and more weight for the European Commission in implementing them, and possibly harsher sanctions both in financial and reputational terms.

Fiscal responsibility will also be encouraged by setting minimum requirements for national fiscal frameworks to make sure they are in line with EU Treaty obligations. Experience with the EU's fiscal rules has revealed the problems of a coordination mechanism that requires peers to sanction each other. National fiscal rules are part of the attempt to improve national adherence to certain objectives. The European Commission has suggested that national budgetary frameworks include standards for public accounting systems, better statistics, better forecasting practices, numerical fiscal rules, independent national budget offices or institutions acting in the field of budgetary policy, budgetary procedures governing all stages of the budget process, medium-term budgetary frameworks, and fiscal relations across government layers.

Furthermore, economic policy co-ordination will probably be improved. It is today widely acknowledged that neither the debt crisis in Spain nor the one in Ireland would have been prevented, even with the new emerging fiscal control mechanisms. Indeed, persistent and large current-account imbalances and diverging competitiveness put the Eurozone under consistent tensions. The large current-account deficits and losses in competitiveness were associated with a misallocation of capital and labor, unsustainable accumulation of debt, and housing bubbles. Conversely, other member-states with external surpluses capitalised on their competitive export sectors, but domestic demand lagged behind, amplifying the gap between deficit and surplus countries within the euro area.

The mechanism that is foreseen in both the Van Rompuy report and the legislative proposals tabled by the European Commission would provide a framework for identifying and addressing macroeconomic imbalances, including deteriorating competitiveness trends. There will probably be an alert mechanism (a kind of scoreboard) that identifies member-states with potentially problematic levels of macroeconomic imbalances through a set of indicators to identify imbalances emerging in different parts of the economy. The Commission's proposal suggests that it would regularly publish the results of the scoreboard and would provide a list of member-states that risk running too large account deficits or surpluses. There would then be a debate in the Council and the Eurogroup, after which the Commission would provide in-depth country reviews. The reviews would take into account the severity of imbalances and possible spill-overs to other member-states, as well as the assessment of findings from stability and convergence programmes and the national reform programs. The Commission has proposed a rather far-reaching procedure: if there is a risk of macroeconomic imbalances, it issues preventive recommendations to the member-states concerned. Ultimately, there could be sanctions in the event of repeated non-compliance. Depending on the nature of the imbalances, the policy prescriptions could address fiscal, wage, and macrostructural, as well as macroprudential, policy aspects under the control of government authorities. The member-state concerned would basically have to set up a road map for implementing policy measures, and the Commission would monitor that state's implementation of corrective action and issue progress reports on a regular basis.

Introducing this kind of surveillance of member-state economic policies would be a big step forward if it obliges both deficit and surplus countries to take economic and budgetary policy choices in line with European objectives. However, without a truly binding mechanism at the EU level, the risk remains that the new rules will turn out to be a 'toothless tiger,' just as most fiscal rules have proven to be since the start of the EMU. Despite the depth and impact of the current crisis, there is currently no political appetite to create a European economic regime that could take binding decisions and have a budget significant enough to underwrite European economic policies and more.

The third major issue in the reform debate that will prove decisive in determining the Eurozone's future is the so-called crisis resolution mechanism. This instrument will probably include a permanent rescue fund for the period after spring 2013, when the current rescue fund will no longer be able to provide credit to member-states because of its limited duration. The European Financial Stability Facility was set up in May 2010 to provide credit to those Eurozone member-states in need of liquidity. Debates currently circle around a second pillar of a permanent crisis mechanism, a kind of orderly insolvency procedure for countries unable to service their debts. The idea is to involve creditors when it comes to sharing the losses if a Eurozone country has to resort to the crisis mechanism. Markets have reacted sceptically to these proposals. Given rising fears (the expanding use of bonds may increase further and the Eurozone may eventually break apart), a far-reaching debate over the question of the extent to which joint guarantees for sovereign debt should go in a monetary union has evolved. In addition to the idea of a much larger rescue fund, several member-states (for instance Luxembourg and Italy) have argued for joint European bonds for a certain percentage of public debt: up to an amount of 40 to 60 percent of GDP. Such a development would be a very important step forward towards integration. Meeting public debt has so far been a unique member-state responsibility and, until the emergence of the rescue packages of spring 2010, member-states were also solely responsible for paying back the debt. With the creation of a rescue fund that can both provide credit and guarantee a member-state's debt, the fundamental principle of individual states coping with their economic and fiscal problems alone has been overhauled. For some observers, introducing Eurobonds would be a logical step forward because the amount of the rescue funds in place are deemed insufficient to calm financial markets.

The current reform process may well lead to a more integrated EMU. The ideal scenario is that national policies are coordinated in such a way that internal divergences are considerably reduced whilst, at the same time, the member-states together implement a useful growth strategy and negotiate the new EU budget in a way that underpins these objectives. Meanwhile, financial markets have calmed, and the sovereign debt crisis was well handled thanks to the new crisis resolution mechanism. The supervision of national budgetary policies and the change of budgetary rules at the national level help member-states regain a course of budgetary consolidation and increase the long-term sustainability of public finances.

But this ideal scenario may not turn out to be the most realistic one. On the one hand, there are internal reasons: it can well be that member-states opt for a weak compromise to protect national sovereignty as far as possible. Moreover, economic recovery may not occur as anticipated; and, in this case, budgetary austerity may not lead to the expected consolidation if growth is too sluggish. On the other hand, there are reasons external to the Eurozone. There is no guarantee that the United States economy might not experience another severe economic downturn or that demand from Asia, mainly China, decrease. This effect can be increased if currencies move in such a way that the euro seriously appreciates whereas other currencies (say, the US\$, the yuan, or the yen) devalue. However, it is unlikely that China will give up the discretionary exchange rate policy that it has followed and that has produced a persistently undervalued exchange rate of the yuan. The low yuan puts other emerging countries under considerable pressure to weaken artificially their own currencies. Against this background, it becomes clear that the EU and, in particular, the Eurozone face important challenges; and they have to tackle them with their international partners, for instance in the G20. But the external representation of the Eurozone and the EU as a whole is fragmented across policy areas, and member-states are unwilling to surrender national influence or even a national seat, especially on the board of the IMF or in the G20. But nevertheless, the recent reform of the IMF board in the course of which the EU has lost two seats has triggered a new debate within the EU on its external representation in economic, financial, and monetary matters.

The EU's external representation in the field of international economics and finance is complex. The division of competencies between the member governments and the Union varies in terms of the different policy areas concerned both for internal decision-making and external representation. For the 17 member states of the Eurozone, the ECB and the Eurosystem formulate and implement monetary policy, whereas fiscal and economic policies remain the responsibility of the member-states with certain limits imposed by European rules and surveillance. With regard to external aspects related to the conduct of monetary policy (such as the sale and acquisition of foreign exchange assets or the conduct of international banking transactions), the statutes of the European System of Central Banks clarify technical matters. The ECB is also present in international financial institutions and organisations such as the IMF and the G20. As far as monetary policy is concerned, therefore, the Eurozone speaks with a single voice. There are further areas in which the external representation of the EU is based on unconditional delegation to the EU level, for instance competition and trade policy, issues related to the single market, and development aid. In these areas, the European Commission speaks for the EU.

Exchange rate policy, in contrast, is a shared responsibility between the ECB and the national finance ministers. Both pursue distinct objectives: whereas the ECB is obliged to ensure price stability, the finance ministers pursue broader fiscal and economic policy objectives that may or may not be compatible with the aim of ensuring low inflation. The EU Treaty leaves some ambiguities over the organisation of exchange rate policies, which reflect precisely this conflict over price-stability orientation and the ECB's independence, on one hand, and other objectives and means for economic policy making, on the other.[5] According to Article 219 of the 'Consolidated Version of the Treaty on the Functioning of the European Union',[6] the Eurozone can enter a system of fixed exchange rates with countries outside the EU, and it can formulate general orientations for exchange rate policy that, however, must not endanger the ECB's objective of price stability. Formal agreements have to be decided with unanimity by the Eurozone Finance Ministers upon proposal by the ECB or the Commission and after consultation of the European Parliament.

Since the euro has been introduced, the formal instruments such as the general orientations have not been applied. Even when preparing the ground for the foreign exchange interventions to strengthen the euro in autumn 2000, the Eurogroup decided to comment on the issue in a *communiqué*. The Eurogroup has still not systemically formulated common positions on exchange rate developments and policies. This situation is partly because views diverge strongly. In spring and summer 2008, when the Euro appreciated strongly against the American dollar and other important currencies, it became particularly clear. Amongst others, the two largest EMU member-states, Germany and France, publicly disagreed over the question about whether there was a need to intervene to weaken the Euro (a French quest) or whether the strong Euro was no problem for the European economy (for a long time the view of the German finance minister). More consistency in opinions and public statements is a prerequisite for a common exchange rate policy and for the Eurogroup to reclaim authority from the ECB, which has practically taken the dominant role in the EMU's first decade.[7] Alternatively, a majority vote on exchange rate issues would enable the Eurogroup to act more decidedly, but this reform would require a change of the EU Treaty and would not receive unanimous support by all member-states.

For fiscal, financial, and economic policies the member-states (especially the large ones present in the G-formats) represent their national interests in international forums and bilateral relationships, even if their governments seek common positions in the Council. In the IMF and the G20, efforts are made to coordinate national positions. But so far, there has been no willingness to merge seats. The 'economic side' remains fragmented for a further reason. Depending on the policy issue at stake, different EU actors have to be involved. So, in addition to the member-states, there may be the Eurogroup President, the rotating Council presidency, which chairs the Ecofin, the Commissioner for Economic and Monetary Affairs, or the Commissioner for Trade.

Most EU member-states hold bilateral relationships with key strategic partners such as the United States, China, or India. In addition, the EU has regular bilateral forums with the world's key economic Powers dealing with macroeconomic and financial issues to complement the multilateral forums. Most dialogue with strategic partners is held by the EU27, and not by the Eurozone, although the ECB President generally participates. An exception was a Eurozone-'troika' trip to China in November 2007 by Eurogroup President Jean-Claude Juncker, European Commissioner Joaquín Almunia, and ECB President Jean-Claude Trichet.[8]

The economic and financial crisis has considerably strengthened the case for an improved external representation of the EU and, in particular, of the Eurozone in international financial and economic matters. In the course of post-2008 crisis management, the insufficiencies of the current arrangements became clear. The volatility of financial markets, and especially the spill-over effects between financial market actors, different segments, and national markets, provides reason for the EU and the Eurozone to act with one voice on international financial matters. Even before the outbreak of the crisis, there were strong arguments for a single European voice.[9] Sharing a single monetary and exchange rate policy makes it logical for the participating member-states also to defend a common position in international forums dealing with macroeconomic matters such as the IMF and the G7–G8. It is especially so as the Eurozone has become more exposed to international portfolio shifts as a result of the substitutability between assets denominated in euros or in American dollars.

Moreover, new approaches to international economic and financial cooperation have emerged. The agenda (for instance in the G20 format) now comprises various policy questions in which the EU or the Eurozone should make their voice heard. On the question of financial market regulation or exchange rate policies, for example, a consolidated representation of the euro area in international forums would strengthen the euro area's negotiating power and could increase its gains from international policy coordination. Given the relative decline of the EU in comparison with emerging markets, pooling the external representation in international financial institutions may become necessary to maintain influence. In addition, many EU partners would prefer dealing with a single interlocutor rather than with a multitude of different actors. Consolidating external representation would not only enable the Eurozone to better defend its interest, but could also increase the interest of other players to cooperate with it. With regard to the international financial institutions, the EU member-states have to face the criticism that the EU is overrepresented. In October 2010, the G20 decided on a reform of the IMF. The package includes a shift of quotas, a change in the Fund's capital stock, and a recomposition of the Executive Board. The European Powers have to give up two of their current eight seats in favor of large emerging market countries.

The reasons why the external representation of the EU or the Eurozone in economic and financial matters is not improved relate mostly to sovereignty concerns. Member-states possibly have strongly diverging views and do not want to run the risk of not being able to make their opinion heard internationally. National representation in global institutions and forums offers influence, and political prestige. As the Commission report puts it: '... some euro countries who find themselves in a privileged situation, holding the Chair or the Alternate Executive Director position of their constituencies, may fear a loss of influence from a consolidation of chairs'.[10] So there is a rather high probability that countries will refrain from giving up their seats for longer-term gains that are perceived as vague.

The economic and financial crisis has revealed the interdependencies and the divergences of the European economies, highlighting insufficiencies in the governance mechanisms. What the sovereign debt crisis has made particularly clear is that those countries that have integrated their currencies share very close ties over the real economies and the financial sectors. They need to strengthen policy coordination and to improve governance instruments. For the first time since the euro's introduction in 1999, there is a widespread consensus that the EMU needs specific governance mechanisms and political integration, which will bring the member states that share a currency closer together both economically and politically. The Eurozone will hence form a more closely integrated core of the EU27. But real political union is still not on the horizon: member-states are extremely prudent to transfer further parts of national sovereignty (for instance in the field of budgetary or economic policy) to the EU level both with regard to internal governance and external representation.

The large member-states such as Germany and France will continue to play a strong role both within the Eurozone and in the interaction with key strategic partners outside Europe. Thanks to its economic weight and large contribution to the rescue packages for those member-states hit by the sovereign debt crisis, Germany in particular has gained a strong leadership role that it uses to pursue reforms of EU governance mechanisms and push other member-states towards national policies that consolidate public finances and improve competitiveness. Meanwhile, Germany's attention in terms of its own economic performance is not solely focused on the Eurozone, but it competes in world markets as a result of its large share of exports to non-European countries.

The years 2010 and 2011 are particularly complex because of the need to manage in parallel the sovereign debt crisis and the reform of economic governance. As recent experience has shown, reform proposals and disputes between member states influence markets and can aggravate sovereign debt crises. But on the other hand, a broad reform of the governance mechanisms of the Eurozone may turn out to be an important condition for the eventual resolution of the current sovereign debt crisis. An institutional shake-up of the EMU along with ambitious national reform and austerity programmes are key to regain market confidence, end contagion, and improve EU competitiveness in global comparison. But the risk of failure is still there, whether because the member-states do not manage to agree on convincing crisis management and governance reform measures or because new economic tensions emerge that aggravate divergence in the Eurozone to such a degree that the single currency is no longer sustainable for all members.

Appendix

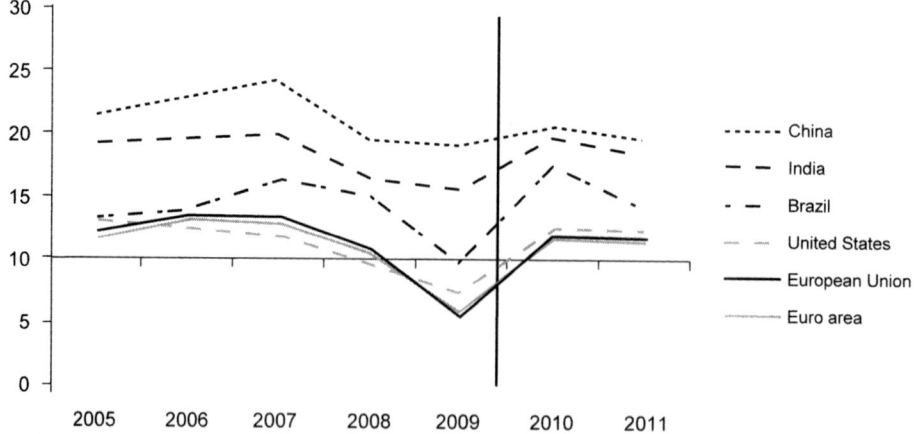

Figure 26.A1 GDP, constant prices, percent change (2005–11 (estimate))
Source: International Monetary Fund, World Economic Outlook Database, October 2010.

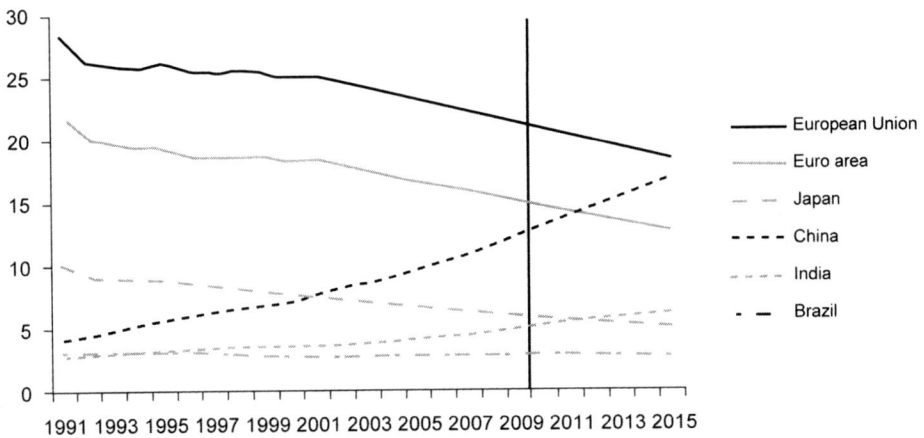

Figure 26.A2 GDP based on purchasing-power-parity (PPP) share of world total
DataSource: International Monetary Fund, 2010.

Notes

1 For a detailed argumentation see S. Dullien and D. Schwarzer, 'Bringing macro-economics into the EU budget debate: Why and How', *Journal of Common Market Studies*, 47(January 2009), 153–74.
2 Sebastian Dullien and Ulrich Fritsche, 'Anhaltende Divergenz bei Inflations–und Lohnentwicklung in der Eurozone: Gefahr für die Währungsunion?', *Vierteljahreshefte zur Wirtschaftsforschung*, 4(2007), 56–76.
3 See for instance: International Monetary Fund, *World Economic Outlook Update, Restoring confidence without harming recovery* (7 July 2010), S.7f: www.imf.org/external/pubs/ft/weo/2010/update/02/pdf/0710.pdf.
4 See, for example, D. Schwarzer, *Fiscal Policy Co-ordination in the EMU. A Preference-Based Explanation of Institutional Change* (Baden-Baden, 2007).
5 For this conflict, see for instance, C.R. Henning, 'Organizing Foreign Exchange Intervention in the Euro Area', *Journal of Common Market Studies*, 45(2007), 317ff.
6 'Consolidated Version of the Treaty on the Functioning of the European Union', (9 May 2008).
7 Ibid., 335.
8 J. Pisani-Ferry, P. Aghion, M. Belka, J. von Hagen, L. Heikensten, and A. Sapir, *Coming of Age: Report on the Euro Area* (Brussels, 2008), 89.
9 A good summary of the arguments for a consolidated external representation is given by the European Commission, *The Euro@ten, Successes and Challenges after ten years of Economic and Monetary Union* (Brussels, 2008), 281ff.
10 Ibid., 146.

27

The Organization of the Petroleum Exporting Countries and contemporary international politics and economy

Houchang Hassan-Yari

Most international regional, political, military, and economic organizations were created during the course of the twentieth century. Some of them like the Warsaw Pact have disappeared. Another, the European Economic Community (or the Common Market), was renamed the European Community (EC) and finally transformed into the European Union. The Organization of African Unity has been superseded by the African Union without introducing significant change in its structures or functions.

The Organization of the Petroleum Exporting Countries (OPEC) has evolved very slowly in adapting to the reality of the international market, whilst maintaining most of its administrative structure. As a permanent, intergovernmental organization concerned with the crude oil policies of its members and the world market, OPEC was created in the context of nationalist claims and the quest for sovereignty by the Third World countries, controlling the seven big multinational oil companies, and protecting member-states' revenue from the volatilities of the oil market caused by lack of discipline and overproduction. It all began in 1949 when Venezuela approached Iran, Iraq, Kuwait, and Saudi Arabia about establishing closer cooperation in managing their energy resources. It took a decade of deliberations and intense negotiations to establish OPEC on 14 September 1960 in Baghdad as a permanent organization with international status by an agreement established between the five founding members: Iran, Iraq, Kuwait, Saudi Arabia, and Venezuela.

Once created, OPEC was approached by new candidates, willing to join. Qatar in 1961, Indonesia[1] and Libya in 1962, Abu Dhabi in 1967, Algeria in 1969, Nigeria in 1971, Ecuador in 1973,[2] Gabon in 1975,[3] and Angola in 2007 became full members. In 1974, Abu Dhabi's full membership was transferred to the United Arab Emirates. Currently, the Organization has twelve member countries. Its initial home was established in Geneva in 1961; four years later, the Organization's Secretariat moved to Vienna.

In 1961, OPEC adopted its original Statute, the constitution of the Organization. Article 7 (C) of the Statute defines the membership of the Organization: 'Any other country with a substantial net export of crude petroleum, which has fundamentally similar interests to those of Member Countries, may become a Full Member of the Organization, if accepted by a majority of three-fourths of Full Members, including the concurrent vote of all Founder Members.' The same article, Section (D), describes another category of membership: 'A net petroleum-exporting country, which does not qualify for membership under paragraph C above, may nevertheless be admitted as an Associate Member by the Conference under such special conditions as may be prescribed by the Conference, if accepted by a majority of three-fourths, including the concurrent vote of all Founder Members.'[4]

The Statute has created three organs that constitute the internal structure of OPEC. They are, the 'Conference' or the supreme authority of the Organization, the Board of Governors, and the Secretariat. Composed of delegations representing the member countries, the Conference periodically elects a President and an Alternate President (Article 14, A). The Secretary-General is the Secretary of the Conference (Article 14, C). Article 15 stipulates that the Conference shall formulate the general policy of the Organization and determine the appropriate ways and means of its implementation; decide upon any application for OPEC membership; confirm the appointment of members of the Board of Governors; direct the Board of Governors to submit reports or make recommendations on any matters of interest to the Organization; consider, or decide upon, the reports and recommendations submitted by the Board of Governors on the affairs of the organization; consider and decide upon the Organization's budget as submitted by the Board of Governors; consider and decide upon the Statement of Accounts and the Auditor's Report, as submitted by the Board of Governors; appoint the Chairman of the Board of Governors and an Alternate Chairman; appoint the Secretary-General; and appoint the Auditor of the Organization for a duration of one year.[5]

Article 20 deals with the responsibilities of the Board of Governors, which assumes the legislative power as in any other constitutional body. The Board of Governors directs the management of the Organization's affairs and the implementation of the decisions of the Conference; considers and decides upon any reports submitted by the Secretary-General; submits reports and makes recommendations to the Conference on the affairs of the Organization; draws up the budget for each calendar year and submits it to the Conference for approval; nominates the Auditor of the Organization for a duration of one year; considers the Statement of Accounts and the Auditor's Report and submits them to the Conference for approval; approves the appointment of Directors of Divisions and Heads of Departments, upon nomination by Member Countries, due consideration being given to the recommendations of the Secretary-General; convenes Extraordinary Meetings of the Conference; and prepares the Agenda for the Conference.[6]

Working at the headquarters in Vienna, the Secretariat is responsible for the executive functions of OPEC in accordance with the provisions of the establishing Statute under the direction of the Board of Governors. The Secretariat is composed of the Secretary-General and staff members. Articles 25–34 of the Statute define the scope of responsibilities of the Secretary-General, who is the legally authorized representative of the Organization. Compared with the Conference (guided by seven articles) and the Board of Governors (eight articles), ten articles are devoted to the duties of the Secretariat and the Secretary-General. The latter organizes and administers the work of the Organization; ensures that the functions and duties assigned to the Secretariat's different departments are carried out; prepares reports for submission to each meeting of the Board of Governors concerning matters that call for consideration and decision; informs the Chairman and other members of the Board of Governors of all activities of the Secretariat, of all studies undertaken, and of the progress of the implementation of the resolutions of the Conference. Finally, he ensures the due performance of the duties that may be assigned to the Secretariat by the Conference or the Board of Governors.[7] The Organization has appointed 27 secretaries-general from 1961 to 2007. The first and last time an Iranian representative occupied that post was from 1961 to 1964. Iraq, Kuwait, Venezuela, and Libya assumed the

Secretary-General position three times, Saudi Arabia and Algeria, Qatar, Ecuador, Gabon once, Indonesia five times, and Nigeria four times.

Why is it that the biggest oil-producing countries, Saudi Arabia and Iran, only once had their candidates selected to serve at the helm of the Organization whereas representatives of marginal states like Indonesia (in terms of oil production and market impact) were nominated Secretary-General five times? Infighting, rivalry, and a lack of trust could explain the anomaly.

As a founding member of the OPEC, Iran has been insisting since 1986 that it should be entitled to the post of Secretary-General, as each of the other member countries had previously held this position. The objection of some member countries, because of political differences, prevented Iran from undertaking this post.[8] The appointment of the twenty-seventh Secretary-General illustrates the state of the relationship between the heavyweights, political divisions, and internal dynamics of the Organization.

At its conference on 14 December 2006, OPEC decided not to select Hossein Kazempour Ardebili, Iran's Governor for OPEC for 20 years and a former minister in the Iranian Government, or his opponent, Adnan Shehab from Kuwait, to be OPEC's Research Manager. It appointed Abdullah Salem El Badri from Libya as its Secretary-General for a period of three years which took effect from 1 January 2007. This Decision brought to a close the impasse which lasted for three years regarding the appointment of a Secretary-General. Political rivalries between Iran and Saudi Arabia continued to divide OPEC members over the process of nominating the Organization's new Secretary-General for many years.

The wave of independence of the Third World territories in the 1950s and 1960s populated the United Nations (UN) with many revolutionary Powers that now claim a new world order in international politics. The most important point in claiming a new world order lay in the adjustment of prices of raw materials and agricultural products from the Third World. The 1973 Arab–Israel October War was a turning point in this and other areas. When the Arab member-states of OPEC decided to boycott any country that supported Israel during the war, the price of oil increased fourfold. The Organization of Arab Petroleum Exporting Countries (OAPEC) is an intergovernmental organization established in 1968 by an agreement amongst Arab countries that rely on the export of petroleum to coordinate their energy policies. OAPEC is concerned with the development of the petroleum industry by fostering cooperation amongst its members: Algeria, Bahrain, Egypt, Iraq, Kuwait, Libya, Qatar, Saudi Arabia, Syria, Tunisia, and the United Arab Emirates. Also, it contributes to the effective use of the resources of member countries through sponsoring joint ventures. It is guided by a belief in the importance of building an integrated petroleum industry as a cornerstone for future economic integration amongst Arab countries.[9] One of the most important actions taken by OAPEC was the use of oil as a weapon in conjunction with OPEC in proclaiming an oil embargo against the United States' decision to resupply the Israeli military during the 1973 war.

The embargo lasted only a few months (October 1973–March 1974) because the Arab states' use of economic coercion to achieve political objectives had its limits.[10] The OPEC and OAPEC embargo resulted in the interruption of oil supply to the United States and its European allies, high oil prices, and an economic crisis with a persistent, long-term political scar. The shock also caused a strong rift within the Western camp, where some Europeans, the Canadians, and the Japanese sought to disassociate themselves from the American pro-Israel Middle East policy. At the European Council in Copenhagen in December 1973, shortly after the October War and onset of the oil embargo, dissension between the Americans and their allies forced the Europeans to launch the Euro-Arab Dialogue as a forum shared by the EC and the League of Arab States. Dialogue arose out of a French initiative. The Euro-Arab Dialogue sought to address different issues for different parties. For Europeans, it was to be a forum to avoid any future surprise in discussing economic affairs, whereas the Arab side saw it as one to discuss political affairs, particularly their conflict with Israel.[11]

Arab oil producers had linked the end of the embargo with successful United States efforts to create peace in the Middle East. Pressured by all sides, the Nixon Administration began parallel negotiations with Arab oil producers to end the embargo, and with Egypt, Syria, and Israel to arrange a withdrawal of Israeli forces from the Sinai and the Golan Heights after the fighting stopped. The shuttle diplomacy of the US Secretary of State, Henry Kissinger, bore fruit. By 18 January 1974, he had negotiated a partial withdrawal of Israeli troops from the Sinai and a promise of a negotiated settlement between Israel and Syria on the Golan Heights. These half-measures were sufficient to convince Arab oil producers to lift the embargo in March 1974. By May, Israel agreed to withdraw from the Golan Heights. To illustrate the actual impact of the American diplomacy, the Israeli commitment to peace, and, most important, Arab resolve, it is sufficient to point out that Israel withdrew from the Sinai after the Camp David peace process with Egypt in 1978–79, the Golan Heights continue to be occupied by the Israel Defence Force, and the Palestinian-occupied territories of the West Bank and Gaza were not even subjects considered by serious Arab, Israel, and American negotiators.

Despite its failure to produce any significant change in the military relationship between the United States and Israel, or to contribute in freeing the Arab land occupied by Israel since the June 1967 war, the Arab oil embargo has showed how much impact a Third World region had on life in the Western countries. The increase of oil prices and the Western countries' panic and dependency on a commodity produced elsewhere emboldened other underdeveloped countries to claim fair prices for their exports.

International trade and financial relations have been regulated and institutionalized since the final phase of the Second World War. The Bretton Woods system created two pivotal regulatory institutions: the International Monetary Fund and the International Bank for Reconstruction and Development (IBRD), one of five World Bank group agencies. They are all part of the UN system. The World Bank mission is to fight poverty through financial and technical assistance to underdeveloped countries. There are three pillars of the World Bank development agenda: results (helping developing countries deliver measurable results); reform (improving investment lending, access to information, and decentralization in assisting governments and communities); and resources (assuring the 187 member-states about their strong financial partner in their endeavors via the IBRD and the International Development Association).[12] The most relevant international agencies in the field of assistance and development have been created in the massive absence of the same countries that had been identified as primary beneficiaries of aid. The decolonization process has changed the demographic face of the UN and its organs without introducing any meaningful reform in the management and decision-making methods of running the same agencies. The OPEC–OAPEC oil embargo and price rise was the first real challenge to the established top to bottom world economic order.

On 1 May 1974, the UN General Assembly adopted the 'Declaration on the Establishment of a New International Economic Order' resolution.[13] For the first time, the Declaration studied the problems of raw materials and development and urged the establishment of a 'New International Economic Order' based on equity, sovereign equality, interdependence, common interest, and cooperation amongst all states, irrespective of their economic and social systems that shall correct inequalities and redress existing injustices, make it possible to eliminate the widening gap between developed and developing countries, and ensure steadily accelerating economic and social development and peace and justice for present and future generations. Article 2 of the resolution asserted:

The present international economic order is in direct conflict with current developments in international political and economic relations. Since 1970 the world economy has experienced a series of grave crises which have had severe repercussions, especially on the developing countries because of their generally greater vulnerability to external economic impulses. The developing world has become a powerful factor that makes its influence felt in all fields of international activity. These irreversible changes in the relationship of forces in the world necessitate the active, full and equal participation of the developing countries in the formulation and application of all decisions that concern the international community.[14]

The oil embargo, and the shock it provoked, was undeniably one of the 'grave crises' that invoked the resolution in claiming partnership instead of assertiveness.

Article 4 of the resolution stipulated that the new international economic order should be founded on full respect for twenty principles.[15] It stems from Principle (a) that the underdeveloped (or as the UN called them, 'developing') countries continued to be traumatized by the sequels of the past colonial rule and fight to prevent a new form of future domination. It sought 'Sovereign equality of States, self-determination of all peoples, inadmissibility of the acquisition of territories by force, territorial integrity and non-interference in the internal affairs of other States'. This principle clearly shows how intertwined the political aspirations and economic issues are and that, without the former, the latter would remain unachievable. Principle (e) laid down very eloquently the interdependence of political and economic spheres in attaining any significant development goal by claiming:

> Full permanent sovereignty of every State over its natural resources and all economic activities. In order to safeguard these resources, each State is entitled to exercise effective control over them and their exploitation with means suitable to its own situation, including the right to nationalization or transfer of ownership to its nationals, this right being an expression of the full permanent sovereignty of the State. No State may be subjected to economic, political or any other type of coercion to prevent the free and full exercise of this inalienable right.

As far as the oil embargo is concerned and its place in the hierarchy of 'grave crisis' that created an environment in which the 'New International Economic Order' was launched, one can only argue that the Arab states have inadvertently become an agent for claiming change. To put it succinctly, they were simply angry at the United States and other Western Powers for their pro-Israeli stance during the 1973 October War. The oil embargo was the only effective weapon that Arabs had in their arsenal to influence the course of war. An analysis of post-embargo events demonstrates that Arab diplomatic weaponry had a limited reach and, in the best case scenario, marginally contributed to the liberation of Arab lands occupied by Israel. It is worth remembering Egypt's expulsion from the Arab League following Cairo's peace treaty with Israel. As for the support to Israel by the United States and other Western states, it will attain new records in the future.

However, the embargo had a real impact on the world economy. It enabled Arab countries to develop some segments of their economies. It also provided Arab state clients with billions of dollars to fuel the military and industrial complex in the United States and its allies, as well as in the Communist camp that had its own Arab clients ready to purchase huge quantities of arms. These weapons will not be used against Israel, because the 1973 War was the last major Arab–Israel clash, but in inter-Arab fighting.

In March 1971, the United States lost control of crude oil prices to OPEC. If the price of oil produced by OPEC began to rise significantly after the 1973 embargo, one needs to recall the role played by the United States in increasing its own oil prices through a complex (and bizarre) oil industry regulation mechanism long before the OPEC move:

By August 1973, regulation of petroleum prices had become complex. There was old oil and new oil, released oil and stripper oil. Old oil was defined in terms of a base production control level, which was the volume of oil produced from reservoirs during 1972. New oil was oil from reservoirs discovered after 1972. Reserved oil was defined as that oil produced from old reservoirs in excess of the 1972 base production control level, plus an equal amount of old oil. Since the price of released oil was uncontrolled, the value of a barrel produced in excess of the base production level exceeded the world price by the difference between the old oil price and the world price. Prices for the old oil were defined in terms of the price existing in May 1972 plus 35 cents. Stripper oil was petroleum from wells producing less than ten barrels per day. New and stripper oil sold at the world prices. . . . As of March 1979, old oil sold for $5.82 a barrel, new oil for $12.84, Naval petroleum reserve oil for $13.97, stripper oil for $14.88, and Alaskan oil at the well head for $6.66 a barrel.[16]

Based on this complex mechanism, the price of American lower tier oil was US$2.85 on 20 June 1960. It jumped to US$5.20, whereas released and stripper oil was US$8.55 in December 1973. The price of lower tier and released and stripper oil in the subsequent years was, respectively, US$5.20 and US$11.20 in December 1974 and US$5.20 and US$13.10 in November 1975. Prices froze at this level until 1 January 1977 (US$5.44 and US$14.95 in December 1977) and were almost the same in 1978.[17] In comparison, in 1972, the price of crude oil was about US$3.00 per barrel. By the end of 1974, the price had quadrupled to over US$12.00. From 1974 to 1978, the world crude oil price was relatively flat, ranging from US$12.21 per barrel to US$13.55 per barrel.[18]

The situation changed dramatically in the late 1970s and early 1980s with the Iran–Iraq war. From a new record high, crude oil prices plummeted below $10.00 by mid-1986. OPEC internal strife, non-observance of quotas and overproduction by member-states, and the end of fear of an Iranian victory over Iraq largely contributed to a free fall in prices. OPEC failed to stabilize prices by setting an $18.00 per barrel target in December 1986. Prices rallied with the invasion of Kuwait by Iraq in August 1990. A steady decline followed the invasion when a large military coalition led by the United States forced the Iraqis out of Kuwait in 1991. A strong American economy and a rapid growth in the Asian Pacific region economies contributed to a short period of oil price recovery that was abruptly interrupted by the economic crisis in Asia and a not very untimely 10 percent increase in OPEC production. After the collapse of prices, another cycle of increases began early in 2000, followed by yet another fall.[19]

A good example of market volatility and OPEC's inability effectively to influence it goes back to Summer 2008. At that time

OPEC . . . failed to prevent oil rising to a record $147.27 a barrel in July, driven by demand from China and other Asian economies and speculative purchases. The oil producers' group has also been unable to stem the plunge in oil to below $40 . . . amid recession in the U.S. and Europe, even with an announced cut of 4.2 million barrels a day in production from its September levels.[20]

From the rollercoaster cycle of price and production, a preliminary lesson could be learned: that OPEC lost its ability to control the oil world market, contrary to what some politicians deny in blaming the Organization for the erratic behavior of the market. Non-OPEC producers in the North Sea, Russia, and consumer conduct with green attempts weigh considerably in the market.

The U.S. Energy Department's Energy Information Agency (EIA) confirmed seven of the world's fifteen largest oil producers are outside of OPEC. As of 2006, those countries were Russia, the United States, China, Mexico, Canada, Norway, and Brazil. Britain had been on the EIA's list as of 2004, but production has continued to decline significantly in the North Sea . . .

Overall in 2007, non-OPEC nations produced roughly 48 million bpd, comprising nearly 60 percent of total production for the year.[21]

Kazakhstan, Azerbaijan, Sudan, and Chad add more oil to the market.

The evaluation of the OPEC share of the world oil production reveals a major discrepancy between the Organization's oil reserves and oil production. Figures 27.1 and 27.2 show the OPEC share of the world crude oil reserves have been significantly improved in 2009 compared with 2004:

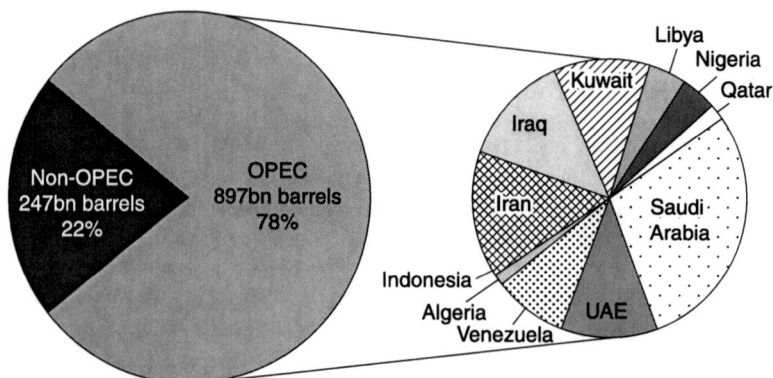

Figure 27.1   OPEC share of world crude oil reserves (2004)
Source: OPEC, www.opec.org/ *and* www.opec.org/opec_web/static_files_project/media/downloads/publications/ ASB2004.pdf

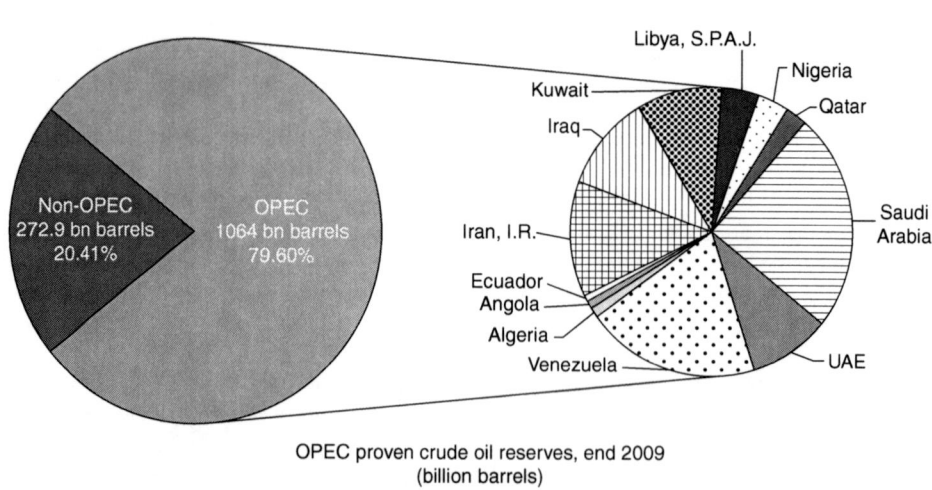

OPEC proven crude oil reserves, end 2009
(billion barrels)

Saudi Arabia	264.59	24.9%	Iraq	115.00	10.8%	Libya, S.P.A.J	46.42	4.4%	Algeria	12.20	1.1%
Venezuela	211.17	19.8%	Kuwait	101.50	9.5%	Nigeria	37.20	3.5%	Angola	9.50	0.9%
Iran, I.R.	137.01	12.9%	UAE	97.80	9.2%	Qatar	25.38	2.4%	Ecuador	6.51	0.6%

Figure 27.2   OPEC shares of world crude oil reserves (2009)
Source: OPEC Annual Statistical Bulletin 2009.

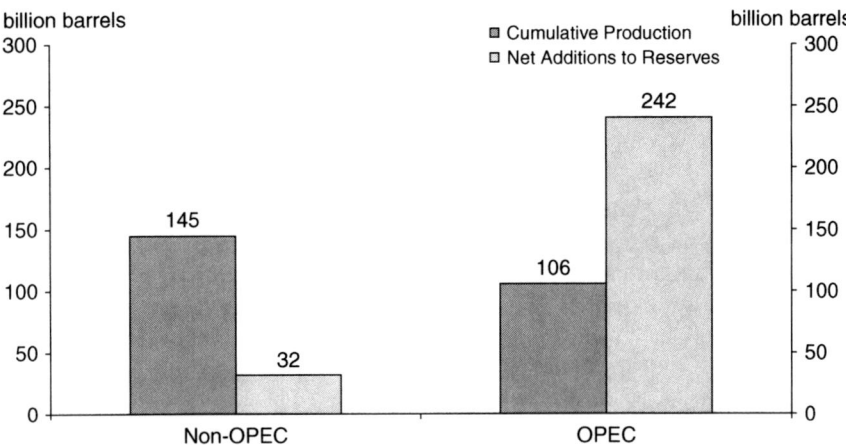

Figure 27.3 World crude oil reserves (2000–2009), cumulative production versus net additions
Source: OPEC Annual Statistical Bulletin 2009.

OPEC's *Annual Statistical Bulletin* published in 2009 estimates more than three-quarters of the world's proven oil reserves are located in its member-states, with 70 percent of total OPEC oil reserves in the Middle East. Organization member-states have made significant additions to their oil reserves in recent years, for example, by adopting the best practices in the industry. As a result, the *Bulletin* confirms, OPEC's proven oil reserves currently stand at well above 1,000 billion barrels.[22]

As Figure 27.3 illustrates, during the period 2000–2009, OPEC member-states added 242 billion barrels to their total oil reserves, substantially more than the reserve additions made by non-OPEC crude oil producers.[23]

OPEC needs to be more active in encouraging its member-states to develop strategies for the diversification of their economies and reducing their reliance on oil revenue. The big improvement in the Organization's crude reserves has created a false sense of confidence amongst its member-states. As long as the current American, Chinese, and other big consumers' addiction to oil goes unchecked,[24] OPEC countries do not see any urgency to prepare for a post-oil world. Currently oil prices remain in a comfortable zone for both suppliers and consumers. This situation facilitates the task of *rentier* states in distributing hydrocarbon revenues amongst their populace, whilst preventing consumers from seriously seeking an alternative clean energy to fuel their economies. If the addiction to oil is denounced by many in the West, the utter dependency of the OPEC members on petro-dollars weakens any chance for a successful transit from authoritarian regimes to democracy. Their vulnerable economies remain at the mercy of a market they do not control. The half measures introduced by Powers such as Iran in developing some aspects of human capital are not sufficient to overcome the bigger failures of the political system in bringing in badly needed structural changes in their economies.

Despite their immense energy resources, all members of OPEC continue to be listed amongst the underdeveloped countries of the world. Comparing them with few other Third World states that elevated their population to a very high level of development, like South Korea, all members of the Organization are at an early stage of development if judged by relevant social and economic indicators.[25] The high gross domestic product of some smaller oil-producing countries hides the larger problem of excessive political underdevelopment, gender inequality, and discrimination of communities based on ethnic background and religious affiliation. In other words, not all citizens in oil-producing countries equally enjoy the hydrocarbon revenues.

The boom of 1973 and subsequent years has generated substantial wealth for OPEC. To lessen criticism about the increase in oil prices and demonstrate its solidarity with the underdeveloped countries, in 1976, OPEC created its own Fund for International Development (OFID). OFID grants low-cost credits to developing states and provides humanitarian aid. As of the end of November 2005, OPEC calculated that it had spent US$7,758.7 million on aid.[26] Technical assistance operations have constituted OFID's core grants activities. The grants accord high priority to women and children in its national and regional development projects that aim at sustainable development and poverty reduction. The Organization also provides funds for research and intellectual activities by increasing South–South and North–South cooperation in the areas of capacity-building, human capital, and advancement of science and technology. Its emergency aid operations assist victims of natural disasters and loans with low interest to reconstruction of devastated regions, in conjunction with international agencies such as UN High Commissioner for Refugees. In June 2001, OFID launched its special grant account for human immunodeficiency virus/acquired immune deficiency syndrome operations. A special grant for Palestine has been created to provide social and economic assistance to the Palestinian-occupied territories of the West Bank and Gaza Strip. The Food Aid account was set up to combat hunger and famine in drought-prone sub-Saharan Africa. The establishment of the International Fund for Agricultural Development benefited from OFID assistance in channelling contributions from the Organization's member states. Albania, Belize, Cambodia, China, Colombia, Cuba, the Dominican Republic, Grenada, Guatemala, the Kyrgyz Republic, Nepal, Turkey, Yemen, and a dozen other countries in Africa are amongst the beneficiaries of the OFID's development projects.[27]

OPEC members have proven wrong a well-known assumption in international relations: that regional organizations are established to create more cohesion amongst their member states. As an intergovernmental organization, OPEC membership comes from Asia, Africa, and Latin America, with the majority of members, production, and reserves being in the Middle East. The relationships amongst the Middle Eastern members of the Organization have never been very cordial. The Iraq–Iran war of 1980–88 lasted eight years and caused hundreds of thousands of casualties and billions of dollars of damages to both Powers. Millions have been internally displaced or forced into exile. The cost of lost opportunities is incalculable. Experts continue to debate the exact number of casualties and the real cost of material destruction. Many regions in Iran and Iraq remain inaccessible because of millions of unmarked mines emplaced during the war. Some regions are still not rebuilt more than two decades after the cessation of hostilities. The war left deep scars on OPEC and disrupted its normal functions. After Iran, the Baathist regime in Baghdad launched a new misadventure by invading Kuwait. The war caused enormous destruction to both countries and the natural environment when Iraqis set fire to dozens of Kuwaiti oil wells.

In both cases, after the absorption of initial shock, other members of the Organization stepped in by providing sufficient oil to relieve the market stress. Saudi Arabia has border problems with a number of its neighbors. Iran is challenged by the United Arab Emirates, which claim three of its islands in the Persian Gulf. Difficult relations between the Middle Eastern members of OPEC are not limited to territorial disputes. Religion is equally divisive. The Shia–Sunni dispute and the excessive politicization of religion appear to be a more agonizing problem to solve.

The aforementioned disputes are just a few examples of deep political and religious issues that separate member-states of OPEC in the Middle East. Based on that account, one can conclude the relative failure of the Organization. However, the criticism on the issue of integration and cohesion of OPEC must be tempered. The Organization was established to regulate the oil market, the level of production, and pricing whilst seeking to protect the interests of its members. Seen from this angle, it can be argued that OPEC has managed to survive several crises, some of which had the potential to paralyze the Organization.

The Organization celebrated its fiftieth anniversary on 14 September 2010.[28] On this occasion, its Secretary-General reiterated the Organization's determination to protect the sovereign interests of members in securing them a steady income, as well as ensuring efficient and regular supplies of oil to consumers at prices that are fair and acceptable. Like the rest of the international community, OPEC was deeply affected by the global financial meltdown after 2008. Demand for petroleum dropped sharply, shaking profoundly the fragile foundations of the Organization's member-states. Smaller members in terms of the size of their population managed the recession better because they could enjoy a cushion of good financial reserves.

Contrary to the post-1973 events, OPEC today is much less politicized and fully conscious about the need to ensure a stable oil market for the benefit of producers and consumers. It needs the market as much as consumers require oil. For this fundamental reason the Organization does its utmost to supply the market at 'fair and reasonable' prices.

The recent political and financial disputes between Russia, Ukraine, and Belarus redeemed the past negative experience of OPEC. When Moscow cut the supply of gas to Europe, European consumers called foul. That action triggered a lot of questioning about the reliability of Russians. Now, as in 1973, shuttle diplomacy succeeded in bringing closure to the interruption of the gas supply. European countries started to look at other providers. The only problem is the absence of adequate infrastructure to carry the large quantity of available gas from the Middle East, the Caspian Basin, and North Africa to Europe. The bad experience with Russia remains a permanent source of concern for Europe.

Because the member-states of OPEC failed to diversify their economies, oil revenues remain their biggest foreign currency provider. A majority of these countries have a young population that seeks to explore and expand its potential. Besides, demography, job creation, housing, and education are a permanent source of tension for non-democratic regimes. OPEC will continue to behave with great responsibility towards the oil market. Another embargo for political reasons is not on the horizon for a foreseeable future. If OPEC as a community is no longer a threat to market stability, social and political unrest in some member-states and the interruption of supply remain a possibility. Because world leaders have shorter electoral concerns, it is difficult to expect a real quest for alternative energy to replace oil. Oil reserves are important, and there is no burning desire to exploit more expensive sources of energy. In not pushing the quest for new energy sources, OPEC will continue to play a low key role and avoid any provocation.

Notes

1 Indonesia withdrew from the cartel in 2008. On 29 May 2008, *Al Jazeera* reported: 'Indonesia has become a net importer because of aging wells and disappointing exploration efforts. Bureaucracy and a weak legal system also drove away investments and Indonesia's oil production of roughly a million barrels a day is at its lowest level in 30 years. However the Government said it has left open the option of re-joining OPEC if it can build up a surplus. In announcing the move, the Indonesian energy minister said the Government was going to focus on increasing domestic production because "we are a consuming country." ': http://english.aljazeera.net/news/asia–pacific/2008/ 05/200861503520814347.html

2 Ecuador left OPEC in 1992 because of membership fee issues and because it felt it needed to produce more oil than permitted under the OPEC quota. Ecuador re-joined OPEC's ranks in 2007. *Kuwait Times* (18 November 2007).

3 Gabon left the organisation in 1994. Not satisfied with its OPEC quota, Gabon decided to disregard its allocated share by increasing its oil production to generate more revenue needed for economic

development projects. See United States Department of Commerce: www.buyusa.gov/westafrica/en/gabon.html.

4 Organization of the Petroleum Exporting Countries, *OPEC Statute* (Vienna, 2008), 3.

5 Articles 10–16, Ibid., 5–8.

6 Ibid., 9–12.

7 Mana Saeed Al-Otaiba, *OPEC and the Petroleum Industry* (London, 1975), 71–76. The author is the former Minister of Petroleum and Mineral Resources of the United Arab Emirates. He became the personal adviser to the President of the United Arab Emirates. Mana Al Otaiba was the President of OPEC for a record six times in the 1970s and 1980s.

8 National Oil Corporation-Libya, 'Mr. Abdullah Salem El Badri Appointed as The Secretary General for the OPEC Organization':http://en.noclibya.com.ly/index.php?option=com_content&task=view&id=183&Itemid=55.

9 For more details, see the official site of the OAPEC: www.oapecorg.org/en/aboutus/establishment.htm.

10 For an assessment of the embargo's effect see A.F. Alhajji, 'Three Decades after the Oil Embargo: Was 1973 Unique?', *Journal of Energy and Development*, 30(2005), 223–37.

11 European Institute for Mediterranean and Euro-Arab Cooperation, 'Euro-Arab Dialogue,' November 1996: www.medea.be/index.html?page=2&lang=en&doc=55.

12 See the World Bank official site: http://web.worldbank.org/WBSITE/EXTERNAL/EXTABOUTUS/0,pagePK:50004410~piPK:36602~theSitePK:29708,00.html

13 UN General Assembly Sixth Special Session, 'Resolutions adopted by the General Assembly, 3201 (S-VI)', *Declaration on the Establishment of a New International Economic Order*, 2229th plenary meeting (1 May 1974).

14 Article 2, Ibid.

15 The rest of this paragraph is based on Article 4, Ibid.

16 Thomas Gale Moore, 'Energy Options,' in Peter Duignan and A. Rabushka, eds, *The United States in the 1980s* (London, 1980), 228–29.

17 The second oil shock in the 1970s was caused by a revolution in Iran and the beginning of the Iraq–Iran war in 1980. The Iranian and Iraqi supply interruptions raised the average OPEC oil price to US$36.00/bbl by 1980. The counter shock of the mid-1980s plunged the price below $10.00/bbl. For an analysis of the oil prices fluctuations, see D.G. Aperjis, 'Oil Export Policy and Economic Development in OPEC,' *Annual Review of Energy*, 9(November 1984). 179–98.

18 WRTG Economics, *Oil Price and Analysis (Updating)*: www.wtrg.com/prices.htm.

19 Ibid.

20 Lucian Kim and Stephen Bierman, '"Gas Producers" Club, Based on OPEC, Will Have Doha Headquarters,' *Bloomberg* (23 December 2008).

21 Toni Johnson, 'Non-OPEC Oil Production', *Council on Foreign Relations Backgrounder* (10 November 2008).

22 *OPEC Annual Statistical Bulletin 2009:* www.opec.org/opec_web/en/data_graphs/330.htm.

23 www.opec.org/opec_web/en/data_graphs/331.htm.

24 In his 2006 State of the Union Address, President George W, Bush warned that the United States must break its addiction to oil: http://news.bbc.co.uk/2/hi/americas/4665758.stm. The United States continuous dependency on oil as important source of energy five years after the addiction speech is as big as ever.

25 Ibrahim F.I. Shihata, *The Other Face of OPEC. Financial Assistance to the Third World* (London, New York, 1982).

26 www.wieninternational.at/en/node/201.

27 For more details see www.ofid.org/projects_operations/commitments_2010.aspx#tech.

28 For the message of the OPEC Secretary-General Abdullah Al-Badri, see www.opec.org/opec_web/en/50th_anniversary/81.htm.

28

From colonies to collective

ALBA, Latin American integration, and the construction of regional political power

Larry Catá Backer

States have long arranged themselves vertically; the fundamental ordering principle of political life remains substantially unchanged, with 'right, as the world goes ... only in question between equals in power, while the strong do what they can and the weak suffer as they must' (Thucydides, 331).[1] Modern international politics, and the system of international law that has been used instrumentally to institutionalise it, is grounded in this foundation of verticality.[2] The state system has, at least since 1945, been formally ordered on the basis of the principle of the equality of states.[3] Yet functionally, the state system is vertically ordered, grounded on a rule of deference by weaker Powers to more powerful ones, and the deference of all to the Great Powers.[4] This fundamental ordering framework, and its repercussions, has been nicely illustrated in the earlier chapters of this collection.

This vertically arranged functional system is replicated in the forms of organisation of the state system at the international level. International institutions from the United Nations (UN) Security Council to the International Monetary Fund (IMF) are organised around the fundamental principle of deference to power. Leaders of less powerful states, like Hugo Chávez of Venezuela, have asserted: 'These organisations only serve the powerful countries to legitimise their aggressions, like the US invasion of Iraq'.[5] Informal institutions with a soft power leadership role, like those of the G20 and the Paris Club, are grounded in the same principle. Even the soft system of transnational constitutionalism that has served as a mechanism for shaping national discretion in the internal construction of domestic legal orders has been shaped by the grand strategies of the Great Powers of the time. Soft interventions through transnational institutions also provide a powerful tool of political, social, and economic acculturation. One argument suggests the powerful disciplining effect of global efforts to inculcate 'good governance' principles in developing states through international organisations like the World Bank and the IMF.[6] These involve 'far reaching transformations, relating to the promotion of democracy, free markets and the rule of law ... directed at reproducing in the Third World a set of principles and institutions which are seen as having been perfected in the West, and which the non-European world must adopt if it is to make progress and achieve stability'.[7] Yet it was also to work on the Great Powers as a means of providing a system of behavior limits for them in dealing with the weaker members of the family of nations.[8]

But weaker Powers had long discovered that the forms of multilateralism could be used as much for defensive purposes for them as it had been used in the construction of the international system for the benefit of the Great Powers. Among others, the Non-Aligned Movement is perhaps the most well known. They declare an intention 'to change the current system of international relations based on injustice, inequality and oppression. We act on international policy as a global independent factor'.[9] Yet the Non-Aligned Movement also represents both the potential of collective action by weaker states against the Great Powers, as well as the inherent weaknesses of these collectives: 'A multilateral trans-national organisation made up of states with differing ideologies and purposes could never create a rational administrative structure to implement its policies that all could accept'.[10] More importantly, the Non-Aligned Movement suggested the impossibility of freeing smaller states from the influence of the Great Powers, even when smaller states sought to act in concert. 'The movement divided against itself over the Soviet invasion of Afghanistan in 1979. This division was an indication that the NAM was indeed aligned, and it is possible that an organization of this nature can never be fully non-aligned'.[11]

Yet the attainment of a measure of political and economic power for small states through collective organisation has remained an ideal for states and theorists.[12] One of the most interesting recent efforts to leverage the power of small states through collective action exists in the form of *Alianza Alternativa para los Pueblos de Nuestra América* (the Bolivarian Alliance for the Peoples of Our Americas [ALBA]); these efforts have produced what may be a viable challenge to the free trade model of globalisation.[13] ALBA serves as a focus of resistance to the conventional trade model of privatisation and globalisation that is assumed to be bad for people, especially for those who live in developing states.[14] It is critically grounded on the idea that internationalisation must be effected through states rather than individuals and private markets.[15] To this process is added a fundamental distrust of private markets, markets not strictly controlled and managed by the state.[16] ALBA thus has been constructed to serve, at least as a matter of theory, as both a system of free trade and as a nexus point for legal and political resistance to economic globalisation and legal internationalism sponsored by developed states. Fernando Bossi, the Secretary of the Bolivarian Peoples' Congress, recently wrote of the ALBA experiment as grounded in the objective of collective independence, the vehicle for which was revolution under the banner of socialism.[17]

ALBA is an expression of a distinct approach to multilateral organisation at once *oppositional* (framed in opposition to the interests of the United States) and *instrumental* (implemented as a workable alternative to a conventional social, economic, and political organisation). ALBA is contextualised within the dense network of trade treaties that mark the realities of economic relations in Latin America.[18] Thus contextualised, ALBA serves as a nexus for competing pressures within both modern trade theory practice and the construction of multistate system frameworks in Latin America beyond the orbit of global Great Powers. ALBA is offered as a successful model of resistance, and as a means of avoiding the consequences of a vertically ordered state system. Fidel Castro declared: 'in this union is our salvation.'[19] ALBA's contribution to that objective is best understood as a function of its history and organisation, ideological framework (theory) and practical expression (praxis).

Integration pits the post-colonial project of state-building against the internationalist project that aims to reduce the sovereign authority of states, both against each other and in their relations with private power. The integration of Latin America and the Caribbean is not a novel idea. This goal, and the ideals guiding it, traces its roots to early nineteenth century conceptions of Latin American independence. The framers of ALBA posited strong connections between their efforts and those that produced the first great wave of Latin American independence movements.[20] ALBA is described as heir to early proponents of integration, especially Simon Bolívar's vision for the newly freed states that had fought for their independence from Spanish rule in the first quarter of the nineteenth century. The expression of these ideas can be found in his 'Letter from Jamaica'.[21] The desire of ALBA to integrate Latin America independent of colonial or neocolonial Powers draws heavily on this effort to connect its activities to those of the founding generation of Latin American independence.[22] ALBA seeks to draw those founders' ideology to those of the revolutionaries of the late nineteenth century: the writings of Jose Martín and later in the work of Augusto Cesar Sandino.[23]

Modern regional integration in Latin America is commonly traced to the period immediately after the Second World War and the work of the UN Commission for Latin America.[24] In 1994, under the leadership of the United States, a Summit of the Americas was held in Miami to develop the capstone to this movement toward hemispheric integration. The intention was to create a Free Trade Area of the Americas (FTAA) by 2005, under which the private market-based model of economic globalisation was to be further institutionalised in the hemisphere.[25] It was in opposition to FTAA that ALBA was born.

Part of the opposition to FTAA was grounded in a well-developed world view that sought to synthesise strong elements of Soviet-style Marxist-Leninist theory, post-colonial theories, especially those coming out of African liberation movements, nineteenth century ethnonationalism, and twentieth century socialist internationalism. Basic to these ideas was the positing of a fundamental opposition between the state and transnational corporations. The former best represented the popular will (and public good); the latter represented private uncontrolled economic power inimical to the interests individuals, states, and society.[26]

Opposition was also grounded in the neocolonialist consequences of asymmetric bargaining among states. The deleterious consequences for small states inherent in the asymmetries produced by current trade integration formulas were elaborated by Fidel Castro. He focused on the function of modern globalisation as a means to preserve asymmetrical trade relations between large and small states. The focus was on sovereign debt and its consequences.[27] Castro also publicly denounced these same concepts during his address to the UN General Assembly in 1979, in which he laid out critical points that now form central guiding principles in the formation of ALBA.[28] Reiterating similar concerns about the strangling effects that foreign debt has on small, impoverished countries, he also emphasised the public side of trade as a fundamental element of globalisation and integration.[29] These ideas served as the ideological basis for what emerged as ALBA.

But ALBA represents a more radical departure from the conventional tactics of hemispheric opposition to perceived overreaching by the United States. That departure is striking in two respects: first by framing ALBA on the basis of a coherent conceptual framework distinct from those espoused by the United States and its allies; and second, by using that oppositional ideology to construct a collective of states meant to be strong enough to challenge American hegemony in the Western hemisphere. While ALBA has failed in its second aim, it has produced a coherent ideology that has proved successful in drawing a number of states into its orbit, and out of that of their traditional patrons.

The idea for ALBA first appeared in 2001 proposals advanced by Chávez.[30] It was developed publicly in a series of speeches and dialogues between Cuba and Venezuela. The idea was to reconstruct and reapply the ideals represented by Bolivar, as understood by Cuban and Venezuelan leaders.[31] The first concrete steps taken to create ALBA occurred after Chávez's electoral success in 2004.[32] ALBA's initial form was memorialised in a bilateral Cuban–Venezuelan agreement, which provided for structuring relations between the two states on principles of solidarity and the exchange of goods and services, at the state-to-state level, in a manner mutually beneficial to the parties. The formal agreement was executed at a ceremony held in Havana in December 2004.[33]

Implementation started in early 2005.[34] Its source in oppositional politics was memorialised in its initial name: the Bolivarian *Alternative*. A variety of additional bilateral accords and joint endeavors were concluded and the ideological basis of the organisation confirmed.[35] These efforts have been followed by a large number of agreements, declarations, and actions to develop the conceptual framework of ALBA, and to construct a number of projects that are supposed to apply those principles in specific sectors and among a variety of shifting groups of ALBA members. And the organisation has grown from the initial bilateral arrangement between Cuba and Venezuela to include Nicaragua, Dominica, Ecuador, Antigua, and Barbuda, and St Vincent and the Grenadines. Honduras, a member after 2008, withdrew after the ousting of President Manuel Zelaya in a controversial action that has yet to be recognised in the ALBA zone. The addition of these members changed the agreement in a number of ways but did not affect the fundamental character of the association.

ALBA might perhaps be better understood as a space through which mutual cooperation on the basis of ALBA principles can be effected, rather than as a heavily institutionalised autonomous supranational organisation. It is comprised of seven commissions focusing on distinct functional areas: political, social, economic, investment and finance, energy, environment and youth. Each commission reports to the Council of ALBA Ministers and Council of ALBA Social Movements, which then reports to the Council of ALBA Presidents. The commissions are headed by the national ministers of the respective areas of each member-state that together form the Council of ALBA Ministers. Because ALBA seeks to respect the national sovereignty of member-states, all ALBA agreements are subject to ratification by the national legislatures of the member-states. The Council of Social Movements was established in 2007 to incorporate organised mass movement actors into the ALBA structure.[36] From 2009, ALBA incorporated a permanent commission to oversee the development of the implementation of ALBA zone commercial activities through the *grannacional* system described below.

ALBA's organisational form has been criticised as insubstantial.[37] Yet, this institutional organisation reflects the objectives of the organisation. The result is substantially less autonomy for the institution at the supranational level and more control at the member-state level. The supranational element of ALBA serves more as a pass through and reflection of member-state consensus than as the locus of an autonomous aggregate power reflecting a ceding of sovereignty up to the supranational level. It emphasises the central position of the state in the construction of internationalist frameworks. This state-centring integration critically affects the underlying theory of its organisation as well as its implementation.

ALBA's ideological framework provides the greatest mark of its distinction from other efforts at integration, which requires harmonisation of an ideological base for action.[38] ALBA is built on the idea of the inherent potential for Latin America development independent of the United States and Europe.[39] But to succeed, that development had to be different from that of the United States, because the founding members do not seek to follow the same path of warfare, genocide, and pillaging that the Americans took to achieve unity.[40] ALBA is grounded on an opposition to capitalism as an economic and political ideology.[41] Early in its formation, ALBA ideology was framed around ten points that defined the ALBA 'line':[42] ALBA is a historic project, a heroic creation, supported by the potential inherent in Latin America and the Caribbean as well by anti-capitalist values. It is a popular construction and a form of integration that is not borne out of mercantile or trade aspects, serves as a political tool and as the programme of Latin American and Caribbean revolution, and in this way represents a strategic step towards a new stage.[43]

The general conceptual basis of ALBA is more specifically elaborated in the development of three organisational lines. The first are the four anti-capitalist values of ALBA; the second are its three pillars and third are its goals. ALBA articulates four so-called anti-capitalist values around which ALBA interventions are built: complementary action based on the strengths that each member may possess; mutual cooperation; solidarity among the member-states; and respect for the national sovereignty of each member.[44] It is not clear whether these are anti-capitalist or anti-colonialist values and, more particularly, whether the solidarity and action suggested is meant to be reactive, that is deployed against the policies and interests of the United States.[45] Indeed, except for the oppositional stance within which ALBA is situated, it would be difficult to suggest that these values are not amenable to capitalist systems.

The difference comes in the form of application of these values, targeting not markets and private activities, but mass social movement programmes and state action. This notion finds expression in the three pillars of ALBA, articulated through the development of a theory of stages of development to which ALBA states are committed: education to inform others about the necessity for ALBA; expanding the distribution of informational material among the masses about the benefits of ALBA; and mobilising and organising concrete steps that will foster the integration of Latin American people.[46] These pillars, in turn, are elaborative of twelve more pragmatic goals to foster progress through the stages of sociopolitical development.[47]

In addition to these goals, ALBA also has four major objectives that seek to weave values and implementation. The first is to promote the integration and development of Latin America through cooperation, solidarity, and unity to place the interests of the people above those of transnational capital.[48] The second aims to promote integration agreements that develop the industrial and social infrastructures of a nation, and the region, with the goal of eliminating poverty, social exclusion, and ensuring better living conditions for all the inhabitants of Latin American nations. The third is to counter neoliberal policies, particularly the attempt by the Americans to create an FTAA, which traditionally benefit developed at the expense of developing nations.[49] The fourth is to use complementary action based on the strengths that each country may possess, mutual cooperation, solidarity, and respect for the national sovereignty of each country.

Together these values, objectives, and goals present a unified ideological position. It serves as a basis for approaching all issues of transnational arrangements. It privileges the state against private actors. It suggests a tighter control of individuals and their arrangements by the state, and it also suggests that those interests must be subordinated to the needs of the states, as understood by those in control of the apparatus of state governance. Private markets are incidental to the development of large sectors of state control. Because neither politics nor economics can be left to the private sector, nor because the private sector might well serve as proxy for the interests of those states from where those private activities originate, then state-to-state arrangements must be the basis of any movement of people, capital, goods, or services. Lastly, the ideological position combines a long tradition of anti-colonialism and nationalism with anti-Americanism to produce an ideological system in which states are essential to combat the direct and indirect interventions of the United States (and to a lesser extent the old European colonial Powers) in the development of adhering states. For many Latin American states the result is an intoxicating mix. It serves to legitimate stronger state control over a private sector that had been relying on the development of global markets to liberate itself from local barriers to development. It shifts power to direct markets from the private to the public sector. It provides an avenue for transferring blame to a demonised 'other' against which state activity is directed. It provides a basis for maintaining control through the form of democratic mass movements by linking state action to the maintenance of the masses, and, by so doing, marginalising the relationship between the masses and other institutional or civil society elements. Most importantly, this ideology preserves state control over the nature and extent of actual arrangements with entities beyond its borders. Packaged in this form, ALBA's ideology has become its most critically successful product.

The importance of ALBA's ideological component is evidenced not merely by the style of its website, but also by efforts to mold popular opinion in other media. Most potent, potentially, are ALBA TV and substantial efforts to use electronic media to publicise ALBA positions on regional political and economic matters. These help establish consensus about political 'facts' through news reporting and related efforts that shape the way in which people receive and understand information and thus exercise their political will in their home states. Important positions of ALBA, and ALBA's political programmes, are given substantial play. These programmes provide a basis for more effective communication well beyond the ALBA zone. A telling example was ALBA's substantially successful effort to delegitimise the current government of Honduras[50] and, less successfully, to put pressure on the United States to abandon its military bases in Colombia.[51]

Yet ALBA's ideological framework has also changed since its creation. Reflecting the growing plausibility of the organisation, its ideology has moved from expression in political revolutionary terms to a revolutionary reorientation of globalisation frameworks within which it seeks to participate.[52] The emphasis after 2009 is still focused on determinism (ALBA as a historic and radical project) but now the emphasis is more structural.[53] ALBA is viewed as a unique model, built on the rejection of conventional forms of economic integration and the embrace of endogenous characteristics of the region. There is also a de-emphasis on the reactive aspects of ALBA. Instead, newly stressed are ALBA's pragmatic and positive contributions to integration, with an increasing focus on praxis through *grannacionales*. These pragmatic containers of revolutionary insight will serve both to preserve the sovereignty of ALBA member-states but also to liberate them from control by the Great Powers, principally the United States. Whether ALBA can deliver remains to be seen. What ALBA ideology has provided, however, is a conceptual base from which opposition can be even marginally maintained and a basis for unity against a greater Power.

Conception, ideology, and organisation can only take a supranational organisation so far. The real value of an organisation beyond its ideological purpose is measured by its implementation. ALBA is a young organisation. However, it has begun to elaborate a series of programmes to provide a basis for understanding how the member-states intend to translate ideology and concept to reality on the ground. Since ALBA's inception, a number of projects have been initiated or announced.[54] These include plans for a fisheries *empresa grannacional* (EG) (an ALBA-wide multinational enterprise), a forestry EG, a coffee EG between Venezuela and Dominica, four energy-related EGs between Venezuela and Bolivia, an ALBA-zone hotels EG, a mining EG between Ecuador and Venezuela, an import–export bank to facilitate trade, an energy EG and a number of mining and mineral extractive EGs among Cuba, Venezuela, Ecuador, and a transport EG between Cuba and Venezuela.[55] The object is to provide an organisational basis for trade stimulation both within the ALBA zone and internationally.[56]

ALBA's most important economic efforts have centered on establishing PETROCARIBE, an energy cooperation agreement proposed by Venezuela to Caribbean nations that aims to resolve the asymmetries that these nations have in having access to energy resources.[57] Its objective is to contribute to the transformation of Latin American and Caribbean societies to become more just, cultured, participatory, and solidarity-minded by removing social inequalities and promoting an improved quality of life through the effective participation of the people in the determination of the affairs of their respective states. The programme has produced a number of trade agreements that represent state-to-state barter relations centered on the provision of Venezuelan petroleum.

One of the most potentially far-reaching ALBA projects has been efforts to build an alternative sovereign finance system around the Banco de ALBA. Its founders' hope is that it will serve as the blueprint for the future financial system through which ALBA's social, cooperative, and *grannnacional* projects are to be funded.[58] In the area of finance, however, Banco del Sur has emerged as another project that, although not within the framework of ALBA, is also being promoted to create a wholly South American source of funding and economic solidarity.[59] In addition to a bank serving as the financial center for ALBA, efforts have begun to develop the *sucre*, an ALBA currency, to replace the American dollar for interstate transactions.[60] The object is to aid efforts at integration in a way that avoids the incidental and perceived detrimental effects of national economies bound by connections to the dollar.

Grannacional projects were newly developed and present one of the most interesting features of ALBA-applied ideological work. Much of ALBA's efforts are now channelled through this device. *Grannacionales* represent an effort of creating a socialist form of multinational enterprise.[61] However, they are also meant to serve as a new means of organising state sector activity not traditionally undertaken through commercial enterprises. The conception of *grannacional* projects is understood as essentially political and is divided into three components: historical and geopolitical, socioeconomic, and ideological. They are meant to apply to the forms of economic organisation of the ALBA zone and the political dimensions used to frame ALBA itself. As a unique form of ideological implementation, the *grannacional* enterprise is understood as experimental.

Grannacionales are meant to serve as the great vehicle for state-directed development through integration. They are the embodiment of an ideology that sees economic activity as a means to satisfy public policy rather than as an end in themselves, that is as a vehicle to maximise individual welfare. That union is bound up in notions of Marxist economic determinism: union will be achieved as the inevitable consequence of global dynamics dominated for the moment by the great industrial Powers and blocs of economically hegemonic states.[62] Even the name of these projects (*grannacional*) is meant to cement the ideological component of the undertaking, suggesting a national grouping cemented through its political-economic relations but that would also respect national peculiarities and sovereignty.

This experimentation manifests in two concrete forms: *proyectos grannacionales* (PGs) and EGs. PGs include all programmes undertaken to benefit the greatest number under the ideological framework and goals of ALBA, approved by ALBA members, and whose execution requires the participation of two or more ALBA member-states. This organisation is grounded in ALBA's normative construction of principles of 'just trade' and solidarity commerce, which is sometimes reduced to three principles (barter transactions, non-reciprocity in trade relations, and differential treatment of trade partners to advance national and development objectives): *comercio compensado, no-reciprocidad*, and *trato diferenciado*.[63]

PGs organise productive activities; EGs implement them in an orderly way. EGs are meant to embody an alternative to the model of the private multinational enterprise, which seeks to maximise the welfare of its shareholders and other important stakeholders.[64] EGs are said to invert the traditional maximisation model by seeking to maximise the welfare of the objects of economic or other activity, embodying what is meant by the ideological focus on 'just commercial zone' within the ALBA region. EGs can be organised under the incorporation rules of any one of the participating ALBA member-states, interest in which is measured through share ownership by participating members. But they might also be organised under special legislation.

PGs and EGs have been used increasingly to organise state sector economic activity within and across ALBA states. In states like Cuba, with minimal private sector activity of any significance, the use of these vehicles merely suggests a rearranging of the economic sectors affected. In other ALBA states, especially Venezuela and Bolivia, the result has been to effect a nationalisation of economic sectors by a process of public privatisation, that is the use of private sector entities 'owned' by the states that also regulate the enterprises operating in that sector. Typical of the hybridity of objective inherent in these projects was the creation of the ALBA Network of Food Trade and the ALBA Food Security Fund in 2008, which were created to 'guarantee food security in the Caribbean, Central, and South American regions'.[65] At the time, Chávez declared: 'We are going to create a supranational company, like a transnational company, but in this case with the concept of a great nation, to produce food with the goal of guaranteeing food sovereignty to our people'.[66]

The principal effect of ALBA has been an increase in state-to-state trade, especially among the ALBA founders, whose commercial trade increased from US$973 million in 2001 to US$2.4 billion in 2005.[67] The primacy of the state-to-state activities in defining the scope of the trade relationships within ALBA was set with the initial agreement, a highlight of which was the agreement to trade Venezuelan petroleum for the services of Cuban doctors to be supplied by the respective states.[68] For its part, Venezuela agreed to similar reciprocal arrangements. This form of agreement has served as a template for the widely publicised social justice element of trade among ALBA states.[69] One group of programmes focuses on education.[70] Another group has focused on programmes of delivery of medical care. Still another group is tied to notions of mass social mobilisations in the service of social justice ideals as conceived by the directing states. One, *Misión Vuelvan Caracas*, seeks to train and educate the Venezuelan people so that they may work alongside the government in transforming the social and economic landscape of the country.

For all of its purported uniqueness, ALBA operates in a regional context richly layered with traditional trade arrangements. Contextualising ALBA within these traditional forms draws in sharper focus those characteristics that make ALBA unique and influential and suggests that though the ideology of integration may be unique to ALBA, its form is not.[71]

The traditional models for integration are well represented in Latin America through MERCOSUR (the *Mercado Común del Sur* or Southern Common Market). MERCOSUR was established in 1990 among Brazil, Argentina, Uruguay, and Paraguay to promote trade among its members. Its history is well known.[72] Through MERCOSUR, these states sought to establish a common market that permits more unimpeded movement of goods, services, modes of production through the elimination of customs duties, and non-tariff restrictions on goods of the member states. The MERCOSUR framework suggests a level of centralisation beyond mere intergovernmentalism; admittedly, it is unrealised to some great extent.[73]

Yet, Latin American integration has also followed a model of unstructured and organic development exemplified in the Latin American Association for Integration (*Asociación Latinoamericana de Integración* [ALADI]). Created in 1980 through the Treaty of Montevideo, ALADI has as a primary objective in the creation of a common Latin American market.[74] The common market is to be created through the use of preferential tariff treatment among member nations, as well as through the signing of regional and bilateral agreements. 'ALADI seems to be primarily a framework within which member states can negotiate and enter into economic integration agreements with each other and a "keeper of the flame" for the ideal of integration in Latin America'.[75] ALADI has set the conceptual stage for the proliferation of a wide variety of arrangements among its members. It, in a sense, made ALBA possible.

ALBA follows a similar decentralised model, even as it furthers an ideological framework inimical to those of these other entities. It has developed a similar set of institutions, all tightly dependent on the will of and serving the interests of the member-states. Divided on functional bases, ALBA is divided into a series of commissions through which common positions might be taken and agreements among ALBA member-states concluded. ALBA is more horizontally constructed than ALADI, but it takes ALADI's intergovernmentalism one step farther. There is no autonomy in the supranational bodies that constitute ALBA. The focus remains on state sovereign rights and tight control of integration. There is little in the construction of these organisations that suggests any move toward the development of autonomous supranational governance institutions with any sort of independent regulatory power. Passive, flow-through organisations, they are more a joint venture than integrative body.

These connections suggest both the singularity of ALBA and its relationship with the now almost ancient tradition of trade integration that has also marked Latin American state-to-state economic relations. That embedding within the great social, political, and cultural movements in

Latin America suggests a contextual complexity that is worth unraveling. ALBA implicates the competing pressures of integration and nationalism and the relationship of both to the maintenance of vertically arranged hierarchies of power among states. ALBA's great innovation is that partial integration under its model is heavily controlled by states. Yet ALBA remains leery of the use of integration as a doorway for the creation of autonomous supranational organs. It seeks to cultivate national power within an integrationist framework powerful enough to stand against the interests of greater Powers. The competing pressures of integration and nationalism parallel that between public and private sector actors for control of economic development and policy. ALBA tilts heavily toward a public market model, grounding its development on the presumption that private markets ought to be incidental to and fill in gaps in public market activity. The engine that drives the economy is the state, even when the state is economically near collapse.[76]

ALBA suggests the difficulties of attempting to overcome patterns of integration within Latin America. Although ALBA presents a conscious inversion of the dominant private markets model on which contemporary trade and investment agreements are framed, that inversion is grounded precisely in the forms adopted for the implementation of that model and its ultimate integrationist aspirations. The partial trade agreements for which ALADI is famous is mimicked by the current crop of ALBA projects. The intergovernmentalism of ALBA is the hallmark of ALADI. This difficulty highlights the problems of mediating state policies between mutual advantage and competition among states. Borders include those within them and exclude those outside them. ALBA's asymmetrical and episodic approach to commercial and trade arrangements constructs borders within borders under its framework of multiple joint venture arrangements, even as ALBA seeks to present a unified ideological and political front.

Still, there is some value to ideological unity in its own right, even in the context of potentially disastrous economic decisions. Cuba exists as a reminder of this sort of power. ALBA stands as a reminder that ideology matters; fundamentals and grounding assumptions about the operation of state and non-state actors, and their powers and prerogatives matter. If one can control the ideological basis for the approach to an issue (like trade and investment) one can effectively control the parameters through which the issue is understood and systems constructed. Indeed, even in the construction of trade arrangements within and outside the ALBA zone, ideology and ideological education may well be its principal aim, at least in its initial stages of development and its most important product.[77]

More problematic, perhaps, is ALBA's unavoidable oppositional orientation. ALBA remains expressed in the negative, as an effort to combat the influence and dominance of the United States. ALBA deepens Latin America's conjunction of anti-Americanism and integration, which has had significant application to Latin American–United States relations.[78] Oppositional politics, and economic policies, has tended to ill-serve its proponents, except perhaps in the short term. Yet in the absence of opposition, it is not clear that ALBA has much meaning. Ironically, however, the focus on opposition leaves its object, the United States, still firmly in control of the destiny of the ALBA zone. Oppositional policies follow, they do not lead.

ALBA has proved compelling for governments increasingly overwhelmed by new sorts of governance power (private, multinational, and governance-based). For small states, ALBA provides a way to combine resources to resist both the public power of large states and the private power of large transnational economic enterprises. It suggests a means to resist exploitation by public and private actors. Equally important, ALBA now serves as a means of aggregating and institutionalising responses to and challenges of American power in the western hemisphere.[79] It also institutionalises opposition to the current framework of economic globalisation and attempts to challenge the hegemony of the current framework for constituting trade among states, grounded in private economic activity and a passive state regulatory role, the so-called Washington

Consensus, based on the assumption that 'growth occurs through liberalization, "freeing up" markets.[80] Privatization, liberalization, and macrostability are supposed to create a climate to attract investment, including from abroad. This investment creates growth'.[81]

There is little consensus on the nature and value of ALBA, even within the Western hemispheric community of public and private actors. Some view ALBA as a major threat to the current system of economic globalisation and to the deepening of global constitutionalism. Most prominent among these is the United States, which views it as essentially a site for anti-democratic, human-rights-violating propaganda combined with an anti-American political agenda.[82] Others view ALBA as little more than an ideologically curious variation on the large number of partial preference free trade agreements that have proliferated in Latin America since the 1980s under the ALADI framework. Still others have suggested that there is little, either institutionally or programatically that distinguishes ALBA from the machinations of the nation states that comprise its various disconnected programmes.[83] ALBA member-states, of course, view the enterprise as the greatest innovation in hemispheric integration since the Soviet Revolution of 1917 by combining European Marxism, Latin American nationalist anti-colonialism, and the vision of integration that has haunted Latin America since the nineteenth century wars of liberation: 'Ricardo Alarcón, president of Cuba's national assembly, has called ALBA the best guarantee for the consolidation of an anti-imperialist front.'[84] There is a little bit of truth in each of these views.

Integration can serve as a proxy for strong state interventions under the cover of private markets internationalism and, in this way, also subvert the post-colonial projects of national liberation. But it can also serve to liberate individuals from the oppression of cliques and ideologies that hijack the apparatus of states by posing supranational norms against narrow assertions of state power. ALBA presents an ideological and functional alternative and challenge to transnational institutions built on the operating assumptions of economic globalisation, and the developing convergence of public and private law. And its potential to provide a public sector variant on private sector globalisation should not be underestimated. It is no longer focused on *eliminating borders* for the production and management of private capital; instead it is focused on *using borders* as a site for the assertion of public authority to control all aspects of social, political, cultural, and economic activity. Yet it is also deeply embedded in the great web of partial economic associations that characterise economic governance in Latin America.

ALBA focuses on changing the terms of debate about trade, the role of states, and the place of private economic activity across borders. In this respect, certainly, ALBA may represent one of Cuba's greatest triumphs and also its greatest challenge to the normative tenets of the current framework of economic globalisation. But the framework within which ALBA can grow also defines the limits of its influence. It is not clear that within a deep system of webs of relationships, one variant (a decidedly socialist and state centered one) will change not merely the framework of discussion about trade but also the economic philosophy of more than a few states in Latin America.

Notes

1 Thucydides [John H. Finley, Jr., translator], *The Peloponnesian War* (New York, 1951), 331.
2 Martti Koskenniemi, *The Gentler Civilizer of Nations: The Rise and Fall of International Law, 1870–1960* (Cambridge, UK, 2001), 238.
3 Jose E. Alvarez, *International Organizations as Law-Makers* (Oxford, 2006), 1–57.
4 Ken Menkhaus, 'Governance Without Government in Somalia: Spoilers, State Building and the Politics of Coping', *International Security*, Volume 31, Number 3(2007), 83–93.
5 James Suggett, 'Latin America's Bolivarian Alliance Grows', *Green Left* (27 June 2009): www.greenleft.org.au/node/41933.

6 Antony Anghie, *Imperialism, Sovereignty and the Making of International Law* (Cambridge, UK, 2004), 245–72.
7 Ibid, 249.
8 Koskenniemi, *Gentler Civilizer*.
9 Fidel Castro Ruz, 'Speech Delivered at the United Nations in his Position as Chairman of the Non-Aligned Countries Movement' (12 October 1979): http://lanic.utexas.edu/la/cb/cuba/castro/1979/19791012.
10 Non-Aligned Movement, 'Background, NAM Structure and Organization' (September 2001): www.nam.gov.za/background/background.htm#1.1%20History.
11 Asian Nuclear Energy, 'The Non-Aligned Movement: A Socio-Political Perspective' (29 January 2009): www.asiannuclearenergy.com/Background/Historical-Perspective/the-non-align-movement-a-socio-political-perspective.html.
12 Makau Mutua, 'What is TWAIL?', *American Society of International Law Proceedings*, 31(2000), 38.
13 Frank J. Garcia, *Trade, Inequality, and Justice: Towards a Liberal Theory of Just Trade* (Ardsley, NY, 2003).
14 Larry C. Backer and Augusto Molina, 'Cuba and the Construction of Alternative Global Trade Systems: ALBA and Free Trade in the Americas', *University of Pennsylvania Journal of International Law*, 31(2010), 679.
15 Fernando Ramon Bossi, '10 Points to Understand the ALBA: Constructing the ALBA from Within the Peoples': www.alianzabolivariana.org/modules.php?name=Content&pa=showpage&pid=1980.
16 ALBA, *ALBA Impulsa lanzamiento del sucre como nueva moneda del sur* (3 March 2009).
17 Fernando Ramon Bossi, 'Qué es el ALBA? Construyendo el ALBA desde los Pueblos', *ALBA TV* (12 August 2009).
18 Victor Bulmer-Thomas, *The Economic History of Latin America Since Independence* (Cambridge, UK, 2003).
19 Bossi, 'Qué es el ALBA?'.
20 ALBA, 'Antecedentes históricos del ALBA' (undated): www.alianzabolivariana.org/modules.php?name=Content&pa=showpage&pid=32.
21 Reply of a South American to a Gentleman of this Island, 6 September 1815: http://faculty.smu.edu/bakewell/BAKEWELL/texts/jamaica-letter.html.
22 Bossi, '10 Points'.
23 See Jose Marti, 'Nuestra América', *La Revista Ilustrada de Nueva York* (10 January 1891); Sandino, 'Manifesto to the Nicaraguan Liberals' (1 January 1929): www.latinamericanstudies.org/sandino/sandino1-1-29.htm
24 See United Nations, *Economic Commission for Latin America. The Economic Development of Latin America and Its Principal Problems* (New York, 1950).
25 See Nicola Philips, 'U.S. Power and the Politics of Economic Governance in the Americas', *Latin American Politics and Society*, Volume 47, Number 4(2005), 1–25.
26 Government of Venezuela, 'Sobre el ALBA: Selección de artículos' (2006): http://alternativabolivariana.org/modules.php?name=Content&pa=showpage&pid=1.
27 Larry C. Backer, 'Ideologies of Globalization and Sovereign Debt: Cuba and the IMF.' *Penn State International Law Review*, 24(2006), 497.
28 Castro, 'Speech Delivered at the United Nations'.
29 Fidel Castro Ruz, 'Discurso pronunciado en el IV Congreso de la FELAP' (7 July 1985): www.cuba.cu/gobierno/discursos/1985/esp/f070785e.html; and idem., 'Una Revolución solo puede ser hija de la cultura y las ideas': www.cuba.cu/gobierno/discursos/1999/esp/f030299e.html; Castro, 'Discurso pronunciado'.
30 ALBA, *Conceptualización de proyecto y empresa grannacional en el marco del ALBA*, VI (24–26 January 2008): http://alternativabolivariana.org/modules.php?name=News&file=article&sid=2668#5.
31 Bossi, '10 Points'.
32 ALBA, *Acuerdo entre el presidente de la República Bolivarina de Venezuela y el presidente del consejo de estado de Cuba para la aplicación de la Alternativa Bolivariana para las Américas* (Havana, 2004).
33 Ibid.
34 ALBA, *Declaración Final De La Primera Reunión Cuba-Venezuela Para La Aplicación De La Alternativa Para Las Américas* (27–28 April, 2005).
35 Ibid.
36 Emir Sader, 'ALBA: From Dream to Reality', *Global Policy Forum* (17 May 2007).
37 Ronald Sanders, 'Time to Care Again for CARICOM' (27 April 2009): BBC Caribbean.com
38 Raúl Castro Ruz 'Cuba Ratifica La Vocación Solidaria Con Los Pueblos De América' (2009).
39 See Bossi, "10 Points', Point 3.
40 Ibid., Point 2.

41 ALBA, 'Fifth Extraordinary Summit of the ALBA Final Declaration' (Cumana, 17 April 2009).
42 See Bossi, '10 Points'.
43 Ibid.
44 Ibid., Point 4.
45 Dennis Paterson and Ari Afilalo, *The New Global Trading Order: The Evolving State and the Future of Trade.* (Cambridge, UK, 2008), 205.
46 Bossi, '10 Points', Point 9.
47 Hugo Chávez, 'Discurso del Presidente de la República Bolivariana de Venezuela, Hugo Chávez, al finalizar la marcha en apoyo a la política latinoamericana y caribeña y contra el imperialismo?' (19 November 2005): http://alternativabolivariana.org/pdf/discurso_chavez.pdf.
48 ALBA, 'Qué es el ALBA?' (undated): http://alianzabolivariana.org/modules.php?name=Content&pa=showpage&pid=2080.
49 Bossi, '10 Points'.
50 ALBA, 'Golpe de estado en Honduras', (undated): www.albatv.org/+Golpe-de-estado-en-Honduras-+.html.
51 ALBA, 'Fuera Bases', (undated): www.albatv.org/+-Contra-las-bases-militares-+.html
52 For example, cf. Bossi, '10 Points' and Bossi, 'Qué es el ALBA?'.
53 Bossi, 'Qué es el ALBA?'.
54 L.M. Regueiro Bello, 'El Nuevo Entorno Latinoamericano. Algunas Reflexiones para el debate. Presentación en la Jornada de Educación Popular', UNRC, Argentina (5–6 October 2007): http://slidefinder.net/e/el_nuevo_entorno/latinoamericano/850771/p2.
55 See Backer and Molina, 'Alternative Global Trade Systems'.
56 Ramierez Cruz et. al., 'Transporte de carga internacional de Cuba: Problemas y perspectivas', (2007): www.eumed.net/libros/2008b/413/Los%20Proyectos%20Grannacionales.html.
57 'PETROCARIBE: Energía para la Unión', Cubahora Revista Informativa (18 November 2010): http://www.cubahora.cu/index.php?tpl=principal/ver-noticias/ver-not_soc.tpl.html&newsid_obj_id=1023274.
58 ALBA, *Conceptualización de proyecto*.
59 Ricardo A. Cardona, 'Banco Sur Financiara Desarrollo Integral Soberano Y Digno De Continente Americano', (22 October 2008): www.alianzabolivariana.org/modules.php?name=News&file=article&sid=2402#1.
60 ALBA, *ALBA Impulsa lanzamiento del sucre como nueva moneda del sur* (3 March 2009).
61 Larry Catá Backer, 'Globalization and the Socialist Multinational: Cuba and ALBA's Grannacional Projects at the Intersection of Business and Human Rights' (2010): http://ssrn.com/abstract=1646962.
62 Ibid.; ALBA, *Conceptualización de proyecto y empresa grannacional*.
63 Norman Girvan, 'ALBA, PetroCaribe and CARICOM: Issues in a New Dynamic' (30 May 2008). www.normangirvan.info/wp-content/uploads/2009/03/alba-petrocaribe-and-caricom.pdf.
64 Backer, 'Globalization and the Socialist Multinational'.
65 Suggett, 'Bolivarian Alliance'.
66 Ibid.
67 Martha Lomas Morales, 'Foreign Investment and Economic Collaboration Minister for the Republic of Cuba', *Firma de Acuerdos en el marco del ALBA entre Bolivia, Cuba y Venezuela: Rueda de Prensa*, Palacio de Convenciones, La Habana, Cuba (Sábado, 29 de abril de 2006).
68 ALBA, *Acuerdo*, Article 12 and propuestos.
69 ALBA, *Declaración Final De La Primera Reunión Cuba-Venezuela*.
70 The rest of this paragraph is based on Morales, 'Foreign Investment'.
71 Backer and Molina, 'Alternative Global Trade Systems'.
72 Rafael A. Porrata-Doria, Jr., *MERCOSUR: The Common Market of the Southern Cone.* (Durham, NC, 2005), 7–21.
73 Welber Barral, 'Dispute Settlement and Legal Harmonization in MERCOSUR', in Larry Catá Backer, ed., *Harmonizing Law in an Era of Globalization: Convergence, Divergence and Resistance* (Durham, NC, 2007).
74 'Tratado de Montevideo 1980, Montevideo, agosto de 1980': http://www.aladi.org/nsfaladi/juridica.nsf/tratadoweb/tm80.
75 Porrata-Doria, *MERCOSUR*, 16.
76 Larry C. Backer, 'Cuba Responds to Globalization and Reorganizes its Political Economy: Revolution, Retrenchment or Small Steps Towards Market Engagement Within a Marxist Framework Under the

Leadership of a Vanguard Party Apparatus', Law at the End of the Day (24 September 2010): http://lcbackerblog.blogspot.com/2010/09/cuba-respondes-to-globalization-opening.html.

77 Max Azicri, 'ALBA y el Renacimiento de la Izquierda en la América Latina,' *Dialago*, 11(Summer 2008).

78 Enrique R. Carrasco, 'Law, Hierarchy, and Vulnerable Groups in Latin America: Towards a Communal Model of Development in a Neoliberal World', *Stanford Journal of International Law*, Volume 30, Number 221(1994).

79 Chávez, 'Discurso del Presidente'.

80 Backer, 'Ideologies of Globalization'; Joseph E. Stiglitz, *Globalization and Its Discontents* (New York, 2003), 16.

81 Ibid, 67.

82 United States Senate Armed Services Committee, *Intelligence Community Annual Threat Assessment, Statement for the Record* (Washington, DC, 2008).

83 Girvan, 'ALBA, PetroCaribe'.

84 Sabrina Johnson, 'The Cuban People Demonstrate Power of Internationalism', *Socialist Voice* (17 July 2006): http://socialistvoice.ca/?p=114.

29

The G8 and the move to a globalised international economy

Andreas Freytag and Leo Wangler

Today's world is highly integrated. International trade (despite the problems caused by the world-wide economic crisis that began in 2008) is at record levels. International capital flows are intense and contribute to global imbalances, on the one hand, as well as to a better allocation of capital, on the other. This world-wide interaction is economically and politically welcome, because it potentially increases welfare and reduces global violence. However, this potential is not everywhere fully used. Instead of contributing to welfare and peace, contemporary globalisation is also increasingly volatile, transferring shocks and, therefore, is perceived as a threat. To materialise its full welfare and peace effects, globalisation needs to be mastered through international agreements and organisations.

This mixture is generally called global or international governance. It is a complex area with varying interests, which often generates different results from what seem to be optimal levels. International rules in many cases turn out to be a compromise between international diplomacy, national interest groups, anti-globalisation campaigns (well meant) of non-governmental organisations (NGOs), and serious liberalisation programmes for goods, services, and capital. Because the number of involved players is high, responsibilities are mostly unclear, and recrimination is common. International enforcement is more or less impossible; often, global rules cannot be enforced. Despite these shortcomings, there is a considerable trust in global governance. Two questions require clarification: first, is this trust justified? And second, can international governance protagonists deliver robust rules and a superior outcome?

The first problem when addressing these questions is the opaque nature of global governance. Who is really in charge? How are global policy assignments organised? How should they be organised? The answer to these questions resides in looking at the changing nature of the Group of Seven, later G8 and nowadays G20, and by laying a normative foundation for their work. The economic framework helps considerably when discussing responsibilities of different players in global governance. It helps to analyze incentives and the constraints on actors, these not only being politicians but also bureaucrats, interest groups, and NGOs. Such a framework can allow discussion of the possibilities, virtues, and constraints of a workable global governance, in particular the chances of the G8 to help bring about welfare and peace. There is a considerable literature about this complex field.[1] However, only a few writings concentrate on rules concerning global governance. This analysis is based mainly on the work of three men working explicitly on the issue of global governance: Cordell Hull, Wilhelm Röpke, and Jan Tumlir.

The politician Hull, the United States Secretary of State from 1933 to 1945, was awarded the Nobel Prize for Peace for founding the United Nations (UN). Unlike many of his coevals, he saw a necessity to include all nations in the global economy after the Second World War;[2] a goal he achieved. Because of his efforts, he is a symbol for peace via integration and, therefore, germane for global policies nowadays. Röpke and Tumlir analyzed the interaction between national and global economic policy, which has been a highly relevant issue for many decades.[3] Their work shows clearly that domestic economic policies in individual Powers are determinants of the success of international cooperation. Of course, the relative weight of a Power is decisive; some Powers may be too small to exert influence. As a working hypothesis, the G20 Powers are potential relevant players.

The fundamental criterion for basic rules for global governance policy is an adequate national policy, which acknowledges the importance of open markets for welfare and peace. In addition, it is based on a logical and consistent assignment of responsibility. International contracts in reverse can be equally important for national policy, with the positive result that it protects them from the demands of national interest groups; in other words, the domestic sovereignty of economic policy can be (re-)established by giving up international sovereignty. Finally, criteria must be found to coordinate politics on an international level.

With the outbreak of the First World War, Hull had already noted that integration and international trade are peace-making processes: 'From then on, to me, unhampered trade dovetailed with peace; high tariffs, trade barriers and unfair economic competition with war'.[4] This insight later led Hull to influence a post-war order after 1945 that was not shaped by isolation and poverty (like the pastoralisation plan suggested for Germany by Henry Morgenthau[5]) but by openness and constitutional rules. This finding is backed empirically and widely approved: international trade not only leads to greater wealth, it also sees more interstate peace.[6] The European example shows the role of economic integration for peace.[7] On 1 January 1940, Hull pointed to the United States peace-making role; after the war, Americans were to exert influence 'in the direction of creating a stable and enduring world order under law'.[8] The consequence of this claim was the foundation of the UN. The discrediting of the Morgenthau plan before the end of the war also goes back to Hull's interventions.

However, an international order that relies on the individual power of a single economy is unlikely to exist permanently. This does not mean that such an international order cannot be initiated and shaped by strong individual Powers (for instance, the United States and probably China). But individual Powers will never have peaceful and legitimate possibilities to force others that do not comply with the order to abide by the rules. The sovereignty of single members must be kept; a functioning mechanism of putting through agreements requires consensus and the will of nation states to comply with a global authority acting as keeper of the rules. Certainly, this mechanism is the most difficult element of global governance. Experience with the dispute settlement mechanism of the General Agreement on Trade and Tariffs (GATT) until 1994, and the World Trade Organization (WTO) thereafter, suggests scepticism.

Thus, a different approach is needed. An international order can work if it is rule-based and fulfils minimum requirements. Part of these basic requirements for a functioning global economic order is that the national economic policies of the individual Powers are compatible with free trade, openness, and integration. Put differently:

> If we claim that the national and international order are insolvably connected and that the former cannot be reached without the latter, then we do not have anything in common with some form of nationalism that merely considers national order to be a programme of ruthlessness and pettiness. What we have in mind is the complete opposite thereof: not a national order that is end in itself and immolates the international one in case of a conflict, but one that adheres to the international one and that prepares and supports it from the lowest

levels of society. We do not complain about too much, but too little internationality, and we demand that it – just like the charity in the formerly cited English saying – starts at home.[9]

Ideally, the national order pursues certain legalities to create this compatibility. Elements include openness, freedom of contract, rule of law, liability, and sound money. Such an order may well be compared with the Augmented Washington Consensus.[10] Since Walter Eucken's fundamental studies in 1952, these institutional prerequisites have often been discussed.[11] In addition, the right policy assignment is needed; that is, each objective needs to be assigned a proper means to achieve consistency in reaching goals.[12] In addition, responsibilities need to be clearly defined so that each goal can be represented only through one responsible organisation. This requirement does not apply only to national economic policy but also within the global order.

Finally, there is an intimate relationship between the international and the national order, since politicoeconomic decision-makers on the national level apparently give away freedom of action in agreeing to international treaties (for instance, the establishment of a global order). Critics speak of an abandoning of sovereignty. Following the logic of collective decision processes, the contrary applies: instead of giving away sovereignty, individual governments gain in capacity to act. Thus, the vital function of GATT consisted in relieving the government from the influence of vested interests.[13] Even if one concedes that it is wise macroeconomically to open markets unilaterally, the danger of backsliding into protectionism remains. Although this is not excluded completely by a binding treaty under international law, it is at least considerably impeded. Insofar, the creation of supranational institutions after the Second World War, co-initiated by Hull, marks an improvement compared with former global orders.[14]

In addition to globally oriented national policies, under specific circumstances, global economic policy needs coordination amongst countries. Therefore, a global order has to establish rules that determine whether coordination is needed and when single countries in competition should enforce their policies.[15] Four prerequisites must be accomplished for political coordination to be useful. First, international coordination requires transnational spill-over; that is, private and public measures in one country must affect other countries. Second, a clearly defined economic problem with a clearly formulated strategy as an answer must be addressed. In case of uncertainty about the best way to progress, the competition of economic policies should find a single solution instead of coordinating diverse national policies. Otherwise decisions will not follow the rule of law, but the rule of force. Third, and a corollary of the second point, partners should be close enough to each other to experience similar problems with comparable preferred solutions, for example, the former G8, or G7. Finally, a group of countries wanting to coordinate their political responses must have proper instruments to do so.

In conclusion, a welfare-enhancing, peace-encouraging and functional global governance demands considerable efforts and a global consensus about principles. This unity is demonstrated best if national economic governance complies with global governance that encourages freedom and openness. Nevertheless, there is a need for international agreements to define the related rules of the game. The G8 may provide such rules.

Originally meant to be a small and one-time meeting of the leaders of the world's six leading Powers in Rambouillet, France, to solve economic problems amongst themselves, the G5, plus Italy, quickly evolved into the G7 and became a permanent institution with a diplomatic procedure. The process started in 1975 with an intimate and personal meeting of six presidents, prime ministers, and chancellors. The topic was macroeconomic policy coordination between the six governments. Twenty-five years later, the G8 governments were discussing the problems of the world and were producing a charter against the global digital divide. Other current issues were debt relief, lifelong learning, global climate change, and the like. On the same token, the number of participants increased. In 1998, with Russia now attending as a full member, the Birmingham summit saw the first official G8 meeting.[16] Critics questioned this extension; India and China were neglected, although they were, respectively, a long-standing WTO member or a Power soon to join. Since 2009, the G8 is cooperating closer with the G20, a group including themselves and 12 other emerging Powers founded in 1999. The reason for this extension is twofold: the emerging economies have increasingly gained influence in the world economy; and the economic crisis that started in the industrialised world has reached the emerging and developing countries. Therefore, the latter have to have a greater say in global affairs.

Despite this formal extension within and, later, outside the G8, one must not overestimate the G8–G20's influence on global economic affairs. Lacking a secretariat, the G8–G20 is not an international organisation. It cannot formally coordinate economic policies nor enforce certain policy measures on its members. It is a means of soft coordination, which may be a good way to bring about globalisation from below and by persuasion.[17] Unfortunately, however, the formalisation of the G8–G20 did not improve the policy coordination process. On the contrary, the G8–G20 seems primarily a huge international 'policy show'. Its summits have more and more been converted into total media events with results prepared beforehand by diplomatic sherpas and shaped in a way that the leaders can report success to their peoples. In fact, the political economy of international organisations suggests that the G8 is used by the leaders to gain a competitive edge over the opposition in their home country.[18] In this setting, the result of the summit as such seems of decreasing importance. It also does not come as a surprise if both the summit itself and the result are increasingly expensive for the G8 countries' taxpayers.

What drives this poor and misguided performance? Three examples demonstrate its opportunities and weaknesses. With the 1999 Cologne Charter, 'Aims and Ambitions for Lifelong Learning',[19] the G8 made a declaration in Cologne with respect to education policy. It had the target of anchoring the issue of lifelong learning into the national awareness, but without any binding promises, especially not for countries outside the group. Measurable success cannot be seen, but at least the issue education is very strong in their agenda, and not only in the G8 countries.

The second example is climate change. Regarding this issue, the German Federal Chancellor persuaded the other leaders in Heiligendamm in June 2007 of the necessity for drastic measures to protect the climate. The second declaration of the meeting conveys that 'In setting a global goal for emissions reductions in the process we have agreed today involving all major emitters, we will consider seriously the decisions made by the European Union, Canada and Japan [to] include at least a halving of global emissions by 2050'.[20] However, the wording cannot be seen as a reliable commitment; at most it is a non-binding declaration of aims. Policy cooperation regarding climate change issues is difficult to reach on an international level, something observed by the failure of the negotiations in Copenhagen in 2009. The negotiation process might have taken a different direction if the G8 acted as a single player. However, this did not happen. For instance, the United States took the position that it made cooperation dependent on the willingness of China (a member of the G20) to cooperate.

The third example (also decided in Heiligendamm) is development policy. The Germans rightly stressed the enormous prominence of governance-structures in African countries and anchored this point in the meeting's declaration.[21] These are basic conditions to solve other problems, like sustainability, peace, security, and health. Without institutional reforms, every other measure is pointless, as the history of development policy shows. However, the G8 has no direct influence on the good conduct of African governments as long as it respects national sovereignty. Thus, conditions for G8 political coordination for the benefit of African countries do not really exist. In addition, not every policy option of development is used, for instance, agricultural trade. Instead of using agricultural liberalisation as an instrument for development policy, it seems that politicians are more interested in focusing further on aid policy. In this context, it seems that politicians have an interest to connect the abatement of climate change with aid transfers and do not attempt to open their markets for developing countries.

It becomes apparent how this mechanism has mostly failed until now. First, every declaration is *non-binding* and will be converted only if it is *politically opportune*. In other cases, there is a benign neglect. Second, the G20 overextends itself if it tries to solve other countries' problems. The extension of the G8 to the G20 implemented additional heterogeneity. On the one hand, it is convenient to take into account that emerging economies like China, Brazil, or India will become more important in the near future. On the other, it seems that a G20-*Pax* will be more difficult to achieve, as this is the case for a G8-*Pax;* and therefore the G20 very likely becomes a stumbling-block instead of a building-block. It counts even more if only half-hearted measures are taken, which in the first place serve the interests of voters in the G20 countries or are due to pressures from NGOs, for example, debt relief without liberalisation of trade.[22]

One can confidently assume that the governments are informed about the cause–effect relationships. Why is the outcome of the G8 summits so unfocused? Another close look at the meeting in Heiligendamm, especially the German agenda, may help to explain this phenomenon. The German G8 presidency developed an agenda without clear priorities and strategies, with randomly chosen issues and targets out of all political fields and with a constantly growing number of issues.[23] A public choice explanation could be that the federal government in 2007 (especially consisting of a so-called grand coalition) needed to assign many issues to grant small political successes to a high number of resort leaders.[24] If the current problems are not solved by implementing binding targets, governments have to use the G8 meetings for crisis management. This was exactly what happened with the G8–G20 meetings in Toyako in 2008 and L'Aquila in 2009. However, highly short-term oriented, such policy is not likely to be sustainable.

Additional topics of the German G8 agenda of Heiligendamm may shed further light: the German Government's aim was to reduce the social burdens that might come along with globalisation. This issue was strongly in the focus of the German federal government, because there was a heated debate about introducing minimum wages. A fixing of higher minimum social standards would have reduced the negative consequences of minimum wages, since all G8 members would have experienced a higher social standard. Second, the transatlantic free trade area has been a German policy objective for a long time, but according to experienced negotiators of transatlantic dialogue it has little chance of success. Progress along these lines would count as the government's success. In addition there are modern fields of policies, but also economically relevant issues like climate change, energy efficiency, and supply of natural resources. In general, the agenda of the federal government for the G8 summit in 2007 was driven by domestic debates. The interest of other governments in many of these issues, e.g. social covering of globalisation, was possibly much lower, so that success was not likely. The same observation with other topics seems to hold for the G8 summits in Toyaoko (2008) and l'Aquila (2009).

To be fair, the G8's occasional successes should not be underestimated. The summits regularly address current topics and support the general international political and economic order. One example is debt relief for developing countries, which started in Cologne in 1999. The Cologne debt relief was well adjusted to the highly indebted poor countries (HIPC) program of the Bretton Woods institutions and supported a shift in the international development policy scheme. The HIPC initiative has the distinctive feature that it only allows debt relief once the country in question has started policy reforms. After 2000, the granting of debt relief positively correlated with improvements in political governance in respective countries, which could not be observed in the 1990s.[25] In this period, the decision to grant debt relief was mainly driven by past debt relief measures. The explanation for such economically irrational behavior lies in the nature of political economy: for governments, it pays to 'help' the poorest, even if it is achieved by spending taxpayers' money instead of opening up markets for Ricardo-or-Heckscher-Ohlin goods. The latter would increase welfare both at home and abroad, but in the long run; in the short run, the government of the industrialised country granting debt relief is better off.[26] In addition to successes like this one, there are other situations when the coordination process helped to harness globalisation, to improve economic policy, or to avoid critical situations. Often, it may be too difficult to trace certain successes back to special G8 summits. So a clear-cut judgement on the virtues of the G8 process is difficult if not impossible.

Apparently, the current global order policy is far from satisfying the basic rules outlined above. Multilateral trade policy is not moving an inch; the multilateral efforts of liberalisation within the Doha Round did not proceed during recent years; instead, bilateral agreements are mushrooming. The international financial crisis shows that it is important to find general rules for the financial markets; maybe the Basle 3 accord can help to mitigate the problems.[27] The development of Africa is proceeding too slowly. Finally, there are free-riders in questions of climate protection. However, most of these problems are not problems of awareness but of convention. It would be naive to think that the governments do not know about the inadequacies of current policy. The reasons for this situation have been discussed above.

During the last few years, the Doha Development Round did not make any progress.[28] This difficulty is due to existing problems within the United States; and in other parts of the world, the process of liberalising trade is slowing down. At the moment it seems that the liberalisation process has come to an end. In China, for instance, the economic reform program, the basis for the comprehensive market-oriented reforms of recent years, has lost speed; whereas in India, the 1990s tendency towards liberalism has made room for a new protectionism. Moreover, the boom of resources leads resource-rich countries towards economic nationalism and beggar-thy-neighbour policies. Europe's multilateral eagerness has noticeably decreased, and the European Commission still has a difficult time taking leadership in the Doha Round. France and Germany particularly block necessary reforms of the Common Agriculture Policy. Nonetheless, a successful outcome of the round remains one of the declared goals of European Union (EU) foreign trade policy. Yet, this supposed dedication to multilateralism in no way reflects the actual economic strategy. In other countries, there are debates about a plurilateral approach if the multilateral avenue is closed.[29]

Meanwhile, the EU has concentrated its trade policy almost exclusively on bilateral free trade agreements, nowadays called Economic Partnership Agreements, and recently started negotiations with 24 countries.[30] In 2008 the EU created a union with Mediterranean countries. Even though each of these free trade contracts might be useful when regarded alone, the liberalisation process lowers the chances for successful multilateral trade liberalisation; and it reduces pressures on national politicians to bring the Doha Round to completion. As mentioned earlier, in 2007 the German Chancellor, Angela Merkel, made use of the German G8 presidency to promote closer economic collaboration on both sides of the Atlantic so that the transatlantic relationship can generally be improved. However, in the meantime, national governments are confronted with the problems of the financial crisis and therefore bilateral collaboration lost priority on the political agenda. From an international perspective, such an agenda is questionable, as a most favoured nation (MFN) agreement between the two biggest trade blocs (the EU and the United States) threatens to undermine international organisations like the WTO significantly.

Finally, it needs to be pointed out that another development in trade policy hardly conforms to good global governance. Instead of applying MFN tariffs, there are a growing number of non-tariff barriers.[31] The EU is no exception: besides tariffs, anti-dumping measures and technical standards are increasingly used. These problems have increased during the financial crisis. Both instruments are discriminatory and impair not only foreign countries but also the EU itself. It is certain that the European Commission should take a leading role internationally in developing a long-term strategy to dismantle global protectionism, regardless of the results of the Doha Round.[32] In any case, the world trade order requires both refreshing as well as new initiatives to resuscitate multilateralism.

The necessity of an international climate agreement is still a young problem of global governance. Economic policy in this field depends on the expertise and research from the natural sciences to make proper political decisions. The necessity for political reaction was given only after the scientific 'diagnosis' that global climate change is caused by human beings had been widely accepted. Important steps towards climate protection were established in the 1990s. A temporary peak of global governance with regard to this issue was the Kyoto Protocol (KP), signed in 1997. The KP was agreed within the framework of the UN climate convention and was enforced in 2005 after Russian ratification.[33] KP's main goal is to reduce the output of greenhouse gases between 2008 and 2012 (based on the reference year 1990) by 5.2 per cent on the global level. After the 2009 world summit for a post-KP in Copenhagen, it seems that international policy coordination related to climate change is confronting severe problems.

Beside those problems related to the future of climate policy, the basic concepts established with the KP contain desirable features. First, the contract considers national aspects in energy policy, which means that every single country has different reduction duties. Second, a worldwide emission certificate trade system was considered.[34] Additional policy instruments aimed at creating incentives for companies to reduce emissions in developing countries are the so-called 'Clean Development Mechanism' (CDM) and/or the 'Joint Implementation' instrument. For a post-KP agreement, it is also planned to integrate the problem of deforestation into the accord.

Although the KP is one of the broadest supranational agreements and contains a number of reasonable policy instruments, problems have occurred with its application. That the United States as one of the two largest emitters of greenhouse gases still has not ratified it seems to point to an international free-rider attitude. Thus, the implementation of the KP, considering national aspects, proceeded heterogeneously.[35] Also the emission certificate trade system could not be established worldwide. CDM is a broad framework; however, it still is of low significance for firms. One reason might be the existence of high transaction costs. Especially with regard to the problems of implementing the agreement and the high transaction costs related to CDM, the positive impact of the KP can be expected to be sub-optimally low.

The media are increasingly focused on global climate change. Prognoses like the 2007 report of the Intergovernmental Panel on Climate Control or studies led by the English economist Sir Nicolas Stern draw alarming conclusions.[36] Despite criticisms of the studies because of concerns about their methodology, the message is clear: mankind is called to action. It can further be observed that politicians (especially in countries where high environmental standards have been introduced) are eager to use these studies to set high environmental standards worldwide: for instance, in the hope of future exports.[37] Some governments seem to connect industrial policy to climate change policy to generate comparative advantages. This incentive seems to be even stronger when other countries free-ride on international environmental agreements. If the government is successful in enforcing the high national standards later at the international level, there would be a competitive advantage for domestic producers of 'clean' technologies. Here lies one explanation for the engagement of the German Government in the implementation of high environmental standards within the EU (in line with the German EU presidency from January to July 2007), within the G8 (the G8 summit in Heiligendamm), and on the global level (the UN General Assembly in New York).

Despite the critique that some international climate policy is also driven by national interests, the political engagement of the German Government has had the positive effect of contributing positively to the global climate debate. Moreover the EU is often seen as an international leader in global governance related to climate problems. For a succession agreement, the general idea is that the existing KP can be used as base. However, the international community has to cooperate more to overcome the described problems and to establish a post-KP agreement. Because of the general dynamics that climate change causes for political decision-makers, there is the danger that interventionist actions become a serious political option.

What to do? The current international policy is inadequate; it barely fulfils the requirements stated above. In many cases seemingly national, but in truth particular, interests are dominating the global policy. From the governments' point of view, an irrational economic policy in economic terms is politically rational. It will be installed against better knowledge; this is not a sign of quality for governments. An economically rational policy often works out only in the long run to enhance welfare and may cause the government to lose the next election.

The previous explanations have made clear that global policy cannot be changed via one single institution. The World Bank and the International Monetary Fund are struggling with their own problems; and the WTO is exclusively concentrating on worldwide trade issues and fighting the drift towards regional agreements and for the success of the Doha Round. Even this relatively small challenge is a huge obstacle because of the heterogeneity of its members and the necessity to reach consensus, which cause high transaction costs. There is no 'global player'. Following the logic of Röpke and Tumlir, a solution to this dilemma could look like the following: a small, but effective group of countries revises global policy: a plurilateral initiative to a multilateral policy. The members of the former G8 adjust their policy at home and scrap their international platform for policy coordination. Further, the G20 can be seen as an extended platform that particularly focuses on development as well as climate change issues and tries to spread the ideas of cooperation agreed by the G8. The countries that now constitute the G20 act closer together with the G8, but their acceptance of all agreed coordination policies is unnecessary. Does the group of the seven leading industrialised nations and Russia (the former G8) have the chance to contribute to an authentic and consistent global policy?

In its first years, G7 meetings were informal and dealt with macroeconomic connections amongst the countries. Over time, the issues became broader and broader, and the meetings more and more bloated. This process did not stop by transforming the G8 into the G20. Nowadays huge diplomatic staffs (the sherpas) prepare the meetings together with explanatory notes, which usually takes months. The decisions have of course no stringent effect on other countries, but they are considered to be important for the global economy. This mechanism could be used in another, welfare-enhancing way. The G8 contains a small number of relatively homogeneous members. If it agrees on small and manageable steps of policy cooperation, which would be binding only on its members, the sovereignty of other states would be left untouched. Nevertheless, there can be a noticeable pull from a G8 initiative, for instance the one-sided cutback of agricultural protectionism. If, for example, the G8 jointly declared the abandonment of export and product subsidies in the agricultural sector under certain conditions (say a plurilateral agreement with some Organisation for Economic Co-operation and Development members) there would be increased pressure on other agricultural protectionists like Switzerland or Norway. Even if a multilateral solution could not be reached, negotiators would have the chance to achieve a unilateral liberalisation via the MFN principle. In any case, the group of the seven most important industrialised nations together with Russia form a strong bloc; they could agree on an order within their group that can be the base of a global order. Instead of a *Pax Americana*, conceived by Hull in 1940, there would be a G8-*Pax*.[38]

This option justifies a closer look at the processes within the G8. The G8 can apparently only contribute to binding global cooperation in the long run, if the production of an agenda is not made by a current presidency. That caveat would both decrease the chances for single actors to abuse the presidency for domestic or election campaign uses and obviate the risk of a misguided agenda. Should such an agenda materialise, the presidency would be devaluated immediately in the eyes of member governments, which would lose faith in setting the G8 agenda for the world economy. However, the possibility of gaining political utility from a reasonable agenda fashioned by all eight Powers would be created. It would even be fair for all the members, including the chairing government, to use such an agreement in domestic election campaigns.

Another alleged disadvantage would be the creation of a small office to set the agenda. After all, it is seen as a great benefit for G8 meetings that they are informal and work without an organised structure. On the other hand, it can be observed that as the organisation of G8–G20 summits increases, ensuring positive political outcomes will ensue. If the G8 takes an organisational form that increases efficiency, gains can be expected. Thus, a permanent office would be valuable. It could collect policy issues from the member-states, group them, and search for inconsistencies. If consistent policy goals were then formulated in a clear way and could be legally confirmed, disadvantages could be transformed into advantages. But the creation of an office with a clear mandate would be only a first step to an international agreement. Informal G8 processes would have to be displaced by a rule-driven system. The potential success of delegating tasks is high, as the example of many independent central banks, the former GATT office, and the present WTO shows. The problem of control seems to be solvable, and the different interests of members can be combined cooperatively.

The questions of how the framework of the G8–G20 is influencing economic policy today and which options are feasible to improve their performance can be answered. Thus, it is possible to find an anchor for a real global policy and secure it in the long run. If and how far the former G8 can use its homogeneity and clearness of purpose to establish an intragroup arrangement, it could be the basis for international comity. This option is based, first, on the well-proven evidence that peace and welfare are linked to each other; second, on the fact that it is impossible to enforce an international order from the top; and, third, that international agreements can be used to keep national interest groups in check. According to this reasoning, this option is an alternative that is superior to the *status quo*.

All depends on the cognition of the governments in the former G8 countries that to be reasonable politically can give economic rationality a higher focus. The alternative discussed here could help to harmonise both political and economic concerns. The political advantages shift from setting the agenda to the actual agreement. With useful declarations in economic terms and their conversion into policy, the G8 presidency could generate political advantages. In fact, the G8 provides an optimal framework to shape the process of a 'globalisation from below'. It leaves all nations with the freedom to pursue their own policy model; and it encourages policy cooperation without strict enforcement, thereby allowing for the competition of ideas. Most importantly, it gives the group of industrialised nations the chance to proceed with innovative and welfare-enhancing policies, which then can be copied by other countries if they prove to be successful.

Notes

1 The websites of the Toronto-based G8 Research Group (www.g7.utoronto.ca/) and G20 Research Group (www.g20.utoronto.ca/), respectively, display an impressive collection of official documents, research papers, and topical comments.
2 For instance, Hull Speech, 9 April 1944, in United States Chamber of Commerce, *Measures to Promote International Law and Order* (New York, 1944), 383–429.

3 For example, Friedrich August von Hayek, Hugo Sieber, Egon Tuchtfeldt, and Hans Willgerodt, eds., *Internationale Ordnung—heute, Wilhelm Röpke—Ausgewählte Werke*, 3 Aufl (Bern, Stuttgart, 1979); Jan Tumlir, 'International Economic Order and Democratic Constitutionalism', *ORDO*, 34(1983), 71–86; idem., *Protectionism: Trade Policy in Democratic Societies* (Washington, DC, 1985).

4 Michael A. Butler, *Cautious Visionary. Cordell Hull and Trade Reform, 1933–1937* (Kent, OH, London, 1998), 7.

5 Henry Morgenthau, *Germany is Our Problem* (New York, 1945).

6 See Jong-Wha Lee and Ju Hyun Pyun, *Does Trade Integration Contribute to Peace?* Asian Development Bank, Working Paper Series: Regional Economic Integration, No.24 (January 2009); Edward D. Mansfield, *Power, Trade, and War* (Princeton, NJ, 1994), Chapter 4. However, it needs to be mentioned that the intensification of international competition, which is often meant by the notion 'globalisation', might well lead to fears and extremist reactions. At least this is what the theoretical analysis shows. Cf. Ronald Wintrobe, *Rational Extremism. The Political Economy of Radicalism* (Cambridge, UK, 2006).

7 Fredrik Erixon, Andreas Freytag, and Gernot Pehnelt, *The Rome Treaty at 50*, ECIPE Policy Briefs No. 4 (Brussels, 2007).

8 Julius W. Pratt, *Cordell Hull* (New York, 1964), 718.

9 Hayeck *et al.*, *Wilhelm Röpke*, 34. Our translation.

10 Center for International Development at Harvard University [CID], 'Global Trade Negotiations Homepage' (2010): www.cid.harvard.edu/cidtrade/issues/washington.html.

11 For a detailed overview see the contributions in Wolfgang Stützel et al., *Standard Text on the Social Market Economy* (Stuttgart, New York, 1982).

12 Jan Tinbergen, *On the Theory of Economic Policy* (Amsterdam, 1952).

13 See Paul R. Krugman, 'What Should Trade Negotiators Negotiate About?', *Journal of Economic Literature*, 35(1997), 113–20; Tumlir, 'International Economic Order'; idem., *Protectionism*.

14 Andreas Freytag and Razeen Sally, 'Globalisation and Trade Policy Response: 1900 and 2000 Compared', *Jahrbuch für Neue Politische Ökonomie*, 19(2000), 191–222.

15 Henning Klodt, *Internationale Politikkoordination—Leitlinien für den globalen Wirtschaftspolitiker*, Institut für Weltwirtschaft, Kieler Diskussionsbeiträge, Number 343(1999).

16 P.I. Hajnal, *The G8 System and the G20: Evolution, Role and Documentation* (Aldershot, 1999).

17 Razeen Sally, 'Looking Askance at Global Governance,' in John J. Kirton, Joseph P. Daniels, and Andreas Freytag, eds., *Guiding Global Order. G8 Governance in the Twenty-First Century* (Aldershot, 2001), 55–76.

18 Roland Vaubel, 'A Public Choice View of International Organization', in Roland Vaubel and Thomas D. Willett, hrsg., *The Political Economy of International Organizations: A Public Choice Approach* (Boulder, CO, San Francisco, CA, Oxford, 1991), 27–45.

19 G8, Köln Charter: 'Aims and Ambitions for Lifelong Learning' (1999): www.g8.utoronto.ca/summit/1999koln/charter.htm.

20 G8, 'Growth and Responsibility in the World Economy, Summit Declaration', Heiligendamm (7 June 2007): www.g-8.de/Webs/G8/EN/G8Summit/SummitDocuments/summit documents.html.

21 G8, 'Growth and responsibility in Africa, Summit Declaration', Heiligendamm, 8 June 2007: www.g-8.de/Content/DE/Artikel/G8Gipfel/Anlage/Abschlusserkl_C3_A4rungen/WV-afrika-en.html.

22 See Edward E. Leamer, *The Heckscher-Ohlin Model in Theory and Practice* (Princeton, NJ, 1995). Cf. M. Morishima, *Ricardo's Economics: A General Equilibrium Theory of Distribution and Growth* (New York, 1989).

23 Bundesregierung, 'Wachstum und Verantwortung—Leitmotiv der deutschen G8-Präsidentschaft', (2007): www.g-8.de/Webs/G8/DE/G8Gipfel/Agenda/agenda.html.

24 Vaubel, 'Public Choice View'.

25 Andreas Freytag and Gernot Pehnelt, 'Debt Relief and Governance Quality in Developing Countries,' *World Development*, Vol. 27(2009), 62–80.

26 Ibid.; Katharina Michaelowa, 'The political economy of the enhanced HIPC-Initiative,' *Public Choice*, 114(2003), 461–76.

27 G. S. Cassidy, 'The Basel III Proposals' Flaws', *American Banker*, Volume 175, Issue 74(2010), 8.

28 Doha Development is the WTO's current trade-negotiation round that began in November 2001. It seeks to lower trade barriers and allow increased global trade. See Rainer Hofmann and Gabriele Tondl, *European Union and the WTO Doha Round* (Baden-Baden, 2007).

29 Peter Draper, 'Whither the Multilateral Trading System? Implications for (South) Africa', SAIIA Occasional Paper Number 64, (July 2010).

30 Peter Draper, 'EU-Africa Trade Relations: The Political Economy of Economic Partnership Agreements', *Jan Tumlir Policy Essay*, Number 2 (Brussels, 2007); Stephen Woolcock, 'European Union Policy Towards Free Trade Agreements,' *ECIPE Working Paper*, No. 3 (Brussels, 2007).

31 M. Bussière, E. Pérez-Barreiro, R. Straub, and D. Taglioni, *Protectionist responses to the Crisis: Global Trends and Implications* (Frankfurt, 2010).

32 Patrick A. Messerlin, 'Assessing the EC Trade Policy in Goods', *Jan Tumlir Policy Essay*, Number 1 (Brussels, 2007).

33 With Russia's signature, the necessary condition was fulfilled; 55 states that together create more than 55 percent of global greenhouse gases signed the Protocol.

34 Emissions trading is ultimately based on the Coase Theorem, since the trade with certificates keeps transaction costs low and sets incentives to reduce emissions. R. H. Coase, 'The Problem of Social Costs', *Journal of Law and Economics*, 3(October 1960), 1–44.

35 Germany likes presenting itself as precursor in climate protection, for example, and has taken some parts of the KP very seriously.

36 Nicholas Stern, *The Economics of Climate Change* (Cambridge, UK, 2007).

37 Andreas Freytag and Leo Wangler, 'Strategic Trade Policy as Response to Climate Change? The Political Economy of Climate', *Jena Economic Research Papers*, 2(2007).

38 There is a similarity to Bergsten's 'Open regionalism', a program that allows participating countries not to fully commit to complete liberalisation packages. The G8 can form the core that commits; other Powers could choose what they like but can learn how beneficial the full program is. See C. Fred Bergsten, 'Open Regionalism', Institute for International Economics, Working Paper 97–3 (Washington, 1997).

30

The opposition to the globalised international economy

Bruno R. Wüest

Over the past three decades, the liberalisation of international trade, finance, and investment has created new opportunities for dynamic business actors. The resulting trends of increased flows of people, goods, services, capital, and information can be subsumed under the term 'economic globalisation'.[1] Some scholars conclude that economic globalisation leads to a Kantian capitalist peace, because economic liberalism is singled out as a commonly shared ideological belief, and war or even protest becomes ever more costly in light of growing economic interdependence.[2] By contrast, popular bestsellers regularly declare that economic globalisation is an irreversible ill for modern societies.[3] However, both of these views overlook that economic globalisation has massive redistributive consequences, which give rise to new societal disparities and new political opposition.[4] And especially since the 2008 global financial, economic, and public debt crises, there is increasing interest in how and by whom the global economy is challenged.

Two basic assumptions guide this chapter. First, increasing economic globalisation is understood as an inherent political phenomenon. To survive, markets must connect organisations and individuals as well as satisfy the needs of their participants. Whilst efficient markets fulfil these functions, they tend to centralise resources and economic power, create inequalities regarding the access of individuals to them, and sometimes produce harmful externalities.[5] In short, markets can provoke considerable contestation, which profoundly affects the political sphere. Second, a comprehensive assessment opposition to the globalised economy is difficult, since causal mechanisms behind the rise and fall of diverse oppositional actors are complex and unclear. Thus, opposition to the globalised economy has to be conceptualised in a fairly broad way. With the end of the Cold War and the global diffusion of neoliberalism, formerly 'frozen' frontlines were resolved but new oppositions emerged. On one hand, both the traditional class-based opposition in Western countries and the real socialist alternatives lost much of their strength and appeal; but they did not entirely vanish. On the other, opposition to the globalised economy is reinforced by populists and social movements.

In the recent past, nation-states have become deeply integrated into a multilevel governance system and a network of bilateral treaties.[6] Integration provided the backbone for the global diffusion of economic liberalism, which found new terrain after the collapse of state socialism in 1989–91. Hence, the spread of economic liberalism was propelled by both socialism's failure and the advocacy of the United States and the Bretton Woods institutions like the International Monetary Fund.[7] Although value changes favoring economic liberalism first captured parties on the right in advanced economies, both the left in these economies and the political elites in many developing countries followed suit after 1989–91.[8]

The most visible consequence of this transformation is the reorganisation of the economies of previous communist one-party systems. Most members of the former Council for Mutual Economic Assistance have successfully transformed their command economies into market ones and have fully integrated into the global economy.[9] Moreover, most of the remaining socialist countries have transformed their economies to competitive sites for the global economy. Most significantly, China has risen from the poverty of Maoist rule to one of the world's economic powerhouses. And even Cuba, one of the last strongholds of a command economy, has recently started to create opportunities for private businesses. Marxian socialism has thus lost much of its appeal as an alternative to capitalism. The few remaining countries with planned economies and socialist one-party systems, like North Korea, and including Cuba, are trapped in a process of protracted decay.[10]

The end of the Cold War also heralded the decline of Marxist rebellions, another form of the socialist counterhegemony to global capitalism. Accordingly, the last two decades brought decisive changes to the scope and intensity of internal conflicts in developing countries.[11] Most importantly, the role of external actors in civil wars has been markedly reduced. During the Cold War, although the United States supported some rebel groups in the developing world, it was much more common for the Soviet Union to side with revolutionary movements. Many rebellions thus stood under the influence of Marxist political groups, directly challenging the Western democratic capitalist model. With Soviet collapse, superpower support ceased and many seemingly intractable civil wars with Marxist rebel participation ended (for example in El Salvador, Nicaragua, and Guatemala).[12] Violent revolutionary opposition therefore seems now a less important threat to global markets than during the twentieth century. Nevertheless, a few remaining Marxist rebellions still affect some countries, notably the Naxalite insurgency in India.

With respect to several developments, the historically contentious division between labor and capital has lost much of its importance in structuring political conflicts in advanced economies. On the organisational level, major left-wing parties have abandoned their once distinct opposition to free markets, and trade unions and radical left parties seem to have severe problems in their capacity to challenge seriously the economically liberal mainstream. The weakening of class cleavage is caused by structural transformations in society. Although exact explanations vary, the decline of class cleavage is mostly ascribed to secularisation, declining materialist values, rising levels of education, improved standards of living, the feminisation of the workforce, sectoral economic change, or a combination of these factors.[13]

Individual economic preferences have therefore undergone major transformations, and some research even suggests that they have become irrelevant for political competition in advanced economies. Argument exists that because of individualisation and alienation, people have become politically indifferent in general and, hence, are not easy to mobilise, which undermines the formation of new cleavages.[14] Others maintain that the most important political conflicts have shifted to cultural issues like immigration, thus leaving economic issues like market liberalisation to be 'valence issues' on which all parties agree.[15] These findings conform to the notion of a more generally widening distance between the citizenry and the political elites. Economic discontent, if existing, is therefore increasingly mis- or underrepresented in politics of advanced economies.[16] Moreover, economic integration weakens electoral support for political incumbents, because voters do not attribute national economic performance to the efforts of governments anymore.[17] And globalisation serves more as a strategic discourse constructed by its supporters to legitimate far-reaching reforms than as programmatic vehicles of oppositional forces.[18]

Not only the structural basis of class cleavage has weakened; one of its main organisational manifestations, trade unions, are in decline. From the end of the Second World War until the late 1970s, labor markets became increasingly organised in advanced economies. More specifically, unions increasingly merged into small numbers of powerful unions, membership grew faster than the workforce, and wage-setting became increasingly centralised. Since the 1980s, however, union density has fallen in most countries, and many centralised systems of wage-setting have been breaking apart.[19] Yet there are important qualifications to this overall finding. There are, first, important differences amongst countries with respect to these trends. In countries where unions administer unemployment insurance and wage-bargaining has remained centralised (Belgium and Scandinavia) unions kept their strength. In Anglo-Saxon countries, by contrast, unionisation was vulnerable in periods of high unemployment and inflation and suffered significant decline.[20] Within the United States, for example, unions have experienced steady setbacks in coverage and density during the past half-century, which began earlier and has been more severe than in all other Western countries.

Further, the number of workers covered by collective agreements has not fallen in lockstep with union density. Except in Anglo-Saxon countries, coverage remained roughly constant. Nevertheless, decreasing union density is a problem for unions even when coverage remains high, because it impairs their ability to mobilise supporters in labor disputes and raise resources.[21] The relationship between social democratic parties and unions in Western Europe, until the 1970s a solid political coalition, has weakened significantly in the last decades. The shift of social democrats towards economic liberalism and their experience that strong ties to unions are an electoral liability have made them reluctant to cooperate strongly with the trade unions.

In addition, unions lost much internal coherence because they have to represent their members' increasingly heterogeneous interests. Regarding room to negotiate, they face continuous pressure to make concessions in light of high unemployment numbers and increasing welfare costs. Nevertheless, unions have proven astonishingly resilient in maintaining social protection (at least for their traditional clientele) at a fairly high level in most advanced economies. In addition, they have begun to repoliticise their strategies in the last decade.[22] Today, labor movement politics goes well beyond relationships with labor-friendly parties and negotiations with social partners and governments. Unions extensively engage in grassroots politics and public campaigns, making them much more visible. Therefore, trade unions, especially from the public sector, remain the main pillar of opposition to economic liberalisation, at least in continental Europe.[23] Moreover, the legacy of unions often decisively shapes the patterns of mobilisation by social movements. Organised labor often helps other civil society actors to articulate their protest potentials.

It has often been maintained that globalisation raises political support for leftist parties, since the political left has historically been distinguishable from its competitors by its defense of the welfare state as compensation for the increasing risks of opening markets.[24] However, this notion contradicts most findings: in established democracies, the plausibility of the left's traditional economic recipes has dramatically eroded during the last decades, and if social democrats win elections then presumably they have abandoned their traditional positions.[25] More specifically, Keynesian economic policies lost much of their viability in the stagflation crisis during the 1970s. Established left parties thus turned from sharp critics of capitalism into pragmatic actors if aspiring for office.[26] Established left parties have often pursued similar or even more vigorous economic reforms than their right counterparts in the recent past. Examples are Bill Clinton's welfare reform and financial market deregulation, the vigorous pursuit of liberalisation policies by the Australian and New Zealand Labour parties in the early 1990s, and the fundamental restructuring of public services by the Tony Blair Government in Britain in the late 1990s. The main consequence of this moderate left transformation is that center-right and center-left parties, those that usually dominate alternate government coalitions, have programmatically converged on the economic dimension.[27] Furthermore, leftist mainstream parties in post-communist countries, chiefly in Eastern Europe, also embraced an economically liberal program because they had to prove their dissociation from socialism and their ability to operate in market economy.[28]

The movement of established left parties to the economic center opens up a niche on the protectionist pole of political space. At least in principle, this program gives radical left parties an opportunity to mobilise the economic losers' potential. However, radical left parties face serious constraints for a successful revival. Most of them lost much of their importance in the 1990s.[29] Similar to the fate of Marxist revolutionaries, the communist collapse was detrimental to the electoral prospects of classical radical left parties; it undermined their ideological coherence and the credibility of their societal project.

Yet communist collapse and the rise of neoliberalism did not completely force liberal values on both populations and political elites. As new divides open up within populations, new forms of opposition to the global economy emerge. Yet these are more heterogeneous and less clear to conceptualise than the all-encompassing Cold War and class conflict, which structured politics for much of the twentieth century.[30] And although radical left parties seem best suited to articulate the losers' potential, it happens only rarely or just to a marginal degree. Instead, the development of globalisation losers has given rise to two distinct political trends: the ascent of populism in several parts of the world and the global appearance of diverse forms of social movements. With respect to new populist forces, Latin American populism has to be separated from European populism. Although such movements challenging economic globalisation can be identified in many parts of the world, these two regions stand out in terms of the populist capacity to reshape domestic and regional politics.[31] Regarding social movements, they differ in their internal structure, durability, and action repertoire. Sometimes protest against the global economy is simply expressed by spontaneous riots. However, spontaneous protest can lead to more organised protest movements with a limited lifetime. Finally, protest movements can institutionalise into transnational networks and non-governmental organisations (NGOs) that exert constant pressure on politics.

Economic inequality and insecurity have increased in most countries; yet there is intense debate about whether and how much globalisation has actually contributed to these developments. For established democracies, other factors like technological change, rising educational levels, work productivity, and deindustrialisation cause inequality.[32] Still other evidence suggests that globalisation has increased inequality in some sectors, mainly because it reduced salaries.[33] Furthermore, in the traditionally generous welfare regimes of continental Western Europe, globalisation eroded the effectiveness of decommodification measures, because welfare regimes were transformed from 'Keynesian welfare states' to 'Schumpeterian workfare states'.[34] This transformation has led to social pacts that contain more market-conforming policies and produce increasingly competitive labor relations between employers and unions.

Regarding developing countries, detailed research on the redistributional consequences of economic globalisation is rare; China is a notable exception.[35] Generally, rapid economic growth over the last two decades has expanded the middle class in many developing countries.[36] Whereas economic prosperity has therefore lifted many people out of poverty and produced a class of wealthy and very wealthy citizens, downward societal mobility for other parts of the population creates new groups of marginalised people. Economic growth and the increasing integration of world markets thus had massive redistributive consequences, broadening the income gap between developing urban areas and stagnating rural regions. And market dynamics have widened disparities between professions demanded by export industries and locally oriented businesses. In China, for example, the gap between wealthy urban centers in the coastal regions and the less-developed interior is a growing concern for the authorities.[37] In addition, large parts of developing country workforces are still informally employed. For example, 2005 estimates concerning Latin America's informal sector suggest that 50 percent of all salaried workers earn their living in the black market.[38]

In sum, economic inequality and insecurity have increased in most countries and the losers of these developments have become more skeptical of globalisation. Thus, whether or not increasing globalisation is the culprit, ample evidence shows that it is often connected to individuals' perception of growing economic and employment insecurity.[39]

Hence, declining class cleavages did not necessarily result in the complete disintegration of all structural divides on economic issues. New antagonisms cut across traditional class conflict. Because of a lack of research on developing countries, however, the new social divides have so far been studied only in advanced economies. A first line of research identifies a structural divide characterised by the increasing share of people with relatively low social protection in industrialised countries. Most decommodification measures (policies to deconnect income streams from market outcomes like employment protection or minimum wages) were established before the restructuring of the labor force by globalisation.[40] Yet labor market regimes were usually not fully adapted to the new conditions, also because established political parties and governments were reluctant to extend social protection to new entrants to the job markets. Across advanced economies there is a trend towards a dualisation of the workforce, leaving ever more people without full-time jobs that are fully insured. Some scholars conceptualise this dualisation as a divide between welfare state insiders and outsiders.[41] Others call it a divide between the protected 'A-team' and a 'B-team' that experiences insecure labor market situations.[42] Female and young workers especially face more volatile employment opportunities and less welfare protection, whereas men working in traditional sectors usually enjoy relatively stable and secure job situations. Hence, the latter are mainly hostile to the global economy: they have more to lose in terms of social protection.

A second attempt to differentiate new structural conflicts regarding globalisation is the distinction between winners and losers. Accordingly, the most distinctive individual characteristic dividing populations in advanced economies is skills.[43] As countries have modernised, cognitive skills and social mobility have become crucial for individuals' status in society. Accordingly, both low-skilled workers in formerly protected industries and small independent business people with relatively little human capital (farmers, craftsmen, and shopkeepers) can be considered as clear losers and should therefore disfavor globalisation the most. Internationalising production can be a sensitive political issue. Although outsourcing enhances the international competitiveness of companies, it becomes controversial in the presence of high unemployment in low-skilled sectors.

There are direct linkages between emerging potential opposition to globalisation and its mobilisation by populist movements. In Latin America, populist support relies on marginalised classes in rural and poor urban areas, which are not amongst the winners of globalisation; in Europe and some other advanced economies, populists mobilise mainly low-skilled and sheltered social groups. To begin with, Latin America is both the region where the global market revolution was launched in the mid-1970s and where the liberal consensus has significantly eroded since the late 1990s. Chilean dictator Augusto Pinochet's reliance on economists from the University of Chicago after 1974 to dismantle his predecessor's democratic socialist experiment marked the beginning of the widespread diffusion of neoliberal orthodoxy to other Latin American countries after the 1980s debt crisis. Most populists in the 1980s and 1990s (notably Carlos Menem in Argentina and Alberto Fujimori in Peru) accepted neoliberal reforms in the context of increasing economic globalisation.[44] Yet this policy consensus began to fall apart after the devastating effects of the Asian financial crisis and the 1999 election of the populist and anti-globalist Hugo Chávez in Venezuela.[45]

Luckily for Chávez, his pronounced position against the economic liberalism advanced by the United States and the Bretton Woods institutions matched the interests of the worldwide alter-globalisation movement. Thus, his foreign policy would have gained much less attention if it had not coincided with internationally growing skepticism towards market globalisation; and his domestic success rests on the credibility of his anti-neoliberalism.[46] Chávez's domestic power depends heavily on the support of *chavista* militants, formerly marginalised classes whose approval he secures by policies of halting or reversing the privatisations of his predecessors and his broad assistance to the poor like subsidised health care and access to education.

Since the late 1990s a diverse array of left-leaning leaders has been elected in eight Latin American countries.[47] Given the constraints of global political and market integration, however, it is too early to conclude if this Latin American 'left turn' constitutes a sustainable alternative to the global economy. The rise of leftist alternatives reflects the crisis of both democratic institutions and market liberalism in some countries, namely Venezuela, Bolivia, and Ecuador. However, in others such as Chile, and most notably Brazil, left electoral success seems to result from the consolidation of democratic regimes and a reconciliation of former radical left forces with market liberalism.[48]

In Europe but also in other stable democracies like Canada, Australia, and New Zealand, right-wing populists have gained significant electoral strength during the past two decades.[49] In Western Europe, the radical right constitutes an established political force at least in France, Belgium, Italy, Austria, Switzerland, and Denmark. Moreover, these parties have participated in governmental coalitions in two Western European countries: Austria in 2000 and Italy in 1994 and 2001. In Eastern Europe, right-wing populists have emerged as important forces, too, for example in Slovakia, Poland, Romania, and Bulgaria. Instead of widespread forms of collective action by social movements found in many developing countries, the dominant pattern of opposition in the Eastern European transition countries is protest voting. This result is due to the historical communist legacy, which created a political climate that discouraged large-scale political unrest as a reaction to market integration.[50] Initially, this situation produced success for pure anti-establishment parties lacking a coherent stance on economic policies. More recently, however, many Eastern European populist parties, like their European Western counterparts, tend to form a culturally framed opposition to globalisation. The 'winning formula', a combination of cultural demarcation and economic liberalism, the preferred strategy of right-wing populists in the 1990s, has lost much of its appeal in the 2000s.[51] In the twenty-first century, by contrast, the right-wing populists increasingly opt for protectionism and are therefore the most successful mobilisers of the economic losers' potential in advanced economies.

Right-wing populist parties mainly take a conservative stance in sociocultural terms, because they put particular emphasis on issues related to national identity. Contrary to the traditional conceptions of nationalism, the central political program of the new radical right can be understood as a doctrine of ethnopluralism: different ethnicities are not necessarily superior or inferior, but simply different and thus incompatible. First adopted by the French National Front, ethnopluralism has been embedded in the political programs and rhetorical profiles of most European right-wing populists.[52] In line with this ideology, most immigrants are singled out as threatening the values of the national community.[53] However, right-wing populists also identify other dangers to the national community, amongst which are increasingly supranational institutions, multinational corporations, and economic globalisation in general. Hence, whereas most populist right parties supported economic liberalisation during the 1980s and early 1990s (often manifest in campaigns for radical tax cuts), newer ones tend toward nationalist capitalism.[54] Accordingly, the most common position of right-wing populists nowadays is to support the capitalist system at the national level, but be fiercely protectionist towards globalisation. Their rationale corresponds to the notion that economic globalisation and the creation of supranational institutions jeopardise the nation-state as the main location of collective identification and well-being. One of the most visible moments of this type of opposition was the 2005 defeat of the French referendum on the European Union (EU) constitution. Although radical left forces also rallied for rejection, the mobilisation of the ultraright National Front proved decisive. However, in some Western countries, for example in the United States and Switzerland, right-wing populist movements have remained distinctly pro-market-oriented concerning the global economy.[55] Yet even in the United States, where conservatives are usually solid advocates of low taxes and limited business regulation, their focus on patriotism and United States superiority over all other countries sometimes fuels grievances against international entities like the World Bank or the World Trade Organization (WTO).[56]

Yet the major part of recent research on the opposition to economic globalisation is not concerned with alter-globalisation movements.[57] Popular resistance to the global economy has intensified since the late 1990s, bringing new voices into public debates about economic globalisation. As a consequence of the democratisation of many countries in Eastern Europe, Asia, and Latin America, social movements and non-governmental actors began mobilising, raising political awareness about growing inequalities and deficient social protection.[58] The opposition of social movements manifests in various forms, not easy to separate from each other.[59] Unfortunately, conceptualisations of such social movements also lack consistency across different studies. Nevertheless, resistance to globalisation from outside the political sphere is divided into three distinct realms: spontaneous rioting; grass roots and international protest movements against highly visible international summits or single nation-state; and transnational networks of actors and NGOs that operate in a comparatively cooperative way in, around, and with governments and international institutions.

In general terms, the combination of rising inequality and popular discontent has fuelled mass protests and riots in developing countries. In China alone, the official number of protests and riots (certainly an underestimate of the real scope of unrest) rose from approximately 10,000 in 1993 to 74,000 in 2004, and the number of participants more than quadrupled.[60] Comparative studies often combine diverse events into a single phenomenon without clarifying the origins and directions of the protests. First, in some contexts, riots erupt in direct response to the beginning of market reforms. For example, Venezuelan urban riots in 1989 targeted government subsidy cuts for gasoline prices.[61] Second, other protests reacted to deteriorating economic conditions. One example is the global wave of protests against rising food prices in 2007–8. Starting with public outcries over corn prices in Mexico, protest spread to such diverse places as Northern Africa, Southern Europe, and Indonesia. And, finally, riots can be spurred by lacking or denied employment protection or wage payments, environmental pollution, and corruption.[62] Most riots are small and localised. However, some can escalate into large-scale revolts by substantive parts of the population. Minor events like traffic accidents in China in 2004, for example, initiated major protests and even riots against local authorities in rural areas like Wanzhou and boom towns like Shenzeng.[63]

Most protest activists do not identify with the label 'anti-globalisation', because they oppose specific forms of economic globalisation, for instance, delocalisation or structural adjustment programs.[64] Rather, seeing their ideas as alternative programs, such protests are better termed 'alter-globalisation movements'. Furthermore, the label 'global justice' can be used to subsume the most important alter-globalisation movements. It has its roots in the reaction to the neoliberal Thatcher and Reagan 'revolutions' after the 1970s. Later, as Bretton Woods institutions became more important for developing countries (as a result of structural adjustment programs and intensified development aid), the global justice movement gained momentum. However, its genesis is usually seen as the early 1990s.[65] In 1992, the first farmer protests accompanied talks on the General Agreement on Tariffs and Trade in Geneva and Strasbourg. In 1994, the founding year of the WTO and North American Free Trade Agreement, the Zapatista insurgency in Southern Mexico began. It sought and rapidly found support amongst radical social movements on a worldwide scale. Coordinating activities by the Zapatista Army of National Liberation resulted in the founding of the Peoples' Global Action (PGA), a network of radical, international grassroots movements ranging from indigenous and farmer groups from developing countries to protest bodies from advanced economies like the original British-based 'Reclaim the Streets' movement. The turn of the new millennium can be considered the peak of the global justice movement. After the 'Battle of Seattle' in November 1999, activism repeatedly galvanised the global elites with violent protests: in 2001, massive protests surrounded the Third Summit of the Americas in Quebec City, the EU summit in Gothenburg, and G8 meetings in Genoa. In these protests, many demonstrators were injured and one killed in clashes with police. Afterwards, however, alter-globalisation protests could not maintain their strength and conflict intensity.

In the years of massive protest, the institutionalisation of the global justice movement began with the founding of the first World Social Forum (WSF) in 2001. Invited by the Brazilian Workers' Party, grassroots movements and activist organisations met at Porto Allegre, Brazil in a countercongress to the annual meeting of economic and political leaders at Davos, Switzerland (the World Economic Forum). Until 2005, the WSF experienced increasing numbers of participants and widely recognised scholars like Joseph Stiglitz, the former chief of the World Bank, were invited as key speakers. Since then, however, its coherence and impact have been put to the test. Initially thought as spin-offs, local, regional, and national Social Forums have begun replacing the WSF as the focus for activists. Hence, the global justice movement seems mainly to have been reintegrated into national politics. Furthermore, besides the charter of principles and a few additional decisions that sketched guidelines for the development of alternatives to neoliberalism and imperialism, coherent messages that could have an impact on everyday politics were rare.

Since the beginning, global justice movement activists have claimed to struggle for a global cause, and their meetings have been distinctly international: at the first PGA meeting, participants from 40 countries attended; at the first WSF, 123 countries were present. Nevertheless, regional centers of activism can be identified. Amongst advanced economies, France and Italy have repeatedly been a preferred base for anti-globalisation movements. Concerning developing countries, Latin America and India are focal regions of contestation by the global justice movement. Here, the WSF meeting in Porto Allegre, the Brazilian Landless Workers Movement, the indigenous movements in Bolivia, Peru, and Mexico, the Argentine Unemployment Workers Movement, and Ekta Parishad, an Indian land reform movement, deserve special mention.[66] Writings by movement sympathisers can give the impression that an all-encompassing backlash against the globalised economy exists.[67] And some scholars once predicted that global social movements would soon create a 'global civil society'.[68] Yet, such views can be misleading. Whilst these conclusions are built on the assumption of a coherent and consistent phenomenon of protest movements, more critical accounts show that most movements, although attaching a global frame to their positions, mainly engage in domestic struggles.[69]

Although NGOs are examined more broadly in Chapter 37, in the context of international opposition to globalisation, these bodies are probably far more successful than protest movements in shaping international politics; they have developed institutionalised relations with the governing bodies of nation-states and international organisations. The same developments that enable corporations to grow beyond national borders have also aided NGOs in building transnational networks. Here, the United States plays a key role, both as major target of NGO politics and the Power most supportive of NGO activities.[70] Many smaller boycotts and protests in the last decades had a strong impact on the behavior of corporations and the course of market processes. NGO activities can significantly harm a company's stock price if they are able to shape the preferences of customers and shareholders.[71] Yet NGO anti-corporate campaigns are not always a curse for business. By contrast, they sometimes evolve into systems of private regulation that strengthen a firm's reputation and decrease investment risks. For example, social movement campaigns in the forest product industry were first conducted to tarnish the image of corporations in this industry. Finally, however, they formed the basis of private regulatory systems like the Forest Stewardship Council, established in 1993.[72] NGO activists were allowed to inspect and certify corporate behavior in the name of a socially and environmentally sensitive clientele, which, in turn, provided incentives for corporations to comply with the standards established by the social movements. Hence, multinational corporations often bring higher standards of labor rights to host developing countries, exactly because they have come under pressure from a variety of actors such as ethically responsive shareholders, NGOs, and consumers.[73]

To conclude, there has been a decline in the classical antagonism that structured conflicts over the global economy along the lines of the class divide and the Cold War. However, when it comes to newer forms of resistance to global economic integration, a lack of scholarly consensus exists on why different forms of opposition are emerging. The dynamics of opposition towards market reforms are certainly complex and vary from country to country, depending on the modes of integration into world markets as well as because of diverging national identities and differing political traditions. Yet much recent work on populism and social movements fails to analyze the variation in outcomes in a systematic fashion.[74]

Nevertheless, some reasonably solid conclusions exist regarding the general trends of these new forms of opposition to economic globalisation. Populism is advancing, notably in Europe and Latin America. Populists are a genuine anti-globalisation movement, because they want to see cultural, political, and economic integration reversed. Most social movements, on the contrary, should be considered as alter-globalisation movements because, in principle, they do not entirely reject internationalisation but strive to realise specific, alternative models of a globalised society. Research that assumes a zero-sum game between governments and business actors, on one side, and social movements, on the other, neglects the complex linkages and interdependencies between political and economic decision-making and the protest arena. Social movements and NGOs can be antagonists to multinational corporations and international organisations, but they can also be a contributive and controlling authority in regulating the global economy. As for protest movements against globalisation, their 'golden age' seems to be over. By contrast, NGOs increasingly help shape international relations.

Beyond these general findings, there is neither consensus about which new divides within societies shape the sociostructural basis of future political conflicts nor the circumstances under which the new identified challengers (populists and social movements) emerge. What, for example, do the Latin American and European styles of populism have in common and where do they differ? More specifically, there are contradicting findings regarding defining characteristics and ideological core beliefs of this supposedly new family of opposition; understanding these contradictions can separate them from other newly emerging parties. Furthermore, why do forceful social movements like the landless or the rubber tapper movements in Brazil emerge in rural regions of some countries whereas, in other countries, old-fashioned Maoist rebels like the Naxalites in Eastern India prevail? More generally, ranging from grassroots mobilisation to top-down populist resistance and institutionalised electoral opposition, how can the overall variety of oppositional reactions to increasing market liberalisation be explained?

Scholarly examination has not thus far established enough causal linkages amongst economic globalisation, social unrest, and its mobilisation. Such paucity comes mainly because they were only rarely the subject of empirical scrutiny in enough case-studies over longer time periods. Hence, there is a fundamental lack of comparative research in this field. Furthermore, interdisciplinary collaborations amongst scholars concerned with structural change, social movements, populism, and civil wars would be valuable to better understand popular resistance to the global economy. But there is little systematic research on changing economic insecurities and related individual preferences in developing countries to provide a basis for the research on the collective articulation of political grievances. Most work simply concludes retrospectively from the reality of popular mobilisation that there must have been significant changing risks for much of the population in developing countries. Real microfoundations for this claim are rare.

Many studies also lack caution when interpreting the scope and intensity of the opposition to economic liberalisation. Populism is on the rise and social movement protests will probably regain strength in the aftermath of the recent economic crisis. However, most studies on protest and populism succumb to simplistic assumptions that economic liberalism is unpopular. Free trade policies, for example, may be perceived as a threat to employment security, but they may just as well be met with popular approval. Free trade potentially induces economic growth, offers new possibilities for business, and widens the variety of available goods for consumers. Many open questions regarding the opposition towards the globalised economy remain. As global markets will keep provoking contestation, populist parties and social movements will continue to shape the political landscape; thus, the study and understanding of opposition to globalisation will continue to be essential to the architecture of international economic relations.

Notes

1 D. Brady, J. Beckfield, and Z. Wei, 'The Consequences of Economic Globalization for Affluent Democracies', *Annual Review of Sociology* 33(2007), 313–34; A. Dreher, N. Gaston, and P. Martens, *Measuring Globalization—Gauging its Consequences* (New York, 2008); D. Held, and A. McGrew, *The Global Transformations Reader* (Cambridge, 2000).

2 F. Fukuyama, *The End of History and the Last Man* (New York, 1992); K. Ohmae, *The End of the Nation State. How Region States Harness the Prosperity of the Global Economy* (New York, 1995).

3 V. Forrester, *L'Horreur Economique* (Paris, 1996); R. Reich, *Supercapitalism* (New York, 2007).

4 A. Przeworski and C. Yebra, 'Globalization and Democracy', in P. Bardhay, S. Bowles, and M. Wallerstein, eds., *Globalization and Egalitarian Distribution* (Princeton, 1995).

5 B. King and N. Pearce, 'The Contentiousness of Markets: Politics, Social Movements, and Institutional Change in Markets', *Annual Review of Sociology*, 36(2010), 249–67.

6 Z. Elkins, A. Guzman, and B. Simmons, 'Competing for Capital: The Diffusion of Bilateral Investment Treaties, 1960–2000', *International Organization*, 60(2006), 811–46; F. Scharpf and V. Schmidt, *Welfare and Work in the Open Economy*. Volume I: *From Vulnerability to Competitiveness* (Oxford, 2000).

7 B. Simmons, F. Dobbin, and G. Garrett, 'The International Diffusion of Liberalism', *International Organization*, 60(2006), 781–810.

8 F. Vandenbroucke, *Globalisation, Inequality, and Social Democracy* (London, 1998).

9 Suzanne Berger, 'Globalization and Politics', *Annual Review of Political Science* 3(2000), 43–62; D.D. Laitin, 'Post-Soviet politics', Ibid., 117–48.

10 S. Kalyvas, 'The Decay and Breakdown of Communist One-Party Systems', *Annual Review of Political Science*, 2(1999), 323–43.

11 S. Kalyvas and L. Balcells, 'International System and Technologies of Rebellion: How the Cold War Shaped Internal Conflict', *American Political Science Review*, 104(2010), 415–29.

12 R. Kanet, 'The Superpower Quest for Empire: The Cold War and Soviet Support for "Wars of National Liberation"', *Cold War History*, 6(2006), 331–52.

13 R. Hardin, 'The Public Trust', in S. Pharr and R. Putnam, ed., *Disaffected Democracies. What's Troubling the Trilateral Countries?* (Princeton, NJ, 2000), 31–51; R. Inglehart and C. Welzel, *Modernization, Cultural Change and Democracy. The Human Development Sequence* (Cambridge, 2005); H. Kriesi, 'The Transformation of Cleavage Politics. The 1997 Stein Rokkan Lecture', *European Journal of Political Research*, 36(1998), 165–85.

14 P. Mair, 'The Challenge to Party Government', *West European Politics* 31(2008), 211–34.

15 H. Kriesi et al., *West European Politics in the Age of Globalization* (Cambridge, 2008).

16 L. Bartels, *Unequal Democracy: The Political Economy of the New Gilded Age* (New York, 2008); P. Beramendi and C. Anderson, *Democracy, Inequality and Representation* (New York, 2008).

17 T. Hellwig and D. Samuels, 'Voting in Open Economies. The Electoral Consequences of Globalization', *Comparative Political Studies*, 40(2007), 283–306.

18 P. Fiss and P. Hirsch, 'The Discourse of Globalization: framing and sensemaking of an emerging concept', *American Sociological Review*, 70(2005), 29–52.

19 M. Golden, P. Lange, and M. Wallerstein, *Dataset on Unions, Employers, Collective Bargaining and Industrial Relations for 16 OECD Countries* (1999): http://dvn.iq.harvard.edu/dvn/dv/golden.

20 J. Godard, 'The Exceptional Decline of the American Labor Movement', *Industrial and Labor Relations Review* 63(2009), 83–108; B. Hirsch and J. Addison, *The Economic Analysis of Unions: New Approaches and Evidence* (London, 1986).

21 M. Upchurch, T. Graham, A. Mathers, *The Crisis of Social Democratic Trade Unionism in Western Europe: The Search for Alternatives* (Burlington, 2009); M. Wallerstein, and B. Western, 'Unions In Decline? What Has Changed and Why?', *Annual Review of Political Science* 3(2000), 355–77.

22 L. Baccaro, K. Hamann, and L. Turner, 'The Politics of Labour Movement Revitalization: The Need for a Revitalized Perspective', *European Journal of Industrial Relations* 9(2003), 119–33.

23 B. Wuest, 'Varieties of Capitalist Debates: How institutions shape public conflicts on economic liberalization in the UK, France, and Germany', *Annual Conference of the Deutsche Vereinigung für Politische Wissenschaft, ETH Züric*, (10 September 2010).

24 G. Garrett, *Partisan Politics in the Global Economy* (Cambridge, 1998).

25 P. Hall, 'Policy Paradigms, Social Learning and the State: The Case of Economic Policymaking in Britain', *Comparative Politics*, 25(1993), 275–96; Kriesi *et al.*, *West European Politics*.

26 A. Giddens, *The Third Way and Its Critics* (Cambridge, 2000); F. Müller-Rommel and T. Poguntke, *Green Parties in National Governments* (London, 2002).

27 C. Boix, 'Partisan Governments, the International Economy, and Macroeconomic Policies in Advanced Nations, 1960–93', *World Politics* 53(2000), 38–73.

28 M. Tavits, and N. Letki, 'When the Left is Right: Party Ideology and Policy in Post-Communist Europe', *American Political Science Review* 103(2003), 555–69.

29 L. March and C. Mudde, 'What's Left of the Radical Left? The European Radical Left After 1989: Decline and Mutation', *Comparative European Politics*, 3(2005), 23–49.

30 S. Bartolini, and P. Mair, *Identity, Competition, and Electoral Availability. The Stabilisation of European Electorates 1885–1985* (Cambridge, UK, 1990); A. Hironaka, *Neverending Wars. The International Community, Weak States, and the Perpetuation of Civil War* (Cambridge, UK, 2005).

31 K. Roberts, 'The Mobilization of Opposition to Economic Liberalization', *Annual Review of Political Science*, 11(2008), 327–49.

32 M. Dewatripont, A. Sapir, and K. Sekkat, *Trade and Jobs in Europe: Much Ado About Nothing?* (New York, 1999); M. Wolf, *Why Globalization Works* (New Haven, CT, 2004).

33 D. Brady and M. Wallace, 'Spatialization, foreign direct investment and labor outcomes in the American states, 1976–96', *Social Forces*, 79(2000), 67–100; I. Dasgupta and T. Osang, 'Globalization and relative wages: further evidence from U.S. manufacturing industries', *International Review Economics and Finance*, 11(2000), 1–16; K. Rees and J. Hathcote, 'The U.S. textile and apparel industry in the age of globalization', *Global Economy Journal*, 4(2004), 1–22.

34 B. Jessop, *The Future of the Capitalist State* (Cambridge, UK, 2002); M. Vail, 'From "welfare without work" to "buttressed liberalization": The shifting dynamics of labor market adjustment in France and Germany', *European Journal of Political Research* 47(2008), 334–58.

35 I. Mares and M. Carnes, 'Social Policy in Developing Countries', *Annual Review of Political Science* 12(2009), 93–113; D. Yang, 'Economic Transformation and Its Political Discontents in China: Authoritarianism, Unequal Growth, and the Dilemmas of Political Development', *Annual Review of Political Science* 9)2006), 143–64.

36 F. Mishkin, *The Next Great Globalization: How Disadvantaged Nations Can Harness Their Financial Systems to Get Rich* (Princeton, NJ, 2008).

37 E. Hung and S. Chiu, 'The lost generation: life course dynamics and Xiagang in China', *Modern China* 29(2003), 204–36.

38 Mares and Carnes, 'Developing Countries'.

39 N. Gaston and D. Nelson, 'Structural change and the labor-market effects of globalization', *Review of International Economics* 12(2004), 769–92.

40 D. Rueda, 'Insider—Outsider Politics in Industrialized Democracies: The Challenge to Social Democratic Parties', *American Political Science Review* 99(2005), 61–74.

41 Ibid.

42 G. Esping-Andersen, 'Politics without Class? Post-industrial Cleavages in Europe and America', in H. Kitschelt, P. Lange, G. Marks and J. Stephens, *eds., Continuity and Change in Contemporary Capitalism* (Cambridge, UK, 1999).

43 M. Kalmijn and G. Kraaykamp, 'Social stratification and attitudes: a comparative analysis of the effects of class and education in Europe', *British Journal of Sociology* 58(2007), 547–76.

44 K. Weyland, 'Neopopulism and Neoliberalism in Latin America: Unexpected Affinities', *Studies in Comparative International Development*, 32(1996), 3–31.

45 Roberts, 'Mobilization of Opposition'.

46 S. Ellner, 'The Contrasting Variants of the Populism of Hugo Chavez and Alberto Fujimori', *Journal of Latin American Studies*, 35(2003), 139–62.

47 E. Hershberg and F. Rosen, *Latin America after Neoliberalism: Turning the tide in the 21st century?* (New York, 2006).

48 J. Mahon, 'Good-bye to the Washington Consensus?', *Current History*, 102(2003), 58–64.

49 Kriesi et al., *West European Politics*; J. Rydgren, 'The Sociology of the radical Right', *Annual Review of Sociology*, 33(2007), 241–62.

50 B. Greskovits, *The Political Economy of Protest and Patience: East European and Latin American Transformations Compared* (Budapest, 1998).

51 H. Kitschelt, 'Review Article: Growth and Persistence of the Radical Right in Postindustrial Democracies: Advances and Challenges in Comparative Research', *West European Politics* 30(2007), 1176–06; H. Kriesi, E. Grande, M. Dolezal, M. Helbling, S. Hutter, D. Hoeglinger, and B. Wuest, *Restructuring Political Conflict in Western Europe* (forthcoming).

52 Rydgren, 'Sociology'.

53 A. Zaslove, 'The dark side of European politics: unmasking the radical right', *European Integration* 26(2004), 61–81.

54 Ibid.; Kitschelt, 'Review Article'.

55 K. Blee and K. Creasap, 'Conservative and Right-Wing Movements', *Annual Review of Sociology* 36(2010), 269–86; Kriesi et al., *West European Politics*.

56 M. Durham, *White Rage: The Extreme Right and American Politics* (New York, 2007).

57 P. Evans, 'Counterhegemonic globalization: transnational social movements in the contemporary global political economy', in T. Janoski, R. Alford, A. Hicks, and M. Schwartz, eds., *The Handbook of Political Sociology* (New York, 2005).

58 Mares and Carnes, 'Social Policy'; C. Mesa-Lago, 'Social Security in Latin America', *Latin American Research Review*, 42(2007), 181–201.

59 J. Smith and H. Johnston, *Globalization and Resistance: Transnational Dimensions of Social Movements* (Lanham, MD, 2002).

60 H. French, 'Land of 74,000 protests', *New York Times* (24 August 2004).

61 J. Walton and D. Seddon, *Free Markets and Food Riots: The Politics of Global Adjustment* (Oxford, 1994).

62 Yang, 'Economic Transformation'.

63 French, '74,000 protests'.

64 T. Mertes, 'Anti-globalization movements: from critiques to alternatives', in B. Turner, ed., *The Routledge International Handbook of Globalization Studies* (London, 2010).

65 M. Kaldor, H. Anheier, and M. Glasius, *Global Civil Society* (New York, 2003).

66 See J. Auyero, *Routine Politics and Violence in Argentina: The Gray Zone of State Power* (Cambridge, UK, 2007); S. Spronk and J. Webber, 'Struggles against accumulation by dispossession in Bolivia: the political economy of natural resource contention', *Latin American Perspective*, 34(2007), 31–47; J. Wolff, '(De-)Mobilizing the marginalized: a comparison of the Argentinean piqueteros and Ecuador's indigenous movement', *Journal of Latin American Studies* 30(2007), 1–29.

67 For example, R. O'Brien, A.M. Goetz, J.A. Scholte, and M. Williams, *Contesting Global Governance: Multilateral Economic Institutions and Global Social Movements* (London, New York, 2000); H. Veltmeyer, (2007) *On the Move: The Politics of Social Change in Latin America* (Toronto, 2007).

68 J. Boli and J. Thomas, *Constructing World Culture: International Nongovernmental Organizations Since 1875* (Stanford, CA, 1995).

69 S. Tarrow, *The New Transnational Activism* (Cambridge, 2005); F. Uggla, 'Between Globalism and Pragmatism: ATTAC in France, Germany, and Sweden', *Mobilization* 11(2006), 51–66.

70 P. Uvin, 'From local organizations to global governance: the role of NGOs in international relations', in K. Stiles, ed., *Global Institutions and Local Empowerment: Competing Theoretical Perspectives* (New York, 2000).

71 B. King and S. Soule, 'Social movements as extrainstitutional entrepreneurs: the effect of protests on stock price returns', *Administrative Science Quarterly* 52(2007), 413–42.

72 T. Bartley, 'Institutional emergence in an era of globalization: the rise of transnational private regulation of labor and environmental conditions', *American Journal of Sociology*, 113(2007), 297–351.

73 T. Moran, E. Graham, and M. Blomstrom, *Does Foreign Direct Investment Promote Development?* (Washington, DC, 2005); A, Prakash, and M. Potoski, 'Investing up: FDI and the Cross-National Diffusion of ISO 14001', *International Studies Quarterly*, 51(2007), 723–44.

74 For notable exceptions, see M. Cleary, 'Democracy and indigenous rebellion in Latin America', *Comparative Political Studies*, 33(2000), 1123–53; Kriesi *et al.*, *West European Politics*.

Part VII

Issues of Conflict and Cooperation

31

International arms control

David Mutimer

Attempts to place some forms of control on the means of warfare have a long, if not always distinguished, history. A recent attempt to place arms control into a historical framework finds examples of such attempts at least as early as the fourth century BC. There is then a fairly significant gap between 188 BC and 1766.[1] Modern arms control is a Cold War social practice, related to the structure of 'Great Powers' in the twentieth century international system. Great Powers can be considered to form the skeletal structure on which the evolving international order is built and, certainly, there are Great, indeed super, Powers at the heart of arms control and its precursors in the first half of the twentieth century. However, arms control is not simply an epiphenomenon of the superpower structure of the Cold War, but rather that structure itself was in part forged in and through the practices of arms control. World order-making, at least in the case of arms control practice, although elsewhere as well, is an iterative process of forming and being formed in and through the practices which constitute the very order being made.

The late nineteenth and early twentieth centuries saw a number of international efforts to regulate the nature and conduct of war. Most notable, perhaps, were the two Hague Conventions of 1899 and 1907, which included amongst various rules for the conduct of wars limitations on particular kinds of weapons, most notably gases and 'dum-dum bullets'.[2] The idea of broad multilateral regulation of warfare was carried over into the first attempt at institutionalised global governance of the twentieth century, the interwar League of Nations.[3] As with a number of other issues, regulation of war and armaments was not far advanced through the League, because it suffered from an unpropitious organisation and a lack of political support.

Modern arms control was a response to the development of nuclear weapons at the end of the Second World War and the belief, captured pithily in Einstein's famous quotation, that they marked a truly qualitative change: 'The unleashed power of the atom has changed everything save our modes of thinking …'.[4] However, arms control was not the first such response, and indeed can be understood in many ways to have developed because of a previous failure to internationalise nuclear arms. In January 1946, the United States Secretary of State, James Byrnes, created a committee, the Acheson-Lilienthal Committee, with the following terms of reference:

> Anticipating favorable action by the United Nations [UN] Organization on the proposal for the establishment of a commission to consider the problems arising as to the control of atomic energy and other weapons of possible mass destruction, the Secretary of State has appointed a Committee of five members to study the subject of controls and safeguards necessary to protect this Government so that the persons hereafter selected to represent the United States on the Commission can have the benefit of the study.[5]

The American representatives were headed by Bernard Baruch, whose name has been attached to the plan that went before the UN. The Baruch Plan called for the creation of a UN agency to control all aspects of atomic energy, and the UN would also hold in trust the world's only legal arsenal of atomic weapons. Based on the findings of the Acheson-Lilienthal Report, the Plan argued for this kind of internationalisation over a simple ban:

> … although nations may agree not to use in bombs the atomic energy developed within their borders the only assurance that a conversion to destructive purposes would not be made would be the pledged word and the good faith of the nation itself. This fact puts an enormous pressure upon national good faith. Indeed it creates suspicion on the part of other nations that their neighbors' pledged word will not be kept. This danger is accentuated by the unusual characteristics of atomic bombs, namely their devastating effect as a surprise weapon, that is, a weapon secretly developed and used without warning. Fear of such surprise violation of pledged word will surely break down any confidence in the pledged word of rival countries developing atomic energy if the treaty obligations and good faith of the nations are the only assurances upon which to rely.[6]

The Plan failed in a vote held on 30 December 1946 in the UN Atomic Energy Commission (UNAEC). Requiring unanimity amongst UNAEC's 12 members, Baruch's plan received ten votes, but the Soviet Union and Poland abstained, killing it.[7] The Russians objected to a number of the Plan's features, including inspections of their facilities and eliminating the veto for permanent members of the UN Security Council over sanctions for prohibited activities. Moscow argued that the Council was already stacked in favor of the United States.[8]

The failure of the Baruch Plan left the development of nuclear energy, and nuclear weaponry, in the hands of individual states. The Soviet Union tested its first atomic explosive in August 1949, four years after the United States had become the only country to use atomic weapons in the twin attacks on Japan. The 1950s, therefore, saw the early development of a nuclear arms race. The two superpowers built their stocks of fission weapons and, then, developed fusion weapons. By the late 1950s, the nuclear age of international diplomacy was under way, with the United States and Soviet Union building arsenals totalling about 20,000 nuclear weapons and both beginning to deploy them on ballistic missiles capable of reaching each other's territories.[9] In this context, the idea of controlling arms was born and raised.

One of the enduring myths of Western civilisation is the story of Icarus, who attempted to escape from the island of Crete. His chosen means of escape was flight, powered by wings that his father built for him of feathers and wax. Ignoring his father's advice, Icarus flew too high, coming too close to the heat of the sun. The sun melted the wax of his wings, and Icarus fell to his death. As with any good myth, the story has served a number of purposes, but perhaps the main one is a cautionary tale of man's relationship to his technology. As the creator of the technology, the father character is vested with wisdom and insight, which his son chooses to ignore and suffers greatly for it. It should be no surprise, therefore, that the American Academy of Arts and Sciences chose to name its flagship journal for the father: *Daedalus*.

In autumn 1960, *Daedalus* published a special issue simply titled *Arms Control*. Its objectives were set out by the editor, Gerald Holton: 'to present the potentially feasible routes as well as the obstacles to arms control as one of the means toward eliminating nuclear warfare and improving national security; to explore the complexity and the magnitude of the task; and to illustrate some of the major considerations bearing on decisions of national policy.'[10] Holton was a physicist, a member of the science that had produced the deadly technology, and he was attempting to follow the model of his journal's namesake in explaining how to fly with nuclear weapons without coming too close to the sun. The fall(out) of this particular Icarus would dwarf even the allegorical power of the original.

Arms control was seen by the contributors to the special issue as providing a means to security through reducing and ultimately eliminating the risk of nuclear war:

> [I]t is useful to think generally of arms control as a cooperative or multilateral approach to armament policy—where 'armament policy' includes not only the amount and kind of weapons and forces in being, but also the development, deployment and utilisation of such forces, whether in periods of relaxation, in periods of tension, or in periods of shooting wars. The approach should be thought of as oriented toward improving the national security of each of the nations involved by adjusting at least some armament capabilities and uses to those 'actually' desirable in the light of the intentions, actions, and adjusted capabilities of the other nations.[11]

The approach adopted and developed by the *Daedalus* authors, therefore, kept with the findings of Acheson-Lilienthal and the practical experience of the Baruch Plan: nuclear disarmament is not an immediately realistic prospect.[12] Arms control, therefore, was proposed as an immediate alternative in the face of the danger of nuclear war: a collaborative exercise between the United States and Soviet Union, either bilaterally or in concert with others, to manage jointly their nuclear weapons for the purposes of living with them safely.

Although the *Daedalus* special issue is an academic publication, the nature of the state in the United States means that such work is not necessarily far removed from power, as it might be in other places. The top levels of the American foreign policy-making bureaucracy cycle between government and the academy, including both universities and 'think tanks'. The 1960 issue on *Arms Control* included authors with significant influence: Edward Teller, the father of the United States fusion weapon; Herman Kahn, a RAND Corporation analyst and soon to found the Hudson Institute; Thomas Schelling, who also spent time at RAND before settling at Harvard; Jerome Wiesner, a science advisor to both Dwight Eisenhower and John F. Kennedy; and Henry Kissinger, who would become National Security Advisor and then Secretary of State at the height of the practice of bilateral arms control. The special issue was therefore not simply the usual reflections of scholars, but a programmatic intervention in the leading policy problem of the day by those with the ear of government.

In the two decades following the *Daedalus* special issue, arms control diplomacy developed as a major practice at the heart of the Cold War. Its goal closely followed the objectives of *Daedalus*: a collaborative practice aimed at shaping nuclear weapons policy for the purposes of reducing, if not eliminating, the chances of a nuclear war. Arms control was an explicit attempt to create peace and security in a world *with* nuclear weapons and, pointedly, not to fashion peace and security by making the world once more without nuclear weapons. This task is not insignificant, and it is one that was pursued through arms control consistently, and relatively successfully, in those two decades; it proceeded on two closely related tracks, both of which speak in important ways to the central themes of this volume.

The special issue of *Daedalus* argued that it made sense to think of 'arms control as a cooperative or multilateral approach to armament policy'. Throughout the 1960s, the United States pursued both approaches, entering into bilateral discussions with the Soviet Union (or with the Soviet Union and Britain) as well as engaging in multilateral discussions around nuclear arms. In many ways, the bilateral practice is more significant, and the one that is more generally imagined when one speaks of 'arms control'. Nevertheless, the attempts at multilateral arms control from the 1960s onwards are important both in terms of their impact on the contemporary shape of weapons and their control and the nature of 'Great Powers' in the global system.

The multilateral practice of arms control sprang from the concern of members of the Kennedy administration that there would be perhaps twenty nuclear powers by the 1980s if nothing was done to limit growth.[13] In 1965 both the United States and the Soviet Union submitted drafts of a treaty designed to prevent the proliferation of nuclear weapons; and in 1966 the UN General Assembly called on the Eighteen Nation Disarmament Conference (ENDC) to give priority to the issue of non-proliferation. On 1 January 1968, the Americans and Russians submitted a joint draft text to the ENDC of a nuclear non-proliferation treaty, which served as the basis for negotiations over the next several months. On 1 July 1968, 62 countries signed the Nuclear Non-Proliferation Treaty (NPT), and it entered into force on 5 March 1970, when the Americans and Russians deposited their instruments of ratification.

Clearly, this process is marked by the influence of the preeminent states of the day: once the United States and the Soviet Union submitted their drafts, and negotiations produced Soviet–American agreement on a joint text, the NPT was able to be settled. The centrality of these two states is seen in the Treaty itself. First of all, the United States, the Soviet Union, and Britain were designated by the Treaty as the depositories. More significantly, no matter how many other states acceded to the NPT, its coming into force depended solely on ratification by these three governments.[14] The treaty has proved remarkably successful by most measures. Roughly 50 percent of the UN membership of the day signed it and, now, only four states remain outside the NPT regime: India, Pakistan, and Israel, which have never signed, and North Korea, which withdrew in 2003. More important than its reach, however, is that there were five nuclear-weapon states when it was signed in 1968 and there are only nine today.[15]

The relationship between the five nuclear-weapon states of 1968 and today's nine, however, points to the way in which the NPT is not just reflective of the distribution of power in the global system, but how it has served to help constitute the Great Power structure of the contemporary world. Article IX.3 of the NPT reads in part: 'For the purposes of this Treaty, a nuclear-weapon State is one which has manufactured and exploded a nuclear weapon or other nuclear explosive device prior to January 1, 1967.' This sentence is tremendously significant because, under the NPT, nuclear-weapon states are permitted to keep their nuclear arms, subject only to a commitment 'to pursue negotiations in good faith on effective measures relating to cessation of the nuclear arms race at an early date and to nuclear disarmament' (Article VI). Non-nuclear-weapon states (NNWSs), by contrast, commit not to acquire these arms and, furthermore, states may only sign as NNWSs. In other words, the NPT freezes the legal possession of nuclear weapons as of 1967, without requiring those states in legal possession to divest themselves in any time-limited way.

In terms of the contemporary world order, the NPT's impact is significant. The five states that had successfully tested nuclear weapons by 1 January 1967 were the United States, the Soviet Union, Britain, France, and, finally, the People's Republic of China (PRC) in 1964. At the time, four of the five also held permanent seats on the UN Security Council; the PRC joined that group in 1971, when it acquired the 'China seat' at the UN. The next state to join the nuclear club was India, which tested a 'nuclear explosive' in 1974 without calling it a weapons test. In contrast to the PRC, whose nuclear possession was legitimised by the NPT, India was sanctioned for its nuclear development. The suppliers of nuclear material formed a cartel to control more tightly access to their technology and, far from being admitted to the inner core of world leaders, India was equated in the international system with Pakistan.[16]

The NPT, therefore, made two contributions to the structuring of the Great Power system in the contemporary world. First, it endorsed the position of the PRC as the fifth of the five global Powers, even before the PRC was formally accepted into that club by its accession to the China seat at the UN. The present international order is one that increasingly will be dominated by the United States and the PRC and, although the NPT did not uniquely produce this outcome, it is an important step on the route to producing the PRC as a Great Power. On the other hand, the NPT drew a line under the system's Great Powers at five. Legal nuclear possession is an extremely important marker of Great Power status in the contemporary world; how else could Britain or France lay claim to continued membership on the Security Council over, for example, Germany, but for their nuclear arsenals? The NPT polices the line between the licit and the illicit, and places those states that do not also hold permanent Security Council seats on the wrong side of it. India is only the most important of those excluded, both by virtue of its having tested nuclear weapons and in having a population to rival China's.

Although limiting the further spread of nuclear weapons was considered important, the centerpiece of arms control was the Soviet–American nuclear relationship. As Holton wrote in the introduction to the *Daedalus* issue, arms control was to be 'a means toward eliminating nuclear warfare and improving national security'. Restricting the number of states capable of fighting a nuclear war mattered, of course, but the preoccupation of those concerned with nuclear conflict was the possibility of a nuclear war between the United States and the Soviet Union. As the practice of arms control developed through the 1960s and into the 1970s, this preoccupation lay at its heart.

The move from multilateral discussion of general and complete disarmament to bilateral discussions of arms control was triggered by the Cuban missile crisis of October 1962. In December 1962, the United States tabled a paper at the ENDC that included a suggestion for a dedicated emergency communication link amongst major capitals. In June 1963, American and Soviet representatives at the ENDC signed a memorandum of understanding establishing a Moscow–Washington link.[17] This memorandum is the famed 'Hotline Agreement' and is generally seen as the first bilateral arms control agreement between the United States and the Soviet Union. Despite its representation in the popular imagination as a 'red phone' on the desks of the respective leaders, the hotline was actually Telex machines in the White House and Kremlin basements. However, it provided the possibility of immediate and direct communication in the time of crisis, which was increasingly important as each side built arsenals of intercontinental ballistic missile (ICBMs) with progressively rapid response times.

In January 1964, the United States proposed disconnecting the bilateral control of nuclear weapons from the multilateral disarmament discussions in the ENDC. It took five more years for the two sides to open negotiations, in which period both developed and began to deploy ballistic missile defense systems.[18] The talks were initially announced by President Lyndon Johnson at the NPT signing ceremony in 1968 but, later that summer, the Soviets invaded Czechoslovakia and the discussions were indefinitely postponed. It took a change in American administrations for the Soviets to come back to the table, with Moscow announcing its willingness to discuss arms limitations on the day of President Richard Nixon's inauguration in January 1969.

Three years of discussion followed, which produced two agreements in May 1972: the ABM Treaty limiting anti-ballistic missiles and an interim agreement limiting strategic arms (SALT I).[19] The ABM Treaty is particularly notable because it illustrates the conditions under which arms control was being conducted. A treaty limiting defenses seems, on the surface, to be an odd way to 'improve national security' in the way foreseen by the *Daedalus* group. Given the potential devastation of nuclear weapons delivered by long-range ballistic missiles, one might imagine that improving national security would involve building defenses, rather than restricting them.[20] However, it is the strange character of nuclear strategy that defenses came to be seen as promoting *in*security. The United States developed a doctrine of nuclear deterrence that essentially argued that each side would be secure to the degree that it could hit back against any attack with a high degree of certainty. This doctrine became known as 'assured destruction' and, given that it was mutual, gave rise to the most infamous of Cold War acronyms: MAD.

Mutual assured destruction (MAD) is at the heart of the Cold War management of nuclear security.[21] Both the Soviet Union and the United States would be deterred from attacking the other (and potentially from a range of other things as well) insofar as each retained the capability to launch a significant retaliatory strike, whatever happened. In terms of nuclear deterrence, this need to ensure a destructive 'second-strike' capability made defenses dangerous, If, for example, the Americans developed a reasonably effective strategic defense (one that could protect the territory of the United States) it might plausibly be able to launch a debilitating first strike against the Soviet Union and repel any subsequent retaliation with those defenses. The first strike would be important, because there was not in the 1960s (and, indeed, there is not now) any prospect of a defensive system that could cope with the scale of a Soviet attack without first severely degrading their capabilities. For mutual deterrence based on MAD to function, strategic defenses needed to be prevented.

The ABM Treaty permitted missile defenses, but it prohibited the development and deployment of strategic or wide-area defense, the kind that could protect the territory of the United States or Soviet Union. The defenses allowed were so-called point-defense systems that can protect a small area: a single city, for example, or a military base. The ABM Treaty allowed each side to protect its capital city and one of its ICBM fields. Where strategic defenses would undermine mutual deterrence, this particular kind of point defense could enhance deterrence by sustaining the ability to launch that all-important second strike. Defending a ballistic missile site would help to ensure that there were weapons that would survive an initial attack and be available for a retaliatory strike; protecting the national capital would make it more likely that someone could order such a strike.

There are two very important points to make about the ABM Treaty as part of this first attempt at bilateral arms control: it demonstrates clearly the relationship of arms control to deterrence theory; and, when arms control discussions started, the Soviet Union did not accept American notions of deterrence based on assured destruction. In the 1960s, Soviet military doctrine located nuclear weapons within a much broader context of the 'correlation of forces'. This concept was not comparable with the narrower notion of 'the balance of power' operative in the West. Rather, the correlation of forces was a broader historical notion of the social relations of power. Grounded in Soviet reading of Marxist social theory, the correlation of forces was a way of thinking about the momentary place of East and West in the overall historical trajectory of change; change that would eventually lead to the revolutionary overthrow of capitalism, as it had previously seen capitalism's emergence from feudalism.[22]

At the operational level, the Soviets had a rather different conception of deterrence:

> Soviet strategic thinking has not made the same doctrinal distinction between deterrence and defense that Western strategists have drawn. In Soviet thinking the one is an extension of the other, or even synonymous. The Soviet conception is the traditional military view, which comprehends deterrence in terms of a threat by an impressive war-fighting capability. The Anglo-American conception, on the other hand, crystallized through the 1950s and 1960s in the idea of mutual deterrence. ...[23]

The United States and Soviet Union, therefore, entered into the discussion of arms limitation with different ideas about the nature of the arms to be limited. The American conception of MAD constructed arms as bulwarks against aggression, which ought never to be used, and the use of which would constitute the profound failure of deterrence. The Soviets, on the other hand, deployed these weapons in a strategy that saw use and deterrence as part of the same doctrine and the unleashing of which would simply be an element of what weapons were built to do.

With its combination of restrictions on strategic defenses and limitations on offensive weapons, the 1972 ABM–SALT I package was underpinned by the Western conception of mutual deterrence, as was the bilateral arms control process that continued during the remaining years of the Cold War, through SALT II (1979) and START I (1991). Through the arms control negotiations, which were ongoing almost constantly for the final twenty years of the Cold War, the United States saw as part of its mission to 'teach' the Soviet Union the 'truths' of deterrence. The sequence of arms control agreements resting on the foundation of deterrence is a testament to the success of that educative process, and the result was a Soviet Union that took on the role of a largely stable superpower competitor in a bipolar international system. Bilateral arms control in the Cold War, therefore, was both a product of the distribution of 'Great Powers' in the system (the United States and the Soviet Union had the largest nuclear arsenals and were recognised as leaders of their respective blocs) but was also productive of that system through the learning and mutual recognition that occurred in and through the negotiating processes.

The 1990s demonstrated the ways in which alterations in the Great Power arrangement of an international system can alter the terrain on which diplomacy in general and arms control in particular are conducted. The end of the Cold War was greeted with euphoria in a variety of fields, including a belief that the way was now open for a more cooperative approach to international security; this would be manifest in the UN Security Council and in international efforts to control arms. It led a leading critic of arms control, Colin Gray, for example, to claim that there would be agreements only because they were not needed. Arms control, he argued, was at best a ratification of what was already produced by state interest.[24]

Gray's criticism misses at least two key points. The first is that arms control is both produced by the organisation of power in the international system and productive of that same organisation. Whereas the Great Power arrangements antecedent of any particular set of negotiations around arms set the conditions for those talks, the processes of discussing arms (regardless of the outcome) in turn shape the contemporary and subsequent international order. The second point is that even if Gray were right that arms control agreements are solely epiphenomenal of Great Power interests, he would still be wrong to suggest they are irrelevant. Once in place treaties (even unratified treaties) constrain the action of states. The ABM Treaty is a signal example of this feature of international life. Thus, the United States twisted its missile defense programme into knots to remain compliant with the treaty after President Ronald Reagan launched his Strategic Defense Initiative in 1983 (a vision clearly in violation of the spirit and letter of the ABM Treaty).[25] It was only in December 2001, with the United States and George W. Bush riding the wave of international and domestic support that followed the 9/11 attacks, that the Americans felt able to walk away from the ABM Treaty.[26]

In keeping with expectations after the end of the Cold War, the early 1990s were productive in terms of arms control, particularly renewed multilateral arms control. The ENDC had both continued and expanded, becoming the Conference on Disarmament (CD) in 1979, mandated by the first UN Special Session on Disarmament as the sole multilateral disarmament negotiating forum.[27] Nevertheless, throughout the 1980s, little of note was accomplished in the CD. With the commitment to cooperation after 1989, however, that changed for several years. The CD was able to negotiate, in short order, the Chemical Weapons Convention (CWC), which was ready for signature in 1993. The CWC had been under discussion in the CD for years but, with the thaw in Soviet–American relations, a series of seemingly intractable stumbling blocks were removed.[28] The result is one of the largest and most complex arms control treaties ever conceived.

The size and complexity of the CWC points to another interesting feature of the relationship between Great Power relations and ongoing arms control discussions. The character of the Soviet–American relationship through much of the 1980s (from the invasion of Afghanistan through Mikhail Gorbachev's transformation of Soviet policy) prevented agreement on the CWC; but the continuous meeting of the CD meant that a great deal of groundwork had been laid for a CWC by the early 1990s. Without the work of the CD in the 1980s, it is unlikely that any CWC, at least one of the nature and scope agreed by 1993, would have been possible. Chemical weapons are intimately tied to the broad range of contemporary chemical industries. Accordingly, verifying a weapons ban whilst permitting industrial use of chemicals is even more complicated than the similar problem posed by the relation of nuclear weapons to nuclear power. Because of this complexity, the verification regime for the CWC is extraordinarily complex: the treaty's text and its annexes run to 181 pages, of which 120 are devoted to setting out verification procedures.[29]

The window of opportunity represented by the end of the Cold War produced a number of important agreements, before largely closing with the (s)election of George W. Bush in 2000 and slamming shut with the terrorist attacks of 9/11. In addition to the CWC, the CD had been discussing a comprehensive nuclear test ban for many years. Although the Americans and Soviets, together with the British, had managed to negotiate some limits on testing, a complete ban proved unobtainable until the 1990s. Again, the opportunity provided by the end of the Cold War combined with the work previously done within the CD produced an agreement for a Comprehensive Test Ban Treaty (CTBT) in 1996. As with the CWC, CTBT monitoring and verification are complex, although in this case not because of close integration with civilian technology, but because of the need for technical data and interpretation.[30] Much of the work of establishing a network for monitoring, based on seismic data, was established whilst the prospects of agreement on CTBT were dim.

The 1996 agreement produced a treaty that has yet to enter into force, but also a monitoring system that functions without a legal treaty. The history of the CTBT, which produced this outcome, points to two of the complexities of arms control and its relation to world order. The United States signed the CTBT when it was first opened for signature, but it has still to ratify the treaty. The failure of the Clinton Administration to achieve CTBT ratification is generally explained by entirely domestic issues within the United States: scandal, the Republican witch hunt that marked Clinton's second term, and political miscalculation by the Administration that led it to put insufficient political capital into the attempt to ratify. None of these issues has much to do with the organisation of greater and lesser states in the international order and, yet, they stand as central to the non-entry-into-force of the CTBT.

Forty-four states must ratify the CTBT to allow entry-into-force; listed in Annex 2 of the Treaty, these states possess nuclear research or power reactors and, thus, could potentially test nuclear weapons. Whereas the United States is one of nine so-called Annex 2 countries that have not ratified, India is the most interesting of the other eight. Particularly disadvantaged by the international nuclear order produced by the NPT, India objected to being relegated to the mass of outsiders whilst its greatest local rival, the PRC, was admitted to the privileged core. India has consistently argued since that it will relinquish its nuclear ambitions, but it will only do so as part of general nuclear disarmament that includes the five NPT states. Until 1996, India also contended that a CTBT was an important step towards that disarmament. However, the nature of the 1996 text led India to claim that it was not a move toward nuclear disarmament but, rather, another discriminatory treaty in the mold of the NPT.[31] India has not signed the CTBT and, furthermore, reacted to its adoption by openly testing a nuclear weapon in 1998.[32] Thus both the present nuclear order and the state of the global arms control regime can be seen as products of the particularities of earlier arms control agreements, in particular the NPT.

The permissive conditions after the end of the Cold War also enabled other multilateral arms control agreements and processes that were less reliant on the participation of the erstwhile superpowers, or even the Great Powers. Most notable was the remarkably rapid conclusion of a treaty outlawing the manufacture and use of anti-personnel landmines, and it was later joined by a treaty on cluster munitions and a global process aimed at controlling the trade in small arms and light weapons. What marks these efforts, plus recent attempts at concluding a general treaty on the arms trade, is that they have been led by groups of states outside the top tier of world-order Great Powers; and they have managed to succeed without, at times, the support of the world's leading states. Through these efforts, a group of states both diverse and diffuse has emerged to play a leading role in advancing the global regulation of arms. Although certainly not Great Powers and often insignificant in other areas, they have developed through their engagement in these arms control processes into world leaders on issues related to arms. Furthermore, they have been joined by a number of NGOs, ranging from the International Committee of the Red Cross to issue-specific coalitions that have grown around each negotiation. These NGOs have been closely involved in the elaboration, and even negotiation, of post-Cold War arms control agreements to a degree never seen in previous decades.

Whilst it is certainly possible to overstate the role of NGOs in the new multilateralism of arms control, they have played a significant and significantly different role in successful discussions around AP landmines, cluster munitions, small arms and light weapons, and even now the Arms Trade Treaty to control conventional weapons.[33] As a consequence, the nature of multilateral arms control has been altered in important ways. States still drive the agenda, because international agreements form the framework of global regulation. However, they increasingly do so in concert with engaged NGOs, which work collaboratively in developing and advancing the arms control agenda. The result is a 'diplomatic' structure around issues of arms that is not dominated by the Great Powers and, indeed, is not an exclusive state practice.

International arms control entered a fallow period during the presidency of George W. Bush, as the United States led its variously willing coalitions in wars more or less unrelated to terror. Nevertheless, by virtue of the arms control practices of the early post-Cold War period, important activity continued that would not previously have been imaginable in the absence of active engagement from the world's leading state. With the change of government in early 2009, the United States appeared to reenter the world of arms control. President Barack Obama announced in 2009 that he would 'seek the security of a world without nuclear weapons' and immediately entered into discussions with Russia, producing a New START agreement in 2010. Although there can be significant doubts about the ability of this process to produce nuclear disarmament, it would seem to mark the return of bilateral nuclear arms control to the panoply of international arms control practices.[34]

Arms control in both its bilateral and multilateral guise has been a centerpiece of the global diplomacy of security since the publication of the seminal *Daedalus* issue in 1960. The diplomatic practice that developed after the publication of the issue has not only been shaped by the involvement and interest (understood in two ways) of the system's Great Powers, it has also shaped that system through the particularities of the arms control negotiations and agreements.

Notes

1 Richard Dean Burns, *The Evolution of Arms Control: From Antiquity to the Nuclear Age* (Santa Barbara, CA, 2009), 20–24. Burns cites the end of the Peloponnesian War (404 BC), the end of the Carthaginian War (202 BC), and the Peace of Apamea (188 BC) as instances of imposed arms limitation agreements from antiquity. The 'evolution' then proceeds to arms reduction proposals of 1766.

2 Ibid., xx; for a recent history of the two conventions, see Frederic Miller, Agnes Vandome, and John McBrewster, *Hague Conventions (1899 and 1907)* (Saarbruken, 2010).

3 Stockholm International Peace Research Institute (SIPRI), *The Arms Trade with the Third World* (New York, 1971), 90–100.

4 'Atomic Education Urged by Einstein: Scientists in Plea for $200,000 to Promote New Type of Essential Thinking', *New York Times* (25 May 1946), 13.

5 United States Department of State, *Report on the International Control of Atomic Energy* (Washington, DC, 1946), vii.

6 Ibid., 4.

7 The UNAEC had six permanent members (the five permanent members of the Security Council, plus Canada) and six rotating members. Baruch wanted a vote before the six non-permanent members rotated after December 1947; it failed.

8 United States Department of State, Office of the Historian, 'The Acheson-Lilienthal & Baruch Plans, 1946': http://history.state.gov/milestones/1945–52/BaruchPlans.

9 The figure comes from the Brooking Institute, 'US Nuclear Weapons Cost Study Project: Global Nuclear Stockpiles 1945–96': www.brookings.edu/projects/archive/nucweapons/stockpile.aspx. In 1960, the United States accounted for the great majority of these weapons, although the Soviet Union caught up in numbers of strategic nuclear weapons by 1970.

10 Gerald Holton, 'Editor's Prefatory Note', *Daedalus: Arms Control*, 89(1960), 675.

11 Donald G. Brennan, 'Setting and Goals of Arms Control', Ibid., 692–93.

12 In his 'Foreword' to the *Daedalus* issue, Jerome Wiesner wrote: 'Obviously, the most important task confronting us today is to find the means of halting the arms race and eliminating the danger of nuclear war. … Like it or not, the nations of the world must make a superhuman effort, working together, to reach agreements leading to some form of rational system of world security.' Weisner, 'Foreword to the issue 'Arms Control', Ibid., 677.

13 Joseph Pilat, 'Introduction: The Nonproliferation Predicament' in idem., ed., *The Nonproliferation Predicament* (Oxford, 1985), 1, reports that the expectation was 'over twenty', but he provides no documentation. William Potter, *Nuclear Power and Nonproliferation: An Interdisciplinary Perspective* (Cambridge, MA, 1982), 41n18, puts the number at 10 and cites three removes from the president. In 1990, Hans Blix attributed a fear of '20–30' to John F. Kennedy, see Tariq Rauf, 'The NPT Article VI Bargain—A Retrospective' in idem., ed., *Regional Approaches to Curbing Nuclear Proliferation in the Middle East and South Asia* Aurora Papers 16 (Ottawa, 1992), 1n6.

14 'Treaty on the Non-Proliferation of Nuclear Weapons', signed at London, Washington, and Moscow (1 July 1968), Article IX 2–3: http://www.fas.org/nuke/control/npt/text/npt2.htm.

15 The four additional states are the four non-parties to the NPT: India, Pakistan, Israel, and North Korea. In addition, South Africa built nuclear weapons but dismantled them with the end of Apartheid in sight. Several other countries have pursued nuclear weapons, but either chose to give up the programme (Argentina, Brazil, and Libya) or were forcibly prevented from completing their programme (Iraq at least twice).

16 See David Mutimer, 'Testing Times: Nuclear Tests, Test Bans and the Framing of Proliferation' *Contemporary Security Policy* 21(2000), 1–22.

17 For a text of the agreement, see 'Memorandum of Understanding Between the United States of America and the Union of Soviet Socialist Republics Regarding the Establishment of a Direct Communications Link; June 20, 1963': Avalon Project [Yale University Law School]: www.yale.edu/lawweb/avalon/diplomacy/soviet/sov003.htm.

18 McGeorge Bundy, *Danger and Survival: Choices about the Bomb in the First Fifty Years* (New York: 1988); Ernest J. Yanarella, *The Missile Defense Controversy: Strategy, Technology, and Politics, 1955–1972* (Lexington, KY, 1977).

19 Raymond Garthoff, *Détente and Confrontation: American-Soviet relations from Nixon to Reagan* Revised edition (Washington, DC, 1994), 146–224.

20 Indeed, this is precisely the argument that has been made by the proponents of the American missile defense programs in the years since. President Reagan argued that defenses were the way to security in his 1983 'Star Wars' speech, and every President since has continued the missile defence program that that speech launched.

21 For a reasonably recent discussion of deterrence theory explaining the centrality of MAD, see Keith Payne and C. Dale Walton, 'Deterrence in the Post-Cold War World', in John Baylis, James Wirtz, Eliot Cohen, and Colin S. Gray, eds., *Strategy in the Contemporary World* (Oxford, 2002), 161–82. It is worth noting that in the third edition of the book (2009), this chapter has been dropped and not replaced with any other discussion of deterrence.

22 Julien Lider, 'The Correlation of World Forces: The Soviet Concept', *Journal of Peace Research*, Volume 17, Number 2(1980), 151–71.

23 Ken Booth, 'Soviet Defense Policy', in John Baylis, Ken Booth, John Garnett, and Phil Williams, eds., *Contemporary Strategy II: The Nuclear Powers* (London, 1987), 92–93.

24 Colin S. Gray, *House of Cards: Why Arms Control Must Fail* (Ithaca, NY, 1992).

25 For a sympathetic recent look at the history of American missile defense policy, although from a perspective focused on Canadian policy, see James Fergusson, *Canada and Ballistic Missile Defence 1954–2009: Déjà vu all over again* (Vancouver, 2010). The relation of missile defenses to the ABM is central to this story, because it is a constant preoccupation of Canadian policy-makers concerned with American missile defense.

26 James Lindsay and Michael O'Hanlon, 'Missile Defense after the ABM Treaty' *Washington Quarterly*, Volume 25, Number 3 (2002), 163–76.

27 United Nations Office at Geneva, 'Conference on Disarmament: Introduction to the Conference':www.unog.ch/80256EE600585943/%28httpPages%29/BF18ABFEFE5D344DC1256F3100311CE9?OpenDocument.

28 See Organisation for the Prohibition of Chemical Weapons (OPCW), 'Chemical Weapons Convention: About the Convention: Genesis and Historical Development': www.opcw.org/chemical-weapons-convention/about-the-convention/genesis-and-historical-development/.

29 OPCW, Convention on the Prohibition of the Development, Production, Stockpiling and Use of Chemical Weapons and on Their Destruction: www.opcw.org/chemical-weapons-convention/download-the-cwc/.

30 Tibor Toth, 'Building up a Regime for Verifying the CTBT', *Arms Control Today*, 39 (September 2009), 6–11.

31 As the CTBT was being adopted, the Indian representative on the CD rose to say: 'I would like to reiterate our position that India cannot and does not accept CD/NTB/WP.330/Rev.1 and now CD/NTB/WP.330/Rev.2 as the CTBT we were mandated to negotiate.' CD/1436, 'Report of the Conference on Disarmament to the General Assembly of the United Nations' 12 September 1996, Section I §20.

32 A CTBT promotes nuclear disarmament because testing is important both for the development of new weapons and to ensure the safety and reliability of an existing stockpile. A truly comprehensive test ban, therefore, will freeze nuclear warhead development and eventually lead to disarmament through attrition. However, the 1996 CTBT enables testing by advanced simulation (which can only work based on data from explosive tests), and so enables the safety and reliability of existing stockpiles to be maintained indefinitely. See Mutimer, *Weapons State*, 150–54; idem., 'Testing Times'.

33 Rebecca Johnson, 'Changing Perceptions and Practice in Multilateral Arms Control Negotiations', in John Borrie and Vanessa Martin Radin, eds. *Thinking Outside the Box in Multilateral Disarmament and Arms Control Negotiations* (Geneva, 2006), 55–87.

34 I have argued elsewhere that the nature of bilateral arms control practiced in the Cold War and continued in the New START agreement precludes the possibility of a negotiated double zero, and so some alternative path to denuclearisation needs to be found. See David Mutimer, 'From Arms Control to Denuclearisation: Governmentality and the Abolitionist Desire', in Neil Cooper and David Mutimer, eds., 'Arms Control for the 21st Century', *Contemporary Security Policy* 32(2011), 57–75.

32

The strategy gap

Contemporary civil–military relations and the use of military power

Michael L. Roi

> The problem of strategy is located along the fault line between policy and the operational level. The consequence of politicians pretending that policy is strategy and of soldiers focusing on operations has been to leave strategy without a home.
>
> Hew Strachan[1]

Contemporary civil–military relations can be examined in the context of Hew Strachan's idea of strategy as the necessary 'bridge' spanning the fault line or chasm between the policy aspirations of politicians and the plans drawn up by military professionals for using military resources. Colin Gray takes a similar view of strategy as 'the bridge that relates military power to political purpose; it is neither military power per se nor political purpose.' He further defines strategy 'as the use that is made of force and the threat of force for the ends of policy.'[2] To be sure, this conception of strategy and the purposive use of force can involve both the actual application of military power in actions such as operations, missions, and tasks as well as the effects that stem in part from the mere existence of what the great maritime strategist, Sir Julian Corbett, referred to as 'forces in being.'[3] Military strategy can, in other words, include both the actual use of military capabilities in discrete actions and also the readiness of forces to undertake activities when called upon to do so. The military instrument is a potent element of national power that a state may bring to bear to attain national strategic objectives. And the absence of strategy and strategic dialogue are at the heart of the problem of civil–military relations in modern democratic states. As a result, more research ought to be focused on developing a new model of civil–military relations, built upon a sustained dialogue between civilians and soldiers that rests ultimately on a more realistic assessment of the military means available to attain policy ends.

There appears to be growing recognition amongst national security scholars and defense analysts that serious deficiencies in current approaches to national strategy formulation, especially the use of military power, continue to undermine the strategic performance of Western Powers in global affairs.[4] A frank assessment of American political and military elites concludes: 'The ability of the US national security establishment to craft, implement, and adapt effective long-term strategies against intelligent adversaries at acceptable costs has been declining for some decades.'[5] A recent British observer came to similar conclusions about his country's strategic performance: 'There is an intellectual vacuum at the heart of British statecraft. The UK doesn't do strategy coherently.'[6] Canada's strategic performance has been equally plagued by poor strategy formulation.[7] Not surprisingly, the question arises: why has strategy formulation become so difficult for Western democracies?

Defense analysts and former government officials have identified time pressures associated with the heavy workload of senior government executives and political decision-makers as a major cause of poor strategy formulation and unsuccessful national security planning. The problem stems from 'the tyranny of the inbox,' which 'often becomes the tyranny of managing today's crises.'[8] The focus on today tends to suit the inclinations of most governments, which remain generally more fixated on dealing with the here and now, managing current political ebbs and flows or even mitigating the political crisis of the moment, than devoting time and energy to developing national strategy for the future. A recent essay on American national strategic planning agrees that time pressures and a focus on current issues are major impediments to better strategy formulation and long-term foreign policy planning.[9] These impediments cannot be easily dismissed. One can bemoan time pressures but it appears extremely difficult to escape them. American Secretaries of State from 1945 to date have all complained about the pressures of what Dean Acheson labeled the 'thundering present.' Time pressures are not likely to disappear in the future and may become more onerous because of the information revolution. The pessimistic conclusion is: 'With so much information being transmitted so quickly, taking the long view has become more important but less likely.'[10] Despite the demands of the 'thundering present,' much can be gained when decision-makers, in Acheson's words, 'look ahead, not into the distant future, but beyond the vision of the operating officers caught in the smoke and crises of the current battle.'[11] It is important to invest time and effort into thinking beyond the crisis of the moment. By not doing so, one risks being perpetually caught in a succession of unfolding events and, in the worst case, committed to a course of action that cannot be sustained over the long term. Whilst devoting time and effort amidst the crush of daily operations and activities will always be challenging, politicians and senior officials need to organise opportunities in their busy schedules to discuss strategic issues beyond current crises.

Notwithstanding the ability of decision-makers to devote the necessary time to think and act more strategically about using military power, other obstacles block the path towards a better approach to strategy formulation, the most important of which is the absence of a sustained dialogue between civil and military leaders in contemporary Western society. In modern democratic states, there has been a strong preference for the 'normal theory' of civil–military relations: the widely accepted ideas prevalent in Western society identified in Samuel Huntington's path-breaking 1957 study of civil–military relations in the post-Second World War era.[12] Huntington's key prescription for ensuring democratic civilian control over the military is the establishment of a sharp division between civilian and military roles. Under the normal theory, politicians set and articulate policy and, once settled, soldiers create military strategy and conduct operations. Each side remains within its own distinct sphere.[13] There is another dimension to the normal theory frequently raised in defense of its virtues: that it enshrines the right of civilian authorities to be 'wrong' about the defense policies and priorities they choose.[14] The implicit assumption here is that tight civilian control over the military remains necessary to safeguard democratic institutions. This assumption is firmly grounded in democratic theory, which asserts that power ultimately rests with the people and their elected representatives and requires that the predilections of the armed services be subordinate to civilian preferences. Tight control ensures that the military does not threaten the political authority of civilian governments. But one has to question the basis of this anxiety especially when looking at Powers where the military has never posed a challenge to civil authorities.[15] These concerns about distinct spheres of civilian and military responsibilities have become essentially an exaggeration of misplaced fears of military encroachments on democratic prerogatives and the politicisation of the officer corps. The result of these exaggerated concerns is policy that does not understand the military instrument and military advice that does not provide policy with the information necessary to form coherent strategy.[16]

In looking at the American military's compliance with democratic theory, one authority makes the important observation: 'The American military has internalised the view that to be professional means that it does not directly challenge civilian political authority for control of the government.' On a practical level (*vice* theoretical one), therefore, little prospect exists of a military coup in the United States or in any other Western democratic state; military forces in modern democracies willingly recognise and accept civilian control. A further *caveat* to the argument exists that civilians have the right to be wrong by pointing out that the military's acceptance of civilian oversight 'is not the same thing as saying that the American military always acts so as to obey without challenge any civil order.'[17] Although generally compliant with the theory of civil control, the actual relationship between civilians and the military, as seen in historical practice, resembles an ongoing dialogue rather than a clear Huntingtonian separation between spheres.

A growing amount of research has pointed to flaws in Huntington's theory.[18] Contrary to its sharp division between civilian and military spheres, an increasing number of scholars such as Strachan insist that '[e]ffective civil-military relations in practice rely on a dialogue.' Strachan adds: 'Policy is ill conceived if it asks the armed forces to do things which are not consistent with their capabilities or with the true nature of war.'[19] It is not simply about politicians heeding the advice of military professionals. Rather, this evolving theory of civil–military relations emphatically argues for deep and sustained civilian political engagement in strategy-making, planning, and overseeing the use of military power. The essence of strategy and modern democratic civil–military relations must be a fulsome and sustained dialogue between statesmen and soldiers for the sake of ensuring coherent policy and military capabilities in the context of the dynamic interaction with adversaries or operational situations that continue to unfold. Sustaining this type of dialogue requires politicians and other civilian leaders to become more knowledgeable of military affairs. This of course remains a major challenge in modern democratic states, where, historically, there has been little political incentive to acquire this type of specialised knowledge.

Recent scholarship highlights the importance of acquiring knowledge of military affairs by democratic leaders in war, exemplified by the critical wartime leadership of President Abraham Lincoln during the American Civil War; his impressive leadership remains a model in many ways for democratic leaders in war.[20] Far from restricting himself to the policy sphere, Lincoln played an active and ongoing role in the Union's evolving strategy, providing and modifying political direction throughout the conflict, appointing and firing key military leaders based on their performances, and shaping the military strategy of Union forces: 'Lincoln exercised a constant oversight of the war effort from beginning to end. … [The President] did not hesitate to overrule his military advisers—not just after he found his feet as commander-in-chief, but at the earliest stage of the war.'[21] As President and Commander-in-Chief, Lincoln set out to become more knowledgeable of military affairs, including familiarising himself with key works of military history and theory and taking a keen interest in weaponry.[22] In short, Lincoln sought and maintained an informed dialogue with his senior commanders over strategy and campaign plans. He did not simply provide direction, sit back, and watch events unfold. He kept a close watch on the progress of the campaigns by visiting the frontlines himself or sending his representatives.

Lincoln's example demonstrates that strategy formulation and national strategic decision-making require a continual and well-informed dialogue and interaction between civilian and military leaders. He grasped that war was dynamic, that circumstances changed, and that he had to remain engaged, as Commander-in-Chief, in fine-tuning strategy:

The 'normal' theory of civil-military relations presents the statesman as the setter of goals and the designer of the outline of the war, but fails to take into account the ways in which the conduct of war causes objectives and strategic methods alike to change. Lincoln's original strategic concept, reasonable though it was, could not and did not stand the test of struggle. The changes that he found necessary reflect not the inadequacy of his original conceptions but the nature of war itself, which compels those who wage it to change their goals and courses of action no less than their techniques.[23]

Successful wartime leaders in the past 'understood that they could not lead if they did not know an enormous amount about the business of war.'[24] Unlike Lincoln, Prime Minister William Lyon Mackenzie King did not attempt to develop a better understanding of the military instrument he wielded as a Canadian wartime leader during the Second World War. His failure to develop a deeper understanding of the military left him in the peculiar circumstances of depending on the advice of his senior military commanders, such as Generals Harry Crerar and Andrew McNaughton, but retaining his distrust and resentment towards their ideas and influence.[25] These generals were certainly prepared to 'stray' beyond Huntington's concept of the rightful 'military sphere' to give advice. Sensing an opportunity to raise the military voice in the civil–military dialogue, Crerar in particular pushed his plans for army expansion forward. In the end, the army view triumphed and a two-corps First Canadian Army of five divisions and two armoured brigades was approved by the Government. Crerar's role in expanding Canada's wartime effort suggests that Canadian civil–military relations have not always in practice adhered to the Huntington ideal and that a more assertive military voice is, at least in part, the result of the absence of a political partner to have an informed dialogue on the use of military power. King's reliance on more knowledgeable military advisors fits a larger pattern of Canadian civil–military relations. Lacking the technical expertise of military professionals, civilians frequently avoid what they perceive as 'specialist' discussions, especially when these deal with military organisation, conduct of operations, planning military missions, equipment, and training. They compensate by focusing on areas in which they believe they possess an advantage such as control of resources and government policy formulation. As mentioned above, this process has not been an entirely successful model of civil–military relations for democratic nations at war, nor arguably in peacetime.

Seventy years later, King's relationship with his military advisers looks very much like the norm for civil–military relations in the twenty-first century. Over the past two centuries, there has been a progressive severing of the connection between the exercise of political power and that of military command. From antiquity to Antietam, political leadership and military command frequently converged in a single ruler or monarch. Roman emperors embodied this convergence. Not all Roman emperors were, of course, brilliant generals. After all, Augustus relied on Agrippa to organise Roman forces and lead them in successful wars and conquests.[26] Nevertheless, Roman emperors had, more often than not, acquired through education and experience the basic skills and perspective for effective strategy formulation and the use of Roman military power. They understood well the vicissitudes of Roman politics and the limitations on imperial resources; most also had a good grasp of the capabilities of Roman legions and warships. Political success was often the prerequisite for senior military command, although most Roman generals would be considered amateur soldiers today because their army service was intermittent, separated by recurrent forays into political office.[27] But, still, 'it is a grave mistake to view the Roman system through modern eyes and to claim that Roman commanders were not really soldiers at all, but politicians, for these men were always both.'[28]

Emperor Hadrian certainly showed more than a little proficiency in exercising political and military power. Known as a soldier's soldier, a reputation acquired by years on campaign in support of imperial expansion, he was comfortable with military life and readily accepted the austere conditions of the legionnaires. Sitting at the acme of Roman political and military power, Hadrian recognised, nonetheless, the need to bring greater coherence between imperial financial and manpower resources and the needs of defending the vast imperial boundaries. He assumed control of an empire that had been rapidly expanded by his predecessor, and these new imperial acquisitions remained, in Hadrian's view, dangerously exposed. The emperor concluded that protecting the recently acquired provinces would place excessive demands on Rome's resources. In response, he adopted a defensive posture, ordering the immediate abandonment of his predecessor's new provinces and a regroup behind more defensible boundaries, making effective use of natural geographic obstacles such as major rivers.[29] But retrenchment did not mean neglect for Roman armies. The historian Dio Cassius portrays an emperor busily working to ensure Rome's armies would remain well prepared and ready for war. Hadrian spent a great deal of time reviewing Roman camps, including trenches, ramparts, and palisades; he closely inspected the troops and their weapons and frequently recommended changes to training and preparations. The emperor, Dio Cassius writes, 'so trained and disciplined the whole military force throughout the empire that even today [a century later] the methods introduced by him are the soldiers' law of campaigning.'[30] It is difficult to disagree with the argument: 'Determined not to squander the advantages he inherited, [Hadrian] made the empire safe, purging it of military adventurism.'[31] The combination of military command, experience in war, and political authority enabled the emperor to devise an effective strategy, ensuring a coherence of Roman ends, ways, and means. His end state was a prosperous and secure empire, his ways were based on a policy of non-aggression and defensive consolidation, and his means were disciplined and trained Roman soldiers.

The convergence of political and military power continued long after the Roman Empire fell. Political authority and military command were concentrated in a single ruler well into the early modern period. Seventeenth century figures like Maurice of Nassau and Gustavus Adolphus effectively combined their roles as military commanders with their responsibilities as heads of state; this practice was fairly common amongst European monarchs until the nineteenth century. 'As late as 1870, King Wilhelm of Prussia accompanied his army against France, took part in the operational decisions of that campaign, and stood on the heights above Sedan whilst Krupp cannon blasted the French army—itself accompanied by Emperor Napoleon III—into ignominious submission.'[32]

In twentieth century democratic states, the separation between military and political power became increasingly pronounced. One exception is President Dwight Eisenhower, who attained the pinnacle of American political power after a career that took him to the highest reaches of military command. There are interesting parallels between Eisenhower's use of military power as Commander-in-Chief and the defensive imperial strategy pursued by Hadrian. Early in his first term, the President had become concerned with the rapid increase in defense expenditures associated with his predecessor's major conventional arms build-up. He feared that these costs would lead to huge deficits and, over the long run, would undermine the American economy and with it the foundations of American global power. In response, Eisenhower launched a major reexamination of American foreign policy and defense posture, engaging his senior officials in an innovative strategy formulation exercise (Operation Solarium) and personally remaining involved in ongoing national security planning.[33] This exercise originated with a discussion on the state of East–West relations in the White House Solarium on 8 May 1953 amongst Eisenhower and a small group of national security advisors.[34] Based on this discussion, Eisenhower gave direction to assemble three teams of what he described as 'bright young fellows', comprised of both civilian and military experts from across the American Government to develop three strategies to deal with the evolving relationship with the Soviet Union.[35] With the creation of these teams, Eisenhower set in motion what has been described as 'an exercise unique in the history of U.S. national security policy making.'[36] The President himself selected some of the key team members, including George F. Kennan, who had been one of the chief architects of the previous administration's containment strategy.

Over several weeks in June–July 1953 at the United States National War College, the teams worked secretly and separately on their respective strategies. On 16 July, they briefed the results of their work to the National Security Council (NSC) at a full-day session in the White House Library with Eisenhower in attendance: 'No president before or after Eisenhower ever received such a systematic and focused briefing on the threats facing the nation's security and the possible strategies for coping with them.'[37] The President listened to all the detailed presentations before intervening with his assessment. Eisenhower's summation impressed many of the participants with its 'mastery' of the subject matter. As Kennan later recalled: 'The president got up at the final [Solarium] meeting on July 16, after the others of us had presented our reports, and spoke about the whole range of these problems. He spoke, I must say, with a mastery of the subject matter and a thoughtfulness and a penetration that were quite remarkable. I came away from it with the conviction (which I have carried to this day) that President Eisenhower was a much more intelligent man than he was given credit for being.'[38]

The Solarium Exercise ultimately produced NSC 162/2—Basic National Security Policy, the so-called 'New Look' strategy, which has been characterised as 'an integrated and reasonably efficient adaptation of resources to objectives, of means to ends.'[39] During the Solarium effort and after, Eisenhower created the conditions for ongoing dialogue amongst civilians and military professionals on his national security decision-making team. He personally chaired NSC meetings, missing only six out of a total of 179 meetings during the first four years of his presidency. Eisenhower's strategy relied heavily on the threat of nuclear weapons and, as some critics have suggested, this limited American policy options in situations in which vital American interests were not at stake. At the same time, however, the President wanted to avoid another global conflict, a view inspired by his awareness of the devastation of the Second World War and the potential destruction of thermonuclear weapons. The result was a cautious but consistent balancing of ends, ways, and means that preserved American financial well-being and maintained United States capabilities to defend its vital interests.

Today, fewer and fewer politicians have served in their nations' militaries, let alone have the vast military experience of leaders like Eisenhower. Adhering consciously or subconsciously to the 'normal theory' of civil–military relations and lacking in-depth knowledge of the military instrument at their disposal, they continue to struggle with strategy formulation and rarely engage in sustained and informed dialogue with their military advisors. As a result, they face difficulties translating military power into political effect in pursuit of national objectives. Military advisors have, for their part, tended to focus their attention on the operational level at the expense of strategic issues. Strachan insists that the British and American militaries in the 1980s embraced the operational level of war as they anticipated fighting in large formations in northwestern Europe against invading Soviet forces. Major war against the Soviet Union, involving high-tempo, high-intensity fighting, placed a premium on speed, maneuver, firepower, and rapid decision-making, requiring a large degree of autonomy by military forces in the field from political leaders at home. A focus on the operational level of war corresponded to a clear delineation of spheres of responsibility as outlined in the 'normal' theory of civil–military relations, allowing officers to appropriate what they saw as the zenith of professional competence (operational excellence) separate from politics and policy-making. In this sense, the operational level of war came to occupy a politics-free zone.[40] The tactical and operational lessons of the 1991 Gulf War appeared to validate maneuverist thinking. Military trends associated with the Revolution in Military Affairs and its successor terms such as 'transformation' tended to reinforce the fixation on the operational level.

But excellence at the operational level has not ensured strategic success. The use of military power has not been conceived holistically, but rather as a way of winning battles as opposed to the winning of wars.[41] Although policy-making has remained the civilian purview and planning and conduct of operations remain the domain of the military as prescribed by the 'normal' theory, contemporary civil–military relations have foundered on the shoals of shallow strategy and the misalignment of military capabilities. Indeed, the absence of a sustained and realistic dialogue between civil authorities and military leaders about military power is at the heart of the strategy formulation gap and the frequently unsuccessful use of military resources by contemporary Western democratic states. As noted above, policy objectives are flawed if they require the armed forces to undertake tasks and missions that are inconsistent with their capabilities or overall capacity. But this is exactly what has happened in Afghanistan over the past decade.

Since 2001, North Atlantic Treaty Organization (NATO) strategy in Afghanistan has been deeply flawed, suffering from ongoing disconnects between ambitious end states and the means allocated to achieve them, including military resources.[42] Most Western governments initially articulated a set of policy objectives that focused on toppling the Taliban regime and rooting out al-Qaeda. After the rapid collapse of the Taliban regime in 2002 and the exodus of surviving Taliban and al-Qaeda leaders to Pakistan, these initial objectives were supplanted by more ambitious goals focused on humanitarian relief and state-building in Afghanistan, which was seen as a worthy cause deserving international assistance. After 2002, lofty humanitarian desires to rebuild the country mixed with fears that an unstable Afghanistan would continue to generate security problems for the rest of the world. Together with lingering concerns about terrorists regaining a foothold in Afghanistan, this humanitarian impulse inspired ambitious thinking about the scale and purpose of reconstruction, which would be more aptly described as transforming Afghanistan rather than restoring a *status quo ante* that never existed. Whatever the worthiness of these aspirations, achieving them will be difficult, requiring a much greater level of commitment and resources by the international community than has been brought to bear to date. In fact, it has been suggested that it will take nothing less than a multiyear commitment (likely decades) of financial resources and troops by Western Powers to ensure Afghanistan's successful transformation.[43]

At some point, the question has to be asked: does this ambitious project justify the enormous investment of national security resources? The answer must not only take into account what has been directly expended but also the opportunity costs as well, that is to say, those other national security issues and national priorities that have been neglected or foreclosed because of the choices made. In terms of American involvement, Richard Haass, the President of the Council on Foreign Relations, doubts that the costs are justified. He estimates that Afghanistan is costing Washington in the order of US$100 billion a year. Beyond financial costs, he points to the lives lost and the inability of the Americans to focus on mounting national security challenges elsewhere. Haass concludes: 'Afghanistan is claiming too many American lives, requiring too much attention, and absorbing too many resources. The sooner we accept that Afghanistan is less a problem to be fixed than a situation to be managed, the better.'[44] Haass and others have begun to question whether the transformation of Afghanistan is unequivocally a vital American national security imperative, which raises doubts about its importance to other Western democratic Powers.

Apart from serious reservations about the requirement for Western Powers to sustain the necessary financial resources and troop numbers over a long period of time, fundamental conceptual problems about Afghanistan transformation and the role of military power in achieving it continue to abound. These problems go deeper than the simple troop-to-task calculus that has recently garnered much media attention. More specifically, the current approach to state-building in Afghanistan rests on profoundly ahistorical assumptions about the process of state formation. No matter how tactically brilliant or skilled in counterinsurgency (COIN) Western armed forces may be, the military can hardly be expected to accelerate economic development and the formation of mature governance structures on the time-lines currently envisaged for a transition to a self-sustaining, stable Afghan security environment. In other words, there are good grounds for skepticism about what can be achieved with the application of military means to what is ostensibly a long-term political, socioeconomic process that occurs over decades, perhaps centuries. A greater familiarity with development studies as well as the work of historians and political scientists who examine the process of state formation would challenge sanguine expectations about the prospects for successful state-building in Afghanistan. Only time will tell whether the recently rescoped American-developed NATO strategy, based on scaling back expectations for ambitious state-building in Afghanistan and a narrower focus on halting the momentum of the Taliban insurgency to enable the transition to Afghan Government security forces, will be successful. Even with the best of luck, the chances for success appear slim and the conclusion remains valid that military forces continue to be asked to accomplish things for which they have not been, nor perhaps should be, prepared. The issue then is not simply a question of whether the military has sufficient resources (force size to population ratio or the proper COIN doctrine) to achieve policy objectives but, rather, if military forces are being asked to do things beyond their training, professional expertise, and mandates. Thus, in the absence of a better-informed and sustained dialogue between civilian authorities and their military advisors about what military capabilities are specifically able to do and what capacity can be brought to bear, it is likely that there will be a continued misalignment of policy ends and the use of military power.

When there is no coherence between policy and military capabilities, policy is unsound even if it is well intentioned. Aside from strategic failure and loss in war, another risk of misaligned policy and capabilities is that policy cannot easily be disaggregated from the manner in which wars are fought when the wars become prolonged because of inadequate resourcing and inappropriate mandates. This dilemma exposes both the policy and the operational conduct of war to the potential of public disapproval. It does Western governments little good to embrace international policies in Afghanistan and elsewhere for which they do not have the military capabilities or capacity. Thus, prolonged military efforts, in which a Power's vital interests are not palpably involved, have the potential to weaken the bonds in the long term between a country's armed forces and its people, making it increasingly difficult to ensure the integration of the military into society (Huntington's desired goal according to his concept of subjective control).

The preference for state-building operations in Afghanistan and, potentially, in other 'failed states' has been inspired by, but not coordinated with, ambitious humanitarian policy. In addition to humanitarian motivation, the assumption behind the need for state-building in the developing world appears to be the supposed link between instability in failed states and the emergence of domestic security threats to Western Powers. Herein lies the origins of a revolutionary though not deeply examined premise guiding current national security thinking. Unsubstantiated assertions about instability everywhere in the world causing security threats to western Powers (this causal chain from instability in far-flung places to actual threats to the homeland has never been adequately explained) leads to expansive thinking about what needs to be done and can be achieved globally by the application of military power. In this abiding sense of humanitarian obligation and its corollary of pervasive threat, there exists the elision of strategy. A proper mission analysis on such an expansive international ambition has never been conducted. There is no way that the military means could be made available for so vast an international agenda. Western democratic states have struggled to use military power effectively in pursuit of their ambitious international objectives. In some instances, force has been applied to situations ill suited for it to be effective and, at others, the amount of military resources deployed has not matched the level of ambition. How did we arrive at this point? Why do Western states have so much trouble using military power, coming perilously close at times to strategic failure?

Sir Rupert Smith believes that the changing character of war challenges existing models of civil–military relations and leads to problems in applying military power because neither the political nor the military sphere understands how outmoded their thinking has become. The military's preference for preparing for and conducting what he calls 'interstate industrial war' remains a key part of the problem. Interstate industrial war is essentially a major conflict involving technologically advanced states, which Smith insists became effectively obsolete with the advent of nuclear weapons. In its place, there is 'war amongst the people,' often an open-ended conflict that has little to do with states and more often deals with individuals or groups, where fighting literally takes place in populated areas and figuratively in the living rooms of people via media coverage.[45] Problems arise when decision-makers pursue the objective of decisive strategic victory, an outcome linked to interstate industrial war, when in reality war amongst the people often leads to interminable fighting. The best that can be hoped for in these circumstances is that military intervention creates acceptable 'conditions' on the ground, laying the foundation for a longer-term resolution of the conflict as opposed to a clear-cut military victory.

Smith puts forward a strong argument, which appears to be borne out, to some degree at least, by the evidence of the ethnic and intrastate conflicts of the post-Cold War period and the frequently mismanaged interventions by Western states in the early stages of these crises. But his argument about the emergence of a new paradigm for war and the failure of decision-makers to respond accordingly is built on several shaky propositions. First, it rests on a false dichotomy between the supposedly opposing paradigms of interstate war and war amongst the people. The Second World War exposed the fallacy of this dichotomy. It was not simply a war of colliding militaries of the states involved. Civilians, who accounted for at least 50 percent of the total casualties in the war, were killed by neighbors as well as by foreign invaders.[46] The second questionable proposition is that interstate wars lead to decisive strategic victories. Although the Second World War certainly witnessed the decisive defeat of Nazi Germany and, to a lesser extent, Japan, the end of the war left much unfinished business and even planted the seeds for future conflicts. As Niall Ferguson points out, 'no one could pretend that Russian occupation was the outcome hoped for by the subject peoples of the Nazi empire.'[47] Massacres, mass rape, and ethnic cleansing continued amongst and between the people across Central and Eastern Europe long after the 'Victory in Europe' celebrations occurred. Germany was divided for 45 years, its once capital city encircled, and the country became a potential trip wire for a new global war. It seems then that interstate war, at least its twentieth century form, is neither completely distinct from war amongst the people nor necessarily crowned with decisive victories.

The final proposition that merits reconsideration is the idea that a failure to understand how war changed is the reason why Western military interventions in the post-Cold War period have been plagued with problems. Smith is certainly right to argue that Western statesmen felt a compassionate urge do something in response to images of violence and suffering but, without delving deeply into the character of these conflicts and how they might be different from other wars, frequently sent forces with equipment and rules of engagement more suited to peace-keeping operations than the dangerous threat environment and military situation that soldiers found. Interestingly, however, the original United States deployment to Somalia in 1992 involved nearly 30,000 American troops and permissive rules of engagement.[48] But as often occurs in war, mission creep happens and initial objectives evolve as circumstances change. All wars are dynamic. They require constant dialogue between soldiers and statesmen about the ends sought, the manner of pursuing those ends, and the means necessary to achieve them. The failure to treat war as dynamic and ensure a sustained dialogue linking military means and ways to policy end states has been the crux of the problem undermining Western military intervention. Civilian authorities and their military advisors have not developed effective strategies to guide military interventions and, consequently, the use of military power frequently suffers from an end-state means gap.

Strachan believes it is time for democratic decision-makers to reappropriate 'the control and direction of war'[49] (the function and purpose of strategy). Reappropriating control and direction of war through the use of strategy faces enormous challenges as a result of the current divide in contemporary civil–military relations. In modern democratic states, political leaders rarely have the level of military knowledge and experience of senior military command that historically was commonplace. One cannot count on the emergence of a 'future Eisenhower.' A more pragmatic way forward is to encourage ongoing dialogue between political leaders and their military advisers towards better strategy formulation. This process will likely establish a stronger foundation upon which to build a new model of civil–military relations. A more effective dialogue requires both politicians and military professionals to think strategically or, to put it another way, of being strategically minded about a country's national security capacity and the ends that can be achieved through the use of military power.[50] Politicians and military advisors must be able to succeed 'in the no man's land where politics/policy and military power meet' (the strategy bridge where national security decisions about using military power for political purposes are made).[51] What is required is the ability to function effectively in the environment where politics and military power converge, orchestrating the use of military capabilities to achieve desired political consequences.[52]

Here the approach of Emperor Hadrian and President Eisenhower has much to teach modern decision-makers. Learning from them involves acceptance of the idea that force will not always be the most appropriate option. Military power retains its utility in today's world, but only when used in situations in which military capabilities match the requirements and nature of the problem at hand and when the level of resources committed are commensurate with the end states sought. Although restraint and focus in using military power are necessary, the examples of Hadrian and Eisenhower also demonstrate the wisdom of ensuring that armed forces continue to be prepared to use deadly force to deter potential adversaries and intervene when called upon to do so. As a recent biographer of Hadrian reminds us: 'Through unremitting energy and skill, he forged a peacetime army into a powerful war machine. Hadrian's legions were one of the most valuable legacies he left to his successors.'[53] Modern civilian democratic leaders and their military advisers would do well to remember this lesson.

Disclaimer

The reported results, their interpretation, and any opinions expressed in this chapter remain those of the author and do not represent or otherwise reflect any official opinion or position of the Department of National Defence or the Government of Canada.

Notes

1 Hew Strachan, 'Making Strategy: Civil-Military Relations after Iraq,' *Survival*, 48(Autumn 2006), 61.

2 Colin S. Gray, *Modern Strategy* (New York, 1999), 17. Italics in the original.

3 Corbett understands forces in being to be 'not merely in existence, but in active and vigorous life.' In essence, Corbett means the necessary measures (such as training, positioning, and exercises) that ensure forces are ready for use. Julian Corbett, *Some Principles of Maritime Strategy* (London, 1911), 214.

4 See Andrew F. Krepinevich and Barry D. Watts, *Regaining Strategic Competence. Strategy for the Long Haul* (Washington, DC, 2009); Patrick Porter, 'Why Britain Doesn't do Grand Strategy,' *RUSI Journal*, 155

(August.-September 2010), 6–12; M.L. Roi and G. Smolynec, 'Canadian Civil-Military Relations: International Leadership, Military Capacity and Overreach,' *International Journal*, 65(2010), 705–24; Hew Strachan, 'The Lost Meaning of Strategy,' *Survival*, 47 (Autumn 2005), 33–54; Hew Strachan, 'The Strategic Gap in British Defence Policy,' *Survival*, 51 (August–September 2009), 49–70; Strachan, 'Making Strategy,' 59–82; Paul Newton, Paul Colley, and Andrew Sharpe, 'Reclaiming the Art of British Strategic Thinking,' *RUSI Journal*, 155(March 2010), 44–51.

5 Krepinevich and Watts, *Regaining Strategic Competence*, vii.

6 Porter, 'Why Britain Doesn't do Grand Strategy,' 6.

7 Roi and Smolynec, 'Canadian Civil-Military Relations,' 720.

8 Michèle A. Flournoy and Shawn W. Brimley, 'Strategic Planning for National Security. A New Project Solarium,' *JFQ*, Volume 41, Number 2 (2006), 81. Flournoy has now become the Under-Secretary for Policy at the United States Department of Defense.

9 Amy B. Zegart, 'Why the Best is Not Yet to Come in Policy Planning,' in Daniel W. Drezner, ed., *Avoiding Trivia. The Role of Strategic Planning in American Foreign Policy* (Washington, DC, 2009), 113.

10 Ibid., 115–16.

11 Acheson quoted in Daniel W. Drezner, 'The Challenging Future of Strategic Planning in Foreign Policy,' in idem., *Avoiding Trivia*, 4.

12 This acceptance of Huntington's theory has been more passive than active because it is unlikely that many politicians and senior civil servants have read Huntington's book. The book represented, in essence, a systematic effort to codify the commonly accepted principles of civil–military relations encapsulated in the expression 'civil control of the military.' Samuel P. Huntington, *The Soldier and the State: The Theory and Politics of Civil-Military Relations* (Cambridge, MA, 1957).

13 Eliot A. Cohen, *Supreme Command: Soldiers, Statesmen, and Leadership in Wartime* (New York, 2003), 4–5, 242–49; Huntington, *Soldier and the State*, 456. Strachan has likewise drawn attention to the predominance of the Huntington theory, which he believes has hampered strategy formulation in Western democratic states because of a slavish devotion to this sharp divide between civil and military leaders. See Strachan, 'Making Strategy,' 66.

14 This view has been argued recently by Philippe Lagassé in assessing current Canadian civil–military relations. Philippe Lagassé, *Accountability for National Defence: Ministerial Responsibility, Military Command and Parliamentary Oversight*, IRPP Study #4 (March 2010), 35. This study amounts to a defense of the normal theory, describing an idealised notion of civilian control of the military, which ought in the author's view to be seriously circumscribed in its participation in national strategic discussions.

15 Peter D. Feaver, *Armed Servants. Agency, Oversight, and Civil-Military Relations* (Cambridge, MA, 2003), 11, 65–68.

16 Strachan, 'Lost Meaning of Strategy,' 47.

17 Feaver, *Armed Servants*, 11.

18 See, for example, Thomas C. Bruneau, Florina Christiana Matei, and Sak Sakoda, 'National Security Councils: Their Potential Functions in Democratic Civil-Military Relations,' *Defense & Security Analysis* 25 (September 2009), 255–69; Cohen, *Supreme Command*, 241–64; Thomas C. Bruneau and Florina Christiana Matei, 'Towards a New Conceptualization of Democratization and Civil-Military Relations,' *Democratization*, 15 (December 2008), 909–29; Feaver, *Armed Servants*; Peter D. Feaver and Richard H. Koln, eds., *Soldiers and Civilians. The Civil-Military Gap and American National Security* (Cambridge, MA, 2001); Peter D. Feaver and Christopher Gelpi, *Choosing Your Battles: American Civil Military Relations and The Use of Force* (Princeton, NJ, 2004); Roi and Smolynec, 'Canadian Civil Military Relations,' 705–24; Strachan, 'Lost Meaning of Strategy,' 49–52; idem., 'Making Strategy,' 78–80.

19 Strachan, 'Making Strategy,' 67.

20 See James M. McPherson, *Tried By War. Abraham Lincoln as Commander-In-Chief* (New York, 2008); Cohen, *Supreme Command*, Chapter 2.

21 Cohen, *Supreme Command*, 17.

22 Ibid., 21–25; McPherson, *Tried By War*, 3–8, 41–48, 191, 265–70.

23 Cohen, *Supreme Command*, 32.

24 Ibid., 214.

25 See Paul Douglas Dickson, *A Thoroughly Canadian General. A Biography of General H.D.G. Crerar* (Toronto, 2007), Chapters 8–10; idem., 'The Politics of Army Expansion: General H.D.G. Crerar and the Creation of the First Canadian Army, 1940–41', *Journal of Military History* 60(April 1996), 271–98; C. P. Stacey, *Arms, Men and Governments: The War Policies of Canada, 1939–1945* (Ottawa, 1970), 111–15, 129; Jack Pickersgill, *The Mackenzie King Record*, Volume 1: *1939–1944* (Toronto, 1960), 129.

26 The critical role of Agrippa in securing the throne for and ensuring the imperial rule of Augustus is well covered in Anthony Everitt, *Augustus: The Life of Rome's First Emperor* (New York, 2006).

27 Adrian Goldsworthy, *In the Name of Rome. The Men Who Won the Roman Empire* (London, 2003), 15. See also in Williamson Murray and Mark Grimsley, 'Introduction. On Strategy,' in Williamson Murray, MacGregor Knox and Alvin H. Bernstein, eds., *The Making of Strategy. Rulers, States, and War* (Cambridge, UK, 1994), 19–20.

28 Goldsworthy, *In the Name of Rome*, 26.

29 For a discussion of Hadrian's strategy of defensive imperialism, see Anthony Everitt, *Hadrian and the Triumph of Rome* (New York, 2009), 172–74, 208–12.

30 Goldsworthy, *In the Name of Rome*, 376–77.

31 Everitt, *Hadrian*, 325.

32 Murray and Grimsley, 'Introduction. On Strategy,' 20.

33 Krepinevich and Watts, *Regaining Strategic Competence*, 7, 46–49; and Flournoy and Brimley, 'Strategic Planning for National Security,' 82–83.

34 See the excellent discussion of the Solarium exercise in Robert R. Bowie and Richard H. Immerman, *Waging Peace: How Eisenhower Shaped an Enduring Cold War Strategy* (New York, 1998), Chapter 8. Bowie had been the Director of Policy Planning in the Department of State at the time of the Solarium exercise.

35 Ibid., 125–26.

36 Ibid., 125.

37 Ibid., 127.

38 General Andrew J. Goodpaster, also involved in the Solarium Exercise, shared Kennan's judgement of the President's summation, describing it as a 'tour de force that has stayed in my mind as well.' The recollections of Kennan and Goodpaster are found in William B. Pickett, ed., *George F. Kennan and the Origins of Eisenhower's New Look. An Oral History of Project Solarium* (Princeton, NJ, 2004), 20, 24.

39 John Lewis Gaddis, *Strategies of Containment. A Critical Appraisal of American Security Policy During the Cold War*, revised and expanded Edition (New York, 2005), 159.

40 Strachan, 'The Meaning of Strategy,' 46–47.

41 Antulio J. Echevarria II, *Toward an American Way of War* (Carlisle, PA, 2004), 16–17. See also Justin Kelly and Mike Brennan, *Alien: how operational art devoured strategy* (Carlisle, PA, September 2009), 60–71.

42 See M.L. Roi and G. Smolynec, 'End States, Resource Allocation and NATO Strategy in Afghanistan,' *Diplomacy & Statecraft* 19(2008), 289–320.

43 Barnett R. Rubin, 'Saving Afghanistan,' *Foreign Affairs* 86(January/February 2007), 73–78.

44 Richard Haass, 'We're Not Winning. It's Not Worth It,' *Newsweek*, (18 July 2010).

45 For a full discussion of Smith's idea of war amongst the people, see General Sir Rupert Smith, *The Utility of Force. The Art of War in the Modern World* (London, 2005), 17, 267–305.

46 Niall Ferguson, *The War of the World. Twentieth-Century Conflict and the Descent of the West* (New York, 2006), xl–xli.

47 Ibid., 588.

48 Feaver, *Armed Servants*, 241–42.

49 Strachan, 'Lost Meaning of Strategy,' 49.

50 For a detailed discussion of what it means to be strategically minded, see Colin S. Gray, *Schools for Strategy: Teaching Strategy for 21st Century Conflict* (Carlisle, PA, November 2009).

51 Ibid., 32. See also Gray, *Modern Strategy*, 17; Echevarria, *American Way of War*, 16.

52 Gray, *Schools for Strategy*, 53. See also Gray, *Modern Strategy*, Chapter 3.

53 Everitt, *Hadrian*, 210.

33

The Middle East
Strategic and military balance of power

Eyal Zisser

In 1967 Malcolm H. Kerr, a leading American scholar on the Middle East, analysed the inter-Arab system and inter-Arab dynamics in the Middle East during the 1950s and 1960s.[1] Kerr described these dynamics as unfolding under the influence of the Cold War and, to a large extent, even imitating the patterns of conduct and dynamics dictated by that Cold War, which saw the United States and the Soviet Union and their respective allies confronting each other all over the world. Kerr argued that just as the world-at-large was divided into two camps so, too, was the Middle East. The radical, revolutionary camp, under the influence of the Soviet Union, was faced by a conservative, moderate, and consequently pro-Western grouping backed by the United States. According to Kerr, the struggle for power in the Middle East during the 1950s and 1960s was an evenly balanced contest between two camps of approximately equal strength that maintained a kind of balance of terror. However, the situation at the time appeared rather differently. To the outside observer, it appeared as if the radical and revolutionary camp had the upper hand. The region seemed to be dominated by the radically nationalistic pan-Arab worldview as expressed by its most prominent and popular exponent, Egyptian President Gamal Abdel Nasser.[2]

Now, fifty years later at the beginning of the twenty-first century, the situation in the Middle East has changed radically. Egypt power has declined, and Cairo has ceased serving as a focal point and center of developments in the region. The Arab nationalist ideology (pan-Arabism) has also declined in popularity, upstaged by an Islamic worldview with a radical version lurking in the wings. In this new situation, the Arab world as a political collective and the Arab territorial states have become weaker and declined in influence. They are in retreat, yielding their place to two old and yet new players: Turkey and, especially, the Islamic Republic of Iran, both of which are now casting their shadow over the Middle Eastern expanse. Over the years, the Arab–Israeli conflict was perceived as a major focal point of trouble with implications for the whole region. In the new scenario, the Jewish state's clash with its neighbors has become just one of a number of conflicts troubling the region, although many continue to view it as a key to dealing with the threat to the region's and the world's stability presented by the chaos spreading in the Middle East.[3]

Iran's rise to power as a regional superpower, maintaining a radical Islamic worldview and aspiring to develop nuclear weapons, has created a new balance of power in the Middle East. On one side is Iran, with its allies, Syria, Hezbollah, and Hamas, an alliance once defined by United States President George W. Bush as 'the axis of evil.' In opposition is a grouping of moderate and pro-Western states, each of which feels threatened by Teheran. As in the 1950s, it seems that the momentum is on the side of the radical axis, which cannot be stopped. In an ironic way, the tragic fate of Malcolm Kerr, the author of *The Arab Cold War*, testifies to this course of events. Kerr, who served as President of the American University in Beirut toward the end of his career, was murdered on 18 January 1984 by radical Lebanese Shi`ites. His murder was one of the harbingers of the rise of radical Islam and the emergence of the Shi`ites both in Lebanon and throughout the Middle East under the inspiration and guidance of Iran.[4]

For nearly four hundred years, from the beginning of the sixteenth century until the beginning of the twentieth, the Middle East was ruled by two Great Powers: the Ottoman Empire, ruled from Istanbul and dominated by an Ottoman dynasty of Turkish origin; and the Persian Empire, ruled from the Iranian plateau and dominated by the Safavid and then the Qajar dynasty.[5] The modern era in the Middle East, the commencement of which can be traced to the beginning of the nineteenth century, was marked by the weakening of the Ottoman and Iranian polities. The two regional empires failed to confront the challenge from the West and could not stand up technologically, economically, militarily, and politically to the more advanced European Powers. This process reached its culmination during the First World War with the collapse of the Ottoman Empire: whereas Arab lands ruled by the Ottomans and the Persians were taken over by Britain and France, Constantinople and Tehran were also compelled to cede other territories in Central Asia.[6] Britain and France ruled the Middle East without restraint from the end of the First World War until the end of the Second. At the beginning of the 1920s, to make it easier to rule the Arab lands that had fallen into their hands, Britain and France established the states of Syria, Trans-Jordan (later called Jordan), Lebanon, Iraq, and others. It goes without saying that these states were artificial, lacking any historical roots. And at the time of their founding, they aroused the opposition of local populations, who aspired to establish a large and united Arab state extending over the whole area or a good part of it.[7]

The Arab world during the 1940s and early 1950s was characterised by intense struggles for influence, control, and leadership. The battle was carried on between two main camps. On one side was Iraq and Jordan, both ruled by members of the Hashemite family. On the other was an axis led by Egypt, ruled by King Farouk, a descendant of the Egyptian royal family. Farouk was joined by the rulers of Saudi Arabia, who viewed the Hashemites as their dangerous enemy, because they had expelled them from the Hejaz. Syria and Lebanon also joined the Egyptian-led axis because they felt threatened by the expansionist intentions of both Hashemite Iraq and Trans-Jordan.[8] Despite these tensions, the interests shared by all the Powers in the Middle East were greater than the issues dividing them; after all, their ruling dynasties were all conservative, moderate, and under the influence of the West, (mainly Britain and later, the United States). On 23 July 1952 a military coup, also known as the 'revolution of the young officers,' took place in Egypt. It brought to power a group of young reformers led by Nasser, who within a few years became the absolute ruler of Egypt. His rise to power intensified the struggle for power in the Arab world.[9]

Following the Second World War, the Middle East became an arena of the Cold War. Its strategic location, oil reserves, and lines of communication all served to turn the region into a strategic asset much coveted by both the East and the West. From the mid-1950s, the Americans worked with British assistance to spread their tutelage over the region and to draft it into the Western camp. However, America's success was only partial, because it could not avoid being identified with the Western colonial Powers that had ruled the region since the beginning of the twentieth century and whose governance had left residues of hostility and disapproval amongst the local populations.[10]

The Suez crisis of 1956 is a striking example of this process. It began with Egypt's drawing closer to the Soviet Union and the Soviet readiness for the first time to supply Nasser with advanced weapons systems (the Czech–Egyptian arms deal of December 1955). The crisis deepened when Nasser nationalised the Suez Canal in July 1956, after the Western powers decided to punish him for joining the Soviet side and denied him the financial aid they had promised for building the Aswan Dam on the Nile River. At the height of the crisis, in October–November 1956, Britain and France worked to strike a blow at Nasser, and even tried to topple him from power using Israel as their agent and ally. It should be noted that Israel, feeling threatened existentially by Nasser's rise to power, entered the confrontation for reasons of its own. The crisis ended after American and Soviet intervention, which aimed at containing the situation and restoring the *status quo ante*.[11]

In the wake of the Suez War of 1956, Nasser became the undisputed leader of the Middle East. Indeed, the closing years of the 1950s were Nasser's zenith as the Arab world's most prominent leader and, perhaps, the leader of all the Arabs. On 22 February 1958, the Egyptian President founded the United Arab Republic with Syria. On 14 July 1958, a *coup d'état* took place in Iraq, which many contemporaries viewed as his work. About the same time, Lebanon sank into civil war, with Nasser again being suspected of responsibility.[12] At that juncture, both Iraq and Lebanon were bastions of the West in the Middle East, so many people felt very threatened by the possibility that Nasser would take control of the entire region.

Whereas the 1950s were Nasser's greatest years (and it may be that the summit he seemed to have reached was only an imagined), the air escaped from the Nasserite balloon in the 1960s. The union between Egypt and Syria broke up in 1961. The next year, having sent Egyptian troops to assist the revolutionary regime that had taken power, Nasser became bogged down in the Yemeni mire. Finally, in 1967, he suffered a crushing and painful defeat in the Six Day War, which in the eyes of many marked his end politically.[13]

The Six Day War is perceived by many as the end of Nasserism and, consequently, the end of the era of pan-Arabism as well. The leftist, socialist, anti-Western, and anti-Israel regimes of revolutionary military officers had proved themselves, in the eyes of their peoples, to be failures. The hopes and expectations they had aroused for economic prosperity and political achievements were dashed. The Arab states lapsed into dealing with their own internal problems and lost interest in, as well as the ability to conduct, policies affecting the whole region. An expression of this trend was Egypt's decision in 1977, four years after the 1973 War, to surrender the crown of leadership of the Arab world. The country now turned inward, addressing its efforts to dealing with the social and economic crisis in which it found itself.[14] In this connection, Egypt changed its international orientation radically. It abandoned its Soviet patron, became friendly with the United States, and signed a peace treaty with Israel.

During the 1980s the Arab world sank into division and fragmentation. During the Iran–Iraq War, which dragged on from 1980 to 1988, a large part of the Arab world backed the Iraqi ruler, Saddam Hussein, because they were fearful of Iran. Only Syria supported Iran. The war broke out in connection with Saddam Hussein's hopes of exploiting the chaos reigning in Iran after the Islamic Revolution of 1979 to gain hegemony over the Persian Gulf. Saddam Hussein also had territorial ambitions; he wanted to acquire lands that all Iraqi rulers had wanted to acquire since the founding of the modern independent state in the 1920s. However, he erred in his calculations and undertook risks without giving them enough thought; this failure led to his downfall. Entangled in a hopeless war with Iran, he only aroused a sleeping monster. The war encouraged and accelerated an arms race in the region, and it probably lay at the root of Iran's recent motivation to develop nuclear weapons.

Another mistake for which Saddam Hussein paid a high price was his rash decision to invade Kuwait in 1990. He took this step without understanding the new international order that had been created with the collapse of the Soviet Union. However, contrary to his expectations in what became the First Gulf War, the United States managed to enlist the support of a broad international coalition and deliver a severe blow to Iraq; it also entailed a severe blow to the radical forces in the Middle East region as a whole. This victory was important for the United States, enabling it to become the leading power in the region and the whole world.[15]

The 1990s witnessed the beginning of a new era in the Middle East, which stood to a large degree under the aegis of a *Pax Americana*.[16] The United States became the leading Power in the region as a result in part of the end of the Cold War, the collapse of the Soviet Union, and the decline of Russia. It also occurred because of victory over Saddam Hussein's Iraq in the First Gulf War and active American efforts to contain the radical threats represented by Iraq and Iran. At the same time, the Americans also worked to bring about a settlement of the Arab–Israeli conflict.

However, American efforts to manage the affairs of the Middle East soon proved to be beyond the reach of even that Great Power. In retrospect, the 'American decade' in the Middle East turned out to be a period of illusions and unfulfilled hopes. The United States failed in its efforts to bring about an all-inclusive regional peace that would serve as an impetus for economic growth and prosperity and inspire a spirit of change towards democratisation throughout the area. Israel and Jordan signed a peace treaty in 1994, but Israeli-Palestinian negotiations quickly reached a dead-end, as did the Israeli-Syrian talks. The hopes for a breakthrough in the peace process and consequently, for the establishment of a new Middle East, were shattered at the beginning of the 2000s by both the outbreak of the Palestinian *intifada* uprising and the 11 September 2001 terror attacks against the United States. The *intifada* inflamed the Arab–Israeli conflict once more, and the 9/11 attacks led President George W. Bush to declare a 'war on terror' on the al-Qaeda organisation and its supporters all over the world. Although not the only factors militating against peace in the Middle East, they were supplemented by the rise of Iran as a regional superpower. Iran came out as a strident opponent of the United States and openly challenged the regional settlement that the Americans were seeking to achieve.[17]

The Middle East met the first decade of the twenty-first century whilst in a chaotic state of disorder and instability. The American hegemony that had prevailed in the 1990s was now weakened and eroded. The United States responded to this new situation in a complex manner and from several different angles. First, with their declaration of a 'war on terror' after the 9/11 attacks, their intention was to fight anyone engaging in terrorism, aiding terrorists, or contributing to instability in the region. The outcome of this policy was the wars in Afghanistan and Iraq and the destruction of the radical regimes ruling those countries (the Taliban in Afghanistan and Saddam Hussein in Iraq). The 9/11 attacks were carried out by the al-Qaeda organisation operating under the auspices of the Taliban regime. The situation provoked US concern in two directions. The first centered on the trouble augured by the very existence of a radical regime that aided major terrorist acts all over the globe. The other was Washington's growing worry that some radical regime would one day develop or acquire nuclear weapons and make them available for the use of terrorist organisations. These concerns, of course, served to sharpen the sense amongst Americans that the radical Middle Eastern regimes presented a severe threat to their national security and, from this point, came their determination to act against those regimes.[18]

As a second response, the United States made efforts to advance the peace process between Israel and the Arab states, although not in a methodical fashion. In fact, the steps taken by America were irresolute and proceeded at a leisurely pace. The process was hindered by American pressures on the Palestine Liberation Organization leader, Yasser Arafat, until his death in December 2003 because of his involvement in terror. Washington was also unwilling to carry on talks with the Syrian regime because of its alliance with Iran and the aid it provided to Palestinian terrorists and to Hezbollah. And it would seem that President George W. Bush's Administration did not apply its full vigor in advancing the peace process because it saw the chances of success as minimal.

Finally, the United States made efforts to advance democracy in the Middle East. Despite some who considered them naive, such steps were taken because it was felt that the advancement of democracy would bring economic prosperity and, in turn, contribute to drying up the swamp of terrorism. This approach actually went against the line taken by earlier American administrations that the United States must act to preserve regional stability even at the price of becoming reconciled to the rule of dictatorial regimes, so long as these regimes were American allies. However, the new American policies, emphasising an all-out 'war on terror' and efforts to advance the ideas of democracy, rather than the path of a peace process, did not bring about the desired results. The hopes of advancing regional stability and founding a New Middle East were disappointed.

After its conquest by the United States in spring 2003, Iraq turned into a quagmire of religious and communal struggles between Sunnis and Shi`ites. The al-Qaeda organisation declared Iraq to be an arena of jihadist struggle against the Americans and the Iraqi Shi`ites. In Lebanon, the Hezbollah organisation grew stronger. It found support from Iran and represented the Shi`ite community of the country, which had become the largest religious group and was seeking to take power over the state. In the Palestinian Authority, the hard-line Hamas organisation won the elections held in January 2006 (forced upon Israel and the Palestinian Authority by the United States). Later, in spring 2007, Hamas used violence to take over the Gaza Strip. Even in Afghanistan, American policy did not fare well; the Taliban continued to exert a heavy hand, and the American-and-Western-supported Government had great difficulty in handling the situation.

What, then, is the character of the Middle East at present in the shadow of the difficulties facing the US and the moderate, pro-American forces in the region? There is no doubt that the area is characterised by the absence of a well-founded regional order. This is in clear contrast to the situation that reigned during the Cold War, when the two superpowers neutralised each other, and to the situation in the 1990s, when the *Pax Americana* promoted stability in the area. The adverse processes noted below serve to reinforce the current feeling that the region lacks a firm political order and faces a period of chaos.

First, the standing of the United States in the Middle East has been eroded. This situation can be attributed to its having become bogged down in the Iraqi and Afghani quagmires, and to what many people in the region perceive as its inability to thwart radical forces, especially in Iran but also with non-state actors like Hezbollah and Hamas. Second, old players have renewed their presence in the Middle East, including China and Russia, and newer ones, like Brazil and other South American countries, see advantage. They are all trying to impair American status in the region or, at least, advance their own interests. In any case, they stimulate the feeling that the United States is no longer all-powerful or the only major outside influence in the arena.

Next, Arabism has declined whereas Islam has risen as a worldview and leading source of identity for individuals, communities, and even amongst the Arab and Muslim collective as a whole throughout the Middle East. Secularism has retreated before religion in most of the region's states, including Turkey (led by the Justice and Development Party [AKP]). But a similar process is also taking place in the Arab states. The result is that all over the region, Islamist forces are rising, growing stronger, and working against existing regimes, most of which are moderate and pro-Western. The fourth issue is that the territorial Arab states are declining in power. These entities emerged or were established in the Middle East during the past one hundred years. Most, if not all, suffer from serious economic and social problems that threaten their stability. As a result, the Arab world has been weakened and, in effect, has lost its role as a central player whether as a collective or as individual states. The vacuum created by the withdrawal of the Arab states into themselves has in many cases been filled by non-state movements (Hezbollah and Hamas for example). They have become important actors even on the regional plane by the role they have assumed in the weak and dysfunctional state entities of Lebanon and the Palestinian Authority. Finally, and most important, two regional Powers have emerged and today set the political tone in the Middle East: Turkey and, especially, Iran. They have advanced themselves to the position of regional superpowers and, in the case of Iran, even to the position of a Power that has hegemonic aspirations.

Iran recovered relatively quickly from the Iran–Iraq Gulf War of the 1980s. In the 2000s, the dramatic rise in oil prices funneled huge amounts of money into the country's coffers and enabled it to grow strong. Wealth made it possible for the regime of the Ayatollahs to survive and even to invest enormous resources in developing Iran's military and nuclear capabilities. It must be admitted that even in the time of the Shah, in power till 1979, Iran had aspirations to regional hegemony; and it was the Shah who first acted to develop nuclear weapons. But this effort was undertaken under the auspices and with the blessing of the West, because, in the Shah's time, Iran was perceived as a major ally of the West.

Iran grew strong also thanks to geostrategic changes taking place in the expanse around it, to which, paradoxically, the United States in particular contributed. In 2000, Iran was surrounded and contained by two rivals. To the east, in Afghanistan, stood the Taliban regime, a radical Sunni government that did not hide its hostility to the Shi'ite regime in Teheran, even reaching the brink of war with it. To the west, in Iraq, was the regime of Saddam Hussein, which had actually come to blows with Iran in the 1980s. Iraq had even used chemical weapons against Iranian soldiers and fired missiles into Iranian cities. After the war, Saddam Hussein's Iraq maintained a balance of terror with its old adversary. However, the United States put an end to Iran's two bitter enemies. In 2001, George W. Bush led the battle to overthrow the Taliban Government; and in 2003, the Bush-led United States invaded Iraq and brought about the fall of Saddam Hussein's regime. Bush probably had good reasons for acting as he did against the Taliban and Saddam Governments, but the result was to let the Iranian genie out of the bottle.[19]

It should be remembered that for many years, Iraq had served as a bulwark blocking Iran's way to the heart of the Arab world. The Iranians thus acted quickly to take advantage of the opening provided by the American overthrow of Saddam. They gained a foothold in Iraq and, thus, sought to penetrate into the Gulf States and the Fertile Crescent on the way to the Levant. The rise in Iran's importance can also be attributed to its nuclear ambitions, the roots of which, as noted above, go back to the 1980s. From 2000, the regime began investing a great deal in its nuclear programme. In 2003, however, after the conquest of Iraq by the United States and the fear that American power would be turned against it, Iran halted the development of its nuclear projects. However, it soon renewed its race to develop nuclear weapons, and, despite desperate efforts by the international community to end this race, it would seem that Iran will reach its goal in just a few years unless it is forced to stop.

The nuclearisation of Iran, even if it is assumed that it will refrain from using nuclear weapons once it has them, will accelerate a Middle Eastern arms race because other states, like Egypt and Saudi Arabia, will try to follow in Iran's footsteps. Furthermore, there is little doubt that a nuclear-armed Iran will be encouraged to conduct belligerent policies towards its Arab neighbors, the West, and Israel. Another aspect of the danger to regional stability and order inherent in Iran's race to nuclearise itself is the concern that nuclear weapons will trickle out to radical movements.

The radical axis headed by Iran, in partnership with Syria, Hezbollah, and Hamas, thus represents a real challenge and threat to the moderate axis, which includes Saudi Arabia, Egypt, and other states enjoying American patronage whilst conducting moderate, pro-Western policies. The latter have proved their ability to survive domestically in the face of social and economic difficulties and an Islamic opposition. Nevertheless, their power and ability to influence affairs at the regional level are in a state of decline. The fact that the radical axis is under Shi'ite hegemony whereas the opposing states are Sunni injects an additional factor that only increases the various tensions at play. The current confrontation thus possesses dimensions and tensions of Shi'ite versus Sunni, Iranian versus Arab, and radical and anti-Western versus moderate and pro-Western, with the former camp aspiring to change the existing order of things in the Middle East fundamentally.

For a long time the Arab–Israeli conflict was routinely viewed as a major focal point of instability in the Middle East. It was indeed the direct cause of a number of wars and violent confrontations that drew in the various regional players. However, in recent years, the weight of the Arab–Israeli clash has subsided, and the violent conflicts raging in Iraq, Afghanistan, Sudan, and elsewhere have advanced to the forefront of the Middle East agenda. Moreover, the Arab world no longer stands solidly against Israel. Thus, the Alliance of the Periphery of the 1950s has been replaced, paradoxically, by dialogue between Israel and the moderate Arab states, Egypt and Saudi Arabia, which are concerned about Iran's rise to power. Even the Second Lebanese War of 2006 between Israel and Hezbollah has been perceived, with good reason, not so much as just another round in the Arab–Israeli conflict, but more as a first round in the battle between Iran and Israel.[20]

At the same time, the Arab–Israeli conflict still fills an emotional need for many people all over the Arab and Muslim world, particularly against the background of the intensification of Islamic sentiments currently being witnessed. For this reason, the Arab–Israeli conflict remains a focus of attention and a destabilising factor and, consequently, a burden on the West. Over and over again, confrontations between Israel and the Palestinians have resonated widely in the Middle East and elsewhere throughout the Arab and Muslim world. Examples of this are the events surrounding Israel's Operation 'Cast Lead' in Gaza at the beginning of 2009 and the flotilla to Gaza at the end of May 2010. The reactions witnessed in the Muslim world are testimony to the fact that the conflict with Israel is no longer strictly an Arab–Israeli matter, but also, and perhaps even mainly, an Islamic–Western confrontation.

Turning now to Turkey, this country has undergone significant changes in recent years, especially since the AKP party took power in 2003. It seems that after long years of waiting to be accepted into the European Union, the Turks came to the conclusion that Europe was not really prepared to accept them as equal partners. Meanwhile, new economic and social elites emerged in the country and began striving to push aside the old ruling classes, especially the secular judicial and military elites that had ruled Turkey with a firm hand for many decades. The AKP gave expression to the aspirations of the new elites. Its declared policy is to return Turkey to its natural place in two respects: as a Muslim entity and an integral member of the Euro-Asiatic expanse as Turkey was in the period before the 1920s. This approach has often been labelled 'Neo-Ottomanism'. However, the Turks prefer to speak about a policy of 'zero problems with our neighbors,' a phrase attributed to the figure who developed this worldview, Turkish Foreign Minister Ahmet Davutoğlu. Israel, in particular, is now paying the price for this new policy. The Jewish state was a close friend and ally of Turkey in the 1990s. Now, however, Ankara is focusing on drawing close to the Arab states, and so it considers Israel superfluous and even an encumbrance on Turkey's path to the Arab and Muslim world. Turkey's treatment of Israel goes far in explaining why, after the events of Operation 'Cast Lead', Turkish Prime Minister Recep Tayyip Erdoğan became the most popular leader in the Middle East, much more popular than most of the Arab rulers themselves.[21]

The balance of power in the Middle East has various military aspects and dimensions and is currently based on two considerations. First, the importance of possessing nuclear weapons has increased greatly in the consciousness of the states of the region. Before this stage, it was considered important to possess non-conventional weapons like missiles with chemical and biological warheads. Insofar as nuclear weapons are concerned, the regimes perceive their possession as a means of gaining immunity from outside attack. This lesson was drawn from the different fates of Saddam Hussein in Iraq and the Stalinist-type regime ruling North Korea. Saddam Hussein's regime had no nuclear weapons, and it was attacked and toppled by the United States in 2003. In contrast the North Korean regime, which pursues the nuclear option, survives, and the Americans have refrained from acting against or attacking it. From this stem Iran's efforts to acquire nuclear capabilities, and the efforts of Syria's leader, Bashar al-Asad, as well. The latter were eliminated by Israel in September 2007, when it bombed the nuclear facilities that Syria was seeking to build in the north of the country.[22] Flowing from the nuclear question is the second consideration: conventional armies and campaigns have declined in importance. They have been replaced by the concept of asymmetrical warfare. In this type of combat, non-state actors employ terrorist attacks and missiles whilst relying on support from a civilian home front that is also exploited as a shield. These tactics are used against the United States and other Western targets as well as Israel.

From the 1940s until the 1980s, and perhaps even into the 1990s, the Middle East witnessed a number of large-scale conventional wars that were decided using conventional armies. Some of these hostilities were between the Arab states and Israel and some were between states of the region without the involvement of Israel. During the largely conventional Iran–Iraq War, for example, millions of soldiers from both sides were killed in battles reminiscent of the trench warfare of the First World War. The campaigns conducted by the United States and its allies in 1991 and 2003 against Iraq were also conventional in character. Now, however, it seems that the feeling in the Middle East is that conventional capabilities have exhausted their potential and their place has been taken by *muqawama*, that is, 'armed resistance' or jihad. The essence of this conception is to pose a challenge to the power of modern, advanced, Western-style states, like Israel, for example, or the United States as in the case of the 9/11 terrorist attacks. These Powers enjoy technological superiority and military power, but find themselves helpless to one degree or another in the face of guerrilla warfare combined with terror; and in the case of Israel, also in the face of missiles like those launched against it by Hamas and Hezbollah.[23]

The following remarks address additional aspects of the Middle East situation as it appears today. For a long time now, the region has been experiencing distress and instability in the social and economic spheres. Population growth is usually blamed as the main cause of the problem. To some extent, the states of the region have found population growth to be uncontrollable and its results difficult to handle. On the eve of the First World War, about 70 million people were living in the region. By 2000, this number had grown to about 400 million. As a result, the infrastructure and resources of the states became overburdened, and they find it difficult to advance their economic development sufficiently to meet the needs of their large populations. Not only have want and poverty led to extremism, they have also led to an accelerated pace of emigration to Europe, which is suffering from a negative natural population growth rate. Meanwhile, the forecasts for the coming decades predict that the Middle East will have tens of millions of additional inhabitants. It is doubtful that they will find possibilities for education, health services, housing, or employment in the region. And this is expected at a time when Europe is already experiencing a shortage of millions of workers.[24]

In addition, there is the factor of globalisation. This revolution has undoubtedly changed the face of the Middle East, although not necessarily in a direction the West would have hoped for or wanted. In 1955, it was the *Sawt al-Arab* (Voice of the Arabs) radio station from Cairo that urged, within the limitations of the radio broadcasts of those years, the masses on the streets of the Arab cities to identify with the regime of Egyptian President Nasser. Today it is the Al-Jazeera satellite TV that reaches the masses. Al Jazeera was established by Qatar, but it became independent and, like the creature that turns upon its creator, advances a pan-Arab agenda. In the late 1980s television helped greatly to encourage the forces and spirit of change in East Germany and Eastern Europe; today the Internet and Arabic-language television stations are inciting the winds of radicalisation and pan-Islam.[25]

For half a century, the Middle East was dominated by an Arabic order. It was replaced by an American order. Today, however, the region finds itself experiencing disorder and chaos, and a political and power vacuum that Iran aspires to fill. But Iran is not alone. The void left by the weakening and decline of the Arab states and the perceived waning of the United States is also being filled by non-state organisations, some of them independent, like al-Qaeda, and some of them working with the encouragement of Iran, like Hezbollah and Hamas.

The Middle East thus finds itself in a power struggle between two camps. One is moderate and pro-Western in orientation and includes Sunni Arab states like Egypt and Saudi Arabia. The opposing camp is radical in orientation and can be characterised as an axis led by Shi`ite Iran, with states like Syria and non-state actors like Hamas and Hezbollah as members. Currently there is a feeling that the radical axis has the momentum, that it is on the move, and that it will be difficult to stop; but only time will tell whether this impression is correct or, as in the case of Egypt and the Soviets in the 1950s and 1960s, the power and impetus of this camp are being greatly exaggerated. Perhaps in practice Iran will not be capable of exerting its rule over the region, even though it may continue to cast its shadow across it for some time. Meanwhile, the Middle East has become a threat to the stability of the whole world and a focal point for terror and nuclear proliferation. The United States and the international community, for their part, are having a hard time finding an answer to this challenge, which, it appears, will become only more severe in the foreseeable future.

Notes

1 Malcolm H. Kerr, *The Arab Cold War, Gamal Abd al-Nasir and his Rivals, 1958–1965* (Oxford, 1967).

2 P.J. Vatikiotis, *Nasser and His Generation* (New York, 1978); James Jankowski, *Nasser's Egypt, Arab Nationalism and the United Arab Republic* (Boulder, CO, 2002).

3 Eyal Zisser, 'Political Trends in the Middle East', *Israel Affairs*, 12(2006), 684–97.

4 *Al-Hayat* [London], 19 January 1984. See also Ann Zwicker Kerr, *Come with Me from Lebanon. An American Family Odyssey* (Syracuse, NY, 1994).

5 For more, see Jane Hathaway, *The Arab Lands under Ottoman Rule, 1516–1800* (Harlow, 2008); Hans J. Kissling, *The Last Great Muslim Empires. The History of the Muslim World* (Princeton, NJ, 1969).

6 Elie Kedourie, *England and the Middle East: The Destruction of the Ottoman Empire 1914–1921* (Boulder, CO, 1987).

7 Elizabeth Monroe, *Britain's Moment in the Middle East, 1914–1956* (London, 1963), 11. See also Elie Kedourie, *The Chatham House version and other Middle-Eastern Studies* (London, 1970); Eliezer Tauber, *The Formation of Modern Syria and Iraq* (London, 1995).

8 Yehoshua Porath, *In Search of Arab Unity, 1930–1945* (London, 1986). See also Bruce Maddy Weitzman, *The Crystallization of the Arab State System, 1945–1954* (Syracuse, NY, 1993).

9 William Roger Louis, *Ends of British Imperialism, the Scramble for Empire, Suez and Decolonization* (London, 2006).

10 For more, see Michael B. Oren, *Power, Faith and Fantasy—America in the Middle East* (New York, 2007), pp. 421–510; Michael J. Cohen, *Fighting World War Three from the Middle East, Allied Contingency Plans, 1945–1954* (London, 1997).

11 Elie Podeh, *The Quest for Hegemony in the Arab World, The Struggle Over the Baghdad Pact* (New York, 1995). See also Keith Kyle, *Suez, Britain. End of Empire in the Middle East* (London, 2003).

12 Roger Louis and Roger Owen, eds., *A Revolutionary Year. The Middle East in 1958* (London, 2002); Elie Podeh, *The Decline of the Arab Unity: the Rise and Fall of the United Arab Republic* (Brighton, 1999). See also Trita Parsi, *Treacherous Alliance: The Secret Dealings of Israel, Iran, and the United States* (New Haven, CT, 2007).

13 Moshe Shemesh, *Arab Politics. Palestinian Nationalism and the Six Day War: The Crystallization of Arab Strategy and Nasir's Descent to War, 1957–1967* (Brighton, 2008); Richard B. Parker, *The Politics of Miscalculation in the Middle East* (Bloomington, IN, 1993); Richard B. Parker, ed., *The Six Day war. A Retrospective* (Gainesville, FL, 1996).

14 Fouad Ajami, *The Arab Predicament, Arab Political Thought and Practice Since 1967* (Cambridge, UK, 1981).

15 See Marion Farouk and Peter Sluglett, *Iraq Since 1958, from Revolution to Dictatorship* (London, 2001); Simon Henderson, *Instant Empire, Saddam Hussein's Ambition for Iraq* (San Francisco, CA, 1991); Said K. Aburish, *Saddam Hussein* (London, 2000).

16 See Bill Clinton, *My Life* (New York, 2004); Madeleine Albright, *Madam Secretary* (New York, 2003); Dennis Ross, *The Missing Pace, the Inside Story of the Fight for the Middle East Peace* (New York, 2008); Martin Indyk, *Innocent Abroad, An Intimate Account of American Peace Diplomacy in the Middle East* (New York, 2009). See also James A. Baker III, *The Politics of Diplomacy, Revolution, War and Peace, 1989–1992* (New York, 1995); William B. Quandt, *Peace Process, America Diplomacy and the Arab-Israeli Conflict since 1967* (Berkeley, CA, 2001).

17 Aaron David Miller, *The Much Too Promised Land, America's Elusive Search for Arab Israeli Peace* (New York, 2008).

18 See Bob Woodward, *Bush at War* (New York, 2003); idem., *State of Denial* (New York, 2006).

19 For more see Dore Gold, *The Rise of Nuclear Iran: How Tehran Defies the West* (Washington, DC, 2010); Ray Takeyh, *Hidden Iran: Paradox and Power in the Islamic Republic* (New York, 2006); David Menashri, *Post-Revolutionary Politics in Iran. Religion, Society and Power* (London, 2001); Alireza Jafarzadeh, *The Iran Threat: President Ahmadinejad and the Coming Nuclear Crisis* (New York, 2007); Kasra Naji, *Ahmadinejad: The Secret History of Iran's Radical Leader* (London, 2008).

20 Shlomo Brom and Meir Elran, eds., *The Second Lebanon War: Strategic Perspectives* (Tel Aviv, 2007).

21 See M. Hakan Yavuz, *Islamic Political Identity in Turkey (Religion and Global Politics)* (Oxford, 2003); idem., *The Emergence of a New Turkey: Democracy and the AK Parti* (Salt Lake City, 2006); Sibel Bozdogan, *Rethinking Modernity and National Identity in Turkey* (Seattle, WA, 1997 (2002).

22 Eyal Zisser, 'An Israeli Watershed: Strike on Syria', *Middle East Quarterly*, Volume 15, Number 3(2008), 57–62.

23 Mark A. Heller, ed., *The Middle East Strategic Balance 2007–2008* (Tel Aviv, 2008): www.inss.org.il/publications. See also Michael Milstein, *Mukawama: The Challenge of Resistance to Israel's National Security Concept* [Hebrew] (Tel Aviv, 2007).

24 Paul Rivlin, *Economic Policy and Performance in the Arab World* (Boulder, CO, 2001); Tareq Y. Ismael and Jacqueline S. Ismael, *Politics and Government in the Middle East and North Africa* (Miami, FL, 1991). See also Bassam Tibi, *The Challenge of Fundamentalism, Political Islam and the New World Order* (Berkeley, CA, 1998).

25 See Hugh Miles, *Al Jazeera: The Inside Story of the Arab News Channel That is Challenging the West* (New York, 2005); Mohammed El-Nawawy and Adel Iskandar, *Al-jazeera: The Story Of The Network That Is Rattling Governments And Redefining Modern Journalism* (Boulder, CO, 2003).

34

The balance of power in South Asia

Sumit Ganguly

Two major strategic fault lines mark South Asia. They are the Indo-Pakistani conflict over Kashmir and the Sino-Indian border dispute.[1] The first dispute involves considerations of power balances as well as profound issues of national identity. The second is rooted in a more straightforward rivalry about status and position in Asia. The People's Republic of China (PRC) has had a long-standing border dispute with India that remains unresolved. The end of the Cold War did not have any discernible effect in terms of ameliorating either of these two deep-seated disputes. In more recent years, the PRC has come to view India as the only serious Great Power competitor in the region and its environs. Despite the increasing disparity in material capabilities between these two states, the PRC remains unreconciled to India's rise and has evinced little or no interest in settling the border dispute.

Beyond these two major and seemingly intractable conflicts, India has minor disputes with Nepal, Bangladesh, and, to a lesser degree, with Sri Lanka. However, these have less to do with relationships of power and influence and more with tangible issues of hydrology, ethnic tensions, and trade. That said, the sheer structural differences of geography, size, economic clout, and military power make its smaller neighbors wary and distrustful of India. Until recently, India's policy-makers have had only limited success in assuaging these misgivings.

Important for the contemporary situation in South Asia is the evolution of the balance of power in the region, its present state, and the likely future of the regional balance. India, in all likelihood, will solidify its position as the dominant Power in the region; however, the future of its competitive relationship with the PRC will remain very much in abeyance. Such a prediction can be made with certainty because of India's very substantial domestic infirmities, the inefficacy of a host of its domestic political institutions, and the rather substantial economic lead that the PRC has over India.

India and Pakistan emerged as independent states from the collapse of the British Indian Empire in 1947.[2] From the very outset, the two new Powers became involved in a conflict-ridden relationship over the status of the former princely state of Jammu and Kashmir, which abutted both nascent countries.[3] The dispute has proved acutely resistant to resolution because, at bottom, it is infused with the self-images of the two states. Pakistan deems its identity as a Muslim homeland incomplete without Kashmir; whereas India sees its control over this Muslim-majority state as a demonstration of its secular credentials.[4] This fractious relationship has resulted in four wars (1947–48, 1965, 1971, and 1999) and multiple crises.[5] Pakistan, which is a revisionist state, has initiated the vast majority of these wars and crises.[6]

A much lesser Power than India, Pakistan has long sought parity with its adversary. In pursuit of this end, it deftly sought to entice the United States into the region from the early Cold War years.[7] It exploited American fears about Communist expansion in Asia and, thereby, forged a military pact with the United States as early as 1954 in an effort to balance Indian power. Subsequently, in the early 1960s, a convergence of interests contributed to a Sino-Pakistani entente.[8] Faced subsequently with what it perceived to be a growing Sino-Pakistani and American nexus in the wake of Henry Kissinger's clandestine trip to Beijing in 1970 to begin normalising Sino-American relations, India chose to sign a treaty of 'peace, friendship and cooperation' with the Soviet Union.[9] And it did so despite its professed non-aligned credentials, shortly thereafter, in the third Indo-Pakistani conflict in 1971, Pakistan broke up both as a consequence of a civil war and subsequent Indian intervention; old East Pakistan, separated by 1,000 miles from West Pakistan, emerged as a new state, Bangladesh.[10] The break-up of Pakistan substantially altered the balance of power in the region because India emerged clearly as the dominant Power in the region.[11] From 1972 until 1979, South Asia remained mostly peaceful and stable because Pakistan was militarily too weak to provoke India.

Even as the United States–Pakistan relationship waned for much of the 1970s, Indo-United States relations, however, remained strained. India's policy-makers, most notably Prime Minister Indira Gandhi, believed that American policy had sought artificially to alter what she believed was the natural balance of power in South Asia with India as the dominant Power. Furthermore, the American tilt toward Pakistan during the 1971 war profoundly colored her views and those of her advisers toward the United States.[12]

Even the Soviet invasion and occupation of Afghanistan beginning in December 1979 did not result in a fundamental shift in India's policies. If anything, the decision of the Republican administration of Ronald Reagan, which took office in January 1981, to rely on Pakistan to prosecute the war against the Soviets in Afghanistan led Washington to significantly bolster Pakistan's military capabilities. To ensure that it could maintain a military edge over Pakistan whilst coping with the capability threat from the PRC, India's policy-makers enhanced New Delhi's arms transfer relationship with the Soviet Union.[13] Throughout much of the 1980s, the United States uncritically backed the military regime in Pakistan because of the exigencies of prosecuting the war in Afghanistan. Because Pakistan was the beneficiary of American military largesse, India came to increasingly rely on the Soviet Union for advanced weaponry. Simultaneously, the Indo-Soviet relationship also rested on a common hostility toward the PRC. Consequently, during the 1980s, improvements in the Indo-United States relationship were mostly fitful and limited, despite some efforts on the part of the Reagan Administration to wean India away from its military dependence on the Soviet Union. Consequently, after India adjusted to the shock of the Soviet invasion and the United States' bolstering of Pakistan's military capabilities, the balance of power in the region again reached an equilibrium. Steady Soviet military assistance to India ensured that the United States–Pakistani security nexus would not significantly affect India's military dominance of the sub-continent. The end of the Cold War would dramatically upset this distribution of power in South Asia.

As noted above, during a significant part of the Cold War and despite its professed commitment to non-alignment, India had a tacit strategic partnership with the Soviet Union. This relationship was not based on ideological affinity. Instead it stemmed from India's strategic necessity to balance the power of the PRC; and the Soviets, in turn, relied on India to act as a strategic bulwark against the PRC. Moscow also found it useful to have friendly ties with one of the few democratic states of any consequence in the Third World. Despite occasional tensions, especially in the aftermath of the Soviet invasion of Afghanistan, this relationship remained remarkably durable.

The end of the Cold War shattered the comfortable assumptions that had long undergirded India's foreign and security policies.[14] Abruptly, the highly reliable Indo-Soviet arms transfer nexus came to a close. Simultaneously, with the collapse of the Soviet Union and its alliance system, it became more than apparent to Indian policy-makers that the principal successor state,

Russia, was far too anemic a Power to serve as an effective counterweight to the PRC. Furthermore, Russia's policy-makers, from Mikhail Gorbachev downwards, made it clear to India that it could not rely on Russian support in the event of an armed conflict with the PRC.[15] Faced with the end of the Indo-Soviet relationship, confronting an uncertain future with the PRC, and viewing the emergence of the United States as the sole surviving superpower, India's policymakers scrambled to reorient Indian foreign policy. Initially, they publicly expressed significant misgivings about the emergence of a United States-dominated, unipolar world order; and they made their preferences well known for a multipolar international system. Their unease about an American-dominated international system was unsurprising. During much of the Cold War, the two Powers had found themselves at odds on a host of bilateral and global issues.[16] To this end, they sought to make common cause with France and, even, on occasion with Russia and China, to call for a multipolar world order.[17]

The dramatic shift in the global power structure forced Indian policy-makers to reappraise India's fundamental foreign-policy orientation and choices. The principal security challenge that they confronted remained the dramatic and seemingly inexorable growth of the PRC's economic and military prowess, especially in an international order where the Soviet Union, its long-standing quasi-ally, had ceased to exist. Consequently, for all practical purposes, New Delhi abandoned the commitment to non-alignment, a doctrine that had been the lodestar of India's foreign policy since independence.[18] Simultaneously, its policy-makers sought to improve relations with the sole surviving superpower, the United States. This task proved to be arduous but Indian diplomacy did demonstrate a degree of dexterity in meeting the challenge. To that end, India's policy-makers ended their propensity to criticise the United States in a range of multilateral forums and also ended their reflexive anti-American rhetoric. At a more substantive level, they also ended their long-standing policy of isolating Israel and chose in 1992 to establish fully fledged diplomatic ties with this key American ally.[19]

Despite an interest in improving relations with the United States, India's policy-makers confronted three important hurdles. First, at a structural level, bureaucracies on both sides remained skeptical about the desirability of altering and improving the relationship. The habits of mind that had been shaped during the Cold War were not easy to discard. Second, two critical policy differences related to questions of nuclear non-proliferation and human rights proved to be important impediments. The United States remained committed to inducing India to abandon its nuclear weapons program and was harshly critical, especially under the first Administration of the Democrat, Bill Clinton, of India's human rights record in suppressing a mostly indigenous insurgency in the Indian-controlled section of the disputed state of Jammu and Kashmir. Third and finally, there was insufficient ballast in the relationship in the form of economic, strategic, or diplomatic ties to enable the two Powers simply to set aside these two issues and concentrate on other areas.

Only in the waning days of the second Clinton administration did Indo-United States relations start to evolve dramatically and in a mostly positive direction. Earlier, an incipient commercial relationship had got under way after India's fitful embrace of the market economy and the American designation of the country as one of the world's 'big emerging markets'. However, it was the Administration's unambiguous condemnation of Pakistan's military misadventure in the Kargil region of the disputed state of Jammu and Kashmir that provided the basis of a transformation of the Indo-United States relationship. For once, India's policy-makers believed that the United States had not equivocated on a critical question involving an Indo-Pakistani dispute.[20] Consequently, despite lingering differences about India's pursuit of a nuclear weapons program, the Indo-United States relationship underwent a profound change as the second Clinton Administration drew to a close in 2000.

The legacy of the Clinton Administration created a political climate conducive to the fundamental transformation of the relationship during the two terms of President George W. Bush, which culminated in the Indo-United States civilian nuclear agreement.[21] Bush saw India as a strategic counterweight to the PRC. India's policy-makers in part shared this concern but were not prepared publicly to admit to a convergence in strategic perspectives on this delicate question for fear of arousing the ire of the PRC. Such fears were hardly unreasonable because of the PRC's extreme displeasure toward any significant improvement of the Indo-United States relationship.

Apart from shared misgivings about the growing military and economic clout of the PRC, Washington and New Delhi saw the strengthening of their bilateral relationship as crucial for other compelling reasons. For example, the Indians were keen on improving Indo-United States ties to legitimise their nuclear weapons program and obtain relief from a raft of controls that had long limited access to dual-use high technology. They managed to forge a viable strategic partnership even though the two Powers could not find much common ground on the question of Pakistan's complicity with terror after the 9/11 al-Qaeda attacks on New York City and Washington, DC and the American-led invasion of Afghanistan. In large part, there was a divergence in American and Indian perspectives on this subject because of the American dependence on Pakistan to prosecute a war against the Taliban and their al-Qaeda associates in Afghanistan. In the wake of President Barack Obama's visit to India in November 2010, some of these differences have been narrowed.[22] However, the United States can ill afford wholly to alienate Pakistan as long as it remains mired in counterinsurgency operations in Afghanistan because of American dependence on Pakistani transit routes to supply the International Security Assistance Forces in Afghanistan.

The question of Afghanistan's future weighs heavily on the minds of India's policy-makers. The United States, in all likelihood, will start drawing down its troops from Afghanistan in 2011 and anticipates a complete withdrawal in 2014. What Indian policy-makers fear most is the reconstitution of the Taliban in Afghanistan in the aftermath of the American and allied military withdrawal. India's concerns are twofold. First, during the Taliban regime, Afghanistan had become a safe haven for a host of anti-Indian terrorist organisations, many of which had organic links with Pakistan's Inter-Services Intelligence Directorate.[23] Indeed, in 1999, the Taliban regime made it possible for the hijackers of an Indian Airlines plane to flee.[24] A resurgent Taliban, consequently, could again prove to be fundamentally inimical to India's national security interests. Second, India's policy-makers fear that a Taliban regime would inevitably gravitate toward Pakistan and allow Pakistan to use Afghan territory for hostile ends. Consequently, New Delhi will keep a close watch on developments within Afghanistan and seek to work with other regional Powers, and especially Russia, to ensure that any regime that emerges within the country is not overly pro-Pakistani and, therefore, anti-Indian.

The key challenge before India's policy-makers is their ability to forge a strategy to cope with the PRC's growth and its recent assertiveness along India's borders and in South Asia. The PRC's rapid economic development requires little or no comment. It is well known that it possesses the world's fastest-growing economy and its per capita income has significantly outstripped that of India despite the latter's own economic development in recent years. What is of much greater concern to India's security analysts and policy-makers is the PRC's successful strategic penetration of Burma/Myanmar, the development of a significant economic presence in Bangladesh, the garnering of a considerable influence in Sri Lanka, its affirmed position in Nepal, and despite much internal turmoil in Pakistan, the bolstered relationship with its 'all-weather ally'. The PRC's growing assertiveness within South Asia has spawned an ongoing debate in India about whether or not the PRC's expanding economic ties and political influence in these states are innocuous or part of an orchestrated and larger strategy to hem in India in South Asia.[25] At another level, the

PRC has had a series of very public disagreements with India on a number of issues of considerable concern. For instance since 2009, the PRC developed the practice of stapling visas on a separate page for all Indian passport-holders hailing from the disputed state of Jammu and Kashmir. This action was a symbolic repudiation of India's legal control over and legitimacy in that segment of the disputed state. Furthermore, it has also recently questioned India's formal, legal control over the northeastern state of Arunachal Pradesh.[26]

These differences have caused much concern on the part of a significant segment of India's attentive public, some of its policy-makers, and important elements of the Indian military. Despite the emergence of these concerns, it is not entirely clear that Indian policy-makers have managed to fashion and evolve a clear-cut policy consensus and, thereby, a long-term strategy to deal with the challenge that its behemoth northern neighbor poses to India's national security and its standing within Asia.[27]

Four factors are likely to shape the future of the balance of power in the region and its environs. First, much will depend on the evolution of the Sino-Indian relationship. If the economic and military gap between the two Powers continues to widen, India's ability to play a role beyond South Asia may well become significantly constrained. On the other hand, if India can manage to sustain economic growth, pursue a balanced program of military modernisation, and restore and strengthen the efficacy of its domestic institutions, it can emerge as a peer competitor to the PRC in Asia. Such a competitive relationship need not necessarily prove to be conflict prone, especially if the PRC's rise in Asia proves to be benign. However, given the uncertainty that surrounds its rise, the PRC's peaceful professions notwithstanding, India's policy-makers have adopted a two-pronged approach in their dealings with Beijing. At one level, they have sought to avoid any outright confrontations with the PRC and have emphasised the significance of diplomatic contacts and continued negotiations on a range of outstanding issues. On the other, they have also recently stepped up defensive preparations along their northern border, continued with a program of naval modernisation, and have proceeded apace with their ballistic missile program. For the foreseeable future, India will proceed with this hedging strategy.[28] It will also continue to improve its ties with the United States by bolstering the strategic partnership as part of a plan designed to cope with potential Chinese recalcitrance.

Second, Pakistan's political fate will also shape the regional order. If the country continues down its present pathway of violent internal discord, political turmoil, and institutional collapse, it may emerge as a greater challenge to India than the one that it currently poses.[29] A nuclear-armed neighbor and adversary facing institutional collapse can pose security challenges on an unimaginable scale because of questions related to the safety and security of its nuclear arsenal.[30] Even if the dire issues of the safety and security of its nuclear arsenal do not arise, a steady erosion of the Pakistani state may lead to the flight of refugees across a porous, if highly militarised, international border. Such population transfers could pose very serious demographic challenges for India and not merely in terms of sheer numbers. Instead, they could well provoke ethnoreligious tensions (Hindu versus Muslim) in extremely fraught border states that have had a history of ethnoreligious discord and violence. On the other hand, if democratic consolidation within Pakistan proves viable, the country may at long last be able to shed the embrace of periodic military rule.[31] In turn, the emergence of a consolidated democratic regime may lead to the beginnings of a political *rapprochement* with India, thereby steadily easing the long-standing hostility and competition that has characterised the relationship.

Third, within the past decade, India has started to forge a wider set of mutually beneficial political and diplomatic ties with both Japan and South Korea.[32] These bilateral relationships, until the past decade, were mostly based on economic and commercial ties. However, with the PRC's growing assertiveness in both South and East Asia, India cannot stand idle. India and these two key

East Asian Powers have, thus, seen it expedient to start widening the scope and dimensions of their relationships. To that end, there have been important high-level exchanges and state visits.[33]

Fourth, and finally, much depends on the future evolution of the Indo-United States strategic partnership. Despite a dramatic improvement in the relationship since the Cold War's end, three critical problems continue to dog the relations between New Delhi and Washington. At the outset, regardless of their political orientation, Indian policy-makers have not articulated a clear vision of what they expect from this strategic partnership barring narrow issues like access to high-technology, relief from sanctions, inclusion in multilateral export control regimes, and support against Pakistan's use of terror.[34] Furthermore, important divisions remain within policy-making circles about both the desirability and the basis of this incipient relationship.[35] Unfortunately, even those within India's policy-making circles who have reservations about the partnership have not spelled out what they would deem to be viable alternatives. Given India's seeming inability to delineate a firm basis of this partnership, some within the American policy-making establishment also remain uncertain about the value and the significance of the emerging Indo-United States nexus.

That said, apart from increased diplomatic, commercial, and other ties, the two states share a common strategic interest; namely that the rise of the PRC does not fundamentally threaten to alter the existing balance of power in Asia, more generally, and in South Asia, particularly. In practical terms, amongst other matters, this strategy involves the pacific settlement of both territorial and maritime disputes and the freedom of navigation on the high seas, including the protection of sea lines of communication. Whether or not India's policy-makers, who have long wanted the country to play a wider role in Asia, can actually meet these challenges remains an open question.[36]

Notes

1 On the Indo-Pakistani conflict see Sumit Ganguly, *Conflict Unending: India-Pakistan Tensions Since 1947* (New York, 2001); on the Sino-Indian border dispute see John W. Garver, *Protracted Contest: Sino-Indian Rivalry in the Twentieth Century* (Seattle, WA, 2010).

2 The literature on this subject is voluminous. However, one important work remains Henry Vincent Hodson, *The Great Divide* (Oxford, 1969); also see G.D. Khosla, David Page and Penderel Moon, *The Partition Omnibus* (New Delhi, 2004).

3 On the status of the 'princely states' in the British Indian Empire see Ian Copland, *The Princes of India in the Endgame of Empire, 1917–1947* (Cambridge, UK, 2002).

4 Sumit Ganguly, 'Stalemate in the Valley: India, Pakistan and the Crisis in Kashmir', *Harvard International Review*, 18(Summer 1996): http://hir.harvard.edu/identity-and-politics-in-south-asia/stalemate-in-the-valley.

5 Ganguly, *Conflict Unending*.

6 For a discussion about Pakistan as a revisionist state, see S. Paul Kapur, *Dangerous Deterrent* (Stanford, CA, 2008).

7 For a mostly descriptive account of the United States–Pakistan relationship, see Dennis Kux, *Disenchanted Allies* (Baltimore, MD, 2001).

8 Anwar H. Syed, *China and Pakistan: The Diplomacy of an Entente Cordiale* (Amherst, MA, 1974).

9 On the Soviet–Indian relationship, see Robert Donaldson, *Soviet Policy Toward India: Ideology and Strategy* (Cambridge, MA, 1974). Also see Robert Horn, *Soviet-Indian Relations: Issues and Influence* (New York, 1982); Linda Racioppi, *Soviet Policy Toward South Asia since the 1970s* (Cambridge, UK, 1994).

10 See Robert Jackson, *South Asia Crisis: India, Pakistan and Bangladesh* (New York, 1975); Richard Sisson and Leo E Rose, *War and Secession* (Berkeley, CA, 1991).

11 Steven Hoffman, 'Anticipation, Disaster, Victory', *Asian Survey*, 12(1972), 960–79.

12 On the 'tilt policy' see Christopher Van Hollen, 'The Tilt Policy Revisited: The Nixon–Kissinger Geopolitics in South Asia', *Asian Survey*, 20(1980), 339–61; for her misgivings about the United States, see Paul H. Kreisberg, 'India After Indira', *Foreign Affairs*, 63(Spring 1985), 884–99.

13 S. Nihal Singh, 'Why India Goes to Moscow for Arms', *Asian Survey*, 24(1984), 707–20; also see P.R. Chari, 'Indo-Soviet Military Cooperation', *Asian Survey*, 19(1979), 230–44.

14 See Sumit Ganguly, 'South Asia After the Cold War', *The Washington Quarterly*, Volume 15, Number 4 (1992), 173–84.

15 John. W. Garver, 'The Indian Factor in Recent Sino-Soviet Relations', *The China Quarterly*, 125 (March 1991), 55–85.

16 For a discussion, see Andrew Rotter, *Comrades at Odds* (Ithaca, NY, 2000).

17 Christian Wagner, 'India's Gradual Rise', *Politics*, Volume 30, Number 1 (2010), 63–70.

18 On this subject, see Sumit Ganguly, 'The Genesis of Nonalignment', in Sumit Ganguly, ed., *India's Foreign Policy: Retrospect and Prospect* (New Delhi, 2010).

19 P.R. Kumaraswamy, *India's Israel Policy* (New York, 2010).

20 See Strobe Talbott, *Engaging India: Democracy, Diplomacy and the Bomb* (Washington, DC, 2004).

21 On the transformation of the Indo-United States relationship, see Sumit Ganguly, 'India and the United States: The Beginning of a Beautiful Friendship?', *World Policy Journal*, Volume 20, Number 1 (2003), 25–0; for a discussion of the Indo-United States civilian nuclear agreement, see Sumit Ganguly and Dinshaw Mistry, 'The US-India Nuclear Pact: A Good Deal', *Current History*, Volume105, Number 694 (2006), 375–78.

22 Sumit Ganguly, 'The Diwali Summit', *The Asian Age* (14 November 2010).

23 Arif Jamal, *Shadow War: The Untold Story of Jihad in Kashmir* (New York, 2009).

24 Indo-Asian News Service, 'Decade after IC-814 hijack, India is prepared', *The Hindustan Times* (24 December 2009).

25 Mohan Guruswamy, ed., *Emerging Trends in India-China Relations* (Gurgaon, 2006).

26 Vikram Sood, 'China asserts itself', *The Deccan Chronicle* (25 August 2010).

27 Sumit Ganguly, 'Structure and Agency in The Making of Indian Foreign Policy', *ISAS Working Paper Number 116* (Singapore, 2010), 1–12.

28 The clandestine release of a very substantial tranche of classified US diplomatic cables in late November 2010, amongst a host of other issues, revealed that the PRC was also responsible for blocking United Nations Security Council sanctions on Pakistan-based terrorist organisations. See Press Trust of India, 'China blocked efforts to put sanctions on JuD, Hafiz Saeed', *The Times of India* (6 December 2010); for a wider discussion of the leaks and their political significance see Jo Becker, C.J. Chivers, James Glanz, Eric Lichtblau, Michael R. Gordon, David E. Sanger, Charlie Savage, Eric Schmitt, Ginger Thompson, and Jane Perlez, 'US diplomacy uncloaked', *International Herald Tribune* (30 November 2010).

29 On Pakistan's dire straits, see Ahmed Rashid, 'The Anarchic Republic of Pakistan', *National Interest* (September-October 2010).

30 See for example the discussion in Pakistan Project Report, *Whither Pakistan? Growing Instability and Implications for India* (New Delhi, 2010).

31 Sumit Ganguly, 'Pakistan's Never-Ending Story: Why The October Coup Was No Surprise', *Foreign Affairs*, 79(April 2000), 2–7.

32 See Walter K. Andersen, 'A Growing Congruence of Interests with Korea', in Ganguly, *Indian Foreign Policy*.

33 Agencies, 'India. South Korea Ink Two MOUs to Boost Defence Cooperation', *The Economic Times*, (3 September 2010).

34 For the purposes of this analysis, the views of the two communist parties, both of which remain as intransigent as ever toward the United States and its policies, are not included. For a discussion of Indian expectations, see Sumit Ganguly, 'What has Delhi Done for Washington Lately?', *Asian Wall Street Journal* (5 October 2010).

35 See for example the sentiments expressed in Rajiv Sikri, *Challenge and Strategy: Rethinking India's Foreign Policy* (New Delhi, 2009).

36 For an intriguing discussion of India's foreign-policy choices, see Rahul Sagar, 'State of mind: what kind of power will India become?' *International Affairs*, 85(2009), 801–16.

35

North Korea

The foreign policy of a 'rogue' state

Balbina Y. Hwang

The Democratic People's Republic of Korea (DPRK), or North Korea, has posed challenges for its regional neighbors and the world almost from the day of its founding on 9 September 1948. Its claim to sovereignty under a communist system emerged from Imperial Japan's defeat in the Second World War, ending a particularly brutal 35-year foreign occupation of the Korean Peninsula. The sudden end to Japanese colonial rule in August 1945 led to the direct involvement by Allied victors (the United States and Soviet Union), who hastily established trusteeship governments in the respective southern and northern halves of Korea. Soon thereafter, United Nations (UN)-monitored elections in 1948 (impeded by the Soviets in the North) were held only in the South on 10 May 1948, leading to the establishment on 15 August of the Republic of Korea (ROK or South Korea). The failure to unify the two occupation zones effectively created two separate states competing for singular legitimacy of the Peninsula.

This competition erupted in a bloody civil war on 25 June 1950, when DPRK military forces invaded the ROK by crossing the demilitarised zone separating the two Koreas. The War lasted three years and ended in stalemate largely where it had begun: dividing the two Koreas along the thirty-eighth parallel with an Armistice agreement governing the cease-fire but with no permanent peace treaty. The War had immense consequences for the region and global politics. It was the first test of the UN and its ability to prevent conflict and enforce 'peace'; and it became the first significant armed conflict of the Cold War. Ultimately the conflict would engage the militaries of the United States and fifteen other countries under the auspices of UN forces supporting the ROK (over one million troops) and nearly one million Chinese forces supporting the DPRK.[1] The human cost was tremendous: an estimated 2.5 million Korean civilians were killed or wounded; over 170,000 ROK soldiers, 330,000 DPRK soldiers, 500,000 Chinese soldiers, and 37,000 American soldiers were killed.

North Korea has remained staunchly communist and the country became one of the most rigidly controlled and isolated in the world under the iron-fisted rule of its founding leader, Kim Il-Sung. Upon his death in 1994, his son Kim Jong-Il became leader; and a succession process began in 2010 that designates Kim Jong-Un, Kim Jong Il's son, as the next ruler. This process confirms that the DPRK is the world's only 'communist dynasty'. Today, treated as a pariah or 'rogue' state, North Korea is considered enigmatic and problematic because of its self-imposed isolation and consistently provocative behavior flaunting international standards and norms. And because outside access to North Korea is so limited, the tendency is to dismiss the country and its leader as 'crazy', 'irrational', and 'unpredictable'. Yet, the state's foreign-policy behaviour and actions belie these descriptions. Indeed, North Korea's pattern of diplomacy, although perhaps morally reprehensible, highly risk-tolerant, and disagreeable internationally, has been consistent, rational, and perhaps the most predictable of all countries in Northeast Asia.

The consistency of North Korea's diplomatic strategy since its founding is due to a logic based on historical, nationalistic, ideological, and pragmatic considerations. The territorial division of the peninsula dominates the political thinking of the North Korean regime, driving its management of internal and external affairs. Centuries of unequal relations, foreign depredation, dependence on foreigners for assorted favors, and, paradoxically, both the emulation of and distancing from foreign cultures and institutions are less the exception than the rule in Pyongyang's perceptions of the outside world. These patterns give rise to the widely shared assumption among Koreans (in the North and South) that their capacity to control their national destiny is limited by geopolitical constraints.[2]

Although every nation's history is instrumental in shaping its present-day identity, perhaps no other country today formulates contemporary actions based on historical precedence more than North Korea. In the century before division, in one assessment, unified Korea had been the last of the major cultures in East Asia to be 'opened' by Western imperialism, not necessarily because it was stronger, but 'perhaps because it was more recalcitrant'.[3] Korea entered into its first international treaty in 1876 because Japan forced it to do so; this settlement marked the beginning of 'modern' Korea, in which its leaders no longer could shape events as they wished and, 'for the first time in its history, the country was shaped from without more strongly than from within'.

Geographically situated at a critical strategic crossroad in Northeast Asia, Korea has over the centuries been coveted by the Great Powers that surround it for its strategic value; its territory was often invaded and fought over. By the turn of the twentieth century, Korea was the prize in Asia's first 'modern' wars: the Sino-Japanese War (1894–95) and the Russo-Japanese War (1904), which marked Japan's international 'debut' as the first industrialised Asian nation to defeat a Western Great Power and set the stage for the Second World War. Yet during this period, Korea remained astonishingly and stubbornly impervious to the growing strength and influence of foreign Powers in the region. Korean kings of the eighteenth and nineteenth centuries 'maintained a rigid policy of seclusion until it was almost too late to learn the art of diplomacy'.[4] In August 1897, King Kojong, the last of the Chosun Dynasty, elevated the status of the dynasty by renaming the country *Taehan Jekuk* ('the Great Han Empire') and took the title of 'Emperor'; 'King' did not sufficiently connote the independent status he claimed and, furthermore, 'Emperor' put Korea on the same level as Japan and China. Although these name changes were meant to declare to the world that as a sovereign state, Korea was the equal of its neighbors, foreigners were unimpressed with mere words.[5] Korea had long been known before the nineteenth century as a country where foreigners were met with mistrust and dispatched as quickly as possible back to their homes.[6] But the modern era ushered in a new fate for Korea in which it was unable to repel foreign force and influence. Indeed, the very existence of the North Korean state today (along with its South Korean counterpart) is an embodiment of the regional dynamic in which Korea, as the 'shrimp' among the 'whales' of Great Powers, is considered incapable of forging its own independent destiny.

Thus, the deeply embedded struggle to retain sovereignty and pursue independent policies is at the heart of North Korean diplomacy, and despite the changing contours in tactics over the years, its strategy has remained remarkably consistent. Since its inception in 1948, the DPRK has pursued three essential foreign-policy goals: national security, economic prosperity, and reunification. In a mirror image of the North, South Korea has pursued precisely these same goals.[7] What is remarkable is that the North's goals and strategy have remained constant despite dramatic changes in the regional and external environment. The end of the Cold War altered the entire landscape of Northeast Asia except in North Korea, a surprise given that conventional wisdom argues that it should have inexorably altered the parameters if not the actual calculations of Korean foreign policies. Shifting regional power relations, after all, are considered the cause for Korea's division. The political characters of the two Koreas were largely determined at the outset by the ideological rivalry between East and West, and each Korean state found an external security guarantor for its own security. Consequently, the foreign policies of both Koreas were largely dominated by the ebb and flow of East–West competition.

Yet, North Korea's foreign-policy goals have largely remained unaltered after the Cold War. This outcome is puzzling. One common supposition about Korea is that certain immutable traits (that it is a small, relatively weak Power sitting at the intersection of interests among the major military and economic Powers in the region) cause foreign policy to be determined in a reactive fashion, responding to the exigencies of the situations thrust upon Korea. According to this capabilities-based argument, the only way Korean (both South and North) foreign-policy formation becomes more proactive is with a corresponding elevation of Korea's status and power in the regional hierarchy.

However, such a viewpoint incorrectly characterises North Korean foreign policies. Although the international system has been an important influence on Pyongyang, it does not have direct causal effect on policy outcomes because norms of identity within Korea affect the responses to external forces in sometimes surprising and even seemingly unpredictable ways. The values, mind-sets, and views that form the North's unique strategic culture are the residue of historical experiences as well as ongoing interactive processes in international and domestic politics. And this framework of strategic culture based on 'nationalistic survival' is the prism through which the regime's grand strategy regarding security is formulated and implemented.[8]

In many ways, North Korea is more of a direct descendant of traditional Korea than the South. The North, like the Choson Dynasty (the last independent rule of a unified Korea) has adopted the traits of the 'Hermit Kingdom': keeping its distance from other nations, including its closest neighbors. During the Cold War, North Korea was largely dependent on the Soviet Union and China as guarantors of security in the face of the US–ROK alliance; but Pyongyang remained at arm's length from Beijing and Moscow, skilfully playing one benefactor against the other. Given the history of foreign intervention, it is unreasonable to characterise North Korean attitudes toward the international community as paranoid.[9] After liberation from Japan, North Korea's struggle for political independence continued by seeking to maintain political autonomy from its two larger allies (China and the Soviet Union) whilst seeking to liberate the southern half of the peninsula, which the North has always considered part of its territory. This second goal entailed not only that the Americans be expelled from South Korea, but that North Korea compete and win a zero-sum game of political legitimacy with South Korea. Unswerving to this day, this goal dominates North Korea's strategic and tactical thinking.

The deathly struggle between the two Koreas to secure singular state legitimacy at the expense of the other essentially ended with the Cold War: the ROK gained UN membership in August 1991; the DPRK followed suit in September. However, the ongoing competition between the two Koreas to gain the upper hand in garnering normative legitimacy in the international community did not abate. Nor did it end the political and social struggle to gain legitimacy among the Korean people as a whole, ironically made easier for North Korea with the democra-tisation of the South. It is easy to assume that given South Korea's transformation into a modern, developed, and democratic society (whilst an impoverished and struggling North Korea has continued its belligerent, provocative behavior in defiance of international norms and standard) the ROK is the clear victor in this arena. However, the South Korean democratic freedoms of expression, assembly, political representation, and more have allowed pro-North Korean ideology that propagates pan-Korean nationalism to flourish, polarising South Korean politics and hindering a coherent policy towards the North.

Meanwhile, the continuation of the North Korean state with its relative ills poses a competitive challenge for South Korea. Since the Armistice in 1953, the nature of the contest between the two Koreas has ebbed and flowed, with brief periods of surprising *rapprochement* interrupting a predominantly tense stand-off that often turned deadly. Episodes of mutual *détente* were driven primarily by external shocks rather than shifts in the strategic objectives of either Koreas. Indeed, what is remarkable is the rigidity of national priorities despite seemingly dramatic gestures of reconciliation, which ultimately explains the lack of any lasting progress towards unification.

The first significant attempt to improve relations between the two Koreas occurred in 1972, a time of great uncertainty in East Asia. In 1969 with the announcement of the 'Nixon Doctrine' (that Asians should provide the manpower for their own wars) the United States appeared to be moving steadily towards disengagement from the region. This perception was cemented in early 1971 when, coupled with the drawdown of the American war effort in Vietnam, Washington withdrew two Army Divisions (approximately 20,000 of the 62,000 American troops) stationed in South Korea since the Korean War, over the vehement objections of ROK President Park Chung Hee. In addition, the breakdown of the Bretton Woods dollar-gold international financial system in 1971 seemed to portend the beginning of the end of the global system of American economic and military hegemony on which both Japan and the ROK depended for their security and stability.[10]

However, the catalytic event that sent shock waves throughout Asia was the historic Sino-American *rapprochement* that permanently divided the communist world. It began on 9 July 1971 when Henry Kissinger, President Richard Nixon's National Security Advisor, landed secretly in Beijing. Korea was probably not a factor in Nixon's desire to end America's two decades of hostility with China, which began with Chinese intervention in the Korean War. Rather, among the most important factors driving Nixon's triangular diplomacy with Beijing and Moscow was its potentially alarming effect on North Vietnam, another Asian client of the two giants of international communism. By simultaneously improving ties with both Hanoi's sponsors, Nixon hoped to demonstrate that North Vietnam was expendable and vulnerable in a larger game being played by major Powers.[11]

It is striking that whilst unintentional, North Korea acutely felt the same set pressures intended for Vietnam, and to Washington's eventual dismay, by South Korea as well. As a result, both Korean regimes felt more insecure than ever before, with fears of abandonment by the Great Powers increased exponentially. As such, both Koreas attempted to parlay their vulnerability by venturing into seemingly more flexible strategies towards reunification, although with little tangible result.

Deeply shaken by the Sino-American *rapprochement*, Kim Il Sung considered China's sudden shift toward amicable relations with the United States as a betrayal of the common struggle against American imperialism, leaving him in an exposed position against the American military power still entrenched in South Korea.[12] And in Seoul, Park was similarly shocked by Nixon's opening to China, reflecting that the two Koreas shared profoundly similar insecurities differing only in their mirror opposite positions. The lack of advance warning from Washington raised profound doubts about the constancy and reliability of American sponsorship. For Park, the *rapprochement* implied American acceptance of a hostile, powerful, and revolutionary Power (China) in South Korea's immediate neighborhood, doubly more dangerous because it was tied with a military alliance to North Korea. Despite the reassuring words of American political leaders and diplomats, Park took these developments as 'a message to the Korean people that we won't rescue you if North Korea invades again'. Reflecting hauntingly similar sentiments of his North Korean adversary, Park later described the maneuvering surrounding the United States *rapprochement* with China: 'this series of developments contained an unprecedented peril to our people's survival. ... [The situation] almost reminded one of the last days of the Korean Empire a century earlier, when European Powers were similarly agitating in rivalry over Korea'.[13]

The acute sense of insecurity because of fears of abandonment by their respective Great Power allies drove both Koreas to relent on long-held positions *vis-à-vis* the other, opening a rare opportunity for dialogue.[14] Thus on 20 August 1971, representatives of the two Korean Red Cross organisations met in Panmunjom for the first exploratory discussions between the two halves of the divided peninsula since the Korean War, marking the first time that the two Koreas attempted settlement of their conflict on their own without external interference or influence.[15] Not surprisingly, the talks were contentious, drawn out, and produced little agreement or *détente*. However, they did lead to secret high-level discussions that were revealed only decades later. From 2 May to 5 May 1972, Lee Hu Rak, Director for the ROK Central Intelligence Agency and widely considered the second most powerful man in South Korea, visited Pyongyang in utmost secrecy and met with Kim Il Sung and his younger brother, Kim Yong Ju. The remarkable meeting was extraordinary for it reveals a deeply shared antipathy to the major Powers and the heavy emphasis by both sides on reaching accords and eventual reunification:[16]

LEE: President Park Chung Hee and I believe unification should be achieved by ourselves without interference of the four powers [the United States, China, Japan, the Soviet Union]. ... We are never front men of the United States or Japan. We believe we should resolve our issues by ourselves.
KIM: Our position is to oppose reliance on external forces on the issue of unification. This is where I agree with Park Chung Hee. ...
LEE: I'd like to tell you that President Park is a person who detests foreign interference most.
KIM: That being so, we are already making progress to solve the issue. Let us exclude foreign offices. Let's not fight. Let's unite as a nation. Let's not take issue with communism or capitalism. ...
LEE: A nation with 40–50 million people is a powerful country. One hundred years ago we yielded to big powers because we were weak. In the future the big powers will yield to us. I'd like to make it clear to you, the big powers only provide lip service to our hope for unification. But in their hearts, they don't want our unification.
KIM: Big powers and imperialism prefer to divide a nation into several nations.

North and South Korea surprised the outside world by publicly issuing a North–South Joint Statement on 4 July 1972, a date that seemed to have been chosen to punctuate the symbolism of declaring independence from a Great Power. The statement declared that the two Koreas had reached an agreement on three principles for achieving unification: independence from foreign interference, peaceful means, and national unity transcending differences in ideology and system:

First, reunification shall be attained independently without either relying upon or tolerating interference from any external power. Second, reunification shall be realized through peaceful means rather than through the use of force against each other. Third, both sides shall promote a great national unity as a homogenous people, transcending differences in ideas, ideologies, and systems.[17]

Indeed, such fundamental agreement over the most basic principles indicate that the driving motive for both Korean leaders in issuing the joint statement was a desperate pragmatism derived from the compelling strategic culture of nationalistic survival that drives both Koreas, each in its own way. Both felt immense pressure and insecurities from the momentous actions taken by their relative Great Power patrons, and the statement was more a declaration of Korean independence from external machinations than any concrete attempt towards reunification.

Thus, although the most common query about the aftermath of the 1972 agreement is, 'why did the initial attempt at North–South dialogue suddenly flower and then wither?', it is the wrong question. The more fundamental and relevant problem is why the seemingly revolutionary agreement did not produce the expected changes in attitude and stance between the two parties. The answer lies in the reality that for both countries, tentative agreement on reunification was the result not of true readiness or willingness to reunify but the attempt to do so on their own terms, and for the first time without external influence that was mutually considered the ultimate threat to their own security.[18]

But violent episodes, such as assassinations, perpetrated by both sides against the other over the years, illustrate the depths of the bitter nature of the competition for legitimacy between the two regimes, which were not likely to be overcome by a tentative agreement, no matter how public.[19] Thus, the significance of the 1972 Joint Statement was not in the watershed moment in intra-Korean relations as many argue; rather, it was the manifestation of a remarkable foreign-policy outcome derived from essentially a singular strategic culture shared by two ideological enemies.

Certainly, Pyongyang may have been harboring some expectations, based on American actions, that the enunciation of the three principles of reunification would lead to the removal of what it perceived as the main obstacle to reunification, namely, American troops stationed in South Korea. Stressing that the most important element of the new accord was the joint commitment 'to solve the problems of our own country by ourselves according to the principles of national self-determination, rejecting outside forces', Pak Sung Chul, Vice-Premier of the DPRK at the time, said that the joint statement was intended to deal 'a powerful blow to those who try to obstruct Korea's reunification and perpetuate the division'.[20]

Thus, notwithstanding the ongoing attempts at intra-Korean dialogue after the 1972 Joint Statement, North and South Korea maintained hostile relations throughout most of the 1970s. Ironically, this initial attempt at dialogue allowed for the further entrenchment and solidification of both regimes, both domestically and internationally, essentially ensuring that future *rapprochement* would be increasingly competitive and thus even more intractable. The dialogue also served to reinforce both leaders' respective hold on political power domestically, as well as proving very useful internationally.[21]

On the international front, intra-Korean dialogue proved beneficial in breaking North Korea out of its diplomatic isolation. Before the talks at the end of 1970, North Korea had diplomatic relations with only thirty-five countries, nearly all of them socialist regimes, whilst South Korea had diplomatic relations with eighty-one countries. Immediately after the start of North–South dialogue, Pyongyang gained recognition from five Western European Powers and many more neutral countries. Within four years, it was recognised by ninety-three countries, on a par with South Korea's relations with ninety-six. The North also gained entry to the UN World Health Organization and, as a result, sent its first permanent UN observer missions to New York and Geneva.[22]

The DPRK's concerted efforts towards gaining diplomatic recognition in the international community underscored the precarious position that Kim Il Sung faced in the early 1970s, given the enormous shift in Great Power dynamics following Sino-American *rapprochement*. He retained a deep and abiding mistrust of the very Great Powers that he relied on, and American *détente* with China in 1971 surely confirmed his suspicions. In essence, *juche* (loosely defined as 'self-reliance'), which has become synonymous with North Korea's infamous autarky, was Kim Il Sung's declaration of political independence from his two communist sponsors. Hailed in North Korea as Kim's original, brilliant, and revolutionary contribution to national and international thought, and a 'creative application of Marxism-Leninism', all references to Marxism would eventually be abandoned. North Korea's commitments to *juche*-style development were tinged by resentment against past interferences, particularly by China and the Soviet Union.[23] Kim's vision of *juche*, which emanates from North Korea's militant nationalism and serves to sanctify all of Kim's decisions, is usually translated as 'self-reliance'; but its meaning is far more profound, complex, and difficult to comprehend: '... *juche* views Korea as a chosen land, as people are told consistently that world civilisation originated from the Korean peninsula'.[24] Indeed, *juche* philosophy has deep traditionalist and neo-Confucian roots and appeals to the Korean antipathy for external domination.[25]

By 1978, the relations between North and South Korea had reverted to the pre-dialogue status. During this period, both Koreas experienced remarkable growth in military power, with each trying to gain a security advantage over the other. At first glance, although the militaristic strategies pursued by both Koreas during this period seem counterintuitive and illogical given the simultaneous move towards a thawing of relations, they make perfect sense considered in the context of the strategic cultures of nationalistic survival. Both Korean leaders formulated and pursued long-term strategies for reunification based on conspicuous strength; it would be achieved by increasing national power through directed efforts towards economic modernisation.

The next breakthrough in intra-Korea relations did not occur until an exchange of separated family members from the North and South in September 1985, the first public reunions since national division in 1945.[26] Yet, this period was also marked by a surprising level of tension and animosity because of several high-profile terrorist attacks perpetrated by North Korea. On 9 October 1983, during the state visit of South Korean President Chun Doo Hwan to Rangoon, Burma, North Korean agents attempted to assassinate Chun, killing instead 17 high-level officials of the South Korean Government.[27]

The Rangoon bombing remains a mystery because it occurred just when Kim Il Sung was meeting with Deng Xiaoping in China in search of a diplomatic breakthrough with the United States. This meeting led to a major DPRK initiative in January 1984, which for the first time called for three-way talks between the United States, the ROK, and the DPRK, a proposal United States President Jimmy Carter had made in 1979 and that had been soundly rejected by North Korea.[28]

North Korea's seemingly schizophrenic behavior during this period can again be explained in part by developments in the strategic environment. In the midst of reemerging of Cold War tensions between the Soviet Union and the United States, Sino-American relations had warmed considerably in 1983, and for the first time China said publicly that it wished to play a role in reducing tension on the Korean peninsula. Meanwhile, in 1982, the Soviets began quietly to engage South Korea in a thawing of diplomatic and economic ties.[29] However, these *rapprochement* efforts were frozen on 1 September 1983, when the Soviets accidentally shot down a civilian Korean Air Lines flight that had strayed inadvertently into Soviet airspace.[30]

Pyongyang took advantage of this fortuitous rift in Moscow–Seoul relations, as well as the growing Washington–Beijing ties, by tilting toward the Soviet Union beginning in 1983. Relations between the DPRK and the USSR improved markedly, with Kim visiting Moscow twice in the ensuing years, his first visit in over a quarter century. The warming trend ended in 1987 with Mikhail Gorbachev's 'new thinking' towards diplomacy and economic reform gaining credence, and the Soviets began systematically to cut back on aid to Pyongyang, admonishing it to use whatever aid remained more wisely.[31]

The Soviet shift towards *perestroika* not only marked the beginning of the end for the Soviet Union, but the first significant economic blow for North Korea from which it would never really recover. 1991 was a very bad year economically and politically for North Korea. Pyongyang's estrangement from the Soviet Union the previous year as a result of Moscow's normalisation with Seoul had cost North Korea a critical alliance and left the country with a painful energy shortage and worsening economic problems. The Soviet Union had been Pyongyang's most important trading partner, providing North Korea with most of its imports of weapons and weapons technology, large amounts of machinery and equipment, and petroleum. But by 1991, North Korean imports from the Soviet Union had dropped precipitously, with energy imports falling 75 percent from the 1990 level.[32]

Moscow's rapid efforts to establish diplomatic relations with Seoul was the most significant blow in a succession of international developments that seemed to strangle and isolate Pyongyang. Within little more than a year, the ROK had established full diplomatic relations and important economic ties with Hungary, Poland, Yugoslavia, Czechoslovakia, Bulgaria, and Romania, all former staunch allies of Kim Il Sung that had previously supported him by spurning Seoul. Romania's communist leader, Nicolae Ceausescu, considered Kim's special friend, had been overthrown and ignominiously executed. As the Berlin Wall crumbled, Kim's other special European friend, East German leader Erich Honnecker, had been deposed, with his communist country in the process of being subsumed by the capitalistic West. As a result of the fall of communism in Europe, intense speculation existed that Kim Il Sung and his regime would be the next to go.[33]

Deepening the sense of crisis in Pyongyang was the reality that reduced Soviet economic support increased North Korea's dependence on China, in particular for more than two-thirds of its energy needs. However, in May 1991, Pyongyang was notified that Beijing would soon discontinue its concessional sales as it aggressively pursued its own normalisation with Seoul. The dire result for North Korea was that in 1991–92, it was forced to abruptly reduce its total petroleum consumption by between one-fourth and one-third, resulting in a dramatic reduction in infrastructure and projects.[34] In fact, by mid-1991, Beijing was already following Moscow's lead by moving towards closer relations with Seoul. The healing of the Sino-Soviet split and Moscow's sharply diminished ties with Pyongyang allowed Chinese leaders to be less concerned that changing their stance towards South Korea would push Kim Il Sung into the arms of the Soviet Union.

But even as Seoul was scoring a series of diplomatic victories as a result of the collapse of the Soviet Union and Eastern Bloc, South Korea and its allies feared that Pyongyang might strike out 'irrationally'. But rather than turn inward or 'lash out', as feared, Pyongyang intensified a flurry of diplomatic activism with China, Japan, and South Korea in an effort to match the diplomatic accomplishments of its rival south of the thirty-eighth parallel.[35] Kim Il Sung initiated this new diplomatic initiative in dramatic fashion with an overture to Japan. On 24 September 1991, as a result of contacts begun earlier in the spring and accelerated after the Gorbachev–Roh meeting in June, forty-four Japanese Diet members (the most important official mission to date) visited Pyongyang. For four days, the Great Leader deployed all his personal charm and diplomatic skill to negotiate an unexpected breakthrough with the country he had fought in the Second World War and had long treated as an 'unregenerate antagonist'.[36]

Japan had normalised its relations with South Korea in 1965, expressing regret for the 'unfortunate period' of Japanese occupation from 1910 to 1945, and providing $800 million in grants and credits as compensation.[37] In the ensuing years, Japanese trade, investment, and technology were important factors in the South's rapid economic development. Allied with both countries, the United States strongly supported South Korean–Japanese *rapprochement* and over the years worked quietly to reduce tensions that might threaten the relationship.[38]

Japan's relations with North Korea had been much more contentious. Kim Il Sung had made modest overtures to Tokyo in the early 1970s, at the time of Sino-American *détente* and the initiation of North–South talks; but a Pyongyang-Tokyo *rapprochement* had been vehemently opposed by Seoul and received no encouragement from Washington. Thus, although stunning in its boldness, Kim Il Sung's overture to Japan in 1991 should not have come as a surprise given the renewed sense of superpower betrayal, this time from the Soviets. During the Japanese visit in 1991 Shin Kanemaru, the head of the delegation, met with Kim Il Sung and recounted that Kim was furious at Moscow and spoke of the necessity for 'yellow skins' to stick together against 'white skins'.[39] He then proposed an immediate normalisation of relations with Japan. Reversing Pyongyang's previous position, this proposal implied forthright Japanese acceptance of two Koreas, which North Korea had always vehemently opposed. in keeping with the precedent of the 1965 Japan–South Korea accord, the pay-off for North Korea would be a large sum of Japanese reparations.[40]

These efforts to ease relations with Japan ultimately proved fruitless because of political mishandling by the Japanese, and they contributed to North Korean suspicions that Japan could not be trusted.[41] It would be a decade before North Korea would attempt another breakthrough in diplomatic relations with Japan. In 2002, North Korea once again found itself under immense pressure as a result of significant changes in the external international environment. The election of George W. Bush as United States President in 2000 signalled a dramatic shift in American policy toward North Korea, which under the previous president, Bill Clinton, had made progress with promising deals on potential diplomatic relations, nuclear energy and arms, and missiles that all advantaged North Korea. Furthermore, a presidential election in South Korea in 2002 raised the possibility that the generous Sunshine Policy that had been coming under increasing criticism might end. And perhaps most significant, the terrorist attacks in the United States on 11 September 2001 fundamentally altered the strategic landscape, elevating threats emanating from Powers that sponsor terrorism as well as those pursuing the development and proliferation of weapons of mass destruction. With the Bush Administration's identification of North Korea in January 2002 as 'an Axis of Evil' country (along with Iran and Iraq) and the subsequent invasion of Iraq in March 2003, North Korea's position as a 'rogue' state made it highly vulnerable and insecure.

Thus, after months of secret negotiations, on 17 September 2002, Japanese Prime Minister Junichiro Koizumi met with Kim Jong Il in Pyongyang to negotiate the normalisation of diplomatic relations between the two countries. The summit resulted in an astonishing breakthrough but, paradoxically, caused shocking repercussions that ultimately impeded progress. During the face-to-face meeting, Kim Jong Il acknowledged and apologised for the kidnapping and deaths of a dozen Japanese citizens during the preceding decades. This lingering issue and North Korean adamant denials to-date had been the singular obstacle to any diplomatic progress, requiring resolution before Japan could agree to any economic reparations, which were widely believed to amount to approximately US$10 billion. Unfortunately, both Tokyo and Pyongyang seem to have miscalculated the level of public backlash at North Korea's admission, which resulted in a worsening of relations between the two countries.[42]

But in 1991, less trusting of Japan and to hedge his bets, Kim Il Sung diversified his options by renewing efforts to restart high-level public and secret talks with South Korea, which lasted for several months.[43] This renewal was an astonishing change from years of sterile negotiations in which the two Koreas had refused to budge from their fixed positions. On 13 December 1991, the two Koreas signed the 'Basic Agreement on Reconciliation, Nonaggression, and Exchanges and Cooperation', by which they came closer than ever before to accepting each other's regime as a legitimate government with a right to exist. This document portrayed the two Koreas as 'recognizing that their relations, not being a relationship between states, constituted a special interim relationship stemming from the process toward unification'.[44] The guidelines of the 'special interim relationship', if implemented, would have meant a nearly complete cessation of the conflict on the peninsula and a reversal of decades of policy on both sides.

The 'Basic Agreement' became effective after ratification in both North and South Korea yet, like previous breakthroughs, it became meaningless as intra-Korean relations quickly deteriorated. Nevertheless, despite the lack of any immediate tangible results, it was the necessary precedent for the later 2000 Presidential summit in Pyongyang. The 'Basic Agreement' is also similar to previous efforts at *rapprochement* in that its fruition was a product of simultaneous efforts by both Koreas, driven by insecurities to seize unique opportunities created in the external environment by the Great Powers. In this case, North Korea's insecure situation was particularly acute, whereas South Korea's insecurities sprang from the novel and paradoxical position of relative confidence.

From 1991 until 2000, relations between the two Koreas made little progress, primarily because of Pyongyang's continued refusal to deal with the Seoul Government as an equal partner. The first opportunity for progress emerged with Kim Dae Jung's inauguration as ROK President in early 1998; his articulation of the Sunshine Policy afforded the opportunity to rekindle efforts to engage North Korea anew. This policy marked the first significant shift in South Korea's policy towards the North, emphasising the pursuit of 'reconciliation and co-operation' through engagement and moving away from the rhetoric of zero-sum confrontation that had marked previous policies.

The symbolic manifestation of the fruits of Sunshine Policy occurred on 15 June 2000 during an unprecedented summit between the two Korean leaders, Kim Jong Il and Kim Dae-Jung, in Pyongyang; they reached agreement on a broad range of issues articulated in the 'June 15 Joint Declaration'.[45] Although touted as the realisation of a dramatic breakthrough in resolving long-standing issues on the Korean peninsula, previous agreements had also included provision for tension reduction and intra-Korean social contacts (the 4 July 1972 Joint Communiqué and 1991 Basic Agreement), although this was the first to be signed by the leaders of the two Koreas. Even the point of agreement, when both Koreas would commit to resolving the question of unification through their own initiative instead of relying on the involvement of foreign countries, was an echo of the two earlier agreements.[46] But it is noteworthy in that it reveals the extent to which the strategic culture of independence from foreign Powers remained dominant and important area of consensus between the two countries.

One of the most significant results of the Korean summit was not a dramatic change in relations (progress has been and continues to be slow) but the nationwide debate it stimulated in South Korea over the potential impact of reconciliation with the North. Although the summit clearly had a significant, if somewhat temporary, impact on South Korean public perceptions of Kim Jong Il,[47] the emergence of a nuclear standoff in 2001 would erode South Korean sympathy for the North in the next decade.

For the last two decades, North Korea's pursuit of nuclear weapons programs in contravention of international protocols, to some of which North Korea has acceded, has dominated the world's focus on the Korean Peninsula. Yet, the two most recent North Korean conventional attacks on South Korea in 2010 (sinking the *Cheonan*, an ROK naval vessel in March, killing 46 sailors, and the November assault on Yeonpyong Island killing four South Koreans) highlight the fundamental reality that instability on the Korean Peninsula stems from a 60-year unresolved conflict between its divided halves. The difficulty of reining in North Korea's nuclear ambitions, although certainly of immense consequence to the international community, has in some ways detracted from finding a permanent solution to conventional military conflict between the two Koreas.

For North Korea, the illicit pursuit of nuclear weapons serves several key state goals that have remained highly consistent for its entire history: to achieve legitimacy as a sovereign state able to retain independence, and to garner enough relative strength to control the future direction of the entire Peninsula. Much of what has guided Pyongyang's diplomatic maneuvers during the nuclear negotiations both in the 1990s (resulting in the Agreed Framework, or Geneva Accords) and the 2000s (manifested in the so-called Six Party Talks) are tactical efforts to extract leverage from a weak position. As the smallest and most impoverished state in Northeast Asia, with its relative position in an inexorable decline compared with the enviable growth of its neighbors, North Korea has few options remaining to achieve its goals other than to become a nuclear state.

Although this is a bold and risky strategy that has served to raise tensions in the region, it is also one entirely consistent with North Korea's appetite for risk and ability to endure hardship at levels greater than most other states. With the succession process under way that will transfer power from current leader Kim Jong Il to his son Kim Jong Un, the North Korean leadership will change its face but not its objectives or strategies. The state has already announced 2012 to be the target year that the DPRK will achieve *Kangsong Taeguk* status, or a 'strong and prosperous Great Power'. Whereas to the outside world such a goal seems absurd or preposterous given the decrepit state of the North Korean economy and society, it is almost poetically reminiscent of King Kojong's declaration of *Taehan Jekuk* a century earlier. And although it might be easy for the world to dismiss North Korea's present aspiration as much of a delusion destined for tragedy as was Kojong's arrogant refusal to accept the reality of his time, this linkage to Korea's past serves to reinforce the fact that Korean reality is very much embedded in its history, and it would serve the world well to heed this lesson.

Notes

1   The Soviet Russians provided armaments and other support to the DPRK, but no direct military forces.
2   Victor Cha and Balbina Hwang, 'Government and Politics', in Robert L. Worden, ed., *North Korea: A Country Study* (Washington, DC, 2008), 217–18.
3   This and the next quote from Bruce Cumings, *Korea's Place in the Sun: A Modern History* (New York, 1997), 86.
4   John K. Fairbank, Edwin O. Reischauer, and Albert M. Craig, *East Asia, Tradition and Transformation*, (Boston, MA, 1978), 610.
5   Balbina Y. Hwang, *Globalization, Strategic Culture and Ideas: Explaining Continuity in Korean Foreign Economic Policy* [Doctoral Dissertation, Georgetown University, 2005], 5.
6   Cumings, *Korea's Place*, 87.
7   See Hwang, 'From Isolation to Sunshine', Chapter 5.
8   Ibid., Chapter 2.
9   Kongdan Oh and Ralph Hassig, *North Korea Through the Looking Glass* (Washington, DC, 2000), 148.
10 Hwang, 'From Isolation to Sunshine', 238.
11 Don Oberdorfer, *The Two Koreas: A Contemporary History* (Reading, MA, 1997), 12–13.
12 Evidence suggests that the astute Chinese were sensitive to Kim Il Sung's position and vulnerability. See Oberdorfer, *Two Koreas*, 11–12.
13 On 6 August 1971 Kim Il Sung announced in a surprise move that 'we are ready to establish contact at any time with all political parties, including the [ruling] Democratic Republican Party, and all social organizations and individual personages in South Korea'. This marked an important departure from Pyongyang's earlier position that it would never negotiate with the 'traitorous Park Chung Hee clique'. In Park Chung Hee, *Korea Reborn* (New York, 1979), 48.
14 Byung Chul Koh, 'Policy Toward Reunification', in Youngnok Koo and Sung-joo Han, eds. *The Foreign Policy of the Republic of Korea* (New York, 1985), 86–87; Oberdorfer, *Two Koreas*, 13–14.
15 Hwang, 'From Isolation to Sunshine', 240.
16 Transcript from *Monthly Joongang*, March 1989 [in Korean]; the North Korean version can be found in *Kim Il Sung Works*, Volume 26 (Pyongyang, 1989), 134ff; Oberdorfer, *Two Koreas*, 23–24.
17 The Joint Statement was issued in the names of Kim Yong Ju and Lee Hu Rak rather than the two Korean leaders but 'pursuant to the intention of their respective superiors'. *Nodong Shinmun* (4 July 1972)l *Dong-A Ilbo* (4 July 1972). For further details, see Yu-Hwan Koh, 'Unification Policies of Two Koreas and the

Outlook for Unity' *Korea Focus*, Volume 8, Number 6 (November–December 2000), 94; B.C. Koh, 'Policy Toward Reunification', 88.

18 Hwang, 'From Isolation to Sunshine', 252–54.

19 B.C. Koh, 'Dilemmas of Korean Reunification', *Asian Survey*, Volume 11, Number 5 (May 1971), 489–91; idem., 'Policy Toward Reunification', 84.

20 Ibid., 90; *Pyongyang Times* (6 July 1972).

21 Park used the argument for national strength and unity in dealing with the North to justify the launching of a new and far more brutally authoritarian *Yushin* ('revitalising reforms') Constitution on October 17, 1972, which gave him the ability to purge his political opponents and guaranteed him an unlimited tenure in the presidency. For his part, Kim Il Sung did not seem to mind Park's shift to a more authoritarian system that was more similar to his own political regime. Y.-H. Koh, 'Unification Policies', 94–95; Oberdorfer, *Two Koreas*, 40–41, 44.

22 Ibid., 44–45.

23 Thomas Bernstein and Andrew Nathan, 'The Soviet Union, China, and Korea', in Gerald Curtis and Sung-Joo Han, eds., *The U.S.-South Korea Alliance: Evolving Patterns in Security Relations*, (Lexington, MA, 1983), 97.

24 Han Park, *North Korea: Ideology, Politics, Economy*, (New York, 1996), 10.

25 For a detailed discussion of *juche*, see Cumings, *Korea's Place*, Chapter 8.

26 Y-.H. Koh, 'Unification Policies', 95.

27 Kim Jong Il, the eldest son of Kim Il Sung, who had emerged as his father's anointed successor two years earlier, had been given control of North Korea's clandestine foreign operations and is believed to have been the mastermind behind these assassination attempts. Don Oberdorfer, 'North Korea Reportedly Set Coordinated Offensives After Rangoon Blast', *Washington Post* (2 December 1983); Oberdorfer interview with Kang Myung Do (11 April 1995).

28 Oberdorfer, *Two Koreas*, 144.

29 Steve Lohr, 'Seoul Likely to Slow Steps Toward Soviet Ties', *New York Times* (5 September 1983).

30 Oberdorfer, *Two Koreas*, 140.

31 Peggy Falkenheim Meyer, 'Gorbachev and Post-Gorbachev Policy Toward the Korean Peninsula: The Impact of Changing Russian Perceptions', *Asian Survey*, 32 (August 1988), 758; Byung-Joon Ahn, 'South Korean-Soviet Relations: Contemporary Issues and Prospects', *Asian Survey*, 31(September 1991), 822.

32 Nicholas Eberstadt, Marc Rubin, and Albina Tretyakova, 'The Collapse of Soviet and Russian Trade with the DPRK, 1989–93', *Korean Journal of National Unification*, Number 4 (1995).

33 Oberdorfer, *Two Koreas*, 218.

34 Chung Sik Lee, 'Prospects for North Korea', in *Democracy and Communism* (Korean Association of international Studies, 1995).

35 Oberdorfer, *Two Koreas*, 248.

36 Ibid., 220–21.

37 Cumings, *Korea's Place*, 321.

38 Ushio Shioda, 'What was Discussed by the "Kanemaru North Korean Mission"?', *Bungei Shunju* (August 1994).

39 Ibid.

40 Maso Okonogi, 'Japan-North Korean Negotiations for Normalization', in M. Lee and R. W. Mansbach, eds., *Changing Order in Northeast Asia* (Boulder, CO, 1993), 195–216.

41 Ibid.

42 For a detailed account of this period, see: Yoichi Funabashi, *The Peninsula Question: A Chronicle of the Second Korean Nuclear Crisis* (Washington, DC, 2007).

43 'Two Koreas Celebrate New Era of Rapprochement', *Korea Annual 1992* (Seoul, 1993), 88–90.

44 'Basic Agreement on Reconciliation, Nonaggression, and Exchanges and Cooperation', February 19, 1992: www.unikorea.go.kr/eg/index.htm.

45 Chong Wa Dae, Office of the President, Republic of Korea (15 June 2000).

46 Y-.W. Koh, 'Unification Policies', 100.

47 *Donga Ilbo* (31 May 2000; 15 June 2000); Geun Lee, 'Political and Economic Consequences of the Inter-Korean Summit', presented at the 2001 KAIS International Conference (22–23 June 22–23, 2001), Seoul, 11.

36

Failed states

Zimbabwe

Jeremy R. Youde

Since 2000, Zimbabwe has undergone a precipitous slide. After achieving majority rule in 1980, it initially developed a reputation for stability and pragmatic economic and political policies. Since the late 1990s, however, the country has become identified with economic decline, political violence, and authoritarian crackdowns against political dissent. The country's education and health care systems have almost completely shut down for a lack of basic supplies and an inability to pay teachers, doctors, and nurses. The annual inflation rate hit 260 million percent. The collapse of the public health and sanitation systems gave rise to Africa's worst cholera epidemic on record. Does this make Zimbabwe a failed state?

In the post-Cold War era, scholars and policy-makers have focused a great deal of attention on identifying failed states and suggesting ways to fix them. Advocates of the failed states paradigm note that some countries (Somalia, Afghanistan, and the Democratic Republic of Congo) cannot provide even the most minimal services and protection for their citizens and threaten international stability. Critics of that paradigm counter that the concept is overly broad, inherently normative, and too ahistorical. It fails to appreciate the historical, political, and economic contexts in these so-called failed states, instead relying on Western liberal models as the ideal. In this context, the Zimbabwean Government has failed in providing basic public goods to its citizenry; but it does not qualify as a failed state as conceptualised by the failed states literature. Zimbabwe's inability to provide public goods stems from an *overabundance*, rather than a lack, of state power.

The state failure paradigm starts from a core belief: an ever-increasing number of states are falling short at fulfilling their basic obligations to their citizens.[1] One study identified 127 instances of state failure between 1955 and 1998.[2] In 2007, the Fund for Peace estimated that two billion people worldwide live in 'insecure' states where there exists a borderline to critical risk of civil violence. Between 25 and 50 states are at a moderate to high risk of political violence that could cause them to fail.[3] This state of affairs threatens not just the failed state itself, but the entire international community. Failed states undermine international peace and security because they can become havens for drug trafficking, criminal syndicates, and terrorist organisations. With no effective government to place a check on them, criminal and terrorist elements can act with impunity and become havens for a host of cross-border ills.[4] Defining the state failure paradigm is based on four prominent understandings: two from prominent academics, one from United States Government policy-makers, and one from collaboration between a non-government organisation (NGO) and a prominent policy-oriented magazine.

Two of the most prominent and prolific authorities on failed states are I. William Zartman and Robert Rotberg. Zartman favors the term 'collapsed states', defining them simply as states that 'can no longer perform the functions required for them to pass as states'.[5] This characterisation means that the state can no longer serve as the arena for politics, provide institutions, serve as a symbol for a national identity, or act as the guarantor of its populace's security. As institutional performance declines over time, the government loses its ability to satisfy societal demands. This situation gives rise to an atmosphere of dissatisfaction, but the state responds by further retrenching its activities and focuses on attempting to satisfy an ever-shrinking base of support. Civil society finds itself unable to operate in the midst of such disarray, and the state gradually loses control over its political and economic space. With the collapse of the state, the government avoids making decisions and practices an increasingly defensive form of politics. Eventually, it loses control over its own agents, heightening the possibility of violence or civil war.[6] Zartman's model provides a qualitative definition that largely centers on the success or failure of institutions to satisfy basic needs and security for the populace. He emphasises that collapsed states are a long time in the making, but they also have opportunities to prevent their demise through taking a variety of actions to resuscitate and relegitimate their institutions.

Rotberg offers an almost Hobbesian vision of failed states, calling them 'tense, deeply conflicted, dangerous, and bitterly contested by warring factions'.[7] States, he argues, exist along a continuum and vary in accordance with their ability to deliver public goods to people within a particular territory, with security being the most important public good. Strong states possess unquestioned control over their territory and consistently deliver a high quality and quantity of public goods. Weak states face constraints on providing public goods, have ethnic or religious tensions that threaten to erupt into violence, and confront decline in economic performance. These constraints impinge upon the quality of life within the state and might lead to greater unrest, but the state still retains some modicum of control. Failed states generally feature sustained violent conflicts, an inability to control their borders, and few if any public goods.[8] The failure to provide political goods like security is particularly important because their provision 'is what states are all about. States only deserve to exist if they perform for their inhabitants'.[9] By failing to provide political goods, failed states become riven with ethnic strife, civil unrest, violence, corruption, repression, poverty, disease, and inequality.[10] Furthermore, because of the connectivity among states, failure in one country has the potential to spill over into others.[11]

Rotberg identifies two defining characteristics of 'failed' states: providing a low quality and quantity of political goods to their citizens, and a loss over the monopoly of the use of violence. Significantly, Rotberg emphasises that state failure is not geographically or historically determined; rather, it is the direct result of tangible actions undertaken by political leaders, largely to benefit themselves at the expense of the population as a whole.[12] 'More than structural or institutional weaknesses,' he emphasises, 'human agency is also culpable, usually in a fatal way'.[13]

Policy-makers have also devised their own definitions of failed states. The United States Agency for International Development (USAID) released a policy paper in 2005, detailing how the United States Government should respond to fragile states. They divided these states into two distinct categories: 'vulnerable' and 'in crisis'. Vulnerable states are those unable or unwilling to provide security, offer basic services to significant portions of the population, and possess questionable legitimacy. By contrast, states in crisis are those in which the central government lacks the ability to exert control over their territory, cannot or will not provide vital services, lack legitimacy, and are at high risk for violent conflict.[14] Such instability arises, according to this view, from ineffective and illegitimate governance as evidenced by economic instability, food insecurity, and violent conflict.[15] More importantly, this negative governance has effects beyond the borders of the state in question. 'Weak states,' USAID notes, 'tend to be vectors for these destabilizing forces, manifesting the dark side of globalisation, and pose a very different kind of national security challenge'.[16]

The Failed States Index, a result of collaboration between the Fund for Peace and *Foreign Policy*, is relatively unique among attempts to define state failure because it creates a quantitative measure.

Using 12 indicators in three broad categories, it makes its assessment about whether a state is failing. The social indicators are demographic pressures (such as high population density or skewed population distributions; large numbers of refugees and/or internally displaced persons); the legacy of group grievances (like scapegoating, institutionalised discrimination against particular groups, or patterns of atrocities); and sustained human flight (through 'brain drain' or the growth of exile communities). The two economic indicators are uneven development, particularly along group lines, and sharp and/or severe economic decline, including the growth of illicit industries, currency devaluation, or failure to pay state salaries. Political indicators include the criminalisation of the state, for instance, widespread corruption or the introduction of crime syndicates within the government; deteriorating public services; arbitrary application of the rule of law and widespread human rights abuses; security services acting with impunity; factionalised elites, especially when combined with nationalist rhetoric; and intervention by external actors.[17] Data are collected by the Fund for Peace's Conflict Assessment System Took programme, giving each country a score of 0 (low intensity) to 10 (high intensity) on each measure. Each state then receives a total score ranging from 0 to 120, with the highest scores being the most at risk for failure. In 2009, Somalia received a score of 114.7, making it the world's most vulnerable state. At the other end of the spectrum, Norway, the state least vulnerable to collapse, received a score of 18.3.[18]

Given these definitions, what common factors help to define failed states? First, state failure definitions emphasise institutional collapse. The state can no longer provide public goods, whether health, education, economic development, or security, because the structures for doing so have degraded too much. Such devastation to a state's institutional capacities does not occur quickly; rather, it occurs after long-term degeneration.[19] Second, definitions of state failure point to the role of violence and the absence of security. The state no longer exists in the Weberian sense because it has lost its monopoly on the use of violence. The presence (or threat) of widespread violence potentially imperils both the government's survival and the ability of the general populace to go about its daily business free of threat and fear. Third, definitions of state failure emphasise economic collapse. Inflation rises, purchasing power decreases, investment flees the country, and the state can no longer afford the basic supplies it requires to provide public goods. Finally, definitions of state failure frequently emphasise the culpability of government leaders. States do not simply collapse under their own weight; they are pushed toward failure specifically because of the actions taken (or not taken) by policy-makers.

Despite its popularity in academic and policy circles, the failed states paradigm has come under a fair amount of scrutiny and opposition. The criticisms largely fall into three categories. First, some authorities argue that the failed states literature starts from an inappropriate foundation for assessment. Second, definitions of failed states are too arbitrary. Third, the failed states paradigm encourages analysis that examines each country abstracted from the larger international context.

The first objection centers on how the definition of failed states imposes inappropriate standards on developing states. The state failure paradigm presents a flawed notion of uniformity among states, highlighting some differences among them and ignoring others.[20] This occurs on two different levels. On the first level, the failed states paradigm is inherently normative. To say that something has failed implies that there must be some standard against which it can be measured. In this case, the failed states definition elevates Western liberal capitalist democracy as the epitome of political development.[21] The problem with this assumption is that it fails to comport with political realities. The truth is that, in many so-called failed states, the institutions that have supposedly collapsed and the loss of control over the use of violence never existed in the first place. These states have been propped up by the international community, superficially adopting these political and economic arrangements without ever really embracing them or allowing them to operate. In one blunt view: 'In vast parts of Africa, state failure is less an objective condition than a permanent mode of political operation'.[22] Jackson and Rosberg highlighted this situation in 1982, when they analyzed the survival of African states, which frequently fail to supply public goods to their citizens. These weak states persist, so this argument goes, not because of their 'own' actions but because they are propped up by the international community.[23] The state failure paradigm parallels this argument. Many failed states have never functioned as liberal capitalist democracies. This inability reflects not problems with the government but, rather, the limitations of the Westphalian state in the modern era. These 'states in crisis' are artificial creations with little to hold them together aside from the collective judgment of the international community.

The second prominent line of criticism regards the standards used to assess state failure. Reflecting on the rankings presented by the Fund for Peace and *Foreign Policy*, one commentator noted: 'Figuring out which faltering states to help depends in large part on what they need. After all, as Tolstoy might have put it, every failing state is failing in its own way.'[24] Methodologically, definitions of state failure rely almost entirely on subjective measurements. Most definitions employ qualitative assessments and assess the situation in a given country through news reports, fieldwork, and expert opinion from scholars and policy-makers familiar with the country. The Fund for Peace–*Foreign Policy* approach is different in that it creates a quantitative index that allows for comparisons between countries and across time. Even here, however, there exists no objective floor. There is no standard of economic collapse, violence, or institutional decay that automatically indicates that a state will fail or has failed. Such subjectivity opens the concept to accusations of bias and political manipulation.

Third, critics of the state failure paradigm object to its tendency to examine problems of governance as pathologies unique to a given state rather than considering the larger international context. No state exists in isolation from others, but the state failure paradigm focuses almost exclusively on individual states without acknowledging its interactions with others. Instead of examining how economic and political relations with Western states have shaped a failed state's institutions, this paradigm focuses its analysis on individual leaders rather than the broader structural situation.[25]

To determine how well the failed state label applies to Zimbabwe, one can apply four elements of the state failure definitions (institutional collapse and inability to provide public goods; economic collapse; violence and the absence of security; and culpability of leaders) to the situation in the country over the past decade.

At one time, Zimbabwe was the beacon of hope and stability in Southern Africa. It boasted strong, vibrant health and education systems, and its infrastructure was among Africa's best. Thanks to this institutional strength, Zimbabwe could provide an array of services and public goods to its citizens, while simultaneously providing support to exiled anti-apartheid activists from South Africa. That reputation for strength and competence has disappeared. The education system is now in utter disarray. The United Nations Children's Fund (UNICEF) declared in 2008 that it was 'seriously concerned' by the 'disturbing results' it found during a monitoring visit. Evaluators found that only 40 percent of teachers and 33 percent of students attended school on a given day, and that the country's educational bureaucracy lacked the capacity to conduct national exams. State-run universities were so short of funds that they could not open for classes in August 2008.[26] During 2008, primary school students received only 23 consecutive days of education in government schools.[27] More than 20,000 teachers left the country between 2007 and 2009, and basic supplies like textbooks are undersupplied. Even in areas where schools are still open, few families can afford US$24 for annual fees.[28]

The health care system has fared little better, and health outcomes today are frequently worse than those experienced at the beginning of Black majority rule in 1980. Life expectancy at birth fell from 62 to 43 years between 1990 and 2006. Between 1990 and 2007, maternal mortality rates quadrupled, whereas childhood vaccination rates declined from 84 percent to 53 percent between 1994 and 2007. Tuberculosis incidence tripled between 1990 and 2006.[29] Reports note that many health care facilities have had to close in the face of Zimbabwe's massive economic disruptions, and patients must provide their own medicines, sutures, and supplies as a result of a 56 percent decline in government health spending: 'Women delivering in rural clinics must bring candles, cotton wool, methylated spirit, gloves, and even fresh water. The physical infrastructure of most government health facilities is decrepit, and ambulances sparse'.[30] Few facilities could stock basic medicines, and most public hospital wards shut completely between September and November 2008.[31] Twenty percent of the country's health care professionals flee the country every year, and those that remain make less than US$1 per day. Compounding the lack of medical personnel, the country's main medical school at the University of Zimbabwe had to close for six months in 2008–9.[32]

The collapse of public services has also affected the water and sanitation infrastructure. In 1998, the Government created the Zimbabwe National Water Authority (ZINWA) to oversee the development and management of national water resources and associated infrastructure.[33] Since ZINWA's creation, water access decreased substantially, and the water and sanitation infrastructure has nearly collapsed. In 1988, the World Health Organization (WHO) and UNICEF reported that 84 percent of Zimbabweans had reliable access to safe drinking water. By 2008, more than 70 percent of Zimbabweans lacked such access, and Harare loses 40 percent of its water supply every day due to pipe bursts and leakage.[34] In August 2008, ZINWA ran out of aluminum sulfate, a key element in water purification, and could not afford to purchase more. When that happened, the Morton Jaffray waterworks, the largest water plant serving Harare, was forced to both stop pumping water from its main station and abandon nearly all efforts to repair burst pipes.[35]

The combination of a deteriorating health system and a collapsing water and sanitation infrastructure led to Africa's worst cholera outbreak on record. Initial reports of a cholera outbreak emerged in August 2008, when 18 cases appeared in Harare and its suburbs. By December, WHO reported 11,735 cases of cholera and 484 deaths throughout the country. In some rural areas, cholera mortality rates reached 20 to 30 percent. Two months later, WHO counted nearly 80,000 suspected cases of cholera and 3,713 deaths. Even with international assistance, WHO officials pessimistically predicted: 'Given the outbreak's dynamic, in the context of a dilapidated water and sanitation infrastructure and a weak health system, the practical implementation of control measures remains a challenge.'[36] By 13 June, WHO and the Zimbabwean Ministry of Health and Child Welfare had recorded 98,531 suspected cases and 4,282 deaths. Although the 2008–9 cholera outbreak largely ended by summer 2009, reports emerged in October 2009 that the disease had returned and claimed at least five lives in a rural district in the northern part of the country.[37]

These indicators all point to the collapse of providing public goods and maintaining governmental institutions throughout the country. The Government has demonstrated a willingness to allow its institutional capacity to wither or hijack it for its own purposes.

Zimbabwe's economic deterioration has imposed huge costs and plunged the country into one of the most severe depressions on record. Problems began in 1998, when high interest rates and inflation led to large demonstrations and riots in major cities against government policies. The economic imbalances arose when the Government promised pensions to veterans of the liberation war and intervened militarily in the conflict in the Democratic Republic of Congo. These demonstrations helped provide support for the Zimbabwe Council of Trade Unions, encouraging the creation of the opposition political party Movement for Democratic Change (MDC). The following year, disagreements between the Government and international financial institutions led the International Monetary Fund (IMF) and World Bank to suspend aid programmes. By 2000, unemployment was at 50 percent, inflation hit 60 percent, and 75 percent of the population was living in poverty.[38]

The economy's downward spiral accelerated throughout the 2000s. The agricultural sector collapsed as a result of a lack of foreign capital, the Government's disastrous policy of expropriating commercial farms without compensation and turning them over to political supporters, and drought. In 2006, the annual inflation rate topped 1000 percent and the Reserve Bank redenominated all banknotes, exchanging 1000ZWD for 1ZWD of the new currency. By the time the new dollar was introduced, annual inflation had reached 782 percent. In response to the worsening economic crisis, the Reserve Bank chose to print more Zimbabwean dollars. It did so in an attempt to pay off its IMF arrears and make good on its promise to increase salaries for soldiers, police, and other civil servants.[39] This policy vastly increased the money supply and wiped out the private savings of most individuals, encouraging even higher rates of inflation. A simultaneous Government order to slash prices of basic goods by 50 percent led to shortages and a thriving black market.[40]

By the end of 2007, the Government declared that it would no longer be able to calculate the annual inflation rate because the stores lacked goods with which to make any such assessments. Estimates pegged the inflation rate in the neighborhood of 15,000 to 20,000 percent.[41] In January 2008, the inflation rate crossed the 100,000 percent threshold, reaching 100,580.2 percent.[42] The economic catastrophe crossed a second threshold that May when the annual inflation rate soared past 1 million percent. As one commentator observed: 'As stores opened for business on Wednesday, a small pack of locally produced coffee beans cost just short of ZWD1 billion. A decade ago, that sum would have bought 60 new cars'.[43] Finally, in October 2008, Government officials announced that the inflation rate in July reached 231 million percent, though many suggested that the actual inflation was higher than the official Government figure.[44] Given the utter collapse of the economy, the Government abandoned the Zimbabwean dollar. Fewer and fewer merchants were willing to accept them, demanding payment instead in United States dollars, South African rand, Euros, or Botswana pula. Responding to this reality, the Government decreed in January 2009 that commercial transactions could occur in any currency.[45]

Early in 2010, the Government (a coalition between President Robert Mugabe's Zimbabwe African National Union–Patriotic Front [ZANU–PF] and the MDC) announced some success at bringing the economy under control. Finance Minister Tendai Biti, a member of the MDC, managed to bring inflation down to an annual rate for 2009 of a mere 1 percent. Abandoning the Zimbabwean dollar significantly contributed to this success, as did restricting the money supply by 1000 percent. Thanks to his aggressive moves, he expects the economy to grow for the first time in a decade; it showed 4 percent gross domestic product (GDP) growth in 2009 and an estimated 6 percent GDP growth rate for 2010.[46] This recent uptick in Zimbabwe's economic fortunes is clearly welcome news, but it will take many years to reestablish some measure of economic security for the people.

Political violence has become disturbingly common in Zimbabwe over the past decade, with beatings, torture, kidnapping, and murder not uncommon. Nonetheless, it would be inaccurate to describe the high rates of violence as a loss of the monopoly of the legitimate use of violence by the Government, as most of the violence occurs at the Government's behest. In some instances, soldiers and police officers are carrying out attacks on political opponents. In others, youth gangs associated with ZANU–PF use violence to target opposition supporters.

After voters rejected Mugabe's proposed constitutional reforms in 2000, which would have strengthened his party and allowed it to seize farmland without compensation from White farmers, he again saw the use of violence as a means for achieving his goals. This time, soldiers, police officers, or youths associated with ZANU–PF carried out most of the violence. In the first half of January 2002 alone, ZANU–PF youths committed four murders, 68 cases of torture, and 22 kidnappings.[47] That March, when the presidential election was held, investigators found 641 cases of torture, nearly 400 property crimes, 83 kidnappings, and 16 deaths.[48] By year's end, a coalition of Zimbabwean human rights NGOs recorded more than 1000 torture cases, nearly 800 politically related property crimes, 227 abductions, 64 death threats, 58 murders, and 29 disappearances.[49]

In 2005, violence directed against political opponents rose to a new level. That year, the Government embarked on Operation Murambatsvina (Operation Remove the Filth), a devastating government program that cleared and flattened numerous high-density suburbs. Approximately 2.4 million people were affected by the Government's program to eliminate shantytowns, markets, and makeshift homes. Government officials claimed that the Operation was an attempt to remove illegal housing and commercial activities and prevent the spread of infectious disease. In reality, by driving so many people out of the city, Operation Murambatsvina sought to displace MDC supporters, who lived predominantly in urban areas. Forcibly and rapidly removing large numbers of people from Harare scattered MDC supporters across the country, making it difficult for the party to organise its supporters.[50] These actions helped make 2005 the most politically violent in Zimbabwe to date. More than 1,300 people were subject to arbitrary arrest or detention, 530 assaults occurred, 136 torture cases were reported, and four people lost their lives.[51] In 2008, the most recent year for which full-year political violence statistics are available, the Zimbabwe Human Rights NGO Forum documented 1,913 assaults, 723 cases of torture, 596 property-related crimes, and 107 murders.[52] These cases offer just a small bit of evidence that Zimbabweans have reason to fear for their safety and that their lives have been made more insecure in recent years.

Still, where the Zimbabwean case differs from most of the literature on state failure is that this violence is not a sign of state weakness, but rather of state strength. The Government is directing the violence. It uses groups either directly or indirectly under its command to carry out attacks on perceived political enemies. Zimbabwe is not a case where the government has lost its control over the use of violence; it is a case where it has strengthened its control. While various Government officials have alleged the existence of domestic or international groups planning to overthrow ZANU–PF, there exists no guerrilla movement or armed rebellions within Zimbabwe. Instead of lawlessness and anarchy promoting this violence, it comes from the overwhelming control the Government holds over the police, soldiers, and its youth supporters.

Without question, Mugabe has been at the apex of power in Zimbabwe since 1980. He has repeatedly taken steps to consolidate power around him and his coterie, and he has demonstrated remarkable success in fending off potential political challengers, both from opposition parties and within ZANU–PF itself. As such, the responsibility for the Government's successes and failures must largely fall on his shoulders. Given his unquestioned dominance within the Zimbabwean political arena, the institutional collapse, failure to provide public goods, and unleashing of terror against political opponents necessarily focuses on Mugabe. He appoints the Cabinet ministers who carry out and implement his policies, and he makes public pronouncements proclaiming his continued dominance. During a speech in the run-up to the 2008 presidential election, Mugabe claimed that the MDC would never rule Zimbabwe and that 'only God who appointed me will remove me, not the MDC, not the British'.[53] His control over the Zimbabwean political apparatus means that he must be culpable for the decisions made. Until 2009's power-sharing agreement with the MDC, Mugabe possessed all the power and all Cabinet members were his appointees.

Evidence of Mugabe's culpability also comes from his use of electoral fraud to ensure electoral success. In 2005, MDC officials presented reports of ballot box stuffing, incorrect vote counts, large numbers of 'ghost voters' on the electoral roll, and unusually long delays in announcing vote tallies. In a number of constituencies, the initial reports of the number of voters and the final results differed greatly, and always in ZANU–PF's favor.[54]

A similar dynamic repeated itself in 2008. Initial reports suggested that Morgan Tsvangirai, MDC's candidate, had won more than 50 percent of the vote and thus the presidency.[55] However, the Zimbabwe Electoral Commission (ZEC), the official vote-counting body, refused to release official tallies for more than a month. This delay raised fears of fraud and vote-rigging. Finally, on 2 May 2008, ZEC announced that Tsvangirai had indeed won more votes than Mugabe, but that he only received 47.9 percent of the vote, necessitating a run-off with the President.[56] In the interim, suspicions about the veracity of the electoral process arose. Despite having only 5.9 million eligible voters, the ZEC ordered 9 million ballots printed. Opposition groups argued that polling places were concentrated in pro-Mugabe areas.[57] Furthermore, ZANU–PF supporters conducted such an intense campaign of violence against MDC supporters that Tsvangirai withdrew from the run-off. He declared that the run-off was a sham and that he could not ask his supporters to risk their lives to support him.[58]

The electoral fraud demonstrates an orchestrated campaign by Mugabe and his supporters to keep him in power so that he can continue to implement the policies that have undermined the basic functioning of the Zimbabwean state. In this way, there is a clear connection between Mugabe's actions and the poor quality of services and the country's economic devastation.

By focusing attention on the public goods and social contract elements of the definition, then Zimbabwe is an exemplar of a failed state. Its economy has gone from being one of the most robust in Southern Africa to setting new records for economic decline. Its political system has devolved into an authoritarian regime largely built around one man. Government agents have assaulted, tortured, kidnapped, and abused opposition supporters. The school system barely exists. More than a million people have fled the country. The sanitation infrastructure has deteriorated such that clean water is a rarity in most of the country. Its demise, combined with the utter destruction of the public health system, has allowed infectious diseases to run rampant. The Zimbabwean Government is obviously not upholding its end of the social contract. People are not receiving even the most basic of services from the Government, and it is nearly impossible to speak of public goods being provided by the Government. From this perspective, Tendai Biti stated in 2009: 'We're basically coming from a situation of a failed state, where for 15 consistent years we have had negative declines in GDP.'[59]

In the Weberian sense, however, Zimbabwe does not qualify as a failed state. Despite all the problems the country has faced, the Government has not lost its monopoly over the use of violence. If anything, it has strengthened its hold here. The youth gangs terrorising MDC supporters do not threaten Mugabe's Government; they do its bidding and use violence in an attempt to solidify ZANU–PF's hold on power. There exist no guerrilla movements within the country that pose a threat to the Government's hold on power, and no neighboring country or external actor considers military intervention a plausible option.

More broadly, Zimbabwe's problems come not from the weakness of the state, but rather from its strength. The collapse of the sanitation system throughout the country was a direct consequence of the Government nationalising the system for its own benefit. Once it had done so, its political designs on the system got in the way of the system itself, allowing it to collapse and preventing the vast majority of Zimbabweans from having access to safe drinking water. It may seem paradoxical, but it takes a strong government to decimate thoroughly such a system. The collapse of the political and economic systems happened not through governmental neglect, but from too great governmental involvement. The Government manipulated the political system, the constitution, and the electoral process to ensure its continued survival. The Government also made economic policy that it calculated would benefit itself and its supporters, regardless of its effects on the larger population. It was able to do both of these things precisely because of the level of control and power it had, and continues to have.

Instead of being a clear-cut case of state failure, Zimbabwe fits awkwardly within this paradigm. Indeed, the Zimbabwean case raises important questions about both the definitions and criticisms of state failure. For supporters of the state failure paradigm, Zimbabwe points to the need for greater conceptual clarity. The literature generally makes no distinction among the different elements that may contribute to state failure. For instance, is economic collapse more important than the monopoly over violence? The definitions of state failure do not make such a distinction, nor do they offer any sort of hierarchy of conditions that lead to state failure. Supporters would likely argue that there can be no such hierarchy, because each state's failure will be unique. If this is the case, it begs the question of what ties these countries together. Are the situations in Somalia, Zimbabwe, and Sudan, the three most at-risk countries in the 2009 Failed States Index, similar enough that it is worthwhile to have them share the same rubric? Without some sort of hierarchy or a way to distinguish among the different elements of failure, it is difficult to say.

Furthermore, repairing economic failure is likely to require different strategies and inputs from a different array of actors than if the security situation in a country has collapsed. As it currently stands, economic and security failures are the same thing. Making distinctions among different types of failure or elements of failure may also clarify the role of internal and external actors in addressing the root problems.

For critics of the state failure paradigm, Zimbabwe challenges a number of their assumptions. Far from being a state that never worked, Zimbabwe did possess many attributes of a liberal capitalist state for many years. Despite initial fears that the country would turn into a bastion of Marxism when Mugabe was elected in 1980, the Government operated as a responsible member of the international community and provided a vast array of public goods to its citizenry after it achieved majority rule. Zimbabwe's current problems, and the country is clearly facing a multitude of problems, are not reflective of the failure of the state as a political institution, but rather of Government decisions. Zimbabwe's strategic importance to the West is marginal at best, and most states have publicly stated their desire to see domestic and regional forces work out the problems. The question for critics then is: how could a country that was seemingly so functional for so long fail so spectacularly? State failure critics tend to focus on how the paradigm awkwardly fits certain normative standards to developing states, but Zimbabwe largely lived up to those standards until the Government undertook specific actions to bolster their grip on power. What should be done when a state like Zimbabwe fails to provide public goods or uphold the social contract?

For both supporters and critics, the big question is what happens next? Robert Gabriel Mugabe turned 86 in 2010 and has been in control of the Zimbabwean Government for 30 years. Most, if not all, governmental institutions are built around him, and he has repeatedly thwarted efforts to name a successor. What happens when Mugabe dies? Will this allow the political process to revive and let the opposition MDC revive the country? Will it throw the country into even greater chaos and turmoil? Will Mugabe's death hasten or hamper the tentative signs of economic growth that started to emerge in 2009? Mugabe's death will mark a huge transformation in Zimbabwe, but it is not at all clear what the effects will be.

Notes

1 Jennifer Milliken and Keith Krause, 'State failure, state collapse, and state reconstruction: concepts, lessons, and strategies', *Development and Change*, 33(2002), 754–55.
2 Gary King and Langche Zeng, 'Improving forecasts of state failure,' *World Politics*, 53 (2001), 625.

3 Pauline H. Baker, 'Fixing failed states: the new security agenda', *Whitehead Journal of Diplomacy and International Relations*, 8(2007), 91–92.

4 Ambassador Richard S. Williamson, 'Nation-building: the dangers of weak, failing, and failed states', Ibid., 13–14.

5 I. William Zartman, 'Introduction: posing the problem of state collapse', in I. William Zartman, ed., *Collapsed States: The Disintegration and Restoration of Legitimate Authority* (Boulder, CO, 1995), 5.

6 Zartman, 'Introduction', 6–11.

7 Robert I. Rotberg, 'The new nature of nation-state failure', *Washington Quarterly*, 25(2002), 85.

8 Robert I. Rotberg, 'Failed states, weak states, collapsed states: causes and indicators,' in Robert I. Rotberg, ed., *State Failure and State Weakness in a Time of Terror* (Washington, DC, 2003), 5–6.

9 Robert I. Rotberg, 'The challenges of frail, failing, and failed states', *Studia Diplomatica*, 58(2005), 42.

10 Branwen Gruffydd Jones, 'The global political economy of social crisis: towards a critique of the 'failed state' ideology,' *Review of International Political Economy*, 15(2008), 180–81.

11 Robert I. Rotberg, 'Failed states in a world of terror', *Foreign Affairs*, 81(July/August 2002), 127.

12 Rotberg, 'The new nature', 93–94.

13 Rotberg, 'Failed states', 127.

14 USAID, *Fragile States Strategy* (Washington, DC, 2005), 1.

15 Ibid., 3–4.

16 Ibid., v.

17 Fund for Peace, 'Failed States Index Score 2007': www.fundforpeace.org/web/index.php?option=com_content&task = view&id = 229&Itemid = 366.

18 http://www.foreignpolicy.com/images/090624_2009_final_data.pdf.

19 Zartman, 'Introduction', 8–9.

20 Morten Boas and Kathleen M. Jennings, ' "*Failed State*" and "State Failure": Threats or Opportunities?', *Globalizations*, 4(2007), 476.

21 Francis Fukuyama, 'The end of history?', *National Interest*, 16(1989), 3–18.

22 Pierre Englebert and Denis M. Tull, 'Postconflict reconstruction in Africa: flawed ideas about failed states', *International Security*, 32(2008), 110.

23 Robert H. Jackson and Carl G. Rosberg, 'Why Africa's weak states persist: the empirical and juridical in statehood', *World Politics*, 35(1982), 1–24.

24 'The 2009 Failed States Index', *Foreign Policy* (22 June 2009): www.foreignpolicy.com/articles/2009/06/22/the_2009_failed_states_index.

25 Anna Gentili, 'Failed states or failed concept?', *Studia Diplomatica*, 62(2009), 10.

26 UNICEF, 'Zimbabwe education system in a state of emergency', 9 October 2008: www.unicef.org/media/media_45950.html.

27 'Zimbabwe's education system crippled on first day of school', Voice of America, 27 January 2009: www1.voanews.com/english/news/a-13hy2009hy01hy27-voa60–68666757.html.

28 Nkepile Mabuse, 'Zimbabwe schools begin fightback,' CNN (6 November 2009): http://edition.cnn.com/2009/WORLD/africa/11/02/zimbabwe.schools/index.

29 Charles Todd, Sunanda Ray, Farai Madzimbamuto, and David Sanders, 'What is the way forward for health in Zimbabwe?', *Lancet*, 375(2010), 606.

30 Todd et al., 'What is the way forward', 606.

31 Physicians for Human Rights, *Health in Ruins: A Man-Made Disaster in Zimbabwe* (Cambridge, MA, 2009), vi.

32 Todd et al., 'What is the way forward', 606–7.

33 M. Musemwa, 'The Politics of Water in Post-Colonial Zimbabwe, 1980–2007', Seminar paper to be presented at the African Studies Centre, University of Leiden, The Netherlands (19 June 2008), 9–10.

34 Ibid., 6.

35 Edgar Gweshe, 'ZINWA admits failure', *Zimbabwe Standard* (17 January 2009): www.allafrica.com/stories/printable/200901190741.html.

36 World Health Organization, 'Cholera in Zimbabwe—Update 2', (20 February 2009): www.who.int/csr/don/2009_02_20/en/index.html.

37 Jan Raath, 'Cholera breaks out in Zimbabwe again amid fears of an epidemic in summer rains', *Times* (21 October 2009): www.timesonline.co.uk/tol/news/world/africa/article6883266.

38 Rachel Rawlins, 'Zimbabwe: economic collapse', *BBC News* (18 October 2000): http://news.bbc.co.uk/2/hi/africa/978768.stm.

39 'Gono ordered to print Z$1 trillion for civil servants and army', *Zimbabwe Daily* (27 June 2007): www.zimbabwesituation.com/jun28_2007.html#Z18.

40 Michael Wines, 'A new plan for Zimbabwe', *New York Times* (27 June 2007); www.zimbabwesituation. com/jun28_2007.html#Z6.

41 'Zimbabwe inflation "incalculable"', *BBC News* (27 November 2007); http://news.bbc.co.uk/2/hi/africa/7115651.stm.

42 'Zimbabwe annual inflation over 100,000 percent', *Sydney Morning Herald* (21 February 2008): www.zimbabwesituation.com/feb21_2008.html#Z1.

43 Tichaona Sibanda, 'Inflation hits one million percent as prices continue to skyrocket', *SW Radio Africa* (21 May 2008): www.zimbabwesituation.com/may24a_2008.html#Z26.

44 Martin Kadzere, 'Inflation soars to 231 million percent,' *The Herald (Harare)* (9 October 2008): www.zimbabwesituation.com/oct9b_2008.html#Z1.

45 'Zimbabwe abandons its currency', *BBC News* (29 January 2009): http://news.bbc.co.uk/2/hi/africa/7859033.stm.

46 Elizabeth Dickinson, 'How to cut inflation by 230 million percent', *Passport. A Blog by the Editors of Foreign Policy* (26 January 2010): http://blog.foreignpolicy.com/posts/2010/01/26/how_to_cut_inflation_by_230_million_percent.

47 'Zimbabwe political violence increases', *BBC News* (24 January 2002): http://news.bbc.co.uk/2/hi/africa/1780206.stm.

48 Zimbabwe Human Rights NGO Forum, 'Political violence report, 16–31 March 2002': www.hrforumzim.com/monthly/march02_02.htm.

49 Zimbabwe Human Rights NGO Forum, 'Political violence report, 1–31 December 2002': www.hrforumzim.com/monthly/dec_02.htm.

50 Michael Bratton, 'Authoritarian resilience and state fragility in Zimbabwe', Paper presented at the American Political Science Association Conference, Toronto (3 September 2009), 6.

51 Zimbabwe Human Rights NGO Forum, 'Political violence report, December 2005': www.hrforumzim.com/monthly/december_2005.htm.

52 Zimbabwe Human Rights NGO Forum, 'Political violence report, December 2008': http://www.hrforumzim.com/monthly/200812MPVR.pdf (accessed 24 February 2010).

53 'Robert Mugabe says "only God" can remove him', *Telegraph* (20 June 2008): www.telegraph.co.uk/news/worldnews/africaandindianocean/zimbabwe/2165171/Robert-Mugabe-says-only-God-can-remove-him.html.

54 'Zimbabwe: electoral fraud report, 4/18/05.', *AfricaFocus Bulletin*: www.africa.upenn.edu/afrfocus/afrfocus041805.html.

55 'Zimbabwe announces first election results', *Telegraph* (31 March 2008): www.telegraph.co.uk/news/worldnews/1583429/Zimbabwe-announces-first-election-results.html.

56 MacDonald Dzirutwe, 'Zim heads for run-off', *IOL* (2 May 2008): www.int.iol.co.za/index.php?set_id=1&click_id=3045&art_id=nw20080502152757558C887809.

57 'Zimbabwe ballot papers spark row', *BBC News* (24 March 2008): http://news.bbc.co.uk/2/hi/africa/7310544.stm.

58 Lee Glendinning and Aidan Jones, 'Tsvangirai pulls out of 'sham' Zimbabwe election', *Guardian* (22 June 2008): www.guardian.co.uk/world/2008/jun/22/zimbabwe4.

59 Elizabeth Dickinson, 'Blame game', *Foreign Policy* (22 June 2009): www.foreignpolicy.com/articles/2009/06/22/2009_failed_states_index_blame_game.

37

Public versus private power

Non-governmental organisations and international security

Jonathan Goodhand and Oliver Walton

Non-governmental organisations (NGOs) have had growing involvement in international security since the end of the Cold War. It is important to explain why and how they have been ascribed and taken on a range of new roles under the rubric of 'international security', including public diplomacy, track-two negotiations, community reconciliation, post-conflict peace-building, and peace advocacy. What have been the key factors behind this trend? What about NGO effectiveness in this policy arena? And what are the wider lessons and implications for those seeking to promote international security?

International security is defined as a pattern of relations among states, multilateral organisations, and non-governmental actors designed to manage risks and maintain the international order. This order was forged by hegemonic Powers, not least the United States and its allies in the West, and sustained by a complex amalgam of actors including intergovernmental organisations like the United Nations (UN), the European Union, international financial institutions, and regional organisations such as the South Asian Association for Regional Cooperation and the African Union. However, since the Cold War this security terrain has expanded, and the security dynamics at the interstate, national, and interpersonal levels have blurred, opening up space for NGOs to play a growing role.

'Peace' is a value-relative and often deeply contested term likely to be defined by more powerful actors. Some believe that peace must be maintained, whereas others consider that it is something that must be strived for.[1] This nicely captures Galtung's differentiation between 'negative peace' (the absence of organised physical violence) and 'positive peace' (eliminating structural violence perpetuated by social inequalities and injustice).[2] Whereas NGOs have tended to understand peace in the 'positive' sense, governments have tended to be more concerned with peace in 'negative' terms.

Peace-building covers an increasingly broad and shifting range of practices and aspirations. Understandings of the term often rely on an uneasy combination of pragmatic problem-solving approaches and idealistic visions based on broad models of societal and political change.[3] Broad concepts such as peace are contested and contain contradictions that 'prevent their being expressed in universally accepted definitions'.[4] Consequently, 'peace and peacebuilding are not terms with a proper descriptive utility and normative value ... but they are political discourses which represent and serve to justify certain political interests and ideas'.[5] Furthermore, the ambiguity and slipperiness of the term 'peace-building' constitutes one of its virtues, allowing organisations with very different objectives and approaches to join in and justify a broad range of interventions.[6]

Straddling the public–private boundary, NGOs have been defined as 'private, non-profit, professional organizations with a distinctive legal character, concerned with public welfare goals'.[7] They work at a range of levels and perform a variety of functions. The literature usually distinguishes amongst three types: international NGOs, usually Western ones working in a number of developing countries but, technically, any based in one country that works in another; national NGOs working only in their country of origin but that have a country-wide focus; and community-based organisations working only in one locality. An important distinction with important implications for the kinds of peace-building roles NGOs are capable of performing is between membership-based organisations (which maintain direct links with their constituencies) and third-party groups (which do not). And NGOs are also often categorised in terms of their objectives. Multimandate organisations like World Vision, Oxfam, Save the Children, and CARE International typically perform activities spanning the humanitarian, development, and peace-building fields; niche organisations focus on a single area, for example, International Alert specializes in the field of peace-building. Another common distinction is between secular and faith-based organisations.

NGO literature tends to be based on assumptions that such third-party organisations are part of civil society, or the 'third sector', which is defined as separate to the public and private sectors. There is also an assumption about the comparative advantage of NGOs over organisations in the two other spheres: NGOs are more flexible, people-centered, innovative, and responsive. They are also perceived to carry over these comparative advantages into security and peace-building. First, they are seen as largely free from the traditional global and sub-national security interests of states, with much of their credibility relying on their capacity to combine a disinterested moral concern with social action. Second, NGOs are valued for their detailed understanding of local political dynamics and awareness of the needs and concerns of communities, often coming from an extended field presence in conflict zones.[8] The access and flexibility of NGOs permits state actors to pursue more intricate security-related goals such as institutionalising bottom-up forms of governance.[9] Moreover, involving civil society has helped fashion a 'peace-building consensus', legitimising otherwise state-driven forms of intervention. Third, NGOs are seen to be uniquely positioned to play a mediating role in conflict; they are archetypal 'mid-level' players that can act as transmission agents between political elites and societal groups. The so-called 'Norwegian model' of peace facilitation, for example, has often drawn upon Norwegian NGOs to establish back-channels between warring parties, who initially would not engage with each other in direct talks. Finally, apparent NGO flexibility means that they may be well placed to exploit peace transition windows of opportunity or critical thresholds, which may occur during the course of a war, which official actors may be slow to recognize and respond to.

This perspective on NGOs is based on an extremely actor-centered view of social change. Individuals and organisations are seen to have power to break free of and transform wider structural constraints. Furthermore, NGO expansion into the peace and international security field has been underpinned by an essentially liberal, cosmopolitan view of politics. From this standpoint, political change promoted by extragovernmental actors is legitimate, so long as these actors pursue goals that conform to liberal norms. This view contrasts with a communitarian or nationalist view of politics, generally more cautious about extragovernmental involvement in the political process, which tends to see foreign political interference as illegitimate. NGOs have struggled to navigate the contrasting demands and expectations that arise from these two positions.

However, this liberal perspective on NGOs is open to critical scrutiny. The notion of clear divisions among states, private sectors, and civil societies is theoretically and empirically problematic. Close links between governments and NGOs are increasingly apparent as NGOs have become more financially reliant on governmental donors, putting in sharp relief the inherent tensions between the public and private aspects of their identities. These tensions have been accentuated further by NGO involvement in politically sensitive activities to reduce, manage, and mitigate the effects of violent conflict. Moreover, the idea that NGO behavior is shaped by declared norms, rather than underlying material interests, is open to question. Several writers argue that NGOs are more akin to private-sector actors, chasing contracts and resources in the aid marketplace.[10] Their expansion into peace-building may partly be understood as a search for market-share in a competitive funding environment.

NGOs have proliferated rapidly since the 1980s; doubling from 19,000 in 1986 to 38,000 in 1996, then rising slightly less rapidly to a total number of around 59,000 in 2004.[11] According to one estimate, the number of development NGOs registered in Organisation for Economic Co-operation and Development (OECD) countries nearly doubled between 1980 and 1990 from 1,600 to 2,500.[12] In the South, NGO expansion has been even more rapid.[13] This overall precipitous growth during the 1980s–1990s was facilitated by an increased availability of financial resources. After tripling during the 1980s, official funding for NGOs doubled again in the 1990s, rising from $47 million (0.18 percent of total overseas development assistance [ODA]) in 1980 to just over $4 billion (6 percent ODA) in 2002.[14] By the mid-1990s, donor funding accounted for an average of 30 percent of NGO total income, compared with 1.5 percent in the early 1970s.[15] Private funding also increased, and net grants made by NGOs have grown steadily since 1990, rising from US$5.2 billion to a peak of US$14.7 billion in 2005.[16]

Donors' growing enthusiasm for NGOs reflects a number of global, political, and ideological shifts. First, these trends were related to donors' mounting dissatisfaction with state-driven development interventions since the 1980s. Many Western governments saw NGOs as useful antidotes to failed state-led development efforts of the 1960–70s, providing flexibility and the capacity to transform societies from the bottom up instead of the perceived inertia and top-down solutions presented by states.[17] NGOs were also linked to an associated need to counterbalance the retreat of the state associated with neoliberal structural reforms.[18] And the rise in funding reflected a growing optimism about the scope for civil society to contribute to political transformation after the Cold War revolutions in Eastern Europe and, later, in the Soviet Union. Finally, NGO growth was linked to a burgeoning interest from Western governments and multilateral institutions in bringing peace to conflict-affected regions, doing so by more intricate hybrid interventions that combined diplomatic and bilateral mediation with measures designed to foster societal transformation.[19]

As NGOs grew in number and geographical range, they began to expand their operational scope beyond traditional humanitarian and developmental roles. This expansion was most conspicuous in conflict-affected regions where NGO developmental and humanitarian work was increasingly supplemented with monitoring, advocacy, and peace-building roles.[20] Over the same period, NGOs also acquired greater prominence in global politics. NGO coalitions such as the International Campaign to Ban Landmines, the World Social Forum, and Jubilee 2000 applied greater pressure on intergovernmental organisations and conferences, encouraging states to sign a treaty banning landmines in 1997, pushing through agreements to ban greenhouse gases at the Earth Summit in 1992, or helping to bring about a dramatic reduction in the debts of poor countries. NGOs were widely seen as sitting at the forefront of an 'associational revolution', capable of disrupting the established hierarchies of world politics by swamping international conferences and promoting new, more participatory forms of bottom-up governance.[21]

This expansion was related to a range of factors including structural shifts in the post-Cold War era, changing understandings and discourses related to security and state sovereignty, in addition to changes and adaptations within the NGO sector itself. This period coincided with a growth in Western governments' geopolitical space for intervention and an unprecedented sense of confidence in the defining ideologies of the West: democracy and capitalism. These factors created a renewed assurance in the West's capacity to intervene in areas of instability, prompting several key actors, including the UN, to take a more active conflict-resolving role.[22] Symptomatic was the threefold increase in UN-led peace operations between 1998 and 2008.[23]

Geopolitical changes prompted several important shifts in the way that war, peace, and interventions were understood and framed. A major underlying factor involved the growing prominence of internal violence. Although the total number of civil wars began to decline after the Cold War, this decline was preceded by a more rapid drop in the number of international conflicts, which fell from an average of six ongoing wars in the 1950s to less than one in the 2000s.[24] The growing significance of civil wars, together with a perceived decline in threats posed by hostile Powers, changed the way security threats were perceived by Western countries. The perceived threat was less rogue states than 'fragile' ones that produced multiple 'public bads', including regional instability, terrorism, and illegal trafficking. So-called 'new wars' characterized by state breakdown, warlordism, and ethnic rivalries were seen rooted in problems of bad governance, underdevelopment, and primordial conflicts.[25] They involved freewheeling non-state actors believed to be less amenable to traditional elite-based diplomacy. Consequently a number of shifts have taken place in relation to intervention strategies.

First, there has been a tendency to view such civil wars as internal problems with external solutions. And the growth of NGO involvement in international security parallels the expansion of the liberal peace-building industry; in this sense, NGOs are part of the growth of international peace promotion's 'supply side'. Second, policy-makers' growing focus on the links between underdevelopment and conflict resulted in an enhanced emphasis on the potential for violence in relatively insignificant regions to endanger the developed world by contributing to immigration pressures or promoting terrorism.[26] Third, the justification and framing of intervention have changed. In the Cold War, intervention was relatively rare in superpower rivalry and the exercise of UN Security Council vetoes; threats were seen to emanate from hostile states, and efforts to prevent or forestall conflict was viewed as the preserve of Powers engaging in 'high politics'. Today's security threats are more diffuse, less state-centered, and more likely to emerge from the developing world and hereto geostrategically insignificant regions on the global periphery. Because of this new political economy of danger, nowhere can be safely left alone; policy-makers make direct connections between conflict on the Afghan–Pakistan frontier and the threat of terrorism in Britain.[27] National security concerns, which may previously have been considered internal issues, became tied to a more expansive international security agenda. And this new agenda has expanded from a more limited concern for the high politics of states towards a growing interest in the 'low politics' of society and, specifically, development processes and governance within the 'Third World'.

Fourth, related to these developments was the emergence of the concept of human security as a challenge to traditional state-centric models of 'hard' security. This notion involved a greater focus on the security and welfare of populations within states, captured in the idea of 'freedom from want and freedom from fear'.[28] This framework questioned the traditional reliance on military forms of intervention to achieve international security. Human security implied a much greater and more active role for citizens and civil society organisations in the security field. It has also blurred established boundaries between the humanitarian, development, and security fields, drawing humanitarian and development NGOs into complex interventions encompassing a wide range of objectives (stabilisation, peace-building, development, humanitarian) and a diverse collection of state, non-governmental, and private actors. Associated with the growth of liberal peace-building has been the emergence of new strategic complexes, global assemblages, or 'epistemic communities' involving complex interrelations between state and non-state, public and private, for-profit and not-for-profit agencies.[29] These further blur the boundaries between the internal and external and throw up important questions related to accountability and the tension between private interests and public good.

This changing understanding of security threats produced a shift in the responses of Western states towards internal conflict from geopolitics to biopolitics. Global governance became more concerned with threats from populations than from states and, therefore, targets these populations in the global South through a range of ameliorative measures including development and humanitarian assistance, civil society support, citizen diplomacy, and more. This framework denotes a 'radicalisation of development', involving a more comprehensive model of societal transformation and a growing focus on conflict issues.[30] These concerns were reflected in the peace-building approaches pursued by Western governments and the UN that increasingly framed peace as an outcome of the simultaneous pursuit of conflict resolution, neoliberal development, and democratisation,[31] and aimed not only to resolve existing conflicts, but to prevent new ones by addressing root causes and in so doing transforming states and societies.

Fifth, the changing nature of international intervention reflected a subtle redefinition of state sovereignty. The commitment to the principles of reciprocity between nations, self-government, and non-intervention that characterised the Cold War eroded quickly in its aftermath. Sovereignty was seen less as a set of rights to be weighed against the right to intervention and was instead increasingly framed as conditional upon upholding certain standards of behavior.[32] These changes were captured in the International Commission on Intervention and State Sovereignty's 'Responsibility to Protect' report, in which sovereignty was seen as dependent upon the state's capacity to protect and provide for populations.[33] The associated rise in 'ethical interventions' that accompanied these ideological developments was also motivated by Western governments' need to boost moral authority and legitimacy at home.[34]

Sixth, linked to all of the above trends, the interventionary model has increasingly emphasised 'multitrack diplomacy' and bottom-up approaches to peace-building. Civil society is assigned a particular role (on the assumption that it constitutes an autonomous sphere separate from the state and private sectors) to promote an enabling environment for peace and reconciliation. This search for bottom-up or more 'emancipatory' approaches to liberal peace-building has been associated with critiques of the top-down and often militarised nature of many contemporary peace operations.[35]

Assessments of liberal peace-building's legitimacy and effectiveness vary radically, as they do regarding the specific role of NGOs within this enterprise. Realists argue that such interventions paradoxically freeze and extend the duration of conflicts by preventing the transformatory effects of military victory from taking place.[36] Critical theorists contend that liberal interventionism is thinly disguised imperialism serving to extend and entrench Western capitalist interests in the global South.[37] Liberals essentially support liberal peace-building, but argue it needs to be pursued more effectively and with greater commitment.[38] Each position leads to different assessments of NGOs, because they are associated with diverging assumptions (implicit or explicit) about the relationships between violent conflict, globalisation, state and non-state public action. Realists are skeptical about the usefulness of soft power and the leverage or legitimacy of NGOs. For them, 'international security' is shaped less by universal norms than the hard security interests of powerful states. Critical theorists, drawing on a Foucauldian analysis, tend to view transnational public action as an extension of the interests of dominant Powers. Universal norms relating to rights, democracy, and peace are part of and help extend this hegemonic order. NGOs are therefore involved in processes of pacification, in which they are seen to be at the forefront of efforts to turn socially and politically peripheral groups into subjects fit for governance.[39] In this sense, NGOs are little more than the 'handmaidens of governmentality'. The 'self association and political will formation characteristic of civil society and non state actors do not stand in opposition to the political power of the state' but has become a central feature of how power operates in contemporary society.[40] The liberal position is more sympathetic to NGO claims of comparative advantage because it is tied to a belief in a more limited role for the state and the transformative potential of civil society. Universal norms are seen to be important and constitutive of power, influencing the choices and behavior of leaders and societal groups caught up in conflict. NGOs as the advocates of such norms (including non-violence) are thus seen to play a number of positive roles in relation to peace-building processes.

NGO involvement in international security issues is not an entirely new phenomenon. The faith-based traditions that informed the work of many NGOs provided a strong normative orientation towards peace work, with Quaker and Gandhian organisations particularly involved.[41] These non-governmental approaches were linked to a peace studies tradition, which argued that strategies to end conflict needed to address not only the needs of the key parties in the conflict but also the 'human needs' of populations or 'structural inequalities' of society.[42] These strategies advocated shifting from a 'conflict management' model that focused on resolving conflict through elite-level negotiations towards a 'conflict transformation' paradigm.[43] Heavily influenced by the work of John Paul Lederach, this perspective posited that building peace relied on a broad portfolio of measures simultaneously focused on top (track one), middle-range (track two), and grassroots leadership (track three).[44] This broad consensus papered over latent tensions inherent in NGO peace-building strategies; for example, between the goal of ending violent conflict and the aim of building just societies. These more emancipatory versions of peace-building pioneered and promoted by NGOs had an important normative influence on developing international peace-building efforts after the Cold War.

Reflecting the broadening notion of 'security' and the profusion of donor efforts to tackle violent conflict, NGO peace-building roles have developed considerably in recent years. They can be divided into five main areas: complementing track-one negotiations; building a more peaceful and prosperous society; policy work designed to improve understanding of and responses to the dynamics of peace and conflict; fostering popular support for peace; and support for justice, rights and reconciliation. These approaches are underpinned by different underlying theories of change, some of which are in tension with one another. Whereas the first area of engagement assumes that 'key people' are the primary drivers of peace-building (without engaging warlords or political leaders, peace cannot be generated), the fourth assumes that mass movements, or constituencies for peace, can play a defining role in the transition from war to peace.[45] Arguably both approaches can be criticised on the grounds that they present an agent-centered and voluntaristic view of power, which ignores the political economy dimensions of peace-building and the way that personal and popular interests intersect with structural factors.

The last twenty years have seen both a rapid growth in international mediation efforts, and a diversification in the kinds of actors involved in mediation. A multidimensional or 'third-generation' model of mediation has emerged, which involves bolstering elite-level 'track-one' negotiations with unofficial peacemaking efforts and the use of incentives and disincentives.[46] Contemporary peace processes typically involve a range of actors including bilateral states, the UN, regional organisations, and NGOs. A number of international NGOs like the Humanitarian Dialogue Centre (HDC), Interpeace, the Community of Sant'Egidio, and International Alert have become engaged in directly facilitating track-one peace negotiations (engaging directly with the leaders of negotiating parties) as well as facilitating informal discussions between other conflict actors, including those excluded from the track-one talks, mid-level leaders, or local actors. National and local NGOs have also played a role in supporting track-one negotiations and in mediating conflicts at the local level. One of the most famous examples came in Aceh, where HDC engineered a 'humanitarian pause' in 2000. Although this ceasefire quickly broke down, HDC is widely credited with building trust amongst key individuals from both sides of the conflict, which underpinned the successful peace agreement facilitated in 2005 by another NGO, the Crisis Management Initiative. The case highlights some NGO strengths and weaknesses in this area; although identifying and responding quickly to a window of opportunity when it occurred, HDC was unable to wield the carrots and sticks needed to sustain the ceasefire.[47]

The scope for NGOs to perform these high-level peace-making roles is largely determined by geopolitics. NGOs tend to be more significant in areas that have less strategic significance to the West such as Aceh (HDC) and Sierra Leone (International Alert). In regions of greater geostrategic importance, such as Bosnia, state and interstate actors (and non-state military actors) tend to monopolize negotiations. NGOs in such cases tend to focus their efforts on the societal level to create an 'enabling environment' for peace-building. Arguably the zenith of NGO mediation at the track-one level has passed: the growing influence of Asian Powers such as China, India, and Iran, all less comfortable with external engagement and more concerned with protecting state sovereignty, places tighter limits on the extent to which Western Powers and their non-governmental allies can exert influence on peace-making.

As the scope and number of international interventions in conflict-affected regions grew in the 1990s, the capacity for humanitarian and development aid to prolong or exacerbate violence became more widely recognised. Humanitarian and development NGOs began to develop 'conflict-sensitive' approaches to deal with these issues. These were supported by operating frameworks such as Mary Anderson's 'Do No Harm' model (determining means by which NGOs could identify and minimise the negative impacts of their work in conflict settings) and the Peace and Conflict Impact Assessment Tool (providing a comprehensive means of anticipating, monitoring, and evaluating how an intervention affects peace and conflict dynamics).[48] Therefore a growing number of multimandate relief and development NGOs have developed programming approaches that explicitly target the 'root causes' and dynamics of violent conflict. This work is based on the assumption that tackling underlying socioeconomic causes of conflict may contribute in the long term to peace-building processes. Working on human security at the community level, with sensitivity to the distributional effects of relief and development aid, may address insecurities and grievances that fuel violent conflict. Capacity building, 'empowerment', and fostering social cohesion within civil society are seen as important peace-building NGO functions.[49] In a post-conflict context, NGO programs may be seen by donors as significant vehicles for delivering a peace dividend; during the Sri Lankan peace negotiations of 2002–06, increased funding was channeled through NGO programs in the northeast with this objective. Furthermore, NGOs may be viewed by international peace-keepers as effective agents of 'stabilisation', taking them into increasingly sensitive programmatic areas in places like Iraq and Afghanistan. The simultaneous pursuit of multiple goals (humanitarian needs, development, peace, justice) within the same organisation or within one peace-building operation has exposed severe tensions, particularly for multimandate NGOs. For example, to what extent does engagement in peace-building compromise neutrality and, therefore, the ability to pursue humanitarian goals? Does the pursuit of justice potentially undermine efforts to consolidate peace? What values and objectives should be given priority and who makes the decision?

A growing number of specialist peace-building organisations combine field-based activities with policy work designed to influence governments and multilateral institutions. Organisations such as International Alert, Saferworld, and Conciliation Resources seek to influence government policy in peace-building and conflict, implement a range of peace-building programs, and improve existing knowledge and understanding about peace-building issues. NGOs have played a leading role in a number of highly successful global advocacy campaigns like the International

Campaign to Ban Landmines and efforts to ban cluster munitions led by the Cluster Munitions Coalition. Many of these roles have been closely linked to the growing activism of middle Powers such as Norway, Canada, and Sweden. Norway's role as a specialist mediator since the 1990s has been supported by the field experience and expertise of a range of Norwegian NGOs. This cooperation was underpinned by a process of 'elite circulation', in which individuals moved between government agencies and research and field-based NGOs.[50] Similarly, the success of NGO advocacy campaigns such as the International Campaign to Ban Landmines relied heavily on support from the political leadership of middle Powers.[51] A number of NGOs have been involved in developing systems designed to prevent conflict by detecting the early escalation of conflict. Established in 1997, the Forum on Early Warning and Early Response sought to establish a global network of organisations committed to observing the Caucasus, the Great Lakes Region of Africa, and West Africa. Other organisations like the International Crisis Group seek to prevent conflict by combining an extensive global network with an influential board capable of mobilising world policy-makers into action.

NGOs and NGO coalitions have been active in promoting peace in a range of interstate and internal conflicts. The Stop the War Coalition, for example, led a campaign against Britain's military involvement in Iraq and Afghanistan. NGO-led peace campaigns have played an important role in a number of conflict-affected countries. 'Peace Now', an Israeli NGO, took a prominent role in promoting peace among the Israeli population. The Women of Liberia Mass Action for Peace proved critical during the peace talks that successfully ended the Liberian civil war in 2003. Hence NGOs are seen to have an important socialization and educative function, countering radicalisation and building wider constituencies for peace. The scope for NGOs to perform this role is heavily contingent both on the historical relationship between state and non-state arenas and on the composition and character of civil society or the NGO sector in any given context.

Although a traditional divide exists between NGOs working on peace and rights, this division has become increasingly blurred as humanitarian and development organisations extend their mandates to incorporate rights and protection. Moreover, many human rights groups explicitly connect their work to peace-building, arguing that the absence of peace is rooted in the absence of justice. Within this broad sphere, there are many different actors and positions, and the tensions between specialist peace and rights groups continue; on the ground, a division of labor often emerges, with the former working on community-level reconciliation processes and the latter speaking out against human rights abuses and for processes of accountability and truth telling.

Measuring the impact of NGO peace-building interventions is extremely challenging. First, processes of peace-building are extremely politicised and complex, typically occurring over a long period and involving numbers of domestic and external actors. This complexity creates attribution issues and difficulties in determining causality, something exacerbated by the growing NGO tendency to collaborate with broad 'strategic complexes' of state, non-governmental, and private actors. Second, NGOs work at a number of levels, making it difficult to determine claims about their impact. Some organisations seek to resolve or manage conflict at the local level, whereas others aim to build peace 'writ large' at the national or regional levels. Third, little consensus exists about what success looks like because different NGOs pursue dissimilar peace-related goals. Whereas some NGOs pursue the narrow goal of containing violence, others desire to transform social and political relationships. These problems are compounded by NGOs often expressing their normative and causal objectives in vague and general terms, a tendency often driven by a need to hedge their bets in environments where donors' funding priorities are liable to shift.[52] Both the critics of NGOs working in conflict and proponents of NGO peace-building have tended to overstate the level of impact that NGOs can have on peace and conflict. The resources controlled by NGOs are typically small compared with other elements of war economies, such as illegal trade. Consequently, they are 'unlikely to be a leading edge in moving towards or consolidating peace', although they can play a vital support role when judiciously implemented.[53]

Some contexts may be more conducive to NGO peace-building than others. 'Peace-building space' is dependent on several factors including the causes of hostility, the local capacities for change, and the scope of the international response. The kind of role NGOs can play is heavily determined by the historical relationship between the state and civil society. As a recent case study of the Sri Lankan peace process has found, Sri Lanka's civil society historically played a role heavily dependent on the patronage of the state. As the ceasefire broke down, although many donors and activists were keen for NGOs to be more politically active, NGOs found it difficult to inhabit or influence the political arena after the election of a government broadly opposed to a negotiated settlement and international engagement.[54]

In recent years, humanitarian and development NGOs have played a growing role in hyper-politicised interventions such as Afghanistan and Iraq, where NGOs are explicitly seen as 'force multipliers' for the intervening Powers; they are seen by the populations on the receiving end of such interventions as little more than 'mendicants of empire'.[55] NGOs' comparatively high levels of legitimacy with local populations have made them appealing partners in a new stabilisation agenda that seeks to win the 'hearts and minds' of local populations and reduce the control and legitimacy of armed groups or extremists. These interventions have prompted considerable debates and dilemmas within the humanitarian community. NGOs' close working relationships with military-led interventions, such as the International Security Assistance Force in Afghanistan, or security-driven governmental programmes like AFRICOM (US Africa Command) in Kenya, have eroded the perceived independence of these NGOs and made them more vulnerable to extremist attacks.[56] Whereas some continue to work within or alongside military actors, others have spoken out openly about the threat these relationships pose to humanitarian space.[57]

Much of the current debate on liberal peace-building centers on questions of local agency. Critical theorists interpret liberal peace-building as 'empire in denial' or a 'hegemonic' project that seeks to 'spread the values and norms of dominant power brokers'. They often see NGOs as part of a broader process wherein international actors have been responsible for hollowing out development states by providing services that had previously been the domain of government, helping to erode links between the state and the population.[58] Such perspectives also ignore the potential for local actors, working alongside or in cooperation with more powerful ones, to undermine, renegotiate, or reinterpret the agendas of international actors. There has been growing concern with understanding these processes of renegotiation, whereby local actors may generate 'hybrid' forms of peace.[59]

The extent to which NGOs and civil society are considered capable of contributing to these hybrid or 'post-liberal' models of peace-building depends on the degree to which they are deemed capable of resisting liberal peace-building agendas. Years of heavy international intervention in countries such as Sri Lanka and the Occupied Palestinian Territories have changed the character of civil society, leading to the dominance of a group of local organisations whose 'DNA is western'.[60] Much of the literature on local and national NGOs describes their capacity of working closely with donors and aligning their priorities with donor programs whilst pursuing their own agendas.[61] Thus, Sri Lanka's Sarvodaya Shramadana Movement, a national NGO with Gandhian and Buddhist roots, received major donor funding. Seen by donors as useful in building popular support for the Sri Lankan peace process and in its capacity to implement a range of community-based peace-building projects, Sarvodaya performed both roles. At the same time, however, it pursued its own vision of peace derived from nationalist and spiritual understandings of peace and development. Although donors allowed a degree of reinterpretation during the relatively stable part of the ceasefire period, tensions between these two approaches emerged as the ceasefire began to break down.[62] It suggests that although opportunities for hybrid versions of peace can arise under certain circumstances, these openings may be fleeting.

Growing NGO involvement in peace-building can partly be understood as a search for profile and market share, which provokes questions about the voluntary and norm-based ethos of such organisations. In the humanitarian marketplace where there are many sellers (aid agencies) and few buyers (donors) it is perfectly rational for aid agencies to act like competing private companies: rent-seeking, information-hoarding, and failing to coordinate.[63] Hard interests tend to trump declared soft interests.[64] In unruly aid markets like Afghanistan and Iraq or post-tsunami Sri Lanka, little difference often exists between the behavior and motivations of NGOs and private-sector companies. Arguably, NGOs are symptomatic of a trend towards the marketisation and privatisation of the public sphere,[65] leading to questions about their legitimacy in helping adjudicate disputes in the absence of a clear legal and ethical framework to take on such a role.

NGO engagement in peace-building has been associated with broader changes in the composition and characteristics of civil society in conflict-affected regions. In various regions where international actors have provided significant amounts of funding to support peace processes (the Occupied Palestinian Territories, Nepal, and Sri Lanka) various studies highlight a professionalisation of the NGO sector.[66] These trends have often been associated with depoliticisation: NGO peace-building in these contexts characterised by a technical, project-based approach that distances organisations from indigenous modes of civil society. In these same cases, NGOs' increasingly close association with governmental donors and their highly interventionist agendas have spawned crises of legitimacy.[67] As the recent ceasefire agreement in Sri Lanka broke down, for example, NGO support of the peace process and their heavy reliance on foreign funding made them prime targets for nationalist political groups keen to critique the heavily internationalised peace process.[68]

On the other hand, far from escaping from politics, the non-governmental label or arena can provide certain groups and individuals with means of doing politics in a political environment where this would otherwise be impossible. In Sri Lanka, again, a number of NGO leaders and organisations have kept questions relating to constitutional change and human rights on the political agenda in a way that would have been impossible if they engaged in formal politics. Furthermore, in many contexts, the divide between state and non-state actors is more blurred and dynamic than either the advocates or critics of NGOs allow. The same actors frequently cross institutional boundaries between the state, private, and non-governmental sectors. In Afghanistan, for instance, many key ministerial positions are occupied by ex-NGO leaders and, when they lose these positions, they frequently return to the NGO or private sectors.[69]

After a period in the 1980s and 1990s characterised by a mounting confidence in NGO capacity to foster political change and perform an expanded array of technical roles, NGOs experienced something of a backlash in the 2000s. Criticism focused on three main areas: growing scrutiny and skepticism about NGOs' effectiveness and performance; questions surrounding NGO legitimacy and accountability; and growing concerns about the close relationships between NGOs and their governmental funders.[70] This broader crisis has been reflected in the field of peace-building. Critical theorists highlight how civil society interventions can represent an escape from and a rejection of the democratic accountability associated with the political realm.[71] They argue that more powerful actors manipulate NGOs to legitimise peace-building interventions that prioritise hard security interests at the expense of the human needs and welfare concerns of local populations.[72] NGO expansion into peace-building is seen as a strategy to capture new sources of donor funding.[73] It is argued that NGOs have become more responsive to international donors than to the communities they aim to serve and represent, forming part of a new globalised comprador elite that ignores indigenous forms of civil society at the expense of NGOs that conform to Western organisational patterns.[74]

Although these criticisms have much validity, a more nuanced picture than outright condemnation or unquestioning championing of NGOs exists. There is certainly a need for more in-depth and comparative research on NGO roles in this arena, but current evidence points to the need for policy-makers and analysts to lower their expectations about NGO potential to engineer peace. Case studies suggest that they may play a role in supporting preexisting trends towards peace, but they have limited capacity to challenge wider power structures and conflict dynamics. There is also a need to understand domestic politics and the complex ways in which legitimacy is mobilized in these contexts. Only by developing a clear understanding of these processes of legitimation and delegitimation can appropriate NGO peace-building roles in any given context be identified. This analysis also highlights the importance of timing; sudden shifts in the political arena can change the rules of the game and the legitimacy or otherwise of particular positions. Developing a detailed understanding of the broader dynamics of the political arena is also therefore required to identify spaces and moments that are conducive to NGO involvement. NGOs have emerged as important actors in international security and, although their significance varies from place to place, they will continue for better or for worse to be influential. The question is not whether to intervene but how to do it more effectively.[75]

Notes

1 M. Howard, *The Invention of Peace: Reflections on War and International Order* (New Haven, CT, 2001).
2 J. Galtung, *Peace by Peaceful Means: Peace and Conflict, Development and Civilization* (Oslo, 1996).
3 J. Heathershaw, 'Unpacking the Liberal Peace: Dividing and Merging of Peacebuilding Discourses', *Millennium*, 36 (2008), 604.
4 Ibid.
5 Ibid.
6 M. Barnett, H. Kim, M. O'Donnell, and L. Sitea, 'Peacebuilding: What's in a name?', *Global Governance*, 13(2007), 35–58.
7 G. Clarke, *The Politics of NGOs in South-East Asia: Participation and Protest in the Philippines* (London, 1998), 2–3.
8 R.L. Bryant, *Nongovernmental Organisations in Environmental Struggles: Politics and the Making of Moral Capital* (New Haven, CT, London, 2005).
9 O. Richmond, *Peace in International Relations* (London, 2008).
10 A. Cooley and J. Ron, 'The NGO Scramble: Organizational Insecurity and the Political Economy of Transnational Action', *International Security*, 1(2001), 5–39.
11 C. Agg, 'Trends in Government Support for Non-Governmental Organizations: Is the "Golden Age" of the NGO Behind Us?', Civil Society and Social Movements Programme Paper Number 23 June 2006, United Nations Research Institute for Social Development, *Yearbook of International Organizations* (Geneva, 2006).
12 M. Lindenberg and C. Bryant, *Going Global: Transforming Relief and Development NGOs* (Bloomfield, CT, 2001), 3.
13 T. Carroll, *Intermediary NGOs: The Supporting Link in Grassroots Development* (West Hartford, CT, 1993); M. Edwards and David Hulme, *NGOs, States and Donors: Too Close for Comfort?* (Basingstoke, 1997).
14 K.D. Reimann, 'Up to No Good? Recent Critics and Critiques of NGOs', in O. Richmond, and H. Carey, eds., *Subcontracting Peace: The Challenges of NGO Peacebuilding* (Aldershot, 2005); Agg, 'Trends in Government Support'.
15 Edwards and Hulme, *NGOs*.
16 OECD, 'Table 2. Total Net Flows from DAC Countries by Type of Flow', *Statistical Annex of the 2009 Development Co-operation Report* (Paris, 2008).
17 Edwards and Hulme, *NGOs*; N.A. Zaidi, 'NGO Failure and the Need to Bring Back the State', *Journal of International Development*, 11(2001), 259–71.

18 See, for instance, Stephen Jackson, 'The State Didn't Even Exist: Non-Governmentality in Kivu, Eastern DR Congo', in J. Igoe and T. Kelsall, eds., *Between a Rock and a Hard Place* (Durham, NC, 2005), 170; Roland Hodson, 'Elephant Loose in the Jungle: The World Bank and NGOs in Sri Lanka', in Hulme and Edwards, *NGOs*.

19 M. Duffield, *Global Governance and the New Wars* (London, 2001); J. Goodhand, *Aiding Peace? The Role of NGOs in Armed Conflict* (Boulder, CO, 2006).

20 Goodhand, *Aiding Peace?*

21 J. Fisher, *The Road From Rio. Sustainable Development and the Nongovernmental Movement in the Third World* (New York, 1993); L. Salamon, 'The rise of the non-profit sector', *Foreign Affairs*, 73 (Summer 1994):109–22.; Edwards and Hulme *NGOs*.

22 See B. Boutros-Ghali, *Report on the Work of the Organisation from the Forty-Seventh to the Forty-Eighth Session of the General Assembly* (New York, 1993).

23 Human Security Centre, 'Human Security Report 2009/2010: The Causes of Peace and the Shrinking Costs of War' (Burnaby, BC, 2010).

24 Ibid.

25 M. Kaldor, *New and Old Wars: Organized Violence in a Global Era* (London, 2001).

26 See White House, *The National Security Strategy of the United States of America* (Washington, DC, 2002); Government of Great Britain. *A Strong Britain in an Age of Uncertainty: the National Security Strategy* (London, 2010).

27 M. Duffield, *Development, Security and Unending War* (Oxford, 2007).

28 UN Development Programme, *Human Development Report, 1994*.

29 Duffield, *Global Governance*.

30 Ibid.

31 M. Pugh and N. Cooper, *War Economies in a Regional Context: Challenges of Transformation* (Boulder, CO, 2004).

32 D. Chandler, 'The responsibility to protect? Imposing the 'Liberal Peace'', *International Peacekeeping*, 11(2004), 59–81.

33 International Commission on Intervention and State Sovereignty, *The Responsibility to Protect: Report of the International Commission on Intervention and State Sovereignty* (Ottawa, 2001).

34 D. Chandler, 'Rhetoric Without Responsibility: the attraction of 'ethical foreign policy'', *British Journal of Politics and International Relations*, 5 (August 2003), 295–16.

35 R. MacGinty, 'Hybrid Peace: The Interaction Between Top-Down and Bottom-Up Peace', *Security Dialogue*, 41(2010), 391; O. Richmond, 'Resistance and the Post Liberal Peace', *Millennium*, 38 (2010), 665–92; D. Roberts, *Liberal Peacebuilding and Global Governance: Beyond the Metropolis*, (London, 2010).

36 E.N. Luttwak, 'Give war a chance', *Foreign Affairs*, 78 (December 1999), 36–44.

37 Duffield, *Global Governance*; Chandler, 'Liberal Peace'.

38 R. Paris, 'Saving Liberal Peacebuilding', *Review of International Studies*, 36(2010), 337–65.

39 Duffield, *Global Governance*.

40 O. Sending and I. Neumann, 'Governance to Governmentality: Analyzing NGOs, States, and Power', *International Studies Quarterly*, 50(2006), 651–72.

41 T. Woodhouse, 'Conflict Resolution and Ethnic Conflict', Bradford, Department of Peace Studies Working Paper (Bradford, 1994).

42 E. Azar and J. Burton, eds., *International Conflict Resolution: Theory and Practice* (Boulder, CO, 1986); J. Galtung, *Peace by Peaceful Means: Peace and Conflict, Development and Civilization* (Oslo, 1996).

43 O. Richmond, 'A Genealogy of Peacemaking: The Creation and Re-Creation of Order', *Alternatives: Global, Local, Political*, 26(2000), 3.

44 J. Lederach, *Building Peace: Sustainable Reconciliation in Divided Societies* (Washington DC, 1997).

45 M. Anderson, *Do No Harm: Supporting Local Capacities for Peace thorough Aid* (Cambridge, MA, 1996).

46 Richmond, *Peace In International Relations*.

47 K. Huber, 'The HDC In Aceh: Promises and Pitfalls of NGO Mediation and Implementation', *Policy Studies*, 9(Washington, DC, 2004).

48 Anderson, *Do No Harm*.

49 T. Paffenholz and C. Spurk. 'Civil Society, Civic Engagement, and Peacebuilding', Conflict Prevention and Reconstruction, Paper No. 36 (October 2006).

50 T. Tvedt, 'International Development Aid and Its Impact on a Donor Country: A Case Study of Norway,' *European Journal of Development Research*, 19(2007), 614–35.

51 J. Davis, 'The Campaign to Ban Landmines: Public Diplomacy, Middle Power Leadership and an Unconventional Negotiating Process', *Journal of Humanitarian Assistance*, (2004); N. Short, 'The Role of NGOs in the Ottawa Process to Ban Landmines', *International Negotiation*, 4(1999), 481–500.

52 O. Walton, 'Between War and the Liberal Peace: National NGOs, legitimacy and the politics of peacebuilding in Sri Lanka 2006–7'. (Doctoral Dissertation, University of London, 2010).

53 Goodhand, *Aiding Peace?*

54 O. Walton, with P. Saravanamuttu, 'In the balance? Civil society and the peace process 2002–8', in J. Goodhand, J. Spencer, and B. Korf, eds., *Caught in the Peace Trap?* (London, 2010).

55 A. Donini, 'The far side: the meta functions of humanitarianism in a globalised world', *Disasters*, 34(2010), S220–37.

56 M. Bradbury and M. Kleinman, *Winning Hearts and Minds? Examining the Relationship Between Aid and Security in Kenya* (Medford, MA, 2010).

57 L. Olson, L., 'Fighting for Humanitarian Space: NGOs in Afghanistan', *Journal for Military and Strategic Studies*, 9(2006).

58 M. Duffield, 'Governing the Borderlands: Decoding the Power of Aid', *Disasters*, Volume 25, Issue 4 (2001), 308–20.

59 J. Goodhand and O. Walton, 'The Limits of Liberal Peacebuilding: International Engagement in the Sri Lankan Peace Process' *Journal of Intervention and Statebuilding*, Volume 3, Issue 3 (2009), 303–23; Richmond, 'Resistance'; MacGinty, 'Hybrid Peace'.

60 MacGinty, 'Hybrid Peace', 399.

61 Richmond, 'Resistance'.

62 Walton, 'Between War and the Liberal Peace'.

63 Cooley and Ron, 'NGO Scramble'.

64 De Waal, *Famine Crimes: Politics and the Disaster Relief Industry in Africa* (Bloomington, IN, 1997).

65 S. Kamat, *Development Hegemony: NGOs and the State in India* (Oxford, 2002).

66 See I. Jad, 'NGOs: between buzzwords and social movements', *Development In Practice*, Vol. 17, Numbers 4–5 (2007); C. Heaton Shrestha, ' "We will not take a single rupee from any donor organisation": exploring the changing conceptions and practices of civil society in Nepal', Paper presented at CLE/CCS Conference, European Development Aid and NGOs: Changing Notions of Civil Society in 'North' and 'South', 12–14 March 2008; S Liyanage, 'The Rise of "Peace" Professionals in Sri Lanka: Rent-Seeking in the peace sector', *Groundviews*, (15 March 2007).

67 Walton, 'Balance?'

68 Ibid.

69 D. Lewis, 'The failure of a liberal peace: Sri Lanka's counter-insurgency in global perspective', *Conflict, Security and Development*, 10(2010), 647–71.

70 I. Smillie, *The Alms Bazaar: Altruism under fire—Non-Profit Organizations and International Development* (London, 1995); H. Slim, 'By What Authority? The Legitimacy and Accountability of Non-governmental Organisations', ICHRP Working Paper (2002); Edwards and Hulme, *NGOs*.

71 D. Chandler, 'Building Global Civil Society "From Below?"', *Millennium*, 32(2004).

72 D. Chandler, 'Race, Culture and Civil Society: Peacebuilding Discourse and the Understanding of Difference', *Security Dialogue* 41(2010), 369.

73 B. Challand, *Palestinian Civil Society: Foreign Donors and the Power to Promote and Exclude* (New York, 2009).

74 Ibid.; S. Hanafi, and L. Tabar, *The Emergence of a Palestinian Globalized Elite: Donors, International Organizations and Local NGOs* (Jerusalem, 2005).

75 S. Woodward, 'Do The Root Causes of Civil War Matter? On Using Knowledge to Improve Peacebuilding Interventions', *Journal of Statebuilding and Intervention*, Volume 1, Issue 2 (2007), 143–70.

38

Soft power

Overcoming the limits of a concept

Kostas Ifantis

Since the end of the Cold War and the subsequent 'opening' of the international system, the pursuit of national interests through traditional hard power has come under intense scrutiny. Using military force on foreign soil has in particular been criticised; and the high-profile examples of Iraq and Afghanistan provide fuel to arguments that such an approach cannot succeed in the complex tasks of nation-building and fighting terrorism. Within this context, the concept of 'soft' power has increasingly been advanced as an alternative or complementary approach. The concept of soft power was introduced by Joseph S. Nye in 1990.[1] He argued that the United States was not only the strongest nation-state in military and economic terms, but also in soft power, that is the capacity to influence other nations to identify American interests as their own. In 2001 with The Paradox of American Power, he placed soft power in the context of a broader argument about multilateralism.[2] And then, in 2004, with *Soft Power: The Means to Success in World Politics*, he provided an in-depth treatise, defining the concept as 'the ability to get what you want through attraction rather than coercion or payments', an ability which 'arises from the attractiveness of a country's culture, political ideals, and policies.'[3] For Nye, soft power is much more than image, public relations, and ephemeral popularity. It constitutes very real power: an ability to gain objectives.

Nye's works on the soft power have achieved great authoritative stature, with a visible impact on American foreign policy as well as on that of other countries. His terminology and concepts are indispensable for analysis of and discourse about this subject. In his definition, there are at least two salient points: soft power falls within the usual conceptions of power; and culture is a new source of power. Nye divides the 'power' to achieve desired ends into three general categories: coercive with threats, inducing with payments, or cooptive. The information age has greatly expanded the effectiveness of the third category and extended the mobility of information and propaganda. Nye's core argument is that soft power resources are increasingly important in the modern age, and it is extremely foolish to ignore them or (with acts of arrogance) heedlessly squander them.

Soft power contrasts with hard power (the use of military and economic force to make others change their position). Understood as resting on inducements or/and threats, hard power is not always a necessary or desirable strategy. Sometimes a Power can achieve its goals without military and economic threats or payoffs by exercising that ability to influence events through persuasion and attraction. Nye uses the analogy of three-dimensional chess played on a stack of three boards. On the top military board, the United States is the only Power with international reach. But even on this level, there are regional and local Powers with enough armed strength to make it difficult for the Americans to act militarily in those regions and localities; China and Russia are the most obvious examples. On the middle board of economic interests, power is multipolar. On vital issues like trade, anti-trust, and financial regulation, agreement must be obtained from the European Union (EU), Japan, and other economic Powers if Washington is to achieve its various objectives. The bottom board is inhabited by diverse issues such as terrorism, international crime, climate change, and the spread of infectious disease. Obviously lacking a unipolar dimension, the bottom board sees power widely distributed and chaotically organised among state and non-state actors.[4] As Nye argues:

> many political leaders still focus almost entirely on military assets and classic military solutions— the top board. They mistake the necessary for the sufficient. They are one-dimensional players in a three-dimensional game. In the long term, that is the way to lose, since obtaining favorable outcomes on the bottom transnational board often requires the use of soft power assets.[5]

Of course, Nye shows that these boards are not mutually exclusive. With relationships and overlaps amongst the various forms of power, distinctions can be fuzzy:

> If I am persuaded to go along with your purposes without any explicit threat or exchange taking place—in short, if my behavior is determined by an observable but intangible attraction—soft power is at work. Soft power uses a different type of currency—not force, not money—to engender cooperation—an attraction to shared values and the justness and duty of contributing to the achievement of those values. ... Command power—the ability to change what others do—can rest on coercion or inducement. Co-optive power—the ability to shape what others want—can rest on the attractiveness of one's culture and values or the ability to manipulate the agenda of political choices in a manner that makes others fail to express some preferences because they seem to be too unrealistic.[6]

Soft power in international politics arises from such nebulous but very real factors like dominant values, internal practices and policies, and the manner of conducting international relations. The states more likely to be attractive and gain soft power in the information age are those with multiple channels of communications that help frame issues; those whose dominant culture and ideas are closer to prevailing global norms (which now emphasise liberalism, pluralism, and autonomy); and those whose credibility is enhanced by their domestic and international values and policies.[7] Many crucial soft-power resources are outside the control of governments (unlike hard power) and their effects depend heavily on receptive audiences. Moreover, soft-power resources often work indirectly by shaping the policy environment and, sometimes, take years to produce desired outcomes; of course, soft power has also occasionally achieved quick results.

As noted above, the attractiveness of a country's culture and how that culture is perceived abroad are among the key foundations of soft power. However, part of the problem is that culture is difficult to define, making it all but impossible to produce a quantified, cost–benefit analysis of cultural spending. Culture is much more than state-funded, brick-and-mortar institutions such as museums, opera houses, and libraries; it encompasses varied matters ranging from cuisine to television programming to fashion. By its nature, culture is never permanent but constantly evolving and, because it is universal rather than narrowly parochial, it is a significant source of soft power. American popular culture is central to Nye's thinking. From McDonald's to Hollywood movies to the heavy American flavor of the internet, United States culture has influence worldwide; and pop culture may be even more powerful than high culture because it can be seen as transmitting on a wide scale 'American values' that are open, mobile, individualistic, anti-establishment, pluralistic, voluntaristic, populist, and free. Although America's pop culture resonates widely in Europe, the Americas, South and East Asia, and more, some resentment and envy attaches to its strength and success. Some is an unavoidable resentment of the United States as the primary driving force of modernity and globalisation that threatens traditional cultures and established vested interests. Global culture flows into the United States and, if successful, is repackaged and commercialised for the rest of the world. That the entire world contributes to modern global culture is obvious but frequently forgotten, hence, in a sense, the United States is often a convenient scapegoat for those that resent some aspects of change.

What is also forgotten is that soft power, and particularly culture as soft power, is often something over which governments have little control but with which they must reckon. In democracies like the United States, soft power is not government-controlled. Although Washington cannot censor the libertine attitudes and sexuality displayed in Hollywood movies that offend Islamic nations, this uncensored exuberance is precisely the source of the inherent attractiveness of American culture. That soft power is determined by civil society does not render it immaterial for public diplomacy. Also relevant is the lure of the American style of government, widely esteemed for its freedoms and for the opportunity it offers immigrants. Domestic policies can have an impact on soft power. Efforts to promote human rights and democracy have enhanced American influence, whereas capital punishment and weak gun control laws have undermined it, especially in Europe. Apparent military, economic, and soft-power influence abroad can both enhance and hinder soft power.

The substance and style of foreign policy is also a powerful factor. Policies based on broadly shared values are more likely to attract cooperation. Federalism, democracy, and open markets were the widely shared values on which the Western Cold War alliances were built. Shared values in the twenty-first century include international order, control of weapons of mass destruction, inhibiting terrorism and illicit drugs, and promoting trade, economic growth, and environmental causes. 'Soft versus hard power' is a false dichotomy. In one estimation, 'neither the advocates of soft power nor the proponents of hard power have adequately integrated their positions into a single framework to advance the national interest.'[8] However, what soft power can accomplish is significant, varied, and even surprising. Although the hard variety remains crucial in an anarchic world of Powers and non-state groups (like terrorist organisations ready and willing to use mass and indiscriminate violence), soft power can be ever more important in preventing such groups from recruiting supporters, and for dealing with transnational issues that require multilateral cooperation. For Nye:

> all power depends on context—who relates to whom under what circumstances—but soft power depends more than hard power upon the existence of willing interpreters and receivers. Moreover, attraction often has a diffuse effect, creating general influence rather than producing an easily observable specific action.[9]

Yet, soft power often grows out of hard power. At a domestic level, power has always consisted of both hard and soft elements; governments need a social base. Legitimacy is not built only through coercive power, it is also based on authority, and, flowing from legitimacy and authority, culture. Attractive cultures enjoy tangible foreign-policy gains. China's spectacular Beijing Olympics in 2008 exemplify soft power as the continuation of hard power by other means. In political practice, soft and hard power are intimately linked. Soft power cannot be understood in isolation; rather, it needs to be understood in terms of hegemony and domination. Otherwise, the approach misses the reason why it matters in the study of international politics: 'It constrains by shaping upstream rather than coercing later'.[10] For instance, international aid is a form of hard, not soft power. It creates dependency, and when it is withdrawn, the effects are felt keenly.

Hard power is of little use with a range of today's security challenges: nuclear proliferation, jihadism, collapsed states, refugees, piracy, suicide bombers, and 'black swan' (high-impact, difficult to foresee, and usually outside customary expectations) events. Because these challenges might be better met by using soft power, two examples present themselves: Washington's effort to contain Iran's nuclear weapons program; and its desire for regime change in Cuba. In the case of Iran, neither economic bans nor political attacks have achieved American aims. In fact, the embargoes and criticism have helped Iran become more self-reliant. It is actually doing better than many Powers that have depended on American assistance. Teheran has upheld oil production quotas set by the Organization of Petroleum Exporting Countries; the Government remains financially sound; and trade and investment with the rest of the world continue. In fact, Iran's economy is healthier than in the early 1990s, with high surpluses, record currency reserves, and making foreign debt payments on time.[11] Respecting Cuba, the international community has been critical of the United States, especially since the passage of the 1996 Helms-Burton Act, which tightened American sanctions against the Island. Canada, Mexico, France, and Britain are major investors in Cuba and are particularly critical of the legislation. These key American allies see Helms-Burton as an extraterritorial attempt to bully sovereign nations into assuming a particular foreign-policy position, and they threatened to bring the case before the World Trade Organization (WTO) before reaching a tenuous last-minute understanding. Still, the EU vows to fight on at the WTO.

The unilateralism demonstrated with Helms-Burton devolves from the United States eminence in the post-Cold War international order. However, the feasibility of American unipolarity and hegemony can be misleading because the international power structure is complex and multilayered. Whereas the United States has unprecedented military strength, economic power is widely shared with Europe and East Asia. Within the realm of a booming world of transnational relations, much lies outside Washington's control. When the United States pursues heavy-handed, unilateral foreign policy, it weakens its political preponderance and ability to shape the global politics.

Thus, foreign perceptions of the United States have declined considerably in the past few years as a result of various unpopular international American actions. From refusing to accede to a variety of international treaties to the conflict in Iraq, the Americans have pursued their own interests despite widespread foreign objections. Hence, President George W. Bush's repudiation of the Kyoto Protocol was widely criticised; and American failure to participate in the International Court of Justice was a further abstention from multilateral cooperation. This substantial loss of soft power has high costs economically, militarily, and diplomatically. Whereas the American people and their culture continue to be viewed favorably, the United States Government is regarded with growing disapproval and finds it ever more difficult and costly to achieve its objectives. When pursuing national interests, one needs to be constantly aware that choices are to be made both about how broadly or narrowly those interests are defined and with what means they are pursued. Because soft power depends on the currency of attraction rather than force or payoffs, it is subject to how objectives are framed: 'Policies based on broadly inclusive and far-sighted definitions of the national interest are easier to make attractive to others than policies that take a narrow and myopic perspective'.[12]

By binding itself to the outside world through multilateral treaties and agreements, Nye admits, the United States may lose some freedom of action. Nevertheless, it gains far more by securing other Powers as predictable and cooperative partners. And Institutions must be seen as enhancing a country's soft power by shaping international rules, norms, and regimes that are consistent with its interests and values; its actions will more likely be 'enforced' by legitimacy and willing acceptance.[13] Supporting democracy and human rights, for example, can help make American policies attractive to others when these values appear genuine and are promoted in a fair-minded way.

Whilst emphasising the importance of spreading democracy in the Middle East, the Bush Administration abjured being held back by institutional constraints.[14] In that sense, it advocated the soft power of democracy, but focused more on substance than process. By downgrading the legitimacy that comes from institutional processes where others are consulted, it squandered American soft power by failing to appreciate all its dimensions.[15]

All power has limits, and soft power is no exception. Cultural features may be attractive in Asia but repulsive in the Middle East. A blind spot within soft power is the confusion over its source. There seems to be a tendency to call anything attractive 'soft power'. However, whether attractiveness 'can become soft power depends on the policy objective itself, of course, and also policy aims and context and the methods employed.'[16] It is problematic that soft power views things from the perspective of the party exercising influence. From the viewpoint of the party being influenced, the question of whether accepting direction accords with its interests is likely a far more important consideration than the attraction of power. Sovereign nations act not on the basis of likes and dislikes but in harmony with their own interests. No matter how attractive a given country may be, others will not accept its attractive power if it obstructs their freedom of action or adversely affects their economic interests.[17] Again, justness and legitimacy in the exercise of power are often an issue. 'Soft power arises from the attractiveness of a country's culture, political ideals, and policies. When policies are seen as legitimate in the eyes of others, a country's soft power is enhanced'.[18]

However, legitimacy will be an issue regardless of whether power is hard or soft. Within the international community, the exercise of military and non-military power is basically the same, or rather, when the power is military in nature, there is a need for strict legitimacy in its use. But whereas military power can exert a coercive influence, however vague, its legitimacy, when the justification for using soft power is tenuous, can prompt the party on the receiving end to resist. That is why it can be problematic to regard the legitimacy of soft power as the source of its clout. In the same context, an important question is what constituent elements comprise soft power, and what are the precise indices for quantifying it. Art, movies, anime, ideas, ideology, language, and education are often cited as concrete examples of soft power. However, regarding cultural attributes as sources of soft power implies approval of the commercialisation of culture and linking it with the power structure. Linking language with the concept of power is tantamount to confusing language as a means of communicating ideas with the ideas that are communicated. Moreover, scholarship and culture are by rights independent of political power. Very often, they are a means of resisting authority. Even if the arts or scholarship have the potential to serve as one facet of power, there remain serious doubts as to whether it is acceptable for governments to use them:

> … it is clear that soft power as an actual political theory is loaded with ideology and riddled with contradictions and hypocrisy. Religion and ideology, for example, are seen by some as potent examples of soft power. Looking back through history, however, one cannot fail to notice that whenever religion and ideology have spread around the world, they have invariably been accompanied by military might. History teaches us that soft power needs to be backed by hard power, and this is something that many soft power theorists are now recognising.[19]

It is possible, therefore, to see soft power as no more than a means of rationalising the exercise of hard power. Describing the use of military force as a 'war on terror' could be regarded as a deft use of soft power. Tying the use of force to the ideology of a righteous struggle against terrorism is a means of legitimising military action undertaken without the consent of the international community. To put it another way, soft power can be a subtle way of rationalising military action that lacks international legitimacy by bringing into play the concept of good and evil.

In this light, although there is much that soft power can accomplish when used appropriately, there is also much that it cannot do: 'the fact that the USA makes good films is probably good for its image generally ... but the connection with American influence is not obvious.'[20] Many people like American values, American society, even American people; but this does not mean they like American policy.[21] For example, government policies have a powerful impact on foreign perceptions of the United States. Some have both positive and negative effects. Patriarchal societies feel threatened by libertine influences that engage their young. Many peoples are attracted by American prosperity, but fear the lack of security and resent the income inequality of the relatively free market system. Moreover, the substance and style of domestic polices have an impact on foreign perceptions. Along with the earlier mentioned policies on gun control and capital punishment, stricter visa procedures and suspicions of Muslims after 9/11 have hurt the American image. Vocal criticism of Islamic beliefs by some Christian clerics has provided grist for anti-American propaganda mills in Muslim nations.Domestic political interests are frequently too strong and fervent to be swayed by criticism from abroad, but the connection between domestic policies and foreign perceptions can certainly have an impact on American public diplomacy.

Ultimately, if soft power is to be regarded as important, its main precondition is legitimacy. Legitimacy allows one to set the agenda, define a crisis, and mobilise support for policies among both countries and non-state forces. 'There is, first and foremost a legitimacy that comes from sustaining the international order. If the USA is seen by others as the guarantor of the international system or the ultimate guarantor of security and if its actions are seen as contributing to sustaining order they will be accepted as legitimate'.[22] Success is also a great legitimiser. A country acquires influence not so much by its own achievements, as by the conviction that these achievements can be turned into success for someone else.[23] The third and most important source of legitimacy is a respectful participation in international institutions. 'The United Nations [UN] remains the most important source of legitimacy because of the (sometimes contradictory) aspirations and norms it represents, because of its established place in the international legal framework but above all because it is a forum in which everyone has a voice'.[24] However,

> a country may be respected and trusted, as for example Norway is; this will bring it influence but not, when the chips are down, power. American supremacy in hard power on the other hand gives it equally enormous potential for soft power. If you want to exercise soft power you must have something to offer – a recipe for success, resources to help others get there, and probably armed force to protect them on the way. Hard power begets soft power.[25]

Soft power has a Chinese pedigree in the form of the seventh-century thinker Lao-Tzu. Well before Washington, Beijing embraced soft power as a prominent part of its comprehensive national power (CNP).[26] Alongside the growth of economic and military resources, Chinese elites have concluded that the development of soft power is a critical element of achieving long-term strategic objectives.[27] The People's Republic of China (PRC) officially stresses China's national identity and the influence over other neighburing countries through the power of its own culture.[28] China is an emerging power but, for now, it prefers to rise quietly and inconspicuously, pursuing foreign-policy aims through soft power. China's grand strategy is currently discussed with reference to a 'peaceful rise', 'peaceful development', or the building of a 'harmonious world'. In more specific terms, three stages have been identified in the process of China's rise: first, by 2010, establish a leading position in East Asia, symbolised by the opening of the China–ASEAN free trade zone; second, by 2020, play a leading role as a 'quasi-world power' in the larger Asia–Pacific region; and, third, by 2050, develop into a 'world-level power'.[29] Reaching these stages is inextricably linked to the growth of China's CNP.[30] The hope is that through soft power, China can achieve its most important goals at the regional and global level to mitigate the 'China threat theory,' earn the understanding of the international community, and enhance support for China's peaceful development and rise to a global Power status.

Soft power has not been elaborated as a competitive tool in itself; nor have the ways in which forms of soft and hard power may be used as parts of more complex foreign-policy strategies been explicated. However, from the conceptual level of soft power as a rubric of CNP, the discourse has evolved into a detailed examination of specific ways through which China's broader ambitions can be achieved:

> First is the project of transmitting traditional Chinese culture to foreign actors, by means of Confucius Institutes and other activities; second is a focus on China's leadership in the developing world and, especially, the use of economic incentives to develop diplomatic goodwill; and third are means through which the PRC may be able to reassure neighboring states and others that its strategic intentions are benign and that it is behaving as a 'responsible great power'.[31]

As far as Chinese culture is concerned, it is defined as an amalgam of Confucian social and political values, folk and high customs, art, and the Chinese language. In that sense, it is widely considered a core component of China's soft power. Its promotion is based on state-run initiatives and state-funded programs that could be regarded as mainstream cultural diplomacy; and it involves efforts to raise the stature and appeal of Chinese civilisation and culture both within the region and in the wider world. It includes cultural and academic exchanges, artistic exhibitions, 'cultural years,' and more, with great attention paid to education: 'Studying Chinese language, history, and culture is viewed not only as a way to engender respect for China, but also as a way to cultivate a pool of foreign talent that will be better equipped to form personal ties with Chinese counterparts.'[32]

Soft-power development to counter the 'China threat' theory has proceeded as a series of tangible programs at three levels. Globally, as a permanent member of the UN Security Council, China has supported efforts to achieve common peace and security. Since 2005, its track record of participation and credible promises in the WTO demonstrate that it is committed to maintaining the international financial status quo. Emphasis has also been placed on other policies that underwrite Beijing's image as a 'responsible Great Power.' At the regional level, Beijing's role in the six-party talks with North Korea has been interpreted as a way for China to bolster its image as a Power interested in the peaceful resolution of threats to international security, despite its historical ties with and narrow security interests touching Pyongyang. And Beijing's efforts following the 1997 Asian financial crisis to support monetarily the governments of Thailand, Indonesia, Malaysia, and others was heralded as an indication of China's benign leadership role.

In the same context, Chinese grand strategy to establish a leadership position in the developing world has been a major priority aimed at both earning 'traditional' diplomatic capital (and securing access to scarce natural resources) whilst stressing at the same time the principle of non-interference. Within this discourse, three mechanisms to enhance China's influence in the developing world have been emphasised: its 'development style', which aims to avoid high social and environmental costs; 'stability'; and 'harmony' (to minimise damage in relations among individuals, society, and the environment and between states). In this context, specific attention has been paid to the notion of a 'Beijing Consensus', which stresses political stability and the flexibility of states to choose a development path based on experimentation and the peculiarities of specific situations. The problem with this notion is that 'due to deficiencies in its own reform process',[33] China's ability to offer an attractive model to emulate is limited.

The second, more promising, mechanism is 'economic diplomacy'. Current foreign aid practices have evolved in ways that facilitate positive ties and minimise friction as a result of China's growing economic involvement in far-flung regions. Africa is a case in point. China's emblematic search for cooperative relations in Africa is symbolised by the establishment in 2000 of the Forum on China–Africa Cooperation, through which Beijing channeled development aid and proceeded with debt-forgiveness policies.[34] Over the past 20 years in particular, trade, aid, and investment have flowed between China and Africa in ever greater volumes. In 2000, bilateral trade for the first time exceeded US$10 billion. By 2008, it reached US$106.8 billion. Twenty African countries now have trade of more than US$1bn with China. Oil from Angola, Sudan, the Democratic Republic of the Congo, and Equatorial Guinea is exported to China, and aid has principally taken the form of development through construction of infrastructure (dams, railways, bridges, and airports). It could be argued that China places its involvement in Africa within a 'South–South' framework, stressing solidarity between developing countries based on respect for sovereignty and non-interference in the internal affairs of its partners. This stance is attractive to African leaders such as Zimbabwe's Robert Mugabe, who have no appetite for lectures from Westerners. China has also sought to propagate its own past as one of peaceful exploration, cooperation, and trade with Africa through the centuries, in contrast with Western imperialism.

More recently, however, China's emergence as a major global player has placed a strain on its solidarity-based approach. With increased influence comes increased responsibility, including the responsibility to criticise the domestic affairs of other countries. China's changing approach to the Darfur conflict in 2004–08 is illustrative. Initially, China was reluctant to breach its principle of non-interference and jeopardise its considerable commercial interests in oil-rich Sudan. But by early 2007, it felt responsible enough, and conscious of its role as a major world Power, to support a UN resolution to deploy peacekeepers to Darfur, albeit with Sudanese consent. And in early 2008, the year of the Beijing Olympics, China's desire to be seen as a responsible Power resulted in informal attempts to persuade Khartoum to heed UN resolutions. China stopped short of advocating compulsion or sanctions, but it no longer observes strict 'non-interference'. In the past, the Chinese would have dismissed a humanitarian crisis such as Darfur as the domestic business of a sovereign country. Today, the combination of an increased (and, thus, threatened) economic stake with a rising sense of international presence has dragged China into active intervention.

The EU remains one of the most unusual and widest-ranging global political actors. Although it has had its share of difficulties, setbacks, and failures, the same holds true of any other global actor. The EU has engaged in a continual process of institutional growth in a wide policy domain, produced some notable policy outputs, and positively influenced various global issues. It has been described as a civilian Power, a soft Power and, more recently, a normative Power.[35] In the literature, normative power encompasses economic, social, diplomatic, and cultural instruments as opposed to military means. Moreover, 'normative' implies a strong linkage to international law and institutions because they represent the most universal 'normative boundary' within which policy is to be assessed. EU enlargement shows a commitment to peace, freedom, and prosperity that has not only served well the six original founding nations, but has continued to stand as an alluring beacon to successive waves of new member-states and aspiring candidates.

Europe is the closest competitor to the United States in terms of soft power. European art, literature, music, design, fashion, and food have long served as global cultural magnets; and in terms of specific resources, France ranks first in Nobel prizes for literature; Britain is first and Germany second in attracting asylum applications; France, Germany, Italy, and Britain have higher life expectancy rates than the United States; almost all European countries outrank the United States in overseas development assistance as a percentage of gross domestic product; and, although much smaller, Britain and France each spend about the same as the US on public diplomacy.[36] EU soft power comes from its common values, namely the principles of democracy, rule of law, social justice, human rights, and commitment to a market economy, plus social solidarity, sustainable development, and the fight against discrimination. At the same time, in the past few years, Europe has quietly been rebranding itself to make political capital out of global anti-Americanism. Where America seems to have reverted to an evangelical Protestantism under-written by George W. Bush and the Republican Party, Europe offers itself as a secular oasis. Where United States forces are used to assert an international Pax Americana, Europe has borrowed Nye's idea to present itself as a connoisseur in the art of soft power. Bogged down in Iraq, America has acquiesced in Europe having its way over Iran, and it has politely exited the ring, occasionally cheering on British, French, and German efforts to find a diplomatic solution.[37]

Aside from its enlargement process, the EU contributes to global governance norms through its leading role on global climate change, international law, and human rights treaties, and in assisting poorer, less developed countries. Given its size, the EU is the largest donor of development aid, providing 56 percent of total global flows; and it leads in the fields of sustainable development, environmental awareness, and tackling climate change. Moreover, showing a strong commitment in encouraging multilateralism, the EU is party to over 700 global, regional, association, and cooperation agreements.

With its arsenal of calibrated relationships, from cooperation and free trade agreements to full membership in its own organisation, the EU exercises immense soft power. Because its institutions and policies have yielded useful lessons for troubled areas of the globe, the EU possesses a strong power of attraction and attempts to lead by example rather than force. In fact, its deliberate efforts to export novel processes and forms of cooperation, governance, and integration comprise, perhaps, its most important soft-power resource.[38] In one assessment, 'without excluding recourse to military force as an instrument of last resort in a messy world where conflicts are, alas, expected to persist for long, the EU will continue to operate essentially as a civilian power—hopefully, a civilian power with a clear voice, more self-confidence and effective instruments at its disposal'.[39] Enlargement has proven to be one of the most important instruments for European security. It reflects the EU essence as a civilian power, extending the area of peace, prosperity, liberty, and democracy, and achieving more through its gravitational pull than it could ever have done with a stick or sword.[40] The process undertaken by national applicants to join the EU entails a long and comprehensive process of reform. Moreover, the processes of institutional development directly result in greater policy integration and, therefore, contribute to the EU's impact on important global problems.

Soft power is nothing new. But it is also difficult to distinguish between soft and hard power when instances of the latter, such as nuclear weapons, can produce soft power. It could be argued that it is pointless to opt for either hard or soft power. They are not mutually exclusive strategies; rather, different conditions lend themselves to different approaches:

> Advocates of soft power and public diplomacy tend to frame their arguments poorly; their positions are often politically naïve and institutionally weak. Meanwhile, hard power pro-ponents, who are politically and institutionally powerful, frequently frame their arguments inadequately because they seem to believe they can safely ignore or simply subsume elements of national power that lay outside their traditional purview. The consequence is that the national interest is being badly served by an imperfect, dichotomous debate.[41]

That line of reasoning has resulted in a strong drive to reconceptualise power in the context of the unifying multidimensional 'smart' power. The quest for smart power reflects an American conviction that the hard power, unilateralist policies of the Bush Administration severely compromised United States diplomatic and security interests, provoked unprecedented international resentment, and greatly diminished America's global position. Not surprisingly, the foolish use of power has provoked a smart-power countermovement.[42]

Another reason to search for smart power is that target populations have become 'smarter'. With the steady spread of secondary and higher education and the availability of more media outlets, Asian, African, and Latin American populations have grown more affluent, more sophisticated, and less easily influenced by the exercise of soft or hard power. Spreading democratic practices have meant that foreign leaders also are less inclined to act as American surrogates and recipients of American power and influence.[43] In 2006, the Center for Strategic and International Studies (CSIS) launched a bipartisan Commission on Smart Power to develop a vision for America's global engagement.[44] Its report laid out recommendations for how the United States President, regardless of political party, could implement a smart power strategy; power neither hard nor soft, but the skilful combination of both. According to CSIS, 'it is an approach that underscores the necessity of a strong military, but also invests heavily in alliances, partnerships, and institutions at all levels to expand American influence and establish the legitimacy of American action.'[45] The United States must become shrewder by again investing in the global good, providing things that people and governments in all quarters of the world want but cannot attain in the absence of American leadership. Specifically, the United States should focus on five critical areas: alliances, partnerships, and institutions; global development; public diplomacy; economic integration; and technology and innovation. By complementing its military and economic might with greater soft-power investments, America can build the framework needed to tackle tough international challenges.

To achieve these objectives, the implementation of a smart power strategy will require a strategic reassessment of how the American Government is organised, coordinated, and budgeted. Going beyond the report's recommendations, a conceptually robust and policy-relevant framework for smart power should first take account of the target over which one seeks to exercise influence, its internal nature and broader global setting. Smart power also requires the wielder to know what its country seeks, as well as its will and capacity to achieve those goals. And strong awareness of the broader regional and global context within which the action will be conducted is essential, whereas how and when the tools are to be used should be subject to firm strategic analysis.[46] Smart power means knowing the strengths and limitations of each hard and soft instrument, the circumstance in which it is to be used, and how to combine the elements of coercion with the power to persuade and inspire emulation: 'Finally, a genuinely sophisticated smart power approach comes with the awareness that hard and soft power constitute separate and distinct institutions and institutional cultures that exert their own normative influences over their members, each with its own attitudes, incentives, and anticipated career paths'.[47] The effectiveness of any foreign policy is ultimately a matter of power and politics. In democracies, priorities are set by elected political leaders, and smart power in foreign policy rests on their savvy as much as it draws on concepts, however robust.[48]

Moving forward, smart power must begin with the assumption that hard power is essential and the national interest is best advanced by combining hard power and soft. Given the complexity of the issues (conceptual, institutional, political, and cultural) smart power will not be easy to achieve, especially in the short term. There are structural imperatives at play and a generational adjustment with which to be reckoned. As Wilson has observed,

> To launch this long march, smart power advocates need to become more sophisticated at soft power and communicate their message more convincingly. Public diplomacy services are

superb at telling everyone's story but their own. ... Soft power advocates need to be more convincing that their particular strengths can advance the national well-being, and be much more Machiavellian about how to do so. The hard power advocates need to be willing to admit publicly what they readily admit in private at conferences and side conversations: good diplomacy can prevent bad military conflicts.[49]

Notes

1 Joseph S. Nye, Jr, *Bound to Lead: The Changing Nature of American Power* (New York, 1990).
2 Joseph S. Nye, Jr, *The Paradox of American Power: Why the World's Only Superpower Can't Go It Alone* (New York, 2002).
3 Joseph S. Nye, Jr, *Soft Power: The Means to Success in World Politics* (New York, 2004), 9.
4 Ibid., 4.
5 Ibid., 5.
6 Ibid., 7.
7 Ibid., 31.
8 E.J. Wilson III, 'Hard Power, Soft Power, Smart Power', *Annals of the American Academy of Political and Social Science*, 616(2008), 110.
9 Nye, *Soft Power*, 16.
10 A. Bohas, 'The Paradox of Anti-Americanism: Reflection on the Shallow Concept of Soft Power', *Global Society*, 20(2006), 410.
11 T. Bohorquez, 'Soft Power', UCLA International Institute: www.international.ucla.edu/print.asp?parentid=34734.
12 Nye, *Soft Power*, 35.
13 Ibid., 10.
14 See E. El-Din Aysha, 'September 11 and the Middle East Failure of US "Soft Power": Globalisation contra Americanisation in the "New" US Century', International Relations, 19(2005), 193–210.
15 Joseph S. Nye, Jr, 'Soft Power and European-American Affairs', in T.L. Ilgen, ed., *Hard Power, Soft Power and the Future of Transatlantic Relations* (Aldershot, 2006), 30.
16 Y. Watanabe, 'Revisiting Soft Power' (2006): www.cgp.org/popups/articleswindow.php?articleid=342.
17 K. Ogoura, 'The Limits of Soft Power' (2006): http://www.cgp.org/popups/articleswindow.php?articleid=341.
18 Nye, 'Soft Power and European-American Affairs', 26.
19 Ogoura, 'Soft Power'.
20 R. Cooper, 'The Goals of Diplomacy: Hard Power and Soft Power', in D. Held and M. Koenig-Archibugi, eds., *American Power in the Twenty-First Century* (Cambridge, 2004), 169.
21 Bohas, 'Paradox', 399.
22 Cooper, 'Goals of Diplomacy', 175.
23 Ibid., 176.
24 Ibid., 178.
25 Ibid., 176.
26 A.L. Vuving, 'How Soft Power Works', Paper presented at the panel "Soft Power and Smart Power", American Political Science Association Annual Meeting, Toronto (3 September 2009), p. 2.
27 J. Wuthnow, 'The Concept of Soft Power in China's Strategic Discourse', *Issues & Studies*, 44(2008), 5.
28 I. D'Hooghe, 'Public Diplomacy in the People's Republic of China', in J. Melissen, ed., *New Public Diplomacy* (New York, 2007), 95.
29 Z. Bijian, 'China's Peaceful Rise to Great-Power Status', *Foreign Affairs*, Volume 84, Number 5(2005), 18–24.
30 CNP was developed in the 1980s as an analytical construct through which progress in China's overall power position could be tracked and measured against other states. See Wuthnow, 'Soft Power', 6.
31 Ibid., 9.
32 Ibid., 10. As of 2006, there were over 140,000 foreign students studying in China, about 75 percent of whom were from East Asian countries. At the same time, there are initiatives undertaken outside the PRC. Here, the most obvious example has been the establishment of 'Confucius Institutes,' which are centers for the teaching of Chinese language and culture sited in universities around the world. The goal

has been that, by 2010, there will be 500 such institutes in operation. More broadly, by 2010, the Chinese Government estimates that there will be as many as 100 million students learning the Chinese language. See Kyoungtaek Lee, 'Towards a New Framework for Soft Power: An Observation of China's Confucius Institute', (2010): https://journal.hass.tsukuba.ac.jp/interfaculty/artcle/view/3/5.

33 Wuthnow, 'Soft Power', 16.

34 Ibid., 17.

35 N. Tocci, 'Profiling Normative Foreign Policy: The European Union and its Global Partners', CEPS Working Document No. 279 (December 2007), 1.

36 Nye, 'Soft Power and European-American Affairs', 30–31.

37 James Harkin, 'Soft Power', Guardian (28 January 2006).

38 R.H. Ginsberg and M.E. Smith, 'Understanding the European Union as a global political actor: Theory, practice and impact', European Union Studies Association, Montreal (17–19 May 2007), 4.

39 L. Tsoukalis, 'Global, Social and Political Europe', ELIAMEP Seminar on Global, Social and Political Europe, Nafplion, Greece (28 June-1 July 2007), 5.

40 'Enlargement as an instrument of the EU's soft power', Speech by EU Commissioner Olli Rehn, Brussels (19 October 2007): www.europa-eu-un.org/articles/en/article_7417_en.htm.

41 Wilson, 'Hard Power, Soft Power', 110–11.

42 Ibid., 113.

43 Ibid.

44 Center for Strategic & International Studies, A Smarter, More Secure America (Washington, DC, 2007).

45 Ibid., 7.

46 Wilson, 'Hard Power, Soft Power', 115.

47 Ibid., 116.

48 Ibid., 118.

49 Ibid., 122.

Bibliography

Official Documents

African Union. *Protocol on Amendments to the Constitutive Act of the African Union* (adopted in Addis Ababa, 3 February 2003 and Maputo, 11 July 2003) (Addis Ababa, 2003).
——. *Protocol Relating to the Establishment of the Peace and Security Council of the African Union* (adopted in Durban, 9 July 2002) (Addis Ababa, 2002).
Alianza Alternativa para los Pueblos de Nuestra América. *ALBA Impulsa lanzamiento del sucre como nueva moneda del sur* (3 March 2009).
——. *Conceptualizacion de proyecto y empresa grannacional en el marco del ALBA*, VI (24–26 January 2008): http://alternativabolivariana.org/modules.php?name=News&file=article&sid=2668#5.
——. *Declaracion Final De La Primera Reunion Cuba-Venezuela Para La Aplicacion De La Alternativa Para Las Americas* (27–28 April, 2005).
——. *Acuerdo entre el presidente de la Republica Bolivarina de Venezuela y el presidente del consejo de estado de Cuba para la aplicacion de la Alternativa Bolivariana para las Americas* (Havana, 2004).
Brazil, Government of. Ministério das Relações Exteriores. *A Inserção Internacional do Brasil: A Gestão do Ministro Celso Lafer no Itamaraty* (Brasília, 1993).
——. *A Inserção Internacional do Brasil: A Gestão do Ministro Celso Lafer no Itamaraty* (Brasília, 1993).
——. *Reflexões Sobre a Política Externa Brasileira* (Brasília, 1993).
Castro Ruz, Fidel. 'Speech Delivered at the United Nations in his Position as Chairman of the Non-Aligned Countries Movement' (12 October 1979): http://lanic.utexas.edu/la/cb/cuba/castro/1979/19791012.
China, Government of. Ministry of Foreign Affairs, *New Concept of Security Advocated by China* (Beijing, 2004).
Chinese Permanent Mission to the United Nations in Geneva. *New Concept of Security Advocated by China* (16 April 2004).
Czech Republic, Government of. Ministerstvo zahraničních věcí. *Zpráva o zahraniční politice České republiky za rok 2009* (Praha, 21 May 2010).
——. *Zpráva o zahraniční politice České republiky za rok 2008* (Praha, 4 April 2009).
——. *Czech Foreign Policy: Points of Departure, Principles, Interests and Objectives* (Praha, 12 August 1998): http://pdc.ceu.hu/archive/00002560/01/conc_basis.pdf.
European Council. 'European Security Strategy. A Secure Europe in a Better World' (2003), 1: www.consilium.europa.eu/uedocs/cmsUpload/78367.pdf.
European Union. 'Consolidated Version of the Treaty on the Functioning of the European Union', (9 May 2008).
European Commission, *The Euro@ten, Successes and Challenges after ten years of Economic and Monetary Union* (Brussels, 2008).
France, Government of. *Constitution de la République française, texte intégral de la Constitution de la Vème République à jour des dernières révisions constitutionnelles* (Paris, 2010).
——. *Défense et Sécurité nationale. Livre Blanc. Les Débats* (Paris, 2008).
——. *Les constitutions de la France de la Révolution à la IVème République*, (Paris, 2009).
——. *Livre Blanc sur la Défense et la Sécurité nationale* (Paris, 2008).
G8. 'Growth and responsibility in Africa, Summit Declaration', Heiligendamm, 8 June 2007: www.g-8.de/Content/DE/Artikel/G8Gipfel/Anlage/Abschlusserkl C3_A4rungen/ WV-afrika-en.html.

——. 'Growth and Responsibility in the World Economy, Summit Declaration', Heiligendamm (7 June 2007): www.g-8.de/Webs/G8/EN/G8Summit/SummitDocuments/ summit-documents.html.

——. Köln Charter: 'Aims and Ambitions for Lifelong Learning' (1999): www.g8.utoronto.ca/summit/ 1999koln/charter.htm.

Germany, Government of. Bundesregierung, 'Wachstum und Verantwortung—4Leitmotiv der deutschen G8-Präsidentschaft', (2007): www.g-8.de/Webs/G8/DE/G8Gipfel/Agenda/agenda.html.

Great Britain, Government of. *A Strong Britain in an Age of Uncertainty: the National Security Strategy* (London, 2010).

——. *Securing Britain in an Age of Uncertainty: The Strategic Defence and Security Review*, (London, 2010).

Great Britain Prime Minister, Cm 7953: *A Strong Britain in an Age of Uncertainty: the National Security Strategy* (London, 2010).

——. Cm 7948: *Securing Britain in an Age of Uncertainty: The Strategic Defence and Security Review*, (London, 2010).

International Monetary Fund. *IMF Board Approves Far-Reaching Governance Reforms* (Washington, DC, 2010).

——. *World Economic Outlook Update, Restoring confidence without harming recovery* (7 July 2010).

Japan, Government of. Ministry of Foreign Affairs.*Roshia ni okeru nihon senta no jigyō* (Tokyo, 2006).

Korea, Republic of. Ministry of Foreign Affairs and Trade. *ODA Korea* (2010): www.odakorea.go.kr/eng/ operations/Europe/Uzbekistan.php.

'Memorandum of Understanding Between the United States of America and the Union of Soviet Socialist Republics Regarding the Establishment of a Direct Communications Link; June 20, 1963': Avalon Project (Yale University Law School): www.yale.edu/lawweb/avalon/diplomacy/soviet/sov003.htm.

Netherlands, Government of the. Ministry of Foreign Affairs, *Turkey and the European Union: From association to accession*: www.sant.ox.ac.uk/ext/knicolaidis/sortedpubs.htm#EUenlargement.

Non-Aligned Movement. *Final Document, XV Summit of Heads of State and Government of the Non-Aligned Movement*, Sharm el Sheikh, Egypt, 1(11–16 July 2009).

——. *Final Document, 14th Summit Conference of Heads of State or Government of the Non-Aligned Movement*, Havana, Cuba (11–16 September 2006): NAM 2006/Doc.1/Rev.3.

——. 'Background, NAM Structure and Organization' (September 2001): www.nam.gov.za/background/ background.htm#1.1%20History.

——. *Conference of Heads of State or Government of Non-Aligned Countries, Programme for Peace and International Co-operation, Declaration as Adopted by the Conference*, NAC-II/Heads/5, Cairo (10 October 1964).

North Atlantic Council. 'Statement by the North Atlantic Council,' NATO Press Release PR/CP(2001) 122, 11 September 2001, www.nato.int/docu/pr/2001/p01–122e.htm.

North Atlantic Treaty Organisation. Parliamentary Assembly. *Russia, the West and the Future of Euro-Atlantic Security* (Brussels, 2009).

——. 'Informal NATO Defence Ministers Meeting, Warsaw,' 24–25 September 2002, www.nato.int/ docu/comm/2002/0209-wrsw.htm.

Obama, Barack. *Remarks by the President in Address to the Nation on the End of Combat Operations in Iraq* (Washington, DC, August 31, 2010).

Organisation for the Prohibition of Chemical Weapons. 'Chemical Weapons Convention: About the Convention: Genesis and Historical Development': www.opcw.org/chemical-weapons-convention/ about-the-convention/genesis-and-historical-development/.

——. *Convention on the Prohibition of the Development, Production, Stockpiling and Use of Chemical Weapons and on Their Destruction*: www.opcw.org/chemical-weapons-convention/download-the-cwc/.

Organization of the Petroleum Exporting Countries. *OPEC Statute* (Vienna, 2008).

——. *OPEC Annual Statistical Bulletin 2009*: www.opec.org/opec_web/en/data_graphs/330.htm.

People's Republic of China, Embassy in the United States of America. *Joint Military Exercises Testify New Concept of Security* (26 August 2005).

Perú, Ministerio de Relaciones Exteriores. *Un Líder sin Fronteras: Diplomacia Presidencial, 2001–2006* (Lima, 2006).

Robertson, George. 'Defence and Security in an Uncertain World,' Keynote Speech, Forum Europe, Brussels, 17 May 2002 www.nato.int/docu/speech/2002/s020517a.htm.

'Treaty on the Non-Proliferation of Nuclear Weapons', signed at London, Washington, and Moscow (1 July 1968), Article IX 2–3: http://www.fas.org/nuke/control/npt/text/npt2.htm.

United Nations. *Ranking of Military and Police Contributions to UN Operations* (2010): www.un.org/en/ peacekeeping/contributors/2010/june10_2.pdf.

———. *UN Mission's Contribution by Country* (New York, 2010): www.un.org/en/peacekeeping/contributors/ 2010/june10_1.pdf.

———. *Economic Commission for Latin America. The Economic Development of Latin America and Its Principal Problems* (New York, 1950).

United Nations General Assembly Sixth Special Session. 'Resolutions adopted by the General Assembly, 3201 (S-VI)', *Declaration on the Establishment of a New International Economic Order*, 2229th plenary meeting (1 May 1974).

United Nations Office at Geneva. 'Conference on Disarmament: Introduction to the Conference': www. unog.ch/80256EE600585943/%28httpPages%29/BF18ABFEFE5D344DC1256F3100311CE9? OpenDocument.

United States Agency for International Development, *Fragile States Strategy* (Washington: USAID, 2005).

United States Congress, Joint Congressional Committee on Inaugural Ceremonies. *Inaugural addresses of the presidents of the United States: from George Washington to George W. Bush* (Washington, DC, 2001).

United States Department of State. *Foreign Relations of the United States, 1958–1960, Volume VI: Cuba* (Washington, DC, 1991).

———. *Report on the International Control of Atomic Energy* (Washington, DC, 1946).

———. Office of the Historian. 'The Acheson-Lilienthal & Baruch Plans, 1946': http://history.state.gov/ milestones/1945–52/BaruchPlans.

United States, Government of. Office of the Secretary of Defense. *Annual Report to Congress: Military and Security Developments Involving the People's Republic of China 2010* (Washington DC, August 2010).

United States Senate Armed Services Committee, *Intelligence Community Annual Threat Assessment, Statement for the Record* (Washington, DC, 2008).

White House. *National Security Strategy* (Washington, DC, 2010).

———. *The National Security Strategy of the United States of America* (Washington, DC, 2002).

World Bank, *The East Asian Miracle: Economic Growth and Public Policy* (Washington DC, 1993).

Wörner, Manfred. 'Opening Statement to the NATO Summit Meeting,' London, 5 July 1990, www.nato. int/docu/speech/1990/s900705a_e.htm.

Books, Memoirs, Dissertations

Aburish, Said K. *Saddam Hussein* (London, 2000).

Adebajo, Adekeye and Raufu Mustapha, eds. *Gulliver's Troubles: Nigeria's Foreign Policy after the Cold War* (Scottsville, 2008).

Adebajo, Akekeye. *Liberia's Civil War: Nigeria, ECOMOG and Regional Security in West Africa* (Boulder, CO, 2002).

Ajami, Fouad. *The Arab Predicament, Arab Political Thought and Practice Since 1967* (Cambridge, UK, 1981).

Alade Fawole, W. *Nigeria's External Relations and Foreign Policy Under Military Rule (1966–1999)* (Ile-Ife, 2003).

Albright, M. *The Mighty and the Almighty* (Basingstoke, 2006).

———. *Madam Secretary* (New York, 2003).

Allain, J.-C., F. Autrand, L. Bély, P. Contamine, P. Guillen, T. Lentz, G.-H. Soutou, L. Theis, M. Vaïsse, *Histoire de la Diplomatie française* (Paris, 2005).

Alonso, Aurelio. *El laberinto tras la caída del muro* (La Habana, 2006).

Al-Otaiba, Mana Saeed. *OPEC and the Petroleum Industry* (London, 1975).

Alverez, Jose E. *International Organizations as Law-Makers* (Oxford, 2006).

Anderson, M.S. *The Origins of the Modern European State System, 1494–1618* (Harlow, 1998).

Anghie, Antony. *Imperialism, Sovereignty and the Making of International Law* (Cambridge, UK, 2004).

Anonymous. *Kim Il Sung Works*, Volume 26 (Pyongyang, 1989).

Anwar, Dewi Fortuna. *Indonesia in ASEAN: Foreign Policy and Regionalism* (Singapore, 1994).

Armstrong, D., L. Lloyd, and J. Redmond. *International Organizations in World Politics* (Basingstoke, 2004).

Aron, R. *Peace and War: A Theory of International Relations* (New York, 1966).

Asmus, Ronald. *Opening NATO's Door; How the Alliance Remade Itself for a New Era* (New York, 2002).

Asmus, Ronald, Stefan Czmur, Chris Donnelly, Aivis Ronis, Tomas Valasek, and Klaus Wittman. *NATO, New Allies and Reassurance* (London 2010).

Autret, Florence. *Sarkozy à Bruxelles* (Paris, 2008).

Bach, D.C., ed. *Regionalization in Africa: Integration and Disintegration* (Oxford, 1999).

Bibliography

Baker III James A. *The Politics of Diplomacy, Revolution, War and Peace, 1989–1992* (New York, 1995).

Bákula, Juan Miguel. *Perú: Entre la Realidad y la Utopía, 180 Años de Política Exterior*, Volume 1 (Lima, 2002).

Barber, P. *Diplomacy* (London, 1979).

Barnett, M. and R. Duvall, eds. *Power in Global Governance* (Cambridge, UK, 2005).

Barston, R.P. *Modern Diplomacy* (London, New York, 1988).

Baylis, John, James Wirtz, Eliot Cohen, and Colin S. Gray, eds. *Strategy in the Contemporary World*, third edition (Oxford, 2009).

Beck, Ulrich. 'The Terrorist Threat: World Risk Society Revisited,' *Theory, Culture and Society* Volume 19, Number 4(2002).

——. *World Risk Society* (Cambridge, 1999).

Bély, L., ed. *L'Europe des Traités de Westphalie: Esprit de la Diplomatie et Diplomatie de l'Esprit* (Paris, 2000).

Bély, L., G.-H. Soutou, L. Theis, M. Vaïsse, eds., *Dictionnaire des Ministres des Affaires étrangères 1589–2004* (Paris, 2005).

Bengtsson, R. *The EU and the European Security order: Interfacing Security Actors* (London, 2009).

Beramendi, P. and C. Anderson, *Democracy, Inequality and Representation* (New York, 2008).

Berger, Thomas U. *Cultures of Antimilitarism: National Security in Germany and Japan* (Baltimore, MD, 1998).

Bernard, Lewis. *The Emergence of Modern Turkey* (Oxford, 2001).

Berridge, G.R. *Return to the UN* (Basingstoke, 1991).

Berridge, G.R., M. Keens-Soper, and T.G. Otte, eds., *Diplomatic Theory from Machiavelli to Kissinger* (Basingstoke, 2001).

Berstein, Serge. *Chef de l'État. L'histoire vivante de 22 présidents à l'épreuve du pouvoir* (Paris, 2002).

Black, Jeremy. *Quest for Power: The World Order Since 1500* (London, 2007).

——. *Eighteenth Century Europe 1700–1789* (New York, 1990).

Blair, Tony. *A Journey* (London, 2010).

Blight, James G., Bruce J. Allyn and David A. Welch, eds., *Cuba on the Brink: Castro, the Missile Crisis, and the Soviet Collapse* (New York, 1993).

Bluth, Christoph. *Britain, Germany and Western Nuclear Strategy* (Oxford, 1995).

Bøås, Morten. *Governance, Leadership and Ownership: the Case of the African Development Bank and the Asian Development Bank 1979–1996* (Doctoral Dissertation, University of Oslo, 2001).

Bøås, Morten and Desmond McNeill, eds. *Global Institutions and Development: Framing the World?* (London, 2004).

Bøås, Morten and Desmond McNeill. *Multilateral Institutions—a Critical Introduction* (London, 2003).

Bobbitt, Philip. *The Shield of Achilles: War, Peace, and the Course of History* (New York, 2003).

Brasil Francisco de Holanda, Mauro. *O Gás no Mercosul: Uma Perspectiva Brasileira* (Brasília, 2001).

Braveboy-Wagner, Jacqueline Anne. *Institutions of the Global South* (London, 2009).

Bretherton C. and J. Vogler, *The European Union as a Global Actor*, 2nd edition (London, 2006).

Brummett, P. *Ottoman Seapower and Levantine Diplomacy in the Age of Discovery* (Albany, NY, 1994).

Bryant, R.L. *Nongovernmental Organisations in Environmental Struggles: Politics and the Making of Moral Capital* (New Haven, CT, London, 2005).

Bukh, A. *Japan's Identity and Foreign Policy: Russia as Japan's "Other"* (London, 2009).

Bull, H. *The Anarchic Society: A Study of Order in World Politics* (London, 1977).

Bulmer-Thomas, Victor. *The Economic History of Latin America Since Independence* (Cambridge, UK, 2003).

Bundy, McGeorge. *Danger and Survival: Choices about the Bomb in the First Fifty Years* (New York: 1988).

Burns, E.Bradford. *The Unwritten Alliance: Rio Branco and Brazilia-American Relations* (New York, 1966).

Burns, Richard Dean. *The Evolution of Arms Control: From Antiquity to the Nuclear Age* (Santa Barbara, CA, 2009).

Bussière, M., E. Pérez-Barreiro, R. Straub and D. Taglioni, *Protectionist Responses to the Crisis: Global Trends and Implications* (Frankfurt, 2010).

Bussmann, K. and H. Schilling, eds. *1648: War and Peace in Europe*, 3 Volumes (Münster, 1998).

Buzan, B. *From International to World Society? English School Theory and the Social Structure of Globalisation* (Cambridge, UK, 2004).

Byers, M. and G. Nolte, eds. *United States Hegemony and the Foundations of International Law* (Cambridge, 2003).

Calleo, David. *Follies of Power, America's Unipolar Fantasy* (Cambridge, UK, New York 2009).

Cameron, F. *US Foreign Policy after the Cold War: Global Hegemon or Reluctant Sheriff* (London, 2002).

Canani, Nev. *Política Externa no Governo Itamar Franco, 1992–1994* (Porto Alegre, 2004).

Cardoso, Fernando Henrique. *Discurso no Almoço com o Presidente do México na Fiesp* (São Paulo, 1999).

Carroll, T. *Intermediary NGOs: the supporting link in grassroots development* (West Hartford, CT, 1993).

Castro, Raúl. *El gobierno cubano insta al Presidente Obama a que sea consecuente con su compromiso en la lucha antiterrorista* (6 de octubre de 2010): www.cubadebate.cu/raul-castro-ruz/2010/10/06/el-gobierno-cubano-insta-al-presidente-obama-a-que-sea-consecuente-con-su-compromiso-en-la-lucha-antiterrorista/.

Center for Strategic & International Studies. *A Smarter, More Secure America* (Washington, DC, 2007).

Cervo, Amado Luiz and Clodoaldo Bueno, *História da Política Exterior do Brasil* (Brasília, 2002).

Chachavalpongpun, Pavin. *Reinventing Thailand: Thaksin and His Foreign Policy* (Singapore, 2010).

Charillon, F. *La France peut-elle encore agir sur le monde? Éléments de réponse* (Paris, 2010).

Chinawanno, Chulacheeb. 'Thai-Chinese Relations: Security and Strategic Partnerships', RSIS Working Paper, Number 155 (Singapore, 2008).

Chinvanno, Anuson. *Thailand's Policies towards China, 1949–1954* (Oxford, 1992).

Chomsky, N. *World Orders, Old and New* (New York, 1994); R.W. Merry, *Sands of Empire: Missionary Zeal, American Foreign Policy, and the Hazards of Global Ambition* (New York, 2005).

Chua, A. *Day of Empire. How Hyperpowers Rise to Global Dominance—And Why They Fail* (New York, 2007).

Clarke, G. *The Politics of NGOs in South-East Asia: Participation and Protest in the Philippines* (London, 1998).

Clarke, Michael. *British External Policy-making the 1990s* (London, 1992).

Clarkson, Stephen. *Does North America Exist? Governing the Continent after NAFTA and 9/11* (Toronto, 2008).

——. *Uncle Sam and US. Globalization, Neoconservatism, and the Canadian State* (Toronto, Washington, DC, 2002).

Claude, Jr., I.L. *Swords into Plowshares*, 4th edition (New York, 1984).

Clayton, Lawrence A. *Peru and the United States: The Condor and the Eagle* (Athens, GA, 1999).

Cleva, G.D. *Henry Kissinger and the American Approach to Foreign Policy* (London, 1989).

Clinton, Bill. *My Life* (New York, 2004).

Cogan, Charles. (with Nicolas Roussellier and Hubert Védrine). *Diplomatie à la française* (Paris, 2008).

Cohen, Eliot A. *Supreme Command: Soldiers, Statesmen, and Leadership in Wartime* (New York, 2003).

Cohen, Stephen P. *India: Emerging Power* (New Delhi, 2001).

Coker, Christopher. *Globalization and Insecurity in the Twenty-First Century: NATO and the Management of Risk.* Adelphi Paper Number 345 (London, 2002).

Cooley, Alexander. *Base Politics: Democratic Change and the U.S. Military Overseas* (Ithaca, NY, 2008).

Cooper, Andrew, Richard Higgott and Kim Richard Nossal, *Relocating Middle Powers: Australia and Canada in a Changing World Order* (Vancouver, 1993).

Cooper, A.F. *Niche Diplomacy: Middle Powers After the Cold War* (Basingstoke, New York, 1997).

Crabtree, John. *Peru under García: An Opportunity Lost* (Pittsburgh, PA, 1992).

Cuadros, Manuel Rodríguez. *Delimitación Marítima con Equidad: El caso de Perú y Chile* (Lima, 2007).

Cumings, Bruce. *Korea's Place in the Sun: A Modern History* (New York, 1997).

Daalder, Ivo H. and James M. Lindsay. *America Unbound: The Bush Revolution in Foreign Policy* (Washington, DC, 2003).

Dale, P.N. *The Myth of Japanese Uniqueness* (New York, 1986).

Danese, Sérgio. *Diplomacia Presidencial: História e Crítica* (Rio de Janeiro, 1999).

Daudelin, Jean. 'Trapped: Brazil, Canada and he Aircraft Dispute'. In Norman Hillmer, and Maureen Appel Molot, eds., *Canada Among Nations 2001: A Fading Power* (Toronto, 2002).

De Magalhães, J.C. *The Pure Concept of Diplomacy* (New York, 1988).

Derrida, J. (P. Knauf, translator). *Specters of Marx, the State of the Debt, the Work of Mourning, and the New International* (London, 1994).

Dickinson, G.Lowes. *The International Anarchy, 1904–1914* (New York, 1926).

Diehl, P.F. *Peace Operations*, Cambridge, 2008).

Diehl, Paul F., ed. *The Politics of Global Governance: International Organizations in An Interdependent World*, (Boulder, CO, 2001).

Dominguez, Jorge I. *La política exterior de Cuba* (Madrid, 2009).

——. *To Make the World Safe for Revolution: Cuba's Foreign Policy* (Cambridge, MA, 1989).

Donaldson, Robert. *Soviet Policy Toward India: Ideology and Strategy* (Cambridge, MA, 1974).

Douglas, Mary and Aaron Wildavsky. *Risk and Culture: An Essay on the Selection of Technical and Environmental Dangers* (Berkeley, CA, 1982).

Dreher, A., N. Gaston and P. Martens. *Measuring Globalization—Gauging its Consequences* (New York, 2008).

Duchhardt, Heinz. *Altes Reich und europäische Staatenwelt, 1648–1806* (München, 1990).

Duchhardt, H.J., ed. *Der Westfälische Friede* (Munich, 1998).

Duffield, M. *Global Governance and the New Wars* (London, 2001).

Dumbrell, John. *A Special Relationship: Anglo-American Relations from the Cold War to Iraq* (Aldershot, 2006).

Dunne, T. *Inventing International Society: A History of the English School* (London, 1998).

Eban, A. *The New Diplomacy* (London, 1983).

Echevarria II, Antulio J. *Toward an American Way of War* (Carlisle, PA, 2004).

Edwards, M. and David Hulme. *NGOs, States and Donors: too close for comfort?* (Basingstoke, 1997).

Erisman, H. Michael. *Cuba's International Relations: The Anatomy of a Nationalistic Foreign Policy* (Boulder, CO, 1985).

Erixon, Fredrik, Andreas Freytag, and Gernot Pehnelt, *The Rome Treaty at 50, ECIPE Policy Briefs No. 4* (Brussels, 2007).

Esposito, John L. *Political Islam: Revolution, Radicalism or Reform* (New York, 1997).

Feaver, Peter D. *Armed Servants. Agency, Oversight, and Civil-Military Relations* (Cambridge, MA, 2003).

Feaver, Peter D. and Christopher Gelpi, *Choosing Your Battles: American Civil Military Relations and The Use of Force* (Princeton, NJ, 2004).

Feinsilver, Julie M. *Healing the Masses: Cuban Health Politics at Home and Abroad* (Berkeley, CA, 1993).

Fergusson, James. *Canada and Ballistic Missile Defence 1954–2009: Déjà vu all over again* (Vancouver, 2010).

Fineman, Daniel. *A Special Relationship: The United States and Military Government in Thailand, 1947–1958* (Honolulu, HI, 1997).

Finlay, R. *Venice Besieged. Politics and Diplomacy in the Italian Wars, 1494–1534* (Farnham, 2008).

Fonseca Júnior, Gelson and Sérgio Henrique Nabuco de Castro, eds. *Temas de Política Externa Brasileira* (São Paulo, 1994).

Foot, R., S.N. MacFarlane, and M. Mastanduno. *US Hegemony and International Organizations* (Oxford, 2003).

Forrester, V. *L'Horreur Economique* (Paris, 1996).

Friedman G. and M. Lebard, *The Coming War with Japan* (New York, 1991).

Fuente, Alejandro de la. *A Nation for All: Race, Inequality and Politics in Twentieth Century Cuba* (Chapel Hill, NC, 2001).

Fürtig, H. *Iran's Rivalry with Saudi Arabia between the Gulf Wars* (Reading, 2002).

Fukuyama, F. *The End of History and the Last Man* (New York, 1992).

Fuller, Graham E. and Ian O. Lesser. *Turkey's New Geopolitics, From the Balkans to Western China* (Boulder, CO, 1993).

Gaddis, John Lewis. *Strategies of Containment. A Critical Appraisal of American National Security Policy During the Cold War*, revised and expanded edition (New York, 2005).

——. *We Now Know: Rethinking Cold War History* (New York, 1997).

Galtung, J. *Peace by peaceful means: peace and conflict, development and civilization* (Oslo, 1996).

Ganguly, Sumit. *Conflict Unending: India-Pakistan Tensions Since 1947* (New York, 2001).

Garcia, Frank J. *Trade, Inequality, and Justice: Towards a Liberal Theory of Just Trade* (Ardsley, NY, 2003).

Garthoff, Raymond. *Détente and Confrontation: American-Soviet relations from Nixon to Reagan*, revised edition (Washington, DC, 1994).

Garver, John W. *Protracted Contest: Sino-Indian Rivalry in the Twentieth Century* (Seattle, WA, 2010).

George, A.L. *Forceful Persuasion: Coercive Diplomacy as an Alternative to War* (Washington, DC, 1991).

Gheciu, Alexandra. *NATO in the 'New Europe': The Politics of International Socialization after the Cold War* (Stanford, CA, 2005).

——. *Securing Civilization?* (Oxford, 2008).

Giddens, A. *The Third Way and Its Critics* (Cambridge, 2000).

Gilpin, Robert. *War and Change in World Politics* (Cambridge, UK, 1981).

Ginsberg, R.H. *The European Union in International Politics: Baptism by Fire* (Lanham, MD, 2001).

Gleijeses, Piero. *Conflicting Missions: Havana, Washington, and Africa, 1959–1976* (Chapel Hill, NC, 2001).

Goertzel, Ted G. *Fernando Henrique Cardoso: Reinventing Democracy for Brazil* (Boulder, CO, 1999).

Goffman, D. *Britons in the Ottoman Empire, 1642–1660* (London, 1998).

Gold, Dore. *The Rise of Nuclear Iran: How Tehran Defies the West* (Washington, DC, 2010).

Goodhand, J. *Aiding Peace? The role of NGOs in armed conflict* (Boulder, CO, 2006).

Gordenker, L. *The UN Secretary-General and Secretariat* (London, 2005).

Gounin, Y. *La France en Afrique. Le combat des Anciens contre les Modernes* (Brussels, 2009).

Grant, J.A. and F. Söderbaum, eds. *The New Regionalism in Africa* (Aldershot, 2003).

Gray, Colin S. *Schools for Strategy: Teaching Strategy for 21st Century Conflict* (Carlisle, PA, November 2009).

——. *Modern Strategy* (New York, 1999).

——. *House of Cards: Why Arms Control Must Fail* (Ithaca, NY, 1992).

Green, M. *Japan's Reluctant Realism* (New York, 2001).

Grevi, G., D. Helly, and D. Keohane, eds. *European Security and Defence Policy: The First Ten Years (1999–2009)* (Paris, 2009).

Griffiths, R.A. and J. Law, eds. *Rawdon Brown and the Anglo-Venetian Relationship* (Stroud, 2005).

Grigoriadis, Ioannis N. *Trials of Europeanization: Turkish Political Culture and the European Union* (New York, 2009).

Guoxing, Ji and Hadi Soesastro, eds. *Sino-Indonesian Relations in the Post-Cold War Era* (Jakarta, 1992).

Guruswamy, Mohan, ed. *Emerging Trends in India-China Relations* (Gurgaon, 2006).

Gwin, Catherine. *U.S. Relations with the World Bank 1945–92* (Washington, DC, 1994).

Haas, Ernst B. *When Knowledge Is Power: Three Models of Change in International Organizations* (Berkeley, CA, 1990).

Hacke, Christian. *Die Außenpolitik der Bundesrepublik Deutschland—von Konrad Adenauer bis Gerhard Schröder* (Berlin 2003).

Haehl, M. *Les affaires étrangères au temps de Richelieu: le secrétariat d'État, les agents diplomatiques, 1624–1642* (Bruxelles, New York, 2006).

Haglund, David G. *The North Atlantic Triangle Revisited. Canadian Grand Strategy at Century's End* (Toronto, 2000).

Hajnal, P.I. *The G8 System and the G20: Evolution, Role and Documentation* (Aldershot, 1999).

Hamilton, K. and R. Langhorne. *The Practice of Diplomacy: Its Evolution, Theory and Administration* (London and New York, 1995).

Hanrieder, Wolfram. *Germany, America, Europe—Forty Years of German Foreign Policy* (New Haven, CT, 1989).

Hara, K. *Cold War Frontiers in the Asia-Pacific* (London, 2007).

Hart, Michael. *A Trading Nation. Canadian Trade Policy from Colonialism to Globalization* (Vancouver, 2002).

Hayek, Friedrich August von, Hugo Sieber, Egon Tuchtfeldt and Hans Willgerodt, eds. *Internationale Ordnung—heute, Wilhelm Röpke—Ausgewählte Werke*, 3 Aufl (Bern, Stuttgart, 1979).

Hazzard, S. *Defeat of an Ideal: the Self-destruction of the United Nations* (London, 1973).

Hee, Park Chung. *Korea Reborn* (New York, 1979).

Held, D. and A. McGrew, *The Global Transformations Reader* (Cambridge, 2000).

Henderson, Simon. *Instant Empire, Saddam Hussein's Ambition for Iraq* (San Francisco, CA, 1991).

Hershberg E. and F. Rosen. *Latin America after Neoliberalism: Turning the tide in the 21st century?* (New York, 2006).

Herz, Monica and João Pontes Nogueira, *Ecuador vs. Peru: Peacemaking Amid Rivalry* (Boulder, CO, 2002).

Hewitt, Steve. *The British War on Terror* (London, 2008).

Hofmann, Rainer and Gabriele Tondl. *European Union and the WTO Doha Round* (Baden-Baden, 2007).

Holsti, K.J. *Peace and War: Armed Conflicts and International Order, 1648–1989* (Cambridge, 1991).

Hook, Steven W. and James M.Scott, *US Foreign Policy Today: American Renewal?* (Washington, DC, 2011).

Howard, M. *The Invention of Peace: Reflections on War and International Order* (New Haven, CT, 2001).

Howorth, Jolyon. *Security and Defence Policy in the European Union* (Basingstoke, 2007).

Huntington, Samuel P. *The Soldier and the State: The Theory and Politics of Civil-Military Relations* (Cambridge, MA, 1957).

Hwang, Balbina Y. *Globalization, Strategic Culture and Ideas: Explaining Continuity in Korean Foreign Economic Policy* (Doctoral Dissertation, Georgetown University, 2005).

Idang, Gordon. *Nigeria's Internal Politics and Foreign Policy (1960–1966)* (Ibadan, 1973).

Ikenberry, G. John. 'America's Imperial Ambition', *Foreign Affairs*, 81(2002).

Indyk, Martin. *Innocent Abroad, An Intimate Account of American Peace Diplomacy in the Middle East* (New York, 2009).

Inglehart, R. and C. Welzel, *Modernization, Cultural Change and Democracy. The Human Development Sequence* (Cambridge, 2005).

Irwin, Rosalind, ed. *Ethics and Security in Canadian Foreign Policy* (Vancouver, 2001).

Jafarzadeh, Alireza. *The Iran Threat: President Ahmadinejad and the Coming Nuclear Crisis* (New York, 2007).

Jamal, Arif. *Shadow War: The Untold Story of Jihad in Kashmir* (New York, 2009).

James, M.E. *English Politics and the Concept of Honour, 1485–1642* (Oxford, 1978).

Jankowski, James. *Nasser's Egypt, Arab Nationalism and the United Arab Republic* (Boulder, CO, 2002).

Jing, Zhong and Pan Zhenqiang, 'Redefining Strategic Stability in a Changing World: A Chinese View', *Contemporary Security Policy*, 25(2004), 123–35.

Jönsson, C. and M. Hall, *Essence of Diplomacy* (Basingstoke, 2005).

Jönsson, C. and R. Langhorne, eds, *Diplomacy*, 3 Volumes (London, 2004).

Jouyet, J.-P. and S. Coignard, *Une présidence de crise: les six mois qui ont bousculé l'Europe* (Paris, 2009).

Juppé, Alain and Louis Schweitzer, eds. *La France et l'Europe dans le monde. Livre blanc sur la politique étrangère et européenne de la France 2008–2020* (Paris, 2008).

Kaldor, Mary. *New and Old Wars: Organised Violence in a Global Era* (Stanford CA, 2007).

Kane, I. and N. Mbelle, *Towards a People-Driven African Union: Current Obstacles and New Opportunities* (London, 2007).

Kapcia, Antoni. *Cuba: Island of Dreams* (Oxford, New York, 2000).

Keddie, N.R.K. and R. Matthee, eds. *Iran and the Surrounding World: Interactions in Culture and Cultural Politics* (Seattle, WA, 2002).

Kedourie, Sylvia, ed. *Turkey, Identity, Democracy, Politics* (London, 1998).

Kelly, Justin and Mike Brennan, *Alien: How Operational Art Devoured Strategy* (Carlisle, PA, September 2009).

Kennedy, Paul M. *The Rise and Fall of the Great Powers: Economic Change and Military Conflict from 1500 to 2000* (New York, 1987).

Keohane, Robert O. *After Hegemony: Cooperation and Discord in the World Political Economy* (Princeton, NJ, 1984).

Keukeleire, S. and J. MacNaughtan. *The Foreign Policy of the European Union* (Basingstoke, 2008).

Khosla, G.D., David Page and Penderel Moon. *The Partition Omnibus* (New Delhi, 2004).

Kirk, John M. and H. Michael Erisman. *Cuban Medical Internationalism: Origins, Evolution, and Goals* (London, 2009).

Kirk, John M. and Peter McKenna, *Canada-Cuba Relations: The Other Good Neighbor Policy* (Gainesville, FL, 1997).

Kissinger, H.A. *Diplomacy* (New York, 1994).

Klarén, Peter Flindell. *Peru: Society and Nationhood in the Andes* (Oxford, 2000).

Klodt, Henning. *Internationale Politikkoordination—Leitlinien für den globalen Wirtschaftspolitiker*, Institut für Weltwirtschaft, Kieler Diskussionsbeiträge, Number 343(1999).

Knight, W.A., ed. *Adapting the United Nations to a Postmodern Era* (Basingstoke, 2001).

Knutsen, Trobjorn L. *The Rise and Fall of World Orders* (Manchester, 1999).

Kořan, Michal, ed. *Česká zahraniční politika v zrcadle sociálně-vědního výzkumu* (Praha, 2009).

Koskenniemi, Martii. *The Gentler Civilizer of Nations: The Rise and Fall of International Law, 1870–1960* (Cambridge, UK, 2001).

Krauske, O. *Die Entwickelung der ständigen Diplomatie* (Leipzig, 1885).

Krepinovich, Andrew F. and Barry D. Watts, *Regaining Strategic Competence. Strategy for the Long Haul* (Washington, DC, 2009).

Kriesi, H. et al., *West European Politics in the Age of Globalization* (Cambridge, 2008).

Kriesi, H., E. Grande, M. Dolezal, M. Helbling, S. Hutter, D. Hoeglinger, and B. Wuest. *Restructuring Political Conflict in Western Europe* (forthcoming).

Kuczynski, Pedro-Pablo. *Peruvian Democracy under Economic Stress: An Account of the Belaúnde Administration, 1963–1968* (Princeton, NJ, 1977).

Kumaraswamy, P.R. *India's Israel Policy* (New York, 2010).

Kux, Dennis. *Disenchanted Allies* (Baltimore, MD, 2001).

Lagassé, Philippe. *Accountability for National Defence: Ministerial Responsibility, Military Command and Parliamentary Oversight*, IRPP Study #4 (March 2010).

Lam, Willy. *Changing of the Guard: Beijing Grooms Sixth-Generation Cadres for 2020s* (Washington DC, 2010).

Langer, H. *1648, der Westfälische Frieden: Pax Europaea und Neuordnung des Reiches* (Berlin, 1994).

Lawson, F.H. *Constructing International Relations in the Arab World* (Stanford, California, 2006).

Lebor, A. *"Complicity with Evil": The United Nations in the Age of Modern Genocide* (New Haven, CT, 2006).

Lechuga, Carlos. *En el Ojo de la Tormenta: F. Castro, N. Jruschov, J.F. Kennedy y la Crisis de los Misiles* (La Habana, North Melbourne, 1995).

Lee, Jong-Wha and Ju Hyun Pyun. *Does Trade Integration Contribute to Peace?* Asian Development Bank, Working Paper Series: Regional Economic Integration, No.24 (January 2009).

Legum, C. *Pan-Africanism* (London, 1962).

Lequesne, C. *La France dans la nouvelle Europe*, (Paris, 2008).

Lesaffer, R., ed. *Peace Treaties and International Law in European History* (Cambridge, 2004).

Lindenberg, M. and C. Bryant. *Going Global: Transforming Relief and Development NGOs* (Bloomfield, CT, 2001).

Luck, E.C. *UN Security Council: Practice and Promise* (London, 2006).

Makinda, S.M. and F.Wafula Okumu, *The African Union: Challenges of Globalization, Security, and Governance* (New York, 2007).

Mandelbaum, Michael. *The Dawn of Peace in Europe* (New York, 1996).

——. *The Fates of Nations: The Search for National Security in the Nineteenth and Twentieth Centuries* (Cambridge, UK, 1988).

Mansfield, Edward D. *Power, Trade, and War* (Princeton, NJ, 1994).

Marek, Dan and Michael Baun. *The Czech Republic and the European Union* (London, New York, 2011).

Marshall, P. *The Dynamics of Diplomacy* (London, 1990).

Martínez, Fernando. *El ejercicio de pensar* (La Habana, 2008).

Mastny, Vojtech and R.Craig Nation, eds. *Turkey Between East and West, New Challenges for a Rising Regional Power* (New York, 1996).

Matheson, J. *Council Unbound* (Washington, DC, 2006).

Mattingly, G. *Renaissance Diplomacy* (London, 1955).

Maull, Hanns, ed. *Germany's Uncertain Power: Foreign Policy of the Berlin Republic* (New York, 2006).

Mazzaoui, M., ed. *Safavid Iran and her neighbors* (Salt Lake City, UT, 2003).

McClintock, Cynthia and Fabian Vallas. *The United States and Peru: Cooperation at a Cost* (London, 2003).

McDowall, David. *The Kurds, A Nation Denied* (London, 1992).

Mearsheimer, John J. *The Tragedy of Great Power Politics* (New York, 2001).

Melakopides, Costas. *Pragmatic Idealism. Canadian Foreign Policy, 1945–1995* (Montréal, 1998).

Melanson, Richard A. *American Foreign Policy since the Vietnam War* (Armonk, NY, 2005).

Miles, Hugh. *Al Jazeera: The Inside Story of the Arab News Channel That is Challenging the West* (New York, 2005).

Mishkin, F. *The Next Great Globalization: How Disadvantaged Nations Can Harness Their Financial Systems to Get Rich* (Princeton, NJ, 2008).

Monteagle, Stearns. *Entangled Allies: U.S. Policy toward Greece, Turkey and Cyprus* (New York, 1992).

Morgenthau, H.J. *Politics Among Nations: The Struggle for Power and Peace*, 3rd edition (New York, 1966).

Müller, K. *1866: Bismarcks deutscher Bruderkrieg: Königgrätz und die Schlachten auf deutschem Boden* (Graz, 2007).

Müller-Rommel, F. and T. Poguntke. *Green Parties in National Governments* (London, 2002).

Murray, L. *Clinton, Peacekeeping and Humanitarian Intervention* (London: 2008).

Nicolson, H. *The Evolution of Diplomatic Method* (London, 1954); reprinted (1998).

Nossal, Kim, Stéphane Roussel, and Stéphane Paquin, *International Policy and Politics in Canada* (Toronto, 2011).

Nye, Jr, Joseph S. *Soft Power: The Means to Success in World Politics* (New York, 1984 and 2004).

——. *The Paradox of American Power: Why the World's Only Superpower Can't Go It Alone* (New York, 2002).

——. *Bound to Lead: The Changing Nature of American Power* (New York, 1990).

Oberdorfer, Don. *The Two Koreas: A Contemporary History* (Reading, MA, 1997).

Ogwu, Joy and Adebayo Olukoshi, eds. *The Economic Diplomacy of the Nigerian State*, revised edition (Lagos, 2002).

Oh, Kongdan and Ralph Hassig, *North Korea Through the Looking Glass* (Washington, DC, 2000).

Ohmae, K. *The End of the Nation State. How Region States Harness the Prosperity of the Global Economy* (New York, 1995).

Oren, Michael B. *Power, Faith and Fantasy—America in the Middle East* (New York, 2007).

Osaghae, Eghosa. *Crippled Giant: Nigeria Since Independence* (London, 1998).

Pakistan Project Report. *Whither Pakistan? Growing Instability and Implications for India* (New Delhi, 2010).

Pant, Harsh V. *Contemporary Debates in Indian Foreign and Security Policy: India Negotiates Its Rise in the International System* (New York, 2008).

Paris, R. *War's End: Building Peace After Civil Conflict* (Cambridge, 2004).

Park, Han. *North Korea: Ideology, Politics, Economy* (New York, 1996).

Parker, Richard B. *The Politics of Miscalculation in the Middle East* (Bloomington, IN, 1993).

Parsi, Trita. *Treacherous Alliance: The Secret Dealings of Israel, Iran, and the United States* (New Haven, CT, 2007).

Parsons, A. *From Cold War to Hot Peace: UN Interventions 1947–1995* (Harmondsworth, 1995).

Paterson, Dennis and Ari Afilalo. *The New Global Trading Order: The Evolving State and the Future of Trade.* (Cambridge, UK, 2008).

Paul Kapur, S. *Dangerous Deterrent* (Stanford, CA, 2008).

Paul, T.V. and John A. Hall, eds. *The International Order and the Future of World Politics* (Cambridge, 1999).

Pérez Jr. Louis A. *Cuba in the American Imagination: Metaphor and Imperial Ethos* (Chapel Hill, NC, 2008).

Phasuk, Sunai. *Nayobai Tang Prathet Khong Thai: Suksa Krabuankarnkamnod Nayobai Khong Ratthaban Pon-ek Chatichai Choonhavan Tor Panha Kumphucha, Si Singhakom 1988–23 Kumphaphan 1991* (Bangkok, 1997).

Physicians for Human Rights. *Health in Ruins: A Man-Made Disaster in Zimbabwe* (Cambridge, MA, 2009).

Pilat, Joseph, ed. *The Nonproliferation Predicament* (Oxford, 1985).

Pisani-Ferry, J., P. Aghion, M. Belka, J. von Hagen, L. Heikensten, and A. Sapir, *Coming of Age: Report on the Euro Area* (Brussels, 2008).

Pope, Nicole and Hugh Pope. *Turkey Unveiled, A History of Modern Turkey* (New York, 1996).

Porath, Yehoshua. *In Search of Arab Unity, 1930–1945* (London, 1986).

Porrata-Doria, Jr., Rafael A. *MERCOSUR: The Common Market of the Southern Cone.* (Durham, NC, 2005).

Potter, Evan H. *Branding Canada: Projecting Canada's Soft Power through Public Diplomacy* (Montreal, Kingston, 2009).

Potter, William. *Nuclear Power and Nonprolifeation: An Interdisciplinary Perspective* (Cambridge, MA, 1982).

Prado, Maria Clara R.M. do. *Real História do Real: Uma Radiografia da Moeda que Mudou o Brasil* (Rio de Janeiro, 2005).

Pyle, K.B. *Japan Rising* (New York, 2007).

Quandt, William B. *Peace Process, America Diplomacy and the Arab-Israeli Conflict since 1967* (Berkeley, CA, 2001).

Racioppi, Linda. *Soviet Policy Toward South Asia since the 1970s* (Cambridge, UK, 1994).

Rao, P.V.R. *India's Defence Policy and Organisation Since Independence* (New Delhi, 1977).

Rauf, Tariq., ed. *Regional Approaches to Curbing Nuclear Proliferation in the Middle East and South Asia* Aurora Papers 16 (Ottawa, 1992).

Reich, R. *Supercapitalism* (New York, 2007).

Reis da Silva, André Luiz. *A Diplomacia Brasileira Entre a Segurança e o Desenvolvimento: A Política Externa do Governo Castelo Branco (1964–1967)* (Porto Alegre, 2004).

Renouvin, P. ed. *Histoire des relations internationals.* 3 volumes (Paris, 1953–55 [new edition 1994]).

Revel, J.-F. *L'obsession anti-americaine: Son fonctionnement, ses causes, ses inconsequences* (Paris, 2002).

Reynolds, D. *Summits. Six Meetings that Shaped the Twentieth Century* (New York, 2007).

Richmond, O. *Peace in International Relations* (London, 2008).

——. *Maintaining Order, Making Peace* (Basingstoke, 2002).

Rosen, Stephen P. *Societies and Military Power: India and Its Armies* (Ithaca, NY, 1996).

Ross, Dennis. *The Missing Pace, the Inside Story of the Fight for the Middle East Peace* (New York, 2008).

Roussel, Stéphane. *The North American Democratic Peace: Absence of War and Security Institution-Building in Canada-US Relations, 1867–1958* (Montreal, Kingston, 2004).

Ryan, S. *The United Nations and International Politics* (Basingstoke, 2000).

Salim, A. *Ushering the OAU into the Next Century: A Programme for Reform and Renewal* (Addis Ababa, 1997).

Sanders, David. *Losing an Empire, Finding a Role* (London, 1990).

Schimmelfennig, Frank. *The EU, NATO and the Integration of Europe. Rules and Rhetoric* (Cambridge, 2003).

Schroeder, P.W. *Metternich's Diplomacy at Its Zenith, 1820–1823* (Austin, TX, 1962).

Schwarz, Hans Peter. *Die Zentralmacht Europas. Deutschlands Rückkehr auf die Weltbühne* (Berlin, 1994).

Schwarzer, D. *Fiscal Policy Co-ordination in the EMU. A Prefence-Based Explanation of Institutional Change* (Baden-Baden, 2007).

Scott, H.M. *The Birth of a Great Power System, 1740–1815* (Essex, UK, 2006).

Scott, James M. *Deciding to Intervene: American Foreign Policy and the Reagan Doctrine* (Durham, NC, 1996).

Scott, James M., ed. *After the End: Making American Foreign Policy in the Post-Cold War World* (Durham, NC, 1998).

Šedivý, Jiří. *Dilema rozšiřování NATO* (Praha, 2001).

Shankland, David. *The Alevis in Turkey: The Emergence of a Secular Islamic Tradition* (London, 2007).

Shaw, T.M., J.A. Grant, and S. Cornelissen, eds. *The Research Companion to Regionalisms* (Aldershot, 2011).

Sheehan, Michael. *The Balance of Power: History and Theory* (London, 1996).

Shihata, Ibrahim F.I. *The Other Face of OPEC. Financial Assistance to the Third World* (London, New York, 1982).

Shinoda, T. *Koizumi Diplomacy* (Seattle, WA, 2007).

Shirk, Susan. *China: Fragile Superpower* (New York, 2007).

Sikri, Rajiv. *Challenge and Strategy: Rethinking India's Foreign Policy* (New Delhi, 2009).

Singh, Jaswant. *Defending India* (New York, 1999).

Singham, A.W. and Shirley Hume. *Non-Alignment in an Age of Alignments* (London, 1986).

SIPRI, *The Arms Trade with the Third World* (New York, 1971).

Smith J. and H. Johnston. *Globalization and Resistance: Transnational Dimensions of Social Movements* (Lanham, MD, 2002).

Smith, General Sir Rupert. *The Utility of Force. The Art of War in the Modern World* (London, 2005).

Smith, Joseph. *Unequal Giants: Diplomatic Relations Between the United States and Brazil, 1889–1930* (Pittsburgh, PA, 1991).

Smith, K.E. *European Union Foreign Policy in a Changing World*, 2nd edition (Cambridge, UK, 2008).

Söderbaum, F. and I. Taylor, eds., *Afro-Regions: The Dynamics of Cross-Border Micro-Regionalism in Africa* (Uppsala, 2008).

Söderbaum, F. and T.M. Shaw, eds. *Theories of New Regionalism: A Palgrave Reader* (Basingstoke, 2003).

Souto, Cíntia Vieira. *A Diplomacia do Interesse Nacional: A Política Externa do Governo Medici* (Porto Alegre, 2003).

St John, Ronald Bruce. *La Política Exterior del Perú* (Lima, 1999).

——. *The Ecuador-Peru Boundary Dispute: The Road to Settlement* (Durham, 2000).

——. *The Foreign Policy of Peru* (Boulder, CO, 1992).

——. *Toledo's Peru: Vision and Reality* (Gainesville, FL, 2010).

Stern, Nichola. *The Economics of Climate Change* (Cambridge, UK, 2007).

Stiglitz, Joseph E. *Globalization and Its Discontents* (New York, 2003).

Stoessinger, J.G. *The United Nations and the Superpowers*, 4th edition (New York, 1977).

Strömvik, Maria. *To Act as a Union: Explaining the Development of the EU's Collective Foreign Policy* (Lund, 2005).

Stützel, Wolfgang et al. *Standard Text on the Social Market Economy* (Stuttgart, New York, 1982).

Subrahmanyam, K. *Indian Security Perspectives* (New Delhi, 1982).

——. *Perspectives in Defence Planning* (New Delhi, 1972).

Suh, J.J., P.J. Katzenstein, and A. Carlson, eds. *Rethinking Security in East Asia* (Stanford, 2004).

Sumption, J. *The Hundred Years War, Volume III: Divided Houses* (London, 2009).

Suryadinata, Leo. *Indonesia's Foreign Policy Under Soeharto: Aspiring to International Leadership* (Singapore, 1996).

Szabo, Stephen F. *Parting Ways. The Crisis in German-American Relations* (Washington, DC, 2004).

Takemae, E. *Inside GHQ: The Allied Occupation of Japan and Its Legacy* (London, 2002).

Takeyh, Ray. *Hidden Iran: Paradox and Power in the Islamic Republic* (New York, 2006).

Talbott, Strobe. *Engaging India: Democracy, Diplomacy and the Bomb* (Washington, DC, 2004).

Tanham, George. *Indian Strategic Thought: An Interpretive Essay* (Santa Monica, CA, 1992).

Tellis, Ashley J. *India's Emerging Nuclear Posture: Between Recessed Deterrent and Ready Arsenal* (New York, 2001).

Telò, M. *Europe: A Civilian Power? European Union, Global Governance, World Order* (Houndsmills, 2006).

Thakur, R. *The United Nations, Peace and Security* (Cambridge, 2006).

Tischer, A. *Französische Diplomatie und Diplomaten auf dem Westfälischen Friedenskongress. Aussenpolitik und Richelieu und Mazarin* (Münster, 1999).

Togan, S. and V.N. Balasubramanyam, eds. *The Economy of Turkey since Liberalization* (New York, 1996).

Trenin, Dmitri, Andrew Kuchins and Thomas Gomart. *Toward a New Euro-Atlantic 'Hard' Security Agenda* (Paris, Washington, 2008).

Tumlir, Jan. *Protectionism: Trade Policy in Democratic Societies* (Washington, DC, 1985).

Ugarteche, Pedro. *Valija de un Diplomático Peruano* (Buenos Aires, 1965).

Upchurch, M., T. Graham, A. Mathers, *The Crisis of Social Democratic Trade Unionism in Western Europe: The Search for Alternatives* (Burlington, 2009).

Urquhart, B. *A Life in Peace and War* (London, 1987).

Vaïsse, Maurice. *La Puissance ou l'Influence? La France dans le monde depuis 1958* (Paris, 2009).

Vatikiotis, Michael. *Indonesian Politics under Suharto*, 3rd edition (London, New York, 1993).

Vatikiotis, P.J. *Nasser and His Generation* (New York, 1978).

Velaochaga, Luis. *Políticas Exteriores del Perú: Sociología, Histórica y Periodismo* (Lima, 2001).

Vogel, E. *Japan as Number One: Lessons for America* (Cambridge, MA, 1979).

Wada, H. *Hoppōryōdo mondai* (Tokyo, 1999).

Wagnsson, C. *Security in a Greater Europe: The Possibility of a Pan-European Approach* (Manchester, 2008).

Walt, Stephen M. *Taming American Power: The Global Response to U.S. Primacy* (New York, 2005).

——. *The Origins of Alliances* (Ithaca, NY, 1987).

Walton, J. and D. Seddon. *Free Markets and Food Riots: The Politics of Global Adjustment* (Oxford, 1994).

Waltz, K.N. *Theory of International Politics* (Reading, MA, 1979).

Watanabe, A., ed. *Sengo nihon no taigai seisaku* (Tokyo, 1985).
Watson, A. *Diplomacy: The Dialogue Between States* (London, 1982).
Weiss, T.G., D.R. Forsythe, and P.A. 1, eds. *The United Nations and Changing World Politics* (Boulder, CO, 1994).
Weitzman, Bruce Maddy. *The Crystallization of the Arab State System, 1945–1954* (Syracuse, NY, 1993).
White, S. *Gorbachev in Power* (Cambridge, 1990).
Willetts, Peter. *The Non-Aligned Movement: The Origins of a Third World Alliance* (New York, 1978).
Williams, Michael J. *NATO, Security and Risk-Management: From Kosovo to Kandahar* (London, 2009).
Windsor, Philip. *Germany and the Management of Detente* (London 1971).
Wolf, M. *Why Globalization Works* (New Haven, CT, 2004).
Woodward, Bob. *Obama's Wars* (New York, NY, 2010).
——. *Plan of Attack* (New York, 2004).
——. *Bush at War* (New York, 2003).
World Bank. *The East Asian Miracle: Economic Growth and Public Policy* (Oxford, 1993).
Yahuda, Michael B. *The International Politics of the Asia Pacific*, second revised edition (London, 2004).
Yanarella, Ernest J. *The Missile Defense Controversy: Strategy, Technology, and Politics, 1955–1972* (Lexington, KY, 1977).
Yavuz, Hakan M., ed. *The Emergence of a New Turkey: Democracy and the AK Party* (Salt Lake City, UT, 2006).
Yokibe, H. *Sengo nihon gaikōshi* (Tokyo, 1999).
Zelikow, Philip and Condoleezza Rice. *Germany Unified And Europe Transformed. A Study in Statecraft* (Cambridge, MA, 1995).

Articles, Chapters, Reports

Abramowitz, Morton and Henri J. Barkey. 'Turkey's Transformers, The AKP Sees Big', *Foreign Affairs*, 87(November/December 2009).
Adediji, Olu. 'Implementation and Administration of Foreign Policy: A Note on the Relationship between the Ministry of External Affairs and the Nigerian Missions Abroad'. In Gabriel Olusanya and Rafiu Akindele, eds., *The Structure and Processes of Foreign Policy Making and Implementation 1960–1990* (Lagos, 1990).
Agg, C. 'Trends in Government Support for Non-Governmental Organizations: Is the "Golden Age" of the NGO Behind Us?', Civil Society and Social Movements Programme Paper Number 23 June 2006, United Nations Research Institute for Social Development, *Yearbook of International Organizations* (Geneva, 2006).
Aggestam, L. 'Introduction: Ethical Power Europe?', *International Affairs*, 84(2008).
Ahn, Byung-Joon. 'South Korean-Soviet Relations: Contemporary Issues and Prospects', *Asian Survey*, 31(September 1991).
Alhajji, A.F. 'Three Decades after the Oil Embargo: Was 1973 Unique?', *Journal of Energy and Development*, 30(2005).
Allen, D. and R. Bengtsson. 'Exploring a triangular drama: Solana, the Commission and the Council presidencies'. In G. Müller-Brandeck-Bocquet, ed., *The High Representative for the Common Foreign and Security Policy 1999–2009: A Strong catalyst for the European Union's International Role?* (forthcoming).
Almeida, Paulo Roberto de. 'A Política Internacional do Partido dos Trabalhadores: Da Fundação à Diplomacia do Governo Lula,' *Revista Sociológica Política*, 20(June 2003).
Alzugaray, Carlos. 'La seguridad nacional de Cuba frente a los Estados Unidos: conflicto y ¿cooperación?' *Temas* 62–63(2010).
——. 'La creación de una Cancillería revolucionaría 1959–65,' in Ana Cairo, ed., *Raúl Roa: Imaginarios* (La Habana, 2008).
——. 'Problems of National Security in the Cuban-U.S. Historic Breach'. In Jorge I. Domínguez and Rafael Hernández, eds., *U.S.-Cuban Relations in the 1990s* (Boulder, CO, 1989).
Anwar, Dewi Fortuna. 'A Journey of Change: Indonesia's Foreign Policy', *Global Asia*, Volume 4, Number 3 (2009).
——. 'The East Timor Crisis: An Indonesian View', in Bruce Brown, ed., *East Timor–the Consequences* (Wellington, 2000).
Audelin, Jean D. 'Joining the Club: Lula and the End of the Periphery for Brazil'. In Peter Birle, Sérgio Costa and Horst Nitschack, eds., *Brazil and the Americas: Convergences and Perspectives* (Madrid, 2008).

Aysha, E. El-Din. 'September 11 and the Middle East Failure of US "Soft Power": Globalisation contra Americanisation in the "New" US Century', *International Relations*, 19(2005).

Azicri, Max. 'ALBA y el Renacimiento de la Izquierda en la America Latina,' *Dialogo*, 11(Summer 2008).

Baccaro, L., K. Hamann, and L. Turner. 'The Politics of Labour Movement Revitalization: The Need for a Revitalized Perspective', *European Journal of Industrial Relations* 9(2003).

Backer, Larry Catá. 'Globalization and the Socialist Multinational: Cuba and ALBA's Grannacional Projects at the Intersection of Business and Human Rights' (2010): http://ssrn.com/abstract=1646962.

——. 'Ideologies of Globalization and Sovereign Debt: Cuba and the IMF.' *Penn State International Law Review*, 24(2006), 497.

Backer, Larry C. and Augusto Molina. 'Cuba and the Construction of Alternative Global Trade Systems: ALBA and Free Trade in the Americas', *University of Pennsylvania Journal of International Law*, 31(2010).

Baker, Pauline H. 'Fixing failed states: the new security agenda', *Whitehead Journal of Diplomacy and International Relations*, 8(2007).

Barnett, M., H. Kim, M. O'Donnell, L. Sitea, 'Peacebuilding: What's in a name?', *Global Governance*, 13(2007).

Barral, Welber. 'Dispute Settlement and Legal Harmonization in MERCOSUR', in Larry Catá Backer, ed., *Harmonizing Law in an Era of Globalization: Convergence, Divergence and Resistance* (Durham, NC, 2007).

Baun, Michael and Dan Marek. 'Czech Foreign Policy and EU Integration: European and Domestic Sources,' *Perspectives on European Politics and Society*, Volume 11, Number 2(2010).

Bély, L. 'Méthodes et perspectives dans l'étude des négociations internationales à l'époque moderne'. In R. Babel, ed., *Frankreich im europäischen Staatensystem der Frühen Neuzeit* (Paris, 1995).

Bembelly, F. R. 'L'évolution juridique et politique de la question Cabindaise', *Revue Juridique et Politique, Indépendance et Coopération*, 50(1996).

Beneš, Vit and Mats Braun. 'Evropský rozměr české zahraniční politiky', in Michal Kořan, ed., *Česká zahraniční politika v roce 2009* (Praha, 2010).

Bengtsson, R. 'Constructing interfaces: The neighbourhood discourse in EU external policy', *Journal of European Integration*, 30(2008).

Bengtsson, R. and O. Elgström. 'Reconsidering the EU's Role in International Relations—do Role Performances Fit to Role Conceptions?'. In S. Harnisch, C. Frank, and H. W. Maull, eds., *Role Theory in International Relations* (forthcoming, 2011).

Bergsten, C. Fred. 'Open Regionalism', Institute for International Economics, Working Paper 97–3 (Washington, 1997).

Bernard, Jr., Prosper. 'Canada and Human security: From the Axworthy Doctrine to Middle Power Internationalism', *American Review of Canadian Studies*, 36(2006).

Bernstein, Thomas and Andrew Nathan. 'The Soviet Union, China, and Korea'. In Gerald Curtis and Sung-Joo Han, eds., *The U.S.-South Korea Alliance: Evolving Patterns in Security Relations*, (Lexington, MA, 1983).

Betts, Richard K. 'The Soft Underbelly of American Primacy: Tactical Advantages of Terror', *Political Science Quarterly*, 117(2002).

Bijian, Z. 'China's Peaceful Rise to Great-Power Status', *Foreign Affairs*, Volume 84, Number 5(2005).

Binet, L. 'Supporting Europe and Voting No?'. In M. Maclean and J. Szarka, eds., *France on the World Stage. Nation State Strategies in the Global Era* (Basingstoke, 2008).

Bluth, Christoph. 'The British Road to War: Blair, Bush and the decision to invade Iraq', *International Affairs*, 80(2004), 851–72.

——. 'Russian Military Policy: Constraints and Capabilities'. In Roy Allison, and Christoph Bluth, eds. *Security Dilemmas in Russia and Eurasia* (London, 1998).

Bøås, Morten. 'Multilateral institutions and the developing world—changes and challenges'. In Vandana Desai and Robert B. Potter, eds. *The Companion to Development Studies*, 2nd edition (London, 2008).

——. 'Multilateral development banks, environmental impact assessments and nongovernmental organizations in U.S. foreign policy'. In Paul G. Harris, ed., *The Environment, International Relations and U.S. Foreign Policy* (Washington D.C, 2001).

Bøås, M., M. H. Marchand, and T. M. Shaw, eds. 'Special Issue: New Regionalisms in the New Millennium', *Third World Quarterly*, 20(1999).

Bohas, A. 'The Paradox of Anti-Americanism: Reflection on the Shallow Concept of Soft Power', *Global Society*, 20(2006).

Bohorquez, T. 'Soft Power', UCLA International Institute: www.international.ucla.edu/print.asp?parentid= 34734.

Bondiguel, Thomas and Thierry Kellner. 'The Impact of China's Foreign Policy Think Tanks', *Asia Papers*, Volume 5, Issue 5(April 2010).

Brady, D., J. Beckfield, and Z. Wei. 'The Consequences of Economic Globalization for Affluent Democracies', *Annual Review of Sociology* 33(2007).

Braun, Mats. 'Understanding Klaus. The Story of Czech Eurorealism,' *EPIN Working Paper*, Number 26(November 2009).

Brown, Kerry. 'The Power Struggle among China's Elite', *Foreign Policy* (14 October 2010).

Bruneau, Thomas C. and Florina Christiana Matei, 'Towards a New Conceptualization of Democratization and Civil-Military Relations,' *Democratization*, 15(December 2008).

Bruneau, Thomas C., Florina Christiana Matei, and Sak Sakoda. 'National Security Councils: Their Potential Functions in Democratic Civil-Military Relations,' *Defense & Security Analysis* 25(September 2009).

Burges, Sean W. '*Auto-Estima* in Brazil: The Logic of Lula's South-South Foreign Policy,' *International Journal*, 60(2005).

Buszynski, Leszek. 'Thailand's Foreign Policy: Management of a Regional Vision', *Asian Survey*, 34(1994).

Cagaptay, Soner. 'Is Turkey Leaving the West? An Islamist Foreign Policy Puts Ankara at Odds With Its Former Allies', *Foreign Affairs*, 57(September/October 2009).

Cardoso, Eliana. 'Monetary and Fiscal Reforms,' in Mauricio A. Font and Anthony Peter Spanakos, eds., *Reforming Brazil* (New York, 2004).

Carrasco, Enrique R. 'Law, Hierarchy, and Vulnerable Groups in Latin America: Towards a Communal Model of Development in a Neoliberal World', *Stanford Journal of International Law*, Volume 30, Number 221(1994).

Cason, Jeffrey. 'Democracy Looks South: Mercosul and the Politics of Brazilian Trade Strategy'. In Peter R. Kingstone and Timothy J. Power, eds., *Democratic Brazil: Actors, Institutions, and Processes* (Pittsburgh, PA, 2000).

——. 'On the Road to Southern Cone Economic Integration,' *Journal of Interamerican Studies and World Affairs*, 42(2002).

Cassidy, G.S. 'The Basel III Proposals' Flaws', *American Banker*, Volume 175, Issue 74(2010), 8.

Cengiz, Aktar. 'The present and future of Turkey's membership negotiations with the EU', Global Political Trends Center, *A Policy Brief* (Istanbul, October 2010).

Cha, Victor and Balbina Hwang. 'Government and Politics', in Robert L. Worden, ed., *North Korea: A Country Study* (Washington, DC, 2008).

Chantasasawat, Busakorn. 'The Burgeoning Sino-Thai Relations: Seeking Sustained Economic Security', *China: An International Journal*, 4(March 2006).

Chari, P.R. 'Civil-Military Relations in India,' *Armed Forces and Society*, 4(1977).

Cohen, E. 'History and the Hyperpower', *Foreign Affairs*, Vol.83, No. 4(2004).

Cohn, R. 'Reflections on the New Global Diplomacy: Statecraft 2500 BC to 2000 AD'. In J. Melissen, ed., *Innovation in Diplomatic Practice* (London, New York, 1999).

Cooley, A. and J. Ron, 'The NGO Scramble: Organizational Insecurity and the Political Economy of Transnational Action', *International Security*, 1(2001).

Cox, Robert W. 'Gramsci, Hegemony and International Relations: An Essay in Method'. In Louis Amoore, ed., *The Global Resistance Reader* (Cambridge, UK, 2005).

——. 'Multilateralism and world order', *Review of International Studies*, Volume 18, Number 2 (1992).

Croxton, D. 'The Peace of Westphalia and the origins of sovereignty', *International History Review*, 21(1999).

Cuellar, J.P. de. 'Reflecting on the Past and Contemplating the Future', *Global Governance*, 1(1969).

D'Hooghe, I. 'Public Diplomacy in the People's Republic of China'. In J. Melissen, ed., *New Public Diplomacy* (New York, 2007).

D'Urso, Dario. 'Shifting Turkey: Ankara's new dynamics under the AKP government.' *Portuguese Journal of International Affairs*, 3(Spring/Summer 2010).

Daalder, I.H., and J.M. Lindsay. 'Bush's foreign policy revolution', in F. Greenstein, ed., *The George W. Bush Presidency* (Baltimore, 2003).

Dariush, Zahedi and Gokhan Bacik. 'Kemalism is Dead, Long Live Kemalism, How the AKP Became Ataturk's Last Defender', *Foreign Affairs*, 88(March/April 2010).

Daudelin, Jean and Sean W. Burges. 'Brazil: How Realists Defend Democracy,' in Thomas Legler, Sharon F. Lean, and Dexter S. Boniface, eds., *Promoting Democracy in the Americas* (Baltimore, MD 2007).

Deibel, Terry L. 'Bush's Foreign Policy: Mastery and Inaction', *Foreign Policy*, 84(1991).

Der Deriam, J. 'Mediating estrangement: a theory for diplomacy', *Review of International Studies*, 13 (1987).

Deudney, Daniel and G. Johnl kenberry. 'The International Sources of Soviet Change', *International Security*, Volume 16, Number 3 (1991).

Dhanapala, J. 'The United Nations' Response to 9/11', *Terrorism and Political Violence*, 17(2005).

Donaghy, Greg. 'All God's Children: Lloyd Axworthy, Human Security and Canadian Foreign Policy, 1996–2000', *Canadian Foreign Policy*, 10(Winter 2003).

Draper, Peter. 'EU-Africa Trade Relations: The Political Economy of Economic Partnership Agreements', *Jan Tumlir Policy Essay*, Number 2 (Brussels, 2007).

Drulák, Petr. 'Jediný národní zájem, na němž jsme se dokázali shodnout a naplnit ho, byl vstup do Evropské unie', *Mezinárodní politika*, Volume 34, Number 5(2010).

——. 'The Czech EU Presidency: Background and Priorities', *Studies & Research*, Number 67(2008).

Dufourcq, J. 'Intérêts stratégiques français', *Revue Défense Nationale*, n° 726(2010).

Dullien, S. and D. Schwarzer. 'Bringing macro-economics into the EU budget debate: Why and How', *Journal of Common Market Studies*, 47(January 2009).

Dullien, Sebastian and Ulrich Fritsche. 'Anhaltende Divergenz bei Inflations-und Lohnentwicklung in der Eurozone: Gefahr für die Währungsunion?', *Vierteljahreshefte zur Wirtschaftsforschung*, 4(2007).

Eberstadt, Nicholas, Marc Rubin, and Albina Tretyakova. 'The Collapse of Soviet and Russian Trade with the DPRK, 1989–93', *Korean Journal of National Unification*, Number 4 (1995).

Elgström, O. 'Outsiders' Perceptions of the European Union in International Trade Negotiations', *Journal of Common Market Studies*, 45(2007).

Elkins, Z., A. Guzman, and B. Simmons. 'Competing for Capital: The Diffusion of Bilateral Investment Treaties, 1960–2000', *International Organization*, 60(2006).

Englebert, Pierre and Denis M. Tull. 'Postconflict reconstruction in Africa: Flawed Ideas about Failed States', *International Security* 32 (2008).

Ferrero Costa, Eduardo. 'Peruvian Foreign Policy: Current Trends, Constraints and Opportunities', *Journal of Interamerican Studies and World Affairs* 29(1987).

Fiss, P. and P. Hirsch.'The Discourse of Globalization: Framing and Sensemaking of an Emerging Concept', *American Sociological Review*, 70(2005).

Flockhart, Trine. '"Masters and Novices": Socialisation and Social Learning through the NATO Parliamentary Assembly', *International Relations*, 18(2004).

Flournoy, Michèle A. and Shawn W. Brimley. 'Strategic Planning for National Security. A New Project Solarium,' *JFQ*, Volume 41, Number 2 (2006).

Fournier, Dominique. 'The Alfonsín Administration and the Promotion of Democratic Values in the Southern Cone and the Andes,' *Journal of Latin American Studies*, 31(1999).

Freytag, Andreas and Leo Wangler. 'Strategic Trade Policy as Response to Climate Change? The Political Economy of Climate', *Jena Economic Research Papers*, 2(2007).

Freytag, Andreas and Razeen Sally. 'Globalisation and Trade Policy Response: 1900 and 2000 Compared', *Jahrbuch für Neue Politische Ökonomie*, 19(2000).

Fubini, R. 'Diplomacy and Government in the Italian City-States of the Fifteenth Century (Florence and Venice)'. In D. Frigo, ed., *Politics and Diplomacy in Early Modern Italy. The Structure of Diplomatic Practice, 1450–1800* (Cambridge, 2000).

Fukuyama, F. 'The End of History?', *National Interest* (Summer 1989).

Funabashi, Yoichi. *The Peninsula Question: A Chronicle of the Second Korean Nuclear Crisis* (Washington, DC, 2007).

Ganguly, Sumit. 'The Genesis of Nonalignment'. In Sumit Ganguly, ed., *India's Foreign Policy: Retrospect and Prospect* (New Delhi, 2010).

——. 'India and the United States: The Beginning of a Beautiful Friendship?', *World Policy Journal*, Volume 20, Number 1 (2003).

——. 'Pakistan's Never-Ending Story: Why The October Coup Was No Surprise', *Foreign Affairs*, 79(April 2000).

——. 'Stalemate in the Valley: India, Pakistan and the Crisis in Kashmir', *Harvard International Review*, 18(Summer 1996): http://hir.harvard.edu/identity-and-politics-in-south-asia/stalemate-in-the-valley.

Ganguly, Sumit and Dinshaw Mistry. 'The US-India Nuclear Pact: A Good Deal', *Current History*, Volume105, Number 694 (2006).

Gat, Azar. 'The Return of Authoritarian Great Powers', *Foreign Affairs*, 86(July/August 2007).

Gehre Galvão, Thiago. 'América do Sul: Construção Pela Reinvenção,' *Revista Brasileira de Política Internacional*, Volume 52, Number 2(2009).

Gentili, Anna. 'Failed states or failed concept?', *Studia Diplomatica* 62 (2009).

Goodhand, J. and O. Walton. 'The Limits of Liberal Peacebuilding: International Engagement in the Sri Lankan Peace Process' *Journal of Intervention and Statebuilding*, Volume 3, Issue 3 (2009).

Bibliography

Grant, J.A. 'Informal Cross-Border Micro-Regionalism in West Africa: The Case of the Parrot's Beak'. In F. Söderbaum and I. Taylor, eds., *Afro-Regions: The Dynamics of Cross-Border Micro-Regionalism in Africa* (Uppsala, 2008).

——. 'New Regionalism and Micro-Regionalism in South-Western Africa: The Oil-Rich Enclave of Cabinda'. In J.A. Grant and F. Söderbaum, eds. *The New Regionalism in Africa* (Aldershot, 2003).

Haber, S., D.M. Kennedy, and S.D. Krasner, 'Brothers Under the Skin: Diplomatic History and International Relations', *International Security*, 22(1997).

Handl, Vladimír and Otto Pick. 'Česká zahraniční politika 1993–2005 od návratu do Evropy kevropeizaci, 1. část,' *Mezinárodní politika*, Volume 29, Number 8(2005).

He, Kai. 'Interpreting China-Indonesia Relations: "Good-Neighborliness," "Mutual Trust", and "All-Round Cooperation"', *SDSC Working Paper*, No. 349 (Canberra, 2000).

Heathershaw, J. 'Unpacking the Liberal Peace: Dividing and Merging of Peacebuilding Discourses', *Millennium*, 36 (2008).

Hélan Jaworski, C. 'Peru: The Military Government's Foreign Policy in Its Two Phases (1968–80)'. In Heraldo Muñoz and Joseph S. Tulchin, eds., *Latin American Nations in World Politics* (Boulder, CO, 1984).

Hellwig, T. and D. Samuels, 'Voting in Open Economies. The Electoral Consequences of Globalization', *Comparative Political Studies*, 40(2007).

Henderson, Robert. 'China's military build-up must be checked', *Taiwan Journal* (27 October 2006).

——. 'China – National Intelligence Community', *Brassey's International Intelligence Yearbook* (Washington DC, 2003).

Henning, C.R. 'Organizing Foreign Exchange Intervention in the Euro Area', *Journal of Common Market Studies*, 45(2007).

Hermet, G. 'Les Nouveaux centres de pouvoir dans le systéme international: Entre l'Utopie et la Stratégie. La hiérarchie des nations dans le systéme mondial', *Revue Française de Science Politique*, 30(1980).

Hettne B. and F. Söderbaum, 'The New Regionalism Approach', *Politeia*, Volume 17, Number 3 (1998).

Hill, C. 'The capability-expectations gap, or conceptualising Europe's international role', *Journal of Common Market Studies*, 31(1993).

Hirsch, Michael. 'Bush and the World', *Foreign Affairs*, 81(2002).

Holton, Gerald et al. 'Special Issue—*Arms Control*': Daedalus: Arms Control, 89(1960).

Howard, D.J. 'Using Europe to Keep the World at Bay: French Policy on EU Economic Governance'. In M. Maclean, and J. Szarka, eds., *France on the World Stage. Nation State Strategies in the Global Era* (Basingstoke, 2008).

Inada, J. 'ODA seisaku ni miru sengo nihon gaikō no "kihan"', in Y. Hasegawa, ed., *Nihon gaikō no aidentiti* (Tokyo, 2004).

Jackson, Robert H. and Carl G. Rosberg. 'Why Africa's Weak States Persist: The Empirical and Juridical in Statehood,' *World Politics* 35 (1982).

Johnson, Rebecca. 'Changing Perceptions and Practice in Multilateral Arms Control Negotiations', in John Borrie and Vanessa Martin Radin, eds. *Thinking Outside the Box in Multilateral Disarmament and Arms Control Negotiations* (Geneva, 2006).

Johnson, Sabrina. 'The Cuban People Demonstrate Power of Internationalism', *Socialist Voice* (17 July 2006): http://socialistvoice.ca/?p=114.

Jones, Branwen Gruffydd. 'The Global Political Economy of Social Crisis: Towards a Critique of the "Failed State" Ideology', *Review of International Political Economy*, 15(2008).

Kalyvas, S. and L. Balcells. 'International System and Technologies of Rebellion: How the Cold War Shaped Internal Conflict', *American Political Science Review*, 104(2010).

Kaplan, Robert D. 'The Geography of Chinese Power: How far can Beijing reach on land and at sea?', *Foreign Affairs*, 89(May-June 2010).

Katzenstein, P.J. 'Coping with Terrorism: Norms and Internal Security in Germany and Japan'. In Judith Goldstein and Robert O. Keohane, eds., *Ideas and Foreign Policy: Beliefs, Institutions and Political Change* (Ithaca, NY, London, 1993).

King, B. and N. Pearce. 'The Contentiousness of Markets: Politics, Social Movements, and Institutional Change in Markets', *Annual Review of Sociology*, 36(2010).

Kislenko, Arne. 'Bending with the Wind: The Continuity and Flexibility of Thai Foreign Policy', *International Journal*, 57(2002).

Klare, Michael and Daniel Volman. 'The African Oil Rush and US National Security', *Third World Quarterly*, 27(2006).

Koh, Byung Chul. 'Policy Toward Reunification', in Youngnok Koo, and Sung-joo Han, eds. *The Foreign Policy of the Republic of Korea* (New York, 1985).

——. 'Dilemmas of Korean Reunification', *Asian Survey*, Volume 11, Number 5 (May 1971).

Koh, Yu-Hwan. 'Unification Policies of Two Koreas and the Outlook for Unity' *Korea Focus*, Volume 8, Number 6 (November-December 2000).

Kratochwil, Fredrich and John G. Ruggie. 'International organization: a state of the art or an art of the state', *International Organization*, 40(1986).

Krauthammer, C. '"The Unipolar Moment", in Council on Foreign Relations', *America and the World 1990/91*, 70(1991).

——. 'The Unipolar Moment.' *Foreign Affairs*, 70(1990).

Krugman, Paul R. 'What Should Trade Negotiators Negotiate About?', *Journal of Economic Literature*, 35(1997).

Kurlantzick, Joshua. 'China's Charm: Implications of Chinese Soft Power', *Policy Brief*, 47(2006).

Laitin, D.D. 'Post-Soviet politics', *Annual Review of Political Science* 3(2000).

Lam, Willy. 'Hawks vs. Doves: Beijing Debates "Core Interests" and Sino-U.S. Relations', *China Brief*, 10 (19 August 2010).

——. 'Is China Afraid of its Own People?'. *Foreign Policy* (28 September 2010).

Lampreia, Luiz Felipe and Ademar Seabra da Cruz Junior. 'Brazil: Coping with Structural Constraints'. In Justin L: Robertson and Maurice A: East, eds., *Diplomacy and Developing Nations: Post-Cold War Foreign Policy-making Structures and Processes* (London, 2005).

Lanti, Irman. 'Indonesia: The Year of Continuing Turbulence', *Southeast Asian Affairs* 2002 (Singapore, 2003).

Lawson, F.H. 'Westphalian Sovereignty and the Emergence of the Arab States System: The Case of Syria', *International History Review*, 22(2000).

Layne, Christopher. 'The Unipolar Illusion: Why New Great Powers Will Rise?', *International Security*, Volume 17, Number 4(1993).

Lee, Chung Sik. 'Prospects for North Korea', in *Democracy and Communism* (Korean Association of international Studies, 1995).

Lee, Kyoungtaek. 'Towards a New Framework for Soft Power: An Observation of China's Confucius Institute', (2010): https://journal.hass.tsukuba.ac.jp/interfaculty/artcle/view/3/5.

Len, C. 'Japan's Central Asian Diplomacy: Motivations, Implications and Prospects for the Region', *China and Eurasia Forum Quarterly*, 3(2005).

Levy, J.S. 'Explaining Events and Developing Theories: History, Political Science, and the Analysis of International Relations'. In C. Elman and M.F. Elman, eds. *Bridges and Boundaries: Historians, Political Scientists, and the Study of International Relations* (Cambridge, MA, 2001).

——. 'Too Important to Leave to the Other: History and Political Science in the Study of International Relations', *International Security*, 22(1997).

Liddle, R. William and Saiful Mujani. 'Indonesia in 2005: A New Multiparty Presidential Democracy.' *Asian Survey* 46, no. 1 (2006).

Liddle, William. 'Indonesia in 1999: Democracy Restored,' *Asian Survey*, 40(2000).

Lider, Julien. 'The Correlation of World Forces: The Soviet Concept', *Journal of Peace Research*, Volume 17, Number 2(1980).

Lindsay, James and Michael O'Hanlon, 'Missile Defense after the ABM Treaty' *Washington Quarterly*, Volume 25, Number 3 (2002).

Linklater, Andrew. 'A European Civilising Process?'. In C.J. Hill and M. Smith, eds., *International Relations and the European Union* (Oxford, 2005).

Maclean, M. and J. Szarka, 'Globalization and the Nation State: Conceptual Lenses on French Ambitions in a Changing World Order'. In idem., eds., *France on the World Stage. Nation State Strategies in the Global Era* (Basingstoke, 2008).

Malley, Michael S. 'Indonesia in 2001: Restoring Stability in Jakarta', *Asian Survey*, 42(2002).

Manarungsan, Sompop. 'Thailand-China Cooperation in Trade, Investment and Official Development Assistance', in Kagami Mitsuhiro, ed., *A China-Japan Comparison of Economic Relations with the Mekong River Basin Countries* (Tokyo, 2009).

Manners, I. 'Normative Power Europe Reconsidered: Beyond the Crossroads', *Journal of European Public Policy*, 13(2006).

——. 'Normative Power Europe: A Contradiction in Terms?', *Journal of Common Market Studies*, 40(2002).

Manners, I. and R. Whitman, 'The "Difference Engine": Constructing and Representing the International Identity of the EU', *Journal of European Public Policy*, 10(2003).

Manzetti, Luigi. 'Argentine-Brazilian Economic Integration: An Early Appraisal,' *Latin American Research Review*, Volume 25, Number 3 (1990).

March, L. and C. Mudde, 'What's Left of the Radical Left? The European Radical Left After 1989: Decline and Mutation', *Comparative European Politics*, 3(2005).

Martin, Lenore L. 'Turkey's Middle East Foreign Policy'. In Lenore G. Martin and Dimitris Keridis, *The Future of Turkish Foreign Policy* (Cambridge, MA, 2004).

Massie, Justin. 'Regional Strategic Subculture? Canadians and the Use of Force in Afghanistan and Iraq', *Canadian Foreign Policy*, 14(Spring 2008).

Massie, Justin and Stéphane Roussel. 'Au service de l'unité: Le rôle des mythes en politique étrangère canadienne', *Canadian Foreign Policy*, 14(Spring 2008).

Mattingly, G, 'The First Resident Embassies: Medieval Italian Origins of Modern Diplomacy', *Speculum*, 12 (1937).

McClintock, Cynthia. 'An Unlikely Comeback in Peru,' *Journal of Democracy*, Volume 17, Number 4(2006).

McKercher, B.J.C. 'Deterrence and the European Balance of Power: The Field Force and British Grand Strategy, 1934–38', *English Historical Review*, 123(2008).

———. 'The League of Nations and the Problem of Collective Security 1919–39'. In U.M. Ruser, ed. *The League of Nations 1920–1946* (New York, Geneva, 1996).

McKercher, B.J.C., and M.R. Roi. ' "Ideal" and "Punch-Bag": Conflicting Views of the Balance of Power and Their Influence on Interwar British Foreign Policy', *Diplomacy & Statecraft*, 12(2001).

Mearsheimer, John J. 'China's Unpeaceful Rise, *Current History*, Volume 105, Issue 690 (2006).

———. 'Back to the Future', *International Security*, 15(1999).

———. 'The False Promise of International Institutions', *International Security*, 19(1995).

———. 'Back to the Future: Instability in Europe after the Cold War,' *International Security*, 14(1990).

Menkhaus, Ken. 'Governance Without Government in Somalia: Spoilers, State Building and the Politics of Coping', *International Security*, Volume 31, Number 3(2007).

Messerlin, Patrick A. 'Assessing the EC Trade Policy in Goods', *Jan Tumlir Policy Essay*, Number 1 (Brussels, 2007).

Meyer, Peggy Falkenheim. 'Gorbachev and Post-Gorbachev Policy Toward the Korean Peninsula: The Impact of Changing Russian Perceptions', *Asian Survey*, 32(August 1988).

Mietzner, Marcus. 'Indonesia in 2009: Electoral Contestation and Economic Resilience', *Asian Survey*, 50(2010).

Milliken, Jennifer and Keith Krause. 'State Failure, State Collapse, and State Reconstruction: Concepts, Lessons, and Strategies,' *Development and Change* 33 (2002).

Mohan, C.R. 'India's Grand Strategy in the Gulf'. In Gulf Research Centre and the Nixon Centre, *India's Growing Role in the Gulf Implications for the Region and the United States* (Dubai, Washington, DC, 2009).

Momani, Bessma. 'American Politicization of the International Monetary Fund', *Review of International Political Economy*, Volume 15, Number 5 (2004).

Moore, Thomas Gale. 'Energy Options,' in Peter Duignan and A. Rabushka, eds, *The United States in the 1980s* (London, 1980).

Morales, Martha Lomas. 'Foreign Investment and Economic Collaboration Minister for the Republic of Cuba', *Firma de Acuerdos en el marco del ALBA entre Bolivia, Cuba y Venezuela: Rueda de Prensa*, Palacio de Convenciones, La Habana, Cuba (Sábado, 29 de abril de 2006).

Motta Veiga, Pedro da. 'Política Comercial no Brasil: Características, Condicionantes Domésticos e Policy-Making'. In Marcos Sawaya Jank and Simão Davi Silber, eds., *Políticas Comerciais Comparadas: Desempenho e Modelos Organizacionais* (São Paulo, 2007).

Moyo, B. 'Civil Society and the African Union Architecture: Institutional Provisions and Invented Interfaces'. In S. Adejumobi and A. Olukoshi, eds., *The African Union and Strategies for Development in Africa* (Amherst, MA, 2008).

Mukherji, Rahul. 'Appraising the Legacy of Bandung: A View from India,' in Seng Tan and Amitav Acharya, eds., *Bandung Revisited: The Legacy of the 1955 Asian-African Conference for International Order* (Singapore, 2008).

Murithi, T. *The African Union: Pan-Africanism, Peacebuilding and Development*, 2nd edition (Aldershot, 2010).

Mustapha, Abdul Raufu. 'The Three Faces of Nigeria's Foreign Policy: Nationhood, Identity and External Relations'. In Adekeye Adebajo and Raufu Mustapha, eds., *Gulliver's Troubles: Nigeria's Foreign Policy after the Cold War* (Scottsville, 2008).

Mutimer, David. 'From Arms Control to Denuclearisation: Governmentality and the Abolitionist Desire'. In Neil Cooper and David Mutimer, eds., *Arms Control for the 21st Century, Contemporary Security Policy* 32 (2011).

——. 'Testing Times: Nuclear Tests, Test Bans and the Framing of Proliferation' *Contemporary Security Policy* 21(2000).

Neumann, I.B. 'To Be a Diplomat', *International Studies Perspectives*, 6(2005).

Newton, Paul Paul Colley and Andrew Sharpe. 'Reclaiming the Art of British Strategic Thinking,' *RUSI Journal*, 155(March 2010).

Nicolaidis, Kalypso. 'Europe's Tainted Mirror: Reflections on Turkey's Candidacy Status after Helsinki', in Dimitris Keridis and Dimitrios Triantaphyllou, eds., *Greek-Turkish Relations in the Era of Globalization* (New York, 2001).

Nossal, Kim. 'Un pays européen? L'histoire de l'atlantisme au Canada'. In J. English and N. Hillmer, eds. *La politique étrangère canadienne dans un ordre international en mutation. Une volonté de se démarquer?* (Québec, 1992).

Nossal, Kim and Stéphane Roussel. 'Canada and the Kosovo War: the Happy Follower', in Pierre Martin and Mark Brawley, eds., *Alliance Politics, Kosovo, and NATO's War: Allied Force or Forced Allies?* (New York, 2000).

Novotný, Lukáš. 'Hodnocení současných vztahů mezi Českou republikou a SRN,' *Mezinárodní politika*, 30(2006).

Nustad, Knut. 'The Development Discourse in the Multilateral System'. In Morten Bøås and Desmond McNeill, eds., *Global Institutions and Development: Framing the World?* (London, 2004).

Nweke, Aforka. 'The Domestic Structure and Processes of Nigeria's Foreign Policy'. In Gabriel Olusanya and Rafiu Akindele, eds., *The Structure and Processes of Foreign Policy Making and Implementation 1960–1990* (Lagos, 1990).

Nye, Jr, Joseph S. 'Security and Smart Power', *American Behavioral Scientist*, 51(2008).

——. 'Soft Power and European-American Affairs'. In T.L. Ilgen, ed., *Hard Power, Soft Power and the Future of Transatlantic Relations* (Aldershot, 2006).

Obi, Cyril. 'African Oil in the Energy and Security Calculations of China and India', in Fantu Cheru and Cyril Obi, eds., *The Rise of China and India in Africa* (London, 2010).

——. 'Economic Community of West African States on the Ground: Comparing Peacekeeping in Liberia, Sierra Leone, Guinea Bissau and Cote D'Ivoire'. In Fredrik Söderbaum and Rodrigo Tavares, eds., *Regional Organizations in African Security* (London, New York, 2010).

——. 'Oil Extraction, Dispossession, Resistance and Conflict in the Niger Delta', *Canadian Journal of International Affairs*, 30(2010).

——. 'Scrambling for Oil in West Africa'. In Roger Southall and Henning Melber, eds., *A New Scramble for Africa* (Scottsville, 2009).

——. 'Nigeria's Foreign Policy and Transnational Security Challenges in West Africa', *Journal of Contemporary African Studies*, 26(2008).

——. 'Terrorism in Africa: Real, Emerging or Imagined Threats?', *African Security Review*, 15(2006).

——. 'The Politics of the Nigerian Oil Industry: Implications for Environmental Governance'. In Akınjıde Osuntokun, ed., *Democracy and Sustainable Development in Nigeria* (Lagos, 2002).

Ogoura, K. 'The Limits of Soft Power' (2006): http://www.cgp.org/popups/articleswindow.php?articleid=341.

Okonogi, Maso. 'Japan-North Korean Negotiations for Normalization'. In M. Lee and R.W. Mansbach, eds., *Changing Order in Northeast Asia* (Boulder, CO, 1993).

Ozcan, Sezer. 'Historical Evolution of the Europeanization Process of Turkey', *Portuguese Journal of International Affairs*, 3(Spring/Summer 2010).

Pahlavi, Pierre. 'La diplomatie publique du Canada: Virage ou figure de style?', *Canadian Foreign Policy*, 14(2007).

Palmer, David Scott. 'Relaciones entre Estados Unidos y el Perú durante el decenio de 1990: dinámicas, antecedentes y proyecciones,' *Política Internacional*, 53(July-September 1998).

Pant, Harsh V. 'China—A Great Power like Any Other', *ISN Security Watch* (15 February 2010).

Payne, Keith and C. Dale Walton. 'Deterrence in the Post-Cold War World'. In John Baylis, James Wirtz, Eliot Cohen and Colin S. Gray, eds., *Strategy in the Contemporary World* (Oxford, 2002).

Philips, Nicola. 'U.S. Power and the Politics of Economic Governance in the Americas', *Latin American Politics and Society*, Volume 47, Number 4(2005).

Pick, Otto. 'Uskutečnění původních priorit české zahraniční politiky,' *Mezinárodní politika*, Volume 28, Number 1(2004).

Porter, Patrick. 'Why Britain Doesn't do Grand Strategy,' *RUSI Journal*, 155(August–September 2010).

Przeworski, A. and C. Yebra. 'Globalization and Democracy', in P. Bardhay, S. Bowles and M. Wallerstein, eds., *Globalization and Egalitarian Distribution* (Princeton, 1995).

R. Cooper, 'The Goals of Diplomacy: Hard Power and Soft Power'. In D. Held and M. Koenig-Archibugi, eds., *American Power in the Twenty-First Century* (Cambridge, 2004).

Rashid, Ahmed. 'The Anarchic Republic of Pakistan', *National Interest* (September-October 2010).

Rasmussen, Mikkel Vedby. 'A Parallel Globalization of Terror: 9–11, Security and Globalization', *Cooperation and Conflict*, 37(2002).

Reimann, K.D. 'Up to No Good? Recent Critics and Critiques of NGOs'. In O. Richmond and H. Carey, eds., *Subcontracting Peace: The Challenges of NGO Peacebuilding* (Aldershot, 2005).

Reytag, Andreas and Gernot Pehnelt. 'Debt Relief and Governance Quality in Developing Countries,' *World Development*, Vol. 27(2009).

Rice, Condolezza. 'Campaign 2000: Promoting the National Interest', *Foreign Affairs*, 79(2000).

Risse-Kappen, Thomas. 'Collective Identity in a Democratic Community'. In Peter Katzenstein, ed. *The Culture of National Security* (New York: 1996).

Roberts, K. 'The Mobilization of Opposition to Economic Liberalization', *Annual Review of Political Science*, 11(2008).

Robinson, Thomas W. 'Chinese Foreign Policy from the 1940s to the 1990s'. In Thomas W. Robinson and David Shambaugh, eds., *Chinese Foreign Policy: Theory and Practice* (Oxford, 1994).

Roi, M.L. and G. Smolynec. 'Canadian Civil-Military Relations: International Leadership, Military Capacity and Overreach,' *International Journal*, 65(2010).

——. 'End States, Resource Allocation and NATO Strategy in Afghanistan,' *Diplomacy & Statecraft* 19 (2008).

Ronald Wintrobe, *Rational Extremism. The Political Economy of Radicalism* (Cambridge, UK, 2006).

Rotberg, Robert I. 'Failed States, Weak States, Collapsed States: Causes and Indicators'. In idem., ed., *State Failure and State Weakness in a Time of Terror* (Washington, DC, 2003).

——. 'Failed States in a World of Terror', *Foreign Affairs*, 81(2002).

Roussel, Stéphane and Jean-Christophe Boucher. 'The Myth of the Pacific Society: Quebec's Contemporary Strategic Culture', *American Review of Canadian Studies*, 38(Summer 2008).

Rupert, Mark. 'Globalizing Common Sense: A Marxian-Gramscian (Re)Vision of the Politics of Governance/Resistance,' *Review of International Studies*, 29(2003).

Ryan, S. 'The United Nations', in M. Buckley and R. Singh, eds., *The Bush Doctrine and the War on Terrorism* (London: 2006).

——. 'United Nations Peacekeeping: A Matter of Principles?', *International Peacekeeping*, 7(2006).

Saaler, S. 'Pan-Asianism in Modern Japanese History' In S. Saaler and V.J. Koschmann, eds., *Pan-Asianism in Modern Japanese History: Colonialism, Regionalism and Borders* (London, 2007).

Sagar, Rahul. 'State of Mind: What Kind of Power will India Become?' *International Affairs*, 85 (2009).

Sahni, S.K. 'The Non-Aligned Movement: Bandung to Durban,' *Non-Aligned World* 26(October 1998).

Sally, Razeen. 'Looking Askance at Global Governance'. In John J. Kirton, Joseph P. Daniels and Andreas Freytag, eds., *Guiding Global Order. G8 Governance in the Twenty-First Century* (Aldershot, 2001).

Sanger, David E. 'Runaway agency or U.S. Pawn?'. In L. John McQuillian and Paul C. Montgomery, eds., *The International Monetary Fund: Financial Medic to the World?* (Stanford, CA, 1999).

Sarkin, J. 'Intervention and the Responsibility to Protect in Africa'. In J. Akokpari and D.S. Zimbler, eds., *Africa's Human Rights Architecture* (Auckland Park, Cape Town, 2008).

Schieder, T. 'Die Mittleren Staaten im System der Grossen Mächte', *Historische Zeitschrift*, 232(1981).

Schmidt, Helmut. 'The 1977 Alastair Buchan Memorial Lecture', *Survival*, 20(1978).

Schneider, Jiří. 'Budoucnost transatlantických vztahů zpohledu České republiky', *Mezinárodní politika*, Volume 29, Number 4(2005).

Schoultz, Lars. 'Politics, Economics and U.S. Participation in Multilateral Development Banks', *International Organization*, 36(1982).

Šedivý, Jiří. 'Czech-NATO Relations: A Dynamic Process'. In Tadayuki Hayashi, ed., *The Emerging New Regional Order in Central and Eastern Europe* (Hokkaido, 1996).

Šedivý, Jiří and Marcin Zaborowski, 'Old Europe, New Europe and Transatlantic Relations,' *European Security*, Volume 13, Number 3(2004).

Shea, Jamie. 'NATO's New Strategic Concept', *Turkish Policy Quarterly*, 9(2010).

Simmons, B., F. Dobbin and G. Garrett, 'The International Diffusion of Liberalism', *International Organization*, 60(2006).

Sjursen, H. 'What Kind of Power?', *Journal of European Public Policy*, vol. 13 (2006).

Smith, Anthony. 'Indonesia's Aceh Problem: Measuring International and Domestic Costs', *Asia-Pacific Security Studies*, 2(2003).

——. 'Indonesia's Foreign Policy under Abdurrahman Wahid: Radical or Status Quo State', *Contemporary Southeast Asia*, 22(2000).

Snitwongse, Kusuma. 'Thai Foreign Policy in the Global Age: Principle of Profit?', *Contemporary Southeast Asia*, 23(2001).

Snyder, S. 'The Korean Peninsula and Northeast Asian Stability'. In D. Shambaugh and M. Yahuda, eds., *International Relations of Asia* (New York, 2008).

Sonntag, Albrecht. 'The Burdensome Heritage of Prestige Politics'. In M. Maclean and J. Szarka, eds., *France on the World Stage. Nation State Strategies in the Global Era* (Basingstoke, 2008).

St John, Ronald Bruce. 'Chile and Peru: The Final Settlement', *Boundary and Security Bulletin* 8(Spring 2000).

——. 'Peru: Atypical External Behavior,' in Gordon Mace and Jean-Philippe Thérien, eds., *Foreign Policy & Regionalism in the Americas*, (Boulder, CO, 1996).

Startin, N. 'The French Rejection of the 2005 EU Constitution in a Global Context: A Public Opinion Perspective'. In M. Maclean and J. Szarka, eds., *France on the World Stage. Nation State Strategies in the Global Era* (Basingstoke, 2008).

Stent, Angela. 'Berlin`s Russia Challenge,' *National Interest*, Number 46(2007).

Storey, Ian. 'China and Indonesia: Military security Ties Fail to Gain Momentum,' *China Brief*, IX, Number 4(2009).

Strachan, Hew. 'The Strategic Gap in British Defence Policy,' *Survival*, 51(August–September 2009).

——. 'Making Strategy: Civil-Military Relations after Iraq,' *Survival*, 48(Autumn 2006).

——. 'The Lost Meaning of Strategy,' *Survival*, 47(Autumn 2005).

Suberu, Rotimi. *Federalism and Ethnic Conflict in Nigeria* (Washington, DC, 2001).

Sukma, Rizal. 'Recent Developments in Sino-Indonesian Relations: An Indonesian View.' *Contemporary Southeast Asia*, 16(1994).

Suzanne Berger, 'Globalization and Politics', *Annual Review of Political Science* 3(2000).

Suzuki, S. 'Japan's Socialization into Janus-Faced European International Society', *European Journal of International Relations*, 11(2005).

Swaine, Michael D. 'Chinese Crisis Management'. In Andrew Scobell and Larry M. Wortzel, eds., *Chinese National Security Decisionmaking under Stress* (Carlisle PA).

Thakur, R. and A. Schnabel. 'Cascading Generations of Peacekeeping: Across the Mogadishu Line to Kosovo and Timor'. In R. Thakur and A. Schnabel, eds., *United Nations Peacekeeping Operations* (Tokyo, 2001).

Todd, Charles, Sunanda Ray, Farai Madzimbamuto and David Sanders. 'What is the Way Forward for Health in Zimbabwe?', *Lancet* 375 (2010).

Toth, Tibor. 'Building up a Regime for Verifying the CTBT', *Arms Control Today*, 39(September 2009).

Townsend, J. and A. King, 'Sino-Japanese Competition for Central Asian Energy: China's Game to Win', *China and Eurasia Forum Quarterly*, 5(2007).

Tumlir, Jan. 'International Economic Order and Democratic Constitutionalism', *ORDO*, 34(1983), 71–86.

Uyama, T. 'Japan's Diplomacy Towards Central Asia in the Context of Japan's Asian Diplomacy and Japan–US Relations'. In C. Len, T. Uyama and T. Hirose, eds., *Japan's Silk Road Diplomacy* (Singapore, 2008).

Vaubel, Roland. 'A Public Choice View of International Organization'. In Roland Vaubel and Thomas D. Willett, hrsg., *The Political Economy of International Organizations: A Public Choice Approach* (Boulder, CO, San Francisco, CA, Oxford, 1991).

Vigevani, Tullo and Marcello Fernandes de Oliveira (2007), 'Brazilian Foreign Policy in the Cardoso Era: The Search for Autonomy Through Integration,' *Latin American Perspecitves*, 34(2007).

Wade, Robert. 'U.S. hegemony and the World Bank: The Fight over People and Ideas,' *Review of International Political Economy*, Volume 9, Number 2 (2002).

——. 'Showdown at the World Bank', *New Left Review*, 7(January/February 2001).

——. 'Is the East Asian Miracle right?'. In Arthur Fishlow, Catherine Gwin, Stephen Haggard, Dani Rodrik and Robert Wade, eds., *Miracle or Design: Lessons from the East Asian Experience* (Washington DC, 1994).

Wagner, Christian. 'India's Gradual Rise', *Politics*, Volume 30, Number 1 (2010).

Wallat, Josefine. 'Czechoslovak/Czech Foreign and Security Policy 1989–99,' *Perspectives—The Central European Review of International Affairs*, Volume 9, Number 17(2001).

Walt, Stephen M. 'Keeping the World Off-balance: Self-Restraint and U.S. Foreign Policy'. In G. John Ikenberry, ed., *America Unrivaled: The Future of the Balance of Power* (Ithaca, NY, 2002).

Walton, O. with P. Saravanamuttu. 'In the Balance? Civil Society and the Peace Process 2002–8'. In J. Goodhand, J. Spencer and B. Korf, eds., *Caught in the Peace Trap?* (London, 2010).

Waltz, Kenneth. 'The Emerging Structure of International Politics.' *International Security*, Volume 18, Number 2 (1990).

Watanabe, Y. 'Revisiting Soft Power' (2006): www.cgp.org/popups/articleswindow.php?articleid=342.

Weiss, T.G. and S. Daws. 'World Politics: Continuity and Change since 1945'. In T.G. Weiss and S. Daws, eds., *The Oxford Handbook on the United Nations* (Oxford, 2007).

Weyland, K. 'Neopopulism and Neoliberalism in Latin America: Unexpected Affinities', *Studies in Comparative International Development*, 32(1996).

Wie, Thee Kian. 'Indonesia's Economic Performance under President Soeharto's New Order,' *Seoul Journal of Economics*, 20(2007).

Williams, Michael C. and Iver Neumann 'From Alliance to Security Community: NATO, Russia and the Power of Identity,' *Millennium: Journal of International Studies*, 29(2000).

Williamson, Richard S. 'Nation-building: The Dangers of Weak, Failing, and Failed States', *Whitehead Journal of Diplomacy and International Relations*, 8(2007).

Wilson, III, E.J. 'Hard Power, Soft Power, Smart Power', *Annals of the American Academy of Political and Social Science*, 616(2008).

Wong, Reuben. 'The Europeanisation of Foreign Policy'. In Christopher Hill and Michael Smith eds., *International Relations and the European Union* (Oxford, 2005).

Woodward, S. 'Do The Root Causes of Civil War Matter? On Using Knowledge to Improve Peacebuilding Interventions', *Journal of Statebuilding and Intervention*, Volume 1, Issue 2 (2007).

Woolcock, Stephen. 'European Union Policy Towards Free Trade Agreements,' *ECIPE Working Paper, No. 3* (Brussels, 2007).

Wright, M.C. 'The Adaptability of Ch'ing Diplomacy: The Case of Korea', *Journal of Asian Studies*, 17(1958).

Wuest, B. 'Varieties of Capitalist Debates: How Institutions Shape Public Conflicts on Economic Liberalization in the UK, France, and Germany', *Annual Conference of the Deutsche Vereinigung für Politische Wissenschaft, ETH Züric*, (10 September 2010).

Wuthnow, J. 'The Concept of Soft Power in China's Strategic Discourse', *Issues & Studies*, 44(2008).

Yahuda, M. *The International Politics of the Asia-Pacific, 1945–1995* (London, 1996).

Zaidi, N.A. 'NGO Failure and the Need to Bring Back the State', *Journal of International Development*, 11(2001).

Zartman, I. William. 'Introduction: Posing the Problem of State Collapse'. In idem., ed, *Collapsed States: The Disintegration and Restoration of Legitimate Authority* (Boulder, CO, 1995).

Zegart, Amy B. 'Why the Best is Not Yet to Come in Policy Planning,' in Daniel W. Drezner, ed., *Avoiding Trivia. The Role of Strategic Planning in American Foreign Policy* (Washington, DC, 2009).

Zelikow, Philip. 'Foreign Policy Engineering: From Theory to Practice and Back Again', *International Security*, Volume 18, Number 4 (1994).

Zisser, Eyal. 'An Israeli Watershed: Strike on Syria', *Middle East Quarterly*, Volume 15, Number 3(2008).

——. 'Political Trends in the Middle East', *Israel Affairs*, 12(2006).

Zutshi, P. 'Proctors acting for English Petitioners in the Chancery of the Avignon Popes (1305–78)', *Journal of Ecclesiastical History*, 35(1984).

Index

Page numbers in *italic* refer to tables

A Guide to Diplomatic Practice (Satow) 17
ABM Treaty: SALT I 369–71; SALT II 371;
  START I 371
Aceh 220, 221, 222, 223, 224, 433–4
Acheson, Dean 376
Acheson-Lilienthal Report 366
actorness 230
Adenauer, Konrad 87–8
Afghanistan 36, 39, 49, 51, 82, 91, 93, 137, 287n3,
  326, 391, 392, 393, 399, 401; and NATO
  256–7, 260, 382–3; and Russia 61; and United
  States of America 48, 382
Africa 80, 83, 174; China and 448; common
  currency 269; and the end of the Cold War
  192–3; G8 development policy 341–2; human
  rights abuses 265; regional organizations 264–5;
  scramble for 193; trade with EU 270–1
African Economic Community [AEC] 270
African Integration Review 273n30
African Union (AU) 192, 195, 264–71; Assembly
  268–9, 271; Executive Council 268–9, 271;
  Peace and Security Council 266; Permanent
  Representatives Committee (PRC) 268–9, 271;
  relations with the EU 270–1, 271; trade
  agreements 269
African Union Commission (AUC) 266
Africrats 264, 266–9
Afro-pessimism 265
aid 99, 148; as hard power 443
Alarcón, Ricardo 335
ALBA 325–34; goals 329; *grannacional* projects 331;
  ideological framework 328–30;
  intergovernmentalism 333; project
  implementation 330–2; *proyectos grannacionales*
  (PGs) 331
Albright, Madeleine 258–60, 261
alliances xxi–xxii, xxvi, 6–7
al-Qaeda 38, 46, 221, 256, 382, 391, 392, 401
Alzugaray, Carlos 169–79
ambassadors, role 17
American Civil War 377
American War of Independence 77
American way, the 33

Amsterdam Treaty 232
An Agenda for Peace 244
Andean Community of Nations (CAN) 187
Anderson, Mary 434
Anderson, Matthew 3
Anglo-Japanese treaty, 1902 10
Angola 176
Annan, Kofi, *In Larger Freedom* 246
anti-Americanism 327, 329, 333
Anti-Ballistic Missile Treaty, 1972 xxiii, 57
anti-globalisation organisations xvii
Anwar, Dewi Fortuna 219
appeasement xxiii, xxv
Arab Cold War, The (Kerr) 388
Arab–Israeli conflict 316–7, 390, 391, 394, 395
Arafat, Yasser 391
arbitration, emergence of faith in 8
Arctic, the, territorial claims xxvi
Argentina 112, 172
armed conflict, risk of 43–4
Armenia 160–1
arms control 365–73
Arms Trade Treaty 373
Aron, Raymond 19
Arthasastra 16
ASEAN Regional Forum (ARF) 210, 214n29, 217
Ashton, Baroness Catherine 233
Asia, decolonisation 274–5
Asia Pacific Economic Cooperation forum 61,
  214n29
Asia Times 211
Asian financial crisis, 1997 295, 300, 301
Asian Relations Conference, 1947 274–5
Asia-Pacific Economic Cooperation (APEC) 210,
  217
Asia-Pacific Economic Cooperation (APEC)
  forum 186
Association of Southeast Asian Nations (ASEAN)
  205, 209–10, 271; Indonesia and 216, 217, 224
Atlanticism 132
Attali, Jacques 80
Augmented Washington Consensus, the 340
Augustine, St. 22

Australia 131, 141, 218, 219, 220
Australia, New Zealand, United States Security
    (ANZUS) Treaty xxi
Austria 147
Austrian Succession, War of the xii, xiii, xix
axis of evil, the 388, 413

Bacevich, A. J. 31
Backer, Larry Cata 325–34
balance of power xxii–xxiii, xxiv–xxv; Middle East
    xxvi, 388–96; South Asia 398–403
Balkans conflict 44, 48, 51
bamboo diplomacy 204–12
Bandung Conference 174, 216, 275–7
Bangladesh 123, 399
Barber, Peter 10
Barnier, Michel 80
Baruch Plan, the 366
Baun, Michael 143–52
Bay of Pigs 171
Beck, Ulrich 254
Bencow, John 10
Bengtsson, Rikard 229–38
Bergsten, C. Fred 348n38
Berlusconi, Silvio 156
Betts, Richard K. 41
bipolarity xvi, 31, 36
Biti, Tendai 424
Black, Jeremy 3–12
Blair, Tony xvi–xvii, 44–4, 46, 48, 50, 82
Blake, Hector (Toe) xxvi
Bluth, Christoph 43–52
Bøås, Morten 293–301
Boer Wars 136
Bolívar, Simon 326–7
Bolivia 115, 174, 187, 189, 331, 354, 356
Bolton, John 246
Bonde, Christer 7–8
Bossi, Fernando 326
Boyce, Ralph 222
Brandt, Willi 88, 92
Brasília Summit, 2000 113
Braveboy-Wagner, Jacqueline Anne 274–87
Brazil 131, 172, 187; defense policy 115;
    diplomatic history 109–10; economic growth
    111–3, 116; engagement strategy 112–3;
    Foreign Ministry 109, 110; foreign policy 109,
    110, 110–1, 113–7; gross domestic product
    (GDP) 312, 313; historical background 109;
    internationalisation 110; and Iran 116–7;
    military capabilities 117; and multilateralism
    111; regionalism 111–2; relations with Peru 188;
    rise of 109–17; stabilisation 110–1; United
    Nations and 109
Bremmer, Ian 210
Bretherton, Charlotte 230–1
Bretton Woods conference 293–4, 297, 317, 349

Briand, Aristide 78
BRIC economies 73
bridging powers 129
British Empire xvii, 136
Brown, Gordon 48, 50
Bukh, Alexander 96–104
Bull, Hedley 20, 22, 23
Burges, Sean W. 109–17
Bush, George, Sr. xvi, 177
Bush, George W. 37–8, 39, 137, 177, 188, 222,
    245, 371, 373, 388, 391, 393, 401, 413, 444
Bush Doctrine 38
Buszynski, Leszek 213n14
Butterfield, Herbert 20
Buzan, Barry 20
Byrnes, James 365

Cabinda 265
Callières, François de, De la manière de négocier avec
    les souverains 17
Cambodia 207
Cameron, David 47, 48, 51
Campbell, Kurt 212
Canada 435; and Afghanistan 137; anti-
    Americanism 138; Atlanticism 132;
    biculturalism 135; and the British Empire 136;
    Canadian–American trade agreements 134, 137,
    140; civil–military relations 378; continentalism
    140–1; critical nationalism 139–40; and Cuba
    176, 177; defense policy 137; demography
    134–5; economy 134; education 135; foreign
    policy 131–41; geographical features 133;
    historical background 132; idealism 132, 133;
    internationalism 138–9; involvement in Iraq
    138; isolationism 132; linguistic divisions 135;
    military deployments 136; multilateralism 132,
    139; NATO and 132, 136–7; peacekeeping
    operations 132; as regional power 133; relations
    with America 133, 134, 137–8, 139; relations
    with Great Powers 135–8; sovereignty 137; as
    stability seeker 134; status 131, 139, 140; values
    132
Canadian-American North American Air Defence
    agreement xxi
Canadian–American Reciprocity Treaty 134
Cardoso, Fernando Henrique 110, 111, 112, 113
Carter, Jimmy 32, 89, 175
Castro, Fidel 171, 174, 327
Castro, Raúl 174
Center for Strategic and International Studies
    (CSIS), Commission on Smart Power 450
Central European Initiative, the 147
Central Intelligence Agency 35, 172–3
Central Treaty Organization (CENTO) 276
Centre for European Reform 257–60
Chachavalpongpun, Pavin 204–12
Chamberlain, Neville xxiii, xxiv, xxv

Chávez, Hugo 11, 178, 187, 189, 325, 327, 331, 353–4
Che Guevara, Ernesto 172, 172–3, 174
Chechnya, Russian invasion of 55
Chemical Weapons Convention (CWC) 371–2
Cheney, Dick 241
Chiang Kai-shek 67
Chile 176, 183–4
China 188; Africa and 448; anti-globalisation riots 355; CCP International Liaison Department 70; Chinese Communist Party (CCP) control 65–8; civil war 275; defense budget 64; democratic reform 67; diplomatic history 8–9; economic diplomacy 448; economic growth 65, 68, 69, 73; economic inequality 352; economic power 64, 73; economic transformation 350; emergence as Great Power xxv; foreign policy xxvi, 65, 68–74; foreign-policy actors 69–72; Four Modernisations' strategy 67, 68; GDP 65, 312, 313; grand strategy 446–8; historical background 66–7; influence 65; interests 68, 72; Leading Small Groups (LSGs) 69–70; military capabilities 64, 65–6, 73; Ministry of Commerce 70; Ministry of Foreign Affairs 70; Ministry of National Defense (MND) 70–1; Ministry of State Security (MSS) 70; and NAM 277; National People's Congress (NPC) 66; National Security Council 69; new security concept 67–8, 69; nuclear weapons 368, 372; peaceful development concept 72; peacekeeping operations 248; People's Liberation Army (PLA) 65–6, 71; public input 72; relations with America 65, 140–1; relations with Cuba 177; relations with India 120–1, 276, 401–2; relations with Indonesia 217, 220 1, 224; relations with Japan 65, 97; relations with Nigeria 201; relations with North Korea 412; relations with Peru 189; relations with Russia 61, 61–2; relations with Thailand 205, 207, 208–12, 213n15; rise of 64–74, 99, 121, 208, 401–2; security policies 69–70; Sino-American rapprochement 408, 410; Sino-Indian border dispute 398; Sino-Pakistani entente 399; soft power 211, 212, 443, 446–8, 451n32; State Constitution 65–6; State Council 70; state owned enterprises (SOEs) 71; status 208; and Taiwan 277–8; territorial claims 65, 66, 68, 209–10; Thai trade 209, 211; threat of 64–5, 74; Tiananmen Square massacre 67, 68, 72; and Tibet 276; trade with America 36; and the UN 247–8; UN seat 67; under the Manchu 8–9; WTO membership 70; Xinhua (New China) News Agency 71–2
Chinese Communist Party (CCP) 65–8; International Liaison Department 70
Chirac, Jacques 79, 80, 82, 83
Chirol, Valentine 10

Christian civilization, values of the 132
Churchill, Winston 81; Three Circles Doctrine 49
citizen-centred diplomacy 195
civil society 264, 418, 429, 432–3, 437, 443
civil wars 431
civil–military relations 376–85; control and direction 384; dialogue 377; national strategy formulation 376–7; normal theory of 376–8, 381; separation between military and political 380–1; wartime leadership and 377–9
Claude, I.L. 248
Clean Development Mechanism (CDM) 344
Clemenceau, Georges 77
climate change 341, 344
Clinton, Bill xvii, 31, 177, 219, 351, 372, 400
Clinton, Hillary 117, 223, 237
coercive diplomacy 16
Cohen, Raymond 24
Cold War xviii, xxi, 5, 43, 56, 87, 122, 158, 204, 215; arms control 365; balance of power xxiv–xxv; bipolarity 31, 36; coercive diplomacy 16; conference diplomacy xxiii–xxiv; and decolonisation 274–5; détente xxiii; end of xv–xvi, xxii, xxv, 36, 90, 206, 253, 282, 350, 371, 372, 399, 412; end of in Africa 192–3; intelligence operations 12; in the Middle East 388, 389–90; and North Korea 407; in South Asia 398–9; UN and 241, 242–4; UN Security Council deadlock xxiv
collapsed states 417–8
collective defense xxv
collective diplomacy 274–87
collective security xxiv, 101
Collor de Mello, Fernando 110
Cologne Charter 341
Colombia 186, 187, 188–9
colonialism 276, 281
coloured revolutions, the 58
Comprehensive Test Ban Treaty (CTBT) 372, 375n32
Concert of Europe xx, xxiii, xxvi
conference diplomacy xxiii–xxiv, xxv
Conference on Disarmament (CD) 371–2
Congress of Europe xx
Congress system, the xx
consensus 41
Constantinou, Costas 22–3
Constitutive Act of the African Union 264, 265, 266, 268
continentalism 140–1, 146
Cooper, R. 446
Corbett, Sir Julian 376
Corfu crisis, 1923 xxi
Council for Mutual Economic Assistance (COMECON) xvii, 175, 350
counterinsurgency (COIN) 383
crimes against humanity 266

Crispin, Shaun 211
critical nationalism 139–40
Cromwell, Oliver 7–8
Cuba 331, 333, 335, 444; Afro-Asian policy 174; *Agrarian Reform Law* 171; American sanctions on 169, 177, 178, 444; and Canada 176, 177; and the collapse of the Soviet Union 177; diplomatic performance 174–5; economic transformation 350; economy 170; foreign policy 178–9; geographical features 169–70; Guantánamo Naval Base 178; medical diplomacy 178; military operations 176; multiethnic culture 170; and NAM 281, 282; national interest 169–71; normalisation of relations with Latin America 175–6; relations with America 171–3, 175, 176, 177–8; relations with China 177; relations with EU 177; relations with Europe 176; relations with Soviet Union 173–4, 175; revolutionary diplomacy 169–79; social justice 170; UN membership 176–7
Cuban missile crisis xxiv, 172, 174, 369
cultural superpowers 103–4
culture, as power 442–3, 445
Cyprus 158, 164n44
Czech Republic, the: Balkan policy 148; *The Conception of Czech Foreign Policy for the 2003–2006 Period* 144; *Conception of the Foreign Policy of the Czech Republic* 143–4; Constitution 150; continentalism 146; contradictory tendencies 148–9; domestic limits in 143–52; EU membership 143, 144, 145–6, 149, 150; EU presidency 145–6, 149–51; foreign development assistance 148; foreign policy 143–52; foreign policy performance 149–52; foreign trade 147–8; historical background 143; influence 151; interests 144, 145, 151; internationalism 146; multilateral cooperation 145; multilateral diplomacy 146–7; national identity 144; NATO membership 143, 146; political environment 149–52; political parties influence 145; public opinion 144–5; relations with America 148; relations with neighbours 147–8; relations with Russia 148; role 151; strategic goals 143–4
Czech–German Declaration 147

Daedalus, Arms Control issue 366–7, 369, 374n12
Dai Bingguo 68, 70
Dalai Lama 120
Davotuglu, Ahmet 160
Daws, S. 245
de Gaulle, General Charles 78, 79–80, 81, 82
De Jure Naturae et Gentium Libri Ócto (Pufendorf) 8
De la manière de négocier avec les souverains (Callières) 17

Declaration on the Establishment of a New International Economic Order (United Nations) 317–8
decolonisation 242, 243, 265, 274–5, 278, 282, 316, 317
defense budgets 44, 64, 260–1
defense in depth xxv
Delcassé, Théophile 78
Delors, Jacques 81
democracy building 255
democratic liberalism 33
Deng Xiaoping 64, 67, 68, 74n12
Der Derian, James 10; *On Diplomacy* 22
Derrida, Jacques xvii, 22
détente xxiii, xxv, 88–9
deterrence xxv, 370
Developing Powers xxvii
diplomacy: bamboo 204–12; citizen-centred 195; coercive 16; collective 274–87; complexity of 10; conceptual limitations to 5; conference xxiii–xxiv, xxv; contested issues 25–6; definition 10, 15–6; dimensions of 21–2; discourse 10–1; dollar 10; dramaturgical approach 24; economic 448; emergence of 4–5; the English School 16, 19–22, 23; Eurasian 98–9; European 5–6; and foreign policy 15; functions 20; genealogy of 22; institutionalisation of 21; Jönsson and Hall on 21–2; literature 16–8; medical 178; modernisation 6; multidisciplinary approaches 26; multitrack 432; neo-realist perspective 19; non-Western 12; post-modern approach 22–3; realist school 16, 18–9; revolutionary 169–79; and security 5; Sharp's theory 23–4; social anthropological approaches 25; and sovereignty 20; and state power 19; theories of 15–26; two-level game metaphor 24
Diplomacy (Nicolson) 18
Diplomacy (Kissinger) 15
diplomatic choice 9–10
diplomatic corps 9, 15, 184–5
diplomatic history 3–12, 16; China 8–9; early-modern period 3; emergence of permanent embassies 3–4, 5; European expansion 5; European international relations 5–6; and information-gathering 11; medieval period 3–6; Middle East 6; modernisation 6; peace congresses 8; the Peace of Westphalia 7–8; Renaissance 4–5; spread of permanent embassies 9–10; Thirty Years War 6–7
diplomatic immunity 11
diplomats 3–4, 10, 11
Dogan, Aydin 159
Doha Development Round 343, 345
dollar diplomacy 10
Dower, J. W. 100
Drulák, Petr 149
Dufourcq, Jean 84n5

Dugin, Aleksandr 58
duplicity 23

East Asia Miracle Report 300–1
East Asia Summit (EAS) 210, 214n29
East Timor 217–8, 218–9, 220, 223
Eastern Question, the xxii–xxiii
Eban, Abba 15, 242, 244
economic aid, dollar diplomacy 10
Economic Community of West African States
   (ECOWAS) 192
economic diplomacy 448
economic interdependence 36
Economist, The 162
Ecuador 186, 188, 323n2, 354
egalitarianism 33
Egypt 156, 388, 389, 389–90, 396
Eighteen Nation Disarmament Conference
   (ENDC) 368, 369, 371
Einstein, Albert 365
Eisenhower, Dwight 32, 380–1, 384
El Embajador (Vera) 16–7
embassies 3–4, 5, 9–10
English Republic, the 7–8
English School, the 16, 19–22, 23
Erdogan, Tayip 155, 156, 159, 160, 161–2
Erhard, Ludwig 88
Erzan, Refik 164n31
Ethiopia 176, 267, 269
ethnopluralism 354–5
Eucken, Walter 340
Eurasian Diplomacy 98–9
Eurasianism 57–8
European Central Bank (ECB) 303, 304, 309, 310
European Convention on Human Rights 50
European Court of Human Rights 50
European Economic Community xvii, xxii, 49,
   81, 88, 176
European External Action Service (EEAS), 81, 234
European Financial Stability Facility 308–9
European Monetary System 81
European Monetary Union (EMU) 50, 81, 89,
   303–4, 307, 309, 312
European Neighbourhood Policy (ENP) 235–6
European Political Cooperation 232
European Security and Defence Policy (ESDP) 43,
   45, 48, 50–1, 91, 232–3
European Security Strategy (ESS) 229
European System of Central Banks 310
European Union: actorness 230–1; African trade
   270–1; and Brazil 112; Britain and 49–50;
   Common Agricultural Policy 81; Common
   Foreign and Security Policy (CFSP) 145;
   Common Security and Defense Policy (CSDP)
   145, 146, 148, 229, 231, 232–3, 234, *238*;
   consistency problems 235; Consolidated
   Version of the Treaty on the Functioning of the

European Union 310; continentalism 146; crisis
   resolution mechanism 308–9; Czech Republic
   membership 143, 144, 145–6, 149, 150; defense
   policy 81–3; diplomatic instruments 234–5;
   disunity 229; Eastern Europe policy 148;
   economic instruments 234; economic
   partnership agreements (EPAs) 270–1, 271;
   economic performance 304; economic policy
   co-ordination 308; economic reform 306–9;
   effectiveness 235; emergence in global politics
   230; enlargement 91, 92, 159, 235–6, 305;
   ESDP 43, 45, 48, 50–1, 91, 232–3; European
   External Action Service (EEAS), 234; European
   Financial Stability Facility 308–9; European
   Neighbourhood Policy (ENP) 235–6; exchange
   rate policy 310; external representation of
   Eurozone 309–11; fiscal rules 307–8; Foreign
   Affairs Council 233; foreign policy cooperation
   232; foreign policy development 229–38;
   foreign policy institutions 233–4; foreign-policy
   instruments 234–5; foreign-policy objectives
   231–2; and Germany 88, 89; and the global
   financial and economic crisis 303–13; as Great
   Power 236, 237; gross domestic product (GDP)
   304–5, *312, 313*; growth rates 306; High
   Representative of the Union for Foreign Affairs
   and Security Policy 233, 234; and the IMF 304;
   international ambitions 231–2; international
   identity 231; the Luxembourg Group 145;
   military instruments 235; and NATO 260–1;
   new economic map 305–6; partnership and
   cooperation agreements (PCA) 234, 236; Polish
   membership 54; presence 230; presidency
   145–6; President 233–4; relations with America
   237; relations with Cuba 177; relations with
   Nigeria 200–1; relations with Russia 236–7;
   relations with the AU 270–1, 271; security and
   defense collaboration 232–3; soft power 448–9;
   sovereign debt problems 305, 306, 307–9,
   311–2; Stability and Growth Pact 307; trade
   policy 343; Turkish membership application
   159; unit labor costs 305; values 231; Van
   Rompuy task Force 306–7
Europe's Common Defense Identity 82
Eurozone crisis, 2010 86n65, 303–4, 305, 306,
   309–11
EU–Russia Partnership and Cooperation
   Agreement 92
Evolution of Diplomatic Method, The
   (Nicolson) 18
Extraordinary Summit of the Americas 187

failed states 383, 417–25; definition 417–8, 419,
   420, 425; indicators 418–9
Failed States Index 418–9, 425
Falklands War 185
Ferguson, Niall 383

First World War xviii, xx–xxi, xxiv, 19, 32, 77, 109, 132, 136, 137, 339, 389
force, limited 16
foreign policy, *see also* individual states: consensus 128; and diplomacy 15; domestic limits on 143–52; economic 49–50; global context 36; Great Powers xxv–xxvi; institutional context 35; and international stability xxiv–xxv; national identity and 144; orientations 33–4; public opinion and 144–5; societal context 33–4; and soft power 443–5
foundational institutions 21
France 312; and Afghanistan 82; African policy 80, 83; anti-globalisation movement 356; Constitution 79; Constitutional Laws, 1875 78–9; de Gaulle's influence 78, 79–80, 81, 82; defense policy 83; ethnopluralism 354–5; and European defense policy 81–3; European policies 81–2; the Fifth Republic 77, 80–3; foreign policy 83; as Great Power xix; heritage 76; historical background 76–7; humanitarian intervention 82–3; interests 76; involvement in Iraq 45; leaves NATO 82; under Louis XIV 8; military capabilities 82–3; Minister of Foreign Affairs 78, 80; Morgenthau on 18–9; NATO participation 80, 85n50; nuclear weapons 47, 76; parliamentary oversight 80–1; political objectives 77; power and influence 76–83; presidential role 78–81; prime minister 79, 84n19; *Revue Défense Nationale* 76; Suez Crisis 390; Third and Fourth Republic legacies 78–80; UN and 243; UN peace-keeping operations 82; White Paper on Defense 83
Frederick the Great xviii
Free Trade Area of the Americas (FTAA) 327, 329
Freedman, Lawrence 44
Freedman doctrine 44–5
French Revolution, the 77
Freytag, Andreas 338–46
Fukuyama, Fukuyama, The End of History xvi
Fund for Peace, Conflict Assessment System 419
Furlan, Luiz Fernando 114–5

G5 85n32, 340
G7 338, 340, 345
G8 xxiv, 121, 271; Cologne debt relief 342–3; development policy 341–2; and globalised international economy 338–46; Heiligendamm summit 116, 341–2; opportunities and weaknesses 341–2; processes within 346
G20 39, 45, 114, 116, 224, 271, 338, 339, 341, 342
Gabon 323n3
Galtung, J. 428
Gandhi, Indira 123
Gandhi, Mahatma 126
Gandhi, Rajiv 124
Gandhi Peace Foundation 120

Ganguly, Sumit 398–403
Garcia, Marco Aurelio 114
Gardner, Richard 242
Gat, Azar 73
Gautier, Louis 83
Gazprom 59
General Agreement on Tariffs and Trade (GATT) xvii, xxii, 37, 109, 134, 339, 340, 355
genocide 266
Georgia 55, 58, 59, 61, 258
German Democratic Republic (GDR) 88, 90, 93–4
Germany 44, 312; and Afghanistan 91, 93; *détente* 88–9; East German legacy 93–4; and ESDP 91; and European Union 88, 89; Federal Republic of 87–90; foreign policy 87–94; GDP 304; and Iraq 93; *Ostpolitik* 88, 88–90, 92; partition of 87; peacekeeping operations 91, 93; post-unification 90–4; pre-unification 87–90; relations with America 89, 91–2; relations with Russia 92; relations with Soviet Union 88–90; relations with the Czech Republic 147; scepticism 94; status 90–1; and the UN 246; unification 90, 92
Gheciu, Alexandra 252–61
Gilpin, Robert 124
Ginsberg, Roy 230
global financial and economic crisis, 2008 36, 39, 55, 295, 303–13, 323, 349
global governance 338–40, 344, 349, 432
global hierarchy, reducing 274
global justice movement 355–6
global South, collective diplomacy 274–87
globalisation 115, 195, 335, 338, 347n6, 349, 357; definition xvii; leftist parties and 351–2; losers 352, 353; and the Middle East 395; opposition to xvii; popular protest against 355–6; winners 353
globalised international economy: coordination 340; decommodification measures 353; economic inequality 352–3; economic transformation and 350; global justice movement 355–6; leftist parties and 351–2; move to 338–46; NGO activist networks 356–7; opposition to 348n38; policy cooperation 341–2; popular dissent 353–7; and trade policy 343–4; and trade unions 350–1
Goodhand, Jonathan 428–38
Goodwin, G.L. 243
Gorbachev, Mikhail 90, 243–4, 400
Grant, J. Andrew 264–71
Gray, Colin 371, 376
Great Britain: 7/7 attacks 49; and Afghanistan 49; alliances xxi; appeasement xxv; and Canada 136; counterterrorism strategy 49; economic foreign policy 49–50; emergence as Great Power xix; and ESDP 45, 48, 50–1; and the EU 49–50; and Europe's Common Defense Identity 82; foreign

policy 43–52; involvement in Iraq 45, 48, 49; Labour Party 44–51; Liberal Democrat (LibDem)–Conservative coalition 46–7, 50; military capabilities 51; Morgenthau on 18; *National Security Review and Defence Review* 51; national strategy formulation 376–7; and nuclear proliferation 46–7; nuclear weapons 46; and regional crises 48; security commitment 51–2; 'special relationship' with the United States 43; status 43, 49, 52; *Strategic Defence and Security Review* 47; strategic defence review 51; strategic priorities 44; Suez Crisis 390; UN and 243; UN Security Council membership 47; and the War on Terror 48–9

Great Depression, the xvii

Great Power system xvii–xxi

Great Powers xv, xvii, 22; and Afghanistan 48; alliance system xxi–xxii, xxvi; appeasement xxiii; balance of power xxii–xxiii, xxv; cooperation xx; domination 122; emergence of new xxv; foreign-policy interests xxv–xxvi; interests xix; involvement in Iraq 45–6; legal constraints xx; persistence xxv; rarity of conflict amongst 43–4; UN Security Council deadlock xxiv

Greece 161, 305, 306

Grey, Sir Edward xx

gross domestic product (GDP) 304–5, *312, 313*

Grotius, Hugo, *On the Laws of War and Peace* xx

Guéant, Claude 80

Guimarães, Samuel Pinheiro 114

Gulf War, 1990–91 xvi, 82, 83, 244, 245, 381–2, 390

Haass, Richard 382

Hacke, Christian 87–94

Hague Conventions, 1899 and 1907 365

Haiti, earthquake, 2010 116

Hall, Martin 21–2

Hamas 162, 223, 392, 395, 396

Hammarskjold, Dag 243

Hanseatic League xvii

hard power 441, 443–4, 445

al-Hariri, Rafiq, assassination of 12

Harootunian, Harry 102

Hashimoto, Ryutaro 98–9

Hassan-Yari, Houchang 314–23

Havel, Václav 145, 150

Hazzard, S. 240

He, Kai 215–25

Hegel, G. W. F. 22

hegemonic Powers, global responses to 40–1

Helsinki Accords, 1975 88

Henderson, Robert D'A. 64–74

historical sociology 21

history, the end of xvi

Hitler, Adolf xviii, xxiii, xxiv

Hoffmann, S. 241, 248

Holbrooke, Richard 282

Holsti, Kalevi 20, 21

Holton, Gerald 366–7, 369

Holy Roman Empire 7

honour 4

Hotline Agreement, the 369

Howard, John 219, 220

Hull, Cordell 338–40, 345

human rights 218, 276, 435

human security 431–2, 434

Humanitarian Dialogue Centre (HDC) 433–4

humanitarian intervention 82–3, 271, 280, 382–3, 432

Hungary 146

Huntington, Samuel 376–7, 378, 385n12

Hwang, Balbina Y. 405–15

idealism 132, 133

Ifantis, Kostas 441–51

In Larger Freedom (Annan) 246

India xxvi, 131, 398; and Afghanistan 401; Asian Relations Conference, 1947 275; as bridging power 129; civil–military relations 125–6; and the Cold War 122; defence policy 125–7; economic growth 402; economic strategy 128; foreign exchange reserves 121; foreign policy 121, 122–9, 400; gross domestic product (GDP) *312, 313*; historical background 122–3; interests 125; lack of foreign policy 129; lack of institutionalisation 127; Mumbai attacks, 2008 120; and NAM 277, 282; National Security Advisor (NSA) 127; National Security Council (NSC) 127–8; Naxalite insurgency 350, 357; nuclear policy 123–4; nuclear weapons 368, 372, 401; political leadership 128–9; and power 121, 125; regional role 124; relations with America 399, 400–1, 403; relations with China 120–1, 276, 401–2; relations with Japan 402–3; relations with Nigeria 201; relations with Pakistan 120, 122, 123; relations with Russia 400; relations with South Korea 402–3; relations with Soviet Union 123, 124; rise of 120–9; Sino-Indian border dispute 398; status 121, 124, 129; strategic culture 126–8; structural constraints on 124–5

India–Brazil–South Africa Dialogue Forum (IBSA) 114

Indian Council of World Affairs 275

Indonesia 275, 277; Aceh 220, 221, 222, 223, 224, 433–4; anti-terrorism policy 221–2; and ASEAN 216, 217, 224; background 215; democratisation, 215, 216, 224; East Timor issue 217–8, 218–9, 220, 223; economic growth 216; foreign policy 215–25; Habibie administration 218–9, 224; human rights record 218; international profile 224; leadership legitimacy

215–6, 218, 222, 224–5; looking towards Asia policy 220–1, 226n27; Megawati administration 221–2, 224; militaries influence 216; and NAM 216–7; and OPEC 323n1; People's Consultative Assembly 225n23; regional leadership 217; relations with America 218, 219, 220, 222, 223–4, 225; relations with China 217, 220–1, 224; Soeharto administration 215, 216–8; status 216; UN Security Council service 224; US military aid 222; Wahid administration 219–21, 224, 226n27; Yudhoyono administration 222–5
influence, definition 77
information-gathering 11
Initiative for Integration of Regional Infrastructure in South America 187
interdependence xvi–xvii
international anarchy, the xix–xx
International Bank for Reconstruction and Development (IBRD) 317
International Commission on Intervention and State Sovereignty, Responsibility to Protect report 432
International Committee of the Red Cross 373
International Criminal Court (ICC) 266
International Development Association 317
International Force for East Timor 218
international institutions 20
international law, origins of xx
International Monetary Fund xxii, 112, 206, 208, 293–301, 294, 317, 325, 345, 349; American role 299–300, 302n6; approaches 296–7; capital construction 294; chain of command 295–6; consensus 296; establishment of xvii, 293–4, 296; and the EU 304; functions 294–5; membership 295; power 301; power relationships 296; quota subscription 295; reform 293, 295; shareholders 302n6
international order xv–xxvii, 339–40
international organisations xxii, xxvi
international relations, diplomacy's role 15, 20
international relations theories xxvi, xxvii
international security: changing understanding of 431–2; definition 428; and NGOs 428–38
International Security Assistance Force (ISAF) 256–7
internationalism 138–9, 146
inter-regional relationships 271
interstate industrial war 383
Iran xxvi, 39, 47, 156, 162, 316, 321, 396; nuclear programme 116–7, 393, 395, 444; revolution 324n17; rise of 388, 391, 393
Iran–Iraq War 322, 324n17, 390, 393, 395
Iraq xxvi, xvi, 36, 389, 393; British involvement in 45, 45–6, 48; Canadian involvement 138; German involvement 93; invasion of, 2003 38, 45–6, 49, 55, 91, 188, 258, 391, 393; occupation of 392; Turkey and 161

Ireland 305, 306
Islam: jihad 395; political 156; radical 388–9, 393–4; rise of 392; Turkish 159–60
isolationism 31, 132
Israel xxvi, 161–2, 223; Arab–Israeli conflicts 316–7, 390, 391, 395
Italian Wars 4, 5, 76
Italy 156, 356

Jackson, Robert H. 420
Jank, Marcos 114
Japan xix; aid 99; American alliance 98, 101–2; and American foreign policy 97; Central Asia diplomacy 98–9; collective security 101; Constitution 98; as cultural superpower 103–4; culture 99–104; defense policy 97–8; diplomacy 98–9; expansionism 100; foreign policy 96–9, 101, 103; as free rider 97; Fukuda Doctrine 97; GDP 313; historical background 96, 100; and the Korean peninsula 99; Law Concerning Cooperation for United Nations 97; militarism 100–1; neutrality 101; nihonjinron (the theory of Japaneseness) 102–3; nuclear weapons 44; relations with America 103; relations with China 65, 97; relations with India 402–3; relations with North Korea 412–3; relations with Russia 98, 104; relations with South Korea 412; relations with Thailand 208; relations with West 103; soft power 103–4; territorial dispute with Russia 60, 98; Tokugawa Shogunate 9; and the UN 246–7; and the World Bank 300–1; Yoshida Doctrine 96
Jiang Zemin 68
John, Eric 212
Jonathan, Goodluck 192
Jönsson, Christer 15–26
Jordan 389
Jospin, Lionel 79
Joyandet, Alain 86n53

Kahn, Herman 133
Kashmir 398, 400
Keiger, John 78, 79
Kennan, George 240–9, 245, 381
Kennedy, John F. 32, 172, 368
Kennedy, Paul, The Rise and Fall of the Great Powers 64
Keridis, Dimitris 155–63
Kerr, Malcolm H. 388–9
Khilnani, Sunil 125
Khrushchev, Nikita 174
Kiat Sitheeamorn 212
Kiesinger, Kurt Georg 88
Kim Il Sung 405, 408, 410–1, 412, 413, 415n13
Kim Jong-Il 405, 415, 416n27
Kim Jong-Un 405, 415
Kirkpatrick, Jean 241

Kislenko, Arne 212
Kissinger, Henry 109, 317, 399; *Diplomacy*, 15
Klaus, Václav 145, 150, 151
Knox, Philander 10
Kodjo, Edem 267
Kofi Annan 45
Kohl, Helmut 81, 89, 89–91, 112
Koizumi, Junichiro 97
Korea 406
Korean War 96, 158, 243, 275, 405
Kosovo 37, 45, 91
Kozyrev, Andrey 56, 57
Kurds 157, 158, 161
Kyoto Protocol (KP) 37, 344, 444

Lafer, Celso 111
Lahoud, Émile 12
L'Ambassadeur et ses fonctions (Wicquefort) 17
landmines 373
Latin America: anti-Americanism 327, 329, 333;
    decolonisation 275; integration 325–34;
    populism 352, 353, 357; UN Commission for
    Latin America 327
Latin American Association for Integration 332
Latin American Free Trade Association 184
leadership legitimacy 215–6, 218, 222, 224–5
League of Nations xxi, xxiv, 32, 184, 365
Lebanon 12, 389, 390, 392
Lederach, John Paul 433
liberal international order 53–4
Libya 46, 266
Lie, Trygve 243
Lincoln, Abraham 377
Lisbon, Treaty of 50, 81, 229, 231, 233–4, 237
Lloyd George, David 11
Lo, B. 249
Lodi, Peace of, 1454 4
Lomé Accords 177
Louis XIV, King of France xix, 8, 77
Ludwig IV, Holy Roman Emperor 4

Maastricht Treaty 49–50, 81, 232, 307
McCargo, Duncan 211
Macedonia 244
McGray, Douglas, 'Japan's Gross National Cool'
    103–4
McKercher, B.J.C. xv–xxvii
Malay 275
Malaysia 216
Mandelbaum, Michael 124
Mankoff, Jeffrey 53–62
Manners, I. 231
Mao Zedong 67, 68, 74n12
Marek, Dan 143–52
market development, state-led model 73
markets 349
Marshall, Sir Peter 15

Martín, Jose 327
Mattingly, Garrett 3, 18
Mearsheimer, John 44, 240
medical diplomacy 178
Medvedev, Dmitry 55, 58, 60, 61
Menon, V.K. Krishna 126
Merchant, Livingston 171
Mercosul (Common Market of the South) 111–2,
    113
MERCOSUR 332
Merkel, Angela 92, 159
Mexico 355, 356
Middle East: American policy 317, 388, 391–2,
    394–5; Arab–Israeli conflict 316–7, 390, 391,
    394, 395; balance of power xxvi, 388–96; and
    the Cold War 388, 389–90; diplomatic history
    6; and globalisation 395; military aspects 394–5;
    Pax Americana 391–2; population growth 395;
    the radical axis 393–4
Middle Powers xxvii, 131; characteristics of 116
military power 64: civil control 376–8; control and
    direction 384; counterinsurgency (COIN) 383;
    humanitarian intervention 382–3; and interstate
    industrial war 383; national strategy formulation
    376–7; operational excellence 381–2; use of
    376–85; wartime leadership and 377–9
military strategy, realist perspective 18
Millennium Development Goals 280
mini-state syndrome 125
money, power of 293–301
moralism/idealism 33
morality xx
Morgenthau, Hans, *Politics Among Nations* 18–9
Morgenthau, Henry 339
Morocco 272n8
multilateralism 111, 132, 139, 325–6
multipolarity 31, 44, 54–5, 193, 206
multitrack diplomacy 432
Murville, Maurice Couve de 80
Mutimer, David 365–73
mutual assured destruction (MAD) 370
mytho-diplomacy 22

Nakasone, Yasuhiro 103
Napoleon I 77
Napoleonic Wars xix
Nasser, Gamal Abdel 388, 389–90
nation building 36, 38
national identity 144
national interest 179n2
National Security Review and Defence Review (Great
    Britain) 51
NATO xxi, 43, 48, 50–1, 82, 88, 252–61; and
    Afghanistan 256–7, 260; Afghanistan strategy
    382–3; the Albright Report 258–60, 261;
    Article 2 253; Article 5 253, 258; Canada and
    132, 136–7; Comprehensive Political Guidance

255; counterinsurgency (COIN) doctrine 383; Czech Republic membership 146; democracy building 255; Double Track policy 89–90; and the end of the Cold War 253; enlargement 90, 92, 143, 255–6; and the EU 260–1; expansion 37, 56–7, 59; French participation 80, 85n50; International Security Assistance Force (ISAF) 256–7; and Iraq 258; Istanbul Cooperation Initiative (ICI) 255; Kosovo campaign 91; logic of exclusion 252–3, 255, 261; logic of inclusion 252, 253, 259, 261; new strategic concept 258–60, 261, 262n43; origins of 252–3; resources 260; Riga Summit 254–5; risk management 254–5, 259; role 253–4; and Russia 259–60, 262n44, 262n45; success 252; and terrorism 253–4, 256; Turkish membership 157, 158

Nazi Germany xviii, xxiii, 87, 383
negotiation, theories of 15
Nehru, Jawaharlal 122–3, 125, 126, 127, 277
neocolonialism 278–9
neoliberalism 349, 352
Neumann, Iver 20, 25
neutrality 274
New Partnership for Africa's Development 195
new regionalisms approach (NRA) 264–5, 271
New World Order 41, 244–6
Nicholas, H.G. 243
Nicolson, Harold 10, 17–8; *Diplomacy* 18; *The Evolution of Diplomatic Method* 18
Nigeria: citizen-centred diplomacy 195; domestic structure and foreign policy 197; economy 196; and the end of the Cold War 192–3; engagement with Asian Powers 194; foreign policy 192–202; foreign policy personnel 193–4; foreign policy principles 194–5; foreign-policy formulation 194; historical context 193–4; leadership 198; manifest destiny 192; Ministry of Foreign Affairs 198–9; multiethnic society 196–7, 198; and multipolarity 193; national interest 193, 195, 201; oil 196, 200, 201; oil exports 192; peacekeeping operations 192, 200; political elite 197–8; Presidential Advisory Council on International Relations (PACIR) 199; pro-Western foreign-policy 194; and regional challenges 200; relations with America 200; relations with China 201; relations with EU 200–1; relations with India 201; socioeconomic structure 197–8; state role 195–6; strategic importance 200
Nigerian Civil War, 1967–70. 194
Nigerian Institute of International Affairs (NIIA) 199–200
nihonjinron (the theory of Japaneseness) 102–3
Nixon, Richard 97, 408
Non-Aligned Movement (NAM) 123, 124, 174, 176, 185, 216–7, 326; adaptability 278–80;

America and 282–3; Bandung Conference 275–7; basic principles 280, 285–6; Belgrade summit 277; Cairo conference 277–8; Chairs 281; cohesion 280–2; collective diplomacy 274–87; credibility 282–4; Economic Declaration and Action Programme 279; enlargement 280; Founding Principles 285; historical background 274–9; ideological tensions within 281–2; Malaysia Summit 279–80; membership 286–7; and non-involvement in military alliances 278; normative successes 282–3; post-Cold War 282; strength 284; triennial summit meetings 278; unity in diversity 281
non-governmental organisations (NGOs) xxii; advantages of 429; area of engagement 433; criticisms 437–8; definition 429; Do No Harm model 434; expansion 430–1; financial resources 430; functions 429; human rights groups 435; humanitarian and development 436; impact 435–6; and international security 428–38; mediation model 433–4; peace campaigns 435; peace-building interventions 433–8; professionalisation 437; profile and market share 437; scope 434
non-nuclear-weapon states (NNWSs) 368
North American Free Trade Agreement (NAFTA) 36, 37, 355–6
North Atlantic Triangle, the 132
North Korea 39, 46, 47, 99; Basic Agreement on Reconciliation, Nonaggression, and Exchanges and Cooperation 413–4; and the Cold War 407; diplomatic relations 410; diplomatic strategy 405–6; foreign policy 405–15; foreign-policy goals 406–7; historical background 405, 406; imports 412; intra-Korean dialogue 409–11; *juche* 410–1; leadership 405, 415; North–South Joint Statement 409–10, 415n17; nuclear weapons program 414–5; rapprochement with South Korea 408; relations with America 413; relations with China 412; relations with Japan 412–3; relations with Soviet Union 407, 411–2; South Korean Sunshine Policy 414; strategic culture 407, 414; and terrorism 411
Norway 435
nuclear disarmament xxiii–xxiv, 365–73, 367
Nuclear Non-Proliferation Treaty (NPT) xxiii, 46, 47, 123, 368–9
nuclear weapons 76; arms control 365–73; deterrence xxv, 370; Indian policy 123–4; North Korean program 414–5; numbers 44; proliferation 39, 44, 46–7, 121, 368, 401; and soft power 444; states 368
Numelin, Ragnar 25
Nweke, Aforka 197
Nye, Joseph 235; *Soft Power: The Means to Success in World Politics* 103, 104, 441–2, 443, 444–5

Obama, Barack 37, 38–41, 48, 49, 55, 60, 82, 92, 116, 178, 180n20, 242, 247, 373, 401
Obi, Cyril I. 192–202
Ogoura, K. 445
oil: embargo, 1973 316–8; Nigerian 192, 196, 200, 201; prices 317, 318–20, 324n17; production quotas 444; reserves *320*, 320–1, *321*; Russian 62
oil pipelines 62
On Diplomacy (Der Derian) 22
On the Laws of War and Peace (Grotius) xx
open regionalism 348n38
Organisation for Economic Co-operation 231
Organisation of African Unity (OAU) 174, 265–8, 271, 278; Charter 267; Commission for Mediation, Arbitration, and Conciliation 267; Secretariat 267–8
Organization for European Economic Development 134
Organization of African Union 176
Organization of American States (OAS) 113, 141n1, 172, 184
Organization of Arab Petroleum Exporting Countries (OAPEC) 316
Organization of Islamic Conference 197
Organization of the Petroleum Exporting Countries (OPEC) 314–23; aid 322; diversification 321–2; Fund for International Development (OFID) 322; and the global financial and economic crisis 323; internal relations 322–3; internal structure 315–6; oil embargo, 1973 316–8; oil reserves *320*, 320–1, *321*; Secretary-General 315–6; Statute 314–5; wealth 322; withdrawals 323n1, 323n2, 323n3
Orient, the 100
Ostpolitik 88, 88–90, 92
Ottoman Empire, the 389

Pacific, War of the 183
Pacific Basin Cooperation Group 102
Pacific Economic Cooperation Council 186
Pakistan xxvi, 39, 402; and Afghanistan 401; civil–military relations 126; relations with America 123, 398–9; relations with India 120, 122, 123; relations with Soviet Union 399; Sino-Pakistani entente 399
Palestine 322, 391, 394
Palestine Liberation Organization 391
Palestinian Authority 392
Palmerston, Lord ix, xv, xx
Pan-Africanism 266
pan-Arabism 388
Pant, Harsh V. 120–9
Paris Peace Conference, 1919 xxiii, xxv, 11, 17
Parsons, A. 241
Partnership for Peace, the 146
Patriota, Antonio 111

peace, definition 428
peace congresses 8
peace facilitation 429
peace studies 433
peace-building 428, 431–8
peacekeeping operations 71, 82, 91, 93, 132, 192, 200, 243, 244, 248, 431
Pearson, Lester B. 132
Persian Empire, the 389
Peru 356; arms spending 186–7; Castilla administrations 182, 183; Consultative Commission of Foreign Relations 183, 184; democracy and 186–7; diplomatic corps 182, 184–5; diplomatic legislation 182; diplomatic relations 181–90; economic growth 184; foreign policy 185–91; foreign policy development 181–4; foreign policy expansion 184; Fujimori administration 185–6; García administration 188–9; international engagement 187; and Iraq 188; Leguía administrations 183–4; national interest 185, 189; Pardo and Prado administrations 182; regional economic cooperation 184, 185, 186; relations with America 184, 185, 186, 188; relations with Chile 183–4, 188; relations with China 189; relations with neighbours 188–9; shortcomings 189; Spanish intervention, 1863–66 182; Toledo administration 186–8; and the UN 184; war of independence 181; the War of the Pacific 183
Peter the Great, Tsar 56
pluralism 33
Poland 131, 141, 147, 148; American missile defence system 57; EU membership 54
Polish question, the xix
Politics Among Nations (Morgenthau) 18–9
Polman, L. 240, 242
popular culture 104, 442–3
populism 352, 357–8
Portugal 305, 306
Powell, Jonathan 44, 50
power 76, 125; *see also* soft power: military power; economic 64, 73; forms of 235; hard 441, 443–4, 445; legitimacy in the exercise of 445; smart 449–51
pragmatism/realism 33–4
presence 230–1
Primakov, Yevgeny 57
Protestant Reformation 7
Protocol Relating to the Establishment of the Peace and Security Council of the African Union 265–6
Prussia–Germany xviii–xix
public opinion, foreign policy and 144–5
Pufendorf, Samuel, Freiherr von, *De Jure Naturae et Gentium Libri Ôcto* 8
Putin, Vladimir 55, 57, 58, 59, 92, 159
Putnam, Robert 24

Rangoon 411
rapprochement 55, 60–1
Rasmussen, Anders Fogh 262n43
Rastatt, Treaty of, 1714 7
Reagan, Ronald xvi, 32, 90, 103, 137, 175, 176, 282, 371, 374n20
Realism 16, 18–9, 33–4
realpolitik x, xvii, 44, 141, 240
Regensburg, Treaty of 7
regional crises 48
regional integration 325–34
regional Powers 131
regionalism 111–2, 264–71
Religion, Wars of 4, 6
Revolution in Military Affairs 382
revolutionary diplomacy 169–79
Ribbentrop–Molotov pact xxiii
Rice, Condoleezza 38
Richelieu, Cardinal xx, 7, 17
Rio Group, the 113, 178
Rise and Fall of the Great Powers, The (Kennedy) 64
Robertson, Lord 256
rogue states, North Korea as 405–15
Roi, Michael L. 376–85
Roman Empire 378–9
Rompuy, Herman Van 233–4, 307, 308
Roosevelt, Franklin D. 32
Roosevelt, Theodore 10
Röpke, Wilhelm 338, 339, 345
Roque, Felipe 280
Rosberg, Carl G. 420
Rosen, Stephen 126
Rosier, Bernard du 18; *Short Treatise About Ambassadors* 16
Rotberg, Robert 417, 418
Roth, Stanley 220
Roussel, Stéphane 131–41
Russia xix; *see also* Soviet Union; and Afghanistan 61; Arctic territorial claims xxvi; cuts gas supplies to Europe 323; economic crisis, 2008-9 59; economic state control 58–9; economy 55; Eurasianism 57–8; foreign assistance capacity 54; foreign policy 53–62; Georgian war 58, 59, 61; identity 53–4; Institute for Contemporary Development (INSOR) 60; interests 55–6; invasion of Chechnya 55; military power 43–4; military reform 61; modernisation 54, 60; and multipolarity 54–5; and NATO 259–60, 262n44, 262n45; nuclear weapons 44, 47; oil and gas industry 62; rapprochement and confrontation 55, 60–1; relations with America 54–5, 57–8, 60, 62; relations with China 61, 61–2; relations with the Czech Republic 148; relations with EU 236–7; relations with Germany 92; relations with India 400; relations with Japan 98, 104; relations with Thailand 207–8; relations with Turkey 158; relations with West 56–7, 60–1, 62; strategic environment 61–2; territorial dispute with Japan 60, 98; UN and 248
Russo-Japanese War (1904) 406
Rwanda 83, 84n30
Ryan, Stephen 240–9

Saakashvili, Mikheil 58
Saddam Hussein xvi, 38, 46, 161, 390, 393, 394
St. John, Ronald Bruce 181–90
Sandino, Augusto Cesar 327
Sarkozy, Nicolas 80, 82, 83, 159
Satow, Sir Ernest 10, 15; *A Guide to Diplomatic Practice* 17
Saudi Arabia 316, 322, 389, 396
Schengen Agreement, the 140
Schmidt, Helmut 81, 89
Schröder, Gerhard 91–2, 92
Schumacher, Kurt 87
Schuman, Robert 78
Schwarzer, Daniela 303–13
Scott, James M. 31–41
Second World War xvii, xviii, xix, 32, 43, 67, 77, 87, 93, 109, 131, 132, 136, 137, 157–8, 204, 339, 383, 389, 405
security, and diplomacy 5
Sellal, Pierre 85n46
Shanghai Cooperation Organization 69
Sharp, Paul 23–4
Short Treatise About Ambassadors (Rosier) 16
Singh, Jaswant 127
Single European Act 81
Sino-Indian border dispute 398
Sino-Indian war, 1962 123, 126
Sino-Japanese War, 1894–95 67, 406
Sino-Thai free trade agreement (FTA) 209
Six Day War 390
Slovak Republic 147, 147–8
small powers: integration 325–34; options 274
Smith, K. E. 231–2
Smith, Sir Rupert 383
social constructions 296
social order 22
soft power 39, 77, 103–4, 211, 212, 235, 325, 441–51; categories 441; China and 446–8, 451n32; control of 443; culture as 442–3, 445; economic diplomacy 448; EU 448–9; and foreign policy 443–5; legitimacy 445, 446; limitations 445; relationships 441–2; resources 442; and smart power 449–51; United States of America 442–3, 444–5, 446
Soft Power: The Means to Success in World Politics (Nye) 103, 104, 441–2, 443, 444–5
Solana, Javier 232
Somalia 383, 419, 425
Sonderweg 90, 95n8

South Africa 131, 176, 280
South American Community of Nations 187
South Asia, balance of power 398–403
South Korea 402–3, 405, 406, 407–8, 409–11, 412, 416n21
South Ossetia 58, 61
South-East Asia Treaty Organization (SEATO) xxi, 276
sovereign debt crisis 305, 306, 307–9, 311–2
sovereignty 7, 20, 137, 339, 340, 432
Soviet Union xix. *see also* Russia; and arms control 368, 370; collapse of xv–xvi, xxv, 37, 43, 44, 53, 90, 124, 177, 244, 253, 279, 350, 412; heritage of 55–6, 61; Middle East policy 388; nuclear weapons 366; relations with America 36; relations with Cuba 173–4, 175; relations with Germany 88–90; relations with India 123, 124; relations with North Korea 407, 411–2; relations with Pakistan 399; Ribbentrop–Molotov pact xxiii; superposer role 54; UN and 243
Spain 304–5, 306, 308
Spanish Succession, War of the xii, 7
stability seekers 134
state, the, realist perspective 18
state failure paradigm 417–20, 425
state power 18–9
state system 325
Stiglitz, Joseph 356
Stoessinger, J.G. 241
Strachan, Hew 376, 377, 381, 384, 385n13
Strategic Defence and Security Review (Great Britain) 47
Strategic Defense Initiative 90, 371, 374n20
strategic environment, structural constraints from 124–5
Strategic Framework of the African Union Commission 268
strategy, definition 376
Straw, Jack 46
Sudan 425
Suez Crisis 132, 389–90
Sukarno, Achmed 275, 278
summit meetings xxiv
Sweden 435
Syria 12, 158, 389, 395

Taiwan 67, 68, 73, 277–8
Taiwan Strait missile crises 68
Tanham, George 126–7
Taylor, Charles 25
terrorism 256, 431; 7/7 attacks 49; 9/11 attacks 36, 37, 41, 91, 222, 253–4, 391; Bali bombing, 2002 221–2; Mumbai attacks, 2008 120; Rangoon bombing 411
Thailand 287n3; and ASEAN 205; balance-of-power strategy 206; Chatichai

administration 206–7; Chinese trade 209, 211; Chinese-language teachers 209; Cold War 204, 206; colonial period 204; crisis 210–2; diplomacy 204–12; economic growth 207; foreign policy 205–7, 213n14; foreign policy flexibility 205; foreign-policy pragmatism 205–6; IMF bailout 206, 208; instability 212n1; national interest 206–7, 209; national security 206; network monarchy 211; open-door policy 206; Phibun Songkhram Government 204; relations with America 204, 206, 207, 210–2; relations with China 205, 207, 208–12, 213n15; relations with Great Powers 206, 207–10; relations with Japan 208; relations with Russia 207–8; Second World War 204; as Siam 205; status 204; and the War on Terror 210
Thatcher, Margaret 49
Theory of International Politics (Waltz) 19
Thirty Years War xii, xiv, xviii, xx, 6–7, 8, 77
Three Circles Doctrine (Churchill) 49
Thucydides 325
Tibet 68, 276
Tieku, Thomas Kwasi 264–71
trade liberalisation 343
trade unions, decline of 350–1
transnationalisation, 195
Treaty on Conventional Armed Forces in Europe 43
Treaty on European Union 81
Truman, Harry 32
Tumlir, Jan 338, 339, 345
Turkey 392, 394; cultural identity 156; democratic tradition 155–6; demography 155; economic growth 155, 164n31; ethnic divisions 157; European policy 159; foreign policy 155–63; GDP 155; geostrategic position 156–7; historical background 157–8, 160; influence 157; and Iraq 161; Islam in 159–60; and Israel 161–2; NATO membership 157, 158; power 162; regional disputes 160–1; relations with America 158, 161; relations with neighbours 158; relations with Russia 158; relations with West 157–8, 163; status 162

Ukraine 59
UN Atomic Energy Commission (UNAEC) 366, 374n7
UN Development Programme 276
UN Preventive Deployment Force (UNPREDEP) 244
UNESCO 243
Union of South American Nations (UNASUR) 114, 187
United Nations: authority 240–1, 249; Brazil and 109; Charter xxiv, 280; China and 73, 247–8; China seat 67; and the Cold War 242–4; collective security measures 242, 244;

Commission for Latin America 327; Cuban membership 176–7; Czech Republic and 146; Declaration on the Establishment of a New International Economic Order 317–8; and East Timor 217, 218; failure 240–1; the future 246–9; and Great Britain 243; and the Great Powers 240–9; humanitarian operations 245; international organisations xxii; and legitimacy 446; and the New World Order 244–6; origins of xxi, 132; Peacebuilding Commission 244; peacekeeping operations 71, 82, 132, 192, 243, 244, 248, 431; Peru and 184; reform 246; role 241–2, 245–6, 249; Russia and 248; Secretary-General 240–1; and the Soviet Union 243; Special Session on Disarmament 371; status 249; and the United States of America 241, 242, 243, 245, 247; the veto 241, 248
United Nations Children's Emergency Fund (UNICEF) 420, 421
United Nations Economic Commission for Africa (UNECA) 268
United Nations Security Council 44–5, 45, 47, 54, 244, 325; Chinese influence 73; Counter-Terrorism Committee 245; Cuban membership 177; Great Power deadlock xxiv; Indonesian service 224; membership 246–7; permanent membership 76; reform 246–9; Resolution 1373 245
United Nations (UN) Transitional Authority for Cambodia 207
United States Agency for International Development (USAID) 418
United States of America: 9/11 attacks 36, 37, 41, 91, 222, 253–4, 391; and Afghanistan 48, 382; and arms control 367–8, 373; Asian policies 74, 210; Basic National Security Policy 381; Canadian–American trade agreements 134, 137, 140; Central Intelligence Agency 35, 172–3; civil–military relations 376–7; Clinton Administration 37; Congress 34–5; Constitution 34; Continental Era (1776–1860s) 32; critics of xvi–xvii; *Cuban Adjustment Act* 175; Defence Department 35; defence expenditure 44; defence policy xvi; *détente* xxiii, xxv; dollar diplomacy 10; economic aid 10; economic interdependence 36; economic power xvii; foreign policy xvi, 31–41, 97; foreign policy challenges 36–7, 39, 40, 41; foreign policy model 34; foreign policy orientation continuum 34; foreign policy role of Presidents 34–5; George W. Bush administration 37–8, 39; global context 36; Global Era (1940s–present) 32; and global governance 339; global military presence 32; gross domestic product (GDP) *312*; Guantánamo Naval Base 178; hegemony xvi–xviii, 67–8; as Hyper Power xvi–xviii, xxv; and the IMF 296, 297, 299–300, 302n6; India

overtakes 121; institutional context 35; interests 33–4; internationalism 31; invasion of Iraq 38, 45, 49, 55, 188, 391, 393; isolationism 31; Japanese alliance 98, 101–2; Latin American opposition to 327, 329, 333; liberal international order 53–4; and MAD 370; manifest destiny 32; Middle East policy 317, 388, 391–2, 394–5; and NAM 282–3; National Security Council (NSC) 381; national security strategy 40; national strategy formulation 376; nuclear weapons 44, 47; Obama Administration 37, 38–41, 49; oil prices 318–9; Operation Solarium 380–1, 386n38; popular culture 442–3; post-Cold War strategy xvi; refusal to join League of Nations xxi; Regional Era (1860s–1940s) 32; relations with Canada 133, 134, 137–8, 139, 140–1; relations with China 65; relations with Cuba 171–3, 175, 176, 177–8, 444; relations with the Czech Republic 148; relations with EU 237; relations with Germany 89, 91–2; relations with India 399, 400–1, 403; relations with Indonesia 218, 219, 220, 222, 223–4, 225; relations with Japan 103; relations with Nigeria 200; relations with North Korea 413; relations with Pakistan 123, 398–9; relations with Peru 184, 185, 186, 188; relations with Russia 54–5, 57–8, 60, 62; relations with Soviet Union 36; relations with Thailand 204, 206, 207, 210–2; relations with Turkey 158, 161; rise of 32; sanctions against Cuba 169, 177, 178; Sino-American rapprochement 408, 410; smart power 449–50; soft power 442–3, 444–5, 446; sole global Power 31–41, 45; Somalia deployment 383; 'special relationship' with Britain 43; State Department 35; Strategic Defense Initiative 90, 371, 374n20; trade unions 351; trade with China 36; and the UN 241, 242, 243, 245, 247; values 34; Vietnam War 32; and the World Bank 296, 297–9, 300–1

Vaïsse, Maurice 77, 79, 81
Vallet, Paul P. 76–83
vassalage 4–5
Vatikiotis, Michael 209
Védrine, Hubert 79
Venezuela 11, 177, 178, 186, 187, 189, 331, 354, 355
Vera, Don Juan Antonio De, *El Embajador* 16–7
Versailles, Treaty of 11, 109
Vienna, Congress of xix, xxiii, xxv
Vietnam War 32, 174, 274, 408
Villepin, Dominique de 85n37
Visegrad Group, the 147
Vision of the African Union and the Mission of the African Union Commission 268
Vogler, John 230–1

Wallat, J. 148–9, 150
Walton, Oliver 428–38
Waltz, Kenneth, *Theory of International Politics* 19
Wangler, Leo 338–46
war 383–4, 431; realist perspective 18, 19
war crimes 266
War on Terror 5, 36–7, 38, 48–9, 210, 222, 391
Warsaw Pact xxi, 56, 88, 143, 253
Washington conference, 1921–22 xxiii
Watson, Adam 15, 20, 21
Wattanayagorn, Panitan 211
weapons of mass destruction (WMD) 38, 46, 133, 242, 254, 280, 365, 413, 443
Weiss, T.G 245
Westphalia, Peace of xviii, xxiii, 7–8
Whitman, R. 231
Wicquefort, Abraham de, *L'Ambassadeur et ses fonctions* 17
Wiesner, James 374n12
Wight, Martin 19, 20, 22, 23
Wilson, E.J. 450–1
Winthrop, John 34
Wolfowitz, Paul xvi
World Bank xxii, 112, 293–301, 317, 325, 345; American role 297–9, 300–1; approaches 296–7; capital construction 294; establishment of xvii, 293–4, 296; Executive Director 293; and Japan 300–1; power 301; power relationships 296; structure 294
World Economic Forum 114

World Health Organization 421
World Social Forum (WSF) 356
World Trade Center, 9/11 attacks 36
World Trade Organisation (WTO) 55, 229–30, 339, 355, 444; Cancun ministerial meetings, 2003 114; Chinese membership 70; Doha round 115; establishment of xvii, 36
Wörner, Manfred 253
Wüest, Bruno R. 349–58
Wuthnow, J. 447

Xinhua (New China) News Agency 71–2

Yeltsin, Boris 55, 56
Yoshida Shigeru 96
Youde, Jeremy R. 417–25
Yushchenko, Viktor 59

Zartman, William 417–8
Zheng Bijian 72
Zhou en Lai 277
Zimbabwe 417, 448; economic deterioration 421–2; education 420; electoral fraud 423–4; as failed state 424–5; health outcomes 420–1; inflation 422; Mugabe's culpability 423–4, 425; Operation Murambatsvina 423; public services 421; violence 422–3, 424
Zisser, Eyal 388–96
zollverein xvii